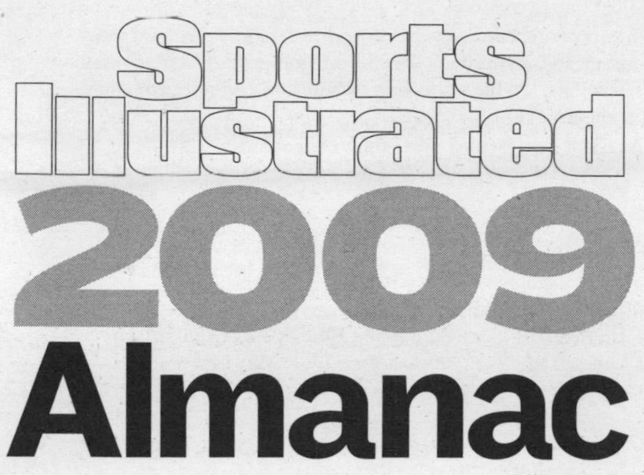

By the Editors of Sports Illustrated

YEAR IN SPORTS CALENDAR
BASEBALL
PRO FOOTBALL
COLLEGE FOOTBALL
PRO BASKETBALL
COLLEGE BASKETBALL
HOCKEY
TENNIS
GOLF
BOXING
HORSE RACING
MOTOR SPORTS

Published by Sports Illustrated Books

Time Inc.
1271 Avenue of the Americas
New York, New York 10020

First Edition
ISBN10: 1-933405-46-5
ISBN 13: 978-1-933405-46-9

Sports Illustrated 2009 Almanac was prepared by
Touchpoint Sports Publishing, of White Plains, N.Y.
Editorial Director: Morin Bishop
Art Director: Barbara Chilenskas
Photo Editor: John Blackmar
Managing Editor: Reed Richardson
Associate Editor: Max Berry

Cover photography credits:
ELI MANNING: Bob Rosato
SERENA WILLIAMS: Bob Martin
MICHAEL PHELPS: Heinz Kluetmeier
TIGER WOODS: Fred Vuich

Back cover photography credits:
MANNY RAMIREZ: Tom DiPace
SIDNEY CROSBY: Lou Capozzola
NASTIA LIUKIN: Peter Read Miller

Spine photography credit: KEVIN GARNETT: AP Photo/Elise Amendola

---

TIME INC. HOME ENTERTAINMENT

Publisher .... Richard Fraiman
General Manager .... Steven Sandonato
Executive Director, Marketing Services .... Carol Pittard
Director, Retail & Special Sales .... Tom Mifsud
Director, New Product Development .... Peter Harper
Assistant Director, Newsstand Marketing .... Laura Adam
Assistant Director, Brand Marketing .... Joy Butts
Associate Counsel .... Helen Wan
Senior Brand Manager, TWRS/M .... Holly Oakes
Brand & Licensing Manager .... Alexandra Bliss
Design & Prepress Manager .... Anne-Michelle Gallero
Book Production Manager .... Susan Chodakiewicz

Special thanks: Glenn Buonocore, Suzanne Janso, Margaret Hess, Brynn Joyce, Robert Marasco, Brooke Reger, Mary Sarro-Waite, Ilene Schreider, Adriana Tierno, Alex Voznesenskiy, Robert Yalen, Joan Lawrence

We welcome your comments and suggestions about Sports Illustrated Books. Please write to us at: Sports Illustrated Books, Attention: Book Editors, P.O. Box 11016, Des Moines, IA 50336-1016
If you would like to order any of our hardcover Collector's Edition books, please call us at 1-800-327-6388. (Monday through Friday, 7:00 a.m.- 8:00 p.m. or Saturday, 7:00 a.m.- 6:00 p.m. Central Time)

CONTENTS

THE YEAR IN SPORTS by Hank Hersch 7

BASEBALL by Merrell Noden 17

PRO FOOTBALL by Hank Hersch 93

COLLEGE FOOTBALL by B.J. Schecter 181

PRO BASKETBALL by Chris Mannix 245

COLLEGE BASKETBALL by B.J. Schecter 281

HOCKEY by B.J. Schecter 321

TENNIS by B.J. Schecter 361

GOLF by Merrell Noden 383

BOXING by Chris Mannix 413

HORSE RACING by Chris Mannix 427

MOTOR SPORTS by B.J. Schecter 441

SOCCER by Hank Hersch 461

NCAA SPORTS by Hank Hersch 471

OLYMPICS by Merrell Noden 485

TRACK AND FIELD by Merrell Noden 521

SWIMMING by Mark Bechtel 535

MISCELLANEOUS SPORTS by Merrell Noden 545

AWARDS 567

OBITUARIES 571

2009 MAJOR EVENTS 575

SOURCES

In compiling the Sports Illustrated 2009 Almanac, the editors would like to extend their gratitude to the media relations offices of the following organizations for their help in providing information and materials relating to their sports: Major League Baseball; Elias Sports Bureau, the Canadian Football League; the National Football League, Arena Football League; the National Collegiate Athletic Association; the National Basketball Association; the National Hockey League; the Association of Tennis Professionals; the Women's Tennis Association; the U.S. Tennis Association; the U.S. Golf Association; the Ladies Professional Golf Association; the Professional Golfers Association; National Thoroughbred Racing Association; the Breeders' Cup; Churchill Downs; the New York Racing Association, Inc.; the Jockey's Guild, Inc.; the Champ Car Auto Racing circuit; the National Hot Rod Association; the International Motor Sports Association; the National Association for Stock Car Auto Racing; the Professional Bowlers Association; the United Soccer Leagues; Major League Soccer; the Fédération Internationale de Futbol Association; the U.S. Soccer Federation; the U.S. Olympic Committee; USA Track & Field; U.S. Swimming; U.S. Diving; U.S. Skiing; U.S. Figure Skating Association; U.S. Curling; the Iditarod Trail Committee; USA Gymnastics; U.S. Handball Association; the Lacrosse Foundation; the American Power Boat Association; the Unlimited Hydroplane Racing Association; the Professional Rodeo Cowboys Association; U.S. Rowing; the Amateur Softball Association of America; U.S. Speed Skating; U.S. Rugby Football Union; USA Triathlon; the National Archery Association; USA Wrestling; the U.S. Squash Racquets Association; the U.S. Polo Association; NBC Sports; and the U.S. Volleyball Association.

The following sources were consulted in gathering information:

SOURCES *(Cont.)*

Baseball mlb.com, worldseries.com, baseballhalloffame.org, baseball-almanac.com, *Associated Press* (LCS, WS game recaps)

Pro Football nfl.com, superbowl.com, nfleurope.com arenafootball.com, arenabowl.com, profootballhof.com

College Football ncaasports.com, heisman.com, *Official 2008 NCAA Division I-A and I-AA Football Records Book, Official 2008 Division II and III Football Records Book*

Pro Basketball nba.com, hoophall.com

College Basketball ncaasports.com, *Official 2009 NCAA Division I Men's Basketball Records Book, Official 2009 NCAA Division I Women's Basketball Records Book, Official 2009 NCAA Division II and III Men's Basketball Records Book*

Hockey nhl.com, hhof.com, ushockeyhall.com

Tennis atptennis.com, sonyericssonwtatour.com, usopen.org, australianopen.com, wimbledon.org, rolandgarros.com, masters-cup.com, daviscup.com, fedcup.com, tennisfame.com

Golf pgatour.com, masters.org, usopen.org, usga.org, opengolf.com, pga.com, randa.org, lpga.com, knc.com, usseniorOpen.com, usamateur.org, rydercup.com, walkercup.org, curtiscup.org, pinggolf.com

Boxing wbaonline.com, wbcboxing.com, ibf-usba-boxing.com, ibhof.com, thering-online.com, usaboxing.org, olympic.org

Horse Racing ntra.com, equibase.com, bloodhorse.com, kentuckyderby.com, , preakness.com, belmontstakes.nyra.com

Motor Sports nascar.com, formula1.com, indycar.com, americanlemans.com, nhra.com, champcarworldseries.com, lemans.org, indy500.com, daytona24hr.com

Soccer fifa.com, fifaworldcup.yahoo.com, mlsnet.com, ussoccer.com, uefa.com, rsssf.com, premierleague.com, uslsoccer.com, soccernet.com

NCAA Sports ncaasports.com

Olympics olympic.org, en.beijing2008.com, usoc.org

Track and Field iaaf.org, usatf.org, usoc.org, fortismarathonrotterdam.nl, *Track and Field News*

Swimming fina.org, usaswimming.org, ishof.org, usoc.org

Miscellaneous Sports letour.fr, usarchery.org, pba.com, fide.com, uschesschampionship.com, worldcurling.org, usacurl.org, usacycling.org, uci.ch, iditarod.com, igfa.org, usfigureskating.org, isu.org, usoc.org, fig-gymnastics.com, usa-gymnastics.org, ushandball.org, uscla.com, nll.com, littleleague.org, abrahydroplanes.com, us-polo.org, prorodeo.org, usrowing.org, usarugby.org, rugbyworldcup.com, amnrl.com, ussailing.org, americascup.com, issf-shooting.org, fis-ski.com, asasoftball.com, isu.org, us-squash.org, ironmanlive.com, usatriathlon.org, fivb.org, usavolleyball.org, themat.com

Obituaries *Associated Press*

SIMON BRUTY

Olympic swimmer Michael Phelps's eight gold medals capped a dramatic 2008

The Year In Sports

The Right Kind of Crazy

Nothing was predictable in 2008, but that made for some of the most memorable moments in sports history

BY HANK HERSCH

THE HELMET CATCH—THAT WAS the first sign. A backup wide receiver doesn't make the most significant play in the history of the Super Bowl and scuttle the NFL's first unbeaten season in 35 years by pinning the ball to his plastic-encased head as he tumbles cleats over teakettle. When such a thing happens, who knows what might come next? A three-pointer as the clock expires to finish off a sublime comeback in the NCAA basketball finals? A chatty everyman forcing the greatest golfer in history to stoically burnish his legend? A record haul of gold medals made possible by two of the most shocking finishes in the annals of Olympic swimming? A laid-back island nation of 2.8 million leaving sprinters from across the planet in its dust?

This wasn't '08—this was Crazy '08, in which down (the Devil Rays, who during their first 10 years in Tampa Bay averaged 64.5 wins) was up (the rechristened 97-win Rays, who went to the World Series) and Roger (as in top-seeded Federer) was over and out (to Rafael Nadal) in a five-set Wimbledon final for the ages. In fact, given the extraordinary challenge each champion faced, whether pulling off or fighting off an upset, and the record-setting performances from Boston to Beijing, an argument can be made that Crazy '08 ranked among the most memorable years ever in sports. Just ask the helmet catcher, whose 32-yard grab on third-and-five with 1:15 to play in Super Bowl XLII set up the decisive touchdown in the New York Giants' 17–14 win. "The more you look at it," said wideout David Tyree of the play that thwarted the New England Patriots' bid to go 19–0, "the more it doesn't make sense from a logical standpoint."

Kansas did not have much hope of overcoming a nine-point deficit in the final 2:12 to win the school's third NCAA hoops title. But factor in Memphis's propensity to clang free throws (1-of-5 from the line down the stretch in regulation) and the boyhood ritual of Jayhawks guard Mario Chalmers (who as a four-year-old in Anchorage practiced buzzer-beaters in his living room with a Nerf basketball) and what appeared unlikely was, well, a mortal lock. After Chalmers's straight-away trey sent the game into overtime, Kansas roared to a 75–68 victory. "As soon as it left my hand it felt good," Chalmers said. "I just waited for it to hit the net."

And why wouldn't a KU alum pick up where Chalmers left off? All Boston forward Paul Pierce did in the NBA Finals was return from a sprained right knee to rally the Celtics past their storied archrival, the Los

BOB ROSATO

The Giants' incredible 17–14 upset over New England in Super Bowl XLII left Patriots QB Tom Brady stunned.

Angeles Lakers, in Game 1; hit the decisive free throws in Game 2; lead a 24-point comeback, the largest in Finals history, in Game 4; outplay league MVP Kobe Bryant over most of the six-game series; and, with newcomers and fellow All-Stars Kevin Garnett and Ray Allen, hang the 17th championship banner—and the first in 22 seasons—in Boston by completing the greatest single-season turnaround the league has ever seen. "Knowing that you were at rock bottom a year ago today, and to climb all the way to the top," said Pierce, his uniform soaked with champagne, his smile as wide as Boston Harbor, "this is a dream come true."

One of Earl Woods's most famous quotes was actually a whisper into his son's ear at a critical juncture of a long-ago U.S. Amateur: "Let the legend grow." At the U.S. Open, over a 7,643-yard Torrey Pines layout in La Jolla, Calif., Tiger Woods won his 14th major despite having to play 91 holes on a left leg so gimpy two months after arthroscopic knee surgery that his leg occasionally buckled mid-swing, and he grimaced and grunted and groaned after many shots. (Afterward, he would announce he had also suffered a double stress fracture, then undergo surgery to repair torn ligaments and miss the rest of the season.) To force a Monday playoff with Rocco Mediate he had to bury a 12-foot birdie putt on the par-five 18th; to send that playoff to a 19th hole, he had to birdie it again. Mediate, a 45-year-old with a bad back, pushed Woods to the limit, rallying from a three-stroke deficit in the playoff. But Tiger's resourcefulness and resolve were too much. "He is so hard to beat," Mediate said. "He's unreal."

Unprecedented accomplisments could only be achieved in mind-bending fashion during Crazy '08. Perhaps fittingly, U.S. swimmer Michael Phelps entered the Beijing Games with the most audacious goal in Olympic history: eight gold medals. Yet two days and one gold in, the 23-year-old from Baltimore stood on the Water Cube deck, watching his dream swirl down the drain. Despite his phenomenal 47.51 split in the sec-

A cold, steady rain turned Game 5 of the 2008 World Series into a mudbath, forcing a suspension of play that lasted for nearly two days.

HEINZ KLUETMEIER

ond leg of the 4 x 100 freestyle relay, the American team trailed the French by almost a body length in the final lap—an insurmountable margin for Jason Lezak to overcome against France's swimmer, Alain Bernard, who had broken the world record in the 100 free during the spring. But riding Bernard's wake, Lezak, 32, steadily closed the gap and with five meters left drew even. His finish was perfect, powering into the wall. When the scoreboard flashed a U.S. victory by .08 seconds, Phelps erupted in a tendon-popping banshee screech. Lezak had swum the fastest split in history, 46.06, and helped lower the world record by four seconds.

This is the thing I love the most," Phelps said. "I love to race." At no time was that more apparent than on Day 8, in the finals of the 100 butterfly. At the turn he was seventh, .62 seconds behind Milorad Cavic, a California-born swimmer representing Serbia. Phelps churned his way back, but he was in mid-stroke as Cavic's fingertips drifted under the surface, inches from the wall. Phelps's longtime coach, Bob Bowman, was resigned to silver. His mom, Debbie, held up two fingers in the stands. But the clock told a different story: Phelps's last stroke had propelled him to a 50.58; Cavic's glide slowed him to a 50.59. And in the 400 medley relay the following day, Phelps bagged that—*yes*—crazy eighth gold, breaking the record set by U.S. swimmer Mark Spitz in 1972. "Dream as big as you can dream," Phelps said, "and anything is possible."

Anything? How about 21-year-old sprinter Usain Bolt lowering the world record in the 100 meters by .03 seconds to 9.69, so blowing away the field in the Olympic finals that he began celebrating 10 long strides from the finish, squandering another tenth of a second? How about three of Bolt's countrywomen—Shelly-Ann Fraser, Sherone Simpson and Kerron Stewart—pulling off the first women's 100-meter medal sweep in the history of the Games? How about Bolt following his 100 record by running 19.30 in the 200, shaving .02 seconds off Michael Johnson's thought-to-be-unassailable 12-year-old mark, then bagging a third gold and a third world record with Jamaica's 4 x 100 relay team? "All I did was relax," Bolt said after the 100. "I ate my nuggets at McDonald's, I chilled, I focused. That's all it is."

Chilled (on a 40-degree night) and focused (despite a nearly 48-hour delay), that was the state of the Phillies when they won the World Series. Tied 2–2 when MLB halted play on Monday night because of rain, Game 5 couldn't resume until Wednesday, an almost unbearable wait for a city leading three games to one and hoping to end an 0-for-99 drought in the four major sports. (Philly's last champion was the 76ers in 1983.) But when the Phils squeezed ahead of the Rays 4–3 in the bottom of the eighth, a premature celebration might almost have been justified. Brad Lidge, their 31-year-old closer, had converted each of his 47 save opportunities in the regular season and the playoffs. And he delivered once again, striking out pinch hitter Eric Hinske to deny Tampa Bay a chance to become the first club to go from having the worst record one season to a title the next.

Maybe that would have been *too* crazy, even for '08.

THE YEAR IN SPORTS CALENDAR

November 2007–February 2008

NOVEMBER

11/1- The Los Angeles Dodgers announce that they have hired Joe Torre as their new manager.

11/4- The 8–0 New England Patriots meet the 7–0 Indianapolis Colts in a clash of unbeaten teams. New England comes back from a 10-point fourth quarter deficit to win 24–20.

11/4- Roger Federer loses to Fernando Gonzalez in round-robin play at the Tennis Masters Cup, marking the first time in over four years Federer has lost back-to-back matches.

11/4- Minnesota Vikings rookie running back Adrian Peterson gains 296 yards against the San Diego Chargers, setting a new NFL single-game rushing record.

11/14- The NFL reinstates Ricky Williams after his having served a ban for violating the league's substance abuse policy. He is quickly re-signed by his former team, the Miami Dolphins.

11/19-Lloyd Carr announces he will retire as head football coach at Michigan at the end of the 2007–08 season.

DECEMBER

12/2- The United States wins tennis's Davis Cup for the first time since 1995.

12/12- Sprinter Marion Jones is officially stripped of her five Olympic medals after confessing that she used performance-enhancing drugs at the 2000 Summer Games in Sydney, Australia.

12/14- Annika Sorenstam wins her LPGA first tournament in a year at the Dubai Ladies Masters.

12/27- The Boston Celtics match their entire previous season's win total with a victory over the Seattle SuperSonics.

JANUARY

1/1- USC, making its third consecutive appearance, defeats Illinois 49–17 in the Rose Bowl in Pasadena.

1/4- The Dakar Rally, a car, truck and motorcycle race across the Sahara desert, is cancelled due to terrorist threats.

1/4- Olympic champion figure skater Dorothy Hamill announces she is being treated for breast cancer.

1/4- Tennis star Martina Hingis is banned from the sport for two years after testing positive for cocaine at Wimbledon in 2007.

JANUARY *(Cont.)*

1/7- The LSU Tigers defeat the Ohio State Buckeyes 38–24 to win the BCS Championship game, becoming first two-loss champion in BCS history.

1/11- Marion Jones is sentenced to six months in prison.

1/14- The IAAF rules that South African sprinter Oscar Pistorious, a double amputee, is ineligible to compete in the Olympics because his prosthetic blades give him an unfair advantage.

1/18- In a game against the Tampa Bay Lightning, Pittsburgh Penguins center Sidney Crosby suffers a high ankle sprain that will force him to miss 29 games.

1/26- Maria Sharapova defeats Ana Ivanovic in the women's Australian Open final.

1/27- In his first PGA tournament of the year, Tiger Woods wins the Buick Invitational by eight strokes.

1/27- Novak Djokovic wins his maiden Grand Slam singles title with a four-set win over Jo-Wilfried Tsonga at the Australian Open.

1/29- The U.S. women's soccer team defeats China to win the Four Nations Cup.

1/29- The New York Mets acquire two-time Cy Young award winner Johan Santana from the Minnesota Twins in a blockbuster trade.

1/30- Kansas State's men's basketball team ends a 24-year home losing streak to rival Kansas with an 84–75 win in Manhattan.

FEBRUARY

2/3- The NFC wild card New York Giants defeat the previously undefeated New England Patriots 17–14 In Super Bowl XLII.

2/4- Former Olympic and U.S. champion sprinter Maurice Greene announces his retirement

2/4- Bob Knight, the winningest men's basketball coach in NCAA history, announces his retirement.

2/6- The Miami Heat trade Shaquille O'Neal to the Phoenix Suns for Shawn Marion and Marcus Banks.

2/9- Dale Earnhardt Jr. makes his debut with Hendrick Motorsports at the Budweiser Shootout.

2/10- In soccer, Egypt defeats Cameroon 1–0 for its sixth Africa Cup of Nations title.

2/13- In a deal involving seven players and two first-round draft picks, the Dallas Mavericks acquire Jason Kidd from the New Jersey Nets.

FEBRUARY (CONT.)

2/16– Kelly Pavlik wins his second world middleweight championship bout against Jermain Taylor.

2/17– Boosted by MVP LeBron James, the East defeats the West 134–128 in the NBA All-Star Game.

2/22– After years of feuding, Champ Car and the Indy Racing League finally agree to merge.

2/23– Wladimir Klitschko defeats Sultan Ibragimov to unify the WBO and IBF heavyweight titles.

2/24– Tiger Woods wins his fifth PGA event in a row at the Accenture Match Play Championship.

2/25– Tennessee's men's basketball team is ranked No. 1 in the USA Today/ESPN Coaches' Poll for the first time in history.

2/26– Hours before the NHL trade deadline, the San Jose Sharks acquire defenseman Brian Campbell while the Dallas Stars get center Brad Richards.

2/28– The FBI opens a probe on pitcher Roger Clemens to determine whether or not he lied to Congress in stating that he never used steroids.

2/29– Quarterback Derek Anderson signs a three-year deal with the Cleveland Browns.

MARCH

3/1– Israel Vazquez defeats Rafael Marquez for the WBC super bantamweight title.

American skier Bode Miller took home the men's overall World Cup skiing title in 2008.

MARCH *(CONT.)*

3/2– Austrian skiier Matthias Lanzinger collides with a gate during a World Cup Super-G race in Norway, causing injuries that will require his left leg to be amputated below the knee.

3/2– Carl Edwards wins his second Sprint Cup race in six days at the UAW-Dodge 400, but is subsequently penalized when it's discovered in a post-race inspection that his car's oil cap was off.

3/4– Brett Favre tearfully announces his retirement from professional football.

3/6– After splitting with coach Jimmy Connors, Andy Roddick beats Rafael Nadal at the Dubai Open, his first victory over a player ranked higher than No. 3 in the world in more than four years.

3/7– Kyle Busch wins the American Commercial Lines 200, notching the first Sprint Cup win for Toyota.

3/10– With a win over the Philadelphia 76ers , the Boston Celtics reach 50 victories in a seaon for the first time since 1992.

3/11– Wide receiver Larry Fitzgerald signs a $40 million contract with the Arizona Cardinals.

3/14– U.S. skiers sweeps the men's and women's overall World Cup titles for the first time since 1983.

3/16– The Houston Rockets extend their epic winning streak to 22 games while Tiger Woods extends his to six straight PGA titles.

3/18– The Celtics stop the Rockets streak at 22—leaving it as the second longest streak in NBA history—with a 94–74 victory.

FABRICE COFFRINI/AFP/GETTY IMAGES

MARCH *(Cont.)*

3/19- Allen Iverson returns to Philladelphia for the first time since being traded to Denver. The 76ers beat the Nuggets 115–113.

3/20- Duke narrowly avoids an enormous upset, beating Belmont 71–70 to reach the second round of the NCAA men's basketball tournament.

3/23- Davidson upsets No. 2 seed Georgetown to advance to the NCAA Sweet 16.

3/24- Geoff Ogilvy stops Tiger Woods' winning streak at the Ford Championship.

3/25- French President Nicolas Sarkozy says that his nation may boycott the Olympics opening ceremony to protest Chinese human rights violations.

3/25- Chris Webber announces his retirement from the NBA.

3/26- Alex Rodriguez offers no comment to Jose Canseco's claims that he introduced the Yankee to a steroid supplier.

3/27- Images of Barry Bonds are removed from AT&T Park.

3/30- All four No. 1 seeds advance to NCAA men's Final Four for the first time in tournament history.

3/31- Max Mosley, president of Formula One Racing, is caught portraying a Nazi guard in an underground London sex club.

3/31- Johan Santana makes a winning start with the Mets in 7–2 victory over the Marlins.

APRIL

4/1- The Yankees defeat the Toronto Blue Jays to win their final home opener in Yankee Stadium.

4/2- Donnie Walsh takes over for Isiah Thomas as President of the New York Knicks.

4/3- Days after announcing his engagement to *Sports Illustrated* swimsuit model Brooklyn Decker, Andy Roddick defeats Roger Federer for the first time since 2003.

4/4- The *Associated Press* names North Carolina power forward Tyler Hansbrough its NCAA men's basketball Player of the Year.

4/6- The Tennessee Lady Vols defeat the LSU Tigers 47–46 to advance to their second consecutive NCAA title game

4/6- Lorena Ochoa wins the second major of her career at the Kraft Nabisco Championship.

4/7- The Olympic torch is extinguished three times in Paris by protestors.

4/7- Kansas defeats Memphis 75–68 in overtime to win the NCAA men's basketball title.

APRIL *(Cont.)*

4/8- The Lady Vols defeat Stanford 64–48 to repeat as NCAA women's basketball champions.

4/10- Marion Jones' 4 x 400 and 4 x 100 relay teammates are stripped of their Olympic medals.

4/13- Trevor Immelman wins The Masters by three strokes over Tiger Woods.

4/14- The Golden State Warriors (48–34) fall just short of a Western Conference playoff while the Atlanta Hawks (37–45) earn the eighth and final playoff seed in the Eastern Conference.

4/15- The Lakers earn the No. 1 seed in the Western Conference with a win over Sacramento.

4/17- The Rockies top the Padres 2–1 after 22 innings, the longest major-league game in 15 years.

4/18- Isiah Thomas is officially relieved of his duties as head coach of the New York Knicks.

4/19- In his first fight in the United States, Joe Calzaghe defeats Bernard Hopkins in a 12-round split decision to take Hopkins' light heavyweight crown.

4/19- Danica Patrick wins the first race of her career at the Japan 300.

4/21- San Antonio Spurs guard Manu Ginobli wins the NBA's Sixth Man award.

4/22- The Miami Dolphins announce they will take Jake Long as the No. 1 pick in the NFL Draft.

4/22- Boston Celtics center Kevin Garnett is named the NBA's Defensive Player of the Year.

4/23- The Tennessee Titans trade suspended return man Adam "Pacman" Jones to Dallas.

4/27- Kyle Busch wins Talladega.

4/27- Chile defeats Brazil to take the Polo World Championship in Mexico.

4/28- Pat Riley steps down as head coach of the Miami Heat.

4/29- The New Orleans Hornets win an NBA playoff series for the first time in franchise history, handing Dallas its second straight first-round loss.

4/30- Avery Johnson is fired as head coach of the Dallas Mavericks.

MAY

5/1- Seattle SuperSonics forward Kevin Durant is named NBA Rookie of the Year.

5/1- The Detroit Tigers sweep New York at Yankee Stadium for first time since 1966.

5/3- Big Brown wins the Kentucky Derby, while runner-up Eight Belles falls after the race and is euthanized on the track.

May–June 2008

MAY *(Cont.)*

5/4– New Hampshire resident and Yankees fan Ivonne Hernandez allegedly runs over and kills a Red Sox fan following a dispute in a bar parking lot.

5/5– Bullet casings from a shooting outside Indianapolis Colts wide receiver Marvin Harrison's Philadelphia car wash are traced to a gun belonging to Harrison.

5/6– Kobe Bryant is named the NBA's regular season MVP.

5/7– At the ATP Masters Series in Rome, Rafael Nadal loses only his second career match on clay to fellow Spaniard Juan Carlos Ferrero.

5/8– A former New England Patriots employee hands over eight tapes to the NFL showing the Patriots recording the play-calling signals of five opponents between 2000 and 2002.

5/9– Rick Carlisle is hired as the new coach of the Dallas Mavericks.

5/11– Sergio Garcia wins The Players Championship.

5/12– Indians second baseman Asdrubal Cabrera makes just the 14th unassisted triple play in major-league history against the Blue Jays.

5/13– Annika Sorenstam announces she will retire from competitive golf at the conclusion of the 2008 season.

5/14– World No. 1 tennis player Justine Henin announces her retirement.

5/15– Suspect Venjah Hunte pleads guilty to the murder of Washington Redskins safety Sean Taylor.

5/16– The Court of Arbirtation for Sport overturns a previous IAAF ruling, making double amputee Oscar Pistorious eligible for the 2008 Olympics.

5/17– Big Brown wins the Preakness.

5/19– Red Sox pitcher Jon Lester throws a no-hitter against Kansas City.

5/21– Manchester United wins the UEFA Champions League by defeating Chelsea 6–5 in a penalty shootout after a 1–1 draw.

5/25– Scott Dixon wins the Indianapolis 500.

5/29– The Lakers eliminate the Spurs in five games to advance to their first NBA Finals since 2004.

5/30– The Celtics eliminate the Pistons in six games to advance to their first NBA Finals since 1987.

JUNE

6/1– Kyle Busch wins the Monster Mile in Dover, Delaware, for his fourth Sprint Cup win of the year.

6/1– Johan Santana gets his 100th career win as the Mets top the Dodgers 6–1.

JUNE *(Cont.)*

6/2– Michael Johnson announces he will return the Olympic gold he won with Antonio Pettigrew, who openly admitted to using performance enhancing drugs at the 2000 Sydney Olympics.

6/2– The Pittsburgh Penguins stave off elimination with a 4–3 triple overtime victory against the Detroit Red Wings in Game 5 of the Stanley Cup Finals, the fifth-longest game in Finals history.

6/3– After losing in the Eastern Conference Finals for the third straight year, the Detroit Pistons fire head coach Flip Saunders.

6/4– The Detroit Red Wings defeat the Pittsburgh Penguins in six games to win their 11th Stanley Cup.

6/7– Alexander Ovechkin becomes the first Washington player ever to win the Hart trophy.

6/7– Serb Ana Ivanovic defeats Russian Dinara Safina to win her first major Grand Slam singles title at the French Open.

6/7– Da' Tara wins Belmont while an injured Big Brown fails to finish.

6/8– Rafael Nadal wins his fourth consecuctive French Open by thrashing top seed Roger Federer in straight sets.

6/8– Yani Tseng wins her first major title at the LPGA Championship.

6/9– Red Wings goaltender Dominik Hasek announces his retirement.

6/12– Martin Brodeur wins the Vezina trophy as the NHL's top goaltender, while Blackhawks forward Patrick Kane wins the Calder trophy as the league's top rookie.

6/15– Dale Earnhardt Jr. wins at the Michigan International Speedway to end a 76-race winless streak.

6/16– Tiger Woods overcomes Rocco Mediate in a sudden death playoff to win his third U.S. Open.

6/17– The Celtics defeat the Lakers in six games to win their first NBA championship since 1986.

6/18– Two days after winning the U.S. Open on an injured leg, Tiger Woods announces he will miss the rest of the season to undergo reconstructive surgery on his left leg.

6/21– Stock car driver Scott Kalitta is killed in a crash during qualifying at a race in Englishtown, New Jersey.

6/22– Candace Parker becomes only the second player ever to dunk in a WNBA game.

6/24– Shaquille O'Neal is stripped of his Arizona deputy's badge after a videotape of his lewd freestyle rap, featuring jabs at former teammate Kobe Bryant, turns up on the Internet.

CHUCK BURTON/AP PHOTO

In 2008, the *Associated Press* named North Carolina forward Tyler Hansbrough (r.) its College Basketball Player of the Year.

JUNE *(Cont.)*

6/25- The Fresno State Bulldogs become the biggest underdogs ever to win the College World Series by beating the Georgia Bulldogs.

6/25- Astros pitcher Shawn Chacon is suspended indefinitely for assaulting Astros GM Ed Wade.

6/26- The Bulls select Derrick Rose with the first pick in the 2008 NBA Draft.

6/29- Spain's soccer team beats Germany 1–0 to win its first major title in 44 years at the Euro Cup.

6/29- Inbee Park wins the U.S. Women's Open.

JULY

7/5- News reports note that Brett Favre is in talks with the Packers to return to the NFL.

7/5- Venus Williams beats her sister Serena in straight sets to win her fifth Wimbledon title.

7/6- Rafael Nadal defeats five-time defending champion Roger Federer in five sets to win his first Wimbledon title in what many go on to call the greatest tennis match ever played.

7/7- After 41 years, the SuperSonics leave Seattle for Oklahoma.

7/8- The Chicago Cubs acquire starting pitcher Rich Harden from Oakland in a mid-season trade.

7/9- Power forward Elton Brand signs with the Philadelphia 76ers.

JULY *(Cont.)*

7/10- The L.A. Clippers acquire Baron Davis from Golden State.

7/10- Brett Favre sends a letter to Packers management asking for his release from his contract.

7/14- Brett Favre appears on *On the Record With Greta Van Susteren* and says he was "never fully committed" to retirement.

7/14- Josh Hamilton sets a record for the most home runs ever hit in one round of the All-Star Home Run Derby with 28, beating Bobby Abreu's 2005 record of 24.

7/14- Justin Mourneau wins the All-Star Game Home Run Derby at Yankee Stadium.

7/15- The Americn League wins the All-Star Game 4–3 and Boston rightfielder J.D. Drew is named the game's MVP after going 2-for-4 and hitting a game-tying two-run homer.

7/16- Double amputee Oscar Pistorious fails to qualify for the South African Olympic team.

7/20- Padraig Harrington wins his second straight British Open.

7/27- The Philadelphia Soul defeat the San Jose Sabrecats 59–56 in Arena Bowl XXII and Philadelphia quarterback Matt D'Orazio is named Arena Bowl MVP.

7/27- Jimmie Johnson wins the Brickyard 400.

7/27- Oakland rookie Brad Ziegler pitches his 27th consecutive scoreless inning to start his career, breaking George McQuillan's 1907 record of 25.

7/29- Disgraced NBA referee Tim Donaghy is sentenced to 15 months in prison.

AUGUST

8/4- Ji-Yai Shin wins the Women's British Open.

8/4- Though no one sees him enter or exit, Brett Favre reports to Packers preseason training camp.

8/7- Brett Favre signs with the New York Jets.

8/10- Padraig Harrington wins his third career major and his second in a row at the PGA Championship.

8/11- Abhinav Bindra wins the first ever individual Olympic gold medal for India in the 10-meter air rifle.

AUGUST *(Cont.)*

8/11- The U.S. men's 4 x 100 free relay team sets a swimming world record (3:08.24) and takes gold on the strength of Jason Lezak's anchor leg.

8/12- American swimmers Michael Phelps (200m freestyle), Aaron Peirsol (100m backstroke) and Natalie Coughlin (100m backstroke) all win Olympic gold.

8/13- With a record 14 gold medals to his name, Michael Phelps becomes the most successful Olympian in history.

8/14- James Blake beats Roger Federer in the quarterfinals of the Olympic tennis tournament.

8/15- U.S. gymnast Nastia Liukin wins gold in the all-around competition.

8/16- Usain Bolt runs the 100-meter dash in 9.69 seconds, easily winning the gold medal and breaking his own world record.

8/17- Jamaican women sprinters Shelly-Ann Fraser, Sherone Williams and Kerron Stewart sweep the Olympic 100-meter dash medals.

8/19- U.S. gymnast Shawn Johnson wins gold in the balance beam.

8/20- Usain Bolt wins Olympic gold in the 200 meter dash, setting another new world record with his time of 19.30 seconds.

8/22- Usain Bolt earns his third gold medal and third world record (37.10 seconds) of the 2008 Summer Games as the third leg of the triumphant Jamaican men's 4 x 100 relay team.

8/31- Two-time Olympic champion beach volleyball team Misty May-Treanor and Kerri Walsh lose their first match since April 2007 to Nicole Branagh and Elaine Youngs at the AVP Shootout in Cincinnati, ending their winning streak at 112 matches.

SEPTEMBER

9/7- Serena Williams wins her third career U.S. Open, defeating Jelena Jankovic in straight sets.

9/7- The New York Jets win their first game with Brett Favre at quarterback, beating the Miami Dolphins 20–14.

9/8- Roger Federer wins his fifth consecutive U.S. Open title.

9/9- Lance Armstrong announces he is coming out of retirement and will race in the 2009 Tour de France.

9/9- Derek Jeter notches his 2,519th hit to pass Babe Ruth on the Yankees' hit list.

9/14- In a game that had to be relocated due to damage to Houston's Minute Maid Park from Hurricane Ike, Carlos Zambrano pitches the first Chicago Cubs no-hitter in 36 years against the Astros at Milwaukee's Miller Park.

9/14- NASCAR's 10-race Chase For the Cup begins in Loudon, New Hampshire, where Greg Biffle takes home the checkered flag.

9/21- Team USA defeats Team Europe 16½–11½ in the Ryder Cup.

9/2- The Yankees beat the Orioles 7–3 in the final home game at Yankee Stadium.

9/26- In their first-ever winning season (97–65), the Tampa Bay Rays clinch the AL Eastern Division and set a new record for most wins by a team that finished with the worst record in the previous year.

9/28- Vijay Singh wins the inaugural FedEx Cup and clinches the $10-million bonus at the PGA's Tour Championship.

OCTOBER

10/4- The Los Angeles Dodgers complete a sweep of the Chicago Cubs in the National League Division Series, handing the top-seeded Cubs their ninth consecutive postseason loss.

10/8- The NBA's new franchise, the Oklahoma City Thunder, loses its home debut 90–88 in a preseason game against the Minnesota Timberwolves.

10/13- After sustaining an injury during a workout, 2008 Kentucky Derby and Preakness champion Big Brown is retired from racing.

10/15- The Philadelphia Phillies eliminate the Los Angeles Dodgers 5–1 in Game 5 of the National League Championship Series.

10/18- Reigning middleweight champion Kelly Pavlik loses for the first time, by unanimous decision to Bernard Hopkins in a light heavyweight bout.

10/19- The Tampa Bay Rays defeat the Boston Red Sox 3–1 in Game 7 of the American League Championship series to win their first pennant in franchise history.

10/19- Rafael Nadal becomes the first Spanish tennis player ever to clinch the year-end ATP world No.1 ranking.

10/23- Robert "Lute" Olson, longtime head basketball coach at the University of Arizona, announces his retirement.

10/29- After a nearly two-day rain delay split World Series Game 5 into two portions, the Philadelphia Phillies finally win the game 4–3 and the Series 4–1.

Baseball

MVP Cole Hamels pitched the Philadelphia Phillies to their first World Series title in 28 years

DAMIAN STROHMEYER

Fall's New Look

The Rays shook off their bedeviled past, but it was the Phillies that shook off 10,000 losses to win the Series

BY MERRELL NODEN

LONG BEFORE THE REGULAR season had even begun, there was no doubt about how it was going to end: on a bittersweet note, with the closing of Yankee Stadium. Say what you will about Wrigley Field and Fenway Park, both ballparks of great charm and history, it is Yankee Stadium, the "House That Ruth Built," that is still synonymous with baseball 85 years after it opened. The roll call of greats who made their names there—Ruth, Gehrig, DiMaggio, Mantle and Maris, Reggie, and now Jeter—has no equal, nor does the Yankees' record of 26 World Series wins in the Stadium. Poor Shea Stadium, across town, was also in its last season, but you'd hardly have known it for all the fevered attention lavished on Yankee Stadium.

Disappointing this year were the injury-ravaged Yankees themselves, who, under new manager Joe Girardi, shared first place for only one game, their first of the season, before sliding back into mid-pack mediocrity and an eventual third-place finish. Not that the Mets fared much better. For the second straight year they waited until the last game of the season to miss making the playoffs, losing at home to the Marlins even as their wildcard rival, Milwaukee, was beating the Cubs to clinch a playoff berth.

Home run king Barry Bonds would have liked to have been playing, but no team was willing to touch the surly slugger. Bonds never saw action in 2008. Of more concern to Bonds, surely, was whether federal prosecutors were planning to pursue perjury charges against him for his testimony in the BALCO drug case. Ditto Roger Clemens, whose testimony during a February appearance before the House Committee on Oversight and Government Reform was contradicted by his former trainer, Brian McNamee. "It's just sad," said Joe Torre, who, before moving to the Dodgers this year, had managed Clemens when he played for the Yankees. "I'd like to see baseball move on right now."

The season opened in Japan, with the Red Sox and Athletics splitting two games in the Tokyo Dome. The defending World Series Champion Red Sox were expected to be the team to beat in the American League East, but they hadn't counted on the biggest surprise of the season, the Tampa Bay Rays. After shedding the demonic half of their nickname, the Rays played like Angels, spending most of the season atop the division, propelled there by an anonymous collection of young talent. Rookie third baseman Evan Longoria was as close to a star as the Rays had, batting .272 with 27 homers and 85 RBIs. It helped that the Rays' starters managed to stay healthy and that their bullpen, which last year had an ERA of 6.16—the major league's worst in 50 years—improved mightily, recording the third-best ERA in the league, 3.55. Tampa Bay passed the franchise record for wins-in-a-season

JOHN IACONO

Rookie third baseman Longoria (r.) was the closest thing to a superstar on a suprising Rays team that took home the AL pennant.

(70) on August 10 and wound up going 97–65 to win the division; never before had the Rays finished higher than fourth. The only thing they lacked was fans: Home attendance at Tropicana Field averaged only 22,370, fifth worst in the majors.

Left in the unexpected role of pursuers were the Red Sox. Boston got great pitching from Daisuke Matsuzaka, who went 18–3 with a major league-leading opponent batting average of .211, and reliever Jonathan Papelbon, who notched 41 saves with an ERA of 2.34. Still, the biggest news out of Beantown was the decision to trade eccentric, disgruntled slugger Manny Ramirez to the Dodgers on July 31. Ramirez joined a team that was a game below .500 and barely keeping pace with Arizona. He immediately justified the Dodgers' faith in him, hitting two home runs in his first three games and finishing the L.A. portion of his year with fantastic numbers: .396 with 17 homers and 53 RBIs in 53 games. "Every time he comes to bat I expect him to get a hit," said Dodgers teammate Clayton Kershaw.

The Brewers made the season's other great trade, acquiring big C.C. Sabathia, the 2007 American League Cy Young Award winner, from the Indians on July 7. Sabathia would go 11–2 with a 1.65 ERA for Milwaukee. On the final day of the season, making his third-straight start on short rest, Sabathia hurled a four-hitter against the Cubs to send the Brewers into the playoffs for the first time since 1982.

Of course, no one knows futility like the Chicago Cubs. This year marked the 100th anniversary of the Cubs' last trip to the World Series. In 1908 they beat Detroit four games to one, and until their shocking exit in the first round of the playoffs, it looked as if this year's Cubs might finally return to the Series. Led by Ryan Dempster and Carlos Zambrano, who went a combined 31-12, their starting pitching was consistently strong, and they had six players with 20 or more homers. The Cubs finished the year 97–64, best record in the National League. So when the White Sox squeezed into the

CHUCK SOLOMON

Yogi Berra and a host of other former Yankees legends bid a final farewell to Yankee Stadium on September 21, 2008.

playoffs by winning first a make-up game with Detroit and then a one-game playoff with Minnesota, it sparked talk of an All-Windy City World Series. But the Cubs were swept by the Dodgers and the White Sox only did one game better against the Rays.

There didn't look to be much drama in store for the Los Angeles Angels either. The Angels enjoyed a six-game lead in the AL West at the All-Star break and never wavered, finishing with 100 wins and a 21-game lead over second-place Texas. Reliever Francisco Rodriguez set a single-season major-league record with 62 saves. But the Red Sox proved that, no matter their record coming into the playoffs, they are a post-season force. Boston beat L.A. in four games.

The National League East once again came down to a seesaw battle between the Mets and the Phillies, with the Marlins lurking as potential spoilers. Phillies' second baseman Chase Utley got off to an incredible start, hitting 20 of his eventual 33 home runs before June 1. Brad Lidge, acquired from the Astros in an offseason trade, was 41-for-41 in save opportunities. But it was first baseman Ryan Howard, the 2006 MVP, who carried the Phillies in the homestretch. On his way to recording major-league-leading totals of 48 home runs and 146 RBIs, Howard was sensational in September, hitting .352 with 11 homers and 32 RBIs in 25 games, moving himself into contention for a second MVP award despite his .251 batting average and 199 strikeouts.

Still, it was hard not to be impressed by the Rays. Led by their seemingly unflappable, delightfully cerebral manager, Joe Maddon, Tampa Bay had youth, power, speed, and a few veterans like Cliff Floyd scattered in amongst the striplings. And after the Rays won the AL pennant by knocking off the defending champion Red Sox, their opponent, the NL-champion Phillies were considered slight underdogs.

If there had been one nagging question about the Phillies all year, it had been their starting pitching, especially when Opening Day starter Brett Meyers got sent down to the minors. But in the Series they all came through. Cole Hamels, the eventual World Series MVP, pitched the Phillies to a Game 1 win in Tampa. Jamie Moyer, at 45 the second oldest starting pitcher in World Series history, pitched 6⅓-strong innings in Game 3, and Joe Blanton, who'd been Oakland's Opening Day pitcher, pitched magnificently in Game 4 to help the Phillies take a three games to one lead.

They needed just one more win, but it seemed Game 5 might take forever. After 5½ innings played in a cold, steady rain, the score stood 2–2, and Commissioner Bud Selig decided to halt the game. Once the weather cleared and the game resumed two days later, the Phillies got to work and took a one-run lead into the ninth. And in 2008 there was no more sure thing in the ninth inning than Brad "Lights Out" Lidge, who ended the torment of Phillies fans when he got Rays pinch hitter Eric Hinske to wave helplessly at a third-strike slider for the final out. For long suffering Phillies fans, the wait was finally over.

FOR THE RECORD•2008

2008 Final Regular Season Standings

National League

EASTERN DIVISION

Team	Won	Lost	Pct	GB	Home	*Away
Philadelphia	92	70	.568	--	48–33	44–37
NY Mets	89	73	.549	3.0	48–33	41–40
Florida	84	77	.522	7.5	39–36	39–41
Atlanta	72	90	.444	20.0	29–38	29–52
Washington	59	102	.366	32.5	34–46	25–56

CENTRAL DIVISION

Team	Won	Lost	Pct	GB	Home	Away
Chicago	97	64	.602	--	42–26	42–38
†Milwaukee	90	72	.556	7.5	41–32	41–40
Houston	86	75	.534	11.0	47–33	39–42
St. Louis	86	76	.531	11.5	46–35	40–41
Cincinnati	74	88	.457	23.5	43–38	31–50
Pittsburgh	67	95	.414	30.5	39–42	28–53

WESTERN DIVISION

Team	Won	Lost	Pct	GB	Home	Away
LA Dodgers	84	78	.519	--	48–33	36–45
Arizona	82	80	.506	2.0	48–33	34–47
Colorado	74	88	.457	10.0	43–38	31–50
San Francisco	72	90	.444	12.0	37–44	35–46
San Diego	63	99	.389	21.0	35–46	28–53

†Wild-card teams.

American League

EASTERN DIVISION

Team	Won	Lost	Pct	GB	Home	Away
Tampa Bay	97	65	.599	--	57–24	40–41
†Boston	95	67	.586	2.0	56–25	39–42
NY Yankees	89	73	.549	8.0	48–33	41–40
Toronto	86	76	.531	11.0	47–34	39–42
Baltimore	68	93	.422	28.5	37–43	31–50

CENTRAL DIVISION

Team	Won	Lost	Pct	GB	Home	Away
*Chicago	89	74	.546	--	54–28	35–46
Minnesota	88	75	.540	1.0	53–28	35–47
Cleveland	81	81	.500	7.5	45–36	36–45
Kansas City	75	87	.463	13.5	38–43	37–44
Detroit	74	88	.457	14.5	40–41	34–47

WESTERN DIVISION

Team	Won	Lost	Pct	GB	Home	Away
LA Angels	100	62	.617	--	50–31	50–31
Texas	79	83	.488	21.0	35–46	26–55
Oakland	75	86	.466	24.5	43–48	32–48
Seattle	61	101	.377	39.0	40–42	39–42

*won division in one-game tiebreaker against Minnesota.

2008 Playoffs

National League Division Playoffs

Oct 1 ....Milwaukee 1 at Philadelphia 3
Oct 2 ....Milwaukee 2 at Philadelphia 5
Oct 4 .... Philadelphia 1 at Milwaukee 4
Oct 5 .... Philadelphia 6 at Milwaukee 2

(Philadelphia won series 3–1)

Oct 1 ....Los Angeles 7 at Chicago 2
Oct 2 ....Los Angeles 10 at Chicago 3
Oct 4 ....Chicago 1 at Los Angeles 3

(LA Dodgers won series 3–0)

National League Championship Series

Oct 9 ....Los Angeles 2 at Philadelphia 3
Oct 10 ....Los Angeles 5 at Philadelphia 8
Oct 12 ....Philadelphia 2 at Los Angeles 7
Oct 13 ....Philadelphia 7 at Los Angeles 5
Oct 15 ....Philadelphia 5 at Los Angeles 1

(Philadelphia won series 4–1)

GAME 1

										R	H	E
LA Dodgers	1	0	0	1	0	0	0	0	0	**2**	**7**	**1**
Philadelphia	0	0	0	0	0	3	0	0	x	**3**	**7**	**0**

W—Phi: Hamels. **L**—LA: Lowe. **SV**—Phi: Lidge. **LOB**—LA: 4; Phi: 6. **2B**—LA: Ethier, Ramirez, Kemp. **HR**—Phi: Utley, Burrell. **RBI**—LA: Ramirez, DeWitt; Phi: Utley (2), Burrell. **GIDP**—LA: Kemp. Phi: Werth, Rollins. **SF**—LA: DeWitt. **E**—LA: Furcal. **T**—2:36. **A**—45,839.

Recap: Pat Burrell and Chase Utley cleared the wall, while Manny Ramirez's drive fell just short and stayed in the park. The pair of Phillies homered off of a tiring Derek Lowe in the sixth inning to back a strong performance by Cole Hamels, and the Philadelphia Phillies were a winner, beating the Los Angeles Dodgers 3–2. Ramirez put the Dodgers ahead with a long RBI double in the first, just missing a two-run homer. But the Phillies' big bats answered in the sixth. Ryan Madson pitched a scoreless eighth, and Brad Lidge finished with his third save of the postseason.

GAME 2

										R	H	E
LA Dodgers	0	1	1	3	0	0	0	0	0	**5**	**8**	**1**
Philadelphia	0	4	4	0	0	0	0	0	x	**8**	**11**	**1**

W—Phi: Myers. **L**—LA: Billingsley. **SV**—Phi: Lidge. **LOB**—LA: 11; Phi: 10. **2B**—LA: Loney; Phi: Ruiz, Werth. **3B**—Phi: Victorino. **HR**—LA: Ramirez. **RBI**—LA: DeWitt, Loney, Ramirez (3); Phi: Ruiz, Myers (3), Victorino (4). **GIDP**—LA: Kent. **IBB**—LA: Blake; Phi: Dobbs. **E**—LA: Kemp; Phi: Dobbs. **T**—3:33. **A**—45,883.

Recap: With so many big hitters in Philadelphia's potent lineup, no one ever expected it would be pitcher Brett Myers who put the Phillies in control of the NLCS with his bat. Myers did better at the plate than on the mound, going 3-for-3 with three RBIs. Shane Victorino drove in four more runs as Philadelphia overcame another homer by Manny Ramirez to beat the Los Angeles Dodgers 8–5 and take a two games to none lead in the best-of-seven series just hours after Phillies manager Charlie Manuel learned that his mother had passed away.

National League Championship Series (Cont.)

GAME 3

										R	H	E
Philadelphia	0	1	0	0	0	0	1	0	0	**2**	**7**	**0**
Los Angeles	5	1	0	1	0	0	0	0	X	**7**	**10**	**0**

W—LA: Kuroda. **L**—Phi: Moyer. **LOB**—Phi 5; LA: 7. **2B**—Phi: Howard, Utley. **3B**— LA: DeWitt. **HR**—LA: Furcal. **RBI**—Phi: Feliz, Burrell; LA: Ramirez, Blake, DeWitt (3), Furcal, Garciaparra. **SB**—LA: Martin. **CS**—Phi: Utley; LA: Kemp. **GIDP**—LA: Martin. **HBP**—Phi: Martin 2. **T**—3:57. **A**—56,800.

Recap: Blake DeWitt's bases-loaded triple off Phillies starter Jamie Moyer capped a five-run first inning, and the feisty Dodgers beat the Phillies 7–2 to trim Philadelphia's lead to 2–1 in the best-of-seven series. The benches and bullpens emptied in the third inning, moments after Los Angeles starter Hiroki Kuroda threw a pitch over Shane Victorino's head, but there were no punches or ejections, and the Dodgers played with poise all night.

GAME 4

										R	H	E
Philadelphia	2	0	0	0	0	1	0	4	0	**7**	**12**	**1**
Los Angeles	1	0	0	0	2	2	0	0	0	**5**	**11**	**0**

W—Phi: Madson. **L**—LA: Wade. **SV**—Phi: Lidge. **LOB**—Phi 7; LA: 12. **2B**—Phi: Utley, Dobbs; LA: Loney, Pierre, Ramirez. **HR**—Phi: Victorino, Stairs; LA: Blake. **RBI**—Phi: Utley, Howard, Victorino (2), Stairs (2); LA: Loney, Ramirez, Martin, Blake. **SB**—Phi: Rollins. **CS**—Phi: Bruntlett; LA: Pierre. **GIDP**—Phi: Victorino. LA: DeWitt, Ethier. **IBB**–LA: Ramirez (2), Loney. **T**—3:44. **A**—56,800.

Recap: Shane Victorino and the Philadelphia Phillies struck back with long balls rather than beanballs to move within one win of the World Series. After ducking a pitch thrown over his head the previous day, Victorino and much-traveled pinch-hitter Matt Stairs delivered two-run homers in the eighth inning Monday night, lifting the Phillies to a 7–5 victory over the Los Angeles Dodgers for a 3–1 lead in the NL championship series. Brad Lidge got his first four-out save for the Phillies, remaining perfect this season.

GAME 5

										R	H	E
Philadelphia	1	0	2	0	2	0	0	0	0	**5**	**8**	**0**
Los Angeles	0	0	0	0	0	1	0	0	0	**1**	**7**	**3**

W—Phi: Hamels. **L**—LA: Billingsley. **LOB**—Phi: 9; LA: 7. **HR**—Phi: Rollins; LA: Ramirez. **RBI**—Phi: Rollins, Howard, Burrell; LA: Ramirez. **SB**—Phi: Rollins. **GIDP**—Phi: Utley, Bruntlett. LA: DeWitt (2). **IBB**-Phi: Victorino (2), Loney. **E**—LA: Furcal. **T**—3:14. **A**—56,800.

Recap: The next stop for the losingest team in pro sports history?—the World Series. Jimmy Rollins got them rollin' with a leadoff home run, Cole Hamels pitched his third gem of the playoffs and Philadelphia beat the bumbling Los Angeles Dodgers 5-1 to win its first pennant since 1993. The NL East champions, who didn't clinch a playoff berth until the final weekend of the season, took advantage of three errors by shortstop Rafael Furcal in the fifth inning and shrugged off another homer by Manny Ramirez. Brad Lidge closed it out for the Phillies, who hope to add to their lone championship, won in 1980 against the Kansas City Royals.

American League Division Playoffs

Oct 1 ....Boston 4 at Los Angeles 1
Oct 3 ....Boston 7 at Los Angeles 5
Oct 4 ....Los Angeles 5 at Boston 4 (12 inn.)
Oct 6 ....Los Angeles 2 at Boston 3

(Boston won series 3–1)

Oct 2 ....Chicago 4 at Tampa Bay 6
Oct 3 ....Chicago 2 at Tampa Bay 6
Oct 5 ....Tampa Bay 3 at Chicago 5
Oct 6 ....Tampa Bay 6 at Chicago 2

(Tampa Bay won series 3–1)

American League Championship Series

Oct 10 ....Boston 2 at Tampa Bay 0
Oct 11 ....Boston 8 at Tampa Bay 9 (11 inn.)
Oct 13 ....Tampa Bay 9 at Boston 1
Oct 14 ....Tampa Bay 13 at Boston 4
Oct 16 ....Tampa Bay 7 at Boston 8
Oct 18 ....Boston 4 at Tampa Bay 2
Oct 19 ....Boston 1 at Tampa Bay 3

(Tampa Bay won series 4–3)

GAME 1

										R	H	E
Boston	0	0	0	0	1	0	0	1	0	**2**	**7**	**0**
Tampa Bay	0	0	0	0	0	0	0	0	0	**0**	**4**	**0**

W—Bos: Matsuzaka. **L**—TB: Shields. **SV**—Bos: Papelbon. **LOB**—Bos: 8; TB: 7. **2B**—Bos: Youkilis, Kotsay. **RBI**—Bos: Lowrie, Youkilis. **SB**—Bos: Pedroia. **SF**—Bos: Lowrie. **GIDP**—Bos: Drew; TB: Longoria. **HBP**—Bos: Drew.

T—3:25. **A**—35,001.

GAME 1 *(CONT.)*

Recap: Red Sox starter Daisuke Matsuzaka struck out nine, gave up four hits and walked four in seven-plus innings to help the Boston Red Sox beat the Tampa Bay Rays 2–0 and take Game 1 of the series. Carl Crawford broke up Matsuzaka's no-hit bid with a single to lead off the sixth. Jed Lowrie delivered the first run with a sac fly in the fifth and Kevin Youkilis drove in an insurance run in the eighth.

American League Championship Series *(Cont.)*

GAME 2

					R	H	E
Boston	2 0 1	0 3 1	0 1 0	0 0	**8**	**12**	**0**
Tampa Bay	2 0 2	1 3 0	0 0 0	0 1	**9**	**12**	**0**

W—TB: Price. **L**—Bos: Timlin. **LOB**—Bos: 13; TB: 6. **2B**—Bos: Bay, Crisp (2); TB: Pena, Longoria (2). **HR**—Bos: Pedroia, Youkilis, Bay; TB: Longoria, Upton, Floyd. **RBI**—Bos: Bay (4), Pedroia (2), Youkilis; TB: Longoria (3), Upton (2), Crawford (2), Floyd, Pena. **SB**—TB: Upton. **SF**—TB: Upton. **GIDP**—Bos: Youkilis. **IBB**–TB: Iwamura. **T**—5:27. **A**—34,904.

Recap: B.J. Upton and the Tampa Bay Rays won a game of home run derby with a shallow fly ball, outlasting the Boston Red Sox 9–8 in a game in which the teams combined for seven home runs, tying a postseason record. The Rays wound up winning a game that lasted 5 hours, 27 minutes when speedy Fernando Perez tagged up on Upton's one-out fly and beat right fielder J.D. Drew's throw home. The Red Sox and Rays matched the postseason record for homers first set in the 1989 World Series.

GAME 3

				R	H	E
Tampa Bay	0 1 4	0 0 0	0 3 1	**9**	**13**	**0**
Boston	0 0 0	0 0 0	1 0 0	**1**	**7**	**0**

W—TB: Garza. **L**—Bos: Lester. **LOB**—TB: 5; Bos: 8. **2B**—TB: Iwamura (2); Bos: Pedroia. **HR**—TB: Upton, Longoria, Baldelli, Pena. **RBI**—TB: Navarro, Upton (3), Longoria, Baldelli, Pena; Bos: Ellsbury. **SB**—TB: Pena. **SF**—Bos: Ellsbury. **GIDP**—Bos: Pedroia. **T**—3:23. **A**—38,301.

Recap: B.J. Upton hit a three-run home run and Evan Longoria also homered off suddenly shaky Red Sox ace Jon Lester, then Rocco Baldelli and Carlos Pena cleared the Green Monster as well to give the Rays a 9–1 victory over the Boston Red Sox. Matt Garza held Boston scoreless through six innings. The four homers in a game tied the ALCS home run record last matched by Boston in Game 2 against Tampa Bay on Saturday. Lester, who hadn't allowed an earned run in four previous postseason outings—including last year's World Series clincher against Colorado—gave up four earned runs on eight hits in 5⅔ innings. He gave up an unearned run on Varitek's passed ball in the second, before yielding Upton's home run in the third.

GAME 4

				R	H	E
Tampa Bay	3 0 2	0 1 5	0 2 0	**13**	**14**	**3**
Boston	0 0 1	0 0 0	1 2 0	**4**	**7**	**0**

W—TB: Sonnanstine. **L**—Bos: Wakefield. **LOB**—TB: 6; Bos: 6. **2B**—TB: Crawford (2); Youkilis. **3B**—TB: Bartlett, Crawford; Bos: Ortiz. **HR**—TB: Pena, Longoria, Aybar; Bos: Cash. **RBI**—TB: Pena (2), Longoria (2), Aybar (5), Upton, Crawford (2), Navarro; Bos: Cash, Youkilis, Pedroia. **SB**—TB: Crawford (2), Upton; **GIDP**—TB: Navarro; Bos: Crisp. **E**—TB: Upton, Longoria (2). **T**—3:07. **A**—38,133.

Recap: Tampa Bay sent three more homers sailing over the Green Monster, and the Rays were on their way to another blowout in Boston. Evan Longoria hit his rookie-record fifth home run of the playoffs, and Carlos Pena and Willy Aybar also homered off aging knuckleballer Tim Wakefield to give Tampa Bay a 13–4 victory over the Red Sox that left the defending champions on the brink of elimination. Aybar had four hits and five RBIs, and Andy Sonnanstine pitched 7⅓ sharp innings as Tampa Bay took a three games to one lead in the best-of-seven playoff.

GAME 5

				R	H	E
Tampa Bay	2 0 3	0 0 0	2 0 0	**7**	**8**	**1**
Boston	0 0 0	0 0 0	4 3 1	**8**	**11**	**1**

W—Bos: Masterson. **L**—TB: Howell. **LOB**—TB: 5; Bos: 8. **2B**—TB: Upton; Bos: Lowrie. **HR**—TB: Upton, Pena, Longoria; Bos: Ortiz, Drew. **RBI**—TB: Upton (4), Pena (2), Longoria; Bos: Pedroia, Ortiz (3), Drew (3), Crisp. **SB**—TB: Gross, Iwamura, Bartlett. **GIDP**—TB: Longoria, Pena. **IBB**—TB: Pena; Bos: Bay. **HBP**—Bos: Varitek. **E**—TB: Longoria. **T**—4:08. **A**—38,437.

Recap: Trailing by seven runs with seven outs left in their season, the Red Sox pulled off the biggest postseason rally since 1929, staving off elimination with an 8–7 victory over the Tampa Bay Rays when J.D. Drew singled home the winning run with two outs in the ninth. Boston had trailed 7–0 with two outs in the seventh, then rallied when Dustin Pedroia hit an RBI single and David Ortiz added a three-run homer against Grant Balfour. Drew hit a two-run homer in the eighth, and Coco Crisp tied it with a two-out RBI single off Dan Wheeler. In the ninth, Kevin Youkilis reached on an infield single with two outs and wound up at second thanks to a Rays error. Jason Bay was intentionally walked, and Drew then lined a single to right off J.P. Howell to drive in the winning run and complete the comeback.

GAME 6

				R	H	E
Boston	0 1 1	0 0 2	0 0 0	**4**	**10**	**0**
Tampa Bay	1 0 0	0 1 0	0 0 0	**2**	**4**	**1**

W—Bos: Beckett. **L**—TB: Shields. **SV**—Bos: Papelbon. **LOB**—Bos: 12; TB: 4. **2B**—Bos: Ortiz, Drew. **HR**—Bos: Youkilis, Varitek; TB: Upton, Bartlett. **RBI**—Bos: Youkilis (2), Varitek, Ortiz; TB: Upton, Bartlett. **SB**—TB: Crawford. **CS**—TB: Navarro. **GIDP**—Bos: Youkilis; TB: Longoria. **IBB**—Bos: Ortiz. **HBP**—Bos: Bay; TB: Bartlett (2). **E**—TB: Bartlett. **T**—3:48. **A**—40,947.

Recap: The Boston Red Sox played like defending World Series champs from the start and beat the Tampa Bay Rays 4–2 to force a Game 7. Slumping Jason Varitek hit a tiebreaking home run in the sixth inning and Red Sox ace Josh Beckett, who struggled in his first two playoff starts, allowed only two runs and four hits in five innings despite reduced velocity. B.J. Upton tied an AL record in the first inning with his seventh home run of the postseason. After Boston went ahead 2-1, Tampa Bay tied it on Jason Bartlett 's fifth-inning homer. But after that, the Rays didn't get another hit.

GAME 7

				R	H	E
Boston	1 0 0	0 0 0	0 0 0	**1**	**3**	**0**
Tampa Bay	0 0 0	1 1 0	1 0 x	**3**	**6**	**1**

W—TB: Garza. **L**—Bos: Lester. **SV**—TB: Price. **LOB**—Bos: 8; TB: 3. **2B**—TB: Longoria, Aybar. **HR**—Bos: Pedroia; TB: Aybar. **RBI**—Bos: Pedroia, TB: Longoria, Baldelli, Aybar. **SB**—Bos: Pedroia. **CS**—Bos: Pedroia. **HBP**—Bos: Pedroia. **E**—TB: Bartlett. **T**—3:31. **A**—40,473.

Recap: Down to their last chance, the Tampa Bay Rays held off the defending champion Boston Red Sox 3–1 behind Matt Garza's masterful pitching. Facing another potential Red Sox comeback, Rays rookie David Price struck out J.D. Drew with the bases loaded to end the eighth inning and the Rays were on their way. Willy Aybar homered and Evan Longoria and Rocco Baldelli also drove in runs.

2008 World Series

Oct 22 ....Philadelphia 3 at Tampa Bay 2
Oct 23 ....Philadelphia 2 at Tampa Bay 4
Oct 25 ....Tampa Bay 4 at Philadelphia 5
Oct 26 ....Tampa Bay 10 at Philadelphia 2
Oct 27/29 ....Tampa Bay 3 at Philadelphia 4

(Philadelphia won series 4–1)

GAME 1

Philadelphia	2 0 0	1 0 0	0 0 0	**3**	**8**	**1**
Tampa Bay	0 0 0	1 1 0	0 0 0	**2**	**5**	**1**

W—Phi: Hamels. **L**—TB: Kazmir. **SV**—Phi: Lidge. **LOB**—Phi: 11; TB: 3. **2B**—Phi: Werth; TB: Iwamura. **HR**—Phi: Utley; TB: Crawford. **RBI**—Phi: Utley (2), Ruiz; TB: Crawford, Iwamura. **SB**—Phi: Utley (2); TB: Bartlett. **CS**—TB: Pena. **GIDP**—TB: Upton (2). **IBB**—Phi: Utley. **E**—Phi: Howard; TB: Pena. **T**—3:23. **A**—40,783.

Recap: The glamorous teams all eliminated, the Philadelphia Phillies and worst-to-first Tampa Bay Rays opened a most unexpected World Series. Cole Hamels escaped trouble to win his fourth postseason start, Chase Utley hit a two-run homer in the first inning and the Phillies beat Tampa Bay 3-2. While the City of Brotherly Love celebrated, the worst-to-first Rays flopped in their first game in baseball's ultimate event, eking out just five hits—none after the fifth inning. Hamels, MVP of the NL championship series, improved to 4–0 with a 1.55 ERA this postseason. He had only a pair of 1-2-3 innings, but the composed 24-year-old left-hander allowed two runs and five hits in seven innings. While the Rays' Carl Crawford homered, playoff stars B.J. Upton, Evan Longoria and Carlos Pena went a combined 0-for-12, striking out five times and hitting into two double plays. Leadoff man Akinori Iwamura had three of his team's five hits.

GAME 2

Philadelphia	0 0 0	0 0 0	0 1 1	**2**	**9**	**2**
Tampa Bay	2 1 0	1 0 0	0 0 X	**4**	**7**	**1**

W—TB: Shields. **L**—Phi: Myers. **LOB**—Phi: 11; TB: 4. **2B**—Phi: Howard, Ruiz (2). **HR**—Phi: Bruntlett. **RBI**—Phi: Bruntlett; TB: Upton, Pena, Longoria, Bartlett. **SAC**—TB: Bartlett. **SB**—Phi: Ruiz. **GIDP**—TB: Upton. **E**—Phi: Werth, Ruiz; TB: Longoria. **T**—3:05. **A**—40,843.

Recap: Big Game James finally lived up to his nickname. After losing two games in the ALCS, Tampa Bay starter James Shields stymied the slumping Philadelphia Phillies, pitching the plucky Rays to a 4–2 victory to tie the World Series at 1-all. Tampa Bay never really got a huge hit, but neither did the Phillies as Jimmy Rollins and crew fell to 1-for-28 with runners in scoring position. The Rays scored on Jason Bartlett's safety squeeze and built another rally when Rocco Baldelli walked on a checked swing that seemed to confuse players and umpires alike. Shields threw shutout ball into the sixth, outpitching Brett Myers and working out of trouble just as Hamels did in Game 1 for the Phillies. The Rays' 23-year-old reliever David Price, called up in September after he was the top pick in last year's draft, struck out Phillies slugger Ryan Howard with two on to end the seventh. The hard-throwing lefty gave up a pinch-hit homer to Eric Bruntlett in the eighth, then stayed on to close it out against Philadelphia's big boppers.

GAME 3

Tampa Bay	0 1 0	0 0 0	2 1 0	**4**	**6**	**1**
Philadelphia	1 1 0	0 0 2	0 0 1	**5**	**7**	**1**

W—Phi: Romero. **L**—TB: Howell. **LOB**—TB: 4; Phi: 6. **2B**—TB: Crawford, Navarro. **HR**—Phi: Ruiz, Utley, Howard. **RBI**—TB: Gross (2), Bartlett; Phi: Utley (2), Ruiz (2), Howard. **SF**—TB: Gross. **SB**—TB: Upton (3), Crawford; Phi: Werth. **CS**—Phi: Rollins. **IBB**—Phi: Victorino, Dobbs. **HBP**—Phi: Bruntlett. **WP**—TB: Garza, Balfour. **E**—TB: Navarro; Phi: Ruiz. **T**—3:41 (1:31 delayed start). **A**—45,900.

Recap: Game 3 was midnight madness, and then some. Carlos Ruiz finished off a wacky ninth inning with an infield single with the bases loaded, and the Phillies outlasted the Tampa Bay Rays 5–4 for a 2–1 Series lead. Ruiz, Chase Utley and Ryan Howard homered for the Phils, but it took three kooky plays to win it on a bases-loaded trickler with no outs. Rays reliever J.P. Howell hit Eric Bruntlett with a pitch to start the ninth. Enter Grant Balfour, who threw a wild pitch that caromed off the backstop to catcher Dioner Navarro, whose throw trying to get Bruntlett skipped into center field. With Bruntlett on third, the Rays issued two intentional walks and brought in right fielder Ben Zobrist for a five-man infield before Ruiz hit the game ender. And the end was almost as bizarre as the 10:06 p.m. start—the latest in Series history. The game's beginning was held up because of a rainstorm that delayed the first pitch of Phillies starter Jamie Moyer, who, at age 45, became the second-oldest player in Series history.

GAME 4

Tampa Bay	0 0 0	1 1 0	0 0 0	**2**	**5**	**2**
Philadelphia	1 0 1	3 1 0	0 4 X	**10**	**12**	**1**

W—Phi: Blanton. **L**—TB: Sonnanstine. **LOB**—TB: 7; Phi: 8. **2B**—Phi: Rollins (2), Werth. **HR**—TB: Crawford, Hinske; Phi: Howard (2), Blanton, Werth. **RBI**—TB: Crawford, Hinske; Phi: Burrell, Feliz, Howard (5), Blanton, Werth (2). **GIDP**—Phi: Burrell. **IBB**—Phi: Howard. **HBP**—TB: Crawford. **E**—TB: Iwamura (2); Phi: Romero. **T**—3:08. **A**—45,903.

Recap: Phillies starter Joe Blanton became the first pitcher in 34 years to homer in the World Series, Ryan Howard drove in five runs with two homers and Philadelphia romped over the Tampa Bay Rays 10–2 to move within one win of its first title since 1980. Jayson Werth also homered as the Phillies took a 3–1 lead in the best-of-seven Series and thrilled their frustrated, long-suffering fans. Rollins made a great escape from a rundown in the first inning -- perhaps with the help of an umpire's blown call -- energizing the Phillies and rattling the Rays. Then in the fourth inning, a day after hitting his first homer of the Series, Howard, the major league leader in homers and RBIs, hit a three-run drive off Andy Sonnanstine that made it 5–1 and sent screams through a whooped-up crowd of 45,903. He added a long, two-run shot against Dan Wheeler in the eighth. Blanton gave up only four hits—solo homers to Carl Crawford and pinch-hitter Eric Hinske—and struck out seven and walked two in six-plus innings.

2008 World Series (Cont.)

GAME 5

										R	H	E
Tampa Bay	0	0	0	1	0	1	1	0	0	**3**	**10**	**0**
Philadelphia	2	0	0	0	0	1	1	0	x	**4**	**8**	**1**

W—Phi: Romero. **L**—TB: Howell. **SV**—Phi: Lidge. **LOB**—TB: 5. Phi: 12. **2B**—TB: Pena; Phi: Jenkins, Burrell. **HR**—TB: Baldelli. **RBI**—TB: Longoria, Pena, Baldelli; Phi: Victorino (2), Werth, Feliz. **SAC**—TB: Howell; Phi: Rollins. **SB**—TB: Upton, Perez; Phi: Werth, Utley. **HBP**—Phi: Utley. **GIDP**—TB: Navarro, Bartlett, Upton. **E**—Phi: Rollins. **T**—3:28. **A**—45,940.

Recap: From losingest team to longest game, the Philadelphia Phillies are World Series champions. Closer Brad Lidge and the Phillies finished off the Tampa Bay Rays 4–3 in a three-inning sprint to win a suspended Game 5 nearly 50 hours after it started. Left in limbo by a two-day rainstorm, the Phillies seesawed to their first championship since 1980. Pedro Feliz singled home the go-ahead run in the seventh and Lidge closed out his perfect season to deliver the title Philly had craved for so long. Bundled in parkas and blankets, fans returned in force to Citizens Bank Park and saw the city claim its first major sports championship in 25 years. No more references needed to those sad-sack Phillies teams in the past and their 10,000-plus losses. But it was among the wackiest endings in baseball history, a best-of-seven series turned into a 3½-inning showdown when play resumed in the bottom of the sixth inning tied at 2. How bizarre? Hamels was a star in Game 5—yet the ace never stepped on the mound in the postponed portion of the game, instead Phillies reliever J.C. Romero got the win, his second of the Series. In addition, two Rays relievers warmed up to

GAME 5 *(CONT.)*

start for their side, and there was a pinch-hitter before a single pitch. All because the game was suspended two days earlier after rain turned the field into a quagmire, washing out the foul lines, creating a puddle at home plate and turning every ball into an adventure. Commissioner Bud Selig eventually suspended play, but he still was booed by the Phillies fans after the game when he presented the MVP trophy to Hamels, who went 4–0 in five postseason starts, beating the Rays in Game 1 and pitching six sharp innings in the rain to start Game 5.

Once play did resume, Philadelphia quickly scored in the bottom of the sixth on an RBI bloop to center that Rays shortstop Akinori Iwamura was unable to glove. Rocco Baldelli's solo home run off Ryan Madson tied it in the top of the seventh, however. Then, Pat Burrell led off the seventh with a drive off the center-field wall against J.P. Howell. Chad Bradford relieved Howell and one out later Feliz singled home pinch-runner Eric Bruntlett. Clinging to a one-run led in the top of the ninth, Lidge, who ended up 48-for-48 on save chances this year, including two during the Series, came in to seal the game. He retired two batters and then with a runner on second, struck out pinch-hitter Eric Hinske to end it. Catcher Carlos Ruiz ran out to grab Lidge, and his Phillies teammates sprinted to the mound to join them as towel-waving fans let loose. For Philly, it was more than a World Series win. It was a bit of redemption for all the losses, the jokes, the slights. "At first, I couldn't believe it. And then the gravity of what happened hit me," Lidge said.

2008 World Series Composite Box Score

TAMPA BAY

BATTING	AB	R	H	HR	RBI	Avg
Longoria	20	0	1	0	2	.050
Upton	20	3	5	0	1	.250
Crawford	19	4	5	2	2	.263
Iwamura	19	1	5	0	1	.263
Navarro	17	2	6	0	0	.353
Pena	17	1	2	0	2	.118
Bartlett	14	1	3	0	2	.214
Zobrist	7	0	1	0	0	.143
Baldelli	6	1	1	1	1	.167
Aybar	4	0	1	0	0	.250
Gross	3	0	0	0	2	.000
Floyd	3	1	1	0	0	.333
Hinske	2	1	1	1	1	.500
Pitchers	4	0	1	0	0	.250
Totals	**156**	**15**	**33**	**4**	**14**	**.212**

PITCHING	G	IP	H	BB	SO	ERA
Kazmir	2	10.0	10	10	9	4.50
Garza	1	6.0	6	2	7	6.00
Shields	1	5.2	7	2	4	0.00
Sonnanstine	1	4.0	6	3	2	6.75
Price	2	3.1	2	2	4	2.70
Balfour	3	3.0	4	3	2	3.00
Wheeler	3	2.2	3	1	3	6.75
Howell	3	2.1	2	1	5	7.72
Bradford	2	2.0	1	1	0	0.00
Jackson	1	2.0	2	1	1	4.50
Miller	2	1.0	1	1	1	18.00
Totals	**5**	**42.0**	**44**	**27**	**38**	**4.50**

PHILADELPHIA

BATTING	AB	R	H	HR	RBI	Avg
Rollins	22	4	5	0	0	.227
Howard	21	3	6	3	6	.286
Victorino	20	1	5	0	2	.250
Feliz	18	0	6	0	2	.333
Utley	18	5	3	2	4	.167
Werth	18	4	8	1	3	.444
Ruiz	16	2	6	1	3	.375
Burrell	14	0	1	0	1	.071
Coste	4	0	0	0	0	.000
Bruntlett	3	3	1	1	1	.333
Dobbs	3	0	1	0	0	.333
Jenkins	2	1	1	0	0	.500
Stairs	1	0	0	0	0	.000
Pitchers	8	1	1	1	1	.125
Totals	**168**	**24**	**44**	**9**	**23**	**.262**

PITCHING	G	IP	H	BB	SO	ERA
Hamels	1	13.0	10	3	8	2.77
Myers	1	7.0	7	3	2	3.86
Moyer	1	6.1	5	1	5	4.26
Blanton	3	6.0	4	2	7	3.00
Romero	3	4.2	2	0	4	0.00
Madson	4	3.2	3	0	6	4.91
Lidge	2	2.0	1	0	3	0.00
Durbin	1	0.2	1	1	0	0.00
Eyre	2	0.2	0	0	1	0.00
Totals	**5**	**44.0**	**33**	**10**	**36**	**2.86**

2008 Individual Leaders

National League Batting

BATTING AVERAGE

Chipper Jones, Atl	.364
Albert Pujols, StL	.357
Matt Holliday, Col	.321
Cristian Guzman, Was	.316
Lance Berkman, Hou	.312
RyanTheriot, Chi	.307
Brian Giles, SD	.306
Randy Winn, SF	.306
Andre Ethier, LAD	.305
Skip Schumaker, StL	.302
David Wright, NYM	.302

HITS

Jose Reyes, NYM	204
David Wright, NYM	189
Albert Pujols, StL	187
Cristian Guzman, Was	183
Randy Winn, SF	183
Derek Lee, CHC	181
Miguel Tejada, Hou	179
Stephen Drew, Ari	178
Ryan Theriot, CHC	178
Hanley Ramirez, Fla	177
Chase Utley, Phi	177

DOUBLES

Lance Berkman, Hou	46
Nate McLouth, Pit	46
Corey Hart, Mil	45
Stephen Drew, Ari	44
Albert Pujols, StL	44
Aramis Ramirez, CHC	44

STOLEN BASES

Willy Taveras, Col	68
Jose Reyes, NYM	56
Jimmy Rollins, Phi	47
Michael Bourn, Hou	41
Juan Pierre, LAD	40

TRIPLES

Jose Reyes, NYM	19
Stephen Drew, Ari	11
Fred Lewis, SF	11
Jimmy Rollins, Phi	9
Shane Victorino, Phi	8

Five tied with 7.

HOME RUNS

Ryan Howard, Phi	48
Adam Dunn, Ari	40
Carlos Delgado, NYM	38
Ryan Braun, Mil	37
Ryan Ludwick, StL	37
Albert Pujols, StL	37
Adrian Gonzalez, SD	36
Prince Fielder, Mil	34
Pat Burrell, Phi	33
Hanley Ramirez, Fla	33
David Wright, NYM	33
Chase Utley, Phi	33

RUNS SCORED

Hanley Ramirez, Fla	125
Carlos Beltran, NYM	116
David Wright, NYM	115
Lance Berkman, Hou	114
Nate McLouth, Pit	113
Jose Reyes, NYM	113
Chase Utley, Phi	113
Matt Holiday, Col	107
Ryan Howard, Phi	105
Ryan Ludwick, StL	104
Mark DeRosa, CHC	103
Adrian Gonzalez, SD	103

RUNS BATTED IN

Ryan Howard, Phi	146
David Wright, NYM	124
Adrian Gonzalez, SD	119
Albert Pujols, StL	116
Carlos Delgado, NYM	115
Ryan Ludwick, StL	113
Carlos Beltran, NYM	112
Aramis Ramirez, CHC	111
Lance Berkman, Hou	106
Ryan Braun, Mil	106

SLUGGING PERCENTAGE

Albert Pujols, StL	.653
Ryan Ludwick, StL	.591
Chipper Jones, Atl	.574
Lance Berkman, Hou	.567
Ryan Braun, Mil	.553

ON-BASE PERCENTAGE

Chipper Jones, Atl	.470
Albert Pujols, StL	.462
Lance Berkman, Hou	.420
Matt Holliday, Col	.409
Hanley Ramirez, Fla	.400
Brian Giles, SD	.398

BASES ON BALLS

Adam Dunn, Ari	122
Albert Pujols, StL	104
Pat Burrell, Phi	102
Lance Berkman, Hou	99
David Wright, NYM	94

National League Pitching

EARNED RUN AVERAGE

Johan Santana, NYM	2.53
Tim Lincecum, SF	2.62
Jake Peavy, SD	2.85
Ryan Dempster, CHC	2.96
Cole Hamels, Phi	3.09
Ben Sheets, Mil	3.09
Chad Billingsley, LAD	3.14
Edinson Volquez, Cin	3.21
Derek Lowe, LAD	3.24
Brandon Webb, Ari	3.30

SAVES

Jose Valverde, Hou	44
Brad Lidge, Phi	41
Brian Wilson, SF	41
Francisco Cordero, Cin	34
Kerry Wood, CHC	34
Brian Fuentes, Col	30
Trevor Hoffman, SD	30
Kevin Gregg, Fla	29
SalomonTorres, Mil	28

WINS

Brandon Webb, Ari	22
Tim Lincecum, SF	18
Ryan Dempster, CHC	17
Ted Lilly, CHC	17
Roy Oswalt, Hou	17
Edinson Volquez, Cin	17

Five tied with 16.

GAMES PITCHED

Pedro Feliciano, NYM	86
Will Ohman, Atl	83
Carlos Marmol, CHC	82
Joe Smith, NYM	82
Luis Ayala, NYM	81
J.C. Romero, Phi	81

INNINGS PITCHED

Johan Santana, NYM	234.1
Cole Hamels, Phi	227.1
Tim Lincecum, SF	227.0
Brandon Webb, Ari	226.2
Matt Cain, SF	217.2

STRIKEOUTS

Tim Lincecum, SF	265
Dan Haren, Ari	206
Johan Santana, NYM	206
Edinson Volquez, Cin	206
Chad Billingsley, LAD	201
Cole Hamels, Phi	196
Ryan Dempster, CHC	187
Matt Cain, SF	186
Ricky Nolasco, Fla	186

COMPLETE GAMES

Player	CG
C.C. Sabathia, Mil	7
Ben Sheets, Mil	5
Roy Oswalt, Hou	3
Johan Santana, NYM	3
Brandon Webb, Ari	3

SHUTOUTS

Player	SHO
C.C. Sabathia, Mil	3
Ben Sheets, Mil	3
Cole Hamels, Phi	2

2008 Individual Leaders *(Cont.)*

American League Batting

BATTING AVERAGE

Joe Mauer, Min .328
Dustin Pedroia, Bos .326
Milton Bradley, Tex .321
Ian Kinsler, Tex .319
Magglio Ordonez, Det .317
Kevin Youkillis, Bos .312
Ichiro Suzuki, Sea .310
David DeJesus, KC .307
Placido Polanco, Det .307
Nick Markakis, Bal .306

HITS

Dustin Pedroia, Bos 213
Ichiro Suzuki, Sea 213
Jose Lopez, Sea 191
Josh Hamilton, Tex 190
Justin Morneau, Min 187
Orlando Cabrera, CWS 186
Raul Ibanez, Sea 186
Alex Rios, Tor 185
Michael Young, Tex 183
Aubrey Huff, Bal 182
Nick Markakis, Bal 182

DOUBLES

Dustin Pedroia, Bos 54
Brian Roberts, Bal 51
Aubrey Huff, Bal 48
Nick Markakis, Bal 48
Justin Morneau, Min 47
Alex Rios, Tor 47

TRIPLES

Curtis Granderson, Det 13
Carl Crawford, TB 10
Akinori Iwamura, TB 9
Alex Rios, Tor 8
Brian Roberts, Bal 8

HOME RUNS

Miguel Cabrera, Det 37
Carlos Quentin, CWS 36
Alex Rodriquez, NYY 35
Jermaine Dye, CWS 34
Jim Thome, CWS 34
Jack Cust, Oak 33
Grady Sizemore, Cle 33
Jason Giambi, NYY 32
Josh Hamilton, Tex 32
Aubrey Huff, Bal 32

RUNS SCORED

Dustin Pedroia, Bos 118
Curtis Granderson, Det 112
Brian Roberts, Bal 107
Nick Markakis, Bal 106
Jhonny Peralta, Cle 104
Alex Rodriquez, NYY 104
Ichiro Suzuki, Sea 103
Ian Kinsler, Tex 102
Michael Young, Tex 102
Grady Sizemore, Cle 101

STOLEN BASES

Jacoby Ellsbury, Bos 50
B.J Upton, TB 44
Ichiro Suzuki, Sea 43
Brian Roberts, Bal 40
Grady Sizemore, Cle 38

RUNS BATTED IN

Josh Hamilton, Tex 130
Justin Morneau, Min 129
Miguel Cabrera, Det 127
Kevin Youkillis, Bos 115
Raul Ibanez, Sea 110
Aubrey Huff, Bal 108
Melvin Mora, Bal 104
Magglio Ordonez, Det 103
Alex Rodriguez, NYY 103
Carlos Pena, TB 102

SLUGGING PERCENTAGE

Alex Rodriguez, NYY .573
Carlos Quentin, CWS .571
Kevin Youkillis, Bos .569
Milton Bradley, Tex .563
Aubrey Huff, Bal .552

ON-BASE PERCENTAGE

Milton Bradley, Tex .436
Joe Mauer, Min .413
Nick Markakis, Bal .406
Carlos Quentin, CWS .394
Alex Rodriguez, NYY .392

BASES ON BALLS

Jack Cust, Oak 111
Nick Markakis, Bal 99
Grady Sizemore, Cle 98
B.J. Upton, TB 97
Carlos Pena, TB 96

American League Pitching

EARNED RUN AVERAGE

Cliff Lee, Cle 2.54
Roy Halladay, Tor 2.78
Daisuke Matsuzaka, Bos 2.90
Jon Lester, Bos 3.21
John Danks, CWS 3.32
Mike Mussina, NYY 3.37
Joe Saunders, LAA 3.41
Scott Baker, Min 3.45
Felix Hernandez, Sea 3.45
Zack Greinke, KC 3.47

SAVES

Francisco Rodriguez, LAA 62
Joakim Soria, KC 42
Jonathan Papelbon, Bos 41
Joe Nathan, Min 39
Mariano Rivera, NYY 39
B.J.Ryan, Tor 32
George Sherrill, Bal 31
Bobby Jenks, CWS 30
Troy Percival, TB 28
C.J. Wilson, Tex 24

WINS

Cliff Lee, Cle 22
Roy Halladay, Tor 20
Mike Mussina, NYY 20
A.J. Burnett, Tor 18
Daisuke Matsuzaka, Bos 18
Gavin Floyd, CWS 17
Joe Saunders, LAA 17

GAMES PITCHED

Matt Guerrier, Min 76
Francisco Rodriguez, LAA 76
Dennys Reyes, Min 75
Jamey Wright, Tex 75
Matt Thornton, CWS 74
Manny Delcarmen, Bos 73

INNINGS PITCHED

Roy Halladay, Tor 246.0
Cliff Lee, Cle 223.1
A.J. Burnett, Tor 221.1
Ervin Santana, LAA 219.0

SHUTOUTS

Matt Garza, TB 2
Roy Halladay, Tor 2
Cliff Lee, Cle 2
Jon Lester, Bos 2

COMPLETE GAMES

Roy Halladay, Tor 9
Cliff Lee, Cle 4

Six tied with 3.

STRIKEOUTS

A.J. Burnett, Tor 231
Ervin Santana, LAA 214
Roy Halladay, Tor 206
Javier Vazquez, CWS 200
Zack Greinke, KC 183
Gil Meche, KC 183
Felix Hernandez, Sea 175
Josh Beckett, Bos 172
Cliff Lee, Cle 170
Scott Kazmir, TB 166

2008 Team Statistics

National League

TEAM BATTING	G	AB	R	H	2B	3B	HR	TB	RBI	BA	OBP	SLG	OPS
St. Louis Cardinals	162	5636	779	1585	283	26	174	2442	744	.281	.350	.433	.783
Chicago Cubs	161	5588	855	1552	329	21	184	2475	811	.278	.354	.443	.797
Atlanta Braves	162	5604	753	1514	316	33	130	2286	721	.270	.345	.408	.753
New York Mets	162	5606	799	1491	274	38	172	2357	751	.266	.340	.420	.761
Los Angeles Dodgers	162	5506	700	1455	271	29	137	2195	659	.264	.333	.399	.732
Colorado Rockies	162	5557	747	1462	310	28	160	2308	714	.263	.336	.415	.751
Houston Astros	161	5451	712	1432	284	22	167	2261	684	.263	.323	.415	.737
San Francisco Giants	162	5543	640	1452	311	37	94	2119	606	.262	.321	.382	.703
Pittsburgh Pirates	162	5628	735	1454	314	21	153	2269	705	.258	.320	.403	.723
Philadelphia Phillies	162	5509	799	1407	291	36	214	2412	762	.255	.332	.438	.770
Florida Marlins	161	5499	770	1397	302	28	208	2379	741	.254	.326	.433	.759
Milwaukee Brewers	162	5535	750	1398	324	35	198	2386	722	.253	.325	.431	.757
Arizona Diamondbacks	162	5409	720	1355	318	47	159	2244	683	.251	.327	.415	.742
Washington Nationals	161	5491	641	1376	269	26	117	2048	608	.251	.323	.373	.696
San Diego Padres	162	5568	637	1390	264	27	154	2170	615	.250	.317	.390	.707
Cincinnati Reds	162	5465	704	1351	269	24	187	2229	677	.247	.321	.408	.729

TEAM PITCHING	GP	W	L	SV	SVO	CG	SHO	R	ERA	IP	Ks	BB
Los Angeles Dodgers	162	84	78	35	55	5	11	648	3.68	1447.1	1205	480
Milwaukee Brewers	162	90	72	45	71	12	10	689	3.85	1455.2	1110	528
Chicago Cubs	161	97	64	44	68	2	8	624	3.87	1450.2	1264	548
Philadelphia Phillies	162	92	70	47	62	4	11	680	3.88	1449.2	1081	533
Arizona Diamondbacks	162	82	80	39	62	6	9	706	3.98	1434.2	1229	451
New York Mets	162	89	73	43	72	5	12	715	4.07	1464.1	1181	590
St. Louis Cardinals	162	86	76	42	73	2	7	725	4.19	1454.0	957	496
Houston Astros	161	86	75	48	65	4	12	743	4.36	1425.1	1095	492
San Francisco Giants	162	72	90	41	60	4	12	759	4.38	1442.0	1240	652
San Diego Padres	162	63	99	30	56	3	6	764	4.41	1458.1	1100	561
Florida Marlins	161	84	77	36	60	2	8	767	4.43	1435.1	1127	586
Atlanta Braves	162	72	90	26	44	2	7	778	4.46	1440.2	1076	586
Cincinnati Reds	162	74	88	34	55	2	6	800	4.55	1442.1	1227	557
Washington Nationals	161	59	102	28	56	2	8	825	4.66	1434.0	1063	588
Colorado Rockies	162	74	88	36	59	3	8	822	4.77	1446.0	1041	562
Pittsburgh Pirates	162	67	95	34	56	3	7	884	5.08	1455.0	963	657

2008 Team Statistics

American League

TEAM BATTING	G	AB	R	H	2B	3B	HR	TB	RBI	BA	OBP	SLG	OPS
Texas Rangers	162	5728	901	1619	376	35	194	2647	867	.283	.354	.462	.816
Boston Red Sox	162	5596	845	1565	353	33	173	2503	807	.280	.358	.447	.805
Minnesota Twins	163	5641	829	1572	298	49	111	2301	791	.279	.340	.408	.748
Detroit Tigers	162	5641	821	1529	293	41	200	2504	780	.271	.340	.444	.784
New York Yankees	162	5572	789	1512	289	20	180	2381	758	.271	.342	.427	.769
Kansas City Royals	162	5608	691	1507	303	28	120	2226	650	.269	.320	.397	.717
Los Angeles Angels	162	5540	765	1486	274	25	159	2287	721	.268	.330	.413	.743
Baltimore Orioles	161	5559	782	1486	322	30	172	2384	750	.267	.333	.429	.762
Seattle Mariners	162	5643	671	1498	285	20	124	2195	631	.265	.318	.389	.707
Toronto Blue Jays	162	5503	714	1453	303	32	126	2198	681	.264	.331	.399	.731
Chicago White Sox	163	5553	811	1458	296	13	235	2485	785	.263	.332	.448	.780
Cleveland Indians	162	5543	805	1455	339	22	171	2351	772	.262	.339	.424	.763
Tampa Bay Rays	162	5541	774	1443	284	37	180	2341	735	.260	.340	.422	.762
Oakland Athletics	161	5451	646	1318	270	23	125	2009	610	.242	.318	.369	.686

TEAM PITCHING	GP	W	L	SV	SVO	CG	SHO	R	ERA	IP	Ks	BB
Toronto Blue Jays	162	86	76	44	56	15	13	610	3.49	1446.2	1184	467
Tampa Bay Rays	162	97	65	52	68	7	12	671	3.82	1457.2	1143	526
Los Angeles Angels	162	100	62	66	89	7	10	697	3.99	1451.1	1106	457
Boston Red Sox	162	95	67	47	69	5	16	694	4.01	1446.1	1185	548
Oakland Athletics	161	75	86	33	52	4	7	690	4.01	1435.0	1061	576
Chicago White Sox	163	89	74	34	52	4	10	729	4.06	1457.2	1147	460
Minnesota Twins	163	88	75	42	65	5	10	745	4.16	1459.0	995	406
New York Yankees	162	89	73	42	51	1	11	727	4.28	1441.2	1141	489
Cleveland Indians	162	81	81	31	51	10	13	761	4.45	1437.0	986	444
Kansas City Royals	162	75	87	44	60	2	8	781	4.48	1445.2	1085	515
Seattle Mariners	162	61	101	36	67	4	4	811	4.73	1435.1	1016	626
Detroit Tigers	162	74	88	34	62	1	2	857	4.90	1445.0	991	644
Baltimore Orioles	161	68	93	35	59	4	4	869	5.13	1422.0	922	687
Texas Rangers	162	79	83	36	64	6	8	967	5.37	1442.0	963	625

National League Team-by-Team Statistical Leaders *(Cont.)*

Arizona Diamondbacks

BATTING	G	AB	R	H	2B	3B	HR	RBI	TB	BB	SO	SB	OBP	SLG	BA
Chris B. Young	160	625	85	155	42	7	22	85	277	62	165	14	.315	.443	.248
Stephen Drew	152	611	91	178	44	11	21	67	307	41	109	3	.333	.502	.291
Conor Jackson	144	540	87	162	31	6	12	75	241	59	61	10	.376	.446	.300
Mark Reynolds	152	539	87	129	28	3	28	97	247	64	204	11	.320	.458	.239
Adam Dunn	158	517	79	122	23	0	40	100	265	122	164	2	.386	.513	.236
Orlando Hudson	107	407	54	124	29	3	8	41	183	40	62	4	.367	.450	.305
Justin Upton	108	356	52	89	19	6	15	42	165	54	121	1	.353	.463	.250
Chris Snyder	115	334	47	79	22	1	16	64	151	56	101	0	.348	.452	.237
Chad Tracy	88	273	25	73	16	0	8	39	113	16	49	0	.308	.414	.267
Augie Ojeda	105	231	27	56	9	2	0	17	69	26	24	0	.343	.299	.242
Eric Byrnes	52	206	28	43	13	1	6	23	76	16	36	4	.272	.369	.209
Miguel Montero	70	184	24	47	16	1	5	18	80	19	49	0	.330	.435	.255
Chris Burke	86	165	20	32	5	1	2	12	45	27	33	5	.310	.273	.194
Tony Clark	108	151	12	34	5	0	3	24	48	31	55	0	.359	.318	.225
Alex Romero	78	135	13	31	8	2	1	12	46	3	20	4	.250	.341	.230

PITCHING	GP	GS	W–L	SV	SHO	R	ERA	IP	Ks	BB
Brandon Webb	34	34	22–7	0	1	95	3.30	226.2	183	65
Dan Haren	33	33	16–8	0	1	86	3.33	216.0	206	40
Randy Johnson	30	30	11–10	0	0	92	3.91	184.0	173	44
Doug Davis	26	26	6–8	0	0	76	4.32	146.0	112	64
Micah Owings	22	18	6–9	0	0	73	5.93	104.2	87	41
Chad Qualls	77	0	4–8	9	17	29	2.81	73.2	71	18
Tony Pena	72	0	3–2	3	8	38	4.33	72.2	52	17
Jon Rauch	26	0	0–6	1	0	18	6.16	23.1	22	9
Brandon Lyon	61	0	3–5	26	0	34	4.70	59.1	44	13
Wilfredo Ledezma	28	6	0–2	0	0	29	4.17	58.1	53	41
Yusmerio Petit	19	8	3–5	0	0	29	4.31	56.1	42	14
Max Scherzer	16	7	0–4	0	0	24	3.05	56.0	66	21
Juan Cruz	57	0	4–0	0	0	17	2.61	51.2	71	31
Enrique Gonzalez	17	6	1–3	0	0	34	6.00	48.0	32	21

Atlanta Braves

BATTING	G	AB	R	H	2B	3B	HR	RBI	TB	BB	SO	SB	OBP	SLG	BA
Jeff Francoeur	155	599	70	143	33	3	11	71	215	39	111	0	.294	.359	.239
Kelly Johnson	150	547	86	157	39	6	12	69	244	52	113	11	.349	.446	.287
Yunel Escobar	136	514	71	148	24	2	10	60	206	59	62	2	.366	.401	.288
Brian McCann	145	509	68	153	42	1	23	87	266	57	64	5	.373	.523	.301
Chipper Jones	128	439	82	160	24	1	22	75	252	90	61	4	.470	.574	.364
Gregor Blanco	144	430	52	108	14	4	1	38	133	74	99	13	.366	.309	.251
Mark Teixeira	103	381	63	108	27	0	20	78	195	65	70	0	.390	.512	.283
Mark Kotsay	88	318	39	92	17	3	6	37	133	25	34	2	.340	.418	.289
Omar Infante	96	317	45	93	24	3	3	40	132	22	44	0	.338	.416	.293
Martin Prado	78	228	36	73	18	4	2	33	105	21	29	3	.377	.461	.320
Greg Norton	111	171	27	42	10	0	7	31	73	31	40	0	.361	.427	.246
Casey Kotchman	43	152	18	36	4	1	2	20	48	18	16	0	.331	.316	.294
Josh Anderson	40	136	21	40	7	1	3	12	58	8	33	10	.338	.426	.294
Matt Diaz	43	135	9	33	2	0	2	14	41	3	32	4	.264	.304	.244

PITCHING	GP	GS	W–L	SV	SHO	R	ERA	IP	Ks	BB
Jair Jurrjens	31	31	13–10	0	0	87	3.68	188.1	139	70
Jorge Campillo	39	35	8–7	0	0	74	3.91	158.2	107	38
Tim Hudson	23	22	11–7	0	1	53	3.17	142.0	85	40
Jo-Jo Reyes	23	22	3–11	0	0	77	5.81	113.0	78	52
Jeff Bennett	72	4	3–7	3	0	44	3.70	97.1	68	47
Mike Hampton	13	13	3–4	0	0	45	4.85	78.0	38	28
Charlie Morton	16	15	4–8	0	0	56	6.15	74.2	48	41
Blaine Boyer	76	0	2–6	1	0	26	3.00	72.0	70	15
Tom Glavine	13	13	2–4	0	0	40	5.54	63.1	37	37
Buddy Carlyle	45	0	2–0	0	0	26	3.59	62.2	59	26
Will Ohman	83	0	4–1	1	0	27	3.68	58.2	53	22
Manny Acosta	46	0	3–5	3	0	25	3.57	53.0	31	26
Julian Tavarez	43	0	1–4	0	0	30	4.71	42.0	45	19
Mike Gonzalez	36	0	0–3	14	0	21	4.28	33.2	44	14
Vladimir Nunez	23	0	1–2	0	0	14	3.86	32.2	24	19

National League Team-by-Team Statistical Leaders *(Cont.)*

Chicago Cubs

BATTING	G	AB	R	H	2B	3B	HR	RBI	TB	BB	SO	SB	OBP	SLG	BA
Derek Lee	155	623	93	181	41	3	20	90	288	71	119	8	.361	.462	.291
Ryan Theriot	149	580	85	178	19	4	1	38	208	73	58	22	.387	.359	.307
Aramis Ramirez	149	554	97	160	44	1	27	111	287	74	94	2	.380	.518	.289
Mark DeRosa	149	505	103	144	30	3	21	87	243	69	106	6	.376	.481	.285
Kosuke Fukudome	150	501	79	129	25	3	10	58	190	81	104	12	.359	.379	.257
Geovany Soto	141	494	66	141	35	2	23	86	249	62	121	0	.364	.504	.285
Alfonso Soriano	109	453	76	127	27	0	29	75	241	43	103	19	.344	.532	.280
Jim Edmonds	111	340	53	80	19	2	20	55	163	55	82	2	.343	.479	.235
Reed Johnson	109	333	52	101	21	0	6	50	140	19	68	5	.358	.420	.303
Mike Fontenot	119	243	42	74	22	1	9	40	125	34	51	2	.395	.514	.305
Ronny Cedeno	99	216	36	58	12	0	2	28	76	18	41	4	.328	.352	.269
Henry Blanco	58	120	15	35	3	3	3	12	47	6	22	0	.325	.392	.292
Daryle Ward	89	102	8	22	7	0	4	17	41	16	24	0	.319	.402	.216

PITCHING	GP	GS	W–L	SV	SHO	R	ERA	IP	Ks	BB
Ryan Dempster	33	33	17–6	0	0	75	2.96	206.2	187	76
Ted Lilly	34	34	17–9	0	0	96	4.09	204.2	184	64
Carlos Zambrano	30	30	14–6	0	1	85	3.91	188.2	130	72
Jason Marquis	29	28	11–9	0	0	87	4.53	167.0	91	70
Carlos Marmol	82	0	2–4	7	0	30	2.68	87.1	114	41
Rich Harden	12	12	5–1	0	0	17	1.77	71.0	89	30
Bob Howry	72	0	7–5	1	0	44	5.35	70.2	59	13
Kerry Wood	65	0	5–4	34	0	24	3.26	66.1	84	18
Sean Marshall	34	7	3–5	1	0	28	3.86	65.1	58	23
Sean Gallagher	12	10	3–4	0	0	31	4.45	58.2	49	22
Jon Lieber	26	1	2–3	0	0	24	4.05	46.2	27	6
Michael Wuertz	45	0	1–1	0	0	23	3.63	44.2	30	20
Neal Cotts	50	0	0–2	0	0	18	4.29	35.2	43	13
Kevin Hart	21	0	2–2	0	0	24	6.51	27.2	23	18

Cincinnati Reds

BATTING	G	AB	R	H	2B	3B	HR	RBI	TB	BB	SO	SB	OBP	SLG	BA
Brandon Phillips	141	559	80	146	24	7	21	78	247	39	93	23	.312	.442	.261
Joey Votto	151	526	69	156	32	3	24	84	266	59	102	7	.368	.506	.297
Edwin Encarnacion	146	506	75	127	29	1	26	68	236	61	102	1	.340	.466	.251
Jeff Keppinger	121	459	45	122	24	2	3	43	159	30	24	3	.310	.346	.266
Jay Bruce	108	413	63	105	17	1	21	52	187	33	110	4	.314	.453	.254
Corey Patterson	135	366	46	75	17	2	10	34	126	16	57	14	.238	.344	.205
Ken Griffey Jr.	102	359	51	88	20	1	15	53	155	61	64	0	.355	.432	.245
Paul Bako	99	299	30	65	11	2	6	35	98	34	90	0	.299	.328	.217
Jerry Hairston Jr.	80	261	47	85	20	2	6	36	127	23	36	15	.384	.487	.326
David Ross	52	134	17	31	9	0	3	13	49	32	36	0	.381	.366	.231
Ryan Freel	48	131	17	39	8	0	0	10	47	8	18	6	.340	.359	.298
Javier Valentin	94	129	10	33	8	0	4	18	53	14	27	0	.326	.411	.256
Jolbert Cabrera	48	115	17	29	6	1	3	12	46	8	29	2	.310	.400	.252
Chris Dickerson	31	102	20	31	9	2	6	15	62	17	35	5	.413	.608	.304

PITCHING	GP	GS	W–L	SV	SHO	R	ERA	IP	Ks	BB
Bronson Arroyo	34	34	15–11	0	0	116	4.77	200.0	163	68
Edinson Volquez	33	32	17–6	0	0	82	3.21	196.0	206	93
Aaron Harang	30	29	6–17	0	1	104	4.78	184.1	153	50
Johnny Cueto	31	31	9–14	0	0	101	4.81	174.0	158	68
Jeremy Affeldt	74	0	1–1	0	0	36	3.33	78.1	80	25
Josh Fogg	22	14	2–7	0	0	69	7.58	78.1	45	27
Francisco Cordero	72	0	5–4	34	0	28	3.33	70.1	78	38
Mike Lincoln	64	0	2–5	0	0	37	4.48	70.1	57	24
David Weathers	72	0	4–6	0	0	27	3.25	69.1	46	30
Jared Burton	54	0	5–1	0	0	24	3.22	58.2	58	25
Bill Bray	63	0	2–2	0	0	19	2.87	47.0	54	24
Gary Majewski	37	0	1–0	0	0	31	6.53	40.0	27	15

National League Team-by-Team Statistical Leaders *(Cont.)*

Colorado Rockies

BATTING	G	AB	R	H	2B	3B	HR	RBI	TB	BB	SO	SB	OBP	SLG	BA
Garrett Atkins	155	611	86	175	32	3	21	99	276	40	100	1	.328	.452	.286
Matt Holliday	139	539	107	173	38	2	25	88	290	74	104	28	.409	.538	.321
Brad Hawpe	133	488	69	138	24	3	25	85	243	76	134	2	.381	.498	.283
Willy Taveras	133	479	64	120	15	2	1	26	142	36	79	68	.308	.296	.251
Clint Barmes	107	393	47	114	25	6	11	44	184	17	69	13	.322	.468	.290
Troy Tulowitzki	101	377	48	99	24	2	8	46	151	38	56	1	.332	.401	.263
Chris Iannetta	104	333	50	88	22	2	18	65	168	56	92	0	.390	.505	.264
Jeff Baker	104	299	55	80	22	1	12	48	140	26	85	4	.322	.468	.268
Todd Helton	83	299	39	79	16	0	7	29	116	61	50	0	.391	.388	.264
Ian Stewart	81	266	33	69	18	2	10	41	121	30	94	1	.349	.455	.259
Yorvit Torrealba	70	236	19	58	17	0	6	31	93	12	44	0	.293	.394	.246
Ryan Spilborghs	89	233	38	73	14	2	6	36	109	38	41	7	.407	.468	.313
Omar Quintanilla	81	210	28	50	17	0	2	15	73	15	46	0	.288	.348	.238
Scott Podsednik	93	162	22	41	8	1	1	15	54	16	28	12	.322	.333	.253
Seth Smith	67	108	13	28	7	0	4	15	47	15	23	1	.350	.435	.259

PITCHING	GP	GS	W–L	SV	SHO	R	ERA	IP	Ks	BB
Aaron Cook	32	32	16–9	0	1	102	3.96	211.1	96	48
Ubaldo Jimenez	34	34	12–12	0	0	97	3.99	198.2	172	103
Jeff Francis	24	24	4–10	0	0	84	5.01	143.2	94	49
Jorge De La Rosa	28	23	10–8	0	0	77	4.92	130.0	128	62
Glendon Rusch	35	9	5–5	0	0	50	5.16	83.2	55	25
Manny Corpas	76	0	3–4	4	0	41	4.52	79.2	50	23
Taylor Buchholz	63	0	6–6	1	0	23	2.17	66.1	56	18
Matt Herges	58	0	3–4	0	0	40	5.04	64.1	46	24
Brian Fuentes	67	0	1–5	30	0	22	2.73	62.2	82	22
Greg Reynolds	14	13	2–8	0	0	58	8.13	62.0	22	26
Jason Grilli	51	0	3–2	1	0	22	2.93	61.1	59	31
Ryan Speier	43	0	2–1	0	0	23	4.06	51.0	33	18
Luis Vizcaino	43	0	1–2	0	0	28	5.28	46.0	49	19
Mark Redman	10	9	2–5	0	0	40	7.54	45.1	20	16

Florida Marlins

BATTING	G	AB	R	H	2B	3B	HR	RBI	TB	BB	SO	SB	OBP	SLG	BA
Jorge Cantu	155	628	92	174	41	0	29	95	302	40	111	6	.327	.481	.277
Hanley Ramirez	153	589	125	177	34	4	33	67	318	92	122	35	.400	.540	.301
Dan Uggla	146	531	97	138	37	1	32	92	273	77	171	5	.360	.514	.260
Jeremy Hermida	142	502	74	125	22	3	17	61	204	48	138	6	.323	.406	.249
Mike Jacobs	141	477	67	118	27	2	32	93	245	36	119	1	.299	.514	.247
Cody Ross	145	461	59	120	29	5	22	73	225	33	116	1	.316	488	.260
Josh Willingham	102	351	54	89	21	5	15	51	165	48	82	3	.364	.470	.254
Luis Gonzalez	136	341	30	89	26	1	8	47	141	41	43	1	.336	.413	.261
Alfredo Amezaga	125	311	41	82	13	5	3	32	114	19	47	8	.312	.367	.264
Wes Helms	132	251	28	61	11	0	5	31	87	17	65	0	.299	.347	.243
Matt Treanor	65	206	18	49	7	0	2	23	62	18	53	1	.306	.301	.238
John Baker	61	197	32	59	14	0	5	32	88	30	48	0	.392	.447	.299
Paul Lo Duca	67	173	16	42	9	0	0	15	51	15	11	1	.321	.295	.243
Mike Rabelo	34	109	9	22	1	0	3	10	32	8	25	0	.256	.294	.202

PITCHING	GP	GS	W–L	SV	SHO	R	ERA	IP	Ks	BB
Ricky Nolasco	34	32	15–8	0	1	88	3.52	212.1	186	42
Scott Olsen	33	33	8–11	0	0	106	4.20	201.2	113	69
Mark Hendrickson	36	19	7–8	0	0	87	5.45	133.2	81	48
Andrew Miller	29	20	6–10	0	0	78	5.87	107.1	89	56
Josh Johnson	14	14	7–1	0	0	36	3.61	87.1	77	27
Chris Volstad	15	14	6–4	0	0	30	2.88	84.1	52	36
Kevin Gregg	72	0	7–8	29	0	30	3.41	68.2	58	37
Renyel Pinto	67	0	2–5	0	0	33	4.45	64.2	56	39
Doug Waechter	48	0	4–2	0	0	29	3.69	63.1	46	21
Matt Lindstrom	66	0	3–3	5	0	21	3.14	57.1	43	26
Logan Kensing	48	0	3–1	0	0	26	4.23	55.1	55	33
Joe Nelson	59	0	3–1	1	0	16	2.00	54.0	60	22

National League Team-by-Team Statistical Leaders *(Cont.)*

Houston Astros

BATTING	G	AB	R	H	2B	3B	HR	RBI	TB	BB	SO	SB	OBP	SLG	BA
Miguel Tejada	158	632	92	179	38	3	13	66	262	24	72	7	.314	.415	.283
Hunter Pence	157	595	78	160	34	4	25	83	277	40	124	11	.318	.466	.269
Lance Berkman	159	554	114	173	46	4	29	106	314	99	108	18	.420	.567	.312
Michael Bourn	138	467	57	107	10	4	5	29	140	37	111	41	.288	.300	.229
Carlos Lee	115	436	61	137	27	0	28	100	248	37	49	4	.368	.569	.314
Jose Castillo	127	426	46	105	29	4	6	37	160	27	81	2	.292	.376	.246
Ty Wigginton	111	386	50	110	22	1	23	58	203	32	69	4	.350	.526	.285
Kazuo Matsui	96	375	58	110	26	3	6	33	160	37	53	20	.354	.427	.293
Geoff Blum	114	325	36	78	14	1	14	53	136	21	54	1	.287	.418	.240
Darren Erstad	140	322	49	89	16	0	4	31	117	14	68	2	.309	.363	.276
Mark Loretta	101	261	27	73	15	0	4	38	100	29	30	0	.350	.383	.280
Brad Ausmus	81	216	15	47	8	0	3	24	64	25	41	0	.303	.296	.218
Humberto Quinero	59	168	16	38	6	0	2	12	50	6	34	0	.270	.298	.226
J.R Towles	54	146	10	20	5	0	4	16	37	16	40	0	.250	.253	.137
David Newhan	64	104	11	27	5	2	2	12	42	6	28	1	.297	.404	.260

PITCHING	GP	GS	W–L	SV	SHO	R	ERA	IP	Ks	BB
Roy Oswalt	32	32	17–10	0	2	89	3.54	208.2	165	47
Randy Wolf	33	33	12–12	0	1	100	4.30	190.1	162	71
Brandon Backe	31	31	9–14	0	0	114	6.05	166.2	127	77
Brian Moehler	31	26	11–8	0	0	79	4.56	150.0	82	36
Wandy Rodriguez	25	25	9–7	0	0	65	3.54	137.1	131	44
Chris Sampson	54	11	6–4	0	0	60	4.22	117.1	61	23
Shawn Chacon	15	15	2–3	0	0	52	5.04	85.2	53	41
Jose Valverde	74	0	6–3	44	0	28	3.38	72.0	83	23
Doug Brocail	72	0	7–5	2	0	30	3.93	68.2	64	21
Geoff Geary	55	0	2–3	0	0	18	2.53	64.0	45	28
Wesley Wright	71	0	4–3	1	0	34	5.01	55.2	57	34
Tim Byrdak	59	0	2–1	0	0	24	3.90	55.1	47	29

Los Angeles Dodgers

BATTING	G	AB	R	H	2B	3B	HR	RBI	TB	BB	SO	SB	OBP	SLG	BA
Matt Kemp	155	606	93	176	38	5	18	76	278	46	153	35	.340	.459	.290
James Loney	161	595	66	172	35	6	13	90	258	45	85	7	.338	.434	.289
Russell Martin	155	553	87	155	25	0	13	69	219	90	83	18	.385	.396	.280
Andre Ethier	141	525	90	160	38	5	20	77	268	59	88	6	.375	.510	.305
Jeff Kent	121	440	42	123	23	1	12	59	184	25	52	0	.327	.418	.280
Juan Pierre	119	375	44	106	10	2	1	28	123	22	24	40	.327	.328	.283
Blake DeWitt	117	368	45	97	13	2	9	52	141	45	68	3	.344	.383	.264
Angel Berroa	84	226	26	52	13	1	1	16	70	20	41	0	.304	.310	.230
Casey Blake	58	211	25	53	12	1	10	23	97	16	52	1	.313	.460	.251
Andruw Jones	75	209	21	33	8	1	3	14	52	27	76	0	.256	.249	.158
Manny Ramirez	53	187	36	74	14	0	17	53	139	35	38	2	.489	.743	.396
Nomar Garciaparra	55	163	24	43	9	0	8	28	76	15	11	1	.326	.466	.264
Rafael Furcal	36	143	34	51	12	2	5	16	82	20	17	8	.439	.573	.357
Delwyn Young	83	126	10	31	9	0	1	7	43	14	34	0	.321	.341	.246
Chin-lung Hu	65	116	16	21	2	2	0	9	27	11	23	2	.252	.233	.181
Mark Sweeney	98	92	2	12	3	0	0	5	15	15	28	0	.250	.163	.130
Luis Maza	45	79	7	18	1	0	1	4	22	5	11	0	.282	.278	.228

PITCHING	GP	GS	W–L	SV	SHO	R	ERA	IP	Ks	BB
Derek Lowe	34	34	14–11	0	0	84	3.24	211.0	147	45
Chad Billingsley	35	32	16–10	0	1	76	3.14	200.2	201	80
Greg Maddux	33	33	8–13	0	0	105	4.22	194.0	98	30
Hiroki Kuroda	31	31	9–10	0	2	85	3.73	183.1	116	42
Clayton Kershaw	22	21	5–5	0	0	51	4.26	107.2	100	52
Chan Ho Park	54	5	4–4	2	0	43	3.40	95.1	79	36
Brad Penny	19	17	6–9	0	0	68	6.27	94.2	51	42
Hong-Chih Kuo	42	3	5–3	1	0	21	2.14	80.0	96	21
Cory Wade	55	0	2–1	0	0	22	2.27	71.1	51	15
Jonathan Broxton	70	0	3–5	14	0	29	3.13	69.0	88	27
Joe Beimel	71	0	5–1	0	0	11	2.02	49.0	32	21
Takashi Saito	45	0	4–4	18	0	14	2.49	47.0	60	16
Scott Proctor	41	0	2–0	0	0	30	6.05	38.2	46	24

National League Team-by-Team Statistical Leaders *(Cont.)*

Milwaukee Brewers

BATTING	G	AB	R	H	2B	3B	HR	RBI	TB	BB	SO	SB	OBP	SLG	BA
Corey Hart	157	612	76	164	45	6	20	91	281	27	109	23	.300	.459	.268
Ryan Braun	151	611	92	174	39	7	37	106	338	42	129	14	.335	.553	.285
Prince Fielder	159	588	86	162	30	2	34	102	298	84	134	3	.372	.507	.276
J.J. Hardy	146	569	78	161	31	4	24	74	272	52	98	2	.343	.478	.283
Jason Kendall	151	516	46	127	30	2	2	49	167	50	45	8	.327	.324	.246
Rickie Weeks	129	475	89	111	22	7	14	46	189	66	115	9	.342	.398	.234
Mike Cameron	120	444	69	108	25	2	25	70	212	54	142	17	.331	.477	.243
Bill Hall	128	404	50	91	22	1	15	55	160	37	124	5	.293	.396	.225
Ray Durham	128	370	64	107	35	0	6	45	160	53	72	8	.380	.432	.289
Craig Counsell	110	248	31	56	14	1	1	14	75	46	42	3	.355	.302	.226
Gabe Kapler	96	229	36	69	17	2	8	38	114	13	39	3	.340	.498	.301
Russell Branyan	50	132	24	33	8	0	12	20	77	19	42	1	.342	.583	.250
Joe Dillon	56	75	13	16	3	0	1	6	22	13	21	1	.337	.293	.213

PITCHING	GP	GS	W–L	SV	SHO	R	ERA	IP	Ks	BB
Ben Sheets	31	31	13–9	0	3	74	3.09	198.1	158	47
Dave Bush	31	29	9–10	0	0	92	4.18	185.0	109	48
Jeff Suppan	31	31	10–10	0	0	110	4.96	177.2	90	67
Manny Parra	32	29	10–8	0	0	91	4.39	166.0	147	75
C.C. Sabathia	17	17	11–2	0	3	31	1.65	130.2	128	25
Carlos Villanueva	47	9	4–7	1	0	53	4.07	108.1	93	30
Seth McClung	37	12	6–6	0	0	47	4.02	105.1	87	55
Salomon Torres	71	0	7–5	28	0	35	3.49	80.0	51	33
Guillermo Mota	58	0	5–6	1	0	28	4.11	57.0	50	28
Brian Shouse	69	0	5–1	2	0	19	2.81	51.1	33	14
Eric Gagne	50	0	4–3	10	0	28	5.44	46.1	38	22
David Riske	45	0	1–2	2	0	25	5.31	42.1	27	25
Todd Coffey	26	0	1–0	0	0	13	4.39	26.2	15	8
Mitch Stetter	30	0	3–1	0	0	9	3.20	25.1	31	19
Yovani Gallardo	4	4	0–0	0	0	5	1.88	24.0	20	8

New York Mets

BATTING	G	AB	R	H	2B	3B	HR	RBI	TB	BB	SO	SB	OBP	SLG	BA
Jose Reyes	159	688	113	204	37	19	16	68	327	66	82	56	.358	.475	.297
David Wright	160	626	115	189	42	2	33	124	334	94	118	15	.390	.534	.302
Carlos Beltran	161	606	116	172	40	5	27	112	303	92	96	25	.376	.500	.284
Carlos Delgado	159	598	96	162	32	1	38	115	310	72	124	1	.353	.518	.271
Brian Schneider	110	335	30	86	10	0	9	38	123	42	53	0	.339	.367	.257
Ryan Church	90	319	54	88	14	1	12	49	140	33	83	2	.346	.439	.276
Damion Easley	113	316	33	85	10	2	6	44	117	19	38	0	.322	.370	.269
Luis Castillo	87	298	46	73	7	1	3	28	91	50	35	17	.355	.305	.245
Fernando Tatis	92	273	33	81	16	1	11	47	132	29	59	3	.369	.484	.297
Endy Chavez	133	270	30	72	10	2	1	12	89	17	22	6	.308	.330	.267
Ramon Castro	52	143	15	35	7	0	7	24	63	13	34	0	.312	.441	.245
Marlon Anderson	87	138	16	29	6	0	1	10	38	9	27	2	.255	.275	.210
Daniel Murphy	49	131	24	41	9	3	2	17	62	18	28	0	.397	.473	.313
Argenis Reyes	49	110	13	24	0	0	1	3	27	4	20	2	.259	.245	.218
Nick Evans	50	109	18	28	10	0	2	9	44	7	24	0	.303	.404	.257
Angel Pagan	31	91	12	25	7	1	0	13	34	11	18	4	.346	.374	.275

PITCHING	GP	GS	W–L	SV	SHO	R	ERA	IP	Ks	BB
Johan Santana	34	34	16–7	0	2	74	2.53	234.1	206	63
Mike Pelfrey	32	32	13–11	0	0	86	3.72	200.2	110	64
Oliver Perez	34	34	10–7	0	0	100	4.22	194.0	180	105
John Maine	25	25	10–8	0	0	70	4.18	140.0	122	67
Pedro Martinez	20	20	5–6	0	0	70	5.61	109.0	87	44
Aaron Heilman	78	0	3–8	3	0	48	5.21	76.0	80	46
Luis Ayala	81	0	2–10	9	0	53	5.71	75.2	50	24
Joe Smith	82	0	6–3	0	0	28	3.55	63.1	52	31
Duaner Sanchez	66	0	5–1	0	0	28	4.32	58.1	44	23
Scott Schoeneweis	73	0	2–6	1	0	23	3.34	56.2	34	23
Pedro Feliciano	86	0	3–4	2	0	24	4.05	53.1	50	26
Billy Wagner	45	0	0–1	27	0	17	2.30	47.0	52	10
Nelson Figueroa	16	6	3–3	0	0	26	4.57	45.1	36	26
Claudio Vargas	11	4	3–2	0	0	20	4.62	37.0	20	11
Brian Stokes	24	1	1–0	1	0	13	3.51	33.1	26	8
Carlos Muniz	18	0	1–1	0	0	14	5.40	23.1	16	7

National League Team-by-Team Statistical Leaders *(Cont.)*

Philadelphia Phillies

BATTING	G	AB	R	H	2B	3B	HR	RBI	TB	BB	SO	SB	OBP	SLG	BA
Ryan Howard	162	610	105	153	26	4	48	146	331	81	199	1	.339	.543	.251
Chase Utley	159	607	113	177	41	4	33	104	325	64	104	14	.380	.535	.292
Shane Victorino	146	570	102	167	30	8	14	58	255	45	69	36	.352	.447	.293
Jimmy Rollins	137	556	76	154	38	9	11	59	243	58	55	47	.349	.437	.277
Pat Burrell	157	536	74	134	33	3	33	86	272	102	136	0	.367	.507	.250
Pedro Feliz	133	425	43	106	19	2	14	58	171	33	54	0	.302	.402	.249
Jayson Werth	134	418	73	114	16	3	24	67	208	57	119	20	.363	.498	.273
Carlos Ruiz	117	320	47	70	14	0	4	31	96	44	38	1	.320	.300	.219
Tadahito Iguchi	85	310	29	72	15	1	2	24	95	26	75	8	.292	.306	.232
Geoff Jenkins	115	293	27	72	16	0	9	29	115	24	68	1	.301	.392	.246
Chris Coste	98	274	28	72	17	0	9	36	116	16	51	0	.325	.423	.263
Greg Dobbs	128	226	30	68	14	1	9	40	111	11	40	3	.333	.491	.301
Eric Bruntlett	120	212	37	46	9	1	2	15	63	21	35	9	.297	.297	.217
So Taguchi	88	91	18	20	5	1	0	9	27	8	14	3	.283	.297	.220

PITCHING	GP	GS	W–L	SV	SHO	R	ERA	IP	Ks	BB
Cole Hamels	33	33	14–10	0	2	89	3.09	227.1	196	53
Jamie Moyer	33	33	16–7	0	0	85	3.71	196.1	123	62
Brett Myers	30	30	10–13	0	1	103	4.55	190.0	163	65
Kyle Kendrick	31	30	11–9	0	0	103	5.49	155.2	68	57
Adam Eaton	21	19	4–8	0	0	71	5.80	107.0	57	44
J.D. Durbin	71	0	5–4	1	0	33	2.87	87.2	63	35
Ryan Madson	76	0	4–2	1	0	29	3.05	82.2	67	23
Joe Blanton	13	13	4–0	0	0	36	4.20	70.2	49	31
Brad Lidge	72	0	2–0	41	0	17	1.95	69.1	92	35
Clay Condrey	56	0	3–4	1	0	26	3.26	69.0	34	19
J.C. Romero	81	0	4–4	1	0	18	2.75	59.0	52	38
Rudy Seanez	42	0	5–4	0	0	24	3.53	43.1	30	25
J.A. Happ	8	4	1–0	0	0	13	3.69	31.2	26	14
Tom Gordon	34	0	5–4	2	0	19	5.16	29.2	26	17

Pittsburgh Pirates

BATTING	G	AB	R	H	2B	3B	HR	RBI	TB	BB	SO	SB	OBP	SLG	BA
Nate McLouth	152	597	113	165	46	4	26	94	297	65	93	23	.356	.497	.276F
Freddy Sanchez	145	569	75	154	26	2	9	52	211	21	63	0	.298	.371	.271
Adam LaRoche	136	492	66	133	32	3	25	85	246	54	122	1	.341	.500	.270
Ryan Doumit	116	431	71	137	34	0	15	69	216	23	55	2	.357	.501	.318
Jason Bay	106	393	72	111	23	2	22	64	204	59	86	7	.375	.519	.282
Xavier Nady	89	327	50	108	26	1	13	57	175	25	55	1	.383	.535	.330
Jose Bautisa	107	314	38	76	15	0	12	44	127	38	77	1	.325	.404	.242
Jack Wilson	87	305	24	83	18	1	1	22	106	13	27	2	.312	.348	.272
Doug Mientkiewicz	125	285	37	79	19	2	2	30	108	44	28	0	.374	.379	.277
Jason Michaels	102	228	25	52	9	1	8	44	87	23	52	1	.300	.382	.228
Andy LaRoche	76	233	17	37	5	0	5	18	57	24	37	2	.252	.256	.166
Luis Rivas	79	206	25	45	6	2	3	20	64	13	27	3	.267	.311	.218
Chris Gomez	90	183	26	50	8	0	1	20	61	13	30	0	.322	.333	.273
Nyjer Morgan	58	160	26	47	13	0	0	7	60	10	32	9	.345	.375	.294
Brandon Moss	45	158	12	35	10	2	6	23	67	15	45	0	.288	.424	.222

PITCHING	GP	GS	W–L	SV	SHO	R	ERA	IP	Ks	BB
Paul Maholm	31	31	9–9	0	0	89	3.71	206.1	139	63
Zach Duke	31	31	5–14	0	1	111	4.82	185.0	87	47
Ian Snell	31	31	7–12	0	0	107	5.42	164.1	135	89
Tom Gorzelanny	21	21	6–9	0	0	79	6.66	105.1	67	70
Phil Dumatrait	21	11	3–4	0	0	48	5.26	78.2	52	42
John Grabow	74	0	6–3	4	0	25	2.84	76.0	62	37
Tyler Yates	72	0	6–3	1	0	39	4.66	73.1	63	41
Franquelis Osoria	43	0	4–3	0	0	43	6.08	60.2	31	12
Sean Burnett	58	0	1–1	0	0	31	4.76	56.2	42	34
Matt Capps	49	0	2–3	21	0	20	3.02	53.2	39	5
Jeff Karstens	9	9	2–6	0	1	32	4.03	51.1	23	13
Damaso Marte	47	0	4–0	5	0	18	3.47	46.2	47	16

National League Team-by-Team Statistical Leaders *(Cont.)*

St. Louis Cardinals

BATTING	G	AB	R	H	2B	3B	HR	RBI	TB	BB	SO	SB	OBP	SLG	BA
Troy Glaus	151	544	69	147	33	1	27	99	263	87	104	0	.372	.483	.270
Skip Schumaker	153	540	87	163	22	5	8	46	219	47	60	8	.359	.406	.302
Ryan Ludwick	152	538	104	161	40	3	37	113	318	62	146	4	.375	.591	.299
Albert Pujols	148	542	100	187	44	0	37	116	342	104	54	7	.462	.653	.357
Felipe Lopez	143	481	64	136	28	2	6	46	186	43	82	8	.343	.387	.283
Yadier Molina	124	444	37	135	18	0	7	56	174	32	29	0	.349	.392	.304
Cesar Izturis	135	414	50	109	10	3	1	24	128	29	26	24	.319	.309	.263
Rick Ankiel	120	413	65	109	21	2	25	71	209	42	100	2	.337	.506	.264
Aaron Miles	134	379	49	120	15	2	4	31	151	23	37	3	.355	398	.317
Adam Kennedy	115	339	42	95	17	4	2	36	126	21	43	7	.321	.372	.280
Chris Duncan	76	222	26	55	8	0	6	27	81	34	52	2	.346	.365	.248
Brendan Ryan	80	197	30	48	9	0	0	10	57	16	31	7	.307	.289	.244
JasonLaRue	61	164	17	35	8	1	4	21	57	15	20	0	.296	.348	.213
Brian Barton	82	153	23	41	9	2	2	13	60	19	39	3	.354	.392	.268
Joe Mather	54	133	20	32	7	0	8	18	63	12	32	1	.306	.474	.241

PITCHING	GP	GS	W–L	SV	SHO	R	ERA	IP	Ks	BB
Kyle Lohse	33	33	15–6	0	0	88	3.78	200.0	119	49
Braden Looper	33	33	12–14	0	1	101	4.16	199.0	108	45
Todd Wellemeyer	32	32	13–9	0	0	84	3.71	191.2	134	62
Joel Pineiro	26	25	7–7	1	0	89	5.15	148.2	81	35
Adam Wainwright	20	20	11–3	0	0	51	3.20	132.0	91	34
Ryan Franklin	74	0	6–6	17	0	34	3.55	78.2	51	30
Kyle McClellan	68	0	2–7	1	0	37	4.04	75.2	59	26
Brad Thompson	26	6	6–3	0	0	38	5.15	64.2	32	19
Russ Springer	70	0	2–1	0	0	14	2.32	50.1	45	18
Ron Villone	74	0	1–2	1	0	27	4.68	50.0	50	37
Jason Isringhausen	42	0	1–5	12	0	28	5.70	42.2	36	22
Chris Perez	41	0	3–3	7	0	18	3.46	41.2	42	22
Mitchell Boggs	8	6	3–2	0	0	29	7.41	34.0	13	22
Randy Flores	43	0	1–0	1	0	16	5.26	25.2	17	20
Kelvin Jimenez	15	0	0–0	0	0	15	5.63	24.0	11	15

San Diego Padres

BATTING	G	AB	R	H	2B	3B	HR	RBI	TB	BB	SO	SB	OBP	SLG	BA
Kevin Kouzmanoff	154	624	71	162	31	4	23	84	270	23	139	0	.299	.433	.260
Adrian Gonzalez	162	616	103	172	32	1	36	119	314	74	142	0	.361	.510	.279
Brian Giles	147	559	81	171	40	4	12	63	255	87	52	2	.398	.456	.306
Khalil Greene	105	389	30	83	15	2	10	35	132	22	100	5	.260	.339	.213
Chase Headley	91	331	34	89	19	2	9	38	139	30	104	4	.337	.420	.269
Jody Gerut	100	328	46	97	15	4	14	43	162	28	52	6	.351	.494	.296
Scott Hairston	112	326	42	81	18	3	17	31	156	28	84	3	.312	.479	.248
Edgar Gonzalez	111	325	38	89	15	0	7	33	125	25	76	1	.329	.385	.274
Luis Rodriguez	64	202	22	58	11	1	0	12	71	13	13	1	.326	.351	.287
Nick Hundley	60	198	21	47	7	1	5	24	71	11	52	0	.278	.359	.237
Josh Bard	57	178	11	36	9	0	1	16	48	18	25	0	.279	.270	.202
Paul McAnulty	66	135	9	28	7	1	3	13	46	26	41	0	.341	.341	.207
Will Venable	28	110	16	29	4	2	2	10	43	13	21	1	.339	.391	.264
Michael Barrett	30	94	9	19	3	0	2	9	28	9	16	0	.274	.298	.202

PITCHING	GP	GS	W–L	SV	SHO	R	ERA	IP	Ks	BB
Jake Peavy	27	27	10–11	0	0	57	2.85	173.2	166	59
Cha Seung Baek	22	20	6–9	0	0	60	4.62	111.0	77	30
Chris R. Young	18	18	7–6	0	0	46	3.96	102.1	93	48
Josh Banks	17	14	3–6	0	0	47	4.75	85.1	43	32
Heath Bell	74	0	6–6	0	0	31	3.58	78.0	71	28
Cla Meredith	73	0	0–3	0	0	34	4.09	70.1	49	24
Mike Adams	54	0	2–3	0	0	18	2.48	65.1	74	19
Trevor Hoffman	48	0	3–6	30	0	19	3.77	45.1	46	9
Shawn Estes	9	8	2–3	0	0	26	4.74	43.2	19	18
Justin Germano	12	6	0–3	0	0	31	5.98	43.2	17	13
Bryan Corey	39	0	1–3	0	0	27	6.23	39.0	18	9
Clay Hensley	32	1	1–2	0	0	27	5.31	39.0	26	25
Justin Hampson	35	0	2–1	0	0	11	2.93	30.2	19	10
Josh Geer	5	5	2–1	0	0	8	2.67	27.0	16	9

National League Team-by-Team Statistical Leaders *(Cont.)*

San Francisco Giants

BATTING	G	AB	R	H	2B	3B	HR	RBI	TB	BB	SO	SB	OBP	SLG	BA
Randy Winn	155	598	84	183	38	2	10	64	255	59	88	25	.363	.426	.306
Aaron Rowand	152	549	57	149	37	0	13	70	225	44	126	2	.339	.410	.271
Bengie Molina	145	530	46	155	33	0	16	95	236	19	38	0	.322	.445	.292
Fred Lewis	133	468	81	132	25	11	9	40	206	51	124	21	.351	.440	.282
Rich Aurilia	140	407	33	115	21	1	10	52	168	30	56	1	.332	.413	.283
John Bowker	111	326	31	83	14	3	10	43	133	19	74	1	.300	.408	.255
Eugenio Velez	98	275	32	72	16	7	1	30	105	14	40	15	.299	.382	.262
Omar Vizquel	92	266	24	59	10	1	0	23	71	24	29	5	.283	.267	.222
Emmanuel Burriss	95	240	37	68	6	1	1	18	79	23	24	13	.357	.329	.283
Pablo Sandoval	41	145	24	50	10	1	3	24	71	4	14	0	.357	.490	.345
Ivan Ochoa	47	120	7	24	8	0	0	3	32	4	28	0	.244	.267	.200
Dave Roberts	52	107	18	24	2	2	0	9	30	20	18	5	.341	.280	.224
Travis Isikawa	33	95	12	26	6	0	3	15	41	9	27	1	.337	.432	.274
Steve Holm	49	84	10	22	9	0	1	6	34	10	16	0	.357	.405	.262

PITCHING	GP	GS	W–L	SV	SHO	R	ERA	IP	Ks	BB
Tim Lincecum	34	33	18–5	0	1	72	2.62	227.0	265	84
Matt Cain	34	34	8–14	0	1	95	3.76	217.2	186	91
Barry Zito	32	32	10–17	0	0	115	5.15	180.0	120	102
Jonathan Sanchez	29	29	9–12	0	0	90	5.01	158.0	157	75
Kevin Correia	25	19	3–8	0	0	80	6.05	110.0	66	47
Keiichi Yabu	60	0	3–6	0	0	33	3.57	68.0	48	32
Brian Wilson	63	0	3–2	41	0	32	4.62	62.1	67	28
Tyler Walker	65	0	5–8	0	0	29	4.56	53.1	49	21
Pat Misch	15	7	0–3	0	0	34	5.68	52.1	38	15
Jack Taschner	67	0	3–2	0	0	27	4.88	48.0	39	24
Billy Sadler	33	0	0–1	0	0	21	4.06	44.1	42	27
Brad Hennessey	17	4	1–2	0	0	35	7.81	40.1	21	15
Alex Hinshaw	48	0	2–1	0	0	16	3.40	39.2	47	29
Sergio Romo	29	0	3–1	0	0	13	2.12	34.0	33	8

Washington Nationals

BATTING	G	AB	R	H	2B	3B	HR	RBI	TB	BB	SO	SB	OBP	SLG	BA
Cristian Guzman	138	579	77	183	35	5	9	55	255	23	57	6	.345	.440	.316
Lastings Milledge	138	523	65	140	24	2	14	61	210	38	96	24	.330	.402	.268
Ryan Zimmerman	106	428	51	121	24	1	14	51	189	31	71	1	.333	.442	.283
Willie Harris	140	367	58	92	14	4	13	43	153	50	66	13	.344	.417	.251
Austin Kearns	866	313	40	68	10	0	7	32	99	35	63	2	.311	.316	.217
Jesus Flores	90	301	23	77	18	1	8	59	121	15	78	0	.296	.402	.256
Ronnie Belliard	96	296	37	85	22	0	11	46	140	37	58	3	.372	.473	.287
Elijah Dukes	81	276	48	73	16	2	13	44	132	50	79	13	.386	.478	.264
Aaron Boone	104	232	23	56	13	1	6	28	89	18	52	0	.299	.384	.241
Wily Mo Pena	64	195	10	40	6	0	2	10	52	10	48	0	.243	.267	.205
Wil Nieves	68	176	15	46	9	1	1	20	60	13	29	0	.309	.341	.261
Emilio Bonifacio	49	169	29	41	6	5	0	14	57	14	46	7	.296	.337	.243
Kory Castro	66	163	15	35	10	0	2	16	51	19	36	1	.297	.313	.215
Dmitri Young	50	150	15	42	6	0	4	10	60	28	28	0	.394	.400	.280
Ryan Langerhans	73	111	17	26	5	2	3	12	44	25	31	2	.380	.396	.234

PITCHING	GP	GS	W–L	SV	SHO	R	ERA	IP	Ks	BB
John Lannan	31	31	9–15	0	0	89	3.91	182.0	117	72
Tim Redding	33	33	10–11	0	0	110	4.95	182.0	120	65
Odalis Perez	30	30	7–12	0	0	87	4.34	159.2	119	55
Jason Bergmann	30	22	2–11	0	0	94	5.09	139.2	96	47
Joel Hanrahan	69	0	6–3	9	0	40	3.95	84.1	93	42
Saul Rivera	76	0	5–6	0	0	41	3.96	84.0	65	35
Collin Balester	15	15	3–7	0	0	53	5.51	80.0	50	28
Jesus Colome	61	0	2–2	0	0	38	4.31	71.0	55	39
Shawn Hill	12	12	1–5	0	0	47	5.83	63.1	39	23
Steven Shell	39	0	2–2	2	0	14	2.16	50.0	41	20
Jon Rauch	48	0	4–2	17	0	18	2.98	48.1	44	7
Matt Chico	11	8	0–6	0	0	34	6.19	48.0	31	17
Charlie Manning	57	0	1–3	0	0	25	5.14	42.0	37	31

American League Team-by-Team Statistical Leaders

Baltimore Orioles

BATTING	G	AB	R	H	2B	3B	HR	RBI	TB	BB	SO	SB	OBP	SLG	BA
Brian Roberts	155	611	107	181	51	8	9	57	275	82	104	40	.378	.450	.296
Aubrey Huff	154	598	96	182	48	2	32	108	330	53	89	4	.360	.552	.304
Nick Markakis	157	595	106	182	48	1	20	87	292	99	113	10	.406	.491	.306
Kevin Millar	145	531	73	124	25	0	20	72	209	71	93	0	.323	.394	.234
Melvin Mora	135	513	77	146	29	2	23	104	248	37	70	3	.342	.483	.285
Adam Jones	132	477	61	129	21	7	9	57	191	23	108	10	.311	.400	.270
Luke Scott	148	475	67	122	29	2	23	65	224	53	102	2	.336	.472	.257
Ramon Hernandez	133	463	49	119	22	1	15	65	188	32	62	0	.308	.406	.257
Jay Payton	127	338	41	82	10	2	7	41	117	22	53	8	.291	.346	.243
Juan Castro	54	151	15	31	6	0	2	16	43	10	26	0	.256	.285	.205
Guillermo Quiroz	56	134	12	25	5	0	2	14	36	12	34	0	.259	.269	.187
Alex Cintron	61	133	12	38	5	1	1	10	48	7	15	0	.321	.361	.286
Freddie Mynum	40	112	13	20	3	1	0	8	25	5	31	2	.220	.223	.179
Lou Montanez	38	112	18	33	6	1	3	14	50	4	20	0	.316	.446	.295
Brandon Fahey	58	106	8	24	9	2	0	12	37	3	25	0	.252	.349	.226
Oscar Salazar	34	81	13	23	3	0	5	15	41	12	13	0	.372	.506	284

PITCHING	GP	GS	W–L	SV	SHO	R	ERA	IP	Ks	BB
Jeremy Guthrie	30	30	10–12	0	0	82	3.63	190.2	120	58
Daniel Cabrera	30	30	8–10	0	0	109	5.25	180.0	95	90
Garrett Olson	26	26	9–10	0	0	100	6.65	132.2	83	62
Brian Burres	31	22	7–10	0	0	90	6.04	129.2	63	50
Brian Bass	49	4	4–4	1	0	55	4.84	89.1	45	31
Radhames Liz	17	17	6–6	0	0	67	6.72	84.1	57	51
Dennis Sarfate	57	4	4–3	0	0	47	4.74	79.2	86	62
Lance Cormier	45	1	3–3	1	0	36	4.02	71.2	46	34
Jim Johnson	54	0	2–4	1	0	18	2.23	68.2	38	28
Chris Waters	11	11	3–5	0	0	38	5.01	64.2	33	29
George Sherrill	57	0	3–5	31	0	28	4.73	53.1	58	33
Matt Albers	28	3	3–3	0	0	21	3.49	49.0	26	22
Steve Trachsel	10	8	2–5	0	0	41	8.39	39.2	16	27
Jamie Walker	59	0	1–3	0	0	31	6.87	38.0	24	11
Randor Bierd	29	0	0–2	0	0	21	4.91	36.2	25	19

Boston Red Sox

BATTING	G	AB	R	H	2B	3B	HR	RBI	TB	BB	SO	SB	OBP	SLG	BA
Dustin Pedroia	157	653	118	213	54	2	17	83	322	50	52	20	.376	.493	.326
Jacoby Ellsbury	145	554	98	155	22	7	9	47	218	41	80	50	.336	.394	.280
Kevin Youkilis	145	538	91	168	43	4	29	115	306	62	108	3	.390	.569	.312
Jason Varitek	131	423	37	93	20	0	13	43	152	52	122	0	.313	.359	.220
Mike Lowell	113	419	58	115	27	0	17	73	193	38	61	2	.338	.461	.274
David Ortiz	109	416	74	110	30	1	23	89	211	70	74	1	.369	.507	.264
J.D. Drew	109	368	79	103	23	4	19	64	191	79	80	4	.408	.519	.280
Manny Ramirez	100	365	66	109	22	1	20	68	193	52	86	1	.398	.529	.299
Coco Crisp	118	361	55	102	18	3	7	41	147	35	59	20	.344	.407	.283
Julio Lugo	82	261	27	70	13	0	1	22	86	34	51	12	.355	.330	.268
Jed Lowrie	81	260	34	67	25	3	2	46	104	35	68	1	.339	.400	.258
Sean Casey	69	199	14	64	14	0	0	17	78	17	25	1	.381	.392	.322
Jason Bay	49	184	39	54	12	2	9	37	97	22	51	3	.370	.527	.293
Alex Cora	75	152	14	41	8	2	0	9	53	16	13	1	.371	.349	.270
Kevin Cash	61	142	11	32	7	0	3	15	48	18	50	0	.309	.338	.225
Mark Kotsay	22	84	6	19	8	1	0	12	29	7	11	0	.286	.345	226

PITCHING	GP	GS	W–L	SV	SHO	R	ERA	IP	Ks	BB
Jon Lester	33	33	16–6	0	2	78	3.21	210.1	152	66
Tim Wakefield	30	30	10–11	0	0	89	4.13	181.0	117	60
Paul Byrd	30	30	11–12	0	0	96	4.60	180.0	82	34
Josh Beckett	27	27	12–10	0	0	80	4.03	174.1	172	34
Daisuke Matsuzaka	29	29	18–3	0	0	58	2.90	167.2	154	94
Justin Masterson	36	9	6–5	0	0	31	3.16	88.1	68	40
Clay Buchholz	16	15	2–9	0	0	63	6.75	76.0	72	41
Manny Delcarmen	73	0	1–2	2	0	28	3.27	74.1	72	28
Jonathan Papelbon	67	0	5–4	41	0	24	2.34	69.1	77	8
Hideki Okajima	64	0	3–2	1	0	18	2.61	62.0	60	23
Javier Lopez	70	0	2–0	0	0	18	2.43	59.1	38	27
Mike Timlin	47	0	4–4	1	0	32	5.66	49.1	32	20
David Aardsma	47	0	4–2	0	0	32	5.55	48.2	49	35
Bartolo Colon	7	7	4–2	0	0	23	3.92	39.0	27	10

Chicago White Sox

BATTING	G	AB	R	H	2B	3B	HR	RBI	TB	BB	SO	SB	OBP	SLG	BA
Orlando Cabrera	161	661	93	186	33	1	8	57	245	56	71	19	.334	.371	.281
Jermaine Dye	154	590	96	172	41	2	34	96	319	44	104	3	.344	.541	292
A.J. Pierzynski	134	534	66	150	31	1	13	60	222	19	71	1	.312	.416	.281
Jim Thome	149	503	93	123	28	0	34	90	253	91	147	1	.362	.503	.245
Nick Swisher	153	497	86	109	21	1	24	69	204	82	135	3	.332	.410	.219
Carlos Quentin	130	480	96	138	26	1	36	100	274	66	80	7	.394	.571	.288
Alexei Ramirez	136	480	65	139	22	2	21	77	228	18	61	13	.317	.475	.290
Paul Konerko	122	438	59	105	19	1	22	62	192	65	80	2	.344	.438	.240
Joe Crede	97	335	41	83	18	1	17	55	154	30	45	0	.314	.460	.248
Juan Uribe	110	324	38	80	22	1	7	40	125	22	64	1	.296	.386	.247
Brian Anderson	109	181	24	42	13	0	8	26	79	10	45	5	.272	.436	.232
Ken Griffey	41	131	16	34	10	0	3	18	53	17	25	0	.347	.405	.260
Dewayne Wise	57	129	20	32	4	2	6	18	58	8	32	9	.293	.450	.248
Toby Hall	41	127	7	33	3	0	2	7	42	6	19	0	.304	.331	.260
Pablo Ozuna	32	64	5	18	3	0	0	6	21	2	3	0	.313	.328	.281

PITCHING	GP	GS	W–L	SV	SHO	R	ERA	IP	Ks	BB
Mark Buehrle	34	34	15–12	0	0	106	3.79	218.2	140	52
Javier Vazquez	33	33	12–16	0	0	113	4.67	208.1	200	61
Gavin Floyd	33	33	17–8	0	0	107	3.84	206.1	145	70
John Danks	33	33	12–9	0	0	74	3.32	195.0	159	57
Jose Contreras	20	20	7–6	0	0	64	4.54	121.0	70	35
Matt Thornton	74	0	5–3	1	0	20	2.67	67.1	77	19
Octavio Dotel	72	0	4–4	1	0	34	3.76	67.0	92	29
Bobby Jenks	57	0	3–1	30	0	18	2.63	61.2	38	17
Clayton Richard	13	8	2–5	0	0	37	6.04	47.2	29	13
Scott Linebrink	50	0	2–2	1	0	20	3.69	46.1	40	9
Nick Masset	32	1	1–0	1	0	26	4.63	44.2	32	21
Boone Logan	55	0	2–3	0	0	31	5.95	42.1	42	14
D.J. Carrasco	31	0	1–0	0	0	17	3.96	38.2	30	14

Cleveland Indians

BATTING	G	AB	R	H	2B	3B	HR	RBI	TB	BB	SO	SB	OBP	SLG	BA
Grady Sizemore	157	634	101	170	39	5	33	90	318	98	130	38	.374	.502	.268
Jhonny Peralta	154	605	104	167	42	4	23	89	286	48	126	3	.331	.473	.276
Ryan Garko	141	495	61	135	21	1	14	90	200	45	86	0	.346	.404	.273
Ben Francisco	121	447	65	119	32	0	15	54	196	40	86	4	.332	.438	.266
Franklin Gutierrez	134	399	54	99	26	2	8	41	153	27	87	9	.307	.383	.248
Asdrubal Cabrera	114	352	48	91	20	0	6	47	129	46	77	4	.346	.366	.259
Kelly Shoppach	112	352	67	92	27	0	21	55	182	36	133	0	.348	.517	.261
Jamey Carroll	113	347	60	96	13	4	1	36	120	34	65	7	.355	.346	.277
David Dellucci	113	336	41	80	19	2	11	47	136	24	76	3	.307	.405	.238
Casey Blake	94	325	46	94	24	0	11	58	151	33	68	2	.365	.465	.289
Shin-Soo Choo	94	317	68	98	28	3	14	66	174	44	78	4	.397	.549	.309
Victor Martinez	73	266	30	74	17	0	2	35	97	24	32	0	.337	.365	.278
Andy Marte	80	235	21	52	11	1	3	17	74	14	52	1	.268	.315	.221
Travis Hafner	57	198	21	39	10	0	5	24	64	27	55	1	.305	.323	.197

PITCHING	GP	GS	W–L	SV	SHO	R	ERA	IP	Ks	BB
Cliff Lee	31	31	22–3	0	2	68	2.54	223.1	170	34
C.C. Sabathia	18	18	6–8	0	2	54	3.83	122.1	123	34
Jeremy Sowers	22	22	4–9	0	0	84	5.58	121.0	64	39
Fausto Carmona	22	22	8–7	0	1	80	5.44	120.2	58	70
Aaron Laffey	16	16	5–7	0	0	52	4.23	93.2	43	31
Rafael Perez	73	0	4–4	2	0	32	3.54	76.1	86	23
Rafael Betancourt	69	0	3–4	0	0	41	5.07	71.0	64	25
Jensen Lewis	51	0	0–4	13	0	29	3.82	66.0	52	27
Masahide Kobayashi	57	0	4–5	6	0	30	4.53	55.2	35	14
Juan Rincon	47	0	3–3	0	0	39	5.86	55.1	39	24
Zach Jackson	9	9	2–3	0	0	36	5.60	54.2	30	14
Edward Mujica	33	0	3–2	0	0	29	6.75	38.2	27	10
Jake Westbrook	5	5	1–2	0	0	13	3.12	34.2	19	7
Anthony Reyes	6	6	2–1	0	0	7	1.83	34.1	15	12
Scott Lewis	4	4	4–0	0	0	9	2.63	24.0	15	6
Matt Ginter	4	4	1–3	0	0	12	5.14	21.0	12	3
Tom Mastny	14	0	2–2	0	0	24	10.80	20.0	19	11
Jorge Julio	15	0	0–0	0	0	11	5.60	17.2	15	11
Joe Borowski	18	0	1–3	6	0	18	7.56	16.2	9	8

American League Team-by-Team Statistical Leaders *(Cont.)*

Detroit Tigers

BATTING	G	AB	R	H	2B	3B	HR	RBI	TB	BB	SO	SB	OBP	SLG	BA
Miguel Cabrera	160	616	85	180	36	2	37	127	331	56	126	1	.349	.537	.292
Placido Polanco	141	580	90	178	34	3	8	58	242	35	43	7	.350	.417	.307
Magglio Ordonez	146	561	72	178	32	2	21	103	277	53	76	1	.376	.494	.317
Curtis Granderson	141	553	112	155	26	13	22	66	273	71	111	12	.365	.494	.280
Edgar Renteria	138	503	69	136	22	2	10	55	192	37	64	6	.317	.382	.270
Carlos Guillen	113	420	68	120	29	2	10	54	183	60	67	9	.376	.436	.286
Gary Sheffield	114	418	52	94	16	0	19	57	167	58	83	9	.326	.400	.225
Brandon Inge	113	347	41	71	16	4	11	51	128	43	94	4	.303	.369	.205
Marcus Thames	103	316	50	76	12	0	25	56	163	24	95	0	.292	.516	.241
Matt Joyce	92	242	40	61	16	3	12	33	119	31	65	0	.339	.492	.252
Ryan Raburn	92	182	26	43	10	1	4	20	67	16	49	3	.298	.368	.236
Ramon Santiago	58	124	30	35	6	2	4	18	57	22	17	1	.411	.460	.282
Clete Thomas	40	116	7	33	9	1	1	9	47	14	26	2	.366	.405	.284
Jeff Larish	42	104	12	27	6	0	2	16	39	7	34	2	.306	.375	.260
Jacque Jones	24	79	10	13	2	1	1	5	20	8	18	0	.244	.253	.165

PITCHING	GP	GS	W–L	SV	SHO	R	ERA	IP	Ks	BB
Justin Verlander	33	33	11–17	0	0	119	4.84	201.0	163	87
Armando Galarraga	30	28	13–7	0	0	83	3.73	178.2	126	61
Kenny Rogers	30	30	9–13	0	0	118	5.70	173.2	82	71
Nate Robertson	32	28	7–11	0	0	124	6.35	168.2	108	62
Zach Miner	45	13	8–5	0	0	60	4.27	118.0	62	46
Aquilino Lopez	48	0	4–1	0	0	33	3.55	78.2	61	22
Jeremy Bonderman	12	12	3–4	0	0	39	4.29	71.1	44	36
Kyle Farnsworth	16	0	1–1	0	0	14	6.75	16.0	18	5
Bobby Seay	60	0	1–2	0	0	28	4.47	56.1	58	25
Gary Glover	47	0	2–3	0	0	33	5.30	54.1	37	22
Freddy Dolsi	42	0	1–5	2	0	21	3.97	47.2	29	28
Todd Jones	45	0	4–1	18	0	30	4.97	41.2	14	18
Casey Fossum	31	0	3–1	0	0	26	5.66	41.1	28	18
Fernando Rodney	38	0	0–6	13	0	22	4.91	40.1	49	30
Eddie Bonnie	5	5	2–1	0	0	19	5.40	26.2	9	5
Dontrelle Willis	8	7	0–2	0	0	25	9.38	24.0	18	35

Kansas City Royals

BATTING	G	AB	R	H	2B	3B	HR	RBI	TB	BB	SO	SB	OBP	SLG	BA
Jose Guillen	153	598	66	158	42	1	20	97	262	23	106	2	.300	.438	.264
Mark Teahen	149	572	66	146	31	4	15	59	230	46	131	4	.313	.402	.255
David DeJesus	135	518	70	159	25	7	12	73	234	46	71	11	.366	.452	.307
Alex Gordon	134	493	72	128	35	1	16	59	213	66	120	9	.351	.432	.260
Billy Butler	124	443	44	122	22	0	11	55	177	33	57	0	.324	.400	.275
Mike Aviles	102	419	68	136	27	4	10	51	201	18	58	8	.354	.480	.325
Ross Gload	122	388	46	106	18	1	3	37	135	23	39	3	.317	.348	.273
John Buck	109	370	48	83	23	1	9	48	135	38	96	0	.304	.365	.224
Mark Grudzielanek	86	331	36	99	24	0	3	24	132	19	41	2	.345	.399	.299
Miguel Olivo	84	306	29	78	22	0	12	41	136	7	82	7	.278	.444	.255
Joey Gathright	105	279	41	71	3	1	0	22	76	20	40	21	.311	.272	.254
Tony Pena	95	225	22	38	4	1	1	14	47	6	49	3	.189	.209	.169
Esteban German	89	216	30	53	14	3	0	22	73	18	42	7	.303	.338	.245
Alberto Callaspo	74	213	21	65	8	3	0	16	79	19	14	2	.361	.371	.305
Mitch Maier	34	91	9	26	1	1	0	9	29	2	18	0	.316	.319	.286

PITCHING	GP	GS	W–L	SV	SHO	R	ERA	IP	Ks	BB
Gil Meche	34	34	14–11	0	0	98	3.98	210.1	183	73
Zack Greinke	32	32	13–10	0	0	87	3.47	202.1	183	56
Brian Bannister	32	32	9–16	0	0	127	5.76	182.2	113	58
Luke Hochevar	22	22	6–12	0	0	84	5.51	129.0	72	47
Kyle Davies	21	21	9–7	0	0	57	4.06	113.0	71	43
Ramon Ramirez	71	0	3–2	1	0	23	2.64	71.2	70	31
Joakim Soria	63	0	2–3	42	0	13	1.60	67.1	66	19
Ron Mahey	57	0	5–0	0	0	27	3.48	64.2	49	29
Brett Tomko	16	10	2–7	0	0	49	6.97	60.2	40	13
Joel Peralta	40	0	1–2	0	0	37	5.98	52.2	38	14
Leo Nunez	45	0	4–1	0	0	19	2.98	48.1	26	15
Robinson Tejeda	29	1	2–2	0	0	23	3.97	45.1	45	24

American League Team-by-Team Statistical Leaders *(Cont.)*

Los Angeles Angels of Anaheim

BATTING	G	AB	R	H	2B	3B	HR	RBI	TB	BB	SO	SB	OBP	SLG	BA
Garret Anderson	145	557	66	163	27	3	15	84	241	29	77	7	.325	.433	.293
Torii Hunter	146	551	85	153	37	2	21	78	257	50	108	19	.344	.466	.278
Vladimir Guerrero	143	541	85	164	31	3	27	91	282	51	77	5	.365	.521	.303
Chone Figgins	116	453	72	125	14	1	1	22	144	62	80	34	.367	.318	.276
Gary Matthews	127	426	53	103	19	3	8	46	152	45	95	8	.319	.357	.242
Casey Kotchman	100	373	47	107	24	0	12	54	167	18	23	2	.327	.448	.287
Erick Aybar	98	346	53	96	18	5	3	39	133	14	45	7	.314	.384	.277
Howie Kendrick	92	340	43	104	26	2	3	37	143	12	58	11	.333	.421	.306
Maicer Izturis	79	290	44	78	14	2	3	37	105	26	27	11	.329	.362	.269
Jeff Mathis	94	283	35	55	8	0	9	42	90	30	90	2	.275	.318	.194
Juan Rivera	89	256	31	63	13	0	12	45	112	16	33	1	.282	.438	.246
Mike Napoli	78	227	39	62	9	1	20	49	133	35	70	7	.374	.586	.273
Mark Teixeira	54	193	39	69	14	0	13	43	122	32	23	2	.449	.632	.358
Sean Rodriguez	59	167	18	34	8	1	3	10	53	14	55	3	.276	.317	.204
Robb Quinlan	68	164	15	43	1	2	1	11	51	14	28	4	.326	.311	.262
Brandon Wood	55	150	13	30	4	0	5	13	49	4	43	4	.224	.327	.200

PITCHING	GP	GS	W-L	SV	SHO	R	ERA	IP	Ks	BB
Ervin Santana	32	32	16–7	0	1	89	3.49	219.0	214	47
Joe Saunders	31	31	17–7	0	0	82	3.41	198.0	103	53
Jon Garland	32	32	14–8	0	0	116	4.90	196.2	90	59
Jered Weaver	30	30	11–10	0	0	88	4.33	176.2	152	54
John Lackey	24	24	12–5	0	0	71	3.75	163.1	130	40
Darren Oliver	54	0	7–1	0	0	24	2.88	72.0	48	16
Francisco Rodriguez	76	0	2–3	62	0	21	2.24	68.1	77	34
Justin Speier	62	0	2–8	0	0	41	5.03	68.0	56	27
Scot Shields	64	0	6–4	4	0	29	2.70	63.1	64	29
Jose Arredondo	52	0	10–2	0	0	15	1.62	61.0	55	22
Dustin Moseley	12	10	2–4	0	0	38	6.79	50.1	37	20
Darren O'Day	30	0	0–1	0	0	24	4.57	43.1	29	14
Chris Bootcheck	10	0	0–1	0	0	18	10.13	16.0	20	9

Minnesota Twins

BATTING	G	AB	R	H	2B	3B	HR	RBI	TB	BB	SO	SB	OBP	SLG	BA
Justin Morneau	163	623	97	187	47	4	23	129	311	76	85	0	.374	.499	.300
Carlos Gomez	153	577	79	149	24	7	7	59	208	25	142	33	.296	.360	.258
Delmon Young	151	575	80	167	28	4	10	69	233	35	105	14	.336	.405	.290
Joe Mauer	146	536	98	176	31	4	9	85	242	84	50	1	.413	.451	.328
Jason Kubel	141	463	74	126	22	5	20	78	218	47	91	0	.335	.471	.272
Brendan Harris	130	434	57	115	29	3	7	49	171	39	98	1	.327	.394	.265
Alexi Casilla	98	385	58	108	15	0	7	50	144	31	45	7	.333	.374	.281
Denard Span	93	347	70	102	16	7	6	47	150	50	60	18	.387	.432	.294
Nick Punto	99	338	43	96	19	4	2	28	129	32	57	15	.344	.382	.284
Michael Cuddyer	71	249	30	62	13	4	3	36	92	25	40	5	.330	.369	.249
Mike Lamb	81	236	20	55	12	3	1	32	76	17	32	0	.276	.322	.233
Brian Buscher	70	218	29	64	9	0	4	47	85	19	42	0	.340	.390	.294
Craig Monroe	58	163	22	3	9	0	8	29	66	16	48	0	.274	.405	.202
Mike Redmond	38	129	14	37	6	0	0	12	43	5	11	0	.321	.333	.287
Adam Everett	48	127	19	27	6	1	2	20	41	12	15	0	.278	.323	.213
Matt Tolbert	41	113	18	32	6	3	0	6	44	7	19	7	.322	.389	.283
Randy Ruiz	22	62	13	17	2	0	1	7	22	6	21	0	.338	.355	.274

PITCHING	GP	GS	W-L	SV	SHO	R	ERA	IP	Ks	BB
Nick Blackburn	33	33	11–11	0	0	102	4.05	193.1	96	39
Scott Baker	28	28	11–4	0	0	66	3.45	172.1	141	42
Kevin Slowey	27	27	12–11	0	2	74	3.99	160.1	123	24
Glen Perkins	26	26	12–4	0	0	81	4.41	151.0	74	39
Livan Hernandez	23	23	10–8	0	0	93	5.48	139.2	54	29
Boof Bonser	47	12	3–7	0	0	87	5.93	118.1	97	36
Matt Guerrier	76	0	6–9	1	0	47	5.19	76.1	59	37
Francisco Liriano	14	14	6–4	0	0	40	3.91	76.0	67	32
Joe Nathan	68	0	1–2	39	0	13	1.33	67.2	74	18
Jesse Crain	66	0	5–4	0	0	29	3.59	62.2	50	24
Eddie Guardado	64	0	4–4	4	0	26	4.15	56.1	33	19
Craig Breslow	49	0	0–2	1	0	12	1.91	47.0	39	19

New York Yankees

BATTING	G	AB	R	H	2B	3B	HR	RBI	TB	BB	SO	SB	OBP	SLG	BA
Bobby Abreu	156	609	100	180	39	4	20	100	287	73	109	22	.371	.471	.296
Robinson Cano	159	597	70	162	35	3	14	72	245	26	65	2	.305	.410	.271
Derek Jeter	150	596	88	179	25	3	11	69	243	52	85	11	.363	.408	.300
Johnny Damon	143	555	95	168	27	5	17	71	256	64	82	29	.375	.461	.303
Alex Rodriguez	138	510	104	154	33	0	35	103	292	65	117	18	.392	.573	.302
Jason Giambi	145	458	68	113	19	1	32	96	230	76	111	2	.373	.502	.247
Melky Cabrera	129	414	42	103	12	1	8	37	141	29	58	9	.301	.341	.249
Ivan Rodriguez	115	398	44	110	20	3	7	35	157	23	67	10	.319	.394	.276
Hideki Matsui	93	337	43	99	17	0	9	45	143	38	47	0	.370	.424	.294
Richie Sexton	96	280	29	62	9	0	12	36	107	43	86	1	.321	.382	.221
Jose Molina	100	268	32	58	17	0	3	18	84	12	52	0	.263	.313	.216
Xavier Nady	59	228	26	61	11	0	12	40	108	14	48	1	.320	.474	.268
Wilson Betemit	87	189	24	50	13	0	6	25	81	6	56	0	.289	.429	.265
Jorge Posada	51	168	18	45	13	1	3	22	69	24	38	0	.364	.411	.268
Brett Gardner	42	127	18	29	5	2	0	16	38	8	30	1	.283	.299	.228

PITCHING	GP	GS	W–L	SV	SHO	R	ERA	IP	Ks	BB
Andy Pettitte	33	33	14–14	0	0	112	4.54	204.0	158	55
Mike Mussina	34	34	20–9	0	0	85	3.37	200.1	150	31
Sidney Ponson	25	24	8–5	0	0	89	5.04	135.2	58	48
Darrell Rasner	24	20	5–10	0	0	74	5.40	113.1	67	39
Joba Chamberlain	42	12	4–3	0	0	32	2.60	100.1	118	39
Chien-Ming Wang	15	15	8–2	0	0	44	4.07	95.0	54	35
Mariano Rivera	64	0	6–5	39	0	11	1.40	70.2	77	6
Jose Veras	60	0	5–3	0	0	23	3.59	57.2	63	29
Edwar Ramirez	55	0	5–1	1	0	25	3.90	55.1	63	24
Kyle Farnsworth	45	0	1–2	1	0	18	3.65	44.1	43	17
Dan Giese	20	3	1–3	0	0	22	3.53	43.1	29	14
La Troy Hawkins	33	0	1–1	0	0	26	5.71	41.0	23	17
Ross Ohlendorf	25	0	1–1	0	0	31	6.53	40.0	36	19
Ian Kennedy	10	9	0–4	0	0	37	8.17	39.2	27	26
Brian Bruney	32	1	3–0	1	0	7	1.83	34.1	33	16
Carl Pavano	7	7	4–2	0	0	23	5.77	34.1	15	10
Phil Hughes	8	8	0–4	0	0	26	6.62	34.0	23	15
David Robertson	25	0	4–0	0	0	18	5.34	30.1	36	15

Oakland Athletics

BATTING	G	AB	R	H	2B	3B	HR	RBI	TB	BB	SO	SB	OBP	SLG	BA
Bobby Crosby	145	556	66	132	39	1	7	91	194	47	96	7	.296	.349	.237
Kurt Suzuki	148	530	54	148	25	1	7	42	196	44	69	2	.346	.370	.279
Jack Cust	148	481	77	111	19	0	33	77	229	111	197	0	.375	.476	.231
Daric Barton	140	446	59	101	17	5	9	47	155	65	99	2	.327	.348	.226
Mark Ellis	117	442	55	103	20	3	12	41	165	53	65	14	.321	.373	.233
Jack Hannahan	143	436	48	95	27	0	9	47	149	55	131	2	.305	.342	.218
Emil Brown	117	402	48	98	14	2	13	59	155	27	65	4	.297	.386	.244
Ryan Sweeney	115	384	53	110	18	2	5	45	147	38	67	9	.350	.383	.286
Carlos Gonzalez	85	302	31	73	22	1	4	26	109	13	81	4	.273	.361	.242
Frank Thomas	71	246	27	59	7	1	8	30	92	39	57	0	.349	.374	.240
Rajai Davis	101	196	28	51	5	4	3	19	73	7	34	25	.288	.372	.260
Travis Buck	38	155	16	35	9	1	7	25	67	11	38	1	.291	.432	.226
Mike Sweeney	42	126	13	36	8	0	2	12	50	7	6	0	.331	.397	.286
Donnie Murphy	46	103	10	19	3	0	3	13	31	11	38	2	.274	.301	.184
Cliff Pennington	36	99	14	24	5	0	0	9	29	13	18	4	.339	.293	.242

PITCHING	GP	GS	W–L	SV	SHO	R	ERA	IP	Ks	BB
Greg Smith	32	32	7–16	0	0	92	4.16	190.1	111	87
Dana Eveland	29	29	9–9	0	0	82	4.34	168.0	118	77
Justin Duchscherer	22	22	10–8	0	1	45	2.54	141.2	95	34
Joe Blanton	20	20	5–12	0	0	74	4.96	127.0	62	35
Rich Harden	13	13	5–1	0	0	21	2.34	77.0	92	31
Dallas Branden	19	10	5–4	0	0	36	4.14	71.2	41	25
Huston Street	63	0	7–5	18	0	29	3.73	70.0	69	27
Chad Gaudin	26	6	5–3	0	0	29	3.59	62.2	44	17
Alan Embree	70	0	2–5	0	0	36	4.96	61.2	57	30
Brad Ziegler	47	0	3–0	11	0	8	1.06	59.2	30	22
Sean Gallagher	11	11	2–3	0	0	42	5.88	56.2	54	36
Santiago Casilla	51	0	2–1	2	0	22	3.93	50.1	43	20
Joey Devine	42	0	6–1	1	0	7	0.59	45.2	49	15

American League Team-by-Team Statistical Leaders *(Cont.)*

Seattle Mariners

BATTING	G	AB	R	H	2B	3B	HR	RBI	TB	BB	SO	SB	OBP	SLG	BA
Ichiro Suzuki	162	686	103	213	20	7	6	42	265	51	65	43	.361	.386	.310
Jose Lopez	159	644	80	191	41	1	17	89	285	27	67	6	.322	.443	.297
Raul Ibanez	162	635	85	186	43	3	23	110	304	64	110	2	.358	.479	.293
Yuniesky Betancourt	153	559	66	156	36	3	7	51	219	17	42	4	.300	.392	.279
Adrian Beltre	143	556	74	148	29	1	25	77	254	50	90	8	.327	.457	.266
Kenji Johjima	112	379	29	86	19	0	7	39	126	19	33	2	.277	.332	.227
Jose Vidro	85	308	28	72	11	0	7	45	104	18	36	2	.274	.338	.234
Jeremy Reed	97	286	30	77	18	1	2	31	103	18	38	2	.314	.360	.269
Wladimir Balentien	71	243	23	49	13	0	7	24	83	16	79	0	.250	.342	.202
Miguel Cairo	108	221	34	55	14	2	0	23	73	18	32	5	.316	.330	.249
Jeff Clement	66	203	17	46	10	1	5	23	73	15	63	0	.295	.360	.227
Willie Bloomquist	71	165	32	46	1	0	0	9	47	25	29	14	.377	.285	.279
Bryan LaHair	45	136	15	34	4	0	3	10	47	13	40	0	.315	.346	.250
Jamie Burke	48	92	10	24	3	0	1	8	30	5	7	0	.303	.326	.261
Tug Hulett	30	49	2	11	1	0	1	2	15	5	17	0	.309	.306	.224

PITCHING	GP	GS	W–L	SV	SHO	R	ERA	IP	Ks	BB
Felix Hernandez	31	31	9–11	0	0	85	3.45	200.2	175	80
Jarrod Washburn	28	26	5–14	1	0	87	4.69	153.2	87	50
Carlos Silva	28	28	4–15	0	0	114	6.46	153.1	69	32
Ryan Rowland-Smith	47	12	5–3	2	0	49	3.42	118.1	77	48
Miguel Batista	44	20	4–14	1	0	89	6.26	115.0	73	79
R.A. Dickey	32	14	5–8	0	0	65	5.21	112.1	58	51
Erik Bedard	15	15	6–4	0	0	38	3.67	81.0	72	37
Sean Green	72	0	4–5	1	0	47	4.67	79.0	62	36
Roy Corcoran	50	0	6–2	3	0	31	3.22	72.2	39	36
Brandon Morrow	45	5	3–4	10	0	26	3.34	64.2	75	34
Mark Lowe	57	0	1–5	1	0	44	5.37	63.2	55	34
J.J. Putz	47	0	6–5	15	0	20	3.88	46.1	56	28
Ryan Feierabend	8	8	1–4	0	0	34	7.71	39.2	26	14
Cesar Jimenez	31	2	0–2	0	0	13	3.41	34.1	26	13
Cha Seung Baek	10	1	0–1	0	0	18	5.40	30.0	15	13

Tampa Bay Devil Rays

BATTING	G	AB	R	H	2B	3B	HR	RBI	TB	BB	SO	SB	OBP	SLG	BA
Akinori Iwamura	152	627	91	172	30	9	6	48	238	70	131	8	.349	.380	.274
B.J. Upton	145	531	85	145	37	2	9	67	213	97	134	44	.383	.401	.273
Carlos Pena	139	490	76	121	24	2	31	102	242	96	166	1	.377	.494	.247
Jason Bartlett	128	454	48	130	25	3	1	37	164	22	69	20	.329	.361	.286
Evan Longoria	122	448	67	122	31	2	27	85	238	46	122	7	.343	.531	.272
Carl Crawford	109	443	69	121	12	10	8	57	177	30	60	25	.319	.400	.273
Dioner Navarro	120	427	43	126	27	0	7	54	174	34	47	0	.349	.407	.295
Eric Hinske	133	381	59	94	21	1	20	60	177	47	88	10	.333	.465	.247
Willy Aybar	95	324	33	82	17	2	10	33	133	32	44	2	.327	.410	.253
Gabe Gross	127	302	40	73	13	3	13	38	131	40	75	2	.333	.434	.242
Cliff Floyd	80	246	32	66	13	0	11	39	112	28	58	1	.349	.455	.268
Ben Zobrist	62	198	32	50	10	2	12	30	100	25	37	3	.339	.505	.253
Jonny Gomes	77	154	23	28	5	1	8	21	59	15	46	8	.282	.383	.182
Shawn Riggans	44	135	21	30	7	0	6	24	55	12	30	0	.287	.407	.222

PITCHING	GP	GS	W–L	SV	SHO	R	ERA	IP	Ks	BB
James Shields	33	33	14–8	0	2	94	3.56	215.0	160	40
Andy Sonnanstine	32	32	13–9	0	1	105	4.38	193.1	124	37
Matt Garza	30	30	11–9	0	2	83	3.70	184.2	128	59
Edwin Jackson	32	31	14–11	0	0	91	4.42	183.1	108	77
Scott Kazmir	27	27	12–8	0	0	61	3.49	152.1	166	70
J.P. Howell	64	0	6–1	3	0	29	2.22	89.1	92	39
Jason Hammel	40	5	4–4	2	0	45	4.60	78.1	44	35
Dan Wheeler	70	0	5–6	13	0	25	3.12	66.1	53	22
Chad Bradford	68	0	4–3	0	0	20	2.12	60.2	70	21
Grant Balfour	51	0	6–2	4	0	10	1.54	58.1	82	24
Troy Percival	50	0	2–1	28	0	26	4.53	45.2	38	27
Trever Miller	68	0	2–0	2	0	21	4.15	43.1	44	20
Al Reyes	26	0	2–2	0	0	12	4.37	22.2	19	10
Jeff Niemann	5	2	2–2	0	0	12	5.06	16.0	14	8
Scott Dohmann	12	0	2–0	0	0	10	6.14	14.2	12	7

American League Team-by-Team Statistical Leaders *(Cont.)*

Texas Rangers

BATTING	G	AB	R	H	2B	3B	HR	RBI	TB	BB	SO	SB	OBP	SLG	BA
Michael Young	155	645	102	183	36	2	12	82	259	55	109	10	.339	.402	.284
Josh Hamilton	156	624	98	190	35	5	32	130	331	64	126	9	.371	.530	.304
Ian Kinsler	121	518	102	165	41	4	18	71	268	45	67	26	.375	.517	.319
David Murphy	108	415	64	114	28	3	15	74	193	31	70	7	.321	.465	.275
Milton Bradley	126	414	78	133	32	1	22	77	233	80	112	5	.436	.563	.321
Marlon Byrd	122	403	70	120	28	4	10	53	186	46	62	7	.380	.462	.298
Gerald Laird	95	344	54	95	24	0	6	41	137	23	63	2	.329	.398	.276
Ramon Vazquez	105	300	44	87	18	3	6	40	129	38	66	0	.365	.430	.290
Chris Davis	80	295	51	84	23	2	17	55	162	20	88	1	.331	.549	.285
Brandon Boggs	101	283	30	64	17	4	8	41	113	44	93	3	.333	.399	.226
Hank Blalock	65	258	37	74	19	1	12	38	131	19	40	1	.338	.508	.287
Frank Catalanotto	88	248	28	68	23	1	2	21	99	20	29	1	.342	.399	.274
Jarrod Saltalamacchia	61	198	27	50	13	0	3	26	72	31	74	0	.352	.364	.253
German Duran	60	143	22	33	6	1	3	16	50	7	32	1	.275	.350	.231
Nelson Cruz	31	115	19	38	9	1	7	26	70	17	28	3	.421	.609	.330
Joaquin Arias	32	110	15	32	7	3	0	9	45	7	12	4	.345	.409	.291
Chris Shelton	41	97	14	21	5	0	2	11	32	17	33	1	.333	.330	.216

PITCHING	GP	GS	W–L	SV	SHO	R	ERA	IP	Ks	BB
Vincente Padilla	29	29	14–8	0	1	100	4.74	171.0	127	65
Kevin Millwood	29	29	9–10	0	0	104	5.07	168.2	125	49
Scott Feldman	28	25	6–8	0	0	103	5.29	151.1	74	56
Josh Rupe	46	0	3–1	0	0	52	5.14	89.1	53	46
Jamey Wright	75	0	8–7	0	0	57	5.12	84.1	60	35
Matt Harrison	15	15	9–3	0	1	57	5.49	83.2	42	31
Dustin Nippert	20	6	3–5	0	0	52	6.40	71.2	55	37
Frank Francisco	58	0	3–5	5	0	24	3.13	63.1	83	26
Luis Mendoza	25	11	3–8	1	0	36	8.67	63.1	35	25
Kason Gabbard	12	12	2–3	0	0	36	4.82	56.0	33	39
C.J. Wilson	50	0	2–2	24	0	35	6.02	46.1	41	27
Joaquin Benoit	44	0	3–2	1	0	28	5.00	45.0	43	35
Warner Madrigal	31	1	0–2	1	0	22	4.75	36.0	22	14
Kameron Loe	14	0	1–0	0	0	18	3.23	30.2	20	8
Jason Jennings	6	6	0–5	0	0	27	8.56	27.1	12	18
Eric Hurley	5	5	1–2	0	0	15	5.47	24.2	13	9

Toronto Blue Jays

BATTING	G	AB	R	H	2B	3B	HR	RBI	TB	BB	SO	SB	OBP	SLG	BA
Alex Rios	155	635	91	185	47	8	15	79	293	44	112	32	.337	.461	.291
Lyle Overbay	158	544	74	147	32	2	15	69	228	74	116	1	.358	.419	.270
Marco Scutaro	145	517	76	138	23	1	7	60	184	57	65	7	.341	.356	.267
Vernon Wells	108	427	63	128	22	1	20	78	212	29	46	4	.343	.496	.300
Scott Rolen	115	408	58	107	30	3	11	50	176	46	71	5	.349	.431	.262
Rod Barajas	104	349	44	87	23	0	11	49	143	17	61	0	.294	.410	.249
Joe Inglett	109	344	45	102	15	7	3	39	140	28	43	9	.355	.407	.297
Adam Lind	88	326	48	92	16	4	9	40	143	16	59	2	.316	.439	.282
Matt Stairs	105	320	42	80	11	1	11	44	126	41	87	1	.342	.394	.250
Brad Wilkerson	104	264	21	58	12	2	4	28	86	35	68	3	.308	.326	.220
David Eckstein	76	260	27	72	18	0	1	23	93	24	27	2	.354	.358	.277
Gregg Zaun	86	245	29	58	12	0	6	30	88	38	38	2	.340	.359	.237
Aaron Hill	55	205	19	54	14	0	2	20	74	16	31	4	.324	.361	.263
John McDonald	84	186	21	39	8	0	1	18	50	10	25	3	.255	.269	.210

PITCHING	GP	GS	W–L	SV	SHO	R	ERA	IP	Ks	BB
Roy Halladay	34	33	20–11	0	2	88	2.78	246.0	206	39
A.J. Burnett	35	34	18–10	0	0	109	4.07	221.1	231	86
Jesse Litsch	29	28	13–9	0	2	79	3.58	176.0	99	39
Shaun Marcum	25	25	9–7	0	0	60	3.39	151.1	123	50
Dustin McGowan	19	19	6–7	0	0	60	4.37	111.1	85	38
Scott Downs	66	0	0–3	5	0	15	1.78	70.2	57	27
David Purcey	12	12	3–6	0	0	41	5.54	65.0	58	29
Jesse Carlson	69	0	7–2	2	0	16	2.25	60.0	55	21
B.J. Ryan	60	0	2–4	32	0	21	2.95	58.0	58	28
Brian Tallet	51	0	1–2	0	0	19	2.88	56.1	47	22
Jason Frasor	49	0	1–2	0	0	23	4.18	47.1	42	32
John Parrish	13	6	1–1	0	0	19	4.04	42.1	21	15
Shawn Camp	40	0	3–1	0	0	18	4.12	39.1	31	11
Brandon League	31	0	1–2	1	0	9	2.18	33.0	23	15

The World Series

Results

1903..............Boston (A) 5, Pittsburgh (N) 3
1904..............No series
1905..............New York (N) 4, Philadelphia (A) 1
1906..............Chicago (A) 4, Chicago (N) 2
1907..............Chicago (N) 4, Detroit (A) 0; 1 tie
1908..............Chicago (N) 4, Detroit (A) 1
1909..............Pittsburgh (N) 4, Detroit (A) 3
1910..............Philadelphia (A) 4, Chicago (N) 1
1911..............Philadelphia (A) 4, New York (N) 2
1912..............Boston (A) 4, New York (N) 3; 1 tie
1913..............Philadelphia (A) 4, New York (N) 1
1914..............Boston (N) 4, Philadelphia (A) 0
1915..............Boston (A) 4, Philadelphia (N) 1
1916..............Boston (A) 4, Brooklyn (N) 1
1917..............Chicago (A) 4, New York (N) 2
1918..............Boston (A) 4, Chicago (N) 2
1919..............Cincinnati (N) 5, Chicago (A) 3
1920..............Cleveland (A) 5, Brooklyn (N) 2
1921..............New York (N) 5, New York (A) 3
1922..............New York (N) 4, New York (A) 0; 1 tie
1923..............New York (A) 4, New York (N) 2
1924..............Washington (A) 4, New York (N) 3
1925..............Pittsburgh (N) 4, Washington (A) 3
1926..............St. Louis (N) 4, New York (A) 3
1927..............New York (A) 4, Pittsburgh (N) 0
1928..............New York (A) 4, St. Louis (N) 0
1929..............Philadelphia (A) 4, Chicago (N) 1
1930..............Philadelphia (A) 4, St. Louis (N) 2
1931..............St. Louis (N) 4, Philadelphia (A) 3
1932..............New York (A) 4, Chicago (N) 0
1933..............New York (N) 4, Washington (A) 1
1934..............St. Louis (N) 4, Detroit (A) 3
1935..............Detroit (A) 4, Chicago (N) 2
1936..............New York (A) 4, New York (N) 2
1937..............New York (A) 4, New York (N) 1
1938..............New York (A) 4, Chicago (N) 0
1939..............New York (A) 4, Cincinnati (N) 0
1940..............Cincinnati (N) 4, Detroit (A) 3
1941..............New York (A) 4, Brooklyn (N) 1
1942..............St. Louis (N) 4, New York (A) 1
1943..............New York (A) 4, St. Louis (N) 1
1944..............St. Louis (N) 4, St. Louis (A) 2
1945..............Detroit (A) 4, Chicago (N) 3
1946..............St. Louis (N) 4, Boston (A) 3
1947..............New York (A) 4, Brooklyn (N) 3
1948..............Cleveland (A) 4, Boston (N) 2
1949..............New York (A) 4, Brooklyn (N) 1
1950..............New York (A) 4, Philadelphia (N) 0
1951..............New York (A) 4, New York (N) 2
1952..............New York (A) 4, Brooklyn (N) 3
1953..............New York (A) 4, Brooklyn (N) 2
1954..............New York (N) 4, Cleveland (A) 0
1955..............Brooklyn (N) 4, New York (A) 3
1956..............New York (A) 4, Brooklyn (N) 3
1957..............Milwaukee (N) 4, New York (A) 3
1958..............New York (A) 4, Milwaukee (N) 3
1959..............Los Angeles (N) 4, Chicago (A) 2
1960..............Pittsburgh (N) 4, New York (A) 3
1961..............New York (A) 4, Cincinnati (N) 1
1962..............New York (A) 4, San Francisco (N) 3
1963..............Los Angeles (N) 4, New York (A) 0
1964..............St. Louis (N) 4, New York (A) 3
1965..............Los Angeles (N) 4, Minnesota (A) 3
1966..............Baltimore (A) 4, Los Angeles (N) 0
1967..............St. Louis (N) 4, Boston (A) 3
1968..............Detroit (A) 4, St. Louis (N) 3
1969..............New York (N) 4, Baltimore (A) 1
1970..............Baltimore (A) 4, Cincinnati (N) 1
1971..............Pittsburgh (N) 4, Baltimore (A) 3
1972..............Oakland (A) 4, Cincinnati (N) 3
1973..............Oakland (A) 4, New York (N) 3
1974..............Oakland (A) 4, Los Angeles (N) 1
1975..............Cincinnati (N) 4, Boston (A) 3
1976..............Cincinnati (N) 4, New York (A) 0
1977..............New York (A) 4, Los Angeles (N) 2
1978..............New York (A) 4, Los Angeles (N) 2
1979..............Pittsburgh (N) 4, Baltimore (A) 3
1980..............Philadelphia (N) 4, Kansas City (A) 2
1981..............Los Angeles (N) 4, New York (A) 2
1982..............St. Louis (N) 4, Milwaukee (A) 3
1983..............Baltimore (A) 4, Philadelphia (N) 1
1984..............Detroit (A) 4, San Diego (N) 1
1985..............Kansas City (A) 4, St. Louis (N) 3
1986..............New York (N) 4, Boston (A) 3
1987..............Minnesota (A) 4, St. Louis (N) 3
1988..............Los Angeles (N) 4, Oakland (A) 1
1989..............Oakland (A) 4, San Francisco (N) 0
1990..............Cincinnati (N) 4, Oakland (A) 0
1991..............Minnesota (A) 4, Atlanta (N) 3
1992..............Toronto (A) 4, Atlanta (N) 2
1993..............Toronto (A) 4, Philadelphia (N) 2
1994..............Series canceled due to players' strike.
1995..............Atlanta (N) 4, Cleveland (A) 2
1996..............New York (A) 4, Atlanta (N) 2
1997..............Florida (N) 4, Cleveland (A) 3
1998..............New York (A) 4, San Diego (N) 0
1999..............New York (A) 4, Atlanta (N) 0
2000..............New York (A) 4 , New York (N) 1
2001..............Arizona (N) 4, New York (A) 3
2002..............Anaheim (A) 4, San Francisco (N) 3
2003..............Florida (N) 4, New York (A) 2
2004..............Boston (A) 4, St. Louis (N) 0
2005..............Chicago (A) 4, Houston (N) 0
2006..............St. Louis (N) 4, Detroit (A) 1
2007..............Boston (A) 4, Colorado (N) 0
2008..............Philadelphia (N) 4, Tampa Bay (A) 1

Most Valuable Players

1955	Johnny Podres, Bklyn
1956	Don Larsen, NY (A)
1957	Lew Burdette, Mil
1958	Bob Turley, NY (A)
1959	Larry Sherry, LA
1960	Bobby Richardson, NY (A)
1961	Whitey Ford, NY (A)
1962	Ralph Terry, NY (A)
1963	Sandy Koufax, LA
1964	Bob Gibson, StL
1965	Sandy Koufax, LA
1966	Frank Robinson, Balt
1967	Bob Gibson, StL
1968	Mickey Lolich, Det
1969	Donn Clendenon, NY (N)
1970	Brooks Robinson, Balt
1971	Roberto Clemente, Pitt
1972	Gene Tenace, Oak
1973	Reggie Jackson, Oak
1974	Rollie Fingers, Oak
1975	Pete Rose, Cin
1976	Johnny Bench, Cin
1977	Reggie Jackson, NY (A)
1978	Bucky Dent, NY (A)
1979	Willie Stargell, Pitt
1980	Mike Schmidt, Phil
1981	Ron Cey, LA; Steve Yeager, LA; Pedro Guerrero, LA
1982	Darrell Porter, StL
1983	Rick Dempsey, Balt
1984	Alan Trammell, Det
1985	Bret Saberhagen, KC
1986	Ray Knight, NY (N)
1987	Frank Viola, Minn
1988	Orel Hershiser, LA
1989	Dave Stewart, Oak
1990	Jose Rijo, Cin
1991	Jack Morris, Minn
1992	Pat Borders, Tor
1993	Paul Molitor, Tor
1994	Series canceled due to strike.
1995	Tom Glavine, Atl
1996	John Wetteland, NY (A)
1997	Livan Hernandez, Fla
1998	Scott Brosius, NY (A)
1999	Mariano Rivera, NY (A)
2000	Derek Jeter, NY (A)
2001	Randy Johnson, Ariz Curt Schilling, Ariz
2002	Troy Glaus, Ana
2003	Josh Beckett, Fla
2004	Manny Ramirez, Bos
2005	Jermaine Dye, Chi (A)
2006	David Eckstein, StL
2007	Mike Lowell, Bos
2008	Cole Hamels, Phi

Career Batting Leaders (Minimum 40 at bats)

GAMES

Yogi Berra	75
Mickey Mantle	65
Elston Howard	54
Hank Bauer	53
Gil McDougald	53
Phil Rizzuto	52
Joe DiMaggio	51
Frankie Frisch	50
Pee Wee Reese	44
Roger Maris	41
Babe Ruth	41

AT BATS

Yogi Berra	259
Mickey Mantle	230
Joe DiMaggio	199
Frankie Frisch	197
Gil McDougald	190
Hank Bauer	188
Phil Rizzuto	183
Elston Howard	171
Pee Wee Reese	169
Roger Maris	152

HITS

Yogi Berra	71
Mickey Mantle	59
Frankie Frisch	58
Joe DiMaggio	54
Pee Wee Reese	46
Hank Bauer	46
Phil Rizzuto	45
Gil McDougald	45
Lou Gehrig	43
Eddie Collins	42
Babe Ruth	42
Elston Howard	42

BATTING AVERAGE

Bobby Brown	.439
Paul Molitor	.418
Pepper Martin	.418
Hal McRae	.400
Lou Brock	.391
Marquis Grissom	.390
Thurman Munson	.373
George Brett	.373
Pat Borders	.372
Hank Aaron	.364

HOME RUNS

Mickey Mantle	18
Babe Ruth	15
Yogi Berra	12
Duke Snider	11
Reggie Jackson	10
Lou Gehrig	10
Frank Robinson	8
Bill Skowron	8
Joe DiMaggio	8
Goose Goslin	7
Hank Bauer	7
Gil McDougald	7

RUNS BATTED IN

Mickey Mantle	40
Yogi Berra	39
Lou Gehrig	35
Babe Ruth	33
Joe DiMaggio	30
Bill Skowron	29
Duke Snider	26
Reggie Jackson	24
Bill Dickey	24
Hank Bauer	24
Gil McDougald	24

RUNS

Mickey Mantle	42
Yogi Berra	41
Babe Ruth	37
Lou Gehrig	30
Joe DiMaggio	27
Derek Jeter	27
Roger Maris	26
Elston Howard	25
Gil McDougald	23
Jackie Robinson	22

STOLEN BASES

Lou Brock	14
Eddie Collins	14
Frank Chance	10
Davey Lopes	10
Phil Rizzuto	10
Honus Wagner	9
Frankie Frisch	9
Kenny Lofton	9
Johnny Evers	8
Roberto Alomar	7
Joe Tinker	7
Pepper Martin	7
Joe Morgan	7
Rickey Henderson	7

Career Batting Leaders (Cont.)

TOTAL BASES

Mickey Mantle	123
Yogi Berra	117
Babe Ruth	96
Lou Gehrig	87
Joe DiMaggio	84
Duke Snider	79
Hank Bauer	75
Reggie Jackson	74
Frankie Frisch	74
Gil McDougald	72

SLUGGING AVERAGE

Player	SA
Reggie Jackson	.755
Babe Ruth	.744
Lou Gehrig	.731
Bobby Brown	.707
Lenny Dykstra	.700
Al Simmons	.658
Lou Brock	.655
Pepper Martin	.636
Paul Molitor	.636
Joe Harris	.625

STRIKEOUTS

Mickey Mantle	54
Elston Howard	37
Duke Snider	33
Derek Jeter	33
Babe Ruth	30
David Justice	30
Gil McDougald	29
Bill Skowron	26
Bernie Williams	26
Hank Bauer	25

Career Pitching Leaders

GAMES

Whitey Ford	22
Mariano Rivera	20
Mike Stanton	19
Jeff Nelson	16
Rollie Fingers	16
Allie Reynolds	15
Bob Turley	15
Clay Carroll	14
Clem Labine	13
Mark Wohlers	13

INNINGS PITCHED

Whitey Ford	146
Christy Mathewson	101⅔
Red Ruffing	85⅔
Chief Bender	85
Waite Hoyt	83⅔
Bob Gibson	81
Art Nehf	79
Allie Reynolds	77
Jim Palmer	65
Catfish Hunter	63

WINS

Whitey Ford	10
Bob Gibson	7
Red Ruffing	7
Allie Reynolds	7
Lefty Gomez	6
Chief Bender	6
Waite Hoyt	6
Jack Coombs	5
Three Finger Brown	5
Herb Pennock	5
Christy Mathewson	5
Vic Raschi	5
Catfish Hunter	5

*Minimum 25 innings pitched.

LOSSES

Whitey Ford	8
Eddie Plank	5
Schoolboy Rowe	5
Joe Bush	5
Rube Marquard	5
Christy Mathewson	5
Andy Pettite	5

SAVES

Mariano Rivera	9
Rollie Fingers	6
Allie Reynolds	4
Johnny Murphy	4
John Wetteland	4
Robb Nen	4

*EARNED RUN AVERAGE

Player	ERA
Jack Billingham	0.36
Harry Brecheen	0.83
Babe Ruth	0.87
Sherry Smith	0.89
Sandy Koufax	0.95
Hippo Vaughn	1.00
Monte Pearson	1.01
Christy Mathewson	1.06
Mariano Rivera	1.16
Babe Adams	1.29

SHUTOUTS

Christy Mathewson	4
Three Finger Brown	3
Whitey Ford	3
Bill Hallahan	2
Lew Burdette	2
Bill Dinneen	2
Sandy Koufax	2
Allie Reynolds	2
Art Nehf	2
Bob Gibson	2

COMPLETE GAMES

Player	CG
Christy Mathewson	10
Chief Bender	9
Bob Gibson	8
Red Ruffing	7
Whitey Ford	7
George Mullin	6
Eddie Plank	6
Art Nehf	6
Waite Hoyt	6

STRIKEOUTS

Whitey Ford	94
Bob Gibson	92
Allie Reynolds	62
Sandy Koufax	61
Red Ruffing	61
Chief Bender	59
George Earnshaw	56
John Smoltz	52
Waite Hoyt	49
Roger Clemens	49
Christy Mathewson	48

BASES ON BALLS

Whitey Ford	34
Allie Reynolds	32
Art Nehf	32
Jim Palmer	31
Bob Turley	29
Paul Derringer	27
Red Ruffing	27
Don Gullett	26
Burleigh Grimes	26
Vic Raschi	25

Alltime Team Rankings, by Championships

Team	W	L	Appearances	Pct.	Most Recent App.	Last Championship
New York Yankees	26	13	39	.666	2003	2000
St. Louis Cardinals	10	7	17	.588	2006	2006
Phila./K.C./Oakland Athletics	9	5	14	.643	1990	1989
Boston Red Sox	7	5	12	.583	2007	2007
Brooklyn/Los Angeles Dodgers	6	12	18	.333	1988	1988
Pittsburgh Pirates	5	2	7	.714	1979	1979
Cincinnati Reds	5	4	9	.556	1990	1990
New York/San Francisco Giants	5	12	17	.294	2002	1954
Detroit Tigers	4	6	10	.400	2006	1984
Chicago White Sox	3	2	5	.600	2005	2005
Wash. Senators/Minnesota Twins	3	3	6	.500	1991	1991
St. Louis Browns/Baltimore Orioles	3	4	7	.429	1983	1983
Boston/Milwaukee/Atlanta Braves	3	6	9	.333	1999	1995

The World Series *(Cont.)*

Alltime Team Rankings, by Championships *(Cont.)*

Team	W	L	Appearances	Pct.	Most Recent App.	Last Championship
Florida Marlins	2	0	2	1.000	2003	2003
Toronto Blue Jays	2	0	2	1.000	1993	1993
New York Mets	2	2	4	.500	2000	1986
Cleveland Indians	2	3	5	.400	1997	1948
Philadelphia Phillies	2	4	6	.333	2008	2008
Chicago Cubs	2	8	10	.200	1945	1908
California/Anaheim/L.A. Angels	1	0	1	1.000	2002	2002
Arizona Diamondbacks	1	0	1	1.000	2001	2001
Kansas City Royals	1	1	2	.500	1985	1985
Tampa Bay Rays	0	1	1	.000	2008	—
Colorado Rockies	0	1	1	.000	2007	—
Houston Astros	0	1	1	.000	2005	—
Seattle Pilots/Milwaukee Brewers	0	1	1	.000	1982	—
San Diego Padres	0	2	2	.000	1998	—

League Pennant Winners

National League

Year	Team	Manager	W	L	Pct	GA
1900	Brooklyn	Ned Hanlon	82	54	.603	4½
1901	Pittsburgh	Fred Clarke	90	49	.647	7½
1902	Pittsburgh	Fred Clarke	103	36	.741	27½
1903	Pittsburgh	Fred Clarke	91	49	.650	6½
1904	New York	John McGraw	106	47	.693	13
1905	New York	John McGraw	105	48	.686	9
1906	Chicago	Frank Chance	116	36	.763	20
1907	Chicago	Frank Chance	107	45	.704	17
1908	Chicago	Frank Chance	99	55	.643	1
1909	Pittsburgh	Fred Clarke	110	42	.724	6½
1910	Chicago	Frank Chance	104	50	.675	13
1911	New York	John McGraw	99	54	.647	7½
1912	New York	John McGraw	103	48	.682	10
1913	New York	John McGraw	101	51	.664	12½
1914	Boston	George Stallings	94	59	.614	10½
1915	Philadelphia	Pat Moran	90	62	.592	7
1916	Brooklyn	Wilbert Robinson	94	60	.610	2½
1917	New York	John McGraw	98	56	.636	10
1918	Chicago	Fred Mitchell	84	45	.651	10½
1919	Cincinnati	Pat Moran	96	44	.686	9
1920	Brooklyn	Wilbert Robinson	93	61	.604	7
1921	New York	John McGraw	94	59	.614	4
1922	New York	John McGraw	93	61	.604	7
1923	New York	John McGraw	95	58	.621	4½
1924	New York	John McGraw	93	60	.608	1½
1925	Pittsburgh	Bill McKechnie	95	58	.621	8½
1926	St. Louis	Rogers Hornsby	89	65	.578	2
1927	Pittsburgh	Donie Bush	94	60	.610	1½
1928	St. Louis	Bill McKechnie	95	59	.617	2
1929	Chicago	Joe McCarthy	98	54	.645	10½
1930	St. Louis	Gabby Street	92	62	.597	2
1931	St. Louis	Gabby Street	101	53	.656	13
1932	Chicago	Charlie Grimm	90	64	.584	4
1933	New York	Bill Terry	91	61	.599	5
1934	St. Louis	Frankie Frisch	95	58	.621	2
1935	Chicago	Charlie Grimm	100	54	.649	4
1936	New York	Bill Terry	92	62	.597	5
1937	New York	Bill Terry	95	57	.625	3
1938	Chicago	Gabby Hartnett	89	63	.586	2
1939	Cincinnati	Bill McKechnie	97	57	.630	4½
1940	Cincinnati	Bill McKechnie	100	53	.654	12
1941	Brooklyn	Leo Durocher	100	54	.649	2½
1942	St. Louis	Billy Southworth	106	48	.688	2
1943	St. Louis	Billy Southworth	105	49	.682	18
1944	St. Louis	Billy Southworth	105	49	.682	14½
1945	Chicago	Charlie Grimm	98	56	.636	3

League Pennant Winners (*Cont.*)

National League (*Cont.*)

Year	Team	Manager	W	L	Pct	GA
1946	St. Louis*	Eddie Dyer	98	58	.628	2
1947	Brooklyn	Burt Shotton	94	60	.610	5
1948	Boston	Billy Southworth	91	62	.595	6½
1949	Brooklyn	Burt Shotton	97	57	.630	1
1950	Philadelphia	Eddie Sawyer	91	63	.591	2
1951	New York†	Leo Durocher	98	59	.624	1
1952	Brooklyn	Chuck Dressen	96	57	.627	4½
1953	Brooklyn	Chuck Dressen	105	49	.682	13
1954	New York	Leo Durocher	97	57	.630	5
1955	Brooklyn	Walter Alston	98	55	.641	13½
1956	Brooklyn	Walter Alston	93	61	.604	1
1957	Milwaukee	Fred Haney	95	59	.617	8
1958	Milwaukee	Fred Haney	92	62	.597	8
1959	Los Angeles‡	Walter Alston	88	68	.564	2
1960	Pittsburgh	Danny Murtaugh	95	59	.617	7
1961	Cincinnati	Fred Hutchinson	93	61	.604	4
1962	San Francisco#	Al Dark	103	62	.624	1
1963	Los Angeles	Walter Alston	99	63	.611	6
1964	St. Louis	Johnny Keane	93	69	.574	1
1965	Los Angeles	Walter Alston	97	65	.599	2
1966	Los Angeles	Walter Alston	95	67	.586	1½
1967	St. Louis	Red Schoendienst	101	60	.627	10½
1968	St. Louis	Red Schoendienst	97	65	.599	9
1969	New York (E)††	Gil Hodges	100	62	.617	8
1970	Cincinnati (W)††	Sparky Anderson	102	60	.630	14½
1971	Pittsburgh (E)††	Danny Murtaugh	97	65	.599	7
1972	Cincinnati (W)††	Sparky Anderson	95	59	.617	10½
1973	New York (E)††	Yogi Berra	82	79	.509	1½
1974	Los Angeles (W)††	Walter Alston	102	60	.630	4
1975	Cincinnati (W)††	Sparky Anderson	108	54	.667	20
1976	Cincinnati (W)††	Sparky Anderson	102	60	.630	10
1977	Los Angeles (W)††	Tommy Lasorda	98	64	.605	10
1978	Los Angeles (W)††	Tommy Lasorda	95	67	.586	2½
1979	Pittsburgh (E)††	Chuck Tanner	98	64	.605	2
1980	Philadelphia (E)††	Dallas Green	91	71	.562	1
1981	Los Angeles (W)††	Tommy Lasorda	63	47	.573	**
1982	St. Louis (E)††	Whitey Herzog	92	70	.568	3
1983	Philadelphia (E)††	Pat Corrales/ Paul Owens	90	72	.556	6
1984	San Diego (W)††	Dick Williams	92	70	.568	12
1985	St. Louis (E)††	Whitey Herzog	101	61	.623	3
1986	New York (E)††	Davey Johnson	108	54	.667	21½
1987	St. Louis (E)††	Whitey Herzog	95	67	.586	3
1988	Los Angeles (W)††	Tommy Lasorda	94	67	.584	7
1989	San Francisco (W)††	Roger Craig	92	70	.568	3
1990	Cincinnati (W)††	Lou Piniella	91	71	.562	5
1991	Atlanta (W)††	Bobby Cox	94	68	.580	1
1992	Atlanta (W)††	Bobby Cox	98	64	.605	8
1993	Philadelphia (E)††	Jim Fregosi	97	65	.599	3
1994	Season ended Aug. 11 due to players' strike.					
1995	Atlanta (E)††	Bobby Cox	90	54	.625	21
1996	Atlanta (E)††	Bobby Cox	96	66	.593	8
1997	Florida (wc)††	Jim Leyland	92	70	.568	-9
1998	San Diego (W)††	Bruce Bochy	98	64	.605	9½
1999	Atlanta (E)††	Bobby Cox	103	59	.636	6½
2000	New York (wc)††	Bobby Valentine	94	68	.580	-6½
2001	Arizona (W)††	Bob Brenly	92	70	.568	2
2002	San Francisco (wc)††	Dusty Baker	95	66	.590	-2½
2003	Florida (wc)††	Jack McKeon	91	71	.562	-10
2004	St. Louis (C)††	Tony LaRussa	105	57	.648	13
2005	Houston (wc)††	Phil Garner	89	73	.549	-11
2006	St. Louis (C)††	Tony LaRussa	83	78	.516	1½
2007	Colorado (wc)††§	Clint Hurdle	89	73	.549	-1
2008	Philadelphia (E)††	Charlie Manuel	92	70	.568	3

*Defeated Brooklyn, two games to none, in playoff for pennant. †Defeated Brooklyn, two games to one, in playoff for pennant. ‡Defeated Milwaukee, two games to none, in playoff for pennant. #Defeated Los Angeles, two games to one, in playoff for pennant. § Defeated San Diego one-game playoff for wild card. ††Won Championship Series. **First half 36–21; second half 27–26, in season split by strike; defeated Houston in playoff for Western Division title.

League Pennant Winners *(Cont.)*

American League

Year	Team	Manager	W	L	Pct	GA
1901	Chicago	Clark Griffith	83	53	.610	4
1902	Philadelphia	Connie Mack	83	53	.610	5
1903	Boston	Jimmy Collins	91	47	.659	14½
1904	Boston	Jimmy Collins	95	59	.617	1½
1905	Philadelphia	Connie Mack	92	56	.622	2
1906	Chicago	Fielder Jones	93	58	.616	3
1907	Detroit	Hughie Jennings	92	58	.613	1½
1908	Detroit	Hughie Jennings	90	63	.588	½
1909	Detroit	Hughie Jennings	98	54	.645	3½
1910	Philadelphia	Connie Mack	102	48	.680	14½
1911	Philadelphia	Connie Mack	101	50	.669	13½
1912	Boston	Jake Stahl	105	47	.691	14
1913	Philadelphia	Connie Mack	96	57	.627	6½
1914	Philadelphia	Connie Mack	99	53	.651	8½
1915	Boston	Bill Carrigan	101	50	.669	2½
1916	Boston	Bill Carrigan	91	63	.591	2
1917	Chicago	Pants Rowland	100	54	.649	9
1918	Boston	Ed Barrow	75	51	.595	2½
1919	Chicago	Kid Gleason	88	52	.629	3½
1920	Cleveland	Tris Speaker	98	56	.636	2
1921	New York	Miller Huggins	98	55	.641	4½
1922	New York	Miller Huggins	94	60	.610	1
1923	New York	Miller Huggins	98	54	.645	16
1924	Washington	Bucky Harris	92	62	.597	2
1925	Washington	Bucky Harris	96	55	.636	8½
1926	New York	Miller Huggins	91	63	.591	3
1927	New York	Miller Huggins	110	44	.714	19
1928	New York	Miller Huggins	101	53	.656	2½
1929	Philadelphia	Connie Mack	104	46	.693	18
1930	Philadelphia	Connie Mack	102	52	.662	8
1931	Philadelphia	Connie Mack	107	45	.704	13½
1932	New York	Joe McCarthy	107	47	.695	13
1933	Washington	Joe Cronin	99	53	.651	7
1934	Detroit	Mickey Cochrane	101	53	.656	7
1935	Detroit	Mickey Cochrane	93	58	.616	3
1936	New York	Joe McCarthy	102	51	.667	19½
1937	New York	Joe McCarthy	102	52	.662	13
1938	New York	Joe McCarthy	99	53	.651	9½
1939	New York	Joe McCarthy	106	45	.702	17
1940	Detroit	Del Baker	90	64	.584	1
1941	New York	Joe McCarthy	101	53	.656	17
1942	New York	Joe McCarthy	103	51	.669	9
1943	New York	Joe McCarthy	98	56	.636	13½
1944	St. Louis	Luke Sewell	89	65	.578	1
1945	Detroit	Steve O'Neill	88	65	.575	1½
1946	Boston	Joe Cronin	104	50	.675	12
1947	New York	Bucky Harris	97	57	.630	12
1948	Cleveland†	Lou Boudreau	97	58	.626	1
1949	New York	Casey Stengel	97	57	.630	1
1950	New York	Casey Stengel	98	56	.636	3
1951	New York	Casey Stengel	98	56	.636	5
1952	New York	Casey Stengel	95	59	.617	2
1953	New York	Casey Stengel	99	52	.656	8½
1954	Cleveland	Al Lopez	111	43	.721	8
1955	New York	Casey Stengel	96	58	.623	3
1956	New York	Casey Stengel	97	57	.630	9
1957	New York	Casey Stengel	98	56	.636	8
1958	New York	Casey Stengel	92	62	.597	10
1959	Chicago	Al Lopez	94	60	.610	5
1960	New York	Casey Stengel	97	57	.630	8
1961	New York	Ralph Houk	109	53	.673	8
1962	New York	Ralph Houk	96	66	.593	5
1963	New York	Ralph Houk	104	57	.646	10½
1964	New York	Yogi Berra	99	63	.611	1
1965	Minnesota	Sam Mele	102	60	.630	7
1966	Baltimore	Hank Bauer	97	63	.606	9
1967	Boston	Dick Williams	92	70	.568	1

League Pennant Winners (*Cont.*)

American League (*Cont.*)

Year	Team	Manager	W	L	Pct	GA
1968	Detroit	Mayo Smith	103	59	.636	12
1969	Baltimore (E)‡	Earl Weaver	109	53	.673	19
1970	Baltimore (E)‡	Earl Weaver	108	54	.667	15
1971	Baltimore (E)‡	Earl Weaver	101	57	.639	12
1972	Oakland (W)‡	Dick Williams	93	62	.600	5½
1973	Oakland (W)‡	Dick Williams	94	68	.580	6
1974	Oakland (W)‡	Al Dark	90	72	.556	5
1975	Boston (E)‡	Darrell Johnson	95	65	.594	4½
1976	New York (E)‡	Billy Martin	97	62	.610	10½
1977	New York (E)‡	Billy Martin	100	62	.617	2½
1978	New York (E)†‡	Billy Martin, Bob Lemon	100	63	.613	1
1979	Baltimore (E)‡	Earl Weaver	102	57	.642	8
1980	Kansas City (W)‡	Jim Frey	97	65	.599	14
1981	New York (E)‡	Gene Michael/Bob Lemon	59	48	.551	#
1982	Milwaukee (E)‡	Buck Rodgers, Harvey Kuenn	95	67	.586	1
1983	Baltimore (E)‡	Joe Altobelli	98	64	.605	6
1984	Detroit (E)‡	Sparky Anderson	104	58	.642	15
1985	Kansas City (W)‡	Dick Howser	91	71	.562	1
1986	Boston (E)‡	John McNamara	95	66	.590	5½
1987	Minnesota (W)‡	Tom Kelly	85	77	.525	2
1988	Oakland (W)‡	Tony LaRussa	104	58	.642	13
1989	Oakland (W)‡	Tony LaRussa	99	63	.611	7
1990	Oakland (W)‡	Tony LaRussa	103	59	.636	9
1991	Minnesota (W)‡	Tom Kelly	95	67	.586	8
1992	Toronto‡	Cito Gaston	96	66	.593	4
1993	Toronto‡	Cito Gaston	95	67	.586	7
1994	Season ended Aug. 11 due to players' strike.					
1995	Cleveland (C)‡	Mike Hargrove	100	44	.694	30
1996	New York (E)‡	Joe Torre	92	70	.568	4
1997	Cleveland (C)‡	Mike Hargrove	86	75	.534	6
1998	New York (E)‡	Joe Torre	114	48	.704	22
1999	New York (E)‡	Joe Torre	98	64	.605	4
2000	New York (E)‡	Joe Torre	87	74	.540	2½
2001	New York (E)‡	Joe Torre	95	65	.594	13½
2002	Anaheim (wc)‡	Mike Scioscia	99	63	.611	-4
2003	New York (E)‡	Joe Torre	101	61	.623	6
2004	Boston (wc)‡	Terry Francona	98	64	.605	-3
2005	Chicago (C)‡	Ozzie Guillen	99	63	.611	6
2006	Detroit (wc)‡	Jim Leyland	95	67	.586	-1
2007	Boston (E)‡	Terry Francona	96	66	.593	2
2008	Tampa Bay (E)‡	Joe Maddon	97	65	.599	2

†Defeated Boston in one-game playoff. ‡Won championship series.
#First half 34–22; second half 25–26, in season split by strike; defeated Milwaukee in playoff for Eastern Divison title.

League Championship Series

National League

1969 ....New York (E) 3, Atlanta (W) 0
1970 ....Cincinnati (W) 3, Pittsburgh (E) 0
1971 ....Pittsburgh (E) 3, San Francisco (W) 1
1972 ....Cincinnati (W) 3, Pittsburgh (E) 2
1973 ....New York (E) 3, Cincinnati (W) 2
1974 ....Los Angeles (W) 3, Pittsburgh (E) 1
1975 ....Cincinnati (W) 3, Pittsburgh (E) 0
1976 ....Cincinnati (W) 3, Philadelphia (E) 0
1977 ....Los Angeles (W) 3, Philadelphia (E) 1
1978 ....Los Angeles (W) 3, Philadelphia (E) 1
1979 ....Pittsburgh (E) 3, Cincinnati (W) 0
1980 ....Philadelphia (E) 3, Houston (W) 2
1981 ....Los Angeles (W) 3, Montreal (E) 2
1982 ....St. Louis (E) 3, Atlanta (W) 0
1983 ....Philadelphia (E) 3, Los Angeles (W) 1
1984 ....San Diego (W) 3, Chicago (E) 2
1985 ....St. Louis (E) 4, Los Angeles (W) 2
1986 ....New York (E) 4, Houston (W) 2
1987 ....St. Louis (E) 4, San Francisco (W) 3
1988 ....Los Angeles (W) 4, New York (E) 3
1989 ....San Francisco (W) 4, Chicago (E) 1
1990 ....Cincinnati (W) 4, Pittsburgh (E) 2
1991 ....Atlanta (W) 4, Pittsburgh (E) 3
1992 ....Atlanta (W) 4, Pitsburgh (E) 3
1993 ....Philadelphia (E) 4, Atlanta (W) 2
1994 ....Playoffs canceled due to players' strike.
1995 ....Atlanta (E) 4, Cincinnati (C) 0
1996 ....Atlanta (E) 4, St. Louis (C) 3
1997 ....Florida (wc) 4, Atlanta (E) 2
1998 ....San Diego (W) 4, Atlanta (E) 2
1999 ....Atlanta (E) 4, New York (wc) 2
2000 ....New York (wc) 4, St. Louis (C) 1
2001 ....Arizona (W) 4, Atlanta (E) 1
2002 ....San Francisco (wc) 4, St. Louis (C) 1
2003 ....Florida (wc) 4, Chicago (C) 3
2004 ....St. Louis (C) 4, Houston (wc) 3
2005 ....Houston (wc) 4, St. Louis (C) 2
2006 ....St. Louis (C) 4, New York (E) 3
2007 ....Colorado (wc) 4, Arizona (W) 0
2008 ....Philadelphia (E) 4, Los Angeles (W) 1

American League

1969 ....Baltimore (E) 3, Minnesota (W) 0
1970 ....Baltimore (E) 3, Minnesota (W) 0
1971 ....Baltimore (E) 3, Oakland (W) 0
1972 ....Oakland (W) 3, Detroit (E) 2
1973 ....Oakland (W) 3, Baltimore (E) 2
1974 ....Oakland (W) 3, Baltimore (E) 1
1975 ....Boston (E) 3, Oakland (W) 0
1976 ....New York (E) 3, Kansas City (W) 2
1977 ....New York (E) 3, Kansas City (W) 2
1978 ....New York (E) 3, Kansas City (W) 1
1979 ....Baltimore (E) 3, California (W) 1
1980 ....Kansas City (W) 3, New York (E) 0
1981 ....New York (E) 3, Oakland (W) 0
1982 ....Milwaukee (E) 3, California (W) 2
1983 ....Baltimore (E) 3, Chicago (W) 1
1984 ....Detroit (E) 3, Kansas City (W) 0
1985 ....Kansas City (W) 4, Toronto (E) 3
1986 ....Boston (E) 4, California (W) 3
1987 ....Minnesota (W) 4, Detroit (E) 1
1988 ....Oakland (W) 4, Boston (E) 0
1989 ....Oakland (W) 4, Toronto (E) 1
1990 ....Oakland (W) 4, Boston (E) 0
1991 ....Minnesota (W) 4, Toronto (E) 1
1992 ....Toronto (E) 4, Oakland (W) 2
1993 ....Toronto (E) 4, Chicago (W) 2
1994 ....Playoffs canceled due to players' strike.
1995 ....Cleveland (C) 4, Seattle (W) 2
1996 ....New York (E) 4, Baltimore (wc) 1
1997 ....Cleveland (C) 4, Baltimore (E) 2
1998 ....New York (E) 4, Cleveland (C) 2
1999 ....New York (E) 4, Boston (wc) 1
2000 ....New York (E) 4, Seattle (wc) 2
2001 ....New York (E) 4, Seattle (W) 1
2002 ....Anaheim (wc) 4, Minnesota (C) 1
2003 ....New York (E) 4, Boston (wc) 3
2004 ....Boston (wc) 4, New York (E) 3
2005 ....Chicago (C) 4, Los Angeles (W) 1
2006 ....Detroit (wc) 4, Oakland (W) 0
2007 ....Boston (E) 4, Cleveland (C) 3
2008 ....Tampa Bay (E) 4, Boston (wc) 3

NLCS Most Valuable Player

1977........Dusty Baker, LA
1978........Steve Garvey, LA
1979........Willie Stargell, Pitt
1980........Manny Trillo, Phi
1981........Burt Hooton, LA
1982........Darrell Porter, StL
1983........Gary Matthews, Phi
1984........Steve Garvey, SD
1985........Ozzie Smith, StL
1986........Mike Scott, Hou
1987........Jeffrey Leonard, SF
1988........Orel Hershiser, LA
1989........Will Clark, SF
1990........R. Myers/R. Dibble, Cin
1991........Steve Avery, Atl
1992........John Smoltz, Atl
1993........Curt Schilling, Phi
1994........Playoffs canceled
1995........Mike Devereaux, Atl
1996........Javier Lopez, Atl
1997........Livan Hernandez, Fla
1998........Sterling Hitchcock, SD
1999........Eddie Perez, Atl
2000........Mike Hampton, NY
2001........Craig Counsell, Ariz
2002........Benito Santiago, SF
2003........Ivan Rodriguez, Fla
2004........Albert Pujols, StL
2005........Roy Oswalt, Hou
2006........Jeff Suppan, StL
2007........Matt Holliday, Col
2008........Cole Hamels, Phi

ALCS Most Valuable Player

1980........Frank White, KC
1981........Graig Nettles, NY
1982........Fred Lynn, Calif
1983........Mike Boddicker, Balt
1984........Kirk Gibson, Det
1985........George Brett, KC
1986........Marty Barrett, Bos
1987........Gary Gaetti, Minn
1988........Dennis Eckersley, Oak
1989........Rickey Henderson, Oak
1990........Dave Stewart, Oak
1991........Kirby Puckett, Minn
1992........Roberto Alomar, Tor
1993........Dave Stewart, Tor
1994........Playoffs canceled
1995........Orel Hershiser, Clev
1996........Bernie Williams, NY
1997........Marquis Grissom, Clev
1998........David Wells, NY
1999........Orlando Hernandez, NY
2000........David Justice, NY
2001........Andy Pettitte, NY
2002........Adam Kennedy, Ana
2003........Mariano Rivera, NY
2004........David Ortiz, Bos
2005........Paul Konerko, Chi
2006........Placido Polanco, Det
2007........Josh Beckett, Bos
2008........Matt Garza, TB

Divisional Playoffs

National League

1995	Atlanta (E) 3, Colorado (wc) 1 Cincinnati (C) 3, Los Angeles (W) 0
1996	St. Louis (C) 3, San Diego (W) 0 Atlanta (E) 3, Los Angeles (wc) 0
1997	Atlanta (E) 3, Houston (C) 0 Florida (wc) 3, San Francisco (W) 0
1998	San Diego (W) 3, Houston (C) 1 Atlanta (E) 3, Chicago (wc) 0
1999	Atlanta (E) 3, Houston (C) 1 New York (wc) 3, Arizona (W) 1
2000	St. Louis (C) 3, Atlanta (E) 0 New York (wc) 3, San Francisco (W) 1
2001	Atlanta (E) 3, Houston (C) 0 Arizona (W) 3, St. Louis (wc) 2
2002	St. Louis (C) 3, Arizona (W) 0 San Francisco (wc) 3, Atlanta (E) 2
2003	Chicago (C) 3, Atlanta (E) 2 Florida (wc) 3, San Francisco (W) 1
2004	St. Louis (C) 3, Los Angeles (W) 1 Houston (wc) 3, Atlanta (E) 2
2005	Houston (wc) 3, Atlanta (E) 1 St. Louis (wc) 3, San Diego (W) 1
2006	St. Louis (C) 3, San Diego (W) 1 New York (E) 3, Los Angeles (wc) 0
2007	Colorado (wc) 3, Philadelphia (E) 0 Arizona (W) 3, Chicago (C) 0
2008	Los Angeles (W) 3, Chicago (C) 0 Philadelphia (E) 3, Milwaukee (wc) 1

American League

1995	Cleveland (C) 3, Boston (E) 0 Seattle (W) 3, New York (wc) 2
1996	Baltimore (wc) 3, Cleveland (C) 1 New York (E) 3, Texas (W) 1
1997	Baltimore (E) 3, Seattle (W) 1 Cleveland (C) 3, New York (wc) 2
1998	New York (E) 3, Texas (W) 0 Cleveland (C) 3, Boston (wc) 1
1999	New York (E) 3, Texas (W) 1 Boston (wc) 3, Cleveland (C) 2
2000	New York (E) 3, Oakland (W) 2 Seattle (wc) 3, Chicago (C) 0
2001	Seattle (W) 3, Cleveland (wc) 2 New York (E) 3, Oakland (wc) 2
2002	Minnesota (C) 3, Oakland (W) 2 Anaheim (wc) 3, New York (E) 1
2003	New York (E) 3, Minnesota (C) 1 Boston (wc) 3, Oakland (W) 2
2004	New York (E) 3, Minnesota (C) 1 Boston (wc) 3 Anaheim (W) 0
2005	Los Angeles (W) 3, New York (E) 2 Chicago (C) 3, Boston (wc) 0
2006	Oakland (W) 3, Minnesota (C) 0 Detroit (wc) 3, New York (E) 1
2007	Boston (E) 3, Los Angeles (W) 0 Cleveland (C) 3, New York (wc) 1
2008	Boston (wc) 3, Los Angeles (W) 1 Tampa Bay (E) 3, Chicago (C) 1

The All-Star Game

Results

Date	Winner	Score	Site
7-6-33	American	4–2	Comiskey Park, Chi
7-10-34	American	9–7	Polo Grounds, NY
7-8-35	American	4–1	Municipal Stadium, Clev
7-7-36	National	4–3	Braves Field, Bos
7-7-37	American	8–3	Griffith Stadium, Wash
7-6-38	National	4–1	Crosley Field, Cin
7-11-39	American	3–1	Yankee Stadium, NY
7-10-40	National	4–0	Sportsman's Park, StL
7-8-41	American	7–5	Briggs Stadium, Det
7-6-42	American	3–1	Polo Grounds, NY
7-13-43	American	5–3	Shibe Park, Phi
7-11-44	National	7–1	Forbes Field, Pitt
1945	No game due to wartime travel restrictions.		
7-9-46	American	12–0	Fenway Park, Bos
7-8-47	American	2–1	Wrigley Field, Chi
7-13-48	American	5–2	Sportsman's Park, StL
7-12-49	American	11–7	Ebbets Field, Bklyn
7-11-50	National	4–3	Comiskey Park, Chi
7-10-51	National	8–3	Briggs Stadium, Det
7-8-52	National	3–2	Shibe Park, Phi
7-14-53	National	5–1	Crosley Field, Cin
7-13-54	American	11–9	Municipal Stadium, Clev
7-12-55	National	6–5	County Stadium, Mil
7-10-56	National	7–3	Griffith Stadium, Wash
7-9-57	American	6–5	Busch Stadium, StL
7-8-58	American	4–3	Memorial Stadium, Balt
7-7-59	National	5–4	Forbes Field, Pitt
8-3-59	American	5–3	Memorial Coliseum, LA
7-11-60	National	5–3	Municipal Stadium, KC
7-13-60	National	6–0	Yankee Stadium, NY
7-11-61	National	5–4	Candlestick Park, SF
7-31-61	Tie*	1–1	Fenway Park, Bos
7-10-62	National	3–1	D.C. Stadium, Wash
7-30-62	American	9–4	Wrigley Field, Chi
7-9-63	National	5–3	Municipal Stadium, Clev
7-7-64	National	7–4	Shea Stadium, NY
7-13-65	National	6–5	Metro. Stadium, Minn
7-12-66	National	2–1	Busch Stadium, StL
7-11-67	National	2–1	Anaheim Stadium, Cal
7-9-68	National	1–0	Astrodome, Hou
7-23-69	National	9–3	R.F.K. Stadium, Wash.
7-14-70	National	5–4	Riverfront Stadium, Cin
7-13-71	American	6–4	Tiger Stadium, Det
7-25-72	National	4–3	Atlanta Stadium, Atl
7-24-73	National	7–1	Royals Stadium, KC
7-23-74	National	7–2	Three Rivers Stadium, Pitt
7-15-75	National	6–3	County Stadium, Mil
7-13-76	National	7–1	Veterans Stadium, Phi
7-19-77	National	7–5	Yankee Stadium, NY
7-11-78	National	7–3	Jack Murphy Stadium, SD
7-17-79	National	7–6	Kingdome, Sea
7-8-80	National	4–2	Dodger Stadium, LA
8-9-81	National	5–4	Municipal Stadium, Clev
7-13-82	National	4–1	Olympic Stadium, Mtl
7-6-83	American	13–3	Comiskey Park, Chi
7-10-84	National	3–1	Candlestick Park, SF
7-16-85	National	6–1	Metrodome, Minn
7-15-86	American	3–2	Astrodome, Hou
7-14-87	National	2–0	Oakland Coliseum, Oak
7-12-88	American	2–1	Riverfront Stadium, Cin
7-11-89	American	5–3	Anaheim Stadium, Cal
7-10-90	American	2–0	Wrigley Field, Chi
7-9-91	American	4–2	SkyDome, Tor
7-14-92	American	13–6	Jack Murphy Stadium, SD
7-13-93	American	9–3	Camden Yards, Balt
7-12-94	National	8–7	Three Rivers Stadium, Pitt
7-11-95	National	3–2	The Ballpark in Arlington, Tex
7-9-96	National	6–0	Veterans Stadium, Phi
7-8-97	American	3–1	Jacobs Field, Cle

*Game called because of rain after nine innings.

The All-Star Game *(Cont.)*

Results *(Cont.)*

Date	Winner	Score	Site
7-7-98	American	13–8	Coors Field, Col
7-13-99	American	4–1	Fenway Park, Bos
7-11-00	American	6–3	Turner Field, Atl
7-10-01	American	4–1	Safeco Field, Sea
7-9-02	Tie (11 inn)	7–7	Miller Park, Mil
7-15-03	American	7–6	Comiskey Park, Chi
7-13-04	American	9–4	Minute Maid Park, Hou
7-12-05	American	7–5	Comerica Park, Det
7-11-06	American	3–2	PNC Park, Pitt
7-10-07	American	5–4	AT&T Park, SF
7-15-08	American	4–3	Yankee Stadium, NY

Most Valuable Players

Year	Player	League
1962	Maury Wills, LA	NL
	Leon Wagner, LA	AL
1963	Willie Mays, SF	NL
1964	Johnny Callison, Phi	NL
1965	Juan Marichal, SF	NL
1966	Brooks Robinson, Balt	AL
1967	Tony Perez, Cin	NL
1968	Willie Mays, SF	NL
1969	Willie McCovey, SF	NL
1970	Carl Yastrzemski, Bos	AL
1971	Frank Robinson, Balt	AL
1972	Joe Morgan, Cin	NL
1973	Bobby Bonds, SF	NL
1974	Steve Garvey, LA	NL
1975	Bill Madlock, Chi	NL
	Jon Matlack, NY	NL
1976	George Foster, Cin	NL
1977	Don Sutton, LA	NL
1978	Steve Garvey, LA	NL
1979	Dave Parker, Pitt	NL
1980	Ken Griffey, Cin	NL
1981	Gary Carter, Mtl	NL
1982	Dave Concepcion, Cin	NL
1983	Fred Lynn, Calif	AL
1984	Gary Carter, Mtl	NL
1985	LaMarr Hoyt, SD	NL
1986	Roger Clemens, Bos	AL
1987	Tim Raines, Mtl	NL
1988	Terry Steinbach, Oak	AL
1989	Bo Jackson, KC	AL
1990	Julio Franco, Tex	AL
1991	Cal Ripken Jr., Balt	AL
1992	Ken Griffey Jr., Sea	AL
1993	Kirby Puckett, Minn	AL
1994	Fred McGriff, Atl	NL
1995	Jeff Conine, Fla	NL
1996	Mike Piazza, LA	NL
1997	Sandy Alomar, Clev	AL
1998	Roberto Alomar, Balt	AL
1999	Pedro Martinez, Bos	AL
2000	Derek Jeter, NY	AL
2001	Cal Ripken Jr., Balt	AL
2002	None selected	
2003	Garret Anderson, Ana	AL
2004	Alfonso Soriano, Tex	AL
2005	Miguel Tejada, Balt	AL
2006	Michael Young, Tex	AL
2007	Ichiro Suzuki, Sea	AL
2008	J.D. Drew, Bos	AL

The Regular Season

Most Valuable Players

NATIONAL LEAGUE

Year	Name and Team	Position	Noteworthy
1911	Wildfire Schulte, Chi	Outfield	21 HR†, 121 RBI†, .300
1912	*Larry Doyle, NY	Second base	10 HR, 90 RBI, .330
1913	Jake Daubert, Bklyn	First base	52 RBI, .350†
1914	*Johnny Evers, Bos	Second base	FA .976†, .279
1915–23	No selection		
1924	Dazzy Vance, Bklyn	Pitcher	28†–6, 2.16 ERA†, 262 K†
1925	Rogers Hornsby, StL	Second base, Manager	39 HR†, 143 RBI†, .403†
1926	*Bob O'Farrell, StL	Catcher	7 HR, 68 RBI, .293
1927	*Paul Waner, Pitt	Outfield	237 hits†, 131 RBI†, .380†
1928	*Jim Bottomley, StL	First base	31 HR†, 136 RBI†, .325
1929	*Rogers Hornsby, Chi	Second base	39 HR, 149 RBI, 156 runs†, .380
1930	No selection		
1931	*Frankie Frisch, StL	Second base	4 HR, 82 RBI, 28 SB†, .311
1932	Chuck Klein, Phi	Outfield	38 HR†, 137 RBI, 226 hits†, .348
1933	*Carl Hubbell, NY	Pitcher	23†–12, 1.66 ERA†, 10 SO†
1934	*Dizzy Dean, StL	Pitcher	30†–7, 2.66 ERA, 195 K†
1935	*Gabby Hartnett, Chi	Catcher	13 HR, 91 RBI, .344
1936	*Carl Hubbell, NY	Pitcher	26†–6, 2.31 ERA†
1937	Joe Medwick, StL	Outfield	31 HR‡, 154 RBI†, 111 runs†, .374†
1938	Ernie Lombardi, Cin	Catcher	19 HR, 95 RBI, .342†
1939	*Bucky Walters, Cin	Pitcher	27†–11, 2.29 ERA†, 137 K‡
1940	*Frank McCormick, Cin	First base	19 HR, 127 RBI, 191 hits†, .309
1941	*Dolph Camilli, Bklyn	First base	34 HR†, 120 RBI†, .285
1942	*Mort Cooper, StL	Pitcher	22†–7, 1.78 ERA†, 10 SO†
1943	*Stan Musial, StL	Outfield	13 HR, 81 RBI, 220 hits†, .357†
1944	*Marty Marion, StL	Shortstop	FA .972†, 63 RBI
1945	*Phil Cavarretta, Chi	First base	6 HR, 97 RBI, .355†
1946	*Stan Musial, StL	First base, Outfield	103 RBI, 124 runs†, 228 hits†, .365†
1947	Bob Elliott, Bos	Third base	22 HR, 113 RBI, .317
1948	Stan Musial, StL	Outfield	39 HR, 131 RBI†, .376†
1949	*Jackie Robinson, Bklyn	Second base	16 HR, 124 RBI, 37 SB†, .342†
1950	*Jim Konstanty, Phi	Pitcher	16–7, 22 saves†, 2.66 ERA
1951	Roy Campanella, Bklyn	Catcher	33 HR, 108 RBI, .325
1952	Hank Sauer, Chi	Outfield	37 HR‡, 121 RBI†, .270

*Played for pennant or, after 1968, division winner. †Led league. ‡Tied for league lead.

Most Valuable Players (Cont.)

NATIONAL LEAGUE (Cont.)

Year	Name and Team	Position	Noteworthy
1953	*Roy Campanella, Bklyn	Catcher	41 HR, 142 RBI†, .312
1954	*Willie Mays, NY	Outfield	41 HR, 110 RBI, 13 3B†, .345†
1955	*Roy Campanella, Bklyn	Catcher	32 HR, 107 RBI, .318
1956	*Don Newcombe, Bklyn	Pitcher	27†–7, 3.06 ERA
1957	*Hank Aaron, Mil	Outfield	44 HR†, 132 RBI†, .322
1958	Ernie Banks, Chi	Shortstop	47 HR†, 129 RBI†, .313
1959	Ernie Banks, Chi	Shortstop	45 HR, 143 RBI†, .304
1960	*Dick Groat, Pitt	Shortstop	2 HR, 50 RBI, .325†
1961	*Frank Robinson, Cin	Outfield	37 HR, 124 RBI, .323
1962	Maury Wills, LA	Shortstop	104 SB†, 208 hits, .299, GG
1963	*Sandy Koufax, LA	Pitcher	25‡–5, 1.88 ERA†, 306 K†
1964	*Ken Boyer, StL	Third Base	24 HR, 119 RBI†, .295
1965	Willie Mays, SF	Outfield	52 HR†, 112 RBI, .317, GG
1966	Roberto Clemente, Pitt	Outfield	29 HR, 119 RBI, 202 hits, .317, GG
1967	*Orlando Cepeda, StL	First base	25 HR, 111 RBI†, .325
1968	*Bob Gibson, StL	Pitcher	22–9, 1.12 ERA†, 268 K†, 13 SO†, GG
1969	Willie McCovey, SF	First base	45 HR†, 126 RBI†, .320
1970	*Johnny Bench, Cin	Catcher	45 HR†, 148 RBI†, .293, GG
1971	Joe Torre, StL	Third base	24 HR, 137 RBI†, .363†
1972	*Johnny Bench, Cin	Catcher	40 HR†, 125 RBI†, .270, GG
1973	*Pete Rose, Cin	Outfield	5 HR, 64 RBI, .338†, 230 hits†
1974	*Steve Garvey, LA	First base	21 HR, 111 RBI, 200 hits, .312, GG
1975	*Joe Morgan, Cin	Second base	17 HR, 94 RBI, 67 SB, .327, GG
1976	*Joe Morgan, Cin	Second base	27 HR, 111 RBI, 60 SB, .320, GG
1977	George Foster, Cin	Outfield	52 HR†, 149 RBI†, .320
1978	Dave Parker, Pitt	Outfield	30 HR, 117 RBI, .334†, GG
1979	Keith Hernandez, StL	First base	11 HR, 105 RBI, 210 hits, .344†, GG
	*Willie Stargell, Pitt	First base	32 HR, 82 RBI, .281
1980	*Mike Schmidt, Phi	Third base	48 HR†, 121 RBI†, .286, GG
1981	Mike Schmidt, Phi	Third base	31 HR†, 91 RBI†, 78 runs†, .316, GG
1982	*Dale Murphy, Atl	Outfield	36 HR, 109 RBI‡, .281, GG
1983	Dale Murphy, Atl	Outfield	36 HR, 121 RBI†, .302, GG
1984	*Ryne Sandberg, Chi	Second base	19 HR, 84 RBI, 114 runs†, .314, GG
1985	*Willie McGee, StL	Outfield	10 HR, 82 RBI, 18 3B†, .353†, GG
1986	Mike Schmidt, Phi	Third base	37 HR†, 119 RBI†, .290, GG
1987	Andre Dawson, Chi	Outfield	49 HR†, 137 RBI†, .287, GG
1988	*Kirk Gibson, LA	Outfield	25 HR, 76 RBI, 106 runs, .290
1989	*Kevin Mitchell, SF	Outfield	47 HR†, 125 RBI†, .291
1990	*Barry Bonds, Pitt	Outfield	33 HR, 114 RBI, .301
1991	*Terry Pendleton, Atl	Third base	23 HR, 86 RBI, .319†
1992	Barry Bonds, Pitt	Outfield	34 HR, 103 RBI, .311
1993	Barry Bonds, SF	Outfield	46 HR†, 123 RBI†, .336
1994	Jeff Bagwell, Hou	First base	39 HR, 116 RBI†, .368
1995	*Barry Larkin, Cin	Shortstop	15 HR, 66 RBI, 51 SB, .319
1996	*Ken Caminiti, SD	Third base	40 HR, 130 RBI, .326
1997	Larry Walker, Col	Outfield	49 HR†, 130 RBI, .452 OBA†, .366, GG
1998	Sammy Sosa, Chi	Outfield	66 HR, 158 RBI†, 134 runs†, 416 TB†, .308
1999	*Chipper Jones, Atl	Third Base	45 HR, 110 RBI, 116 runs, .319
2000	*Jeff Kent, SF	Second Base	33 HR, 125 RBI, 114 runs, .334
2001	Barry Bonds, SF	Outfield	73 HR†, 137 RBI. 177 BB†, .328, .863 SLG†
2002	Barry Bonds, SF	Outfield	46 HR, 110 RBI, .582 OBP, 198 BB† .370
2003	Barry Bonds, SF	Outfield	45 HR, .341, .529 OBP†, .749 SLG†
2004	Barry Bonds, SF	Outfield	45HR, 101 RBI, .609 OBP, .812 SLG
2005	Albert Pujols, StL	First Base	41 HR, 117 RBI, .330, .430 OBP†, .609 SLG†
2006	Ryan Howard, Phi	First Base	58 HR†, 149 RBI†, .313, .425 OBP, .659 SLG
2007	Jimmy Rollins, Phi	Shortstop	30 HR, 94 RBI, .296, 139 runs, 41 SB

*Played for pennant or, after 1968, division winner. †Led league. ‡Tied for league lead.

Most Valuable Players (Cont.)

AMERICAN LEAGUE

Year	Name and Team	Position	Noteworthy
1911	Ty Cobb, Det	Outfield	8 HR, 144 RBI†, 24 3B†, .420†
1912	*Tris Speaker, Bos	Outfield	10 HR‡, 98 RBI, 53 2B†, .383
1913	Walter Johnson, Wash	Pitcher	36†–7, 1.09 ERA†, 11 SO†, 243 K†
1914	*Eddie Collins, Phi	Second base	2 HR, 85 RBI, 122 runs†, .344
1915–21	No selection		
1922	George Sisler, StL	First base	8 HR, 105 RBI, 246 hits†, .420†
1923	*Babe Ruth, NY	Outfield	41 HR†, 131 RBI†, .393
1924	*Walter Johnson, Wash	Pitcher	23†–7, 2.72 ERA†, 158 K†
1925	*Roger Peckinpaugh, Wash	Shortstop	4 HR, 64 RBI, .294
1926	George Burns, Clev	First base	114 RBI, 216 hits‡, 64 2B†, .358
1927	*Lou Gehrig, NY	First base	47 HR, 175 RBI†, 52 2B†, .373
1928	Mickey Cochrane, Phi	Catcher	10 HR, 57 RBI, .293
1929	No selection		
1930	No selection		
1931	*Lefty Grove, Phi	Pitcher	31†–4, 2.06 ERA†, 175 K†
1932	Jimmie Foxx, Phi	First base	58 HR†, 169 RBI†, 151 runs†, .364
1933	Jimmie Foxx, Phi	First base	48 HR†, 163 RBI†, .356†
1934	*Mickey Cochrane, Det	Catcher	2 HR, 76 RBI, .320
1935	*Hank Greenberg, Det	First base	36 HR‡, 170 RBI†, 203 hits, .328
1936	*Lou Gehrig, NY	First base	49 HR†, 152 RBI, 167 runs†, .354
1937	Charlie Gehringer, Det	Second base	14 HR, 96 RBI, 133 runs, .371†
1938	Jimmie Foxx, Bos	First base	50 HR, 175 RBI†, .349†
1939	*Joe DiMaggio, NY	Outfield	30 HR, 126 RBI, .381†
1940	*Hank Greenberg, Det	Outfield	41 HR†, 150 RBI†, 50 2B†, .340
1941	*Joe DiMaggio, NY	Outfield	30 HR, 125 RBI†, .357
1942	*Joe Gordon, NY	Second base	18 HR, 103 RBI, .322
1943	*Spud Chandler, NY	Pitcher	20†–4, 1.64 ERA†, 5 SO‡
1944	Hal Newhouser, Det	Pitcher	29†–9, 2.22 ERA†, 187 K†
1945	*Hal Newhouser, Det	Pitcher	25†–9, 1.81 ERA†, 8 SO†, 212 K†
1946	*Ted Williams, Bos	Outfield	38 HR, 123 RBI, 142 runs†, .342
1947	*Joe DiMaggio, NY	Outfield	20 HR, 97 RBI, .315
1948	*Lou Boudreau, Clev	Shortstop	18 HR, 106 RBI, .355
1949	Ted Williams, Bos	Outfield	43 HR†, 159 RBI‡, 150 runs†, .343
1950	*Phil Rizzuto, NY	Shortstop	125 runs, 200 hits, .324
1951	*Yogi Berra, NY	Catcher	27 HR, 88 RBI, .294
1952	Bobby Shantz, Phi	Pitcher	24†–7, 2.48 ERA
1953	Al Rosen, Clev	Third base	43 HR†, 145 RBI†, 115 runs†, .336
1954	Yogi Berra, NY	Catcher	22 HR, 125 RBI, .307
1955	*Yogi Berra, NY	Catcher	27 HR, 108 RBI, .272
1956	*Mickey Mantle, NY	Outfield	52 HR†, 130 RBI†, 132 runs†, .353†
1957	*Mickey Mantle, NY	Outfield	34 HR, 94 RBI, 121 runs†, .365
1958	Jackie Jensen, Bos	Outfield	35 HR, 122 RBI†, .286
1959	*Nellie Fox, Chi	Second base	2 HR, 70 RBI, .306, GG
1960	*Roger Maris, NY	Outfield	39 HR, 112 RBI†, .283, GG
1961	*Roger Maris, NY	Outfield	61 HR†, 142 RBI†, .269
1962	*Mickey Mantle, NY	Outfield	30 HR, 89 RBI, .321, GG
1963	*Elston Howard, NY	Catcher	28 HR, 85 RBI, .287, GG
1964	Brooks Robinson, Balt	Third base	28 HR, 118 RBI†, .317, GG
1965	*Zoilo Versalles, Minn	Shortstop	126 runs†, 45 2B‡, 12 3B‡, GG
1966	*Frank Robinson, Balt	Outfield	49 HR†, 122 RBI†, 122 runs†, .316†
1967	*Carl Yastrzemski, Bos	Outfield	44 HR‡, 121 RBI†, 112 runs†, .326†, GG
1968	*Denny McLain, Det	Pitcher	31†–6, 1.96 ERA, 280 K
1969	*Harmon Killebrew, Minn	Third base, First base	49 HR†, 140 RBI†, .276
1970	*Boog Powell, Balt	First base	35 HR, 114 RBI, .297
1971	*Vida Blue, Oak	Pitcher	24–8, 1.82 ERA†, 8 SO†, 301 K
1972	Dick Allen, Chi	First base	37 HR†, 113 RBI†, .308
1973	*Reggie Jackson, Oak	Outfield	32 HR†, 117 RBI†, 99 runs†, .293
1974	Jeff Burroughs, Tex	Outfield	25 HR, 118 RBI†, .301
1975	*Fred Lynn, Bos	Outfield	21 HR, 105 RBI, 103 runs†, .331, GG
1976	*Thurman Munson, NY	Catcher	17 HR, 105 RBI, .302
1977	Rod Carew, Minn	First base	100 RBI, 128 runs†, 239 hits†, .388†
1978	Jim Rice, Bos	Outfield, DH	46 HR†, 139 RBI†, 213 hits†, .315
1979	*Don Baylor, Calif	Outfield, DH	36 HR, 139 RBI†, 120 runs†, .296
1980	*George Brett, KC	Third base	24 HR, 118 RBI, .390†
1981	*Rollie Fingers, Mil	Pitcher	6–3, 28 saves†, 1.04 ERA
1982	*Robin Yount, Mil	Shortstop	29 HR, 114 RBI, 210 hits†, .331, GG

The Regular Season (*Cont.*)

Most Valuable Players (*Cont.*)

AMERICAN LEAGUE (*Cont.*)

Year	Name and Team	Position	Noteworthy
1983	*Cal Ripken Jr., Balt	Shortstop	27 HR, 102 RBI, 121 runs†, 211 hits†, .318
1984	*Willie Hernandez, Det	Pitcher	9–3, 32 saves, 1.92 ERA
1985	Don Mattingly, NY	First base	35 HR, 145 RBI†, 48 2B†, .324, GG
1986	*Roger Clemens, Bos	Pitcher	24†–4, 2.48 ERA†, 238 K
1987	George Bell, Tor	Outfield	47 HR, 134 RBI†, .308
1988	*Jose Canseco, Oak	Outfield	42 HR†, 124 RBI†, 40 SB, .307
1989	Robin Yount, Mil	Outfield	21 HR, 103 RBI, 101 runs, .318
1990	*Rickey Henderson, Oak	Outfield	28 HR, 119 runs†, 65 SB†, .325
1991	Cal Ripken Jr., Balt	Shortstop	34 HR, 114 RBI, .323
1992	Dennis Eckersley, Oak	Pitcher	7–1, 1.91 ERA, 51 saves
1993	Frank Thomas, Chi	First base	41 HR, 128 RBI, .317
1994	Frank Thomas, Chi	First base	38 HR, 101 RBI, .353
1995	*Mo Vaughn, Bos	First base	39 HR, 126 RBI, .300
1996	*Juan Gonzalez, Tex	Outfield	47 HR, 144 RBI, .314
1997	*Ken Griffey Jr., Sea	Outfield	56 HR†, 125 runs†, 393 TB†, 147 RBI†, .304
1998	*Juan Gonzalez, Tex	Outfield	45 HR, 157 RBI†, 50 2B†, .318
1999	*Ivan Rodriguez, Tex	Catcher	35 HR, 113 RBI, 116 runs, .332, GG
2000	*Jason Giambi, Oak	First Base	43 HR, 137 RBI, .333
2001	*Ichiro Suzuki, Sea	Outfield	.350†, 242 H†, 127 R, 56 SB†
2002	*Miguel Tejada, Oak	Shortstop	34 HR, 131 RBI, .308
2003	Alex Rodriguez, Tex	Shortstop	47 HR†, 118 RBI, .600 SLG†
2004	*Vladimir Guerrero, Ana	Outfield	39 HR, 126 RBI, .598 SLG
2005	*Alex Rodriguez, NYY	Third Base	48 HR†, 130 RBI, .610 SLG†
2006	Justin Morneau, Min	First Base	30HR, 130 RBI, .321, 190 hits
2007	Alex Rodriguez, NYY	Third Base	54 HR, 156 RBI, .314, 183 hits, 24 SB

*Played for pennant or, after 1968, division winner. †Led league. ‡Tied for league lead.
Notes: 2B=doubles; 3B=triples; FA=fielding average; GG=won Gold Glove, award begun in 1957; K=strikeouts; O=shutouts; SB=stolen bases; TB=total bases.

Rookies of the Year

NATIONAL LEAGUE

1947*	Jackie Robinson, Bklyn (1B)
1948*	Alvin Dark, Bos (SS)
1949	Don Newcombe, Bklyn (P)
1950	Sam Jethroe, Bos (OF)
1951	Willie Mays, NY (OF)
1952	Joe Black, Bklyn (P)
1953	Junior Gilliam, Bklyn (2B)
1954	Wally Moon, StL (OF)
1955	Bill Virdon, StL (OF)
1956	Frank Robinson, Cin (OF)
1957	Jack Sanford, Phi (P)
1958	Orlando Cepeda, SF (1B)
1959	Willie McCovey, SF (1B)
1960	Frank Howard, LA (OF)
1961	Billy Williams, Chi (OF)
1962	Ken Hubbs, Chi (2B)
1963	Pete Rose, Cin (2B)
1964	Dick Allen, Phi (3B)
1965	Jim Lefebvre, LA (2B)
1966	Tommy Helms, Cin (2B)
1967	Tom Seaver, NY (P)
1968	Johnny Bench, Cin (C)
1969	Ted Sizemore, LA (2B)
1970	Carl Morton, Mtl(P)
1971	Earl Williams, Atl (C)
1972	Jon Matlack, NY (P)
1973	Gary Matthews, SF (OF)
1974	Bake McBride, StL (OF)
1975	John Montefusco, SF (P)
1976	Pat Zachry, Cin (P)
	Butch Metzger, SD (P)
1977	Andre Dawson, Mtl (OF)
1978	Bob Horner, Atl (3B)
1979	Rick Sutcliffe, LA (P)
1980	Steve Howe, LA (P)

AMERICAN LEAGUE

1949	Roy Sievers, StL (OF)
1950	Walt Dropo, Bos (1B)
1951	Gil McDougald, NY (3B)
1952	Harry Byrd, Phi (P)
1953	Harvey Kuenn, Det (SS)
1954	Bob Grim, NY (P)
1955	Herb Score, Clev (P)
1956	Luis Aparicio, Chi (SS)
1957	Tony Kubek, NY (OF, SS)
1958	Albie Pearson, Wash (OF)
1959	Bob Allison, Wash (OF)
1960	Ron Hansen, Balt (SS)
1961	Don Schwall, Bos (P)
1962	Tom Tresh, NY (SS)
1963	Gary Peters, Chi (P)
1964	Tony Oliva, Minn (OF)
1965	Curt Blefary, Balt (OF)
1966	Tommie Agee, Chi (OF)
1967	Rod Carew, Minn (2B)
1968	Stan Bahnsen, NY (P)
1969	Lou Piniella, KC (OF)
1970	Thurman Munson, NY (C)
1971	Chris Chambliss, Clev (1B)
1972	Carlton Fisk, Bos (C)
1973	Al Bumbry, Balt (OF)
1974	Mike Hargrove, Tex (1B)
1975	Fred Lynn, Bos (OF)
1976	Mark Fidrych, Det (P)
1977	Eddie Murray, Balt (DH)
1978	Lou Whitaker, Det (2B)
1979	Alfredo Griffin, Tor (SS)
	John Castino, Minn (3B)
1980	Joe Charboneau, Clev (OF)
1981	Dave Righetti, NY (P)
1982	Cal Ripken Jr., Balt (SS)

*Just one selection for both leagues.

Rookies of the Year *(Cont.)*

NATIONAL LEAGUE *(Cont.)*

1981 .... Fernando Valenzuela, LA (P)
1982 .... Steve Sax, LA (2B)
1983 .... Darryl Strawberry, NY (OF)
1984 .... Dwight Gooden, NY (P)
1985 .... Vince Coleman, StL (OF)
1986 .... Todd Worrell, StL (P)
1987 .... Benito Santiago, SD (C)
1988 .... Chris Sabo, Cin (3B)
1989 .... Jerome Walton, Chi (OF)
1990 .... Dave Justice, Atl (OF)
1991 .... Jeff Bagwell, Hou (3B)
1992 .... Eric Karros, LA (1B)
1993 .... Mike Piazza, LA (C)
1994 .... Raul Mondesi, LA (OF)
1995 .... Hideo Nomo, LA (P)
1996 .... Todd Hollandsworth, LA (OF)
1997 .... Scott Rolen, Phi (3B)
1998 .... Kerry Wood, Chi (P)
1999 .... Scott Williamson, Cin (P)
2000 .... Rafael Furcal, Atl (SS)
2001 .... Albert Pujols, StL (OF)
2002 .... Jason Jennings, Col (P)
2003 .... Dontrelle Willis, Fla (P)
2004 .... Jason Bay, Pit (OF)
2005 .... Ryan Howard, Phi (1B)
2006 .... Hanley Ramirez, Fla (SS)
2007 .... Ryan Braun, Mil (OF)

AMERICAN LEAGUE *(Cont.)*

1983 .... Ron Kittle, Chi (OF)
1984 .... Alvin Davis, Sea (1B)
1985 .... Ozzie Guillen, Chi (SS)
1986 .... Jose Canseco, Oak (OF)
1987 .... Mark McGwire, Oak (1B)
1988 .... Walt Weiss, Oak (SS)
1989 .... Gregg Olson, Balt (P)
1990 .... Sandy Alomar Jr, Clev (C)
1991 .... Chuck Knoblauch, Minn (2B)
1992 .... Pat Listach, Mil (SS)
1993 .... Tim Salmon, Calif (OF)
1994 .... Bob Hamelin, KC (DH)
1995 .... Marty Cordova, Minn (OF)
1996 .... Derek Jeter, NY (SS)
1997 .... Nomar Garciaparra, Bos (SS)
1998 .... Ben Grieve, Oak (OF)
1999 .... Carlos Beltran, KC (OF)
2000 .... Kazuhiro Sasaki, Sea (P)
2001 .... Ichiro Suzuki, Sea (OF)
2002 .... Eric Hinske, Tor (3B)
2003 .... Angel Berroa, KC (SS)
2004 .... Bobby Crosby, Oak (SS)
2005 .... Huston Street, Oak (P)
2006 .... Justin Verlander, Det (P)
2007 .... Dustin Pedroia, Bos (2B)

Cy Young Award

Year	W–L	Sv	ERA
1956....*Don Newcombe, Bklyn (NL)	27–7	0	3.06
1957....Warren Spahn, Mil (NL)	21–11	3	2.69
1958....Bob Turley, NY (AL)	21–7	1	2.97
1959....Early Wynn, Chi (AL)	22–10	0	3.17
1960....Vernon Law, Pitt (NL)	20–9	0	3.08
1961....Whitey Ford, NY (AL)	25–4	0	3.21
1962....Don Drysdale, LA (NL)	25–9	1	2.83
1963....*Sandy Koufax, LA (NL)	25–5	0	1.88
1964....Dean Chance, LA (AL)	20–9	4	1.65
1965....Sandy Koufax, LA (NL)	26–8	2	2.04
1966....Sandy Koufax, LA (NL)	27–9	0	1.73

NATIONAL LEAGUE

Year	W–L	Sv	ERA
1967.....Mike McCormick, SF	22–10	0	2.85
1968.....*Bob Gibson, StL	22–9	0	1.12
1969.....Tom Seaver, NY	25–7	0	2.21
1970.....Bob Gibson, StL	23–7	0	3.12
1971.....Ferguson Jenkins, Chi	24–13	0	2.77
1972.....Steve Carlton, Phi	27–10	0	1.97
1973.....Tom Seaver, NY	19–10	0	2.08
1974.....Mike Marshall, LA	15–12	21	2.42
1975.....Tom Seaver, NY	22–9	0	2.38
1976.....Randy Jones, SD	22–14	0	2.74
1977.....Steve Carlton, Phi	23–10	0	2.64
1978.....Gaylord Perry, SD	21–6	0	2.72
1979.....Bruce Sutter, Chi	6–6	37	2.23
1980.....Steve Carlton, Phi	24–9	0	2.34
1981.....Fernando Valenzuela, LA	13–7	0	2.48
1982.....Steve Carlton, Phi	23–11	0	3.10
1983.....John Denny, Phi	19–6	0	2.37
1984.....†Rick Sutcliffe, Chi	16–1	0	2.69
1985.....Dwight Gooden, NY	24–4	0	1.53
1986.....Mike Scott, Hou	18–10	0	2.22
1987.....Steve Bedrosian, Phi	5–3	40	2.83
1988.....Orel Hershiser, LA	23–8	1	2.26
1989.....Mark Davis, SD	4–3	44	1.85
1990.....Doug Drabek, Pitt	22–6	0	2.76
1991.....Tom Glavine, Atl	20–11	0	2.55
1992.....Greg Maddux, Chi	20–11	0	2.18
1993.....Greg Maddux, Atl	20–10	0	2.36
1994.....Greg Maddux, Atl	16–6	0	1.56

AMERICAN LEAGUE

Year	W–L	Sv	ERA
1967.....Jim Lonborg, Bos	22–9	0	3.16
1968.....*Denny McLain, Det	31–6	0	1.96
1969.....Denny McLain, Det	24–9	0	2.80
Mike Cuellar, Balt	23–11	0	2.38
1970.....Jim Perry, Minn	24–12	0	3.03
1971.....*Vida Blue, Oak	24–8	0	1.82
1972.....Gaylord Perry, Clev	24–16	1	1.92
1973.....Jim Palmer, Balt	22–9	1	2.40
1974.....Catfish Hunter, Oak	25–12	0	2.49
1975.....Jim Palmer, Balt	23–11	1	2.09
1976.....Jim Palmer, Balt	22–13	0	2.51
1977.....Sparky Lyle, NY	13–5	26	2.17
1978.....Ron Guidry, NY	25–3	0	1.74
1979.....Mike Flanagan, Balt	23–9	0	3.08
1980.....Steve Stone, Balt	25–7	0	3.23
1981.....*Rollie Fingers, Mil	6–3	28	1.04
1982.....Pete Vuckovich, Mil	18–6	0	3.34
1983.....LaMarr Hoyt, Chi	24–10	0	3.66
1984.....*Willie Hernandez, Det	9–3	32	1.92
1985.....Bret Saberhagen, KC	20–6	0	2.87
1986.....*Roger Clemens, Bos	24–4	0	2.48
1987.....Roger Clemens, Bos	20–9	0	2.97
1988.....Frank Viola, Minn	24–7	0	2.64
1989.....Bret Saberhagen, KC	23–6	0	2.16
1990.....Bob Welch, Oak	27–6	0	2.95
1991.....Roger Clemens, Bos	18–10	0	2.62
1992.....*Dennis Eckersley, Oak	7–1	51	1.91
1993.....Jack McDowell, Chi	22–10	0	3.37

Cy Young Award

NATIONAL LEAGUE

Year		W–L	Sv	ERA
1995	Greg Maddux, Atl	19–2	0	1.63
1996	John Smoltz, Atl	24–8	0	2.94
1997	Pedro Martinez, Mtl	17–8	0	1.90
1998	Tom Glavine, Atl	20–6	0	2.47
1999	Randy Johnson, Ariz	17–9	0	2.48
2000	Randy Johnson, Ariz	19–7	0	2.64
2001	Randy Johnson, Ariz	21-6	0	2.49
2002	Randy Johnson, Ariz	24–5	0	2.32
2003	Eric Gagne, LA	2–3	55	1.20
2004	Roger Clemens, Hou	18-4	0	2.98
2005	Chris Carpenter, StL	21-5	0	2.83
2006	Brandon Webb, Ariz	16–8	0	3.10
2007	Jake Peavy, SD	19–6	0	2.54

AMERICAN LEAGUE

Year		W–L	Sv	ERA
1994	David Cone, KC	16–4	0	2.94
1995	Randy Johnson, Sea	18–2	0	2.48
1996	Pat Hentgen, Tor	20–10	0	3.22
1997	Roger Clemens, Tor	21–7	0	2.05
1998	Roger Clemens, Tor	20–6	0	2.65
1999	Pedro Martinez, Bos	23–4	0	1.55
2000	Pedro Martinez, Bos	18–6	0	1.74
2001	Roger Clemens, NY	20–3	0	3.51
2002	Barry Zito, Oak	23–5	0	2.75
2003	Roy Halladay, Tor	22–7	0	3.25
2004	Johan Santana, Min	20-6	0	2.61
2005	Bartolo Colon, LAA	21-8	0	3.48
2006	Johan Santana, Min	19-6	0	2.77
2007	C.C. Sabathia, Cle	19–7	0	3.21

*Won the MVP and Cy Young awards in the same season.
†NL games only. Sutcliffe pitched 15 games with Cleveland before being traded to the Cubs.

Career Individual Batting

GAMES

Pete Rose	3562
Carl Yastrzemski	3308
Hank Aaron	3298
Rickey Henderson	3081
Ty Cobb	3034
Eddie Murray	3026
Stan Musial	3026
Cal Ripken Jr.	3001
Willie Mays	2992
Barry Bonds	2986
Dave Winfield	2973
Rusty Staub	2951
Brooks Robinson	2896
Robin Yount	2856
Craig Biggio	2850
Al Kaline	2834
Rafael Palmeiro	2831
Harold Baines	2830
Eddie Collins	2826
Reggie Jackson	2820
Frank Robinson	2808
Honus Wagner	2792
Tris Speaker	2789

RUNS

Rickey Henderson	2295
Ty Cobb	2245
Barry Bonds	2227
Hank Aaron	2174
Babe Ruth	2174
Pete Rose	2165
Willie Mays	2062
Cap Anson	1996
Stan Musial	1949
Lou Gehrig	1888
Tris Speaker	1882
Mel Ott	1859
Craig Biggio	1834
Frank Robinson	1829
Eddie Collins	1821
Carl Yastrzemski	1816
Ted Williams	1798
Paul Molitor	1782
Charlie Gehringer	1774
Jimmie Foxx	1751
Honus Wagner	1736

HOME RUNS

Barry Bonds	762
Hank Aaron	755
Babe Ruth	714
Willie Mays	660
*Ken Griffey Jr.	611
Sammy Sosa	609
Frank Robinson	586
Mark McGwire	583
Harmon Killebrew	573
Rafael Palmeiro	569
Reggie Jackson	563
*Alex Rodriguez	553
Mike Schmidt	548
*Jim Thome	541
Mickey Mantle	536
Jimmie Foxx	534
*Manny Ramirez	527
Willie McCovey	521
Ted Williams	521
*Frank Thomas	521
Ernie Banks	512
Eddie Mathews	512
Mel Ott	511
Eddie Murray	504

BATTING AVERAGE (5,000 AB)

Ty Cobb	.367
Rogers Hornsby	.358
Ed Delahanty	.346
Tris Speaker	.345
Billy Hamilton	.344
Ted Williams	.344
Dan Brouthers	.342
Harry Heilmann	.342
Babe Ruth	.342
Willie Keeler	.341
Bill Terry	.341
Lou Gehrig	.340
George Sisler	.340
Jesse Burkett	.338
Tony Gwynn	.338
Nap Lajoie	.338
Al Simmons	.334
Cap Anson	.333
Eddie Collins	.333
Paul Waner	.333

HITS

Pete Rose	4256
Ty Cobb	4189
Hank Aaron	3771
Stan Musial	3630
Tris Speaker	3515
Carl Yastrzemski	3419
Cap Anson	3418
Honus Wagner	3415
Paul Molitor	3319
Eddie Collins	3313
Willie Mays	3283
Eddie Murray	3255
Nap Lajoie	3251
Cal Ripken Jr.	3184
George Brett	3154
Paul Waner	3152
Robin Yount	3142
Tony Gwynn	3141
Dave Winfield	3110
Craig Biggio	3060
Rickey Henderson	3055
Rod Carew	3053
Lou Brock	3023
Rafael Palmeiro	3020
Wade Boggs	3010
Al Kaline	3007
Roberto Clemente	3000

AT BATS

Pete Rose	14053
Hank Aaron	12364
Carl Yastrzemski	11988
Cal Ripken Jr.	11551
Ty Cobb	11429
Eddie Murray	11336
Robin Yount	11008
Dave Winfield	11003
Stan Musial	10972
Rickey Henderson	10961
Willie Mays	10881
Craig Biggio	10876
Paul Molitor	10835
Brooks Robinson	10654
Rafael Palmeiro	10472
Honus Wagner	10430
George Brett	10349
Lou Brock	10332

* Active in 2008.

Career Individual Batting (Cont.)

DOUBLES

Tris Speaker	792
Pete Rose	746
Stan Musial	725
Ty Cobb	724
Craig Biggio	668
George Brett	665
Nap Lajoie	657
Carl Yastrzemski	646
Honus Wagner	640
Hank Aaron	624
Paul Molitor	605
Paul Waner	605
Cal Ripken Jr.	603
Barry Bonds	601
*Luis Gonzalez	596
Rafael Palmeiro	585
Robin Yount	583
Cap Anson	581
Wade Boggs	578
Charlie Gehringer	574

TRIPLES

Sam Crawford	309
Ty Cobb	295
Honus Wagner	252
Jake Beckley	243
Roger Connor	233
Tris Speaker	222
Fred Clarke	220
Dan Brouthers	205
Joe Kelley	194
Paul Waner	191
Bid McPhee	188
Eddie Collins	187
Ed Delahanty	185
Sam Rice	184
Jesse Burkett	182
Ed Konetchy	182
Edd Roush	182
Buck Ewing	178
Rabbit Maranville	177
Stan Musial	177

BASES ON BALLS

Barry Bonds	2558
Rickey Henderson	2190
Babe Ruth	2062
Ted Williams	2021
Joe Morgan	1865
Carl Yastrzemski	1845
Mickey Mantle	1733
Mel Ott	1708
*Frank Thomas	1667
Eddie Yost	1614
Darrell Evans	1605
Stan Musial	1599
Pete Rose	1566
Harmon Killebrew	1559
*Jim Thome	1550
Lou Gehrig	1508
Mike Schmidt	1507
Eddie Collins	1499
Willie Mays	1464
Jimmie Foxx	1452
Eddie Mathews	1444
*Gary Sheffield	1435

RUNS BATTED IN

Hank Aaron	2297
Babe Ruth	2213
Cap Anson	2076
Barry Bonds	1996
Lou Gehrig	1995
Stan Musial	1951
Ty Cobb	1937
Jimmie Foxx	1922
Eddie Murray	1917
Willie Mays	1903
Mel Ott	1860
Carl Yastrzemski	1844
Ted Williams	1839
Rafael Palmeiro	1835
Dave Winfield	1833
Al Simmons	1827
Frank Robinson	1812
*Ken Griffey Jr.	1772
Honus Wagner	1732
*Manny Ramirez	1725
*Frank Thomas	1704

SLUGGING AVERAGE (5,000 AB)

Babe Ruth	.690
Ted Williams	.634
Lou Gehrig	.632
Jimmie Foxx	.609
Barry Bonds	.607
Hank Greenberg	.605
*Manny Ramirez	.593
Mark McGwire	.588
*Todd Helton	.583
Joe Dimaggio	.579
*Alex Rodriguez	.578
Rogers Hornsby	.577
*Vladimir Guerrero	.575
Larry Walker	.565
Albert Belle	.564
Johnny Mize	.562
Juan Gonzalez	.561
*Jim Thome	.560
Stan Musial	.559
Mickey Mantle	.557
Willie Mays	.557

STOLEN BASES

Rickey Henderson	1406
Lou Brock	938
Billy Hamilton	912
Ty Cobb	892
Tim Raines	808
Vince Coleman	752
Eddie Collins	745
Max Carey	738
Honus Wagner	722
Joe Morgan	689
Willie Wilson	668
Bert Campaneris	649
*Kenny Lofton	622
Otis Nixon	620
George Davis	616
Tom Brown	615
Dummy Hoy	594
Maury Wills	586
George Van Haltren	583
Ozzie Smith	580

ON-BASE PERCENTAGE (5,000 AB)

Ted Williams	.482
Babe Ruth	.469
Barry Bonds	.444
Lou Gehrig	.442
*Todd Helton	.428
Jimmie Foxx	.425
Ty Cobb	.424
Rogers Hornsby	.424
Mickey Mantle	.422
*Frank Thomas	.419
Edgar Martinez	.418
Stan Musial	.417
Tris Speaker	.417
Wade Boggs	.415
*Manny Ramirez	.411
Mel Ott	.410
Mickey Cochrane	.409
Hank Greenberg	.409
Jeff Bagwell	.408
*Jason Giambi	.408
*Chipper Jones	.408

TOTAL BASES

Hank Aaron	6856
Stan Musial	6134
Willie Mays	6066
Barry Bonds	5976
Ty Cobb	5859
Babe Ruth	5793
Pete Rose	5752
Carl Yastrzemski	5539
Eddie Murray	5397
Rafael Palmeiro	5388
Frank Robinson	5373
Dave Winfield	5221
Cal Ripken Jr.	5168
Tris Speaker	5101
*Ken Griffey Jr.	5092
Lou Gehrig	5060
George Brett	5044
Mel Ott	5041
Jimmie Foxx	4956
Ted Williams	4884
Honus Wagner	4862

STRIKEOUTS

Reggie Jackson	2597
Sammy Sosa	2306
*Jim Thome	2190
Andres Galarraga	2003
Jose Canseco	1942
Willie Stargell	1936
Mike Schmidt	1883
Fred McGriff	1882
Tony Perez	1867
Dave Kingman	1816
Bobby Bonds	1757
Craig Biggio	1753
Dale Murphy	1748
Lou Brock	1730
*Carlos Delgado	1725
Mickey Mantle	1710
Harmon Killebrew	1699
Chili Davis	1698
Dwight Evans	1697
Rickey Henderson	1694

*Active in 2008.

The 30–30 Club (30 HR, 30 SB in single season)

Year		HR	SB
1922	Kenny Williams, StL	39	37
1956	Willie Mays, NYG	36	40
1957	Willie Mays, NYG	35	38
1963	Hank Aaron, Mil	44	31
1969	Bobby Bonds, SF	32	45
1970	Tommy Harper, Mil	31	38
1973	Bobby Bonds, SF	39	43
1975	Bobby Bonds, NYY	32	30
1977	Bobby Bonds, Cal	37	41
1978	Bobby Bonds, Chi/Tex	31	43
1983	Dale Murphy, Atl	36	30
1987	Joe Carter, Clev	32	31
1987	Eric Davis, Cin	37	50
1987	Darryl Strawberry, NYM	39	36
1987	Howard Johnson, NYM	36	32
1988	Jose Canseco, Oak	42	40
1989	Howard Johnson, NYM	36	41
1990	Ron Gant, Atl	32	33
1990	Barry Bonds, Pitt	33	52
1991	Ron Gant, Atl	32	34
1991	Howard Johnson, NYM	38	30
1992	Barry Bonds, Pitt	34	39
1993	Sammy Sosa, ChiC	33	36
1995	Barry Bonds, SF	33	31
1995	Sammy Sosa, ChiC	36	34
1996	Barry Bonds, SF	42	40
1996	Ellis Burks, Col	40	32
1996	Barry Larkin, Cin	33	36
1996	Dante Bichette, Col	31	31
1997	Larry Walker, Col	49	33
1997	Jeff Bagwell, Hou	43	31
1997	Raul Mondesi, LA	30	32
1997	Barry Bonds, SF	40	37
1998	Alex Rodriguez, Sea	42	46
1998	Shawn Green, Tor	35	35
1999	Jeff Bagwell, Hou	42	30
1999	Raul Mondesi, LA	33	36
2000	Preston Wilson, Fla	31	36
2001	Vladimir Guerrero, Mtl	34	37
2001	Jose Cruz Jr., Tor	34	32
2001	Bobby Abreu, Phi	31	36
2002	Alfonso Soriano, NYY	39	41
2002	Vladimir Guerrero, Mtl	39	40
2003	Alfonso Soriano, NYY	38	35
2004	Carlos Beltran, KC/Hou	38	42
2004	Bobby Abreu, Phi	30	40
2005	Alfonso Soriano, Tex	36	30
2006	Alfonso Soriano, Wash	46	41
2007	Brandon Phillips, Cin	30	32
2007	Jimmy Rollins, Phi	30	41
2007	David Wright, NYM	30	34
2008	Grady Sizemore, Cle	33	38
2008	Hanley Ramirez, Fla	33	35

Career Individual Pitching

GAMES

Jesse Orosco	1251
Mike Stanton	1178
John Franco	1119
Dennis Eckersley	1071
Hoyt Wilhelm	1070
Dan Plesac	1064
*Mike Timlin	1058
Kent Tekulve	1050
Jose Mesa	1022
Lee Smith	1022
Roberto Hernandez	1010
Mike Jackson	1005
Goose Gossage	1002
Lindy McDaniel	987
*Todd Jones	982
Rollie Fingers	944
Gene Garber	931
*Trevor Hoffman	929
Cy Young	906
Sparky Lyle	899
Jim Kaat	898
*David Weathers	896
*Tom Gordon	887

INNINGS PITCHED

Cy Young	7356.0
Pud Galvin	6003.1
Walter Johnson	5914.1
Phil Niekro	5404.1
Nolan Ryan	5386.0
Gaylord Perry	5350.1
Don Sutton	5282.1
Warren Spahn	5243.1
Steve Carlton	5217.1
Grover Alexander	5190.0
Kid Nichols	5056.1
Tim Keefe	5049.2
*Greg Maddux	5008.1
Bert Blyleven	4970.0
Bobby Mathews	4956.0
Roger Clemens	4916.2
Mickey Welch	4802.0
Tom Seaver	4782.2
Christy Mathewson	4780.2
Tommy John	4710.1
Robin Roberts	4688.2
Early Wynn	4564.0
John Clarkson	4536.1

WINS

Cy Young	511
Walter Johnson	417
Grover Alexander	373
Christy Mathewson	373
Pud Galvin	365
Warren Spahn	363
Kid Nichols	361
*Greg Maddux	355
Roger Clemens	354
Tim Keefe	342
Steve Carlton	329
John Clarkson	328
Eddie Plank	326
Nolan Ryan	324
Don Sutton	324
Phil Niekro	318
Gaylord Perry	314
Tom Seaver	311
Charley Radbourn	309
Mickey Welch	307
*Tom Glavine	305
Lefty Grove	300
Early Wynn	300

* Active in 2008.

Career Individual Pitching *(Cont.)*

LOSSES

Cy Young	316
Pud Galvin	310
Nolan Ryan	292
Walter Johnson	279
Phil Niekro	274
Gaylord Perry	265
Don Sutton	256
Jack Powell	254
Eppa Rixey	251
Bert Blyleven	250
Bobby Mathews	248
Robin Roberts	245
Warren Spahn	245
Steve Carlton	244
Early Wynn	244
Jim Kaat	237
Frank Tanana	236
Gus Weyhing	232
Tommy John	231
Bob Friend	230
Ted Lyons	230

WINNING PERCENTAGE**

Al Spalding	.795
Spud Chandler	.717
Whitey Ford	.690
Dave Foutz	.690
Bob Caruthers	.688
Don Gullett	.686
*Pedro Martinez	.684
Lefty Grove	.680
Joe Wood	.672
Vic Raschi	.667
Roger Clemens	.667
Larry Corcoran	.665
Christy Mathewson	.665
Sam Leever	.660
Sal Maglie	.657
Dick McBride	.656
Sandy Koufax	.655
*Tim Hudson	.655
Johnny Allen	.654

SAVES

*Trevor Hoffman	554
*Mariano Rivera	482
Lee Smith	478
John Franco	424
Dennis Eckersley	390
*Billy Wagner	385
Jeff Reardon	367
*Troy Percival	352
Randy Myers	347
Rollie Fingers	341
John Wetteland	330
Roberto Hernandez	326
Jose Mesa	321
*Todd Jones	319
Rick Aguilera	318
Robb Nen	314
Tom Henke	311
Goose Gossage	310
Jeff Montgomery	304
Doug Jones	303
Bruce Sutter	300

EARNED RUN AVERAGE (2,000 IP)

Ed Walsh	1.82
Addie Joss	1.89
Al Spalding	2.04
Three Finger Brown	2.06
John Ward	2.10
Christy Mathewson	2.13
Tommy Bond	2.14
Rube Waddell	2.16
Walter Johnson	2.17
Ed Reulbach	2.28
Will White	2.28
Eddie Plank	2.35
Larry Corcoran	2.36
Eddie Cicotte	2.38
Candy Cummings	2.39
Doc White	2.39
Nap Rucker	2.42
George Bradley	2.43
Jim McCormick	2.43
Chief Bender	2.46

SHUTOUTS

Walter Johnson	110
Grover Alexander	90
Christy Mathewson	79
Cy Young	76
Eddie Plank	69
Warren Spahn	63
Nolan Ryan	61
Tom Seaver	61
Bert Blyleven	60
Don Sutton	58
Pud Galvin	57
Ed Walsh	57
Bob Gibson	56
Three Finger Brown	55
Steve Carlton	55
Jim Palmer	53
Gaylord Perry	53
Juan Marichal	52
Rube Waddell	50
Vic Willis	50

COMPLETE GAMES

Cy Young	749
Pud Galvin	639
Tim Keefe	554
Walter Johnson	531
Kid Nichols	531
Mickey Welch	525
Bobby Mathews	525
Charley Radbourn	489
John Clarkson	485
Tony Mullane	468
Jim McCormick	466
Gus Weyhing	448
Grover Alexander	437
Christy Mathewson	434
Jack Powell	422
Eddie Plank	410
Will White	394
Amos Rusie	392
Vic Willis	388
Tommy Bond	386

STRIKEOUTS

Nolan Ryan	5714
*Randy Johnson	4789
Roger Clemens	4672
Steve Carlton	4136
Bert Blyleven	3701
Tom Seaver	3640
Don Sutton	3574
Gaylord Perry	3534
Walter Johnson	3509
*Greg Maddux	3371
Phil Niekro	3342
Ferguson Jenkins	3192
Bob Gibson	3117
*Pedro Martinez	3117
*Curt Schilling	3116
*John Smoltz	3011
Jim Bunning	2855
Mickey Lolich	2832
*Mike Mussina	2813
Cy Young	2803

BASES ON BALLS

Nolan Ryan	2795
Steve Carlton	1833
Phil Niekro	1809
Early Wynn	1775
Bob Feller	1764
Bobo Newsom	1732
Amos Rusie	1707
Charlie Hough	1665
Roger Clemens	1580
Gus Weyhing	1566
Red Ruffing	1541
*Tom Glavine	1500
*Randy Johnson	1466
Bump Hadley	1442
Warren Spahn	1434
Earl Whitehill	1431
Tony Mullane	1408
Sad Sam Jones	1396
Jack Morris	1390
Tom Seaver	1390

* Active in 2008. ** Minumum 100 victories.

The Regular Season (*Cont.*)

Alltime Winningest Managers

CAREER

	W	L	Pct	Yrs
Connie Mack	3755	3967	.486	53
John McGraw	2810	1987	.586	33
*Tony LaRussa	2518	2190	.535	30
*Bobby Cox	2393	1918	.555	27
Sparky Anderson	2238	1855	.547	26
*Joe Torre	2227	1898	.540	27
Bucky Harris	2168	2228	.493	29
Joe McCarthy	2155	1346	.616	24
Walter Alston	2063	1634	.558	23
Leo Durocher	2015	1717	.540	24
Casey Stengel	1942	1868	.510	25
Gene Mauch	1907	2044	.483	26
Bill McKechnie	1904	1737	.523	25
*Lou Piniella	17TK	15TK	.517	21
Ralph Houk	1627	1539	.514	20
Fred Clarke	1609	1189	.575	19
Dick Williams	1592	1474	.519	21
Tommy Lasorda	1589	1434	.526	20
Earl Weaver	1506	1080	.582	17
Clark Griffith	1491	1367	.522	20

REGULAR SEASON

	W	L	Pct	Yrs
Connie Mack	3731	3948	.486	53
John McGraw	2784	1959	.587	33
*Tony LaRussa	2461	2146	.534	30
*Bobby Cox	2327	1854	.557	27
Sparky Anderson	2194	1834	.545	26
Bucky Harris	2157	2218	.493	29
*Joe Torre	2151	1848	.538	27
Joe McCarthy	2125	1333	.615	24
Walter Alston	2040	1613	.558	23
Leo Durocher	2008	1709	.540	24
Casey Stengel	1905	1842	.508	25
Gene Mauch	1902	2037	.483	26
Bill McKechnie	1896	1723	.524	25
*Lou Piniella	1701	1561	.521	21
Ralph Houk	1619	1531	.514	20
Fred Clarke	1602	1181	.576	19
Dick Williams	1571	1451	.520	21
Tommy Lasorda	1558	1404	.526	20
Lou Piniella	1519	1420	.523	19
Clark Griffith	1491	1367	.522	20

WORLD SERIES

	W	L	T	Pct	App	WS
Casey Stengel	37	26	0	.587	10	7
Joe McCarthy	30	13	0	.698	9	7
John McGraw	26	28	2	.482	9	2
Connie Mack	24	19	0	.558	8	5
*Joe Torre	21	11	0	.657	6	4
Walter Alston	20	20	0	.500	7	4
Miller Huggins	18	15	1	.544	6	3
Sparky Anderson	16	12	0	.571	5	3
Tommy Lasorda	12	11	0	.522	4	2
Dick Williams	12	14	0	.462	4	2
Frank Chance	11	9	1	.548	4	2
Bucky Harris	11	10	0	.524	3	2
Billy Southworth	11	11	0	.500	4	2
Earl Weaver	11	13	0	.458	4	1
*Bobby Cox	11	18	0	.379	5	1
Whitey Herzog	10	11	0	.476	3	1
*Tony LaRussa	9	13	0	.409	5	2
*Terry Francona	8	0	0	1.000	2	2
Bill Carrigan	8	2	0	.800	2	2
Cito Gaston	8	4	0	.667	2	2
Danny Murtaugh	8	6	0	.571	2	2
Tom Kelly	8	6	0	.571	2	2
Ralph Houk	8	8	0	.500	3	2
Bill McKechnie	8	14	0	.364	4	2

* Active in 2008.

Individual Batting Records (Single Season)

HITS

Ichiro Suzuki, 2004 262
George Sisler, 1920 257
Lefty O'Doul, 1929 254
Bill Terry, 1930 254
Al Simmons, 1925 253
Rogers Hornsby, 1922 250
Chuck Klein, 1930 250
Ty Cobb, 1911 248
George Sisler, 1922 246
Ichiro Suzuki, 2001 242

BATTING AVERAGE

Levi Meyerle, 1871 .... .492
Hugh Duffy, 1894 .... .440
Tip O'Neill, 1887 .... .435
Ross Barnes, 1872 .... .432
Cal McVey, 1871 .... .431
Ross Barnes, 1876 .... .429
Nap Lajoie, 1901 .... .426
Ross Barnes, 1873 .... .425
Willie Keeler, 1897 .... .424
Rogers Hornsby, 1924 .... .424

DOUBLES

Earl Webb, 1931 67
George Burns, 1926 64
Joe Medwick, 1936 64
Hank Greenberg, 1934 63
Paul Waner, 1932 62
Charlie Gehringer, 1936 60
Tris Speaker, 1923 59
Chuck Klein, 1930 59
Todd Helton, 2000 59
Billy Herman, 1936 57
Billy Herman, 1935 57
Carlos Delgado, 2000 57

TOTAL BASES

Babe Ruth, 1921 457
Rogers Hornsby, 1922 450
Lou Gehrig, 1927 447
Chuck Klein, 1930 445
Jimmie Foxx, 1932 438
Stan Musial, 1948 429
Sammy Sosa, 2001 425
Hack Wilson, 1930 423
Chuck Klein, 1932 420
Luis Gonzalez, 2001 419
Lou Gehrig, 1930 419

TRIPLES

Chief Wilson, 1912 36
Dave Orr, 1886 31
Heinie Reitz, 1894 31
Perry Werden, 1893 29
Harry Davis, 1897 28
George Davis, 1893 27
Sam Thompson, 1894 27
Jimmy Williams, 1899 27
Sam Crawford, 1914 26
Kiki Cuyler, 1925 26
Joe Jackson, 1912 26
John Reilly, 1890 26
George Treadway 26

HOME RUNS

Barry Bonds, 2001 73
Mark McGwire, 1998 70
Sammy Sosa, 1998 66
Mark McGwire, 1999 65
Sammy Sosa, 2001 64
Sammy Sosa, 1999 63
Roger Maris, 1961 61
Babe Ruth, 1927 60
Babe Ruth, 1921 59
Jimmie Foxx, 1932 58
Hank Greenberg, 1938 58
Mark McGwire, 1997 58
Ryan Howard, 2006 58

RUNS BATTED IN

Hack Wilson, 1930 191
Lou Gehrig, 1931 184
Hank Greenberg, 1937 183
Lou Gehrig, 1927 175
Jimmie Foxx, 1938 175
Lou Gehrig, 1930 174
Babe Ruth, 1921 171
Chuck Klein, 1930 170
Hank Greenberg, 1935 170
Jimmie Foxx, 1932 169

STRIKEOUTS

Mark Reynolds, 2008 204
Ryan Howard, 2008 199
Ryan Howard, 2007 199
Jack Cust, 2008 197
Adam Dunn, 2004 195
Bobby Bonds, 1970 189
Jose Hernandez, 2002 188
Bobby Bonds, 1969 187
Preston Wilson, 2000 187
Rob Deer, 1987 186
Jose Hernandez, 2001 185
Pete Incaviglia, 1986 185
Jim Thome, 2001 185
Cecil Fielder, 1990 182
Jim Thome, 2003 182

RUNS

Billy Hamilton, 1894 192
Tom Brown, 1891 177
Babe Ruth, 1921 177
Lou Gehrig, 1936 167
Tip O'Neill, 1887 167
Billy Hamilton, 1895 166
Willie Keeler, 1894 165
Joe Kelley, 1894 165
Lou Gehrig, 1931 163
Arlie Latham, 1887 163
Babe Ruth, 1928 163

STOLEN BASES

Hugh Nicol, 1887 138
Rickey Henderson, 1982 130
Arlie Latham, 1887 129
Lou Brock, 1974 118
Charlie Comiskey, 1887 117
Billy Hamilton, 1891 111
Billy Hamilton, 1889 111
John Ward, 1887 111
Vince Coleman, 1985 110
Vince Coleman, 1987 109
Arlie Latham, 1888 109

BASES ON BALLS

Barry Bonds, 2004 232
Barry Bonds, 2002 198
Barry Bonds, 2001 177
Babe Ruth, 1923 170
Ted Williams, 1947 162
Ted Williams, 1949 162
Mark McGwire, 1998 162
Ted Williams, 1946 156
Barry Bonds, 1996 151
Eddie Yost, 1956 151
Babe Ruth, 1920 150

SLUGGING AVERAGE

Barry Bonds, 2001 .... .863
Babe Ruth, 1920 .... .847
Babe Ruth, 1921 .... .846
Barry Bonds, 2004 .... .812
Barry Bonds, 2002 .... .799
Babe Ruth, 1927 .... .772
Lou Gehrig, 1927 .... .765
Babe Ruth, 1923 .... .764
Rogers Hornsby, 1925 .... .756
Mark McGwire, 1998 .... .752

The Regular Season *(Cont.)*

Individual Pitching Records (Single Season)

GAME APPEARANCES

Mike Marshall, 1974	106
Kent Tekulve, 1979	94
Salomon Torres, 2006	94
Mike Marshall, 1973	92
Kent Tekulve, 1978	91
Wayne Granger, 1969	90
Mike Marshall, 1979	90
Kent Tekulve, 1987	90
Steve Kline, 2001	89
Jim Brower, 2004	89
Mark Eichhorn, 1987	89
Steve Kline, 2001	89

GAMES STARTED

Will White, 1879	75
Pud Galvin, 1883	75
Jim McCormick, 1880	74
Charley Radbourn, 1884	73
Guy Hecker, 1884	73
Jim Galvin, 1884	72
John Clarkson, 1889	72
Bill Hutchison, 1892	71
John Clarkson, 1885	70
Bobby Mathews, 1875	70

INNINGS PITCHED

Will White, 1878	680.0
Charley Radbourn, 1884	678.2
Guy Hecker, 1884	670.2
Jim McCormick, 1880	657.2
Jim Galvin, 1883	656.1
Jim Galvin, 1884	636.1
Charley Radbourn, 1883	632.1
Bill Hutchison, 1892	627.0
Bobby Mâthews, 1875	626.2
John Clarkson, 1885	623.0

WINS

Charley Radbourn, 1884	59
Al Spalding, 1875	55
John Clarkson, 1885	53
Guy Hecker, 1884	52
Al Spalding, 1874	52
John Clarkson, 1889	49
Charlie Buffinton, 1884	48
Charley Radbourn, 1883	48
Al Spalding, 1876	47
John Ward, 1879	47
Matt Kilroy, 1887	46

LOSSES

John Coleman, 1883	48
Will White, 1880	42
Larry McKeon, 1884	41
George Bradley, 1879	40
Jim McCormick, 1879	40
Bobby Mathews, 1875	38
Kid Carsey, 1891	37
George Cobb, 1892	37
Henry Porter, 1888	37

WINNING PERCENTAGE

Roy Face, 1959	.947
Johnny Allen, 1937	.938
Greg Maddux, 1995	.905
Randy Johnson, 1995	.900
Ron Guidry, 1978	.893
Freddie Fitzsimmons, 1940	.889
Lefty Grove, 1931	.886
Bob Stanley, 1978	.882
Preacher Roe, 1951	.880
Cliff Lee, 2008	.880
Fred Goldsmith, 1880	.875
Tom Seaver, 1981	.875

SAVES

Francisco Rodriguez, 2008	62
Bobby Thigpen, 1990	57
Eric Gagne, 2003	55
John Smoltz, 2002	55
Mariano Rivera, 2004	53
Randy Myers, 1993	53
Trevor Hoffman, 1998	53
Eric Gagne, 2002	52
Rod Beck, 1998	51
Dennis Eckersley, 1992	51
Mariano Rivera, 2001	50

EARNED RUN AVERAGE

Tim Keefe, 1880	0.86
Dutch Leonard, 1914	0.96
Three Finger Brown, 1906	1.04
Bob Gibson, 1968	1.12
Christy Mathewson, 1909	1.14
Walter Johnson, 1913	1.15
Jack Pfiester, 1907	1.15
Addie Joss, 1908	1.16
Carl Lundgren, 1907	1.17
Denny Driscoll, 1882	1.21

SHUTOUTS

Grover Alexander, 1916	16
George Bradley, 1876	16
Jack Coombs, 1910	13
Bob Gibson, 1968	13
Grover Alexander, 1915	12
Jim Galvin, 1884	12
Ed Morris, 1886	12
Tommy Bond, 1879	11
Dean Chance, 1964	11
Dave Foutz, 1886	11
Walter Johnson, 1913	11
Sandy Koufax, 1963	11
Christy Mathewson, 1908	11
Charles Radbourn, 1884	11
Ed Walsh, 1908	11

COMPLETE GAMES

Will White, 1879	75
Charley Radbourn, 1884	73
Pud Galvin, 1883	72
Guy Hecker, 1884	72
Jim McCormick, 1880	72
Pud Galvin, 1884	71
Bobby Mathews, 1875	69
John Clarkson, 1885	68
John Clarkson, 1889	68

STRIKEOUTS

Matt Kilroy, 1886	513
Toad Ramsey, 1886	499
Hugh Daily, 1884	483
Dupee Shaw, 1884	451
Charley Radbourn, 1884	441
Charlie Buffinton, 1884	417
Guy Hecker, 1884	385
Nolan Ryan, 1973	383
Sandy Koufax, 1965	382

BASES ON BALLS

Pitcher	BB
Amos Rusie, 1890	289
Mark Baldwin, 1889	274
Amos Rusie, 1892	267
Amos Rusie, 1891	262
Mark Baldwin, 1890	249
Jack Stivetts, 1891	232
Mark Baldwin, 1891	227
Phil Knell, 1891	226
Bob Barr, 1890	219

Manager of the Year

NATIONAL LEAGUE

1983	Tommy Lasorda, LA
1984	Jim Frey, Chi
1985	Whitey Herzog, StL
1986	Hal Lanier, Hou
1987	Buck Rodgers, Mtl
1988	Tommy Lasorda, LA
1989	Don Zimmer, Chi
1990	Jim Leyland, Pitt
1991	Bobby Cox, Atl
1992	Jim Leyland, Pitt
1993	Dusty Baker, SF
1994	Felipe Alou, Mtl
1995	Don Baylor, Col
1996	Bruce Bochy, SD
1997	Dusty Baker, SF
1998	Larry Dierker, Hou

AMERICAN LEAGUE

1983	Tony LaRussa, Chi
1984	Sparky Anderson, Det
1985	Bobby Cox, Tor
1986	John McNamara, Bos
1987	Sparky Anderson, Det
1988	Tony LaRussa, Oak
1989	Frank Robinson, Balt
1990	Jeff Torborg, Chi
1991	Tom Kelly, Minn
1992	Tony LaRussa, Oak
1993	Gene Lamont, Chi
1994	Buck Showalter, NY
1995	Lou Piniella, Sea
1996	Joe Torre, NY/Johnny Oates, Tex
1997	Davey Johnson, Balt
1998	Joe Torre, NY

Manager of the Year (Cont.)

NATIONAL LEAGUE

1999 ....Jack McKeon, Cin
2000 ....Dusty Baker, SF
2001 ....Larry Bowa, Phi
2002 ....Tony LaRussa, StL
2003 ....Jack McKeon, Fla
2004 ....Bobby Cox, Atl
2005 ....Bobby Cox, Atl
2006 ....Joe Girardi, Fla
2007 ....Bob Melvin, Ari

AMERICAN LEAGUE

1999 ....Jimy Williams, Bos
2000 ....Jerry Manuel, Chi
2001 ....Lou Piniella, Sea
2002 ....Mike Scioscia, Ana
2003 ....Tony Pena, KC
2004 ....Buck Showalter, Tex
2005 ....Ozzie Guillen, Chi
2006 ....Jim Leyland, Det
2007 ....Eric Wedge, Cle

Individual Batting Records (Single Game)

MOST RUNS

7 ....Guy Hecker, Lou Aug 15, 1886

MOST HITS

7 ....Wilbert Robinson, Balt June 10, 1892
Rennie Stennett, Pitt Sept 16, 1975

MOST HOME RUNS

4 ....Bobby Lowe, Bos (N) May 30, 1894
Ed Delahanty, Phi July 13, 1896
Lou Gehrig, NY (A) June 3, 1932
Gil Hodges, Bklyn Aug 31, 1950
Joe Adcock, Mil (N) July 31, 1954
Rocky Colavito, Clev June 10, 1959
Willie Mays, SF April 30, 1961
Mike Schmidt, Phi April 17, 1976
Bob Horner, Atl July 6, 1986
Mark Whiten, StL Sept 7, 1993
Mike Cameron, Sea May 2, 2002
Shawn Green, LA May 23, 2002
Carlos Delgado, Tor Sept 25, 2003

MOST GRAND SLAMS

2 ....Tony Lazzeri, NY (A) May 24, 1936
Jim Tabor, Bos (A) July 4, 1939
Rudy York, Bos (A) July 27, 1946
Jim Gentile, Balt May 9, 1961
Tony Cloninger, Atl July 3, 1966
Jim Northrup, Det June 24, 1968
Frank Robinson, Balt June 26, 1970
Robin Ventura, Chi (A) Sept 4, 1995
Chris Hoiles, Balt Aug 14, 1998
Fernando Tatis, StL Apr 23, 1999
N. Garciaparra, Bos May 10, 1999
Bill Mueller, Bos July 29, 2003

MOST RBIs

12 .....Jim Bottomley, StL Sept 16, 1924
Mark Whiten, StL Sept 7, 1993

Note: All single-game hitting records for a nine-inning game.

Individual Batting Records (Single Inning)

MOST RUNS

3 ....Tommy Burns, Chi (N) Sept 6, 1883, 7th inning
Ned Williamson, Chi (N) Sept 6, 1883, 7th inning
Sammy White, Bos (A) June 18, 1953, 7th inning

MOST HITS

3 ....Tommy Burns, Chi (N) Sept 6, 1883, 7th inning
Fred Pfeiffer, Chi (N) Sept 6, 1883, 7th inning
Ned Williamson, Chi (N) Sept 6, 1883, 7th inning
Gene Stephens, Bos (A) June 18, 1953, 7th inning
Johnny Damon, Bos (A), June 27, 2003, 1st inning

MOST RBIs

8.......Fernando Tatis, StL Apr 23, 1999, 3rd inning

Individual Pitching Records (Single Game)

MOST INNINGS PITCHED

26 .....Leon Cadore, Bklyn May 1, 1920, tie 1–1
Joe Oeschger, Bos (N) May 1, 1920, tie 1–1

MOST RUNS ALLOWED

24 .....Al Travers, Det May 18, 1912

MOST HITS ALLOWED

36 .....Jack Wadsworth, Lou Aug 17, 1894

MOST STRIKEOUTS

20 .....Roger Clemens, Bos April 29, 1986
20 .....Roger Clemens, Bos Sept 18, 1996
20 .....Kerry Wood, Chi (N) May 6, 1998
20 .....Randy Johnson, Ariz May 8, 2001

MOST WALKS ALLOWED

16 .....Bill George, NY (N) May 30, 1887
George Van Haltren, Chi (N) June 27, 1887
Henry Gruber, Clev Apr 19, 1890
Bruno Haas, Phi (A) June 2, 1915

MOST WILD PITCHES

6 .......J.R. Richard, Hou April 10, 1979
Phil Niekro, Atl Aug 14, 1979
Bill Gullickson, Mtl April 10, 1982

Individual Pitching Records (Single Inning)

MOST RUNS ALLOWED

13 .....Lefty O'Doul, Bos (A) July 7, 1923

MOST WALKS ALLOWED

8 ....Dolly Gray, Wash Aug 28, 1909

MOST WILD PITCHES

4 ....Walter Johnson, Wash Sept 21, 1914
Phil Niekro, Atl Aug 14, 1979
Kevin Gregg, Ana July 25, 2004
Ryan Madson, Phi July 25, 2006

Miscellaneous Records

LONGEST GAME, BY INNINGS

26 .....Brooklyn 1, Boston 1 May 1, 1920

LONGEST NINE-INNING GAME, BY TIME

4:45...New York (A) 14, Boston 11 Aug 18, 2006

Baseball Hall of Fame

Players

	Position	Career	Selected
Hank Aaron	OF	1954–76	1982
Grover Alexander	P	1911–30	1938
Cap Anson	1B	1876–97	1939
Luis Aparicio	SS	1956–73	1984
Luke Appling	SS	1930–50	1964
Richie Ashburn	OF	1948–62	1995
Earl Averill	OF	1929–41	1975
Jose Mendez Baez*	P	1908–26	2006
Frank Baker	3B	1908–22	1955
Dave Bancroft	SS	1915–30	1971
Ernie Banks	SS-1B	1953–71	1977
Jake Beckley	1B	1888–1907	1971
Cool Papa Bell*	OF		1974
Johnny Bench	C	1967–83	1989
Chief Bender	P	1903–25	1953
Yogi Berra	C	1946–65	1972
Wade Boggs	3B	1982–99	2005
Jim Bottomley	1B	1922–37	1974
Lou Boudreau	SS	1938–52	1970
Roger Bresnahan	C	1897–1915	1945
George Brett	3B	1973–93	1999
Lou Brock	OF	1961–79	1985
Dan Brouthers	1B	1879–1904	1945
Ray Brown*	P	1930–48	2006
Three Finger Brown	P	1903–16	1949
Willard Jesse Brown*	OF	1935–58	2006
Jim Bunning	P	1955–71	1996
Jesse Burkett	OF	1890–1905	1946
Roy Campanella	C	1948–57	1969
Rod Carew	1B-2B	1967–85	1991
Max Carey	OF	1910–29	1961
Steve Carlton	P	1965–88	1994
Gary Carter	C	1974–92	2003
Orlando Cepeda	1B	1958–74	1999
Frank Chance	1B	1898–1914	1946
Oscar Charleston*	OF		1976
Jack Chesbro	P	1899–1909	1946
Fred Clarke	OF	1894–1915	1945
John Clarkson	P	1882–94	1963
Roberto Clemente	OF	1955–72	1973
Ty Cobb	OF	1905–28	1936
Mickey Cochrane	C	1925–37	1947
Eddie Collins	2B	1906–30	1939
Jimmy Collins	3B	1895–1908	1945
Earle Combs	OF	1924–35	1970
Roger Connor	1B	1880–97	1976
Andrew Cooper*	P	1920–41	2006
Stan Coveleski	P	1912–28	1969
Sam Crawford	OF	1899–1917	1957
Joe Cronin	SS	1926–45	1956
Candy Cummings	P	1872–77	1939
Kiki Cuyler	OF	1921–38	1968
Ray Dandridge*	3B		1987
George Davis	SS	1890–1909	1998
Leon Day*	P		1995
Dizzy Dean	P	1930–47	1953
Ed Delahanty	OF	1888–1903	1945
Bill Dickey	C	1928–46	1954
Martin Dihigo*	P-OF		1977
Joe DiMaggio	OF	1936–51	1955
Larry Doby	OF	1947–59	1998
Bobby Doerr	2B	1937–51	1986
Don Drysdale	P	1956–69	1984
Hugh Duffy	OF	1888–1906	1945
Dennis Eckersley	P	1975–98	2004
Johnny Evers	2B	1902–29	1939
Buck Ewing	C	1880–97	1946
Red Faber	P	1914–33	1964
Bob Feller	P	1936–56	1962
Rick Ferrell	C	1929–47	1984
Rollie Fingers	P	1968–85	1992
Carlton Fisk	C	1969–93	2000
Elmer Flick	OF	1898–1910	1963
Whitey Ford	P	1950–67	1974
Bill Foster*	P		1996
Nellie Fox	2B	1947–65	1997
Jimmie Foxx	1B	1925–45	1951
Frankie Frisch	2B	1919–37	1947
Pud Galvin	P	1879–92	1965
Lou Gehrig	1B	1923–39	1939
Charlie Gehringer	2B	1924–42	1949
Bob Gibson	P	1959–75	1981
Josh Gibson*	C		1972
Lefty Gomez	P	1930–43	1972
Goose Goslin	OF	1921–38	1968
Rich "Goose" Gossage	P	1972-94	2008
Ulysses F. Grant*	2B	1886–1903	2006
Hank Greenberg	1B	1930–47	1956
Burleigh Grimes	P	1916–34	1964
Lefty Grove	P	1925–41	1947
Tony Gwynn	OF	1982–2001	2007
Chick Hafey	OF	1924–37	1971
Jesse Haines	P	1918–37	1970
Billy Hamilton	OF	1888–1901	1961

Note: Career dates indicate first and last appearances in the majors.
*Elected on the basis of their career in the Negro leagues.

Baseball Hall of Fame (*Cont.*)

Players (*Cont.*)

	Position	Career	Selected
Gabby Hartnett	C	1922–41	1955
Harry Heilmann	OF	1914–32	1952
Billy Herman	2B	1931–47	1975
Jospeh Hill*	OF	1899–1925	2006
Harry Hooper	OF	1909–25	1971
Rogers Hornsby	2B	1915–37	1942
Waite Hoyt	P	1918–38	1969
Carl Hubbell	P	1928–43	1947
Catfish Hunter	P	1965–79	1987
Monte Irvin*	OF	1949–56	1973
Reggie Jackson	OF	1967–87	1993
Travis Jackson	SS	1922–36	1982
Ferguson Jenkins	P	1965–83	1991
Hugh Jennings	SS	1891–1918	1945
Judy Johnson*	3B		1975
Walter Johnson	P	1907–27	1936
Addie Joss	P	1902–10	1978
Al Kaline	OF	1953–74	1980
Tim Keefe	P	1880–93	1964
Willie Keeler	OF	1892–1910	1939
George Kell	3B	1943–57	1983
Joe Kelley	OF	1891–1908	1971
George Kelly	1B	1915–32	1973
King Kelly	C	1878–93	1945
Harmon Killebrew	1B-3B	1954–75	1984
Ralph Kiner	OF	1946–55	1975
Chuck Klein	OF	1928–44	1980
Sandy Koufax	P	1955–66	1972
Nap Lajoie	2B	1896–1916	1937
Tony Lazzeri	2B	1926–39	1991
Bob Lemon	P	1941–58	1976
Buck Leonard*	1B		1977
Fred Lindstrom	3B	1924–36	1976
Pop Lloyd*	SS-1B		1977
Ernie Lombardi	C	1931–47	1986
Ted Lyons	P	1923–46	1955
James Mackey*	C	1920–47	2006
Mickey Mantle	OF	1951–68	1974
Heinie Manush	OF	1923–39	1964
Rabbit Maranville	SS-2B	1912–35	1954
Juan Marichal	P	1960–75	1983
Rube Marquard	P	1908–25	1971
Eddie Mathews	3B	1952–68	1978
Christy Mathewson	P	1900–16	1936
Willie Mays	OF	1951–73	1979
Bill Mazeroski	2B	1956–72	2001
Tommy McCarthy	OF	1884–96	1946
Willie McCovey	1B	1959–80	1986
Joe McGinnity	P	1899–1908	1946
Bid McPhee	2B	1882–99	2000
Joe Medwick	OF	1932–48	1968
Johnny Mize	1B	1936–53	1981
Paul Molitor	3B	1978–98	2004
Joe Morgan	2B	1963–84	1990
Eddie Murray	1B	1977–97	2003
Stan Musial	OF-1B	1941–63	1969
Hal Newhouser	P	1939–55	1992
Kid Nichols	P	1890–1906	1949
Phil Niekro	P	1964–87	1997
Jim O'Rourke	OF	1876–1904	1945
Mel Ott	OF	1926–47	1951
Satchel Paige*	P	1948–65	1971
Jim Palmer	P	1965–84	1990
Herb Pennock	P	1912–34	1948
Tony Perez	1B	1964–86	2000
Gaylord Perry	P	1962–83	1991
Eddie Plank	P	1901–17	1946
Kirby Puckett	OF	1984–95	2001
Charley Radbourn	P	1880–91	1939
Pee Wee Reese	SS	1940–58	1984
Sam Rice	OF	1915–35	1963
Cal Ripken Jr.	SS	1981–2001	2007
Eppa Rixey	P	1912–33	1963
Phil Rizzuto	SS	1941–56	1994
Robin Roberts	P	1948–66	1976
Brooks Robinson	3B	1955–77	1983
Frank Robinson	OF	1956–76	1982
Jackie Robinson	2B	1947–56	1962
Joe (Bullet) Rogan*	P		1998
Edd Roush	OF	1913–31	1962
Red Ruffing	P	1924–47	1967
Amos Rusie	P	1889–1901	1977
Babe Ruth	OF	1914–35	1936
Nolan Ryan	P	1966–93	1999
Ryne Sandberg	2B	1981–97	2005
Louis Santop*	C	1909–26	2006
Ray Schalk	C	1912–29	1955
Mike Schmidt	3B	1972–89	1995
Red Schoendienst	2B	1945–63	1989
Tom Seaver	P	1967–86	1992
Joe Sewell	SS	1920–33	1977
Al Simmons	OF	1924–44	1953
George Sisler	1B	1915–30	1939
Enos Slaughter	OF	1938–59	1985
Hilton Smith*	P		2001
Ozzie Smith	SS	1978–96	2002
Duke Snider	OF	1947–64	1980
Warren Spahn	P	1942–65	1973
Al Spalding	P	1871–78	1939
Tris Speaker	OF	1907–28	1937
Willie Stargell	OF-1B	1962–82	1988
Turkey Stearns*	CF		2000
Don Sutton	P	1966–88	1998
Bruce Sutter	P	1976–88	2006
George Suttles*	C	1923–44	2006
Benjamin Harrison Taylor*	P-1B	1908–29	2006
Bill Terry	1B	1923–36	1954
Sam Thompson	OF	1885–1906	1974
Joe Tinker	SS	1902–16	1946
Cristóbal Torriente*	OF	1913–32	2006
Pie Traynor	3B	1920–37	1948
Dazzy Vance	P	1915–35	1955
Arky Vaughan	SS	1932–48	1985
Rube Waddell	P	1897–1910	1946
Honus Wagner	SS	1897–1917	1936
Bobby Wallace	SS	1894–1918	1953
Ed Walsh	P	1904–17	1946
Lloyd Waner	OF	1927–45	1967
Paul Waner	OF	1926–45	1952
John Ward	2B-P	1878–94	1964
Mickey Welch	P	1880–92	1973
Willie Wells*	SS	1924–49	1997
Zach Wheat	OF	1909–27	1959
Hoyt Wilhelm	P	1952–72	1985
Billy Williams	OF	1959–76	1987
Ted Williams	OF	1939–60	1966
Vic Willis	P	1898–1910	1995
Ernest Judson Wilson*	3B	1922–45	2006
Hack Wilson	OF	1923–34	1979
Dave Winfield	OF	1973–95	2001
Early Wynn	P	1939–63	1972
Carl Yastrzemski	OF	1961–83	1989
Cy Young	P	1890–1911	1937
Ross Youngs	OF	1917–26	1972
Robin Yount	SS	1974–93	1999

*Elected on the basis of their career in the Negro leagues.

Baseball Hall of Fame *(Cont.)*

Pioneers/Executives

	Selected
Ed Barrow (manager-executive)	1953
Morgan Bulkeley (executive)	1937
Alexander Cartwright (executive)	1938
Henry Chadwick (writer-executive)	1938
Happy Chandler (commissioner)	1982
Charles Comiskey (manager-executive)	1939
Barney Dreyfuss (executive)	2008
Ford Frick (commissioner-executive)	1970
Warren Giles (executive)	1979
Clark Griffith (executive)	1946
Will Harridge (executive)	1972
William Hulbert (executive)	1995
Ban Johnson (executive)	1937
Kenesaw M. Landis (commissioner)	1944
Bowie Kuhn (commissioner)	2008
Larry MacPhail Sr. (executive)	1978
Lee MacPhail Jr. (executive)	1998
Effa Manley (executive)	2006
Walter O'Malley (executive)	2008
Alex Pompez (executive)	2006
Cum Posey (player-manager-owner)	2006
Branch Rickey (manager-executive)	1967
Al Spalding (player-executive)	1939
Bill Veeck Jr. (owner)	1991
George Weiss (executive)	1971
Sol White (player-manager)	2006
J.L. Wilkinson (executive)	2006
George Wright (player-manager)	1937
Harry Wright (player-manager-executive)	1953
Tom Yawkey (executive)	1980

Managers

	Managed	Selected
Walter Alston	1954–76	1983
Sparky Anderson	1970–94	2000
Leo Durocher	1939–73	1994
Rube Foster	1907–26	1981
Bucky Harris	1924–56	1975
Ned Hanlon	1899–1907	1996
Miller Huggins	1913–29	1964
Tommy Lasorda	1977–96	1997
Al Lopez	1951–69	1977
Connie Mack	1894–1950	1937
Joe McCarthy	1926–50	1957
John McGraw	1899–1932	1937
Bill McKechnie	1915–46	1962
Wilbert Robinson	1902–31	1945
Frank Selee	1890–1905	1999
Billy Southworth	1929, 1940–51	2008
Casey Stengel	1934–65	1966
Earl Weaver	1968–82, 85–86	1996
Dick Williams	1967–69, 1971–88	2008

Umpires

	Selected
Al Barlick	1989
Nestor Chylak	1999
Jocko Conlan	1974
Tom Connolly	1953
Billy Evans	1973
Cal Hubbard	1976
Bill Klem	1953
Bill McGowan	1992

Notable Achievements

No-Hit Games, Nine Innings or More

NATIONAL LEAGUE

Date		Pitcher and Game
1876	July 15	George Bradley, StL vs Hart 2–0
1880	June 12	John Richmond, Wor vs Clev 1–0 (perfect game)
	June 17	Monte Ward, Prov vs Buff 5–0 (perfect game)
	Aug 19	Larry Corcoran, Chi vs Bos 6–0
	Aug 20	Pud Galvin, Buff vs Wor 1–0
1882	Sept 20	Larry Corcoran, Chi vs Wor 5–0
	Sept 22	Tim Lovett, Bklyn vs NY 4–0
1883	July 25	Hoss Radbourn, Prov vs Clev 8–0
	Sept 13	Hugh Daily, Clev vs Phi 1–0
1884	June 27	Larry Corcoran, Chi vs Prov 6–0
	Aug 4	Pud Galvin, Buff vs Det 18–0
1885	July 27	John Clarkson, Chi vs Prov 4–0
	Aug 29	Charles Ferguson, Phi vs Prov 1–0
1891	July 31	Amos Rusie, NY vs Bklyn 6–0
	June 22	Tom Lovett, Bklyn vs NY 4–0
1892	Aug 6	Jack Stivetts, Bos vs Bklyn 11–0
	Aug 22	Alex Sanders, Lou vs Balt 6–2
1892	Oct 15	Bumpus Jones, Cin vs Pitt 7–1 (first major league game)
1893	Aug 16	Bill Hawke, Balt vs Wash 5–0
1897	Sept 18	Cy Young, Clev vs Cin 6–0
1898	Apr 22	Ted Breitenstein, Cin vs Pitt 11–0
	Apr 22	Jim Hughes, Balt vs Bos 8–0
	July 8	Frank Donahue, Phi vs Bos 5–0
	Aug 21	Walter Thornton, Chi vs Bklyn 2–0
1899	May 25	Deacon Phillippe, Lou vs NY 7–0
	Aug 7	Vic Willis, Bos vs Wash 7–1
1900	July 12	Noodles Hahn, Cin vs Phi 4–0
1901	July 15	Christy Mathewson, NY vs StL 5–0
1903	Sept 18	Chick Fraser, Phi vs Chi 10–0
1904	June 11	Bob Wicker, Chi at NY 1–0 (hit in 10th; won in 12th)
1905	June 13	Christy Mathewson, NY vs Chi 1–0
1906	May 1	John Lush, Phi vs Bklyn 6–0
	July 20	Mal Eason, Bklyn vs StL 2–0
1906	Aug 1	Harry McIntire, Bklyn vs Pitt 0–1 (hit in 11th; lost in 13th)
1907	May 8	Frank Pfeffer, Bos vs Cin 6–0
	Sept 20	Nick Maddox, Pitt vs Bklyn 2–1
1908	July 4	George Wiltse, NY vs Phi 1–0 (10 innings)
	Sept 5	Nap Rucker, Bklyn vs Bos 6–0
1909	Apr 15	Leon Ames, NY vs Bklyn 0–3 (hit in 10th; lost in 13th)
1912	Sept 6	Jeff Tesreau, NY vs Phi 3–0
1914	Sept 9	George Davis, Bos vs Phi 7–0
1915	Apr 15	Rube Marquard, NY vs Bklyn 2–0
	Aug 31	Jimmy Lavender, Chi vs NY 2–0
1916	June 16	Tom Hughes, Bos vs Pitt 2–0
1917	May 2	Jim Vaughn, Chi vs Cin 0–1 (hit in 10th; lost in 10th)
	May 2	Fred Toney, Cin vs Chi 1–0 (10 innings)

No-Hit Games, Nine Innings or More (Cont.)

NATIONAL LEAGUE (Cont.)

Date	Pitcher and Game
1919......May 11	Hod Eller, Cin vs StL 6–0
1922......May 7	Jesse Barnes, NY vs Phi 6–0
1924......July 17	Jesse Haines, StL vs Bos 5–0
1925......Sept 13	Dazzy Vance, Bklyn vs Phi 10–1
1929......May 8	Carl Hubbell, NY vs Pitt 11–0
1934......Sept 21	Paul Dean, StL vs Bklyn 3–0
1938......June 11	Johnny Vander Meer, Cin vs Bos 3–0
June 15	Johnny Vander Meer, Cin vs Bklyn 6–0
1940......Apr 30	Tex Carleton, Bklyn vs Cin, 3–0
1941......Aug 30	Lon Warneke, StL vs Cin 2–0
1944......Apr 27	Jim Tobin, Bos vs Bklyn 2–0
May 15	Clyde Shoun, Cin vs Bos 1–0
1946......Apr 23	Ed Head, Bklyn vs Bos 5–0
1947......June 18	Ewell Blackwell, Cin vs Bos 6–0
1948......Sept 9	Rex Barney, Bklyn vs NY 2–0
1950......Aug 11	Vern Bickford, Bos vs Bklyn 7–0
1951......May 6	Cliff Chambers, Pitt vs Bos 3–0
1952......June 19	Carl Erskine, Bklyn vs Chi 5–0
1954......June 12	Jim Wilson, Mil vs Phi 2–0
1955......May 12	Sam Jones, Chi vs Pitt 4–0
1956......May 12	Carl Erskine, Bklyn vs NY 3–0
Sept 25	Sal Maglie, Bklyn vs Phi 5–0
1959......May 26	Harvey Haddix, Pitt vs Mil 0–1 (hit in 13th; lost in 13th)
1960......May 15	Don Cardwell, Chi vs StL 4–0
Aug 18	Lew Burdette, Mil vs Phi 1–0
Sept 16	Warren Spahn, Mil vs Phi 4–0
1961......Apr 28	Warren Spahn, Mil vs SF 1–0
1962......June 30	Sandy Koufax, LA vs NY 5–0
1963......May 11	Sandy Koufax, LA vs SF 8–0
May 17	Don Nottebart, Hou vs Phi 4–1
June 15	Juan Marichal, SF vs Hou 1–0
1964......Apr 23	Ken Johnson, Hou vs Cin 0–1
June 4	Sandy Koufax, LA vs Phi 3–0
June 21	Jim Bunning, Phi vs NY 6–0 (perfect game)
1965......June 14	Jim Maloney, Cin vs NY 0–1 (hit in 11th; lost in 11th)
Aug 19	Jim Maloney, Cin vs Chi 1–0 (10 innings)
Sept 9	Sandy Koufax, LA vs Chi 1–0 (perfect game)
1967......June 18	Don Wilson, Hou vs Atl 2–0
1968......July 29	George Culver, Cin vs Phi 6–1
Sept 17	Gaylord Perry, SF vs StL 1–0
Sept 18	Ray Washburn, StL vs SF 2–0
1969......Apr 17	Bill Stoneman, Mtl vs Phi 7–0
Apr 30	Jim Maloney, Cin vs Hou 10–0
May 1	Don Wilson, Hou vs Cin 4–0
Aug 19	Ken Holtzman, Chi vs Atl 3–0
Sept 20	Bob Moose, Pitt vs NY 4–0
1970......June 12	Dock Ellis, Pitt vs SD 2–0
July 20	Bill Singer, LA vs Phi 5–0
1971......June 3	Ken Holtzman, Chi vs Cin 1–0
June 23	Rick Wise, Phi vs Cin 4–0
Aug 14	Bob Gibson, StL vs Pitt 11–0
1972......Apr 16	Burt Hooton, Chi vs Phi 4–0
Sept 2	Milt Pappas, Chi vs SD 8–0
Oct 2	Bill Stoneman, Mtl vs NY 7–0
1973......Aug 5	Phil Niekro, Atl vs SD 9–0
1975......Aug 24	Ed Halicki, SF vs NY 6–0
1976......July 9	Larry Dierker, Hou vs Mtl 6–0
Aug 9	John Candelaria, Pitt vs LA 2–0
Sept 29	John Montefusco, SF vs Atl 9–0
1978......Apr 16	Bob Forsch, StL vs Phi 5–0
June 16	Tom Seaver, Cin vs StL 4–0
1979......Apr 7	Ken Forsch, Hou vs Atl 6–0
1980......June 27	Jerry Reuss, LA vs SF 8–0
1981......May 10	Charlie Lea, Mtl vs SF 4–0
Sept 26	Nolan Ryan, Hou vs LA 5–0
1983......Sept 26	Bob Forsch, StL vs Mtl 3–0
1986......Sept 25	Mike Scott, Hou vs SF 2–0
1988......Sept 16	Tom Browning, Cin vs LA 1–0 (perfect game)
1990......June 29	Fernando Valenzuela, LA vs StL 6–0
1990......Aug 15	Terry Mulholland, Phi vs SF 6–0
1991......May 23	Tommy Greene, Phi vs Mtl 2–0
July 26	Mark Gardner, Mtl vs LA 0–1 (hit in 10th, lost in 10th)
July 28	Dennis Martinez, Mtl vs LA 2–0 (perfect game)
Sept 11	Kent Mercker (6), Mark Wohlers (2), and Alejandro Pena (1), Atl vs SD 1–0
1992......Aug 17	Kevin Gross, LA vs SF 2–0
1993......Sept 8	Darryl Kile, Hou vs NY 7–1
1994......Apr 8	Kent Mercker, Atl vs LA 6–0
1995......June 3	Pedro Martinez, Mtl vs SD 1–0 (perfect through nine, hit in 10th)
July 14	Ramon Martinez, LA vs Fla 7–0
1996......May 11	Al Leiter, Fla vs Col 11–0
Sept 17	Hideo Nomo, LA vs Col 9–0
1997......June 10	Kevin Brown, Fla vs SF 9–0
July 12	Francisco Cordova (9) and Ricardo Rincon (1), Pitt vs Col 3–0
1999......June 25	Jose Jimenez, StL vs Ariz 1–0
2001......May 12	A.J. Burnett, Fla vs SD 3–0
Sept 3	Bud Smith, StL vs SD 4–0
2003......June 11	R. Oswalt (1), P. Munro (2.2), K. Saarloos (1.1), B. Lidge (2), O. Dotel (1), B. Wagner (1), Hou vs NYY 8–0
April 27	Kevin Millwood, Phi vs SF 1–0
2004......May 18	Randy Johnson, Ariz vs Atl 2–0 (perfect game)
2006......Sept 6	Anibal Sanchez, Fla vs Ariz 2–0
2008......Sept 14	†Carlos Zambrano, Chi vs Hou 5–0

Note: Includes the games struck from the official record book on Sept. 4, 1991, when baseball's committee on statistical accuracy voted to define no-hitters as games of nine innings or more that end with a team getting no hits.

†Game played in Milwaukee due to weather-related closure of Houston's home field.

Notable Achievements (*Cont.*)

No-Hit Games, Nine Innings or More (*Cont.*)

AMERICAN LEAGUE

Date		Pitcher and Game
1901	May 9	Earl Moore, Clev vs Chi 2–4 (hit in 10th; lost in 10th)
1902	Sept 20	Jimmy Callahan, Chi vs Det 3–0
1904	May 5	Cy Young, Bos vs Phi 3–0 (perfect game)
	Aug 17	Jesse Tannehill, Bos vs Chi 6–0
1905	July 22	Weldon Henley, Phi vs StL 6–0
	Sept 6	Frank Smith, Chi vs Det 15–0
	Sept 27	Bill Dinneen, Bos vs Chi 2–0
1908	June 30	Cy Young, Bos vs NY 8–0
	Sept 18	Bob Rhoades, Clev vs Bos 2–1
	Sept 20	Frank Smith, Chi vs Phi 1–0
1908	Oct 2	Addie Joss, Clev vs Chi 1–0 (perfect game)
1910	Apr 20	Addie Joss, Clev vs Chi 1–0
	May 12	Chief Bender, Phi vs Clev 4–0
	Aug 30	Tom Hughes, NY vs Clev 0–5 (hit in 10th; lost in 11th)
1911	July 29	Joe Wood, Bos vs StL 5–0
	Aug 27	Ed Walsh, Chi vs Bos 5–0
1912	July 4	George Mullin, Det vs StL 7–0
	Aug 30	Earl Hamilton, StL vs Det 5–1
1914	May 14	Jim Scott, Chi vs Wash 0–1 (hit in 10th; lost in 10th)
	May 31	Joe Benz, Chi vs Clev 6–1
1916	June 21	George Foster, Bos vs NY 2–0
	Aug 26	Joe Bush, Phi vs Clev 5–0
	Aug 30	Dutch Leonard, Bos vs StL 4–0
1917	Apr 14	Ed Cicotte, Chi vs StL 11–0
	Apr 24	George Mogridge, NY vs Bos 2–1
	May 5	Ernie Koob, StL vs Chi 1–0
	May 6	Bob Groom, StL vs Chi 3–0
	June 23	Ernie Shore, Bos vs Wash 4–0 (perfect game)
1918	June 3	Dutch Leonard, Bos vs Det 5–0
1919	Sept 10	Ray Caldwell, Clev vs NY 3–0
1920	July 1	Walter Johnson, Wash vs Bos 1–0
1922	Apr 30	Charlie Robertson, Chi vs Det 2–0 (perfect game)
1923	Sept 4	Sam Jones, NY vs Phi 2–0
	Sept 7	Howard Ehmke, Bos vs Phi 4–0
1926	Aug 21	Ted Lyons, Chi vs Bos 6–0
1931	Apr 29	Wes Ferrell, Clev vs StL 9–0
	Aug 8	Bob Burke, Wash vs Bos 5–0
1934	Sept 18	Bobo Newsom, StL vs Bos 1–2 (hit in 10th; lost in 10th)
1935	Aug 31	Vern Kennedy, Chi vs Clev 5–0
1937	June 1	Bill Dietrich, Chi vs StL 8–0
1938	Aug 27	Mtle Pearson, NY vs Clev 13–0
1940	Apr 16	Bob Feller, Clev vs Chi 1–0 (opening day)
1945	Sept 9	Dick Fowler, Phi vs StL 1–0
1946	Apr 30	Bob Feller, Clev vs NY 1–0
1947	July 10	Don Black, Clev vs Phi 3–0
	Sep 3	Bill McCahan, Phi vs Wash 3–0
1948	June 30	Bob Lemon, Clev vs Det 2–0
1951	July 1	Bob Feller, Clev vs Det 2–1
	July 12	Allie Reynolds, NY vs Clev 1–0
	Sept 28	Allie Reynolds, NY vs Bos 8–0
1952	May 15	Virgil Trucks, Det vs Wash 1–0
	Aug 25	Virgil Trucks, Det vs NY 1–0
1953	May 6	Bobo Holloman, StL vs Phi 6–0 (first major league start)
1956	July 14	Mel Parnell, Bos vs Chi 4–0
1966	Oct 8	Don Larsen, NY (A) vs Bklyn (N) 2–0 (World Series) (perfect game)
1957	Aug 20	Bob Keegan, Chi vs Wash 6–0
1958	July 20	Jim Bunning, Det vs Bos 3–0
	Sept 20	Hoyt Wilhelm, Balt vs NY 1–0
1962	May 5	Bo Belinsky, LA vs Balt 2–0
	June 26	Earl Wilson, Bos vs LA 2–0
	Aug 1	Bill Monbouquette, Bos vs Chi 1–0
	Aug 26	Jack Kralick, Minn vs KC 1–0
1965	Sept 16	Dave Morehead, Bos vs Clev 2–0
1966	June 10	Sonny Siebert, Clev vs Wash 2–0
1967	Apr 30	Steve Barber (8⅔) and Stu Miller (⅓), Balt vs Det 1–2
	Aug 25	Dean Chance, Minn vs Clev 2–1
	Sept 10	Joel Horlen, Chi vs Det 6–0
1968	Apr 27	Tom Phoebus, Balt vs Bos 6–0
	May 8	Catfish Hunter, Oak vs Minn 4–0 (perfect game)
1969	Aug 13	Jim Palmer, Balt vs Oak 8–0
1970	July 3	Clyde Wright, Cal vs Oak 4–0
	Sept 21	Vida Blue, Oak vs Minn 6–0
1973	Apr 27	Steve Busby, KC vs Det 3–0
	May 15	Nolan Ryan, Cal vs KC 3–0
	July 15	Nolan Ryan, Cal vs Det 6–0
	July 30	Jim Bibby, Tex vs Oak 6–0
1974	June 19	Steve Busby, KC vs Mil 2–0
	July 19	Dick Bosman, Clev vs Oak 4–0
	Sept 28	Nolan Ryan, Cal vs Minn 4–0
1975	June 1	Nolan Ryan, Cal vs Balt 1–0
	Sept 28	Vida Blue (5), Glenn Abbott and Paul Lindblad (1), Rollie Fingers (2), Oak vs Cal 5–0
1976	July 28	John Odom (5) and Francisco Barrios (4), Chi vs Oak 2–1
1977	May 14	Jim Colborn, KC vs Tex 6–0
	May 30	Dennis Eckersley, Clev vs Cal 1–0
	Sept 22	Bert Blyleven, Tex vs Cal 6–0
1981	May 15	Len Barker, Clev vs Tor 3–0 (perfect game)
1983	July 4	Dave Righetti, NY vs Bos 4–0
	Sept 29	Mike Warren, Oak vs Chi 3–0
1984	Apr 7	Jack Morris, Det vs Chi 4–0
	Sept 30	Mike Witt, Cal vs Tex 1–0 (perfect game)
1986	Sept 19	Joe Cowley, Chi vs Cal 7–1
1987	Apr 15	Juan Nieves, Mil vs Balt 7–0
1990	Apr 11	Mark Langston (7), Mike Witt (2), Cal vs Sea 1–0
	June 2	Randy Johnson, Sea vs Det 2–0
	June 11	Nolan Ryan, Tex vs Oak 5–0
	June 29	Dave Stewart, Oak vs Tor 5–0
1990	July 1	Andy Hawkins, NY vs Chi 0–4 (pitched eight of nine–innning game)
	Sept 2	Dave Stieb, Tor vs Clev 3–0
1991	May 1	Nolan Ryan, Tex vs Tor 3–0
	July 13	Bob Milacki (6), Mike Flanagan (1), Mark Williamson (1), and Gregg Olson (1), Balt vs Oak 2–0
	Aug 11	Wilson Alvarez, Chi vs Balt 7–0
	Aug 26	Bret Saberhagen, KC vs Chi 7–0
1993	Apr 22	Chris Bosio, Sea vs Bos 7–0
	Sept 4	Jim Abbott, NY vs Clev 4–0

No-Hit Games, Nine Innings or More *(Cont.)*

AMERICAN LEAGUE *(Cont.)*

Date		Pitcher and Game
1994	Apr 27	Scott Erickson, Minn vs Mil 6–0
	July 28	Kenny Rogers, Texas vs Cal 4–0 (perfect game)
1996	May 14	Dwight Gooden, NY vs Sea 2–0
1998	May 17	David Wells, NY vs Minn 4–0 (perfect game)
1999	July 18	David Cone, NY vs Mtl 6–0 (perfect game)
	Sept 11	Eric Milton, Minn vs Ana 7–0
2001	Apr 4	Hideo Nomo, Bos vs Balt 3–0
2002	Apr 27	Derek Lowe, Bos vs TB 10–0
2007	Apr 19	Mark Buehrle, Chi vs Tex, 6–0
	June 12	Justin Verlander, Det vs Mil 4–0
	Sep 1	Clay Buchholz, Bos vs Balt 10–0
2008	May 19	Jon Lester, Bos vs KC 7–0

Longest Hitting Streaks

NATIONAL LEAGUE

Player and Team	Year	G
Willie Keeler, Balt	1897	44
Pete Rose, Cin	1978	44
Bill Dahlen, Chi	1894	42
Tommy Holmes, Bos	1945	37
Billy Hamilton, Phi	1894	36
Jimmy Rollins, Phi	2005–06	36
Luis Castillo, Fla	2002	35
Fred Clarke, Lou	1895	35
Chase Utley, Phi	2006	35
Benito Santiago, SD	1987	34
George Davis, NY	1893	33
Rogers Hornsby, StL	1922	33

AMERICAN LEAGUE

Player and Team	Year	G
Joe DiMaggio, NY	1941	56
George Sisler, StL	1922	41
Ty Cobb, Det	1911	40
Paul Molitor, Mil	1987	39
Ty Cobb, Det	1917	35
George Sisler, StL	1925	34
George McQuinn, StL	1938	34
Dom DiMaggio, Bos	1949	34
Hal Chase, NY	1907	33
Heinie Manush, Wash	1933	33

Triple Crown Hitters

NATIONAL LEAGUE

Player and Team	Year	HR	RBI	BA
Paul Hines, Prov	1878	4	50	.358
Hugh Duffy, Bos	1894	18	145	.438
Heinie Zimmerman*, Chi	1912	14	103	.372
Rogers Hornsby, StL	1922	42	152	.401
	1925	39	143	.403
Chuck Klein, Phi	1933	28	120	.368
Joe Medwick, StL	1937	31	154	.374

*Zimmerman ranked first in RBIs as calculated by Ernie Lanigan, but only third as calculated by Information Concepts Inc.

AMERICAN LEAGUE

Player and Team	Year	HR	RBI	BA
Nap Lajoie, Phi	1901	14	125	.422
Ty Cobb, Det	1909	9	115	.377
Jimmie Foxx, Phi	1933	48	163	.356
Lou Gehrig, NY	1934	49	165	.363
Ted Williams, Bos	1942	36	137	.356
	1947	32	114	.343
Mickey Mantle, NY	1956	52	130	.353
Frank Robinson, Balt	1966	49	122	.316
Carl Yastrzemski, Bos	1967	44	121	.326

Notable Achievements *(Cont.)*

Triple Crown Pitchers

NATIONAL LEAGUE

Player and Team	Year	W	L	SO	ERA
Tommy Bond, Bos	1877	40	17	170	2.11
Hoss Radbourn, Prov	1884	60	12	441	1.38
Tim Keefe, NY	1888	35	12	333	1.74
John Clarkson, Bos	1889	49	19	284	2.73
Amos Rusie, NY	1894	36	13	195	2.78
Christy Mathewson, NY	1905	31	8	206	1.27
	1908	37	11	259	1.43
Grover Alexander, Phi	1915	31	10	241	1.22
	1916	33	12	167	1.55
	1917	30	13	201	1.86
Hippo Vaughn, Chi	1918	22	10	148	1.74
Dazzy Vance, Bklyn	1924	28	6	262	2.16
Bucky Walters, Cin	1939	27	11	137	2.29
Sandy Koufax, LA	1963	25	5	306	1.88
	1965	26	8	382	2.04
	1966	27	9	317	1.73
Steve Carlton, Phi	1972	27	10	310	1.97
Dwight Gooden, NY	1985	24	4	268	1.53
Randy Johnson, Ariz	2002	24	5	334	2.32

AMERICAN LEAGUE

Player and Team	Year	W	L	SO	ERA
Cy Young, Bos	1901	33	10	158	1.62
Rube Waddell, Phi	1905	26	11	287	1.48
Walter Johnson, Wash	1913	36	7	303	1.09
	1918	23	13	162	1.27
	1924	23	7	158	2.72
Lefty Grove, Phi	1930	28	5	209	2.54
	1931	31	4	175	2.06
Lefty Gomez, NY	1934	26	5	158	2.33
	1937	21	11	194	2.33
Hal Newhouser, Det	1945	25	9	212	1.81
Roger Clemens, Tor	1997	21	7	292	2.05
	1998	20	6	271	2.64
Pedro Martinez, Bos	1999	23	4	313	2.07
*Johan Santana, Min	2006	19	6	245	2.77

*Tied with another pitcher for wins

Consecutive Games Played, 500 or More Games

Player	Games
Cal Ripken Jr.	2,632
Lou Gehrig	2,130
Everett Scott	1,307
Steve Garvey	1,207
Miguel Tejada	1,152
Billy Williams	1,117
Joe Sewell	1,103
Stan Musial	895
Eddie Yost	829
Gus Suhr	822
Nellie Fox	798
Pete Rose	745
Dale Murphy	740
Richie Ashburn	730
Ernie Banks	717
Pete Rose	678
Earl Averill	673
Frank McCormick	652
Sandy Alomar Sr.	648
Eddie Brown	618
Roy McMillan	585
George Pinckney	577
Steve Brodie	574
Aaron Ward	565
Alex Rodriguez	546
Candy LaChance	540
Buck Freeman	535
Fred Luderus	533
Hideki Matsui	518
Clyde Milan	511
Charlie Gehringer	511
Vada Pinson	508
Tony Cuccinello	504
Charlie Gehringer	504

Unassisted Triple Plays

Player and Team	Date	Pos	Opp	Opp Batter
Neal Ball, Clev	7-19-09	SS	Bos	Amby McConnell
Bill Wambsganss, Clev	10-10-20	2B	Bklyn	Clarence Mitchell
George Burns, Bos	9-14-23	1B	Clev	Frank Brower
Ernie Padgett, Bos	10-6-23	SS	Phi	Walter Holke
Glenn Wright, Pitt	5-7-25	SS	StL	Jim Bottomley
Jimmy Cooney, Chi	5-30-27	SS	Pitt	Paul Waner
Johnny Neun, Det	5-31-27	1B	Clev	Homer Summa
Ron Hansen, Wash	7-30-68	SS	Clev	Joe Azcue
Mickey Morandini, Phi	9-20-92	2B	Pitt	Jeff King
John Valentin, Bos	7-15-94	SS	Minn	Marc Newfield
Randy Velarde, Oak	5-29-00	2B	NYY	Shane Spencer
Rafael Furcal, Atl	8-10-03	SS	StL	Woody Williams
Troy Tulowitzki, Col	4-29-07	SS	Atl	Chipper Jones
Asdrubal Cabrera, Cle	5-12-08	2B	Tor	Lyle Overbay

National League

Leading Batsmen

Year	Player and Team	BA
1900	Honus Wagner, Pitt	.381
1901	Jesse Burkett, StL	.382
1902	Ginger Beaumtl, Pitt	.357
1903	Honus Wagner, Pitt	.355
1904	Honus Wagner, Pitt	.349
1905	Cy Seymour, Cin	.377
1906	Honus Wagner, Pitt	.339
1907	Honus Wagner, Pitt	.350
1908	Honus Wagner, Pitt	.354
1909	Honus Wagner, Pitt	.339
1910	Sherry Magee, Phi	.331
1911	Honus Wagner, Pitt	.334
1912	Heinie Zimmerman, Chi	.372
1913	Jake Daubert, Bklyn	.350
1914	Jake Daubert, Bklyn	.329
1915	Larry Doyle, NY	.320
1916	Hal Chase, Cin	.339
1917	Edd Roush, Cin	.341
1918	Zach Wheat, Bklyn	.335
1919	Edd Roush, Cin	.321
1920	Rogers Hornsby, StL	.370
1921	Rogers Hornsby, StL	.397
1922	Rogers Hornsby, StL	.401
1923	Rogers Hornsby, StL	.384
1924	Rogers Hornsby, StL	.424
1925	Rogers Hornsby, StL	.403
1926	Bubbles Hargrave, Cin	.353
1927	Paul Waner, Pitt	.380
1928	Rogers Hornsby, Bos	.387
1929	Lefty O'Doul, Phi	.398
1930	Bill Terry, NY	.401
1931	Chick Hafey, StL	.349
1932	Lefty O'Doul, Bklyn	.368
1933	Chuck Klein, Phi	.368
1934	Paul Waner, Pitt	.362
1935	Arky Vaughan, Pitt	.385
1936	Paul Waner, Pitt	.373
1937	Joe Medwick, StL	.374
1938	Ernie Lombardi, Cin	.342
1939	Johnny Mize, StL	.349
1940	Debs Garms, Pitt	.355
1941	Pete Reiser, Bklyn	.343
1942	Ernie Lombardi, Bos	.330
1943	Stan Musial, StL	.357
1944	Dixie Walker, Bklyn	.357
1945	Phil Cavarretta, Chi	.355
1946	Stan Musial, StL	.365
1947	Harry Walker, StL-Phi	.363
1948	Stan Musial, StL	.376
1949	Jackie Robinson, Bklyn	.342
1950	Stan Musial, StL	.346
1951	Stan Musial, StL	.355
1952	Stan Musial, StL	.336
1953	Carl Furillo, Bklyn	.344
1954	Willie Mays, NY	.345
1955	Richie Ashburn, Phi	.338
1956	Hank Aaron, Mil	.328
1957	Stan Musial, StL	.351
1958	Richie Ashburn, Phi	.350
1959	Hank Aaron, Mil	.355
1960	Dick Groat, Pitt	.325
1961	Roberto Clemente, Pitt	.351
1962	Tommy Davis, LA	.346
1963	Tommy Davis, LA	.326
1964	Roberto Clemente, Pitt	.339
1965	Roberto Clemente, Pitt	.329
1966	Matty Alou, Pitt	.342
1967	Roberto Clemente, Pitt	.357
1968	Pete Rose, Cin	.335
1969	Pete Rose, Cin	.348
1970	Rico Carty, Atl	.366
1971	Joe Torre, StL	.363
1972	Billy Williams, Chi	.333
1973	Pete Rose, Cin	.338
1974	Ralph Garr, Atl	.353
1975	Bill Madlock, Chi	.354
1976	Bill Madlock, Chi	.339
1977	Dave Parker, Pitt	.338
1978	Dave Parker, Pitt	.334
1979	Keith Hernandez, StL	.344
1980	Bill Buckner, Chi	.324
1981	Bill Madlock, Pitt	.341
1982	Al Oliver, Mtl	.331
1983	Bill Madlock, Pitt	.323
1984	Tony Gwynn, SD	.351
1985	Willie McGee, StL	.353
1986	Tim Raines, Mtl	.334
1987	Tony Gwynn, SD	.370
1988	Tony Gwynn, SD	.313
1989	Tony Gwynn, SD	.336
1990	Willie McGee, StL	.335
1991	Terry Pendleton, Atl	.319
1992	Gary Sheffield, SD	.330
1993	Andres Galarraga, Col	.370
1994	Tony Gwynn, SD	.394
1995	Tony Gwynn, SD	.368
1996	Tony Gwynn, SD	.353
1997	Tony Gwynn, SD	.372
1998	Larry Walker, Col	.363
1999	Larry Walker, Col	.379
2000	Todd Helton, Col	.372
2001	Larry Walker, Col	.350
2002	Barry Bonds, SF	.370
2003	Albert Pujols, StL	.359
2004	Barry Bonds, SF	.362
2005	Derrek Lee, Chi	.335
2006	Freddy Sanchez, Pitt	.334
2007	Matt Holliday, Col	.340*
2008	Chipper Jones, Atl	.364

*includes NL play-in tiebreaker

Leaders in Runs Scored

Year	Player and Team	Runs
1900	Roy Thomas, Phi	131
1901	Jesse Burkett, StL	139
1902	Honus Wagner, Pitt	105
1903	Ginger Beaumont, Pitt	137
1904	George Browne, NY	99
1905	Mike Donlin, NY	124
1906	Honus Wagner, Pitt	103
	Frank Chance, Chi	103
1907	Spike Shannon, NY	104
1908	Fred Tenney, NY	101
1909	Tommy Leach, Pitt	126
1910	Sherry Magee, Phi	110
1911	Jimmy Sheckard, Chi	121
1912	Bob Bescher, Cin	120
1913	Tommy Leach, Chi	99
	Max Carey, Pitt	99
1914	George Burns, NY	100
1915	Gavvy Cravath, Phi	89
1916	George Burns, NY	105
1917	George Burns, NY	103
1918	Heinie Groh, Cin	88
1919	George Burns, NY	86
1920	George Burns, NY	115
1921	Rogers Hornsby, StL	131
1922	Rogers Hornsby, StL	141
1923	Ross Youngs, NY	121
1924	Frankie Frisch, NY	121
	Rogers Hornsby, StL	121
1925	Kiki Cuyler, Pitt	144
1926	Kiki Cuyler, Pitt	113
1927	Lloyd Waner, Pitt	133
	Rogers Hornsby, NY	133
1928	Paul Waner, Pitt	142
1929	Rogers Hornsby, Chi	156
1930	Chuck Klein, Phi	158
1931	Bill Terry, NY	121
	Chuck Klein, Phi	121
1932	Chuck Klein, Phi	152
1933	Pepper Martin, StL	122
1934	Paul Waner, Pitt	122
1935	Augie Galan, Chi	133
1936	Arky Vaughan, Pitt	122
1937	Joe Medwick, StL	111
1938	Mel Ott, NY	116
1939	Billy Werber, Cin	115
1940	Arky Vaughan, Pitt	113
1941	Pete Reiser, Bklyn	117
1942	Mel Ott, NY	118
1943	Arky Vaughan, Bklyn	112
1944	Bill Nicholson, Chi	116
1945	Eddie Stanky, Bklyn	128
1946	Stan Musial, StL	124
1947	Johnny Mize, NY	137
1948	Stan Musial, StL	135
1949	Pee Wee Reese, Bklyn	132
1950	Earl Torgeson, Bos	120
1951	Stan Musial, StL	124
	Ralph Kiner, Pitt	124
1952	Stan Musial, StL	105
	Solly Hemus, StL	105
1953	Duke Snider, Bklyn	132
1954	Stan Musial, StL	120
	Duke Snider, Bklyn	120
1955	Duke Snider, Bklyn	126
1956	Frank Robinson, Cin	122
1957	Hank Aaron, Mil	118
1958	Willie Mays, SF	121
1959	Vada Pinson, Cin	131
1960	Bill Bruton, Mil	112
1961	Willie Mays, SF	129
1962	Frank Robinson, Cin	134
1963	Hank Aaron, Mil	121
1964	Dick Allen, Phi	125
1965	Tommy Harper, Cin	126
1966	Felipe Alou, Atl	122
1967	Hank Aaron, Atl	113
	Lou Brock, StL	113
1968	Glenn Beckert, Chi	98
1969	Bobby Bonds, SF	120
	Pete Rose, Cin	120
1970	Billy Williams, Chi	137
1971	Lou Brock, StL	126
1972	Joe Morgan, Cin	122
1973	Bobby Bonds, SF	131
1974	Pete Rose, Cin	110
1975	Pete Rose, Cin	112
1976	Pete Rose, Cin	130
1977	George Foster, Cin	124
1978	Ivan DeJesus, Chi	104
1979	Keith Hernandez, StL	116
1980	Keith Hernandez, StL	111
1981	Mike Schmidt, Phi	78
1982	Lonnie Smith, StL	120
1983	Tim Raines, Mtl	133
1984	Ryne Sandberg, Chi	114
1985	Dale Murphy, Atl	118
1986	Von Hayes, Phi	107
	Tony Gwynn, SD	107
1987	Tim Raines, Mtl	123
1988	Brett Butler, SF	109
1989	Howard Johnson, NY	104
	Will Clark, SF	104
	Ryne Sandberg, Chi	104
1990	Ryne Sandberg, Chi	116
1991	Brett Butler, LA	112
1992	Barry Bonds, Pitt	109
1993	Lenny Dykstra, Phi	143
1994	Jeff Bagwell, Hou	104
1995	Craig Biggio, Hou	123
1996	Ellis Burks, Col	142
1997	Craig Biggio, Hou	146
1998	Sammy Sosa, Chi	134
1999	Jeff Bagwell, Hou	143
2000	Jeff Bagwell, Hou	152
2001	Sammy Sosa, Chi	146
2002	Sammy Sosa, Chi	122
2003	Albert Pujols, StL	137
2004	Albert Pujols, StL	133
2005	Albert Pujols, StL	129
2006	Chase Utley, Phi	131
2007	Jimmy Rollins, Phi	139
2008	Hanley Ramirez, Fla	125

Leaders in Hits

*includes NL Wild Card tiebreaker

Year	Player and Team	Hits
1900	Willie Keeler, Bklyn	208
1901	Jesse Burkett, StL	228
1902	Ginger Beaumont, Pitt	194
1903	Ginger Beaumont, Pitt	209
1904	Ginger Beaumont, Pitt	185
1905	Cy Seymour, Cin	219
1906	Harry Steinfeldt, Chi	176
1907	Ginger Beaumont, Bos	187
1908	Honus Wagner, Pitt	201
1909	Larry Doyle, NY	172
1910	Honus Wagner, Pitt	178
	Bobby Byrne, Pitt	178
1911	Doc Miller, Bos	192
1912	Heinie Zimmerman, Chi	207
1913	Gavvy Cravath, Phi	179
1914	Sherry Magee, Phi	171
1915	Larry Doyle, NY	189
1916	Hal Chase, Cin	184
1917	Heinie Groh, Cin	182
1918	Charlie Hollocher, Chi	161
1919	Ivy Olson, Bklyn	164
1920	Rogers Hornsby, StL	218
1921	Rogers Hornsby, StL	235
1922	Rogers Hornsby, StL	250
1923	Frankie Frisch, NY	223
1924	Rogers Hornsby, StL	227
1925	Jim Bottomley, StL	227
1926	Eddie Brown, Bos	201
1927	Paul Waner, Pitt	237
1928	Freddy Lindstrom, NY	231
1929	Lefty O'Doul, Phi	254
1930	Bill Terry, NY	254
1931	Lloyd Waner, Pitt	214
1932	Chuck Klein, Phi	226
1933	Chuck Klein, Phi	223
1934	Paul Waner, Pitt	217
1935	Billy Herman, Chi	227
1936	Joe Medwick, StL	223
1937	Joe Medwick, StL	237
1938	Frank McCormick, Cin	209
1939	Frank McCormick, Cin	209
1940	Stan Hack, Chi	191
	Frank McCormick, Cin	191
1941	Stan Hack, Chi	186
1942	Enos Slaughter, StL	188
1943	Stan Musial, StL	220
1944	Stan Musial, StL	197
	Phil Cavarretta, Chi	197
1945	Tommy Holmes, Bos	224
1946	Stan Musial, StL	228
1947	Tommy Holmes, Bos	191
1948	Stan Musial, StL	230
1949	Stan Musial, StL	207
1950	Duke Snider, Bklyn	199
1951	Richie Ashburn, Phi	221
1952	Stan Musial, StL	194
1953	Richie Ashburn, Phi	205
1954	Don Mueller, NY	212
1955	Ted Kluszewski, Cin	192
1956	Hank Aaron, Mil	200
1957	Red Schoendienst, NY-Mil	200
1958	Richie Ashburn, Phi	215
1959	Hank Aaron, Mil	223
1960	Willie Mays, SF	190
1961	Vada Pinson, Cin	208
1962	Tommy Davis, LA	230
1963	Vada Pinson, Cin	204
1964	Roberto Clemente, Pitt	211
	Curt Flood, StL	211
1965	Pete Rose, Cin	209
1966	Felipe Alou, Atl	218
1967	Roberto Clemente, Pitt	209
1968	Felipe Alou, Atl	210
	Pete Rose, Cin	210
1969	Matty Alou, Pitt	231
1970	Pete Rose, Cin	205
	Billy Williams, Chi	205
1971	Joe Torre, StL	230
1972	Pete Rose, Cin	198
1973	Pete Rose, Cin	230
1974	Ralph Garr, Atl	214
1975	Dave Cash, Phi	213
1976	Pete Rose, Cin	215
1977	Dave Parker, Pitt	215
1978	Steve Garvey, LA	202
1979	Garry Templeton, StL	211
1980	Steve Garvey, LA	200
1981	Pete Rose, Phi	140
1982	Al Oliver, Mtl	204
1983	Jose Cruz, Hou	189
	Andre Dawson, Mtl	189
1984	Tony Gwynn, SD	213
1985	Willie McGee, StL	216
1986	Tony Gwynn, SD	211
1987	Tony Gwynn, SD	218
1988	Andres Galarraga, Mtl	184
1989	Tony Gwynn, SD	203
1990	Brett Butler, SF	192
	Lenny Dykstra, Phi	192
1991	Terry Pendleton, Atl	187
1992	Terry Pendleton, Atl	199
	Andy Van Slyke, Pitt	199
1993	Lenny Dykstra, Phi	194
1994	Tony Gwynn, SD	165
1995	Dante Bichette, Col	197
	Tony Gwynn, SD	197
1996	Lance Johnson, NY	227
1997	Tony Gwynn, SD	220
1998	Dante Bichette, Col	219
1999	Luis Gonzalez, Ariz	206
2000	Todd Helton, Col	216
2001	Rich Aurilia, SF	206
2002	Vladimir Guerrero	206
2003	Albert Pujols, StL	212
2004	Juan Pierre, Fla	221
2005	Derrek Lee, Chi	199
2006	Juan Pierre, Chi	204
2007	Matt Holliday, Col	216*
2008	Jose Reyes, NYM	204

Home Run Leaders

Year	Player and Team	HR
1900	Herman Long, Bos	12
1901	Sam Crawford, Cin	16
1902	Tommy Leach, Pitt	6
1903	Jimmy Sheckard, Bklyn	9
1904	Harry Lumley, Bklyn	9
1905	Fred Odwell, Cin	9
1906	Tim Jordan, Bklyn	12
1907	Dave Brain, Bos	10
1908	Tim Jordan, Bklyn	12
1909	Red Murray, NY	7
1910	Fred Beck, Bos	10
	Wildfire Schulte, Chi	10
1911	Wildfire Schulte, Chi	21
1912	Heinie Zimmerman, Chi	14
1913	Gavvy Cravath, Phi	19
1914	Gavvy Cravath, Phi	19
1915	Gavvy Cravath, Phi	24
1916	Dave Robertson, NY	12
	Cy Williams, Chi	12
1917	Dave Robertson, NY	12
	Gavvy Cravath, Phi	12
1918	Gavvy Cravath, Phi	8
1919	Gavvy Cravath, Phi	12
1920	Cy Williams, Phi	15
1921	George Kelly, NY	23
1922	Rogers Hornsby, StL	42
1923	Cy Williams, Phi	41
1924	Jack Fournier, Bklyn	27
1925	Rogers Hornsby, StL	39
1926	Hack Wilson, Chi	21
1927	Hack Wilson, Chi	30
	Cy Williams, Phi	30
1928	Hack Wilson, Chi	31
	Jim Bottomley, StL	31
1929	Chuck Klein, Phi	43
1930	Hack Wilson, Chi	56
1931	Chuck Klein, Phi	31
1932	Chuck Klein, Phi	38
	Mel Ott, NY	38
1933	Chuck Klein, Phi	28
1934	Ripper Collins, StL	35
	Mel Ott, NY	35
1935	Wally Berger, Bos	34
1936	Mel Ott, NY	33
1937	Mel Ott, NY	31
	Joe Medwick, StL	31
1938	Mel Ott, NY	36
1939	Johnny Mize, StL	28
1940	Johnny Mize, StL	43
1941	Dolph Camilli, Bklyn	34
1942	Mel Ott, NY	30
1943	Bill Nicholson, Chi	29
1944	Bill Nicholson, Chi	33
1945	Tommy Holmes, Bos	28
1946	Ralph Kiner, Pitt	23
1947	Ralph Kiner, Pitt	51
	Johnny Mize, NY	51
1948	Ralph Kiner, Pitt	40
	Johnny Mize, NY	40
1949	Ralph Kiner, Pitt	54
1950	Ralph Kiner, Pitt	47
1951	Ralph Kiner, Pitt	42
1952	Ralph Kiner, Pitt	37
	Hank Sauer, Chi	37
1953	Eddie Mathews, Mil	47
1954	Ted Kluszewski, Cin	49
1955	Willie Mays, NY	51
1956	Duke Snider, Bklyn	43
1957	Hank Aaron, Mil	44
1958	Ernie Banks, Chi	47
1959	Eddie Mathews, Mil	46
1960	Ernie Banks, Chi	41
1961	Orlando Cepeda, SF	46
1962	Willie Mays, SF	49
1963	Hank Aaron, Mil	44
	Willie McCovey, SF	44
1964	Willie Mays, SF	47
1965	Willie Mays, SF	52
1966	Hank Aaron, Atl	44
1967	Hank Aaron, Atl	39
1968	Willie McCovey, SF	36
1969	Willie McCovey, SF	45
1970	Johnny Bench, Cin	45
1971	Willie Stargell, Pitt	48
1972	Johnny Bench, Cin	40
1973	Willie Stargell, Pitt	44
1974	Mike Schmidt, Phi	36
1975	Mike Schmidt, Phi	38
1976	Mike Schmidt, Phi	38
1977	George Foster, Cin	52
1978	George Foster, Cin	40
1979	Dave Kingman, Chi	48
1980	Mike Schmidt, Phi	48
1981	Mike Schmidt, Phi	31
1982	Dave Kingman, NY	37
1983	Mike Schmidt, Phi	40
1984	Dale Murphy, Atl	36
	Mike Schmidt, Phi	36
1985	Dale Murphy, Atl	37
1986	Mike Schmidt, Phi	37
1987	Andre Dawson, Chi	49
1988	Darryl Strawberry, NY	39
1989	Kevin Mitchell, SF	47
1990	Ryne Sandberg, Chi	40
1991	Howard Johnson, NY	38
1992	Fred McGriff, SD	35
1993	Barry Bonds, SF	46
1994	Matt Williams, SF	43
1995	Dante Bichette, Col	40
1996	Andres Galarraga, Col	47
1997	Larry Walker, Col	49
1998	Mark McGwire, StL	70
1999	Mark McGwire, StL	65
2000	Sammy Sosa, Chi	50
2001	Barry Bonds, SF	73
2002	Sammy Sosa, Chi	49
2003	Jim Thome, Phi	47
2004	Adrian Beltre, LA	48
2005	Andruw Jones, Atl	51
2006	Ryan Howard, Phi	58
2007	Prince Fielder, Mil	50
2008	Ryan Howard, Phi	48

Runs Batted In Leaders

Year	Player and Team	RBI
1900	Elmer Flick, Phi	110
1901	Honus Wagner, Pitt	126
1902	Honus Wagner, Pitt	91
1903	Sam Mertes, NY	104
1904	Bill Dahlen, NY	80
1905	Cy Seymour, Cin	121
1906	Jim Nealon, Pitt	83
	Harry Steinfeldt, Chi	83
1907	Sherry Magee, Phi	85
1908	Honus Wagner, Pitt	109
1909	Honus Wagner, Pitt	100
1910	Sherry Magee, Phi	123
1911	Wildfire Schulte, Chi	121
1912	Heinie Zimmerman, Chi	103
1913	Gavvy Cravath, Phi	128
1914	Sherry Magee, Phi	103
1915	Gavvy Cravath, Phi	115
1916	Heinie Zimmerman, Chi-NY	83
1917	Heinie Zimmerman, NY	102
1918	Sherry Magee, Phi	76
1919	Hi Myers, Bklyn	73
1920	George Kelly, NY	94
	Rogers Hornsby, StL	94
1921	Rogers Hornsby, StL	126
1922	Rogers Hornsby, StL	152
1923	Irish Meusel, NY	125
1924	George Kelly, NY	136
1925	Rogers Hornsby, StL	143
1926	Jim Bottomley, StL	120
1927	Paul Waner, Pitt	131
1928	Jim Bottomley, StL	136
1929	Hack Wilson, Chi	159
1930	Hack Wilson, Chi	190
1931	Chuck Klein, Phi	121
1932	Don Hurst, Phi	143
1933	Chuck Klein, Phi	120
1934	Mel Ott, NY	135
1935	Wally Berger, Bos	130
1936	Joe Medwick, StL	138
1937	Joe Medwick, StL	154
1938	Joe Medwick, StL	122
1939	Frank McCormick, Cin	128
1940	Johnny Mize, StL	137
1941	Dolph Camilli, Bklyn	120
1942	Johnny Mize, NY	110
1943	Bill Nicholson, Chi	128
1944	Bill Nicholson, Chi	122
1945	Dixie Walker, Bklyn	124
1946	Enos Slaughter, StL	130
1947	Johnny Mize, NY	138
1948	Stan Musial, StL	131
1949	Ralph Kiner, Pitt	127
1950	Del Ennis, Phi	126
1951	Monte Irvin, NY	121
1952	Hank Sauer, Chi	121
1953	Roy Campanella, Bklyn	142
1954	Ted Kluszewski, Cin	141
1955	Duke Snider, Bklyn	136
1956	Stan Musial, StL	109
1957	Hank Aaron, Mil	132
1958	Ernie Banks, Chi	129
1959	Ernie Banks, Chi	143
1960	Hank Aaron, Mil	126
1961	Orlando Cepeda, SF	142
1962	Tommy Davis, LA	153
1963	Hank Aaron, Mil	130
1964	Ken Boyer, StL	119
1965	Deron Johnson, Cin	130
1966	Hank Aaron, Atl	127
1967	Orlando Cepeda, StL	111
1968	Willie McCovey, SF	105
1969	Willie McCovey, SF	126
1970	Johnny Bench, Cin	148
1971	Joe Torre, StL	137
1972	Johnny Bench, Cin	125
1973	Willie Stargell, Pitt	119
1974	Johnny Bench, Cin	129
1975	Greg Luzinski, Phi	120
1976	George Foster, Cin	121
1977	George Foster, Cin	149
1978	George Foster, Cin	120
1979	Dave Winfield, SD	118
1980	Mike Schmidt, Phi	121
1981	Mike Schmidt, Phi	91
1982	Dale Murphy, Atl	109
	Al Oliver, Mtl	109
1983	Dale Murphy, Atl	121
1984	Gary Carter, Mtl	106
	Mike Schmidt, Phi	106
1985	Dave Parker, Cin	125
1986	Mike Schmidt, Phi	119
1987	Andre Dawson, Chi	137
1988	Will Clark, SF	109
1989	Kevin Mitchell, SF	125
1990	Matt Williams, SF	122
1991	Howard Johnson, NY	117
1992	Darren Daulton, Phi	109
1993	Barry Bonds, SF	123
1994	Jeff Bagwell, Hou	116
1995	Dante Bichette, Col	128
1996	Andres Galarraga, Col	150
1997	Andres Galarraga, Col	140
1998	Sammy Sosa, Chi	158
1999	Mark McGwire, StL	147
2000	Todd Helton, Col	147
2001	Sammy Sosa, Chi	160
2002	Lance Berkman, Hou	128
2003	Preston Wilson, Col	141
2004	Vinny Castilla, Col	131
2005	Andruw Jones, Atl	128
2006	Ryan Howard, Phi	149
2007	Matt Holliday, Col	137*
2008	Ryan Howard, Phi	146

*includes NL play-in tiebreaker

Leading Base Stealers

Year	Player and Team	SB
1900	George Van Haltren, NY	45
	Patsy Donovan, StL	45
1901	Honus Wagner, Pitt	48
1902	Honus Wagner, Pitt	43
1903	Jimmy Sheckard, Bklyn	67
	Frank Chance, Chi	67
1904	Honus Wagner, Pitt	53
1905	Billy Maloney, Chi	59
	Art Devlin, NY	59
1906	Frank Chance, Chi	57
1907	Honus Wagner, Pitt	61
1908	Honus Wagner, Pitt	53
1909	Bob Bescher, Cin	54
1910	Bob Bescher, Cin	70
1911	Bob Bescher, Cin	80
1912	Bob Bescher, Cin	67
1913	Max Carey, Pitt	61
1914	George Burns, NY	62
1915	Max Carey, Pitt	36
1916	Max Carey, Pitt	63
1917	Max Carey, Pitt	46
1918	Max Carey, Pitt	58
1919	George Burns, NY	40
1920	Max Carey, Pitt	52
1921	Frankie Frisch, NY	49
1922	Max Carey, Pitt	51
1923	Max Carey, Pitt	51
1924	Max Carey, Pitt	49
1925	Max Carey, Pitt	46
1926	Kiki Cuyler, Pitt	35
1927	Frankie Frisch, StL	48
1928	Kiki Cuyler, Chi	37
1929	Kiki Cuyler, Chi	43
1930	Kiki Cuyler, Chi	37
1931	Frankie Frisch, StL	28
1932	Chuck Klein, Phi	20
1933	Pepper Martin, StL	26
1934	Pepper Martin, StL	23
1935	Augie Galan, Chi	22
1936	Pepper Martin, StL	23
1937	Augie Galan, Chi	23
1938	Stan Hack, Chi	16
1939	Stan Hack, Chi	17
	Lee Handley, Pitt	17
1940	Lonny Frey, Cin	22
1941	Danny Murtaugh, Phi	18
1942	Pete Reiser, Bklyn	20
1943	Arky Vaughan, Bklyn	20
1944	Johnny Barrett, Pitt	28
1945	Red Schoendienst, StL	26
1946	Pete Reiser, Bklyn	34
1947	Jackie Robinson, Bklyn	29
1948	Richie Ashburn, Phi	32
1949	Jackie Robinson, Bklyn	37
1950	Sam Jethroe, Bos	35
1951	Sam Jethroe, Bos	35
1952	Pee Wee Reese, Bklyn	30
1953	Bill Bruton, Mil	26
1954	Bill Bruton, Mil	34
1955	Bill Bruton, Mil	35
1956	Willie Mays, NY	40
1957	Willie Mays, NY	38
1958	Willie Mays, SF	31
1959	Willie Mays, SF	27
1960	Maury Wills, LA	50
1961	Maury Wills, LA	35
1962	Maury Wills, LA	104
1963	Maury Wills, LA	40
1964	Maury Wills, LA	53
1965	Maury Wills, LA	94
1966	Lou Brock, StL	74
1967	Lou Brock, StL	52
1968	Lou Brock, StL	62
1969	Lou Brock, StL	53
1970	Bobby Tolan, Cin	57
1971	Lou Brock, StL	64
1972	Lou Brock, StL	63
1973	Lou Brock, StL	70
1974	Lou Brock, StL	118
1975	Davey Lopes, LA	77
1976	Davey Lopes, LA	63
1977	Frank Taveras, Pitt	70
1978	Omar Moreno, Pitt	71
1979	Omar Moreno, Pitt	77
1980	Ron LeFlore, Mtl	97
1981	Tim Raines, Mtl	71
1982	Tim Raines, Mtl	78
1983	Tim Raines, Mtl	90
1984	Tim Raines, Mtl	75
1985	Vince Coleman, StL	110
1986	Vince Coleman, StL	107
1987	Vince Coleman, StL	109
1988	Vince Coleman, StL	81
1989	Vince Coleman, StL	65
1990	Vince Coleman, StL	77
1991	Marquis Grissom, Mtl	76
1992	Marquis Grissom, Mtl	78
1993	Chuck Carr, Fla	58
1994	Craig Biggio, Hou	39
1995	Quilvio Veras, Fla	56
1996	Eric Young, Col	53
1997	Tony Womack, Pitt	60
1998	Tony Womack, Pitt	58
1999	Tony Womack, Ariz	72
2000	Luis Castillo, Fla	62
2001	Juan Pierre, Col	46
2002	Luis Castillo, Fla	48
2003	Juan Pierre, Fla	65
2004	Scott Podsednik, Mil	70
2005	Jose Reyes, NY	60
2006	Jose Reyes, NY	64
2007	Jose Reyes, NY	78
2008	Willy Taveras, Hou	68

National League *(Cont.)*

Leading Pitchers—Winning Percentage

Year	Pitcher and Team	W	L	Pct
1900	Jesse Tannehill, Pitt	20	6	.769
1901	Jack Chesbro, Pitt	21	10	.677
1902	Jack Chesbro, Pitt	28	6	.824
1903	Sam Leever, Pitt	25	7	.781
1904	Joe McGinnity, NY	35	8	.814
1905	Sam Leever, Pitt	20	5	.800
1906	Ed Reulbach, Chi	19	4	.826
1907	Ed Reulbach, Chi	17	4	.810
1908	Ed Reulbach, Chi	24	7	.774
1909	Christy Mathewson, NY	25	6	.806
	Howie Camnitz, Pitt	25	6	.806
1910	King Cole, Chi	20	4	.833
1911	Rube Marquard, NY	24	7	.774
1912	Claude Hendrix, Pitt	24	9	.727
1913	Bert Humphries, Chi	16	4	.800
1914	Bill James, Bos	26	7	.788
1915	Grover Alexander, Phi	31	10	.756
1916	Tom Hughes, Bos	16	3	.842
1917	Ferdie Schupp, NY	21	7	.750
1918	Claude Hendrix, Chi	19	7	.731
1919	Dutch Ruether, Cin	19	6	.760
1920	Burleigh Grimes, Bklyn	23	11	.676
1921	Bill Doak, StL	15	6	.714
1922	Pete Donohue, Cin	18	9	.667
1923	Dolf Luque, Cin	27	8	.771
1924	Emil Yde, Pitt	16	3	.842
1925	Bill Sherdel, StL	15	6	.714
1926	Ray Kremer, Pitt	20	6	.769
1927	Larry Benton, Bos-NY	17	7	.708
1928	Larry Benton, NY	25	9	.735
1929	Charlie Root, Chi	19	6	.760
1930	Freddie Fitzsimmons, NY	19	7	.731
1931	Paul Derringer, StL	18	8	.692
1932	Lon Warneke, Chi	22	6	.786
1933	Ben Cantwell, Bos	20	10	.667
1934	Dizzy Dean, StL	30	7	.811
1935	Bill Lee, Chi	20	6	.769
1936	Carl Hubbell, NY	26	6	.813
1937	Carl Hubbell, NY	22	8	.733
1938	Bill Lee, Chi	22	9	.710
1939	Paul Derringer, Cin	25	7	.781
1940	Freddie Fitzsimmons, Bklyn	16	2	.889
1941	Elmer Riddle, Cin	19	4	.826
1942	Larry French, Bklyn	15	4	.789
1943	Mort Cooper, StL	21	8	.724
1944	Ted Wilks, StL	17	4	.810
1945	Harry Brecheen, StL	15	4	.789
1946	Murray Dickson, StL	15	6	.714
1947	Larry Jansen, NY	21	5	.808
1948	Harry Brecheen, StL	20	7	.741
1949	Preacher Roe, Bklyn	15	6	.714
1950	Sal Maglie, NY	18	4	.818
1951	Preacher Roe, Bklyn	22	3	.880
1952	Hoyt Wilhelm, NY	15	3	.833
1953	Carl Erskine, Bklyn	20	6	.769
1954	Johnny Antonelli, NY	21	7	.750
1955	Don Newcombe, Bklyn	20	5	.800
1956	Don Newcombe, Bklyn	27	7	.794
1957	Bob Buhl, Mil	18	7	.720
1958	Warren Spahn, Mil	22	11	.667
	Lew Burdette, Mil	20	10	.667
1959	Roy Face, Pitt	18	1	.947
1960	Ernie Broglio, StL	21	9	.700
1961	Johnny Podres, LA	18	5	.783
1962	Bob Purkey, Cin	23	5	.821
1963	Ron Perranoski, LA	16	3	.842
1964	Sandy Koufax, LA	19	5	.792
1965	Sandy Koufax, LA	26	8	.765
1966	Juan Marichal, SF	25	6	.806
1967	Dick Hughes, StL	16	6	.727
1968	Steve Blass, Pitt	18	6	.750
1969	Tom Seaver, NY	25	7	.781
1970	Bob Gibson, StL	23	7	.767
1971	Don Gullett, Cin	16	6	.727
1972	Gary Nolan, Cin	15	5	.750
1973	Tommy John, LA	16	7	.696
1974	Andy Messersmith, LA	20	6	.769
1975	Don Gullett, Cin	15	4	.789
1976	Steve Carlton, Phi	20	7	.741
1977	John Candelaria, Pitt	20	5	.800
1978	Gaylord Perry, SD	21	6	.778
1979	Tom Seaver, Cin	16	6	.727
1980	Jim Bibby, Pitt	19	6	.760
1981*	Tom Seaver, Cin	14	2	.875
1982	Phil Niekro, Atl	17	4	.810
1983	John Denny, Phi	19	6	.760
1984	Rick Sutcliffe, Chi	16	1	.941
1985	Orel Hershiser, LA	19	3	.864
1986	Bob Ojeda, NY	18	5	.783
1987	Dwight Gooden, NY	15	7	.682
1988	David Cone, NY	20	3	.870
1989	Mike Bielecki, Chi	18	7	.720
1990	Doug Drabeck, Pitt	22	6	.786
1991	John Smiley, Pitt	20	8	.714
	Jose Rijo, Cin	15	6	.714
1992	Bob Tewksbury, StL	16	5	.762
1993	Tom Glavine, Atl	22	6	.786
1994	Ken Hill, Mtl	16	5	.762
1995	Greg Maddux, Atl	19	2	.905
1996	John Smoltz, Atl	24	8	.750
1997	Denny Neagle, Atl	20	5	.800
1998	John Smoltz, Atl	17	3	.850
1999	Mike Hampton, Hou	22	4	.846
2000	Randy Johnson, Ariz	19	7	.730
2001	Curt Schilling, Ariz	22	6	.786
2002	Randy Johnson, Ariz	24	5	.828
2003	Jason Schmidt, SF	17	5	.773
2004	Roger Clemens, Hou	18	4	.818
2005	Chris Carpenter, StL	21	5	.808
2006	Carlos Zambrano, Chi	16	7	.695
2007	Brad Penny, LA	16	4	.800
2008	Tim Lincecum, SF	18	5	.783

*1981 percentages based on 10 or more victories. Note: Percentages based on 15 or more victories in all other years.

Leading Pitchers—Earned Run Average

Year	Player and Team	ERA
1900	Rube Waddell, Pitt	2.37
1901	Jesse Tannehill, Pitt	2.18
1902	Jack Taylor, Chi	1.33
1903	Sam Leever, Pitt	2.06
1904	Joe McGinnity, NY	1.61
1905	Christy Mathewson, NY	1.27
1906	Three Finger Brown, Chi	1.04
1907	Jack Pfiester, Chi	1.15
1908	Christy Mathewson, NY	1.43
1909	Christy Mathewson, NY	1.14
1910	George McQuillan, Phi	1.60
1911	Christy Mathewson, NY	1.99
1912	Jeff Tesreau, NY	1.96
1913	Christy Mathewson, NY	2.06
1914	Bill Doak, StL	1.72
1915	Grover Alexander, Phi	1.22
1916	Grover Alexander, Phi	1.55
1917	Grover Alexander, Phi	1.83
1918	Hippo Vaughn, Chi	1.74
1919	Grover Alexander, Chi	1.72
1920	Grover Alexander, Chi	1.91
1921	Bill Doak, StL	2.58
1922	Rosy Ryan, NY	3.00
1923	Dolf Luque, Cin	1.93
1924	Dazzy Vance, Bklyn	2.16
1925	Dolf Luque, Cin	2.63
1926	Ray Kremer, Pitt	2.61
1927	Ray Kremer, Pitt	2.47
1928	Dazzy Vance, Bklyn	2.09
1929	Bill Walker, NY	3.08
1930	Dazzy Vance, Bklyn	2.61
1931	Bill Walker, NY	2.26
1932	Lon Warneke, Chi	2.37
1933	Carl Hubbell, NY	1.66
1934	Carl Hubbell, NY	2.30
1935	Cy Blanton, Pitt	2.59
1936	Carl Hubbell, NY	2.31
1937	Jim Turner, Bos	2.38
1938	Bill Lee, Chi	2.66
1939	Bucky Walters, Cin	2.29
1940	Bucky Walters, Cin	2.48
1941	Elmer Riddle, Cin	2.24
1942	Mort Cooper, StL	1.77
1943	Howie Pollet, StL	1.75
1944	Ed Heusser, Cin	2.38
1945	Hank Borowy, Chi	2.14
1946	Howie Pollet, StL	2.10
1947	Warren Spahn, Bos	2.33
1948	Harry Brecheen, StL	2.24
1949	Dave Koslo, NY	2.50
1950	Jim Hearn, StL-NY	2.49
1951	Chet Nichols, Bos	2.88
1952	Hoyt Wilhelm, NY	2.43
1953	Warren Spahn, Mil	2.10
1954	Johnny Antonelli, NY	2.29
1955	Bob Friend, Pitt	2.84
1956	Lew Burdette, Mil	2.71
1957	Johnny Podres, Bklyn	2.66
1958	Stu Miller, SF	2.47
1959	Sam Jones, SF	2.82
1960	Mike McCormick, SF	2.70
1961	Warren Spahn, Mil	3.01
1962	Sandy Koufax, LA	2.54
1963	Sandy Koufax, LA	1.88
1964	Sandy Koufax, LA	1.74
1965	Sandy Koufax, LA	2.04
1966	Sandy Koufax, LA	1.73
1967	Phil Niekro, Atl	1.87
1968	Bob Gibson, StL	1.12
1969	Juan Marichal, SF	2.10
1970	Tom Seaver, NY	2.81
1971	Tom Seaver, NY	1.76
1972	Steve Carlton, Phi	1.98
1973	Tom Seaver, NY	2.08
1974	Buzz Capra, Atl	2.28
1975	Randy Jones, SD	2.24
1976	John Denny, StL	2.52
1977	John Candelaria, Pitt	2.34
1978	Craig Swan, NY	2.43
1979	J.R. Richard, Hou	2.71
1980	Don Sutton, LA	2.21
1981	Nolan Ryan, Hou	1.69
1982	Steve Rogers, Mtl	2.40
1983	Atlee Hammaker, SF	2.25
1984	Alejandro Pena, LA	2.48
1985	Dwight Gooden, NY	1.53
1986	Mike Scott, Hou	2.22
1987	Nolan Ryan, Hou	2.76
1988	Joe Magrane, StL	2.18
1989	Scott Garrelts, SF	2.28
1990	Danny Darwin, Hou	2.21
1991	Dennis Martinez, Mtl	2.39
1992	Bill Swift, SF	2.08
1993	Greg Maddux, Atl	2.36
1994	Greg Maddux, Atl	1.56
1995	Greg Maddux, Atl	1.63
1996	Kevin Brown, Fla	1.89
1997	Pedro Martinez, Mtl	1.90
1998	Greg Maddux, Atl	1.98
1999	Randy Johnson, Ariz	2.48
2000	Kevin Brown, LA	2.58
2001	Randy Johnson, Ariz	2.49
2002	Randy Johnson, Ariz	2.32
2003	Jason Schmidt, SF	2.34
2004	Jake Peavy, SD	2.27
2005	Roger Clemens, Hou	1.87
2006	Roy Oswalt, Hou	2.98
2007	Jake Peavy, SD	2.54*
2008	Johan Santana, NYM	2.53

*includes NL play-in tiebreaker

Note: Based on 10 complete games through 1950, then 154 innings until National League expanded in 1962, when it became 162 innings. In strike-shortened 1981, one inning per game required.

Leading Pitchers—Strikeouts

Year	Player and Team	SO
1900	Rube Waddell, Pitt	133
1901	Noodles Hahn, Cin	233
1902	Vic Willis, Bos	226
1903	Christy Mathewson, NY	267
1904	Christy Mathewson, NY	212
1905	Christy Mathewson, NY	206
1906	Fred Beebe, Chi-StL	171
1907	Christy Mathewson, NY	178
1908	Christy Mathewson, NY	259
1909	Orval Overall, Chi	205
1910	Christy Mathewson, NY	190
1911	Rube Marquard, NY	237
1912	Grover Alexander, Phi	195
1913	Tom Seaton, Phi	168
1914	Grover Alexander, Phi	214
1915	Grover Alexander, Phi	241
1916	Grover Alexander, Phi	167
1917	Grover Alexander, Phi	200
1918	Hippo Vaughn, Chi	148
1919	Hippo Vaughn, Chi	141
1920	Grover Alexander, Chi	173
1921	Burleigh Grimes, Bklyn	136
1922	Dazzy Vance, Bklyn	134
1923	Dazzy Vance, Bklyn	197
1924	Dazzy Vance, Bklyn	262
1925	Dazzy Vance, Bklyn	221
1926	Dazzy Vance, Bklyn	140
1927	Dazzy Vance, Bklyn	184
1928	Dazzy Vance, Bklyn	200
1929	Pat Malone, Chi	166
1930	Bill Hallahan, StL	177
1931	Bill Hallahan, StL	159
1932	Dizzy Dean, StL	191
1933	Dizzy Dean, StL	199
1934	Dizzy Dean, StL	195
1935	Dizzy Dean, StL	182
1936	Van Lingle Mungo, Bklyn	238
1937	Carl Hubbell, NY	159
1938	Clay Bryant, Chi	135
1939	Claude Passeau, Phi-Chi	137
	Bucky Walters, Cin	137
1940	Kirby Higbe, Phi	137
1941	Johnny Vander Meer, Cin	202
1942	Johnny Vander Meer, Cin	186
1943	Johnny Vander Meer, Cin	174
1944	Bill Voiselle, NY	161
1945	Preacher Roe, Pitt	148
1946	Johnny Schmitz, Chi	135
1947	Ewell Blackwell, Cin	193
1948	Harry Brecheen, StL	149
1949	Warren Spahn, Bos	151
1950	Warren Spahn, Bos	191
1951	Warren Spahn, Bos	164
	Don Newcombe, Bklyn	164
1952	Warren Spahn, Bos	183
1953	Robin Roberts, Phi	198
1954	Robin Roberts, Phi	185
1955	Sam Jones, Chi	198
1956	Sam Jones, Chi	176
1957	Jack Sanford, Phi	188
1958	Sam Jones, StL	225
1959	Don Drysdale, LA	242
1960	Don Drysdale, LA	246
1961	Sandy Koufax, LA	269
1962	Don Drysdale, LA	232
1963	Sandy Koufax, LA	306
1964	Bob Veale, Pitt	250
1965	Sandy Koufax, LA	382
1966	Sandy Koufax, LA	317
1967	Jim Bunning, Phi	253
1968	Bob Gibson, StL	268
1969	Ferguson Jenkins, Chi	273
1970	Tom Seaver, NY	283
1971	Tom Seaver, NY	289
1972	Steve Carlton, Phi	310
1973	Tom Seaver, NY	251
1974	Steve Carlton, Phi	240
1975	Tom Seaver, NY	243
1976	Tom Seaver, NY	235
1977	Phil Niekro, Atl	262
1978	J.R. Richard, Hou	303
1979	J.R. Richard, Hou	313
1980	Steve Carlton, Phi	286
1981	Fernando Valenzuela, LA	180
1982	Steve Carlton, Phi	286
1983	Steve Carlton, Phi	275
1984	Dwight Gooden, NY	276
1985	Dwight Gooden, NY	268
1986	Mike Scott, Hou	306
1987	Nolan Ryan, Hou	270
1988	Nolan Ryan, Hou	228
1989	Jose DeLeon, StL	201
1990	David Cone, NY	233
1991	David Cone, NY	241
1992	John Smoltz, Atl	215
1993	Jose Rijo, Cin	227
1994	Andy Benes, SD	189
1995	Hideo Nomo, LA	236
1996	John Smoltz, Atl	276
1997	Curt Schilling, Phi	319
1998	Curt Schilling, Phi	300
1999	Randy Johnson, Ariz	364
2000	Randy Johnson, Ariz	347
2001	Randy Johnson, Ariz	372
2002	Randy Johnson, Ariz	334
2003	Kerry Wood, Chi	266
2004	Randy Johnson, Ariz	290
2005	Jake Peavy, SD	216
2006	Aaron Harang, Cin	216
2007	Jake Peavy, SD	240*
2008	Tim Lincecum, SF	265

*includes NL play-in tiebreaker

National League *(Cont.)*

Leading Pitchers—Saves

Year	Player and Team	SV
1947	Hugh Casey, Bklyn	18
1948	Harry Gumpert, Cin	17
1949	Ted Wilks, StL	9
1950	Jim Konstanty, Phi	22
1951	Ted Wilks, StL, Pitt	13
1952	Al Brazle, StL	16
1953	Al Brazle, StL	18
1954	Jim Hughes, Bklyn	24
1955	Jack Meyer, Phi	16
1956	Clem Labine, Bklyn	19
1957	Clem Labine, Bklyn	17
1958	Roy Face, Pitt	20
1959	Lindy McDaniel, StL	15
	Don McMahon, Mil	15
1960	Lindy McDaniel, StL	26
1961	Stu Miller, SF	17
	Roy Face, Pitt	17
1962	Roy Face, Pitt	28
1963	Lindy McDaniel, Chi	22
1964	Hal Woodeshick, Hou	23
1965	Ted Abernathy, Chi	31
1966	Phil Regan, LA	21
1967	Ted Abernathy, Cin	28
1968	Phi Regan, Chi, LA	25
1969	Fred Gladding, Hou	29
1970	Wayne Granger, Cin	35
1971	Dave Giusti, Pitt	30
1972	Clay Carroll, Cin	37
1973	Mike Marshall, Mtl	13
1974	Mike Marshall, LA	21
1975	Al Hrabosky, StL	22
	Rawly Eastwick, Cin	22
1976	Rawly Eastwick, Cin	26
1977	Rollie Fingers, SD	
35		
1978	Rollie Fingers, SD	37
1979	Bruce Sutter, Chi	37
1980	Bruce Sutter, Chi	28
1981	Bruce Sutter, StL	25
1982	Bruce Sutter, StL	36
1983	Lee Smith, Chi	29
1984	Bruce Sutter, StL	45
1985	Jeff Reardon, Mtl	41
1986	Todd Worrell, StL	36
1987	Steve Bedrosian, Phi	40
1988	John Franco, Cin	39
1989	Mark Davis, SD	44
1990	John Franco, NY	33
1991	Lee Smith, StL	47
1992	Lee Smith, StL	42
1993	Randy Myers, Chi	53
1994	John Franco, NY	30
1995	Randy Myers, Chi	38
1996	Jeff Brantley, Cin	44
	Todd Worrell, LA	44
1997	Jeff Shaw, Cin	42
1998	Trevor Hoffman, SD	53
1999	Ugueth Urbina, Mtl	41
2000	Antonio Alfonseca, Fla	45
2001	Robb Nen, SF	45
2002	John Smoltz, Atl	55
2003	Eric Gagne, LA	55
2004	Armando Benitez, Fla	47
	Jason Isringhausen, StL	47
2005	Chad Cordero, Wash	47
2006	Trevor Hoffman, SD	46
2007	Jose Valverde, Ariz	47
2008	Jose Valverde, Hou	44

American League

Leading Batsmen

Year	Player and Team	BA	Year	Player and Team	BA
1901	Nap Lajoie, Phi	.422	1955	Al Kaline, Det	.340
1902	Ed Delahanty, Wash	.376	1956	Mickey Mantle, NY	.353
1903	Nap Lajoie, Clev	.355	1957	Ted Williams, Bos	.388
1904	Nap Lajoie, Clev	.381	1958	Ted Williams, Bos	.328
1905	Elmer Flick, Clev	.306	1959	Harvey Kuenn, Det	.353
1906	George Stone, StL	.358	1960	Pete Runnels, Bos	.320
1907	Ty Cobb, Det	.350	1961	Norm Cash, Det	.361
1908	Ty Cobb, Det	.324	1962	Pete Runnels, Bos	.326
1909	Ty Cobb, Det	.377	1963	Carl Yastrzemski, Bos	.321
1910	Nap Lajoie, Clev*	.383	1964	Tony Oliva, Minn	.323
1911	Ty Cobb, Det	.420	1965	Tony Oliva, Minn	.321
1912	Ty Cobb, Det	.410	1966	Frank Robinson, Balt	.316
1913	Ty Cobb, Det	.390	1967	Carl Yastrzemski, Bos	.326
1914	Ty Cobb, Det	.368	1968	Carl Yastrzemski, Bos	.301
1915	Ty Cobb, Det	.369	1969	Rod Carew, Minn	.332
1916	Tris Speaker, Clev	.386	1970	Alex Johnson, Cal	.329
1917	Ty Cobb, Det	.383	1971	Tony Oliva, Minn	.337
1918	Ty Cobb, Det	.382	1972	Rod Carew, Minn	.318
1919	Ty Cobb, Det	.384	1973	Rod Carew, Minn	.350
1920	George Sisler, StL	.407	1974	Rod Carew, Minn	.364
1921	Harry Heilmann, Det	.394	1975	Rod Carew, Minn	.359
1922	George Sisler, StL	.420	1976	George Brett, KC	.333
1923	Harry Heilmann, Det	.403	1977	Rod Carew, Minn	.388
1924	Babe Ruth, NY	.378	1978	Rod Carew, Minn	.333
1925	Harry Heilmann, Det	.393	1979	Fred Lynn, Bos	.333
1926	Heinie Manush, Det	.378	1980	George Brett, KC	.390
1927	Harry Heilmann, Det	.398	1981	Carney Lansford, Bos	.336
1928	Goose Goslin, Wash	.379	1982	Willie Wilson, KC	.332
1929	Lew Fonseca, Clev	.369	1983	Wade Boggs, Bos	.361
1930	Al Simmons, Phi	.381	1984	Don Mattingly, NY	.343
1931	Al Simmons, Phi	.390	1985	Wade Boggs, Bos	.368
1932	Dale Alexander, Det-Bos	.367	1986	Wade Boggs, Bos	.357
1933	Jimmie Foxx, Phi	.356	1987	Wade Boggs, Bos	.363
1934	Lou Gehrig, NY	.363	1988	Wade Boggs, Bos	.366
1935	Buddy Myer, Wash	.349	1989	Kirby Puckett, Minn	.339
1936	Luke Appling, Chi	.388	1990	George Brett, KC	.329
1937	Charlie Gehringer, Det	.371	1991	Julio Franco, Tex	.341
1938	Jimmie Foxx, Bos	.349	1992	Edgar Martinez, Sea	.343
1939	Joe DiMaggio, NY	.381	1993	John Olerud, Tor	.363
1940	Joe DiMaggio, NY	.352	1994	Paul O'Neill, NY	.359
1941	Ted Williams, Bos	.406	1995	Edgar Martinez, Sea	.356
1942	Ted Williams, Bos	.356	1996	Alex Rodriguez, Sea	.358
1943	Luke Appling, Chi	.328	1997	Frank Thomas, Chi	.347
1944	Lou Boudreau, Clev	.327	1998	Bernie Williams, NY	.339
1945	Snuffy Stirnweiss, NY	.309	1999	Nomar Garciaparra, Bos	.357
1946	Mickey Vernon, Wash	.353	2000	Nomar Garciaparra, Bos	.372
1947	Ted Williams, Bos	.343	2001	Ichiro Suzuki, Sea	.350
1948	Ted Williams, Bos	.369	2002	Manny Ramirez, Bos	.349
1949	George Kell, Det	.343	2003	Bill Mueller, Bos	.326
1950	Billy Goodman, Bos	.354	2004	Ichiro Suzuki, Sea	.372
1951	Ferris Fain, Phi	.344	2005	Michael Young, Tex	.331
1952	Ferris Fain, Phi	.327	2006	Joe Mauer, Minn	.347
1953	Mickey Vernon, Wash	.337	2007	Magglio Ordonez, Det	.363
1954	Bobby Avila, Clev	.341	2008	Joe Mauer, Minn	.330

*League president Ban Johnson declared Ty Cobb batting champion with a .385 average, beating Lajoie's .384. However, subsequent research has led to the revision of Lajoie's average to .383 and Cobb's to .382.

Leaders in Runs Scored

Year	Player and Team	Runs
1901	Nap Lajoie, Phi	145
1902	Dave Fultz, Phi	110
1903	Patsy Dougherty, Bos	108
1904	Patsy Dougherty, Bos-NY	113
1905	Harry Davis, Phi	92
1906	Elmer Flick, Clev	98
1907	Sam Crawford, Det	102
1908	Matty McIntyre, Det	105
1909	Ty Cobb, Det	116
1910	Ty Cobb, Det	106
1911	Ty Cobb, Det	147
1912	Eddie Collins, Phi	137
1913	Eddie Collins, Phi	125
1914	Eddie Collins, Phi	122
1915	Ty Cobb, Det	144
1916	Ty Cobb, Det	113
1917	Donie Bush, Det	112
1918	Ray Chapman, Clev	84
1919	Babe Ruth, Bos	103
1920	Babe Ruth, NY	158
1921	Babe Ruth, NY	177
1922	George Sisler, StL	134
1923	Babe Ruth, NY	151
1924	Babe Ruth, NY	143
1925	Johnny Mostil, Chi	135
1926	Babe Ruth, NY	139
1927	Babe Ruth, NY	158
1928	Babe Ruth, NY	163
1929	Charlie Gehringer, Det	131
1930	Al Simmons, Phi	152
1931	Lou Gehrig, NY	163
1932	Jimmie Foxx, Phi	151
1933	Lou Gehrig, NY	138
1934	Charlie Gehringer, Det	134
1935	Lou Gehrig, NY	125
1936	Lou Gehrig, NY	167
1937	Joe DiMaggio, NY	151
1938	Hank Greenberg, Det	144
1939	Red Rolfe, NY	139
1940	Ted Williams, Bos	134
1941	Ted Williams, Bos	135
1942	Ted Williams, Bos	141
1943	George Case, Wash	102
1944	Snuffy Stirnweiss, NY	125
1945	Snuffy Stirnweiss, NY	107
1946	Ted Williams, Bos	142
1947	Ted Williams, Bos	125
1948	Tommy Henrich, NY	138
1949	Ted Williams, Bos	150
1950	Dom DiMaggio, Bos	131
1951	Dom DiMaggio, Bos	113
1952	Larry Doby, Clev	104
1953	Al Rosen, Clev	115
1954	Mickey Mantle, NY	129
1955	Al Smith, Clev	123
1956	Mickey Mantle, NY	132
1957	Mickey Mantle, NY	121
1958	Mickey Mantle, NY	127
1959	Eddie Yost, Det	115
1960	Mickey Mantle, NY	119
1961	Mickey Mantle, NY	132
	Roger Maris, NY	132
1962	Albie Pearson, LA	115
1963	Bob Allison, Minn	99
1964	Tony Oliva, Minn	109
1965	Zoilo Versalles, Minn	126
1966	Frank Robinson, Balt	122
1967	Carl Yastrzemski, Bos	112
1968	Dick McAuliffe, Det	95
1969	Reggie Jackson, Oak	123
1970	Carl Yastrzemski, Bos	125
1971	Don Buford, Balt	99
1972	Bobby Murcer, NY	102
1973	Reggie Jackson, Oak	99
1974	Carl Yastrzemski, Bos	93
1975	Fred Lynn, Bos	103
1976	Roy White, NY	104
1977	Rod Carew, Minn	128
1978	Ron LeFlore, Det	126
1979	Don Baylor, Cal	120
1980	Willie Wilson, KC	133
1981	Rickey Henderson, Oak	89
1982	Paul Molitor, Mil	136
1983	Cal Ripken, Balt	121
1984	Dwight Evans, Bos	121
1985	Rickey Henderson, NY	146
1986	Rickey Henderson, NY	130
1987	Paul Molitor, Mil	114
1988	Wade Boggs, Bos	128
1989	Rickey Henderson, NY-Oak	113
	Wade Boggs, Bos	113
1990	Rickey Henderson, Oak	119
1991	Paul Molitor, Mil	133
1992	Tony Philips, Det	114
1993	Rafael Palmeiro, Tex	124
1994	Frank Thomas, Chi	106
1995	Albert Belle, Clev	121
	Edgar Martinez, Sea	121
1996	Alex Rodriguez, Sea	141
1997	Ken Griffey Jr., Sea	125
1998	Derek Jeter, NY	127
1999	Roberto Alomar, Clev	138
2000	Johnny Damon, KC	136
2001	Alex Rodriguez, Tex	133
2002	Alfonso Soriano, NY	128
2003	Alex Rodriguez, Tex	124
2004	Vladimir Guerrero, Ana	124
2005	Alex Rodriguez, NY	124
2006	Grady Sizemore, Clev	134
2007	Alex Rodriguez, NY	143
2008	Dustin Pedroia, Bos	118

Leaders in Hits

Year	Player and Team	Hits
1901	Nap Lajoie, Phi	229
1902	Piano Legs Hickman, Bos-Clev	194
1903	Patsy Dougherty, Bos	195
1904	Nap Lajoie, Clev	211
1905	George Stone, StL	187
1906	Nap Lajoie, Clev	214
1907	Ty Cobb, Det	212
1908	Ty Cobb, Det	188
1909	Ty Cobb, Det	216
1910	Nap Lajoie, Clev	227
1911	Ty Cobb, Det	248
1912	Ty Cobb, Det	227
1913	Joe Jackson, Clev	197
1914	Tris Speaker, Bos	193
1915	Ty Cobb, Det	208
1916	Tris Speaker, Clev	211
1917	Ty Cobb, Det	225
1918	George Burns, Phi	178
1919	Ty Cobb, Det	191
	Bobby Veach, Det	191
1920	George Sisler, StL	257
1921	Harry Heilmann, Det	237
1922	George Sisler, StL	246
1923	Charlie Jamieson, Clev	222
1924	Sam Rice, Wash	216
1925	Al Simmons, Phi	253
1926	George Burns, Clev	216
	Sam Rice, Wash	216
1927	Earle Combs, NY	231
1928	Heinie Manush, StL	241
1929	Dale Alexander, Det	215
	Charlie Gehringer, Det	215
1930	Johnny Hodapp, Clev	225
1931	Lou Gehrig, NY	211
1932	Al Simmons, Phi	216
1933	Heinie Manush, Wash	221
1934	Charlie Gehringer, Det	214
1935	Joe Vosmik, Clev	216
1936	Earl Averill, Clev	232
1937	Beau Bell, StL	218
1938	Joe Vosmik, Bos	201
1939	Red Rolfe, NY	213
1940	Rip Radcliff, StL	200
	Barney McCosky, Det	200
	Doc Cramer, Bos	200
1941	Cecil Travis, Wash	218
1942	Johnny Pesky, Bos	205
1943	Dick Wakefield, Det	200
1944	Snuffy Stirnweiss, NY	205
1945	Snuffy Stirnweiss, NY	195
1946	Johnny Pesky, Bos	208
1947	Johnny Pesky, Bos	207
1948	Bob Dillinger, StL	207
1949	Dale Mitchell, Clev	203
1950	George Kell, Det	218
1951	George Kell, Det	191
1952	Nellie Fox, Chi	192
1953	Harvey Kuenn, Det	209
1954	Nellie Fox, Chi	201
	Harvey Kuenn, Det	201
1955	Al Kaline, Det	200
1956	Harvey Kuenn, Det	196
1957	Nellie Fox, Chi	196
1958	Nellie Fox, Chi	187
1959	Harvey Kuenn, Det	198
1960	Minnie Minoso, Chi	184
1961	Norm Cash, Det	193
1962	Bobby Richardson, NY	209
1963	Carl Yastrzemski, Bos	183
1964	Tony Oliva, Minn	217
1965	Tony Oliva, Minn	185
1966	Tony Oliva, Minn	191
1967	Carl Yastrzemski, Bos	189
1968	Bert Campaneris, Oak	177
1969	Tony Oliva, Minn	197
1970	Tony Oliva, Minn	204
1971	Cesar Tovar, Minn	204
1972	Joe Rudi, Oak	181
1973	Rod Carew, Minn	203
1974	Rod Carew, Minn	218
1975	George Brett, KC	195
1976	George Brett, KC	215
1977	Rod Carew, Minn	239
1978	Jim Rice, Bos	213
1979	George Brett, KC	212
1980	Willie Wilson, KC	230
1981	Rickey Henderson, Oak	135
1982	Robin Yount, Mil	210
1983	Cal Ripken Jr., Balt	211
1984	Don Mattingly, NY	207
1985	Wade Boggs, Bos	240
1986	Don Mattingly, NY	238
1987	Kirby Puckett, Minn	207
	Kevin Seitzer, KC	207
1988	Kirby Puckett, Minn	234
1989	Kirby Puckett, Minn	215
1990	Rafael Palmeiro, Tex	191
1991	Paul Molitor, Mil	216
1992	Kirby Puckett, Minn	210
1993	Paul Molitor, Tor	211
1994	Kenny Lofton, Clev	160
1995	Lance Johnson, Chi	186
1996	Paul Molitor, Minn	225
1997	Nomar Garciaparra, Bos	209
1998	Alex Rodriguez, Sea	213
1999	Derek Jeter, NY	219
2000	Darin Erstad, Ana	240
2001	Ichiro Suzuki, Sea	242
2002	Alfonso Soriano, NY	209
2003	Vernon Wells, Tor	215
2004	Ichiro Suzuki, Sea	262
2005	Michael Young, Tex	221
2006	Ichiro Suzuki, Sea	224
2007	Ichiro Suzuki, Sea	238
2008	Dustin Pedroia, Bos	213
	Ichiro Suzuki, Sea	213

American League *(Cont.)*

Home Run Leaders

Year	Player and Team	HR
1901	Nap Lajoie, Phi	13
1902	Socks Seybold, Phi	16
1903	Buck Freeman, Bos	13
1904	Harry Davis, Phi	10
1905	Harry Davis, Phi	8
1906	Harry Davis, Phi	12
1907	Harry Davis, Phi	8
1908	Sam Crawford, Det	7
1909	Ty Cobb, Det	9
1910	Jake Stahl, Bos	10
1911	Frank Baker, Phi	9
1912	Frank Baker, Phi	10
	Tris Speaker, Bos	10
1913	Frank Baker, Phi	13
1914	Frank Baker, Phi	9
1915	Braggo Roth, Chi-Clev	7
1916	Wally Pipp, NY	12
1917	Wally Pipp, NY	9
1918	Babe Ruth, Bos	11
	Tilly Walker, Phi	11
1919	Babe Ruth, Bos	29
1920	Babe Ruth, NY	54
1921	Babe Ruth, NY	59
1922	Ken Williams, StL	39
1923	Babe Ruth, NY	41
1924	Babe Ruth, NY	46
1925	Bob Meusel, NY	33
1926	Babe Ruth, NY	47
1927	Babe Ruth, NY	60
1928	Babe Ruth, NY	54
1929	Babe Ruth, NY	46
1930	Babe Ruth, NY	49
1931	Babe Ruth/ Lou Gehrig NY	46
1932	Jimmie Foxx, Phi	58
1933	Jimmie Foxx, Phi	48
1934	Lou Gehrig, NY	49
1935	Jimmie Foxx, Phi	36
	Hank Greenberg, Det	36
1936	Lou Gehrig, NY	49
1937	Joe DiMaggio, NY	46
1938	Hank Greenberg, Det	58
1939	Jimmie Foxx, Bos	35
1940	Hank Greenberg, Det	41
1941	Ted Williams, Bos	37
1942	Ted Williams, Bos	36
1943	Rudy York, Det	34
1944	Nick Etten, NY	22
1945	Vern Stephens, StL	24
1946	Hank Greenberg, Det	44
1947	Ted Williams, Bos	32
1948	Joe DiMaggio, NY	39
1949	Ted Williams, Bos	43
1950	Al Rosen, Clev	37
1951	Gus Zernial, Chi-Phi	33
1952	Larry Doby, Clev	32
1953	Al Rosen, Clev	43
1954	Larry Doby, Clev	32
1955	Mickey Mantle, NY	37
1956	Mickey Mantle, NY	52
1957	Roy Sievers, Wash	42
1958	Mickey Mantle, NY	42
1959	Rocky Colavito, Clev	42
	Harmon Killebrew, Wash	42
1960	Mickey Mantle, NY	40
1961	Roger Maris, NY	61
1962	Harmon Killebrew, Minn	48
1963	Harmon Killebrew, Minn	45
1964	Harmon Killebrew, Minn	49
1965	Tony Conigliaro, Bos	32
1966	Frank Robinson, Balt	49
1967	Harmon Killebrew, Minn	44
	Carl Yastrzemski, Bos	44
1968	Frank Howard, Wash	44
1969	Harmon Killebrew, Minn	49
1970	Frank Howard, Wash	44
1971	Bill Melton, Chi	33
1972	Dick Allen, Chi	37
1973	Reggie Jackson, Oak	32
1974	Dick Allen, Chi	32
1975	Reggie Jackson, Oak	36
	George Scott, Mil	36
1976	Graig Nettles, NY	32
1977	Jim Rice, Bos	39
1978	Jim Rice, Bos	46
1979	Gorman Thomas, Mil	45
1980	Reggie Jackson, NY	41
	Ben Oglivie, Mil	41
1981	Tony Armas, Oak	22
1981	Dwight Evans, Bos	22
	Bobby Grich, Cal	22
	Eddie Murray, Balt	22
1982	Reggie Jackson, Cal	39
	Gorman Thomas, Mil	39
1983	Jim Rice, Bos	39
1984	Tony Armas, Bos	43
1985	Darrell Evans, Det	40
1986	Jesse Barfield, Tor	40
1987	Mark McGwire, Oak	49
1988	Jose Canseco, Oak	42
1989	Fred McGriff, Tor	36
1990	Cecil Fielder, Det	51
1991	Jose Canseco, Oak	44
	Cecil Fielder, Det	44
1992	Juan Gonzalez, Tex	43
1993	Juan Gonzalez, Tex	46
1994	Ken Griffey Jr., Sea	40
1995	Albert Belle, Clev	50
1996	Mark McGwire, Oak	52
1997	Ken Griffey Jr., Sea	56
1998	Ken Griffey Jr., Sea	56
1999	Ken Griffey Jr., Sea	48
2000	Troy Glaus, Ana	47
2001	Alex Rodriguez, Tex	52
2002	Alex Rodriguez, Tex	57
2003	Alex Rodriguez, Tex	47
2004	Manny Ramirez, Bos	43
2005	Alex Rodriguez, NY	48
2006	David Ortiz, Bos	54
2007	Alex Rodriguez, NY	54
2008	Miguel Cabrera, Det	37

American League *(Cont.)*

Runs Batted In Leaders

Year	Player and Team	RBI
1907	Ty Cobb, Det	116
1908	Ty Cobb, Det	108
1909	Ty Cobb, Det	107
1910	Sam Crawford, Det	120
1911	Ty Cobb, Det	144
1912	Frank Baker, Phi	133
1913	Frank Baker, Phi	126
1914	Sam Crawford, Det	104
1915	Sam Crawford, Det	112
	Bobby Veach, Det	112
1916	Del Pratt, StL	103
1917	Bobby Veach, Det	103
1918	Bobby Veach, Det	78
1919	Babe Ruth, Bos	114
1920	Babe Ruth, NY	137
1921	Babe Ruth, NY	171
1922	Ken Williams, StL	155
1923	Babe Ruth, NY	131
1924	Goose Goslin, Wash	129
1925	Bob Meusel, NY	138
1926	Babe Ruth, NY	145
1927	Lou Gehrig, NY	175
1928	Babe Ruth/ Lou Gehrig, NY	142
1929	Al Simmons, Phi	157
1930	Lou Gehrig, NY	174
1931	Lou Gehrig, NY	184
1932	Jimmie Foxx, Phi	169
1933	Jimmie Foxx, Phi	163
1934	Lou Gehrig, NY	165
1935	Hank Greenberg, Det	170
1936	Hal Trosky, Clev	162
1937	Hank Greenberg, Det	183
1938	Jimmie Foxx, Bos	175
1939	Ted Williams, Bos	145
1940	Hank Greenberg, Det	150
1941	Joe DiMaggio, NY	125
1942	Ted Williams, Bos	137
1943	Rudy York, Det	118
1944	Vern Stephens, StL	109
1945	Nick Etten, NY	111
1946	Hank Greenberg, Det	127
1947	Ted Williams, Bos	114
1948	Joe DiMaggio, NY	155
1949	Ted Williams, Bos	159
	Vern Stephens, Bos	159
1950	Walt Dropo, Bos	144
	Vern Stephens, Bos	144
1951	Gus Zernial, Chi-Phi	129
1952	Al Rosen, Clev	105
1953	Al Rosen, Clev	145
1954	Larry Doby, Clev	126
1955	Ray Boone, Det	116
	Jackie Jensen, Bos	116
1956	Mickey Mantle, NY	130
1957	Roy Sievers, Wash	114
1958	Jackie Jensen, Bos	122
1959	Jackie Jensen, Bos	112
1960	Roger Maris, NY	112
1961	Roger Maris, NY	142
1962	Harmon Killebrew, Minn	126
1963	Dick Stuart, Bos	118
1964	Brooks Robinson, Balt	118
1965	Rocky Colavito, Clev	108
1966	Frank Robinson, Balt	122
1967	Carl Yastrzemski, Bos	121
1968	Ken Harrelson, Bos	109
1969	Harmon Killebrew, Minn	140
1970	Frank Howard, Wash	126
1971	Harmon Killebrew, Minn	119
1972	Dick Allen, Chi	113
1973	Reggie Jackson, Oak	117
1974	Jeff Burroughs, Tex	118
1975	George Scott, Mil	109
1976	Lee May, Balt	109
1977	Larry Hisle, Minn	119
1978	Jim Rice, Bos	139
1979	Don Baylor, Cal	139
1980	Cecil Cooper, Mil	122
1981	Eddie Murray, Balt	78
1982	Hal McRae, KC	133
1983	Cecil Cooper, Mil	126
	Jim Rice, Bos	126
1984	Tony Armas, Bos	123
1985	Don Mattingly, NY	145
1986	Joe Carter, Clev	121
1987	George Bell, Tor	134
1988	Jose Canseco, Oak	124
1989	Ruben Sierra, Tex	119
1990	Cecil Fielder, Det	132
1991	Cecil Fielder, Det	133
1992	Cecil Fielder, Det	124
1993	Albert Belle, Clev	129
1994	Kirby Puckett, Minn	112
1995	Albert Belle, Clev	126
	Mo Vaughn, Bos	126
1996	Albert Belle, Clev	148
1997	Ken Griffey Jr., Sea	147
1998	Juan Gonzales, Tex	157
1999	Manny Ramirez, Clev	165
2000	Edgar Martinez, Sea	145
2001	Bret Boone, Sea	141
2002	Alex Rodriguez, Tex	142
2003	Carlos Delgado, Tor	145
2004	Miguel Tejada, Balt	150
2005	David Ortiz, Bos	148
2006	David Ortiz, Bos	137
2007	Alex Rodriguez, NY	156
2008	Josh Hamilton, Tex	130

Leading Base Stealers

Year	Player and Team	SB
1901	Frank Isbell, Chi	48
1902	Topsy Hartsel, Phi	54
1903	Harry Bay, Clev	46
1904	Elmer Flick, Clev	42
	Harry Bay, Clev	42
1905	Danny Hoffman, Phi	46
1906	Elmer Flick, Clev	39
	John Anderson, Wash	39
1907	Ty Cobb, Det	49
1908	Patsy Dougherty, Chi	47
1909	Ty Cobb, Det	76
1910	Eddie Collins, Phi	81
1911	Ty Cobb, Det	83
1912	Clyde Milan, Wash	88
1913	Clyde Milan, Wash	75
1914	Fritz Maisel, NY	74
1915	Ty Cobb, Det	96
1916	Ty Cobb, Det	68
1917	Ty Cobb, Det	55
1918	George Sisler, StL	45
1919	Eddie Collins, Chi	33
1920	Sam Rice, Wash	63

Note: Runs Batted In not compiled before 1907; officially adopted in 1920.

Leading Base Stealers (Cont.)

Year	Player and Team	SB
1921	George Sisler, StL	35
1922	George Sisler, StL	51
1923	Eddie Collins, Chi	49
1924	Eddie Collins, Chi	42
1925	John Mostil, Chi	43
1926	John Mostil, Chi	35
1927	George Sisler, StL	27
1928	Buddy Myer, Bos	30
1929	Charlie Gehringer, Det	27
1930	Marty McManus, Det	23
1931	Ben Chapman, NY	61
1932	Ben Chapman, NY	38
1933	Ben Chapman, NY	27
1934	Bill Werber, Bos	40
1935	Bill Werber, Bos	29
1936	Lyn Lary, StL	37
1937	Bill Werber, Phi	35
	Ben Chapman, Wash-Bos	35
1938	Frank Crosetti, NY	27
1939	George Case, Wash	51
1940	George Case, Wash	35
1941	George Case, Wash	33
1942	George Case, Wash	44
1943	George Case, Wash	61
1944	Snuffy Stirnweiss, NY	55
1945	Snuffy Stirnweiss, NY	33
1946	George Case, Clev	28
1947	Bob Dillinger, StL	34
1948	Bob Dillinger, StL	28
1949	Bob Dillinger, StL	20
1950	Dom DiMaggio, Bos	15
1951	Minnie Minoso, Clev-Chi	31
1952	Minnie Minoso, Chi	22
1953	Minnie Minoso, Chi	25
1954	Jackie Jensen, Bos	22
1955	Jim Rivera, Chi	25
1956	Luis Aparicio, Chi	21
1957	Luis Aparicio, Chi	28
1958	Luis Aparicio, Chi	29
1959	Luis Aparicio, Chi	56
1960	Luis Aparicio, Chi	51
1961	Luis Aparicio, Chi	53
1962	Luis Aparicio, Chi	31
1963	Luis Aparicio, Balt	40
1964	Luis Aparicio, Balt	57
1965	Bert Campaneris, KC	51
1966	Bert Campaneris, KC	52
1967	Bert Campaneris, KC	55
1968	Bert Campaneris, Oak	62
1969	Tommy Harper, Sea	73
1970	Bert Campaneris, Oak	42
1971	Amos Otis, KC	52
1972	Bert Campaneris, Oak	52
1973	Tommy Harper, Bos	54
1974	Bill North, Oak	54
1975	Mickey Rivers, Cal	70
1976	Bill North, Oak	75
1977	Freddie Patek, KC	53
1978	Ron LeFlore, Det	68
1979	Willie Wilson, KC	83
1980	Rickey Henderson, Oak	100
1981	Rickey Henderson, Oak	56
1982	Rickey Henderson, Oak	130
1983	Rickey Henderson, Oak	108
1984	Rickey Henderson, Oak	66
1985	Rickey Henderson, NY	80
1986	Rickey Henderson, NY	87
1987	Harold Reynolds, Sea	60
1988	Rickey Henderson, NY	93
1989	Rickey Henderson, NY-Oak	77
1990	Rickey Henderson, Oak	65
1991	Rickey Henderson, Oak	58
1992	Kenny Lofton, Clev	66
1993	Kenny Lofton, Clev	70
1994	Kenny Lofton, Clev	60
1995	Kenny Lofton, Clev	54
1996	Kenny Lofton, Clev	75
1997	Brian Hunter, Det	74
1998	Rickey Henderson, Oak	66
1999	Brian Hunter, Sea	44
2000	Johnny Damon, KC	46
2001	Ichiro Suzuki, Sea	56
2002	Alfonso Soriano, NY	41
2003	Carl Crawford, TB	55
2004	Carl Crawford, TB	59
2005	Chone Figgins, LA	62
2006	Carl Crawford, TB	58
2007	Carl Crawford, TB	50
	Brian Roberts, Balt	50
2008	Jacoby Ellsbury, Bos	50

Leading Pitchers—Winning Percentage

Year	Pitcher and Team	W	L	Pct
1901	Clark Griffith, Chi	24	7	.774
1902	Bill Bernhard, Phi-Clev	18	5	.783
1903	Earl Moore, Clev	22	7	.759
1904	Jack Chesbro, NY	41	12	.774
1905	Jess Tannehill, Bos	22	9	.710
1906	Eddie Plank, Phi	19	6	.760
1907	Wild Bill Donovan, Det	25	4	.862
1908	Ed Walsh, Chi	40	15	.727
1909	George Mullin, Det	29	8	.784
1910	Chief Bender, Phi	23	5	.821
1911	Chief Bender, Phi	17	5	.773
1912	Smoky Joe Wood, Bos	34	5	.872
1913	Walter Johnson, Wash	36	7	.837
1914	Chief Bender, Phi	17	3	.850
1915	Smoky Joe Wood, Bos	15	5	.750
1916	Eddie Cicotte, Chi	15	7	.682
1917	Reb Russell, Chi	15	5	.750
1918	Sad Sam Jones, Bos	16	5	.762
1919	Eddie Cicotte, Chi	29	7	.806
1920	Jim Bagby, Clev	31	12	.721
1921	Carl Mays, NY	27	9	.750
1922	Joe Bush, NY	26	7	.788
1923	Herb Pennock, NY	19	6	.760
1924	Walter Johnson, Wash	23	7	.767
1925	Stan Coveleski, Wash	20	5	.800
1926	George Uhle, Clev	27	11	.711
1927	Waite Hoyt, NY	22	7	.759
1928	General Crowder, StL	21	5	.808
1929	Lefty Grove, Phi	20	6	.769
1930	Lefty Grove, Phi	28	5	.848
1931	Lefty Grove, Phi	31	4	.886
1932	Johnny Allen, NY	17	4	.810
1933	Lefty Grove, Phi	24	8	.750
1934	Lefty Gomez, NY	26	5	.839
1935	Eldon Auker, Det	18	7	.720
1936	Monte Pearson, NY	19	7	.731
1937	Johnny Allen, Clev	15	1	.938
1938	Red Ruffing, NY	21	7	.750

Leading Pitchers—Winning Percentage (Cont.)

Year	Pitcher and Team	W	L	Pct
1939	Lefty Grove, Bos	15	4	.789
1940	Schoolboy Rowe, Det	16	3	.842
1941	Lefty Gomez, NY	15	5	.750
1942	Ernie Bonham, NY	21	5	.808
1943	Spud Chandler, NY	20	4	.833
1944	Tex Hughson, Bos	18	5	.783
1945	Hal Newhouser, Det	25	9	.735
1946	Boo Ferriss, Bos	25	6	.806
1947	Allie Reynolds, NY	19	8	.704
1948	Jack Kramer, Bos	18	5	.783
1949	Ellis Kinder, Bos	23	6	.793
1950	Vic Raschi, NY	21	8	.724
1951	Bob Feller, Clev	22	8	.733
1952	Bobby Shantz, Phi	24	7	.774
1953	Ed Lopat, NY	16	4	.800
1954	Sandy Consuegra, Chi	16	3	.842
1955	Tommy Byrne, NY	16	5	.762
1956	Whitey Ford, NY	19	6	.760
1957	Dick Donovan, Chi	16	6	.727
	Tom Sturdivant, NY	16	6	.727
1958	Bob Turley, NY	21	7	.750
1959	Bob Shaw, Chi	18	6	.750
1960	Jim Perry, Clev	18	10	.643
1961	Whitey Ford, NY	25	4	.862
1962	Ray Herbert, Chi	20	9	.690
1963	Whitey Ford, NY	24	7	.774
1964	Wally Bunker, Balt	19	5	.792
1965	Mudcat Grant, Minn	21	7	.750
1966	Sonny Siebert, Clev	16	8	.667
1967	Joel Horlen, Chi	19	7	.731
1968	Denny McLain, Det	31	6	.838
1969	Jim Palmer, Balt	16	4	.800
1970	Mike Cuellar, Balt	24	8	.750
1971	Dave McNally, Balt	21	5	.808
1972	Catfish Hunter, Oak	21	7	.750
1973	Catfish Hunter, Oak	21	5	.808
1974	Mike Cuellar, Balt	22	10	.688
1975	Mike Torrez, Balt	20	9	.690
1976	Bill Campbell, Minn	17	5	.773
1977	Paul Splittorff, KC	16	6	.727
1978	Ron Guidry, NY	25	3	.893
1979	Mike Caldwell, Mil	16	6	.727
1980	Steve Stone, Balt	25	7	.781
1981*	Pete Vuckovich, Mil	14	4	.778
1982	Pete Vuckovich, Mil	18	6	.750
	Jim Palmer, Balt	15	5	.750
1983	Richard Dotson, Chi	22	7	.759
1984	Doyle Alexander, Tor	17	6	.739
1985	Ron Guidry, NY	22	6	.786
1986	Roger Clemens, Bos	24	4	.857
1987	Roger Clemens, Bos	20	9	.690
1988	Frank Viola, Minn	24	7	.774
1989	Bret Saberhagen, KC	23	6	.793
1990	Bob Welch, Oak	27	6	.818
1991	Scott Erickson, Minn	20	8	.714
1992	Mike Mussina, Balt	18	5	.783
1993	Jimmy Key, NY	18	6	.750
1994	Jimmy Key, NY	17	4	.810
1995	Randy Johnson, Sea	18	2	.900
1996	Charles Nagy, Clev	17	5	.773
1997	Randy Johnson, Sea	20	4	.833
1998	David Wells, NY	18	4	.818
1999	Pedro Martinez, Bos	23	4	.852
2000	Tim Hudson, Oak	20	6	.769
2001	Roger Clemens, NY	20	3	.870
2002	Pedro Martinez, Bos	20	4	.833
2003	Roy Halladay, Tor	22	7	.759
2004	Curt Schilling, Bos	21	6	.778
2005	Cliff Lee, Cle	18	5	.783
2006	Roy Halladay, Tor	16	5	.762
2007	Justin Verlander, Det	18	6	.750
2008	Cliff Lee, Cle	22	3	.880

*1981 percentages based on 10 or more victories. Note: Percentages based on 15 or more victories in all other years.

Leading Pitchers—Earned Run Average

Year	Player and Team	ERA
1913	Walter Johnson, Wash	1.14
1914	Dutch Leonard, Bos	1.01
1915	Smoky Joe Wood, Bos	1.49
1916	Babe Ruth, Bos	1.75
1917	Eddie Cicotte, Chi	1.53
1918	Walter Johnson, Wash	1.27
1919	Walter Johnson, Wash	1.49
1920	Bob Shawkey, NY	2.46
1921	Red Faber, Chi	2.47
1922	Red Faber, Chi	2.80
1923	Stan Coveleski, Clev	2.76
1924	Walter Johnson, Wash	2.72
1925	Stan Coveleski, Wash	2.84
1926	Lefty Grove, Phi	2.51
1927	Wilcy Moore, NY#	2.28
1928	Garland Braxton, Wash	2.52
1929	Lefty Grove, Phi	2.81
1930	Lefty Grove, Phi	2.54
1931	Lefty Grove, Phi	2.06
1932	Lefty Grove, Phi	2.84
1933	Monte Pearson, Clev	2.33
1934	Lefty Gomez, NY	2.33
1935	Lefty Grove, Bos	2.70
1936	Lefty Grove, Bos	2.81
1937	Lefty Gomez, NY	2.33
1938	Lefty Grove, Bos	3.07
1939	Lefty Grove, Bos	2.54
1940	Bob Feller, Clev†	2.62
1941	Thornton Lee, Chi	2.37
1942	Ted Lyons, Chi	2.10
1943	Spud Chandler, NY	1.64
1944	Dizzy Trout, Det	2.12
1945	Hal Newhouser, Det	1.81
1946	Hal Newhouser, Det	1.94
1947	Spud Chandler, NY	2.46
1948	Gene Bearden, Clev	2.43
1949	Mel Parnell, Bos	2.78
1950	Early Wynn, Clev	3.20
1951	Saul Rogovin, Det-Chi	2.78
1952	Allie Reynolds, NY	2.07
1953	Ed Lopat, NY	2.43
1954	Mike Garcia, Clev	2.64
1955	Billy Pierce, Chi	1.97
1956	Whitey Ford, NY	2.47
1957	Bobby Shantz, NY	2.45
1958	Whitey Ford, NY	2.01
1959	Hoyt Wilhelm, Balt	2.19
1960	Frank Baumann, Chi	2.68
1961	Dick Donovan, Wash	2.40
1962	Hank Aguirre, Det	2.21
1963	Gary Peters, Chi	2.33
1964	Dean Chance, LA	1.65
1965	Sam McDowell, Clev	2.18
1966	Gary Peters, Chi	1.98

Leading Pitchers—Earned Run Average (*Cont.*)

Year	Player and Team	ERA
1967	Joe Horlen, Chi	2.06
1968	Luis Tiant, Clev	1.60
1969	Dick Bosman, Wash	2.19
1970	Diego Segui, Oak	2.56
1971	Vida Blue, Oak	1.82
1972	Luis Tiant, Bos	1.91
1973	Jim Palmer, Balt	2.40
1974	Catfish Hunter, Oak	2.49
1975	Jim Palmer, Balt	2.09
1976	Mark Fidrych, Det	2.34
1977	Frank Tanana, Cal	2.54
1978	Ron Guidry, NY	1.74
1979	Ron Guidry, NY	2.78
1980	Rudy May, NY	2.47
1981	Steve McCatty, Oak	2.32
1982	Rick Sutcliffe, Clev	2.96
1983	Rick Honeycutt, Tex	2.42
1984	Mike Boddicker, Balt	2.79
1985	Dave Stieb, Tor	2.48
1986	Roger Clemens, Bos	2.48
1987	Jimmy Key, Tor	2.76
1988	Allan Anderson, Minn	2.45
1989	Bret Saberhagen, KC	2.16
1990	Roger Clemens, Bos	1.93
1991	Roger Clemens, Bos	2.62
1992	Roger Clemens, Bos	2.41
1993	Kevin Appier, KC	2.56
1994	Steve Ontiveros, Oak	2.65
1995	Randy Johnson, Sea	2.48
1996	Juan Guzman, Tor	2.93
1997	Roger Clemens, Tor	2.05
1998	Roger Clemens, Tor	2.64
1999	Pedro Martinez, Bos	2.07
2000	Pedro Martinez, Bos	1.74
2001	Freddy Garcia, Sea	3.05
2002	Pedro Martinez, Bos	2.26
2003	Pedro Martinez, Bos	2.22
2004	Johan Santana, Minn	2.61
2005	Kevin Millwood, Cle	2.86
2006	Johan Santana, Minn	2.77
2007	John Lackey, LA	3.01
2008	Cliff Lee, Cle	2.54

Note: Based on 10 complete games through 1950, then 154 innings until the American League expanded in 1961, when it became 162 innings. In strike-shortened 1981, one inning per game required. Earned runs not tabulated in American League prior to 1913.

#Wilcy Moore pitched only six complete games—he started 12—in 1927 but was recognized as leader because of 213 innings pitched. †Ernie Bonham, New York, had 1.91 ERA and 10 complete games in 1940 but appeared in only 12 games and 99 innings, and Bob Feller was recognized as leader.

Leading Pitchers—Strikeouts

Year	Player and Team	SO
1901	Cy Young, Bos	159
1902	Rube Waddell, Phi	210
1903	Rube Waddell, Phi	301
1904	Rube Waddell, Phi	349
1905	Rube Waddell, Phi	286
1906	Rube Waddell, Phi	203
1907	Rube Waddell, Phi	226
1908	Ed Walsh, Chi	269
1909	Frank Smith, Chi	177
1910	Walter Johnson, Wash	313
1911	Ed Walsh, Chi	255
1912	Walter Johnson, Wash	303
1913	Walter Johnson, Wash	243
1914	Walter Johnson, Wash	225
1915	Walter Johnson, Wash	203
1916	Walter Johnson, Wash	228
1917	Walter Johnson, Wash	188
1918	Walter Johnson, Wash	162
1919	Walter Johnson, Wash	147
1920	Stan Coveleski, Clev	133
1921	Walter Johnson, Wash	143
1922	Urban Shocker, StL	149
1923	Walter Johnson, Wash	130
1924	Walter Johnson, Wash	158
1925	Lefty Grove, Phi	116
1926	Lefty Grove, Phi	194
1927	Lefty Grove, Phi	174
1928	Lefty Grove, Phi	183
1929	Lefty Grove, Phi	170
1930	Lefty Grove, Phi	209
1931	Lefty Grove, Phi	175
1932	Red Ruffing, NY	190
1933	Lefty Gomez, NY	163
1934	Lefty Gomez, NY	158
1935	Tommy Bridges, Det	163
1936	Tommy Bridges, Det	175
1937	Lefty Gomez, NY	194
1938	Bob Feller, Clev	240
1939	Bob Feller, Clev	246
1940	Bob Feller, Clev	261
1941	Bob Feller, Clev	260
1942	Bobo Newsom, Wash	
	Tex Hughson, Bos	113
1943	Allie Reynolds, Clev	151
1944	Hal Newhouser, Det	187
1945	Hal Newhouser, Det	212
1946	Bob Feller, Clev	348
1947	Bob Feller, Clev	196
1948	Bob Feller, Clev	164
1949	Virgil Trucks, Det	153
1950	Bob Lemon, Clev	170
1951	Vic Raschi, NY	164
1952	Allie Reynolds, NY	160
1953	Billy Pierce, Chi	186
1954	Bob Turley, Balt	185
1955	Herb Score, Clev	245
1956	Herb Score, Clev	263
1957	Early Wynn, Clev	184
1958	Early Wynn, Chi	179
1959	Jim Bunning, Det	201
1960	Jim Bunning, Det	201
1961	Camilo Pascual, Minn	221
1962	Camilo Pascual, Minn	206
1963	Camilo Pascual, Minn	202
1964	Al Downing, NY	217
1965	Sam McDowell, Clev	325
1966	Sam McDowell, Clev	225
1967	Jim Lonborg, Bos	246
1968	Sam McDowell, Clev	283
1969	Sam McDowell, Clev	279
1970	Sam McDowell, Clev	304
1971	Mickey Lolich, Det	308
1972	Nolan Ryan, Cal	329
1973	Nolan Ryan, Cal	383
1974	Nolan Ryan, Cal	367
1975	Frank Tanana, Cal	269

American League *(Cont.)*

Leading Pitchers—Strikeouts *(Cont.)*

Year	Player and Team	SO
1976	Nolan Ryan, Cal	327
1977	Nolan Ryan, Cal	341
1978	Nolan Ryan, Cal	260
1979	Nolan Ryan, Cal	223
1980	Len Barker, Clev	187
1981	Len Barker, Clev	127
1982	Floyd Bannister, Sea	209
1983	Jack Morris, Det	232
1984	Mark Langston, Sea	204
1985	Bert Blyleven, Clev-Minn	206
1986	Mark Langston, Sea	245
1987	Mark Langston, Sea	262
1988	Roger Clemens, Bos	291
1989	Nolan Ryan, Tex	301
1990	Nolan Ryan, Tex	232
1991	Roger Clemens, Bos	241
1992	Randy Johnson, Sea	241

Year	Player and Team	SO
1993	Randy Johnson, Sea	308
1994	Randy Johnson, Sea	204
1995	Randy Johnson, Sea	294
1996	Roger Clemens, Bos	257
1997	Roger Clemens, Tor	292
1998	Roger Clemens, Tor	271
1999	Pedro Martinez, Bos	313
2000	Pedro Martinez, Bos	284
2001	Hideo Nomo, Bos	220
2002	Pedro Martinez, Bos	239
2003	Esteban Loaiza, Chi	207
2004	Johan Santana, Minn	265
2005	Johan Santana, Minn	238
2006	Johan Santana, Minn	245
2007	Scott Kazmir, TB	239
2008	A.J. Burnett, Tor	231

Leading Pitchers—Saves

FYear	Player and Team	SV
1947	Joe Page, NY	17
1948	Russ Christopher, Clev	17
1949	Joe Page, NY	29
1950	Mickey Harris, Wash	15
1951	Ellis Kinder, Bos	14
1952	Harry Dorish, Chi	11
1953	Ellis Kinder, Bos	27
1954	Johnny Sain, NY	22
1955	Ray Narleski, Clev	19
1956	George Zuverink, Bal	16
1957	Bob Grim, NY	19
1958	Ryne Duren, NY	20
1959	Turk Lown, Chi	15
1960	Mike Fornieles, Bos	14
	Johnny Klippstein, Clev	14
1961	Luis Arroyo, NY	29
1962	Dick Radatz, Bos	24
1963	Stu Miller, Bal	27
1964	Dick Radatz, Bos	29
1965	Ron Kline, Wash	29
1966	Jack Aker, KC	32
1967	Minnie Rojas, Cal	27
1968	Al Worthington, Minn	18
1969	Ron Perranoski, Minn	31
1970	Ron Perranoski, Minn	34
1971	Ken Sanders, Mil	31
1972	Sparky Lyle, NY	35
1973	John Hiller, Det	38
1974	Terry Forster, Chi	24
1975	Goose Gossage, Chi	26
1976	Sparky Lyle, NY	23
1977	Bill Campbell, Bos	31
1978	Goose Gossage, NY	27

Year	Player and Team	SV
1979	Mike Marshall, Minn	32
1980	Dan Quisenberry, KC	33
1981	Rollie Fingers, Mil	28
1982	Dan Quisenberry, KC	35
1983	Dan Quisenberry, KC	35
1984	Dan Quisenberry, KC	44
1985	Dan Quisenberry, KC	37
1986	Dave Righetti, NY	46
1987	Tom Henke, Tor	34
1988	Dennis Eckersley, Oak	45
1989	Jeff Russell, Tex	38
1990	Bobby Thigpen, Chi	57
1991	Bryan Harvey, Cal	46
1992	Dennis Eckersley, Oak	51
1993	Jeff Montgomery, KC	45
	Duane Ward, Tor	45
1994	Lee Smith, Bal	33
1995	Jose Mesa, Clev	46
1996	John Wetteland, NY	43
1997	Randy Myers, Balt	45
1998	Tom Gordon, Bos	46
1999	Mariano Rivera, NY	45
2000	Todd Jones, Det	42
2001	Mariano Rivera, NY	50
2002	Eddie Guardado, Minn	45
2003	Keith Foulke, Oak	43
2004	Mariano Rivera, NY	53
2005	Francisco Rodríguez, LA	45
	Bob Wickman, Cle	45
2006	Francisco Rodriguez, LA	47
2007	Joe Borowski, Cle	45
2008	Francisco Rodriguez, LA	62

The Commissioners of Baseball

Kenesaw Mountain Landis.....Elected Nov. 12, 1920. Served until his death on Nov. 25, 1944.

Happy Chandler.....Elected April 24, 1945. Served until July 15, 1951.

Ford Frick.....Elected Sept. 20, 1951. Served until Nov. 16, 1965.

William Eckert.....Elected Nov. 17, 1965. Served until Dec. 20, 1968.

Bowie Kuhn.....Elected Feb. 8, 1969. Served until Sept. 30, 1984.

Peter Ueberroth.....Elected March 3, 1984. Took office Oct. 1, 1984. Served through March 31, 1989.

A. Bartlett Giamatti.....Elected Sept. 8, 1988. Took office April 1, 1989. Served until his death on Sept. 1, 1989.

Francis Vincent Jr. .....Appointed Acting Commissioner Sept. 2, 1989. Elected Commissioner Sept. 13, 1989. Served through Sept. 7, 1992.

Allan H. (Bud) Selig.....Elected chairman of the executive council and given the powers of interim commissioner on Sept. 9, 1992. Unanimously elected Commissioner July 9, 1998.

Pro Football

WR David Tyree's incredible, improbable catch helped the New York Giants win Super Bowl XLII

DAMIAN STROHMEYER

One-defeated

A year after his brother proved he had what it takes to win on the big stage, Eli Manning and a Cinderella Giants team thwarted the New England Patriots' run at 19–0 perfection

BY HANK HERSCH

ON NOV. 25 AT GIANTS STADIUM, Eli Manning delivered a performance that exceeded what even the most jaded New York fans had come to expect. In a game with playoff implications, with his older brother Peyton watching, against the NFL's worst pass defense, which was also missing its best cornerback, the 26-year-old Manning became the first NFL quarterback in 23 years to have three interceptions returned for touchdowns—not to mention a fourth pick that Minnesota brought back to the 8-yard line and the two more passes that the Vikings' defense dropped in their 41–17 victory.

"If Giants Stadium was the Roman Coliseum," wrote *The Asbury Park Press*, Manning "wouldn't have survived the afternoon."

Adam Sandler does not become Robert DeNiro. William Hung doesn't turn into Placido Domingo. And in a season marked by the brilliance of Brett Favre, the proficiency of Peyton Manning and the transcendent play of Tom Brady, Eli Manning does not become the last word in quarterbacks. Not when he's reeling under the weight of a fabled franchise that mortgaged its future to acquire him with the No. 1 pick in 2004 draft. Not when he has only once had back-to-back games with a passer efficiency rating of more than 100. Not when his hangdog demeanor is fodder for caricature, and his impassioned reaction to a four-pick day that put his team's season in jeopardy is, "You know, just disappointed."

But in a fairy-tale transformation from clutz to clutch as sudden as Dumbo's, Manning guided the Giants to three wins in their last five regular season games. He then engineered three NFC playoff victories on the road, throwing 85 passes without an interception. And finally, with his team a 13½-point underdog, he made the most scintillating and significant heave in Super Bowl history, a scrambling 32-yard completion to reserve receiver David Tyree that propelled New York to a 17–14 win over the Patriots. That didn't just give the Manning family another MVP trophy to bookend the one Peyton earned a year earlier with the Indianapolis Colts' Super Bowl XLI victory. It also capped one of the most monumental upsets ever and denied New England its chance to be considered the greatest team in the 88-year history of the NFL.

The Patriots entered Glendale, Ariz. without a loss in 18 games; the last team to go unbeaten was the 1972 Miami Dolphins, who went 17–0. Brady was the runaway MVP in 2007, setting a record for touchdown passes (50) while amassing the second-best passer rating ever (117.2) and the third-most yardage (4,806). Wide receiver Randy Moss, picked up from the Oakland Raiders in the off-season for a fourth-round pick, had 23 TD catches, breaking Jerry Rice's 20-year-old single-season mark. The offense set a single-season record for points

BILL FRAKES

The New England Patriots QB-WR tandem of Tom Brady and Randy Moss became a scoring juggernaut in 2008.

(589) while the defense, characteristically opportunistic, gave up just 17.1 per game. And all this was accomplished under the cloud of scandal; in Week 1, the league determined that the Patriots had illegally taped opposing team's defensive signals. New England had to pay a $2,500 fine and surrender a first-round draft choice, while coach Bill Belichick was fined $500,000.

The Pats' quest for perfection became the primary storyline for the season, leaving room for only minor subplots: the breathtaking rushing of Vikings rookie Adrian Peterson, who rambled for a record 296 yards in a Week 9 victory, en route to gaining 1,341 yards for the season on 5.6 yards per carry; the Dolphins, avoiding the ignominy of becoming the first team to go winless since the 1976 Tampa Bay Buccaneers with a 22–16 overtime defeat of Baltimore Ravens in Week 15; and Chicago Bears return man Devin Hester, who tied the NFL mark he set as a rookie by returning six kicks for TDs. About the only other story as compelling as Brady & Co. was the magnificence of Favre.

Not much was expected of the Green Bay Packers entering 2007. They had gone 8–8 the year before and Favre, after a record 234 straight starts, seemed to be on the decline. But taking charge of second-year coach Mike McCarthy's offense, Favre, at age 38, completed a career-high 66.5 percent of his passes and by season's end had toppled Dan Marino's career marks for touchdowns (442) and total yardage (61,655). More important: The Pack finished 13–3, tying the Dallas Cowboys for the best record in the NFC.

"I've always shown up, I've always been prepared, I practice every day," Favre said. "I practice hard. I study. No matter what happens on the field, I never point blame at anybody else. Everything I do comes back to leadership, the example I want to set."

When the Giants knocked off Dallas 21–17 in the divisional championships, Favre seemed poised to make his first Super Bowl appearance in a decade. Not only would the NFC title game take place at Lambeau Field, but the conditions were also Packer-perfect: It was the third-coldest game in NFL history, registering -1°F with a -23°F windchill at kickoff. Still, Favre had his frigid hands full with the Giants' pass rush. He had to rally his team from two deficits before tying the score at 20 in the fourth quarter; it remained that way after Giants kicker Lawrence Tynes botched a 36-yard try with four seconds left. When the Packers won the coin toss before overtime, the frozen faithful sensed that Favre's magnificent ride would continue.

But just 47 seconds into OT, Favre

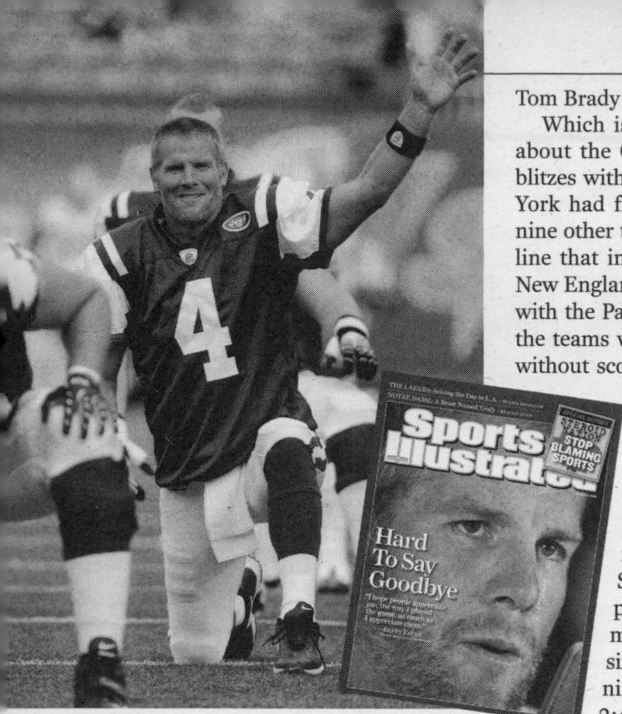

After a tearful retirement press conference in March, Brett Favre changed his mind in July, and was then traded to the New York Jets.

LEFT: JOHN IACONO; INSET: JONATHAN DANIEL/GETTY IMAGES

attempted an out to Donald Driver—they'd earlier connected on a 90-yard TD—that wasn't out enough. New York cornerback Corey Webster picked off the throw and after Manning drove the Giants five yards, Tynes nailed the longest playoff field goal by an opponent in Lambeau history, a 47-yarder. "What a football game," said Archie Manning, Eli's dad. "I don't care who you were rooting for. If you're a football fan in Idaho, you're saying, 'That's one of the best games I've ever seen.'"

No sense of destiny accompanied New York into the University of Phoenix Stadium for the Super Bowl "Everywhere you went, it was all about the Patriots and 19–0," said Giants cornerback R.W. McQuarters after the game. "We go into the city, and there's Tom Brady on the buildings. We get to the stadium today, and there's a Super Bowl program in our locker, and it's like a Tom Brady magazine. We come out to warm up, and Tom Brady is on the big screen. It's like Tom Brady was everywhere."

Which is exactly how Brady would feel about the Giants' defensive front. Mixing blitzes with steady four-man pressure, New York had five sacks of Brady and hit him nine other times, manhandling an offensive line that included three Pro Bowl players. New England's D was equally stout, though; with the Pats up 7–3 in the second quarter, the teams went a Super Bowl record 33:52 without scoring. But then they compressed a game's worth of action into the final 15 minutes of the quarter.

With 11:50 left Manning hit Tyree for a five-yard TD. Three series later Brady flashed the form that had already won three Super Bowls, completing 8 of 11 passes to lead an 80-yard scoring march, which he capped with a six-yard toss to Moss. When Manning returned to the field he had 2:42 remaining, a 14–10 deficit and 83 yards to pay dirt.

Six plays later, the Giants faced third-and-five on their own 44. Manning took a snap out of the shotgun and was quickly swarmed, for an instant disappearing under the rush. Somehow, he popped free and lofted a pass into the middle of the field to Tyree, who leaped for the ball against safety Rodney Harrison. Outmuscling the four-time All-Pro, Tyree made the grab between his right hand and his helmet. "Some things just don't make sense," said Tyree, "and I guess you could put that catch right up there with them."

After another first-down pass to Steve Smith, Manning found Plaxico Burress in the end zone from 13 yards out with 35 seconds to play, and the Giants were champions. Manning wasn't spectacular—he completed 19 of 34 passes for 255 yards—but he delivered when it mattered most. "I've had a lot of downs in New York," he said. "A lot of times I've thought, 'Why have I gotten this treatment? Do I deserve this?' So to come out here and win, not just for me but for our whole team, is really special. And for me personally, I'd have to say it is kind of sweet."

FOR THE RECORD•2007–2008

2007 NFL Final Standings

American Football Conference

EAST DIVISION

	W	L	T	Pct	Pts	OP
New England	16	0	0	1.000	589	274
Buffalo	7	9	0	.438	252	354
NY Jets	4	12	0	.250	268	355
Miami	1	15	0	.063	267	437

NORTH DIVISION

	W	L	T	Pct	Pts	OP
Pittsburgh	10	6	0	.625	393	269
Cleveland	10	6	0	.625	402	382
Cincinnati	7	9	0	.438	380	385
Baltimore	5	11	0	.313	275	384

SOUTH DIVISION

	W	L	T	Pct	Pts	OP
Indianapolis	13	3	0	.813	450	262
*Jacksonville	11	5	0	.688	411	304
*Tennessee	10	6	0	.625	301	297
Houston	8	8	0	.500	379	384

WEST DIVISION

	W	L	T	Pct	Pts	OP
San Diego	11	5	0	.688	412	284
Denver	7	9	0	.438	320	409
Kansas City	4	12	0	.250	226	335
Oakland	4	12	0	.250	286	398

* Wild-card team.

National Football Conference

EAST DIVISION

	W	L	T	Pct	Pts	OP
Dallas	13	3	0	.813	455	325
*NY Giants	10	6	0	.625	373	351
*Washington	9	7	0	.563	334	310
Philadelphia	8	8	0	.500	336	300

NORTH DIVISION

	W	L	T	Pct	Pts	OP
Green Bay	13	3	0	.813	435	291
Minnesota	8	8	0	.500	365	311
Detroit	7	9	0	.438	346	444
Chicago	7	9	0	.438	334	348

SOUTH DIVISION

	W	L	T	Pct	Pts	OP
Tampa Bay	9	7	0	.563	334	270
Carolina	7	9	0	.438	267	347
New Orleans	7	9	0	.438	379	388
Atlanta	4	12	0	.250	259	414

WEST DIVISION

	W	L	T	Pct	Pts	OP
Seattle	10	6	0	.625	393	291
Arizona	8	8	0	.500	404	399
San Francisco	5	11	0	.313	219	364
St. Louis	3	13	0	.188	263	438

* Wild-card team.

2007–08 NFL Playoffs

AFC FIRST ROUND	AFC DIVISIONAL PLAYOFF	AFC CHAMPIONSHIP	NFC CHAMPIONSHIP	NFC DIVISIONAL PLAYOFF	NFC FIRST ROUND

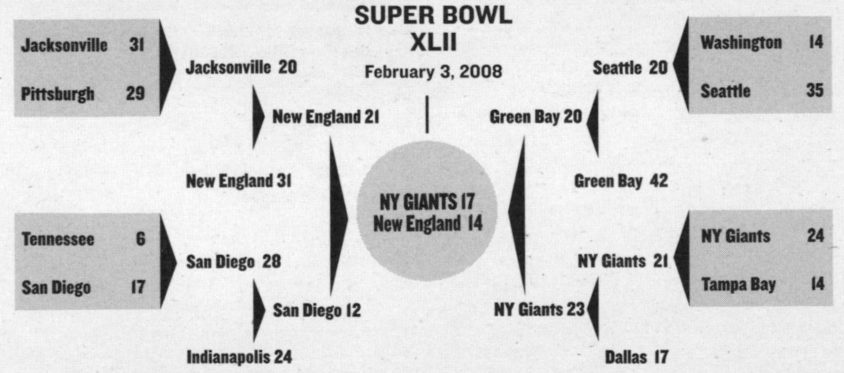

NFL Playoff Recaps

AFC Wild-card Games

Jacksonville	**7**	**14**	**7**	**3—31**
Pittsburgh	**7**	**0**	**3**	**19—29**

FIRST QUARTER: Pittsburgh: TD Davenport 1 run (Reed Kick), 10:03.

Jacksonville: TD Taylor 1 run (Scobee Kick), 9:39.

SECOND QUARTER: Jacksonville: TD Mathis 63 Intercept (Scobee Kick), 10:19.

Jacksonville : TD Jones-Drew 43 pass from Garrard (Scobee Kick), 8:34.

THIRD QUARTER: Pittsburgh: FG Reed 28, 9:24.

Jacksonville: TD Jones-Drew 10 run (Scobee Kick), 4:39.

FOURTH QUARTER: Pittsburgh: TD Holmes 37 pass from Roethlisberger (Reed Kick), 14:53.

Pittsburgh: TD Miller 14 pass from Roethlisberger run failed, 10:25.

Pittsburgh: TD Davenport 1 run pass failed, 6:21.

Jacksonville: FG Scobee 25, 0:37.

A: 63,629; 3:24.

Tennessee	**3**	**3**	**0**	**0—6**
San Diego	**0**	**0**	**10**	**7—17**

FIRST QUARTER: Tennessee: FG Bironas 30, 9:37.

SECOND QUARTER: Tennessee: FG Bironas 44, 0:00.

THIRD QUARTER: San Diego: FG Kaeding 20, 9:41.

San Diego: TD Jackson 25 pass from Rivers (Kaeding Kick), 2:35.

FOURTH QUARTER: San Diego: TD Tomlinson 1 run (Kaeding Kick), 8:45.

A: 65,640; 3:04.

NFC Wild-card Games

Washington	**0**	**0**	**0**	**14—14**
Seattle	**7**	**3**	**3**	**22—35**

FIRST QUARTER: Seattle: TD Weaver 17 run (Brown Kick), 3:45.

SECOND QUARTER: Seattle: FG Brown 50, 8:58.

THIRD QUARTER: Seattle: FG Brown 33, 4:30.

FOURTH QUARTER: Washington: TD Randle El 7 pass from Collins (Suisham Kick), 14:53.

Washington: TD Moss 30 pass from Collins (Suisham Kick), 12:38.

Seattle: TD Hackett 20 pass from Hasselbeck (Pollard pass from Hasselbeck for 2-pt. conversion), 6:06.

Seattle: TD Trufant 78 interception return (Brown Kick), 5:38.

Seattle: TD Babineaux 57 interception return (Brown Kick), 0:27.

A: 68,297; 3:18.

NY Giants	**0**	**14**	**3**	**7—24**
Tampa Bay	**7**	**0**	**0**	**7—14**

FIRST QUARTER: Tampa Bay: TD Graham 1 run (Bryant Kick), 1:49.

SECOND QUARTER: New York: TD Jacobs 5 pass from Manning (Tynes Kick), 10:02.

New York: TD Jacobs 8 run (Tynes Kick), 4:06.

THIRD QUARTER: New York: FG Tynes 25, 9:56.

FOURTH QUARTER: New York: TD Toomer 4 pass from Manning (Tynes Kick), 8:03.

Tampa Bay: TD Smith 6 pass from Garcia (Bryant Kick), 3:25.

A: 65,621; 2:53.

NFL Playoff Recaps *(Cont.)*

AFC Divisional Games

Jacksonville	**7**	**7**	**3**	**3—20**
New England	**7**	**7**	**14**	**3—31**

FIRST QUARTER: Jacksonville: TD Jones 8 pass from Garrard (Scobee Kick), 10:50.

New England: TD Watson 3 pass from Brady (Gostkowski Kick), 5:01.

SECOND QUARTER: New England: TD Maroney 1 run (Gostkowski Kick), 14:57.

Jacksonville: TD Wilford 6 pass from Garrard (Scobee Kick), 7:46.

THIRD QUARTER: New England: TD Welker 6 pass from Brady (Gostkowski Kick), 8:49.

Jacksonville: FG Scobee 39, 4:04

New England: TD Watson 9 pass from Brady (Gostkowski Kick), 0:49.

FOURTH QUARTER: Jacksonville: FG Scobee 25, 9:44.

New England: FG Gostkowski 35, 6:39.

A: 68,756; 2:48.

San Diego	**0**	**7**	**14**	**7—28**
Indianapolis	**7**	**3**	**7**	**7—24**

FIRST QUARTER: Indianapolis: TD Clark 25 pass from Manning (Vinatieri Kick), 9:13.

SECOND QUARTER: San Diego: TD Jackson 14 pass from Rivers (Kaeding Kick), 11:33.

Indianapolis: FG Vinatieri 46, 5:10.

THIRD QUARTER: San Diego: TD Chambers 30 pass from Rivers (Kaeding Kick), 11:33.

Indianapolis: TD Wayne 9 pass from Manning (Vinatieri Kick), 2:53.

San Diego: TD Sproles 56 pass from Rivers (Kaeding Kick), 0:00.

FOURTH QUARTER: Indianapolis: TD Gonzalez 55 pass from Manning (Vinatieri Kick), 10:07.

San Diego: TD Volek 1 run (Kaeding Kick), 4:50.

A: 56,590 3:12.

NFC Divisional Games

NY Giants	**7**	**7**	**0**	**7—21**
Dallas	**0**	**14**	**3**	**0—17**

FIRST QUARTER: New York: TD Toomer 52 pass from Manning (Tynes Kick), 11:50.

SECOND QUARTER: Dallas: TD Owens 5 pass from Romo (Folk Kick), 14:56.

Dallas: TD Barber 1 run (Folk Kick), 0:53.

New York: TD Toomer 4 pass from Manning (Tynes Kick), 0:07.

THIRD QUARTER: Dallas: FG Folk 34, 6:53.

FOURTH QUARTER: New York: TD Jacobs 1 run (Tynes Kick), 13:29.

A: 63,660; 3:05.

Seattle	**14**	**3**	**3**	**0—20**
Green Bay	**14**	**14**	**7**	**7—42**

FIRST QUARTER: Seattle: TD Alexander 1 run (Brown Kick), 14:40.

Seattle: TD Engram 11 pass fro Hasselbeck (Brown Kick), 10:59.

Green Bay: TD Jennings 15 pass from Favre (Crosby Kick), 7:08.

Green Bay: TD Grant 1 run (Crosby Kick), 1:02.

SECOND QUARTER: Green Bay: TD Jennings 2 pass from Favre (Crosby Kick), 13:22.

Seattle: FG Brown 29, 7:18.

Green Bay: TD Grant 3 run (Crosby Kick), 0:26.

THIRD QUARTER: Green Bay: TD Jackson 13 pass from Favre (Crosby Kick), 10:25.

Seattle: FG Brown 27, 2:46.

FOURTH QUARTER: Green Bay: TD Grant 1 run (Crosby Kick), 13:26.

A: 72,168; 2:58.

NFL Playoff Recaps *(Cont.)*

AFC Championship

San Diego	**3**	**6**	**3**	**0—12**
New England	**0**	**14**	**0**	**7—21**

FIRST QUARTER: San Diego: FG Kaeding 26, 2:55.

SECOND QUARTER: New England: TD Maroney 1 run (Gostkowski Kick), 13:48.

San Diego: FG Kaeding 23, 9:14.

New England: TD Gaffney 12 pass from Brady (Gostkowski Kick), 3:51.

San Diego: FG Kaeding 40, 0:08.

THIRD QUARTER: San Diego: FG Kaeding 24, 8:36.

FOURTH QUARTER: New England: TD Welker 6 pass from Brady (Gostkowski Kick), 12:15.

A: 68,756; 2:55.

NFC Championship

NY Giants	**3**	**3**	**14**	**0**	**3—23**
Green Bay	**0**	**10**	**7**	**3**	**0—20**

FIRST QUARTER: New York: FG Tynes 29, 4:50.

SECOND QUARTER: New York: FG Tynes 37. 11:41.

Green Bay: TD Driver 90 pass from Favre (Crosby Kick), 11:18

Green Bay: FG Crosby 36, 1:30.

THIRD QUARTER: New York: TD Jacobs 1 run (Tynes Kick), 7:56.

Green Bay: TD Lee 12 pass from Favre (Crosby Kick), 5:00.

New York: TD Bradshaw 4 run (Tynes Kick), 2:12.

FOURTH QUARTER: Green Bay: FG Crosby 37, 11:46.

OVERTIME: New York: FG Tynes 47, 12:25.

A: 72,740; 3:33.

Super Bowl XLII Recap

NY Giants	**3**	**0**	**0**	**14—17**
New England	**0**	**7**	**0**	**7—14**

FIRST QUARTER: New York: FG Tynes 32, 5:01.
NY Giants 3-0.

SECOND QUARTER: New England: TD Maroney 1 run (Gostkowski Kick), 14.57.
New England 7-3.

FOURTH QUARTER: New York: TD Tyree 5 pass from Manning (Tynes Kick), 11:05.
NY Giants 10-7.
New England: TD Moss 6 pass from Brady (Gostkowski Kick), 2:42.
New England 14-10.

New York: TD Burress 13 pass from Manning (Tynes Kick), 0:35.
NY Giants 17-14

A: 71,101; 3:35.

Super Bowl XLII Box Score

Team Statistics

	NY Giants	New England
FIRST DOWNS	17	22
Rushing	4	3
Passing	13	17
Penalty	0	2
THIRD DOWN EFF	8-16	7-14
FOURTH DOWN EFF	1-1	0-2
TOTAL NET YARDS	338	274
Total plays	63	69
Avg gain	5.4	4.0
NET YARDS RUSHING	91	45
Rushes	26	16
Avg per rush	3.5	2.8
NET YARDS PASSING	247	229
Completed–Att–Int.	19-34-1	29-48-0
Yards per pass	6.7	4.3
Sacked–yards lost	3-8	5-37
Had intercepted	1	0
PUNTS–Avg	4-39.0	4-43.8
PENALTIES–Yds	4-36	5-35
FUMBLES–Lost	2-0	1-1

Passing

NY GIANTS

	Comp	Att	Yds	Int	TD
Manning	19	34	255	1	2

NEW ENGLAND

	Comp	Att	Yds	Int	TD
Brady	29	48	266	0	1

Rushing

NY GIANTS

	No.	Yds	Lg	TD
Bradshaw	9	45	13	0
Jacobs	14	42	7	0
Manning	3	4	5	0

NEW ENGLAND

	No.	Yds	Lg	TD
Maroney	14	36	9	1
Faulk	1	7	7	0
Evans	1	2	2	0

Receiving

NY GIANTS

	No.	Yds	Lg	TD
Toomer	6	84	38	0
Smith	5	50	17	0
Boss	1	45	45	0
Tyree	3	43	32	1
Burress	2	27	14	1
Bradshaw	1	3	3	0
Hedgecock	1	3	3	0

NEW ENGLAND

	No.	Yds	Lg	TD
Welker	11	103	19	0
Moss	5	62	18	1
Faulk	7	52	14	0
Stallworth	3	34	18	0
Maroney	2	12	8	0
Brady	1	3	3	0

Defense

NY GIANTS

	Tck	Ast	Int	Sack
Butler	9	1	0	0
Pierce	7	3	0	0
Tuck	5	1	0	2
Dockery	3	0	0	0
Mitchell	3	5	0	1
Robbins	3	0	0	0
Umenyiora	3	1	0	0
Wilson	3	2	0	0
Alford	2	0	0	1
Madison	2	0	0	0
Strahan	2	1	0	1
Torbor	2	0	0	0
Cofield	1	0	0	0
Johnson	1	0	0	0
Ross	1	1	0	0
Webster	1	1	0	0

NEW ENGLAND

	Tck	Ast	Int	Sack
Harrison	11	1	0	0
Bruschi	5	3	0	0
Thomas	5	0	0	2
Warren	4	2	0	0
Wilfork	4	1	0	0
Meriweather	3	0	0	0
Sanders	3	1	0	0
Seymour	3	4	0	0
Seau	2	0	0	0
Green	1	0	0	1
Samuel	1	1	0	0
Vrabel	1	1	0	0
Woods	1	0	0	0
Hobbs	0	1	1	0

2007 Associated Press All-Pro Team

OFFENSE

Tom Brady, New England	Quarterback
LaDainian Tomlinson, San Diego	Running Back
Brian Westbrook, Philadelphia	Running Back
Lorenzo Neal, San Diego	Fullback
Jason Witten, Dallas	Tight End
Terrell Owens, Dallas	Wide Receiver
Randy Moss, New England	Wide Receiver
Walter Jones, Seattle	Tackle
Matt Light, New England	Tackle
Alan Faneca, Pittsburgh	Guard
Steve Hutchinson, Minnesota	Guard
Jeff Saturday, Indianapolis	Center

DEFENSE

Jared Allen, Kansas City	Defensive End
Patrick Kerney, Seattle	Defensive End
Kevin Williams, Minnesota	Defensive Tackle
Albert Haynesworth, Tennessee	Defensive Tackle
DeMarcus Ware, Dallas	Linebacker
Mike Vrabel, New England	Linebacker
Patrick Willis, San Francisco	Linebacker
Lofa Tatupu, Seattle	Linebacker
Asante Samuel, New England	Cornerback
Antonio Cromartie, San Diego	Cornerback
Ed Reed, Baltimore	Safety
Bob Sanders, Indianapolis	Safety

SPECIALISTS

Rob Bironas, Tennessee	Kicker
Devin Hester, Chicago	Kick Returner
Andy Lee, San Francisco	Punter

2007 AFC Team-by-Team Results

BALTIMORE RAVENS (5-11)

20	at Cincinnati	27
20	NY JETS	13
26	ARIZONA	23
13	at Cleveland	27
9	at San Francisco	7
22	ST. LOUIS	3
14	at Buffalo	19
7	at Pittsburgh	38
7	CINCINNATI	21
*30	CLEVELAND	33
14	at San Diego	32
24	NEW ENGLAND	27
20	INDIANAPOLIS	44
*16	at Miami	22
6	at Seattle	27
27	PITTSBURGH	21
275		384

BUFFALO BILLS (7-9)

14	DENVER	15
3	at Pittsburgh	26
7	at New England	38
17	NY JETS	14
24	DALLAS	25
19	BALTIMORE	14
13	at NY Jets	3
33	CINCINNATI	21
13	at Miami	10
10	NEW ENGLAND	56
14	at Jacksonville	36
17	at Washington	16
38	MIAMI	17
0	at Cleveland	8
21	NY GIANTS	38
9	at Philadelphia	17
252		354

CINCINNATI BENGALS (7-9)

27	BALTIMORE	20
45	at Cleveland	51
21	at Seattle	24
13	NEW ENGLAND	34
20	at Kansas City	27
38	NY JETS	31
13	PITTSBURGH	24
21	at Buffalo	33
21	at Baltimore	7
27	ARIZONA	35
35	TENNESSEE	6
10	at Pittsburgh	24
19	ST. LOUIS	10
13	at San Francisco	20
19	CLEVELAND	14
38	at Miami	25
380		385

CLEVELAND BROWNS (10-6)

7	PITTSBURGH	34
51	CINCINNATI	45
24	at Oakland	26
27	BALTIMORE	13
17	at New England	34
41	MIAMI	31
27	at St. Louis	20
*33	SEATTLE	30
28	at Pittsburgh	31
*33	at Baltimore	30
27	HOUSTON	17
21	at Arizona	27
24	at NY Jets	18
8	BUFFALO	0
14	at Cincinnati	19
20	SAN FRANCISCO	7
402		382

*overtime

2007 AFC Team-by-Team Results *(Cont.)*

DENVER BRONCOS (7-9)

15	at Buffalo	14
23	OAKLAND	20
14	JACKSONVILLE	23
20	at Indianapolis	38
3	SAN DIEGO	41
31	PITTSBURGH	28
*13	GREEN BAY	19
7	at Detroit	44
27	at Kansas City	11
34	TENNESSEE	20
*34	at Chicago	37
20	at Oakland	34
41	KANSAS CITY	7
13	at Houston	31
3	at San Diego	23
*22	MINNESOTA	19
320		409

JACKSONVILLE JAGUARS (11-5)

10	TENNESSEE	13
13	ATLANTA	7
23	at Denver	14
17	at Kansas City	7
37	HOUSTON	17
7	INDIANAPOLIS	29
24	at Tampa Bay	23
24	at New Orleans	41
28	at Tennessee	13
24	SAN DIEGO	17
36	BUFFALO	14
25	at Indianapolis	28
37	CAROLINA	6
29	at Pittsburgh	22
49	OAKLAND	11
28	at Houston	42
411		304

NEW ENGLAND PATRIOTS (16-0)

38	at NY Jets	14
38	SAN DIEGO	14
38	BUFFALO	7
34	at Cincinnati	13
34	CLEVELAND	17
48	at Dallas	27
49	at Miami	28
52	WASHINGTON	7
24	at Indianapolis	20
56	at Buffalo	10
31	PHILADELPHIA	28
27	at Baltimore	24
34	PITTSBURGH	13
20	NY JETS	10
28	at Miami	7
38	at NY Giants	35
589		274

HOUSTON TEXANS (8-8)

20	KANSAS CITY	3
34	at Carolina	21
24	INDIANAPOLIS	30
16	at Atlanta	26
22	MIAMI	19
17	at Jacksonville	37
36	TENNESSEE	38
10	at San Diego	35
24	at Oakland	17
23	NEW ORLEANS	10
17	at Cleveland	27
20	at Tennessee	28
28	TAMPA BAY	14
31	DENVER	13
15	at Indianapolis	38
42	JACKSONVILLE	28
379		384

KANSAS CITY CHIEFS (4-12)

3	at Houston	20
10	at Chicago	20
13	MINNESOTA	10
30	at San Diego	16
7	JACKSONVILLE	17
27	CINCINNATI	20
12	at Oakland	10
22	GREEN BAY	33
11	DENVER	27
10	at Indianapolis	13
17	OAKLAND	20
10	SAN DIEGO	24
7	at Denver	41
17	TENNESSEE	26
20	at Detroit	25
*10	at NY Jets	13
226		335

NEW YORK JETS (4-12)

14	NEW ENGLAND	38
13	at Baltimore	20
31	MIAMI	28
14	at Buffalo	17
24	at NY Giants	35
9	PHILADELPHIA	16
31	at Cincinnati	38
3	BUFFALO	13
*20	WASHINGTON	23
*19	PITTSBURGH	16
3	at Dallas	34
40	at Miami	13
18	CLEVELAND	24
10	at New England	20
6	at Tennessee	10
*13	KANSAS CITY	10
268		355

INDIANAPOLIS COLTS (13-3)

41	NEW ORLEANS	10
22	at Tennessee	20
30	at Houston	24
38	DENVER	20
33	TAMPA BAY	14
29	at Jacksonville	7
31	at Carolina	7
20	NEW ENGLAND	24
21	at San Diego	23
13	KANSAS CITY	10
31	at Atlanta	13
28	JACKSONVILLE	25
44	at Baltimore	20
21	at Oakland	14
38	HOUSTON	15
10	TENNESSEE	16
450		262

MIAMI DOLPHINS (1-15)

*13	at Washington	16
20	DALLAS	37
28	at NY Jets	31
17	OAKLAND	35
19	at Houston	22
31	at Cleveland	41
28	NEW ENGLAND	49
10	NY GIANTS	13
10	BUFFALO	13
7	at Philadelphia	17
0	at Pittsburgh	3
13	NY JETS	40
17	at Buffalo	38
*22	BALTIMORE	16
7	at New England	28
25	CINCINNATI	38
267		437

OAKLAND RAIDERS (4-12)

21	DETROIT	36
*20	at Denver	23
26	CLEVELAND	24
35	at Miami	17
14	at San Diego	28
10	KANSAS CITY	12
9	at Tennessee	13
17	HOUSTON	24
6	CHICAGO	17
22	at Minnesota	29
20	at Kansas City	17
34	DENVER	20
7	at Green Bay	38
14	INDIANAPOLIS	21
11	at Jacksonville	49
17	SAN DIEGO	30
283		398

*overtime

2007 AFC Team-by-Team Results *(Cont.)*

PITTSBURGH STEELERS (10-6)

34	at Cleveland	7
26	BUFFALO	3
37	SAN FRANCISCO	16
14	at Arizona	21
21	SEATTLE	0
28	at Denver	31
24	at Cincinnati	13
38	BALTIMORE	7
31	CLEVELAND	28
*16	at NY Jets	19
3	MIAMI	0
24	CINCINNATI	10
13	at New England	34
22	JACKSONVILLE	29
41	at St. Louis	24
21	at Baltimore	27
393		269

SAN DIEGO CHARGERS (11-5)

14	CHICAGO	3
14	at New England	38
24	at Green Bay	31
16	KANSAS CITY	30
41	at Denver	3
28	OAKLAND	14
35	HOUSTON	10
17	at Minnesota	35
23	INDIANAPOLIS	21
17	at Jacksonville	24
32	BALTIMORE	14
24	at Kansas City	10
*23	at Tennessee	17
51	DETROIT	14
23	DENVER	3
30	at Oakland	17
412		284

TENNESSEE TITANS (10-6)

13	at Jacksonville	10
20	INDIANAPOLIS	22
31	at New Orleans	14
20	ATLANTA	13
10	at Tampa Bay	13
38	at Houston	36
13	OAKLAND	9
20	CAROLINA	7
13	JACKSONVILLE	28
20	at Denver	34
6	at Cincinnati	35
28	HOUSTON	20
*17	SAN DIEGO	23
26	at Kansas City	17
10	NY JETS	6
16	at Indianapolis	10
301		297

2007 NFC Team-by-Team Results

ARIZONA CARDINALS (8-8)

17	at San Francisco	20
23	SEATTLE	20
23	at Baltimore	26
21	PITTSBURGH	14
34	at St. Louis	31
10	CAROLINA	25
19	at Washington	21
10	at Tampa Bay	17
31	DETROIT	21
35	at Cincinnati	27
31	SAN FRANCISCO	37
27	CLEVELAND	21
21	at Seattle	42
24	at New Orleans	31
30	ATLANTA	27
48	ST. LOUIS	19
404		399

ATLANTA FALCONS (4-12)

3	at Minnesota	24
7	at Jacksonville	13
20	CAROLINA	27
26	HOUSTON	16
13	at Tennessee	20
10	NY GIANTS	31
16	at New Orleans	22
20	SAN FRANCISCO	16
20	at Carolina	13
7	TAMPA BAY	31
13	INDIANAPOLIS	31
16	at St. Louis	28
14	NEW ORLEANS	34
3	at Tampa Bay	37
*27	at Arizona	30
44	SEATTLE	41
259		414

CAROLINA PANTHERS (7-9)

27	at St. Louis	13
21	HOUSTON	34
27	at Atlanta	20
7	TAMPA BAY	20
16	at New Orleans	13
25	at Arizona	10
7	INDIANAPOLIS	31
7	at Tennessee	20
13	ATLANTA	20
17	at Green Bay	31
6	NEW ORLEANS	31
31	SAN FRANCISCO	14
6	at Jacksonville	37
13	SEATTLE	10
13	DALLAS	20
31	at Tampa Bay	23
267		347

CHICAGO BEARS (7-9)

3	at San Diego	14
20	KANSAS CITY	10
10	DALLAS	34
27	at Detroit	37
27	at Green Bay	20
31	MINNESOTA	34
19	at Philadelphia	16
7	DETROIT	16
17	at Oakland	6
23	at Seattle	30
*37	DENVER	34
16	NY GIANTS	21
16	at Washington	24
13	at Minnesota	20
35	GREEN BAY	7
33	NEW ORLEANS	25
334		348

DALLAS COWBOYS (13-3)

45	NY GIANTS	35
37	at Miami	20
34	at Chicago	10
35	ST. LOUIS	7
25	at Buffalo	24
27	NEW ENGLAND	48
24	MINNESOTA	14
38	at Philadelphia	17
31	at NY Giants	20
28	WASHINGTON	23
34	NY JETS	3
37	GREEN BAY	27
28	at Detroit	27
6	PHILADELPHIA	10
20	at Carolina	13
6	at Washington	27
455		325

DETROIT LIONS (7-9)

36	at Oakland	21
*20	MINNESOTA	17
21	at Philadelphia	56
37	CHICAGO	27
3	at Washington	34
23	TAMPA BAY	16
16	at Chicago	7
44	DENVER	7
21	at Arizona	31
10	NY GIANTS	16
26	GREEN BAY	37
10	at Minnesota	42
27	DALLAS	28
14	at San Diego	51
25	KANSAS CITY	20
13	at Green Bay	34
346		444

*overtime

2007 NFC Team-by-Team Results *(Cont.)*

GREEN BAY PACKERS (13-3)

16	PHILADELPHIA	13
35	at NY Giants	13
31	SAN DIEGO	24
23	at Minnesota	16
20	CHICAGO	27
17	WASHINGTON	14
*19	at Denver	13
33	at Kansas City	22
34	MINNESOTA	0
31	CAROLINA	17
37	at Detroit	26
27	at Dallas	37
38	OAKLAND	7
33	at St. Louis	14
7	at Chicago	35
34	DETROIT	13
435		291

MINNESOTA VIKINGS (8-8)

24	ATLANTA	3
*17	at Detroit	20
10	at Kansas City	13
16	GREEN BAY	23
34	at Chicago	31
14	at Dallas	24
16	PHILADELPHIA	23
35	SAN DIEGO	17
0	at Green Bay	34
29	OAKLAND	22
41	at NY Giants	17
42	DETROIT	10
27	at San Francisco	7
20	CHICAGO	13
21	WASHINGTON	32
*19	at Denver	22
365		311

NEW ORLEANS SAINTS (7-9)

10	at Indianapolis	41
14	at Tampa Bay	31
14	TENNESSEE	31
13	CAROLINA	16
28	at Seattle	17
22	ATLANTA	16
31	at San Francisco	10
41	JACKSONVILLE	24
29	ST. LOUIS	37
10	at Houston	23
31	at Carolina	6
23	TAMPA BAY	27
34	at Atlanta	14
31	ARIZONA	24
23	PHILADELPHIA	38
25	at Chicago	33
379		388

NEW YORK GIANTS (10-6)

35	at Dallas	45
13	GREEN BAY	35
24	at Washington	17
16	PHILADELPHIA	3
35	NY JETS	24
31	at Atlanta	10
33	SAN FRANCISCO	15
13	at Miami	10
20	DALLAS	31
16	at Detroit	10
17	MINNESOTA	41
21	at Chicago	16
16	at Philadelphia	13
10	WASHINGTON	22
38	at Buffalo	21
35	NEW ENGLAND	38
373		351

PHILADELPHIA EAGLES (8-8)

13	at Green Bay	16
12	WASHINGTON	20
56	DETROIT	21
3	at NY Giants	16
16	at NY Jets	9
16	CHICAGO	19
23	at Minnesota	16
17	DALLAS	38
33	at Washington	25
17	MIAMI	7
28	at New England	31
24	SEATTLE	28
13	NY GIANTS	16
10	at Dallas	6
38	at New Orleans	23
17	BUFFALO	9
336		300

ST. LOUIS RAMS (3-13)

13	CAROLINA	27
16	SAN FRANCISCO	17
3	at Tampa Bay	24
7	at Dallas	35
31	ARIZONA	34
3	at Baltimore	22
6	at Seattle	33
20	CLEVELAND	27
37	at New Orleans	29
13	at San Francisco	9
19	SEATTLE	24
28	ATLANTA	16
10	at Cincinnati	19
14	GREEN BAY	33
24	PITTSBURGH	41
19	at Arizona	48
263		438

SAN FRANCISCO 49ERS (5-11)

20	ARIZONA	17
17	at St. Louis	16
16	at Pittsburgh	37
3	SEATTLE	23
7	BALTIMORE	9
15	at NY Giants	33
10	NEW ORLEANS	31
16	at Atlanta	20
0	at Seattle	24
9	ST. LOUIS	13
*37	at Arizona	31
14	at Carolina	31
7	MINNESOTA	27
20	CINCINNATI	13
21	TAMPA BAY	19
7	at Cleveland	20
219		364

SEATTLE SEAHAWKS (10-6)

20	TAMPA BAY	6
20	at Arizona	23
24	CINCINNATI	21
23	at San Francisco	3
0	at Pittsburgh	21
17	NEW ORLEANS	28
33	ST. LOUIS	6
*30	at Cleveland	33
24	SAN FRANCISCO	0
30	CHICAGO	23
24	at St. Louis	19
28	at Philadelphia	24
42	ARIZONA	21
10	at Carolina	13
27	BALTIMORE	6
41	at Atlanta	44
393		291

TAMPA BAY BUCCANEERS (9-7)

6	at Seattle	20
31	NEW ORLEANS	14
24	ST. LOUIS	3
20	at Carolina	7
14	at Indianapolis	33
13	TENNESSEE	10
16	at Detroit	23
23	JACKSONVILLE	24
17	ARIZONA	10
31	at Atlanta	7
19	WASHINGTON	13
27	at New Orleans	23
14	at Houston	28
37	ATLANTA	3
19	at San Francisco	21
23	CAROLINA	31
334		270

WASHINGTON REDSKINS (9-7)

*16	MIAMI	13
20	at Philadelphia	12
17	NY GIANTS	24
34	DETROIT	3
14	at Green Bay	17
21	ARIZONA	19
7	at New England	52
*23	at NY Jets	20
25	PHILADELPHIA	33
23	at Dallas	28
13	at Tampa Bay	19
16	BUFFALO	17
24	CHICAGO	16
22	at NY Giants	10
32	at Minnesota	21
27	DALLAS	6
334		310

*overtime

2007 NFL Individual Leaders

American Football Conference

Scoring

TOUCHDOWNS	TD	Rush	Rec	Ret	2PT	Pts
Moss, NE	23	0	23	0	0	138
Tomlinson, SD	18	15	3	0	0	108
Edwards, Cle	16	0	16	0	0	96
Addai, Ind	15	12	3	0	1	92
H'mandzadeh, Cin	12	0	12	0	0	72
Clark, Ind	11	0	11	0	0	66
Lewis, Cle	11	9	2	0	0	66
Jones-Drew, Jac	10	9	0	1	0	60
Wayne, Ind	10	0	10	0	0	60
Williams, Jac	10	0	10	0	0	60

KICKING	PAT	FG	Pts
Bironas, Ten	28	35	133
Graham, Cin	37	31	130
Nugent, NYJ	23	29	110
Elam, Den	33	27	114
Stover, Bal	26	27	107
Dawson, Cle	42	26	120
Brown, Hou	40	25	115
Kaeding, SD	46	24	118
Lindell, Buff	24	24	96
Janikowski, Oak	28	23	97

Passing

	Att	Comp	Yds	TD	Int	Lg	Rating Pts
Brady, NE	578	398	4806	50	8	69	117.2
Roethlisberger, Pitt	404	264	3154	32	11	83	104.1
Garrard, Jac	325	208	2509	18	3	59	102.2
Manning, Ind	515	337	4040	31	14	73	98.0
Cutler, Den	467	297	3497	20	14	68	88.1
Schaub, Hou	289	192	2241	9	9	77	87.2
Palmer, Cin	575	373	4131	26	20	70	86.7
Pennington, NYJ	260	179	1765	10	9	57	86.1
Rosenfels, Hou	240	154	1684	15	12	53	84.8
Anderson, Cle	527	298	3787	29	19	78	82.5

Pass Receiving

RECEPTIONS	No.	Yds	Avg	Lg	TD
Houshmandzadeh, Cin	112	1143	10.2	42	12
Welker, NE	112	1175	10.5	42	8
Wayne, Ind	104	1510	14.5	64	10
Mason, Bal	103	1087	10.6	79	5
Marshall, Den	102	1325	13.0	68	7
Gonzalez, KC	99	1172	11.8	31	5
Moss, NE	98	1493	15.2	65	23
C. Johnson, Cin	93	1440	15.5	70	8
Cotchery, NYJ	82	1130	13.8	50	2
Winslow, Cle	82	1106	13.5	49	5
Edwards, Cle	80	1289	16.1	78	16

YARDS	Yds	No.	Avg	Lg	TD
Wayne, Ind	1510	104	14.5	64	10
Moss, NE	1493	98	15.2	65	23
C. Johnson, Cin	1440	93	15.5	70	8
Marshall, Den	1325	102	13.0	68	7
Edwards, Cle	1289	80	16.1	78	16
Welker, NE	1175	112	10.5	42	8
Gonzalez, KC	1172	99	11.8	31	5
Houshmandzadeh, Cin	1143	112	10.2	42	12
Cotchery, NYJ	1130	82	13.8	50	2
Winslow, Cle	1106	82	13.5	49	5
Mason, Balt	1087	103	10.6	79	5

Rushing

	Att	Yds	Avg	Lg	TD
Tomlinson, SD	315	1474	4.7	49	15
Parker, Pitt	321	1316	4.1	32	2
Lewis, Cle	298	1304	4.4	66	9
McGahee, Balt	294	1207	4.1	46	7
Taylor, Jac	223	1202	5.4	80	5
Jones, NYJ	310	1119	3.6	36	1
Lynch, Buff	280	1115	4.0	56	7
White, Tenn	303	1110	3.7	28	7
Addai, Ind	261	1072	4.1	23	12
Fargas, Oak	222	1009	4.5	48	4

Interceptions

	No.	Yds	Lg	TD
Cromartie, SD	10	144	70	1
Reed, Balt	7	130	32	0
Bodden, Cle	6	75	26	0
Howard, Oak	6	172	66	2
Samuel, NE	6	89	42	1

Sacks

Allen, KC	15.5
Williams, Hou	14.0
Dumervil, Den	12.5
Merriman, SD	12.5
Vrabel, NE	12.5

American Football Conference (Cont.)

Punting

	No.	Yds	Avg	Net Avg	TB	In 20	Lg	Blk	Ret	Ret Avg
Lechler, Oak	73	3585	49.1	41.1	7	25	70	0	40	11.1
Sauerbrun, Den	47	2200	46.8	36.1	6	14	65	2	28	11.2
Scifres, SD	81	3735	46.1	39.6	9	36	70	1	29	10.7
Player, Cle	13	593	45.6	40.3	2	6	57	0	6	4.8
Colquitt, KC	95	4322	45.5	39.1	9	27	81	1	50	7.7

Punt Returns

	No.	Yds	Avg	Lg	TD
Parrish, Buff	27	440	16.3	74	1
Cribbs, Cle	30	405	13.5	76	1
Welker, NE	25	249	10.0	35	0
Ginn, Mia	24	230	9.6	87	1

Three tied at 9.5 yds/ret.

Kickoff Returns

	No.	Yds	Avg	Lg	TD
Cribbs, Cle	59	1809	30.7	100	2
Davis, Hou	32	968	30.3	104	3
Washington, NYJ	47	1291	27.5	98	3
Sproles, SD	37	1008	27.2	89	1
Jones-Drew, Jac	31	811	26.2	100	1

National Football Conference

Scoring

TOUCHDOWNS	TD	Rush	Rec	Ret	2PT	Pts
Owens, Dal	15	0	15	0	0	90
Peterson, Min	13	12	1	0	0	78
Burress, NYG	12	0	12	0	1	72
Westbrook, Phi	12	7	5	0	0	72
Barber, Dal	12	10	2	0	0	72
Jennings, GB	12	0	12	0	0	72
Portis, Was	11	11	0	0	0	66
Burleson, Sea	11	0	9	2	0	66
Colston, NO	11	0	11	0	0	66
Graham, TB	10	10	0	0	0	60
Fitzgerald, Ari	10	0	10	0	0	60

KICKING	PAT	FG	Pts
Crosby, GB	48	31	141
Gould, Chi	33	31	126
Hanson, Det	36	29	122
Suisham, Was	30	29	116
Brown, Sea	43	28	127
Bryant, TB	34	28	118
Folk, Dal	53	26	131
Andersen, Atl	24	25	99
Akers, Phi	36	24	108
Kasay, Car	27	24	99
Wilkins, StL	25	24	97

Passing

	Att	Comp	Yds	TD	Int	Lg	Rating Pts
Romo, Dal	520	335	4211	36	19	59	97.4
Favre, GB	535	356	4155	28	15	82	95.7
Garcia, TB	327	209	2440	13	4	69	94.6
Hasselbeck, Sea	562	352	3966	28	12	65	91.4
McNabb, Phi	473	291	3324	19	7	75	89.9
Warner, Ari	451	281	3417	27	17	62	89.8
Brees, NO	652	440	4423	28	18	58	89.4
Kitna, Det	561	355	4068	18	20	91	80.9
Campbell, Was	417	250	2700	12	11	54	77.6
Harrington, Atl	348	215	2215	7	8	69	77.2

Pass Receiving

RECEPTIONS	No.	Yds	Avg	Lg	TD
Fitzgerald, Ari	100	1409	14.1	48	10
Colston, NO	98	1202	12.3	45	11
Witten, Dal	96	1145	11.9	53	7
Engram, Sea	94	1147	12.2	49	6
Holt, StL	93	1189	12.8	40	7
Westbrook, Phi	90	771	8.6	57	5
Smith, Car	87	1002	11.5	74	7
White, Atl	83	1202	14.5	69	6
Driver, GB	82	1048	12.8	47	2
Owens, Dal	81	1355	16.7	52	15

YARDS	Yds	No.	Avg	Lg	TD
Fitzgerald, Ari	1409	100	14.1	48	10
Owens, Dal	1355	81	16.7	52	15
White, Atl	1202	83	14.5	69	6
Colston, NO	1202	98	12.3	45	11
Holt, StL	1189	93	12.8	40	7
Engram, Sea	1147	94	12.2	49	6
Witten, Dal	1145	96	11.9	53	7
Curtis, Phi	1110	77	14.4	75	6
Driver, GB	1048	82	12.8	47	2
Burress, NYG	1025	70	14.6	60	12

National Football Conference (Cont.)

Rushing

	Att	Yds	Avg	Lg	TD
Peterson, Min	238	1341	5.6	73	12
Westbrook, Phi	278	1333	4.8	36	7
Portis, Was	325	1262	3.9	32	11
James, Ari	324	1222	3.8	27	7
Gore, SF	260	1102	4.2	43	5
Jacobs, NYG	202	1009	5.0	43	4
Jackson, StL	237	1002	4.2	54	5
Barber, Dal	204	975	4.8	54	10
Grant, GB	188	956	5.1	66	8
Graham, TB	222	898	4.0	28	10

Interceptions

	No.	Yds	Lg	TD
Atogwe, StL	8	125	52	1
Trufant, Sea	7	150	84	1
Henry, Dal	6	81	28	1

Seven tied with five ints.

Sacks

Kerney, Sea	14.5
Ware, Dal	14.0
Umenyiora, NYG	13.0
Cole, Phi	12.5
Ellis, Dal	12.5

Punting

	No.	Yds	Avg	Net Avg	TB	In 20	Lg	Blk	Ret	Ret Avg
Lee, SF	105	4968	47.3	41.0	13	42	74	0	53	7.6
Jones, StL	78	3684	47.2	39.3	9	18	80	0	48	9.1
McBriar, Dal	63	2970	47.1	38.5	7	17	64	0	35	11.6
Kluwe, Min	81	3621	44.7	37.0	9	34	70	0	43	10.2
Ryan, GB	60	2664	44.4	38.9	11	18	72	2	19	5.9

Punt Returns

	No.	Yds	Avg	Lg	TD
Hester, Chi	42	651	15.5	89	4
Burleson, Sea	58	658	11.3	94	1
Breaston, Ari	42	395	9.4	73	1
Crayton, Dal	22	201	9.1	49	0
Moore, NO	20	185	9.3	48	0

Kickoff Returns

	No.	Yds	Avg	Lg	TD
Allison, Min	20	574	28.7	104	1
Cartwright, Was	52	1339	25.8	80	0
Norwood, Atl	52	1317	25.3	76	0
Austin, Dal	24	612	25.5	60	0
Stanley, StL	20	509	25.5	49	0

2007 NFL Team Leaders

AFC Total Offense

	Total Plays	Yds/ Game	Yds/ Play	Ist Dwns/ Game	Time of Poss
New England	1058	411.2	6.2	24.6	32:31
Indianapolis	1020	358.7	5.6	22.3	29:49
Jacksonville	1022	357.4	5.6	20.5	32:08
Cleveland	1004	351.3	5.6	19.7	29:31
Cincinnati	1008	348.0	5.5	20.0	29:24
Denver	976	346.3	5.7	19.1	29:35
Houston	968	333.6	5.5	18.4	29:41
Pittsburgh	1000	327.4	5.2	18.6	33:29
San Diego	980	315.2	5.1	17.4	30:04
Tennessee	1037	311.7	4.8	19.1	31:53
Baltimore	1042	302.0	4.6	18.2	31:10
Oakland	1000	294.8	4.7	16.7	31:27
NY Jets	1011	294.7	4.7	17.9	29:07
Miami	989	287.5	4.7	17.7	29:27
Buffalo	919	277.1	4.8	15.5	28:51
Kansas City	1001	276.8	4.4	15.9	30:02

AFC Total Defense

	Opp Total Plays	Opp Yds/ Game	Opp Yds/ Play	Opp Time of Poss
Pittsburgh	933	266.4	4.6	26:50
Indianapolis	980	279.7	4.6	30:11
New England	933	288.3	4.9	27:25
Tennessee	978	291.6	4.8	28:36
Baltimore	968	301.6	5.0	29:37
Jacksonville	970	313.8	5.2	27:52
Kansas City	980	319.4	5.2	30:18
San Diego	1013	320.2	5.1	30:25
NY Jets	1016	331.9	5.2	31:59
Denver	992	336.0	5.4	31:18
Oakland	952	341.6	5.7	29:08
Miami	983	342.2	5.6	31:19
Houston	994	344.2	5.5	30:19
Cincinnati	1011	348.8	5.5	30:31
Cleveland	1066	359.6	5.4	31:12
Buffalo	1047	362.9	5.5	31:09

NFC Total Offense

	Total Plays	Yds/ Game	Yds/ Play	Ist Dwns/ Game	Time of Poss
Green Bay	985	370.1	6.0	19.2	30:19
Dallas	975	365.7	6.0	20.1	30:34
New Orleans	1060	361.2	5.5	21.6	31:09
Philadelphia	1047	358.1	5.5	20.2	30:56
Seattle	1056	348.9	5.3	20.2	29:59
Arizona	1016	344.1	5.4	19.2	30:40
Minnesota	964	336.2	5.6	18.4	29:35
Washington	1052	333.4	5.1	19.2	31:11
NY Giants	1041	331.4	5.1	20.1	31:22
Tampa Bay	975	326.8	5.4	17.6	30:27
Detroit	965	322.9	5.4	18.9	27:43
Atlanta	987	301.0	4.9	15.5	28:43
St. Louis	1026	297.5	4.6	17.6	30:08
Chicago	1035	293.2	4.5	16.6	28:29
Carolina	989	284.9	4.6	15.9	28:44
San Francisco	925	237.3	4.1	13.6	27:08

NFC Total Defense

	Opp Total Plays	Opp Yds/ Game	Opp Yds/ Play	Opp Time of Poss
Tampa Bay	977	278.4	4.6	29:33
NY Giants	984	305.0	5.0	28:38
Washington	1026	305.2	4.8	29:38
Dallas	1008	307.6	4.9	29:26
Philadelphia	979	311.4	5.1	29:04
Green Bay	994	313.3	5.0	29:42
Seattle	1035	321.8	5.0	30:22
Carolina	1032	324.8	5.0	31:16
Arizona	1013	330.2	5.2	30:19
Minnesota	1063	338.1	5.1	30:51
St. Louis	999	341.1	5.5	29.52
San Francisco	1078	346.2	5.1	33:31
New Orleans	964	348.1	5.8	28:51
Chicago	1036	354.7	5.5	31:45
Atlanta	1042	355.5	5.5	31:37
Detroit	1087	377.6	5.6	32:40

Takeaways/Giveaways

American Football Conference

	Takeaways			Giveaways			Net
	Int	Fum	Total	Int	Fum	Total	Diff
San Diego	30	18	48	16	8	24	24
Indianapolis	22	15	37	14	5	19	18
New England	19	12	31	9	6	15	16
Jacksonville	20	10	30	8	13	21	9
Buffalo	18	12	30	14	7	21	9
Cincinnati	19	16	35	20	10	30	5
Pittsburgh	11	14	25	14	8	22	3
Denver	14	16	30	15	14	29	1
Tennessee	22	12	34	17	17	34	0
Cleveland	17	10	27	20	9	29	-2
NY Jets	15	6	21	19	6	25	-4
Miami	14	8	22	16	13	29	-7
Oakland	18	8	26	20	17	37	-11
Kansas City	14	8	22	20	13	33	-11
Houston	11	14	25	21	17	38	-13
Baltimore	17	6	23	14	26	40	-17

National Football Conference

	Takeaways			Giveaways			Net
	Int	Fum	Total	Int	Fum	Total	Diff
Tampa Bay	16	19	35	8	12	20	15
Seattle	20	14	34	13	11	24	10
Dallas	19	10	29	19	5	24	5
Green Bay	19	9	28	15	9	24	4
Atlanta	16	12	28	15	9	24	4
Minnesota	15	16	31	14	16	30	1
Carolina	14	16	30	17	12	29	1
Detroit	17	18	35	22	14	36	-1
Chicago	16	17	33	21	13	34	-1
Washington	14	10	24	11	18	29	-5
New Orleans	13	10	23	18	12	30	-7
Arizona	18	11	29	24	12	36	-7
Philadelphia	11	8	19	15	12	27	-8
NY Giants	15	10	25	20	14	34	-9
St.Louis	18	9	27	28	9	37	-10
San Francisco	12	10	22	17	17	34	-12

2007 AFC Team-by-Team Statistical Leaders

Baltimore Ravens

SCORING	TD Rush	TD Rec	TD Ret	PAT	FG	S	Pts
Stover	0	0	0	26	27	0	107
McGahee	7	1	0	0	0	0	48
Mason	0	5	5	0	0	0	30
Darling	0	3	3	0	0	0	18
Smith	2	0	0	0	0	0	12
Figurs	0	0	2	0	0	0	12

RUSHING	No.	Yds	Avg	Lg	TD
McGahee	294	1207	4.1	46	7
Smith	75	264	3.5	24	2

PASSING	Att	Comp	Pct Comp	Yds	Avg Gain	TD	Int	Rating Pts
Boller	275	168	61.1	1743	6.34	9	10	75.2
McNair	205	133	64.9	1113	5.43	2	4	73.9

RECEIVING	No.	Yds	Avg	Lg	TD
Mason	103	1087	10.6	79	5
Clayton	48	531	11.1	52	0
Darling	18	326	18.1	53	3
Wiliams	20	290	14.5	34	0
Sypniewski	34	246	7.2	13	1
Heap	23	239	10.4	37	1

INTERCEPTIONS: Reed, 7

PUNTING	No.	Yds	Avg	Net Avg	TB	In 20	Lg	Blk
Koch	78	3397	43.6	36.0	9	20	64	1

SACKS: Suggs, 5

Buffalo Bills

SCORING	TD Rush	TD Rec	TD Ret	PAT	FG	S	Pts
Lindell	0	0	0	24	24	0	96
Lynch	7	0	0	0	0	0	44
Evans	0	5	0	0	0	0	30
Royal	0	3	0	0	0	0	18
Parrish	1	1	1	0	0	0	18
Gaines	0	2	0	0	0	0	12

RUSHING	No.	Yds	Avg	Lg	TD
Lynch	280	1115	4.0	56	7
Jackson	58	300	5.2	27	0

PASSING	Att	Comp	Pct Comp	Yds	Avg Gain	TD	Int	Rating Pts
Edwards	269	151	56.1	1630	6.06	7	8	70.4
Losman	175	111	63.4	1204	6.88	4	6	76.9

RECEIVING	No.	Yds	Avg	Lg	TD
Evans	55	849	15.4	85	5
Reed	51	578	11.3	30	0
Parrish	35	352	10.1	47	1
Royal	25	248	9.9	28	3
Gaines	25	215	8.6	20	2

INTERCEPTIONS: McGee, 4

PUNTING	No.	Yds	Avg	Net Avg	TB	In 20	Lg	Blk
Moorman	81	3302	40.8	38.3	3	30	75	0

SACKS: Schobel, 6.5

Cincinnati Bengals

SCORING	TD Rush	TD Rec	TD Ret	PAT	FG	S	Pts
Graham	0	0	0	37	31	0	130
Houshmandzadeh	0	12	0	0	0	0	72
C. Johnson	0	8	0	0	0	0	48
Watson	7	0	0	0	0	0	42
R. Johnson	3	1	0	0	0	0	24
Henry	0	2	0	0	0	0	12

RUSHING	No.	Yds	Avg	Lg	TD
Watson	178	763	4.3	24	7
R. Johnson	170	497	2.9	22	3

PASSING	Att	Comp	Pct Comp	Yds	Avg Gain	TD	Int	Rating Pts
Palmer	575	373	64.9	4131	7.18	26	20	86.7

RECEIVING	No.	Yds	Avg	Lg	TD
C. Johnson	93	1440	15.5	70	8
Houshmandzadeh	112	1143	10.2	42	12
Watson	52	374	7.2	43	0
Henry	21	343	16.3	52	2
Kelly	20	211	10.5	26	0
Chatman	19	149	7.8	15	1

INTERCEPTIONS: Hall, 5

PUNTING	No.	Yds	Avg	Net Avg	TB	In 20	Lg	Blk
Larson	59	2437	41.3	35.2	3	21	55	0

SACKS: Geathers, 3.5

Cleveland Browns

SCORING	TD Rush	TD Rec	TD Ret	PAT	FG	S	Pts
Dawson	0	0	0	42	26	0	120
Edwards	0	16	0	0	0	0	96
Lewis	9	2	0	0	0	0	66
Winslow	0	5	0	0	0	0	32
Jurevicius	0	3	0	1*	0	0	20
Anderson	3	0	0	0	0	0	18

RUSHING	No.	Yds	Avg	Lg	TD
Lewis	298	1304	4.4	66	9
Wright	60	277	4		

PASSING	Att	Comp	Pct Comp	Yds	Avg Gain	TD	Int	Rating Pts
Anderson	527	298	56.5	3787	7.19	29	19	82.5

RECEIVING	No.	Yds	Avg	Lg	TD
Edwards	80	1289	16.1	78	16
Winslow	82	1106	13.5	49	5
Jurevicius	50	614	12.3	50	3
Lewis	30	248	8.3	34	2
Wright	24	233	9.7	23	0
Carter	8	117	14.6	22	1
Heiden	12	104	8.7	27	0

INTERCEPTIONS: Bodden, 6

PUNTING	No.	Yds	Avg	Net Avg	TB	In 20	Lg	Blk
Zastudil	49	2046	41.8	34.6	4	14	64	0

SACKS: Wimbley, 5

*2-pt. conversion.

2007 AFC Team-by-Team Statistical Leaders *(Cont.)*

Denver Broncos

SCORING	TD Rush	TD Rec	TD Ret	PAT	FG	S	Pts
Elam	0	0	0	33	27	0	114
Marshall	0	7	0	0	0	0	42
Stokley	0	5	0	0	0	0	30
Scheffler	0	5	0	0	0	0	30
Henry	4	0	0	0	0	0	24

RUSHING	No.	Yds	Avg	Lg	TD
Young	140	729	5.2	50	1
Henry	167	691	4.1	33	4
Hall	44	216	4.9	62	2

PASSING	Att	Comp	Pct Comp	Yds	Avg Gain	TD	Int	Rating Pts
Cutler	467	297	63.6	3497	7.49	20	14	88.1

RECEIVING	No.	Yds	Avg	Lg	TD
Marshall	102	1325	13.0	68	7
Stokley	40	635	15.9	58	5
Scheffler	49	549	11.2	41	5
Walker	26	287	11.0	24	0
Graham	24	246	10.3	28	2
Young	35	231	6.6	24	0

INTERCEPTIONS: Bly, 5

PUNTING	No.	Yds	Avg	Net Avg	TB	In 20	Lg	Blk
Sauerbrun	47	2200	46.8	37.6	6	14	65	0

SACKS: Dumervil, 12

Indianapolis Colts

SCORING	TD Rush	TD Rec	TD Ret	PAT	FG	S	Pts
Vinatieri	0	0	0	49	23	0	118
Addai	12	3	0	1*	0	0	92
Clark	0	11	0	0	0	0	66
Wayne	0	10	0	0	0	0	60
Keith	3	1	0	0	0	0	24
Manning	3	0	0	0	0	0	18

RUSHING	No.	Yds	Avg	Lg	TD
Addai	261	1072	4.1	23	12
Keith	121	533	4.4	22	3

PASSING	Att	Comp	Pct Comp	Yds	Avg Gain	TD	Int	Rating Pts
Manning	515	337	65.4	4040	7.85	31	14	98.0

RECEIVING	No.	Yds	Avg	Lg	TD
Wayne	104	1510	14.5	64	10
Clark	58	616	10.6	39	11
Gonzalez	37	576	15.6	57	3
Addai	41	364	8.9	73	3
Utecht	31	364	11.7	30	1
Harrison	20	247	12.4	42	1

INTERCEPTIONS: Brackett, Bethea 4

PUNTING	No.	Yds	Avg	Net Avg	TB	In 20	Lg	Blk
Smith	52	2181	41.9	34.2	5	18	63	0

SACKS: Mathis, 7

* 2-pt. conversion.

Houston Texans

SCORING	TD Rush	TD Rec	TD Ret	PAT	FG	S	Pts
Brown	0	0	0	40	25	0	115
Johnson	0	8	0	0	0	0	48
Davis	0	3	3	0	0	0	38
Dayne	6	0	0	0	0	0	36
Walter	0	4	1†	0	0	0	30

RUSHING	No.	Yds	Avg	Lg	TD
Dayne	194	773	4.0	39	6
Walker	58	264	4.6	41	1
Green	70	260	3.7	18	2

PASSING	Att	Comp	Pct Comp	Yds	Avg Gain	TD	Int	Rating Pts
Schaub	289	192	66.4	2241	7.75	9	9	87.2
Rosenfels	240	154	64.2	1684	7.02	15	12	84.8

RECEIVING	No.	Yds	Avg	Lg	TD
Johnson	60	851	14.2	77	8
Walter	65	800	12.3	46	4
Daniels	63	768	12.2	29	3
Davis	33	583	17.7	53	3
Jones	15	149	9.9	26	0
Anderson	12	131	10.9	24	1

INTERCEPTIONS: Bennett, 3

PUNTING	No.	Yds	Avg	Net Avg	TB	In 20	Lg	Blk
Turk	55	2296	41.7	37.9	3	24	59	0

SACKS: Williams, 14

Jacksonville Jaguars

SCORING	TD Rush	TD Rec	TD Ret	PAT	FG	S	Pts
Scobee	0	0	0	26	12	0	62
Williams	0	10	0	0	0	0	60
Jones-Drew	9	0	1	0	0	0	60
Carney	0	0	0	20	9	0	47
Taylor	5	0	0	0	0	0	30
Northcutt	0	4	0	0	0	0	24

RUSHING	No.	Yds	Avg	Lg	TD
Taylor	223	1202	5.4	80	5
Jones-Drew	167	768	4.6	57	9

PASSING	Att	Comp	Pct Comp	Yds	Avg Gain	TD	Int	Rating Pts
Garrard	325	208	64.0	2509	7.72	18	3	102.2
Gray	144	80	55.6	986	6.85	10	5	85.6

RECEIVING	No.	Yds	Avg	Lg	TD
Williams	38	629	16.6	80	10
Northcutt	44	601	13.7	55	4
Wilford	45	518	11.5	35	3
Jones-Drew	40	407	10.2	43	0
Lewis	37	391	10.6	25	2

INTERCEPTIONS: Nelson, 5

PUNTING	No.	Yds	Avg	Ne Avg	TB	In 20	Lg	Blk
Podlesh	54	2249	41.6	36.9	2	14	76	0

SACKS: Spicer, 7.5

†fumble return for TD.

Kansas City Chiefs

SCORING	TD Rush	TD Rec	TD Ret	PAT	FG	S	Pts
Rayner	0	0	0	14	15	0	59
Gonzalez	0	5	0	0	0	0	30
Bowe	0	5	0	0	0	0	30
L. Johnson	3	1	0	0	0	0	24
Carney	0	0	0	7	3	0	16
Parker	0	2	0	0	0	0	12

RUSHING	No.	Yds	Avg	Lg	TD
L. Johnson	158	559	3.5	54	3
Smith	112	407	3.6	19	2

PASSING	Att	Comp	Pct Comp	Yds	Avg Gain	TD	Int	Rating Pts
Huard	332	206	62.0	2257	6.80	11	13	76.8
Croyle	224	127	56.7	1227	5.48	6	6	69.9

RECEIVING	No.	Yds	Avg	Lg	TD
Gonzalez	99	1172	11.8	31	5
Bowe	70	995	14.2	58	5
Webb	28	313	11.2	32	1
Parker	24	298	12.4	24	2
L. Johnson	30	186	6.2	30	1
Wilson	24	180	7.5	31	1

INTERCEPTIONS: Page, 3

PUNTING	No.	Yds	Avg	Net Avg	TB	In 20	Lg	Blk
Colquitt	95	4322	45.5	39.1	9	27	81	1

SACKS: Allen, 15.5

New England Patriots

SCORING	TD Rush	TD Rec	TD Ret	PAT	FG	S	Pts
Moss	0	23	0	0	0	0	138
Gostkowski	0	0	0	74	21	0	137
Welker	0	8	0	0	0	0	48
Maroney	6	0	0	1*	0	0	38
Watson	0	6	0	0	0	0	36

RUSHING	No.	Yds	Avg	Lg	TD
Maroney	185	835	4.5	59	6
Morris	85	384	4.5	49	3

PASSING	Att	Comp	Pct Comp	Yds	Avg Gain	TD	Int	Rating Pts
Brady	578	398	68.9	4806	8.32	50	8	117.2

RECEIVING	No.	Yds	Avg	Lg	TD
Moss	98	1493	15.2	65	23
Welker	112	1175	10.5	42	8
Stallworth	46	697	15.2	69	3
Gaffney	36	449	12.5	56	5
Watson	36	389	10.8	35	6
Faulk	47	383	8.1	23	1

INTERCEPTIONS: Samuel, 6

PUNTING	No.	Yds	Avg	Net Avg	TB	In 20	Lg	Blk
Hanson	44	1821	41.4	36.1	6	13	64	1

SACKS: Vrabel, 12.5

Miami Dolphins

SCORING	TD Rush	TD Rec	TD Ret	PAT	FG	S	Pts
Feely	0	0	0	26	21	0	89
Brown	4	1	0	1*	0	0	32
Lemon	4	0	0	0	0	2	24
Gado	3	0	0	0	0	0	18
Ginn Jr.	0	2	1	0	0	0	18
Hagan	0	2	0	1*	0	0	14

RUSHING	No.	Yds	Avg	Lg	TD
Brown	119	602	5.1	60	4
Chatman	128	515	4.0	30	1

PASSING	Att	Comp	Pct Comp	Yds	Avg Gain	TD	Int	Rating Pts
Lemon	309	173	56.0	1773	5.74	6	6	71.0
Green	141	85	60.3	987	7.00	5	7	72.6
Beck	107	60	56.1	559	5.22	1	3	62.0

RECEIVING	No.	Yds	Avg	Lg	TD
Booker	50	556	11.1	26	1
Ginn Jr.	34	420	12.4	54	2
Chambers	31	415	13.4	28	0
Brown	39	389	10.0	43	1
Hagan	29	373	12.9	22	2
Martin	34	303	8.9	28	2

INTERCEPTIONS: Allen, 3

PUNTING	No.	Yds	Avg	Net Avg	TB	In 20	Lg	Blk
Fields	77	3327	43.2	36.6	6	10	61	0

SACKS: Taylor, 11

New York Jets

SCORING	TD Rush	TD Rec	TD Ret	PAT	FG	S	Pts
Nugent	0	0	0	23	29	0	110
Washington	3	0	3	1*	0	0	38
Coles	0	6	0	0	0	0	36
Baker	0	3	0	0	0	0	18
Jones	1	1	0	0	0	0	12
Cotchery	0	2	0	0	0	0	12
Smith	0	2	0	0	0	0	12

RUSHING	No.	Yds	Avg	Lg	TD
Jones	310	1119	3.6	36	1
Washington	71	353	5.0	49	3

PASSING	Att	Comp	Pct Comp	Yds	Avg Gain	TD	Int	Rating Pts
Pennington	260	179	68.8	1765	6.79	10	9	86.1
Clemens	250	130	52.0	1529	6.12	5	10	60.9

RECEIVING	No.	Yds	Avg	Lg	TD
Cotchery	82	1130	13.8	50	2
Coles	55	646	11.7	57	6
Baker	41	409	10.0	22	3
Smith	32	325	10.2	29	2
McCareins	19	232	12.2	51	1

INTERCEPTIONS: Rhodes, 5

PUNTING	No.	Yds	Avg	Net Avg	TB	In 20	Lg	Blk
Graham	66	2855	43.3	36.6	7	23	62	1

SACKS: Harris, Ellis 5.0

*2-pt conversion.

2007 AFC Team-by-Team Statistical Leaders *(Cont.)*

Oakland Raiders

SCORING	TD Rush	TD Rec	TD Ret	PAT	FG	S	Pts
Janikowski	0	0	0	28	23	0	97
Porter	0	6	0	0	0	0	36
Curry	0	4	0	2*	0	0	28
Fargas	4	0	0	0	0	0	24
Culpepper	3	0	0	0	0	0	18
Jordan	3	0	0	0	0	0	18

RUSHING	No.	Yds	Avg	Lg	TD
Fargas	222	1009	4.5	48	4
Jordan	144	549	3.8	33	3
Rhodes	75	302	4.0	25	1

PASSING	Att	Comp	Pct Comp	Yds	Avg Gain	TD	Int	Rating Pts
Culpepper	186	108	58.1	1331	7.16	5	5	78.0
McCown	190	111	58.4	1151	6.06	10	11	69.4
Russell	66	36	54.5	373	5.65	2	4	55.9

RECEIVING	No.	Yds	Avg	Lg	TD
Curry	55	717	13.0	49	4
Porter	44	705	16.0	59	6
Miller	44	444	10.1	28	3
Jordan	28	247	8.8	27	0
Fargas	23	188	8.2	17	0

INTERCEPTIONS: Howard, 6

PUNTING	No.	Yds	Avg	Net Avg	TB	In 20	Lg	Blk
Lechler	73	3585	49.1	41.1	7	25	70	0

SACKS: Burgess, Clemons 8

San Diego Chargers

SCORING	TD Rush	TD Rec	TD Ret	PAT	FG	S	Pts
Kaeding	0	0	0	46	24	0	118
Tomlinson	15	3	0	0	0	0	108
Gates	0	9	0	0	0	0	54
Chambers	0	4	0	0	0	0	24
Sproles	2	0	2	0	0	0	24
Jackson	0	3	0	0	0	0	18

RUSHING	No.	Yds	Avg	Lg	TD
Tomlinson	315	1474	4.7	49	15
Turner	71	316	4.5	74	1

PASSING	Att	Comp	Pct Comp	Yds	Avg Gain	TD	Int	Rating Pts
Rivers	460	277	60.2	3152	6.85	21	15	82.4

RECEIVING	No.	Yds	Avg	Lg	TD
Gates	75	984	13.1	49	9
Jackson	41	623	15.2	45	3
Chambers	35	555	15.9	44	4
Tomlinson	60	475	7.9	36	3
Davis	20	188	9.4	18	1
Floyd	7	97	13.9	25	0

INTERCEPTIONS: Cromartie, 10

PUNTING	No.	Yds	Avg	Net Avg	TB	In 20	Lg	Blk
Scifres	81	3735	46.1	39.6	9	36	70	1

SACKS: Merriman, 12.5

Pittsburgh Steelers

SCORING	TD Rush	TD Rec	TD Ret	PAT	FG	S	Pts
Reed	0	0	0	44	23	0	113
Holmes	0	8	0	1*	0	0	50
Ward	0	7	0	1*	0	0	44
Davenport	5	2	0	0	0	0	42
Miller	0	7	0	0	0	0	42

RUSHING	No.	Yds	Avg	Lg	TD
Parker	321	1316	4.1	32	2
Davenport	107	499	4.7	45	5
Roethlisberger	35	204	5.8	30	2

PASSING	Att	Comp	Pct Comp	Yds	Avg Gain	TD	Int	Rating Pts
Roethlisberger	404	264	65.3	3154	7.81	32	11	104.1
Batch	36	17	47.2	232	6.44	2	3	52.1

RECEIVING	No.	Yds	Avg	Lg	TD
Holmes	52	942	18.1	83	8
Ward	71	732	10.3	25	7
Miller	47	566	12.0	29	7
Washington	29	450	15.5	40	5
Wilson	18	207	11.5	18	1

INTERCEPTIONS: Taylor, 3

PUNTING	No.	Yds	Avg	Net Avg	TB	In 20	Lg	Blk
Sepulveda	68	2880	42.4	37.9	2	28	59	0

SACKS: Harrison, 8.5

Tennessee Titans

SCORING	TD Rush	TD Rec	TD Ret	PAT	FG	S	Pts
Bironas	0	0	0	28	35	0	133
White	7	0	0	0	0	0	42
Brown	5	0	0	0	0	0	30
Williams	0	4	0	0	0	0	24

RUSHING	No.	Yds	Avg	Lg	TD
White	303	1110	3.7	28	7
Brown	102	462	4.5	42	5
Young	93	395	4.2	21	3

PASSING	Att	Comp	Pct Comp	Yds	Avg Gain	TD	Int	Rating Pts
Young	382	238	62.3	2546	6.67	9	17	71.1
Collins	82	50	61.0	531	6.48	0	0	79.9

RECEIVING	No.	Yds	Avg	Lg	TD
Gage	55	750	13.6	73	2
Williams	55	719	13.1	48	4
Scaife	46	421	9.2	26	1
Moulds	32	342	10.7	46	0
Jones	21	248	11.8	35	2
Hartsock	12	138	11.5	27	0
Brown	19	128	6.7	16	0
White	20	114	5.7	15	0

INTERCEPTIONS: Bulluck, 5

PUNTING	No.	Yds	Avg	Net Avg	TB	In 20	Lg	Blk
Hentrich	70	2939	42.0	36.5	6	24	66	0

SACKS: Vanden Bosch, 12

*2-pt conversion.

Arizona Cardinals

SCORING	TD Rush	TD Rec	TD Ret	PAT	FG	S	Pts
Rackers	0	0	0	47	21	0	110
Fitzgerald	0	10	0	0	0	0	60
Boldin	0	9	0	0	0	0	54
James	7	0	0	0	0	0	42
Pope	0	5	0	0	0	0	30

RUSHING	No.	Yds	Avg	Lg	TD
James	324	1222	3.8	27	7
Arrington	26	78	3.0	12	0

PASSING	Att	Comp	Pct Comp	Yds	Avg Gain	TD	Int	Rating Pts
Warner	451	281	62.3	3417	7.58	27	17	89.8
Leinart	112	60	53.6	647	5.78	2	4	61.9

RECEIVING	No.	Yds	Avg	Lg	TD
Fitzgerald	100	1409	14.1	48	10
Boldin	71	853	12.0	44	9
Johnson	46	528	11.5	30	2
Urban	22	329	15.0	42	2
Arrington	29	241	8.3	32	1
Pope	23	238	10.3	31	5

INTERCEPTIONS: Rolle, Hood, 5

PUNTING	No.	Yds	Avg	Net Avg	TB	In 20	Lg	Blk
Barr	59	2385	40.4	31.7	5	15	61	1
Berger	20	813	40.7	33.0	2	6	56	0

SACKS: Dockett, 9

Atlanta Falcons

SCORING	TD Rush	TD Rec	TD Ret	PAT	FG	S	Pts
Andersen	0	0	0	24	25	0	99
White	0	6	0	0	0	0	36
Crumpler	0	5	0	0	0	0	30
Dunn	4	0	0	0	0	0	24
Jenkins	0	4	0	0	0	0	24

RUSHING	No.	Yds	Avg	Lg	TD
Dunn	227	720	3.2	38	4
Norwood	103	613	6.0	67	1

PASSING	Att	Comp	Pct Comp	Yds	Avg Gain	TD	Int	Rating Pts
Harrington	348	215	61.8	2215	6.37	7	8	77.2
Redman	149	89	59.7	1079	7.24	10	5	90.4
Leftwich	58	32	55.2	279	4.81	1	2	59.5

RECEIVING	No.	Yds	Avg	Lg	TD
White	83	1202	14.5	69	6
Jenkins	53	532	10.0	29	4
Crumpler	42	444	10.6	55	5
Robinson	37	437	11.8	74	1
Norwood	28	277	9.9	46	0
Horn	27	243	9.0	26	1

INTERCEPTIONS: Hall, 5

PUNTING	No.	Yds	Avg	Net Avg	TB	In 20	Lg	Blk
Koenen	88	3824	43.5	38.8	5	30	63	0

SACKS: Abraham, 10

Carolina Panthers

SCORING	TD Rush	TD Rec	TD Ret	PAT	FG	S	Pts
Kasay	0	0	0	27	24	0	99
Smith	0	7	0	0	0	0	42
Williams	4	1	0	0	0	0	30
Foster	3	1	0	0	0	0	24
Carter	0	4	0	0	0	0	24

RUSHING	No.	Yds	Avg	Lg	TD
Foster	247	876	3.5	20	3
Williams	144	717	5.0	75	4

PASSING	Att	Comp	Pct Comp	Yds	Avg Gain	TD	Int	Rating Pts
Testaverde	172	94	54.7	952	5.54	5	6	65.8
Carr	136	73	53.7	635	4.67	3	5	58.3
Moore	111	63	56.8	730	6.58	3	5	67.0
Delhomme	86	55	64.0	624	7.26	8	1	111.8

RECEIVING	No.	Yds	Avg	Lg	TD
Smith	87	1002	11.5	74	7
Carter	38	517	13.6	49	4
King	46	406	8.8	29	2
Colbert	32	332	10.4	43	0
Foster	25	182	7.3	23	1

INTERCEPTIONS: Cooper, Marshall, 3

PUNTING	No.	Yds	Avg	Net Avg	TB	In 20	Lg	Blk
Baker	90	3978	44.2	37.7	5	22	64	0

SACKS: Diggs, Lewis 3.5

Chicago Bears

SCORING	TD Rush	TD Rec	TD Ret	PAT	FG	S	Pts
Gould	0	0	0	33	31	0	126
Hester	0	2	6	0	0	0	48
Berrian	0	5	0	0	0	0	30
Clark	0	4	0	0	0	0	24
Benson	4	0	0	0	0	0	24

RUSHING	No.	Yds	Avg	Lg	TD
Benson	196	674	3.4	43	4
Peterson	151	510	3.4	21	3

PASSING	Att	Comp	Pct Comp	Yds	Avg Gain	TD	Int	Rating Pts
Griese	262	161	61.5	1803	6.88	10	12	75.6
Grossman	225	122	54.2	1411	6.27	4	7	66.4
Orton	80	43	53.8	478	5.98	3	2	73.9

RECEIVING	No.	Yds	Avg	Lg	TD
Berrian	71	951	13.4	59	5
Muhammad	40	570	14.3	44	3
Clark	44	545	12.4	52	4
Peterson	51	420	8.2	30	0
Olsen	39	391	10.0	31	2

INTERCEPTIONS: Urlacher, 5

PUNTING	No.	Yds	Avg	Net Avg	TB	In 20	Lg	Blk
Maynard	88	3682	41.8	37.4	9	27	56	0

SACKS: Ogunleye, 9

2007 NFC Team-by-Team Statistical Leaders *(Cont.)*

Dallas Cowboys

SCORING	TD Rush	TD Rec	TD Ret	PAT	FG	S	Pts
Folk	0	0	0	53	26	0	131
Owens	0	15	0	0	0	0	90
Barber	10	2	0	0	0	0	72
Witten	0	7	0	0	0	0	42
Crayton	0	7	0	0	0	0	42
Curtis	0	3	0	0	0	0	18

RUSHING	No.	Yds	Avg	Lg	TD
Barber	204	975	4.8	54	10
Jones	164	588	3.6	25	2

PASSING	Att	Comp	Pct Comp	Yds	Avg Gain	TD	Int	Rating Pts
Romo	520	335	64.4	4211	8.10	36	19	97.4

RECEIVING	No.	Yds	Avg	Lg	TD
Owens	81	1355	16.7	52	15
Witten	96	1145	11.9	53	7
Crayton	50	697	13.9	59	7
Hurd	19	314	16.5	51	1
Barber	44	282	6.4	29	2

INTERCEPTIONS: Henry, 6

PUNTING	No.	Yds	Avg	Net Avg	TB	In 20	Lg	Blk
McBriar	63	2970	47.1	38.5	7	17	64	0

SACKS: Ware, 14

Green Bay Packers

SCORING	TD Rush	TD Rec	TD Ret	PAT	FG	S	Pts
Crosby	0	0	0	48	31	0	141
Jennings	0	12	0	0	0	0	72
Grant	8	0	0	0	0	0	48
Lee	0	6	0	0	0	0	36
Martin	0	4	0	0	0	0	24
Wynn	4	0	0	0	0	0	24

RUSHING	No.	Yds	Avg	Lg	TD
Grant	188	956	5.1	66	8
Jackson	75	267	3.6	46	1
Wynn	50	203	4.1	44	4

PASSING	Att	Comp	Pct Comp	Yds	Avg Gain	TD	Int	Rating Pts
Favre	535	356	66.5	4155	7.77	28	15	95.7
Rodgers	28	20	71.4	218	7.79	1	0	106.0

RECEIVING	No.	Yds	Avg	Lg	TD
Driver	82	1048	12.8	47	2
Jennings	53	920	17.4	82	12
Jones	47	676	14.4	79	2
Lee	48	575	12.0	60	6
Martin	16	242	15.1	36	4
Robinson	21	241	11.5	43	1

INTERCEPTIONS: Bigby, 5

PUNTING	No.	Yds	Avg	Net Avg	TB	In 20	Lg	Blk
Ryan	60	2664	44.4	37.6	11	18	72	2

SACKS: Kampman, 12

Detroit Lions

SCORING	TD Rush	TD Rec	TD Ret	PAT	FG	S	Pts
Hanson	0	0	0	35	29	0	122
Jones	8	0	0	0	0	0	48
McDonald	0	6	0	0	0	0	36
R. Williams	0	5	0	0	0	0	30
Johnson	1	4	0	0	0	0	30

RUSHING	No.	Yds	Avg	Lg	TD
Jones	153	581	3.8	34	8
Duckett	65	335	5.2	53	3
Bell	44	182	4.1	24	1

PASSING	Att	Comp	Pct Comp	Yds	Avg Gain	TD	Int	Rating Pts
Kitna	561	355	63.3	4068	7.25	18	20	80.9

RECEIVING	No.	Yds	Avg	Lg	TD
McDonald	79	943	11.9	49	6
R. Williams	64	838	13.1	91	5
Johnson	48	756	15.8	49	4
Furrey	61	664	10.9	49	1
McHugh	17	252	14.8	46	0

INTERCEPTIONS: Smith, 3

PUNTING	No.	Yds	Avg	Net Avg	TB	In 20	Lg	Blk
Harris	68	3010	44.3	36.4	5	26	58	0

SACKS: Rogers, 7

Minnesota Vikings

SCORING	TD Rush	TD Rec	TD Ret	PAT	FG	S	Pts
Longwell	0	0	0	39	20	0	99
Peterson	12	1	0	0	0	0	78
C. Taylor	7	0	0	0	0	0	42
Rice	0	4	0	0	0	0	24
Jackson	3	0	0	0	0	0	22
Wade	0	3	0	0	0	0	18

RUSHING	No.	Yds	Avg	Lg	TD
Peterson	238	1341	5.6	73	12
C. Taylor	157	844	5.4	84	7
T. Jackson	54	260	4.8	32	3

PASSING	Att	Comp	Pct Comp	Yds	Avg Gain	TD	Int	Rating Pts
T. Jackson	294	171	58.2	1911	6.50	9	12	70.8
Holcomb	83	42	50.6	515	6.21	2	1	73.1
Bollinger	50	33	66.0	390	7.82	1	1	88.0

RECEIVING	No.	Yds	Avg	Lg	TD
Wade	54	647	12.0	40	3
Rice	31	396	12.8	60	4
Ferguson	32	391	12.2	71	1
Shiancoe	27	323	12.0	79	1
Taylor	29	281	9.7	50	0
Peterson	19	268	14.1	60	1
Williamson	18	240	13.3	60	1

INTERCEPTIONS: Sharper, Smith, 4

PUNTING	No.	Yds	Avg	Net Avg	TB	In 20	Lg	Blk
Kluwe	81	3621	44.7	37.0	9	34	70	0

SACKS: Leber, Udeze, Edwards 5

2007 NFC Team-by-Team Statistical Leaders *(Cont.)*

New Orleans Saints

SCORING	TD Rush	TD Rec	TD Ret	PAT	FG	S	Pts
Colston	0	11	0	0	0	0	66
Mare	0	0	0	34	10	0	64
Bush	4	2	0	0	0	0	36
Stecker	5	0	0	0	0	0	30
Gramatica	0	0	0	8	5	0	23

RUSHING	No.	Yds	Avg	Lg	TD
Bush	157	581	3.7	22	4
Stecker	115	448	3.9	26	5
Thomas	52	252	4.8	24	1

PASSING	Att	Comp	Pct Comp	Yds	Avg Gain	TD	Int	Rating Pts
Brees	652	440	67.5	4423	6.78	28	18	89.4

RECEIVING	No.	Yds	Avg	Lg	TD
Colston	98	1202	12.3	45	11
Patten	54	792	14.7	58	3
Bush	73	417	5.7	25	2
Henderson	20	409	20.5	54	3
Johnson	48	378	7.9	22	2
Miller	27	328	12.1	57	2

INTERCEPTIONS: Harper, McKenzie, David 3

PUNTING	No.	Yds	Avg	Net Avg	TB	In 20	Lg	Blk
Weatherford	63	2757	43.8	36.1	4	20	61	0

SACKS: Smith, 7

Philadelphia Eagles

SCORING	TD Rush	TD Rec	TD Ret	PAT	FG	S	Pts
Akers	0	0	0	36	24	0	108
Westbrook	7	5	0	0	0	0	72
Curtis	0	6	2	0	0	1	48
Buckhalter	4	0	0	0	0	0	24
Brown	0	4	0	0	0	0	24

RUSHING	No.	Yds	Avg	Lg	TD
Westbrook	278	1333	4.8	36	7
Buckhalter	62	313	5.0	30	4
McNabb	50	236	4.7	40	0

PASSING	Att	Comp	Pct Comp	Yds	Avg Gain	TD	Int	Rating Pts
McNabb	473	291	61.5	3324	7.03	19	7	89.9
Feeley	103	59	57.3	681	6.61	5	8	61.2

RECEIVING	No.	Yds	Avg	Lg	TD
Curtis	77	1110	14.4	75	6
Brown	61	780	12.8	45	4
Westbrook	90	771	8.6	57	5
Avant	23	267	11.6	31	2
Lewis	13	265	20.4	50	3

INTERCEPTIONS: Brown, 3

PUNTING	No.	Yds	Avg	Net Avg	TB	In 20	Lg	Blk
Rocca	73	3066	42.0	34.5	7	24	65	0

SACKS: Cole, 12.5

New York Giants

SCORING	TD Rush	TD Rec	TD Ret	PAT	FG	S	Pts
Tynes	0	0	0	40	23	0	109
Burress	0	12	0	0	0	0	72
Droughns	6	0	0	0	0	0	36
Jacobs	4	2	0	0	0	0	36
Ward	3	1	0	0	0	0	24
Toomer	0	3	0	0	0	0	18
Shockey	0	3	0	0	0	0	18

RUSHING	No.	Yds	Avg	Lg	TD
Jacobs	202	1009	5.0	43	4
Ward	125	602	4.8	44	3
Droughns	85	275	3.2	45	6

PASSING	Att	Comp	Pct Comp	Yds	Avg Gain	TD	Int	Rating Pts
Manning	529	297	56.1	3336	6.31	23	20	73.9

RECEIVING	No.	Yds	Avg	Lg	TD
Burress	70	1025	14.6	60	12
Toomer	59	760	12.9	40	3
Shockey	57	619	10.9	29	3
Moss	21	225	10.7	20	0

INTERCEPTIONS: Wilson, Madison 4

PUNTING	No.	Yds	Avg	Net Avg	TB	In 20	Lg	Blk
Feagles	71	2865	40.4	36.0	5	25	60	1

SACKS: Umenyiora, 13

St. Louis Rams

SCORING	TD Rush	TD Rec	TD Ret	PAT	FG	S	Pts
Wilkins	0	0	0	25	24	0	97
Holt	0	7	0	1*	0	0	44
Jackson	5	1	0	0	0	0	36
Bruce	0	4	0	0	0	0	24
Bennett	0	3	0	0	0	0	18

RUSHING	No.	Yds	Avg	Lg	TD
Jackson	237	1002	4.2	54	5
Leonard	86	303	3.5	31	0

PASSING	Att	Comp	Pct Comp	Yds	Avg Gain	TD	Int	Rating Pts
Bulger	378	221	58.5	2392	6.33	11	15	70.3
Frerotte	167	94	56.3	1014	6.07	7	12	58.3

RECEIVING	No.	Yds	Avg	Lg	TD
Holt	93	1189	12.8	40	7
Bruce	55	733	13.3	37	4
McMichael	39	429	11.0	29	3
Bennett	33	375	11.4	24	3
Jackson	38	271	7.1	37	1

INTERCEPTIONS: Atogwe, 8

PUNTING	No.	Yds	Avg	Net Avg	TB	In 20	Lg	Blk
Jones	78	3684	47.2	39.3	9	18	80	0

SACKS: Witherspoon, 7

*2-pt. conversion.

San Francisco 49ers

SCORING	TD Rush	TD Rec	TD Ret	PAT	FG	S	Pts
Nedney	0	0	0	22	17	0	73
Battle	1	5	0	0	0	0	36
Gore	5	1	0	0	0	0	36
Davis	0	4	0	0	0	0	24
Jackson	0	3	0	0	0	0	18

RUSHING	No.	Yds	Avg	Lg	TD
Gore	260	1102	4.2	43	5
Robinson	26	121	4.7	28	0
Hicks	21	117	5.6	18	1

PASSING	Att	Comp	Pct Comp	Yds	Avg Gain	TD	Int	Rating Pts
Dilfer	219	113	51.6	1166	5.32	7	12	55.1
Smith	193	94	48.7	914	4.74	2	4	57.2
Hill	79	54	68.4	501	6.34	5	1	101.3

RECEIVING	No.	Yds	Avg	Lg	TD
Battle	50	600	12.0	57	5
Davis	52	509	9.8	31	4
Jackson	46	497	10.8	34	3
Gore	53	436	8.2	23	1

INTERCEPTIONS: Clements, Harris, 4

PUNTING	No.	Yds	Avg	Net Avg	TB	In 20	Lg	Blk
Lee	105	4968	47.3	41.0	13	42	74	0

SACKS: Young, 6

Tampa Bay Buccaneers

SCORING	TD Rush	TD Rec	TD Ret	PAT	FG	S	Pts
Bryant	0	0	0	34	28	0	118
Graham	10	0	0	0	0	0	60
Galloway	0	6	0	0	0	0	36
Stevens	0	4	0	0	0	0	24
Williams	3	0	0	0	0	0	18
Smith	0	3	0	0	0	0	18

RUSHING	No.	Yds	Avg	Lg	TD
Graham	222	898	4.0	28	10
Pittman	68	286	4.2	29	0
Williams	54	208	3.9	20	3

PASSING	Att	Comp	Pct Comp	Yds	Avg Gain	TD	Int	Rating Pts
Garcia	327	209	63.9	2440	7.46	13	4	94.6
McCown	139	94	67.6	1009	7.26	5	3	91.7

RECEIVING	No.	Yds	Avg	Lg	TD
Galloway	57	1014	17.8	69	6
Hilliard	62	722	11.6	56	1
Smith	32	385	12.0	33	3
Graham	49	324	6.6	21	0
Clayton	22	301	13.7	39	0
Pittman	26	191	7.3	16	0

INTERCEPTIONS: Phillips, 4

PUNTING	No.	Yds	Avg	Net Avg	TB	In 20	Lg	Blk
Bidwell	77	3382	43.9	37.2	10	30	61	1

SACKS: White, 8

Seattle Seahawks

SCORING	TD Rush	TD Rec	TD Ret	PAT	FG	S	Pts
Brown	0	0	0	43	28	0	127
Burleson	0	0	9	0	0	0	54
Engram	0	0	6	0	0	0	36
Alexander	4	1	0	0	0	0	30
Morris	4	1	0	0	0	0	30
Branch	0	0	4	0	0	0	24

RUSHING	No.	Yds	Avg	Lg	TD
Alexander	207	716	3.5	25	4
Morris	140	628	4.5	46	4

PASSING	Att	Comp	Pct Comp	Yds	Avg Gain	TD	Int	Rating Pts
Hasselbeck	562	352	62.6	3966	7.06	28	12	91.4

RECEIVING	No.	Yds	Avg	Lg	TD
Engram	94	1147	12.2	49	6
Burleson	50	694	13.9	45	9
Branch	49	661	13.5	65	4
Hackett	32	384	12.0	59	3
Weaver	39	313	8.0	46	0
Pollard	28	273	9.8	22	2

INTERCEPTIONS: Trufant, 7

PUNTING	No.	Yds	Avg	Net Avg	TB	In 20	Lg	Blk
Plackemeier	86	3436	40.0	34.3	6	30	62	0

SACKS: Kerney, 14.5

Washington Redskins

SCORING	TD Rush	TD Rec	TD Ret	PAT	FG	S	Pts
Suisham	0	0	0	29	29	0	116
Portis	11	0	0	0	0	0	66
Cooley	0	8	0	1*	0	0	50
Sellers	2	1	0	0	0	0	18
Moss	0	3	0	0	0	0	18

RUSHING	No.	Yds	Avg	Lg	TD
Portis	325	1262	3.9	32	11
Betts	93	335	3.6	20	1
Campbell	36	185	5.1	29	1
Sellers	26	78	3.0	15	2

PASSING	Att	Comp	Pct Comp	Yds	Avg Gain	TD	Int	Rating Pts
Campbell	417	250	60.0	2700	6.48	12	11	77.6
Collins	105	67	63.8	888	8.46	5	0	106.4

RECEIVING	No.	Yds	Avg	Lg	TD
Moss	61	808	13.2	49	3
Cooley	66	786	11.9	39	8
Randle El	51	728	14.3	54	1
Portis	47	389	8.3	54	0
McCardell	22	256	11.6	32	1

INTERCEPTIONS: Taylor, 5

PUNTING	No.	Yds	Avg	Net Avg	TB	In 20	Lg	Blk
Frost	75	3072	41.0	36.4	7	23	64	0

SACKS: Carter, 10.5

*2-pt. conversion.

2008 NFL Draft

First two rounds of the 72nd annual NFL Draft, held April 26–27, 2008 in New York City.

First Round

	Team	Selection	Position
1.	Miami	Jake Long, Michigan	OT
2.	St. Louis	Chris Long, Virginia	DE
3.	Atlanta	Matt Ryan, Boston College	QB
4.	Oakland	Darren McFadden, Arkansas	RB
5.	Kansas City	Glenn Dorsey, LSU	DT
6.	NY Jets	Vernon Gholston, Ohio St	DE
7.	New Orleans (from San Francisco through New England)	Sedrick Ellis, USC	DT
8.	Jacksonville (from Baltimore)	Derrick Harvey, Florida	DE
9.	Cincinnati	Keith Rivers, USC	LB
10.	New England (from New Orleans)	Jerod Mayo, Tennessee	OLB
11.	Buffalo	Leodis McKelvin, Troy	CB
12.	Denver	Ryan Clady, Boise St	OT
13.	Carolina	Jonathan Stewart, Oregon	RB
14.	Chicago	Chris Williams, Vanderbilt	OT
15.	Kansas City (from Detroit)	Branden Albert, Virginia	OG
16.	Arizona	Dominique Rodgers-Cromartie, Tennessee St	CB
17.	Detroit (from Minnesota through Kansas City)	Gosder Cherilus, Boston College	OT
18.	Baltimore (from Houston)	Joe Flacco, Delaware	QB
19.	Carolina (from Philadelphia)	Jeff Otah, Pittsburgh	OT
20.	Tampa Bay	Aqib Talib, Kansas	CB
21.	Atlanta (from Washington)	Sam Baker, USC	OT
22.	Dallas (from Cleveland)	Felix Jones, Arkansas	RB
23.	Pittsburgh	Rashard Mendenhall, Illinois	RB
24.	Tennessee	Chris Johnson, East Carolina	RB
25.	Dallas (from Seattle)	Mike Jenkins, South Florida	CB
26.	Houston (from Jacksonville through Baltimore)	Duane Brown, Virginia Tech	OT
27.	San Diego	Antoine Cason, Arizona	CB
28.	Seattle (from Dallas)	Lawrence Jackson, USC	DE
29.	San Francisco (from Indianapolis)	Kentwan Balmer, North Carolina	DE
30.	NY Jets (from Green Bay)	Dustin Keller, Purdue	TE
31.	NY Giants	Kenny Phillips, Miami (Fla.)	FS

Note: New England's 2008 first-round pick was revoked by the NFL for violating league videotaping rules.

Second Round

	Team	Selection	Position
32.	Miami	Phillip Merling, Clemson	DE
33.	St. Louis	Donnie Avery, Houston	WR
34.	Washington (from Oakland through Atlanta)	Devin Thomas, Michigan St	WR
35.	Kansas City	Brandon Flowers, Virginia Tech	CB
36.	Green Bay (from NY Jets)	Jordy Nelson, Kansas St	WR
37.	Atlanta	Curtis Lofton, Oklahoma	LB
38.	Seattle (from Baltimore)	John Carlson, Notre Dame	TE
39.	San Francisco	Chilo Rachal, USC	OG
40.	New Orleans	Tracy Porter, Indiana	CB
41.	Buffalo	James Hardy, Indiana	WR
42.	Denver	Eddie Royal, Virginia Tech	WR
43.	Minnesota (from Carolina through Philadelphia)	Tyrell Johnson, Arkansas St	FS
44.	Chicago	Matt Forte, Tulane	RB
45.	Detroit	Jordon Dizon, Colorada	LB
46.	Cincinnati	Jerome Simpson, Coastal Carolina	WR
47.	Philadelphia (from Minnesota)	Trevor Laws, Notre Dame	DT
48.	Washington (from Houston through Atlanta)	Fred Davis, USC	TE
49.	Philadelphia	DeSean Jackson, California	WR
50.	Arizona	Calais Campbell, Miami (Fla.)	DE
51.	Washington	Malcolm Kelly, Oklahoma	WR
52.	Jacksonville (from Tampa Bay)	Quentin Groves, Auburn	DE
53.	Pittsburgh	Limas Sweed, Texas	WR
54.	Tennessee	Jason Jones, Eastern Michigan	DT
55.	Baltimore (from Seattle)	Ray Rice, Rutgers	RB
56.	Green Bay (from Cleveland)	Brian Brohm, Louisville	QB
57.	Miami (from San Diego)	Chad Henne, Michigan	QB
58.	Tampa Bay (from Jacksonville)	Dexter Jackson, Appalachian St	WR
59.	Indianapolis	Mike Pollak, Arizona St	C
60.	Green Bay	Patrick Lee, Auburn	CB
61.	Dallas	Martellus Bennett, Texas A&M	TE
62.	New England	Terrence Wheatley, Colorado	CB
63.	NY Giants	Terrell Thomas, USC	CB

2007 Canadian Football League

EASTERN DIVISION

	W	L	T	Pts	PF	PA
†Toronto	11	7	0	22	440	336
*Winnipeg	10	7	1	21	439	404
*Montreal	8	10	0	16	398	433
Hamilton	3	15	0	6	315	514

WESTERN DIVISION

	W	L	T	Pts	PF	PA
†British Columbia	14	3	1	29	542	379
*Saskatchewan	12	6	0	24	530	434
*Calgary	7	10	1	15	473	527
Edmonton	5	12	1	11	399	409

†Clinched division title.

*Clinched playoff berth.

2007 Playoff Results

DIVISION SEMI-FINALS

WINNIPEG 24, Montreal 22
SASKATCHEWAN 26, Calgary 24

DIVISION FINALS

Winnipeg 19, TORONTO 9
Saskatchewan 26, BRITISH COLUMBIA 17

Home team in caps.

2007 Grey Cup Championship

November 25, 2007 at Toronto, Ontario

Saskatchewan Roughriders	0	10	6	7	23
Winnipeg Blue Bombers	3	4	7	5	19

A: 52,230.

2008 Arena Football League

AMERICAN CENTRAL DIVISION

	W	L	T	PF	PA
†Chicago	11	5	0	926	765
*Grand Rapids	6	10	0	952	968
Colorado	6	10	0	847	909
Kansas City	3	13	0	752	923

AMERICAN WESTERN DIVISION

	W	L	T	PF	PA
†San Jose	11	5	0	945	875
*Arizona	8	8	0	842	907
*Utah	6	10	0	941	959
Los Angeles	5	11	0	847	1,004

NATIONAL EASTERN DIVISION

	W	L	T	PF	PA
†Philadelphia	13	3	0	992	810
*Dallas	12	4	0	861	798
*Cleveland	9	7	0	901	895
New York	8	8	0	822	819
Columbus	3	13	0	750	909

NATIONAL SOUTHERN DIVISION

	W	L	T	PF	PA
†Georgia	10	6	0	927	848
*Orlanda	9	7	0	881	898
Tampa Bay	8	8	0	903	895
New Orleans	8	8	0	893	935

†Clinched division title.*Clinched playoff berth.

2008 AFL Playoff Results

WILD CARD ROUND

CLEVELAND 69, Orlando 66
New York 77, DALLAS 63
Grand Rapids 48, ARIZONA 41
Colorado 49, UTAH 44

DIVISIONAL ROUND

Cleveland 73, GEORGIA 70
PHILADELPHIA 49, New York 48
Grand Rapids 58, CHICAGO 41
SAN JOSE 64, Colorado 51

CONFERENCE CHAMPIONSHIPS

PHILADELPHIA 70, Cleveland 35
SAN JOSE 81, Grand Rapids 55

Home team in caps.

Arena Bowl XXII

July 27, 2008 at New Orleans

San Jose	**14**	**13**	**7**	**22–56**
Philadelphia	**14**	**23**	**9**	**13–59**

FIRST QUARTER

SJ: Wright 8 pass (Haglund kick), 11:21. **San Jose 7-0.**
Phi: Holmes 34 pass from D'Orazio (Hughes kick), 9:30. **7-7.**
SJ: Geathers 5 pass from Grieb (Haglund kick), 5:30. **San Jose 14-7.**
Phi: Jackson 34 pass from D'Orazio (Hughes kick), 2:59. **14-14.**

SECOND QUARTER

SJ: Geathers 22 pass from Grieb (Haglund kick failed), 14:54. **San Jose 20-14.**
Phi: Jackson 13 pass from D'Orazio (Hughes kick failed), 8:59. **20-20.**
Phi: Brackins 20 pass from D'Orazio (Hughes kick), 5:31. **Phi 27-20.**
Phi: D'Orazio 8 run (Highes kick), 0:54. **Phi 34-20.**
SJ: Geather 23 pass from Grieb (Haglund kick) 0:29. **Phi 34-27.**

THIRD QUARTER

Phi: Jackson 32 pass from D'Orazio (Hughes kick), 7:56. **Phi 44-27.**
Phi: Grieb safety, tackled by Orr in end zone, 3:48. **Phi 46-27.**
SJ: Geathers 12 pass from Grieb (Haglund kick), 0:00. **Phi 46-34.**

FOURTH QUARTER

Phi: Brackins 7 pass from D'Orazio (Hughes kick failed), 6:49. **Phi 52-34.**
SJ: Johnson 3 pass from Grieb (Grieb pass to Saintil for two-point conversion), 2:13. **Phi 52-42.**
Phi: Bogle 2 pass from D'Orazio (Hughes kick), 0:39. **Phi 59-42.**
SJ: Wright 26 pass from Grieb (Grieb pass failed), 0:28. **Phi 59-48.**
SJ: Geathers 14 pass from Grieb (Geathers run for two-point conversion), 0:17. **Phi 59-56.**

A: 17,244.

Season-by-Season NFL Final Standings

1920*

	W	L	T	Pct	Pts	OP
Akron Pros	8	0	3	1.000	95	7
Decatur Staleys	10	1	2	.909	67	14
Buffalo All-Americans	9	1	1	.900	74	19
Chicago Cardinals	6	2	2	.750	34	26
Rock Island Independents	6	2	2	.750	98	35
Dayton Triangles	5	2	2	.714	127	47
Rochester Jeffersons	6	3	2	.667	6	17
Canton Bulldogs	7	4	2	.636	72	44
Detroit Heralds	2	3	3	.400	6	61
Cleveland Tigers	2	4	2	.333	22	63
Chicago Tigers	2	5	1	.286	22	63
Hammond Pros	2	5	0	.286	7	98
Columbus Panhandles	2	6	2	.250	7	107
Muncie Flyers	0	1	0	.000	0	45

*no official standings kept

1921

	W	L	T	Pct	Pts	OP
Chicago Staleys	9	1	1	.900	128	53
Buffalo All-Americans	9	1	2	.900	211	29
Akron Pros	8	3	1	.727	148	31
Canton Bulldogs	5	2	3	.714	106	55
Rock Island Independents	4	2	1	.667	65	30
Evansville Crimson Giants	3	2	0	.600	89	46
Green Bay Packers	3	2	1	.600	70	55
Dayton Triangles	4	4	1	.500	96	67
Chicago Cardinals	3	3	2	.500	54	53
Rochester Jeffersons	2	3	0	.400	85	76
Cleveland Tigers	3	5	0	.375	95	58
Washington Senators	1	2	0	.333	21	43
Cincinnati Celts	1	3	0	.250	14	117
Hammond Pros	1	3	1	.250	17	45
Minneapolis Marines	1	3	0	.250	37	41
Detroit Tigers	1	5	1	.167	19	109
Columbus Panhandles	1	8	0	.111	47	222
Tonawanda Kardex	0	1	0	.000	0	45
Muncie Flyers	0	2	0	.000	0	28
Louisville Brecks	0	2	0	.000	0	27
New York Giants	0	2	0	.000	0	72

1922

	W	L	T	Pct	Pts	OP
Canton Bulldogs	10	0	2	1.000	184	15
Chicago Bears	9	3	0	.750	123	44
Chicago Cardinals	8	3	0	.727	96	50
Toledo Maroons	5	2	2	.714	94	59
Rock Island Independents	4	2	1	.667	154	27
Racine Legion	6	4	1	.600	122	56
Dayton Triangles	4	3	1	.571	80	62
Green Bay Packers	4	3	3	.571	70	54
Buffalo All-Americans	5	4	1	.556	87	41
Akron Pros	3	5	2	.375	146	95
Milwaukee Badgers	2	4	3	.333	51	71
Oorang Indians	3	6	0	.333	69	190
Minneapolis Marines	1	3	0	.250	19	40
Louisville Brecks	1	3	0	.250	13	140
Evansville Crimson Giants	0	3	0	.000	6	88
Rochester Jeffersons	0	4	1	.000	13	76
Hammond Pros	0	5	1	.000	0	69
Columbus Panhandles	0	8	0	.000	24	174

1923

	W	L	T	Pct	Pts	OP
Canton Bulldogs	11	0	1	1.000	246	19
Chicago Bears	9	2	1	.818	123	35
Green Bay Packers	7	2	1	.778	85	34
Milwaukee Badgers	7	2	3	.778	100	49
Cleveland Indians	3	1	3	.750	52	49
Chicago Cardinals	8	4	0	.667	139	37
Duluth Kelleys	4	3	0	.571	35	33
Buffalo All-Americans	5	4	3	.556	94	43
Columbus Tigers	5	4	1	.556	119	35
Racine Legion	4	4	2	.500	86	76
Toledo Maroons	3	3	2	.500	35	66
Rock Island Independents	2	3	2	.400	83	62
Minneapolis Marines	2	5	1	.286	48	80
St. Louis All-Stars	1	4	2	.200	14	32
Hammond Pros	1	5	1	.167	14	59
Dayton Triangles	1	6	1	.143	16	95
Akron Pros	1	6	0	.143	25	74
Oorang Indians	1	10	0	.091	24	235
Louisville Brecks	0	3	0	.000	0	90
Rochester Jeffersons	0	4	0	.000	6	141

1924

	W	L	T	Pct	Pts	OP
Cleveland Bulldogs	7	1	1	.875	229	60
Chicago Bears	6	1	4	.857	136	55
Frankfort Yellow Jackets	11	2	1	.846	326	109
Duluth Kelleys	5	1	0	.833	56	16
Rock Island Independents	5	2	2	.714	81	15
Green Bay Packers	7	4	0	.636	108	38
Racine Legion	4	3	3	.571	69	47
Chicago Cardinals	5	4	1	.556	90	67
Buffalo Bisons	6	5	0	.545	120	140
Columbus Tigers	4	4	0	.500	91	68
Hammond Pros	2	2	1	.500	18	45
Milwaukee Badgers	5	8	0	.385	142	188
Akron Pros	2	6	0	.250	59	132
Dayton Triangles	2	6	0	.250	45	148
Kansas City Blues	2	7	0	.222	46	124
Kenosha Maroons	0	4	1	.000	12	117
Minneapolis Marines	0	6	0	.000	14	108
Rochester Jeffersons	0	7	0	.000	14	179

1925

	W	L	T	Pct	Pts	OP
Chicago Cardinals	11	2	1	.846	230	65
Pottsville Maroons	10	2	0	.833	280	45
Detroit Panthers	8	2	2	.800	118	42
New York Giants	8	4	0	.667	122	67
Akron Pros	4	2	2	.650	65	51
Frankfort Yellow Jackets	13	7	0	.643	196	189
Chicago Bears	9	5	3	.625	158	96
Rock Island Independents	5	3	3	.615	99	58
Green Bay Packers	8	5	0	.545	151	120
Providence Steam Roller	6	5	1	.500	131	108
Canton Bulldogs	4	4	0	.385	50	73
Cleveland Bulldogs	5	8	1	.286	75	134
Kansas City Cowboys	2	5	1	.200	68	106
Hammond Pros	1	4	0	.143	23	87

Season-by-Season NFL Final Standings *(Cont.)*

1925 (Cont.)

	W	L	T	Pct	Pts	OP
Buffalo Bisons	1	6	2	.143	33	113
Duluth Kelleys	0	3	0	.000	6	25
Rochester Jeffersons	0	6	1	.000	26	91
Milwaukee Badgers	0	6	0	.000	7	191
Dayton Triangles	0	7	1	.000	3	84
Columbus Tigers	0	9	0	.000	28	124

1926

	W	L	T	Pct	Pts	OP
Frankfort Yellow Jackets	14	1	2	.765	223	43
Chicago Bears	12	1	3	.844	216	63
Pottsville Maroons	10	2	2	.714	155	29
Kansas City Cowboys	8	3	0	.727	76	54
Green Bay Packers	7	3	3	.462	144	68
Los Angeles Buccaneers	6	3	1	.600	67	57
NY Giants	8	4	1	.583	140	45
Duluth Eskimos	6	5	3	.429	114	81
Buffalo Rangers	4	4	2	.400	53	62
Chicago Cardinals	5	6	1	.417	67	86
Providence Steam Roller	5	7	1	.417	94	96
Detroit Panthers	4	6	2	.500	115	52
Hartford Blues	3	7	0	.300	57	99
Brooklyn Lions	3	8	0	.273	60	150
Milwaukee Badgers	2	7	0	.222	41	66
Akron Indians	1	4	3	.125	23	89
Dayton Triangles	1	4	1	.167	15	82
Racine Tornadoes	1	4	0	.200	8	92
Columbus Tigers	1	6	0	.143	26	93
Canton Bulldogs	1	9	3	.077	46	172
Hammond Pros	0	4	0	.000	3	56
Louisville Colonels	0	4	0	.000	0	108

1927

	W	L	T	Pct	Pts	OP
NY Giants	11	1	1	.917	197	20
Green Bay Packers	7	2	1	.778	113	43
Chicago Bears	9	3	2	.750	149	98
Cleveland Bulldogs	8	4	1	.667	209	107
Providence Steam Roller	8	5	1	.615	105	88
New York Yankees	7	8	1	.467	142	174
Frankfort Yellow Jackets	6	9	3	.400	152	166
Pottsville Maroons	5	8	0	.385	80	163
Chicago Cardinals	3	7	1	.300	69	134
Dayton Triangles	1	6	1	.143	15	57
Duluth Eskimos	1	8	0	.111	68	134
Buffalo Bisons	0	5	0	.000	8	123

1928

	W	L	T	Pct	Pts	OP
Providence Steam Roller	8	1	1	.889	128	36
Frankfort Yellow Jackets	11	3	1	.786	169	84
Detroit Wolverines	7	2	1	.778	189	76
Green Bay Packers	6	4	3	.600	120	92
Chicago Bears	7	5	1	.583	182	85
NY Giants	4	7	2	.364	79	137
NY Yankees	4	8	1	.333	104	179
Pottsville Maroons	2	8	0	.200	74	134
Chicago Cardinals	1	5	0	.167	7	107
Dayton Triangles	0	7	0	.000	9	131

1929

	W	L	T	Pct	Pts	OP
Green Bay Packers	12	0	1	1.000	198	22
NY Giants	13	1	1	.929	312	86
Frankfort Yellow Jackets	10	4	5	.714	139	128
Chicago Cardinals	6	6	1	.500	154	83
Boston Bulldogs	4	4	0	.500	98	73
Staten Island Stapletons	3	6	3	.429	89	62
Providence Steam Roller	4	5	2	.400	107	117
Orange Tornadoes	3	6	4	.375	32	90
Chicago Bears	4	9	2	.308	119	227
Buffalo Bisons	1	7	1	.125	48	142
Minneapolis Red Jackets	1	9	0	.100	48	185
Dayton Triangles	0	6	0	.000	7	136

1930

	W	L	T	Pct	Pts	OP
Green Bay Packers	10	3	1	.769	234	111
NY Giants	13	4	0	.765	308	98
Chicago Bears	9	4	1	.692	169	71
Brooklyn Dodgers	7	4	1	.636	154	59
Providence Steam Roller	6	4	1	.600	90	125
Staten Island Stapletons	5	5	2	.500	95	112
Chicago Cardinals	5	6	2	.455	128	132
Portsmouth Spartans	5	6	3	.455	176	161
Frankfort Yellow Jackets	4	13	1	.222	113	321
Minneapolis Red Jackets	1	7	1	.125	27	165
Newark Tornadoes	1	10	1	.091	51	190

1931

	W	L	T	Pct	Pts	OP
Green Bay Packers	12	2	0	.857	318	94
Portsmouth Spartans	11	3	0	.786	161	77
Chicago Bears	8	5	0	.615	145	92
Chicago Cardinals	5	4	0	.556	120	128
NY Giants	7	6	1	.538	161	127
Providence Steam Roller	4	4	3	.500	78	127
Staten Island Stapletons	4	6	1	.400	79	118
Cleveland Indians	2	8	0	.200	45	137
Brooklyn Dodgers	2	12	0	.143	64	199
Frankfort Yellow Jackets	1	6	1	.143	13	85

1932

	W	L	T	Pct	Pts	OP
Chicago Bears	7	1	6	.875	160	44
Green Bay Packers	10	3	1	.769	152	63
Portsmouth Spartans	6	2	4	.750	116	71
Boston Braves	4	4	2	.500	55	79
NY Giants	4	6	2	.400	93	113
Brooklyn Dodgers	3	9	0	.250	63	131
Chiago Cardinals	2	6	2	.250	72	114
Staten Island Stapletons	2	7	3	.222	77	173

1933

EAST	W	L	T	Pct	Pts	OP
NY Giants	11	3	0	.786	244	101
Brooklyn Dodgers	5	4	1	.556	93	54
Boston Redskins	5	5	2	.500	103	97
Philadelphia Eagles	3	5	1	.375	77	158
Pittsburgh Pirates	3	6	2	.333	67	208

Season-by-Season NFL Final Standings *(Cont.)*

1933 (Cont.)

WEST	W	L	T	Pct	Pts	OP
Chicago Bears	10	2	1	.833	133	82
Portsmouth Spartans	6	5	0	.545	128	87
Green Bay Packers	5	7	1	.417	170	107
Cincinnati Reds	3	6	1	.333	38	110
Chicago Cardinals	1	9	1	.100	52	101

1934

EAST	W	L	T	Pct	Pts	OP
NY Giants	8	5	0	.615	147	107
Boston Redskins	6	6	0	.500	107	93
Brooklyn Dodgers	4	7	0	.364	60	153
Philadelphia Eagles	4	7	0	.364	127	85
Pittsburgh Pirates	2	10	0	.167	51	206

WEST	W	L	T	Pct	Pts	OP
Chicago Bears	13	0	0	1.000	286	86
Detroit Lions	10	3	0	.769	238	59
Green Bay Packers	7	6	0	.538	156	112
Chicago Cardinals	5	6	0	.455	80	84
St. Louis Gunners	1	2	0	.333	27	61
Cincinnati Reds	0	8	0	.000	10	243

1935

EAST	W	L	T	Pct	Pts	OP
NY Giants	9	3	0	.750	180	96
Brooklyn Dodgers	5	6	1	.455	90	141
Pittsburgh Pirates	4	8	0	.333	99	209
Boston Redskins	2	8	1	.200	65	122
Philadelphia Eagles	2	9	0	.182	60	179

WEST	W	L	T	Pct	Pts	OP
Detroit Lions	7	3	2	.700	191	111
Green Bay Packers	8	4	0	.667	181	96
Chicago Bears	6	4	2	.600	192	106
Chicago Cardinals	6	4	2	.600	99	97

1936

EAST	W	L	T	Pct	Pts	OP
Boston Redskins	7	5	0	.583	149	110
Pittsburgh Pirates	6	6	0	.500	98	187
NY Giants	5	6	1	.455	115	163
Brooklyn Dodgers	3	8	1	.273	92	161
Philadelphia Eagles	1	11	0	.083	51	206

WEST	W	L	T	Pct	Pts	OP
Green Bay	10	1	1	.909	248	118
Chicago Bears	9	3	0	.750	222	94
Detroit Lions	8	4	0	.667	235	102
Chicago Cardinals	3	8	1	.273	74	143

1937

EAST	W	L	T	Pct	Pts	OP
Washington Redskins	8	3	0	.727	195	120
NY Giants	6	3	2	.667	128	109
Pittsburgh Pirates	4	7	0	.364	122	145
Brooklyn Dodgers	3	7	1	.300	82	174
Philadelphia Eagles	2	8	1	.200	86	177

WEST	W	L	T	Pct	Pts	OP
Chicago Bears	9	1	1	.900	201	100
Green Bay Packers	7	4	0	.636	220	122
Detroit Lions	7	4	0	.636	180	105
Chicago Cardinals	5	5	1	.500	135	165
Cleveland Rams	1	10	0	.091	75	207

1938

EAST	W	L	T	Pct	Pts	OP
NY Giants	8	2	1	.800	194	79
Washington Redskins	6	3	2	.667	148	154
Brooklyn Dodgers	4	4	3	.500	131	161
Philadelphia Eagles	5	6	0	.455	154	164
Pittsburgh Pirates	2	9	0	.182	79	169

WEST	W	L	T	Pct	Pts	OP
Green Bay Packers	8	3	0	.727	223	118
Detroit Lions	7	4	0	.636	119	108
Chicago Bears	6	5	0	.545	194	148
Cleveland Rams	4	7	0	.364	131	215
Chicago Cardinals	2	9	0	.182	111	168

1939

EAST	W	L	T	Pct	Pts	OP
NY Giants	9	1	1	.168	168	85
Washington Redskins	8	2	1	.242	242	94
Brooklyn Dodgers	4	6	1	.108	108	219
Philadelphia Eagles	1	9	1	.105	105	200
Pittsburgh Pirates	1	9	1	.114	114	216

WEST	W	L	T	Pct	Pts	OP
Green Bay Packers	9	2	0	.818	233	153
Chicago Bears	8	3	0	.727	298	157
Detroit Lions	6	5	0	.545	145	150
Cleveland Rams	5	5	1	.195	195	164
Chicago Cardinals	1	10	0	.091	84	254

1940

EAST	W	L	T	Pct	Pts	OP
Washington Redskins	9	2	0	.818	245	142
Brooklyn Dodgers	8	2	0	.800	179	110
NY Giants	6	4	1	.545	131	133
Pittsburgh Pirates	2	7	2	.182	67	174
Philadelphia Eagles	1	10	0	.091	121	200

WEST	W	L	T	Pct	Pts	OP
Chicago Bears	8	3	0	.727	238	152
Green Bay Packers	6	4	1	.600	238	155
Detroit Lions	5	5	1	.500	120	177
Cleveland Rams	4	6	1	.400	181	191
Chicago Cardinals	2	7	2	.222	139	222

Season-by-Season NFL Final Standings *(Cont.)*

1941

EAST	W	L	T	Pct	Pts	OP
NY Giants	8	3	0	.727	238	114
Brooklyn Dodgers	7	4	0	.636	158	127
Washington	6	5	0	.545	176	174
Philadelphia	2	8	1	.200	119	218
Pittsburgh Steelers	1	9	1	.100	103	276

WEST	W	L	T	Pct	Pts	OP
Green Bay	10	1	0	.909	258	120
Chicago Bears	10	1	0	.909	396	147
Detroit	4	6	1	.400	121	195
Chicago Cardinals	3	7	1	.300	127	197
Cleveland Rams	2	9	0	.182	116	244

1942

EAST	W	L	T	Pct	Pts	OP
Washington	10	1	0	.909	227	102
Pittsburgh Steelers	7	4	0	.636	167	119
NY Giants	5	5	1	.500	155	139
Brooklyn Dodgers	3	8	0	.273	100	168
Philadelphia	2	9	0	.182	134	239

WEST	W	L	T	Pct	Pts	OP
Chicago Bears	11	0	0	1.000	376	84
Green Bay	8	2	1	.800	300	215
Cleveland Rams	5	6	0	.455	150	207
Chicago Cardinals	3	8	0	.273	98	209
Detroit	0	11	0	.000	38	263

1943

EAST	W	L	T	Pct	Pts	OP
Washington	6	3	1	.667	229	137
NY Giants	6	3	1	.667	197	170
Phi/Pitt Eagles/Steelers	5	4	1	.556	225	230
Brooklyn Dodgers	2	8	0	.200	65	234

WEST	W	L	T	Pct	Pts	OP
Chicago Bears	8	1	1	.889	303	157
Green Bay	7	2	1	.778	264	172
Detroit	3	6	1	.333	178	218
Chicago Cardinals	0	10	0	.000	95	238

1944

EAST	W	L	T	Pct	Pts	OP
NY Giants	8	1	1	.889	206	75
Philadelphia	7	1	2	.875	267	131
Washington	6	3	1	.667	169	180
Boston Yanks	2	8	0	.200	82	233
Brooklyn Tigers	0	10	0	.000	69	166

WEST	W	L	T	Pct	Pts	OP
Green Bay	8	2	0	.800	238	141
Chicago Bears	6	3	1	.667	258	172
Detroit	6	3	1	.667	216	151
Cleveland Rams	4	6	0	.400	188	224
Chi/Pitt Cards/Steelers	0	10	0	.000	116	336

1945

EAST	W	L	T	Pct	Pts	OP
Washington	8	2	0	.800	209	121
Philadelphia	7	3	0	.700	272	133
NY Giants	3	6	1	.333	179	198
Bos/Bkn Yanks/Tigers	3	6	1	.333	123	211
Pittsburgh	2	8	0	.200	79	220

WEST	W	L	T	Pct	Pts	OP
Cleveland Rams	9	1	0	.900	244	136
Detroit	7	3	0	.700	195	194
Green Bay	6	4	0	.600	258	173
Chicago Bears	3	7	0	.300	192	235
Chicago Cardinals	1	9	0	.100	98	228

1946

EAST	W	L	T	Pct	Pts	OP
NY Giants	7	3	1	.700	236	162
Philadelphia	6	5	0	.545	231	220
Washington	5	5	1	.500	171	191
Pittsburgh	5	5	1	.500	136	117
Boston Yanks	2	8	1	.200	189	273

WEST	W	L	T	Pct	Pts	OP
Chicago Bears	8	2	1	.800	289	193
Los Angeles Rams	6	4	1	.600	277	257
Chicago Cardinals	6	5	0	.545	260	198
Green Bay	6	5	0	.545	148	158
Detroit	1	10	0	.091	142	310

1947

EAST	W	L	T	Pct	Pts	OP
Pittsburgh	8	4	0	.667	240	259
Philadelphia	8	4	0	.667	308	242
Boston Yanks	4	7	1	.364	168	256
Washington	4	8	0	.333	295	367
NY Giants	2	8	2	.200	190	309

WEST	W	L	T	Pct	Pts	OP
Chicago Cardinals	9	3	0	.750	306	231
Chicago Bears	8	4	0	.667	363	241
Green Bay	6	5	1	.542	274	210
LA Rams	6	6	0	.500	259	214
Detroit Lions	3	9	0	.250	231	305

1948

EAST	W	L	T	Pct	Pts	OP
Philadelphia	9	2	1	.818	376	156
Washington	7	5	0	.583	291	287
Pittsburgh	4	8	0	.333	200	243
NY Giants	4	8	0	.333	297	388
Boston Yanks	3	9	0	.250	174	372

WEST	W	L	T	Pct	Pts	OP
Chicago Cardinals	11	1	0	.917	395	226
Chicago Bears	10	2	0	.833	375	151
LA Rams	6	5	1	.545	327	269
Green Bay	3	9	0	.250	154	290
Detroit Lions	2	10	0	.167	200	407

1949

EAST	W	L	T	Pct	Pts	OP
Philadelphia	11	1	0	.917	364	134
Pittsburgh	6	5	1	.545	224	214
NY Giants	6	6	0	.500	287	298
Washington	4	7	1	.364	268	339
New York Bulldogs	1	10	1	.091	153	368

WEST	W	L	T	Pct	Pts	OP
LA Rams	8	2	2	.800	360	239
Chicago Bears	9	3	0	.750	332	218
Chicago Cardinals	6	5	1	.545	360	301
Detroit Lions	4	8	0	.333	237	259
Green Bay	2	10	0	.167	114	329

1950

EAST	W	L	T	Pct	Pts	OP
Cleveland Browns	10	2	0	.833	310	144
NY Giants	10	2	0	.833	268	150
Philadelphia	6	6	0	.500	254	141
Pittsburgh	6	6	0	.500	180	195
Chicago Cardinals	5	7	0	.417	233	287
Washington	3	9	0	.250	232	326

WEST	W	L	T	Pct	Pts	OP
Chicago Bears	9	3	0	.750	279	207
LA Rams	9	3	0	.750	466	309
New York Yanks	7	5	0	.583	366	367
Detroit	6	6	0	.500	321	285
San Francisco 49ers	3	9	0	.250	213	300
Green Bay	3	9	0	.250	244	406
Baltimore Colts	1	11	0	.067	213	462

1951

AMERICAN	W	L	T	Pct	Pts	OP
Cleveland	11	1	0	.917	331	152
NY Giants	9	2	1	.818	254	161
Washington	5	7	0	.417	183	296
Pittsburgh	4	7	1	.364	183	235
Philadelphia	4	8	0	.333	234	264
Chicago Cardinals	3	9	0	.250	210	287

NATIONAL	W	L	T	Pct	Pts	OP
LA Rams	8	4	0	.667	392	261
Detroit Lions	7	4	1	.636	336	259
San Francisco 49ers	7	4	1	.636	255	205
Chicago Bears	7	5	0	.583	286	282
Green Bay	3	9	0	.250	254	375
New York Yanks	1	9	2	.100	241	382

1952

AMERICAN	W	L	T	Pct	Pts	OP
Cleveland	8	4	0	.667	310	213
Philadelphia	7	5	0	.583	252	271
NY Giants	7	5	0	.583	234	231
Pittsburgh	5	7	0	.417	300	273
Washington	4	8	0	.333	240	287
Chicago Cardinals	4	8	0	.333	172	221

NATIONAL	W	L	T	Pct	Pts	OP
Detroit	9	3	0	.750	344	192
LA Rams	9	3	0	.750	349	234
San Francisco	7	5	0	.583	285	221
Green Bay	6	6	0	.500	295	312
Chicago Bears	5	7	0	.417	245	326
Dallas Texans	1	11	0	.083	182	427

1953

EAST	W	L	T	Pct	Pts	OP
Cleveland	11	1	0	.917	348	162
Philadelphia	7	4	1	.636	352	215
Washington	6	5	1	.545	208	215
Pittsburgh	5	7	0	.417	211	272
NY Giants	4	8	0	.333	188	277
Chicago Cardinals	1	10	1	.091	190	337

WEST	W	L	T	Pct	Pts	OP
Detroit	10	2	0	.833	271	205
San Francisco	9	3	0	.750	372	237
LA Rams	8	3	1	.727	366	236
Chicago Bears	3	8	1	.273	218	262
Baltimore Colts	3	9	0	.250	182	350
Green Bay	2	9	1	.182	200	338

1954

EAST	W	L	T	Pct	Pts	OP
Cleveland	9	3	0	.750	336	162
Philadelphia	7	4	1	.636	284	230
NY Giants	7	5	0	.583	293	184
Pittsburgh	5	7	0	.417	219	263
Washington	3	9	0	.250	207	432
Chicago Cardinals	2	10	0	.167	183	347

WEST	W	L	T	Pct	Pts	OP
Detroit	9	2	1	.818	337	189
Chicago Bears	8	4	0	.667	301	279
San Francisco	7	4	1	.636	313	251
LA Rams	6	5	1	.545	314	285
Green Bay	4	8	0	.333	234	251
Baltimore	3	9	0	.250	131	279

1955

EAST	W	L	T	Pct	Pts	OP
Cleveland	9	2	1	.818	349	218
Washington	8	4	0	.667	246	222
NY Giants	6	5	1	.545	267	223
Philadelphia	4	7	1	.364	248	231
Chicago Cardinals	4	7	1	.364	224	252
Pittsburgh	4	8	0	.333	195	285

WEST	W	L	T	Pct	Pts	OP
LA Rams	8	3	1	.727	260	231
Chicago Bears	8	4	0	.667	294	251
Green Bay	6	6	0	.500	258	276
Baltimore	5	6	1	.455	214	239
San Francisco	4	8	0	.333	216	298
Detroit	3	9	0	.250	230	275

1956

EAST	W	L	T	Pct	Pts	OP
NY Giants	8	3	1	.727	264	197
Chicago Cardinals	7	5	0	.583	240	182
Washington	6	6	0	.500	183	225
Pittsburgh	5	7	0	.417	217	250
Cleveland	5	7	0	.417	167	177
Philadelphia	3	8	1	.273	143	215

WEST	W	L	T	Pct	Pts	OP
Chicago Bears	9	2	1	.818	269	169
Detroit	9	3	0	.750	300	188
San Francisco	5	6	1	.455	233	284
Baltimore	5	7	0	.417	270	322
Green Bay	4	8	0	.333	264	342
LA Rams	4	8	0	.333	291	307

1957

EAST	W	L	T	Pct	Pts	OP
Cleveland	9	2	1	.818	269	169
NY Giants	7	5	0	.583	251	211
Pittsburgh	6	6	0	.500	155	178
Washington	5	6	1	.455	251	230
Philadelphia	4	8	0	.333	173	224
Chicago Cardinals	3	9	0	.250	200	299

WEST	W	L	T	Pct	Pts	OP
San Francisco	8	4	0	.667	260	264
Detroit	8	4	0	.667	251	231
Baltimore	7	5	0	.583	303	235
LA Rams	6	6	0	.500	307	278
Chicago Bears	5	7	0	.417	203	211
Green Bay	3	9	0	.250	218	311

1958

EAST	W	L	T	Pct	Pts	OP
Cleveland	9	3	0	.750	302	217
NY Giants	9	3	0	.750	246	183
Pittsburgh	7	4	1	.636	261	230
Washington	4	7	1	.364	214	268
Chicago Cardinals	2	9	1	.182	261	356
Philadelphia	2	9	1	.182	235	306

WEST	W	L	T	Pct	Pts	OP
Baltimore	9	3	0	.750	381	203
LA Rams	8	4	0	.667	344	278
Chicago Bears	8	4	0	.667	298	230
San Francisco	6	6	0	.500	257	324
Detroit	4	7	1	.364	261	276
Green Bay	1	10	1	.091	193	382

1959

EAST	W	L	T	Pct	Pts	OP
NY Giants	10	2	0	.833	284	167
Philadelphia	7	5	0	.583	268	278
Cleveland	7	5	0	.583	270	214
Pittsburgh	6	5	1	.545	257	216
Washington	3	9	0	.250	185	350
Chicago Cardinals	2	10	0	.167	231	324

WEST	W	L	T	Pct	Pts	OP
Baltimore	9	3	0	.750	374	251
Chicago Bears	8	4	0	.667	246	196
Green Bay	7	5	0	.583	248	240
San Francisco	7	5	0	.583	255	237
Detroit	3	8	1	.273	203	275
LA Rams	2	10	0	.167	242	315

1960

NFL EAST	W	L	T	Pct	Pts	OP
Philadelphia	10	2	0	.833	321	246
Cleveland	8	3	1	.727	362	217
NY Giants	6	4	2	.600	271	261
St. Louis Cardinals	6	5	1	.545	288	230
Pittsburgh	5	6	1	.455	240	275
Washington	1	9	2	.100	178	309

NFL WEST	W	L	T	Pct	Pts	OP
Green Bay	8	4	0	.667	332	209
Detroit	7	5	0	.583	239	212
San Francisco	7	5	0	.583	208	205
Baltimore	6	6	0	.500	288	234
Chicago Bears	5	6	1	.455	194	299
LA Rams	4	7	1	.364	265	297
Dallas Cowboys	0	11	1	.000	177	369

AFL EAST	W	L	T	Pct	Pts	OP
Houston Oilers	10	4	0	.714	379	285
NY Titans	7	7	0	.500	382	399
Buffalo Bills	5	8	1	.385	296	303
Boston Patriots	5	9	0	.357	286	349

AFL WEST	W	L	T	Pct	Pts	OP
Los Angeles Chargers	10	4	0	.714	373	336
Dallas Texans	8	6	0	.571	361	253
Oakland Raiders	6	8	0	.429	319	388
Denver Broncos	4	9	1	.308	309	393

1961

NFL EAST	W	L	T	Pct	Pts	OP
NY Giants	10	3	1	.769	368	220
Philadelphia	10	4	0	.714	361	297
Cleveland	8	5	1	.615	319	270
St. Louis Cardinals	7	7	0	.500	279	267
Pittsburgh	6	8	0	.429	295	287
Dallas Cowboys	4	9	1	.308	236	380
Washington	1	12	1	.077	174	392

NFL WEST	W	L	T	Pct	Pts	OP
Green Bay	11	3	0	.786	391	223
Detroit	8	5	1	.615	270	258
Baltimore	8	6	0	.571	302	307
Chicago	8	6	0	.571	326	302
San Francisco	7	6	1	.538	346	272
LA Rams	4	10	0	.286	263	407
Minnesota Vikings	3	11	0	.214	285	407

AFL EAST	W	L	T	Pct	Pts	OP
Houston Oilers	10	3	1	.769	513	242
Boston Patriots	9	4	1	.692	413	313
New York Titans	7	7	0	.500	301	390
Buffalo Bills	6	8	0	.429	294	342

AFL WEST	W	L	T	Pct	Pts	OP
San Diego Chargers	12	2	0	.857	396	219
Dallas Texans	6	8	0	.429	334	343
Denver	3	11	0	.214	251	432
Oakland	2	12	0	.143	237	458

Season-by-Season NFL Final Standings *(Cont.)*

1962

NFL EAST	W	L	T	Pct	Pts	OP
NY Giants	12	2	0	.857	398	283
Pittsburgh	9	5	0	.642	312	363
Cleveland	7	6	1	.538	291	257
Washington	5	7	2	.417	305	376
Dallas Cowboys	5	8	1	.385	398	402
St. Louis Cardinals	4	9	1	.308	287	361
Philadelphia	3	10	1	.231	282	356

NFL WEST	W	L	T	Pct	Pts	OP
Green Bay	13	1	0	.929	415	148
Detroit	11	3	0	.786	315	177
Chicago	9	5	0	.643	321	287
Baltimore	7	7	0	.500	293	288
San Francisco	6	8	0	.429	282	331
Minnesota	2	11	1	.154	254	410
LA Rams	1	12	1	.077	220	334

AFL EAST	W	L	T	Pct	Pts	OP
Houston	11	3	0	.786	387	270
Boston	9	4	1	.692	346	295
Buffalo	7	6	1	.538	309	272
NY Titans	5	9	0	.357	278	423

AFL WEST	W	L	T	Pct	Pts	OP
Dallas Texans	11	3	0	.786	389	233
Denver	6	7	0	.462	323	313
San Diego	4	9	0	.308	293	362
Oakland	1	13	0	.071	213	370

1963

NFL EAST	W	L	T	Pct	Pts	OP
NY Giants	11	3	0	.786	448	280
Cleveland	10	4	0	.714	343	262
St. Louis	9	5	0	.643	341	283
Pittsburgh	7	4	3	.636	321	295
Dallas Cowboys	4	10	0	.286	305	378
Washington	3	11	0	.214	279	398
Philadelphia	2	10	2	.214	242	381

NFL WEST	W	L	T	Pct	Pts	OP
Chicago	11	1	2	.917	301	144
Green Bay	11	2	1	.846	369	206
Baltimore	8	6	0	.571	316	285
Minnesota	5	8	1	.385	309	390
Detroit	5	8	1	.385	32	265
LA Rams	5	9	0	.357	210	350
San Francisco	2	12	0	.143	198	391

AFL EAST	W	L	T	Pct	Pts	OP
Boston	7	6	1	.538	327	257
Buffalo	7	6	1	.538	304	291
Houston	6	8	0	.429	302	372
NY Jets	5	8	1	.385	249	399

AFL WEST	W	L	T	Pct	Pts	OP
San Diego	11	3	0	.786	399	255
Oakland	10	4	0	.714	363	282
Kansas City Chiefs	5	7	2	.417	347	263
Denver	2	11	1	.154	301	473

1964

NFL EAST	W	L	T	Pct	Pts	OP
Cleveland	10	3	1	.769	415	293
St. Louis	9	3	2	.750	357	331
Philadelphia	6	8	0	.429	312	313
Washington	6	8	0	.429	307	305
Dallas	5	8	1	.385	250	289
Pittsburgh	5	9	0	.357	253	315
NY Giants	2	10	2	.167	241	399

NFL WEST	W	L	T	Pct	Pts	OP
Baltimore	12	2	0	.857	428	225
Green Bay	8	5	1	.615	342	245
Minnesota	8	5	1	.615	355	296
Detroit	7	5	2	.583	280	260
LA Rams	5	7	2	.417	283	339
Chicago	5	9	0	.357	260	379
San Francisco	4	10	0	.286	236	330

AFL EAST	W	L	T	Pct	Pts	OP
Buffalo	12	2	0	.857	400	242
Boston	10	3	1	.769	365	297
NY Jets	5	8	1	.385	278	315
Houston	4	10	0	.286	310	355

AFL WEST	W	L	T	Pct	Pts	OP
San Diego	8	5	1	.615	341	300
Kansas City Chiefs	7	7	0	.500	366	306
Oakland	5	7	2	.417	303	350
Denver	2	11	1	.154	240	438

1965

NFL EAST	W	L	T	Pct	Pts	OP
Cleveland	11	3	0	.786	363	325
NY Giants	7	7	0	.500	270	338
Dallas	7	7	0	.500	325	280
Washington	6	8	0	.429	257	301
St. Louis	5	9	0	.357	296	309
Philadelphia	5	9	0	.357	363	359
Pittsburgh	2	12	0	.143	202	397

NFL WEST	W	L	T	Pct	Pts	OP
Green Bay	10	3	1	.769	316	224
Baltimore	9	3	1	.769	389	263
Chicago	9	5	0	.643	409	275
San Francisco	7	6	1	.538	421	402
Minnesota	7	6	0	.500	383	362
Detroit	6	7	1	.462	257	295
LA Rams	4	10	0	.286	269	328

AFL EAST	W	L	T	Pct	Pts	OP
Buffalo	10	3	1	.769	313	226
NY Jets	5	8	1	.385	285	303
Boston	4	8	2	.333	244	302
Houston	4	10	0	.286	298	429

AFL WEST	W	L	T	Pct	Pts	OP
San Diego	9	2	3	.818	340	227
Oakland	8	5	1	.615	298	239
Kansas City	7	5	2	.583	322	285
Denver	4	10	0	.286	303	392

Season-by-Season NFL Final Standings *(Cont.)*

1966

NFL EAST	W	L	T	Pct	Pts	OP
Dallas	10	3	1	.769	445	239
Cleveland	9	5	0	.643	403	259
Philadelphia	9	5	0	.643	326	340
St. Louis	8	5	1	.625	264	265
Washington	7	7	0	.500	351	355
Pittsburgh	5	8	1	.385	316	347
Atlanta Falcons	3	11	0	.214	204	437
NY Giants	1	12	1	.077	263	501

NFL WEST	W	L	T	Pct	Pts	OP
Green Bay	12	2	0	.857	335	163
Baltimore	9	5	0	.643	314	226
LA Rams	8	6	0	.571	289	212
San Francisco	6	6	2	.500	320	325
Chicago	5	7	2	.417	234	272
Detroit	4	9	1	.308	206	317
Minnesota	4	9	1	.308	292	304

AFL EAST	W	L	T	Pct	Pts	OP
Buffalo	9	4	1	.692	358	255
Boston	8	4	2	.677	315	283
NY Jets	6	6	2	.500	322	312
Houston	3	11	0	.214	335	396
Miami Dolphins	3	11	0	.214	213	362

AFL WEST	W	L	T	Pct	Pts	OP
Kansas City	11	2	1	.846	448	276
Oakland	8	5	1	.615	315	288
San Diego	7	6	1	.538	335	284
Denver	4	10	0	.286	196	381

1967

NFL CAPITOL	W	L	T	Pct	Pts	OP
Dallas	9	5	0	.643	342	268
Philadelphia	6	7	1	.462	351	409
Washington	5	6	3	.455	347	353
New Orleans Saints	3	11	0	.214	233	379

NFL CENTURY	W	L	T	Pct	Pts	OP
Cleveland	9	5	0	.643	334	297
NY Giants	7	7	0	.500	369	379
St. Louis	6	7	1	.462	333	356
Pittsburgh	4	9	1	.308	281	320

NFL COASTAL	W	L	T	Pct	Pts	OP
LA Rams	11	1	2	.917	398	196
Baltimore	11	1	2	.917	394	198
San Francisco	7	7	0	.500	273	337
Atlanta	1	12	1	.077	175	422

NFL CENTRAL	W	L	T	Pct	Pts	OP
Green Bay	9	4	1	.692	332	209
Chicago	7	6	1	.538	239	218
Detroit	5	7	2	.417	260	259
Minnesota	3	8	3	.273	233	294

AFL EAST	W	L	T	Pct	Pts	OP
Houston	9	4	1	.692	258	199
NY Jets	8	5	1	.615	371	329
Buffalo	4	10	0	.286	237	285
Miami	4	10	0	.286	219	407
Boston	3	10	1	.231	280	389

1967 (Cont.)

AFL WEST	W	L	T	Pct	Pts	OP
Oakland	13	1	0	.929	468	233
Kansas City	9	5	0	.643	408	254
San Diego	8	5	1	.615	360	352
Denver	3	11	0	.214	256	409

1968

NFL CAPITOL	W	L	T	Pct	Pts	OP
Dallas	12	2	0	.857	431	186
NY Giants	7	7	0	.500	294	325
Washington	5	9	0	.357	249	358
Philadelphia	2	12	0	.143	202	351

NFL CENTURY	W	L	T	Pct	Pts	OP
Cleveland	10	4	0	.714	394	273
St. Louis	9	4	1	.692	325	289
New Orleans	4	9	1	.308	246	327
Pittsburgh	2	11	1	.154	244	397

NFL COASTAL	W	L	T	Pct	Pts	OP
Baltimore	13	1	0	.929	402	144
LA Rams	10	3	1	.769	312	200
San Francisco	7	6	1	.538	303	310
Atlanta	2	12	0	.143	202	351

NFL CENTRAL	W	L	T	Pct	Pts	OP
Minnesota	8	6	0	.571	282	242
Chicago	7	7	0	.500	250	333
Green Bay	6	7	1	.462	281	227
Detroit	4	8	2	.333	207	241

AFL EAST	W	L	T	Pct	Pts	OP
NY Jets	11	3	0	.786	419	280
Houston	7	7	0	.500	303	248
Miami	5	8	1	.385	276	355
Boston	4	10	0	.286	229	406
Buffalo	1	12	1	.077	199	367

AFL WEST	W	L	T	Pct	Pts	OP
Oakland	12	2	0	.857	453	233
Kansas City	12	2	0	.857	371	170
San Diego	9	5	0	.643	382	310
Denver	5	9	0	.357	255	404
Cincinnati Bengals	3	11	0	.214	215	329

1969

NFL CAPITOL	W	L	T	Pct	Pts	OP
Dallas	11	2	1	.846	369	223
Washington	7	5	2	.583	307	319
New Orleans	5	9	0	.357	311	393
Philadelphia	4	9	1	.308	279	377

NFL CENTURY	W	L	T	Pct	Pts	OP
Cleveland	10	3	1	.769	351	300
NY Giants	6	8	0	.429	264	298
St. Louis	4	9	1	.308	314	389
Pittsburgh	1	13	0	.071	218	404

NFL COASTAL	W	L	T	Pct	Pts	OP
LA Rams	11	3	0	.786	320	243
Baltimore	7	5	2	.615	307	319
Atlanta	6	8	0	.429	276	268
San Francisco	4	8	2	.333	277	319

1969 (Cont.)

NFL CENTRAL	W	L	T	Pct	Pts	OP
Minnesota	12	2	0	.857	379	133
Detroit	9	4	1	.692	259	188
Green Bay	8	6	0	.571	269	221
Chicago	1	13	0	.071	210	339

AFL EAST	W	L	T	Pct	Pts	OP
NY Jets	10	4	0	.714	353	269
Houston	6	6	2	.500	278	279
Buffalo	4	10	0	.286	230	359
Boston	4	10	0	.286	266	316
Miami	3	10	1	.231	233	332

AFL WEST	W	L	T	Pct	Pts	OP
Oakland	12	1	1	.923	377	242
Kansas City	11	3	0	.786	359	177
San Diego	8	6	0	.571	288	276
Denver	5	8	1	.385	297	344
Cincinnati	4	9	1	.308	280	367

1970

AFC EAST	W	L	T	Pct	Pts	OP
Baltimore	11	2	1	.846	321	234
Miami	10	4	0	.714	297	228
NY Jets	4	10	0	.286	255	286
Buffalo	3	10	1	.231	204	337
Boston	2	12	0	.143	149	361

AFC CENTRAL	W	L	T	Pct	Pts	OP
Cincinnati	8	6	0	.571	312	255
Cleveland	7	7	0	.500	286	265
Pittsburgh	5	9	0	.357	210	272
Houston	3	10	1	.231	217	352

AFC WEST	W	L	T	Pct	Pts	OP
Oakland	8	4	2	.667	300	293
Kansas City	7	5	2	.583	272	244
San Diego	5	6	3	.455	282	278
Denver	5	8	1	.385	253	264

NFC EAST	W	L	T	Pct	Pts	OP
Dallas	10	4	0	.714	299	221
NY Giants	9	5	0	.643	301	270
St. Louis	8	5	1	.615	325	228
Washington	6	8	0	.429	297	314
Philadelphia	3	10	1	.231	241	332

NFC CENTRAL	W	L	T	Pct	Pts	OP
Minnesota	12	2	0	.857	335	143
Detroit	10	4	0	.714	347	202
Green Bay	6	8	0	.429	196	293
Chicago	6	8	0	.429	256	261

NFC WEST	W	L	T	Pct	Pts	OP
San Francisco	10	3	1	.769	352	267
LA Rams	9	4	1	.692	325	202
Atlanta	4	8	2	.333	206	261
New Orleans	2	11	1	.154	172	347

1971

AFC EAST	W	L	T	Pct	Pts	OP
Miami	10	3	1	.769	315	174
Baltimore	10	4	0	.714	313	140
New England Patriots	6	8	0	.429	238	325
NY Jets	6	8	0	.429	212	299
Buffalo	1	13	0	.071	184	394

AFC CENTRAL	W	L	T	Pct	Pts	OP
Cleveland	9	5	0	.643	285	273
Pittsburgh	6	8	0	.429	246	292
Houston	4	9	1	.308	251	330
Cincinnati	4	10	0	.286	284	265

AFC WEST	W	L	T	Pct	Pts	OP
Kansas City	10	3	1	.769	302	208
Oakland	8	4	2	.667	344	278
San Diego	6	8	0	.429	311	341
Denver	4	9	1	.308	203	275

NFC EAST	W	L	T	Pct	Pts	OP
Dallas	11	3	0	.786	406	222
Washington	9	4	1	.692	276	190
Philadelphia	6	7	1	.462	221	302
St. Louis	4	9	1	.308	231	279
NY Giants	4	10	0	.286	228	362

NFC CENTRAL	W	L	T	Pct	Pts	OP
Minnesota	11	3	0	.786	245	139
Detroit	7	6	1	.538	341	286
Chicago	6	8	0	.429	185	276
Green Bay	4	8	2	.333	274	298

NFC WEST	W	L	T	Pct	Pts	OP
San Francisco	9	5	0	.643	300	216
LA Rams	8	5	1	.615	313	260
Atlanta	7	6	1	.538	274	277
New Orleans	4	8	2	.333	266	347

1972

AFC EAST	W	L	T	Pct	Pts	OP
Miami	14	0	0	1.000	385	171
NY Jets	7	7	0	.500	367	324
Baltimore	5	9	0	.357	235	252
Buffalo	4	9	1	.321	257	377
New England	3	11	0	.214	192	446

AFC CENTRAL	W	L	T	Pct	Pts	OP
Pittsburgh	11	3	0	.786	343	175
Cleveland	10	4	0	.714	268	249
Cincinnati	8	6	0	.571	299	229
Houston	1	13	0	.071	164	380

AFC WEST	W	L	T	Pct	Pts	OP
Oakland	10	3	1	.750	365	248
Kansas City	8	6	0	.571	287	254
Denver	5	9	0	.357	325	350
San Diego	4	9	1	.321	264	344

NFC EAST	W	L	T	Pct	Pts	OP
Washington	11	3	0	.786	336	218
Dallas	10	4	0	.286	319	240
NY Giants	8	6	0	.571	331	247
St. Louis	4	9	1	.321	193	303
Philadelphia	2	11	1	.179	145	352

Season-by-Season NFL Final Standings *(Cont.)*

1972 (Cont.)

NFC CENTRAL	W	L	T	Pct	Pts	OP
Green Bay	10	4	0	.714	304	226
Detroit	8	5	1	.607	339	290
Minnesota	7	7	0	.500	301	252
Chicago	4	9	1	.321	225	275

NFC WEST	W	L	T	Pct	Pts	OP
San Francisco	8	5	1	.607	353	249
Atlanta	7	7	0	.500	269	274
LA Rams	6	7	1	.464	291	286
New Orleans	2	11	1	.179	215	361

1973

AFC EAST	W	L	T	Pct	Pts	OP
Miami	12	2	0	.857	343	150
Buffalo	9	5	0	.643	259	230
New England	5	9	0	.357	258	300
Baltimore	4	10	0	.286	226	341
NY Jets	4	10	0	.286	240	306

AFC CENTRAL	W	L	T	Pct	Pts	OP
Pittsburgh	10	4	0	.714	347	210
Cincinnati	10	4	0	.714	286	231
Cleveland	7	5	2	.571	234	255
Houston	1	13	0	.071	199	447

AFC WEST	W	L	T	Pct	Pts	OP
Oakland	9	4	1	.679	292	175
Kansas City	7	5	2	.571	231	192
Denver	7	5	2	.571	354	296
San Diego	2	11	1	.179	188	386

NFC EAST	W	L	T	Pct	Pts	OP
Washington	10	4	0	.714	325	198
Dallas	10	4	0	.714	325	198
Philadelphia	5	8	1	.393	310	393
St. Louis	4	9	1	.321	286	365
NY Giants	2	11	1	.179	226	362

NFC CENTRAL	W	L	T	Pct	Pts	OP
Minnesota	12	2	0	.857	296	168
Detroit	6	7	1	.464	271	247
Green Bay	5	7	2	.429	202	259
Chicago	3	11	0	.214	195	334

NFC WEST	W	L	T	Pct	Pts	OP
LA Rams	12	2	0	.857	388	178
Atlanta	9	5	0	.643	318	224
New Orleans	5	9	0	.357	163	312
San Francisco	5	9	0	.357	262	319

1974

AFC EAST	W	L	T	Pct	Pts	OP
Miami	11	3	0	.786	327	216
Buffalo	9	5	0	.643	264	244
NY Jets	7	7	0	.500	279	300
New England	7	7	0	.500	348	289
Baltimore	2	12	0	.143	190	329

AFC CENTRAL	W	L	T	Pct	Pts	OP
Pittsburgh	10	3	1	.750	305	189
Houston	7	7	0	.500	236	282
Cincinnati	7	7	0	.500	283	259
Cleveland	4	10	0	.283	251	344

1974 (Cont.)

AFC WEST	W	L	T	Pct	Pts	OP
Oakland	12	2	0	.857	355	228
Denver	7	6	1	.536	302	294
Kansas City	5	9	0	.357	233	293
San Diego	5	9	0	.357	212	285

NFC EAST	W	L	T	Pct	Pts	OP
Washington	10	4	0	.714	320	196
St. Louis	10	4	0	.714	285	218
Dallas	8	6	0	.571	297	235
Philadelphia	7	7	0	.500	242	217
NY Giants	2	12	0	.143	195	299

NFC CENTRAL	W	L	T	Pct	Pts	OP
Minnesota	10	4	0	.714	310	195
Detroit	7	7	0	.500	256	270
Green Bay	6	8	0	.429	210	206
Chicago	4	10	0	.286	152	279

NFC WEST	W	L	T	Pct	Pts	OP
LA Rams	10	4	0	.714	263	181
San Francisco	6	8	0	.429	226	236
New Orleans	5	9	0	.357	166	263
Atlanta	3	11	0	.214	111	271

1975

AFC EAST	W	L	T	Pct	Pts	OP
Miami	10	4	0	.714	357	222
Baltimore	10	4	0	.714	395	269
Buffalo	8	6	0	.571	420	355
NY Jets	3	11	0	.214	258	433
New England	3	11	0	.214	258	358

AFC CENTRAL	W	L	T	Pct	Pts	OP
Pittsburgh	12	2	0	.857	373	162
Cincinnati	11	3	0	.786	340	246
Houston	10	4	0	.714	293	226
Cleveland	3	11	0	.214	218	372

AFC WEST	W	L	T	Pct	Pts	OP
Oakland	11	3	0	.786	375	255
Denver	6	8	0	.429	254	307
Kansas City	5	9	0	.357	282	341
San Diego	2	12	0	.143	189	345

NFC EAST	W	L	T	Pct	Pts	OP
St. Louis	11	3	0	.786	356	276
Dallas	10	4	0	.714	350	268
Washington	8	6	0	.571	325	276
NY Giants	5	9	0	.357	216	306
Philadelphia	4	10	0	.286	225	302

NFC CENTRAL	W	L	T	Pct	Pts	OP
Minnesota	12	2	0	.857	377	180
Detroit	7	7	0	.500	245	262
Green Bay	4	10	0	.286	226	285
Chicago	4	10	0	.286	191	379

NFC WEST	W	L	T	Pct	Pts	OP
LA Rams	12	2	0	.857	312	135
San Francisco	5	9	0	.357	255	286
Atlanta	4	10	0	.286	240	289
New Orleans	2	12	0	.143	165	360

1976

AFC EAST	W	L	T	Pct	Pts	OP
Baltimore	11	3	0	.786	417	246
New England	11	3	0	.786	376	236
Miami	6	8	0	.429	263	264
NY Jets	3	11	0	.214	169	383
Buffalo	2	12	0	.143	246	363

AFC CENTRAL	W	L	T	Pct	Pts	OP
Cincinnati	10	4	0	.714	335	210
Pittsburgh	10	4	0	.714	342	138
Cleveland	9	5	0	.643	267	287
Houston	5	9	0	.357	222	273

AFC WEST	W	L	T	Pct	Pts	OP
Oakland	13	1	0	.929	350	237
Denver	9	5	0	.643	315	206
San Diego	6	8	0	.429	248	285
Kansas City	5	9	0	.357	290	376
Tampa Bay Buccaneers	0	14	0	.000	125	412

NFC EAST	W	L	T	Pct	Pts	OP
Dallas	11	3	0	.786	296	194
Washington	10	4	0	.714	291	217
St. Louis	10	4	0	.714	309	267
Philadelphia	4	10	0	.286	165	286
NY Giants	3	11	0	.214	170	250

NFC CENTRAL	W	L	T	Pct	Pts	OP
Minnesota	11	2	1	.821	305	176
Chicago	7	7	0	.500	253	216
Detroit	6	8	0	.429	218	299
Green Bay	5	9	0	.357	218	299

NFC WEST	W	L	T	Pct	Pts	OP
LA Rams	10	3	1	.750	351	190
San Francisco	8	6	0	.571	270	190
Atlanta	4	10	0	.286	172	312
New Orleans	4	10	0	.286	253	346
Seattle Seahawks	2	12	0	.143	229	429

1977

AFC EAST	W	L	T	Pct	Pts	OP
Miami	10	4	0	.714	313	197
Baltimore	10	4	0	.714	295	221
New England	9	5	0	.643	279	217
Buffalo	3	11	0	.214	160	313
NY Jets	3	11	0	.214	191	313

AFC CENTRAL	W	L	T	Pct	Pts	OP
Pittsburgh	9	5	0	.643	283	243
Houston	8	6	0	.571	299	230
Cincinnati	8	6	0	.571	238	235
Cleveland	6	8	0	.429	269	267

AFC WEST	W	L	T	Pct	Pts	OP
Denver	12	2	0	.857	274	148
Oakland	11	3	0	.786	351	230
San Diego	7	7	0	.500	222	205
Seattle	5	9	0	.357	282	373
Kansas City	2	12	0	.143	225	349

1977 (Cont.)

NFC EAST	W	L	T	Pct	Pts	OP
Dallas	12	2	0	.857	345	212
Washington	9	5	0	.643	196	189
St. Louis	7	7	0	.500	272	287
NY Giants	5	9	0	.357	181	265
Philadelphia	5	9	0	.357	220	207

NFC CENTRAL	W	L	T	Pct	Pts	OP
Chicago	9	5	0	.643	255	253
Minnesota	9	5	0	.643	231	227
Detroit	6	8	0	.429	183	252
Green Bay	4	10	0	.286	134	219
Tampa Bay	2	12	0	.143	103	223

NFC WEST	W	L	T	Pct	Pts	OP
LA Rams	10	4	0	.714	302	146
Atlanta	7	7	0	.500	179	129
San Francisco	5	9	0	.357	220	260
New Orleans	3	11	0	.214	232	336

1978

AFC EAST	W	L	T	Pct	Pts	OP
New England	11	5	0	.688	358	286
Miami	11	5	0	.688	372	254
NY Jets	8	8	0	.500	359	364
Buffalo	5	11	0	.313	302	354
Baltimore	5	11	0	.313	239	421

AFC CENTRAL	W	L	T	Pct	Pts	OP
Pittsburgh	14	2	0	.875	356	195
Houston	10	6	0	.625	283	298
Cleveland	8	8	0	.500	334	356
Cincinnati	4	12	0	.250	252	284

AFC WEST	W	L	T	Pct	Pts	OP
Denver	10	6	0	.625	282	198
Seattle	9	7	0	.563	345	358
Oakland	9	7	0	.563	311	283
San Diego	9	7	0	.563	355	309
Kansas City	4	12	0	.250	243	327

NFC EAST	W	L	T	Pct	Pts	OP
Dallas	12	4	0	.750	384	208
Philadelphia	9	7	0	.563	270	250
Washington	8	8	0	.500	273	283
St. Louis	6	10	0	.375	248	296
NY Giants	6	10	0	.375	264	298

NFC CENTRAL	W	L	T	Pct	Pts	OP
Green Bay	8	7	1	.531	249	269
Minnesota	8	7	1	.531	294	306
Detroit	7	9	0	.438	290	300
Chicago	7	9	0	.438	253	274
Tampa Bay	5	11	0	.313	241	259

NFC WEST	W	L	T	Pct	Pts	OP
LA Rams	12	4	0	.750	316	245
Atlanta	9	7	0	.563	240	290
New Orleans	7	9	0	.438	281	298
San Francisco	2	14	0	.125	219	350

1979

AFC EAST	W	L	T	Pct	Pts	OP
Miami	10	6	0	.625	341	257
New England	9	7	0	.563	411	326
NY Jets	8	8	0	.500	337	383
Buffalo	7	9	0	.438	268	279
Baltimore	5	11	0	.313	271	351

AFC CENTRAL	W	L	T	Pct	Pts	OP
Pittsburgh	12	4	0	.750	416	262
Houston	11	5	0	.688	362	331
Cleveland	9	7	0	.563	359	352
Cincinnati	4	12	0	.250	337	421

AFC WEST	W	L	T	Pct	Pts	OP
San Diego	12	4	0	.750	411	246
Denver	10	6	0	.625	289	262
Seattle	9	7	0	.563	378	372
Oakland	9	7	0	.563	365	337
Kansas City	7	9	0	.438	238	262

NFC EAST	W	L	T	Pct	Pts	OP
Dallas	11	5	0	.688	371	313
Philadelphia	11	5	0	.688	339	282
Washington	10	6	0	.625	348	295
NY Giants	6	10	0	.375	237	323
St. Louis	5	11	0	.313	307	358

NFC CENTRAL	W	L	T	Pct	Pts	OP
Chicago	10	6	0	.625	306	249
Tampa Bay	10	6	0	.625	273	237
Minnesota	7	9	0	.438	259	337
Green Bay	5	11	0	.313	246	316
Detroit	2	14	0	.125	219	365

NFC WEST	W	L	T	Pct	Pts	OP
LA Rams	9	7	0	.563	323	309
New Orleans	8	8	0	.500	370	360
Atlanta	6	10	0	.375	300	388
San Francisco	2	14	0	.125	308	416

1980

AFC EAST	W	L	T	Pct	Pts	OP
Buffalo	11	5	0	.688	320	260
New England	10	6	0	.625	441	325
Miami	8	8	0	.500	266	305
Baltimore	7	9	0	.438	355	387
NY Jets	4	12	0	.250	302	395

AFC CENTRAL	W	L	T	Pct	Pts	OP
Cleveland	11	5	0	.688	357	310
Houston	11	5	0	.688	295	251
Pittsburgh	9	7	0	.563	352	313
Cincinnati	6	10	0	.375	244	312

AFC WEST	W	L	T	Pct	Pts	OP
San Diego	11	5	0	.688	418	327
Oakland	11	5	0	.688	364	306
Denver	8	8	0	.500	310	323
Kansas City	8	8	0	.500	319	336
Seattle	4	12	0	.250	291	408

NFC EAST	W	L	T	Pct	Pts	OP
Dallas	12	4	0	.750	454	311
Philadelphia	12	4	0	.750	384	222
Washington	6	10	0	.375	261	293
St. Louis	5	11	0	.313	299	350
NY Giants	4	12	0	.250	249	425

1980 (Cont.)

NFC CENTRAL	W	L	T	Pct	Pts	OP
Detroit	9	7	0	.563	334	272
Minnesota	9	7	0	.563	317	308
Chicago	7	9	0	.438	304	264
Tampa Bay	5	10	1	.344	271	341
Green Bay	5	10	1	.344	231	371

NFC WEST	W	L	T	Pct	Pts	OP
Atlanta	12	4	0	.750	405	272
LA Rams	11	5	0	.688	424	289
San Francisco	6	10	0	.375	320	415
New Orleans	1	15	0	.063	291	487

1981

AFC EAST	W	L	T	Pct	Pts	OP
Miami	11	4	1	.719	345	275
NY Jets	10	5	1	.656	355	287
Buffalo	10	6	0	.625	311	276
Baltimore	2	14	0	.125	259	533
New England	2	14	0	.125	322	370

AFC CENTRAL	W	L	T	Pct	Pts	OP
Cincinnati	12	4	0	.750	421	304
Pittsburgh	8	8	0	.500	356	297
Houston	7	9	0	.438	281	355
Cleveland	5	11	0	.313	276	375

AFC WEST	W	L	T	Pct	Pts	OP
Denver	10	6	0	.625	321	289
San Diego	10	6	0	.625	478	390
Kansas City	9	7	0	.563	343	290
Oakland	7	9	0	.438	273	343
Seattle	6	10	0	.375	322	388

NFC EAST	W	L	T	Pct	Pts	OP
Dallas	12	4	0	.750	367	277
Philadelphia	10	6	0	.625	368	221
NY Giants	9	7	0	.563	295	257
Washington	8	8	0	.500	347	349
St. Louis	7	9	0	.438	315	407

NFC CENTRAL	W	L	T	Pct	Pts	OP
Tampa Bay	9	7	0	.563	315	268
Detroit	8	8	0	.500	397	322
Green Bay	8	8	0	.500	324	361
Minnesota	7	9	0	.438	325	369
Chicago	6	10	0	.375	253	324

NFC WEST	W	L	T	Pct	Pts	OP
San Francisco	13	3	0	.813	357	250
Atlanta	7	9	0	.438	426	355
LA Rams	6	10	0	.375	303	351
New Orleans	4	12	0	.250	207	378

1982

AFC EAST	W	L	T	Pct	Pts	OP
Miami	7	2	0	.778	198	131
NY Jets	6	3	0	.667	245	166
New England	5	4	0	.556	143	157
Buffalo	4	5	0	.444	150	154
Baltimore	0	8	1	.056	113	236

Season-by-Season NFL Final Standings *(Cont.)*

1982 (Cont.)

AFC CENTRAL	W	L	T	Pct	Pts	OP
Cincinnati	7	2	0	.778	232	177
Pittsburgh	6	3	0	.667	204	146
Cleveland	4	5	0	.444	140	182
Houston	1	8	0	.111	136	245

AFC WEST	W	L	T	Pct	Pts	OP
Los Angeles Raiders	8	1	0	.889	260	200
San Diego	6	3	0	.667	288	221
Seattle	4	5	0	.444	127	147
Kansas City	3	6	0	.333	176	184
Denver	2	7	0	.222	148	226

NFC EAST	W	L	T	Pct	Pts	OP
Washington	8	1	0	.889	190	128
Dallas	6	3	0	.667	226	145
St. Louis	5	4	0	.556	135	170
NY Giants	4	5	0	.444	164	160
Philadelphia	3	6	0	.333	191	195

NFC CENTRAL	W	L	T	Pct	Pts	OP
Green Bay	5	3	1	.611	226	169
Tampa Bay	5	4	0	.556	158	178
Minnesota	5	4	0	.556	187	198
Detroit	4	5	0	.444	181	176
Chicago	3	6	0	.333	141	174

NFC WEST	W	L	T	Pct	Pts	OP
Atlanta	5	4	0	.556	183	199
New Orleans	4	5	0	.444	129	160
San Francisco	3	6	0	.333	209	206
Los Angeles Rams	2	7	0	.222	200	250

1983

AFC EAST	W	L	T	Pct	Pts	OP
Miami	12	4	0	.750	389	250
Buffalo	8	8	0	.500	283	351
New England	8	8	0	.500	274	289
Baltimore	7	9	0	.438	264	354
NY Jets	7	9	0	.438	313	331

AFC CENTRAL	W	L	T	Pct	Pts	OP
Pittsburgh	10	6	0	.625	355	303
Cleveland	9	7	0	.563	356	342
Cincinnati	7	9	0	.438	346	302
Houston	2	14	0	.125	288	460

AFC WEST	W	L	T	Pct	Pts	OP
LA Raiders	12	4	0	.750	442	338
Seattle	9	7	0	.563	403	397
Denver	9	7	0	.563	302	327
San Diego	6	10	0	.375	358	462
Kansas City	6	10	0	.375	386	367

NFC EAST	W	L	T	Pct	Pts	OP
Washington	14	2	0	.875	541	332
Dallas	12	4	0	.750	479	360
St. Louis	8	7	1	.531	374	428
Philadelphia	5	11	0	.313	233	322
NY Giants	3	12	1	.219	267	347

NFC CENTRAL	W	L	T	Pct	Pts	OP
Detroit	9	7	0	.563	47	286
Minnesota	8	8	0	.500	316	348
Chicago	8	8	0	.500	311	301
Green Bay	8	8	0	.500	429	439
Tampa Bay	2	14	0	.125	241	380

1983 (Cont.)

NFC WEST	W	L	T	Pct	Pts	OP
San Francisco	10	6	0	.625	432	293
LA Rams	9	7	0	.563	361	344
New Orleans	8	8	0	.500	319	337
Atlanta	7	9	0	.438	370	389

1984

AFC EAST	W	L	T	Pct	Pts	OP
Miami	14	2	0	.875	513	298
New England	9	7	0	.563	362	352
NY Jets	7	9	0	.438	332	364
Indianapolis Colts	4	12	0	.250	239	414
Buffalo	2	14	0	.125	250	454

AFC CENTRAL	W	L	T	Pct	Pts	OP
Pittsburgh	9	7	0	.563	387	310
Cincinnati	8	8	0	.500	339	339
Cleveland	5	11	0	.313	250	297
Houston	3	13	0	.188	240	437

AFC WEST	W	L	T	Pct	Pts	OP
Denver	13	3	0	.813	353	241
Seattle	12	4	0	.750	418	282
LA Raiders	11	5	0	.313	368	278
Kansas City	8	8	0	.500	314	324
San Diego	7	9	0	.438	394	413

NFC EAST	W	L	T	Pct	Pts	OP
Washington	11	5	0	.688	426	310
NY Giants	9	7	0	.563	299	301
Dallas	9	7	0	.563	308	308
St. Louis	9	7	0	.563	423	345
Philadelphia	6	9	1	.406	278	320

NFC CENTRAL	W	L	T	Pct	Pts	OP
Chicago	10	6	0	.625	325	248
Green Bay	8	8	0	.500	390	309
Tampa Bay	6	10	0	.375	335	380
Detroit	4	11	1	.281	283	408
Minnesota	3	13	0	.188	276	484

	W	L	T	Pct	Pts	OP
San Francisco	15	1	0	.938	475	227
LA Rams	10	6	0	.625	346	316
New Orleans	7	9	0	.438	298	361
Atlanta	4	12	0	.20	281	382

Season-by-Season NFL Final Standings *(Cont.)*

1985

AFC EAST	W	L	T	Pct	Pts	OP
Miami	12	4	0	.750	428	320
New England	11	5	0	.688	362	290
NY Jets	11	5	0	.688	393	264
Indianapolis	5	11	0	.313	320	386
Buffalo	2	14	0	.125	200	381

AFC CENTRAL	W	L	T	Pct	Pts	OP
Cleveland	8	8	0	.500	287	294
Cincinnati	7	9	0	.438	441	437
Pittsburgh	7	9	0	.438	379	355
Houston	5	11	0	.313	284	412

AFC WEST	W	L	T	Pct	Pts	OP
LA Raiders	12	4	0	.750	354	308
Denver	11	5	0	.688	380	329
Seattle	8	8	0	.500	349	303
San Diego	8	8	0	.500	467	435
Kansas City	6	10	0	.375	317	360

NFC EAST	W	L	T	Pct	Pts	OP
Washington	10	6	0	.625	297	312
NY Giants	10	6	0	.625	399	283
Dallas	10	6	0	.625	357	333
Philadelphia	7	9	0	.438	286	310
St. Louis	5	11	0	.313	278	414

NFC CENTRAL	W	L	T	Pct	Pts	OP
Chicago	15	1	0	.938	456	198
Green Bay	8	8	0	.500	337	355
Detroit	7	9	0	.438	307	366
Minnesota	7	9	0	.438	346	359
Tampa Bay	2	14	0	.125	294	448

NFC WEST	W	L	T	Pct	Pts	OP
LA Rams	11	5	0	.688	340	277
San Francisco	10	6	0	.625	411	263
New Orleans	5	11	0	.313	294	401
Atlanta	4	12	0	.250	282	452

1986

AFC EAST	W	L	T	Pct	Pts	OP
New England	11	5	0	.688	412	307
NY Jets	10	6	0	.625	364	386
Miami	8	8	0	.500	430	405
Buffalo	4	12	0	.250	287	348
Indianapolis	3	13	0	.188	299	400

AFC CENTRAL	W	L	T	Pct	Pts	OP
Cleveland	12	4	0	.750	391	310
Cincinnati	10	6	0	.625	409	394
Pittsburgh	6	10	0	.375	307	336
Houston	5	11	0	.313	274	329

AFC WEST	W	L	T	Pct	Pts	OP
Denver	11	5	0	.688	378	327
Kansas City	10	6	0	.625	358	326
Seattle	10	6	0	.625	366	293
LA Raiders	8	8	0	.500	323	346
San Diego	4	12	0	.250	335	396

NFC EAST	W	L	T	Pct	Pts	OP
NY Giants	14	2	0	.875	371	236
Washington	12	4	0	.750	368	296
Dallas	7	9	0	.438	346	337
Philadelphia	5	10	1	.344	256	312
St. Louis	4	11	1	.281	518	351

1986 (Cont.)

NFC CENTRAL	W	L	T	Pct	Pts	OP
Chicago	14	2	0	.875	352	187
Minnesota	9	7	0	.563	398	271
Detroit	5	11	0	.313	277	326
Green Bay	4	12	0	.250	254	418
Tampa Bay	2	14	0	.125	239	473

NFC WEST	W	L	T	Pct	Pts	OP
San Francisco	10	5	1	.656	374	247
LA Rams	10	6	0	.625	309	267
Atlanta	7	8	1	.469	280	280
New Orleans	7	9	0	.438	288	287

1987

AFC EAST	W	L	T	Pct	Pts	OP
Indianapolis	9	6	0	.643	300	238
Miami	8	7	0	.533	362	335
New England	8	7	0	.533	320	293
Buffalo	7	8	0	.467	320	293
NY Jets	6	9	0	.400	334	360

AFC CENTRAL	W	L	T	Pct	Pts	OP
Cleveland	10	5	0	.700	390	239
Houston	9	6	0	.600	345	349
Pittsburgh	8	7	0	.533	285	299
Cincinnati	4	11	0	.267	285	370

AFC WEST	W	L	T	Pct	Pts	OP
Denver	10	4	1	.667	379	288
Seattle	9	6	0	.600	371	314
San Diego	8	7	0	.563	253	317
LA Raiders	5	10	0	.333	301	289
Kansas City	4	11	0	.267	276	388

NFC EAST	W	L	T	Pct	Pts	OP
Washington	11	4	0	.733	379	285
Dallas	7	8	0	.467	340	348
St. Louis	7	8	0	.467	362	368
Philadelphia	7	8	0	.467	337	380
NY Giants	6	9	0	.400	280	312

NFC CENTRAL	W	L	T	Pct	Pts	OP
Chicago	11	4	0	.733	356	282
Minnesota	8	7	0	.533	336	335
Green Bay	5	9	1	.367	255	300
Tampa Bay	4	11	0	.267	286	360
Detroit	4	11	0	.267	269	384

NFC WEST	W	L	T	Pct	Pts	OP
San Francisco	13	2	0	.867	459	253
New Orleans	12	3	0	.800	422	283
LA Rams	6	9	0	.400	317	361
Atlanta	3	12	0	.200	205	436

Season-by-Season NFL Final Standings *(Cont.)*

1988

AFC EAST	W	L	T	Pct	Pts	OP
Buffalo	12	4	0	.750	329	237
New England	9	7	0	.563	250	284
Indianapolis	9	7	0	.563	354	315
NY Jets	8	7	1	.531	372	354
Miami	6	10	0	.375	319	380

AFC CENTRAL	W	L	T	Pct	Pts	OP
Cincinnati	12	4	0	.750	448	329
Cleveland	10	6	0	.625	304	288
Houston	10	6	0	.625	424	365
Pittsburgh	5	1	0	.313	336	421

AFC WEST	W	L	T	Pct	Pts	OP
Seattle	9	7	0	.563	339	329
Denver	8	8	0	.500	327	352
LA Raiders	7	9	0	.438	325	369
San Diego	6	10	0	.375	231	332
Kansas City	4	11	1	.281	254	320

NFC EAST	W	L	T	Pct	Pts	OP
NY Giants	10	6	0	.625	359	304
Philadelphia	10	6	0	.625	379	319
Phoenix Cardinals	7	9	0	.438	344	398
Washington	7	9	0	.438	345	387
Dallas	3	13	0	.188	265	381

NFC CENTRAL	W	L	T	Pct	Pts	OP
Chicago	12	4	0	.750	312	215
Minnesota	11	5	0	.688	406	233
Tampa Bay	5	11	0	.313	261	350
Detroit	4	12	0	.250	220	313
Green Bay	4	12	0	.250	240	315

NFC WEST	W	L	T	Pct	Pts	OP
New Orleans	10	6	0	.625	312	283
San Francisco	10	6	0	.625	369	294
LA Rams	10	6	0	.625	407	293
Atlanta	5	11	0	.313	244	315

1989

AFC EAST	W	L	T	Pct	Pts	OP
Buffalo	9	7	0	.563	407	317
Miami	8	8	0	.500	331	379
Indianapolis	8	8	0	.500	298	301
New England	5	11	0	.313	297	391
NY Jets	4	12	0	.250	253	411

AFC CENTRAL	W	L	T	Pct	Pts	OP
Cleveland	9	6	1	.594	334	254
Houston	9	7	0	.563	365	412
Pittsburgh	9	7	0	.563	265	326
Cincinnati	8	8	0	.500	404	285

AFC WEST	W	L	T	Pct	Pts	OP
Denver	11	5	0	.688	362	226
Kansas City	8	7	1	.531	318	286
LA Raiders	8	8	0	.500	315	297
Seattle	7	9	0	.438	241	327
San Diego	6	10	0	.375	266	290

1989 (Cont.)

NFC EAST	W	L	T	Pct	Pts	OP
NY Giants	12	4	0	.750	348	252
Philadelphia	11	5	0	.688	342	274
Washington	10	6	0	.625	386	308
Phoenix	5	11	0	.313	258	377
Dallas	1	15	0	.063	204	393

NFC CENTRAL	W	L	T	Pct	Pts	OP
Green Bay	10	6	0	.625	362	356
Minnesota	10	6	0	.625	351	275
Detroit	7	9	0	.438	312	364
Chicago	6	10	0	.375	358	377
Tampa Bay	5	11	0	.313	320	419

NFC WEST	W	L	T	Pct	Pts	OP
San Francisco	14	2	0	.875	442	253
LA Rams	11	5	0	.688	426	344
New Orleans	9	7	0	.563	386	301
Atlanta	3	13	0	.188	279	437

1990

AFC EAST	W	L	T	Pct	Pts	OP
Buffalo	13	3	0	.813	428	263
Miami	12	4	0	.750	336	242
Indianapolis	7	9	0	.438	281	353
NY Jets	6	10	0	.375	295	345
New England	1	15	0	.063	181	446

AFC CENTRAL	W	L	T	Pct	Pts	OP
Pittsburgh	9	7	0	.563	292	240
Cincinnati	9	7	0	.563	360	352
Houston	9	7	0	.563	405	307
Cleveland	3	13	0	.188	228	462

AFC WEST	W	L	T	Pct	Pts	OP
LA Raiders	12	4	0	.750	337	268
Kansas City	11	5	0	.688	369	257
Seattle	9	7	0	.563	306	286
San Diego	6	10	0	.375	315	281
Denver	5	11	0	.313	331	374

NFC EAST	W	L	T	Pct	Pts	OP
NY Giants	13	3	0	.813	335	211
Washington	10	6	0	.625	381	301
Philadelphia	10	6	0	.625	396	299
Dallas	7	9	0	.438	244	308
Phoenix	5	11	0	.313	268	396

NFC CENTRAL	W	L	T	Pct	Pts	OP
Chicago	11	5	0	.688	348	280
Green Bay	6	10	0	.375	271	347
Minnesota	6	10	0	.375	351	326
Detroit	6	10	0	.375	373	413
Tampa Bay	6	10	0	.375	264	367

NFC WEST	W	L	T	Pct	Pts	OP
San Francisco	14	2	0	.875	353	239
New Orleans	8	8	0	.500	274	275
LA Rams	5	11	0	.313	345	412
Atlanta	5	11	0	.313	348	365

1991

AFC EAST	W	L	T	Pct	Pts	OP
Buffalo	13	3	0	.813	458	318
Miami	8	8	0	.500	343	349
NY Jets	8	8	0	.500	314	293
New England	6	10	0	.375	211	305
Indianapolis	1	15	0	.063	143	381

AFC CENTRAL	W	L	T	Pct	Pts	OP
Houston	11	5	0	.688	386	251
Pittsburgh	7	9	0	.438	292	344
Cleveland	6	10	0	.375	293	298
Cincinnati	3	13	0	.188	263	435

AFC WEST	W	L	T	Pct	Pts	OP
Denver	12	4	0	.750	304	235
Kansas City	10	6	0	.625	322	252
LA Raiders	9	7	0	.563	298	297
Seattle	7	9	0	.438	276	261
San Diego	4	12	0	.250	274	342

NFC EAST	W	L	T	Pct	Pts	OP
Washington	14	2	0	.875	485	224
Dallas	11	5	0	.688	342	310
Philadelphia	10	6	0	.625	285	244
NY Giants	8	8	0	.500	281	297
Phoenix	4	12	0	.250	196	344

NFC CENTRAL	W	L	T	Pct	Pts	OP
Detroit	12	4	0	.750	339	295
Chicago	11	5	0	.688	299	269
Minnesota	8	8	0	.500	301	306
Green Bay	4	12	0	.250	273	313
Tampa Bay	3	13	0	.188	199	365

NFC WEST	W	L	T	Pct	Pts	OP
New Orleans	11	5	0	.688	341	211
Atlanta	10	6	0	.625	361	338
San Francisco	10	6	0	.625	393	239
LA Rams	3	13	0	.188	234	390

1992

AFC EAST	W	L	T	Pct	Pts	OP
Buffalo	11	5	0	.688	381	283
Miami	11	5	0	.688	340	281
Indianapolis	9	7	0	.563	216	302
NY Jets	4	12	0	.250	220	315
New England	2	14	0	.125	205	363

AFC CENTRAL	W	L	T	Pct	Pts	OP
Pittsburgh	11	5	0	.688	299	225
Houston	10	6	0	.625	352	258
Cleveland	7	9	0	.438	272	275
Cincinnati	5	11	0	.313	274	364

AFC WEST	W	L	T	Pct	Pts	OP
San Diego	11	5	0	.688	335	241
Kansas City	10	6	0	.625	348	282
Denver	8	8	0	.500	262	329
LA Raiders	7	9	0	.438	249	281
Seattle	2	14	0	.125	140	312

1992 (Cont.)

NFC EAST	W	L	T	Pct	Pts	OP
Dallas	13	3	0	.813	409	243
Philadelphia	11	5	0	.688	354	245
Washington	9	7	0	.563	300	255
NY Giants	6	10	0	.375	306	367
Phoenix	4	12	0	.250	243	332

NFC CENTRAL	W	L	T	Pct	Pts	OP
Minnesota	11	5	0	.688	374	249
Green Bay	9	7	0	.563	276	296
Tampa Bay	5	11	0	.313	267	365
Detroit	5	11	0	.313	273	332
Chicago	5	11	0	.313	295	361

NFC WEST	W	L	T	Pct	Pts	OP
San Francisco	14	2	0	.875	431	236
New Orleans	12	4	0	.750	330	202
Atlanta	6	10	0	.375	327	414
LA Rams	6	10	0	.375	313	383

1993

AFC EAST	W	L	T	Pct	Pts	OP
Buffalo	12	4	0	.750	329	242
Miami	9	7	0	.563	349	351
NY Jets	8	8	0	.500	270	247
New England	5	11	0	.313	238	286
Indianapolis	4	12	0	.250	189	378

AFC CENTRAL	W	L	T	Pct	Pts	OP
Houston	12	4	0	.750	368	238
Pittsburgh	9	7	0	.563	308	281
Cleveland	7	9	0	.438	304	307
Cincinnati	3	13	0	.188	187	319

AFC WEST	W	L	T	Pct	Pts	OP
Kansas City	11	5	0	.688	328	291
LA Raiders	10	6	0	.625	306	326
Denver	9	7	0	.563	373	284
San Diego	8	8	0	.500	322	290
Seattle	6	10	0	.375	280	314

NFC EAST	W	L	T	Pct	Pts	OP
Dallas	12	4	0	.750	376	229
NY Giants	11	5	0	.688	288	205
Philadelphia	8	8	0	.500	293	315
Phoenix	7	9	0	.438	326	269
Washington	4	12	0	.250	230	345

NFC CENTRAL	W	L	T	Pct	Pts	OP
Detroit	10	6	0	.625	298	292
Green Bay	9	7	0	.563	340	282
Minnesota	9	7	0	.563	277	290
Chicago	7	9	0	.438	234	230
Tampa Bay	5	11	0	.313	237	375

NFC WEST	W	L	T	Pct	Pts	OP
San Francisco	10	6	0	.625	473	295
New Orleans	8	8	0	.500	317	343
Atlanta	6	10	0	.375	316	385
LA Rams	5	11	0	.313	221	367

Season-by-Season NFL Final Standings *(Cont.)*

1994

AFC EAST	W	L	T	Pct	Pts	OP
Miami	10	6	0	.625	389	327
New England	10	6	0	.625	351	312
Indianapolis	8	8	0	.500	307	320
Buffalo	7	9	0	.438	340	356
NY Jets	6	10	0	.375	264	320

AFC CENTRAL	W	L	T	Pct	Pts	OP
Pittsburgh	12	4	0	.750	316	234
Cleveland	11	5	0	.688	340	204
Cincinnati	3	13	0	.188	276	406
Houston	2	14	0	.125	226	352

AFC WEST	W	L	T	Pct	Pts	OP
San Diego	11	5	0	.688	384	306
LA Raiders	9	7	0	.563	303	327
Kansas City	9	7	0	.563	319	298
Denver	7	9	0	.438	347	396
Seattle	6	10	0	.375	287	323

NFC EAST	W	L	T	Pct	Pts	OP
Dallas	12	4	0	.750	414	248
NY Giants	9	7	0	.563	279	305
Arizona Cardinals	8	8	0	.500	235	267
Philadelphia	7	9	0	.438	308	308
Washington	3	13	0	.188	320	412

NFC CENTRAL	W	L	T	Pct	Pts	OP
Minnesota	10	6	0	.625	356	314
Green Bay	9	7	0	.563	382	287
Detroit	9	7	0	.563	357	342
Chicago	9	7	0	.563	271	307
Tampa Bay	6	10	0	.375	251	351

NFC WEST	W	L	T	Pct	Pts	OP
San Francisco	13	3	0	.813	505	296
New Orleans	7	9	0	.438	348	407
Atlanta	7	9	0	.438	317	385
LA Rams	4	12	0	.250	286	365

1995

AFC EAST	W	L	T	Pct	Pts	OP
Buffalo	10	6	0	.625	350	335
Miami	9	7	0	.563	398	332
Indianapolis	9	7	0	.563	331	316
New England	6	10	0	.375	294	377
NY Jets	3	13	0	.188	233	384

AFC CENTRAL	W	L	T	Pct	Pts	OP
Pittsburgh	11	5	0	.688	407	327
Houston	7	9	0	.438	348	324
Cincinnati	7	9	0	.438	349	374
Cleveland	5	11	0	.313	289	356
Jacksonville Jaguars	4	12	0	.250	275	404

AFC WEST	W	L	T	Pct	Pts	OP
Kansas City	13	3	0	.813	358	241
San Diego	9	7	0	.563	321	323
Oakland Raiders	8	8	0	.500	348	332
Denver	8	8	0	.500	388	345
Seattle	8	8	0	.500	363	366

1995 (Cont.)

NFC EAST	W	L	T	Pct	Pts	OP
Dallas	12	4	0	.750	435	291
Philadelphia	10	6	0	.625	318	338
Washington	6	10	0	.375	326	359
NY Giants	5	11	0	.313	290	340
Arizona	4	12	0	.250	275	422

NFC CENTRAL	W	L	T	Pct	Pts	OP
Green Bay	11	5	0	.688	404	314
Detroit	10	6	0	.625	436	336
Chicago	9	7	0	.563	392	360
Minnesota	8	8	0	.500	412	385
Tampa Bay	7	9	0	.438	238	335

NFC WEST	W	L	T	Pct	Pts	OP
San Francisco	11	5	0	.688	457	258
Atlanta	9	7	0	.563	362	349
St. Louis Rams	7	9	0	.438	309	418
Carolina Panthers	7	9	0	.438	289	325
New Orleans	7	9	0	.438	319	348

1996

AFC EAST	W	L	T	Pct	Pts	OP
New England	11	5	0	.688	418	313
Buffalo	10	6	0	.625	319	266
Indianapolis	9	7	0	.563	317	334
Miami	8	8	0	.500	339	325
NY Jets	1	15	0	.063	279	454

AFC CENTRAL	W	L	T	Pct	Pts	OP
Pittsburgh	10	6	0	.625	344	257
Jacksonville	9	7	0	.563	325	334
Houston	8	8	0	.500	345	319
Cincinnati	8	8	0	.500	372	369
Baltimore Ravens	4	12	0	.250	371	441

AFC WEST	W	L	T	Pct	Pts	OP
Denver	13	3	0	.813	391	275
Kansas City	9	7	0	.563	297	300
San Diego	8	8	0	.500	310	376
Seattle	7	9	0	.438	317	375
Oakland	7	9	0	.438	340	293

NFC EAST	W	L	T	Pct	Pts	OP
Dallas	10	6	0	.625	286	250
Philadelphia	10	6	0	.625	363	341
Washington	9	7	0	.563	364	312
Arizona	7	9	0	.438	300	397
NY Giants	6	10	0	.375	242	297

NFC CENTRAL	W	L	T	Pct	Pts	OP
Green Bay	13	3	0	.813	456	210
Minnesota	9	7	0	.563	298	315
Chicago	7	9	0	.438	283	305
Tampa Bay	6	10	0	.375	221	293
Detroit	5	11	0	.313	302	368

NFC WEST	W	L	T	Pct	Pts	OP
San Francisco	12	4	0	.750	398	257
Carolina	12	4	0	.750	367	218
St. Louis	6	10	0	.375	303	409
New Orleans	3	13	0	.188	229	339
Atlanta	3	13	0	.188	309	461

1997

AFC EAST	W	L	T	Pct	Pts	OP
New England	10	6	0	.625	369	289
Miami	9	7	0	.563	339	327
NY Jets	9	7	0	.563	348	287
Buffalo	6	10	0	.375	255	367
Indianapolis	3	13	0	.188	313	401

AFC CENTRAL	W	L	T	Pct	Pts	OP
Jacksonville	11	5	0	.688	394	318
Pittsburgh	11	5	0	.688	372	307
Tennessee Oilers	8	8	0	.500	333	310
Cincinnati	7	9	0	.438	355	405
Baltimore	6	9	1	.375	326	345

AFC WEST	W	L	T	Pct	Pts	OP
Kansas City	13	3	0	.813	375	232
Denver	12	4	0	.750	472	287
Seattle	8	8	0	.500	365	362
Oakland	4	12	0	.250	324	419
San Diego	4	12	0	.250	266	425

NFC EAST	W	L	T	Pct	Pts	OP
NY Giants	10	5	1	.656	307	265
Washington	8	7	1	.531	327	289
Philadelphia	6	9	1	.406	317	372
Dallas	6	10	0	.375	304	314
Arizona	4	12	0	.250	283	379

NFC CENTRAL	W	L	T	Pct	Pts	OP
Green Bay	13	3	0	.813	422	282
Tampa Bay	10	6	0	.625	299	263
Detroit	9	7	0	.563	379	306
Minnesota	9	7	0	.563	354	359
Chicago	4	12	0	.250	263	421

NFC WEST	W	L	T	Pct	Pts	OP
San Francisco	13	3	0	.813	375	265
Carolina	7	9	0	.438	265	314
Atlanta	7	9	0	.438	320	361
New Orleans	6	10	0	.375	237	327
St. Louis	5	11	0	.313	299	359

1998

AFC EAST	W	L	T	Pct	Pts	OP
NY Jets	12	4	0	.750	416	266
Miami	10	6	0	.625	321	265
Buffalo	10	6	0	.625	400	333
New England	9	7	0	.563	337	329
Indianapolis	3	13	0	.188	310	444

AFC CENTRAL	W	L	T	Pct	Pts	OP
Jacksonville	11	5	0	.688	392	338
Tennessee	8	8	0	.500	330	320
Pittsburgh	7	9	0	.438	263	303
Baltimore	6	10	0	.375	269	335
Cincinnati	3	13	0	.188	268	452

AFC WEST	W	L	T	Pct	Pts	OP
Denver	14	2	0	.875	501	309
Oakland	8	8	0	.500	288	356
Seattle	8	8	0	.500	372	310
Kansas City	7	9	0	.438	327	363
San Diego	5	11	0	.313	241	342

1998 (Cont.)

NFC EAST	W	L	T	Pct	Pts	OP
Dallas	10	6	0	.625	381	275
Arizona	9	7	0	.563	325	378
NY Giants	8	8	0	.500	287	309
Washington	6	10	0	.375	319	421
Philadelphia	3	13	0	.188	161	344

NFC CENTRAL	W	L	T	Pct	Pts	OP
Minnesota	15	1	0	.938	556	296
Green Bay	11	5	0	.688	408	319
Tampa Bay	8	8	0	.500	314	295
Detroit	5	11	0	.313	306	378
Chicago	4	12	0	.250	276	368

NFC WEST	W	L	T	Pct	Pts	OP
Atlanta	14	2	0	.875	442	289
San Francisco	12	4	0	.750	479	328
New Orleans	6	10	0	.375	305	359
Carolina	4	12	0	.250	336	413
St. Louis	4	12	0	.250	285	378

1999

AFC EAST	W	L	T	Pct	Pts	OP
Indianapolis	13	3	0	.813	423	333
Buffalo	11	5	0	.688	320	229
Miami	9	7	0	.563	326	336
NY Jets	8	8	0	.500	309	309
New England	8	8	0	.500	299	284

AFC CENTRAL	W	L	T	Pct	Pts	OP
Jacksonville	14	2	0	.875	396	217
Tennessee Titans	13	3	0	.813	392	324
Baltimore	8	8	0	.500	324	277
Pittsburgh	6	10	0	.375	317	320
Cincinnati	4	12	0	.250	283	460
Cleveland Browns	2	14	0	.125	217	437

AFC WEST	W	L	T	Pct	Pts	OP
Seattle	9	7	0	.563	338	298
Kansas City	9	7	0	.563	390	322
Oakland	8	8	0	.500	390	329
San Diego	8	8	0	.500	269	316
Denver	6	10	0	.375	314	318

NFC EAST	W	L	T	Pct	Pts	OP
Washington	10	6	0	.625	443	377
Dallas	8	8	0	.500	352	276
NY Giants	7	9	0	.438	299	358
Arizona	6	10	0	.375	245	382
Philadelphia	5	11	0	.313	272	357

NFC CENTRAL	W	L	T	Pct	Pts	OP
Tampa Bay	11	5	0	.688	270	235
Minnesota	10	6	0	.625	399	335
Green Bay	8	8	0	.500	357	341
Detroit	8	8	0	.500	322	323
Chicago	6	10	0	.375	272	341

NFC WEST	W	L	T	Pct	Pts	OP
St. Louis	13	3	0	.813	526	242
Carolina	8	8	0	.500	421	381
Atlanta	5	11	0	.313	285	380
San Francisco	4	12	0	.250	295	453
New Orleans	3	13	0	.188	260	434

Season-by-Season NFL Final Standings *(Cont.)*

2000

AFC EAST	W	L	T	Pct	Pts	OP
Miami	11	5	0	.688	323	226
Indianapolis	10	6	0	.625	429	326
NY Jets	9	7	0	.563	321	321
Buffalo	8	8	0	.500	315	350
New England	5	11	0	.313	276	338

AFC CENTRAL	W	L	T	Pct	Pts	OP
Tennessee	13	3	0	.813	346	191
Baltimore	12	4	0	.750	333	165
Pittsburgh	9	7	0	.563	321	255
Jacksonville	7	9	0	.438	367	327
Cincinnati	4	12	0	.250	185	359
Cleveland	3	13	0	.188	161	419

AFC WEST	W	L	T	Pct	Pts	OP
Oakland	12	4	0	.750	479	299
Denver	11	5	0	.688	485	369
Kansas City	7	9	0	.438	355	354
Seattle	6	10	0	.375	320	405
San Diego	1	15	0	.063	269	440

NFC EAST	W	L	T	Pct	Pts	OP
NY Giants	12	4	0	.750	328	246
Philadelphia	11	5	0	.688	351	245
Washington	8	8	0	.500	281	269
Dallas	5	11	0	.313	294	361
Arizona	3	13	0	.188	210	443

NFC CENTRAL	W	L	T	Pct	Pts	OP
Minnesota	11	5	0	.688	397	371
Tampa Bay	10	6	0	.625	388	269
Green Bay	9	7	0	.563	353	323
Detroit	9	7	0	.563	307	307
Chicago	5	11	0	.313	216	355

NFC WEST	W	L	T	Pct	Pts	OP
New Orleans	10	6	0	.625	354	306
St. Louis	10	6	0	.625	540	471
Carolina	7	9	0	.438	310	310
San Francisco	6	10	0	.375	388	422
Atlanta	4	12	0	.250	252	413

2001

AFC EAST	W	L	T	Pct	Pts	OP
New England	11	5	0	.688	371	272
Miami	11	5	0	.688	344	290
NY Jets	10	6	0	.625	413	486
Indianapolis	6	10	0	.375	413	486
Buffalo	3	13	0	.188	265	420

AFC CENTRAL	W	L	T	Pct	Pts	OP
Pittsburgh	13	3	0	.813	352	212
Baltimore	10	6	0	.625	303	265
Cleveland	7	9	0	.438	285	319
Tennessee	7	9	0	.438	336	388
Jacksonville	6	10	0	.375	294	286
Cincinnati	6	10	0	.375	226	309

AFC WEST	W	L	T	Pct	Pts	OP
Oakland	10	6	0	.625	399	327
Seattle	9	7	0	.563	301	324
Denver	8	8	0	.500	340	339
Kansas City	6	10	0	.375	320	344
San Diego	5	11	0	.313	332	321

2001 (Cont.)

NFC EAST	W	L	T	Pct	Pts	OP
Philadelphia	11	5	0	.688	343	208
Washington	8	8	0	.500	256	303
NY Giants	7	9	0	.438	294	321
Arizona	7	9	0	.438	295	343
Dallas	5	11	0	.313	246	338

NFC CENTRAL	W	L	T	Pct	Pts	OP
Chicago	13	3	0	.813	338	203
Green Bay	12	4	0	.750	390	266
Tampa Bay	9	7	0	.563	324	280
Minnesota	5	11	0	.313	290	390
Detroit	2	14	0	.125	270	424

NFC WEST	W	L	T	Pct	Pts	OP
St. Louis	14	2	0	.875	503	273
San Francisco	12	4	0	.750	409	282
Atlanta	7	9	0	.438	291	377
New Orleans	7	9	0	.438	333	409
Carolina	1	15	0	.938	253	410

2002

AFC EAST	W	L	T	Pct	Pts	OP
New England	9	7	0	.563	384	346
Miami	9	7	0	.563	378	301
NY Jets	9	7	0	.563	359	336
Buffalo	8	8	0	.500	379	397

AFC NORTH	W	L	T	Pct	Pts	OP
Pittsburgh	10	5	1	.656	390	345
Cleveland	9	7	0	.563	344	320
Baltimore	7	9	0	.438	316	354
Cincinnati	2	14	0	.125	279	456

AFC SOUTH	W	L	T	Pct	Pts	OP
Tennessee	11	5	0	.688	367	324
Indianapolis	10	6	0	.625	349	313
Jacksonville	6	10	0	.375	328	315
Houston Texans	4	12	0	.250	213	356

AFC WEST	W	L	T	Pct	Pts	OP
Oakland	11	5	0	.688	450	304
Denver	9	7	0	.563	392	344
Kansas City	8	8	0	.500	467	399
San Diego	8	8	0	.500	333	367

NFC EAST	W	L	T	Pct	Pts	OP
Philadelphia	12	4	0	.750	415	241
NY Giants	10	6	0	.625	320	279
Washington	7	9	0	.438	307	365
Dallas	5	11	0	.313	217	329

NFC NORTH	W	L	T	Pct	Pts	OP
Green Bay	12	4	0	.750	398	328
Minnesota	6	10	0	.375	390	442
Chicago	4	12	0	.250	281	379
Detroit	3	13	0	.188	306	451

2002 (Cont.)

NFC SOUTH	W	L	T	Pct	Pts	OP
Tampa Bay	12	4	0	.750	346	196
Atlanta	9	6	1	.594	402	314
New Orleans	9	7	0	.563	432	388
Carolina	7	9	0	.438	258	302

NFC WEST	W	L	T	Pct	Pts	OP
San Francisco	10	6	0	.625	367	351
St. Louis	7	9	0	.438	316	367
Seattle	7	9	0	.438	355	369
Arizona	5	11	0	.313	262	417

2003

AFC EAST	W	L	T	Pct	Pts	OP
New England	14	2	0	.875	348	238
Miami	10	6	0	.625	311	261
Buffalo	6	10	0	.375	243	279
NY Jets	6	10	0	.375	283	299

AFC NORTH	W	L	T	Pct	Pts	OP
Baltimore	10	6	0	.625	391	281
Cincinnati	8	8	0	.500	346	384
Pittsburgh	6	10	0	.375	300	327
Cleveland	5	11	0	.313	254	322

AFC SOUTH	W	L	T	Pct	Pts	OP
Indianapolis	12	4	0	.750	447	336
Tennessee	12	4	0	.750	435	324
Houston	5	11	0	.313	255	380
Jacksonville	5	11	0	.313	276	331

AFC WEST	W	L	T	Pct	Pts	OP
Kansas City	13	3	0	.813	484	332
Denver	10	6	0	.625	381	301
Oakland	4	12	0	.250	270	379
San Diego	4	12	0	.250	313	441

NFC EAST	W	L	T	Pct	Pts	OP
Philadelphia	12	4	0	.750	374	287
Dallas	10	6	0	.625	289	260
Washington	5	11	0	.313	287	372
NY Giants	4	12	0	.250	243	387

NFC NORTH	W	L	T	Pct	Pts	OP
Green Bay	10	6	0	.625	442	307
Minnesota	9	7	0	.563	416	353
Chicago	7	9	0	.438	283	346
Detroit	5	11	0	.313	270	379

NFC SOUTH	W	L	T	Pct	Pts	OP
Carolina	11	5	0	.688	325	304
New Orleans	8	8	0	.500	340	326
Tampa Bay	7	9	0	.438	301	264
Atlanta	5	11	0	.313	299	422

NFC WEST	W	L	T	Pct	Pts	OP
St. Louis	12	4	0	.750	447	328
Seattle	10	6	0	.625	404	327
San Francisco	7	9	0	.438	384	337
Arizona	4	12	0	.250	225	452

2004

AFC EAST	W	L	T	Pct	Pts	OP
New England	14	2	0	.875	437	260
NY Jets	10	6	0	.625	333	261
Buffalo	9	7	0	.562	395	284
Miami	4	12	0	.250	275	354

AFC NORTH	W	L	T	Pct	Pts	OP
Pittsburgh	15	1	0	.938	372	251
Baltimore	9	7	0	.562	317	268
Cincinnati	8	8	0	.500	374	372
Cleveland	4	12	0	.250	275	354

AFC SOUTH	W	L	T	Pct	Pts	OP
Indianapolis	12	4	0	.750	522	351
Jacksonville	9	7	0	.562	261	280
Houston	7	9	0	.438	309	339
Tennessee	5	11	0	.312	344	439

AFC WEST	W	L	T	Pct	Pts	OP
San Diego	12	4	0	.750	446	313
Denver	10	6	0	.625	381	304
Kansas City	7	9	0	.438	483	435
Oakland	5	11	0	.312	320	442

NFC EAST	W	L	T	Pct	Pts	OP
Philadelphia	13	3	0	.812	386	260
NY Giants	6	10	0	.375	303	347
Dallas	6	10	0	.375	293	405
Washington	6	10	0	.375	240	265

NFC NORTH	W	L	T	Pct	Pts	OP
Green Bay	10	6	0	.625	424	380
Minnesota	8	8	0	.500	405	395
Detroit	6	10	0	.375	296	350
Chicago	5	11	0	.312	231	331

NFC SOUTH	W	L	T	Pct	Pts	OP
Atlanta	11	5	0	.688	340	337
New Orleans	8	8	0	.500	348	405
Carolina	7	9	0	.438	355	339
Tampa Bay	5	11	0	.312	301	304

NFC WEST	W	L	T	Pct	Pts	OP
Seattle	9	7	0	.562	371	373
St. Louis	8	8	0	.500	319	392
Arizona	6	10	0	.375	284	322
San Francisco	2	14	0	.125	259	452

Season-by-Season NFL Final Standings *(Cont.)*

2005

AFC EAST	W	L	T	Pct	Pts	OP
New England	10	6	0	.625	379	338
Miami	9	7	0	.562	318	317
Buffalo	5	11	0	.312	271	367
NY Jets	4	12	0	.250	240	355

AFC NORTH	W	L	T	Pct	Pts	OP
Cincinnati	11	5	0	.688	421	350
Pittsburgh	11	5	0	.688	389	258
Cleveland	6	10	0	.375	232	301
Baltimore	6	10	0	.375	265	299

AFC SOUTH	W	L	T	Pct	Pts	OP
Indianapolis	14	2	0	.875	439	247
Jacksonville	12	4	0	.750	361	269
Tennessee	4	12	0	.250	299	421
Houston	2	14	0	.125	260	431

AFC WEST	W	L	T	Pct	Pts	OP
Denver	13	3	0	.812	395	258
Kansas City	10	6	0	.625	403	325
San Diego	9	7	0	.562	418	312
Oakland	4	12	0	.250	290	383

NFC EAST	W	L	T	Pct	Pts	OP
NY Giants	11	5	0	.688	422	314
Washington	10	6	0	.625	359	293
Dallas	9	7	0	.562	325	308
Philadelphia	6	10	0	.375	310	388

NFC NORTH	W	L	T	Pct	Pts	OP
Chicago	11	5	0	.688	260	202
Minnesota	9	7	0	.562	306	344
Detroit	5	11	0	.312	254	345
Green Bay	4	12	0	.250	298	344

NFC SOUTH	W	L	T	Pct	Pts	OP
Carolina	11	5	0	.688	391	259
Tampa Bay	11	5	0	.688	300	274
Atlanta	8	8	0	.500	351	341
New Orleans	3	13	0	.188	235	398

NFC WEST	W	L	T	Pct	Pts	OP
Seattle	13	3	0	.812	452	271
St. Louis	6	10	0	.375	363	429
Arizona	5	11	0	.312	311	387
San Francisco	4	12	0	.250	239	428

2006

AFC EAST	W	L	T	Pct	Pts	OP
New England	12	4	0	.750	385	237
NY Jets	10	6	0	.625	316	295
Buffalo	7	9	0	.438	300	311
Miami	6	10	0	.375	260	283

AFC NORTH	W	L	T	Pct	Pts	OP
Baltimore	13	3	0	.812	353	201
Cincinnati	8	8	0	.500	373	331
Pittsburgh	8	8	0	.500	353	315
Cleveland	4	12	0	.250	238	356

AFC SOUTH	W	L	T	Pct	Pts	OP
Indianapolis	12	4	0	.750	427	360
Tennessee	8	8	0	.500	324	400
Jacksonville	8	8	0	.500	371	274
Houston	6	10	0	.375	267	366

AFC WEST	W	L	T	Pct	Pts	OP
San Diego	14	2	0	.875	492	303
Kansas City	9	7	0	.562	331	315
Denver	9	7	0	.562	319	305
Oakland	2	14	0	.125	168	332

NFC EAST	W	L	T	Pct	Pts	OP
Philadelphia	10	6	0	.625	398	328
Dallas	9	7	0	.562	425	350
NY Giants	8	8	0	.500	355	362
Washington	5	11	0	.312	307	376

NFC NORTH	W	L	T	Pct	Pts	OP
Chicago	13	3	0	.812	427	255
Green Bay	8	8	0	.500	301	366
Minnesota	6	10	0	.375	282	327
Detroit	3	13	0	.188	305	398

NFC SOUTH	W	L	T	Pct	Pts	OP
New Orleans	10	6	0	.625	413	322
Carolina	8	8	0	.500	270	305
Atlanta	7	9	0	.438	292	328
Tampa Bay	4	12	0	.250	211	353

NFC WEST	W	L	T	Pct	Pts	OP
Seattle	9	7	0	.562	335	341
St. Louis	8	8	0	.500	367	381
San Francisco	7	9	0	.438	298	412
Arizona	5	11	0	.312	314	389

The Super Bowl

Results

	Date	Winner (Share)	Loser (Share)	Score	Site (Attendance)
I	1-15-67	Green Bay ($15,000)	Kansas City ($7,500)	35–10	Los Angeles (61,946)
II	1-14-68	Green Bay ($15,000)	Oakland ($7,500)	33–14	Miami (75,546)
III	1-12-69	NY Jets ($15,000)	Baltimore ($7,500)	16–7	Miami (75,389)
IV	1-11-70	Kansas City ($15,000)	Minnesota ($7,500)	23–7	New Orleans (80,562)
V	1-17-71	Baltimore ($15,000)	Dallas ($7,500)	16–13	Miami (79,204)
VI	1-16-72	Dallas ($15,000)	Miami ($7,500)	24–3	New Orleans (81,023)
VII	1-14-73	Miami ($15,000)	Washington ($7,500)	14–7	Los Angeles (90,182)
VIII	1-13-74	Miami ($15,000)	Minnesota ($7,500)	24–7	Houston (71,882)
IX	1-12-75	Pittsburgh ($15,000)	Minnesota ($7,500)	16–6	New Orleans (80,997)
X	1-18-76	Pittsburgh ($15,000)	Dallas ($7,500)	21–17	Miami (80,187)
XI	1-9-77	Oakland ($15,000)	Minnesota ($7,500)	32–14	Pasadena (103,438)
XII	1-15-78	Dallas ($18,000)	Denver ($9,000)	27–10	New Orleans (76,400)
XIII	1-21-79	Pittsburgh ($18,000)	Dallas ($9,000)	35–31	Miami (79,484)
XIV	1-20-80	Pittsburgh ($18,000)	Los Angeles ($9,000)	31–19	Pasadena (103,985)
XV	1-25-81	Oakland ($18,000)	Philadelphia ($9,000)	27–10	New Orleans (76,135)
XVI	1-24-82	San Francisco ($18,000)	Cincinnati ($9,000)	26–21	Pontiac, Mich. (81,270)
XVII	1-30-83	Washington ($36,000)	Miami ($18,000)	27–17	Pasadena (103,667)
XVIII	1-22-84	LA Raiders ($36,000)	Washington ($18,000)	38–9	Tampa (72,920)
XIX	1-20-85	San Francisco ($36,000)	Miami ($18,000)	38–16	Stanford, Calif. (84,059)
XX	1-26-86	Chicago ($36,000)	New England ($18,000)	46–10	New Orleans (73,818)
XXI	1-25-87	NY Giants ($36,000)	Denver ($18,000)	39–20	Pasadena (101,063)
XXII	1-31-88	Washington ($36,000)	Denver ($18,000)	42–10	San Diego (73,302)
XXIII	1-22-89	San Francisco ($36,000)	Cincinnati ($18,000)	20–16	Miami (75,129)
XXIV	1-28-90	San Francisco ($36,000)	Denver ($18,000)	55–10	New Orleans (72,919)
XXV	1-27-91	NY Giants ($36,000)	Buffalo ($18,000)	20–19	Tampa (73,813)
XXVI	1-26-92	Washington ($36,000)	Buffalo ($18,000)	37–24	Minneapolis (63,130)
XXVII	1-31-93	Dallas ($36,000)	Buffalo ($18,000)	52–17	Pasadena (98,374)
XXVIII	1-30-94	Dallas ($38,000)	Buffalo ($23,500)	30–13	Atlanta (72,817)
XXIX	1-29-95	San Francisco ($42,000)	San Diego ($26,000)	49–26	Miami (74,107)
XXX	1-28-96	Dallas ($42,000)	Pittsburgh ($27,000)	27–17	Tempe, Ariz. (76,347)
XXXI	1-26-97	Green Bay ($48,000)	New England ($29,000)	35–21	New Orleans (72,301)
XXXII	1-25-98	Denver ($48,000)	Green Bay ($27,500)	31–24	San Diego (68,912)
XXXIII	1-31-99	Denver ($53,000)	Atlanta ($32,500)	34–19	Miami (74,803)
XXXIV	1-30-00	St. Louis ($58,000)	Tennessee ($33,000)	23–16	Atlanta (72,625)
XXXV	1-28-01	Baltimore ($58,000)	NY Giants ($34,500)	34–7	Tampa (71,921)
XXXVI	2-3-02	New England ($63,000)	St. Louis ($34,500)	20–17	New Orleans (72,922)
XXXVII	1-26-03	Tampa Bay ($64,000)	Oakland ($35,000)	48–21	San Diego (67,603)
XXXVIII	2-1-04	New England ($64,000)	Carolina ($35,000)	32–29	Houston (71,525)
XXXIX	2-6-05	New England ($68,000)	Philadelphia ($36,500)	24–21	Jacksonville (78,125)
XL	2-5-06	Pittsburgh ($73,000)	Seattle ($38,000)	21–10	Detroit (68,206)
XLI	2-4-07	Indianapolis ($78,000)	Chicago ($40,000)	29–17	Miami (74,512)
XLII	2-3-08	NY Giants ($78,000)	New England ($40,000)	17–14	Glendale, Ariz. (71,101)

Most Valuable Players

Super Bowl	Player/ Team	Position
I	Bart Starr, GB	QB
II	Bart Starr, GB	QB
III	Joe Namath, NYJ	QB
IV	Len Dawson, KC	QB
V	Chuck Howley, Dal	LB
VI	Roger Staubach, Dal	QB
VII	Jake Scott, Mia	S
VIII	Larry Csonka, Mia	RB
IX	Franco Harris, Pitt	RB
X	Lynn Swann, Pitt	WR
XI	Fred Biletnikoff, Oak	WR
XII	Randy White, Dal	DT
	Harvey Martin, Dal	DE
XIII	Terry Bradshaw, Pitt	QB
XIV	Terry Bradshaw, Pitt	QB
XV	Jim Plunkett, Oak	QB
XVI	Joe Montana, SF	QB
XVII	John Riggins, Wash	RB
XVIII	Marcus Allen, LA Rai	RB
XIX	Joe Montana, SF	QB
XX	Richard Dent, Chi	DE
XXI	Phil Simms, NYG	QB
XXII	Doug Williams, Wash	QB
XXIII	Jerry Rice, SF	WR
XXIV	Joe Montana, SF	QB
XXV	Ottis Anderson, NYG	RB
XXVI	Mark Rypien, Wash	QB
XXVII	Troy Aikman, Dal	QB
XXVIII	Emmitt Smith, Dal	RB
XXIX	Steve Young, SF	QB
XXX	Larry Brown, Dal	CB
XXXI	Desmond Howard, GB	KR
XXXII	Terrell Davis, Den	RB
XXXIII	John Elway, Den	QB
XXXIV	Kurt Warner, StL	QB
XXXV	Ray Lewis, Balt	LB
XXXVI	Tom Brady, NE	QB
XXXVII	Dexter Jackson, TB	S
XXXVIII	Tom Brady, NE	QB
XXXIX	Deion Branch, NE	WR
XL	Hines Ward, Pitt	WR
XLI	Peyton Manning, Ind	QB
XLII	Eli Manning, NYG	QB

Composite Standings

	W	L	Pct	Pts	Opp Pts
San Francisco 49ers	5	0	1.000	188	89
Baltimore Ravens	1	0	1.000	34	7
New York Jets	1	0	1.000	16	7
Tampa Bay Buccaneers	1	0	1.000	48	21
Pittsburgh Steelers	5	1	.833	141	110
Green Bay Packers	3	1	.750	127	76
New York Giants	3	1	.750	83	87
Baltimore/Indianapolis Colts	2	1	.667	52	46
Dallas Cowboys	5	3	.625	221	132
Oakland/LA Raiders	3	2	.600	132	114
Washington Redskins	3	2	.600	122	103
New England Patriots	3	3	.500	121	165
Chicago Bears	1	1	.500	63	39
Kansas City Chiefs	1	1	.500	33	42
Miami Dolphins	2	3	.400	74	103
Denver Broncos	2	4	.333	115	206
Los Angeles/St. Louis Rams	1	2	.333	59	67
Atlanta Falcons	0	1	.000	19	34
Carolina Panthers	0	1	.000	29	32
San Diego Chargers	0	1	.000	26	49
Seattle Seahawks	0	1	.000	10	21
Tennessee Titans	0	1	.000	16	23
Cincinnati Bengals	0	2	.000	37	46
Philadelphia Eagles	0	2	.000	31	51
Buffalo Bills	0	4	.000	73	139
Minnesota Vikings	0	4	.000	34	95

Career Leaders

Passing

	GP	Att	Comp	Pct Comp	Yds	Avg Gain	TD	Pct TD	Int	Pct Int	Lg	Rating Pts
Joe Montana, SF	4	122	83	68.0	1142	9.36	11	9.0	0	0.0	44	127.8
Jim Plunkett, Oak/LA Rai	2	46	29	63.0	433	9.41	4	8.7	0	0.0	t80	122.8
Terry Bradshaw, Pitt	4	84	49	58.3	932	11.10	9	10.7	4	4.8	t75	112.8
Troy Aikman, Dal	3	80	56	70.0	689	8.61	5	6.3	1	1.3	t56	111.9
Bart Starr, GB	2	47	29	61.7	452	9.62	3	6.4	1	2.1	t62	106.0
Brett Favre, GB	2	69	39	56.5	502	7.28	5	7.2	1	1.4	t81	97.7
Roger Staubach, Dal	4	98	61	62.2	734	7.49	8	8.2	4	4.1	t45	95.4
Tom Brady, NE	4	156	100	64.1	1001	6.42	7	4.5	1	0.1	52	94.5
Kurt Warner, StL	2	89	52	58.4	779	8.75	3	3.4	2	1.1	t73	93.8
Len Dawson, KC	2	44	28	63.6	353	8.02	2	4.5	2	4.5	t46	84.8

Note: Minimum 40 attempts.

Rushing

	GP	Yds	Att	Avg	Lg	TD
Franco Harris, Pitt	4	354	101	3.5	25	4
Larry Csonka, Mia	3	297	57	5.2	49	2
Emmitt Smith, Dal	3	289	70	4.1	38	5
Terrell Davis, Den	2	259	55	4.7	27	3
John Riggins, Wash	2	230	64	3.6	43	2
Timmy Smith, Wash	1	204	22	9.3	58	2
Thurman Thomas, Buff	4	204	52	3.9	31	4
Roger Craig, SF	3	217	44	4.9	20	3
Marcus Allen, LA Rai	1	191	20	9.6	t74	2
Antowain Smith, NE	2	175	44	4.0	17	1

Receiving

	GP	No.	Yds	Avg	Lg	TD
Jerry Rice, SF	4	33	589	17.9	t48	8
Andre Reed, Buff	4	27	323	12.0	40	0
Deion Branch, NE	2	21	276	13.1	52	1
Roger Craig, SF	3	20	212	10.6	40	2
Thurman Thomas, Buff	4	20	144	7.2	24	0
Jay Novacek, Dal	3	17	148	8.7	23	2
Lynn Swann, Pitt	4	16	364	22.8	t74	3
Michael Irvin, Dal	3	16	256	16.0	25	2
Troy Brown, NE	3	16	182	11.4	23	0
Chuck Foreman, Minn	3	15	139	9.3	26	0

t-scored touchdown

Single-Game Leaders

Scoring

	Pts
Roger Craig: XIX, San Francisco vs Miami (1 rush, 2 rec)	18
Jerry Rice: XXIV, San Francisco vs Denver (3 rec); XXIX, SF vs San Diego (3 rec)	18
Ricky Watters: XXIX, San Francisco vs San Diego (1 rush, 2 rec)	18
Terrell Davis: XXXII, Denver vs Green Bay (3 rec)	18

Rushing Yards

	Yds
Timmy Smith: XXII, Washington vs Denver	204
Marcus Allen: XVIII, LA Raiders vs Washington	191
John Riggins: XVII, Washington vs Miami	166
Franco Harris: IX, Pittsburgh vs Minnesota	158
Terrell Davis: XXXII, Denver vs Green Bay	157
Larry Csonka: VIII, Miami vs Minnesota	145
Clarence Davis: XI, Oakland vs Minnesota	137
Thurman Thomas: XXV, Buffalo vs NY Giants	135
Emmitt Smith: XXVIII, Dallas vs Buffalo	132
Michael Pittman: XXXVII, Tampa Bay vs Oakland	124

Receptions

	No.
Deion Branch: XXXIX, New England vs Phila.	11
Jerry Rice: XXIII, San Francisco vs Cincinnati	11
Dan Ross: XVI, Cincinnati vs San Francisco	11
Wes Welker: XLII, New England vs NY Giants	11
Joseph Addai: XLI, Indianapolis vs Chicago	10
Deion Branch: XXXVIII, New England vs Carolina	10
Andre Hastings: XXX, Pittsburgh vs Dallas	10
Tony Nathan: XIX, Miami vs San Francisco	10
Jerry Rice: XXIX, San Francisco vs San Diego	10
Antonio Freeman: XXXII, Green Bay vs Denver	9
Terrell Owens: XXXIX, Philadelphia vs New England	9
Ricky Sanders: XXII, Washington vs Denver	9

Seven tied with eight.

Touchdown Passes

	No.
Steve Young: XXIX, San Francisco vs San Diego	6
Joe Montana: XXIV, San Francisco vs Denver	5
Terry Bradshaw: XIII, Pittsburgh vs Dallas	4
Doug Williams: XXII, Washington vs Denver	4
Troy Aikman: XXVII, Dallas vs Buffalo	4

Seven tied with three.

Passing Yards

	Yds
Kurt Warner: XXXIV, St. Louis vs Tennessee	414
Kurt Warner: XXXVI, St. Louis vs New England	365
Donovan McNabb, XXXIX, Phila vs. New England	357
Joe Montana: XXIII, San Francisco vs Cincinnati	357
Tom Brady: XXXVIII, New England vs. Carolina	354
Doug Williams: XXII, Washington vs Denver	340
John Elway: XXXIII, Denver vs Atlanta	336
Joe Montana: XIX, San Francisco vs Miami	331
Steve Young: XXIX, San Francisco vs San Diego	325
Jake Delhomme: XXXVIII Carolina vs New England	323
Terry Bradshaw: XIII, Pittsburgh vs Dallas	318
Dan Marino: XIX, Miami vs San Francisco	318

Receiving Yards

	Yds
Jerry Rice: XXIII, San Francisco vs Cincinnati	215
Ricky Sanders: XXII, Washington vs Denver	193
Isaac Bruce: XXXIV, St. Louis vs Tennessee	162
Lynn Swann: X, Pittsburgh vs Dallas	161
Andre Reed: XXVII, Buffalo vs Dallas	152
Rod Smith: XXXIII, Denver vs Atlanta	152
Jerry Rice: XXIX, San Francisco vs San Diego	149
Jerry Rice: XXIV, San Francisco vs Denver	148
Deion Branch: XXXVIII, New England vs Carolina	143

Super Bowl History Recaps*

I - 1967

Green Bay	7	7	14	7—35
Kansas City	0	10	0	0—10

FIRST QUARTER: GB: McGee 37 pass from Starr (Chandler kick), 8:56. **Green Bay 7-0.**

SECOND QUARTER: KC: McClinton 7 pass from Dawson (Mercer kick), 4:20. **7-7.**
GB: Taylor 14 run (Chandler kick), 10:23. **Green Bay 14-7.**
KC: FG Mercer 31, 14:06. **Green Bay 14-10.**

THIRD QUARTER: GB: Pitts 5 run (Chandler kick), 2:27. **Green Bay 21-10.**
GB: McGee 13 pass from Starr (Chandler kick), 14:09. **Green Bay 28-10.**

FOURTH QUARTER: GB: Pitts 1 run (Chandler kick), 8:25. **Green Bay 35-10.**

A: 61,946

II - 1968

Green Bay	3	13	10	7—33
Oakland	0	7	0	7—14

FIRST QUARTER: GB: FG Chandler 39 5:07. **Green Bay 3-0.**

SECOND QUARTER: GB: FG Chandler, 20, 3:08. **Green Bay 6-0.**
GB: Dowler 62 pass from Starr (Chandler kick), 4:10. **Green Bay 13-0.**
Oak: Miller 23 pass from Lamonica (Blanda kick), 8:45. **Green Bay 13-7.**
GB: FG Chandler 43, 14:59. **Green Bay 16-7.**

THIRD QUARTER: GB: Anderson 2 run (Chandler kick), 9:06. **Green Bay 23-7.**
GB: FG Chandler 31, 14:58. **Green Bay 26-7.**

FOURTH QUARTER:
GB: Adderley 60 int return (Chandler kick), 3:57. **Green Bay 33-7.**
Oak: Miller 23 pass from Lamonica (Blanda kick), 5:47. **Green Bay 33-14.**

A: 75,546

III - 1969

NY Jets	0	7	6	3—16
Baltimore	0	0	0	7—7

SECOND QUARTER: Jets: Snell 4 run (Turner kick), 5:57. **Jets: 7-0.**

THIRD QUARTER: Jets: FG Turner 32, 4:52. **Jets: 10-0.**
Jets: FG Turner 30, 11:02. **Jets: 13-0.**

FOURTH QUARTER: Jets: FG Turner 9, 1:34. **Jets: 16-0.**
Balt: Hill 1 run (Michaels kick), 11:41. **Jets: 16-7.**

A: 75,389

IV - 1970

Kansas City	3	13	7	0—23
Minnesota	0	0	7	0—7

FIRST QUARTER: KC: FG Stenerud 48, 8:08. **Kansas City 3-0.**

SECOND QUARTER: KC: FG Stenerud 32, 1:40. **Kansas City 6-0.**
KC: FG Stenerud 25, 7:08. **Kansas City 9-0.**
KC: Garrett 5 run (Stenerud kick), 9:26. **Kansas City 16-0.**

THIRD QUARTER: Minn: Osborn 4 run (Cox kick), 10:28. **Kansas City 16-7.**
KC: Taylor 46 pass from Dawson (Stenerud kick), 13:38. **Kansas City 23-7.**

A: 80,562

V - 1971

Baltimore	0	6	0	10—16
Dallas	3	10	0	0—13

FIRST QUARTER: Dal (9:28): FG Clark 14, 9:28. **Dallas 3-0.**

SECOND QUARTER: Dal: FG Clark 30, 0:08. **Dallas 6-0.**
Balt: Mackey 75 pass from Unitas (kick blocked). 0:50. **6-6.**
Dal: Thomas 7 pass from Morton (Clark kick), 7:07. **Dallas 13-6.**

FOURTH QUARTER: Balt: Nowatzke 2 run (O'Brien kick), 7:25. **13-13.**
Balt: FG O'Brien 32, 14:55. **Baltimore 16-13.**

A: 79,204

VI - 1972

Dallas	3	7	7	7—24
Miami	0	3	0	0—3

FIRST QUARTER: Dal: FG Clark 9, 13:37. **Dallas 3-0.**

SECOND QUARTER: Dal: Alworth 7 pass from Staubach (Clark kick), 13:45. **Dallas 10-0.**
Mia: FG Yepremian, 31, 14:56. **Dallas 10-3.**

THIRD QUARTER: Dal: D. Thomas 3 run (Clark kick), 5:17. **Dallas 17-3.**

FOURTH QUARTER: Dal: Ditka 7 pass from Staubach (Clark kick), 3:18. **Dallas 24-3.**

A: 81,023

VII - 1973

Miami	7	7	0	0—14
Washington	0	0	0	7—7

FIRST QUARTER: Mia: Twilley 28 pass from Griese (Yepremian kick), 14:59. **Miami 7-0.**

SECOND QUARTER: Mia: Kiick 1 run (Yepremian kick), 14:42. **Miami 14-0.**

FOURTH QUARTER: Wash: Bass 49 fumble recovery return (Knight kick), 12:53. **Miami 14-7.**

A: 90,182

*From 1967 to 1999, Super Bowl scoring times indicate the time elapsed in each quarter. Starting in 2000, times listed give the time remaining in each quarter.

VIII - 1974

Miami	14	3	7	0—24
Minnesota	0	0	0	7—7

FIRST QUARTER: Mia: Csonka 5 run (Yepremian kick), 5:27. **Miami 7-0.**
Mia: Kiick 1 run (Yepremian kick), 13:38. **Miami 14-0.**

SECOND QUARTER: Mia: FG Yepremian 28, 8:58. **Miami 17-0.**

THIRD QUARTER: Mia: Csonka 2 run (Yepremian kick), 6:16. **Miami 24-0.**

FOURTH QUARTER: Minn: Tarkenton 4 run (Cox kick), 1:35. **Miami 24-7.**

A: 71,882

IX - 1975

Pittsburgh	0	2	7	7—16
Minnesota	0	0	0	6—6

SECOND QUARTER: Pit: White tackled Tarkenton for safety, 7:49. **Pittsburgh 2-0.**

THIRD QUARTER: Pit: Harris 9 run (Gerela kick), 1:35. **Pittsburgh 9-0.**

FOURTH QUARTER: Minn: T. Brown recovered blocked punt in end zone (kick failed), 4:27. **Pittsburgh 9-6.**
Pit: L. Brown 4 pass from Bradshaw (Gerela kick), 11:29. **Pittsburgh 16-6.**

A: 80,997

X - 1976

Pittsburgh	7	0	0	14—21
Dallas	7	3	0	7—17

FIRST QUARTER: Dal: D. Pearson 29 pass from Staubach (Fritsch kick), 4:36. **Dallas 7-0.**
Pit: Grossman 7 pass from Bradshaw (Gerela kick), 9:03. **7-7.**

SECOND QUARTER: Dal: FG Fritsch 36, 0:15. **Dallas 10-7.**

FOURTH QUARTER: Pit: Harrison blocked Hoopes's punt for safety, 3:32. **Dallas 10-9.**
Pit: FG Gerela 36, 6:19. **Pittsburgh 12-10.**
Pit: FG Gerela 18, 8:32. **Pittsburgh 15-10.**
Pit: Swann 64 pass from Bradshaw (kick failed), 11:58. **Pittsburgh 21-10.**
Dal: P. Howard 34 pass from Staubach (Fritsch kick), 13:12. **Pittsburgh 21-17.**

A: 80,187

XI - 1977

Oakland	0	16	3	13—32
Minnesota	0	0	7	7—14

SECOND QUARTER: Oak: FG Mann, 24, 0:48. **Oakland 3-0.**
Oak: Casper 1 pass from Stabler (Mann kick), 7:50. **Oakland 10-0.**
Oak: Banaszak 1 run (kick failed), 11:27. **Oakland 16-0.**

THIRD QUARTER: Oak: FG Mann, 40, 9:44. **Oakland 19-0.**
Min: S. White 8 pass from Tarkenton (Cox kick), 14:13. **Oakland 19-7.**

FOURTH QUARTER: Oak: Banaszak 2 run (Mann kick), 7:21. **Oakland 26-7.**
Oak: Brown 75 int return (kick failed), 9:17. **Oakland 32-7.**
Min: Voigt 13 pass from Lee (Cox kick), 14:35. **Oakland 32-14.**

A: 103,438

XII - 1978

Dallas	10	3	7	7—27
Denver	0	0	10	0—10

FIRST QUARTER: FIRST QUARTER: Dal: Dorsett 3 run (Herrera kick), 10:31. **Dallas 7-0.**
Dal: FG Herrera 35, 13:29. **Dallas 10-0.**

SECOND QUARTER: Dal: FG Herrera 43, 3:44. **Dallas 13-0.**

THIRD QUARTER: Den: FG Turner 47, 2:28. **Dallas 13-3.**
Dal: Johnson 45 pass from Staubach (Herrera kick), 8:01. **Dallas 20-3.**
Den: Lytle 1 run (Turner kick), 9:21. **Dallas 20-10.**

FOURTH QUARTER: Dal: Richards 29 pass from Newhouse (Herrera kick), 7:56. **Dallas 27-10.**

A: 76,400

XIII - 1979

Pittsburgh	7	14	0	14—35
Dallas	7	7	3	14—31

FIRST QUARTER: Pit: Stallworth 28 pass from Bradshaw (Gerela kick), 5:13. **Pittsburgh 7-0.**
Dal: Hill 39 pass from Staubach (Septien kick), 15:00. **7-7.**

SECOND QUARTER: Dal: Hegman 37 fumble recovery return (Septien kick), 2:52. **Dallas 14-7.**
Pit: Stallworth 75 pass from Bradshaw (Gerela kick), 4:35. **14-14.**
Pit: Bleier 7 pass from Bradshaw (Gerela kick), 14:34. **Pittsburgh 21-14.**

THIRD QUARTER: Dal: FG Septien 27, 12:24. **Pittsburgh 21-17.**

FOURTH QUARTER: Pit: Harris 22 run (Gerela kick), 7:50. **Pittsburgh 28-17.**
Pit: Swann 18 pass from Bradshaw (Gerela kick), 8:09. **Pittsburgh 35-17.**
Dal: DuPree 7 pass from Staubach (Septien kick), 12:33. **Pittsburgh 35-24.**
Dal: B. Johnson 4 pass from Staubach (Septien kick), 14:38. **Pittsburgh 35-31.**

A: 79,484

XIV - 1980

Pittsburgh	**3**	**7**	**7**	**14—31**
LA Rams	**7**	**6**	**6**	**0—19**

FIRST QUARTER: Pit: FG Bahr, 41, 7:29. **Pittsburgh 3-0.**
LA: Bryant 1 run (Corral kick), 12:16. **LA Rams 7-3.**

SECOND QUARTER: Pit: Harris 1 run (Bahr kick), 2:08. **Pittsburgh 10-7.**
LA: FG Corral 31, 7:39. **10-10.**
LA: FG Corral 45, 14:46. **LA Rams 13-10.**

THIRD QUARTER: Pit: Swann 47 pass from Bradshaw (Bahr kick), 2:48. **Pittsburgh 17-13.**
LA: Smith 24 pass from McCutcheon (kick failed), 4:45. **LA Rams 19-17.**

FOURTH QUARTER: Pit: Stallworth 73 pass from Bradshaw (Bahr kick), 2:56. **Pittsburgh 24-19.**
Pit: Harris 1 run (Bahr kick), 13:11. **Pittsburgh 31-19.**

A: 103,985

XV - 1981

Oakland	**14**	**0**	**10**	**3—27**
Philadelphia	**0**	**3**	**0**	**7—10**

FIRST QUARTER: Oak: Branch 2 pass from Plunkett (Bahr kick), 6:04. **Oakland 7-0.**
Oak: King 80 pass from Plunkett (Bahr kick), 14:51. **Oakland 14-0.**

SECOND QUARTER: Phi: FG Franklin 30, 4:32. **Oakland 14-3.**

THIRD QUARTER: Oak: Branch 29 pass from Plunkett (Bahr kick), 2:36. **Oakland 21-3.**
Oak: FG Bahr 46, 10:25. **Oakland 24-3.**

FOURTH QUARTER: Phi: Krepfle 8 pass from Jaworski (Franklin kick), 1:01. **Oakland 24-10.**
Oak: FG Bahr, 35, 6:31. **Oakland 27-10.**

A: 76,135

XVI - 1982

San Francisco	**7**	**13**	**0**	**6—26**
Cincinnati	**0**	**0**	**7**	**14—21**

FIRST QUARTER: SF: Montana 1 run (Wersching kick), 9:08. **San Francisco 7-0.**

SECOND QUARTER: SF: E. Cooper 11 pass from Montana (Wersching kick), 8:07. **San Francisco 14-0.**
SF: FG Wersching 22, 14:45. **San Francisco 17-0.**
SF: FG Wersching 26, 14:58. **San Francisco 20-0.**

THIRD QUARTER: Cin: Anderson 5 run (Breech kick), 3:35. **San Francisco 20-7.**

FOURTH QUARTER: Cin: Ross 4 pass from Anderson (Breech kick), 4:54. **San Francisco 20-14.**
SF: FG Wersching 40, 9:35. **San Francisco 23-14.**
SF: FG Wersching 23, 13:03. **San Francisco 26-14.**
Cin: Ross 3 pass from Anderson (Breech kick), 14:44. **San Francisco 26-21.**

A: 81,270

XVII - 1983

Washington	**0**	**10**	**3**	**14—27**
Miami	**7**	**10**	**0**	**0—17**

FIRST QUARTER: Mia: Cefalo 76 pass from Woodley (Von Schamann kick), 6:49. **Miami 7-0.**

SECOND QUARTER: Wash: FG Moseley 31, 0:21. **Miami 7-3.**
Mia: FG Von Schamann 20, 9:00. **Miami 10-3.**
Wash: Garrett 4 pass from Theismann (Moseley kick), 13:09. **10-10.**
Mia: Walker 98 kick return (Von Schamann kick), 13:22. **Miami 17-10.**

THIRD QUARTER: Wash: FG Moseley 20, 6:51. **Miami 17-13.**

FOURTH QUARTER: Wash: Riggins 43 run (Moseley kick), 4:59. **Washington 20-17.**
Wash: Brown 6 pass from Theismann (Moseley kick), 13:05. **Washington 27-17.**

A: 103,667

XVIII - 1984

LA Raiders	**7**	**14**	**14**	**3—38**
Washington	**0**	**3**	**6**	**0—9**

FIRST QUARTER: LA: Jensen 0 blocked punt return (Bahr kick), 4:52. **LA Raiders 7-0.**

SECOND QUARTER: LA: Branch 12 pass from Plunkett (Bahr kick), 5:46. **LA Raiders 14-0.**
Wash: FG Moseley 24, 11:55. **LA Raiders 14-3.**
LA: Squirek 5 int return (Bahr kick), 14:53. **LA Raiders 21-3.**

THIRD QUARTER: Wash: Riggins 1 run (kick blocked), 4:08. **LA Raiders 21-9.**
LA: Allen 5 run (Bahr kick), 7:54. **LA Raiders 28-9.**
LA: Allen 74 run (Bahr kick), 15:00. **LA Raiders 35-9.**

FOURTH QUARTER: LA: FG Bahr 21, 12:36. **LA Raiders 38-9.**

A: 72,920

XIX - 1985

San Francisco	**7**	**21**	**10**	**0–38**
Miami	**10**	**6**	**0**	**0–16**

FIRST QUARTER: Mia: FG Von Schamann 37, 7:36. **Miami 3–0.**
SF: Monroe 33 pass from Montana (Wersching kick), 11:48. **San Francisco 7–3.**
Mia: D. Johnson 2 pass from Marino (Von Schamann kick), 14:15. **Miami 10–7.**

SECOND QUARTER: SF: Craig 8 pass from Montana (Wersching kick), 3:26. **San Francisco 14–10.**
SF: Montana 6 run (Wersching kick), 8:02. **San Francisco 21–10.**
SF: Craig 2 run (Wersching kick), 12:55. **San Francisco 28–10.**
Mia: FG Von Schamann 31, 14:48. **San Francisco 28–13.**
Mia: FG Von Schamann 30, 15:00. **San Francisco 28–16.**

THIRD QUARTER: SF: FG Wersching 27, 4:48. **San Francisco 31–16.**
SF: Craig 16 pass from Montana (Wershing kick), 8:42. **San Francisco 38–16.**

A: 84,059

XX - 1986

Chicago	**13**	**10**	**21**	**2–46**
New England	**3**	**0**	**0**	**7–10**

FIRST QUARTER: NE: FG Franklin 36, 1:19. **New England 3–0.**
Chi: FG Butler 28, 5:40. **3–3.**
Chi: FG Butler 24, 13:34. **Chicago 6–3.**
Chi: Suhey 11 run (Butler kick), 14:37. **Chicago 13–3.**

SECOND QUARTER: Chi: McMahon 2 run (Butler kick), 7:36. **Chicago 20–3.**
Chi: FG Butler 24, 15:00. **Chicago 23–3.**

THIRD QUARTER: Chi: McMahon 1 run (Butler kick), 7:38. **Chicago 30–3.**
Chi: Phillips 28 int return (Butler kick), 8:44. **Chicago 37–3.**
Chi: Perry 1 run (Butler kick), 11:38. **Chicago 44–3.**

FOURTH QUARTER: NE: Fryar 8 pass from Grogan (Franklin kick), 1:46. **Chicago 44–10.**
Chi: Waechter safety, 9:24. **Chicago 46–10.**

A: 73,818

XXI - 1987

NY Giants	**7**	**2**	**17**	**13–39**
Denver	**10**	**0**	**0**	**10–20**

FIRST QUARTER: Den: FG Karlis 48, 4:09. **Denver 3–0.**
NYG: Mowatt 6 pass from Simms (Allegre kick), 9:33. **NY Giants 7–3.**
Den: Elway 4 run (Karlis kick), 12:54. **Denver 10–7.**

SECOND QUARTER: NYG: Martin safety, 12:14. **Denver 10–9.**

THIRD QUARTER: NYG: Bavaro 13 pass from Simms (Allegre kick), 4:52. **NY Giants 16–10.**
NYG: FG Allegre 21, 11:06. **NY Giants 19–10.**
NYG: Morris 1 run (Allegre kick), 14:36. **NY Giants 26–10.**

FOURTH QUARTER: NYG: McConkey 6 pass from Simms (Allegre kick), 4:04. **NY Giants 33–10.**
Den: FG Karlis 28, 8:59. **NY Giants 33–13.**
NYG: Anderson 2 run (kick failed), 11:42. **NY Giants 39–13.**
Den: Johnson 47 pass from Elway (Karlis kick), 12:54. **NY Giants 39–20.**

A: 101,063

XXII - 1988

Washington	**0**	**35**	**0**	**7–42**
Denver	**10**	**0**	**0**	**0–10**

FIRST QUARTER: Den: Nattiel 56 pass from Elway (Karlis kick), 1:57. **Denver 7–0.**
Den: FG Karlis 24, 5:51. **Denver 10–0.**

SECOND QUARTER: Wash: Sanders 80 pass from D. Williams (Haji-Sheikh kick), 0:53. **Denver 10–7.**
Wash: Clark 27 pass from D. Williams (Haji-Sheikh kick), 4:45. **Washington 14–10.**
Wash: Smith 58 run (Haji-Sheikh kick), 8:33. **Washington 21–10.**
Wash: Sanders 50 pass from D. Williams (Haji-Sheikh kick), 11:18. **Washington 28–10.**
Wash: Didier 8 pass from D. Williams (Haji-Sheikh kick), 13:56. **Washington 35–10.**

FOURTH QUARTER: Wash: Smith 4 run (Haji-Sheikh kick), 1:51. **Washington 42–10.**

A: 73,302

XXIII - 1989

San Francisco	**3**	**0**	**3**	**14–20**
Cincinnati	**0**	**3**	**10**	**3–16**

FIRST QUARTER: SF: FG Cofer 41, 11:46. **San Francisco 3–0.**

SECOND QUARTER: Cin: FG Breech 34, 13:41. **3–3.**

THIRD QUARTER: Cin: FG Breech 43, 9:15. **Cincinnati 6–3.**
SF: FG Cofer 32, 14:10. **6–6.**
Cin: Jennings 93 kick return (Breech kick), 14:26. **Cincinnati 13–6.**

FOURTH QUARTER: SF: Rice 14 pass from Montana (Cofer kick), 0:57. **13–13.**
Cin: FG Breech 40, 11:40. **Cincinnati 16–13.**
SF: Taylor 10 pass from Montana (Cofer kick), 14:26. **San Francisco 20–16.**

A: 75,129

XXIV - 1990

San Francisco	**13**	**14**	**14**	**14—55**
Denver	**3**	**0**	**7**	**0—10**

FIRST QUARTER: SF: Rice 20 pass from Montana (Cofer kick), 4:54. **San Francisco 7-0.**
Den: FG Treadwell 42, 8:13. **San Francisco 7-3.**
SF: Jones 7 pass from Montana (kick failed), 14:57. **San Francisco 13-3.**

SECOND QUARTER: SF: Rathman 1 run (Cofer kick), 7:45. **San Francisco 20-3.**
SF: Rice 38 pass from Montana (Cofer kick), 14:26. **San Francisco 27-3.**

THIRD QUARTER: SF: Rice 28 pass from Montana (Cofer kick), 2:12. **San Francisco 34-3.**
SF: Taylor 35 pass from Montana (Cofer kick), 5:16. **San Francisco 41-3.**
Den: Elway 3 run (Treadwell kick), 8:07. **San Francisco 41-10.**

FOURTH QUARTER: SF: Rathman 3 run (Cofer kick), 0:03. **San Francisco 48-10.**
SF: Craig 1 run (Cofer kick), 1:13. **San Francisco 55-10.**

A: 72,919

XXV - 1991

NY Giants	**3**	**7**	**7**	**3—20**
Buffalo	**3**	**9**	**0**	**7—19**

FIRST QUARTER: NYG: FG Bahr 28, 7:46. **NY Giants 3-0.**
Buff: FG Norwood 23, 9:09. **3-3.**

SECOND QUARTER: Buff: D. Smith 1 run (Norwood kick), 2:30. **Buffalo 10-3.**
Buff: B. Smith safety 0, 6:33. **Buffalo 12-3.**
NYG: Baker 14 pass from Hostetler (Bahr kick), 14:35. **Buffalo 12-10.**

THIRD QUARTER: NYG: Anderson 1 run (Bahr kick), 9:29. **NY Giants 17-12.**

FOURTH QUARTER: Buff: Thomas 31 run (Norwood kick), 0:08. **Buffalo 19-17.**
NYG: FG Bahr 21, 7:40. **NY Giants 20-19.**

A: 73,813

XXVI - 1992

Washington	**0**	**17**	**14**	**6—37**
Buffalo	**0**	**0**	**10**	**14—24**

SECOND QUARTER: Wash: FG Lohmiller 34, 1:58. **Washington 3-0.**
Wash: Byner 10 pass from Rypien (Lohmiller kick), 5:06. **Washington 10-0.**
Wash: Riggs 1 run (Lohmiller kick), 7:43. **Washington 17-0.**

THIRD QUARTER: Wash: Riggs 2 run (Lohmiller kick), 0:16. **Washington 24-0.**
Buff: FG Norwood 21, 3:01. **Washington 24-3.**
Buff: Thomas 1 run (Norwood kick), 9:02. **Washington 24-10.**
Wash: Clark 30 pass from Rypien (Lohmiller kick), 13:36. **Washington 31-10.**

FOURTH QUARTER: Wash: FG Lohmiller 25, 0:06. **Washington 34-10.**
Wash: FG Lohmiller 39, 3:24. **Washington 37-10.**
Buff: Metzelaars 2 pass from Kelly (Norwood kick), 9:01. **Washington 37-17.**
Buff: Beebe 4 pass from Kelly (Norwood kick), 11:05. **Washington 37-24.**

A: 63,130.

XXVII - 1993

Dallas	**14**	**14**	**3**	**21—52**
Buffalo	**7**	**3**	**7**	**0—17**

FIRST QUARTER: Buff: Thomas 2 run (Christie kick), 5:00. **Buffalo 7-0.**
Dal: Novacek 23 pass from Aikman (Elliott kick), 13:24. **7-7.**
Dal: J.Jones 2 fumble return (Elliott kick), 13:39. **Dallas 14-7.**

SECOND QUARTER: Buff: FG Christie 21, 11:36. **Dallas 14-10.**
Dal: Irvin 19 pass from Aikman (Elliott kick)13:06. **Dallas 21-10.**
Dal: Irvin 18 pass from Aikman (Elliott kick), 13:24. **Dallas 28-10.**

THIRD QUARTER: Dal: FG Elliott 20, 6:39. **Dallas 31-10.**
Buff: Beebe 40 pass from Reich (Christie kick), 15:00. **Dallas 31-17.**

FOURTH QUARTER: Dal: Harper 45 pass from Aikman (Elliott kick), 4:56. **Dallas 38-17.**
Dal: E. Smith 10 run (Elliott kick), 6:48. **Dallas 45-17.**
Dal: Norton 9 fumble return (Elliott kick), 7:29. **Dallas 52-17.**

A: 98,374

XXVIII - 1994

Dallas	**6**	**0**	**14**	**10—30**
Buffalo	**3**	**10**	**0**	**0—13**

FIRST QUARTER: Dal: FG Murray 41, 2:19. **Dallas 3-0.**
Buff: FG Christie 54: 4:41. **3-3.**
Dal: FG Murray 24, 11:05. **Dallas 6-3.**

SECOND QUARTER: Buff: Thomas 4 run (Christie kick), 2:34. **Buffalo 10-6.**
Buff: FG Christie 28, 15:00. **Buffalo 13-6.**

THIRD QUARTER: Dal: Washington fumble return (Murray kick), 0:55. **13-13.**
Dal: Smith15 run (Murray kick), 0:55. **Dallas 20-13.**

FOURTH QUARTER: Dal: Smith1 run (Murray kick), 5:10. **Dallas 27-13.**
Dal: FG Murray 20, 12:10. **Dallas 30-13.**

A: 72,817

XXIX - 1995

San Francisco	**14**	**14**	**14**	**7—49**
San Diego	**7**	**3**	**8**	**8—26**

FIRST QUARTER: SF: Rice 44 pass from Young (Brien kick), 1:24.
San Francisco 7-0.
SF: Watters 51 pass from Young (Brien kick, 4:55.
San Francisco 14-0.
SD: Means 1 run (Carney kick), 12:16.
San Francisco 14-7.

SECOND QUARTER: SF: Floyd 5 pass from Young (Brien kick), 1:58.
San Francisco 21-7.
SF: Watters 8 pass from Young (Brien kick), 10:16.
San Francisco 28-7.
SD: FG Carney 31, 13:16. **San Francisco 28-10.**

THIRD QUARTER: SF: Watters 9 run (Brien kick), 5:25.
San Francisco 35-10.
SF: Rice 15 pass from Young (Brien kick), 11:42.
San Francisco 42-10.
SD: Coleman 98 kickoff return (Humphries 2-pt conv pass to Seay), 11:59. **San Francisco 42-18.**

FOURTH QUARTER: SF: Rice 7 pass from Young (Brien kick), 1:11.
San Francisco 49-18.
SD: Martin 30 pass from Humphries (Humphries 2 pt-conv pass to Pupunu), 12:35. **San Francisco 49-26.**

A: 74,107.

XXX - 1996

Dallas	**10**	**3**	**7**	**7—27**
Pittsburgh	**0**	**7**	**0**	**10—17**

FIRST QUARTER: Dal: FG Boniol 42, 2:55. **Dallas 3-0.**
Dal: Novacek 3 pass from Aikman (Boniol kick), 9:37.
Dallas 10-0.

SECOND QUARTER: Dal: FG Boniol 35, 8:57.
Dallas 13-0.
Pitt: Thigpen 6 pass from O'Donnell (N. Johnson kick), 14:47. **Dallas 13-7.**

THIRD QUARTER: Dal: E. Smith 1 run (Boniol kick), 8:18.
Dallas 20-7.

FOURTH QUARTER: Pitt: FG N. Johnson 46, 3:40.
Dallas 20-10.
Pitt: Morris 1 run (N. Johnson kick), 8:24. **Dallas 20-17.**
Dal: E. Smith 4 run (Boniol kick), 11:17. **Dallas 27-17.**

A: 76,347.

XXXI - 1997

Green Bay	**10**	**17**	**8**	**0—35**
New England	**14**	**0**	**7**	**0—21**

FIRST QUARTER: GB: Rison 54 pass from Favre (Jacke kick), 3:32. **Green Bay 7-0.**
GB: FG Jacke 37, 6:18. **Green Bay 10-0.**
NE: Byars 1 pass from Bledsoe (Vinatieri kick), 8:25.
Green Bay 10-7.
NE: Coates 4 pass from Bledsoe (Vinatieri kick), 12:27. **New England 14-10.**

SECOND QUARTER: GB: Freeman 81 pass from Favre (Jacke kick), 0:56. **Green Bay 17-14.**
GB: FG Jacke 31, 6:45. **Green Bay 20-14.**
GB: Favre 2 run (Jacke kick), 13:49. **Green Bay 27-14.**

THIRD QUARTER: NE: Martin 18 run (Vinatieri kick), 11:33.
Green Bay 27-21.
GB: Howard 99 kickoff return (Favre 2 pt conv pass to Chmura), 11:50. **Green Bay 35-21.**

A: 72,301.

XXXII - 1998

Denver	**7**	**10**	**7**	**7—31**
Green Bay	**7**	**7**	**3**	**7—24**

FIRST QUARTER: GB: Freeman 22 pass from Favre (Longwell kick), 4:02. **Green Bay 7-0.**
Den: Davis 1 run (Elam kick), 9:21. **7-7.**

SECOND QUARTER: Den: Elway 1 run (Elam kick), 0:05.
Denver 14-7.
Den: FG Elam 51, 2:39. **Denver 17-7.**
GB: Chmura 6 pass from Favre (Longwell kick), 14:48. **Denver 17-14.**

THIRD QUARTER: GB: FG Longwell 27, 3:01. **17-17.**
Den: Davis 1 run (Elam kick), 14:26. **Denver 24-17.**

FOURTH QUARTER: GB: Freeman 13 pass from Favre (Longwell kick), 1:28. **24-24.**
Den: Davis 1 run (Elam kick), 13:15. **Denver 31-24.**

A: 68,912

XXXIII - 1999

Denver	**7**	**10**	**0**	**17—34**
Atlanta	**3**	**3**	**0**	**13—19**

FIRST QUARTER: Atl: FG Andersen 32, 5:25. **Atlanta 3–0.**
Den: Griffith 1 run (Elam kick), 11:05. **Denver 7–3.**

SECOND QUARTER: Den: FG Elam 26, 5:43. **Denver 10–3.**
Den: Smith 80 pass from Elway (Elam kick), 10:06. **Denver 17–3.**
Atl: FG Andersen 28, 12:35. **Denver 17–6.**

FOURTH QUARTER: Den: Griffith 1 run (Elam kick), 0:04. **Denver 24–6.**
Den: Elway 3 run (Elam kick), 3:40. **Denver 31–6.**
Atl: Dwight 94 kickoff return (Andersen kick), 3:59. **Denver 31–13.**
Den: FG Elam 37, 7:52. **Denver 34–13.**
Atl: Mathis 3 pass from Chandler (2-pt conv failed), 12:56. **Denver 34–19.**

A: 74,803

XXXIV - 2000

St. Louis	**3**	**6**	**7**	**7—23**
Tennessee	**0**	**0**	**6**	**10—16**

FIRST QUARTER: StL: FG Wilkins 27, 3:00. **St. Louis 3–0.**

SECOND QUARTER: StL: FG Wilkins 29, 4:16. **St. Louis 6–0.**
StL: FG Wilkins 28, 0:15. **St. Louis 9–0.**

THIRD QUARTER: StL: Holt 9 pass from Warner (Wilkins kick), 7:20. **St. Louis 16–0.**
Tenn: George 1 run (2-pt conv failed), 0:14. **St. Louis 16–6.**

FOURTH QUARTER: Tenn: George 2 run (Del Greco kick), 7:21. **St. Louis 16–13.**
Tenn: FG Del Greco 43, 2:15. **16–16.**
StL: : Bruce 73 pass from Warner, 1:54. **St. Louis 23–16.**

A: 72,265

XXXV - 2001

Baltimore	**7**	**3**	**14**	**10—34**
NY Giants	**0**	**0**	**7**	**0—7**

FIRST QUARTER: Balt: Stokely 38 pass from Dilfer (Stover kick), 6:50. **Baltimore 7-0.**

SECOND QUARTER: Balt: FG Stover 47, 1:41. **Baltimore 10-0.**

THIRD QUARTER: Balt: Starks 49 int return (Stover kick), 3:49. **Baltimore 17-0.**
NYG: Dixon 97 kickoff return (Daluiso kick), 3:31. **Baltimore 17-7.**
Balt: Je. Lewis 84 kickoff return (Stover kick), 3:13. **Baltimore 24-7.**

FOURTH QUARTER: Balt: Ja. Lewis 3 run (Stover kick), 8:45. **Baltimore 31-7.**
Balt: FG Stover 34, 5:28. **Baltimore 34-7.**

A: 71,921

XXXVI - 2002

New England	**0**	**14**	**3**	**3—20**
St. Louis	**3**	**0**	**0**	**14—17**

FIRST QUARTER: StL: FG Wilkins 50, 3:50. **St. Louis 3–0.**

SECOND QUARTER: NE: Law 47 int return (Vinatieri kick), 8:49. **New England 7–3.**
NE: Patten 8 pass from Brady (Vinatieri kick), 0:31. **New England 14–3.**

THIRD QUARTER: NE: FG Vinatieri 37, 1:18. **New England 17–3.**

FOURTH QUARTER: StL: Warner 2 run (Wilkins kick), 9:31. **New England 17-10.**
StL: Proehl 26 pass from Warner (Wilkins kick), 1:30. **17-17.**
NE: FG Vinatieri 48, 0:00. **New England 20-17.**

A: 72,922

XXXVII - 2003

Tampa Bay	**3**	**17**	**14**	**14—48**
Oakland	**3**	**0**	**6**	**12—21**

FIRST QUARTER: Oak: FG Janikowski 40, 10:20. **Oakland 3–0.**
TB: FG Gramatica 31, 7:51. **3–3.**

SECOND QUARTER: TB: FG Gramatica 43, 11:16. **Tampa Bay 6–3.**
TB: Alstott 2 run (Gramatica kick), 6:24. **Tampa Bay 13–3.**
TB: McCardell 5 pass from B. Johnson (Gramatica kick), 0:30. **Tampa Bay 20–3.**

THIRD QUARTER: TB: McCardell 8 pass from B. Johnson (Gramatica kick), 5:30. **Tampa Bay 27–3.**
TB: Smith 44 int. return (Gramatica kick), 4:47. **Tampa Bay 34–3.**
Oak: Porter 39 pass from Gannon (2-pt conv failed), 2:14. **Tampa Bay 34–9.**

FOURTH QUARTER: Oak: Johnson 13 return of blocked punt (two-pt. conversion failed), 14:14. **Tampa Bay 34–15.**
Oak: Rice 48 pass from Gannon (2-pt conv failed), 6:06. **Tampa Bay 34–21.**
TB: Brooks 44 int. return (Gramatica kick), 1:18. **Tampa Bay 41–21.**
TB: Smith 50 int. return (Gramatica kick), 0:02. **Tampa Bay 48–21.**

A: 67,603

XXXVIII - 2004

New England	**0**	**14**	**0**	**18—32**
Carolina	**0**	**10**	**0**	**19—29**

SECOND QUARTER: NE: Branch 5 pass from Brady (Vinatieri kick), 3:11. **New England 7-0.**

Car: Smith 39 pass from Delhomme (Kasay kick), 1:17. **7-7.**

NE: Givens 5 pass from Brady (Vinatieri kick), 0:28. **New England 14-7.**

Car: FG Kasay 50, 0:00. **New England 14-10.**

FOURTH QUARTER: NE: Smith 2 run (Vinatieri kick), 14:49. **New England 21-10.**

Car: Foster 33 run (2-pt conv failed), 12:49. **New England 21-16.**

Car: Muhammad 85 pass from Delhomme (2-pt conv failed), 7:13. **Carolina 22-21.**

NE: Vrabel 1 pass from Brady (Faulk ran for 2-pt conv), 2:51. **New England 29-22.**

Car: Proehl 12 pass from Delhomme (Kasay kick), 1:18. **29-29.**

NE: FG Vinatieri 41, 0:04. **New England 32-29.**

A: 71,525

XXXIX - 2005

New England	**0**	**7**	**7**	**10—24**
Philadelphia	**0**	**7**	**7**	**7—21**

SECOND QUARTER: Phil: Smith 6 pass from McNabb (Akers kick), 10:05. **Philadelphia 7-0.**
NE: Givens 4 pass from Brady (Vinatieri kick), 1:10. **7-7.**

THIRD QUARTER: NE: Vrabel 2 pass from Brady (Vinatieri kick), 11:04. **New England 14-7.**
Phil: Westbrook 10 pass from McNabb (Akers kick), 3:45. **14-14.**

FOURTH QUARTER: NE: Dillon 2 run (Vinatieri kick), 13:44. **New England 21-14.**

NE: FG Vinatieri 22, 9:40. **New England 24-14.**
Phil: Lewis 30 pass from McNabb (Akers kick), 13:12. **New England 24-21.**

A: 78,125

XL - 2006

Pittsburgh	**0**	**7**	**7**	**7—21**
Seattle	**3**	**0**	**7**	**0—10**

FIRST QUARTER: Sea: FG Brown 47, 0:22. **Seattle 3-0.**

SECOND QUARTER: Pit: Roethlisberger 1 run (Reed kick), 1:55. **Pittsburgh 7-3.**

THIRD QUARTER: Pit: Parker 75 run (Reed kick) , 14:38. **Pittsburgh 14-3.**
Sea: Stevens 16 pass from Hasselbeck (Brown kick), 6:45. **Pittsburgh 14-10.**

FOURTH QUARTER: Pit: Ward 43 pass from Randle El (Reed kick), 8:56. **Pittsburgh 21-10.**

A: 68,206

XLI - 2007

Indianapolis	**6**	**10**	**6**	**7—29**
Chicago	**14**	**0**	**3**	**0—17**

FIRST QUARTER: Chicago: TD Hester 92 kick return (Gould kick)14:46. **Chicago 7-0.**
Indianapolis: TD Wayne 53 pass from Manning, 6:50 (Vinatieri kick failed). **Chicago 7-6.**
Chicago: TD Muhammad 4 pass from Grossman (Gould kick), 4:34. **Chicago 14-6.**

SECOND QUARTER: Indianapolis: FG Vinatieri 29, 11:17. **Chicago 14-9.**
Indianapolis: TD Rhodes 1 run (Vinatieri kick), 6:09. **Indianapolis 16-14.**

THIRD QUARTER: Indianapolis: FG Vinatieri 24, 7:26. **Indianapolis 19-14.**
Indianapolis: FG Vinatieri 20, 3:16. **Indianapolis 22-14.**
Chicago: FG Gould 44, 1:14. **Indianapolis 22-17.**

FOURTH QUARTER: Indianapolis: TD Hayden 56 interception return (Vinatieri kick) 11:44. **Indianapolis 29-17.**

A: 74,512

XLII - 2008

NY Giants	**3**	**0**	**0**	**14—17**
New England	**0**	**7**	**0**	**7—14**

FIRST QUARTER: NY Giants: FG Tynes 32, 5:01. **NY Giants 3-0.**

SECOND QUARTER: New England: TD Maroney 1 run (Gostkowski kick), 14:57. **New England 7-3.**

FOURTH QUARTER: NY Giants: TD Tyree 5 pass from Manning (Tynes kick), 11:05. **NY Giants 10-7.**
New England: TD Moss 6 pass from Brady (Gostkowski kick), 02:42. **New England 14-10.**
NY Giants: TD Burress 13 pass from Manning (Tynes kick), 00:35. **NY Giants 17-14.** .

A: 71,101

NFL Playoff History

1933

NFL championship	Chicago Bears 23, NY Giants 21

1934

NFL championship	NY Giants 30, Chicago Bears 13

1935

NFL championship	Detroit 26, NY Giants 7

1936

NFL championship	Green Bay 21, Boston 6

1937

NFL championship	Washington 28, Chicago Bears 21

1938

NFL championship	NY Giants 23, Green Bay 17

1939

NFL championship	Green Bay 27, NY Giants 0

1940

NFL championship	Chicago Bears 73, Washington 0

1941

W. div. playoff	Chicago Bears 33, Green Bay 14
NFL championship	Chicago Bears 37, NY Giants 9

1942

NFL championship	Washington 14, Chicago Bears 6

1943

E. div. playoff	Washington 28, NY Giants 0
NFL championship	Chicago Bears 41, Washington 21

1944

NFL championship	Green Bay 14, NY Giants 7

1945

NFL championship	Cleveland 15, Washington 14

1946

NFL championship	Chicago Bears 24, NY Giants 14

1947

E. div. playoff	Philadelphia 21, Pittsburgh 0
NFL championship	Chi Cardinals 28, Philadelphia 21

1948

NFL championship	Philadelphia 7, Chi Cardinals 0

1949

NFL championship	Philadelphia 14, Los Angeles 0

1950

Am. Conf. playoff	Cleveland 8, NY Giants 3
Nat. Conf. playoff	Los Angeles 24, Chicago Bears 14
NFL championship	Cleveland 30, Los Angeles 28

1951

NFL championship	Los Angeles 24, Cleveland 17

1952

Nat. Conf. playoff	Detroit 31, Los Angeles 21
NFL championship	Detroit 17, Cleveland 7

1953

NFL championship	Detroit 17, Cleveland 16

1954

NFL championship	Cleveland 56, Detroit 10

1955

NFL championship	Cleveland 38, Los Angeles 14

1956

NFL championship	NY Giants 47, Chicago Bears 7

1957

W. Conf. playoff	Detroit 31, San Francisco 27
NFL championship	Detroit 59, Cleveland 14

1958

E. Conf. playoff	NY Giants 10, Cleveland 0
NFL championship	Baltimore 23, NY Giants 17

1959

NFL championship	Baltimore 31, NY Giants 16

1960

NFL championship	Philadelphia 17, Green Bay 13
AFL championship	Houston 24, LA Chargers 16

1961

NFL championship	Green Bay 37, NY Giants 0
AFL championship	Houston 10, San Diego 3

1962

NFL championship	Green Bay 16, NY Giants 7
AFL championship	Dallas Texans 20, Houston 17

1963

NFL championship	Chicago 14, NY Giants 10
AFL E. div. playoff	Boston 26, Buffalo 8
AFL championship	San Diego 51, Boston 10

1964

NFL championship	Cleveland 27, Baltimore 0
AFL championship	Buffalo 20, San Diego 7

1965

NFL W. Conf. playoff	Green Bay 13, Baltimore 10
NFL championship	Green Bay 23, Cleveland 12
AFL championship	Buffalo 23, San Diego 0

1966

NFL championship	Green Bay 34, Dallas 27
AFL championship	Kansas City 31, Buffalo 7

1967

NFL E. Conf. championship	Dallas 52, Cleveland 14
NFL W. Conf. championship	Green Bay 28, Los Angeles 7
NFL championship	Green Bay 21, Dallas 17
AFL championship	Oakland 40, Houston 7

1968

NFL E. Conf. championship	Cleveland 31, Dallas 20
NFL W. Conf. championship	Baltimore 24, Minnesota 14
NFL championship	Baltimore 34, Cleveland 0
AFL W. div. playoff	Oakland 41, Kansas City 6
AFL championship	NY Jets 27, Oakland 23

1969

NFL E. Conf. championship	Cleveland 38, Dallas 14
NFL W. Conf. championship	Minnesota 23, Los Angeles 20
NFL championship	Minnesota 27, Cleveland 7
AFL div. playoffs	Kansas City 13, NY Jets 6 Oakland 56, Houston 7
AFL championship	Kansas City 17, Oakland 7

NFL Playoff History *(Cont.)*

1970

AFC div. playoffs	Baltimore 17, Cincinnati 0
	Oakland 21, Miami 14
AFC championship	Baltimore 27, Oakland 17
NFC div. playoffs	Dallas 5, Detroit 0
	San Francisco 17, Minnesota 14
NFC championship	Dallas 17, San Francisco 10

1971

AFC div. playoffs	Miami 27, Kansas City 24
	Baltimore 20, Cleveland 3
AFC championship	Miami 21, Baltimore 0
NFC div. playoffs	Dallas 20, Minnesota 12
	San Francisco 24, Washington 20
NFC championship	Dallas 14, San Francisco 3

1972

AFC div. playoffs	Pittsburgh 13, Oakland 7
	Miami 20, Cleveland 14
AFC championship	Miami 21, Pittsburgh 17
NFC div. playoffs	Dallas 30, San Francisco 28
	Washington 16, Green Bay 3
NFC championship	Washington 26, Dallas 3

1973

AFC div. playoffs	Oakland 33, Pittsburgh 14
	Miami 34, Cincinnati 16
AFC championship	Miami 27, Oakland 10
NFC div. playoffs	Minnesota 27, Washington 20
	Dallas 27, Los Angeles 16
NFC championship	Minnesota 27, Dallas 10

1974

AFC div. playoffs	Oakland 28, Miami 26
	Pittsburgh 32, Buffalo 14
AFC championship	Pittsburgh 24, Oakland 13
NFC div. playoffs	Minnesota 30, St Louis 14
	Los Angeles 19, Washington 10
NFC championship	Minnesota 14, Los Angeles 10

1975

AFC div. playoffs	Pittsburgh 28, Baltimore 10
	Oakland 31, Cincinnati 28
AFC championship	Pittsburgh 16, Oakland 10
NFC div. playoffs	Los Angeles 35, St Louis 23
	Dallas 17, Minnesota 14
NFC championship	Dallas 37, Los Angeles 7

1976

AFC div. playoffs	Oakland 24, New England 21
	Pittsburgh 40, Baltimore 14
AFC championship	Oakland 24, Pittsburgh 7
NFC div. playoffs	Minnesota 35, Washington 20
	Los Angeles 14, Dallas 12
NFC championship	Minnesota 24, Los Angeles 13

1977

AFC div. playoffs	Denver 34, Pittsburgh 21
	Oakland 37, Baltimore 31
AFC championship	Denver 20, Oakland 17
NFC div. playoffs	Dallas 37, Chicago 7
	Minnesota 14, Los Angeles 7
NFC championship	Dallas 23, Minnesota 6

1978

AFC 1st-rd. playoff	Houston 17, Miami 9
AFC div. playoffs	Houston 31, New England 14
	Pittsburgh 33, Denver 10
AFC championship	Pittsburgh 34, Houston 5
NFC 1st-rd. playoff	Atlanta 14, Philadelphia 13
NFC div. playoffs	Dallas 27, Atlanta 20
	Los Angeles 34, Minnesota 10
NFC championship	Dallas 28, Los Angeles 0

1979

AFC 1st-rd. playoff	Houston 13, Denver 7
AFC div. playoffs	Houston 17, San Diego 14
	Pittsburgh 34, Miami 14
AFC championship	Pittsburgh 27, Houston 13
NFC 1st-rd. playoff	Philadelphia 27, Chicago 17
NFC div. playoffs	Tampa Bay 24, Philadelphia 17
	Los Angeles 21, Dallas 19
NFC championship	Los Angeles 9, Tampa Bay 0

1980

AFC 1st-rd. playoff	Oakland 27, Houston 7
AFC div. playoffs	San Diego 20, Buffalo 14
	Oakland 14, Cleveland 12
AFC championship	Oakland 34, San Diego 27
NFC 1st-rd. playoff	Dallas 34, Los Angeles 13
NFC div. playoffs	Philadelphia 31, Minnesota 16
	Dallas 30, Atlanta 27
NFC championship	Philadelphia 20, Dallas 7

1981

AFC 1st-rd. playoff	Buffalo 31, NY Jets 27
AFC div. playoffs	San Diego 41, Miami 38
	Cincinnati 28, Buffalo 21
AFC championship	Cincinnati 27, San Diego 7
NFC 1st-rd. playoff	NY Giants 27, Philadelphia 21
NFC div. playoffs	Dallas 38, Tampa Bay 0
	San Francisco 38, NY Giants 24
NFC championship	San Francisco 28, Dallas 27

1982

AFC 1st-rd. playoffs	Miami 28, New England 13
	LA Raiders 27, Cleveland 10
	NY Jets 44, Cincinnati 17
	San Diego 31, Pittsburgh 28
AFC div. playoffs	NY Jets 17, LA Raiders 14
	Miami 34, San Diego 13
AFC championship	Miami 14, NY Jets 0
NFC 1st-rd. playoffs	Washington 31, Detroit 7
	Green Bay 41, St Louis 16
	Minnesota 30, Atlanta 24
	Dallas 30, Tampa Bay 17
NFC div. playoffs	Washington 21, Minnesota 7
	Dallas 37, Green Bay 26
NFC championship	Washington 31, Dallas 17

1983

AFC 1st-rd. playoff	Seattle 31, Denver 7
AFC div. playoffs	Seattle 27, Miami 20
	LA Raiders 38, Pittsburgh 10
AFC championship	LA Raiders 30, Seattle 14
NFC 1st-rd. playoff	LA Rams 24, Dallas 17
NFC div. playoffs	San Francisco 24, Detroit 23
	Washington 51, LA Rams 7
NFC championship	Washington 24, San Francisco 21

1984

AFC 1st-rd. playoff	Seattle 13, LA Raiders 7
AFC div. playoffs	Miami 31, Seattle 10
	Pittsburgh 24, Denver 17
AFC championship	Miami 45, Pittsburgh 28
NFC 1st-rd. playoff	NY Giants 16, LA Rams 13
NFC div. playoffs	San Francisco 21, NY Giants 10
	Chicago 23, Washington 19
NFC championship	San Francisco 23, Chicago 0

1985

AFC 1st-rd. playoff	New England 26, NY Jets 14
AFC div. playoffs	Miami 24, Cleveland 21
	New England 27, LA Raiders 20
AFC championship	New England 31, Miami 14
NFC 1st-rd. playoff	NY Giants 17, San Francisco 3
NFC div. playoffs	LA Rams 20, Dallas 0
	Chicago 21, NY Giants 0
NFC championship	Chicago 24, LA Rams 0

NFL Playoff History *(Cont.)*

1986

AFC 1st-rd. playoff	NY Jets 35, Kansas City 15
AFC div. playoffs	Cleveland 23, NY Jets 20
	Denver 22, New England 17
AFC championship	Denver 23, Cleveland 20
NFC 1st-rd. playoff	Washington 19, LA Rams 7
NFC div playoffs	Washington 27, Chicago 13
	NY Giants 49, San Francisco 3
NFC championship	NY Giants 17, Washington 0

1987

AFC 1st-rd. playoff	Houston 23, Seattle 20
AFC div. playoffs	Cleveland 38, Indianapolis 21
	Denver 34, Houston 10
AFC championship	Denver 38, Cleveland 33
NFC 1st-rd. playoff	Minnesota 44, New Orleans 10
NFC div playoffs	Minnesota 36, San Francisco 24
	Washington 21, Chicago 17
NFC championship	Washington 17, Minnesota 10

1988

AFC 1st-rd. playoff	Houston 24, Cleveland 23
AFC div. playoffs	Cincinnati 21, Seattle 13
	Buffalo 17, Houston 10
AFC championship	Cincinnati 21, Buffalo 10
NFC 1st-rd. playoff	Minnesota 28, LA Rams 17
NFC div. playoffs	Chicago 20, Philadelphia 12
	San Francisco 34, Minnesota 9
NFC championship	San Francisco 28, Chicago 3

1989

AFC 1st-rd. playoff	Pittsburgh 26, Houston 23
AFC div. playoffs	Cleveland 34, Buffalo 30
	Denver 24, Pittsburgh 23
AFC championship	Denver 37, Cleveland 21
NFC 1st-rd. playoff	LA Rams 21, Philadelphia 7
NFC div. playoffs	LA Rams 19, NY Giants 13
	San Francisco 41, Minnesota 13
NFC championship	San Francisco 30, LA Rams 3

1990

AFC 1st-rd. playoffs	Miami 17, Kansas City 16
	Cincinnati 41, Houston 14
AFC div. playoffs	Buffalo 44, Miami 34
	LA Raiders 20, Cincinnati 10
AFC championship	Buffalo 51, LA Raiders 3
NFC 1st-rd. playoffs	Chicago 16, New Orleans 6
NFC 1st-rd playoffs	Washington 20, Philadelphia 6
NFC div. playoffs	NY Giants 31, Chicago 3
	San Francisco 28, Washington 10
NFC championship	NY Giants 15, San Francisco 13

1991

AFC 1st-rd. playoffs	Houston 17, NY Jets 10
	Kansas City 10, LA Raiders 6
AFC div. playoffs	Denver 26, Houston 24
	Buffalo 37, Kansas City 14
AFC championship	Buffalo 10, Denver 7
NFC 1st-rd. playoffs	Atlanta 27, New Orleans 20
	Dallas 17, Chicago 13
NFC div. playoffs	Washington 24, Atlanta 7
	Detroit 38, Dallas 6
NFC championship	Washington 41, Detroit 10

1992

AFC 1st-rd. playoffs	San Diego 17, Kansas City 0
	Buffalo 41, Houston 38 (OT)
AFC div. playoffs	Buffalo 24, Pittsburgh 3
	Miami 31, San Diego 0
AFC championship	Buffalo 29, Miami 10
NFC 1st-rd. playoffs	Washington 24, Minnesota 7
	Philadelphia 36, New Orleans 20
NFC div. playoffs	San Francisco 20, Washington 13
	Dallas 34, Philadelphia 10
NFC championship	Dallas 30, San Francisco 20

1993

AFC 1st-rd. playoffs	LA Raiders 42, Denver 24
	Kansas City 27, Pittsburgh 24 (OT)
AFC div. playoffs	Buffalo 29, LA Raiders 23
	Kansas City 28, Houston 20
AFC championship	Buffalo 30, Kansas City 13
NFC 1st-rd. playoffs	NY Giants 17, Minnesota 10
	Green Bay 28, Detroit 24
NFC div. playoffs	San Francisco 44, NY Giants 3
	Dallas 27, Green Bay 17
NFC championship	Dallas 38, San Francisco 21

1994

AFC 1st-rd. playoffs	Miami 27, Kansas City 17
	Cleveland 20, New England 13
AFC div. playoffs	San Diego 22, Miami 21
	Pittsburgh 29, Cleveland 9
AFC championship	San Diego 17, Pittsburgh 13
NFC 1st-rd. playoffs	Green Bay 16, Detroit 12
	Chicago 35, Minnesota 18
NFC div. playoffs	Dallas 35, Green Bay 9
	San Francisco 44, Chicago 15
NFC championship	San Francisco 38, Dallas 28

1995

AFC 1st-rd. playoffs	Buffalo 37, Miami 22
	Indianapolis 35, San Diego 20
AFC div. playoffs	Pittsburgh 40, Buffalo 21
	Indianapolis 10, Kansas City 7
AFC championship	Pittsburgh 20, Indianapolis 16
NFC 1st-rd. playoffs	Philadelphia 58, Detroit 37
	Green Bay 37, Atlanta 20
NFC div. playoffs	Dallas 30, Philadelphia 11
	Green Bay 27, San Francisco 17
NFC championship	Dallas 38, Green Bay 27

1996

AFC 1st-rd. playoffs	Jacksonville 30, Buffalo 27
	Pittsburgh 42, Indianapolis 14
AFC div. playoffs	Jacksonville 30, Denver 27
	New England 28, Pittsburgh 3
AFC championship	New England 20, Jacksonville 6
NFC 1st-rd. playoffs	Dallas 40, Minnesota 15
	San Francisco 14, Philadelphia 0
NFC div. playoffs	Green Bay 35, San Francisco 14
	Carolina 26, Dallas 17
NFC championship	Green Bay 30, Carolina 13

1997

AFC 1st-rd. playoffs	Denver 42, Jacksonville 17
	New England 17, Miami 3
AFC div. playoffs	Denver 14, Kansas City 0
	Pittsburgh 7, New England 6
AFC championship	Denver 24, Pittsburgh 21
NFC 1st-rd. playoffs	Minnesota 23, NY Giants 22
	Tampa Bay 20, Detroit 10
NFC div. playoffs	Green Bay 21, Tampa Bay 7
	San Francisco 38, Minnesota 22
NFC championship	Green Bay 23, San Francisco 10

1998

AFC 1st-rd. playoffs	Miami 24, Buffalo 17
	Jacksonville 25, New England 10
AFC div. playoffs	Denver 38, Miami 3
	NY Jets 34, Jacksonville 24
AFC championship	Denver 23, NY Jets 10
NFC 1st-rd. playoffs	Arizona 20, Dallas 7
	San Francisco 30, Green Bay 27
NFC div. playoffs	Atlanta 20, San Francisco 18
	Minnesota 41, Arizona 21
NFC championship	Atlanta 30, Minnesota 27 (OT)

NFL Playoff History (*Cont.*)

1999

AFC 1st-rd. playoffs	Tennessee 22, Buffalo 16
	Miami 20, Seattle 17
AFC div. playoffs	Jacksonville 62, Miami 7
	Tennessee 19, Indianapolis 16
AFC championship	Tennessee 33, Jacksonville 14
NFC 1st-rd. playoffs	Washington 27, Detroit 13
	Minnesota 27, Dallas 10
NFC div. playoffs	Tampa Bay 14, Washington 13
	St Louis 49, Minnesota 37
NFC championship	St Louis 11, Tampa Bay 6

2000

AFC 1st-rd. playoffs	Baltimore 21, Denver 3
	Miami 23, Indianapolis 17 (OT)
AFC div. playoffs	Baltimore 24, Tennessee 10
	Oakland 27, Miami 0
AFC championship	Baltimore 16, Oakland 3
NFC 1st-rd. playoffs	New Orleans 31, St. Louis 28
	Philadelphia 21, Tampa Bay 3
NFC div. playoffs	NY Giants 20, Philadelphia 10
	Minnesota 34, New Orleans 16
NFC championship	NY Giants 41, Minnesota 0

2001

AFC 1st-rd. playoffs	Oakland 38, NY Jets 24
	Baltimore 20, Miami 3
AFC div. playoffs	New England 16, Oakland 13(OT)
	Pittsburgh 27, Baltimore 10
AFC championship	New England 24, Pittsburgh 17
NFC 1st-rd. playoffs	Philadelphia 31, Tampa Bay 9
	Green Bay 25, San Francisco 15
NFC div. playoffs	Philadelphia 33, Chicago 19
	St. Louis 45, Green Bay 17
NFC championship	St. Louis 29, Philadelphia 24

2002

AFC 1st-rd. playoffs	NY Jets 41, Indianapolis 0
	Pittsburgh 36, Cleveland 33
AFC div. playoffs	Tennessee 34, Pittsburgh 31 (OT)
	Oakland 30, NY Jets 10
AFC championship	Oakland 41, Tennessee 24
NFC 1st-rd. playoffs	Atlanta 27, Green Bay 7
	San Francisco 39, NY Giants 38
NFC div. playoffs	Philadelphia 20, Atlanta 6
	Tampa Bay 31, San Francisco 6
NFC championship	Tampa Bay 27, Philadelphia 10

2003

AFC 1st-rd. playoffs	Tennessee 20, Baltimore 17
	Indianapolis 41, Denver 10
AFC div. playoffs	New England 17, Tennessee 14
	Indianapolis 38, Kansas City 31
AFC championship	New England 24, Indianapolis 14
NFC 1st-rd. playoffs	Carolina 29, Dallas 10
	Green Bay 37, Seattle 31 (OT)
NFC div. playoffs	Carolina 29, St. Louis 23
	Philadelphia 20, Green Bay 17 (OT)
NFC championship	Carolina 14, Philadelphia 3

2004

AFC 1st-rd. playoffs	Indianapolis 49, Denver 24
	NY Jets 20, San Diego 17
AFC div. playoffs	New England 20, Indianapolis 3
	Pittsburgh 20, NY Jets 17
AFC championship	New England 41, Pittsburgh 27
NFC 1st-rd. playoffs	Minnesota 31, Green Bay 17
	St. Louis 27, Seattle 20
NFC div. playoffs	Atlanta 47, St. Louis 17
	Philadelphia 27, Minnesota 14
NFC championship	Philadelphia 27, Atlanta 10

2005

AFC 1st-rd. playoffs	Pittsburgh 31, Cincinnati 17
	New England 28, Jacksonville 3
AFC div. playoffs	Pittsburgh 21, Indianapolis 18
	Denver 27, New England 13
AFC championship	Pittsburgh 34, Denver 17
NFC 1st-rd. playoffs	Washington 17, Tampa Bay 10
	Carolina 23, NY Giants 0
NFC div. playoffs	Seattle 20, Washington 10
	Carolina 29, Chicago 21
NFC championship	Seattle 34, Carolina 14

2006

AFC 1st-rd. playoffs	Indianapolis 23, Kansas City 8
	New England 37, NY Jets 16
AFC div. playoffs	Indianapolis 15, Baltimore 6
	New England 24, San Diego 21
AFC championship	Indianapolis 38, New England 34
NFC 1st-rd. playoffs	Seattle 21, Dallas 20
	Philadelphia 23, NY Giants 20
NFC div. playoffs	Chicago 27, Seattle 24
	New Orleans 27, Philadelphia 24
NFC championship	Chicago 39, New Orleans 14

2007

AFC 1st-rd. playoffs	Jacksonville 31, Pittsburgh 29
	San Diego 17, Tennessee 6
AFC Div. Playoffs	New England 31, Jacksonville 20
	San Diego 28, Indianapolis 24
AFC Championship	New England 21, San Diego 12
NFC 1st-rd. playoffs	Seattle 35, Washington 14
	NY Giants 24, Tampa Bay 14
NFC Div. Playoffs	NY Giants 21, Dallas 17
	Green Bay 42, Seattle 20
NFC Championship	NY Giants 23, Green Bay 20 (OT)

Alltime NFL Individual Statistical Leaders

Career Leaders

Scoring

	Yrs	TD	FG	PAT	Pts
†Morten Andersen	25	0	565	849	2,544
Gary Anderson	23	0	538	820	2,434
George Blanda	26	9	335	943	2,002
†Matt Stover	17	0	435	517	1,822
†John Carney	19	0	425	537	1,812
†Jason Elam	15	0	395	601	1,786
Norm Johnson	18	0	366	638	1,736
Nick Lowery	18	0	383	562	1,711
Jan Stenerud	19	0	373	580	1,699
†Jason Hanson	16	0	385	504	1,659
Lou Groza	21	1	264	810	1,608
Eddie Murray	19	0	352	538	1,594
Al Del Greco	17	0	347	543	1,584
†John Kasay	16	0	358	430	1,504
Steve Christie	15	0	336	468	1,476

Rushing

	Yrs	Att	Yds	Avg	Lg	TD
Emmitt Smith	15	4,409	18,355	4.2	75	164
Walter Payton	13	3,838	16,726	4.4	76	110
Barry Sanders	10	3,062	15,269	5.0	85	99
Curtis Martin	11	3,518	14,101	4.0	70	90
Jerome Bettis	13	3,479	13,662	3.9	71	91
Eric Dickerson	11	2,996	13,259	4.4	85	90
Tony Dorsett	12	2,936	12,739	4.3	99	77
Jim Brown	9	2,359	12,312	5.2	80	106
Marshall Faulk	12	2,836	12,279	4.3	71	100
Marcus Allen	16	3,022	12,243	4.1	61	123
Franco Harris	13	2,949	12,120	4.1	75	91
Thurman Thomas	13	2,877	12,074	4.2	80	66
†Edgerrin James	9	2,849	11,607	4.1	72	77
John Riggins	14	2,916	11,352	3.9	66	104
Corey Dillon	10	2,618	11,241	4.3	96	82

Touchdowns

	Yrs	Rush	Rec	Ret	Total TD
Jerry Rice	20	10	197	0	207
Emmitt Smith	15	164	11	0	175
Marcus Allen	16	123	21	0	144
Marshall Faulk	12	100	36	0	136
†Terrell Owens	12	2	129	0	131
Cris Carter	16	0	130	0	130
†LaDainian Tomlinson	7	115	14	0	129
Jim Brown	9	106	20	0	126
Walter Payton	13	110	15	0	125
†Randy Moss	10	0	124	1	125
†Marvin Harrison	12	0	123	0	123
John Riggins	14	104	12	0	116
Lenny Moore	12	63	48	1	112
†Shaun Alexander	8	100	12	0	112
Barry Sanders	10	99	10	0	109
Tim Brown	17	1	100	4	105
Don Hutson	11	3	99	0	102
Steve Largent	14	1	100	0	101
Curtis Martin	12	90	10	0	100
Franco Harris	13	91	9	0	100

Combined Yards Gained

	Yrs	Total	Rush	Rec	Int Ret	Punt Ret	Kickoff Ret	Fum Ret
Jerry Rice	20	23,546	645	22,895	0	0	6	0
Brian Mitchell	14	23,330	1,967	2,336	0	4,999	14,014	14
Walter Payton	13	21,803	16,726	4,538	0	0	539	0
Emmitt Smith	15	21,564	18,355	3,224	0	0	0	-15
Tim Brown	17	19,682	190	14,934	0	3,320	1,235	3
Marshall Faulk	12	19,154	12,279	6,875	0	0	18	18
Barry Sanders	10	18,308	15,269	2,921	0	0	118	0
Herschel Walker	12	18,168	8,225	4,859	0	0	5,084	0
Marcus Allen	16	17,648	12,243	5,411	0	0	0	-6
Curtis Martin	11	17,430	14,101	3,329	0	0	0	-9
Tiki Barber	10	17,359	10,449	5,183	0	1,181	544	2
Eric Metcalf	13	17,230	2,392	5,572	0	3,453	5,813	0
Thurman Thomas	13	16,532	12,074	4,458	0	0	0	0
Tony Dorsett	12	16,326	12,739	3,554	0	0	0	33
Henry Ellard	16	15,718	50	13,777	0	1,527	364	0

†-active player in 2007.

Alltime NFL Individual Statistical Leaders *(Cont.)*

Career Leaders *(Cont.)*

Passing

PASSER RATING*

	Yrs	Att	Comp	Pct Comp	Yds	Avg Gain	TD	Pct TD	Int	Pct Int	Rating Pts
Steve Young	15	4,149	2,667	64.3	33,124	8.0	232	5.6	107	2.6	96.8
†Peyton Manning	10	5,405	3,468	64.2	41,626	7.7	306	5.7	153	2.8	94.7
†Kurt Warner	10	2,959	1,908	65.1	24,008	8.1	152	5.1	100	3.4	93.2
†Tom Brady	8	3,642	2,294	63.0	26,370	7.2	197	5.4	86	2.4	92.9
Joe Montana	15	5,391	3,409	63.2	40,551	7.5	273	5.2	139	2.6	92.3
†Carson Palmer	5	2,036	1,305	64.1	14,899	7.3	104	5.1	63	3.1	90.1
†Daunte Culpepper	9	2,927	1,867	63.8	22,422	7.7	142	4.9	94	3.2	89.9
†Chad Pennington	8	1,919	1,259	65.6	13,738	7.2	82	4.3	55	2.9	88.9
†Marc Bulger	7	2,484	1,578	63.5	18,625	7.5	106	4.3	74	3.0	88.1
†Drew Brees	7	3,015	1,921	63.7	21,189	7.0	134	4.4	82	2.7	87.9
†Jeff Garcia	9	3,300	2,020	61.2	22,825	6.9	149	4.5	77	2.3	87.2
†Trent Green	14	3,668	2,228	60.7	27,950	7.6	162	4.4	108	2.9	86.9
†Matt Hasselbeck	9	3,138	1,904	60.7	22,333	7.1	142	4.5	84	2.7	86.2
†Donovan McNabb	9	3,732	2,189	58.7	25,404	6.8	171	4.6	79	2.1	85.8
†Brett Favre	17	8,758	5,377	61.4	61,655	7.0	442	5.0	288	3.3	85.7
†Jake Delhomme	10	2,020	1,206	59.7	14,589	7.2	100	5.0	64	3.2	85.2
Dan Marino	17	8,358	4,967	59.4	61,361	7.3	420	5.0	252	3.0	85.1
Rich Gannon	18	4,206	2,533	60.2	28,743	6.8	180	4.3	104	2.3	84.7
Jim Kelly	11	4,779	2,874	60.1	35,467	7.4	237	5.0	175	3.7	84.4
†Mark Brunell	15	4,594	2,738	59.6	31,826	6.9	182	4.0	106	2.3	84.2
†Brian Griese	10	2,612	1,642	62.9	18,367	7.0	114	4.4	92	3.5	83.6
Roger Staubach	11	2,958	1,685	57.0	22,700	7.7	153	5.2	109	3.7	83.4
†Brad Johnson	16	4,248	2,627	61.8	28,627	6.7	164	4.1	117	2.7	83.1

*1,500 or more attempts. The passer ratings are based on performance standards established for completion percentage, interception percentage, touchdown percentage and average gain. Passers are allocated points according to how their marks compare with those standards.

YARDS

	Yrs	Att	Comp	Pct Comp	Yds
†Brett Favre	17	8,758	5,377	61.4	61,655
Dan Marino	17	8,358	4,967	59.4	61,361
John Elway	16	7,250	4,123	56.9	51,475
Warren Moon	17	6,823	3,988	58.5	49,325
Fran Tarkenton	18	6,467	3,686	57.0	47,003
†Vinny Testaverde	21	6,701	3,787	56.5	46,233
Drew Bledsoe	14	6,717	3,839	57.2	44,611
Dan Fouts	15	5,604	3,297	58.8	43,040
†Peyton Manning	10	5,405	3,468	64.4	41,626
Joe Montana	15	5,391	3,409	63.2	40,551
Johnny Unitas	18	5,186	2,830	54.6	40,239
Dave Krieg	19	5,311	3,105	58.5	38,147
Boomer Esiason	14	5,205	2,969	57.0	37,920
Jim Kelly	11	4,779	2,874	60.1	35,467
Jim Everett	12	4,923	2,841	57.7	34,837
†Kerry Collins	13	5,254	2,918	55.5	34,717
Jim Hart	19	5,076	2,593	51.1	34,665
Steve DeBerg	17	4,746	2,924	61.6	34,241
John Hadl	16	4,687	2,363	50.4	33,503
Phil Simms	14	4,647	2,576	55.4	33,462
Steve Young	15	4,149	2,667	64.3	33,124
Troy Aikman	12	4,715	2,898	61.5	32,942

TOUCHDOWNS

	No.
†Brett Favre	442
Dan Marino	420
Fran Tarkenton	342
†Peyton Manning	306
John Elway	300
Warren Moon	291
Johnny Unitas	290
†Vinny Testaverde	275
Joe Montana	273
Dave Krieg	261
Sonny Jurgensen	255
Dan Fouts	254
Drew Bledsoe	251
Boomer Esiason	247
John Hadl	244
Len Dawson	239
Jim Kelly	237
George Blanda	236
Steve Young	232
John Brodie	214
Terry Bradshaw	212
Y.A. Tittle	212
Jim Hart	209
Randall Cunningham	207
Jim Everett	203
Roman Gabriel	201
Phil Simms	199
Ken Anderson	197
†Tom Brady	197
Joe Ferguson	196
Bobby Layne	196

† Active in 2007.

Alltime NFL Individual Statistical Leaders *(Cont.)*

Career Leaders *(Cont.)*

Receiving

RECEPTIONS

	Yrs	No.	Yds	Avg	Lg	TD
Jerry Rice	20	1,549	22,895	14.8	96	197
Cris Carter	16	1,101	13,899	12.6	80	130
Tim Brown	17	1,094	14,934	13.7	80	100
†Marvin Harrison	12	1,042	13,944	13.4	80	123
Andre Reed	16	951	13,198	13.9	83	87
†Isaac Bruce	14	942	14,109	15.0	80	84
Art Monk	16	940	12,721	13.5	79	68
†Keenan McCardell	17	883	11,373	12.9	76	63
†Terrell Owens	12	882	13,070	14.8	91	129
Jimmy Smith	13	862	12,287	14.3	75	67
Irving Fryar	17	851	12,785	15.0	80	84
Rod Smith	12	849	11,389	13.4	85	68
Larry Centers	14	826	6,797	8.2	54	28
†Tony Gonzalez	11	820	9,882	12.1	73	66
Steve Largent	14	819	13,089	16.0	74	100
Shannon Sharpe	15	815	10,060	12.3	82	62
Henry Ellard	16	814	13,777	16.9	81	65
Keyshawn Johnson	11	814	10,571	13.0	76	64
†Torry Holt	9	805	11,864	14.7	85	71
†Randy Moss	10	774	12,193	15.8	82	124
Marshall Faulk	11	767	6,875	9.0	85	36
James Lofton	16	764	14,004	18.3	80	75
†Eric Moulds	12	764	9,995	13.1	84	49
Michael Irvin	12	750	11,904	15.9	87	65
Charlie Joiner	18	750	12,146	16.2	87	65
Andre Rison	12	743	10,205	13.7	80	84

YARDS

Jerry Rice	22,895
Tim Brown	14,934
†Isaac Bruce	14,109
James Lofton	14,004
†Marvin Harrison	13,944
Cris Carter	13,899
Henry Ellard	13,777
Andre Reed	13,198
Steve Largent	13,089
†Terrell Owens	13,070
Irving Fryar	12,785
Art Monk	12,721
Jimmy Smith	12,287
†Randy Moss	12,193
Charlie Joiner	12,146
Michael Irvin	11,904
†Torry Holt	11,864
Don Maynard	11,834
Rod Smith	11,389
†Keenan McCardell	11,373
Gary Clark	10,856

SACKS

Bruce Smith	200.0
Reggie White	198.0
Kevin Greene	160.0
Chris Doleman	150.5
†Michael Strahan	141.5
John Randle	137.5
Richard Dent	137.5

Note: Officially compiled since 1982.

Interceptions

	Yrs	No.	Yds	Avg	Lg	TD
Paul Krause	16	81	1185	14.6	81	3
Emlen Tunnell	14	79	1282	16.2	55	4
Rod Woodson	17	71	1483	20.9	98	17
Dick (Night Train) Lane	14	68	1207	17.8	80	5
Ken Riley	15	65	596	9.2	66	5

Punting

	Yrs	No.	Yds	Avg	Lg	Blk
†Shane Lechler	8	592	27,511	49.1	73	0
Sammy Baugh	16	338	15,245	45.1	85	9
†Mat McBriar	4	275	12,288	44.7	75	0
Tommy Davis	11	511	22,833	44.7	82	2
Yale Lary	11	503	22,279	44.3	74	4
†Todd Sauerbrun	13	889	39,208	44.1	73	9

Note: 250 or more punts.

Punt Returns

	Yrs	No.	Yds	Avg	Lg	TD
†Devin Hester	2	89	1,251	14.1	89	7
George McAfee	8	112	1,431	12.8	74	2
Jack Christiansen	8	85	1,084	12.8	89	8
Claude Gibson	5	110	1,381	12.6	85	3
Bill Dudley	9	124	1,515	12.2	96	3

Note: 75 or more returns.

Kickoff Returns

	Yrs	No.	Yds	Avg	Lg	TD
Gale Sayers	7	91	2,781	30.6	103	6
Lynn Chandnois	7	92	2,720	29.6	93	3
Abe Woodson	9	193	5,538	28.7	105	5
Claude (Buddy) Young	6	90	2,514	27.9	104	2
Travis Williams	5	102	2,801	27.5	105	6

Note: 75 or more returns.

† Active in 2007.

Alltime NFL Individual Statistical Leaders *(Cont.)*

Single-Season Leaders

Scoring

POINTS

	Year	TD	PAT	FG	Pts
†LaDainian Tomlinson, SD	2006	31	0	0	186
Paul Hornung, GB	1960	15	41	15	176
†Shaun Alexander, Sea	2005	28	0	0	168
Gary Anderson, Minn	1998	0	59	35	164
†Jeff Wilkins, StL	2003	0	46	39	163
†Priest Holmes, KC	2003	27	0	0	162
Mark Moseley, Wash	1983	0	62	33	161
†Mike Vanderjagt, Ind	2003	0	46	37	157
†Marshall Faulk, StL	2000	26	0	0	156
Gino Cappelletti, Bos	1964	7	38	25	155
Emmitt Smith, Dal	1995	25	0	0	150
Chip Lohmiller, Wash	1991	0	56	31	149
†Jay Feely, NYG	2005	0	43	35	148

Note: Cappelletti's total includes a two-point conversion.

TOUCHDOWNS

	Year	Rush	Rec	Ret	Total
†LaDainian Tomlinson, SD	2006	28	3	0	31
†Shaun Alexander, Sea	2005	27	1	0	28
†Priest Holmes, KC	2003	27	0	0	27
†Marshall Faulk, StL	2000	18	8	0	26
Emmitt Smith, Dal	1995	25	0	0	25
John Riggins, Wash	1983	24	0	0	24
†Priest Holmes, KC	2002	21	3	0	24
O.J. Simpson, Buff	1975	16	7	0	23
Jerry Rice, SF	1987	1	22	0	23
Terrell Davis, Den	1998	21	2	0	23
†Randy Moss, NE	2007	0	0	23	23

FIELD GOALS

	Year	FGA	FGM
†Neil Rackers, Ari	2005	42	40
†Olindo Mare, Mia	1999	46	39
†Jeff Wilkins, StL	2003	42	39
†John Kasay, Car	1996	45	37
†Mike Vanderjagt, Ind	2003	37	37
Cary Blanchard, Ind	1996	40	36
Al Del Greco, Tenn	1998	39	36

Rushing

YARDS GAINED

	Year	Att	Yds	Avg
Eric Dickerson, LA Rams	1984	379	2,105	5.6
†Jamal Lewis, Balt	2003	387	2,066	5.3
Barry Sanders, Det	1997	335	2,053	6.1
Terrell Davis, Den	1998	392	2,008	5.1
O.J. Simpson, Buff	1973	332	2,003	6.0
Earl Campbell, Hou	1980	373	1,980	5.2
†Ahman Green, GB	2003	355	1,883	5.3
Barry Sanders, Det	1994	331	1,883	5.7
†Shaun Alexander, Sea	2005	370	1,880	5.1
Jim Brown, Clev	1963	291	1,863	6.4
†Tiki Barber, NYG	2005	357	1,860	5.2
Ricky Williams, Mia	2002	383	1,853	4.8

AVERAGE GAIN

	Year	Avg
Beattie Feathers, Chi	1934	8.44
Randall Cunningham, Phil	1990	7.98
†Michael Vick, Atl	2004	7.50
†Michael Vick, Atl	2002	6.88
Bobby Douglass, Chi	1972	6.87

Minimum 100 attempts.

TOUCHDOWNS

	Year	No.
†LaDainian Tomlinson, SD	2006	28
†Shaun Alexander, Sea	2005	27
†Priest Holmes, KC	2003	27
Emmitt Smith, Dal	1995	25
John Riggins, Wash	1983	24
†Priest Holmes, KC	2002	24
Emmitt Smith, Dal	1994	21
Joe Morris, NYG	1985	21
Terry Allen, Wash	1996	21
Terrell Davis, Den	1998	21

Passing

YARDS GAINED

	Year	Att	Comp	Pct	Yds
Dan Marino, Mia	1984	564	362	64.2	5,084
†Kurt Warner, StL Rams	2001	546	375	68.7	4,830
†Tom Brady, NE	2007	578	398	68.9	4,806
Dan Fouts, SD	1981	609	360	59.1	4,802
Dan Marino, Mia	1986	623	378	60.7	4,746
†Daunte Culpepper	2004	548	379	69.2	4,717
Dan Fouts, SD	1980	589	348	59.1	4,715
Warren Moon, Hou	1991	655	404	61.7	4,690
Warren Moon, Hou	1990	584	362	62.0	4,689
Rich Gannon, Oak	2002	618	418	67.6	4,689
Neil Lomax, StL Cards	1984	560	345	61.6	4,614
†Trent Green, StL Rams	2004	556	369	66.4	4,591
†Peyton Manning, Ind.	2004	497	336	67.6	4,557
†Drew Bledsoe, NE	1994	691	400	57.9	4,555

† Active in 2007.

PASSER RATING

	Year	Rat.
†Peyton Manning, Ind	2004	121.1
†Tom Brady, NE	2007	117.2
Steve Young, SF	1994	112.8
Joe Montana, SF	1989	112.4
†Daunte Culpepper, Minn	2004	110.9
Milt Plum, Clev	1960	110.4
Sammy Baugh, Wash	1945	109.9

TOUCHDOWNS

	Year	No.
†Tom Brady, NE	2007	50
†Peyton Manning, Ind	2004	49
Dan Marino, Mia	1984	48
Dan Marino, Mia	1986	44
†Kurt Warner, StL	1999	41
†Daunte Culpepper, Minn	2004	39
†Brett Favre, GB	1995	38

Five tied with 36.

Single-Season Leaders (Cont.)

Receiving

RECEPTIONS

	Year	No.	Yds
†Marvin Harrison, Ind	2002	143	1,722
Herman Moore, Det	1995	123	1,686
Cris Carter, Minn	1994	122	1,256
Jerry Rice, SF	1995	122	1,848
Cris Carter, Minn	1995	122	1,371
†Isaac Bruce, StL Rams	1995	119	1,781
†Torry Holt, StL Rams	2003	117	1,696
Jimmy Smith, Jac	1999	116	1,636
†Marvin Harrison, Ind	1999	115	1,663
Rod Smith, Den	2001	113	1,343

YARDS GAINED

	Year	Yds
Jerry Rice, SF	1995	1,848
†Isaac Bruce, StL Rams	1995	1,781
Charley Hennigan, Hou	1961	1,746
†Marvin Harrison, Ind	2002	1,722
†Torry Holt, StL	2003	1,696

TOUCHDOWNS

	Year	No.
†Randy Moss, NE	2007	23
Jerry Rice, SF	1987	22
Mark Clayton, Mia	1984	18
Sterling Sharpe, GB	1994	18

Seven tied with 17.

All-Purpose Yards

	Year	Run	Rec	Ret	Total
Derrick Mason, Tenn	2000	1	895	1794	2690
Michael Lewis, NO	2002	15	200	2432	2647
Lionel James, SD	1985	516	1027	992	2535
Terry Metcalf, StL Cards	1975	816	378	1268	2462
Mack Herron, NE	1974	824	474	1146	2444
Gale Sayers, Chi	1966	1231	447	762	2440
Marshall Faulk, StL Rams	1999	1381	1048	0	2429
Timmy Brown, Phil	1963	841	487	1100	2428
Tiki Barber, NYG	2005	1860	530	0	2390
Barry Sanders, Det	1997	2053	305	0	2358
Tim Brown, LA Rai	1988	50	725	1542	2317
†Josh Cribbs, Cle	2007	61	37	2214	2312
Marcus Allen, LA Rai	1985	1759	555	-6	2308

Interceptions

	Year	No.
Dick (Night Train) Lane, LA Rams	1952	14
Dan Sandifer, Wash	1948	13
Spec Sanders, NY Yanks	1950	13
Lester Hayes, Oak	1980	13

Nine tied with 12.

Punt Returns

	Year	Avg
Herb Rich, Balt Colts	1950	23.0
Jack Christiansen, Det	1952	21.5
Dick Christy, NY Titans	1961	21.3
Bob Hayes, Dal	1968	20.8

Punting

	Year	No.	Yds	Avg
Sammy Baugh, Wash	1940	35	1,799	51.4
†Shane Lechler, Oak	2007	73	3,585	49.1
Yale Lary, Det	1963	35	1,713	48.9
Sammy Baugh, Wash	1941	30	1,462	48.7
Yale Lary, Det	1961	52	2,519	48.4
Sammy Baugh, Wash	1942	37	1,785	48.2

Sacks

	Year	No.
†Michael Strahan, NYG	2001	22.5
Mark Gastineau, NYJ	1984	22
Reggie White, Phil	1987	21
Chris Doleman, Minn	1989	21
Lawrence Taylor, NYG	1986	20.5

Kickoff Returns

	Year	Avg
Travis Williams, GB	1967	41.1
Gale Sayers, Chi	1967	37.7
Ollie Matson, Chi Cards	1958	35.5
Jim Duncan, Balt Colts	1970	35.4
Lynn Chandnois, Pitt	1952	35.2

Single-Game Leaders

Scoring

POINTS

	Date	Pts
Ernie Nevers, Chi Cards vs Chi	11-28-29	40
Dub Jones, Clev vs Chi	11-25-51	36
Gale Sayers, Chi vs SF	12-12-65	36
Paul Hornung, GB vs Balt Colts	10-8-61	33

On Thanksgiving Day, 1929, Nevers scored all the Cardinals' points on six rushing TDs and four PATs. The Cards defeated Red Grange and the Bears, 40–6. Jones and Sayers each rushed for four touchdowns and scored two more on returns in their teams' victories. Hornung scored four touchdowns and kicked 6 PATs and a field goal in a 45-7 win over the Colts.

FIELD GOALS

	Date	No.
†Rob Bironas, Tenn vs Hou	10-21-07	8
Jim Bakken, StL Cards vs Pitt	9-24-67	7
Rich Karlis, Minn vs Rams	11-5-89	7
Chris Boniol, Dal vs GB	11-18-96	7
†Billy Cundiff, Dal vs NYG	9-15-03	7

Bironas was 8 for 8.

Bakken was 7 for 9; Cundiff was 7 for 8; and Karlis and Boniol went 7 for 7.

† Active in 2007.

Single-Game Leaders (Cont.)

Scoring (Cont.)

TOUCHDOWNS

	Date	No.
Ernie Nevers, Chi Cards vs Chi	11-28-29	6
Dub Jones, Clev vs Chi	11-25-51	6
Gale Sayers, Chi vs SF	12-12-65	6
Bob Shaw, Chi Cards vs Balt Colts	10-2-50	5
Jim Brown, Clev vs Balt Colts	11-1-59	5
Abner Haynes, Dal Texans vs Oak	11-26-61	5
Billy Cannon, Hou vs NY Titans	12-10-61	5
Cookie Gilchrist, Buff vs NYJ	12-8-63	5
Paul Hornung, GB vs Balt Colts	12-12-65	5
Kellen Winslow, SD vs Oak	11-22-81	5
Jerry Rice, SF vs Atl	10-14-90	5
James Stewart, Jac vs Phil	10-12-97	5
†Shaun Alexander, Sea vs Minn	9-29-02	5
†Clinton Portis, Den vs KC	12-07-03	5

Rushing

YARDS GAINED

	Date	Yds
†Adrian Peterson, Minn vs SD	11-4-07	296
†Jamal Lewis, Balt vs Clev	9-14-03	295
Corey Dillon, Cin vs Den	10-22-00	278
Walter Payton, Chi vs Minn	11-20-77	275
O.J. Simpson, Buff vs Det	11-25-76	273

TOUCHDOWNS

	Date	No.
Ernie Nevers, Chi Cards vs Chi	11-28-29	6
Jim Brown, Clev vs Balt Colts	11-1-59	5
Cookie Gilchrist, Buff vs NYJ	12-8-63	5
James Stewart, Jac vs Phil	10-12-97	5
†Clinton Portis, Den vs KC	12-7-03	5

CARRIES

	Date	No.
Jamie Morris, Wash vs Cin	12-17-88	45
Butch Woolfolk, NYG vs Phil	11-20-83	43
James Wilder, TB vs GB	9-30-84	43
†Rudi Johnson, Cin vs Hou	11-9-03	43
James Wilder, TB vs Pitt	10-30-83	42
Terrell Davis, Den vs Buff (OT)	10-26-97	42
Ricky Williams, Mia vs Buff	9-21-03	42

Passing

YARDS GAINED

	Date	Yds
N. Van Brocklin, Rams vs NY Yanks	9-28-51	554
Warren Moon, Hou vs KC	12-16-90	527
Boomer Esiason, Ariz vs Wash	11-10-96	522
Dan Marino, Mia vs NYJ	10-23-88	521
Phil Simms, NYG vs Cin	10-13-85	513

TOUCHDOWNS

	Date	No.
Sid Luckman, Chi vs NYG	11-14-43	7
Adrian Burk, Phil vs Wash	10-17-54	7
George Blanda, Hou vs NY Titans	11-19-61	7
Y. A. Tittle, NYG vs Wash	10-28-62	7
Joe Kapp, Minn vs Balt Colts	9-28-69	7

COMPLETIONS

	Date	No.
†Drew Bledsoe, NE vs Minn	11-13-94	45
Rich Gannon, Oak vs Pitt	9-15-02	43
Richard Todd, NYJ vs SF	9-21-80	42
†Vinny Testaverde, NYJ vs Sea	12-6-98	42
Warren Moon, Hou vs Dal	11-10-91	41
Ken Anderson, Cin vs SD	12-20-82	40
Phil Simms, NYG vs Cin	10-13-85	40
†Brad Johnson, TB vs Chi	11-18-01	40
†Marc Bulger, StL Rams vs. NYG	10-02-05	40

Receiving

YARDS GAINED

	Date	Yds
Flipper Anderson, Rams vs NO	11-26-89	336
Stephone Paige, KC vs SD	12-22-85	309
Jim Benton, Clev vs Det	11-22-45	303
Cloyce Box, Det vs Balt Colts	12-3-50	302
Jimmy Smith, Jac vs Balt Ravens	9-10-00	291

† Active in 2007.

RECEPTIONS

	Date	No.
†Terrell Owens, SF vs Chi	12-17-00	20
Tom Fears, Rams vs GB	12-3-50	18
Clark Gaines, NYJ vs SF	9-21-80	17
Sonny Randle, StL Cards vs NYG	11-4-62	16
Jerry Rice, SF vs Rams	11-20-94	16
†Keenan McCardell, Jac vs Rams	10-20-96	16
†Troy Brown, NE vs KC	9-22-02	16

Six tied with 15.

Single-Game Leaders (Cont.)

Receiving (Cont.)

TOUCHDOWNS

	Date	No.
Bob Shaw, Chi Cards vs Balt Colts	10-2-50	5
Kellen Winslow, SD vs Oak	11-22-81	5
Jerry Rice, SF vs Atl	10-14-90	5

All-Purpose Yards

	Date	Yds
Glyn Milburn, Den vs Sea	12-10-95	404
Billy Cannon, Hou vs NY Titans	12-10-61	373
Tyrone Hughes, NO vs LA Rams	10-23-94	347
Lionel James, SD vs LA Rai	11-10-85	345
Timmy Brown, Phi vs StL Cards	12-16-62	341

Longest Plays

RUSHING	Opponent	Year	Yds
Tony Dorsett, Dal	Minn	1983	99
Ahman Green, GB	Den	2003	98
Andy Uram, GB	Chi Cards	1939	97
Bob Gage, Pitt	Chi	1949	97
Jim Spavital, Balt Colts	GB	1950	96
Bob Hoernschemeyer, Det	NY Yanks	1950	96
Garrison Hearst, SF	NYJ	1998	96
Corey Dillon, Cin	Det	2001	96

PASSING	Opponent	Year	Yds
Frank Filchock to Andy Farkas, Wash	Pitt	1939	99
George Izo to Bobby Mitchell, Wash	Clev	1963	99
Karl Sweetan to Pat Studstill, Det	Balt Colts	1966	99
Sonny Jurgensen to Gerry Allen, Wash	Chi	1968	99
Jim Plunkett to Cliff Branch, LA Rai	Wash	1983	99
Ron Jaworski to Mike Quick, Phil	Atl	1985	99
Stan Humphries to Tony Martin, SD	Sea	1994	99
Brett Favre to Robert Brooks, GB	Chi	1995	99
Trent Green to Marc Boerigter, KC	SD	2002	99
Jeff Garcia to Andre Davis, Cle	Cin	2004	99

FIELD GOALS	Opponent	Year	Yds
Tom Dempsey, NO	Det	1970	63
Jason Elam, Den	Jax	1998	63
Matt Bryant, TB	Phi	2006	62
Rob Bironas, Ten	Ind	2006	62

PUNTS	Opponent	Year	Yds
Steve O'Neal, NYJ	Den	1969	98
Joe Lintzenich, Chi	NYG	1931	94
Shawn McCarthy, NE	Buff	1991	93
Randall Cunningham, Phil	NYG	1989	91

INTERCEPTION RETURNS	Opponent	Year	Yds
Ed Reed, Balt	Clev	2004	106
Vencie Glenn, SD	Den	1987	103
Louis Oliver, Mia	Buff	1992	103
Nine players tied at 102.			

KICKOFF RETURNS	Opponent	Year	Yds
Ellis Hobbs, NE	NYJ	2007	108
Al Carmichael, GB	Chi	1956	106
Noland Smith, KC	Den	1967	106
Roy Green, StL Cards	Dal	1979	106

PUNT RETURNS	Opponent	Year	Yds
Robert Bailey, LA Rams	NO	1994	103
Gil LeFebvre, Cin	Brooklyn	1933	98
Charlie West, Minn	Wash	1968	98
Dennis Morgan, Dal	StL Cards	1974	98
Terance Mathis, NYJ	Dal	1990	98

MISSED FIELD GOAL RETURNS	Opponent	Year	Yds
Antonio Cromartie, SD	Minn	2007	109
Devin Hester, Chi	NYG	2006	108
Nathan Vasher, Chi	SF	2005	108
Chris McAllister, Balt	Den	2002	107
Aaron Glenn, NYJ	Ind	1998	104

Annual NFL Individual Statistical Leaders

Rushing

Year	Player, Team	Att	Yards	Avg	TD
1932	Cliff Battles, Bos	148	576	3.9	3
1933	Jim Musick, Bos	173	809	4.7	5
1934	Beattie Feathers, Chi	119	1,004	8.4	8
1935	Doug Russell, Chi Cards	140	499	3.6	0
1936	Alphonse Leemans, NY	206	830	4.0	2
1937	Cliff Battles, Wash	216	874	4.0	5
1938	Byron White, Pitt	152	567	3.7	4
1939	Bill Osmanski, Chi	121	699	5.8	7
1940	Byron White, Det	146	514	3.5	5
1941	Clarence Manders, Bklyn	111	486	4.4	5
1942	Bill Dudley, Pitt	162	696	4.3	5
1943	Bill Paschal, NY	147	572	3.9	10
1944	Bill Paschal, NY	196	737	3.8	9
1945	Steve Van Buren, Phil	143	832	5.8	15
1946	Bill Dudley, Pitt	146	604	4.1	3
1947	Steve Van Buren, Phil	217	1,008	4.6	13
1948	Steve Van Buren, Phil	201	945	4.7	10
1949	Steve Van Buren, Phil	263	1,146	4.4	11
1950	Marion Motley, Clev	140	810	5.8	3
1951	Eddie Price, NY	271	971	3.6	7
1952	Dan Towler, LA	156	894	5.7	10
1953	Joe Perry, SF	192	1,018	5.3	10
1954	Joe Perry, SF	173	1,049	6.1	8
1955	Alan Ameche, Balt	213	961	4.5	9
1956	Rick Casares, Chi	234	1,126	4.8	12
1957	Jim Brown, Clev	202	942	4.7	9
1958	Jim Brown, Clev	257	1,527	5.9	17
1959	Jim Brown, Clev	290	1,329	4.6	14
1960	Jim Brown, Clev, NFL	215	1,257	5.8	9
	Abner Haynes, Dallas Texans, AFL	156	875	5.6	9
1961	Jim Brown, Clev, NFL	305	1,408	4.6	8
	Billy Cannon, Hou, AFL	200	948	4.7	6
1962	Jim Taylor, GB, NFL	272	1,474	5.4	19
	Cookie Gilchrist, Buff, AFL	214	1,096	5.1	13
1963	Jim Brown, Clev, NFL	291	1,863	6.4	12
	Clem Daniels, Oak, AFL	215	1,099	5.1	3
1964	Jim Brown, Clev, NFL	280	1,446	5.2	7
	Cookie Gilchrist, Buff, AFL	230	981	4.3	6
1965	Jim Brown, Clev, NFL	289	1,544	5.3	17
	Paul Lowe, SD, AFL	222	1,121	5.0	7
1966	Jim Nance, Bos, AFL	299	1,458	4.9	11
	Gale Sayers, Chi, NFL	229	1,231	5.4	8
1967	Jim Nance, Bos, AFL	269	1,216	4.5	7
	Leroy Kelly, Clev, NFL	235	1,205	5.1	11
1968	Leroy Kelly, Clev, NFL	248	1,239	5.0	16
	Paul Robinson, Cin, AFL	238	1,023	4.3	8
1969	Gale Sayers, Chi, NFL	236	1,032	4.4	8
	Dickie Post, SD, AFL	182	873	4.8	6
1970	Larry Brown, Wash, NFC	237	1,125	4.7	5
	Floyd Little, Den, AFC	209	901	4.3	3
1971	Floyd Little, Den, AFC	284	1,133	4.0	6
	John Brockington, GB, NFC	216	1,105	5.1	4
1972	O.J. Simpson, Buff, AFC	292	1,251	4.3	6
	Larry Brown, Wash, NFC	285	1,216	4.3	8
1973	O.J. Simpson, Buff, AFC	332	2,003	6.0	12
	John Brockington, GB, NFC	265	1,144	4.3	3
1974	Otis Armstrong, Den, AFC	263	1,407	5.3	9
	Lawrence McCutcheon, LA, NFC	236	1,109	4.7	3
1975	O.J. Simpson, Buff, AFC	329	1,817	5.5	16
	Jim Otis, StL, NFC	269	1,076	4.0	5
1976	O.J. Simpson, Buff, AFC	290	1,503	5.2	8
	Walter Payton, Chi, NFC	311	1,390	4.5	13
1977	Walter Payton, Chi, NFC	339	1,852	5.5	14
	Mark van Eeghen, Oak, AFC	324	1,273	3.9	7
1978	Earl Campbell, Hou, AFC	302	1,450	4.8	13
	Walter Payton, Chi, NFC	333	1,395	4.2	11
1979	Earl Campbell, Hou, AFC	368	1,697	4.6	19
	Walter Payton, Chi, NFC	369	1,610	4.4	14
1980	Earl Campbell, Hou, AFC	373	1,934	5.2	13
	Walter Payton, Chi, NFC	317	1,460	4.6	6
1981	George Rogers, NO, NFC	378	1,674	4.4	13
	Earl Campbell, Hou, AFC	361	1,376	3.8	10
1982	Freeman McNeil, NYJ, AFC	151	786	5.2	6
	Tony Dorsett, Dal, NFC	177	745	4.2	5
1983	Eric Dickerson, LA, NFC	390	1,808	4.6	18
	Curt Warner, Sea, AFC	335	1,449	4.3	13
1984	Eric Dickerson, LA, NFC	379	2,105	5.6	14
	Earnest Jackson, SD, AFC	296	1,179	4.0	8
1985	Marcus Allen, LA, AFC	380	1,759	4.6	11
	Gerald Riggs, Atl, NFC	397	1,719	4.3	10
1986	Eric Dickerson, LA, NFC	404	1,821	4.5	11
	Curt Warner, Sea, AFC	319	1,481	4.6	13
1987	Charles White, LA, NFC	324	1,374	4.2	11
	Eric Dickerson, Ind, AFC	223	1,011	4.5	5
1988	Eric Dickerson, Ind, AFC	388	1,659	4.3	14
	Herschel Walker, Dal, NFC	361	1,514	4.2	5
1989	Christian Okoye, KC, AFC	370	1,480	4.0	12
	Barry Sanders, Det, NFC	280	1,470	5.3	14
1990	Barry Sanders, Det, NFC	255	1,304	5.1	13
	Thurman Thomas, Buff, AFC	271	1,297	4.8	11
1991	Emmitt Smith, Dal, NFC	365	1,563	4.3	12
	Thurman Thomas, Buff, AFC	288	1,407	4.9	7
1992	Emmitt Smith, Dal, NFC	373	1,713	4.6	18
	Barry Foster, Pitt, AFC	390	1,690	4.3	11
1993	Emmitt Smith, Dal, NFC	283	1,486	5.3	9
	Thurman Thomas, Buff, AFC	355	1,315	3.7	6

Annual NFL Individual Statistical Leaders (Cont.)

Rushing (Cont.)

Year	Player, Team	Att	Yards	Avg	TD
1994	Barry Sanders, Det, NFC	331	1,883	5.7	7
	Chris Warren, Sea, AFC	333	1,545	4.6	9
1995	Emmitt Smith, Dal, NFC	377	1,773	4.7	25
	Curtis Martin, NE, AFC	368	1,487	4.0	14
1996	Barry Sanders, Det, NFC	307	1,553	5.1	11
	Terrell Davis, Den, AFC	345	1,538	4.5	13
1997	Barry Sanders, Det, NFC	335	2,053	6.1	11
	Terrell Davis, Den, AFC	369	1,750	4.7	15
1998	Terrell Davis, Den, AFC	392	2,008	5.1	21
	Jamal Anderson, Atl, NFC	410	1,846	4.5	14
1999	Edgerrin James, Ind, AFC	369	1,553	4.2	13
	Stephen Davis, Wash, NFC	290	1,405	4.8	17
2000	Edgerrin James, Ind, AFC	387	1,709	4.4	13
	Robert Smith, Minn, NFC	295	1,521	5.2	7
2001	Priest Holmes, Kan, AFC	327	1,555	4.8	8
	Stephen Davis, Wash, NFC	356	1,432	4.0	5
2002	Ricky Williams, Mia, AFC	383	1,853	4.8	16
	Deuce McAllister, NO, NFC	325	1,388	4.3	13
2003	Jamal Lewis, Balt, AFC	387	2,066	5.3	14
	Ahman Green, GB, NFC	355	1,883	5.3	15
2004	Curtis Martin, NY Jets, AFC	371	1,697	4.6	12
	Shaun Alexander, Sea, NFC	353	1,696	4.8	16
2005	Shaun Alexander, Sea, NFC	370	1,880	5.1	27
	Larry Johnson, KC, AFC	336	1,750	5.2	20
2006	LaDainian Tomlinson, SD, AFC	348	1,815	5.2	28
	Frank Gore, SF, NFC	312	1,695	5.4	8
2007	LaDainian Tomlinson, SD, AFC	315	1,474	4.7	15
	Adrian Peterson Minn, NFC	238	1,341	5.6	12

Passing

Year	Player, Team	Att	Comp	Yards	TD	Int
1932	Arnie Herber, GB	101	37	639	9	9
1933	Harry Newman, NYG	136	53	973	11	17
1934	Arnie Herber, GB	115	42	799	8	12
1935	Ed Danowski, NYG	113	57	794	10	9
1936	Arnie Herber, GB	173	77	1,239	11	13
1937	Sammy Baugh, Wash	171	81	1,127	8	14
1938	Ed Danowski, NYG	129	70	848	7	8
1939	Parker Hall, Clev	208	106	1,227	9	13
1940	Sammy Baugh, Wash	177	111	1,367	12	10
1941	Cecil Isbell, GB	206	117	1,479	15	11
1942	Cecil Isbell, GB	268	146	2,021	24	14
1943	Sammy Baugh, Wash	239	133	1,754	23	19
1944	Frank Filchock, Wash	147	84	1,139	13	9
1945	Sammy Baugh, Wash	182	128	1,669	11	4
	Sid Luckman, Chi	217	117	1,725	14	10
1946	Bob Waterfield, LA	251	127	1,747	18	17
1947	Sammy Baugh, Wash	354	210	2,938	25	15
1948	Tommy Thompson, Phil	246	141	1,965	25	11
1949	Sammy Baugh, Wash	255	145	1,903	18	14
1950	Norm Van Brocklin, LA	233	127	2,061	18	14
1951	Bob Waterfield, LA	176	88	1,566	13	10
1952	Norm Van Brocklin, LA	205	113	1,736	14	17
1953	Otto Graham, Clev	258	167	2,722	11	9
1954	Norm Van Brocklin, LA	260	139	2,637	13	21
1955	Otto Graham, Clev	185	98	1,721	15	8
1956	Ed Brown, Chi	168	96	1,667	11	12
1957	Tommy O'Connell, Clev	110	63	1,229	9	8
1958	Eddie LeBaron, Wash	145	79	1,365	11	10
1959	Charlie Conerly, NYG	194	113	1,706	14	4
1960	Milt Plum, Clev, NFL	250	151	2,297	21	5
	Jack Kemp, LA, AFL	406	211	3,018	20	25
1961	George Blanda, Hou, AFL	362	187	3,330	36	22
	Milt Plum, Clev, NFL	302	177	2,416	18	10
1962	Len Dawson, Dal, AFL	310	189	2,759	29	17
	Bart Starr, GB, NFL	285	178	2,438	12	9
1963	Y.A. Tittle, NY, NFL	367	221	3,145	36	14
	Tobin Rote, SD, AFL	286	170	2,510	20	17
1964	Len Dawson, KC, AFL	354	199	2,879	30	18
	Bart Starr, GB, NFL	272	163	2,144	15	4
1965	Rudy Bukich, Chi, NFL	312	176	2,641	20	9
	John Hadl, SD, AFL	348	174	2,798	20	21
1966	Bart Starr, GB, NFL	251	156	2,257	14	3
	Len Dawson, KC, AFL	284	159	2,527	26	10
1967	Sonny Jurgensen, Wash, NFL	508	288	3,747	31	16
	Daryle Lamonica, Oak, AFL	425	220	3,228	30	20
1968	Len Dawson, KC, AFL	224	131	2,109	17	9
	Earl Morrall, Balt, NFL	317	182	2,909	26	17
1969	S. Jurgensen, Wash, NFL	442	274	3,102	22	15
	Greg Cook, Cin, AFL	197	106	1,854	15	11
1970	John Brodie, SF, NFC	378	223	2,941	24	10
	Daryle Lamonica, Oak, AFC	356	179	2,516	22	15
1971	Roger Staubach, Dal, NFC	211	126	1,882	15	4
	Bob Griese, Mia, AFC	263	145	2,089	19	9
1972	Norm Snead, NY, NFC	325	196	2,307	17	12
	Earl Morrall, Mia, AFC	150	83	1,360	11	7

Annual NFL Individual Statistical Leaders *(Cont.)*

Passing* *(Cont.)*

*Since 1973, the annual passing NFL leaders have been determined by a passer rating system that compares individual performances to a fixed performance standard. Before 1973, total passing yards gained was used.

Year	Player, Team	Comp%	Yds	TD	Int	Rating
1973	Roger Staubach, Dal, NFC	62.6	2,428	23	15	94.6
	Ken Stabler, Oak, AFC	62.7	1,997	14	10	88.3
1974	Ken Anderson, Cin, AFC	64.9	2,667	18	10	95.7
	Sonny Jurgensen, Wash, NFC	64.1	1,185	11	5	94.5
1975	Ken Anderson, Cin, AFC	60.5	3,169	21	11	93.9
	Fran Tarkenton, Minn, NFC	64.2	2,994	25	13	91.8
1976	Ken Stabler, Oak, AFC	66.7	2,737	27	17	103.4
	James Harris, LA, NFC	57.6	1,460	8	6	89.6
1977	Bob Griese, Mia, AFC	58.6	2,252	22	13	87.8
	Roger Staubach, Dal, NFC	58.2	2,620	18	9	87.0
1978	Roger Staubach, Dal, NFC	55.9	3,190	25	16	84.9
	Terry Bradshaw, Pitt, AFC	56.3	2,915	28	20	84.7
1979	Roger Staubach, Dal, NFC	57.9	3,586	27	11	92.3
	Dan Fouts, SD, AFC	62.6	4,082	24	24	82.6
1980	Brian Sipe, Clev, AFC	60.8	4,132	30	14	91.4
	Ron Jaworski, Phi, NFC	57.0	3,529	27	12	91.0
1981	Ken Anderson, Cin, AFC	62.6	3,754	29	10	98.4
	Joe Montana, SF, NFC	63.7	3,565	19	12	88.4
1982	Ken Anderson, Cin, AFC	70.6	2,495	12	9	95.3
	Joe Theismann, Wash, NFC	63.9	2,033	13	9	91.3
1983	Steve Bartkowski, Atl, NFC	63.4	3,167	22	5	97.6
	Dan Marino, Mia AFC	58.4	2,210	20	6	96.0
1984	Dan Marino, Mia, AFC	64.2	5,084	48	17	108.9
	Joe Montana, SF, NFC	64.6	3,630	28	10	102.9
1985	Ken O'Brien, NY, AFC	60.9	3,888	25	8	96.2
	Joe Montana, SF, NFC	61.3	3,653	27	13	91.3
1986	Tommy Kramer, Minn, NFC	55.9	3,000	24	10	92.6
	Dan Marino, Mia, AFC	60.7	4,746	44	23	92.5
1987	Joe Montana, SF, NFC	66.8	3,054	31	13	102.1
	Bernie Kosar, Clev, AFC	61.9	3,033	22	9	95.4
1988	Boomer Esiason, Cin, AFC	57.5	3,572	28	14	97.4
	Wade Wilson, Minn, NFC	61.4	2,746	15	9	91.5
1989	Joe Montana, SF, NFC	70.2	3,521	26	8	112.4
	Boomer Esiason, Cin, AFC	56.7	3,525	28	11	92.1
1990	Jim Kelly Buffalo, AFC	63.3	2,829	24	9	101.2
	Phil Simms, NY, NFC	59.2	2,284	15	4	92.7
1991	Steve Young, SF, NFC	64.5	2,517	17	8	101.8
	Jim Kelly, Buff, AFC	64.1	3,844	33	17	97.6
1992	Steve Young, SF, NFC	66.7	3,465	25	7	107.0
	Warren Moon, Hou, AFC	64.7	2,521	18	12	89.3
1993	Steve Young, SF, NFC	68.0	4,023	29	16	101.5
	John Elway Den, AFC	63.2	4,030	25	10	92.8
1994	Steve Young, SF, NFC	70.3	3,969	35	10	112.8
	Dan Marino, Mia, AFC	62.0	4,453	30	17	89.2
1995	Brett Favre, GB, NFC	62.9	4,413	38	13	99.5
	Jim Harbaugh, Ind, AFC	61.2	2,575	17	5	100.7
1996	John Elway, Den, AFC	61.6	3,328	26	14	89.2
	Steve Young, SF, NFC	67.7	2,410	14	6	97.2
1997	Steve Young, SF, NFC	67.7	3,029	19	6	104.7
	Mark Brunell, Jax, AFC	60.7	3,281	18	7	91.2
1998	Randall Cunningham, Minn, NFC	60.9	3,704	34	10	106.0
	Vinny Testaverde, NYJ, AFC	61.5	3,256	29	7	101.6
1999	Kurt Warner, StL, NFC	65.1	4,353	41	13	109.2
	Peyton Manning, Ind, AFC	62.1	4,135	26	15	90.7
2000	Trent Green, StL, NFC	60.4	2,063	16	5	101.8
	Brian Griese, Den, AFC	64.3	2,688	19	4	102.9
2001	Kurt Warner, StL, NFC	68.7	4,830	36	22	101.4
	Rich Gannon, Oak, AFC	65.8	3,828	27	9	95.5
2002	Brad Johnson, TB, NFC	62.3	3,049	22	6	92.9
	Chad Pennington, NY, AFC	68.9	3,120	22	6	104.2

Passing *(Cont.)*

Year	Player, Team	Comp%	Yds	TD	Int	Rating
2003	Steve McNair, Tenn, AFC	62.5	3,215	24	7	100.4
	Daunte Culpepper, Minn, NFC	65.0	3,479	25	11	96.4
2004	Peyton Manning, Ind, AFC	67.6	4,557	49	10	121.1
	Daunte Culpepper, Minn, NFC	69.2	4,717	39	11	110.9
2005	Peyton Manning, Ind, AFC	67.3	3,747	28	10	104.1
	Matt Hasselbeck, GB, NFC	65.5	3,459	24	9	98.2
2006	Peyton Manning, Ind, AFC	65.0	4,397	31	9	101.0
	Drew Brees, NO, NFC	64.3	4,418	26	11	96.2
2007	Tom Brady, NE, AFC	68.9	4,806	50	8	117.2
	Tony Romo Dal, NFC	64.4	4,211	36	19	97.4

Pass Receiving†

Year	Player, Team	No.	Yds	Avg	TD
1932	Ray Flaherty, NY	21	350	16.7	3
1933	John Kelly, Brooklyn	22	246	11.2	3
1934	Joe Carter, Phil	16	238	14.9	4
	Morris Badgro, NY	16	206	12.9	1
1935	Tod Goodwin, NY	26	432	16.6	4
1936	Don Hutson, GB	34	536	15.8	8
1937	Don Hutson, GB	41	552	13.5	7
1938	Gaynell Tinsley, Chi Cards	41	516	12.6	1
1939	Don Hutson, GB	34	846	24.9	6
1940	Don Looney, Phil	58	707	12.2	4
1941	Don Hutson, GB	58	738	12.7	10
1942	Don Hutson, GB	74	1,211	16.4	17
1943	Don Hutson, GB	47	776	16.5	11
1944	Don Hutson, GB	58	866	14.9	9
1945	Don Hutson, GB	47	834	17.7	9
1946	Jim Benton, LA	63	981	15.6	6
1947	Jim Keane, Chi	64	910	14.2	10
1948	Tom Fears, LA	51	698	13.7	4
1949	Tom Fears, LA	77	1,013	13.2	9
1950	Tom Fears, LA	84	1,116	13.3	7
1951	Elroy Hirsch, LA	66	1,495	22.7	17
1952	Mac Speedie, Clev	62	911	14.7	5
1953	Pete Pihos, Phil	63	1,049	16.7	10
1954	Pete Pihos, Phil	60	872	14.5	10
	Billy Wilson, SF	60	830	13.8	5
1955	Pete Pihos, Phil	62	864	13.9	7
1956	Billy Wilson, SF	60	889	14.8	5
1957	Billy Wilson, SF	52	757	14.6	6
1958	Raymond Berry, Balt	56	794	14.2	9
	Pete Retzlaff, Phil	56	766	13.7	2
1959	Raymond Berry, Balt	66	959	14.5	14
1960	Lionel Taylor, Den, AFL	92	1,235	13.4	12
	Raymond Berry, Balt, NFL	74	1,298	17.5	10
1961	Lionel Taylor, Den, AFL	100	1,176	11.8	4
	Jim Phillips, LA, NFL	78	1,092	14.0	5
1962	Lionel Taylor, Den, AFL	77	908	11.8	4
	Bobby Mitchell, Wash, NFL	72	1,384	19.2	11
1963	Lionel Taylor, Den, AFL	78	1,101	14.1	10
	Bobby Joe Conrad, St. Louis, NFL	73	967	13.2	10
1964	Charley Hennigan, Houston, AFL	101	1,546	15.3	8
	Johnny Morris, Chi, NFL	93	1,200	12.9	10
1965	Lionel Taylor, Den, AFL	85	1,131	13.3	6
	Dave Parks, SF, NFL	80	1,344	16.8	12
1966	Lance Alworth, SD, AFL	73	1,383	18.9	13
	Charley Taylor, Wash, NFL	72	1,119	15.5	12
1967	George Sauer, NY, AFL	75	1,189	15.9	6
	Charley Taylor, Wash, NFL	70	990	14.1	9
1968	Clifton McNeil, SF, NFL	71	994	14.0	7
	Lance Alworth, SD, AFL	68	1,312	19.3	10
1969	Dan Abramowicz, NO, NFL	73	1,015	13.9	7
	Lance Alworth, SD, AFL	64	1,003	15.7	4
1970	Dick Gordon, Chi, NFC	71	1,026	14.5	13
	Marlin Briscoe, Buff, AFC	57	1,036	18.2	8
1971	Fred Biletnikoff, Oak, AFC	61	929	15.2	9
	Bob Tucker, NY, NFC	59	791	13.4	4
1972	Harold Jackson, Phil, NFC	62	1,048	16.9	4
	Fred Biletnikoff, Oak, AFC	58	802	13.8	7
1973	Harold Carmichael, Phil, NFC	67	1,116	16.7	9
	Fred Willis, Hou, AFC	57	371	6.5	1
1974	Lydell Mitchell, Balt, AFC	72	544	7.6	2
	Charles Young, Phil, NFC	63	696	11.0	3
1975	Chuck Foreman, Minn, NFC	73	691	9.5	9
	Reggie Rucker, Clev, AFC	60	770	12.8	3
	Lydell Mitchell, Balt, AFC	60	544	9.1	4
1976	MacArthur Lane, KC, AFC	66	686	10.4	1
	Drew Pearson, Dal, NFC	58	806	13.9	6
1977	Lydell Mitchell, Balt, AFC	71	620	8.7	4
	Ahmad Rashad, Minn, NFC	51	681	13.4	2
1978	Rickey Young, Minn, NFC	88	704	8.0	5
	Steve Largent, Sea, AFC	71	1,168	16.5	8

†Most catches.

Pass Receiving† (Cont.)

Year	Player, Team	No.	Yds	Avg	TD
1979	Joe Washington, Balt, AFC	82	750	9.1	3
	Ahmad Rashad, Minn, NFC	80	1,156	14.5	9
1980	Kellen Winslow, SD, AFC	89	1,290	14.5	9
	Earl Cooper, SF, NFC	83	567	6.8	4
1981	Kellen Winslow, SD, AFC	88	1,075	12.2	10
	Dwight Clark, SF, NFC	85	1,105	13.0	4
1982	Dwight Clark, SF, NFC	60	913	15.2	5
	Kellen Winslow, SD, AFC	54	721	13.4	6
1983	Todd Christensen, LA, AFC	92	1,247	13.6	12
	Roy Green, StL, NFC	78	1,227	15.7	14
	Charlie Brown, Wash, NFC	78	1,225	15.7	8
	Earnest Gray, NY, NFC	78	1,139	14.6	5
1984	Art Monk, Wash, NFC	106	1,372	12.9	7
	Ozzie Newsome, Clev, AFC	89	1,001	11.2	5
1985	Roger Craig, SF, NFC	92	1,016	11.0	6
	Lionel James, SD, AFC	86	1,027	11.9	6
1986	Todd Christensen, LA, AFC	95	1,153	12.1	8
	Jerry Rice, SF, NFC	86	1,570	18.3	15
1987	J.T. Smith, StL Card, NFC	91	1,117	12.3	8
	Al Toon, NY, AFC	68	976	14.4	5
1988	Al Toon, NY, AFC	93	1,067	11.5	5
	Henry Ellard, LA, NFC	86	1,414	16.4	10
1989	Sterling Sharpe, GB, NFC	90	1,423	15.8	12
	Andre Reed, Buff, AFC	88	1,312	14.9	9
1990	Jerry Rice, SF, NFC	100	1,502	15.0	13
	Haywood Jeffires, Hou, AFC	74	1,048	14.2	8
	Drew Hill, Hou, AFC	74	1,019	13.8	5
1991	Haywood Jeffires, Hou, AFC	100	1,181	11.8	7
	Michael Irvin, Dal, NFC	93	1,523	16.4	8
1992	Sterling Sharpe, GB, NFC	108	1,461	13.5	13
	Haywood Jeffires, Hou, AFC	90	913	10.1	9
1993	Sterling Sharpe, GB, NFC	112	1,274	11.4	11
	Reggie Langhorne, Ind, AFC	85	1,038	12.2	3
1994	Cris Carter, Minn, NFC	122	1,256	10.3	7
	Ben Coates, NE, AFC	96	1,174	12.2	7
1995	Herman Moore, Det, NFC	123	1,686	13.7	14
	Carl Pickens, Cin, AFC	99	1,234	12.5	17
1996	Jerry Rice, SF, NFC	108	1,254	11.6	8
	Carl Pickens, Cin, AFC	100	1,180	11.8	12
1997	Herman Moore, Det, NFC	104	1,293	12.4	8
	Tim Brown, Oak, AFC	104	1,408	13.5	5
1998	Frank Sanders, Ariz, NFC	89	1,145	12.9	3
	O.J. McDuffie, Mia, AFC	90	1,050	11.7	7
1999	Muhsin Muhammad, Car, NFC	96	1,253	13.1	8
	Jimmy Smith, Jax, AFC	116	1,636	14.1	6
2000	Mushin Muhammad, Car, NFC	102	1,183	11.6	6
	Marvin Harrison, Ind, AFC	102	1,413	13.9	14
2001	Rod Smith, Den, AFC	113	1,343	11.9	11
	Keyshawn Johnson, TB, NFC	106	1,266	11.9	1
2002	Marvin Harrison, Ind, AFC	143	1,722	12.0	11
	Randy Moss, Minn, NFC	106	1,347	12.7	7
2003	LaDainian Tomlinson, SD, AFC	100	725	7.3	4
	Torry Holt, StL, NFC	117	1,696	14.5	12
2004	Tony Gonzalez, KC, AFC	102	1,258	12.3	7
	Joe Horn, NO, NFC	94	1,399	14.9	11
2005	Chad Johnson, Cin, AFC	97	1,432	14.8	9
	Steve Smith, Car, NFC	103	1,563	15.2	12
2006	Chad Johnson, Cin, AFC	87	1,369	15.7	7
	Roy Williams, Det, NFC	82	1,310	16.0	7
2007	Reggie Wayne, Ind, AFC	104	1,510	14.5	10
	Larry Fitzgerald, Ari, NFC	100	1,409	14.1	10

†Most catches.

Scoring

Year	Player, Team	TD	FG	PAT	TP
1932	Earl Clark, Portsmouth	6	3	10	55
1933	Ken Strong, NY	6	5	13	64
	Glenn Presnell, Ports	6	6	10	64
1934	Jack Manders, Chi	3	10	31	79
1935	Earl Clark, Det	6	1	16	55
1936	Earl Clark, Det	7	4	19	73
1937	Jack Manders, Chi	5	18	15	69
1938	Clarke Hinkle, GB	7	3	7	58
1939	Andy Farkas, Wash	11	0	2	68
1940	Don Hutson, GB	7	0	15	57
1941	Don Hutson, GB	12	1	20	95
1942	Don Hutson, GB	17	1	33	138
1943	Don Hutson, GB	12	3	36	117
1944	Don Hutson, GB	9	0	31	85
1945	Steve Van Buren, Phil	18	0	2	110
1946	Ted Fritsch, GB	10	9	13	100
1947	Pat Harder, Chicago Cards	7	7	39	102
1948	Pat Harder, Chicago Cards	6	7	53	110
1949	Pat Harder, Chicago Cards	8	3	45	102
	Gene Roberts, NY	17	0	0	102
1950	Doak Walker, Det	11	8	38	128
1951	Elroy Hirsch, LA	17	0	0	102

Scoring (Cont.)

Year	Player, Team	TD	FG	PAT	TP
1952	Gordy Soltau, SF	7	6	34	94
1953	Gordy Soltau, SF	6	10	48	114
1954	Bobby Walston, Phil	11	4	36	114
1955	Doak Walker, Det	7	9	27	96
1956	Bobby Layne, Det	5	12	33	99
1957	Sam Baker, Wash	1	14	29	77
	Lou Groza, Clev	0	15	32	77
1958	Jim Brown, Clev	18	0	0	108
1959	Paul Hornung, GB	7	7	31	94
1960	Paul Hornung, GB, NFL	15	15	41	176
	Gene Mingo, Den, AFL	6	18	33	123
1961	Gino Cappelletti, Bos, AFL	8	17	48	147
	Paul Hornung, GB, NFL	10	15	41	146
1962	Gene Mingo, Den, AFL	4	27	32	137
	Jim Taylor, GB, NFL	19	0	0	114
1963	Gino Cappelletti, Bos, AFL	2	22	35	113
	Don Chandler, NY, NFL	0	18	52	106
1964	Gino Cappelletti, Bos, AFL	7	25	36	155
	Lenny Moore, Balt, NFL	20	0	0	120
1965	Gale Sayers, Chi, NFL	22	0	0	132
	Gino Cappelletti, Bos, AFL	9	17	27	132
1966	Gino Cappelletti, Bos, AFL	6	16	35	119
	Bruce Gossett, LA, NFL	0	28	29	113
1967	Jim Bakken, StL, NFL	0	27	36	117
	George Blanda, Oak, AFL	0	20	56	116
1968	Jim Turner, NY, AFL	0	34	43	145
	Leroy Kelly, Clev, NFL	20	0	0	120
1969	Jim Turner, NY, AFL	0	32	33	129
	Fred Cox, Minn, NFL	0	26	43	121
1970	Fred Cox, Minn, NFC	0	30	35	125
	Jan Stenerud, KC, AFC	0	30	26	116
1971	Garo Yepremian, Mia, AFC	0	28	33	117
	Curt Knight, Wash, NFC	0	29	27	114
1972	Chester Marcol, GB, NFC	0	33	29	128
	Bobby Howfield, NY AFC	0	27	40	121
1973	David Ray, LA, NFC	0	30	40	130
	Roy Gerela, Pitt, AFC	0	29	36	123
1974	Chester Marcol, GB, NFC	0	25	19	94
	Roy Gerela, Pitt, AFC	0	20	33	93
1975	O.J. Simpson, Buff, AFC	23	0	0	138
	Chuck Foreman, Minn, NFC	22	0	0	132
1976	Toni Linhart, Balt, AFC	0	20	49	109
	Mark Moseley, Wash, NFC	0	22	31	97
1977	Errol Mann, Oak, AFC	0	20	39	99
	Walter Payton, Chi, NFC	16	0	0	96
1978	Frank Corral, LA, NFC	0	29	31	118
	Pat Leahy, NY, AFC	0	22	41	107
1979	John Smith, NE, AFC	0	23	46	115
	Mark Moseley, Wash, NFC	0	25	39	114
1980	John Smith, NE, AFC	0	26	51	129
	Ed Murray, Det, NFC	0	27	35	116
1981	Ed Murray, Det, NFC	0	25	46	121
	Rafael Septien, Dal, NFC	0	27	40	121
	Jim Breech, Cin, AFC	0	22	49	115
	Nick Lowery, KC, AFC	0	26	37	115
1982	Marcus Allen, LA, AFC	14	0	0	84
	Wendell Tyler, LA, NFC	13	0	0	78
1983	Mark Moseley, Wash, NFC	0	33	62	161
	Gary Anderson, Pitt, AFC	0	27	38	119
1984	Ray Wersching, SF, NFC	0	25	56	131
	Gary Anderson, Pitt, AFC	0	24	45	117
1985	Kevin Butler, Chi, NFC	0	31	51	144
	Gary Anderson, Pitt, AFC	0	33	40	139
1986	Tony Franklin, NE, AFC	0	32	44	140
	Kevin Butler, Chi, NFC	0	28	36	120
1987	Jerry Rice, SF, NFC	23	0	0	138
	Jim Breech, Cin, AFC	0	24	25	97
1988	Scott Norwood, Buff, AFC	0	32	33	129
	Mike Cofer, SF, NFC	0	27	40	121
1989	Mike Cofer, SF, NFC	0	29	49	136
	David Treadwell, Den, AFC	0	27	39	120
1990	Nick Lowery, KC, AFC	0	34	37	139
	Chip Lohmiller, Wash, NFC	0	30	41	131
1991	Chip Lohmiller, Wash, NFC	0	31	56	149
	Pete Stoyanovich, Mia, AFC	0	31	28	121
1992	Pete Stoyanovich, Mia, AFC	0	30	34	124
	Morten Anderson, NO, NFC	0	29	33	120
	Chip Lohmiller, Wash, NFC	0	30	30	120
1993	Jeff Jaeger, Rai, AFC	0	35	27	132
	Jason Hanson, Det, NFC	0	34	28	130
1994	John Carney, SD, AFC	0	34	33	135
	Fuad Reveiz, Minn, NFC	0	34	30	132
	Emmitt Smith, Dal, NFC	22	0	0	132
1995	Emmitt Smith, Dal, NFC	25	0	0	150
	Norm Johnson, Pitt, AFC	0	34	39	141
1996	John Kasay, Car, NFC	0	37	34	145
	Cary Blanchard, Ind, AFC	0	36	27	135
1997	Richie Cunningham, Dal, NFC	0	34	24	126
	Mike Hollis, Jax, AFC	0	41	31	134
1998	Gary Anderson, Minn, NFC	0	35	59	164
	Steve Christie, Buff, AFC	0	33	41	140
1999	Jeff Wilkins, StL, NFC	0	20	64	124
	Mike Vanderjagt, Ind, AFC	0	34	43	145
2000	Marshall Faulk, StL, NFC	26	0	0	160
	Matt Stover, Balt, AFC	0	35	30	135
2001	Marshall Faulk, StL, NFC	21	0	0	128
	Mike Vanderjagt, Ind, AFC	0	28	41	125
2002	Jay Feely. Atl, NFC	0	32	42	138
	Priest Holmes, KC, AFC	24	0	0	144
2003	Jeff Wilkins StL, NFC	0	39	46	163
	Priest Holmes, KC, AFC	27	0	0	162
2004	Adam Vinatieri, NE, AFC	0	31	48	141
	David Akers, Phil, NFC	0	27	41	122
2005	Shayne Graham, Cin, AFC	0	28	47	131
	Shaun Alexander, Sea, NFC	28	0	0	168
2006	LaDainian Tomlinson. SD, AFC	31	0	0	186
	Robbie Gould, Chi, NFC	0	32	47	143
2007	Randy Moss, NE, AFC	23	0	0	138
	Mason Crosby, GB, NFC	0	31	48	141

Interceptions

Year	Player, Team	Int	Yds
1940	Clarence Parker, Brooklyn	6	146
	Kent Ryan, Det	6	65
	Don Hutson, GB	6	24
1941	Marshall Goldberg, Chicago Card	7	54
	Art Jones, Pitt	7	35
1942	Clyde Turner, Chicago Bears	8	96
1943	Sammy Baugh, Wash	11	112
1944	Howard Livingston, NYG	9	172
1945	Ray Zimmerman, Phil	7	90
1946	Bill Dudley, Pittsburgh	10	242
1947	Frank Reagan, NYG	10	203
	Frank Seno, Bos	10	100
1948	Dan Sandifier, Wash	13	258
1949	Bob Nussbaumer, Chicago Car	12	157
1950	Orban Sanders, NY Yanks	13	199
1951	Otto Schnellbacher, NYG	11	194
1952	Dick Lane, LA	14	298
1953	Jack Christiansen, Det	12	238
1954	Dick Lane, Chicago Card	10	181
1955	Will Sherman, LA	11	101
1956	Lindon Crow, Chicago Card	11	170
1957	Milt Davis, Balt	10	219
	Jack Christiansen, Det	10	137
	Jack Butler, Pitt	10	85
1958	Jim Patton, NYG	11	183
1959	Dean Derby, Pitt	7	127
	Milt Davis, Balt	7	119
	Don Shinnick, Balt	7	70
1960	Goose Gonsoulin, Den, AFL	11	98
	Dave Baker, SF, NFL	10	96
	Jerry Norton, StL, NFL	10	96
1961	Billy Atkins, Buff, AFL	10	158
	Dick Lynch, NYG, NFL	9	60
1962	Lee Riley, NY Titans, AFL	11	122
	Willie Wood, GB, NFL	9	132
1963	Fred Glick, Hous, AFL	12	180
	Dick Lynch, NYG, NFL	9	251
	Roosevelt Taylor, Chi, NFL	9	172
1964	Dainard Paulson, NYJ, AFL	12	157
	Paul Krause, Wash, NFL	12	140
1965	W. K. Hicks, Hous, AFL	9	156
	Bobby Boyd, Balt, NFL	9	78
1966	Larry Wilson, StL, NFL	10	180
	Johnny Robinson, KC, AFL	10	136
	Bobby Hunt, KC, AFL	10	113
1967	Lem Barney, Det, NFL	10	232
	Dave Whitsell, NO, NFL	10	178
	Miller Farr, Hous, AFL	10	264
	Tom Janik, Buff, AFL	10	222
	Dick Westmoreland, Mia, AFL	10	127
1968	Dave Grayson, Oak, AFL	10	195
	Willie Williams, NYG, NFL	10	103
1969	Mel Renfro, Dal, NFL	10	118
	Emmitt Thomas, KC, AFL	9	146
1970	Johnny Robinson, KC, AFC	10	155
	Dick LeBeau, Det, NFC	9	96
1971	Bill Bradley, Phil, NFC	11	248
	Ken Houston, Hou, AFC	9	220
1972	Bill Bradley, Phil, NFC	9	73
	Mike Sensibaugh, KC, AFC	8	65
1973	Dick Anderson, Mia, AFC	8	163
	Mike Wagner, Pitt, AFC	8	134
	Bobby Bryant, Minn, NFC	7	105
1974	Emmitt Thomas, KC, AFC	12	214
	Ray Brown, Atl, NFC	8	164
1975	Mel Blount, Pitt, AFC	11	121
	Paul Krause, Minn, NFC	10	201
1976	Monte Jackson, LA, NFC	10	173
	Ken Riley, Cin, AFC	9	141
1977	Lyle Blackwood, Balt, AFC	10	163
	Rolland Lawrence, Atl, NFC	7	138
1978	Thom Darden, Clev, AFC	10	200
	Ken Stone, StL, NFC	9	139
	Willie Buchanon, GB, NFC	9	93
1979	Mike Reinfeldt, Hou, AFC	12	205
	Lemar Parrish, Wash, NFC	9	65
1980	Lester Hayes, Oak, AFC	13	273
	Nolan Cromwell, LA, NFC	8	140
1981	Everson Walls, Dal, NFC	11	133
	John Harris, Sea, AFC	10	155
1982	Everson Walls, Dal, NFC	7	61
	Ken Riley, Cin, AFC	5	88
	Bobby Jackson, NYJ, AFC	5	84
	Dwayne Woodruff, Pitt, AFC	5	53
	Donnie Shell, Pitt, AFC	5	27
1983	Mark Murphy, Wash, NFC	9	127
	Ken Riley, Cin, AFC	8	89
	Vann McElroy, LA, AFC	8	68
1984	Ken Easley, Sea, AFC	10	126
	Tom Flynn, GB, NFC	9	106
1985	Everson Walls, Dal, NFC	9	31
	Albert Lewis, KC, AFC	8	59
	Eugene Daniel, Ind, AFC	8	53
1986	Ronnie Lott, SF, NFC	10	134
	Deron Cherry, KC, AFC	9	150
1987	Barry Wilburn, Wash, NFC	9	135
	Mike Prior, Ind, AFC	6	57
	Mark Kelso, Buff, AFC	6	25
	Keith Bostic, Hou, AFC	6	-14
1988	Scott Case, Atl, NFC	10	47
	Erik McMillan, NYJ, AFC	8	168
1989	Felix Wright, Clev, AFC	9	91
	Eric Allen, Phil, NFC	8	38
1990	Mark Carrier, Chi, NFC	10	39
	Richard Johnson, Hou, AFC	8	100
1991	Ronnie Lott, LA, AFC	8	52
	Ray Crockett, Det, NFC	6	141
	Deion Sanders, Atl, NFC	6	119
	Aeneas Williams, Phoenix, NFC	6	60
	Tim McKyer, Atl, NFC	6	24
1992	Henry Jones, Buff, AFC	8	263
	Audray McMillian, Minn, NFC	8	157
1993	Eugene Robinson, Sea, AFC	9	80
	Nate Odomes, Buff, AFC	9	65
	Deion Sanders, Atl, NFC	7	91
1994	Eric Turner, Clev, AFC	9	199
	Aeneas Williams, Ariz, NFC	9	89

Interceptions (Cont.)

Year	Player, Team	Int	Yds
1995	Orlando Thomas, Minn, NFC	9	108
	Willie Williams, Pitt, AFC	7	122
1996	Tyrone Braxton, Den, AFC	9	128
	Keith Lyle, StL, NFC	9	152
1997	Ryan McNeil, StL, NFC	9	127
	Mark McMillian, KC, AFC	8	274
	Darryl Williams, Sea, AFC	8	172
1998	Ty Law, NE, AFC	9	133
	Kwamie Lassiter, Ariz, NFC	8	80
1999	Rod Woodson, Balt, AFC	7	195
	Sam Madison, Mia, AFC	7	164
	James Hasty, KC, AFC	7	98
	Donnie Abraham, TB, NFC	7	115
	Troy Vincent, Phil, NFC	7	91
2000	Darren Sharper, GB, NFC	9	109
	Samari Rolle, Tenn, AFC	7	140
	Brian Walker, Mia, AFC	7	80
2001	Ronde Barber, TB, NFC	10	86
	Anthony Henry, Clev, AFC	10	177
2002	Rod Woodson, Oak, AFC	8	225
	Brian Kelly, TB, NFC	8	68
2003	Brian Russell, Minn, NFC	9	185
	Tony Parrish, SFo, NFC	9	202
	Patrick Surtain, Mia, AFC	7	59
	Ed Reed, Balt, AFC	7	132
	Marcus Coleman, Hou, AFC	7	95
2004	Ed Reed, Balt, AFC	9	358
	Chris Gamble, Car, NFC	6	15
	Ken Lucas, Sea, NFC	6	46
2005	Ty Law, NYJ, AFC	10	195
	Deltha O'Neal, Cin, AFC	10	103
	Darren Sharper, Minn, NFC	9	276
2006	Champ Bailey, Den, AFC	10	162
	Asante Samuel, NE, AFC	10	120
	Walt Harris, SF, NFC	8	84
	Charles Woodson, GB, NFC	8	61
2007	Antonio Cromartie, SD, AFC	10	144
	O. J. Atogwe, StL, NFC	8	125

Sacks*

Year	Player, Team	Sacks
1982	Doug Martin, Minn, NFC	11.5
	Jesse Baker, Hou, AFC	7.5
1983	Mark Gastineau, NYJ, AFC	19.0
	Fred Dean, SF, NFC	17.5
1984	Mark Gastineau, NYJ, AFC	22.0
	Richard Dent, Chi, NFC	17.5
1985	Richard Dent, Chi, NFC	17.0
	Andre Tippett, NE, AFC	16.5
1986	Lawrence Taylor, NYG, NFC	20.5
	Sean Jones, LA, AFC	15.5
1987	Reggie White, Phil, NFC	21.0
	Andre Tippett, NE, AFC	12.5
1988	Reggie White, Phil, NFC	18.0
	G. Townsend, LA, AFC	11.5
1989	Chris Doleman, Minn, NFC	21.0
	Lee Williams, SD, AFC	14.0
1990	Derrick Thomas, KC, AFC	20.0
	Charles Haley, SF, NFC	16.0
1991	Pat Swilling, NO, NFC	17.0
	William Fuller, Hou, AFC	15.0
1992	Clyde Simmons, Phil, NFC	19.0
	Leslie O'Neal, SD, AFC	17.0
1993	Neil Smith, KC, AFC	15.0
	Renaldo Turnbull, NO, NFC	13.0
	Reggie White, GB, NFC	13.0
1994	Kevin Greene, Pitt, AFC	14.0
	Ken Harvey, Wash, NFC	13.5
	John Randle, Minn, NFC	13.5
1995	Bryce Paup, Buff, AFC	17.5
	William Fuller, Phil, NFC	13.0
	Wayne Martin, NO, NFC	13.0

Year	Player, Team	Int	Yds
1996	Kevin Greene, Car, NFC		14.5
	Michael McCrary, Sea, AFC		13.5
	Bruce Smith, Buff, AFC		13.5
1997	John Randle, Minn, NFC		15.5
	Bruce Smith, Buff, AFC		14.0
1998	Michael Sinclair, Sea, AFC		16.5
	Reggie White, GB, NFC		16.0
1999	Kevin Carter, StL, NFC		17.0
	Jevon Kearse, Tenn, AFC		14.5
2000	La'Roi Glover, NO, NFC		17.0
	Trace Armstrong, Mia, AFC		16.5
2001	Michael Strahan, NYG, NFC		22.5
	Peter Boulware, Balt, AFC		15.0
2002	Jason Taylor, Mia, AFC		18.5
	Simeon Rice, TB, NFC		15.5
2003	Michael Strahan, NYG, NFC		18.5
	Adewale Ogunleye, Mia, AFC		15.0
2004	Dwight Freeney, Ind, AFC		16.0
	Bertrand Berry, Ariz, NFC		14.5
2005	Derrick Burgess, Oak, AFC		16.0
	Osi Umenyiora, NYG, NFC		14.5
2006	Shawne Merriman, SD, AFC		17.0
	Aaron Kampman, GB, NFC		15.5
2007	Jared Allen, KC, AFC		15.5
	Patrick Kerney, Sea, NFC		14.5

*Sacks were not kept as an official NFL statistic until 1982.

Pro Bowl Alltime Results

Date	Result
1-15-39	NY Giants 13, Pro All-Stars 10
1-14-40	Green Bay 16, NFL All-Stars 7
12-29-40	Chi Bears 28, NFL All-Stars 14
1-4-42	Chi Bears 35, NFL All-Stars 24
12-27-42	NFL All-Stars 17, Washington 14
1-14-51	A. Conf. 28, N. Conf. 27
1-12-52	N. Conf. 30, A. Conf. 13
1-10-53	N. Conf. 27, A. Conf. 7
1-17-54	East 20, West 9
1-16-55	West 26, East 19
1-15-56	East 31, West 30
1-13-57	West 19, East 10
1-12-58	West 26, East 7
1-11-59	East 28, West 21
1-17-60	West 38, East 21
1-15-61	West 35, East 31
1-7-62	AFL West 47, East 27
1-14-62	NFL West 31, East 30
1-13-63	AFL West 21, East 14
1-13-63	NFL East 30, West 20
1-12-64	NFL West 31, East 17
1-19-64	AFL West 27, East 24
1-10-65	NFL West 34, East 14
1-16-65	AFL West 38, East 14
1-15-66	AFL All-Stars 30, Buffalo 19
1-15-66	NFL East 36, West 7
1-21-67	AFL East 30, West 23
1-22-67	NFL East 20, West 10
1-21-68	AFL East 25, West 24
1-21-68	NFL West 38, East 20
1-19-69	AFL West 38, East 25
1-19-69	NFL West 10, East 7
1-17-70	AFL West 26, East 3
1-18-70	NFL West 16, East 13
1-24-71	NFC 27, AFC 6
1-23-72	AFC 26, NFC 13
1-21-73	AFC 33, NFC 28
1-20-74	AFC 15, NFC 13
1-20-75	NFC 17, AFC 10
1-26-76	NFC 23, AFC 20
1-17-77	AFC 24, NFC 14
1-23-78	NFC 14, AFC 13
1-29-79	NFC 13, AFC 7
1-27-80	NFC 37, AFC 27
2-1-81	NFC 21, AFC 7
1-31-82	AFC 16, NFC 13
2-6-83	NFC 20, AFC 19
1-29-84	NFC 45, AFC 3
1-27-85	AFC 22, NFC 14
2-2-86	NFC 28, AFC 24
2-1-87	AFC 10, NFC 6
2-7-88	AFC 15, NFC 6
1-29-89	NFC 34, AFC 3
2-4-90	NFC 27, AFC 21
2-3-91	AFC 23, NFC 21
2-2-92	NFC 21, AFC 15
2-7-93	AFC 23, NFC 20
2-6-94	NFC 17, AFC 3
2-5-95	AFC 41, NFC 13
2-4-96	NFC 20, AFC 13
2-2-97	AFC 26, NFC 23
2-1-98	AFC 29, NFC 24
2-7-99	AFC 23, NFC 10
2-6-00	NFC 51, AFC 31
2-4-01	AFC 38, NFC 17
2-10-02	AFC 38, NFC 30
2-2-03	AFC 45, NFC 20
2-8-04	NFC 55, AFC 52
2-13-05	AFC 38, NFC 27
2-12-06	NFC 23, AFC 17
2-10-07	AFC 31, NFC 28
2-10-08	NFC 42, AFC 30

Chicago All-Star Game* Results

Date	Result (Attendance)
8-31-34	Chi Bears 0, All-Stars 0 (79,432)
8-29-35	Chi Bears 5, All-Stars 0 (77,450)
9-2-36	All-Stars 7, Detroit 7 (76,000)
9-1-37	All-Stars 6, Green Bay 0 (84,560)
8-31-38	All-Stars 28, Washington 16 (74,250)
8-30-39	NY Giants 9, All-Stars 0 (81,456)
8-29-40	Green Bay 45, All-Stars 28 (84,567)
8-28-41	Chi Bears 37, All-Stars 13 (98,203)
8-28-42	Chi Bears 21, All-Stars 0 (101,100)
8-25-43	All-Stars 27, Washington 7 (48,471)
8-30-44	Chi Bears 24, All-Stars 21 (48,769)
8-30-45	Green Bay 19, All-Stars 7 (92,753)
8-23-46	All-Stars 16, Los Angeles 0 (97,380)
8-22-47	All-Stars 16, Chi Bears 0 (105,840)
8-20-48	Chi Cardinals 28, All-Stars 0 (101,220)
8-12-49	Philadelphia 38, All-Stars 0 (93,780)
8-11-50	All-Stars 17, Philadelphia 7 (88,885)
8-17-51	Cleveland 33, All-Stars 0 (92,180)
8-15-52	Los Angeles 10, All-Stars 7 (88,316)
8-14-53	Detroit 24, All-Stars 10 (93,818)
8-13-54	Detroit 31, All-Stars 6 (93,470)
8-12-55	All-Stars 30, Cleveland 27 (75,000)
8-10-56	Cleveland 26, All-Stars 0 (75,000)
8-9-57	NY Giants 22, All-Stars 12 (75,000)
8-15-58	All-Stars 35, Detroit 19 (70,000)
8-14-59	Baltimore 29, All-Stars 0 (70,000)
8-12-60	Baltimore 32, All-Stars 7 (70,000)
8-4-61	Philadelphia 28, All-Stars 14 (66,000)
8-3-62	Green Bay 42, All-Stars 20 (65,000)
8-2-63	All-Stars 20, Green Bay 17 (65,000)
8-7-64	Chicago 28, All-Stars 17 (65,000)
8-6-65	Cleveland 24, All-Stars 16 (68,000)
8-5-66	Green Bay 38, All-Stars 0 (72,000)
8-4-67	Green Bay 27, All-Stars 0 (70,934)
8-2-68	Green Bay 34, All-Stars 17 (69,917)
8-1-69	NY Jets 26, All-Stars 24 (74,208)
7-31-70	Kansas City 24, All-Stars 3 (69,940)
7-30-71	Baltimore 24, All-Stars 17 (52,289)
7-28-72	Dallas 20, All-Stars 7 (54,162)
7-27-73	Miami 14, All-Stars 3 (54,103)
1974	No game
8-1-75	Pittsburgh 21, All-Stars 14 (54,562)
7-23-76	Pittsburgh 24, All-Stars 0 (52,895)

*Discontinued.

Alltime Winningest NFL Coaches

Most Career Wins

Coach	Yrs	Teams	Regular Season W	L	T	Pct	Career W	L	T	Pct
Don Shula	33	Colts, Dolphins	328	156	6	.676	347	173	6	.665
George Halas	40	Bears	318	148	31	.671	324	151	31	.671
Tom Landry	29	Cowboys	250	162	6	.605	270	178	6	.601
Curly Lambeau	33	Packers, Cardinals, Redskins	226	132	22	.624	229	134	22	.623
Chuck Noll	23	Steelers	193	148	1	.566	209	156	1	.572
M. Schottenheimer	20	Browns, Chiefs, Redskins, Chargers	200	126	1	.613	205	139	1	.596
Dan Reeves	23	Broncos, Giants, Falcons	190	165	2	.535	201	174	2	.536
Chuck Knox	22	Rams, Bills, Seahawks	186	147	1	.558	193	158	1	.550
Bill Parcells	18	Giants, Patriots, Jets, Cowboys	172	130	1	.569	183	138	1	.570
†Joe Gibbs	15	Redskins	154	94	0	.621	171	101	0	.629
Paul Brown	21	Browns, Bengals	166	100	6	.621	170	108	6	.609
†Mike Holmgren	15	Packers, Seahawks	157	99	0	.613	170	110	0	.607
Bud Grant	18	Vikings	158	96	5	.620	168	108	5	.607
Bill Cowher	14	Steelers	149	90	1	.623	161	99	1	.619
Marv Levy	17	Chiefs, Bills	143	112	0	.561	154	120	0	.562
Steve Owen	23	Giants	151	100	17	.595	153	108	17	.581
Hank Stram	17	Chiefs, Saints	131	97	10	.571	136	100	10	.573
Weeb Ewbank	20	Colts, Jets	130	129	7	.502	134	130	7	.507
Mike Ditka	14	Bears, Saints	121	95	0	.560	127	101	0	.557
Jim Mora	15	Saints, Colts	125	106	0	.541	125	112	0	.527

Top Winning Percentages

	W	L	T	Pct
Vince Lombardi	105	35	6	.740
John Madden	112	39	7	.731
George Allen	118	54	5	.681
George Halas	324	151	31	.671
Don Shula	347	173	6	.665
George Seifert	124	67	0	.650
†Joe Gibbs	162	93	0	.629
Curly Lambeau	229	134	22	.623
Bill Cowher	161	99	1	.619
Paul Brown	170	108	6	.609

Note: Minimum 100 victories.

†Active in 2007.

Pro Football Most Valuable Players

Year	Player/ Team	Position
1938	Mel Hein, NYG (NFL)	C
1939	Parker Hall, Clev (NFL)	HB
1940	Ace Parker, Brooklyn (NFL)	QB
1941	Don Hutson, GB (NFL)	E
1942	Don Hutson, GB (NFL)	E
1943	Sid Luckman, Chi Bears (NFL)	QB
1944	Frank Sinkwich, Det (NFL)	HB
1945	Bob Waterfield, Clev (NFL)	QB
1946	Bill Dudley, Pitt (NFL)	HB
	Glenn Dobbs, Brooklyn (AAFC)	HB
1947	No Selection (NFL)	
	Otto Graham, Clev (AAFC)	QB
1948	No Selection (NFL)	
	Otto Graham, Clev (AAFC-tie)	QB
	Frankie Albert, SF (AAFC-tie)	QB
1949	No Selection (NFL)	
1950	No Selection (NFL)	
1951	Otto Graham, Clev (UP)	QB
1952	No Selection (NFL)	
1953	Otto Graham, Clev (UP)	QB
1954	Joe Perry, SF (UP)	FB
	Lou Groza, Clev (TSN)	OT/K
1955	Otto Graham, Clev (UP, TSN)	QB
	Harlon Hill, Chi Bears (NEA)	E
1956	Frank Gifford, NYG (UP, NEA, TSN)	HB
1957	Y.A. Tittle, SF (UP)	QB
	Jim Brown, Clev (AP, TSN)	FB
	John Unitas, Balt (NEA)	QB
1958	Jim Brown, Clev (UP, AP, NEA, TSN)	FB
1959	John Unitas, Balt (UP, MCP, TSN)	QB
	Charley Conerly, NYG (AP, NEA)	QB
1960	Norm Van Brocklin, Phil, NFL (UP, AP, NEA, TSN, MCP)	QB
	Joe Schmidt, Det, NFL (UP- tie)	LB
	Abner Haynes, Dal Texans, AFL (UP, TSN)	HB
1961	Paul Hornung, GB, NFL (UP, AP, TSN, MCP)	HB
	Y.A. Tittle, NYG, NFL (NEA)	QB
	George Blanda, Hous, AFL (UP, TSN)	QB
1962	Y.A. Tittle, NYG, NFL (UP, TSN)	QB
	Jim Taylor, GB, NFL (AP, NEA)	FB
	Andy Robustelli, NYG, NFL (MCP)	DE
	Cookie Gilchrist, Buff, AFL (UP)	FB
	Len Dawson, Dal Texans, AFL (TSN)	QB
1963	Jim Brown, Clev, NFL (UP, NEA (tie), MCP)	FB
	Y.A. Tittle, NYG, NFL (AP, NEA (tie), TSN)	QB
	Lance Alworth, SD, AFL (UP)	WR
	Clem Daniels, Oak, AFL (TSN)	HB

Pro Football Most Valuable Players *(Cont.)*

Year	Player/ Team	Position
1964	Johnny Unitas, Balt, NFL (UP, AP, TSN, MCP)	QB
	Lenny Moore, Balt, NFL (NEA)	HB
	Gino Cappelletti, Boston, AFL (UP, TSN)	WR
1965	Jim Brown, Clev, NFL (UP, AP, TSN, NEA)	FB
	Pete Retzlaff, Phil, NFL (MCP)	TE
	Jack Kemp, Buff, AFL (UP)	QB
	Paul Lowe, SD, AFL (TSN)	RB
1966	Bart Starr, GB, NFL (UP, AP, NEA, TSN)	QB
	Don Meredith, Dal, NFL (MCP)	QB
	Jim Nance, Boston, AFL (UP, AP, TSN)	FB
1967	Johnny Unitas, Balt, NFL (UP, AP, NEA, TSN, MCP)	QB
	Daryl Lamonica, Oak, AFL (UP, AP, TSN)	QB
1968	Earl Morrall, Balt, NFL (UP, AP, NEA, TSN, PFW)	QB
	Leroy Kelly, Clev, AFL (MCP)	HB
	Joe Namath, NY Jets, AFL (UP, TSN, PFW)	QB
1969	Roman Gabriel, LA Rams, NFL (UP, AP, NEA, MCP, TSN, PFW)	QB
	Daryle Lamonica, Oak, AFL (UP, TSN, PFW)	QB
	Joe Namath, NY Jets, AFL (AP)	QB
1970	John Brodie, SF (AP, NEA)	QB
	George Blanda, Oak (MCP)	QB/K
1971	Alan Page, Minn (AP)	DT
	Bob Griese, Miami (NEA)	QB
	Roger Staubach, Dal (MCP)	QB
1972	Larry Brown, Washington (AP, NEA, MCP)	RB
1973	O.J. Simpson, Buff (AP, NEA, MCP)	RB
1974	Ken Stabler, Oak (AP, NEA)	QB
	Merlin Olsen, LA Rams (MCP)	DT
1975	Fran Tarkenton, Minn (PFWA, AP, NEA, MCP)	QB
1976	Bert Jones, Balt (PFWA, AP, NEA)	QB
	Ken Stabler, Oak (MCP)	QB
1977	Walter Payton, Chi (PFWA, AP, NEA)	RB
	Bob Griese, Miami (MCP)	QB
1978	Earl Campbell, Hous (PFWA, NEA)	RB
	Terry Bradshaw, Pitt (AP, MCP)	QB
1979	Earl Campbell, Hous (PFWA, AP, NEA, MCP)	RB
1980	Brian Sipe, Clev (PFWA, AP, TSN)	QB
	Earl Campbell, Hous (NEA)	RB
	Ron Jaworski, Phil (MCP)	QB
1981	Ken Anderson, Cin (PFWA, AP, NEA, TSN, MCP)	QB
1982	Dan Fouts, SD (PFWA, NEA)	QB
	Mark Moseley, Washington (AP, TSN)	K
	Joe Theismann, Washington (MCP)	QB
1983	Joe Theismann, Washington (PFWAA, AP, NEA)	QB
	Eric Dickerson, LA Rams (TSN)	RB
	John Riggins, Washington (MCP)	RB
1984	Dan Marino, Miami (PFWAA, AP, NEA, MCP, TSN)	QB
1985	Marcus Allen, LA Raiders (PFWAA, AP, TSN)	RB
	Walter Payton, Chi Bears (NEA, MCP)	RB
1986	Lawrence Taylor, NYG (PFWAA, AP, MCP, TSN)	LB
	Phil Simms, NYG (NEA)	QB
1987	Jerry Rice, SF (PFWAA, NEA, MCP, TSN)	WR
	John Elway, Den (AP)	QB
1988	Boomer Esiason, Cin (PFWAA, AP, TSN)	QB
	Roger Craig, SF (NEA)	RB
	Randall Cunningham, Phil (MCP)	QB
1989	Joe Montana, SF (PFWAA, AP, NEA, MCP, TSN)	QB
1990	Randall Cunningham, Phil (PFWAA)	QB
	Joe Montana, SF (AP)	QB
	Jerry Rice, SF (TSN)	WR
1991	Thurman Thomas, Buff (PFWAA, AP, TSN)	RB
	Barry Sanders, Det (MCP)	RB
1992	Steve Young, SF (PFWAA, AP, MCP, TSN)	QB
1993	Emmitt Smith, Dal (PFWAA, AP, MCP, TSN)	RB
1994	Steve Young, SF (PFWAA, AP, MCP, TSN)	QB
1995	Brett Favre, GB (PFWAA, AP, MCP, TSN)	QB
1996	Brett Favre, GB (PFWAA, AP, MCP, TSN)	QB
1997	Brett Favre, GB (AP – tie)	QB
	Barry Sanders, Det (PFWAA, AP (tie), MCP, TSN)	RB
1998	Terrell Davis, Den (PFWAA, AP, TSN)	RB
	Randall Cunningham, Minn (MCP)	QB
1999	Kurt Warner, StL (AP, PFWAA, MCP)	QB
2000	Marshall Faulk, StL (AP, PFWAA)	RB
	Rich Gannon, Oak (MCP)	QB
2001	Kurt Warner, StL (AP)	QB
	Marshall Faulk, StL (PFWAA, MCP, TSN)	RB
2002	Rich Gannon, Oak (AP)	QB
2003	Peyton Manning, Ind (AP - tie)	QB
	Steve McNair, Tenn (AP - tie)	QB
2004	Peyton Manning, Ind (AP)	QB
2005	Shaun Alexander, Sea (AP)	RB
2006	LaDainian Tomlinson, SD (AP)	RB
2007	Tom Brady, NE (AP)	QB

NOTE: AP-Associated Press, UP-United Press, PFW-*Pro Football Weekly*, TSN-*The Sporting News*, PFWAA-Pro Football Writers Association of America, PFWA-Pro Football Writers of America, MCP-Maxwell Club of Philadelphia, NEA-Newspaper Enterprise Association.

The NFL began awarding its MVP award, the Joe F. Carr Trophy (Carr was league president from 1921-39), in 1938, and continued to do so until 1946. Since that time, the NFL's Most Valuable Players and Players of the Year have been named by a variety of sources, among them, the United Press, the Associated Press, the Maxwell Club of Philadelphia, and the Pro Football Writers Association of America as well as magazines such as *Pro Football Weekly* and *The Sporting News*.

Pro Football Rookies of the Year

Year	Player/ Team	Position
1955	Alan Ameche, Balt (UP, TSN)	FB
1956	Lenny Moore, Balt (UP)	HB
	J.C. Caroline, Chi Bears (TSN)	DB
1957	Jim Brown, Clev (UP, AP, TSN)	FB
1958	Jimmy Orr, Pitt (UP, AP)	OE
	Bobby Mitchell, Cleveland (TSN)	HB
1959	Nick Pietrosante, Det (AP, TSN)	FB
	Boyd Dowler, GB (UP)	OE
1960	Gail Cogdill, Det, NFL (AP, UP, TSN)	OE
	Abner Haynes, Dal Texans, AFL (UP, TSN)	HB
1961	Mike Ditka, Chi Bears, NFL (AP, UP, TSN)	OE
	Earl Faison, SD, AFL (UP, TSN)	DE
1962	Ronnie Bull, Chi Bears, NFL (AP, UP, TSN)	HB
	Curtis McClinton, Dal, AFL (UP, TSN)	FB
1963	Paul Flatley, Minn, NFL (AP, UP, TSN)	OE
	Billy Joe, Den, AFL (UP, TSN)	FB
1964	Charley Taylor, Wash,	HB
	NFL (AP, UP, TSN, NEA)	
	Matt Snell, NYJ, AFL (UP, TSN)	FB
1965	Gale Sayers, Chi, NFL (AP, UP, TSN, NEA)	HB
	Joe Namath, NYJ, AFL (UP, TSN)	QB
1966	Johnny Roland, StL, NFL (UP)	HB
	Tommy Nobis, Atl, NFL (AP, TSN, NEA)	LB
	Bobby Burnett, Buff, AFL (UP, TSN)	HB
1967	Mel Farr, Det, NFL (AP-Off, UP, TSN, NEA)	HB
	Lem Barney, Det NFL (AP-Def)	CB
	George Webster, Hous, AFL (UP)	LB
	Dickie Post, SD, AFL (TSN)	HB
1968	Earl McCullouch, Det, NFL	OE
	(AP-Off, UP, TSN, NEA)	
	Claude Humphrey NFL (AP-Def)	DE
	Paul Robinson, Cin, AFL (UP, TSN)	HB
1969	Calvin Hill, Dal, NFL	HB
	(AP-Off, UP, TSN, NEA)	RB
	Joe Greene NFL (AP-Def)	DT
	Greg Cook, Cin, AFL (UP)	QB
	Carl Garrett, Boston, AFL (TSN)	HB
1970	Raymond Chester, Oak (NEA)	TE
	Dennis Shaw Buff (AP-Off, UP-AFC)	QB
	Bruce Taylor, DB SF (AP-Def, UP-NFC)	DB
1971	Jim Plunkett NE (UP-AFC)	QB
	John Brockington GB (AP-Off, UP-NFC)	RB
	Isiah Robertson, SF (AP-Def)	LB
1972	Franco Harris, Pitt (AP-Off, PFW, UP-AFC)	RB
	Chester Marcol, GB (UP-NFC)	PK
	Willie Buchanan, GB (AP-Def)	CB
1973	Chuck Foreman, Minn (AP-Off, PFW)	RB
	Wally Chambers, Chi (AP-Def)	DT
	Bobbie Clark, Cin (UP-AFC)	RB
	Charle Young Phil (UP-NFC)	TE
1974	Don Woods, SD (AP-Off, PFW, UP-AFC)	RB
	John Hicks, NYG (UP-NFC)	G
	Jack Lambert, Pitt (AP-Def)	LB
1975	Steve Bartkowski, Atl (PFW)	QB
	Robert Brazile, Hous (AP-Def, UP-AFC)	LB
	Mike Thomas, Wash (AP-Off, UP-NFC)	RB
1976	Mike Haynes, DB NE (AP-Def, UP-AFC)	DB
	Sammy White, Minn (AP-Off, UP-NFC)	WR
1977	Tony Dorsett, Dal (NEA, AP-Off, UP-NFC)	RB
	A.J. Duhe, Mia (AP-Def, UP-AFC)	DE
1978	Earl Campbell, Hous Oilers	RB
	(NEA, PFWA, AP-Off, UP-AFC)	
	Al "Bubba" Baker, Det (AP-Def, UP-NFC)	DE
1979	Ottis Anderson, StL Card	RB
	(NEA, PFWA, AP-Off, UP-NFC)	
	Jerry Butler, Buff (UP-AFC)	WR
	Jim Haslett, Buff (AP-Def	LB
1980	Billy Sims, Det	RB
	(NEA, TSN, PFWA, AP-Off, UP-NFC)	
	Joe Cribbs Buff (UP-AFC)	RB
	Buddy Curry, Atl (AP-Def tie)	LB
	Al Richardson, Atl (AP-Def tie)	LB
1981	Lawrence Taylor, NYG (NEA, AP-Def)	LB
	George Rogers, NO	RB
	(TSN, PFWA, AP-Off, UP-NFC)	
	Joe Delaney, KC (UP-AFC)	RB
1982	Marcus Allen, LA Raiders	RB
	(NEA, TSN, PFWA, AP-Off, UP-AFC)	
	Jim McMahon, Chi (UP-NFC)	QB
	Chip Banks, Cle (AP-Def)	LB
1983	Eric Dickerson, LA Rams	RB
	(NEA, PFWA, AP-Off, UP-NFC)	
	Dan Marino, Mia (TSN)	QB
	Curt Warner, Sea (UP-AFC)	RB
	Vernon Maxwell, Balt (AP-Def)	LB
1984	Louis Lipps, Pitt	WR
	(NEA, TSN, PFWA, AP-Off, UP-AFC)	
	Paul McFadden, Phil (UP-NFC)	PK
	Bill Maas, KC (AP-Def)	DT
1985	Eddie Brown, Cin (NEA, TSN, AP-Off, PFWA)	WR
	Kevin Mack, Clev (UP-AFC)	RB
	Jerry Rice, SF (UP-NFC)	WR
	Duane Bickett, Ind (AP-Def)	LB
1986	Reuben Mayes, NO	RB
	(NEA, TSN, PFWA, AP-Off, UP-NFC)	
	Leslie O'Neal, SD (AP-Def, UP-AFC)	DE
1987	Shane Conlan, Buff (PFWA, AP-Def, UP-AFC)	LB
	Bo Jackson, LA Raiders (NEA)	RB
	Robert Awalt, StL Card (TSN, UP-NFC)	TE
	Troy Stradford, Mia (AP-Off)	RB
1988	John Stephens, NE (NEA, AP-Off, PFWA)	RB
	Keith Jackson, Phil (TSN, UP-NFC)	TE
	Eric McMillan, NYJ (AP-Def)	S
1989	Barry Sanders, Det	RB
	(NEA, TSN, PFWA, AP-Off, UP-NFC)	
	Derrick Thomas KC (AP-Def, UP-AFC)	LB
1990	Mark Carrier, Chi (PFWA, UP-NFC, AP-Def)	S
	Emmitt Smith, Dal (AP-Off)	RB
	Richmond Webb, Mia (TSN, UP-AFC)	OT
1991	Mike Croel, Den	LB
	(PFWA, TSN, AP-Def, UP-AFC)	
	Lawrence Dawsey TB (UP-NFC)	WR
	Leonard Russell, NE (AP-Off)	RB
1992	Dale Carter, KC (PFWA, AP-Def, UP-AFC)	CB
	Carl Pickens, Cin (AP-Off)	WR
	Santana Dotson, TB (TSN)	DE
	Robert Jones, Dal (UP-NFC)	LB
1993	Jerome Bettis, LA Rams	RB
	(PFWA, TSN, AP-Off, UP-NFC)	
	Rick Mirer, Sea (UP-AFC)	QB
	Dana Stubblefield, SF (AP-Def)	DT
1994	Marshall Faulk, Ind	RB
	(PFWA, TSN, AP-Off, UP-AFC)	
	Bryant Young, SF (UP-NFC)	DT
	Tim Bowens, Mia (AP-Def)	DT
1995	Curtis Martin, NE	RB
	(PFWA, TSN, AP-Off, UP-AFC)	
	Rashaan Salaam Chi (UP-NFC)	RB
	Hugh Douglas, NYJ (AP-Def)	DE

Pro Football Rookies of the Year *(Cont.)*

Year	Player/ Team	Position
1996	Eddie George, Tenn (AP, PFWA, AP-Off, TSN)	RB
	Terry Glenn, NE (UP-AFC)	WR
	Simeon Rice, Ariz (AP-Def, UP-NFC)	DE
1997	Warrick Dunn, TB (PFWA, AP-Off, TSN)	RB
	Peter Boulware, Balt (AP-Def)	LB
1998	Randy Moss, Minn (PFWA, AP-Off, TSN)	WR
	Charles Woodson LA Raiders (AP-Def)	CB
1999	Edgerrin James, Ind (AP-Off, TSN)	RB
	Jevon Kearse, Tenn (AP-Def)	DE
2000	Mike Anderson, Den (AP-Off, TSN)	RB
	Brian Urlacher, Chi (AP-Def)	LB
2001	Anthony Thomas, Chi (AP-Off)	RB
	Kendrell Bell, Pitt (AP-Def)	LB
2002	Clinton Ports, Den (AP-Off)	RB
	Julius Peppers, Car (AP-Def)	DE
2003	Anquan Boldin, Ariz (AP-Off)	WR
	Terrell Suggs, Bal (AP-Def)	LB
2004	Ben Roethlisberger, Pitt (AP-Off)	QB
	Jonathan Vilma, NYJ (AP-Def)	LB
2005	Carnell Williams, TB (AP-Off)	RB
	Shawne Merriman, SD (AP-Def)	LB
2006	Vince Young, Tenn (AP-Off)	QB
	DeMeco Ryans, Hou (AP-Def)	LB
2007	Adrian Peterson, Min (AP-Off)	RB
	Patrick Willis, SF (AP-Def)	LB

NOTE: AP-Associated Press, UP-United Press, PFW-*Pro Football Weekly*, TSN-*The Sporting News*, PFWAA-Pro Football Writers Association of America, PFWA-Pro Football Writers of America, MCP-Maxwell Club of Philadelphia, NEA-Newspaper Enterprise Association
Starting in1960, the United Press annually awarded two Rookie of the Year awards, one to an AFL player and one to a NFL player. After the AFL-NFL merger, the UP kept the two-award format for the AFC and NFC. The UP stopped awarding RoY awards after the 1996 season.
Starting in 1967, the Associated Press began announcing two annual Rookie of the Year awards, as well. One went to the best offensive rookie in the NFL, the other to the best defensive rookie.

Alltime Number-One Draft Choices

Year	Team	Selection	Position
1936	Philadelphia	Jay Berwanger, Chicago	HB
1937	Philadelphia	Sam Francis, Nebraska	FB
1938	Cleveland	Corbett Davis, Indiana	FB
1939	Chicago Cardinals	Ki Aldrich, Texas Christian	C
1940	Chicago Cardinals	George Cafego, Tennessee	HB
1941	Chicago Bears	Tom Harmon, Michigan	HB
1942	Pittsburgh	Bill Dudley, Virginia	HB
1943	Detroit	Frank Sinkwich, Georgia	HB
1944	Boston	Angelo Bertelli, Notre Dame	QB
1945	Chicago Cardinals	Charley Trippi, Georgia	HB
1946	Boston	Frank Dancewicz, Notre Dame	QB
1947	Chicago Bears	Bob Fenimore, Oklahoma A&M	HB
1948	Washington	Harry Gilmer, Alabama	QB
1949	Philadelphia	Chuck Bednarik, Pennsylvania	C
1950	Detroit	Leon Hart, Notre Dame	E
1951	New York Giants	Kyle Rote, SMU	HB
1952	Los Angeles	Bill Wade, Vanderbilt	QB
1953	San Francisco	Harry Babcock, Georgia	E
1954	Cleveland	Bobby Garrett, Stanford	QB
1955	Baltimore	George Shaw, Oregon	QB
1956	Pittsburgh	Gary Glick, Colorado A&M	DB
1957	Green Bay	Paul Hornung, Notre Dame	HB
1958	Chicago Cardinals	King Hill, Rice	QB
1959	Green Bay	Randy Duncan, Iowa	QB
1960	Los Angeles	Billy Cannon, LSU	RB
1961	Minnesota	Tommy Mason, Tulane	RB
	Buffalo (AFL)	Ken Rice, Auburn	G
1962	Washington	Ernie Davis, Syracuse	RB
	Oakland (AFL)	Roman Gabriel, North Carolina St	QB
1963	LA Rams	Terry Baker, Oregon St	QB
	Kansas City (AFL)	Buck Buchanan, Grambling	DT
1964	San Francisco	Dave Parks, Texas Tech	E
	Boston (AFL)	Jack Concannon, Boston College	QB
1965	NY Giants	Tucker Frederickson, Auburn	RB
	Houston (AFL)	Lawrence Elkins, Baylor	E
1966	Atlanta	Tommy Nobis, Texas	LB
	Miami (AFL)	Jim Grabowski, Illinois	RB

Alltime Number-One Draft Choices *(Cont.)*

Year	Team	Selection	Position
1967	Baltimore	Bubba Smith, Michigan St	DT
1968	Minnesota	Ron Yary, USC	T
1969	Buffalo (AFL)	O.J. Simpson, USC	RB
1970	Pittsburgh	Terry Bradshaw, Louisiana Tech	QB
1971	New England	Jim Plunkett, Stanford	QB
1972	Buffalo	Walt Patulski, Notre Dame	DE
1973	Houston	John Matuszak, Tampa	DE
1974	Dallas	Ed Jones, Tennessee St	DE
1975	Atlanta	Steve Bartkowski, California	QB
1976	Tampa Bay	Lee Roy Selmon, Oklahoma	DE
1977	Tampa Bay	Ricky Bell, USC	RB
1978	Houston	Earl Campbell, Texas	RB
1979	Buffalo	Tom Cousineau, Ohio St	LB
1980	Detroit	Billy Sims, Oklahoma	RB
1981	New Orleans	George Rogers, South Carolina	RB
1982	New England	Kenneth Sims, Texas	DT
1983	Baltimore	John Elway, Stanford	QB
1984	New England	Irving Fryar, Nebraska	WR
1985	Buffalo	Bruce Smith, Virginia Tech	DE
1986	Tampa Bay	Bo Jackson, Auburn	RB
1987	Tampa Bay	Vinny Testaverde, Miami (Fla.)	QB
1988	Atlanta	Aundray Bruce, Auburn	LB
1989	Dallas	Troy Aikman, UCLA	QB
1990	Indianapolis	Jeff George, Illinois	QB
1991	Dallas	Russell Maryland, Miami (Fla.)	DT
1992	Indianapolis	Steve Emtman, Washington	DT
1993	New England	Drew Bledsoe, Washington St	QB
1994	Cincinnati	Dan Wilkinson, Ohio St	DT
1995	Cincinnati	Ki-Jana Carter, Penn St	RB
1996	New York Jets	Keyshawn Johnson, USC	WR
1997	St Louis	Orlando Pace, Ohio St	OT
1998	Indianapolis	Peyton Manning, Tennessee	QB
1999	Cleveland	Tim Couch, Kentucky	QB
2000	Cleveland	Courtney Brown, Penn St	DE
2001	Atlanta	Michael Vick, Virginia Tech	QB
2002	Houston	David Carr, Fresno St	QB
2003	Cincinnati	Carson Palmer, USC	QB
2004	San Diego	Eli Manning, Mississippi	QB
2005	San Francisco	Alex Smith, Utah	QB
2006	Houston	Mario Williams, North Carolina St	DE
2007	Oakland	JaMarcus Russell, LSU	QB
2008	Miami	Jake Long, Michigan	OT

From 1947 through 1958, the first selection in the draft was a bonus pick, awarded to the winner of a random draw. That club, in turn, forfeited its last-round draft choice. The winner of the bonus choice was eliminated from future draws. The system was abolished after 1958, by which time all clubs had received a bonus choice.

Members of the Pro Football Hall of Fame

Herb Adderley
Troy Aikman
George Allen
Marcus Allen
Lance Alworth
Doug Atkins
Morris (Red) Badgro
Lem Barney
Cliff Battles
Sammy Baugh
Chuck Bednarik
Bert Bell
Bobby Bell
Raymond Berry
Elvin Bethea
Charles W. Bidwill Sr.
Fred Biletnikoff
George Blanda
Mel Blount
Terry Bradshaw
Bob (the Boomer) Brown
Jim Brown
Paul Brown
Roosevelt Brown
Willie Brown
Junios (Buck) Buchanan
Nick Buoniconti
Dick Butkus
Earl Campbell
Tony Canadeo
Joe Carr
Harry Carson
Dave Casper
Guy Chamberlin
Jack Christiansen
Earl (Dutch) Clark
George Connor
Jimmy Conzelman
Lou Creekmur
Larry Csonka
Al Davis
Willie Davis
Len Dawson
Fred Dean
Joe DeLamielleure
Eric Dickerson
Dan Dierdorf
Mike Ditka
Art Donovan
Tony Dorsett
John (Paddy) Driscoll
Bill Dudley
Albert Glen (Turk) Edwards
Carl Eller
John Elway
Weeb Ewbank
Tom Fears
Jim Finks
Ray Flaherty
Len Ford
Dan Fortmann
Dan Fouts
Benny Friedman
Frank Gatski
Bill George
Joe Gibbs
Frank Gifford
Sid Gillman
Otto Graham
Harold (Red) Grange
Bud Grant
Darrell Green
Joe Greene
Forrest Gregg
Bob Griese
Lou Groza
Joe Guyon
George Halas
Jack Ham
Dan Hampton
John Hannah
Franco Harris
Mike Haynes
Ed Healey
Mel Hein
Ted Hendricks
Wilbur (Pete) Henry
Arnie Herber
Bill Hewitt
Gene Hickerson
Clarke Hinkle
Elroy (Crazylegs) Hirsch
Paul Hornung
Ken Houston
Robert (Cal) Hubbard
Sam Huff
Lamar Hunt
Don Hutson
Michael Irvin
Jimmy Johnson
John Henry Johnson
Charlie Joiner
David (Deacon) Jones
Stan Jones
Henry Jordan
Sonny Jurgensen
Jim Kelly
Leroy Kelly
Walt Kiesling
Frank (Bruiser) Kinard
Paul Krause
Earl (Curly) Lambeau
Jack Lambert
Tom Landry
Dick (Night Train) Lane
Jim Langer
Willie Lanier
Steve Largent
Yale Lary
Dante Lavelli
Bobby Layne
Alphonse (Tuffy) Leemans
Marv Levy
Bob Lilly
Larry Little
James Lofton
Vince Lombardi
Howie Long
Ronnie Lott
Sid Luckman
William Roy (Link) Lyman
Tom Mack
John Mackey
John Madden
Tim Mara
Wellington Mara
Gino Marchetti
Dan Marino
George Preston Marshall
Ollie Matson
Bruce Matthews
Don Maynard
George McAfee
Mike McCormack
Tommy McDonald
Hugh McElhenny
John (Blood) McNally
Mike Michalske
Wayne Millner
Bobby Mitchell
Ron Mix
Art Monk
Joe Montana
Warren Moon
Lenny Moore
Marion Motley
Mike Munchak
Anthony Munoz
George Musso
Bronko Nagurski
Joe Namath
Earle (Greasy) Neale
Ernie Nevers
Ozzie Newsome
Ray Nitschke
Chuck Noll
Leo Nomellini
Merlin Olsen
Jim Otto
Steve Owen
Alan Page
Clarence (Ace) Parker
Jim Parker
Walter Payton
Joe Perry
Pete Pihos
Fritz Pollard
Hugh (Shorty) Ray
Dan Reeves
Mel Renfro
John Riggins
Jim Ringo
Andy Robustelli
Art Rooney
Dan Rooney
Pete Rozelle
Bob St. Clair
Barry Sanders
Charlie Sanders
Gale Sayers
Joe Schmidt
Tex Schramm
Lee Roy Selmon
Billy Shaw
Art Shell
Don Shula
O.J. Simpson
Mike Singletary
Jackie Slater
Jackie Smith
John Stallworth
Bart Starr
Roger Staubach
Ernie Stautner
Jan Stenerud
Dwight Stephenson
Hank Stram
Ken Strong
Joe Stydahar
Lynn Swann
Fran Tarkenton
Charley Taylor
Jim Taylor
Lawrence Taylor
Emmitt Thomas
Thurman Thomas
Jim Thorpe
Andre Tippett
Y.A. Tittle
George Trafton
Charley Trippi
Emlen Tunnell
Clyde (Bulldog) Turner
Johnny Unitas
Gene Upshaw
Norm Van Brocklin
Steve Van Buren
Doak Walker
Bill Walsh
Paul Warfield
Bob Waterfield
Mike Webster
Roger Wehrli
Arnie Weinmeister
Randy White
Reggie White
Dave Wilcox
Bill Willis
Larry Wilson
Kellen Winslow
Alex Wojciechowicz
Willie Wood
Rayfield Wright
Ron Yary
Steve Young
Jack Youngblood
Gary Zimmerman

Champions of Other Leagues

Canadian Football League Grey Cup

Year	Results	Site	Attendance
1909	U of Toronto 26, Parkdale 6	Toronto	3,807
1910	U of Toronto 16, Hamilton Tigers 7	Hamilton	12,000
1911	U of Toronto 14, Toronto 7	Toronto	13,687
1912	Hamilton Alerts 11, Toronto 4	Hamilton	5,337
1913	Hamilton Tigers 44, Parkdale 2	Hamilton	2,100
1914	Toronto 14, U of Toronto 2	Toronto	10,500
1915	Hamilton Tigers 13, Toronto RAA 7	Toronto	2,808
1916–19	No game	—	—
1920	U of Toronto 16, Toronto 3	Toronto	10,088
1921	Toronto 23, Edmonton 0	Toronto	9,558
1922	Queen's U 13, Edmonton 1	Kingston	4,700
1923	Queen's U 54, Regina 0	Toronto	8,629
1924	Queen's U 11, Balmy Beach 3	Toronto	5,978
1925	Ottawa Senators 24, Winnipeg 1	Ottawa	6,900
1926	Ottawa Senators 10, Toronto U 7	Toronto	8,276
1927	Balmy Beach 9, Hamilton Tigers 6	Toronto	13,676
1928	Hamilton Tigers 30, Regina 0	Hamilton	4,767
1929	Hamilton Tigers 14, Regina 3	Hamilton	1,906
1930	Balmy Beach 11, Regina 6	Toronto	3,914
1931	Montreal AAA 22, Regina 0	Montreal	5,112
1932	Hamilton Tigers 25, Regina 6	Hamilton	4,806
1933	Toronto 4, Sarnia 3	Sarnia	2,751
1934	Sarnia 20, Regina 12	Toronto	8,900
1935	Winnipeg 18, Hamilton Tigers 12	Hamilton	6,405
1936	Sarnia 26, Ottawa RR 20	Toronto	5,883
1937	Toronto 4, Winnipeg 3	Toronto	11,522
1938	Toronto 30, Winnipeg 7	Toronto	18,778
1939	Winnipeg 8, Ottawa 7	Ottawa	11,738
1940	Ottawa 8, Balmy Beach 2	Toronto	4,998
1940	Ottawa 12, Balmy Beach 5	Ottawa	1,700
1941	Winnipeg 18, Ottawa 16	Toronto	19,065
1942	Toronto RCAF 8, Winnipeg RCAF 5	Toronto	12,455
1943	Hamilton F Wild 23, Winnipeg RCAF 14	Toronto	16,423
1944	Montreal St H-D Navy 7, Hamilton F Wild 6	Hamilton	3,871
1945	Toronto 35, Winnipeg 0	Toronto	18,660
1946	Toronto 28, Winnipeg 6	Toronto	18,960
1947	Toronto 10, Winnipeg 9	Toronto	18,885
1948	Calgary 12, Ottawa 7	Toronto	20,013
1949	Montreal Als 28, Calgary 15	Toronto	20,087
1950	Toronto 13, Winnipeg 0	Toronto	27,101
1951	Ottawa 21, Saskatchewan 14	Toronto	27,341
1952	Toronto 21, Edmonton 11	Toronto	27,391
1953	Hamilton Ticats 12, Winnipeg 6	Toronto	27,313
1954	Edmonton 26, Montreal 25	Toronto	27,321
1955	Edmonton 34, Montreal 19	Vancouver	39,417
1956	Edmonton 50, Montreal 27	Toronto	27,425
1957	Hamilton 32, Winnipeg 7	Toronto	27,051
1958	Winnipeg 35, Hamilton 28	Vancouver	36,567
1959	Winnipeg 21, Hamilton 7	Toronto	33,133
1960	Ottawa 16, Edmonton 6	Vancouver	38,102
1961	Winnipeg 21, Hamilton 14	Toronto	32,651
1962	Winnipeg 28, Hamilton 27	Toronto	32,655
1963	Hamilton 21, British Columbia 10	Vancouver	36,545
1964	British Columbia 34, Hamilton 24	Toronto	32,655
1965	Hamilton 22, Winnipeg 16	Toronto	32,655
1966	Saskatchewan 29, Ottawa 14	Vancouver	36,553
1967	Hamilton 24, Saskatchewan 1	Ottawa	31,358
1968	Ottawa 24, Calgary 21	Toronto	32,655
1969	Ottawa 29, Saskatchewan 11	Montreal	33,172
1970	Montreal 23, Calgary 10	Toronto	32,669
1971	Calgary 14, Toronto 11	Vancouver	34,484
1972	Hamilton 13, Saskatchewan 10	Hamilton	33,993
1973	Ottawa 22, Edmonton 18	Toronto	36,653
1974	Montreal 20, Edmonton 7	Vancouver	34,450
1975	Edmonton 9, Montreal 8	Calgary	32,454
1976	Ottawa 23, Saskatchewan 20	Toronto	53,467
1977	Montreal 41, Edmonton 6	Montreal	68,318

Champions of Other Leagues *(Cont.)*

Canadian Football League Grey Cup

Year	Results	Site	Attendance
1978	Edmonton 20, Montreal 13	Toronto	54,695
1979	Edmonton 17, Montreal 9	Montreal	65,113
1980	Edmonton 48, Hamilton 10	Toronto	54,661
1981	Edmonton 26, Ottawa 23	Montreal	52,478
1982	Edmonton 32, Toronto 16	Toronto	54,741
1983	Toronto 18, British Columbia 17	Vancouver	59,345
1984	Winnipeg 47, Hamilton 17	Edmonton	60,081
1985	British Columbia 37, Hamilton 24	Montreal	56,723
1986	Hamilton 39, Edmonton 15	Vancouver	59,621
1987	Edmonton 38, Toronto 36	Vancouver	59,478
1988	Winnipeg 22, British Columbia 21	Ottawa	50,604
1989	Saskatchewan 43, Hamilton 40	Toronto	54,088
1990	Winnipeg 50, Edmonton 11	Vancouver	46,968
1991	Toronto 36, Calgary 21	Winnipeg	51,985
1992	Calgary 24, Winnipeg 10	Toronto	45,863
1993	Edmonton 33, Winnipeg 23	Calgary	50,035
1994	British Columbia 26, Baltimore 23	Vancouver	55,097
1995	Baltimore 37, Calgary 20	Regina, Saskatchewan	52,564
1996	Toronto 43, Edmonton 37	Hamilton, Ontario	38,595
1997	Toronto 47, Saskatchewan 23	Edmonton	60,431
1998	Calgary 26, Hamilton 24	Winnipeg	34,157
1999	Hamilton 32, Calgary 21	Vancouver	45,118
2000	British Columbia 28, Montreal 26	Calgary	43,822
2001	Calgary 27, Winnipeg 19	Montreal	65,255
2002	Montreal 25, Edmonton 16	Edmonton	62,531
2003	Edmonton 34, Montreal 22	Regina, Saskatchewan	50,909
2004	Toronto 27, British Columbia 19	Ottawa	51,242
2005	Edmonton 38, Montreal 35 (OT)	Vancouver	59,157
2006	British Columbia 25, Montreal 14	Winnipeg	44,786
2007	Saskatchewan 23, Winnipeg 19	Toronto	52,230

In 1909, Earl Grey, the Governor-General of Canada, donated a trophy for the Rugby Football Championship of Canada. The trophy, which subsequently became known as the Grey Cup, was originally open only to teams registered with the Canada Rugby Union. Since 1954, it has been awarded to the winner of the Canadian Football League's championship game.

AMERICAN FOOTBALL LEAGUE I

Year	Champion	Record
1926	Philadelphia Quakers	7-2

AMERICAN FOOTBALL LEAGUE II

Year	Champion	Record
1936	Boston Shamrocks	8-3
1937	LA Bulldogs	8-0

AMERICAN FOOTBALL LEAGUE III

Year	Champion	Record
1940	Columbus Bullies	8-1-1
1941	Columbus Bullies	5-1-2

ALL-AMERICAN FOOTBALL CONFERENCE

Year	Championship Game
1946	Cleveland 14, NY Yankees 9
1947	Cleveland 14, NY Yankees 3
1948	Cleveland 49, Buffalo 7
1949	Cleveland 21, San Francisco 7

WORLD FOOTBALL LEAGUE

Year	World Bowl Championship
1974	Birmingham 22, Florida 21
1975	Disbanded midseason

UNITED STATES FOOTBALL LEAGUE

Year	Championship Game
1983	Michigan 24, Philadelphia 22
1984	Philadelphia 23, Arizona 3
1985	Baltimore 28, Oakland 24

X FOOTBALL LEAGUE

Year	Championship Game
2001	Los Angeles 38, San Francisco 6

NFL EUROPE

Year Record	Champion	
1991	London	9-1-0
1992	Sacramento	8-2-0
1995	Frankfurt	6-4-0
1996	Scotland	7-3-0
1997	Barcelona	5-5-0
1998	Rhein	7-3-0
1999	Frankfurt	6-4-0
2000	Rhein	7-3-0
2001	Berlin	6-4-0
2002	Berlin	6-4-0
2003	Frankfurt	6-4-0
2004	Berlin	9-1-0
2005	Amsterdam	6-4-0
2006	Frankfurt	7-3-0
2007	Hamburg	7-3-0

Known as World League of American Football until 1998.

College Football

Head coach Les Miles (r.) and his national champion LSU Tigers

BOB ROSATO/SPORTS ILLUSTRATED

Bowl Chaos

Nothing was predictable in a season that saw LSU reign supreme, a sophomore take the Heisman and the BCS confound fans as much as it enthralled them

BY B.J. SCHECTER

WHO KNEW WATCHING A system go up in smoke could be so much fun? The Bowl Championship Series (BCS) was introduced in 1998 with the sole purpose of creating a No. 1 vs. No. 2 matchup for the national title. But lost in the convoluted computer formulas, human polls and parity was a giant mess that left fans clamoring for a playoff. The 2007 season will go down as the year the BCS blew up. It was a wild ride that turned on its ear the final week of the season with not one but two top teams falling, opening the door for pandemonium. But it was riveting theater nonetheless.

To review: LSU was No. 1 for most of the year but lost to Kentucky in triple overtime, giving Ohio State the opportunity to return to No. 1, where it stood for most of the 2006 season. The Buckeyes were then upset by Illinois, giving LSU the top spot again. But the Tigers fell to Arkansas—in triple overtime—vaulting Kansas (yes, Kansas) to the top spot. Kansas lost to rival Missouri the following week, making the Tigers No. 1 and one-loss West Virginia No. 2. Then it got really interesting.

On the final Saturday of the regular season, all Missouri and West Virginia had to do to play for the national title in New Orleans was win. Both teams lost. The first spot in the title game subsequently went to Ohio State, which was idle but had beaten Michigan two weeks earlier. That left one slot open with seven teams vying for it. Oklahoma, which had beaten No. 1 Missouri in the Big 12 title game, LSU, which had won the SEC title with a victory over Tennessee, and red-hot Georgia and USC had the strongest claims. But it was LSU that earned the nod, making the gargantuan leap from No. 7 in the BCS standings to No. 2. It was settled: LSU vs. Ohio State for the national title.

"We always talk to our guys about the fact you better win all your games," said Ohio State coach Jim Tressel. "We didn't do that but we still have an opportunity in a crazy football season."

If fans outside Ohio weren't crazy about the Buckeyes backing into the title game, they had good reason. A year earlier, Ohio State went into the BCS championship game as the prohibitive favorite before getting drilled by Florida 41–14.

LSU came into the year as the preseason favorite and early on lived up to the hype with a 48–7 demolition of Virginia Tech, which went on to win the ACC, in September. But slowly the Tigers began to show nicks in their armor, first with injuries then with some great escapes against Florida and Auburn. Behind it all was fiery and unpredictable coach Les Miles. Miles took a jab at the USC and the Pac-10 before the season began. "They have a much easier road to

AP PHOTO/ DAVID GARD

travel," he said, sarcastically. "They're going to play real knock-down, drag-outs with UCLA and Washington, Cal-Berkeley, Stanford—some real juggernauts."

In 2007, no one could stop runnin' and gunnin' Florida QB Tim Tebow, the first sophomore to win the Heisman Trophy.

Throughout the season there were rumors that Miles was next in line at Michigan, his alma mater (during the year there were rumblings that the 2007 season would be Wolverines coach Lloyd Carr's last and he resigned in November). Then, just before the SEC championship game, there was a report that Miles was going to leave LSU for Ann Arbor. Miles was incensed and called an improptu press conference in the bowels of the Georgia Dome two hours before kickoff. "I'm the head coach at LSU. I will be the head coach at LSU," Miles said. "I have no interest in talking to anybody else. I'm busy. Have a great day."

On the field, Miles was equally bold. He wasn't afraid to gamble and on the season was successful on a pair of fake field goals and a fake punt and was 12-of-15 in fourth down conversions, including a head-scratching five against Florida. If any one of them had failed, LSU would likely have lost. "If there's a way to steal a possession, I'm certainly going to invest in that thought," Miles said.

Buyoyed by their audacious coach, LSU was unfazed when Ohio State jumped to a 10–0 lead in the title game. The Tigers were used to playing from behind, as they trailed in six of their first 11 wins. And, true to form, LSU kicked into high gear, exploding for 31 unanswered points en route to a 38–24 victory. After giving up a 65-yard touchdown run by Ohio State star tailback Chris Wells on the fourth play from scrimmage, LSU locked down both sides of the line and dominated, proving that no matter the mess the BCS created, LSU was clearly the No. 1 team. No controversy there.

West Virgina fans won't soon forget the wild end to the Mountaineers' season,

Coach Lloyd Carr, who led Michigan to five Big Ten titles, announced his retirement in 2007.

though. Picked to win the Big East and vie for a national championship behind the dynamic duo of quarterback Pat White and running back Steve Slaton, West Virginia dazzled from the start. The Mountaineers lost early to South Florida, but slowly worked their way back to the top of the polls before the roof caved in. West Virginia had a clear path to the title game, but layed an egg at home to rival Pittsburgh, losing 13–9 and falling to the Fiesta Bowl.

The following day news leaked that Mountaineers coach Rich Rodriguez was leaving for Michigan. Rodriguez went from favorite son to eternal villan. West Virigina still had a game to play and interim coach Bill Stewart, another lifelong West Virginian, would lead the Mountaineers against Big 12 champ Oklahoma. West Virginia wasn't given much of a chance against the Sooners, but the Mountaineers came out hungry and rolled to a 48–28 victory, earning Stewart the permanent job.

"He deserves it," White said of Stewart. "A great man. A great coach. You couldn't ask for a better man to lead us to victory."

While Kansas and Missouri piled up victories in the Big 12, Florida quarterback Tim Tebow made history. A one-man offensive wrecking crew, the 6'3", 225-pound sophomore became a cult hero in Gainesville. In short yardage situations opponents knew exactly what was coming but Tebow still delivered, bulldozing everything in his trail.

Florida fans developed a website featuring anecdotes about his supernatural feats:

When Google can't find something, it asks Tim Tebow for help.

Before the bogeyman goes to sleep, he checks his closet for Tim Tebow.

Some people wear Superman pajamas. Superman wears Tim Tebow pajamas.

Tebow, who finished the season by throwing for 3,286 yards and 32 touchdowns and rushing for 895 yards and 23 TDs, had a couple of things going against him in the Heisman race. First, Florida wasn't a national title contender; the Gators fell to 9–4 a year after they won the championship. And Tebow was a sophomore and no sophomore had ever won the Heisman. But Tebow was no ordinary sophomore and that wasn't lost on coaches and voters. "I've seen quarterbacks who can run, but not with that kind of power and toughness," said Georgia coach Mark Richt. "He's a freak of nature."

In a freakish season, it was fitting that Tebow broke the mold and became the first sophomore to win the Heisman Trophy, edging out Arkansas running back Darren McFadden. The implosion of the BCS prompted talk of a plus-one game among conference commissioners but not a playoff. But with television deals, a plus-one couldn't be instituted until 2011 at the earliest. That means several more years of chaos is on the horizon, which in college football isn't always a bad thing.

Final Polls

Associated Press

		Record	Pts	Head Coach	SI Preseason Rank
1.	LSU (60)	12-2	1620	Les Miles	2
2.	Georgia (3)	11-2	1515	Mark Richt	19
3.	USC (1)	11-2	1500	Pete Carroll	1
4.	Missouri	12-2	1347	Gary Pinkel	26
5	Ohio St	11-2	1346	Jim Tressel	11
6.	West Virginia	11-2	1342	Rich Rodriguez	4
7.	Kansas (1)	12-1	1303	Mark Mangino	49
8.	Oklahoma	11-3	1139	Bob Stoops	9
9.	Viginia Tech	11-3	1096	Frank Beamer	7
10.	Texas	10-3	962	Mack Brown	8
10.	Boston College	11-3	962	Jeff Jagodzinkski	21
12.	Tennessee	10-4	904	Phillip Fulmer	17
13.	Florida	9-4	685	Urban Meyer	3
14.	BYU	11-2	654	Bronco Mendenhall	35
15.	Auburn	9-4	648	Tommy Tuberville	16
16.	Arizona St	10-3	587	Dennis Erickson	48
17.	Cincinnati	10-3	566	Brian Kelly	56
18.	Michigan	9-4	508	Lloyd Carr	6
19.	Hawaii	12-1	460	June Jones	24
20.	Illinois	9-4	443	Ron Zook	51
21.	Clemson	9-4	353	Tommy Bowden	37
22.	Texas Tech	9-4	308	Mike Leach	34
23.	Oregon	9-4	253	Mike Bellotti	45
24.	Wisconsin	9-4	202	Bret Bielema	10
25.	Oregon St	9-4	110	Mike Riley	38

Note: As voted by a panel of 65 sportswriters and broadcasters following bowl games (1st place votes in parentheses).

USA Today/ESPN

		Pts	SI Preseason Rank
1.	LSU (60)	1500	2
2.	USC	1380	1
3.	Georgia	1370	19
4.	Ohio St	1287	11
5.	Missouri	1241	26
6.	West Virginia	1239	4
7.	Kansas	1217	49
8	Oklahoma	1016	9
9.	Virginia Tech	979	7
10.	Texas	924	8
11.	Boston College	898	21
12.	Tennessee	826	17
13.	Arizona St	635	48
14.	Auburn	624	16
14.	BYU	624	35
16.	Florida	567	3
17.	Hawaii	427	24
18.	Illinois	416	51
19.	Michigan	413	6
20.	Cincinnati	376	56
21.	Wisconsin	333	10
22.	Clemson	319	37
23.	Texas Tech	242	34
24.	Oregon	192	45
25.	Penn St	127	14

Note: Voted by a panel of 60 Div. I-A head coaches; 25 points for 1st, 24 for 2nd, etc. (First place votes in parentheses).

Bowls and Playoffs

NCAA Division I-A Bowl Results

Date	Bowl	Result	Payout/Team ($)	Attendance
12-20-07	Poinsettia	Utah 35, Navy 32	750,000	39,129
12-21-07	New Orleans	Florida Atlantic 44, Memphis 27	325,000	25,146
12-22-07	PapaJohns.com	Cincinnati 31, Southern Miss 21	300,000	35,258
12-22-07	New Mexico	New Mexico 23, Nevada 0	750,000	30,223
12-22-07	Las Vegas	BYU 17, UCLA 16	1 million	40,712
12-23-07	Hawaii	East Carolina 41, Boise St 38	750,000	30,467
12-26-07	Motor City	Purdue 51, Central Michigan 48	750,000	60,624
12-27-07	Holiday	Texas 52, Arizona St 34	2.2 million	64.020
12-28-07	Texas	TCU 20, Houston 13	750,000	62,097
12-28-07	Champs Sports	Boston College 24, Michigan St 21	2.25 million	46,554

NCAA Division I-A Bowl Results (Cont.)

Date	Bowl	Result	Payout/Team($)	Attendance
12-28-07	Emerald	Oregon St 21, Maryland 14	750,000	32,517
12-29-07	Meineke Car Care	Wake Forest 24, Connecticut 10	750,000	53,126
12-29-07	Liberty	Mississippi St 10, Central Florida 3	1.7 million	63,816
12-29-07	Alamo	Penn St 24, Texas A&M 17	2.2 million	66,166
12-30-07	Independence	Alabama 30, Colorado 24	1.1 million	47,043
12-31-07	Armed Forces	California 42, Air Force 36	750,000	44,009
12-31-07	Humanitarian	Fresno St 40, Georgia Tech 28	250,000	27,062
12-31-07	Sun	Oregon 56, South Florida 21	1.9 million	49,867
12-31-07	Music City	Kentucky 35, Florida St 28	1.6 million	68,661
12-31-07	Chick-Fil-A	Auburn 23, Clemson 20 (OT)	3.25 million (ACC) 2.4 million (SEC)	74,413
12-31-07	Insight	Oklahoma St 49, Indiana 33	1.2 million	48,892
01-01-08	Outback	Tennessee 21, Wisconsin 17	3 million	60,121
01-01-08	Cotton	Missouri 38, Arkansas 7	3 million	73,114
01-01-08	Gator	Texas Tech 31, Virginia 28	2.5 million	60,243
01-01-08	Capital One	Michigan 41, Florida 35	4.25 million	69,748
01-01-08	Rose	USC 49, Illinois 17	17 million	93,923
01-01-08	Sugar	Georgia 41, Hawaii 10	17 million	74,383
01-02-08	Fiesta	West Virginia 48, Oklahoma 28	17 million	70,016
01-03-08	Orange	Kansas 24, Virginia Tech 21	17 million	74,111
01-05-08	International	Rutgers 52, Ball St 30	750,000	31,455
01-06-08	GMAC	Tulsa 63, Bowling Green 7	750,000	36,932
01-08-08	BCS Nat'l Championship	LSU 38, Ohio St 24	17 million	79,651

NCAA FCS (I-AA) Championship Box Score

Delaware	**0**	**7**	**7**	**7—21**
Appalachian St	**14**	**14**	**7**	**14—49**

FIRST QUARTER

Appalachian St: TD Richardson 19 pass from Edwards (Rauch kick), 10:47.
Appalachian St: TD Moore 46 run (Rauch kick) 4:15.

SECOND QUARTER

Appalachian St: TD Kilgore recovered fumble (Rauch kick) 10:22.
Delaware: TD Duncan 39 pass from Flacco (Striefsky kick), 1:10.
Appalachian St:TD Jackson 60 pass from Edwards (Rauch kick) 0:44.

THIRD QUARTER

Appalachian St: TD Richardson 8 pass from Edwards (Rauch kick) 4:56.
Delaware: TD Cuff 1 run (Striefsky kick) 10:54.

FOURTH QUARTER

Appalachian St: TD Richardson 6 run (Rauch kick) 6:02.
Appalachian St: TD Elder 53 run (Rauch kick), 3:29.
Delaware: TD Duncan 75 kickoff return (Striefsky kick), 3:18.

	DELAWARE	APPALACHIAN ST
First downs	24	26
Rushes–yards	31-98	51-358
Passing yards	334	198
Comp/Att/Int	23-48-0	9-15-0
Punts	4-32.8	4-38.3
Fumbles-lost	0-0	0-0
Penalties-yards	9-94	9-87
Time of possession	27:53	32:07

12-14-07, Chattanooga, Tennessee; Att: 23,010.

Small College Championship Summaries

NCAA DIVISION II

First round: Central Washington 40, Ashland 24; North Dakota 44, Winona St 2; Abilene Christian 56, Mesa St 12; West Texas A&M 40, Washburn 39; Catawba 66, Albany St 35; Delta St 45, Shaw 7; So. Conn St 45, Bryant 28; Indiana 45, West Chester 35.
Second Round: Central Washington 20, Neb.-Omaha 17; Grand Valley St 21, North Dakota 14; Chadron St 76, Abilene Christian 73; NW Mo. St 56, West Texas 28; Valdosta St 55, Catawba 29; North Alabama 20, Delta St 17; California (Pa.) 43, So. Conn. St 7; Shepherd 41, Indiana 34.
Quarterfinals: Grand Valley St 41, Central Washington 21; NW Mo. St 26, Chadron St 13; Valdosta St 37, North Alabama 23; California (Pa.) 58, Shepherd 38.
Semifinals: NW Mo. St 34, Grand Valley St 16; Valdosta St 28, California (Pa.) 24.

NCAA DIVISION II

Championship: 12-15-07, Florence, Alabama

NW Missouri St	0	14	0	6—20
Valdosta St	3	0	7	15—25

NCAA DIVISION III

First round: Mount Union 42, Ithaca 18; TCNJ 17, Rensselaer 14; Curry 42, Hartwick 21; St. John Fisher 24, Hobart 7; Central College 38, Olivet 17; St. John's 41, Redlands 13; UW-Eau Claire 24, St. Norbert 20; Bethel 28, Concordia 0; N.C. Wesleyan 35, Wash & Jeff 34; Mary Hardin-Baylor 52, Trinity 23; Muhlenberg 31, Salisbury 21; Wesley 45, Hampden-Sydney 17; UW-Whitewater 34, Capital 14; North Central 44, Franklin 42; Wabash 31, Mt. St. Joseph 21; Case Reserve 21, Widener 20.

Bowls and Playoffs (*Cont.*)

NCAA DIVISION III (*CONT.*)

Second Round: Mount Union 59, TCNJ 7; St. John Fisher 38, Curry 7; Central 37, St. Johns 7; Bethel 21, UW-Eau Claire 12; Mary Hardin-Baylor 64, N.C. Wesleyan 0; Wesley 38, Muhlenberg 21; UW-Whitewater 59, No. Central 28; Wabash 38, Case Reserve 23.
Quarterfinals: Mount Union 52, St. John Fisher 10; Bethel 27, Central 13; Mary Hardin-Baylor 27, Wesley 10; UW-Whitewater 47, Wabash 7.
Semifinals: Mt. Union 62, Bethel 14; UW-Whitewater 16, Mary Hardin-Baylor 7.

NCAA DIVISION III

Championship: 12-15-07, Salem, Virginia

Mount Union	0	0	14	7—21
UW-Whitewater	7	3	7	14—31

NAIA CHAMPIONSHIP

12-15-07, Hardin County, Tennessee

Sioux Falls (S.D.)	0	0	6	3—9
Carroll (Mont.)	3	0	14	0—17

Awards

Heisman Memorial Trophy

Player, School	Class	Pos	1st	2nd	3rd	Total
Tim Tebow, Florida	So.	QB	462	229	113	1957
Darren McFadden, Arkansas	Jr.	RB	291	355	120	1703
Colt Brennan, Hawaii	Sr.	QB	54	114	242	632
Chase Daniel, Missouri	Jr.	QB	25	84	182	425
Dennis Dixon, Oregon	Sr.	QB	17	31	65	178

Note: Former Heisman winners and the media vote, with ballots allowing for three names (3 points for 1st, 2 for 2nd, 1 for 3rd).

Other Awards

Maxwell Award (Player) .... Tim Tebow, Florida, QB
Sporting News Player of the Year .... Tim Tebow, Florida, QB
Walter Camp Player of the Year .... Darren McFadden, Arkansas, RB
Chuck Bednarik Award (Defense) .... Dan Connor, Penn St, LB
Vince Lombardi/Rotary Award (Lineman/LB) .... Glenn Dorsey, LSU, DT
Outland Trophy (Interior Lineman) .... Glenn Dorsey, LSU, DT
Davey O'Brien Award (QB) .... Tim Tebow, Florida, QB
Unitas Golden Arm Award (Senior QB) .... Matt Ryan, Boston College, QB
Doak Walker Award (RB) .... Darren McFadden, Arkansas, RB
Biletnikoff Award (WR) .... Michael Crabtree, Texas Tech, WR
Butkus Award (Linebacker) .... James Laurinaitis, Ohio St, LB
Jim Thorpe Award (Defensive Back) .... Antoine Cason, Arizona, CB
Associated Press Player of the Year .... Troy Smith, Ohio St, QB
Walter Payton Award (FCS Player) .... Jayson Foster, Georgia Southern, QB
Harlon Hill Trophy (Div II Player) .... Danny Woodhead, Chadron St, RB
Gagliardi Trophy (Div III Player) .... Justin Beaver, UW-Whitewater, RB

Coaches' Awards

Walter Camp Award .... Mark Mangino ,Kansas
Eddie Robinson Award (FCS) .... Mark Farley, Northern Iowa
Bobby Dodd Award .... Lloyd Carr, Michigan
Bear Bryant Award .... Mark Mangino, Kansas

AFCA COACHES OF THE YEAR

FBS (Division I-A) .... Mark Mangino, Kansas
FCS (Division I-AA) .... Jerry Moore, UAB
Division II .... David Dean, Valdosta
Division III .... Lance Leipold, UW-Whitewater

Football Writers Association of America All-America Team

OFFENSE

QB .... Tim Tebow, Florida, So.
RB .... Darren McFadden, Arkansas, Jr.
RB .... Kevin Smith, Central Florida, Jr.
WR .... Michael Crabtree, Texas Tech, Fr..
WR .... Jordy Nelson, Kansas St, Sr.
TE .... Martin Rucker, Missouri, Sr.
OL .... Anthony Collins, Kansas, Jr.
OL .... Jake Long, Michigan, Sr.
OL .... Hercules Satele, Hawaii, Sr..
OL .... Ryan Stanchek, West Virginia, Jr.
C .... Jonathan Luigs, Arkansas, Jr.
K .... Daniel Lincoln, Tennessee, Fr.
RS .... Jeremy Maclin, Missouri, Fr.

DEFENSE

DL .... Glenn Dorsey, LSU, Sr.
DL .... Sedrick Ellis, USC, Sr.
DL .... Chris Long, Virginia, Sr.
DL .... George Selvie, South Florida, So.
LB .... James Laurinaitis, Ohio St, Jr.
LB .... J Leman, Illinois, Sr.
LB .... Curtis Lofton, Oklahoma, Jr.
DB .... Mike Mickens, Cincinnati, Jr.
DB .... Jamie Silva, Boston College, Sr.
DB .... Craig Stelz, LSU, Sr.
DB .... Aqib Talib, Kansas, Jr.
P .... Louis Sakoda, Utah, Jr.

2007 NCAA Conference Standings

Football Bowl Subdivision (I-A)

ATLANTIC COAST CONFERENCE

ATLANTIC	Conference W	Conference L	Full Season W	Full Season L	Pct
Boston College	6	2	11	3	.786
Wake Forest	5	3	9	4	.692
Clemson	5	3	9	4	.692
Florida St	4	4	7	6	.538
Maryland	3	5	6	7	.462
North Carolina St	3	5	5	7	.417
COASTAL					
Virginia Tech	7	1	11	3	.786
Virginia	6	2	9	4	.692
Georgia Tech	4	4	7	6	.538
North Carolina	3	5	4	8	.333
Miami (Fla.)	2	6	5	7	.417
Duke	0	8	1	11	.083

BIG EAST CONFERENCE

	Conference W	Conference L	Full Season W	Full Season L	Pct
West Virginia	5	2	11	2	.846
Connecticut	5	2	9	4	.692
Cincinnati	4	3	10	3	.769
South Florida	4	3	9	4	.692
Rutgers	3	4	8	5	.615
Louisville	3	4	6	6	.500
Pittsburgh	3	4	5	7	.417
Syracuse	1	6	2	10	.167

BIG TEN CONFERENCE

	Conference W	Conference L	Full Season W	Full Season L	Pct
Ohio St	7	1	11	2	.846
Illinois	6	2	9	4	.692
Michigan	6	2	9	4	.692
Wisconsin	5	3	9	4	.692
Penn St	4	4	9	4	.692
Iowa	4	4	6	6	.500
Purdue	3	5	8	5	.615
Indiana	3	5	7	6	.538
Michigan St	3	5	7	6	.538
Northwestern	3	5	6	6	.500
Minnesota	0	8	1	11	.083

BIG 12 CONFERENCE

NORTH	Conference W	Conference L	Full Season W	Full Season L	Pct
Kansas	7	1	12	1	.923
Missouri	7	1	12	2	.857
Colorado	4	4	6	7	.462
Kansas St	3	5	5	7	.417
Nebraska	2	6	5	7	.417
Iowa St	2	6	3	9	.250
SOUTH					
Oklahoma	6	2	11	3	.786
Texas	5	3	10	3	.769
Texas Tech	4	4	9	4	.692
Oklahoma St	4	4	7	6	.538
Texas A&M	4	4	7	6	.538
Baylor	0	8	3	9	.250

Football Bowl Subdivision (I-A) *(Cont.)*

CONFERENCE USA

EAST	Conference W	Conference L	Full Season W	Full Season L	Pct
Central Florida	7	1	10	4	.714
East Carolina	6	2	8	5	.615
Memphis	6	2	7	6	.538
Southern Miss	5	3	7	6	.538
Marshall	3	5	3	9	.250
UAB	1	7	2	10	.167
WEST					
Tulsa	6	2	10	4	.714
Houston	6	2	8	5	.615
Tulane	3	5	4	8	.333
Rice	3	5	3	9	.250
UTEP	2	6	4	8	.333
SMU	0	8	1	11	.083

MID-AMERICAN ATHLETIC CONFERENCE

EAST	Conference W	Conference L	Full Season W	Full Season L	Pct
Bowling Green	6	2	8	5	.615
Miami (Ohio)	5	2	6	7	.462
Buffalo	5	3	5	7	.417
Ohio	4	4	6	6	.500
Temple	4	4	4	8	.333
Akron	3	5	4	8	.333
Kent St	1	7	3	9	.250
WEST					
Central Michigan	6	1	8	6	.571
Ball St	5	2	7	6	.538
Western Michigan	3	4	5	7	.417
Eastern Michigan	3	4	4	8	.333
Toledo	3	5	5	7	.417
Northern Illinois	1	6	2	10	.167

MOUNTAIN WEST CONFERENCE

	Conference W	Conference L	Full Season W	Full Season L	Pct
BYU	8	0	11	2	.846
Air Force	6	2	9	4	.692
Utah	5	3	9	4	.692
New Mexico	5	3	9	4	.692
TCU	4	4	8	5	.615
San Diego St	3	5	4	8	.333
Wyoming	2	6	5	7	.417
Colorado St	2	6	3	9	.250
UNLV	1	7	2	10	.167

PACIFIC 10 CONFERENCE

	Conference W	Conference L	Full Season W	Full Season L	Pct
USC	7	2	11	2	.846
Arizona St	7	2	10	3	.769
Oregon St	6	3	9	4	.692
Oregon	5	4	9	4	.692
UCLA	5	4	6	7	.462
Arizona	4	5	5	7	.417
California	3	6	7	6	.538
Washington St	3	6	5	7	.417
Stanford	3	6	4	8	.333
Washington	2	7	4	9	.308

Football Bowl Subdivision (I-A) *(Cont.)*

SOUTHEASTERN CONFERENCE

EAST	Conference W	Conference L	Full Season W	Full Season L	Pct
Georgia	6	2	11	2	.846
Tennessee	6	2	10	4	.714
Florida	5	3	9	4	.692
Kentucky	3	5	8	5	.615
South Carolina	3	5	6	6	.500
Vanderbilt	2	6	5	7	.417
WEST					
LSU	6	2	12	2	.857
Auburn	5	3	9	4	.692
Arkansas	4	4	8	5	.615
Mississippi St	4	4	8	5	.615
Alabama	4	4	7	6	.538
Mississippi	0	8	3	9	.250

SUN BELT CONFERENCE

	Conference W	Conference L	Full Season W	Full Season L	Pct
Troy	6	1	8	4	.667
Florida Atlantic	6	1	8	5	.615
La.-Monroe	4	3	6	6	.500
Middle Tennessee St	4	3	5	7	.417
Arkansas St	3	4	5	7	.417
La.-Lafayette	3	4	3	9	.250
North Texas	1	6	2	10	.167
Florida International	1	6	1	11	.083

WESTERN ATHLETIC CONFERENCE

	Conference W	Conference L	Full Season W	Full Season L	Pct
Hawaii	8	0	12	1	.923
Boise St	7	1	10	3	.769
Fresno St	6	2	9	4	.692
Nevada	4	4	6	7	.462
Louisiana Tech	4	4	5	7	.417
San Jose St	4	4	5	7	.417
Utah St	2	6	2	10	.167
New Mexico St	1	7	4	9	.308
Idaho	0	8	1	11	.083

INDEPENDENTS

	Full Season W	Full Season L	Pct
Navy	8	5	.615
Western Kentucky	7	5	.583
Army	3	9	.250
Notre Dame	3	9	.250

Football Championship Subdivision (I-AA)

BIG SKY CONFERENCE

	Conference W	Conference L	Full Season W	Full Season L	Pct
Montana	8	0	11	1	.917
Eastern Washington	6	2	9	4	.692
Northern Arizona	5	3	6	5	.545
Montana St	4	4	6	5	.545
Weber St	4	4	5	6	.455
Sacramento St	3	5	3	8	.273
Portland St	3	5	3	8	.273
Idaho St	2	6	3	8	.273
Northern Colorado	1	7	1	11	.083

BIG SOUTH CONFERENCE

	Conference W	Conference L	Full Season W	Full Season L	Pct
Liberty	4	0	8	3	.727
Coastal Carolina	3	1	5	6	.455
Gardner-Webb	2	2	5	6	.455
Charleston Southern	1	3	5	6	.455
Va. Military Inst	0	4	2	9	.182

COLONIAL CONFERENCE

NORTH	Conference W	Conference L	Full Season W	Full Season L	Pct
Massachusetts	7	1	10	3	.769
Hofstra	4	4	7	4	.636
New Hampshire	4	4	7	5	.583
Maine	3	5	4	7	.364
Northeastern	2	6	3	8	.273
Rhode Island	2	6	3	8	.273
SOUTH					
Richmond	7	1	11	3	.786
James Madison	6	2	8	4	.667
Delaware	5	3	11	4	.733
Villanova	5	3	7	4	.636
William & Mary	2	6	4	7	.364
Towson	1	7	3	8	.273

MISSOURI VALLEY CONFERENCE

	Conference W	Conference L	Full Season W	Full Season L	Pct
Northern Iowa	6	0	12	1	.923
Southern Illinois	5	1	12	2	.857
Youngstown St	3	3	7	4	.636
Western Illinois	3	3	6	5	.545
Missouri St	2	4	6	5	.545
Illinois St	2	4	4	7	.364
Indiana St	0	6	0	11	.000

IVY LEAGUE

	Conference W	Conference L	Full Season W	Full Season L	Pct
Harvard	7	0	8	2	.800
Yale	6	1	9	1	.900
Brown	4	3	5	5	.500
Pennsylvania	3	4	4	6	.400
Princeton	3	4	4	6	.400
Dartmouth	3	4	3	7	.300
Cornell	2	5	5	5	.500
Columbia	0	7	1	9	.100

2007 NCAA Conference Standings *(Cont.)*

Football Championship Subdivision *(Cont.)*

METRO ATLANTIC ATHLETIC CONFERENCE

	Conference		Full Season		
	W	L	W	L	Pct
Iona	2	1	7	4	.636
Duquesne	2	1	6	4	.600
Marist	2	1	3	8	.273
LaSalle	0	3	0	10	.000

MID-EASTERN ATHLETIC CONFERENCE

	Conference		Full Season		
	W	L	W	L	Pct
Delaware St	9	0	10	2	.833
Norfolk St	7	2	8	3	.727
South Carolina St	7	2	7	4	.636
Winston-Salem	5	4	6	5	.545
Hampton	5	4	6	5	.545
Morgan St	4	5	5	6	.455
Bethune-Cookman	3	6	5	6	.455
Howard	3	6	4	7	.364
Florida A&M	2	7	3	8	.273
North Carolina A&T	0	9	0	11	.000

NORTHEAST CONFERENCE

	Conference		Full Season		
	W	L	W	L	Pct
Albany	6	0	8	4	.667
Central Connecticut St	4	2	6	5	.545
Wagner	3	3	7	4	.636
Monmouth (N.J.)	3	3	4	6	.400
Robert Morris	3	3	4	6	.400
St. Francis (Pa.)	2	4	3	7	.300
Sacred Heart	0	6	3	8	.273

OHIO VALLEY CONFERENCE

	Conference		Full Season		
	W	L	W	L	Pct
Eastern Kentucky	8	0	9	3	.750
Eastern Illinois	7	1	8	4	.667
Austin Peay	5	3	7	4	.636
Jacksonville St	5	3	6	5	.545
Tennessee St	4	3	5	6	.455
Tenn.-Martin	4	4	4	7	.364
Tennessee Tech	2	6	4	7	.364
Samford	2	6	4	7	.364
SE Missouri St	1	6	3	8	.273
Murray St	1	7	2	9	.182

PATRIOT LEAGUE

	Conference		Full Season		
	W	L	W	L	Pct
Fordham	5	1	8	4	.667
Holy Cross	4	2	7	4	.636
Lafayette	4	2	7	4	.636
Colgate	4	2	7	4	.636
Lehigh	2	4	5	6	.455
Bucknell	1	5	3	8	.273
Georgetown	1	5	1	10	.091

Football Championship Subdivision *(Cont.)*

PIONEER LEAGUE

	Conference		Full Season		
	W	L	W	L	Pct
Dayton	6	1	11	1	.917
San Diego	6	1	9	2	.818
Morehead St	5	2	7	4	.636
Davidson	4	3	6	4	.600
Drake	3	4	6	5	.545
Valparaiso	2	5	5	6	.455
Jacksonville	2	5	3	8	.273
Butler	0	7	4	7	.364

SOUTHERN CONFERENCE

	Conference		Full Season		
	W	L	W	L	Pct
Appalachian St	5	2	13	2	.867
Wofford	5	2	9	4	.692
Georgia Southern	4	3	7	4	.636
Elon	4	3	7	4	.636
Citadel	4	3	7	4	.636
Furman	4	3	6	5	.545
Chattanooga	2	5	2	9	.182
Western Carolina	0	7	1	10	.091

SOUTHLAND CONFERENCE

	Conference		Full Season		
	W	L	W	L	Pct
McNeese St	7	0	11	1	.917
Sam Houston St	5	2	7	4	.636
Central Arkansas	5	2	6	5	.545
Nicholls St	3	4	6	5	.545
Texas St	3	4	4	7	.364
Northwestern St	3	4	4	7	.364
SE Louisiana	2	5	3	8	.273
Stephen F. Austin	0	7	0	11	.000

SOUTHWESTERN ATHLETIC CONFERENCE

	Conference		Full Season		
EAST	W	L	W	L	Pct
Jackson St	7	2	8	4	.667
Alabama A&M	6	3	8	3	.727
Alabama St	4	5	5	6	.455
Mississippi Valley St	2	7	3	8	.273
Alcorn St	2	7	2	8	.200
WEST					
Grambling St	8	1	8	4	.667
Southern Univ.	6	3	8	3	.727
Prairie View A&M	6	3	7	3	.700
Ark.-Pine Bluff	4	5	4	7	.364
Texas Southern	0	9	0	11	.000

INDEPENDENTS

	Full Season		
	W	L	Pct
North Carolina Central	6	4	.600
Presbyterian	6	5	.545
Stony Brook	6	5	.545
Savannah St	1	9	.100

2007 NCAA Individual Leaders

Football Bowl Subdivision (Division I-A)

SCORING

	Class	GP	TD	XP	FG	Pts	Pts/Game
Kevin Smith, Central Florida	Jr.	14	30	0	0	180	12.86
Ray Rice, Rutgers	Jr.	13	25	0	0	150	11.54
Colt David, LSU	Jr.	14	1	63	26	147	10.50
Chris Johnson, East Carolina	Sr.	13	24	0	0	144	11.08
Matt Forte, Tulane	Sr.	12	23	0	0	140	11.67
Tim Tebow, Florida	So.	13	23	0	0	138	10.62
Michael Crabtree, Texas Tech	Fr.	13	22	0	0	132	10.15
Jeff Wolfert, Missouri	Jr.	14	0	67	21	130	9.29
Jehuu Caulcrick, Michigan St	Sr.	13	21	0	0	126	9.69
Kalvin McRae, Ohio	Sr.	12	20	0	0	120	10.00
Scott Webb, Kansas	Sr.	13	0	66	18	120	9.23
Jeremy Ito, Rutgers	Sr.	13	0	51	23	120	9.23

FIELD GOALS

	Class	GP	FGA	FG	Pct	FG/Game
John Sullivan, New Mexico	Sr.	12	35	29	.829	2.42
Gary Cismesia, Florida St	Sr.	13	34	27	.794	2.08
Colt David, LSU	Jr.	14	33	26	.788	1.86
Kai Forbath, UCLA	Fr.	13	30	25	.833	1.92
Leigh Tiffin, Alabama	So.	13	34	25	.735	1.92

TOTAL OFFENSE

			Rushing		Passing		Total Offense		
	Class	GP	Car	Net	Att	Yds	Yds	Yds/Play	Yds/Game
Graham Harrell, Texas Tech	Jr..	13	38	-91	713	5705	5614	7.48	431.8
Paul Smith, Tulsa	Sr.	14	105	119	544	5065	5184	7.99	370.3
Colt Brennan, Hawaii	Sr.	12	82	27	510	4343	4370	7.38	364.2
Dan LeFevour, Central Michigan	So.	14	188	1122	543	3652	4774	6.53	341.0
Brian Brohm, Louisville	Sr.	12	57	-46	473	4024	3978	7.51	331.5
Chase Clement, Rice	Jr.	12	144	535	508	3377	3912	6.00	326.0
Chase Daniel, Missouri	Jr.	14	109	253	563	4306	4559	6.78	325.6
Chase Holbrook, New Mexico St	Jr.	12	55	5	543	3866	3871	6.47	322.6
Matt Ryan, Boston College	Sr.	14	68	2	654	4507	4509	6.25	322.1
Tim Tebow, Florida	So.	13	210	895	350	3286	4181	7.47	321.6

RUSHING

	Class	GP	Car	Yds	TD	Avg	Yds/Game
Kevin Smith, Central Florida	Jr.	14	450	2567	29	5.70	183.36
Matt Forte, Tulane	Sr.	12	361	2127	23	5.89	177.25
Ray Rice, Rutgers	Jr.	13	380	2012	24	5.29	154.77
Darren McFadden, Arkansas	Jr.	13	325	1830	16	5.63	140.77
Jonathan Stewart, Oregon	Jr.	13	280	1722	11	6.15	132.46
Rashard Mendenhall, Illinois	Jr.	13	262	1681	17	6.42	129.31
Eugene Jarvis, Kent St	So.	12	279	1669	10	5.98	139.08
Jamaal Charles, Texas	Jr.	13	258	1619	18	6.28	124.54
Chris Wells, Ohio St	So.	13	274	1609	15	5.87	123.77
Anthony Aldridge, Houston	Sr.	13	259	1597	14	6.17	122.85

PASSING EFFICIENCY

	Class	GP	Att	Comp	Pct Comp	Yds	Yds/Att	TD	Int	Rating Pts
Sam Bradford, Oklahoma	Fr.	14	341	237	69.5	3121	9.2	36	8	176.5
Tim Tebow, Florida	So.	13	350	234	66.9	3286	9.4	32	6	172.5
Dennis Dixon, Oregon	Sr.	10	254	172	67.7	2136	8.4	20	4	161.2
Paul Smith, Tulsa	Sr.	14	544	327	60.1	5065	9.3	47	19	159.8
Colt Brennan, Hawaii	Sr.	12	510	359	70.4	4343	8.5	38	17	159.8
Graham Harrell, Texas Tech	Jr.	13	713	512	71.8	5705	8.0	48	14	157.3
Taylor Tharp, Boise St	Sr.	13	423	289	68.3	3340	7.9	30	11	152.9
Brian Brohm, Louisville	Sr.	12	473	308	65.1	4024	8.5	30	12	152.4
Patrick White, West Virginia	Jr.	13	216	144	66.7	1724	8.0	14	4	151.4
Colin Kaepernick, Nevada	Fr.	11	247	133	53.9	2175	8.8	19	3	150.8

Note: Minimum 15 attempts per game.

Football Bowl Subdivision (Division I-A) *(Cont.)*

RECEPTIONS PER GAME

	Class	GP	No.	Yds	TD	R/Game
Michael Crabtree, Texas Tech	Fr.	13	134	1962	22	10.3
Jordy Nelson, Kansas St.	Sr.	12	122	1606	11	10.2
Casey Fitzgerald, North Texas	Jr.	12	111	1322	12	9.3
Danny Amendola, Texas Tech	Sr.	13	109	1245	6	8.4
Davone Bess, Hawaii	Jr.	13	108	1266	12	8.3

RECEIVING YARDS PER GAME

	Class	GP	No.	Yds	TD	Yds/Game
Michael Crabtree, Texas Tech	Fr..	13	134	1962	22	150.9
Jordy Nelson, Kansas St	Sr.	12	122	1606	11	133.8
Harry Douglas, Louisville	Sr.	10	71	1159	7	115.9
Donnie Avery, Houston	Sr.	13	91	1456	7	112.0
Casey Fitzgerald, North Texas	Jr.	12	111	1322	12	110.2

ALL-PURPOSE RUNNERS

	Class	GP	Rush	Rec	PR	KOR	Yds	Yds/Game
Chris Johnson, East Carolina	Sr.	13	1423	528	0	1009	2960	227.69
Dante Love, Ball St.	Jr.	13	192	1398	0	1100	2690	206.92
Chad Hall, Air Force	Sr.	13	1478	524	176	505	2683	206.38
Matt Forte, Tulane	Sr.	12	2127	282	0	11	2420	201.67
Kevin Smith, Central Florida	Jr.	14	2567	242	0	0	2809	200.64

INTERCEPTIONS

	Class	GP	No.	Int/Game
Elbert Mack, Troy	Sr.	12	8	.67
DeAngelo Smith, Cincinnati	Jr.	13	8	.62
Alphonso Smith, Wake Forest	Jr.	13	8	.62
Robert Vaughn, Connecticut	So.	12	7	.58
P.J. Mahone, Bowling Green	So.	12	7	.58
Reggie Corner, Akron	Sr.	12	7	.58

PUNTING

	Class	No.	Avg
Kevin Huber, Cincinnati	Jr.	57	46.88
Brett Kern, Toledo	Sr.	52	46.13
Chris Miller, Ball St.	Jr.	61	45.44
Ryan Weigand, Virginia	Sr.	52	45.23
Durant Brooks, Georgia Tech	Sr.	65	45.06

Note: Minimum of 3.6 per game.

PUNT RETURNS

	Class	No.	Yds	TD	Avg
Kevin Robinson, Utah St	Sr.	20	378	1	18.90
Brandon James, Florida	So.	14	254	1	18.14
Deon Murphy, Kansas St	Jr.	26	454	1	17.46
Leodis McKelvin, Troy	Sr.	25	436	3	17.44
Philip Beck, Louisiana Tech	Jr.	18	313	0	17.39

Note: Minimum 1.2 per game.

KICKOFF RETURNS

	Class	No.	Yds	TD	Avg
A.J. Jefferson, Fresno St	So.	26	930	2	35.77
Bryan Williams, Akron	Jr.	21	670	1	31.90
Kevin Marion, Wake Forest	Sr.	28	876	1	31.29
Felix Jones, Arkansas	Jr.	22	652	2	29.64
Ryan Mouton, Hawaii	Jr.	14	414	1	29.57

Note: Minimum of 1.2 per game.

Football Bowl Subdivision (Div. I-A) Team Single-Game Highs

RUSHING AND PASSING

Rushing and passing yards: 643—Graham Harrell, Texas Tech, QB, Sep 22, 2007 (vs Oklahoma St)
Rushing and passing plays: 90—Colt Brennan, Hawaii, QB, Oct. 12, 2007 (vs San Jose St)
Rushing plays: 46—Kevin Smith, Central Florida, RB, Nov. 24, 2007 (vs UTEP)
Net rushing yards: 342—Matt Forte, Tulane, RB, Oct 20, 2007 (vs SMU)
Passes attempted: 75—Colt Brennan, Hawaii, QB, Oct 12, 2007 (vs San Jose St)
Passes completed: 48—Graham Harrell, Texas Tech, QB, Sept 8, 2007 (vs UTEP)
Passing yards: 646—Graham Harrell, Texas Tech, QB, Sept 22, 2007 (vs Oklahoma St)

RECEIVING AND RETURNS

Passes caught: 18—Casey Fitzgerald, North Texas, WR, Sep 8, 2007 (vs SMU)
Receiving yards: 346—Donnie Avery, Houston, WR, Oct 13, 2007 (vs Rice)
Punt return Yards: 146—Shiloh Keo, Idaho, Sept 22, 2007 (vs Northern Ill.)
Kickoff return yards: 266—Dante Love, Ball St, Oct 6, 2007 (vs Central Michigan)

2007 NCAA Individual Leaders *(Cont.)*

Football Championship Subdivision (Division I-AA)

SCORING

	Class	GP	TD	XP	FG	Pts	Pts/Game
Omar Cuff, Delaware	Sr.	15	39	0	0	234	15.60
Jayson Foster, Georgia Southern	Sr.	11	24	0	0	148	13.45
Mike McLeod, Yale	Jr.	10	23	0	0	138	13.80
Jon Striefsky, Delaware	So.	15	0	64	21	127	8.47
Julian Rauch, Appalachian St	Sr.	15	0	76	17	127	8.47

FIELD GOALS

	Class	GP	FGA	FG	Pct	FG/Game
Gavin Hallford, Jacksonville St	Jr.	11	29	22	.759	2.00
Jon Striefsky, Delaware	So.	15	24	21	.875	1.40
Taylor Rowan, Western Illinois	Jr.	11	31	19	.613	1.73
Dan Carpenter, Montana	Sr.	12	23	19	.826	1.58
Peter Gaertner, Delaware St	Sr.	12	25	19	.760	1.58

TOTAL OFFENSE

			Rushing		Passing		Total Offense		
	Class	GP	Car	Net	Att	Yds	Yds	Yds/Play	Yds/Game
Josh Johnson, San Diego	Sr.	10	101	726	301	2988	3714	9.2	371.4
Dominic Randolph, Holy Cross	Jr.	11	51	137	482	3604	3741	7.0	340.1
Scott Riddle, Elon	Fr.	11	114	-79	508	3817	3738	6.0	339.8
Kevin Hoyng, Dayton.	Sr.	12	163	640	384	3317	3957	7.2	329.8
Matt Nichols, Eastern Washington	So.	13	129	392	440	3744	4136	7.2	318.2

RUSHING

	Class	GP	Car	Yds	Avg	TD	Yds/Game
Omar Cuff, Delaware	Sr.	15	398	1945	4.9	35	129.7
Tim Hightower, Richmond	Sr.	14	327	1924	5.9	20	137.4
Jordan Scott, Colgate	Jr.	11	409	1875	4.6	20	170.5
Jayson Foster, Georgia Southern.	Sr.	11	261	1844	7.1	24	167.6
Jason Butler, Wagner	Sr.	11	316	1713	5.4	12	155.7

PASSING EFFICIENCY

	Class	GP	Att	Comp	Pct Comp	Yds	Yds/Att	TD	Int	Rating Pts
Josh Johnson, San Diego	Sr.	10	301	206	68.4	2988	9.9	43	1	198.3
Jonathan Dally, Cal Poly	Jr.	11	192	104	54.2	2238	11.7	29	5	196.7
Nick Hill, Southern Illinois	Sr.	14	361	258	71.5	3175	8.8	28	7	167.1
Eric Sanders, Northern Iowa	Sr.	13	315	237	75.2	2842	9.0	17	6	165.0
Ricky Santos, New Hampshire.	Sr.	11	350	256	73.1	2972	8.5	24	7	163.1

Note: Minimum 15 attempts per game.

RECEPTIONS PER GAME

	Class	GP	No.	Yds	TD	R/G
Terrell Hudgins, Elon	So.	11	117	1474	18	10.6
Tremayne Kirkland, Portland St	Sr.	10	84	1059	10	8.4
Michael Mayers, Elon	Sr.	11	90	1064	3	8.2
Ryan Hubbard, Davidson	Sr.	8	64	886	6	8.0
Charles Sullivan, Hofstra	Sr.	11	86	991	7	7.8

RECEIVING YARDS PER GAME

	Class	GP	No.	Yds	TD	Yds/G
Terrell Hudgins, Elon	So.	11	117	1474	18	134.0
Ramses Barden, Cal Poly	Jr.	11	57	1467	18	133.4
Ryan Hubbard, Davidson	Sr.	8	64	886	6	110.8
Eddie Cohen, Western Carolina	Sr.	11	67	1208	9	109.8
Tremayne Kirkland, Portland St	Sr.	10	84	1059	10	105.9

INTERCEPTIONS

	Class	GP	No.	Yds	TD	Int/G
Derrick Huff, E. Kentucky	Sr.	11	9	120	1	.82
Al Donaldson, Alabama	Jr.	11	9	91	0	.82
David Hyland, Morehead St	Jr.	9	8	57	1	.89
Steven Williams, Harvard	Sr.	10	8	113	1	.80
Al Phillips, Wagner	Sr.	11	7	106	0	.64

PUNTING

	Class	No.	Avg
Chris MacDonald, Texas St	Sr.	49	45.9
Tyson Johnson, Montana	Sr.	54	44.7
Benjamin Dato, Fordham.	Sr.	67	44.7
Kevin Cook, Eastern Illinois	Fr.	36	44.6
Robbie Dehaze, Northern Arizona	Jr.	55	43.3

2007 NCAA Individual Leaders *(Cont.)*

Football Championship Subdivision (Division I-AA) (Cont)

ALL-PURPOSE RUNNERS

	Class	GP	Rush	Rec	PR	KOR	Yds	Yds/Game
Bryant Eteuati, Weber St.	Jr.	11	19	720	345	1199	2283	207.6
J.T. Rogan, San Diego	Jr.	11	1021	331	0	897	2249	204.5
Jason Butler, Wagner	Sr.	11	1713	175	12	271	2171	197.4
Mike Malone, Western Carolina	Sr.	11	563	197	0	1383	2143	194.8
Jayson Foster, Georgia Southern	Sr.	11	1844	65	133	38	2080	189.1

Division II

SCORING

	Class	GP	TD	XP	FG	Pts	Pts/Game
Bernard Scott, Abilene Christian	Jr.	13	39	0	0	234	18.0
Xavier Omon, NW Missouri St.	Sr.	14	38	0	0	228	16.3
Joique Bell, Wayne St (Mich.)	So.	11	28	0	0	168	15.3
Dervon Wallace, Shepherd	Sr.	12	26	0	0	158	13.2
Jerom Freeman, Southern Conn. St	So.	13	24	0	0	144	11.1

FIELD GOALS

	Class	GP	FGA	FG	Pct	FG/Game
Jared Keating, Mesa St.	Jr.	12	33	22	.666	1.8
Tyler Lorenz, California (Pa.)	So.	14	27	21	.777	1.5
Jared Guberman, Western Georgia	Jr.	11	17	15	.882	1.4
Ryne Powell, Shaw	Jr.	11	27	15	.555	1.4
Brandon Hellevang, North Dakota	So.	12	25	15	.600	1.3

TOTAL OFFENSE

	Class	GP	Yds	Yds/Game
Keith Null, West Texas A&M	Jr.	11	4067	369.7
Ben King, Minn. St-Mankato	Sr.	11	4060	369.1
David Knighton, Harding	Jr.	10	3310	331.0
Daniel Polk, Midwestern St.	Sr.	11	3549	322.6
Mark Nicolet, Hillsdale	Sr.	11	3541	321.9

RUSHING

	Class	GP	Car	Yds	TD	Yds/Game
Xavier Omon, NW Missouri St.	Sr.	14	370	2337	37	166.9
Bernard Scott, Abilene Christian	Jr.	13	251	2165	35	166.5
Dervon Wallace, Shepherd	Sr.	12	342	2138	24	178.2
Amos Allen, South Dakota	Sr.	11	265	1961	15	178.3
Jerom Freeman, Southern Conn. St	So.	13	280	1906	15	146.6

PASSING EFFICIENCY

	Class	GP	Att	Comp	Pct Comp	Yds	TD	Int	Rating Pts
Jacary Atkinson, Tuskegee	Jr.	12	266	158	.594	2777	31	9	178.8
Brad Iciek, Grand Valley St	So.	13	303	185	.610	2850	30	7	168.1
Danny Freund, North Dakota	Jr.	12	308	209	.679	2860	24	6	167.7
Billy Cundiff, Ashland	So.	9	222	136	.613	2278	16	4	167.6
Billy Malone, Abilene Christian	Jr.	13	411	264	.642	3914	37	14	167.1

Note: Minimum 15 attempts per game.

RECEPTIONS PER GAME

	Class	GP	No.	Yds	TD	R/G
Nick Smart, Southwest Baptist	Sr.	11	143	1263	9	13.0
Jabari Taylor, Minn St.-Moorehead	So.	11	90	1147	13	8.2
Rod Windsor, Western New Mexico.	Sr.	10	81	1119	6	8.1
Almonzo Banks, West Liberty St.	Sr.	11	88	1331	18	8.0
Ashton Gronewold, Missouri S&T	Sr.	11	87	1009	13	7.9

RECEIVING YARDS PER GAME

	Class	GP	No.	Yds	TD	Yds/G
Almonzo Banks, West Liberty St.	Sr.	11	88	1331	18	121.0
Elfren Quiles, Kutztown	Sr.	10	64	1187	8	118.7
Nick Smart, Southwest Baptist	Sr.	11	143	1263	9	114.8
Rod Windsor, Western New Mexico	Sr.	10	81	1119	6	111.9
Scott Peters, Winona St.	Sr.	12	73	1299	13	108.3

2007 NCAA Individual Leaders (*Cont.*)

Division II (*Cont.*)

INTERCEPTIONS

	Class	GP	No.	Yds	Int/ Game
Darren Banks, West Liberty St.	Sr.	11	13	260	1.2
Dre'Mail Hardin, Stillman	So.	11	9	171	0.8
Paul Tetzel, Bentley	Sr.	10	7	86	0.7
Cary Williams, Washburn	Sr.	12	7	164	0.6
Jamarcus Wiggins, Delta St.	Sr.	12	7	132	0.6
Roderick Mosley, Tex. A&M-Kngvl.	Sr.	11	7	89	0.6
Sherard Reynolds, Valdosta St	Jr.	14	7	76	0.5

PUNTING

	Class	No.	Avg
Michael Podobnik, Arkansas Tech.	Jr.	43	45.2
Wayne Durham, Adams St	Sr.	59	43.8
Brandon Larkin, Clark Atlanta	Sr.	73	43.6
Mike Whitcher, Western New Mexico	Sr.	38	42.3
Kurtis Fournier, Saginaw Valley	So.	41	42.0

Note: Minimum 3.6 per game.

Division III

SCORING

	Class	GP	TD	XP	FG	Pts	Pts/Game
Nate Kmic, Mount Union	Jr.	15	39	0	0	234	15.6
Josh Simpson, Hampden-Sydney	Jr.	8	27	0	0	164	20.5
Robert Heller, Waynesburg	Fr.	11	27	0	0	162	14.7
Mike Zimmerman, Mount Union	Sr.	15	0	100	0	148	9.9
Jack Phelan, Hartwick	Jr.	11	23	0	0	138	12.5
Jarvis Thrasher, Mary Hardin-Baylor	Sr.	14	23	0	0	138	9.9

FIELD GOALS

	Class	GP	FGA	FG	Pct	FG/Game
Jeff Schebler, UW-Whitewater	So.	12	27	21	.727	1.8
Mike Zimmerman, Mount Unioin	Sr.	15	20	16	.800	1.1
Matt Spitz, Capital	Sr.	11	23	15	.705	1.4
Peter Licalzi, Trinity (Tex)	Sr.	11	18	15	.833	1.4

Three tied at 14.

TOTAL OFFENSE

	Class	GP	Yds	Yds/Game
Jason Boltus, Hartwick	Jr.	11	4397	399.7
Josh Vogelbach, Guilford	Jr.	10	3600	360.0
Jordan Berg, Augsburg	Jr.	10	3390	339.0
Adam Shaffer, Mississippi Coll.	Jr.	10	3356	335.6
Juan Joseph, Millsaps	Jr.	9	2893	321.4

RUSHING

	Class	GP	Car	Yds	TD	Yds/Game
Justin Beaver, UW-Whitewater	Sr.	15	444	2455	15	163.7
Robert Heller, Waynesburg	Fr.	11	383	2176	26	197.8
Jarvis Thrasher, Mary Hardin-Baylor	Sr.	14	212	1899	26	135.6
Nate Kmic, Mount Union	Jr.	15	274	1695	38	113.0
Andy Moriarty, UW-Oshkosh	Sr.	10	300	1690	16	169.0

PASSING EFFICIENCY

	Class	GP	Att	Comp	Pct Comp	Yds	TD	Int	Rating Pts
Chad Rupp, Franklin	Jr.	11	302	212	.702	3250	35	6	194.9
Greg Micheli, Mount Union	Jr.	15	327	238	.728	3515	34	6	193.7
Bobby Swallow, Washington & Jefferson	Jr.	11	331	229	.736	3106	46	3	192.1
Justin Feaster, Hardin-Simmons	So.	10	316	207	.655	2946	30	9	169.5
Paul Keeley, Alfred	Sr.	11	343	221	.644	3015	34	8	166.3

Note: Minimum 15 attempts per game.

RECEPTIONS PER GAME

	Class	GP	No.	Yds	TD	Rec/Game
Hagen Miller, Guilford	So.	10	103	976	11	10.3
Royce Winford, Augsburg	Jr.	10	101	1403	16	10.1
Chad Arlt, Gustavus Adolphus	Jr.	10	100	1294	11	10.0
Drew Smith, Hampden-Sydney	Sr.	11	110	1616	8	10.0
Michael Zweifel, UW-River Falls	Fr.	10	97	1056	9	9.7

RECEIVING YARDS PER GAME

	Class	GP	No.	Yds	TD	Yds/Game
Jack Phelan, Hartwick	Jr.	11	73	1628	23	148.0
Drew Smith, Hampden-Sydney	Sr.	11	110	1616	8	146.9
Royce Winford, Augsburg	Jr.	10	101	1403	16	140.3
Chad Arlt, Gustavus Adolphus	Jr.	10	100	1294	11	129.4
Jake Allen, Mississippi Coll.	Sr.	10	61	1254	12	125.4

2007 NCAA Individual Leaders *(Cont.)*

Division III *(Cont.)*

INTERCEPTIONS

	Class	GP	No.	Yds	Int/G
Phil Schroer, Neb. Wesleyan	Jr.	8	8	221	1.0
Zach Sloan, Centre	So.	10	8	48	0.8
Orlando Brown, Widener	Sr.	11	8	131	0.7
James Alexander, Hobart	Sr.	11	8	67	0.7
Guy Dierikx, Central (Ia.)	Sr.	13	8	136	0.6

PUNTING

	Class	No.	Avg
Alex Groh, Occidental	So.	36	45.9
Ryan Patten, Olivet	Fr.	59	43.0
Kevin Soflkiancs, Baldwin-Wallace	Sr.	45	43.0
Matt Barcus, Chris. Newport	Jr.	40	42.8
Justin Ellerman, Lake Forest	Sr.	41	42.2

Note: Minimum 3.6 per game.

2007 NCAA FBS (Div. I-A) Team Leaders

Offense

SCORING

	GP	Pts	Avg
Hawaii	13	564	43.38
Kansas	13	556	42.77
Florida	13	552	42.46
Boise St	13	551	42.38
Oklahoma	14	592	42.29
Tulsa	14	576	41.14
Texas Tech	13	532	40.92
Missouri	14	558	39.86
West Virginia	13	515	39.62
Navy	13	511	39.31

RUSHING

	GP	Car	Yds	Avg	TD	Yds/Game
Navy	13	804	4534	5.64	53	348.77
Air Force	13	721	3894	5.40	36	299.54
West Virginia	13	628	3864	6.15	49	297.23
Arkansas	13	625	3725	5.96	33	286.54
Illinois	13	595	3338	5.61	28	256.77
Oregon	13	615	3272	5.32	32	251.69
La.-Lafayette	12	542	3019	5.57	23	251.58
Oklahoma St	13	592	3161	5.34	30	243.15
Central Florida	14	670	3287	4.91	41	234.79
Houston	13	599	2911	4.86	32	223.92

TOTAL OFFENSE

	GP	Plays	Yds	Avg	TD	Yds/Game
Tulsa	14	1126	7615	6.76	79	543.93
Texas Tech	13	1009	6885	6.82	70	529.62
Hawaii	13	942	6657	7.07	76	512.08
Houston	13	1036	6525	6.30	59	501.92
Missouri	14	1112	6864	6.17	70	490.29
Louisville	12	909	5856	6.44	55	488.00
Oklahoma St.	13	978	6322	6.46	60	486.31
Kansas	13	988	6237	6.31	72	479.77
Nebraska	12	898	5619	6.26	53	468.25
Oregon	13	1028	6078	5.91	62	467.54

PASSING

	GP	Att	Comp	Int	Pct Comp	Yds	Yds/Gm	TD
Texas Tech	13	763	544	15	71.30	6114	470.3	51
Hawaii	13	663	459	23	69.23	5713	439.5	51
Tulsa	14	564	336	19	59.57	5194	371.0	49
Louisville	12	491	316	14	64.36	4103	341.9	30
New Mexico St	13	623	429	22	68.86	4315	331.9	28
Boston College	14	659	390	19	59.18	4535	323.9	31
Nebraska	12	481	296	17	61.54	3886	323.8	31
Washington St	12	524	308	18	58.78	3835	319.6	26
Missouri	14	582	394	13	67.70	4397	314.1	34
Arizona	12	531	332	12	62.52	3702	308.5	28

Single-Game Highs

Points Scored: 79—Oklahoma, Sep 1, 2007 (vs North Texas)
Net Rushing Yards: 572—Navy, Nov 10, 2007 (vs North Texas)
Passing Yards: 646—Texas Tech, Sep 22, 2007 (vs Oklahoma St)
Rushing and Passing Yards: 812—Toledo, Oct 27, 2007 (vs Northern Illinois)
Fewest Rushing and Passing Yards Allowed: 69—Ohio St, Sep 8, 2007 (vs Akron)

Defense

SCORING

	GP	Pts	Avg
Ohio St.	13	166	12.8
USC	13	208	16.0
Virginia Tech	14	225	16.1
Kansas	13	213	16.4
Utah	13	219	16.8
Auburn	13	220	16.9
Penn St	13	228	17.5
West Virginia	13	235	18.1
BYU	13	241	18.5
TCU	13	243	18.7

TOTAL DEFENSE

	GP	Plays	Yds	Avg Y/Play	Avg Y/G
Ohio St	13	832	3029	3.64	233.00
USC	13	875	3551	4.06	273.15
LSU	14	915	4043	4.42	288.79
Virginia Tech	14	960	4157	4.33	296.93
Pittsburgh	12	808	3572	4.42	297.67
Auburn	13	855	3873	4.53	297.92
West Virginia	13	871	3922	4.50	301.69
Oregon St	13	891	3980	4.47	306.15
Clemson	13	877	3988	4.55	306.77
BYU	13	877	4002	4.56	307.85

RUSHING

	GP	Car	Yds	Avg	TD	Yds/Game
Oregon St.	13	447	918	2.05	12	70.6
Boston College	14	436	1057	2.42	8	75.5
Ohio St.	13	426	1077	2.53	3	82.8
USC	13	431	1094	2.54	13	84.2
Virginia Tech	14	442	1213	2.74	14	86.6
Texas	13	425	1214	2.86	12	93.4
Penn St	13	449	1219	2.71	9	93.8
Kansas	13	401	1232	3.07	8	94.8
BYU	13	429	1267	2.95	12	97.5
Florida	13	442	1343	3.04	18	103.3

TURNOVER MARGIN

		Turnovers Gained			Turnovers Lost			
	GP	Fum	Int	Total	Fum	Int	Total	Mar/Gm
Kansas	13	12	23	35	7	7	14	1.62
LSU	14	13	23	36	3	13	16	1.43
Fla. Atlantic	13	14	19	33	4	11	15	1.38
Ball St.	13	9	19	28	5	6	11	1.31
East Carolina	13	14	17	31	5	9	14	1.31
Cincinnati	13	16	26	42	14	12	26	1.23
San Jose St	12	7	20	27	3	11	14	1.08
Connecticut	13	6	23	29	9	6	15	1.08
Clemson	13	9	16	25	6	6	12	1.00
West Virginia	13	18	16	34	15	6	21	1.00

PASSING EFFICIENCY

	GP	Att	Comp	Pct Comp	Int	Pct Int	Yds	Yds/Att	TD	Pct TD	Rating Pts
Utah	13	428	216	50.47	17	3.97	2395	5.60	9	2.10	96.50
Arkansas	13	485	220	45.36	20	4.12	2670	5.51	21	4.33	97.68
LSU	14	451	212	47.01	23	5.10	2558	5.67	19	4.21	98.35
Ohio St	13	406	216	53.20	11	2.71	1952	4.81	13	3.20	98.73
Virginia Tech	14	518	277	53.47	22	4.25	2944	5.68	10	1.93	99.12
USC	13	444	241	54.28	12	2.70	2457	5.53	9	2.03	102.07
Auburn	13	403	223	55.33	14	3.47	2252	5.59	11	2.73	104.30
South Florida	13	474	244	51.48	23	4.85	2757	5.82	21	4.43	105.27
Kansas	13	528	303	57.39	23	4.36	2893	5.48	17	3.22	105.34
Connecticut	13	430	255	59.30	23	5.35	2522	5.87	12	2.79	107.08

NCAA Football Bowl Subdivision* National Champions

Year	Champion	Record	Bowl Game	Head Coach
1883	Yale	8-0-0	No bowl	Ray Tompkins (Captain)
1884	Yale	9-0-0	No bowl	Eugene L. Richards (Captain)
1885	Princeton	9-0-0	No bowl	Charles DeCamp (Captain)
1886	Yale	9-0-1	No bowl	Robert N. Corwin (Captain)
1887	Yale	9-0-0	No bowl	Harry W. Beecher (Captain)
1888	Yale	13-0-0	No bowl	Walter Camp
1889	Princeton	10-0-0	No bowl	Edgar Poe (Captain)
1890	Harvard	11-0-0	No bowl	George A. Stewart/George C. Adams
1891	Yale	13-0-0	No bowl	Walter Camp
1892	Yale	13-0-0	No bowl	Walter Camp
1893	Princeton	11-0-0	No bowl	Tom Trenchard (Captain)
1894	Yale	16-0-0	No bowl	William C. Rhodes
1895	Pennsylvania	14-0-0	No bowl	George Woodruff
1896	Princeton	10-0-1	No bowl	Garrett Cochran
1897	Pennsylvania	15-0-0	No bowl	George Woodruff
1898	Harvard	11-0-0	No bowl	W. Cameron Forbes
1899	Harvard	10-0-1	No bowl	Benjamin H. Dibblee
1900	Yale	12-0-0	No bowl	Malcolm McBride
1901	Michigan	11-0-0	Won Rose	Fielding Yost
1902	Michigan	11-0-0	No bowl	Fielding Yost
1903	Princeton	11-0-0	No bowl	Art Hillebrand
1904	Pennsylvania	12-0-0	No bowl	Carl Williams
1905	Chicago	11-0-0	No bowl	Amos Alonzo Stagg
1906	Princeton	9-0-1	No bowl	Bill Roper
1907	Yale	9-0-1	No bowl	Bill Knox
1908	Pennsylvania	11-0-1	No bowl	Sol Metzger
1909	Yale	10-0-0	No bowl	Howard Jones
1910	Harvard	8-0-1	No bowl	Percy Houghton
1911	Princeton	8-0-2	No bowl	Bill Roper
1912	Harvard	9-0-0	No bowl	Percy Houghton
1913	Harvard	9-0-0	No bowl	Percy Houghton
1914	Army	9-0-0	No bowl	Charley Daly
1915	Cornell	9-0-0	No bowl	Al Sharpe
1916	Pittsburgh	8-0-0	No bowl	Pop Warner
1917	Georgia Tech	9-0-0	No bowl	John Heisman
1918	Pittsburgh	4-1-0	No bowl	Pop Warner
1919	Harvard	9-0-1	Won Rose	Bob Fisher
1920	California	9-0-0	Won Rose	Andy Smith
1921	Cornell	8-0-0	No bowl	Gil Dobie
1922	Cornell	8-0-0	No bowl	Gil Dobie
1923	Illinois	8-0-0	No bowl	Bob Zuppke
1924	Notre Dame	10-0-0	Won Rose	Knute Rockne
1925	Alabama (H)	10-0-0	Won Rose	Wallace Wade
	Dartmouth (D)	8-0-0	No bowl	Jesse Hawley
1926	Alabama (H)	9-0-1	Tied Rose	Wallace Wade
	Stanford (D)(H)	10-0-1	Tied Rose	Pop Warner
1927	Illinois	7-0-1	No bowl	Bob Zuppke
1928	Georgia Tech (H)	10-0-0	Won Rose	Bill Alexander
	USC (D)	9-0-1	No bowl	Howard Jones
1929	Notre Dame	9-0-0	No bowl	Knute Rockne
1930	Notre Dame	10-0-0	No bowl	Knute Rockne
1931	USC	10-1-0	Won Rose	Howard Jones
1932	USC (H)	10-0-0	Won Rose	Howard Jones
	Michigan (D)	8-0-0	No bowl	Harry Kipke
1933	Michigan	7-0-1	No bowl	Harry Kipke
1934	Minnesota	8-0-0	No bowl	Bernie Bierman
1935	Minnesota (H)	8-0-0	No bowl	Bernie Bierman
	SMU (D)	12-1-0	Lost Rose	Matty Bell
1936	Minnesota	7-1-0	No bowl	Bernie Bierman
1937	Pittsburgh	9-0-1	No bowl	Jock Sutherland
1938	TCU (AP)	11-0-0	Won Sugar	Dutch Meyer
	Notre Dame (D)	8-1-0	No bowl	Elmer Layden

*In 2007, the NCAA renamed division I-A as the "Football Bowl Subdivision" and division I-AA as the "Football Championship Subdivision."

NCAA FBS (Div. I-A) National Champions *(Cont.)*

Year	Champion	Record	Bowl Game	Head Coach
1939	USC (D)	8-0-2	Won Rose	Howard Jones
	Texas A&M (AP)	11-0-0	Won Sugar	Homer Norton
1940	Minnesota	8-0-0	No bowl	Bernie Bierman
1941	Minnesota	8-0-0	No bowl	Bernie Bierman
1942	Ohio St	9-1-0	No bowl	Paul Brown
1943	Notre Dame	9-1-0	No bowl	Frank Leahy
1944	Army	9-0-0	No bowl	Red Blaik
1945	Army	9-0-0	No bowl	Red Blaik
1946	Notre Dame	8-0-1	No bowl	Frank Leahy
1947	Notre Dame	9-0-0	No bowl	Frank Leahy
	Michigan*	10-0-0	Won Rose	Fritz Crisler
1948	Michigan	9-0-0	No bowl	Bennie Oosterbaan
1949	Notre Dame	10-0-0	No bowl	Frank Leahy
1950	Oklahoma	10-1-0	Lost Sugar	Bud Wilkinson
1951	Tennessee	10-1-0	Lost Sugar	Bob Neyland
1952	Michigan St	9-0-0	No bowl	Biggie Munn
1953	Maryland	10-1-0	Lost Orange	Jim Tatum
1954	Ohio St	10-0-0	Won Rose	Woody Hayes
	UCLA (UPI)	9-0-0	No bowl	Red Sanders
1955	Oklahoma	11-0-0	Won Orange	Bud Wilkinson
1956	Oklahoma	10-0-0	No bowl	Bud Wilkinson
1957	Auburn	10-0-0	No bowl	Shug Jordan
	Ohio St (UPI)	9-1-0	Won Rose	Woody Hayes
1958	LSU	11-0-0	Won Sugar	Paul Dietzel
1959	Syracuse	11-0-0	Won Cotton	Ben Schwartzwalder
1960	Minnesota	8-2-0	Lost Rose	Murray Warmath
1961	Alabama	11-0-0	Won Sugar	Bear Bryant
1962	USC	11-0-0	Won Rose	John McKay
1963	Texas	11-0-0	Won Cotton	Darrell Royal
1964	Alabama	10-1-0	Lost Orange	Bear Bryant
1965	Alabama	9-1-1	Won Orange	Bear Bryant
	Michigan St (UPI)	10-1-0	Lost Rose	Duffy Daugherty
1966	Notre Dame	9-0-1	No bowl	Ara Parseghian
1967	USC	10-1-0	Won Rose	John McKay
1968	Ohio St	10-0-0	Won Rose	Woody Hayes
1969	Texas	11-0-0	Won Cotton	Darrell Royal
1970	Nebraska	11-0-1	Won Orange	Bob Devaney
	Texas (UPI)	10-1-0	Lost Cotton	Darrell Royal
1971	Nebraska	13-0-0	Won Orange	Bob Devaney
1972	USC	12-0-0	Won Rose	John McKay
1973	Notre Dame	11-0-0	Won Sugar	Ara Parseghian
	Alabama (UPI)	11-1-0	Lost Sugar	Bear Bryant
1974	Oklahoma	11-0-0	No bowl	Barry Switzer
	USC (UPI)	10-1-1	Won Rose	John McKay
1975	Oklahoma	11-1-0	Won Orange	Barry Switzer
1976	Pittsburgh	12-0-0	Won Sugar	Johnny Majors
1977	Notre Dame	11-1-0	Won Cotton	Dan Devine
1978	Alabama	11-1-0	Won Sugar	Bear Bryant
	USC (UPI)	12-1-0	Won Rose	John Robinson
1979	Alabama	12-0-0	Won Sugar	Bear Bryant
1980	Georgia	12-0-0	Won Sugar	Vince Dooley
1981	Clemson	12-0-0	Won Orange	Danny Ford
1982	Penn St	11-1-0	Won Sugar	Joe Paterno
1983	Miami (Fla.)	11-1-0	Won Orange	Howard Schnellenberger
1984	BYU	13-0-0	Won Holiday	LaVell Edwards
1985	Oklahoma	11-1-0	Won Orange	Barry Switzer
1986	Penn St	12-0-0	Won Fiesta	Joe Paterno
1987	Miami (Fla.)	12-0-0	Won Orange	Jimmy Johnson
1988	Notre Dame	12-0-0	Won Fiesta	Lou Holtz
1989	Miami (Fla.)	11-1-0	Won Sugar	Dennis Erickson
1990	Colorado	11-1-1	Won Orange	Bill McCartney
	Georgia Tech (UPI)	11-0-1	Won Citrus	Bobby Ross
1991	Miami (Fla.)	12-0-0	Won Orange	Dennis Erickson
	Washington (CNN)	12-0-0	Won Rose	Don James
1992	Alabama	13-0-0	Won Sugar	Gene Stallings
1993	Florida St	12-1-0	Won Orange	Bobby Bowden
1994	Nebraska	13-0-0	Won Orange	Tom Osborne
1995	Nebraska	12-0-0	Won Fiesta	Tom Osborne
†1996	Florida	12–1	Won Sugar	Steve Spurrier

NCAA FBS National Champions *(Cont.)*

Year	Champion	Record	Bowl Game	Head Coach
1997	Michigan	12–0	Won Rose	Lloyd Carr
	Nebraska (ESPN)	13–0	Won Orange	Tom Osborne
1998	Tennessee	13–0	Won Fiesta	Phillip Fulmer
1999	Florida St	12–0	Won Sugar	Bobby Bowden
2000	Oklahoma	13–0	Won Orange	Bob Stoops
2001	Miami (Fla.)	12–0	Won Rose	Larry Coker
2002	Ohio St	14–0	Won Fiesta	Jim Tressel
2003	LSU	13–1	Won Sugar	Nick Saban
	USC	12–1	Won Rose	Pete Carroll
2004	USC	13–0	Won Orange	Pete Carroll
2005	Texas	13–0	Won Rose	Mack Brown
‡2006	Florida	13–1	Won BCS Nat'l Championship	Urban Meyer
2007	LSU	12–2	Won BCS Nat'l Championship	Les Miles

*The AP, which had voted Notre Dame No. 1, took a second vote, giving the national title to Michigan after its 49–0 win over USC in the Rose Bowl. Note: Selectors: Helms Athletic Foundation (H) 1883–1935, The Dickinson System (D) 1924–40, The Associated Press (AP) 1936–present, United Press International (UPI) 1958–90, *USA Today*/CNN (CNN) 1991–96, and *USA Today*/ESPN (ESPN) 1997–present. †In 1996 the NCAA introduced overtime to break ties. ‡In 2006, the BCS established a separate national championship game in addition to its existing four-bowl structure.

Results of Major Bowl Games

Rose Bowl

1-1-02 .... Michigan 49, Stanford 0
1-1-16 .... Washington St 14, Brown 0
1-1-17 .... Oregon 14, Pennsylvania 0
1-1-18 .... Mare Island 19, Camp Lewis 7
1-1-19 .... Great Lakes 17, Mare Island 0
1-1-20 .... Harvard 7, Oregon 6
1-1-21 .... California 28, Ohio St 0
1-2-22 .... Washington & Jefferson 0, California 0
1-1-23 .... USC 14, Penn St 3
1-1-24 .... Navy 14, Washington 14
1-1-25 .... Notre Dame 27, Stanford 10
1-1-26 .... Alabama 20, Washington 19
1-1-27 .... Alabama 7, Stanford 7
1-2-28 .... Stanford 7, Pittsburgh 6
1-1-29 .... Georgia Tech 8, California 7
1-1-30 .... USC47, Pittsburgh 14
1-1-31 .... Alabama 24, Washington St 0
1-1-32 .... USC 21, Tulane 12
1-2-33 .... USC 35, Pittsburgh 0
1-1-34 .... Columbia 7, Stanford 0
1-1-35 .... Alabama 29, Stanford 13
1-1-36 .... Stanford 7, Southern Methodist 0
1-1-37 .... Pittsburgh 21, Washington 0
1-1-38 .... California 13, Alabama 0
1-2-39 .... USC 7, Duke 3
1-1-40 .... USC 14, Tennessee 0
1-1-41 .... Stanford 21, Nebraska 13
1-1-42 .... Oregon St 20, Duke 16
1-1-43 .... Georgia 9, UCLA 0
1-1-44 .... USC 29, Washington 0
1-1-45 .... USC 25, Tennessee 0
1-1-46 .... Alabama 34, USC 14
1-1-47 .... Illinois 45, UCLA 14
1-1-48 .... Michigan 49, USC 0
1-1-49 .... Northwestern 20, California 14
1-2-50 .... Ohio St 17, California 14
1-1-51 .... Michigan 14, California 6
1-1-52 .... Illinois 40, Stanford 7
1-1-53 .... USC 7, Wisconsin 0
1-1-54 .... Michigan St 28, UCLA 20
1-1-55 .... Ohio St 20, USC 7
1-2-56 .... Michigan St 17, UCLA 14
1-1-57 .... Iowa 35, Oregon St 19
1-1-58 .... Ohio St 10, Oregon 7
1-1-59 .... Iowa 38, California 12
1-1-60 .... Washington 44, Wisconsin 8
1-2-61 .... Washington 17, Minnesota 7
1-1-62 .... Minnesota 21, UCLA 3
1-1-63 .... USC 42, Wisconsin 37
1-1-64 .... Illinois 17, Washington 7
1-1-65 .... Michigan 34, Oregon St 7
1-1-66 .... UCLA 14, Michigan St 12
1-2-67 .... Purdue 14, USC 13
1-1-68 .... USC 14, Indiana 3
1-1-69 .... Ohio St 27, USC16
1-1-70 .... USC 10, Michigan 3
1-1-71 .... Stanford 27, Ohio St 17
1-1-72 .... Stanford 13, Michigan 12
1-1-73 .... USC 42, Ohio St 17
1-1-74 .... Ohio St 42, USC 21
1-1-75 .... USC 18, Ohio St 17
1-1-76 .... UCLA 23, Ohio St 10
1-1-77 .... USC 14, Michigan 6
1-2-78 .... Washington 27, Michigan 20
1-1-79 .... USC 17, Michigan 10
1-1-80 .... USC 17, Ohio St 16
1-1-81 .... Michigan 23, Washington 6
1-1-82 .... Washington 28, Iowa 0
1-1-83 .... UCLA 24, Michigan 14
1-2-84 .... UCLA 45, Illinois 9

Note: The Fiesta, Orange, Rose and Sugar Bowls constitute the Bowl Alliance, formed in 1995 and running through the 2009 regular season and 2010 bowl season. Starting in January 2007, it will include a separate BCS National Championship game as well. The four other BCS Bowls will host the following conference champions with consideration for the following conference tie-ins: the ACC or Big East champion in the FedEx Orange Bowl, the SEC champion in the Allstate Sugar Bowl, the Big Ten and the Pac-10 champions in the Rose Bowl and the Big 12 champion in the Tostitos Fiesta Bowl. rankings. There are also four at-large positions in the BCS that are open to any Division I-A team. This allows any Division I-A school in the nation the opportunity to play in a BCS bowl game.

Rose Bowl (Cont.)

1-1-85............USC 20, Ohio St 17
1-1-86............UCLA 45, Iowa 28
1-1-87............Arizona St 22, Michigan 15
1-1-88............Michigan St 20, USC 17
1-2-89............Michigan 22, USC 14
1-1-90............USC 17, Michigan 10
1-1-91............Washington 46, Iowa 34
1-1-92............Washington 34, Michigan 14
1-1-93............Michigan 38, Washington 31
1-1-94............Wisconsin 21, UCLA 16
1-2-95............Penn St 38, Oregon 20
1-1-96............USC 41, Northwestern 32
1-1-97............Ohio St 20, Arizona St 17
1-1-98............Michigan 21, Washington St 16
1-1-99............Wisconsin 38, UCLA 31
1-1-2000.........Wisconsin 17, Stanford 9
1-1-2001.........Washington 34, Purdue 24
1-3-2002.........Miami 37, Nebraska 14
1-1-2003.........Oklahoma 34, Washington St 14
1-1-2004.........USC 28, Michigan 14
1-1-2005.........Texas 38, Michigan 37
1-4-2006.........Texas 41, USC 38
1-1-2007.........USC 32, Michigan 18
1-1-2008.........USC 49, Illinois 17

City: Pasadena. Stadium: Rose Bowl, capacity 96,576. Playing Sites: Tournament Park (1902, 1916–22), Rose Bowl (1923–41, since 1943), Duke Stadium, Durham, NC (1942).

Orange Bowl

1-1-35............Bucknell 26, Miami (Fla.) 0
1-1-36............Catholic 20, Mississippi 19
1-1-37............Duquesne 13, Mississippi St 12
1-1-38............Auburn 6, Michigan St 0
1-2-39............Tennessee 17, Oklahoma 0
1-1-40............Georgia Tech 21, Missouri 7
1-1-41............Mississippi St 14, Georgetown 7
1-1-42............Georgia 40, TCU 26
1-1-43............Alabama 37, Boston College 21
1-1-44............LSU 19, Texas A&M 14
1-1-45............Tulsa 26, Georgia Tech 12
1-1-46............Miami (Fla.) 13, Holy Cross 6
1-1-47............Rice 8, Tennessee 0
1-1-48............Georgia Tech 20, Kansas 14
1-1-49............Texas 41, Georgia 28
1-2-50............Santa Clara 21, Kentucky 13
1-1-51............Clemson 15, Miami (Fla.) 14
1-1-52............Georgia Tech 17, Baylor 14
1-1-53............Alabama 61, Syracuse 6
1-1-54............Oklahoma 7, Maryland 0
1-1-55............Duke 34, Nebraska 7
1-2-56............Oklahoma 20, Maryland 6
1-1-57............Colorado 27, Clemson 21
1-1-58............Oklahoma 48, Duke 21
1-1-59............Oklahoma 21, Syracuse 6
1-1-60............Georgia 14, Missouri 0
1-2-61............Missouri 21, Navy 14
1-1-62............LSU 25, Colorado 7
1-1-63............Alabama 17, Oklahoma 0
1-1-64............Nebraska 13, Auburn 7
1-1-65............Texas 21, Alabama 17
1-1-66............Alabama 39, Nebraska 28
1-2-67............Florida 27, Georgia Tech 12
1-1-68............Oklahoma 26, Tennessee 24
1-1-69............Penn St 15, Kansas 14
1-1-70............Penn St 10, Missouri 3

Orange Bowl (Cont.)

1-1-71............Nebraska 17, LSU 12
1-1-72............Nebraska 38, Alabama 6
1-1-73............Nebraska 40, Notre Dame 6
1-1-74............Penn St 16, LSU 9
1-1-75............Notre Dame 13, Alabama 11
1-1-76............Oklahoma 14, Michigan 6
1-1-77............Ohio St 27, Colorado 10
1-2-78............Arkansas 31, Oklahoma 6
1-1-79............Oklahoma 31, Nebraska 24
1-1-80............Oklahoma 24, Florida St 7
1-1-81............Oklahoma 18, Florida St 17
1-1-82............Clemson 22, Nebraska 15
1-1-83............Nebraska 21, LSU 20
1-2-84............Miami (Fla.) 31, Nebraska 30
1-1-85............Washington 28, Oklahoma 17
1-1-86............Oklahoma 25, Penn St 10
1-1-87............Oklahoma 42, Arkansas 8
1-1-88............Miami (Fla.) 20, Oklahoma 14
1-2-89............Miami (Fla.) 23, Nebraska 3
1-1-90............Notre Dame 21, Colorado 6
1-1-91............Colorado 10, Notre Dame 9
1-1-92............Miami (Fla.) 22, Nebraska 0
1-1-93............Florida St 27, Nebraska 14
1-1-94............Florida St 18, Nebraska 16
1-1-95............Nebraska 24, Miami (Fla.) 17
1-1-96............Florida St 31, Notre Dame 26
12-31-96.........Nebraska 41, Virginia Tech 21
1-2-98............Nebraska 42, Tennessee 17
1-2-99............Florida 31, Syracuse 10
1-1-00............Michigan 35, Alabama 34 (ot)
1-3-01............Oklahoma 13, Florida St 2
1-2-02............Florida 56, Maryland 23
1-2-03............USC 38, Iowa 17
1-1-04............Miami (Fla.) 16, Florida St 15
1-4-05............USC 55, Oklahoma 19
1-3-06............Penn State 26, Florida State 23 (3OT)
1-2-07............Louisville 24, Wake Forest 13
1-3-08............Kansas 24, Virginia Tech 21

City: Miami. Stadium: Pro Player Stadium, capacity 75,192. Playing Sites: Orange Bowl (1935–96), Pro Player Stadium (since 1996).

Sugar Bowl

1-1-35............Tulane 20, Temple 14
1-1-36............TCU 3, LSU 2
1-1-37............Santa Clara 21, LSU 14
1-1-38............Santa Clara 6, LSU 0
1-2-39............TCU 15, Carnegie Tech 7
1-1-40............Texas A&M 14, Tulane 13
1-1-41............Boston Col 19, Tennessee 13
1-1-42............Fordham 2, Missouri 0
1-1-43............Tennessee 14, Tulsa 7
1-1-44............Georgia Tech 20, Tulsa 18
1-1-45............Duke 29, Alabama 26
1-1-46............Oklahoma St 33, St. Mary's (Ca.) 13
1-1-47............Georgia 20, North Carolina 10
1-1-48............Texas 27, Alabama 7
1-1-49............Oklahoma 14, North Carolina 6
1-2-50............Oklahoma 35, LSU 0
1-1-51............Kentucky 13, Oklahoma 7
1-1-52............Maryland 28, Tennessee 13
1-1-53............Georgia Tech 24, Mississippi 7
1-1-54............Georgia Tech 42, W Virginia 19
1-1-55............Navy 21, Mississippi 0
1-2-56............Georgia Tech 7, Pittsburgh 0

Results of Major Bowl Games *(Cont.)*

Sugar Bowl *(Cont.)*

1-1-57 ....Baylor 13, Tennessee 7
1-1-58 ....Mississippi 39, Texas 7
1-1-59 ....LSU 7, Clemson 0
1-1-60 ....Mississippi 21, LSU 0
1-2-61 ....Mississippi 14, Rice 6
1-1-62 ....Alabama 10, Arkansas 3
1-1-63 ....Mississippi 17, Arkansas 13
1-1-64 ....Alabama 12, Mississippi 7
1-1-65 ....LSU 13, Syracuse 10
1-1-66 ....Missouri 20, Florida 18
1-2-67 ....Alabama 34, Nebraska 7
1-1-68 ....LSU 20, Wyoming 13
1-1-69 ....Arkansas 16, Georgia 2
1-1-70 ....Mississippi 27, Arkansas 22
1-1-71 ....Tennessee 34, Air Force 13
1-1-72 ....Oklahoma 40, Auburn 22
12-31-72 ....Oklahoma 14, Penn St 0
12-31-73 ....Notre Dame 24, Alabama 23
12-31-74 ....Nebraska 13, Florida 10
12-31-75 ....Alabama 13, Penn St 6
1-1-77 ....Pittsburgh 27, Georgia 3
1-2-78 ....Alabama 35, Ohio St 6
1-1-79 ....Alabama 14, Penn St 7
1-1-80 ....Alabama 24, Arkansas 9
1-1-81 ....Georgia 17, Notre Dame 10
1-1-82 ....Pittsburgh 24, Georgia 20
1-1-83 ....Penn St 27, Georgia 23
1-2-84 ....Auburn 9, Michigan 7
1-1-85 ....Nebraska 28, LSU 10
1-1-86 ....Tennessee 35, Miami (Fla.) 7
1-1-87 ....Nebraska 30, LSU 15
1-1-88 ....Syracuse 16, Auburn 16
1-2-89 ....Florida St 13, Auburn 7
1-1-90 ....Miami (Fla.) 33, Alabama 25
1-1-91 ....Tennessee 23, Virginia 22
1-1-92 ....Notre Dame 39, Florida 28
1-1-93 ....Alabama 34, Miami (Fla.) 13
1-1-94 ....Florida 41, West Virginia 7
1-2-95 ....Florida St 23, Florida 17
12-31-95 ....Virginia Tech 28, Texas 10
1-2-97 ....Florida 52, Florida St 20
1-1-98 ....Florida St 31, Ohio St 14
1-1-99 ....Ohio St 24, Texas A&M 14
1-4-00 ....Florida St 46, Virginia Tech 29
1-2-01 ....Miami (Fla.) 37, Florida 20
1-1-02 ....LSU 47, Illinois 34
1-1-03 ....Georgia 26, Florida St 13
1-4-04 ....LSU 21, Oklahoma 14
1-3-05 ....Auburn 16, Virginia Tech 13
1-2-06 ....West Virginia 38, Georgia 35
1-3-07 ....LSU 41, Notre Dame 14
1-1-08 ....Georgia 41, Hawaii 10

City: New Orleans. Stadium: Louisiana Superdome, capacity 76,791. Playing Sites: Tulane Stadium (1935–74), Louisiana Superdome (since 1975). Due to Hurricane Katrina, 2006 Sugar Bowl played in Atlanta's Georgia Dome.

Cotton Bowl

1-1-37 ....TCU 16, Marquette 6
1-1-38 ....Rice 28, Colorado 14
1-2-39 ....St. Mary's (Ca.) 20, Texas Tech 13
1-1-40 ....Clemson 6, Boston Col 3
1-1-41 ....Texas A&M 13, Fordham 12
1-1-42 ....Alabama 29, Texas A&M 21

Cotton Bowl *(Cont.)*

1-1-43 ....Texas 14, Georgia Tech 7
1-1-44 ....Texas 7, Randolph Field 7
1-1-45 ....Oklahoma St 34, TCU 0
1-1-46 ....Texas 40, Missouri 27
1-1-47 ....Arkansas 0, LSU 0
1-1-48 ....Southern Methodist 13, Penn St 13
1-1-49 ....Southern Methodist 21, Oregon 13
1-2-50 ....Rice 27, North Carolina 13
1-1-51 ....Tennessee 20, Texas 14
1-1-52 ....Kentucky 20, TCU 7
1-1-53 ....Texas 16, Tennessee 0
1-1-54 ....Rice 28, Alabama 6
1-1-55 ....Georgia Tech 14, Arkansas 6
1-2-56 ....Mississippi 14, TCU 13
1-1-57 ....TCU 28, Syracuse 27
1-1-58 ....Navy 20, Rice 7
1-1-59 ....TCU 0, Air Force 0
1-1-60 ....Syracuse 23, Texas 14
1-2-61 ....Duke 7, Arkansas 6
1-1-62 ....Texas 12, Mississippi 7
1-1-63 ....LSU 13, Texas 0
1-1-64 ....Texas 28, Navy 6
1-1-65 ....Arkansas 10, Nebraska 7
1-1-66 ....LSU 14, Arkansas 7
12-31-66 ....Georgia 24, Southern Methodist 9
1-1-68 ....Texas A&M 20, Alabama 16
1-1-69 ....Texas 36, Tennessee 13
1-1-70 ....Texas 21, Notre Dame 17
1-1-71 ....Notre Dame 24, Texas 11
1-1-72 ....Penn St 30, Texas 6
1-1-73 ....Texas 17, Alabama 13
1-1-74 ....Nebraska 19, Texas 3
1-1-75 ....Penn St 41, Baylor 20
1-1-76 ....Arkansas 31, Georgia 10
1-1-77 ....Houston 30, Maryland 21
1-2-78 ....Notre Dame 38, Texas 10
1-1-79 ....Notre Dame 35, Houston 34
1-1-80 ....Houston 17, Nebraska 14
1-1-81 ....Alabama 30, Baylor 2
1-1-82 ....Texas 14, Alabama 12
1-1-83 ....SMU 7, Pittsburgh 3
1-2-84 ....Georgia 10, Texas 9
1-1-85 ....Boston Col 45, Houston 28
1-1-86 ....Texas A&M 36, Auburn 16
1-1-87 ....Ohio St 28, Texas A&M 12
1-1-88 ....Texas A&M 35, Notre Dame 10
1-2-89 ....UCLA 17, Arkansas 3
1-1-90 ....Tennessee 31, Arkansas 27
1-1-91 ....Miami (Fla.) 46, Texas 3
1-1-92 ....Florida St 10, Texas A&M 2
1-1-93 ....Notre Dame 28, Texas A&M 3
1-1-94 ....Notre Dame 24, Texas A&M 21
1-2-95 ....USC 55, Texas Tech 14
1-1-96 ....Colorado 38, Oregon 6
1-1-97 ....BYU 19, Kansas St 15
1-1-98 ....UCLA 29, Texas A&M 23
1-1-99 ....Texas 38, Mississippi St 11
1-1-00 ....Arkansas 27, Texas 6
1-1-01 ....Kansas St 35, Tennessee 21
1-1-02 ....Oklahoma 10, Arkansas 3
1-1-03 ....Texas 35, LSU 20
1-2-04 ....Mississippi 31, Oklahoma St 28
1-1-05 ....Tennessee 38, Texas A&M 7
1-2-06 ....Alabama 13, Texas Tech 10
1-1-07 ....Auburn 17, Nebraska 14
1-1-08 ....Missouri 38, Arkansas 7

City: Dallas. Stadium: Cotton Bowl, capacity 68,252.

Sun Bowl

1-1-36..............Hardin-Simmons 14, New Mexico St 14
1-1-37..............Hardin-Simmons 34, UTEP 6
1-1-38..............W Virginia 7, Texas Tech 6
1-2-39..............Utah 26, New Mexico 0
1-1-40..............Catholic 0, Arizona St 0
1-1-41..............Case Reserve 26, Arizona St 13
1-1-42..............Tulsa 6, Texas Tech 0
1-1-43..............2nd Air Force 13, Hardin-Simmons 7
1-1-44..............Southwestern (Tex.) 7, New Mexico 0
1-1-45..............Southwestern (Tex.) 35, New Mexico 0
1-1-46..............New Mexico 34, Denver 24
1-1-47..............Cincinnati 18, Virginia Tech 6
1-1-48..............Miami (OH) 13, Texas Tech 12
1-1-49..............W Virginia 21, UTEP 12
1-2-50..............UTEP 33, Georgetown 20
1-1-51..............W Texas St 14, Cincinnati 13
1-1-52..............Texas Tech 25, Pacific 14
1-1-53..............Pacific 26, Southern Miss 7
1-1-54..............UTEP 37, Southern Miss 14
1-1-55..............UTEP 47, Florida St 20
1-2-56..............Wyoming 21, Texas Tech 14
1-1-57..............George Washington 13, UTEP 0
1-1-58..............Louisville 34, Drake 20
12-31-58..........Wyoming 14, Hardin-Simmons 6
12-31-59..........New Mexico St 28, N Texas 8
12-31-60..........New Mexico St 20, Utah St 13
12-30-61..........Villanova 17, Wichita St 9
12-31-62..........W Texas St 15, Ohio 14
12-31-63..........Oregon 21, Southern Methodist 14
12-26-64..........Georgia 7, Texas Tech 0
12-31-65..........UTEP 13, TCU 12
12-24-66..........Wyoming 28, Florida St 20
12-30-67..........UTEP 14, Mississippi 7
12-28-68..........Auburn 34, Arizona 10
12-20-69..........Nebraska 45, Georgia 6
12-19-70..........Georgia Tech 17, Texas Tech 9
12-18-71..........LSU 33, Iowa St 15
12-30-72..........North Carolina 32, Texas Tech 28
12-29-73..........Missouri 34, Auburn 17
12-28-74..........Mississippi St 26, North Carolina 24
12-26-75..........Pittsburgh 33, Kansas 19
1-2-77..............Texas A&M 37, Florida 14
12-31-77..........Stanford 24, LSU 14
12-23-78..........Texas 42, Maryland 0
12-22-79..........Washington 14, Texas 7
12-27-80..........Nebraska 31, Mississippi St 17
12-26-81..........Oklahoma 40, Houston 14
12-25-82..........North Carolina 26, Texas 10
12-24-83..........Alabama 28, Southern Methodist 7
12-22-84..........Maryland 28, Tennessee 27
12-28-85..........Georgia 13, Arizona 13
12-25-86..........Alabama 28, Washington 6
12-25-87..........Oklahoma St 35, W Virginia 33
12-24-88..........Alabama 29, Army 28
12-30-89..........Pittsburgh 31, Texas A&M 28
12-31-90..........Michigan St 17, USC 16
12-31-91..........UCLA 6, Illinois 3
12-31-92..........Baylor 20, Arizona 15
12-24-93..........Oklahoma 41, Texas Tech 10
12-30-94..........Texas 35, North Carolina 31
12-29-95..........Iowa 38, Washington 18
12-31-96..........Stanford 38, Michigan St 0
12-31-97..........Arizona St 17, Iowa 7
12-31-98..........TCU 28, USC 19
12-31-99..........Oregon 24, Minnesota 20
12-29-00..........Wisconsin 21, UCLA 20
12-31-01..........Washington St 33, Purdue 27
12-31-02..........Purdue 34, Washington 24

Sun Bowl

12-31-03..........Minnesota 31, Oregon 30
12-31-04..........Arizona State 27, Purdue 23
12-30-05..........UCLA 50, Northwestern 39
12-29-06..........Oregon State 39, Missouri 38
12-31-07..........Oregon 56, South Florida 21

City: El Paso. Stadium: Sun Bowl, capacity 51,270. Name Changes: Sun Bowl (1936–86; 94–), John Hancock Sun Bowl (1987–88), John Hancock Bowl (1989–93). Playing Sites: Kidd Field (1936–62), Sun Bowl (since 1963).

Gator Bowl

1-1-46..............Wake Forest 26, South Carolina 14
1-1-47..............Oklahoma 34, North Carolina St 13
1-1-48..............Maryland 20, Georgia 20
1-1-49..............Clemson 24, Missouri 23
1-2-50..............Maryland 20, Missouri 7
1-1-51..............Wyoming 20, Washington & Lee 7
1-1-52..............Miami (Fla.) 14, Clemson 0
1-1-53..............Florida 14, Tulsa 13
1-1-54..............Texas Tech 35, Auburn 13
12-31-54..........Auburn 33, Baylor 13
12-31-55..........Vanderbilt 25, Auburn 13
12-29-56..........Georgia Tech 21, Pittsburgh 14
12-28-57..........Tennessee 3, Texas A&M 0
12-27-58..........Mississippi 7, Florida 3
1-2-60..............Arkansas 14, Georgia Tech 7
12-31-60..........Florida 13, Baylor 12
12-30-61..........Penn St 30, Georgia Tech 15
12-29-62..........Florida 17, Penn St 7
12-28-63..........North Carolina 35, Air Force 0
1-2-65..............Florida St 36, Oklahoma 19
12-31-65..........Georgia Tech 31, Texas Tech 21
12-31-66..........Tennessee 18, Syracuse 12
12-30-67..........Penn St 17, Florida St 17
12-28-68..........Missouri 35, Alabama 10
12-27-69..........Florida 14, Tennessee 13
1-2-71..............Auburn 35, Mississippi 28
12-31-71..........Georgia 7, North Carolina 3
12-30-72..........Auburn 24, Colorado 3
12-29-73..........Texas Tech 28, Tennessee 19
12-30-74..........Auburn 27, Texas 3
12-29-75..........Maryland 13, Florida 0
12-27-76..........Notre Dame 20, Penn St 9
12-30-77..........Pittsburgh 34, Clemson 3
12-29-78..........Clemson 17, Ohio St 15
12-28-79..........North Carolina 17, Michigan 15
12-29-80..........Pittsburgh 37, South Carolina 9
12-28-81..........North Carolina 31, Arkansas 27
12-30-82..........Florida St 31, W Virginia 12
12-30-83..........Florida 14, Iowa 6
12-28-84..........Oklahoma St 21, South Carolina 14
12-30-85..........Florida St 34, Oklahoma St 23
12-27-86..........Clemson 27, Stanford 21
12-31-87..........LSU 30, South Carolina 13
1-1-89..............Georgia 34, Michigan St 27
12-30-89..........Clemson 27, W Virginia 7
1-1-91..............Michigan 35, Mississippi 3
12-29-91..........Oklahoma 48, Virginia 14
12-31-92..........Florida 27, North Carolina St 10
12-31-93..........Alabama 24, North Carolina 10
12-30-94..........Tennessee 45, Virginia Tech 23
1-1-96..............Syracuse 41, Clemson 0
1-1-97..............North Carolina 20, W Virginia 13

Gator Bowl (*Cont.*)

1-1-98..............North Carolina 42, Viginia Tech 13
1-1-99..............Georgia Tech 35, Notre Dame 28
1-1-00..............Miami 27, Georgia Tech 13
1-1-01..............Virginia Tech 41, Clemson 20
1-1-02..............Florida St 30, Virginia Tech 17
1-1-03..............North Carolina St 28, Notre Dame 6
1-1-04..............Maryland 41, W Virginia 7
1-1-05..............Florida State 30, West Virginia 18
1-2-06..............Virginia Tech 35, Louisville 24
1-1-07..............West Virginia 38, Georgia Tech 35
1-1-08..............Texas Tech 31, Virginia 28

City: Jacksonville, FL. Stadium: Alltel Stadium, capacity 76,976.

Florida Citrus Bowl

1-1-47..............Catawba 31, Maryville (Tenn.) 6
1-1-48..............Catawba 7, Marshall 0
1-1-49..............Murray St 21, Sul Ross St 21
1-2-50..............St. Vincent 7, Emory & Henry 6
1-1-51..............Morris Harvey 35, Emory & Henry 14
1-1-52..............Stetson 35, Arkansas St 20
1-1-53..............E Texas St 33, Tennessee Tech 0
1-1-54..............E Texas St 7, Arkansas St 7
1-1-55..............NE-Omaha 7, Eastern Kentucky 6
1-2-56..............Juniata 6, Missouri Valley 6
1-1-57..............W Texas St 20, Southern Miss 13
1-1-58..............E Texas St 10, Southern Miss 9
12-27-58..........E Texas St 26, Missouri Valley 7
1-1-60..............Middle Tennessee St 21, Presbyterian 12
12-30-60..........Citadel 27, Tennessee Tech 0
12-29-61..........Lamar 21, Middle Tennessee St 14
12-22-62..........Houston 49, Miami (Ohio) 21
12-28-63..........Western Kentucky 27, Coast Guard 0
12-12-64..........E Carolina 14, Massachusetts 13
12-11-65..........E Carolina 31, Maine 0
12-10-66..........Morgan St 14, W Chester 6
12-16-67..........TN-Martin 25, W Chester 8
12-27-68..........Richmond 49, Ohio 42
12-26-69..........Toledo 56, Davidson 33
12-28-70..........Toledo 40, William & Mary 12
12-28-71..........Toledo 28, Richmond 3
12-29-72..........Tampa 21, Kent St 18
12-22-73..........Miami (Ohio) 16, Florida 7
12-21-74..........Miami (Ohio) 21, Georgia 10
12-20-75..........Miami (Ohio) 20, South Carolina 7
12-18-76..........Oklahoma St 49, BYU 21
12-23-77..........Florida St 40, Texas Tech 17
12-23-78..........North Carolina St 30, Pittsburgh 17
12-22-79..........LSU 34, Wake Forest 10
12-20-80..........Florida 35, Maryland 20
12-19-81..........Missouri 19, Southern Miss 17
12-18-82..........Auburn 33, Boston Col 26
12-17-83..........Tennessee 30, Maryland 23
12-22-84..........Georgia 17, Florida St 17
12-28-85..........Ohio St 10, BYU 7
1-1-87..............Auburn 16, USC 7
1-1-88..............Clemson 35, Penn St 10
1-2-89..............Clemson 13, Oklahoma 6
1-1-90..............Illinois 31, Virginia 21
1-1-91..............Georgia Tech 45, Nebraska 21
1-1-92..............California 37, Clemson 13
1-1-93..............Georgia 21, Ohio State 14
1-1-94..............Penn State 31, Tennessee 13
1-2-95..............Alabama 24, Ohio St 17

Florida Citrus Bowl (*Cont.*)

1-1-96..............Tennessee 20, Ohio St 14
1-1-97..............Tennessee 48, Northwestern 28
1-1-98..............Florida 21, Penn St 6
1-1-99..............Michigan 45, Arkansas 31
1-1-00..............Michigan St 37, Florida 34
1-1-01..............Michigan 31, Auburn 28
1-1-02..............Tennessee 45, Michigan 17
1-1-03..............Auburn 13, Penn St 9
1-1-04..............Georgia 34, Purdue 27 (OT)
1-1-05..............Iowa 30, LSU 25
1-2-06..............Wisconsin 24, Auburn 10
1-1-07..............Wisconsin 17, Arkansas 14
1-1-08..............Michigan 41, Florida 35

City: Orlando, FL. Stadium: Florida Citrus Bowl, capacity 70,000. Name Change: Tangerine Bowl (1947–82). Capital One Bowl (since 2008). Playing Sites: Tangerine Bowl (1947–72, 1974–82); Florida Field, Gainesville (1973); Orlando Stadium/Florida Citrus Bowl-Orlando (1983–2007).

Liberty Bowl

12-19-59..........Penn St 7, Alabama 0
12-17-60..........Penn St 41, Oregon 12
12-16-61..........Syracuse 15, Miami (Fla.) 14
12-15-62..........Oregon St 6, Villanova 0
12-21-63..........Mississippi St 16, North Carolina St 12
12-19-64..........Utah 32, W Virginia 6
12-18-65..........Mississippi 13, Auburn 7
12-10-66..........Miami (Fla.) 14, Virginia Tech 7
12-16-67..........North Carolina St 14, Georgia 7
12-14-68..........Mississippi 34, Virginia Tech 17
12-13-69..........Colorado 47, Alabama 33
12-12-70..........Tulane 17, Colorado 3
12-20-71..........Tennessee 14, Arkansas 13
12-18-72..........Georgia Tech 31, Iowa St 30
12-17-73..........North Carolina St 31, Kansas 18
12-16-74..........Tennessee 7, Maryland 3
12-22-75..........USC 20, Texas A&M 0
12-20-76..........Alabama 36, UCLA 6
12-19-77..........Nebraska 21, North Carolina 17
12-23-78..........Missouri 20, LSU 15
12-22-79..........Penn St 9, Tulane 6
12-27-80..........Purdue 28, Missouri 25
12-30-81..........Ohio St 31, Navy 28
12-29-82..........Alabama 21, Illinois 15
12-29-83..........Notre Dame 19, Boston Col 18
12-27-84..........Auburn 21, Arkansas 15
12-27-85..........Baylor 21, LSU 7
12-29-86..........Tennessee 21, Minnesota 14
12-29-87..........Georgia 20, Arkansas 17
12-28-88..........Indiana 34, South Carolina 10
12-28-89..........Mississippi 42, Air Force 29
12-27-90..........Air Force 23, Ohio St 11
12-29-91..........Air Force 38, Mississippi St 15
12-31-92..........Mississippi 13, Air Force 0
12-28-93..........Louisville 18, Michigan St 7
12-31-94..........Illinois 30, E Carolina 0
12-30-95..........East Carolina 19, Stanford 13
12-27-96..........Syracuse 30, Houston 17
12-31-97..........Southern Miss 41, Pittsburgh 7
12-31-98..........Tulane 41, BYU 27
12-31-99..........Southern Miss 23, Colorado St 17
12-29-01..........Colorado St 22, Louisville 17
12-31-01..........Louisville 28, BYU 10
12-31-02..........TCU 17, Colorado St 3
12-31-03..........Utah 17, Southern Mississippi 0

Liberty Bowl (Cont.)

12-31-04..........Louisville 44, Boise State 40
12-31-05..........Tulsa 31, Fresno State 24
12-29-06..........South Carolina 44, Houston 36
12-29-07..........Mississippi St 10, Central Florida 3

City: Memphis (since 1965). Stadium: Liberty Bowl Memorial Stadium, capacity 62,921.
Playing Sites: Philadelphia (Municipal Stadium, 1959–63), Atlantic City (Convention Center, 1964).

Bluebonnet Bowl

12-19-59..........Clemson 23, TCU 7
12-17-60..........Texas 3, Alabama 3
12-16-61..........Kansas 33, Rice 7
12-22-62..........Missouri 14, Georgia Tech 10
12-21-63..........Baylor 14, LSU 7
12-19-64..........Tulsa 14, Mississippi 7
12-18-65..........Tennessee 27, Tulsa 6
12-17-66..........Texas 19, Mississippi 0
12-23-67..........Colorado 31, Miami (Fla.) 21
12-31-68..........Southern Methodist 28, Oklahoma 27
12-31-69..........Houston 36, Auburn 7
12-31-70..........Alabama 24, Oklahoma 24
12-31-71..........Colorado 29, Houston 17
12-30-72..........Tennessee 24, LSU 17
12-29-73..........Houston 47, Tulane 7
12-23-74..........North Carolina St 31, Houston 31
12-27-75..........Texas 38, Colorado 21
12-31-76..........Nebraska 27, Texas Tech 24
12-31-77..........USC 47, Texas A&M 28
12-31-78..........Stanford 25, Georgia 22
12-31-79..........Purdue 27, Tennessee 22
12-31-80..........North Carolina 16, Texas 7
12-31-81..........Michigan 33, UCLA 14
12-31-82..........Arkansas 28, Florida 24
12-31-83..........Oklahoma St 24, Baylor 14
12-31-84..........W Virginia 31, TCU 14
12-31-85..........Air Force 24, Texas 16
12-31-86..........Baylor 21, Colorado 9
12-31-87..........Texas 32, Pittsburgh 27

City: Houston. Playing sites: Rice Stadium (1959–67; 1985–86), Astrodome (1968–84, 1987).
Name change: Astro-Bluebonnet Bowl (1968–76). Bowl was discontinued after 1987.

Peach Bowl

12-30-68..........LSU 31, Florida St 27
12-30-69..........W Virginia 14, South Carolina 3
12-30-70..........Arizona St 48, North Carolina 26
12-30-71..........Mississippi 41, Georgia Tech 18
12-29-72..........North Carolina St 49, W Virginia 13
12-28-73..........Georgia 17, Maryland 16
12-28-74..........Vanderbilt 6, Texas Tech 6
12-31-75..........W Virginia 13, North Carolina St 10
12-31-76..........Kentucky 21, North Carolina 0
12-31-77..........North Carolina St 24, Iowa St 14
12-25-78..........Purdue 41, Georgia Tech 21
12-31-79..........Baylor 24, Clemson 18
1-2-81..............Miami (Fla.) 20, Virginia Tech 10
12-31-81..........W Virginia 26, Florida 6
12-31-82..........Iowa 28, Tennessee 22
12-30-83..........Florida St 28, North Carolina 3
12-31-84..........Virginia 27, Purdue 24
12-31-85..........Army 31, Illinois 29
12-31-86..........Virginia Tech 25, North Carolina St 24

Peach Bowl (Cont.)

1-2-88..............Tennessee 27, Indiana 22
12-31-88..........North Carolina St 28, Iowa 23
12-30-89..........Syracuse 19, Georgia 18
12-29-90..........Auburn 27, Indiana 23
1-1-92..............E Carolina 37, North Carolina St 34
1-2-93..............North Carolina 21, Mississippi St 17
12-31-93..........Clemson 14, Kentucky 13
1-1-95..............North Carolina St 28, Mississippi St 24
12-30-95..........Virginia 34, Georgia 27
12-28-96..........LSU 10, Clemson 7
1-2-98..............Auburn 21, Clemson 17
12-31-98..........Georgia 35, Virginia 33
12-30-99..........Mississippi St 17, Clemson 7
12-29-00..........LSU 28, Georgia Tech 14
12-31-01..........North Carolina 16, Auburn 10
12-31-02..........Maryland 30, Tennessee 3
1-2-04..............Clemson 27, Tennessee 14
12-31-04..........Miami (Fla.) 27, Florida 10
12-30-05..........LSU 40, Miami (Fla.) 3
12-30-06..........Georgia 31, Virginia Tech 24
12-31-07..........Auburn 23, Clemson 20 (OT)

City: Atlanta. Stadium: Georgia Dome, capacity 71,500.
Name change: Chick-fil-A Bowl (2006–).Playing Sites: Grant Field (1968–70), Atlanta–Fulton County Stadium (1971–92), Georgia Dome (since 1993).

Fiesta Bowl

12-27-71..........Arizona St 45, Florida St 38
12-23-72..........Arizona St 49, Missouri 35
12-21-73..........Arizona St 28, Pittsburgh 7
12-28-74..........Oklahoma St 16, BYU 6
12-26-75..........Arizona St 17, Nebraska 14
12-25-76..........Oklahoma 41, Wyoming 7
12-25-77..........Penn St 42, Arizona St 30
12-25-78..........Arkansas 10, UCLA 10
12-25-79..........Pittsburgh 16, Arizona 10
12-26-80..........Penn St 31, Ohio St 19
1-1-82..............Penn St 26, USC 10
1-1-83..............Arizona St 32, Oklahoma 21
1-2-84..............Ohio St 28, Pittsburgh 23
1-1-85..............UCLA 39, Miami (Fla.) 37
1-1-86..............Michigan 27, Nebraska 23
1-2-87..............Penn St 14, Miami (Fla.) 10
1-1-88..............Florida St 31, Nebraska 28
1-2-89..............Notre Dame 34, W Virginia 21
1-1-90..............Florida St 41, Nebraska 17
1-1-91..............Louisville 34, Alabama 7
1-1-92..............Penn St 42, Tennessee 17
1-1-93..............Syracuse 26, Colorado 22
1-1-94..............Arizona 29, Miami (Fla.) 0
1-2-95..............Colorado 41, Notre Dame 24
1-2-96..............Nebraska 62, Florida 24
1-1-97..............Penn St 38, Texas 15
12-31-97..........Kansas St 35, Syracuse 18
1-4-99..............Tennessee 23, Florida St 16
1-2-00..............Nebraska 31, Tennessee 21
1-1-01..............Oregon St 41, Notre Dame 9
1-1-02..............Oregon 38, Colorado 16
1-3-03..............Ohio St 31, Miami (Fla.) 24 [2 OT]
1-2-04..............Ohio St 35, Kansas St 28
1-1-05..............Utah 35, Pittsburgh 7
1-2-06..............Ohio State 34, Notre Dame 20
1-1-07..............Boise State 43, Oklahoma 42
1-2-08..............West Virginia 48, Oklahoma 28

City: Tempe, AZ. Stadium: Sun Devil Stadium, capacity 73,471.

Independence Bowl

12-13-76..........McNeese St 20, Tulsa 16
12-17-77..........Louisiana Tech 24, Louisville 14
12-16-78..........E Carolina 35, Louisiana Tech 13
12-15-79..........Syracuse 31, McNeese St 7
12-13-80..........Southern Miss 16, McNeese St 14
12-12-81..........Texas A&M 33, Oklahoma St 16
12-11-82..........Wisconsin 14, Kansas St 3
12-10-83..........Air Force 9, Mississippi 3
12-15-84..........Air Force 23, Virginia Tech 7
12-21-85..........Minnesota 20, Clemson 13
12-20-86..........Mississippi 20, Texas Tech 17
12-19-87..........Washington 24, Tulane 12
12-23-88..........Southern Miss 38, UTEP 18
12-16-89..........Oregon 27, Tulsa 24
12-15-90..........Louisiana Tech 34, Maryland 34
12-29-91..........Georgia 24, Arkansas 15
12-31-92..........Wake Forest 39, Oregon 35
12-31-93..........Virginia Tech 45, Indiana 20
12-28-94..........Virginia 20, TCU 10
12-29-95..........LSU 45, Michigan St 26
12-31-96..........Auburn 32, Army 29
12-28-97..........LSU 27, Notre Dame 9
12-31-98..........Mississippi 35, Texas Tech 18
12-31-99..........Mississippi 27, Oklahoma 25
12-31-00..........Mississippi St 43, Texas A&M 41
12-27-01..........Alabama 14, Iowa St 13
12-27-02..........Mississippi 27, Nebraska 23
12-31-03..........Arkansas 27, Missouri 14
12-28-04..........Iowa State 17, Miami (Ohio) 13
12-30-05..........Missouri 38, South Carolina 31
12-28-06..........Oklahoma State 34, Alabama 31
12-30-07..........Alabama 30, Colorado 24

City: Shreveport, LA. Stadium: Independence Stadium, capacity 50,459.

All-American Bowl

12-22-77..........Maryland 17, Minnesota 7
12-20-78..........Texas A&M 28, Iowa St 12
12-29-79..........Missouri 24, South Carolina 14
12-27-80..........Arkansas 34, Tulane 15
12-31-81..........Mississippi St 10, Kansas 0
12-31-82..........Air Force 36, Vanderbilt 28
12-22-83..........W Virginia 20, Kentucky 16
12-29-84..........Kentucky 20, Wisconsin 19
12-31-85..........Georgia Tech 17, Michigan St 14
12-31-86..........Florida St 27, Indiana 13
12-22-87..........Virginia 22, BYU 16
12-29-88..........Florida 14, Illinois 10
12-28-89..........Texas Tech 49, Duke 21
12-28-90..........North Carolina St 31, Southern Miss 27

City: Birmingham, AL. Stadium: Legion Field. Name Change: Hall of Fame Classic (1977–84). Bowl was discontinued after 1990.

Holiday Bowl

12-22-78..........Navy 23, BYU 16
12-21-79..........Indiana 38, BYU 37
12-19-80..........BYU 46, SMU45
12-18-81..........BYU 38, Washington St 36
12-17-82..........Ohio St 47, BYU 17
12-23-83..........BYU 21, Missouri 17
12-21-84..........BYU 24, Michigan 17
12-22-85..........Arkansas 18, Arizona St 17
12-30-86..........Iowa 39, San Diego St 38

Holiday Bowl *(Cont.)*

12-30-87..........Iowa 20, Wyoming 19
12-30-88..........Oklahoma St 62, Wyoming 14
12-29-89..........Penn St 50, BYU 39
12-29-90..........Texas A&M 65, BYU 14
12-30-91..........Iowa 13, BYU 13
12-30-92..........Hawaii 27, Illinois 17
12-30-93..........Ohio St 28, BYU 21
12-30-94..........Michigan 24, Colorado St 14
12-29-95..........Kansas St 54, Colorado St 21
12-30-96..........Colorado 33, Washington 21
12-29-97..........Colorado St 35, Missouri 24
12-30-98..........Arizona 23, Nebraska 20
12-29-99..........Kansas St 24, Washington 20
12-29-00..........Oregon 35, Texas 30
12-28-01..........Texas 47, Washington 43
12-27-02..........Kansas St 34, Arizona St 27
12-30-03..........Washington St 28, Texas 20
12-30-04..........Texas Tech 45, California 31
12-29-05..........*Oklahoma 17, Oregon 14
12-28-06..........California 45, Texas A&M 10
12-27-07..........Texas 52, Arizona St 34

*victory vacated in 2007

City: San Diego. Stadium: Qualcomm Stadium, capacity 70,000.

Las Vegas Bowl

12-19-81..........Toledo 27, San Jose St 25
12-18-82..........Fresno St 29, Bowling Green 28
12-17-83 Northern Illinois 20, Cal St–Fullerton 13
12-15-84..........UNLV 30, Toledo 13*
12-14-85..........Fresno St 51, Bowling Green 7
12-13-86..........San Jose St 37, Miami (Ohio) 7
12-12-87..........Eastern Michigan 30, San Jose St 27
12-10-88..........Fresno St 35, Western Michigan 30
12-9-89..........Fresno St 27, Ball St 6
12-8-90..........San Jose St 48, Central Michigan 24
12-14-91..........Bowling Green 28, Fresno St 21
12-18-92..........Bowling Green 35, Nevada 34
12-17-93..........Utah St 42, Ball St 33
12-15-94..........UNLV 52, Central Michigan 24
12-14-95..........Toledo 40, Nevada 37
12-19-96..........Nevada 18, Ball St 15
12-19-97..........Oregon 41, Air Force 13
12-19-98..........North Carolina 20, San Diego St 13
12-18-99..........Utah 17, Fresno St 16
12-21-00..........UNLV 31, Arkansas 14
12-25-01..........Utah 10, USC 6
12-25-02..........UCLA 27, New Mexico 13
12-24-03..........Oregon St 55, New Mexico 14
12-23-04..........Wyoming 24, UCLA, 21
12-22-05..........California 35, BYU 28
12-21-06..........BYU 38, Oregon 8
12-22-07..........BYU 17, UCLA 16

* Toledo won later by forfeit. City: Las Vegas (since 1992). Stadium: Sam Boyd Silver Bowl Stadium, capacity 40,000. Name change: California Bowl (1981–91).
Playing sites: Fresno, CA (Bulldog Stadium, 1981–91), Las Vegas.

Aloha Bowl

12-25-82..........Washington 21, Maryland 20
12-26-83..........Penn St 13, Washington 10
12-29-84..........Southern Methodist 27, Notre Dame 20

Results of Major Bowl Games *(Cont.)*

Aloha Bowl *(Cont.)*

12-28-85..........Alabama 24, USC 3
12-27-86..........Arizona 30, North Carolina 21
12-25-87..........UCLA 20, Florida 16
12-25-88..........Washington St 24, Houston 22
12-25-89..........Michigan St 33, Hawaii 13
12-25-90..........Syracuse 28, Arizona 0
12-25-91..........Georgia Tech 18, Stanford 17
12-25-92..........Kansas 23, BYU 20
12-25-93..........Colorado 41, Fresno St 30
12-25-94..........Boston College 12, Kansas St 7
12-25-95..........Kansas 51, UCLA 30
12-25-96..........Navy 42, California 38
12-25-97..........Washington 51, Michigan St 23
12-25-98..........Colorado 51, Oregon 43
12-25-99..........Wake Forest 23, Arizona St 3
12-25-00..........Boston College 31, Arizona St 17

City: Honolulu. Stadium: Aloha Stadium. Bowl was discontinued after 2000.

Freedom Bowl

12-16-84..........Iowa 55, Texas 17
12-30-85..........Washington 20, Colorado 17
12-30-86..........UCLA 31, BYU 10
12-30-87..........Arizona St 33, Air Force 28
12-29-88..........BYU 20, Colorado 17
12-30-89..........Washington 34, Florida 7
12-29-90..........Colorado St 32, Oregon 31
12-30-91..........Tulsa 28, San Diego St 17
12-29-92..........Fresno St 24, USC 7
12-30-93..........USC 28, Utah 21
12-29-94..........Utah 16, Arizona 13

City: Anaheim. Stadium: Anaheim Stadium. Bowl was discontinued after 1994.

Outback Bowl

12-23-86..........Boston College 27, Georgia 24
1-2-88..............Michigan 28, Alabama 24
1-2-89..............Syracuse 23, LSU 10
1-1-90..............Auburn 31, Ohio St 14
1-1-91..............Clemson 30, Illinois 0
1-1-92..............Syracuse 24, Ohio St 17
1-1-93..............Tennessee 38, Boston College 23
1-1-94..............Michigan 42, North Carolina St 7
1-2-95..............Wisconsin 34, Duke 20
1-1-96..............Penn St 43, Auburn 14
1-1-97..............Alabama 17, Michigan 14
1-1-98..............Georgia 33, Wisconsin 6
1-1-99..............Penn St 26, Kentucky 14
1-1-00..............Georgia 28, Purdue 25
1-1-01..............South Carolina 24, Ohio St 7
1-1-02..............South Carolina 31, Ohio St 28
1-1-03..............Michigan 38, Florida 30
1-1-04..............Iowa 37, Florida 17
1-1-05..............Georgia 24, Wisconsin 21
1-2-06..............Florida 31, Iowa 24
1-1-07..............Penn State 20, Tennessee 10
1-1-08..............Tennessee 21, Wisconsin 17

City: Tampa. Stadium: Raymond James Stadium, capacity 75,000. Name change: Hall of Fame Bowl (1986–95).

Insight.com Bowl

12-31-89..........Arizona 17, North Carolina St 10
12-31-90..........California 17, Wyoming 15

Insight.com Bowl *(Cont.)*

12-31-91..........Indiana 24, Baylor 0
12-29-92..........Washington St 31, Utah 28
12-29-93..........Kansas St 52, Wyoming 17
12-29-94..........BYU 31, Oklahoma 6
12-27-95..........Texas Tech 55, Air Force 41
12-27-96..........Wisconsin 38, Utah 10
12-27-97..........Arizona 20, New Mexico 14
12-26-98..........Missouri 34, W Virginia 31
12-31-99..........Colorado 62, Boston College 28
12-28-00..........Iowa St 37, Pittsburgh 29
12-29-01..........Syracuse 26, Kansas St 3
12-26-02..........Pittsburgh 38, Oregon St 13
12-26-03..........California 52, Virginia Tech 49
12 28 04..........Oregon State 38, Notre Dame 21
12-27-05..........Arizona State 45, Rutgers 40
12-29-06..........Texas Tech 44, Minnesota 41
12-31-07..........Oklahoma St 49, Indiana 33

City: Tucson. Stadium: Arizona Stadium, capacity 55,883. Name change: Copper Bowl 1989–97. Insight Bowl (since 2001).

Tangerine Bowl

12-28-90..........Florida St 24, Penn St 17
12-28-91..........Alabama 30, Colorado 25
1-1-93..............Stanford 24, Penn St 3
1-1-94..............Boston College 31, Virginia 13
1-2-95..............South Carolina 24, W Virginia 21
12-30-95..........North Carolina 20, Arkansas 10
12-27-96..........Miami (Fla.) 31, Virginia 21
12-29-97..........Georgia Tech 35, W Virginia 30
12-29-98..........Miami (Fla.) 46, North Carolina St 23
12-30-99..........Illinois 62, Virginia 21
12-28-00..........North Carolina St 38, Minnesota 30
12-20-01..........Pittsburgh 34, North Carolina St 19
12-23-02..........Texas Tech 55, Clemson 15
12-22-03..........North Carolina St 56, Kansas 26

City: Miami. Stadium: Pro Player Stadium, capacity 75,192. Name change: Blockbuster Bowl (1990–93), Carquest Bowl (1994–97), Micron PC Bowl (1998–01). Discontinued after 2003.

Alamo Bowl

12-31-93..........California 37, Iowa 3
12-31-94..........Washington St 10, Baylor 3
12-28-95..........Texas A&M 22, Michigan 20
12-29-96..........Iowa 27, Texas Tech 0
12-30-97..........Purdue 33, Oklahoma St 20
12-29-98..........Purdue 37, Kansas St 34
12-28-99..........Penn St 24, Texas A&M 0
12-30-00..........Nebraska 66, Northwestern 17
12-29-01..........Iowa 16, Texas Tech 13
12-28-02..........Wisconsin 31, Colorado 28 (OT)
12-29-03..........Nebraska 17, Michigan St 3
12-29-04..........Ohio State 33, Oklahoma State 7
12-28-05..........Nebraska 32, Michigan 28
12-30-06..........Texas 26, Iowa 24
12-29-07..........Penn St 24, Texas A&M 17

City: San Antonio, TX. Stadium: Alamodome, capaciity 67,000.

Annual Associated Press Top 20

1936

		Record	Coach
1.	Minnesota	7-1-0	Bernie Bierman
2.	LSU	9-0-1	Bernie Moore
3.	Pittsburgh	7-1-1	Jock Sutherland
4.	Alabama	8-0-1	Frank Thomas
5.	Washington	7-1-1	Jimmy Phelan
6.	Santa Clara	7-1-0	Buck Shaw
7.	Northwestern	7-1-0	Pappy Waldorf
8.	Notre Dame	6-2-1	Elmer Layden
9.	Nebraska	7-2-0	Dana X. Bible
10.	Pennsylvania	7-1-0	Harvey Harman
11.	Duke	9-1-0	Wallace Wade
12.	Yale	7-1-0	Ducky Pond
13.	Dartmouth	7-1-1	Red Blaik
14.	Duquesne	7-2-0	John Smith
15.	Fordham	5-1-2	Jim Crowley
16.	TCU	8-2-2	Dutch Meyer
17.	Tennessee	6-2-2	Bob Neyland
18.	Arkansas	7-3-0	Fred Thomsen
19.	Navy	6-3-0	Tom Hamilton
20.	Marquette	7-1-0	Frank Murray

1937

		Record	Coach
1.	Pittsburgh	9-0-1	Jock Sutherland
2.	California	9-0-1	Stub Allison
3.	Fordham	7-0-1	Jim Crowley
4.	Alabama	9-0-0	Frank Thomas
5.	Minnesota	6-2-0	Bernie Bierman
6.	Villanova	8-0-1	Clipper Smith
7.	Dartmouth	7-0-2	Red Blaik
8.	LSU	9-1-0	Bernie Moore
9.	Notre Dame	6-2-1	Elmer Layden
	Santa Clara	8-0-0	Buck Shaw
11.	Nebraska	6-1-2	Biff Jones
12.	Yale	6-1-1	Ducky Pond
13.	Ohio St	6-2-0	Francis Schmidt
14.	Holy Cross	8-0-2	Eddie Anderson
	Arkansas	6-2-2	Fred Thomsen
16.	TCU	4-2-2	Dutch Meyer
17.	Colorado	8-0-0	Bunnie Oakes
18.	Rice	5-3-2	Jimmy Kitts
19.	North Carolina	7-1-1	Ray Wolf
20.	Duke	7-2-1	Wallace Wade

1938

		Record	Coach
1.	TCU	10-0-0	Dutch Meyer
2.	Tennessee	10-0-0	Bob Neyland
3.	Duke	9-0-0	Wallace Wade
4.	Oklahoma	10-0-0	Tom Stidham
5.	#Notre Dame	8-1-0	Elmer Layden
6.	Carnegie Tech	7-1-0	Bill Kern
7.	USC	8-2-0	Howard Jones
8.	Pittsburgh	8-2-0	Jock Sutherland
9.	Holy Cross	8-1-0	Eddie Anderson
10.	Minnesota	6-2-0	Bernie Bierman
11.	Texas Tech	10-0-0	Pete Cawthon
12.	Cornell	5-1-1	Carl Snavely
13.	Alabama	7-1-1	Frank Thomas
14.	California	10-1-0	Stub Allison
15.	Fordham	6-1-2	Jim Crowley
16.	Michigan	6-1-1	Fritz Crisler
17.	Northwestern	4-2-2	Pappy Waldorf

1938 *(Cont.)*

		Record	Coach
18.	Villanova	8-0-1	Clipper Smith
19.	Tulane	7-2-1	Red Dawson
20.	Dartmouth	7-2-0	Red Blaik

#Selected No. 1 by the Dickinson System.

1939

		Record	Coach
1.	Texas A&M	10-0-0	Homer Norton
2.	Tennessee	10-0-0	Bob Neyland
3.	#USC	7-0-2	Howard Jones
4.	Cornell	8-0-0	Carl Snavely
5.	Tulane	8-0-1	Red Dawson
6.	Missouri	8-1-0	Don Faurot
7.	UCLA	6-0-4	Babe Horrell
8.	Duke	8-1-0	Wallace Wade
9.	Iowa	6-1-1	Eddie Anderson
10.	Duquesne	8-0-1	Buff Donelli
11.	Boston College	9-1-0	Frank Leahy
12.	Clemson	8-1-0	Jess Neely
13.	Notre Dame	7-2-0	Elmer Layden
14.	Santa Clara	5-1-3	Buck Shaw
15.	Ohio St	6-2-0	Francis Schmidt
16.	Georgia Tech	7-2-0	Bill Alexander
17.	Fordham	6-2-0	Jim Crowley
18.	Nebraska	7-1-1	Biff Jones
19.	Oklahoma	6-2-1	Tom Stidham
20.	Michigan	6-2-0	Fritz Crisler

#Selected No. 1 by the Dickinson System.

1940

		Record	Coach
1.	Minnesota	8-0-0	Bernie Bierman
2.	Stanford	9-0-0	C. Shaughnessy
3.	Michigan	7-1-0	Fritz Crisler
4.	Tennessee	10-0-0	Bob Neyland
5.	Boston College	10-0-0	Frank Leahy
6.	Texas A&M	8-1-0	Homer Norton
7.	Nebraska	8-1-0	Biff Jones
8.	Northwestern	6-2-0	Pappy Waldorf
9.	Mississippi St	9-0-1	Allyn McKeen
10.	Washington	7-2-0	Jimmy Phelan
11.	Santa Clara	6-1-1	Buck Shaw
12.	Fordham	7-1-0	Jim Crowley
13.	Georgetown	8-1-0	Jack Hagerty
14.	Pennsylvania	6-1-1	George Munger
15.	Cornell	6-2-0	Carl Snavely
16.	SMU	8-1-1	Matty Bell
17.	Hard.-Simmons	9-0-0	Abe Woodson
18.	Duke	7-2-0	Wallace Wade
19.	Lafayette	9-0-0	Hooks Mylin
20.	—		

Only 19 teams selected.

1941

		Record	Coach
1.	Minnesota	8-0-0	Bernie Bierman
2.	Duke	9-0-0	Wallace Wade
3.	Notre Dame	8-0-1	Frank Leahy
4.	Texas	8-1-1	Dana X. Bible
5.	Michigan	6-1-1	Fritz Crisler

Note: Except where indicated with an asterisk, the polls from 1936 through 1964 were taken before the bowl games and those from 1965 through the present were taken after the bowl games.

1941 (Cont.)

	Record	Coach
6. Fordham	7-1-0	Jim Crowley
7. Missouri	8-1-0	Don Faurot
8. Duquesne	8-0-0	Buff Donelli
9. Texas A&M	9-1-0	Homer Norton
10. Navy	7-1-1	Swede Larson
11. Northwestern	5-3-0	Pappy Waldorf
12. Oregon St	7-2-0	Lon Stiner
13. Ohio St	6-1-1	Paul Brown
14. Georgia	8-1-1	Wally Butts
15. Pennsylvania	7-1-1	George Munger
16. Mississippi St	8-1-1	Allyn McKeen
17. Mississippi	6-2-1	Harry Mehre
18. Tennessee	8-2-0	John Barnhill
19. Washington St	6-4-0	Babe Hollingbery
20. Alabama	8-2-0	Frank Thomas

1942

	Record	Coach
1. Ohio St	9-1-0	Paul Brown
2. Georgia	10-1-0	Wally Butts
3. Wisconsin	8-1-1	H. Stuhldreher
4. Tulsa	10-0-0	Henry Frnka
5. Georgia Tech	9-1-0	Bill Alexander
6. Notre Dame	7-2-2	Frank Leahy
7. Tennessee	8-1-1	John Barnhill
8. Boston College	8-1-0	Denny Myers
9. Michigan	7-3-0	Fritz Crisler
10. Alabama	7-3-0	Frank Thomas
11. Texas	8-2-0	Dana X. Bible
12. Stanford	6-4-0	Marchie Schwartz
13. UCLA	7-3-0	Babe Horrell
14. William & Mary	9-1-1	Carl Voyles
15. Santa Clara	7-2-0	Buck Shaw
16. Auburn	6-4-1	Jack Meagher
17. Washington St	6-2-2	Babe Hollingbery
18. Mississippi St	8-2-0	Allyn McKeen
19. Minnesota	5-4-0	George Hauser
Holy Cross	5-4-1	Ank Scanlon
Penn St	6-1-1	Bob Higgins

1943

	Record	Coach
1. Notre Dame	9-1-0	Frank Leahy
2. Iowa Pre-Flight	9-1-0	Don Faurot
3. Michigan	8-1-0	Fritz Crisler
4. Navy	8-1-0	Billick Whelchel
5. Purdue	9-0-0	Elmer Burnham
6. Great Lakes	10-2-0	Tony Hinkle
7. Duke	8-1-0	Eddie Cameron
8. Del Monte P-F	7-1-0	Bill Kern
9. Northwestern	6-2-0	Pappy Waldorf
10. March Field	9-1-0	Paul Schissler
11. Army	7-2-1	Red Blaik
12. Washington	4-0-0	Ralph Welch
13. Georgia Tech	7-3-0	Bill Alexander
14. Texas	7-1-0	Dana X. Bible
15. Tulsa	6-0-1	Henry Frnka
16. Dartmouth	6-1-0	Earl Brown
17. Bainbridge NTS	7-0-0	Joe Maniaci
18. Colorado College	7-0-0	Hal White
19. Pacific	7-2-0	Amos A. Stagg
20. Pennsylvania	6-2-1	George Munger

1944

	Record	Coach
1. Army	9-0-0	Red Blaik
2. Ohio St	9-0-0	Carroll Widdoes
3. Randolph Field	11-0-0	Frank Tritico
4. Navy	6-3-0	Oscar Hagberg
5. Bainbridge NTS	9-0-0	Joe Maniaci
6. Iowa Pre-Flight	10-1-0	Jack Meagher
7. USC	7-0-2	Jeff Cravath
8. Michigan	8-2-0	Fritz Crisler
9. Notre Dame	8-2-0	Ed McKeever
10. March Field	7-1-2	Paul Schissler
11. Duke	5-4-0	Eddie Cameron
12. Tennessee	8-0-1	John Barnhill
13. Georgia Tech	8-2-0	Bill Alexander
Norman P-F	6-0-0	John Gregg
15. Illinois	5-4-1	Ray Eliot
16. El Toro Marines	8-1-0	Dick Hanley
17. Great Lakes	9-2-1	Paul Brown
18. Fort Pierce	9-0-0	Hamp Pool
19. St. Mary's P-F	4-4-0	Jules Sikes
20. 2nd Air Force	7-2-1	Bill Reese

1945

	Record	Coach
1. Army	9-0-0	Red Blaik
2. Alabama	9-0-0	Frank Thomas
3. Navy	7-1-1	Oscar Hagberg
4. Indiana	9-0-1	Bo McMillan
5. Oklahoma A&M	8-0-0	Jim Lookabaugh
6. Michigan	7-3-0	Fritz Crisler
7. St. Mary's (CA)	7-1-0	Jimmy Phelan
8. Pennsylvania	6-2-0	George Munger
9. Notre Dame	7-2-1	Hugh Devore
10. Texas	9-1-0	Dana X. Bible
11. USC	7-3-0	Jeff Cravath
12. Ohio St	7-2-0	Carroll Widdoes
13. Duke	6-2-0	Eddie Cameron
14. Tennessee	8-1-0	John Barnhill
15. LSU	7-2-0	Bernie Moore
16. Holy Cross	8-1-0	John DeGrosa
17. Tulsa	8-2-0	Henry Frnka
18. Georgia	8-2-0	Wally Butts
19. Wake Forest	4-3-1	Peahead Walker
20. Columbia	8-1-0	Lou Little

1946

	Record	Coach
1. Notre Dame	8-0-1	Frank Leahy
2. Army	9-0-1	Red Blaik
3. Georgia	10-0-0	Wally Butts
4. UCLA	10-0-0	B. LaBrucherie
5. Illinois	7-2-0	Ray Eliot
6. Michigan	6-2-1	Fritz Crisler
7. Tennessee	9-1-0	Bob Neyland
8. LSU	9-1-0	Bernie Moore
9. North Carolina	8-1-1	Carl Snavely
10. Rice	8-2-0	Jess Neely
11. Georgia Tech	8-2-0	Bobby Dodd
12. Yale	7-1-1	Howard Odell
13. Pennsylvania	6-2-0	George Munger
14. Oklahoma	7-3-0	Jim Tatum
15. Texas	8-2-0	Dana X. Bible
16. Arkansas	6-3-1	John Barnhill
17. Tulsa	9-1-0	J.O. Brothers
18. North Carolina St	8-2-0	Beattie Feathers
19. Delaware	9-0-0	Bill Murray
20. Indiana	6-3-0	Bo McMillan

1947

		Record	Coach
1.	Notre Dame	9-0-0	Frank Leahy
2.	#Michigan	9-0-0	Fritz Crisler
3.	SMU	9-0-1	Matty Bell
4.	Penn St	9-0-0	Bob Higgins
5.	Texas	9-1-0	Blair Cherry
6.	Alabama	8-2-0	Red Drew
7.	Pennsylvania	7-0-1	George Munger
8.	USC	7-1-1	Jeff Cravath
9.	North Carolina	8-2-0	Carl Snavely
10.	Georgia Tech	9-1-0	Bobby Dodd
11.	Army	5-2-2	Red Blaik
12.	Kansas	8-0-2	George Sauer
13.	Mississippi	8-2-0	Johnny Vaught
14.	William & Mary	9-1-0	Rube McCray
15.	California	9-1-0	Pappy Waldorf
16.	Oklahoma	7-2-1	Bud Wilkinson
17.	North Carolina St	5-3-1	Beattie Feathers
18.	Rice	6-3-1	Jess Neely
19.	Duke	4-3-2	Wallace Wade
20.	Columbia	7-2-0	Lou Little

#The AP, which had voted Notre Dame No. 1 before the bowl games, took a second vote, giving the title to Michigan after its 49–0 win over USC in the Rose Bowl.

1948

		Record	Coach
1.	Michigan	9-0-0	Bennie Oosterbaan
2.	Notre Dame	9-0-1	Frank Leahy
3.	North Carolina	9-0-1	Carl Snavely
4.	California	10-0-0	Pappy Waldorf
5.	Oklahoma	9-1-0	Bud Wilkinson
6.	Army	8-0-1	Red Blaik
7.	Northwestern	7-2-0	Bob Voigts
8.	Georgia	9-1-0	Wally Butts
9.	Oregon	9-1-0	Jim Aiken
10.	SMU	8-1-1	Matty Bell
11.	Clemson	10-0-0	Frank Howard
12.	Vanderbilt	8-2-1	Red Sanders
13.	Tulane	9-1-0	Henry Frnka
14.	Michigan St	6-2-2	Biggie Munn
15.	Mississippi	8-1-0	Johnny Vaught
16.	Minnesota	7-2-0	Bernie Bierman
17.	William & Mary	6-2-2	Rube McCray
18.	Penn St	7-1-1	Bob Higgins
19.	Cornell	8-1-0	Lefty James
20.	Wake Forest	6-3-0	Peahead Walker

1949

		Record	Coach
1.	Notre Dame	10-0-0	Frank Leahy
2.	Oklahoma	10-0-0	Bud Wilkinson
3.	California	10-0-0	Pappy Waldorf
4.	Army	9-0-0	Red Blaik
5.	Rice	9-1-0	Jess Neely
6.	Ohio St	6-1-2	Wes Fesler
7.	Michigan	6-2-1	Bennie Oosterbaan
8.	Minnesota	7-2-0	Bernie Bierman
9.	LSU	8-2-0	Gaynell Tinsley
10.	Pacific	11-0-0	Larry Siemering
11.	Kentucky	9-2-0	Bear Bryant
12.	Cornell	8-1-0	Lefty James
13.	Villanova	8-1-0	Jim Leonard
14.	Maryland	8-1-0	Jim Tatum

1949 (*Cont.*)

		Record	Coach
15.	Santa Clara	7-2-1	Len Casanova
16.	North Carolina	7-3-0	Carl Snavely
17.	Tennessee	7-2-1	Bob Neyland
18.	Princeton	6-3-0	Charlie Caldwell
19.	Michigan St	6-3-0	Biggie Munn
20.	Missouri	7-3-0	Don Faurot
	Baylor	8-2-0	Bob Woodruff

1950

		Record	Coach
1.	Oklahoma	10-0-0	Bud Wilkinson
2.	Army	8-1-0	Red Blaik
3.	Texas	9-1-0	Blair Cherry
4.	Tennessee	10-1-0	Bob Neyland
5.	California	9-0-1	Pappy Waldorf
6.	Princeton	9-0-0	Charlie Caldwell
7.	Kentucky	10-1-0	Bear Bryant
8.	Michigan St	8-1-0	Biggie Munn
9.	Michigan	5-3-1	Bennie Oosterhaan
10.	Clemson	8-0-1	Frank Howard
11.	Washington	8-2-0	Howard Odell
12.	Wyoming	9-0-0	Bowden Wyatt
13.	Illinois	7-2-0	Ray Eliot
14.	Ohio St	6-3-0	Wes Fesler
15.	Miami (FL)	9-0-1	Andy Gustafson
16.	Alabama	9-2-0	Red Drew
17.	Nebraska	6-2-1	Bill Glassford
18.	Washington & Lee	8-2-0	George Barclay
19.	Tulsa	9-1-1	J.O. Brothers
20.	Tulane	6-2-1	Henry Frnka

1951

		Record	Coach
1.	Tennessee	10-0-0	Bob Neyland
2.	Michigan St	9-0-0	Biggie Munn
3.	Maryland	9-0-0	Jim Tatum
4.	Illinois	8-0-1	Ray Eliot
5.	Georgia Tech	10-0-1	Bobby Dodd
6.	Princeton	9-0-0	Charlie Caldwell
7.	Stanford	9-1-0	Chuck Taylor
8.	Wisconsin	7-1-1	Ivy Williamson
9.	Baylor	8-1-1	George Sauer
10.	Oklahoma	8-2-0	Bud Wilkinson
11.	TCU	6-4-0	Dutch Meyer
12.	California	8-2-0	Pappy Waldorf
13.	Virginia	8-1-0	Art Guepe
14.	San Francisco	9-0-0	Joe Kuharich
15.	Kentucky	7-4-0	Bear Bryant
16.	Boston University	6-4-0	Buff Donelli
17.	UCLA	5-3-1	Red Sanders
18.	Washington St	7-3-0	Forest Evashevski
19.	Holy Cross	8-2-0	Eddie Anderson
20.	Clemson	7-2-0	Frank Howard

1952

		Record	Coach
1.	Michigan St	9-0-0	Biggie Munn
2.	Georgia Tech	11-0-0	Bobby Dodd
3.	Notre Dame	7-2-1	Frank Leahy
4.	Oklahoma	8-1-1	Bud Wilkinson
5.	USC	9-1-0	Jess Hill
6.	UCLA	8-1-0	Red Sanders
7.	Mississippi	8-0-2	Johnny Vaught

1952 (Cont.)

		Record	Coach
8.	Tennessee	8-1-1	Bob Neyland
9.	Alabama	9-2-0	Red Drew
10.	Texas	8-2-0	Ed Price
11.	Wisconsin	6-2-1	Ivy Williamson
12.	Tulsa	8-1-1	J.O. Brothers
13.	Maryland	7-2-0	Jim Tatum
14.	Syracuse	7-2-0	Ben Schwartzwalder
15.	Florida	7-3-0	Bob Woodruff
16.	Duke	8-2-0	Bill Murray
17.	Ohio St	6-3-0	Woody Hayes
18.	Purdue	4-3-2	Stu Holcomb
19.	Princeton	8-1-0	Charlie Caldwell
20.	Kentucky	5-4-2	Bear Bryant

1953

		Record	Coach
1.	Maryland	10-0-0	Jim Tatum
2.	Notre Dame	9-0-1	Frank Leahy
3.	Michigan St	8-1-0	Biggie Munn
4.	Oklahoma	8-1-1	Bud Wilkinson
5.	UCLA	8-1-0	Red Sanders
6.	Rice	8-2-0	Jess Neely
7.	Illinois	7-1-1	Ray Eliot
8.	Georgia Tech	8-2-1	Bobby Dodd
9.	Iowa	5-3-1	Forest Evashevski
10.	W Virginia	8-1-0	Art Lewis
11.	Texas	7-3-0	Ed Price
12.	Texas Tech	10-1-0	DeWitt Weaver
13.	Alabama	6-2-3	Red Drew
14.	Army	7-1-1	Red Blaik
15.	Wisconsin	6-2-1	Ivy Williamson
16.	Kentucky	7-2-1	Bear Bryant
17.	Auburn	7-2-1	Shug Jordan
18.	Duke	7-2-1	Bill Murray
19.	Stanford	6-3-1	Chuck Taylor
20.	Michigan	6-3-0	Bennie Oosterbaan

1954

		Record	Coach
1.	Ohio St	9-0-0	Woody Hayes
2.	#UCLA	9-0-0	Red Sanders
3.	Oklahoma	10-0-0	Bud Wilkinson
4.	Notre Dame	9-1-0	Terry Brennan
5.	Navy	7-2-0	Eddie Erdelatz
6.	Mississippi	9-1-0	Johnny Vaught
7.	Army	7-2-0	Red Blaik
8.	Maryland	7-2-1	Jim Tatum
9.	Wisconsin	7-2-0	Ivy Williamson
10.	Arkansas	8-2-0	Bowden Wyatth
11.	Miami (FL)	8-1-0	Andy Gustafson
12.	W Virginia	8-1-0	Art Lewis
13.	Auburn	7-3-0	Shug Jordan
14.	Duke	7-2-1	Bill Murray
15.	Michigan	6-3-0	Bennie Oosterbaan
16.	Virginia Tech	8-0-1	Frank Moseley
17.	USC	8-3-0	Jess Hill
18.	Baylor	7-3-0	George Sauer
19.	Rice	7-3-0	Jess Neely
20.	Penn St	7-2-0	Rip Engle

#Selected No. 1 by UP.

1955

		Record	Coach
1.	Oklahoma	10-0-0	Bud Wilkinson
2.	Michigan St	8-1-0	Duffy Daugherty
3.	Maryland	10-0-0	Jim Tatum
4.	UCLA	9-1-0	Red Sanders
5.	Ohio St	7-2-0	Woody Hayes
6.	TCU	9-1-0	Abe Martin
7.	Georgia Tech	8-1-1	Bobby Dodd
8.	Auburn	8-1-1	Shug Jordan
9.	Notre Dame	8-2-0	Terry Brennan
10.	Mississippi	9-1-0	Johnny Vaught
11.	Pittsburgh	7-3-0	John Michelosen
12.	Michigan	7-2-0	Bennie Oosterbaan
13.	USC	6-4-0	Jess Hill
14.	Miami (FL)	6-3-0	Andy Gustafson
15.	Miami (OH)	9-0-0	Ara Parseghian
16.	Stanford	6-3-1	Chuck Taylor
17.	Texas A&M	7-2-1	Bear Bryant
18.	Navy	6-2-1	Eddie Erdelatz
19.	W Virginia	8-2-0	Art Lewis
20.	Army	6-3-0	Red Blaik

1956

		Record	Coach
1.	Oklahoma	10-0-0	Bud Wilkinson
2.	Tennessee	10-0-0	Bowden Wyatt
3.	Iowa	8-1-0	Forest Evashevski
4.	Georgia Tech.	9-1-0	Bobby Dodd
5.	Texas A&M	9-0-1	Bear Bryant
6.	Miami (FL)	8-1-1	Andy Gustafson
7.	Michigan	7-2-0	Bennie Oosterbaan
8.	Syracuse	7-1-0	Ben Schwartzwalder
9.	Michigan St	7-2-0	Duffy Daugherty
10.	Oregon St	7-2-1	Tommy Prothro
11.	Baylor	8-2-0	Sam Boyd
12.	Minnesota	6-1-2	Murray Warmath
13.	Pittsburgh	7-2-1	John Michelosen
14.	TCU	7-3-0	Abe Martin
15.	Ohio St	6-3-0	Woody Hayes
16.	Navy	6-1-2	Eddie Erdelatz
17.	Geo Washington	7-1-1	Gene Sherman
18.	USC	8-2-0	Jess Hill
19.	Clemson	7-1-2	Frank Howard
20.	Colorado	7-2-1	Dallas Ward
	Penn St	6-2-1	Rip Engle

1957

		Record	Coach
1.	Auburn	10-0-0	Shug Jordan
2.	#Ohio St	8-1-0	Woody Hayes
3.	Michigan St	8-1-0	Duffy Daugherty
4.	Oklahoma	9-1-0	Bud Wilkinson
5.	Navy	8-1-1	Eddie Erdelatz
6.	Iowa	7-1-1	Forest Evashevski
7.	Mississippi	8-1-1	Johnny Vaught
8.	Rice	7-3-0	Jess Neely
9.	Texas A&M	8-2-0	Bear Bryant
10.	Notre Dame	7-3-0	Terry Brennan
11.	Texas	6-3-1	Darrell Royal
12.	Arizona St	10-0-0	Dan Devine
13.	Tennessee	7-3-0	Bowden Wyatt
14.	Mississippi St	6-2-1	Wade Walker
15.	North Carolina St	7-1-2	Earle Edwards
16.	Duke	6-2-2	Bill Murray

1957 (Cont.)

	Record	Coach
17. Florida	6-2-1	Bob Woodruff
18. Army	7-2-0	Red Blaik
19. Wisconsin	6-3-0	Milt Brunt
20. VMI	9-0-1	John McKenna

#Selected No. 1 by UP.

1958

	Record	Coach
1. LSU	10-0-0	Paul Dietzel
2. Iowa	7-1-1	Forest Evashevski
3. Army	8-0-1	Red Blaik
4. Auburn	9-0-1	Shug Jordan
5. Oklahoma	9-1-0	Bud Wilkinson
6. Air Force	9-0-1	Ben Martin
7. Wisconsin	7-1-1	Milt Bruhn
8. Ohio St	6-1-2	Woody Hayes
9. Syracuse	8-1-0	Ben Schwartzwalder
10. TCU	8-2-0	Abe Martin
11. Mississippi	8-2-0	Johnny Vaught
12. Clemson	8-2-0	Frank Howard
13. Purdue	6-1-2	Jack Mollenkopf
14. Florida	6-3-1	Bob Woodruff
15. South Carolina	7-3-0	Warren Giese
16. California	7-3-0	Pete Elliott
17. Notre Dame	6-4-0	Terry Brennan
18. SMU	6-4-0	Bill Meek
19. Oklahoma St	7-3-0	Cliff Speegle
20. Rutgers	8-1-0	John Stiegman

1959

	Record	Coach
1. Syracuse	10-0-0	Ben Schwartzwalder
2. Mississippi	9-1-0	Johnny Vaught
3. LSU	9-1-0	Paul Dietzel
4. Texas	9-1-0	Darrell Royal
5. Georgia	9-1-0	Wally Butts
6. Wisconsin	7-2-0	Milt Bruhn
7. TCU	8-2-0	Abe Martin
8. Washington	9-1-0	Jim Owens
9. Arkansas	8-2-0	Frank Broyles
10. Alabama	7-1-2	Bear Bryant
11. Clemson	8-2-0	Frank Howard
12. Penn St	8-2-0	Rip Engle
13. Illinois	5-3-1	Ray Eliot
14. USC	8-2-0	Don Clark
15. Oklahoma	7-3-0	Bud Wilkinson
16. Wyoming	9-1-0	Bob Devaney
17. Notre Dame	5-5-0	Joe Kuharich
18. Missouri	6-4-0	Dan Devine
19. Florida	5-4-1	Bob Woodruff
20. Pittsburgh	6-4-0	John Michelosen

1960

	Record	Coach
1. Minnesota	8-1-0	Murray Warmath
2. Mississippi	9-0-1	Johnny Vaught
3. Iowa	8-1-0	Forest Evashevski
4. Navy	9-1-0	Wayne Hardin
5. Missouri	9-1-0	Dan Devine
6. Washington	9-1-0	Jim Owens
7. Arkansas	8-2-0	Frank Broyles
8. Ohio St	7-2-0	Woody Hayes
9. Alabama	8-1-1	Bear Bryant

1960 (Cont.)

	Record	Coach
10. Duke	7-3-0	Bill Murray
11. Kansas	7-2-1	Jack Mitchell
12. Baylor	8-2-0	John Bridgers
13. Auburn	8-2-0	Shug Jordan
14. Yale	9-0-0	Jordan Oliver
15. Michigan St	6-2-1	Duffy Daugherty
16. Penn St	6-3-0	Rip Engle
17. New Mexico St	10-0-0	Warren Woodson
18. Florida	8-2-0	Ray Graves
19. Syracuse	7-2-0	Ben Schwartzwalder
Purdue	4-4-1	Jack Mollenkopf

1961

	Record	Coach
1. Alabama	10-0-0	Bear Bryant
2. Ohio St	8-0-1	Woody Hayes
3. Texas	9-1-0	Darrell Royal
4. LSU	9-1-0	Paul Dietzel
5. Mississippi	9-1-0	Johnny Vaught
6. Minnesota	7-2-0	Murray Warmath
7. Colorado	9-1-0	Sonny Grandelius
8. Michigan St	7-2-0	Duffy Daugherty
9. Arkansas	8-2-0	Frank Broyles
10. Utah St	9-0-1	John Ralston
11. Missouri	7-2-1	Dan Devine
12. Purdue	6-3-0	Jack Mollenkopf
13. Georgia Tech	7-3-0	Bobby Dodd
14. Syracuse	7-3-0	Ben Schwartzwalder
15. Rutgers	9-0-0	John Bateman
16. UCLA	7-3-0	Bill Barnes
17. Rice	7-3-0	Jess Neely
Penn St	7-3-0	Rip Engle
Arizona	8-1-1	Jim LaRue
20. Duke	7-3-0	Bill Murray

1962

	Record	Coach
1. USC	10-0-0	John McKay
2. Wisconsin	8-1-0	Milt Bruhn
3. Mississippi	9-0-0	Johnny Vaught
4. Texas	9-0-1	Darrell Royal
5. Alabama	9-1-0	Bear Bryant
6. Arkansas	9-1-0	Frank Broyles
7. LSU	8-1-1	Charlie McClendon
8. Oklahoma	8-2-0	Bud Wilkinson
9. Penn St	9-1-0	Rip Engle
10. Minnesota	6-2-1	Murray Warmath
11–20: UPI		
11. Georgia Tech	7-2-1	Bobby Dodd
12. Missouri	7-1-2	Dan Devine
13. Ohio St	6-3-0	Woody Hayes
14. Duke	8-2-0	Bill Murray
Washington	7-1-2	Jim Owens
16. Northwestern	7-2-0	Ara Parseghian
Oregon St	8-2-0	Tommy Prothro
18. Arizona St	7-2-1	Frank Kush
Miami (FL)	7-3-0	Andy Gustafson
Illinois	2-7-0	Pete Elliott

1963

	Record	Coach
1. Texas	10-0-0	Darrell Royal
2. Navy	9-1-0	Wayne Hardin
3. Illinois	7-1-1	Pete Elliott

1963 (Cont.)

	Record	Coach
4. Pittsburgh	9-1-0	John Michelosen
5. Auburn	9-1-0	Shug Jordan
6. Nebraska	9-1-0	Bob Devaney
7. Mississippi	7-0-2	Johnny Vaught
8. Alabama	8-2-0	Bear Bryant
9. Oklahoma	8-2-0	Bud Wilkinson
10. Michigan St	6-2-1	Duffy Daugherty
11–20: UPI		
11. Mississippi St	6-2-2	Paul Davis
12. Syracuse	8-2-0	Ben Schwartzwalder
13. Arizona St	8-1-0	Frank Kush
14. Memphis St	9-0-1	Billy J. Murphy
15. Washington	6-4-0	Jim Owens
16. Penn St	7-3-0	Rip Engle
USC	7-3-0	John McKay
Missouri	7-3-0	Dan Devine
19. North Carolina	8-2-0	Jim Hickey
20. Baylor	7-3-0	John Bridgers

1964

	Record	Coach
1. Alabama	10-0-0	Bear Bryant
2. Arkansas	10-0-0	Frank Broyles
3. Notre Dame	9-1-0	Ara Parseghian
4. Michigan	8-1-0	Bump Elliott
5. Texas	9-1-0	Darrell Royal
6. Nebraska	9-1-0	Bob Devaney
7. LSU	7-2-1	Charlie McClendon
8. Oregon St	8-2-0	Tommy Prothro
9. Ohio St	7-2-0	Woody Hayes
10. USC	7-3-0	John McKay
11–20: UPI		
11. Florida St	8-1-1	Bill Peterson
12. Syracuse	7-3-0	Ben Schwartzwalder
13. Princeton	9-0-0	Dick Colman
14. Penn St	6-4-0	Rip Engle
Utah	8-2-0	Ray Nagel
16. Illinois	6-3-0	Pete Elliott
New Mexico	9-2-0	Bill Weeks
18. Tulsa	8-2-0	Glenn Dobbs
19. Missouri	6-3-1	Dan Devine
20. Mississippi	5-4-1	Johnny Vaught
Michigan St	4-5-1	Duffy Daugherty

1965

	Record	Coach
1. Alabama	9-1-1	Bear Bryant
2. #Michigan St	10-1-0	Duffy Daugherty
3. Arkansas	10-1-0	Frank Broyles
4. UCLA	8-2-1	Tommy Prothro
5. Nebraska	10-1-0	Bob Devaney
6. Missouri	8-2-1	Dan Devine
7. Tennessee	8-1-2	Doug Dickey
8. LSU	8-3-0	Charlie McClendon
9. Notre Dame	7-2-1	Ara Parseghian
10. USC	7-2-1	John McKay
11–20: UPI		
11. Texas Tech	8-2-0	J.T. King
12. Ohio St	7-2-0	Woody Hayes
13. Florida	7-3-0	Ray Graves
14. Purdue	7-2-1	Jack Mollenkopf
15. Georgia	6-4-0	Vince Dooley
16. Tulsa	8-2-0	Glenn Dobbs
17. Mississippi	6-4-0	Johnny Vaught

1965 (Cont.)

	Record	Coach
18. Kentucky	6-4-0	Charlie Bradshaw
19 Syracuse	7-3-0	Ben Schwartzwalder
20. Colorado	6-2-2	Eddie Crowder

#Selected No. 1 by UPI.

1966*

	Record	Coach
1. Notre Dame	9-0-1	Ara Parseghian
2. Michigan St	9-0-1	Duffy Daugherty
3. Alabama	10-0-0	Bear Bryant
4. Georgia	9-1-0	Vince Dooley
5. UCLA	9-1-0	Tommy Prothro
6. Nebraska	9-1-0	Bob Devaney
7. Purdue	8-2-0	Jack Mollenkopf
8. Georgia Tech	9-1-0	Bobby Dodd
9. Miami (FL)	7-2-1	Charlie Tate
10. SMU	8-2-0	Hayden Fry
11–20: UPI		
11. Florida	8-2-0	Ray Graves
12. Mississippi	8-2-0	Johnny Vaught
13. Arkansas	8-2-0	Frank Broyles
14. Tennessee	7-3-0	Doug Dickey
15. Wyoming	9-1-0	Lloyd Eaton
16. Syracuse	8-2-0	Ben Schwartzwalder
17. Houston	8-2-0	Bill Yeoman
18. USC	7-3-0	John McKay
19. Oregon St	7-3-0	Dee Andros
20. Virginia Tech	8-1-1	Jerry Claiborne

1967*

	Record	Coach
1. USC	9-1-0	John McKay
2. Tennessee	9-1-0	Doug Dickey
3. Oklahoma	9-1-0	Chuck Fairbanks
4. Indiana	9-1-0	John Pont
5. Notre Dame	8-2-0	Ara Parseghian
6. Wyoming	10-0-0	Lloyd Eaton
7. Oregon St	7-2-1	Dee Andros
8. Alabama	8-1-1	Bear Bryant
9. Purdue	8-2-0	Jack Mollenkopf
10. Penn St	8-2-0	Joe Paterno
11–20: UPI†		
11. UCLA	7-2-1	Tommy Prothro
12. Syracuse	8-2-0	Ben Schwartzwalder
13. Colorado	8-2-0	Eddie Crowder
14. Minnesota	8-2-0	Murray Warmath
15. Florida St	7-2-1	Bill Peterson
16. Miami (FL)	7-3-0	Charlie Tate
17. North Carolina St	8-2-0	Earle Edwards
18. Georgia	7-3-0	Vince Dooley
19. Houston	9-2-0	Bill Yeoman
20. Arizona St	8-2-0	Frank Kush

†UPI ranked Penn St 11th and did not rank Alabama, which was on probation.

1968

	Record	Coach
1. Ohio St	10-0-0	Woody Hayes
2. Penn St	11-0-0	Joe Paterno
3. Texas	9-1-1	Darrell Royal
4. USC	9-1-1	John McKay
5. Notre Dame	7-2-1	Ara Parseghian

Annual Associated Press Top 20 (*Cont.*)

1968 (*Cont.*)

		Record	Coach
6.	Arkansas	10-1-0	Frank Broyles
7.	Kansas	9-2-0	Pepper Rodgers
8.	Georgia	8-1-2	Vince Dooley
9.	Missouri	8-3-0	Dan Devine
10.	Purdue	8-2-0	Jack Mollenkopf
11.	Oklahoma	7-4-0	Chuck Fairbanks
12.	Michigan	8-2-0	Bump Elliott
13.	Tennessee	8-2-1	Doug Dickey
14.	SMU	8-3-0	Hayden Fry
15.	Oregon St	7-3-0	Dee Andros
16.	Auburn	7-4-0	Shug Jordan
17.	Alabama	8-3-0	Bear Bryant
18.	Houston	6-2-2	Bill Yeoman
19.	LSU	8-3-0	Charlie McClendon
20.	Ohio	10-1-0	Bill Hess

1969

		Record	Coach
1.	Texas	11-0-0	Darrell Royal
2.	Penn St	11-0-0	Joe Paterno
3.	USC	10-0-1	John McKay
4.	Ohio St	8-1-0	Woody Hayes
5.	Notre Dame	8-2-1	Ara Parseghian
6.	Missouri	9-2-0	Dan Devine
7.	Arkansas	9-2-0	Frank Broyles
8.	Mississippi	8-3-0	Johnny Vaught
9.	Michigan	8-3-0	Bo Schembechler
10.	LSU	9-1-0	Charlie McClendon
11.	Nebraska	9-2-0	Bob Devaney
12.	Houston	9-2-0	Bill Yeoman
13.	UCLA	8-1-1	Tommy Prothro
14.	Florida	9-1-1	Ray Graves
15.	Tennessee	9-2-0	Doug Dickey
16.	Colorado	8-3-0	Eddie Crowder
17.	W Virginia	10-0-1	Jim Carlen
18.	Purdue	8-2-0	Jack Mollenkopf
19.	Stanford	7-2-1	John Ralston
20.	Auburn	8-3-0	Shug Jordan

1970

		Record	Coach
1.	Nebraska	11-0-1	Bob Devaney
2.	Notre Dame	10-1-0	Ara Parseghian
3.	#Texas	10-1-0	Darrell Royal
4.	Tennessee	11-0-1	Bill Battle
5.	Ohio St	9-1-0	Woody Hayes
6.	Arizona St	11-0-0	Frank Kush
7.	LSU	9-3-0	Charlie McClendon
8.	Stanford	9-3-0	John Ralston
9.	Michigan	9-1-0	Bo Schembechler
10.	Auburn	9-2-0	Shug Jordan
11.	Arkansas	9-2-0	Frank Broyles
12.	Toledo	12-0-0	Frank Lauterbur
13.	Georgia Tech	9-3-0	Bud Carson
14.	Dartmouth	9-0-0	Bob Blackman
15.	USC	6-4-1	John McKay
16.	Air Force	9-3-0	Ben Martin
17.	Tulane	8-4-0	Jim Pittman
18.	Penn St	7-3-0	Joe Paterno
19.	Houston	8-3-0	Bill Yeoman
20.	Oklahoma	7-4-1	Chuck Fairbanks
	Mississippi	7-4-0	Johnny Vaught

#Selected No. 1 by UPI.

1971

		Record	Coach
1.	Nebraska	13-0-0	Bob Devaney
2.	Oklahoma	11-1-0	Chuck Fairbanks
3.	Colorado	10-2-0	Eddie Crowder
4.	Alabama	11-1-0	Bear Bryant
5.	Penn St	11-1-0	Joe Paterno
6.	Michigan	11-1-0	Bo Schembechler
7.	Georgia	11-1-0	Vince Dooley
8.	Arizona St	11-1-0	Frank Kush
9.	Tennessee	10-2-0	Bill Battle
10.	Stanford	9-3-0	John Ralston
11.	LSU	9-3-0	Charlie McClendon
12.	Auburn	9-2-0	Shug Jordan
13.	Notre Dame	8-2-0	Ara Parseghian
14.	Toledo	12-0-0	John Murphy
15.	Mississippi	10-2-0	Billy Kinard
16.	Arkansas	8-3-1	Frank Broyles
17.	Houston	9-3-0	Bill Yeoman
18.	Texas	8-3-0	Darrell Royal
19.	Washington	8-3-0	Jim Owens
20.	USC	6-4-1	John McKay

1972

		Record	Coach
1.	USC	12-0-0	John McKay
2.	Oklahoma	11-1-0	Chuck Fairbanks
3.	Texas	10-1-0	Darrell Royal
4.	Nebraska	9-2-1	Bob Devaney
5.	Auburn	10-1-0	Shug Jordan
6.	Michigan	10-1-0	Bo Schembechler
7.	Alabama	10-2-0	Bear Bryant
8.	Tennessee	10-2-0	Bill Battle
9.	Ohio St	9-2-0	Woody Hayes
10.	Penn St	10-2-0	Joe Paterno
11.	LSU	9-2-1	Charlie McClendon
12.	North Carolina	11-1-0	Bill Dooley
13.	Arizona St	10-2-0	Frank Kush
14.	Notre Dame	8-3-0	Ara Parseghian
15.	UCLA	8-3-0	Pepper Rodgers
16.	Colorado	8-4-0	Eddie Crowder
17.	North Carolina St	8-3-1	Lou Holtz
18.	Louisville	9-1-0	Lee Corso
19.	Washington St	7-4-0	Jim Sweeney
20.	Georgia Tech	7-4-1	Bill Fulch

1973

		Record	Coach
1.	Notre Dame	11-0-0	Ara Parseghian
2.	Ohio St	10-0-1	Woody Hayes
3.	Oklahoma	10-0-1	Barry Switzer
4.	#Alabama	11-1-0	Bear Bryant
5.	Penn St	12-0-0	Joe Paterno
6.	Michigan	10-0-1	Bo Schembechler
7.	Nebraska	9-2-1	Tom Osborne
8.	USC	9-2-1	John McKay
9.	Arizona St	11-1-0	Frank Kush
	Houston	11-1-0	Bill Yeoman
11.	Texas Tech	11-1-0	Jim Carlen
12.	UCLA	9-2-0	Pepper Rodgers
13.	LSU	9-3-0	Charlie McClendon
14.	Texas	8-3-0	Darrell Royal
15.	Miami (OH)	11-0-0	Bill Mallory
16.	North Carolina St	9-3-0	Lou Holtz
17.	Missouri	8-4-0	Al Onofrio
18.	Kansas	7-4-1	Don Fambrough

Annual Associated Press Top 20 (Cont.)

1973 (Cont.)

		Record	Coach
19.	Tennessee	8-4-0	Bill Battle
20.	Maryland	8-4-0	Jerry Claiborne
	Tulane	9-3-0	Bennie Ellender

#Selected No. 1 by UPI.

1974

		Record	Coach
1.	Oklahoma	11-0-0	Barry Switzer
2.	#USC	10-1-1	John McKay
3.	Michigan	10-1-0	Bo Schembechler
4.	Ohio St	10-2-0	Woody Hayes
5.	Alabama	11-1-0	Bear Bryant
6.	Notre Dame	10-2-0	Ara Parseghian
7.	Penn St	10-2-0	Joe Paterno
8.	Auburn	10-2-0	Shug Jordan
9.	Nebraska	9-3-0	Tom Osborne
10.	Miami (Ohio)	10-0-1	Dick Crum
11.	North Carolina St	9-2-1	Lou Holtz
12.	Michigan St	7-3-1	Denny Stolz
13.	Maryland	8-4-0	Jerry Claiborne
14.	Baylor	8-4-0	Grant Teaff
15.	Florida	8-4-0	Doug Dickey
16.	Texas A&M	8-3-0	Emory Ballard
17.	Mississippi St	9-3-0	Bob Tyler
	Texas	8-4-0	Darrell Royal
19.	Houston	8-3-1	Bill Yeoman
20.	Tennessee	7-3-2	Bill Battle

#Selected No. 1 by UPI

1975

		Record	Coach
1.	Oklahoma	11-1-0	Barry Switzer
2.	Arizona St	12-0-0	Frank Kush
3.	Alabama	11-1-0	Bear Bryant
4.	Ohio St	11-1-0	Woody Hayes
5.	UCLA	9-2-1	Dick Vermeil
6.	Texas	10-2-0	Darrell Royal
7.	Arkansas	10-2-0	Frank Broyles
8.	Michigan	8-2-2	Bo Schembechler
9.	Nebraska	10-2-0	Tom Osborne
10.	Penn St	9-3-0	Joe Paterno
11.	Texas A&M	10-2-0	Emory Bellard
12.	Miami (OH)	11-1-0	Dick Crum
13.	Maryland	9-2-1	Jerry Claiborne
14.	California	8-3-0	Mike White
15.	Pittsburgh	8-4-0	Johnny Majors
16.	Colorado	9-3-0	Bill Mallory
17.	USC	8-4-0	John McKay
18.	Arizona	9-2-0	Jim Young
19.	Georgia	9-3-0	Vince Dooley
20.	W Virginia	9-3-0	Bobby Bowden

1976

		Record	Coach
1.	Pittsburgh	12-0-0	Johnny Majors
2.	USC	11-1-0	John Robinson
3.	Michigan	10-2-0	Bo Schembechler
4.	Houston	10-2-0	Bill Yeoman
5.	Oklahoma	9-2-1	Barry Switzer
6.	Ohio St	9-2-1	Woody Hayes
7.	Texas A&M	10-2-0	Emory Bellard
8.	Maryland	11-1-0	Jerry Claiborne

1976 (Cont.)

		Record	Coach
9.	Nebraska	9-3-1	Tom Osborne
10.	Georgia	10-2-0	Vince Dooley
11.	Alabama	9-3-0	Bear Bryant
12.	Notre Dame	9-3-0	Dan Devine
13.	Texas Tech	10-2-0	Steve Sloan
14.	Oklahoma St	9-3-0	Jim Stanley
15.	UCLA	9-2-1	Terry Donahue
16.	Colorado	8-4-0	Bill Mallory
17.	Rutgers	11-0-0	Frank Burns
18.	Kentucky	9-3-0	Fran Curci
19.	Iowa St	8-3-0	Earle Bruce
20.	Mississippi St	9-2-0	Bob Tyler

1977

		Record	Coach
1.	Notre Dame	11-1-0	Dan Devine
2.	Alabama	11-1-0	Bear Bryant
3.	Arkansas	11-1-0	Lou Holtz
4.	Texas	11-1-0	Fred Akers
5.	Penn St	11-1-0	Joe Paterno
6.	Kentucky	10-1-0	Fran Curci
7.	Oklahoma	10-2-0	Barry Switzer
8.	Pittsburgh	9-2-1	Jackie Sherrill
9.	Michigan	10-2-0	Bo Schembechler
10.	Washington	10-2-0	Don James
11.	Ohio St	9-3-0	Woody Hayes
12.	Nebraska	9-3-0	Tom Osborne
13.	USC	8-4-0	John Robinson
14.	Florida St	10-2-0	Bobby Bowden
15.	Stanford	9-3-0	Bill Walsh
16.	San Diego St	10-1-0	Claude Gilbert
17.	North Carolina	8-3-1	Bill Dooley
18.	Arizona St	9-3-0	Frank Kush
19.	Clemson	8-3-1	Charley Pell
20.	BYU	9-2-0	LaVell Edwards

1978

		Record	Coach
1.	Alabama	11-1-0	Bear Bryant
2.	#USC	12-1-0	John Robinson
3.	Oklahoma	11-1-0	Barry Switzer
4.	Penn St	11-1-0	Joe Paterno
5.	Michigan	10-2-0	Bo Schembechler
6.	Clemson	11-1-0	Charley Pell
7.	Notre Dame	9-3-0	Dan Devine
8.	Nebraska	9-3-0	Tom Osborne
9.	Texas	9-3-0	Fred Akers
10.	Houston	9-3-0	Bill Yeoman
11.	Arkansas	9-2-1	Lou Holtz
12.	Michigan St	8-3-0	Darryl Rogers
13.	Purdue	9-2-1	Jim Young
14.	UCLA	8-3-1	Terry Donahue
15.	Missouri	8-4-0	Warren Powers
16.	Georgia	9-2-1	Vince Dooley
17.	Stanford	8-4-0	Bill Walsh
18.	North Carolina St	9-3-0	Bo Rein
19.	Texas A&M	8-4-0	Emory Bellard (4–2) Tom Wilson (4–2)
20.	Maryland	9-3-0	Jerry Claiborne

#Selected No. 1 by UPI.

Annual Associated Press Top 20 (*Cont.*)

1979

		Record	Coach
1.	Alabama	12-0-0	Bear Bryant
2.	USC	11-0-1	John Robinson
3.	Oklahoma	11-1-0	Barry Switzer
4.	Ohio St	11-1-0	Earle Bruce
5.	Houston	11-1-0	Bill Yeoman
6.	Florida St	11-1-0	Bobby Bowden
7.	Pittsburgh	11-1-0	Jackie Sherrill
8.	Arkansas	10-2-0	Lou Holtz
9.	Nebraska	10-2-0	Tom Osborne
10.	Purdue	10-2-0	Jim Young
11.	Washington	10-1-0	Don James
12.	Texas	9-3-0	Fred Akers
13.	BYU	11-1-0	LaVell Edwards
14.	Baylor	8-4-0	Grant Teaff
15.	North Carolina	8-3-1	Dick Crum
16.	Auburn	8-3-0	Doug Barfield
17.	Temple	10-2-0	Wayne Hardin
18.	Michigan	8-4-0	Bo Schembechler
19.	Indiana	8-4-0	Lee Corso
20.	Penn St	8-4-0	Joe Paterno

1980

		Record	Coach
1.	Georgia	12-0-0	Vince Dooley
2.	Pittsburgh	11-1-0	Jackie Sherrill
3.	Oklahoma	10-2-0	Barry Switzer
4.	Michigan	10-2-0	Bo Schembechler
5.	Florida St	10-2-0	Bobby Bowden
6.	Alabama	10-2-0	Bear Bryant
7.	Nebraska	10-2-0	Tom Osborne
8.	Penn St	10-2-0	Joe Paterno
9.	Notre Dame	9-2-1	Dan Devine
10.	North Carolina	11-1-0	Dick Crum
11.	USC	8-2-1	John Robinson
12.	BYU	12-1-0	LaVell Edwards
13.	UCLA	9-2-0	Terry Donahue
14.	Baylor	10-2-0	Grant Teaff
15.	Ohio St	9-3-0	Earle Bruce
16.	Washington	9-3-0	Don James
17.	Purdue	9-3-0	Jim Young
18.	Miami (FL)	9-3-0	H. Schnellenberger
19.	Mississippi St	9-3-0	Emory Bellard
20.	SMU	8-4-0	Ron Meyer

1981

		Record	Coach
1.	Clemson	12-0-0	Danny Ford
2.	Texas	10-1-1	Fred Akers
3.	Penn St	10-2-0	Joe Paterno
4.	Pittsburgh	11-1-0	Jackie Sherrill
5.	SMU	10-1-0	Ron Meyer
6.	Georgia	10-2-0	Vince Dooley
7.	Alabama	9-2-1	Bear Bryant
8.	Miami (FL)	9-2-0	H. Schnellenberger
9.	North Carolina	10-2-0	Dick Crum
10.	Washington	10-2-0	Don James
11.	Nebraska	9-3-0	Tom Osborne
12.	Michigan	9-3-0	Bo Schembechler
13.	BYU	11-2-0	LaVell Edwards
14.	USC	9-3-0	John Robinson
15.	Ohio St	9-3-0	Earle Bruce
16.	Arizona St	9-2-0	Darryl Rogers
17.	W Virginia	9-3-0	Don Nehlen

1981 (*Cont.*)

		Record	Coach
18.	Iowa	8-4-0	Hayden Fry
19.	Missouri	8-4-0	Warren Powers
20.	Oklahoma	7-4-1	Barry Switzer

1982

		Record	Coach
1.	Penn St	11-1-0	Joe Paterno
2.	SMU	11-0-1	Bobby Collins
3.	Nebraska	12-1-0	Tom Osborne
4.	Georgia	11-1-0	Vince Dooley
5.	UCLA	10-1-1	Terry Donahue
6.	Arizona St	10-2-0	Darryl Rogers
7.	Washington	10-2-0	Don James
8.	Clemson	9-1-1	Danny Ford
9.	Arkansas	9-2-1	Lou Holtz
10.	Pittsburgh	9-3-0	Foge Fazio
11.	LSU	8-3-1	Jerry Stovall
12.	Ohio St	9-3-0	Earle Bruce
13.	Florida St	9-3-0	Bobby Bowden
14.	Auburn	9-3-0	Pat Dye
15.	USC	8-3-0	John Robinson
16.	Oklahoma	8-4-0	Barry Switzer
17.	Texas	9-3-0	Fred Akers
18.	North Carolina	8-4-0	Dick Crum
19.	W Virginia	9-3-0	Don Nehlen
20.	Maryland	8-4-0	Bobby Ross

1983

		Record	Coach
1.	Miami (Fla.)	11-1-0	H. Schnellenberger
2.	Nebraska	12-1-0	Tom Osborne
3.	Auburn	11-1-0	Pat Dye
4.	Georgia	10-1-1	Vince Dooley
5.	Texas	11-1-0	Fred Akers
6.	Florida	9-2-1	Charlie Pell
7.	BYU	11-1-0	LaVell Edwards
8.	Michigan	9-3-0	Bo Schembechler
9.	Ohio St	9-3-0	Earle Bruce
10.	Illinois	10-2-0	Mike White
11.	Clemson	9-1-1	Danny Ford
12.	SMU	10-2-0	Bobby Collins
13.	Air Force	10-2-0	Ken Hatfield
14.	Iowa	9-3-0	Hayden Fry
15.	Alabama	8-4-0	Ray Perkins
16.	W Virginia	9-3-0	Don Nehlen
17.	UCLA	7-4-1	Terry Donahue
18.	Pittsburgh	8-3-1	Foge Fazio
19.	Boston College	9-3-0	Jack Bicknell
20.	E Carolina	8-3-0	Ed Emory

1984

		Record	Coach
1.	BYU	13-0-0	LaVell Edwards
2.	Washington	11-1-0	Don James
3.	Florida	9-1-1	Chas Pell (0-1-1) Galen Hall (9-0)
4.	Nebraska	10-2-0	Tom Osborne
5.	Boston College	10-2-0	Jack Bicknell
6.	Oklahoma	9-2-1	Barry Switzer
7.	Oklahoma St	10-2-0	Pat Jones
8.	SMU	10-2-0	Bobby Collins
9.	UCLA	9-3-0	Terry Donahue

Annual Associated Press Top 20 (Cont.)

1984 (Cont.)

	Record	Coach
10. USC	10-3-0	Ted Tollner
11. South Carolina	10-2-0	Joe Morrison
12. Maryland	9-3-0	Bobby Ross
13. Ohio St	9-3-0	Earle Bruce
14. Auburn	9-4-0	Pat Dye
15. LSU	8-3-1	Bill Arnsparger
16. Iowa	8-4-1	Hayden Fry
17. Florida St	7-3-2	Bobby Bowden
18. Miami (Fla.)	8-5-0	Jimmy Johnson
19. Kentucky	9-3-0	Jerry Claiborne
20. Virginia	8-2-2	George Welsh

1985

	Record	Coach
1. Oklahoma	11-1-0	Barry Switzer
2. Michigan	10-1-1	Bo Schembechler
3. Penn St	11-1-0	Joe Paterno
4. Tennessee	9-1-2	Johnny Majors
5. Florida	9-1-1	Galen Hall
6. Texas A&M	10-2-0	Jackie Sherrill
7. UCLA	9-2-1	Terry Donahue
8. Air Force	12-1-0	Fisher DeBerry
9. Miami (Fla.)	10-2-0	Jimmy Johnson
10. Iowa	10-2-0	Hayden Fry
11. Nebraska	9-3-0	Tom Osborne
12. Arkansas	10-2-0	Ken Hatfield
13. Alabama	9-2-1	Ray Perkins
14. Ohio St	9-3-0	Earle Bruce
15. Florida St	9-3-0	Bobby Bowden
16. BYU	11-3-0	LaVell Edwards
17. Baylor	9-3-0	Grant Teaff
18. Maryland	9-3-0	Bobby Ross
19. Georgia Tech.	9-2-1	Bill Curry
20. LSU	9-2-1	Bill Arnsparger

1986

	Record	Coach
1. Penn St	12-0-0	Joe Paterno
2. Miami (Fla.)	11-1-0	Jimmy Johnson
3. Oklahoma	11-1-0	Barry Switzer
4. Arizona St	10-1-1	John Cooper
5. Nebraska	10-2-0	Tom Osborne
6. Auburn	10-2-0	Pat Dye
7. Ohio St	10-3-0	Earle Bruce
8. Michigan	11-2-0	Bo Schembechler
9. Alabama	10-3-0	Ray Perkins
10. LSU	9-3-0	Bill Arnsparger
11. Arizona	9-3-0	Larry Smith
12. Baylor	9-3-0	Grant Teaff
13. Texas A&M	9-3-0	Jackie Sherrill
14. UCLA	8-3-1	Terry Donahue
15. Arkansas	9-3-0	Ken Hatfield
16. Iowa	9-3-0	Hayden Fry
17. Clemson	8-2-2	Danny Ford
18. Washington	8-3-1	Don James
19. Boston College	9-3-0	Jack Bicknell
20. Virginia Tech.	9-2-1	Bill Dooley

†In 1989 the AP expanded its final poll to 25 teams.

1987

	Record	Coach
1. Miami (Fla.)	12-0-0	Jimmy Johnson
2. Florida St	11-1-0	Bobby Bowden
3. Oklahoma	11-1-0	Barry Switzer
4. Syracuse	11-0-1	Dick MacPherson
5. LSU	10-1-1	Mike Archer
6. Nebraska	10-2-0	Tom Osborne
7. Auburn	9-1-2	Pat Dye
8. Michigan St	9-2-1	George Perles
9. UCLA	10-2-0	Terry Donahue
10. Texas A&M	10-2-0	Jackie Sherrill
11. Oklahoma St	10-2-0	Pat Jones
12. Clemson	10-2-0	Danny Ford
13. Georgia	9-3-0	Vince Dooley
14. Tennessee	10-2-1	Johnny Majors
15. South Carolina	8-4-0	Joe Morrison
16. Iowa	10-3-0	Hayden Fry
17. Notre Dame	8-4-0	Lou Holtz
18. USC	8-4-0	Larry Smith
19. Michigan	8-4-0	Bo Schembechler
20. Arizona St	7-4-1	John Cooper

1988

	Record	Coach
1. Notre Dame	12-0-0	Lou Holtz
2. Miami (Fla.)	11-1-0	Jimmy Johnson
3. Florida St	11-1-0	Bobby Bowden
4. Michigan	9-2-1	Bo Schembechler
5. West Virginia	11-1-0	Don Nehlen
6. UCLA	10-2-0	Terry Donahue
7. USC	10-2-0	Larry Smith
8. Auburn	10-2-0	Pat Dye
9. Clemson	10-2-0	Danny Ford
10. Nebraska	11-2-0	Tom Osborne
11. Oklahoma St	10-2-0	Pat Jones
12. Arkansas	10-2-0	Ken Hatfield
13. Syracuse	10-2-0	Dick MacPherson
14. Oklahoma	9-3-0	Barry Switzer
15. Georgia	9-3-0	Vince Dooley
16. Washington St	9-3-0	Dennis Erickson
17. Alabama	9-3-0	Bill Curry
18. Houston	9-3-0	Jack Pardee
19. LSU	8-4-0	Mike Archer
20. Indiana	8-3-1	Bill Mallor

†1989

	Record	Coach
1. Miami (Fla.)	11-1-0	Dennis Erickson
2. Notre Dame	12-1-0	Lou Holtz
3. Florida St	10-2-0	Bobby Bowden
4. Colorado	11-1-0	Bill McCartney
5. Tennessee	11-1-0	Johnny Majors
6. Auburn	10-2-0	Pat Dye
7. Michigan	10-2-0	Bo Schembechler
8. USC	9-2-1	Larry Smith
9. Alabama	10-2-0	Bill Curry
10. Illinois	10-2-0	John Mackovic
11. Nebraska	10-2-0	Tom Osborne
12. Clemson	10-2-0	Danny Ford
13. Arkansas	10-2-0	Ken Hatfield
14. Houston	9-2-0	Jack Pardee
15. Penn St	8-3-1	Joe Paterno
16. Michigan St	8-4-0	George Perles
17. Pittsburgh	8-3-1	Mike Gottfried
18. Virginia	10-3-0	George Welsh

†1989 (Cont.)

	Record	Coach
19. Texas Tech	9-3-0	Spike Dykes
20. Texas A&M	8-4-0	R.C. Slocum
21. W Virginia	8-3-1	Don Nehlen
22. BYU	10-3-0	LaVell Edwards
23. Washington	8-4-0	Don James
24. Ohio St	8-4-0	John Cooper
25. Arizona	8-4-0	Dick Tomey

1990

	Record	Coach
1. Colorado	11-1-1	Bill McCartney
2. #Ga. Tech (UPI)	11-0-1	Bobby Ross
3. Miami (Fla.)	10-2-0	Dennis Erickson
4. Florida St	10-2-0	Bobby Bowden
5. Washington	10-2-0	Don James
6. Notre Dame	9-3-0	Lou Holtz
7. Michigan	9-3-0	Gary Moeller
8. Tennessee	9-2-2	Johnny Majors
9. Clemson	10-2-0	Ken Hatfield
10. Houston	10-1-0	John Jenkins
11. Penn St	9-3-0	Joe Paterno
12. Texas	10-2-0	David McWilliams
13. Florida	9-2-0	Steve Spurrier
14. Louisville	10-1-1	H. Schnellenberger
15. Texas A&M	9-3-1	R.C. Slocum
16. Michigan St	8-3-1	George Perles
17. Oklahoma	8-3-0	Gary Gibbs
18. Iowa	8-4-0	Hayden Fry
19. Auburn	8-3-1	Pat Dye
20. USC I	8-4-1	Larry Smith
21. Mississippi	9-3-0	Billy Brewer
22. BYU	10-3-0	LaVell Edwards
23. Virginia	8-4-0	George Wells
24. Nebraska	9-3-0	Tom Osborne
25. Illinois	8-4-0	John Mackovic

1991

	Record	Coach
1. Miami (Fla.)	12-0-0	Dennis Erickson
2. #Washington	12-0-0	Don James
3. Penn St	11-2-0	Joe Paterno
4. Florida St	11-2-0	Bobby Bowden
5. Alabama	11-1-0	Gene Stallings
6. Michigan	10-2-0	Gary Moeller
7. Florida	10-2-0	Steve Spurrier
8. California	10-2-0	Bruce Snyder
9. E Carolina	11-1-0	Bill Lewis
10. Iowa	10-1-1	Hayden Fry
11. Syracuse	10-2-0	Paul Pasqualoni
12. Texas A&M	10-2-0	R.C. Slocum
13. Notre Dame	10-3-0	Lou Holtz
14. Tennessee	9-3-0	Johnny Majors
15. Nebraska	9-2-1	Tom Osborne
16. Oklahoma	9-3-0	Gary Gibbs
17. Georgia	9-3-0	Ray Goff
18. Clemson	9-2-1	Ken Hatfield
19. UCLA	9-3-0	Terry Donahue
20. Colorado	8-3-1	Bill McCartney
21. Tulsa	10-2-0	David Rader
22. Stanford	8-4-0	Dennis Green
23. BYU	8-3-2	LaVell Edwards
24. North Carolina St	9-3-0	Dick Sheridan
25. Air Force	10-3-0	Fisher DeBerry

#Selected No. 1 by *USA Today*/CNN.

1992

	Record	Coach
1. Alabama	13-0-0	Gene Stallings
2. Florida St	11-1-0	Bobby Bowden
3. Miami	11-1-0	Dennis Erickson
4. Notre Dame	10-1-1	Lou Holtz
5. Michigan	9-0-3	Gary Moeller
6. Syracuse	10-2-0	Paul Pasqualoni
7. Texas A&M	12-1-0	R.C. Slocum
8. Georgia	10-2-0	Ray Goff
9. Stanford	10-3-0	Bill Walsh
10. Florida	9-4-0	Steve Spurrier
11. Washington	9-3-0	Don James
12. Tennessee	9-3-0	Johnny Majors
13. Colorado	9-2-1	Bill McCartney
14. Nebraska	9-3-0	Tom Osborne
15. Washington St	9-3-0	Mike Price
16. Mississippi	9-3-0	Billy Brewer
17. North Carolina St	9-3-1	Dick Sheridan
18. Ohio St	8-3-1	John Cooper
19. North Carolina	9-3-0	Mack Brown
20. Hawaii	11-2-0	Bob Wagner
21. Boston College	8-3-1	Tom Coughlin
22. Kansas	8-4-0	Glen Mason
23. Mississippi St	7-5-0	Jackie Sherrill
24. Fresno St	9-4-0	Jim Sweeney
25. Wake Forest	8-4-0	Bill Dooley

1993

	Record	Coach
1. Florida St	12-1-0	Bobby Bowden
2. Notre Dame	11-1-0	Lou Holtz
3. Nebraska	11-1-0	Tom Osborne
4. Auburn	11-0-0	Terry Bowden
5. Florida	11-2-0	Steve Spurrier
6. Wisconsin	10-1-1	Barry Alvarez
7. W Virginia	11-1-0	Don Nehlen
8. Penn St	10-2-0	Joe Paterno
9. Texas A&M	10-2-0	R.C. Slocum
10. Arizona	10-2-0	Dick Tomey
11. Ohio St	10-1-1	John Cooper
12. Tennessee	9-2-1	Phil Fulmer
13. Boston College	9-3-0	Tom Coughlin
14. Alabama	9-3-1	Gene Stallings
15. Miami	9-3-0	Dennis Erickson
16. Colorado	8-3-1	Bill McCartney
17. Oklahoma	9-3-0	Gary Gibbs
18. UCLA	8-4-0	Terry Donahue
19. North Carolina	10-3-0	Mack Brown
20. Kansas St	9-2-1	Bill Snyder
21. Michigan	8-4-0	Gary Moeller
22. Virginia Tech	9-3-0	Frank Beamer
23. Clemson	9-3-0	Ken Hatfield
24. Louisville	9-3-0	H. Schnellenberger
25. California	9-4-0	Keith Gilbertson

1994

	Record	Coach
1. Nebraska	13-0-0	Tom Osborne
2. Penn St	12-0-0	Joe Paterno
3. Colorado	11-1-0	Bill McCartney
4. Florida St	10-1-1	Bobby Bowden
5. Alabama	12-1-0	Gene Stallings
6. Miami (Fla.)	10-2-0	Dennis Erickson
7. Florida	10-2-1	Steve Spurrier
8. Texas A&M	10-0-1	R.C. Slocum

†In 1989 the AP expanded its final poll to 25 teams.

Annual Associated Press Top 25 (Cont.)

1994 (Cont.)

		Record	Coach
9.	Auburn	9-1-1	Terry Bowden
10.	Utah	10-2-0	Ron McBride
11.	Oregon	9-4-0	Rich Brooks
12.	Michigan	8-4-0	Gary Moeller
13.	USC	8-3-1	John Robinson
14.	Ohio St	9-4-0	John Cooper
15.	Virginia	9-3-0	George Welsh
16.	Colorado St	10-2-0	Sonny Lubick
17.	North Carolina St	9-3-0	Mike O'Cain
18.	BYU	10-3-0	LaVell Edwards
19.	Kansas St	9-3-0	Bill Snyder
20.	Arizona	8-4-0	Dick Tomey
21.	Washington St	8-4-0	Mike Price
22.	Tennessee	8-4-0	Phillip Fulmer
23.	Boston College	7-4-1	Dan Henning
24.	Mississippi St	8-4-0	Jackie Sherrill
25.	Texas	8-4-0	John Mackovic

1995

		Record	Coach
1.	Nebraska	12-0-0	Tom Osborne
2.	Florida	12-1-0	Steve Spurrier
3.	Tennessee	11-1-0	Phillip Fulmer
4.	Florida St	10-2-0	Bobby Bowden
5.	Colorado	10-2-0	Rick Neuheisel
6.	Ohio St	11-2-0	John Cooper
7.	Kansas St	10-2-0	Bill Snyder
8.	Northwestern	10-2-0	Gary Barnett
9.	Kansas	10-2-0	Glen Mason
10.	Virginia Tech	10-2-0	Frank Beamer
11.	Notre Dame	9-3-0	Lou Holtz
12.	USC	9-2-1	John Robinson
13.	Penn St	9-3-0	Joe Paterno
14.	Texas	10-2-1	John Mackovic
15.	Texas A&M	9-3-0	S.C. Slocum
16.	Virginia	9-4-0	George Welsh
17.	Michigan	9-4-0	Lloyd Carr
18.	Oregon	9-3-0	Mike Bellotti
19.	Syracuse	9-3-0	Paul Pasqualoni
20.	Miami (Fla.)	8-3-0	Butch Davis
21.	Alabama	8-3-0	Gene Stallings
22.	Auburn	8-4-0	Terry Bowden
23.	Texas Tech	9-3-0	Spike Dykes
24.	Toledo	11-0-1	Gary Pinkel
25.	Iowa	8-4-0	Hayden Fry

1996

		Record*	Coach
1.	Florida	12–1	Steve Spurrier
2.	Ohio St	11–1	John Cooper
3.	Florida St	11–1	Bobby Bowden
4.	Arizona St	11–1	Bruce Snyder
5.	BYU	14–1	LaVell Edwards
6.	Nebraska	11–2	Tom Osborne
7.	Penn St	11–2	Joe Paterno
8.	Colorado	10–2	Rick Neuheisel
9.	Tennessee	10–2	Phillip Fulmer
10.	North Carolina	10–2	Mack Brown
11.	Alabama	10–3	Gene Stallings
12.	LSU	10–2	Gerry DiNardo
13.	Virginia Tech	10–2	Frank Beamer
14.	Miami (Fla.)	9–3	Butch Davis
15.	Northwestern	9–3	Gary Barnett

*In 1996 the NCAA introduced overtime to break ties.

1996 (Cont.)

		Record	Coach
16.	Washington	9–3	Jim Lambright
17.	Kansas St	9–3	Bill Snyder
18.	Iowa	9–3	Hayden Fry
19.	Notre Dame	8–3	Lou Holtz
20.	Michigan	8–4	Lloyd Carr
21.	Syracuse	9–3	Paul Pasqualoni
22.	Wyoming	10–2	Joe Tiller
23.	Texas	8–5	John Mackovic
24.	Auburn	8–4	Terry Bowden
25.	Army	10–2	Bob Sutton

1997

		Record	Coach
1.	Michigan	12–0	Lloyd Carr
2.	Nebraska	13–0	Tom Osborne
3.	Florida St	11–1	Bobby Bowden
4.	Florida	10–2	Steve Spurrier
5.	UCLA	10–2	Bob Toledo
6.	North Carolina	11–1	Mack Brown
7.	Tennessee	11–2	Phillip Fulmer
8.	Kansas St	11–1	Bill Snyder
9.	Washington St	10–2	Mike Price
10.	Georgia	10–2	Jim Donnan
11.	Auburn	10–3	Terry Bowden
12.	Ohio St	10–3	John Cooper
13.	LSU	9–3	Gerry DiNardo
14.	Arizona St	8–3	Bruce Snyder
15.	Purdue	9–3	Joe Tiller
16.	Penn St	9–3	Joe Paterno
17.	Colorado St	11–2	Sonny Lubick
18.	Washington	8–4	Jim Lambright
19.	Southern Mississippi	9–3	Jeff Bower
20.	Texas A&M	9–4	R. C. Slocum
21.	Syracuse	9–4	Paul Pasqualoni
22.	Mississippi	8–4	Tommy Tuberville
23.	Missouri	7–5	Larry Smith
24.	Oklahoma St	8–4	Bob Simmons
25.	Georgia Tech	7–5	George O'Leary

1998

		Record	Coach
1.	Tennessee	13–0	Phillip Fulmer
2.	Ohio St	11–1	John Cooper
3.	Florida St	11–2	Bobby Bowden
4.	Arizona	12–1	Dick Tomey
5.	Florida	10–2	Steve Spurrier
6.	Wisconsin	11–1	Barry Alvarez
7.	Tulane	12–0	Tommy Bowden
8.	UCLA	10–2	Bob Toledo
9.	Georgia Tech	10–2	George O'Leary
10.	Kansas St	11–2	Bill Snyder
11.	Texas A&M	11–3	R.C. Slocum
12.	Michigan	10–3	Lloyd Carr
13.	Air Force	12–1	Fisher DeBerry
14.	Georgia	9–3	Jim Donnan
15.	Texas	9–3	Mack Brown
16.	Arkansas	9–3	Houston Nutt
17.	Penn St	9–3	Joe Paterno
18.	Virginia	9–3	George Welsh
19.	Nebraska	9–4	Frank Solich
20.	Miami (Fla.)	9–3	Butch Davis
21.	Missouri	8–4	Larry Smith
22.	Notre Dame	9–3	Bob Davie
23.	Virginia Tech	9–3	Frank Beamer

1998 (Cont.)

		Record	Coach
24.	Purdue	9–4	Joe Tiller
25.	Syracuse	8–4	Paul Pasqualoni

1999

		Record	Coach
1.	Florida St	12–0	Bobby Bowden
2.	Virginia Tech	11–1	Frank Beamer
3.	Nebraska	12–1	Frank Solich
4.	Wisconsin	10–2	Barry Alvarez
5.	Michigan	10–2	Lloyd Carr
6.	Kansas St	11–1	Bill Snyder
7.	Michigan St	10–2	Nick Saban
8.	Alabama	10–3	Mike DuBose
9.	Tennessee	9–3	Phillip Fulmer
10.	Marshall	13–0	Bob Pruett
11.	Penn St	10–3	Joe Paterno
12.	Florida	9–4	Steve Spurrier
13.	Mississippi St	10–2	Jackie Sherrill
14.	Southern Miss	9–3	Jeff Bower
15.	Miami (Fla.)	9–4	Butch Davis
16.	Georgia	8–4	Jim Donnan
17.	Arkansas	8–4	Houston Nutt
18.	Minnesota	8–4	Glen Mason
19.	Oregon	9–3	Mike Bellotti
20.	Georgia Tech	8–4	Goerge O'Leary
21.	Texas	9–5	Mack Brown
22.	Mississippi	8–4	David Cutcliffe
23.	Texas A&M	8–4	R.C. Slocum
24.	Illinois	8–4	Ron Turner
25.	Purdue	7–5	Joe Tiller

2000

		Record	Coach
1.	Oklahoma	13–0	Bob Stoops
2.	Miami (Fla.)	11–1	Butch Davis
3.	Washington	11–1	Rick Neuheisel
4.	Oregon St	11–1	Dennis Erickson
5.	Florida St	11–2	Bobby Bowden
6.	Virginia Tech	11–1	Frank Beamer
7.	Oregon	10–2	Mike Belotti
8.	Nebraska	10–2	Frank Solich
9.	Kansas St	11–3	Bill Snyder
10.	Florida	10–3	Steve Spurrier
11.	Michigan	9–3	Lloyd Carr
12.	Texas	9–3	Mack Brown
13.	Purdue	8–4	Joe Tiller
14.	Colorado St	10–2	Sonny Lubeck
15.	Notre Dame	9–3	Bob Davie
16.	Clemson	9–3	Tommy Bowden
17.	Georgia Tech	9–3	George O'Leary
18.	Auburn	9–4	Tommy Tuberville
19.	South Carolina	8–4	Lou Holtz
20.	Georgia	8–4	Jim Donnan
21.	TCU	10–2	Dennis Franchione
22.	LSU	8–4	Nick Saban
23.	Wisconsin	9–4	Barry Alvarez
24.	Mississippi St	8–4	Jackie Sherrill
25.	Iowa St	9–3	Dan McCarney

2001

		Record	Coach
1.	Miami (Fla.)	12–0	Larry Coker
2.	Oregon	11–1	Mike Belotti
3.	Florida	10–2	Steve Spurrier
4.	Tennessee	11–2	Phillip Fulmer

2001

		Record	Coach
5.	Texas	11–2	Mack Brown
6.	Oklahoma	11–2	Bob Stoops
7.	LSU	10–3	Nick Saban
8.	Nebraska	11–2	Frank Solich
9.	Colorado	10–3	Gary Barnett
10.	Washington St	10–2	Mike Price
11.	Maryland	10–2	Ralph Friedgen
12.	Illinois	10–2	Ron Turner
13.	South Carolina	9–3	Lou Holtz
14.	Syracuse	10–3	Paul Pasqualoni
15.	Florida St	8–4	Bobby Bowden
16.	Stanford	9–3	Tyrone Willingham
17.	Louisville	11–2	John Smith
18.	Virginia Tech	8–4	Frank Beamer
19.	Washington	8–4	Rick Neuheisel
20.	Michigan	8–4	Lloyd Carr
21.	Boston College	8–4	Tom O'Brien
22.	Georgia	8–4	Mark Richt
23.	Toledo	10–2	Tom Amstutz
24.	Georgia Tech	8–5	George O'Leary
25.	BYU	12–2	Gary Crowton

2002

		Record	Coach
1.	Ohio St	14–0	Jim Tressel
2.	Miami (Fla.)	12–1	Larry Coker
3.	Georgia	13–1	Mark Richt
4.	USC	11–2	Pete Carroll
5.	Oklahoma	12–2	Bob Stoops
6.	Texas	11–2	Mack Brown
7.	Kansas St	11–2	Bill Snyder
8.	Iowa	11–2	Kirk Ferentz
9.	Michigan	10–3	Lloyd Carr
10.	Washington St	10–3	Mike Price
11.	Alabama	10–3	Dennis Franchione
12.	North Carolina St	11–3	Chuck Amato
13.	Maryland	11–3	Ralph Friedgen
14.	Auburn	9–4	Tommy Tuberville
15.	Boise St	12–1	Dan Hawkins
16.	Penn St	9–4	Joe Paterno
17.	Notre Dame	10–3	Tyrone Willingham
18.	Virginia Tech	10–4	Frank Beamer
19.	Pittsburgh	9–4	Walt Harris
20.	Colorado	9–5	Gary Barnett
21.	Florida St	9–5	Bobby Bowden
22.	Viriginia	9–5	Al Groh
23.	TCU	10–2	Gary Patterson
24.	Marshall	11–2	Bob Pruett
25.	W Virginia	9–4	Rich Rodriguez

2003

		Record	Coach
1.	USC	12–1	Pete Carroll
2.	LSU*	13–1	Nick Saban
3.	Oklahoma	12–2	Bob Stoops
4.	Ohio St	11–2	Jim Tressel
5.	Miami (Fla.)	11–2	Larry Coker
6.	Michigan	10–3	Lloyd Carr
7.	Georgia	11–3	Mark Richt
8.	Iowa	10–3	Kirk Ferentz
9.	Washington St	10–3	Bill Doba
10.	Miami (Ohio)	13–1	Terry Hoeppner
11.	Florida St	10–3	Bobby Bowden
12.	Texas	10–3	Mack Brown
13.	Kansas St	11–4	Bill Snyder
	Mississippi	10–3	David Cutcliffe

Annual Associated Press Top 25 *(Cont.)*

2003

	Team	Record	Coach
15.	Tennessee	10–3	Phillip Fulmer
16.	Boise St	13–1	Dan Hawkins
17.	Maryland	10–3	Ralph Friedgen
18.	Nebraska	10–3	Frank Solich/Bo Pelini
	Purdue	9–4	Joe Tiller
20.	Minnesota	10–3	Glen Mason
21.	Utah	10–2	Urban Meyer
22.	Clemson	9–4	Tommy Bowden
23.	Bowling Green	11–3	Gregg Brandon
24.	Florida	8–5	Ron Zook
25.	TCU	11–2	Gary Patterson

*Ranked No. 1 in *USAToday*/ESPN Poll.

2004

	Team	Record	Coach
1.	USC	13-0	Pete Carroll
2.	Auburn	13-0	Tommy Tuberville
3.	Oklahoma	12-1	Bob Stoops
4.	Utah	12-0	Kyle Whittingham
5.	Texas	11-1	Mack Brown
6.	Louisville	11-1	Bobby Petrino
7.	Georgia	10-2	Mark Richt
8.	Iowa	10-2	Kirk Ferentz
9.	California	10-2	Jeff Tedford
10.	Virginia Tech	10-3	Frank Beamer
11.	Miami	9-3	Larry Coker
12.	Tennessee	10-3	Phillip Fulmer
13.	Michigan	9-3	Lloyd Carr
14.	Florida	8-5	Ron Zook
15.	Michigan	9-3	Lloyd Carr
16.	LSU	9-3	Les Miles
17.	Wisconsin	9-3	Barry Alvarez
18.	Texas Tech	8-4	Mike Leach
19.	Arizona St	9-3	Dirk Koetter
20.	Ohio St	8-4	Jim Tressel
21.	Boston College	9-3	Tom O'Brien
22.	Fresno St	9-3	Pat Hill
23.	Virginia	8-4	Al Groh
24.	Navy	10-2	Paul Johnson
25.	Pittsburgh	8-4	Walt Harris

2005

	Team	Record	Coach
1.	Texas	13-0	Mack Brown
2.	USC	12-1	Pete Carroll
3.	Penn St	11-1	Joe Paterno
4.	Ohio St	10-2	Jim Tressel
5.	Texas	11-1	Mack Brown
6.	LSU	11-2	Les Miles
7.	Virginia Tech	10-3	Frank Beamer
8.	Alabama	10-2	Mike Shula
9.	Notre Dame	9-3	Charlie Weis
10.	Georgia	10-3	Mark Richt
11.	TCU	11-1	Gary Patterson
12.	Florida	9-3	Urban Meyer
12.	Oregon	10-2	Mike Bellotti
14.	Auburn	9-3	Tommy Tuberville
15.	Wisconsin	9-3	Barry Alvarez
15.	Michigan	9-3	Lloyd Carr
16.	UCLA	10-2	Karl Dorrell
17.	Miami (Fla.)	9-3	Larry Coker
18.	Boston College	9-3	Tom O'Brien
19.	Louisville	9-3	Bobby Petrino
20.	Texas Tech	9-3	Mike Leach
21.	Clemson	8-4	Tommy Bowden
22.	Oklahoma	8-4	Bob Stoops

2005

	Team	Record	Coach
23.	Florida St	8-5	Bobby Bowden
24.	Nebraska	8-4	Bill Callahan
25.	California	8-4	Jeff Tedford

2006

	Team	Record	Coach
1.	Florida	13-1	Urban Meyer
2.	Ohio St	12-1	Jim Tressel
3.	LSU	11-2	Les Miles
4.	USC	11-2	Pete Carroll
5.	Boise St	13-0	Chris Petersen
6.	Louisville	12-1	Steve Kragthorpe
7.	Wisconsin	12-1	Bret Bielema
8.	Michigan	11-2	Lloyd Carr
9.	Auburn	11-2	Tommy Tuberville
10.	West Virginia	11-2	Rich Rodriguez
11.	Oklahoma	11-3	Bob Stoops
12.	Rutgers	11-2	Greg Schiano
13.	Texas	10-3	Mack Brown
14.	California	10-3	Jeff Tedford
15.	Arkansas	10-4	Houston Nutt
16.	BYU	11-2	Bronco Mendenhall
17.	Notre Dame	10-3	Charlie Weis
18.	Wake Forest	11-3	Jim Grobe
19.	Virginia Tech	10-3	Frank Beamer
20.	Boston College	10-3	Jeff Jagodzinski
21.	Oregon St	10-4	Mike Riley
22.	TCU	11-2	Gary Patterson
23.	Georgia	9-4	Mark Richt
24.	Penn St	9-4	Joe Paterno
25.	Tennessee	9-4	Phillip Fulmer

2007

	Team	Record	Coach
1.	LSU	12-2	Les Miles
2.	Georgia	11-2	Mark Richt
3.	USC	11-2	Pete Carroll
4.	Missouri	12-2	Gary Pinkell
5.	Ohio St	11-2	Jim Tressel
6.	West Virginia	11-2	Rich Rodriguez
7.	Kansas	12-1	Mark Mangino
8.	Oklahoma	11-3	Bob Stoops
9.	Virginia Tech	11-3	Frank Beamer
10.	Texas	10-3	Mack Brown
10.	Boston College	11-3	Jeff Jagodzinski
12.	Tennessee	10-4	Philip Fulmer
13.	Florida	9-4	Urban Meyer
14.	BYU	11-2	Bronco Mendenhall
15.	Auburn	9-4	Tommy Tuberville
16.	Arizona St	10-3	Dennis Erickson
17.	Cincinnati	10-3	Brian Kelly
18.	Michigan	9-4	Lloyd Carr
19.	Hawaii	12-1	June Jones
20.	Illinois	9-4	Ron Zook
21.	Clemson	9-4	Tommy Bowden
22.	Texas Tech	9-4	Mike Leach
23.	Oregon	9-4	Mike Bellotti
24.	Wisconsin	9-4	Bret Bielema
25.	Oregon St	9-4	Mike Riley

NCAA Divisional Championships

Football Championship Subdivision (Div. I-AA)

Year	Winner	Runner-Up	Score
1978	Florida A&M	Massachusetts	35–28
1979	Eastern Kentucky	Lehigh	30–7
1980	Boise St	Eastern Kentucky	31–29
1981	Idaho St	Eastern Kentucky	34–23
1982	Eastern Kentucky	Delaware	17–14
1983	Southern Illinois	Western Carolina	43–7
1984	Montana St	Louisiana Tech	19–6
1985	Georgia Southern	Furman	44–42
1986	Georgia Southern	Arkansas St	48–21
1987	NE Louisiana	Marshall	43–42
1988	Furman	Georgia Southern	17–12
1989	Georgia Southern	Stephen F. Austin St	37–34
1990	Georgia Southern	Nevada-Reno	36–13
1991	Youngstown St	Marshall	25–17
1992	Marshall	Youngstown St	31–28
1993	Youngstown St	Marshall	17–5
1994	Youngstown St	Boise St	28–14
1995	Montana	Marshall	22–20
1996	Marshall	Montana	49–29
1997	Youngstown St	McNesse St	10–9
1998	Massachusetts	Georgia Southern	55–43
1999	Georgia Southern	Youngstown St	59–24
2000	Georgia Southern	Montana	27–25
2001	Montana	Furman	13–6
2002	Western Kentucky	McNeese St	34–14
2003	Delaware	Colgate	40–0
2004	James Madison	Montana	31–21
2005	Appalachian St	Northern Iowa	21–16
2006	Appalachian St	Massachusetts	28–17
2007	Appalachian St	Delaware	49–21

Division II

Year	Winner	Runner-Up	Score
1973	Louisiana Tech	Western Kentucky	34–0
1974	Central Michigan	Delaware	54–14
1975	Northern Michigan	Western Kentucky	16–14
1976	Montana St	Akron	24–13
1977	Lehigh	Jacksonville St	33–0
1978	Eastern Illinois	Delaware	10–9
1979	Delaware	Youngstown St	38–21
1980	Cal Poly SLO	Eastern Illinois	21–13
1981	SW Texas St	North Dakota St	42–13
1982	SW Texas St	UC–Davis	34–9
1983	North Dakota St	Central St (Ohio)	41–21
1984	Troy St	North Dakota St	18–17
1985	North Dakota St	North Alabama	35–7
1986	North Dakota St	South Dakota	27–7
1987	Troy St	Portland St	31–17
1988	North Dakota St	Portland St	35–21
1989	Mississippi College	Jacksonville St	3–0
1990	N Dakota St	Indiana (Pa.)	51–11
1991	Pittsburg St	Jacksonville St	23–6
1992	Jacksonville St	Pittsburg St	17–13
1993	North Alabama	Indiana (Pa.)	41–34
1994	North Alabama	Texas A&M–Kingsville	16–10
1995	North Alabama	Pittsburg St	27–7
1996	Northern Colorado	Carson-Newman	23–14
1997	Northern Colorado	New Haven	51–0
1998	NW Missouri St	Carson-Newman	24–6
1999	NW Missouri St	Carson-Newman	58–52 (OT)
2000	Delta St	Bloomsburg	63–34
2001	Grand Valley St	North Dakota	17–14
2002	Grand Valley St	Valdosta St	31–24
2003	Grand Valley St	North Dakota	10–3
2004	Valdosta State	Pittsburg State	36–31
2005	Grand Valley St	NW Missouri St	21–17

NCAA Divisional Championships *(Cont.)*

Division II *(Cont.)*

Year	Winner	Runner-Up	Score
2006	Grand Valley St	NW Missouri St	17–14
2007	Valdosta St	NW Missouri St.	25-20

Division III

Year	Winner	Runner-Up	Score
1973	Wittenberg	Juniata	41–0
1974	Central (Iowa)	Ithaca	10–8
1975	Wittenberg	Ithaca	28–0
1976	St. John's (Minn.)	Towson St	31–28
1977	Widener	Wabash	39–36
1978	Baldwin-Wallace	Wittenberg	24–10
1979	Ithaca	Wittenberg	14–10
1980	Dayton	Ithaca	63–0
1981	Widener	Dayton	17–10
1982	W Georgia	Augustana (Ill.)	14–0
1983	Augustana (Ill.)	Union (N.Y.)	21–17
1984	Augustana (Ill.)	Central (Iowa)	21–12
1985	Augustana (Ill.)	Ithaca	20–7
1986	Augustana (Ill.)	Salisbury St	31–3
1987	Wagner	Dayton	19–3
1988	Ithaca	Central (Iowa)	39–24
1989	Dayton	Union (N.Y.)	17–7
1990	Allegheny	Lycoming	21–14 (OT)
1991	Ithaca	Dayton	34–20
1992	WI-LaCrosse	Washington & Jefferson	16–12
1993	Mount Union	Rowan	34–24
1994	Albion	Washington & Jefferson	38–15
1995	WI-LaCrosse	Rowan	36–7
1996	Mount Union	Rowan	56–24
1997	Mount Union	Lycoming	61–12
1998	Mount Union	Rowan	44–24
1999	Pacific Lutheran	Rowan	42–13
2000	Mount Union	St. John's (Minn.)	10–7
2001	Mount Union	Bridgewater	30–27
2002	Mount Union	Trinity (Tex.)	48–7
2003	St. John's (Minn.)	Mount Union	24–6
2004	Linfield	Mary Hardin-Baylor	28–21
2005	Mount Union	UW-Whitewater	35–28
2006	Mount Union	UW-Whitewater	35–16
2007	UW-Whitewater	Mount Union	31–21

NAIA Divisional Championships

Division I

Year	Winner	Runner-Up	Score
1956	St. Joseph's (Ind.)/Montana St		0–0
1957	Pittsburg St (Kan.)	Hillsdale	27–26
1958	NE Oklahoma	Northern Arizona	19–13
1959	Texas A&I	Lenoir-Rhyne	20–7
1960	Lenoir-Rhyne	Humboldt St	15–14
1961	Pittsburg St (Kan.)	Linfield	12–7
1962	Central St (Okla.)	Lenoir-Rhyne	28–13
1963	St. John's (Minn.)	Prairie View	33–27
1964	Concordia-Moorhead/ Sam Houston St		7–7
1965	St. John's (Minn.)	Linfield	33–0
1966	Waynesburg	UW-Whitewater	42–21
1967	Fairmont St	Eastern Washington	28–21
1968	Troy St (Mich.)	Texas A&I	43–35
1969	Texas A&I	Concordia-Moorhead (Minn.)	32–7
1970	Texas A&I	Wofford	48–7
1971	Livingston (Ala.)	Arkansas Tech	14–12
1972	E Texas St	Carson-Newman	21–18
1973	Abilene Christian	Elon	42–14

NAIA Divisional Championships (Cont.)

Division I (Cont.)

Year	Winner	Runner-Up	Score
1974	Texas A&I	Henderson St	34–23
1975	Texas A&I	Salem (W.V.)	37–0
1976	Texas A&I	Central Arkansas	26–0
1977	Abilene Christian	SW Oklahoma	24–7
1978	Angelo St	Elon	34–14
1979	Texas A&I	Central St (Okla.)	20–14
1980	Elon	NE Oklahoma	17–10
1981	Elon	Pittsburg St	3–0
1982	Central St (Okla.)	Mesa	14–11
1983	Carson-Newman	Mesa	36–28
1984	Carson-Newman/Central Arkansas		19–19
1985	Central Arkansas/Hillsdale		10–10
1986	Carson-Newman	Cameron	17–0
1987	Cameron	Carson-Newman	30–2
1988	Carson-Newman	Adams St (Col.)	56–21
1989	Carson-Newman	Emporia St	34–20
1990	Central St (Ohio)	Mesa St	38–16
1991	Central Arkansas	Central St (Ohio)	19–16
1992	Central St (Ohio)	Gardner-Webb	19–16
1993	E Central (Okla.)	Glenville St	49–35
1994	Northeastern St (Okla.)	Arkansas–Pine Bluff	13–12
1995	Central St (Ohio)	Northeastern St (Okla.)	37–7
1996	SW Oklahoma St	Montana Tech	33–31
1997	Findlay	Willamette	14–7
1998	Azusa Pacific	Olivet Nazarene	17–14
1999	Northwestern Oklahoma St	Georgetown (Ky.)	34–26
2000	Georgetown (Ken.)	Northwestern Oklahoma St	20–0
2001	Georgetown (Ken.)	Sioux Falls	49–27
2002	Carroll (Mont.)	Georgetown (Ky.)	28–7
2003	Carroll (Mont.)	Northwestern Oklahoma St	41–28
2004	Carroll (Mont.)	St. Francis (Ind.)	15–13
2005	Carroll (Mont.)	St. Francis (Ind.)	27–10
2006	Sioux Falls (S.D.)	St. Francis (Ind.)	23–19
2007	Carroll (Mont.)	Sioux Falls (S.D.)	17–9

Division II†

Year	Winner	Runner-Up	Score
1970	Westminster (Pa.)	Anderson	21–16
1971	California Lutheran	Westminster (Pa.)	30–14
1972	Missouri Southern	Northwestern (Iowa)	21–14
1973	Northwestern (Iowa)	Glenville St	10–3
1974	Texas Lutheran	Missouri Valley	42–0
1975	Texas Lutheran	California Lutheran	34–8
1976	Westminster (Pa.)	Redlands	20–13
1977	Westminster (Pa.)	California Lutheran	17–9
1978	Concordia-Moorhead (Minn.)	Findlay	7–0
1979	Findlay	Northwestern (Iowa)	51–6
1980	Pacific Lutheran	Wilmington (Ohio)	38–10
1981	Austin Coll./Conc.-Moorhead (Minn.)		24–24
1982	Linfield	William Jewell	33–15
1983	Northwestern (Iowa)	Pacific Lutheran	25–21
1984	Linfield	Northwestern (Iowa)	33–22
1985	WI-La Crosse	Pacific Lutheran	24–7
1986	Linfield	Baker	17–0
1987	Pacific Lutheran	UW-Stevens Point*	16–16
1988	Westminster (Pa.)	UW-La Crosse	21–14
1989	Westminster (Pa.)	UW-La Crosse	51–30
1990	Peru St	Westminster (Pa.)	17–7
1991	Georgetown (Ky.)	Pacific Lutheran	28–20
1992	Findlay	Linfield	26–13
1993	Pacific Lutheran	Westminster (Pa.)	50–20
1994	Westminster (Pa.)	Pacific Lutheran	27–7
1995	Findlay	Central Washington	21–21
1996	Sioux Falls (S.D.)	Western Washington	47–25

*Forfeited 1987 season due to use of an ineligible player. †In 1997 the NAIA consolidated its two divisions into one.

Heisman Memorial Trophy

Awarded to the best college player by the Downtown Athletic Club of New York City. The trophy is named after John W. Heisman, who coached Georgia Tech to the national championship in 1917 and later served as DAC athletic director.

Year	Winner, College, Position	Winner's Season Statistics	Runner-Up, College
1935	...Jay Berwanger, Chicago, HB	Rush: 119 Yds: 577 TD: 6	Monk Meyer, Army
1936	...Larry Kelley, Yale, E	Rec: 17 Yds: 372 TD: 6	Sam Francis, Nebraska
1937	...Clint Frank, Yale, HB	Rush: 157 Yds: 667 TD: 11	Byron White, Colorado
1938	...†Davey O'Brien, TCU, QB	Att/Comp: 194/110 Yds: 1733 TD: 19	Marshall Goldberg, Pittsburgh
1939	...Nile Kinnick, Iowa, HB	Rush: 106 Yds: 374 TD: 5	Tom Harmon, Michigan
1940	...Tom Harmon, Michigan, HB	Rush: 191 Yds: 852 TD: 16	John Kimbrough, Texas A&M
1941	...†Bruce Smith, Minnesota, HB	Rush: 98 Yds: 480 TD: 6	Angelo Bertelli, Notre Dame
1942	...Frank Sinkwich, Georgia, HB	Att/Comp: 166/84 Yds: 1392 TD: 10	Paul Governali, Columbia
1943	...Angelo Bertelli, Notre Dame, QB	Att/Comp: 36/25 Yds: 511 TD: 10	Bob Odell, Pennsylvania
1944	...Les Horvath, Ohio State, QB	Rush: 163 Yds: 924 TD: 12	Glenn Davis, Army
1945	...*†Doc Blanchard, Army, FB	Rush: 101 Yds: 718 TD: 13	Glenn Davis, Army
1946	...Glenn Davis, Army, HB	Rush: 123 Yds: 712 TD: 7	Charley Trippi, Georgia
1947	...†John Lujack, Notre Dame, QB	Att/Comp: 109/61 Yds: 777 TD: 9	Bob Chappius, Michigan
1948	...*Doak Walker, SMU, HB	Rush: 108 Yds: 532 TD: 8	Charlie Justice, North Carolina
1949	...†Leon Hart, Notre Dame, E	Rec: 19 Yds: 257 TD: 5	Charlie Justice, North Carolina
1950	...*Vic Janowicz, Ohio St, HB	Att/Comp: 77/32 Yds: 561 TD: 12	Kyle Rote, SMU
1951	...Dick Kazmaier, Princeton, HB	Rush: 149 Yds: 861 TD: 9	Hank Lauricella, Tennessee
1952	...Billy Vessels, Oklahoma, HB	Rush: 167 Yds: 1072 TD: 17	Jack Scarbath, Maryland
1953	...John Lattner, Notre Dame, HB	Rush: 134 Yds: 651 TD: 6	Paul Giel, Minnesota
1954	...Alan Ameche, Wisconsin, FB	Rush: 146 Yds: 641 TD: 9	Kurt Burris, Oklahoma
1955	...Howard Cassady, Ohio St, HB	Rush: 161 Yds: 958 TD: 15	Jim Swink, TCU
1956	...Paul Hornung, Notre Dame, QB	Att/Comp: 111/59 Yds: 917 TD: 3	Johnny Majors, Tennessee
1957	...John David Crow, Texas A&M, HB	Rush: 129 Yds: 562 TD: 10	Alex Karras, Iowa
1958	...Pete Dawkins, Army, HB	Rush: 78 Yds: 428 TD: 6	Randy Duncan, Iowa
1959	...Billy Cannon, LSU, HB	Rush: 139 Yds: 598 TD: 6	Rich Lucas, Penn St
1960	...Joe Bellino, Navy, HB	Rush: 168 Yds: 834 TD: 18	Tom Brown, Minnesota
1961	...Ernie Davis, Syracuse, HB	Rush: 150 Yds: 823 TD: 15	Bob Ferguson, Ohio St
1962	...Terry Baker, Oregon St, QB	Att/Comp: 203/112 Yds: 1738 TD: 15	Jerry Stovall, LSU
1963	...*Roger Staubach, Navy, QB	Att/Comp: 161/107 Yds: 1474 TD: 7	Billy Lothridge, Georgia Tech
1964	...John Huarte, Notre Dame, QB	Att/Comp: 205/114 Yds: 2062 TD: 16	Jerry Rhome, Tulsa
1965	...Mike Garrett, USC, HB	Rush: 267 Yds: 1440 TD: 16	Howard Twilley, Tulsa
1966	...Steve Spurrier, Florida, QB	Att/Comp: 291/179 Yds: 2012 TD: 16	Bob Griese, Purdue
1967	...Gary Beban, UCLA, QB	Att/Comp: 156/87 Yds: 1359 TD: 8	O.J. Simpson, USC
1968	...O.J. Simpson, USC, HB	Rush: 383 Yds: 1880 TD: 23	Leroy Keyes, Purdue
1969	...Steve Owens, Oklahoma, FB	Rush: 358 Yds: 1523 TD: 23	Mike Phipps, Purdue
1970	...Jim Plunkett, Stanford, QB	Att/Comp: 358/191 Yds: 2715 TD: 18	Joe Theismann, Notre Dame
1971	...Pat Sullivan, Auburn, QB	Att/Comp: 281/162 Yds: 2012; 20 TD	Ed Marinaro, Cornell
1972	...Johnny Rodgers, Nebraska, FL	Rec: 55 Yds: 942 TD: 17	Greg Pruitt, Oklahoma
1973	...John Cappelletti, Penn St, HB	Rush: 286 Yds: 1522 TD: 17	John Hicks, Ohio St
1974	...*Archie Griffin, Ohio St, HB	Rush: 256 Yds: 1695 TD: 12	Anthony Davis, USC
1975	...Archie Griffin, Ohio St, HB	Rush: 262 Yds: 1450 TD: 4	Chuck Muncie, California
1976	...†Tony Dorsett, Pittsburgh, HB	Rush: 370 Yds: 2150 TD: 23	Ricky Bell, USC
1977	...Earl Campbell, Texas, FB	Rush: 267 Yds: 1744 TD: 19	Terry Miller, Oklahoma St
1978	...*Billy Sims, Oklahoma, HB	Rush: 231 Yds: 1762 TD: 20	Chuck Fusina, Penn St
1979	...Charles White, USC, HB	Rush: 332 Yds: 1803 TD: 19	Billy Sims, Oklahoma
1980	...George Rogers, South Carolina, HB	Rush: 324 Yds: 1894 TD: 14	Hugh Green, Pittsburgh
1981	...Marcus Allen, USC, HB	Rush: 433 Yds: 2427 TD: 23	Herschel Walker, Georgia
1982	...*Herschel Walker, Georgia, HB	Rush: 335 Yds: 1752 TD: 17	John Elway, Stanford
1983	...Mike Rozier, Nebraska, HB	Rush: 275 Yds: 2148 TD: 29	Steve Young, BYU
1984	...Doug Flutie, Boston College, QB	Att/Comp: 396/233 Yds: 3454 TD: 27	Keith Byars, Ohio St
1985	...Bo Jackson, Auburn, HB	Rush: 278 Yds: 1786 TD: 17	Chuck Long, Iowa
1986	...Vinny Testaverde, Miami (Fla.), QB	Att/Comp: 276/175 Yds: 2557 TD: 26	Paul Palmer, Temple

Heisman Memorial Trophy (Cont.)

Year	Winner, College, Position	Winner's Season Statistics	Runner-Up, College
1987	...Tim Brown, Notre Dame, WR	Rec: 39 Yds: 846 TD: 7	Don McPherson, Syracuse
1988	...*Barry Sanders, Oklahoma St, RB	Rush: 344 Yds: 2628 TD: 39	Rodney Peete, USC
1989	...*Andre Ware, Houston, QB	Att/Comp: 578/365 Yds: 4699 TD: 46	Anthony Thompson, Indiana
1990	...*Ty Detmer, BYU, QB	Att/Comp: 562/361 Yds: 5188 TD: 41	Raghib Ismail, Notre Dame
1991	...*Desmond Howard, Michigan, WR	Rec: 61 Yds: 950 TD: 23	Casey Weldon, Florida St
1992	...Gino Torretta, Miami (FL), QB	Att/Comp: 402/228 Yds: 3060 TD: 19	Marshall Faulk, San Diego St
1993	...†Charlie Ward, Florida St, QB	Att/Comp: 380/264 Yds: 3032 TD: 27	Heath Shuler, Tennessee
1994	...Rashaan Salaam, Colorado, RB	Rush: 298 Yds: 2055 TD: 24	Ki-Jana Carter, Penn St
1995	...Eddie George, Ohio State, RB	Rush: 303 Yds: 1826 TD: 23	Tommie Frazier, Nebraska
1996	...†Danny Wuerffel, Florida, QB	Att/Comp: 360/207 Yds: 3625 TD: 39	Troy Davis, Iowa St
1997	...†Charles Woodson, Michigan, CB/ WR	7 interceptions; Rec: 11 Yds: 231 TD: 4	Peyton Manning, Tennessee
1998	...Ricky Williams, Texas, RB	Rush: 361 Yds: 2124 TD: 28	Michael Bishop, Kansas St
1999	...Ron Dayne, Wisconsin, RB	Rush: 303 Yds: 1834 TD: 19	Joe Hamilton, Georgia Tech
2000	...Chris Weinke, Florida St, QB	Att/Comp: 431/266 Yds: 4167 TD: 33	Josh Heupel, Oklahoma
2001	...Eric Crouch, Nebraska, QB	Att/Comp: 189/105 Yds: 1510 TD: 7; Rush: 1115 Yds, 18 TD	Rex Grossman, Florida
2002	...Carson Palmer, USC, QB	Att/Comp: 450/228 Yds: 3639 TD: 32	Brad Banks, Iowa
2003	... Jason White, Oklahoma, QB	Pct. Comp: 64; 3744 Yds; TD: 40	Larry Fitzgerald, Pittsburgh
2004	... *†Matt Leinart, USC, QB	Att/Comp: 269/412 Yds: 2990 TD: 28	Adrian Peterson, Oklahoma
2005	... *Reggie Bush, USC, RB	Rush: 200 Rec:478 Ret:179 Yds:1,740 TD: 16	Vince Young, Texas
2006	... Troy Smith, Ohio State, QB	Att/Comp: 311/203 Yds: 2542 TD: 30	Darren McFadden, Arkansas
2007	... ^Tim Tebow, Florida, QB	Att/Comp: 234/350 Yds: 3286 TD: 32 Rush: 210 Yds: 895 TD: 23	Darren McFadden, Arkansas

*Juniors; ^Sophomore; (all others seniors). †Winners who played for national championship teams the same year. Note: Former Heisman winners and national media cast votes, with ballots allowing for three names (3 points for first, 2 for second and 1 for third).

Maxwell Award

Given to the nation's outstanding college football player by the Maxwell Football Club of Philadelphia.

Year	Player, College, Position
1937	Clint Frank, Yale, HB
1938	Davey O'Brien, TCU, QB
1939	Nile Kinnick, Iowa, HB
1940	Tom Harmon, Michigan, HB
1941	Bill Dudley, Virginia, HB
1942	Paul Governali, Columbia, QB
1943	Bob Odell, Pennsylvania, HB
1944	Glenn Davis, Army, HB
1945	Doc Blanchard, Army, FB
1946	Charley Trippi, Georgia, HB
1947	Doak Walker, SMU, HB
1948	Chuck Bednarik, Pennsylvania, C
1949	Leon Hart, Notre Dame, E
1950	Reds Bagnell, Pennsylvania, HB
1951	Dick Kazmaier, Princeton, HB
1952	John Lattner, Notre Dame, HB
1953	John Lattner, Notre Dame, HB
1954	Ron Beagle, Navy, E
1955	Howard Cassady, Ohio St, HB
1956	Tommy McDonald, Oklahoma, HB
1957	Bob Reifsnyder, Navy, T
1958	Pete Dawkins, Army, HB
1959	Rich Lucas, Penn St, QB
1960	Joe Bellino, Navy, HB

Year	Player, College, Position
1961	Bob Ferguson, Ohio St, FB
1962	Terry Baker, Oregon St, QB
1963	Roger Staubach, Navy, QB
1964	Glenn Ressler, Penn St, C
1965	Tommy Nobis, Texas, LB
1966	Jim Lynch, Notre Dame, LB
1967	Gary Beban, UCLA, QB
1968	O.J. Simpson, USC, RB
1969	Mike Reid, Penn St, DT
1970	Jim Plunkett, Stanford, QB
1971	Ed Marinaro, Cornell, RB
1972	Brad Van Pelt, Michigan St, DB
1973	John Cappelletti, Penn St, RB
1974	Steve Joachim, Temple, QB
1975	Archie Griffin, Ohio St, RB
1976	Tony Dorsett, Pittsburgh, RB
1977	Ross Browner, Notre Dame, DE
1978	Chuck Fusina, Penn St, QB
1979	Charles White, USC, RB
1980	Hugh Green, Pittsburgh, DE
1981	Marcus Allen, USC, RB
1982	Herschel Walker, Georgia, RB
1983	Mike Rozier, Nebraska, RB
1984	Doug Flutie, Boston College, QB

Maxwell Award (Cont.)

Year	Player, College, Position
1985	Chuck Long, Iowa, QB
1986	Vinny Testaverde, Miami (Fla.), QB
1987	Don McPherson, Syracuse, QB
1988	Barry Sanders, Oklahoma St, RB
1989	Anthony Thompson, Indiana, RB
1990	Ty Detmer, BYU, QB
1991	Desmond Howard, Michigan, WR
1992	Gino Torretta, Miami (Fla.), QB
1993	Charlie Ward, Florida St, QB
1994	Kerry Collins, Penn St, QB
1995	Eddie George, Ohio St, RB
1996	Danny Wuerffel, Florida, QB
1997	Peyton Manning, Tennessee, QB
1998	Ricky Williams, Texas, RB
1999	Ron Dayne, Wisconsin, RB
2000	Drew Brees, Purdue, QB
2001	Ken Dorsey, Miami (Fla.), QB
2002	Larry Johnson, Penn St, RB
2003	Eli Manning, Mississippi, QB
2004	Jason White, Oklahoma, QB
2005	Vince Young, Texas, QB
2006	Brady Quinn, Notre Dame, QB
2007	Tim Tebow, Florida, QB

Davey O'Brien National Quarterback Award

Given to the top quarterback in the nation by the Davey O'Brien Educational and Charitable Trust of Fort Worth. Named for TCU Hall of Fame quarterback Davey O'Brien (1936–38).

Year	Player, College
1981	Jim McMahon, BYU
1982	Todd Blackledge, Penn St
1983	Steve Young, BYU
1984	Doug Flutie, Boston College
1985	Chuck Long, Iowa
1986	Vinny Testaverde, Miami (Fla.)
1987	Don McPherson, Syracuse
1988	Troy Aikman, UCLA
1989	Andre Ware, Houston
1990	Ty Detmer, BYU
1991	Ty Detmer, BYU
1992	Gino Torretta, Miami (Fla.)
1993	Charlie Ward, Florida St
1994	Kerry Collins, Penn St
1995	Danny Wuerffel, Florida
1996	Danny Wuerffel, Florida
1997	Peyton Manning, Tennessee
1998	Michael Bishop, Kansas St
1999	Joe Hamilton, Georgia Tech
2000	Chris Weinke, Florida St
2001	Eric Crouch, Nebraska
2002	Brad Banks, Iowa
2003	Jason White, Oklahoma
2004	Jason White, Oklahoma
2005	Vince Young, Texas
2006	Troy Smith, Ohio St
2007	Tim Tebow, Florida

Note: Originally honored the outstanding football player in the Southwest as follows: 1977—Earl Campbell, Texas, RB; 1978—Billy Sims, Oklahoma, RB; 1979—Mike Singletary, Baylor, LB; 1980—Mike Singletary, Baylor, LB.

Vince Lombardi/Rotary Award

Given to the outstanding college lineman of the year, the award is sponsored by the Rotary Club of Houston.

Year	Player, College, Position
1970	Jim Stillwagon, Ohio St, MG
1971	Walt Patulski, Notre Dame, DE
1972	Rich Glover, Nebraska, MG
1973	John Hicks, Ohio St, OT
1974	Randy White, Maryland, DT
1975	Lee Roy Selmon, Oklahoma, DT
1976	Wilson Whitley, Houston, DT
1977	Ross Browner, Notre Dame, DE
1978	Bruce Clark, Penn St, DT
1979	Brad Budde, USC, G
1980	Hugh Green, Pittsburgh, DE
1981	Kenneth Sims, Texas, DT
1982	Dave Rimington, Nebraska, C
1983	Dean Steinkuhler, Nebraska, G
1984	Tony Degrate, Texas, DT
1985	Tony Casillas, Oklahoma, NG
1986	Cornelius Bennett, Alabama, LB
1987	Chris Spielman, Ohio St, LB
1988	Tracy Rocker, Auburn, DT
1989	Percy Snow, Michigan St, LB
1990	Chris Zorich, Notre Dame, NG
1991	Steve Emtman, Washington, DT
1992	Marvin Jones, Florida St, LB
1993	Aaron Taylor, Notre Dame, OT
1994	Warren Sapp, Miami (Fla.), DT
1995	Orlando Pace, Ohio St, OT
1996	Orlando Pace, Ohio St, OT
1997	Grant Wistrom, Nebraska, DE
1998	Dat Nguyen, Texas A&M, LB
1999	Corey Moore, Virginia Tech, DE
2000	Jamal Reynolds, Florida St, DE
2001	Julius Peppers, North Carolina, DE
2002	Terrell Suggs, Arizona St, DL
2003	Tommie Harris, Oklahoma, DT
2004	David Pollack, Georgia, DE
2005	A.J. Hawk, Ohio St, LB
2006	LaMarr Woodley, Michigan, DE
2007	Glenn Dorsey, LSU, DT

Outland Trophy

Given to the outstanding interior lineman, selected by the Football Writers Association of America.

Year	Player, College, Position
1946	George Connor, Notre Dame, T
1947	Joe Steffy, Army, G
1948	Bill Fischer, Notre Dame, G
1949	Ed Bagdon, Michigan St, G
1950	Bob Gain, Kentucky, T
1951	Jim Weatherall, Oklahoma, T

Outland Trophy *(Cont.)*

Year	Player, College, Position
1952	Dick Modzelewski, Maryland, T
1953	J.D. Roberts, Oklahoma, G
1954	Bill Brooks, Arkansas, G
1955	Calvin Jones, Iowa, G
1956	Jim Parker, Ohio St, G
1957	Alex Karras, Iowa, T
1958	Zeke Smith, Auburn, G
1959	Mike McGee, Duke, T
1960	Tom Brown, Minnesota, G
1961	Merlin Olsen, Utah St, T
1962	Bobby Bell, Minnesota, T
1963	Scott Appleton, Texas, T
1964	Steve DeLong, Tennessee, T
1965	Tommy Nobis, Texas, G
1966	Loyd Phillips, Arkansas, T
1967	Ron Yary, USC, T
1968	Bill Stanfill, Georgia, T
1969	Mike Reid, Penn St, DT
1970	Jim Stillwagon, Ohio St, MG
1971	Larry Jacobson, Nebraska, DT
1972	Rich Glover, Nebraska, MG
1973	John Hicks, Ohio St, OT
1974	Randy White, Maryland, DE
1975	Lee Roy Selmon, Oklahoma, DT
1976	Ross Browner, Notre Dame, DE
1977	Brad Shearer, Texas, DT
1978	Greg Roberts, Oklahoma, G
1979	Jim Ritcher, North Carolina St, C
1980	Mark May, Pittsburgh, OT

Year	Player, College, Position
1981	Dave Rimington, Nebraska, C
1982	Dave Rimington, Nebraska, C
1983	Dean Steinkuhler, Nebraska, G
1984	Bruce Smith, Virginia Tech, DT
1985	Mike Ruth, Boston College, NG
1986	Jason Buck, BYU, DT
1987	Chad Hennings, Air Force, DT
1988	Tracy Rocker, Auburn, DT
1989	Mohammed Elewonibi, BYU, G
1990	Russell Maryland, Miami (Fla.), DT
1991	Steve Emtman, Washington, DT
1992	Will Shields, Nebraska, G
1993	Rob Waldrop, Arizona, NG
1994	Zach Wiegert, Nebraska, G
1995	Jonathan Ogden, UCLA, OT
1996	Orlando Pace, Ohio St, OT
1997	Aaron Taylor, Nebraska, G
1998	Kris Farris, UCLA, OL
1999	Chris Samuels, Alabama, OL
2000	John Henderson, Tennessee, DT
2001	Bryant McKinnie, Miami (Fla.), OT
2002	Rien Long, Washington St, DL
2003	Robert Gallery, Iowa, OT
2004	Jammal Brown, Oklahoma, OT
2005	Greg Eslinger, Minnesota, LB
2006	Joe Thomas, Wisconsin, OT
2007	Glenn Dorsey, LSU, DT

Butkus Award

Given to the top collegiate linebacker, the award was established by the Downtown Athletic Club of Orlando and named for college Hall of Famer Dick Butkus of Illinois.

Year	Player, College
1985	Brian Bosworth, Oklahoma
1986	Brian Bosworth, Oklahoma
1987	Paul McGowan, Florida St
1988	Derrick Thomas, Alabama
1989	Percy Snow, Michigan St
1990	Alfred Williams, Colorado
1991	Erick Anderson, Michigan
1992	Marvin Jones, Florida St
1993	Trev Alberts, Nebraska
1994	Dana Howard, Illinois
1995	Kevin Hardy, Illinois
1996	Matt Russell, Colorado

Year	Player, College
1997	Andy Katzenmoyer, Ohio St
1998	Chris Claiborne, USC
1999	LaVar Arrington, Penn St
2000	Dan Morgan, Miami (Fla.)
2001	Rocky Calmus, Oklahoma
2002	E.J. Henderson, Maryland
2003	Teddy Lehman, Oklahoma
2004	Derrick Johnson, Texas
2005	Paul Posluszny, Penn State
2006	Patrick Willis, Mississippi
2007	James Laurinaitis, Ohio St

Jim Thorpe Award

Given to the best defensive back of the year, the award is presented by the Jim Thorpe Athletic Club of Oklahoma City.

Year	Player, College
1986	Thomas Everett, Baylor
1987	Bennie Blades, Miami (Fla.)
	Rickey Dixon, Oklahoma
1988	Deion Sanders, Florida St
1989	Mark Carrier, USC
1990	Darryl Lewis, Arizona
1991	Terrell Buckley, Florida St
1992	Deon Figures, Colorado
1993	Antonio Langham, Alabama
1994	Chris Hudson, Colorado
1995	Greg Myers, Colorado St
1996	Lawrence Wright, Florida

Year	Player, College
1997	Charles Woodson, Michigan
1998	Antoine Winfield, Ohio St
1999	Tyrone Carter, Minnesota
2000	Jamar Fletcher, Wisconsin
2001	Roy Williams, Oklahoma
2002	Terence Newman, Kansas St
2003	Derrick Strait, Oklahoma
2004	Carlos Rogers, Auburn
2005	Michael Huff, Texas
2006	Aaron Ross, Texas
2007	Antoine Cason, Arizona

Awards (*Cont.*)

Walter Payton Player of the Year Award

Given to the top FCS (I-AA) player, voted by Div. I-AA sports information directors. Sponsored by Sports Network.

Year	Player, College, Position
1987	Kenny Gamble, Colgate, RB
1988	Dave Meggett, Towson St, RB
1989	John Friesz, Idaho, QB
1990	Walter Dean, Grambling, RB
1991	Jamie Martin, Weber St, QB
1992	Michael Payton, Marshall, QB
1993	Doug Nussmeier, Idaho, QB
1994	Steve McNair, Alcorn St, QB
1995	Dave Dickenson, Montana, QB
1996	Archie Amerson, Northern Arizona, RB
1997	Brian Finneran, Villanova, WR
1998	Jerry Azumah, New Hampshire, RB
1999	Adrian Peterson, Georgia Southern, RB
2000	Louis Ivory, Furman, RB
2001	Brian Westbrook, Villanova, RB
2002	Tony Romo, Eastern Ilinois, QB
2003	Jamaal Branch, Colgate, RB
2004	Lang Campbell, William & Mary, QB
2005	Erik Meyer, Eastern Washington, QB
2006	Ricky Santos, New Hampshire, QB
2007	Jayson Foster, Georgia Southern, QB

NCAA Football Bowl Subdivision (I-A) Individual Records

Career

SCORING

Most Points Scored: 468—Travis Prentice, Miami (Ohio), 1996–99
Most Points Scored per Game: 12.1—Marshall Faulk, San Diego St, 1991–93
Most Touchdowns Scored: 78—Travis Prentice, Miami (Ohio), 1996–99
Most Touchdowns Scored per Game: 2.0—Marshall Faulk, San Diego St, 1991–93
Most Touchdowns Scored, Rushing: 73—Travis Prentice, Miami (Ohio), 1996–99
Most Touchdowns Scored, Passing: 131—Colt Brennan, Hawaii, 2005–07
Most Touchdowns Scored, Receiving: 50—Troy Edwards, Louisiana Tech, 1996–98
Most Touchdowns Scored, Interception Returns: 5—Ken Thomas, San Jose St, 1979–82; Jackie Walker, Tennessee, 1969–71; Deltha O'Neal, California, 1996–99; Darrent Williams, Okla St 2001–04
Most Touchdowns Scored, Punt Returns: 8—Wes Walker, Texas Tech, 2000–03; Antonio Perkins, Oklahoma, 2001–04
Most Touchdowns Scored, Kickoff Returns: 6—Anthony Davis, USC, 1972–74

TOTAL OFFENSE

Most Plays: 2,587—Timmy Chang, Hawaii, 2000–04
Most Plays per Game: 50.1—Kliff Kingsbury, Texas Tech, 1999–2002
Most Yards Gained: 16,910—Timmy Chang, Hawaii, 2000–04 (17,072 passing, -162 rushing)
Most Yards Gained per Game: 387.9—Colt Brennan, Hawaii, 2005–07
Most 300+ Yard Games: 33 —Ty Detmer, BYU, 1988–91

RUSHING

Most Rushes: 1,215—Steve Bartalo, Colorado St, 1983–86 (4813 yds)
Most Rushes per Game: 34.0—Ed Marinaro, Cornell, 1969–71
Most Yards Gained: 6,397—Ron Dayne, Wisconsin, 1996–99
Most Yards Gained per Game: 174.6—Ed Marinaro, Cornell, 1969–71
Most 100+ Yard Games: 34—DeAngelo Williams, Memphis, 2002–05
Most 200+ Yard Games: 11—Marcus Allen, USC, 1978–81; Ricky Williams, Texas, 1995–98; Ron Dayne, Wisconsin, 1996–99

PASSING

Highest Passing Efficiency Rating: 168.9—Ryan Dinwiddie, Boise St, 2000–03
Most Passes Attempted: 2,436—Timmy Chang, Hawaii, 2000–04
Most Passes Attempted per Game: 47.0—Tim Rattay, Louisiana Tech, 1997–99
Most Passes Completed: 1,388—Timmy Chang, Hawaii, 2000–04
Most Passes Completed per Game: 30.8—Tim Rattay, Louisiana Tech, 1997–99
***Highest Completion Percentage:** 70.4—Colt Brennan, Hawaii, 2005–07
Most Yards Gained: 17,072—Timmy Chang, Hawaii, 2000–04
Most Yards Gained per Game: 386.2—Tim Rattay, Louisiana Tech, 1997–99 (3 years); 326.8—Ty Detmer, BYU, 1988–91 (4 years)

RECEIVING

Most Passes Caught: 316—Taylor Stubblefield, Purdue, 2001–04
Most Passes Caught per Game: 10.5—Emmanuel Hazard, Houston, 1989–90
Most Yards Gained: 5,005—Trevor Insley, Nevada, 1996–99
Most Yards Gained per Game: 140.9—Alex Van Dyke, Nevada, 1994–95
†Highest Average Gain per Reception: 22.0—Herman Moore, Virginia, 198–90

ALL-PURPOSE RUNNING

Most Plays: 1,347—Steve Bartalo, Colorado St, 1983-86 (1,215 rushes, 132 receptions)
Most Yards Gained: 7,573—DeAngelo Williams, Memphis, 2002–05 (6,026 rushing, 723 receiving, 824 KO retrurns)
Most Yards Gained per Game: 237.8—Ryan Benjamin, Pacific, 1990–92
Highest Average Gain per Play: 17.4—Anthony Carter, Michigan, 1979–82

*Minimum 1,000 attempts.
†Minimum 105 receptions.

Career (Cont.)

INTERCEPTIONS

Most Passes Intercepted: 29—Al Brosky, Illinois, 1950–52

Most Passes Intercepted per Game: 1.1—Al Brosky, Illinois, 1950–52

Most Yards on Interception Returns: 501—Terrell Buckley, Florida St, 1989–91

Highest Average Gain per Interception: 26.5—Tom Pridemore, West Virginia, 1975–77

SPECIAL TEAMS

Highest Punt Return Average: 23.6—Jack Mitchell, Oklahoma, 1946–48

Highest Kickoff Return Average: 35.1—Anthony Davis, USC, 1972–74

Highest Average Yards per Punt: 46.3—Todd Sauerbrun, West Virginia, 1991–93 (150–199 punts). 45.3—Ryan Plackemeier, Wake Forest, 2002–05 (200-250 punts). 45.2—Daniel Sepulveda, Baylor, 2003–06 (250+ punts).

Single Season

SCORING

Most Points Scored: 234—Barry Sanders, Oklahoma St, 1988

Most Points Scored per Game: 21.3—Barry Sanders, Oklahoma St, 1988

Most Touchdowns Scored: 39—Barry Sanders, Oklahoma St, 1988

Most Touchdowns Scored, Rushing: 37—Barry Sanders, Oklahoma St, 1988

Most Touchdowns Scored, Passing: 58—Colt Brennan, Hawaii, 2006

Most Touchdowns Scored, Receiving: 27—Troy Edwards, Louisiana Tech, 1998

Most Touchdowns Scored, Interception Returns: 4—Deltha O'Neal, California, 1999

Most Touchdowns Scored, Punt Returns: 5—Chad Owens, Hawaii, 2004

Most Touchdowns Scored, Kickoff Returns: 5—Ashlan Davis, Tulsa, 2004

TOTAL OFFENSE

Most Plays: 814—Kliff Kingsbury, Texas Tech, 2002

Most Yards Gained: 5,976—B.J. Symons, Texas Tech, 2003

Most Yards Gained per Game: 474.6—David Klingler, Houston, 1990

Most 300+ Yard Games: 14—Colt Brennan, Hawaii, 2006; Paul Smith, Tulsa, 2007

RUSHING

Most Rushes: 450—Kevin Smith, UCF, 2007

Most Rushes per Game: 39.6—Ed Marinaro, Cornell, 1971

Most Yards Gained: 2,628—Barry Sanders, Oklahoma St, 1988

Most Yards Gained per Game: 238.9—Barry Sanders, Oklahoma St, 1988

Most 100+ Yard Games: 12—Quentin Griffin, Oklahoma, 2002

PASSING

Highest Passing Efficiency Rating: 186.0—Colt Brennan, Hawaii, 2006

Most Passes Attempted: 719—B.J. Symons, Texas Tech, 2003

Most Passes Attempted per Game: 58.5—David Klingler, Houston, 1990

Most Passes Completed: 512—Graham Harrell, Texas Tech, 2007

PASSING (Cont.)

Most Passes Completed per Game: 39.4—Graham Harrell, Texas Tech, 2007

Highest Completion Percentage: 73.6—Daunte Culpepper, Central Florida, 1998

Most Yards Gained: 5,833—B.J. Symons, Texas Tech, 2003

Most Yards Gained per Game: 467.3—David Klingler, Houston, 1990

RECEIVING

Most Passes Caught: 142—Emmanuel Hazard, Houston, 1989

Most Passes Caught per Game: 13.4—Howard Twilley, Tulsa, 1965

Most Yards Gained: 2,060—Trevor Insley, Nevada, 1999

Most Yards Gained per Game: 187.3—Trevor Insley, Nevada, 1999

Highest Average Gain per Reception: 31.9—Brennan Marion, Tulsa, 2007 (min. 30 receptions)

ALL-PURPOSE RUNNING

Most Plays: 432—Marcus Allen, USC, 1981

Most Yards Gained: 3,250—Barry Sanders, Oklahoma St, 1988

Most Yards Gained per Game: 295.5—Barry Sanders, Oklahoma St, 1988

Highest Average Gain per Play: 18.5—Henry Bailey, UNLV, 1992

INTERCEPTIONS

Most Passes Intercepted: 14 — Al Worley, Washington, 1968

Most Yards on Interception Returns: 302 — Charles Phillips, USC, 1974

Highest Average Gain per Interception: 51.8 — Norm Thompson, Utah, 1969

SPECIAL TEAMS

Highest Punt Return Average: 28.5—Maurice Drew, UCLA, 2005

Highest Kickoff Return Average: 40.1 — Paul Allen, BYU, 1961

Highest Average Yards per Punt: 50.3 — Chad Kessler, LSU, 1997

*Minimum 1,000 attempts.

NCAA FBS (Div. I-A) Individual Records *(Cont.)*

Single Game

SCORING

Most Points Scored: 48—Howard Griffith, Illinois, 1990 (vs Southern Illinois)
Most Field Goals: 7—Dale Klein, Nebraska, 1985 (vs Missouri); Mike Prindle, Western Michigan, 1984 (vs Marshall)
Most Extra Points (Kick): 13—Derek Mahoney, Fresno St, 1991 (vs New Mexico); Terry Leiweke, Houston, 1968 (vs Tulsa)
Most Extra Points (2-Pts): 6—Jim Pilot, New Mexico St, 1961 (vs Hardin-Simmons)

TOTAL OFFENSE

Most Yards Gained: 732—David Klingler, Houston, 1990 (vs Arizona St); (716 pass, 16 rush)

RUSHING

Most Yards Gained: 406—LaDainian Tomlinson, TCU, 1999 (vs UTEP)
Most Touchdowns Rushed: 8—Howard Griffith, Illinois, 1990 (vs Southern Illinois)

PASSING

Most Passes Completed: 55—Rusty LaRue, Wake Forest, 1995 (vs Duke); Drew Brees, Purdue, 1998 (vs Wisconsin)
Most Yards Gained: 716—David Klingler, Houston, 1990 (vs Arizona St)
Most Touchdown Passes: 11—David Klingler, Houston, 1990 [vs Eastern Washington (I-AA)]

RECEIVING

Most Passes Caught: 23—Randy Gatewood, UNLV, 1994 (vs Idaho)
Most Yards Gained: 405—Troy Edwards, Louisiana Tech, 1998 (vs Nebraska)
Most Touchdown Catches: 7—Rashaun Woods, Oklahoma St, 2003 (vs SMU)

NCAA Football Championship Subdivision (I-AA) Ind. Records

Career

SCORING

Most Points Scored: 544—Brian Westbrook, Villanova, 1997–98, 2000-01
Most Touchdowns Scored: 89—Brian Westbrook, Villanova, 1997–98, 2000-01
Most Touchdowns Scored, Rushing: 84—Adrian Peterson, Georgia Southern, 1998–2001
Most Touchdowns Scored, Passing: 140—Bruce Eugene, Grambling St, 2001–05
Most Touchdowns Scored, Receiving: 58—David Ball, New Hampshire, 2003–06

RUSHING

Most Rushes: 1,124—Charles Roberts, Cal St-Sacramento, 1997–2000
Most Rushes per Game: 38.2—Arnold Mickens, Butler, 1994–95
Most Yards Gained: 6,559—Adrian Peterson, Georgia Southern, 1998–2001
Most Yards Gained per Game: 190.7—Arnold Mickens, Butler, 1994–95 (2 years); 164.5—Adrian Peterson, Georgia Southern, 1998–2000 (3 years); 156.2—Adrian Peterson, Georgia Southern, 1998–2001 (4 years)

PASSING

Highest Passing Efficiency Rating: 170.8—Shawn Knight, William & Mary, 1991–94 (3 years); 176.7—Josh Johnson, San Diego, 2004–07 (4 years)
Most Passes Attempted: 1,680—Marcus Brady, Cal St-Northridge, 1998–2001; Steve McNair, Alcorn St, 1991–94
Most Passes Completed: 1,122—Ricky Santos, New Hampsire, 2004–07
Most Passes Completed per Game: 26.5—Chris Sanders, Chattanooga, 1999–2000
Highest Completion Percentage: 69.6—Eric Sanders, Northern Iowa, 2004–07
Most Yards Gained: 14,496—Steve McNair, Alcorn St, 1991–94
Most Yards Gained per Game: 350.0—Neil Lomax, Portland St, 1978–80

RECEIVING

Most Passes Caught: 317—Jacquay Nunnally, Florida A&M, 1997–2000
Most Yards Gained: 4,693—Jerry Rice, Mississippi Valley St, 1981–84
Most Yards Gained per Game: 114.5—Jerry Rice, Mississippi Valley St, 1981–84 (min. 3,000 yds)
Highest Average Gain per Reception: 22.0—Dedric Ward, Northern Iowa, 1993–96 (min. 125 rec.)

Single Season

SCORING

Most Points Scored: 234—Omar Cuff, Delaware, 2007
Most Touchdowns Scored: 39—Omar Cuff, Delaware, 2007
Most Touchdowns Scored, Rushing: 35—Omar Cuff, Delaware, 2007
Most Touchdowns Scored, Passing: 56—Willie Totten, Mississippi Valley St, 1984; Bruce Eugene, Grambling St, 2005
Most Touchdowns Scored, Receiving: 27—Jerry Rice, Mississippi Valley St, 1984

RUSHING

Most Rushes: 450—Jamaal Branch, Colgate, 2003
Most Rushes per Game: 40.9—Arnold Mickens, Butler, 1994
Most Yards Gained: 2,326—Jamaal Branch, Colgate, 2003
Most Yards Gained per Game: 225.5—Arnold Mickens, Butler, 1994

NCAA FCS (Div. I-AA) Individual Records *(Cont.)*

Single Season *(Cont.)*

PASSING

Highest Passing Efficiency Rating: 204.6—Shawn Knight, William & Mary, 1993
Most Passes Attempted: 592—Martin Hankins, SE Louisiana, 2003
Most Passes Completed: 385—Brett Gordon, Villanova, 2002
Most Passes Completed per Game: 32.4—Willie Totten, Mississippi Valley St, 1984
Highest Completion Percentage: 75.2—Eric Sanders, Northern Iowa, 2007
Most Yards Gained: 4,863—Steve McNair, Alcorn St, 1994
Most Yards Gained per Game: 455.7—Willie Totten, Mississippi Valley St, 1984

RECEIVING

Most Passes Caught: 120—Stephen Campbell, Brown, 2000
Most Yards Gained: 1,712—Eddie Conti, Delaware, 1998
Most Yards Gained per Game: 168.2—Jerry Rice, Mississippi Valley St, 1984
Highest Average Gain per Reception: 28.9—Mikhael Ricks, Stephen F. Austin, 1997; (min. 35 receptions)

Single Game

SCORING

Most Points Scored: 42—Jesse Burton, McNeese, St, 1998 (vs Southern Utah); Archie Amerson, Northern Arizona, 1996 (vs Weber St); Omar Cuff, Delaware, 2007 (vs William & Mary)
Most Field Goals: 8—Goran Lingmerth, Northern Arizona, 1986 (vs Idaho)

RUSHING

Most Yards Gained: 437—Maurice Hicks, North Carolina A&T, 2001 (vs Morgan St)
Most Touchdowns Rushed: 7—Archie Amerson, Northern Arizona, 1996 (vs Weber St)

PASSING

Most Passes Completed: 50—Martin Hankins, SE Louisiana, 2004, (vs. Jacksonville)
Most Yards Gained: 624—Jamie Martin, Weber St, 1991 (vs Idaho St)
Most Touchdown Passes: 9—Willie Totten, Mississippi Valley St, 1984 (vs Kentucky St); Drew Hubel, Portland St, 2007 (vs Weber St)

RECEIVING

Most Passes Caught: 24—Chas Gessner, Brown, 2002, (vs Rhode Island); Jerry Rice, Mississippi Valley St, 1983 (vs Southern-Birmingham)
Most Yards Gained: 376—Kassim Osgood, Cal Poly, 2000 (vs Northern Iowa)
Most Touchdown Catches: 6—Cos DeMatteo, Chattanooga, 2000 (vs Mississippi Valley St)

NCAA Division II Individual Records

Career

SCORING

Most Points Scored: 656—Germaine Rice, Pittsburg St, 2003–06
Most Touchdowns Scored: 109—Germaine Rice, Pittsburg St, 2003–06
Most Touchdowns Scored, Rushing: 107—Germaine Rice, Pittsburg St, 2003–06
Most Touchdowns Scored, Passing: 148—Jimmy Terwilliger, East Stroudsburg, 2003–06
Most Touchdowns Scored, Receiving: 78—Dallas Mall, Bentley, 2001–04

RUSHING

Most Rushes: 1,271—Xavier Omon, NW Missouri St, 2004–07
Most Rushes per Game: 29.8—Bernie Peeters, Luther, 1968–71
Most Yards Gained: 7,962—Danny Woodhead, Chadron St, 2004–07
Most Yards Gained per Game: 183.4—Anthony Gray, Western New Mexico, 1997–98

PASSING

Highest Passing Efficiency Rating: 170.7—Jimmy Terwilliger, East Stroudsburg, 2003–06 (Min. 750 comp.)
Most Passes Attempted: 1,898—Andrew Webb, Fort Lewis, 2000–03

PASSING *(Cont.)*

Most Passes Completed: 1,007—Andrew Webb, Fort Lewis, 2000–03
Most Passes Completed per Game: 25.9—Evan Gray, Missouri-Rolla, 2003–05
Highest Completion Percentage: 69.0—Chris Hatcher, Valdosta St, 1991–94 (min. 1,000 att.)
Most Yards Gained: 14,350—Jimmy Terwilliger, East Stroudsburg, 2003–06
Most Yards Gained per Game: 323.7—Dusty Bonner, Valdosta St, 2000–01

RECEIVING

Most Passes Caught: 323—Clarence Coleman, Ferris St, 1998–2001
Most Yards Gained: 4,983—Clarence Coleman, Ferris St, 1998–2001
Most Yards Gained per Game: 160.8—Chris George, Glenville St, 1993–94
Highest Average Gain per Reception: 23.2—Romar Crenshaw, SE Oklahoma, 2000–03

NCAA Division II Individual Records *(Cont.)*

Single Season

SCORING

Most Points Scored: 234—Bernard Scott, Abilene Christian, 2007

Most Touchdowns Scored: 39—Bernard Scott, Abilene Christian, 2007

Most Touchdowns Scored, Rushing: 37—Xavier Omon, NW Missouri St, 2007

Most Touchdowns Scored, Passing: 54—Dusty Bonner, Valdosta St, 2000

Most Touchdowns Scored, Receiving: 35—David Kircus, Grand Valley St, 2002

RUSHING

Most Rushes: 385—Joe Gough, Wayne St (Mich.), 1994

Most Rushes per Game: 38.6—Mark Perkins, Hobart, 1968

Most Yards Gained: 2,756—Danny Woodhead, Chadron St, 2006

Most Yards Gained per Game: 222.0—Anthony Gray, Western New Mexico, 1997

PASSING

Highest Passing Efficiency Rating: 221.63—Curt Anes, Grand Valley St, 2001 (min. 100 comp.)

Most Passes Attempted: 583—Dalton Bell, West Texas A&M 2006

Most Passes Completed: 386—Dalton Bell, West Texas A&M 2006

Most Passes Completed per Game: 32.4—Lance Funderburk, Valdosta St, 1995

Highest Completion Percentage: 74.7—Chris Hatcher, Valdosta St, 1994

Most Yards Gained: 4,646—Chad Friehauf, Colorado Mines 2004

Most Yards Gained per Game: 393.4—Grady Benton, West Texas A&M, 1994

RECEIVING

Most Passes Caught: 143—Nick Smart, Southwest Baptist, 2007

Most Yards Gained: 1,876—Chris George, Glenville St, 1993

Most Yards Gained per Game: 187.6—Chris George, Glenville St, 1993

Highest Average Gain per Reception: 32.5—Tyrone Johnson, Western St, 1991 (min. 30 receptions)

Single Game

SCORING

Most Points Scored: 48—Paul Zaeske, North Park, 1968 (vs North Central [Ill.]); Junior Wolf, Panhandle St, 1958 (vs St. Mary [Ks.])

Most Field Goals: 6—Steve Huff, Central Missouri St, 1985 (vs SE Missouri St); Austin Wellock, Ashland, 2002 (vs. Wayne St)

RUSHING

Most Yards Gained: 418—Jarom Freeman, Southern Connecticut St, 2007 (vs Bryant)

Most Touchdowns Rushed: 8—Junior Wolf, Panhandle St, 1958 (vs St. Mary [Ks.])

PASSING

Most Passes Completed: 56—Jarrod DeGeorgia, Wayne St (Neb.),1996 (vs Drake)

Most Yards Gained: 645—Matt Kohn, Indianapolis, 2003 (vs Michigan Tech)

Most Touchdowns Passed: 10—Bruce Swanson, North Park, 1968 (vs North Central [Ill.])

RECEIVING

Most Passes Caught: 23—Chris George, Glenville St, 1994 (vs W.V. Wesleyan); Barry Wagner, Alabama A&M, 1989 (vs Clark Atlanta)

Most Yards Gained: 401—Kevin Ingram, West Chester, 1998 (vs Clarion)

Most Touchdown Catches: 8—Paul Zaeske, North Park, 1968 (vs North Central [Ill.])

NCAA Division III Individual Records

Career

SCORING

Most Points Scored: 562—R.J. Bowers, Grove City, 1997–00

Most Touchdowns Scored: 92—R.J. Bowers, Grove City, 1997–00

Most Touchdowns Scored, Rushing: 91—R.J. Bowers, Grove City, 1997–00

Most Touchdowns Scored, Passing: 148—Justin Peery, Westminster (Mo.), 1996–99

Most Touchdowns Scored, Receiving: 75—Scott Pingel, Westminster (Mo.), 1996–99

RUSHING

Most Rushes: 1,190—Steve Tardif, Maine Maritime, 1996–99

Most Rushes per Game: 32.7—Chris Sizemore, Bridgewater (Va.), 1972–74

RUSHING *(Cont.)*

Most Yards Gained: 7,353—R.J. Bowers, Grove City, 1997–00

Most Yards Gained per Game: 187.1—Tony Sutton, Wooster, 2002–04

PASSING

Highest Passing Efficiency Rating: 194.2—Bill Borchert, Mount Union, 1994–97

Most Passes Attempted: 1,696—Kirk Baumgartner, UW–Stevens Point, 1986–89

Most Passes Completed: 1,012—Justin Peery, Westminster (Mo.), 1996–99

Most Passes Completed per Game: 25.9—Justin Peery, Westminster (Mo.), 1996–99

Highest Completion Percentage: 66.5—Bill Borchert, Mount Union, 1994–97 (min. 1,000 att.)

Career *(Cont.)*

PASSING *(Cont.)*

Most Yards Gained: 13,262—Justin Peery, Westminster (Mo.), 1996–99

Most Yards Gained per Game: 358.9—Brett Elliott, Linfield, 2004–05

RECEIVING

Most Passes Caught: 436—Scott Pingel, Westminster (Mo.), 1996–99

Most Yards Gained: 6,108—Scott Pingel, Westminster (Mo.), 1996–99

Most Yards Gained per Game: 156.6—Scott Pingel, Westminster (Mo.), 1996–99

Highest Average Gain per Reception: 23.4—Michael Coleman, Widener, 1998–2001

Single Season

SCORING

Most Points Scored: 248—Dan Pugh, Mount Union, 2002

Most Points Scored per Game: 20.8—James Regan, Pomona-Pitzer, 1997

Most Touchdowns Scored: 41—Dan Pugh Mount Union, 2002

Most Touchdowns Scored, Rushing: 35—Chris Sharpe, Springfield, 2006; Dan Pugh, Mount Union, 2002

Most Touchdowns Scored, Passing: 61—Brett Elliott, Linfield, 2004

Most Touchdowns Scored, Receiving: 26—Scott Pingel, Westminster (Mo.), 1998

RUSHING

Most Rushes: 463—Dante Washington, Carthage, 2004

Most Rushes per Game: 38.0—Mike Birosak, Dickinson, 1989

Most Yards Gained: 2,455—Justin Beaver, UW–Whitewater, 2007

PASSING

Highest Passing Efficiency Rating: 225.0—Mike Simpson, Eureka, 1994

Most Passes Attempted: 575—Brett Dietz, Hanover, 2003

Most Passes Completed: 360—Brett Dietz, Hanover, 2003

Most Passes Completed per Game: 32.9—Justin Peery, Westminster (Mo.), 1999

Highest Completion Percentage: 73.6—Mitch Tanney, Monmouth (Ill.), 2005

Most Yards Gained: 4,595—Brett Elliott, Linfield, 2004

Most Yards Gained per Game: 450.1—Justin Peery, Westminster (Mo.), 1998

RECEIVING

Most Passes Caught: 136—Scott Pingel, Westminster (Mo.), 1999

Most Yards Gained: 2,157—Scott Pingel, Westminster, (Mo.), 1998

Most Yards Gained per Game: 215.7—Scott Pingel, Westminster, (Mo.), 1998

Highest Average Gain per Reception: 26.9—Marty Redlawsk, Concordia (Ill.), 1985

Single Game

SCORING

Most Field Goals: 6—Jim Hever, Rhodes, 1984 (vs Millsaps)

PASSING

Most Passes Completed: 51—Scott Kello, Sul Ross St, 2002 (vs Howard Payne)

Most Yards Gained: 731—Zamir Amin, Menlo, 2000 (vs California Lutheran)

Most Touchdown Passes: 9—Joe Zarlinga, Ohio Northern, 1998 (vs Capital)

RUSHING

Most Yards Gained: 441—Dante Brown, Marietta, 1996 (vs Baldwin-Wallace)

Most Touchdowns Rushed: 8—Carey Bender, Coe, 1994 (vs Beloit)

RECEIVING

Most Passes Caught: 23—Sean Munroe, Mass-Boston, 1992 (vs Mass-Maritime)

Most Yards Gained: 418—Lewis Howes, Principia, 2002 (vs Martin Luther)

Most Touchdown Catches: 7—Matt Perceval, Wesleyan (Conn.), 1998 (vs Middlebury)

NCAA FBS (Div. I-A) Alltime Individual Leaders

Career

Scoring

POINTS (KICKERS)	Years	Pts
Art Carmody, Louisville	2004–07	433
Roman Anderson, Houston	1988–91	423
Billy Bennett, Georgia	2000–03	409
Jeremy Ito, Rutgers	2004–07	400
Carlos Huerta, Miami (Fla.)	1988–91	397

POINTS (NON-KICKERS)	Years	Pts
Travis Prentice, Miami (Ohio)	1996–99	468
Ricky Williams, Texas	1995–98	452
Taurean Henderson, Texas Tech	2002–05	414
Brock Forsey, Boise St	1999–02	408
Cedric Benson, Texas	2001–04	404

POINTS PER GAME (NON-KICKERS)	Years	Pts/Game
Marshall Faulk, San Diego St	1991–93	12.1
Ed Marinaro, Cornell	1969–71	11.8
Bill Burnett, Arkansas	1968–70	11.3
Steve Owens, Oklahoma	1967–69	11.2
Eddie Talboom, Wyoming	1948–50	10.8

Total Offense

YARDS GAINED	Years	Yds
Timmy Chang, Hawaii	2000–04	16,910
Colt Brennan, Hawaii	2005–07	14,740
Ty Detmer, BYU	1988–91	14,665
Kevin Kolb, Houston	2003–06	13,715
Philip Rivers, North Carolina St	2000–03	13,582

YARDS PER GAME	Years	Yds/Game
Colt Brennan, Hawaii	2005–07	387.9
Tim Rattay, Louisiana Tech	1997–99	382.4
Chris Vargas, Nevada	1992–93	320.9
Timmy Chang, Hawaii	2000–04	319.1
Ty Detmer, BYU	1988–91	318.8

Rushing

YARDS GAINED	Years	Yds
Ron Dayne, Wisconsin	1996–99	6,397
Ricky Williams, Texas	1995–98	6,279
Tony Dorsett, Pittsburgh	1973–76	6,082
DeAngelo Williams, Memphis	2002–05	6,026
Charles White, USC	1976–79	5,598
Travis Prentice, Miami (Ohio)	1996–99	5,596

YARDS PER GAME	Years	Yds/Game
Ed Marinaro, Cornell	1969–71	174.6
O.J. Simpson, USC	1967–68	164.4
Herschel Walker, Georgia	1980–82	159.4
Garrett Wolfe, Northern Illinois	2004–06	156.6
LeShon Johnson, Northern Illinois	1992–93	150.6

TOUCHDOWNS RUSHING	Years	TD
Travis Prentice, Miami (Ohio)	1996–99	73
Ricky Williams, Texas	1995–98	72
Anthony Thompson, Indiana	1986–89	64
Cedric Benson, Texas	2001–04	64
Ron Dayne, Wisconsin	1996–99	63

Passing

PASSING EFFICIENCY	Years	Rating
Ryan Dinwiddie, Boise St	2000–03	168.4
Colt Brennan, Hawaii	2005–07	167.7
Danny Wuerffel, Florida	1993–96	163.6
Omar Jacobs, Bowling Green	2003–05	163.5
Ty Detmer, BYU	1988–91	162.7

Note: Minimum 500 completions.

YARDS GAINED	Years	Yds
Timmy Chang, Hawaii	2000–04	17,072
Ty Detmer, BYU	1988–91	15,031
Colt Brennan, Hawaii	2005–07	14,193
Philip Rivers, North Carolina St	2000–03	13,484
Kevin Kolb, Houston	2003-06	12,964

COMPLETIONS	Years	Comp
Timmy Chang, Hawaii	2000–04	1,388
Kliff Kingsbury, Texas Tech	1999–02	1,231
Philip Rivers, North Carolina St	2000–03	1,147
Colt Brennan, Hawaii	2005–07	1,115
Luke McCown, Louisiana Tech	2000–03	1,063

TOUCHDOWNS PASSING	Years	TD
Colt Brennan, Hawaii	2005–07	131
Ty Detmer, BYU	1988–91	121
Timmy Chang, Hawaii	2000–04	117
Tim Rattay, Louisiana Tech	1997–99	115
Danny Wuerffel, Florida	1993–96	114

Receiving

CATCHES	Years	No.
Taylor Stubblefield, Purdue	2001–04	316
Josh Davis, Marshall	2001–04	306
Taurean Henderson, Texas Tech	2002–05	303
Arnold Jackson, Louisville	1997–00	300
Trevor Insley, Nevada	1996–99	298

CATCHES PER GAME	Years	No./Game
Emmanuel Hazard, Houston	1989–90	10.5
Alex Van Dyke, Nevada	1994–95	10.3
Howard Twilley, Tulsa	1963–65	10.0
Jason Phillips, Houston	1987–88	9.4
Troy Edwards, Louisiana Tech	1996–98	8.2
Bryan Reeves, Nevada	1992–93	8.2

YARDS GAINED	Years	Yds
Trevor Insley, Nevada	1996–99	5,005
Marcus Harris, Wyoming	1993–96	4,518
Rashaun Woods, Oklahoma St	2000–03	4,412
Ryan Yarborough, Wyoming	1990–93	4,357
Troy Edwards, Louisiana Tech	1996–98	4,352

TOUCHDOWN CATCHES	Years	TD
Troy Edwards, Louisiana Tech	1996–98	50
Darius Watts, Marshall	2000–03	47
Aaron Turner, Pacific	1989–92	43
Ryan Yarborough, Wyoming	1990–93	42
Rashaun Woods, Oklahoma St	2000–03	42
Dwayne Jarrett, South Califonia	2004-06	41
Davone Bess, Hawaii	2005–07	41

NCAA FBS (Div. I-A) Alltime Individual Leaders *(Cont.)*

Career *(Cont.)*

All-Purpose Running

YARDS GAINED	Years	Yds
DeAngelo Williams, Memphis	2002–05	7,573
Ricky Williams, Texas	1996–98	7,206
Napoleon McCallum, Navy	1981–85	7,172
Chris Johnson, East Carolina	2004–07	6,993
Darrin Nelson, Stanford	1977–78, 80–81	6,885

YARDS PER GAME	Years	Yds/Game
Ryan Benjamin, Pacific	1990–92	237.8
Sheldon Canley, San Jose St	1988–90	205.8
Howard Stevens, Louisville	1971–72	193.7
O.J. Simpson, USC	1967–68	192.9
Alex Van Dyke, Nevada	1994–95	188.5

Interceptions

PLAYER/SCHOOL	Years	Int
Al Brosky, Illinois	1950–52	29
John Provost, Holy Cross	1972–74	27
Martin Bayless, Bowling Green	1980–83	27
Tom Curtis, Michigan	1967–69	25
Tony Thurman, Boston College	1981–84	25
Tracy Saul, Texas Tech	1989–92	25

Punting Average

PLAYER/SCHOOL	Years	Avg
Daniel Sepulveda, Baylor	2003–06	45.2
Shane Lechler, Texas A&M	1996–99	44.7
Bill Smith, Mississippi	1983–88	44.3
Jim Arnold, Vanderbilt	1979–82	43.9
Ralf Mojsiejenko, Michigan St	1981–84	43.6

Note: 250+ punts.

Punt Return Average

PLAYER/SCHOOL	Years	Avg
Jack Mitchell, Oklahoma	1946–48	23.6
Gene Gibson, Cincinnati	1949–50	20.5
Eddie Macon, Pacific	1949–51	18.9
Jackie Robinson, UCLA	1939–40	18.8
Dan Shelton, Illinois	2001–04	17.9

Note: Minimum 30 returns.

Kickoff Return Average

PLAYER/SCHOOL	Years	Avg
Anthony Davis, USC	1972–74	35.1
Eric Booth, Southern Miss	1994–97	32.4
Overton Curtis, Utah St	1957–58	31.0
Fred Montgomery, New Mexico St	1991–92	30.5
Altie Taylor, Utah St	1966–68	29.3

Note: Minimum 30 returns.

Single Season

Scoring

POINTS	Year	Pts
Barry Sanders, Oklahoma St	1988	234
Brock Forsey, Boise St	2002	192
Troy Edwards, Louisiana Tech	1998	186
Kevin Smith, Central Florida	2007	180
Mike Rozier, Nebraska	1983	174
Lydell Mitchell, Penn St	1971	174

FIELD GOALS	Year	FG
Billy Bennett, Georgia	2003	31
John Lee, UCLA	1984	29
John Sullivan, New Mexico	2007	29
Paul Woodside, West Virginia	1982	28
Luis Zendejas, Arizona St	1983	28
Nick Browne, TCU	2003	28
Justin Medlock, UCLA	2006	28

Three tied with 27.

All-Purpose Running

YARDS GAINED	Year	Yds
Barry Sanders, Oklahoma St	1988	3,250
Ryan Benjamin, Pacific	1991	2,995
Chris Johnson, East Carolina	2007	2,960
Reggie Bush, USC	2005	2,890
Kevin Smith, Central Florida	2007	2,809

YARDS PER GAME	Year	Yds/Game
Barry Sanders, Oklahoma St	1988	295.5
Ryan Benjamin, Pacific	1991	249.6
Byron (Whizzer) White, Colorado	1937	246.3
Mike Pringle, Fullerton St	1989	244.6
Paul Palmer, Temple	1986	239.4

Total Offense

YARDS GAINED	Year	Yds
B.J. Symons, Texas Tech	2003	5,976
Colt Brennan, Hawaii	2006	5,915
Graham Harrell, Texas Tech	2007	5,614
David Klingler, Houston	1990	5,221
Paul Smith, Tulsa	2007	5,184

YARDS PER GAME	Year	Yds/Game
David Klingler, Houston	1990	474.6
B.J. Symons, Texas Tech	2003	459.7
Graham Harrell, Texas Tech	2007	431.8
Andre Ware, Houston	1989	423.7
Colt Brennan, Hawaii	2006	422.5

Rushing

YARDS GAINED	Year	Yds
Barry Sanders, Oklahoma St	1988	2,628
Kevin Smith, UCF	2007	2,567
Marcus Allen, USC	1981	2,342
Troy Davis, Iowa St	1996	2,185
LaDainian Tomlinson, TCU	2000	2,158

YARDS PER GAME	Year	Yds/Game
Barry Sanders, Oklahoma St	1988	238.9
Marcus Allen, USC	1981	212.9
Ed Marinaro, Cornell	1971	209.0
Troy Davis, Iowa St	1996	198.6
LaDainian Tomlinson, TCU	2000	196.2

Single Season (*Cont.*)

Rushing (*Cont.*)

TOUCHDOWNS RUSHING	Year	TD
Barry Sanders, Oklahoma St	1988	37
Mike Rozier, Nebraska	1983	29
Willis McGahee, Miami (Fla.)	2002	28
Ricky Williams, Texas	1998	27
Lee Suggs, Virginia Tech	2000	27

Passing

PASSING EFFICIENCY	Year	Rating
Colt Brennan, Hawaii	2006	186.0
Shaun King, Tulane	1998	183.3
Stefan Lefors, Louisville	2004	181.7
Michael Vick, Virginia Tech	1999	180.4
Danny Wuerffel, Florida	1995	178.4

YARDS GAINED	Year	Yds
B.J. Symons, Texas Tech	2003	5,833
Graham Harrell, Texas Tech	2007	5,705
Colt Brennan, Hawaii	2006	5,549
Ty Detmer, BYU	1990	5,188
David Klingler, Houston	1990	5,140

COMPLETIONS	Year	Att	Comp
Graham Harrell, Texas Tech	2007	713	512
Kliff Kingsbury, Texas Tech	2002	712	479
B.J. Symons, Texas Tech	2003	719	470
Sonny Cumbie, Texas Tech	2004	642	421
Colt Brennan, Hawaii	2006	559	406

TOUCHDOWNS PASSING	Year	TD
Colt Brennan, Hawaii	2006	58
David Klingler, Houston	1990	54
B.J. Symons, Texas Tech	2003	52
Graham Harrell, Texas Tech	2007	48
Jim McMahon, BYU	1980	47

Receiving

CATCHES	Year	GP	No.
Emmanuel Hazard, Houston	1989	11	142
Troy Edwards, Louisiana Tech	1998	12	140
Nate Burleson, Nevada	2002	12	138
Howard Twilley, Tulsa	1965	10	134
Trevor Insley, Nevada	1999	11	134

CATCHES PER GAME	Year	No.	No./Game
Howard Twilley, Tulsa	1965	134	13.4
Emmanuel Hazard, Houston	1989	142	12.9
Trevor Insley, Nevada	1999	134	12.2
Troy Edwards, Louisiana Tech	1998	140	11.7
Alex Van Dyke, Nevada	1995	129	11.7

YARDS GAINED	Year	Yds
Trevor Insley, Nevada	1999	2,060
Troy Edwards, Louisiana Tech	1998	1,996
Michael Crabtree, Texas Tech	2007	1,962
Alex Van Dyke, Nevada	1995	1,854
J.R. Tolver, San Diego St	2002	1,785

TOUCHDOWN CATCHES	Year	TD
Troy Edwards, Louisiana Tech	1998	27
Randy Moss, Marshall	1997	25
Emmanuel Hazard, Houston	1989	22
Larry Fitzgerald, Pittsburgh	2003	22
Michael Crabtree, Texas Tech	2007	22

Single Game

Scoring

POINTS	Opponent	Year	Pts
Howard Griffith, Illinois	Southern Illinois	1990	48
Marshall Faulk, San Diego St	Pacific	1991	44
Jim Brown, Syracuse	Colgate	1956	43
Fred Wendt, UTEP*	New Mexico St	1948	42
Arnold Boykin, Mississippi	Mississippi St	1951	42
Rashaun Woods, Okla. St	SMU	2003	42

*UTEP was Texas Mines in 1948.

FIELD GOALS	Opponent	Year	FG
Dale Klein, Nebraska	Missouri	1985	7
Mike Prindle, Western Michigan	Marshall	1984	7

Note: 15 tied with 6.

Klein's distances were 32-22-43-44-29-43-43.
Prindle's distances were 32-44-42-23-48-41-27.

Total Offense

YARDS GAINED	Opponent	Year	Yds
David Klingler, Houston	Arizona St	1990	732
Matt Vogler, TCU	Houston	1990	696
B.J. Symons, Texas Tech	Mississippi	2003	681
Brian Lindgren, Idaho	Middle Tenn St	2001	657
David Klingler, Houston	TCU	1990	625
Scott Mitchell, Utah	Air Force	1988	625

Passing

YARDS GAINED	Opponent	Year	Yds
David Klingler, Houston	Arizona St	1990	716
Matt Vogler, TCU	Houston	1990	690
B.J. Symons, Texas Tech	Mississippi	2003	661
Graham Harrell, Texas Tech	Oklahoma St	2007	646
Cody Hodges, Texas Tech	Kansas St	2005	643

COMPLETIONS	Opponent	Year	Comp
Drew Brees, Purdue	Wisconsin	1998	55
Rusty LaRue, Wake Forest	Duke	1995	55
Rusty LaRue, Wake Forest	NC St	1995	50
C. Holbrook, New Mexico St	Boise St	2006	49
Brian Lindgren, Idaho	Middle Tenn St	2001	49
Kliff Kingsbury, Texas Tech	Missouri	2002	49
Kliff Kingsbury, Texas Tech	Texas A&M	2002	49
Bruce Gradkowski, Toledo	Pittsburgh	2003	49

TOUCHDOWNS PASSING	Opponent	Year	TD
David Klingler, Houston	E Wash	1990	11

Note: Klingler's TD passes were 5-48-29-7-3-7-40-10-7-8-51.

Single Game (*Cont.*)

Rushing

YARDS GAINED	Opponent	Year	Yds
LaDainian Tomlinson, TCU	UTEP	1999	406
Tony Sands, Kansas	Missouri	1991	396
Marshall Faulk, San Diego St	Pacific	1991	386
Troy Davis, Iowa St	Missouri	1996	378
Anthony Thompson, Indiana	Wisconsin	1989	377
Robbie Mixon, Cent. Mich	Eastern Mich	2002	377

TOUCHDOWNS RUSHING	Opponent	Year	TD
Howard Griffith, Illinois	Southern Illinois	1990	8

Note: Griffith's TD runs were 5-51-7-41-5-18-5-3.

Receiving

CATCHES	Opponent	Year	No.
Randy Gatewood, UNLV	Idaho	1994	23
Jay Miller, BYU	New Mexico	1973	22
Troy Edwards, La. Tech	Nebraska	1998	21
Chris Daniels, Purdue	Michigan St	1999	21
Rick Eber, Tulsa	Idaho St	1967	20
Kenny Christian, East. Mich	Temple	2000	20

Receiving (Cont.)

YARDS GAINED	Opponent	Year	Yds
Troy Edwards, Louisiana Tech	Nebraska	1998	405
Randy Gatewood, UNLV	Idaho	1994	363
Chuck Hughes, UTEP*	N Texas St	1965	349
Donnie Avery, Houston	Rice	2007	346
Casey Fitzgerald, North Texas	SMU	2007	327

*UTEP was Texas Western in 1965.

TOUCHDOWN CATCHES	Opponent	Year	TD
Rashaun Woods, Okla. St	SMU	2003	7
Tim Delaney, San Diego St	New Mex. St	1969	6

Longest Plays (since 1941)

PASSING	Opponent	Year	Yds
Fred Owens to Jack Ford, Portland	St. Mary's (Ca.)	1947	99
Bo Burris to Warren McVea, Houston	Washington St	1966	99
Colin Clapton to Eddie Jenkins, Holy Cross	Boston Univ.	1970	99
Terry Peel to Robert Ford, Houston	Syracuse	1970	99
Terry Peel to Robert Ford, Houston	San Diego St	1972	99
Cris Collinsworth to Derrick Gaffney, Florida	Rice	1977	99
Scott Ankrom to James Maness, TCU	Rice	1984	99
Gino Toretta to Horace Copeland, Miami (Fla.)	Arkansas	1991	99
John Paci to Thomas Lewis, Indiana	Penn St	1993	99
Troy DeGar to Wes Caswell Tulsa	Oklahoma	1996	99
Drew Brees to Vinny Sutherland, Purdue	Northwestern	1999	99
Dan Urban to Justin McCariens, Northern Illinois	Ball St	2000	99
Jason Johnson to Brandon Marshall, Arizona	Idaho	2001	99
Dondrial Pinkins to Troy Williamson, South Carolina	Virginia	2003	99
Jim Sorgi to Lee Evans, Wisconsin	Akron	2003	99
Giovanni Vizza to Casey Fitzgerald, North Texas	La.-Monroe	2007	99

RUSHING	Opponent	Year	Yd
Gale Sayers, Kansas	Nebraska	1963	99
Max Anderson, Arizona St	Wyoming	1967	99
Ralph Thompson, West Texas St	Wichita St	1970	99
Kelsey Finch, Tennessee	Florida	1977	99
Eric Vann, Kansas	Oklahoma	1997	99
Terry Caulley, Connecticut	Army	2006	99

FIELD GOALS	Opponent	Year	Yds
Steve Little, Arkansas	Texas	1977	67
Russell Erxleben, Texas	Rice	1977	67
Joe Williams, Wichita St	Southern Ill.	1978	67
Martin Gramatica, Kansas St	Northern Ill.	1998	65
Tony Franklin, Texas A&M	Baylor	1976	65

PUNTS	Opponent	Year	Yds
Pat Brady, Nevada*	Loyola (Ca.)	1950	99
George O'Brien, Wisconsin	Iowa	1952	96
John Hadl, Kansas	Oklahoma	1959	94
Carl Knox, TCU	Oklahoma St	1947	94
Preston Johnson, SMU	Pittsburgh	1940	94

*Nevada was Nevada-Reno in 1950.

FOOTBALL BOWL SUBDIVISION (DIV. I-A) WINNINGEST TEAMS

Alltime Winning Percentage

	Yrs	W	L	T	Pct	GP	Bowl Record
Michigan	128	869	286	36	.745	1,191	19-20-0
Notre Dame	119	824	278	42	.739	1,144	13-15-0
Texas	115	820	316	33	.716	1,169	24-21-2
Oklahoma	113	779	295	53	.715	1,127	24-16-1
Ohio St	118	798	304	53	.714	1,155	18-21-0
Alabama	113	787	314	43	.707	1,144	31-21-3
USC	115	754	302	54	.704	1,110	30-16-0
Nebraska	118	808	333	40	.701	1,181	22-22-0
Tennessee	111	770	320	53	.697	1,143	25-22-0
Boise St	40	327	143	2	.695	472	5-3-0
Penn St	121	789	347	41	.688	1,177	26-12-2
Florida St	61	450	217	17	.670	684	20-14-2
Georgia	114	713	381	54	.645	1,148	24-16-3
LSU	114	692	378	47	.641	1,117	20-18-1
Miami (Fla.)	81	537	304	19	.635	860	18-13-0
Miami (Ohio)	119	647	369	44	.631	1,060	6-3-0
Auburn	115	676	388	47	.630	1,111	19-13-2
South Florida	11	79	47	0	.627	126	1-2-0
Florida	101	628	372	40	.623	1,040	16-19-0
Washington	118	650	388	50	.620	1,088	14-14-1
Arizona St	95	540	327	24	.620	891	12-11-1
Central Michigan	107	550	348	36	.608	934	1-3-0
Colorado	118	658	419	36	.607	1,113	12-16-0
*Western Kentucky	88	509	327	30	.605	866	0–0–0
Texas A&M	113	655	425	48	.602	1,128	13-17-0

Note: Includes bowl games. *Reclassified as FBS (Div. I-A) on November 2, 2006.

Alltime Victories

Team	W	Team	W	Team	W
Michigan	869	Georgia	713	Virginia Tech	647
Notre Dame	824	LSU	692	Arkansas	646
Texas	820	Auburn	676	Pittsburgh	644
Nebraska	808	Syracuse	671	Army	634
Ohio St	798	West Virginia	664	North Carolina	631
Penn St	789	Colorado	658	Minnesota	630
Alabama	787	Texas A&M	655	Florida	628
Oklahoma	779	Georgia Tech	653	Clemson	625
Tennessee	770	Washington	650	Navy	624
USC	754	Miami (Ohio)	647	Virginia	606

NUMBER ONE VS NUMBER TWO

The No. 1 and No. 2 teams, according to the Associated Press Poll, have met 33 times, including 13 bowl games, since the poll's inception in 1936. The No. 1 teams have a 20-11-2 record in these matchups. Notre Dame (4-3-2) has played in nine of the games.

Date	Results	Stadium
10-9-43	No. 1 Notre Dame 35, No. 2 Michigan 12	Michigan (Ann Arbor)
11-20-43	No. 1 Notre Dame 14, No. 2 Iowa Pre-Flight 13	Notre Dame (South Bend)
12-2-44	No. 1 Army 23, No. 2 Navy 7	Municipal (Baltimore)
11-10-45	No. 1 Army 48, No. 2 Notre Dame 0	Yankee (New York)
12-1-45	No. 1 Army 32, No. 2 Navy 13	Municipal (Philadelphia)
11-9-46	No. 1 Army 0, No. 2 Notre Dame 0	Yankee (New York)
1-1-63	No. 1 USC 42, No. 2 Wisconsin 37 (Rose Bowl)	Rose Bowl (Pasadena)
10-12-63	No. 2 Texas 28, No. 1 Oklahoma 7	Cotton Bowl (Dallas)
1-1-64	No. 1 Texas 28, No. 2 Navy 6 (Cotton Bowl)	Cotton Bowl (Dallas)
11-19-66	No. 1 Notre Dame 10, No. 2 Michigan St 10	Spartan (East Lansing)
9-28-68	No. 1 Purdue 37, No. 2 Notre Dame 22	Notre Dame (South Bend)
1-1-69	No. 1 Ohio St 27, No. 2 USC 16 (Rose Bowl)	Rose Bowl (Pasadena)
12-6-69	No. 1 Texas 15, No. 2 Arkansas 14	Razorback (Fayetteville)
11-25-71	No. 1 Nebraska 35, No. 2 Oklahoma 31	Owen Field (Norman)
1-1-72	No. 1 Nebraska 38, No. 2 Alabama 6 (Orange Bowl)	Orange Bowl (Miami)
1-1-79	No. 2 Alabama 14, No. 1 Penn St 7 (Sugar Bowl)	Sugar Bowl (New Orleans)
9-26-81	No. 1 USC 28, No. 2 Oklahoma 24	Coliseum (Los Angeles)
1-1-83	No. 2 Penn St 27, No. 1 Georgia 23 (Sugar Bowl)	Sugar Bowl (New Orleans)
10-19-85	No. 1 Iowa 12, No. 2 Michigan 10	Kinnick (Iowa City)

NUMBER ONE VS NUMBER TWO (Cont.)

Date	Results	Stadium
9-27-86	No. 2 Miami (Fla.) 28, No. 1 Oklahoma 16	Orange Bowl (Miami)
1-2-87	No. 2 Penn St 14, No. 1 Miami (FL) 10 (Fiesta Bowl)	Sun Devil (Tempe)
11-21-87	No. 2 Oklahoma 17, No. 1 Nebraska 7	Memorial (Lincoln)
1-1-88	No. 2 Miami (Fla.) 20, No. 1 Oklahoma 14 (Orange Bowl)	Orange Bowl (Miami)
11-26-88	No. 1 Notre Dame 27, No. 2 USC 10	Coliseum (Los Angeles)
9-16-89	No. 1 Notre Dame 24, No. 2 Michigan 19	Michigan (Ann Arbor)
11-16-91	No. 2 Miami (Fla.) 17, No. 1 Florida St 16	Campbell (Tallahassee)
1-1-93	No. 2 Alabama 34, No. 1 Miami (Fla.) 13 (Sugar Bowl)	Superdome (New Orleans)
11-13-93	No. 2 Notre Dame 31, No. 1 Florida St 24	Notre Dame (South Bend)
1-1-94	No. 1 Florida St 18, No. 2 Nebraska 16 (Orange Bowl)	Orange Bowl (Miami)
1-2-96	No. 1 Nebraska 62, No. 2 Florida 24 (Fiesta Bowl)	Sun Devil (Tempe)
11-30-96	No. 2 Florida St 24, No. 1 Florida 21	Campbell (Tallahassee)
1-4-99	No. 1 Tennessee 23, No. 2 Florida St 16 (Fiesta Bowl)	Sun Devil (Tempe)
1-4-00	No. 1 Florida St 46, No. 2 Virginia Tech 29 (Sugar Bowl)	Superdome (New Orleans)
1-3-03	No. 2 Ohio St 31, No. 1 Miami (Fla.) 24 [2OT] (Fiesta Bowl)	Sun Devil (Tempe)
1-4-05	No. 1 USC 55, No. 2 Oklahoma 19 (Orange Bowl)	Pro Player Stadium (Miami)
1-5-06	No. 2 Texas 41, No. 1 USC 38 (Rose Bowl)	Rose Bowl (Pasadena)
9-9-06	No. 1 Ohio St 24, No. 2 Texas 7	Texas Memorial (Austin)
11-18-06	No. 1 Ohio St 42, No. 2 Michigan 39	Ohio (Columbus)
1-8-07	No. 2 Florida 41, No. 1 Ohio St 14 (BCS Championship)	Univ. of Phoenix (Glendale)
1-7-08	No. 2 LSU 38, No. 1 Ohio St. 24 (BCS Championship)	Superdome (New Orleans)

LONGEST FBS (DIV. I-A) WINNING STREAKS

Wins	Team	Yrs	Ended by	Score
47	Oklahoma	1953–57	Notre Dame	7–0
39	Washington	1908–14	Oregon St	0–0
37	Yale	1890–93	Princeton	6–0
37	Yale	1887–89	Princeton	10–0
35	Toledo	1969–71	Tampa	21–0
34	USC	2003–05	Texas	41–38
34	Miami	2000–03	Ohio St	31–24 (2ot)
34	Pennsylvania	1894–96	Lafayette	6–4
31	Oklahoma	1948–50	Kentucky	13–7
31	Pittsburgh	1914–18	Cleveland Naval Reserve	10–9
31	Pennsylvania	1896–98	Harvard	10–0
30	Texas	1968–70	Notre Dame	24–11

LONGEST FBS (DIV. I-A) UNBEATEN STREAKS

No.	W	T	Team	Yrs	Ended by	Score
63	59	4	Washington	1907–17	California	27–0
56	55	1	Michigan	1901–05	Chicago	2–0
50	46	4	California	1920–25	Olympic Club	15–0
48	47	1	Oklahoma	1953–57	Notre Dame	7–0
48	47	1	Yale	1885–89	Princeton	10–0
47	42	5	Yale	1879–85	Princeton	6–5
44	42	2	Yale	1894–96	Princeton	24–6
42	39	3	Yale	1904–08	Harvard	4–0
39	37	2	Notre Dame	1946–50	Purdue	28–14
37	36	1	Oklahoma	1972–75	Kansas	23–3
37	37	0	Yale	1890–93	Princeton	6–0
35	35	0	Toledo	1969–71	Tampa	21–0
35	34	1	Minnesota	1903–05	Wisconsin	16–12
34	34	0	USC	2003–05	Texas	41–38
34	34	0	Miami	2000–03	Ohio St	31–24 (2ot)
34	33	1	Nebraska	1912–16	Kansas	7–3
34	34	0	Pennsylvania	1894–96	Lafayette	6–4
34	32	2	Princeton	1884–87	Harvard	12–0
34	29	5	Princeton	1877–82	Harvard	1–0
33	30	3	Tennessee	1926–30	Alabama	18–6
33	31	2	Georgia Tech	1914–18	Pittsburgh	32–0
33	30	3	Harvard	1911–15	Cornell	10–0
32	31	1	Nebraska	1969–71	UCLA	20–17
32	30	2	Army	1944–47	Columbia	21–20
32	31	1	Harvard	1898–1900	Yale	28–0

Note: Includes bowl games.

Notable Achievements *(Cont.)*

LONGEST DIVISION I-A LOSING STREAKS

Losses		Seasons	Ended Against	Score
34	Northwestern	1979–82	Northern Illinois	31–6
28	Virginia	1958–61	William & Mary	21–6
28	Kansas St	1945–48	Arkansas St	37–6
27	New Mexico St	1988–90	Cal St–Fullerton	43–9
27	Eastern Michigan	1980–82	Kent St	9–7

MOST-PLAYED DIVISION I-A RIVALRIES

GP	Opponents (Series Leader Listed First)	Record	First Game
117	Minnesota–Wisconsin	59-50-8	1890
116	Kansas–Missouri	55-52-9	1891
114	Nebraska-Kansas	88-23-3	1892
114	Texas–Texas A&M	73-36-5	1894
112	Miami (Ohio)–Cincinnati	59-46-7	1888
112	North Carolina–Virginia	†57-51-4	1892
111	Auburn–Georgia	53-50-8	1892
111	Oregon–Oregon St	55-46-10	1894
110	Purdue–Indiana	68-36-6	1891
110	Stanford–California	55-44-11	1892
108	Navy–Army	52-49-7	1890
107	Utah–Utah St	75-28-4	1892
105	Baylor–TCU	49-49-7	1899
105	Clemson–South Carolina	64-37-4	1896
105	Kansas–Kansas St	64-36-5	1902
104	Michigan–Ohio St	57-41-6	1897
104	Mississippi–Miss St	59-39-6	1901
103	North Carolina–Wake Forest	67-34-2	1897
103	Tennessee–Kentucky	71-23-9	1893
102	Georgia–Georgia Tech	59-38-5	1893
102	Nebraska–Iowa St	84-16-2	1896
102	Texas–Oklahoma	57-40-5	1900
102	Oklahoma–Oklahoma St	79-16-7	1904

†Disputed series record: Virginia claims North Carolina leads series 55-51-4 based on a forfeited game in 1956.

NCAA Coaches' Records

ALLTIME WINNINGEST FBS (DIV. I-A) COACHES

By Percentage

Coach (Alma Mater)	Colleges Coached	Yrs	W	L	T	Pct
Knute Rockne (Notre Dame '14)†	Notre Dame 1918–30	13	105	12	5	.881
Frank W. Leahy (Notre Dame '31)†	Boston College 1939–40; Notre Dame 1941–43, 1946–53	13	107	13	9	.864
George W. Woodruff (Yale 1889)†	Pennsylvania 1892–01; Illinois 1903; Carlisle 1905	12	142	25	2	.846
Barry Switzer (Arkansas '60)	Oklahoma 1973–88	16	157	29	4	.837
Tom Osborne (Hastings '59)†	Nebraska 1973–97	25	255	49	3	.836
Percy D. Haughton (Harvard 1899)†	Cornell 1899–1900; Harvard 1908–16; Columbia 1923–24	13	96	17	6	.832
Bob Neyland (Army '16)†	Tennessee 1926–34, 1936–40, 1946–52	21	173	31	12	.829
Fielding Yost (West Virginia 1895)†	Ohio Wesleyan 1897; Nebraska 1898; Kansas 1899; Stanford 1900; Michigan 1901–23, 1925–26	29	196	36	12	.828
Bud Wilkinson (Minnesota '37)†	Oklahoma 1947–63	17	145	29	4	.826
Jock Sutherland (Pittsburgh '18)†	Lafayette 1919–23; Pittsburgh 1924–38	20	144	28	14	.812
Bob Devaney (Alma [Mich] '39)†	Wyoming 1957–61; Nebraska 1962–72	16	136	30	7	.806
Frank W. Thomas (Notre Dame '23)†	Tenn.-Chattanooga 1925–28; Alabama 1931–42, 1944–46	19	141	33	9	.795
Henry L. Williams (Yale 1891)†	Army 1891; Minnesota 1900–21	23	141	34	12	.786
Gil Dobie (Minnesota '02)†	North Dakota St 1906–07; Washington 1908-16; Navy 1917–19; Cornell 1920–35; Boston College 1936–38	33	180	45	15	.781
Bear Bryant (Alabama '36)†	Maryland 1945, Kentucky 1946–53,	38	323	85	17	.780
Fred Folsom (Dartmouth 1895)	Colorado 1895–99, 1901–02; Dartmouth 1903–06; Colorado 1908–15	19	106	28	6	.779
Bo Schembechler (Miami [Ohio] '51)	Miami (Ohio) 1963–68; Michigan 1969–89	27	234	65	8	.775
Fritz Crisler (Chicago '22)	Minnesota 1930–31, Princeton 1931–37–Michigan 1938–47	18	116	32	9	.768
*Phillip Fulmer (Tennessee, '72)	Tennessee 1992–	16	147	65	0	.766

*Active in 2007. †Hall of Fame member.

Note: Minimum 10 years as head coach at Division I institutions; record at four-year colleges only; bowl games included; ranked by percentage, ties computed as half won, half lost.

ALLTIME WINNINGEST FBS (DIV. I-A) COACHES (Cont.)

By Victories

	Yrs	W	L	T	Pct
*Bobby Bowden	42	373	119	4	.762
*Joe Paterno	42	372	125	3	.747
Paul (Bear) Bryant	38	323	85	17	.780
Glenn (Pop) Warner	44	319	106	32	.733
Amos Alonzo Stagg	57	314	199	35	.605
LaVell Edwards	29	257	100	3	.718
Tom Osborne	25	255	49	3	.836
Lou Holtz	33	249	132	7	.651
Woody Hayes	33	238	72	10	.759
Bo Schembechler	27	234	65	8	.775
Hayden Fry	37	232	178	10	.564
*Frank Beamer	27	209	108	4	.657
Jim Tressel	22	208	73	2	.739
Jess Neely	40	207	176	19	.539
Warren Woodson	31	203	95	14	.673
Don Nehlen	30	202	128	8	.609
Vince Dooley	25	201	77	10	.715
Eddie Anderson	39	201	128	15	.606

*Active in 2007. Minimum of five years of coaching at FBS level. Record at four-year colleges only.

Most Bowl Victories

	W	L	T
*Joe Paterno	23	10	1
*Bobby Bowden	20	10	1
Paul (Bear) Bryant	15	12	2
Lou Holtz	12	8	2
Tom Osborne	12	13	0
Don James	10	5	0
*Mack Brown	10	6	0
John Vaught	10	8	0
Bobby Dodd	9	4	0
Johnny Majors	9	7	0
John Robinson	8	1	0
Barry Alvarez	8	3	0
Terry Donahue	8	4	1
Barry Switzer	8	5	0
Jackie Sherrill	8	6	0
Darrell Royal	8	7	1
*Philip Fulmer	8	7	0
Vince Dooley	8	10	2
Pat Dye	7	2	1
Bob Devaney	7	3	0
Dan Devine	7	3	0
Earle Bruce	7	5	0
Charlie McClendon	7	6	0
*Steve Spurrier	7	7	0
Hayden Fry	7	9	1

*Active in 2007.

WINNINGEST ACTIVE FBS (DIV. I-A) COACHES

By Percentage

Coach, College	Yrs	W	L	T	Pct.	Bowls W	Bowls L	Bowls T
Pete Carroll, USC	7	76	14	0	.844	5	2	0
Urban Meyer, Florida	7	70	16	0	.814	4	1	0
*Bob Stoops, Oklahoma	9	97	22	0	.815	4	5	0
Mark Richt, Georgia	7	72	19	0	.791	5	2	0
Phillip Fulmer, Tennessee	16	147	45	0	.766	8	7	0
Bobby Bowden, Florida St	42	373	119	4	.756	20	10	1
Joe Paterno, Penn St	42	372	125	3	.747	23	10	1
Steve Spurrier, South Carolina	18	163	56	2	.742	7	7	0
Jim Tressel, Ohio St	22	208	73	2	.739	4	3	0
Paul Johnson, Georgia Tech	11	107	39	0	.733	2	2	0
Brian Kelly, Cincinnati	18	148	54	2	.730	2	0	0
Dan Hawkins, Colorado	12	100	40	1	.713	2	3	0
Gary Patterson, TCU	8	62	25	0	.713	4	3	0
Dennis Erickson, Arizona St	19	158	68	1	.698	5	6	0
Les Miles, LSU	7	62	27	0	.697	4	2	0
Chris Ault, Nevada	23	191	85	1	.691	1	4	0
Rick Neuheisel, UCLA	8	66	30	0	.688	4	3	0
Frank Solich, Ohio	9	77	37	0	.675	2	4	0
Nick Saban, Alabama	12	98	48	1	.670	4	5	0
Tommy Tuberville, Auburn	13	105	53	0	.665	7	3	0

#Bowl games included. Ties computed as half win, half loss. Note: Min. five years as Div. I-A head coach at four-year collges only. *Seven regular season wins and one bowl victory from Stoops' 2005 season at Oklahoma were vacated in 2007 due to NCAA rules violations and then restored on February 28, 2008.

By Victories

Coach, College	W
Bobby Bowden, Florida St	373
Joe Paterno, Penn St	372
Frank Beamer, Viginia Tech	209
Jim Tressel, Ohio St	208
Chris Ault, Nevada	191
Mack Brown, Texas	189
Joe Glenn, Wyoming	183
Dick Tomey, San Jose St	175
Steve Spurrier, South Carolina	163
Dennis Erickson, Arizona St	158
Mike Price, UTEP	154
Brian Kelly, Cincinnati	148
Phillip Fulmer, Tennessee	137
Howard Schellenberger, Fla. Atlantic	133
Larry Blakeney, Troy	127
Mike Bellotti, Oregon	118

WINNINGEST ACTIVE FCS (DIV. I-AA) COACHES

By Percentage

Coach, College	Yrs	W	L	T	Pct*
Bob Hauck, Montana	5	52	14	0	.788
David Bennett, Coastal Carolina	12	102	34	0	.750
K.C. Keeler, Delaware	15	150	47	1	.747
Al Bagnoli, Pennsylvania	26	194	69	0	.738
Joe Taylor, Florida A&M	25	197	76	4	.718
Mark Farley, Northern Iowa	7	63	25	0	.716
Pete Richardson, Southern Univ.	20	163	66	1	.711
Pete Lembo, Elon	7	56	24	0	.700
Buddy Pough, South Carolina St	6	47	21	0	.691
Don Brown, Massachusetts	11	88	40	0	.688
Dick Biddle, Colgate	12	95	46	0	.674

*Playoff games included.
Note: Minimum five years as a Division I-A and/or Division I-AA head coach; record at four-year colleges only.

By Victories

Bob Ford, Albany St....225
Joe Taylor, Florida A&M....197
Al Bagnoli, Pennsylvania....194
Jerry Moore, Appalachian St....194
Walt Hameline, Wagner....186
Rob Ash, Montana St....182
Andy Talley, Villanova....182
Jimmye Laycock, William & Mary....182
Pete Richardson, Southern U.....163
Mike Ayers, Wofford....143

WINNINGEST ACTIVE DIVISION II COACHES

By Percentage

Coach, College	Yrs	W	L	T	Pct*
Chuck Broyles, Pittsburg St (Kan.)	18	182	39	2	.821
Ken Sparks, Carson-Newman	28	269	63	2	.808
Bryan Collins, LIU-C.W. Post	10	84	26	0	.764
Bill Zwaan, West Chester	11	99	31	0	.762
John Luckhardt, California (Pa.)	23	182	59	2	.753
Danny Hale, Bloomsburg	20	165	57	1	.742
Mark Hudspeth, North Alabama	6	54	19	0	.740
Tom Sawyer, Winona St	12	103	37	0	.736
Peter Yetten, Bentley	20	146	54	1	.730
Mel Tjeerdsma, NW Missouri St	24	203	77	4	.722

*Ties computed as half win, half loss. Playoff games included.
Note: Minimum five years as a college head coach; record at four-year colleges only.

By Victories

Ken Sparks, Carson-Newman....269
Willard Bailey, St. Paul's....219
Dennis Douds, East Stroudsburg....209
Mel Tjeerdsma, NW Missouri St....203
Chuck Broyles, Pittsburg St....182
John Luckhardt, California (Pa.)....182
Monte Cater, Shepherd....179
Danny Hale, Bloomsburg....165
Peter Yetten, Bentley....146
Rocky Rees, Shippensburg....141

NCAA Coaches' Records *(Cont.)*

WINNINGEST ACTIVE DIVSION III COACHES

By Percentage

Coach, College	Yrs	W	L	T	Pct*
Larry Kehres, Mount Union	22	260	21	3	.921
Jim Purthill, St. Norbert	9	84	13	0	.866
Mike Sirianni, Washington and Jefferson	5	50	8	0	.862
Joe Fincham, Wittenberg	12	108	25	0	.812
John Gagliardi, St. John's (Minn.)	59	453	122	11	.782
Jimmie Keeling, Hardin-Simmons	18	149	45	0	.768
Mike Swider, Wheaton (Ill.)	12	96	29	0	.768
Pete Fredenberg, Mary Hardin-Baylor	10	87	27	0	.763
†Dean Paul, Ohio Northern	8	61	21	0	.744
Mike Drass, Wesley	15	120	41	1	.744

*Ties computed as half won, half lost. Playoff games included. †Dean Paul's 8–2 season with Ohio Northern in 2004 was later vacated.

Note: Minimum five years as a college head coach; record at four-year colleges only.

By Victories

John Gagliardi, St John's (Minn.)	453
Larry Kehres, Mount Union	260
Eric Hamilton, College of New Jersey	188
Rick Giancola, Montclair St.	173
Rich Lackner, Carnegie Mellon	155
Dale Widolff, Occidental	153
Michael DeLong, Springfield	150
Jimmie Keeling, Hardin-Simmons	149
Larry Kindbom, Wash U.-St. Louis	149
Barry Streeter, Gettysburg	147
Steve Mohr, Trinity (Texas)	145
Mike Hollway, Ohio Wesleyan	139

NAIA Coaches' Records

WINNINGEST ACTIVE NAIA COACHES

By Percentage

Coach, College	Yrs	W	L	T	Pct*
Mike Van Diest, Carroll (Mont.)	9	104	18	0	.852
Bill Cronin, Georgetown (Ky.)	11	112	23	0	.830
Mike Cochran, Southern Nazarene (Okla.)	7	59	19	0	.756
Hank Biesiot, Dickinson St (N.D.)	32	228	85	1	.728
Patrick Ross, Lindenwood (Mo.)	6	47	20	0	.701
Orv Otten, Northwestern (Ia.)	13	98	42	0	.700
Carl Poelker, McKendree (Ill.)	26	176	76	1	.698
Mac Bryan, Pikeville (Ky.)	7	52	23	1	.691
Steve Ryan, Morningside (Ia.)	6	46	22	0	.676
Mike Feminis, St. Xavier (Ill.)	9	69	34	0	.670
Kevin Donley, St. Francis (Ind.)	29	217	107	1	.669
Paul Troth, Missouri Valley	12	81	40	0	.669
Keith Barefield, Northwestern Oklahoma St.	11	74	37	2	.664
Monty Lewis, Friends (Kan.)	15	94	48	0	.662
Chris Welch, Graceland (Ia.)	5	34	18	0	.654

*Playoff games included.

Note: Minimum five years as a collegiate head coach and includes record against four-year institutions only.

By Victories

Hank Biesiot, Dickinson St (N.D.)	228
Kevin Donley, St. Francis (Ind.)	217
Larry Wilcox, Benedictine (Kan.)	200
Carl Poelker, McKendree (Ill.)	176
Jim Dennison, Walsh (Ohio)	173
Fran Schwenk, William Jewell (Mo.)	131
Bob Green, Montana Tech	123
Bill Cronin, Georgetown (Ky.)	112
Mike Van Dienst, Carroll (Mont.)	104
Courtney Meyer, Concordia (Neb.)	104

Pro Basketball

BOB ROSATO/SPORTS ILLUSTRATED

MVP Paul Pierce led the Boston Celtics to that team's first NBA title since 1986

Triumphant Returns

Thanks to the resurgence of two storied franchises, the NBA rebounded in the 2007–08 season

BY CHRIS MANNIX

A GAMBLING SCANDAL. TELEVISION ratings that weren't rivaling other sports so much as re-runs of Matlock. A flagship Eastern Conference franchise in the toilet and its counterpart out west circling the bowl. These were not the best of times for the NBA entering the 2007–08 season.

Add to this the scandal that broke the previous summer when Tim Donaghy, a 13-year veteran referee, pleaded guilty to placing tens of thousands of dollars in bets on games he officiated during the 2005–06 and 2006–07 seasons. "I can tell you that this is the most serious situation and worst situation that I have ever experienced either as a fan of the NBA, a lawyer for the NBA or a commissioner of the NBA," said Commissioner David Stern shortly after the allegations against Donaghy became public. "I feel betrayed by what happened on behalf of the sport."

Even without the point shaving allegations, the league was struggling. For proof, you needed to look no further than the NBA's two marquee franchises. In Boston, where 16 of the NBA's 61 championship banners hang from the rafters, the Celtics had hit rock bottom. It had been 22 years since Boston last hoisted a banner and by the end of the '06–'07 season it looked like it would take at least 22 more. Boston had finished the regular season an abysmal 24–58, the second-worst record in the NBA and the second-worst in franchise history. In Los Angeles, the Lakers weren't bottoming out but there were no plans for a parade either. The 2006–07 Lakers were a far cry from the team that advanced to four NBA Finals earlier in the decade. The superstar, Kobe Bryant, was still there but his cast of characters—a group that included Shaquille O'Neal—had long since abandoned him. By the end of 2007, the Lakers were ousted from the playoffs in the first round, the third straight season the Artists Formerly Known as Showtime failed to advance past the postseason's opening frame. Making matters worse, Bryant was caught on a cell phone camera in the offseason ripping management for refusing to part with second-year center Andrew Bynum in order to acquire Jason Kidd. In the aftermath of his ill-timed rant, Bryant went public demanding a trade from the only franchise he has ever played for.

Perhaps then it is fitting that the NBA and its marquee franchises experienced revivals in the same season. For Boston, the resurgence began on draft night when general manager Danny Ainge—who had become arguably the most maligned figure in the Hub since Bill Buckner—engineered a draft day trade that netted Boston seven-time All-Star guard Ray Allen. A little over a month

Averaging 28.3 points per game for the season, Lakers guard Bryant earned the first regular season MVP award of his career.

STEPHEN DUNN/GETTY IMAGES

later, Ainge shocked the basketball world again when he shipped seven players to Minnesota for former league MVP Kevin Garnett. The seven-for-one swap was the largest deal for one player in NBA history and completed the Celtics rapid transformation from NBA doormat to title contenders. "This is a tremendous day," said Paul Pierce. "I feel like a rookie again."

With a new Big 3 on board, Boston won 20 of their first 22 games and finished the regular season with 66 wins, good for the greatest single-season turnaround in NBA history. Defense was Boston's calling card: Anchored by Garnett, who won his first Defensive Player of the Year award, the Celtics ranked first in the NBA in opponents field goal percentage (41.9%) and second in points allowed (90.3).

Still, while the Celtics rolled through the regular season, the Eastern Conference playoffs would prove an especially tough challenge. In the first round the Celtics were stretched to seven games against eighth-seeded (and sub .500) Atlanta and needed seven more to defeat Cleveland in the conference semifinals. In an epic Game 7, Pierce and LeBron James engaged in an old-fashioned shootout with James (45 points) edging out Pierce (41) on the stat sheet but the Celtics coming away with the win. "I love games like this," said James. "I love going against the best, and Paul Pierce is one of the best." Riding a new wave of momentum, Boston hammered Detroit in six games in the conference finals to advance to their first NBA Finals in 21 years. "This is what we worked for," said Pierce. "This is why they brought us all together."

Meanwhile in Los Angeles, Lakers GM Mitch Kupchak had an ace of his own up his sleeve. Despite the turbulent offseason, the Lakers jumped out to a strong start and with the calendar turning to February, LA found themselves in a dogfight with New Orleans (which was led by the scintillating Chris Paul) and San Antonio (which had the less than scintillating Tim Duncan) in the

GREG NELSON

New Orleans Hornets point guard Chris Paul had a breakout season in 2007–08, leading the league in assists and steals.

Western Conference. However when Bynum went down with a season-ending knee injury in January, it appeared the Lakers would go down with him. But two weeks after losing Bynum, Kupchak dispatched Kwame Brown, Javaris Crittenton and a pair of first round picks to Memphis for All-Star center Pau Gasol. It was a move that instantly bolstered the Laker lineup—they won nine of their first ten with Gasol—but was universally panned by the rest of the league as highway robbery. "What they did in Memphis is beyond comprehension," said Spurs coach Gregg Popovich. "There should be a trade committee that scratches all trades that make no sense." With Gasol on board the Lakers breezed through the Western Conference, dispatching Denver in four games and Utah in six before sending San Antonio (and Popovich) packing in five games. Bryant scored 39 points in the clincher.

Less than a year after facing its darkest hour, the NBA had its dream scenario: the Celtics versus the Lakers, the two most storied franchises in the league. Highlights from the 1980's rivalry filled the airwaves in the days leading up to Game 1 as both teams trotted out nearly every former player with a pulse. But the dream nearly became a nightmare for Boston in Game 1 when, in the third quarter, Pierce crumpled to the floor and had to be carried off the court with a knee injury. Pierce, however, returned to score 15 points in the quarter and propel the Celtics to a 98–88 win. A victory by Boston in Game 2 had LA teetering on the brink of elimination.

While the Lakers rallied to win Game 3, it was the fourth game that served as the defining moment of the series. Trailing by 24 points in the third quarter, Boston staged a furious rally to come back and win, the largest comeback in an NBA Finals game since 1971 and one that put the Lakers in an insurmountable 3–1 hole. Not even a Game 5 win by Los Angeles could slow the Celtics momentum. Returning home, Boston buried LA early in Game 6, building a 39-point lead before going on to win 131–92. As Stern handed Celtics owner Wyc Grousbeck the Larry O'Brien trophy on the Garden floor, he couldn't help but smile. A storied franchise. An exciting postseason. A first step to putting the past behind him.

NBA Final Standings

Western Conference

NORTHWEST DIVISION

Team	W	L	Pct	GB
†Utah	54	28	.659	—
*Denver	50	32	.610	4
Portland	41	41	.500	13
Minnesota	22	60	.268	32
Seattle	20	62	.244	34

PACIFIC DIVISION

Team	W	L	Pct	GB
‡LA Lakers	57	25	.695	—
*Phoenix	55	27	.671	2
Golden State	48	34	.585	9
Sacramento	38	44	.463	19
LA Clippers	23	59	.280	34

SOUTHWEST DIVISION

Team	W	L	Pct	GB
†New Orleans	56	26	.683	—
*San Antonio	56	26	.683	—
*Houston	55	27	.671	1
*Dallas	51	31	.622	5
Memphis	22	60	.268	34

Eastern Conference

ATLANTIC DIVISION

Team	W	L	Pct	GB
‡Boston	66	16	.805	—
*Toronto	41	41	.500	25
*Philadelphia	40	42	.488	26
New Jersey	34	48	.415	32
New York	23	59	.280	43

CENTRAL DIVISION

Team	W	L	Pct	GB
†Detroit	59	23	.720	—
*Cleveland	45	37	.549	14
Indiana	36	46	.439	23
Chicago	33	49	.402	26
Milwaukee	26	56	.317	33

SOUTHEAST DIVISION

Team	W	L	Pct	GB
†Orlando	52	30	.634	—
*Washington	43	39	.524	9
*Atlanta	37	45	.451	15
Charlotte	32	50	.390	20
Miami	15	67	.183	37

†Clinched division title. *Clinched playoff berth. ‡Clinched conference title.

2008 NBA Playoffs

2007 NBA Playoff Results

Eastern Conference First Round

Game	Visitor	Score	Home	Score
Game 1	Toronto	100	at Orlando	114
Game 2	Toronto	103	at Orlando	104
Game 3	Orlando	94	at Toronto	108
Game 4	Orlando	106	at Toronto	94
Game 5	Toronto	92	at Orlando	102

Orlando won series 4–1.

Game	Visitor	Score	Home	Score
Game 1	Washington	86	at Cleveland	93
Game 2	Washington	86	at Cleveland	116
Game 3	Cleveland	72	at Washington	108
Game 4	Cleveland	100	at Washington	97
Game 5	Washington	88	at Cleveland	87
Game 6	Cleveland	105	at Washington	88

Cleveland won series 4–2.

Game	Visitor	Score	Home	Score
Game 1	Atlanta	81	at Boston	104
Game 2	Atlanta	77	at Boston	96
Game 3	Boston	93	at Atlanta	102
Game 4	Boston	92	at Atlanta	97
Game 5	Atlanta	85	at Boston	110
Game 6	Boston	100	at Atlanta	103
Game 7	Atlanta	65	at Boston	99

Boston won series 4–3.

Game	Visitor	Score	Home	Score
Game 1	Philadelphia	90	at Detroit	86
Game 2	Philadelphia	88	at Detroit	105
Game 3	Detroit	75	at Philadelphia	95
Game 4	Detroit	93	at Philadelphia	84
Game 5	Philadelphia	81	at Detroit	98
Game 6	Detroit	100	at Philadelphia	77

Detroit won series 4–2.

Western Conference First Round

Game	Visitor	Score	Home	Score
Game 1	Dallas	92	at New Orleans	104
Game 2	Dallas	103	at New Orleans	127
Game 3	New Orleans	87	at Dallas	97
Game 4	New Orleans	97	at Dallas	84
Game 5	Dallas	94	at New Orleans	99

New Orleans won series 4–1.

Game	Visitor	Score	Home	Score
Game 1	Phoenix	115	at San Antonio	117†
Game 2	Phoenix	96	at San Antonio	102
Game 3	San Antonio	115	at Phoenix	99
Game 4	San Antonio	86	at Phoenix	105
Game 5	Phoenix	87	at San Antonio	92

San Antonio won series 4–1.

Game	Visitor	Score	Home	Score
Game 1	Denver	114	at LA Lakers	128
Game 2	Denver	107	at LA Lakers	122
Game 3	LA Lakers	102	at Denver	84
Game 4	LA Lakers	107	at Denver	101

LA Lakers won series 4–0.

Game	Visitor	Score	Home	Score
Game 1	Utah	93	at Houston	82
Game 2	Utah	90	at Houston	84
Game 3	Houston	94	at Utah	92
Game 4	Houston	82	at Utah	86
Game 5	Utah	69	at Houston	95
Game 6	Houston	91	at Utah	113

Utah won series 4–2.

Eastern Conference Semifinals

Game	Visitor	Score	Home	Score
Game 1	Cleveland	72	at Boston	76
Game 2	Cleveland	73	at Boston	89
Game 3	Boston	84	at Cleveland	108
Game 4	Boston	77	at Cleveland	88
Game 5	Cleveland	89	at Boston	96
Game 6	Boston	69	at Cleveland	74
Game 7	Cleveland	92	at Boston	97

Boston won series 4–3.

Game	Visitor	Score	Home	Score
Game 1	Orlando	72	at Detroit	91
Game 2	Orlando	93	at Detroit	100
Game 3	Detroit	86	at Orlando	111
Game 4	Detroit	90	at Orlando	89
Game 5	Orlando	86	at Detroit	91

Detroit won series 4–1.

Western Conference Semifinals

Game	Visitor	Score	Home	Score
Game 1	Utah	98	at LA Lakers	109
Game 2	Utah	110	at LA Lakers	120
Game 3	LA Lakers	99	at Utah	104
Game 4	LA Lakers	115	at Utah	123*
Game 5	Utah	104	at LA Lakers	111
Game 6	LA Lakers	108	at Utah	105

LA Lakers won series 4–2.

Game	Visitor	Score	Home	Score
Game 1	San Antonio	82	at New Orleans	101
Game 2	San Antonio	84	at New Orleans	102
Game 3	New Orleans	99	at San Antonio	110
Game 4	New Orleans	80	at San Antonio	100
Game 5	San Antonio	79	at New Orleans	101
Game 6	New Orleans	80	at San Antonio	99
Game 7	San Antonio	91	at New Orleans	82

San Antonio won series 4–3.

Eastern Conference Finals

Game	Visitor	Score	Home	Score
Game 1	Detroit	79	at Boston	88
Game 2	Detroit	103	at Boston	97
Game 3	Boston	94	at Detroit	80
Game 4	Boston	75	at Detroit	94
Game 5	Detroit	102	at Boston	106
Game 6	Boston	89	at Detroit	81

Boston won series 4–2.

Western Conference Finals

Game	Visitor	Score	Home	Score
Game 1	San Antonio	85	at LA Lakers	89
Game 2	San Antonio	71	at LA Lakers	101
Game 3	LA Lakers	84	at San Antonio	103
Game 4	LA Lakers	93	at San Antonio	91
Game 5	San Antonio	92	at LA Lakers	100

LA Lakers won series 4–1.

NBA Finals

Game	Visitor	Score	Home	Score
Game 1	LA Lakers	88	at Boston	98
Game 2	LA Lakers	102	at Boston	108
Game 3	Boston	81	at LA Lakers	87
Game 4	Boston	97	at LA Lakers	91
Game 5	Boston	98	at LA Lakers	103
Game 6	LA Lakers	92	at Boston	131

Boston won series 4–2.

* Overtime. †Double overtime.

NBA Finals Composite Box Score

BOSTON CELTICS

Player	GP	Mpg	FG%	3FG%	FT%	Reb./per game Off.	Reb./per game Total	Apg	Spg	Bpg	TOpg	Ppg
Paul Pierce	6	38.8	.432	.393	.830	0.5	4.5	6.3	1.2	0.3	3.7	21.8
Ray Allen	6	41.0	.507	.524	.867	1.3	5.0	2.5	1.3	0.7	1.8	20.3
Kevin Garnett	6	37.9	.429	.000	.760	3.7	13.0	3.0	1.7	1.0	2.7	18.2
Rajon Rondo	6	27.0	.377	.000	.593	1.2	3.8	6.7	1.5	0.5	1.5	9.3
James Posey	6	25.2	.500	.500	1.000	0.5	3.8	0.5	1.3	0.2	0.8	8.7
Eddie House	4	18.5	.357	.412	.833	0.0	2.5	2.5	0.3	0.0	0.5	8.0
Leon Powe	6	8.9	.550	.000	.714	1.2	3.2	0.0	0.0	0.0	0.3	6.2
P.J. Brown	6	19.5	.391	.000	.750	0.8	3.2	0.7	0.5	0.5	0.3	4.0
Kendrick Perkins	5	18.4	.571	.000	.667	1.6	3.6	0.4	0.6	1.0	1.2	4.0
Sam Cassell	5	10.1	.375	.000	1.000	0.0	0.2	1.2	0.4	0.0	0.4	3.8
Glen Davis	1	14.6	.500	.000	.500	2.0	4.0	0.0	0.0	0.0	0.0	3.0
Tony Allen	3	6.3	.667	.000	.000	0.0	0.3	0.7	0.3	0.0	0.0	2.7
Avg/Total	**6**	**240.0**	**.444**	**.430**	**.768**	**10.8**	**42.2**	**23.0**	**14.8**	**4.2**	**13.3**	**102.2**

LOS ANGELES LAKERS

Player	GP	Mpg	FG%	3FG%	FT%	Reb./per game Off.	Reb./per game Total	Apg	Spg	Bpg	TOpg	Ppg
Kobe Bryant	6	43.0	.405	.321	.796	1.3	4.7	5.0	2.7	0.2	3.8	25.7
Pau Gasol	6	39.0	.532	.000	.647	2.0	10.2	3.3	0.5	0.5	2.2	14.7
Lamar Odom	6	36.6	.517	.200	.643	2.0	9.0	3.0	0.3	1.0	2.7	13.5
Derek Fisher	6	31.2	.405	.188	.624	0.3	1.5	3.2	1.5	0.0	1.5	10.8
Sasha Vujacic	6	22.0	.391	.348	.857	0.5	2.0	0.8	0.5	0.2	0.8	8.3
Vasha Radmanovic	6	21.3	.390	.385	1.000	1.0	4.8	1.3	0.7	0.0	0.7	7.3
Jordan Farmar	6	19.2	.484	.529	.750	0.2	1.8	1.3	0.3	0.5	0.8	7.0
Trevor Ariza	5	7.0	.556	.333	.500	0.6	1.8	0.2	0.2	0.2	0.2	2.6
Luke Walton	6	11.0	.313	.333	.750	0.3	1.0	1.2	0.2	0.2	0.5	2.5
Ronny Turiaf	6	10.4	.500	.000	.250	0.0	0.7	0.0	0.0	0.5	0.2	1.8
Chris Mihm	1	2.8	.000	.000	.000	0.0	0.0	0.0	0.0	0.0	1.0	0.0
Avg/Total	**6**	**240.0**	**.441**	**.347**	**.729**	**8.2**	**37.2**	**19.3**	**6.9**	**3.2**	**13.6**	**94.2**

NBA Finals Game Box Scores

Game 1

LOS ANGELES 88

Player	Min	FG M–A	FT M–A	Reb O–T	A	PF	S	TO	TP
V. Radmanovic	17	2–5	0–0	2–5	2	5	2	0	5
L. Odom	39	6–11	2–5	2–6	1	5	1	0	14
P. Gasol	41	6–11	3–4	2–8	4	3	1	1	15
K. Bryant	42	9–26	6–6	0–3	6	3	1	4	24
D. Fisher	41	4–9	6–8	0–4	6	2	3	2	15
S. Vujacic	27	2–7	3–3	0–2	1	4	0	0	8
J. Farmar	7	1–1	0–0	0–1	0	1	0	1	2
L. Walton	14	0–2	0–0	0–2	1	3	0	0	0
R. Turiaf	12	2–5	1–2	1–2	0	3	0	0	5
Totals	240	32–77	21–28	7–26	21	29	8	8	88

Percentages: FG—.416, FT—.750. 3-pt goals: 3–14, .214 (Radmanovic 1–4, Odom 0–1, Bryant 0–3, Vujacic 1–3, Fisher 1–3). Team rebounds: 9. Blocked shots: 2 (Gasol, Bryant).

BOSTON 98

Player	Min	FG M–A	FT M–A	Reb O–T	A	PF	S	TO	TP
P. Pierce	31	7–10	5–7	0–4	2	4	1	3	22
K. Garnett	41	9–22	6–6	4–13	3	3	1	1	24
K. Perkins	23	0–1	1–2	1–4	0	4	0	1	1
R. Allen	44	5–13	7–8	1–8	5	2	1	4	19
R. Rondo	35	4–10	7–10	1–5	7	1	0	2	15
P. Brown	21	1–4	0–0	1–6	2	3	0	0	2
J. Posey	23	1–6	0–0	0–2	0	3	2	2	3
S. Cassell	13	4–9	0–0	0–0	1	1	1	0	8
L. Powe	9	1–1	2–2	2–4	0	1	0	0	4
Totals	240	32–76	28–35	10–46	20	22	6	13	98

Percentages: FG—.421, FT—.800. 3-pt goals: 6–19, .316 (Pierce 3–4, Allen 2–6, Rondo 0–2, Posey 1–5, Cassell 0–2). Team rebounds: 15. Blocked shots: 3 (Perkins, Allen, Brown).

A: 18,624. Officials: Bavetta, Foster, Rush.

NBA Finals Game Box Scores

Game 2

LOS ANGELES 102

Player	Min	FG M–A	FT M–A	Reb O–T	A	PF	S	TO	TP
V. Radmanovic	31	5–12	0–0	3–10	2	3	1	1	13
L. Odom	32	5–11	0–0	3–8	2	5	0	2	10
P. Gasol	40	8–12	1–1	3–10	4	3	1	1	17
K. Bryant	40	11–23	7–7	3–8	8	3	3	4	30
D. Fisher	30	3–8	2–2	0–0	3	5	3	0	9
T. Ariza	7	0–1	0–0	0–2	0	2	0	1	0
L. Walton	13	1–2	0–0	0–1	0	1	0	2	2
S. Vujacic	20	3–6	0–0	0–0	1	3	0	2	8
J. Farmar	18	3–6	0–0	1–1	0	1	0	0	9
R. Turiaf	9	2–2	0–0	0–0	0	2	0	0	4
Totals	240	41–83	10–10	11–36	20	28	8	13	102

Percentages: FG—.494, FT—1.000. 3-pt goals: 10–21 .476 (Radmanovic 3–7, Bryant 1–3, Fisher 1–4, Vujacic 2–3, Farmar 3–4). Technical Fouls: 1 (Bryant). Team rebounds: 3. Blocked shots: 1 (Farmar).

BOSTON 108

Player	Min	FG M–A	FT M–A	Reb O–T	A	PF	S	TO	TP
P Pierce	41	9–16	6–7	0–4	8	4	1	5	28
K. Garnett	39	7–19	3–4	3–14	3	1	1	4	17
K. Perkins	14	2–2	3–3	3–3	1	4	0	2	7
R. Allen	41	6–11	2–3	1–2	2	3	0	2	17
R. Rondo	42	1–4	2–6	1–6	16	3	2	2	4
L. Powe	15	6–7	9–13	1–2	0	4	0	0	21
P. Brown	23	3–4	0–0	1–3	0	1	1	0	6
J. Posey	20	2–3	2–2	0–3	0	1	1	0	8
S. Cassell	6	0–2	0–0	0–0	1	1	1	0	0
Totals	240	36–68	27–38	10–37	31	21	7	15	108

Percentages: FG—.529, FT—.711. 3-pt goals: 9–14, .643 (Pierce 4–4, Allen 3–6, Posey 2–3, Cassell 0–1). Technical Fouls: 1 (Garnett). Team rebounds: 9. Blocked shots: 3 (Pierce, Garnett, Rondo).

A: 18,624. Officials: Crawford, Delaney, Mauer

Game 3

BOSTON 81

Player	Min	FG M–A	FT M–A	Reb O–T	A	PF	S	TO	TP
P. Pierce	32	2–14	2–3	1–6	3	5	1	3	6
K. Garnett	42	6–21	1–2	3–12	5	2	1	3	13
K. Perkins	28	4–5	0–1	2–6	1	4	3	1	8
R. Allen	41	8–13	4–6	3–5	2	3	1	1	25
R. Rondo	22	4–8	0–0	2–2	4	4	0	2	8
P. Brown	17	1–4	1–2	0–2	0	4	0	2	3
S. Cassell	7	1–4	0–0	0–0	2	1	0	0	2
J. Posey	25	1–3	6–6	1–7	0	2	1	0	9
L. Powe	6	0–3	1–2	2–2	0	1	0	1	1
E. House	20	2–8	0–0	0–3	2	2	1	0	6
Totals	240	29–83	15–22	14–45	19	28	8	13	81

Percentages: FG—.349, FT—.682. 3-pt goals: 8–18, .444 (Pierce 0–4, Allen, 5–7. Cassell 0–1, Posey 1–3, House 2–3). Technical Fouls: 1 (Brown). Team rebounds: 11. Blocked shots: 8 (Garnett 3, Perkins 2, Allen, Rondo, Brown).

LOS ANGELES 87

Player	Min	FG M–A	FT M–A	Reb O–T	A	PF	S	TO	TP
V. Radmanovic	13	1–4	0–0	0–1	0	4	0	0	3
L. Odom	28	2–9	0–0	1–9	4	5	1	5	4
P. Gasol	39	3–9	3–8	3–12	2	3	0	3	9
K. Bryant	45	12–20	11–18	3–7	1	4	2	3	36
D. Fisher	28	1–6	4–4	1–3	1	1	1	1	6
R. Turiaf	19	0–1	0–0	0–0	0	3	0	0	0
S. Vujacic	28	7–10	3–4	0–4	1	2	0	0	20
J. Farmar	20	2–4	0–0	0–4	5	0	0	0	5
L. Walton	11	0–3	0–0	1–3	2	1	0	0	0
T. Ariza	9	2–3	0–0	0–1	1	0	0	0	4
Totals	240	30–69	21–34	9–44	17	23	4	12	87

Percentages: FG—.435, FT—.618. 3-pt goals: 6–14, .429 (Radmanovic 1–2, Odom 0–1, Bryant 1–2, Fisher 0–1, Vujacic 3–5, Farmar 1–2, Ariza 0–1). Technical Fouls: 2 (Farmar, Bryant). Team rebounds: 13. Blocked shots: 6 (Turiaf 2, Odom, Vujacic, Farmar, Walton).

A: 18,997. Officials: Crawford, Salvatore, Wunderlich.

Game 4

BOSTON 97

Player	Min	FG M–A	FT M–A	Reb O–T	A	PF	S	TO	TP
P. Pierce	42	6–13	8–9	0–4	7	4	1	4	20
K. Garnett	37	7–14	2–2	2–11	3	3	2	4	16
K. Perkins	13	1–3	0–0	0–1	0	4	0	0	2
R. Allen	48	6–11	5–5	2–9	2	2	3	1	19
R. Rondo	17	2–4	1–2	0–1	2	1	0	0	5
P. Brown	15	1–4	1–2	1–2	0	2	1	0	3
E. House	25	4–9	1–2	0–4	1	0	0	0	11
J. Posey	25	5–10	4–4	0–2	0	5	0	0	18
S. Cassell	7	0–1	0–0	0–0	0	2	0	1	0
L. Powe	9	1–4	1–2	1–5	0	1	0	1	3
T. Allen	2	0–0	0–0	0–1	0	0	0	0	0
Totals	240	33–73	22–28	6–40	15	24	7	11	97

Percentages: FG—.452, FT—.821. 3-pt goals: 8–22, .364 (Pierce 0–3, Allen 2–6, House 2–4, Posey 4–8, Cassell 0–1). Technical Fouls: 1 (Coach Rivers). Team rebounds: 8. Blocked shots: 4 (Pierce, Garnett, Perkins, Allen).

LOS ANGELES 91

Player	Min	FG M–A	FT M–A	Reb O–T	A	PF	S	TO	TP
V. Radmanovic	27	3–8	2–2	1–5	2	3	0	0	10
L. Odom	39	8–11	3–4	4–10	4	1	0	2	19
P. Gasol	38	6–13	5–7	1–10	2	5	0	3	17
K. Bryant	43	6–19	5–6	0–4	10	4	4	2	17
D. Fisher	25	4–5	5–6	0–0	3	2	0	3	13
S. Vujacic	24	1–9	0–0	1–3	1	3	1	1	3
T. Ariza	9	2–2	1–2	3–5	0	2	1	0	6
J. Farmar	21	1–6	0–0	0–3	1	0	0	0	3
L. Walton	4	1–3	0–0	0–0	2	1	0	1	3
R. Turiaf	10	0–1	0–2	0–0	0	2	0	0	0
Totals	240	32–77	21–29	10–41	23	23	6	12	91

Percentages: FG—.416, FT—.724. 3-pt goals: 6–21, .286 (Radmanovic 2–5, Odom 0–1, Bryant 0–2, Fisher 0–1, Vujacic 1–5, Ariza 1–1, Farmar 1–3, Walton 1–3). Team rebounds: 9. Blocked shots: 3 (Odom, Ariza, Turiaf).

A: 18,997. Officials: DeRosa, Javie, Washington.

NBA Finals Game Box Scores *(Cont.)*

Game 5

BOSTON 98

Player	Min	FG M–A	FT M–A	Reb O–T	A	PF	S	TO	TP
P. Pierce	48	10–22	16–19	1–6	8	5	1	5	38
K. Garnett	33	6–11	1–4	7–14	0	5	2	4	13
L. Powe	5	0–0	0–0	0–2	0	1	0	0	0
R. Allen	39	4–13	5–5	0–2	2	6	0	2	16
R. Rondo	15	1–7	1–2	1–2	3	1	1	2	3
P. Brown	25	2–5	0–0	1–3	0	5	0	0	4
E. House	14	2–5	0–0	0–1	2	2	0	2	6
T. Allen	11	3–4	0–0	0–0	1	0	1	0	6
J. Posey	32	1–2	0–0	1–6	2	3	1	2	3
S. Cassell	18	4–8	1–1	0–1	2	0	0	1	9
Totals	240	33–77	22–28	11–37	20	28	6	18	98

Percentages: FG—.429, FT—.774. 3-pt goals: 8–22, .364 (Pierce 2–6, Allen 3–8, House 2–5, Posey 1–2, Cassell 0–1). Technical Fouls: 1 (Allen). Team rebounds: 14. Blocked shots: 2 (Allen, Rondo).

LOS ANGELES 103

Player	Min	FG M–A	FT M–A	Reb O–T	A	PF	S	TO	TP
V. Radmanovic	19	3–6	0–0	0–5	2	2	1	3	7
L. Odom	41	8–10	3–3	2–11	2	3	0	4	20
P. Gasol	42	6–10	7–10	3–13	6	3	1	0	19
K. Bryant	44	8–21	5–7	3–7	4	4	5	6	25
D. Fisher	35	3–10	8–11	1–2	2	2	2	2	15
L. Walton	10	1–2	0–0	0–0	2	5	0	0	2
S. Vujacic	20	2–10	0–0	1–1	0	2	1	0	4
J. Farmar	22	5–9	0–0	0–1	1	3	1	0	11
C. Mihm	3	0–1	0–0	0–0	0	2	0	1	0
T. Ariza	1	0–0	0–0	0–0	0	1	0	0	0
R. Turiaf	1	0–0	0–0	0–0	0	1	0	1	0
Totals	240	36–79	23–31	10–40	19	28	11	17	103

Percentages: FG—.456, FT—.742. 3-pt goals: 8–27, .296 (Radmanovic 1–2, Odom 1–1, Bryant 4–9, Fisher 1–5, Walton 0–1, Vujacic 0–5, Farmar 1–4). Technical Fouls: 2 (Fisher, Radmanovic). Team rebounds: 11. Blocked shots: 7 (Odom 4, Gasol 2, Farmar).

A: 18,997. Officials: Bavetta, Foster, Mauer.

Game 6

LOS ANGELES 92

Player	Min	FG M–A	FT M–A	Reb O–T	A	PF	S	TO	TP
V. Radmanovic	22	2–6	0–0	0–3	0	5	0	0	6
L. Odom	40	2–8	10–16	0–10	5	4	0	3	14
P. Gasol	32	4–7	3–4	0–8	2	3	0	5	11
K. Bryant	43	7–22	5–5	1–3	1	1	1	4	22
D. Fisher	28	3–3	3–3	0–0	4	5	0	1	7
L. Walton	14	2–4	3–4	0–0	2	2	1	0	8
J. Farmar	26	3–5	3–4	0–1	1	2	1	4	12
S. Vujacic	15	3–4	0–0	1–2	1	2	1	2	7
R. Turiaf	11	1–1	0–0	0–1	0	2	0	0	2
T. Ariza	9	1–1	1–2	0–1	0	1	0	0	3
Totals	240	27–64	28–38	2–29	16	25	4	19	92

Percentages: FG—.422, FT—.737. 3-pt goals: 10–27, .370 (Radmanovic 2–6, Odom 0–1, Bryant 3–9, Fisher 0–2, Walton 1–2, Farmar 3–4, Vujacic 1–2, Ariza 0–1). Team rebounds: 11. Blocked shots: None.

BOSTON 131

Player	Min	FG M–A	FT M–A	Reb O–T	A	PF	S	TO	TP
P. Pierce	39	4–13	7–8	1–3	10	2	2	2	17
K. Garnett	36	10–18	6–7	3–14	4	2	3	0	26
K. Perkins	13	1–3	0–0	2–4	0	5	0	2	2
R. Allen	32	8–12	3–3	1–4	2	0	3	1	26
R. Rondo	32	8–20	5–7	2–7	8	3	6	1	21
P. Brown	16	1–2	4–4	1–3	2	4	1	0	6
J. Posey	26	4–4	0–0	1–3	1	2	3	1	11
L. Powe	9	3–5	2–2	1–4	0	5	0	0	8
E. House	16	2–6	4–4	0–2	5	2	0	0	9
G. Davis	15	1–2	1–2	2–4	0	2	0	0	3
T. Allen	6	1–2	0–0	0–0	1	0	0	0	2
Totals	240	43–87	32–37	14–48	33	25	18	7	131

Percentages: FG—.494, FT—.865. 3-pt goals: 13–26, .500 (Pierce 2–7, Garnett 0–1, Allen 7–9, Rondo 0–1, Posey 3–3, House 1–5). Team rebounds: 8. Blocked shots: 4 (Allen, Rondo, Brown, Posey).

A: 18,624. Officials: Crawford, Rush, Salvatore.

2007–08 All-NBA Teams

FIRST TEAM
F LeBron James, Cle
F Kevin Garnett, Bos
C Dwight Howard, Orl
G Kobe Bryant, LAL
G Chris Paul, NO

SECOND TEAM
F Tim Duncan, SA
F Dirk Nowitzki, Dal
C Amare Stoudemire, Phx
G Steve Nash, Phx
G Deron Williams, Utah

THIRD TEAM
F Carlos Boozer, Utah
F Paul Pierce, Bos
C Yao Ming, Hou
G Tracy McGrady, Hou
G Manu Ginobili, SA

All-Rookie Teams

FIRST TEAM
Al Horford, Atl
Kevin Durant, Sea
Luis Scola, Hou
Al Thornton, LAC
Jeff Green, Sea

SECOND TEAM
Jamario Moon, Tor
Juan Carlos Navarro, Mem
Thaddeus Young, Phil
Rodney Stuckey, Det
Carl Landry, Hou

All-Defensive Team

FIRST TEAM
F Tim Duncan, SA
F Kevin Garnett, Bos
C Marcus Camby, Den
G Kobe Bryant, LAL
G/F Bruce Bowen, SA

SECOND TEAM
F Tayshaun Prince, Det
F Shane Battier, Hou
C Dwight Howard, Orl
G Chris Paul, NO
G Raja Bell, Phx

2007–08 NBA Regular Season Individual Leaders

Scoring

	GP	Pts	Avg
LeBron James, Cle	75	2,250	30.0
Kobe Bryant LAL	82	2,323	28.3
Allen Iverson, Den	82	2,164	26.4
Carmelo Anthony, Den	77	1,978	25.7
Amare Stoudemire, Phx	79	1,989	25.2
Dwyane Wade, Mia	51	1,254	24.6
Kevin Martin, Sac	61	1,443	23.7
Dirk Nowitzki, Dal	77	1,817	23.6
Michael Redd, Mil	72	1,632	22.7
Richard Jefferson, NJ	82	1,857	22.6

Assists

	GP	Asst	Avg
Chris Paul, NO	80	925	11.6
Steve Nash, Phx	81	898	11.1
Deron Williams, Utah	82	862	10.5
Jason Kidd, NJ/Dal	80	806	10.1
Jose Calderon, Tor	82	678	8.3
Baron Davis, GS	82	623	7.6
Raymond Felton, Cha	79	583	7.4
LeBron James, Cle	78	539	7.2
Allen Iverson, Den	75	586	7.1
Dwyane Wade, Mia	51	354	6.9

Free-Throw Percentage

	FTA	FTM	Pct
Peja Stojakovic, NO	140	130	.929
Chauncey Billups, Det	437	401	.918
Kyle Korver, Utah/Phil	130	119	.915
Jose Calderon, Tor	120	109	.908
Ben Gordon, Chi	293	266	.908
Ray Allen, Bos	237	215	.907
Steve Nash, Phx	245	222	.906
Caron Butler, Wash	262	236	.901
Jerry Stackhouse, Dal	148	132	.892
Derek Fisher, LAL	188	166	.883

Steals

	GP	Steals	Avg
Chris Paul, NO	80	217	2.71
Ron Artest, Sac	57	133	2.33
Baron Davis, GS	82	191	2.33
Caron Butler, Was	58	128	2.21
Gerald Wallace, Cha	62	131	2.11
Andre Iguodala, Phil	82	171	2.08
Shawn Marion, Phx/Mia	63	125	1.98
Allen Iverson, Den	82	160	1.95
Kobe Bryant, LAL	82	151	1.84
LeBron James, Cle	75	138	1.84

Rebounds

	GP	Reb	Avg
Dwight Howard, Orl	82	1,161	14.2
Marcus Camby, Den	79	1,037	13.1
Chris Kaman, LAC	56	711	12.7
Tyson Chandler, NO	79	928	11.7
Tim Duncan, SA	78	881	11.3
Al Jefferson, Min	82	911	11.1
Yao Ming, Hou	55	594	10.8
Emeka Okafor, Cha	82	876	10.7
Lamar Odom, LAL	77	819	10.6
Carlos Boozer, Utah	81	844	10.4

Field-Goal Percentage

	FGA	FGM	Pct
Andris Biedrins, GS	543	340	.626
Tyson Chandler, NO	605	377	.623
Dwight Howard, Orl	974	583	.599
Shaquille O'Neal, Mia/Phx	558	331	.593
Amare Stoudemire, Phx	1,211	714	.590
Josh Childress, Atl	573	327	.571
Craig Smith, Min	528	297	.563
Ronnie Brewer, Utah	634	354	.558
David Lee, NY	618	341	.552
Carlos Boozer, Utah	1,297	709	.547

Three-Point Field-Goal Percentage

	3FGA	3FGM	Pct
Jason Kapono, Tor	118	57	.483
Steve Nash, Phx	381	179	.470
James Jones, Por	205	91	.444
Peja Stojakovic, NO	524	231	.441
Daniel Gibson, Cle	268	118	.440
Richard Hamilton, Det	141	62	.440
Anthony Parker, Tor	304	133	.438
Sasha Vujacic, LAL	270	118	.437
Matt Carroll, Cha	241	105	.436
Mike Miller, Mem	359	155	.432

Blocked Shots

	GP	BS	Avg
Marcus Camby, Den	79	285	3.61
Josh Smith, Atl	81	227	2.80
Chris Kaman, LAC	56	155	2.77
Samuel Dalembert, Phil	82	192	2.34
Dwight Howard, Orl	82	176	2.15
Amare Stoudemire, Phx	79	163	2.06
Yao Ming, Hou	55	111	2.02
Tim Duncan, SA	78	152	1.95
Andrew Bogut, Mil	78	135	1.73
Emeka Okafor, Cha	82	138	1.68
Rasheed Wallace, Det	77	129	1.68

2007–08 NBA Regular Season Team Statistics

Offense

Team	FG Pct	3FG Pct	FT Pct	Rebound Avg Off	Rebound Avg Total	A	TO	Stl	Scoring Avg
Golden State	46.0	34.8	75.3	12.7	43.2	22.4	13.0	9.1	111.0
Denver	47.0	35.5	75.1	11.2	44.1	24.7	14.4	9.2	110.7
Phoenix	50.0	39.3	78.3	8.8	41.5	26.7	13.9	6.5	110.1
LA Lakers	47.6	37.8	76.9	11.0	44.1	24.4	13.6	8.0	108.6
Utah	49.7	37.2	75.9	11.5	40.9	26.4	14.3	8.7	106.2
Orlando	47.4	38.6	72.1	9.4	42.0	20.8	13.8	6.3	104.5
Indiana	44.3	37.4	76.8	11.0	43.1	22.7	14.7	7.6	104.0
Sacramento	46.4	37.3	79.8	10.1	40.1	19.1	15.3	7.9	102.5
New Orleans	46.6	38.9	76.9	11.4	41.8	21.8	11.3	7.8	100.9
Memphis	45.4	34.9	72.3	10.3	41.6	19.2	14.8	6.1	100.7
Boston	47.5	38.1	77.1	10.1	42.0	22.4	14.4	8.5	100.5
Dallas	46.4	35.2	81.5	10.8	43.0	21.0	12.0	6.0	100.4
Toronto	46.8	39.2	81.2	9.6	40.1	23.8	11.2	7.0	100.2
Washington	44.6	35.6	78.2	12.3	41.6	19.6	12.6	7.7	98.8
Atlanta	45.4	35.6	77.2	12.3	42.2	22.0	14.3	7.3	98.2
Seattle	44.4	33.3	77.0	11.8	44.6	21.3	15.2	6.5	97.5
Detroit	45.8	36.6	76.7	11.9	41.4	22.3	11.1	7.1	97.5
Chicago	43.5	36.3	75.6	12.8	43.0	22.1	14.1	7.7	97.3
Charlotte	45.2	36.7	71.4	10.9	40.6	21.3	13.8	7.5	97.1
Milwaukee	44.9	34.4	73.3	12.9	41.7	21.5	14.3	6.6	97.0
New York	43.9	33.7	72.8	12.5	42.5	18.7	13.8	6.4	96.9
Houston	44.8	34.2	72.6	12.2	44.6	21.4	13.1	7.3	96.7
Philadelphia	46.0	31.7	70.6	13.0	41.9	20.4	13.6	8.7	96.6
Cleveland	43.9	35.8	71.7	13.3	44.6	20.0	13.2	7.1	96.4
New Jersey	44.3	34.8	73.6	11.1	41.9	23.5	14.4	6.4	95.8
Minnesota	45.1	35.0	73.6	11.8	41.4	19.9	13.9	7.5	95.6
San Antonio	45.7	37.7	76.1	9.4	41.3	21.0	12.0	6.4	95.4
Portland	44.8	36.9	76.7	11.0	40.7	21.1	12.1	5.5	95.4
LA Clippers	43.8	32.4	78.2	9.8	40.1	21.1	13.8	6.8	93.8
Miami	44.3	35.8	72.7	9.1	37.6	20.0	14.0	7.2	91.4

Defense (Opponents' Statistics)

Team	FG Pct	3FG Pct	FT Pct	Rebound Avg. Off	Rebound Avg. Total	A	TO	Stl	Scoring Avg
Detroit	43.7	33.2	74.4	10.5	39.1	19.1	12.8	5.8	90.1
Boston	41.9	31.6	74.3	11.0	38.9	18.8	15.3	7.2	90.3
San Antonio	44.4	34.2	75.6	9.5	40.3	18.2	12.3	6.9	90.6
Houston	43.3	36.5	73.7	10.9	40.7	18.9	12.9	7.6	92.0
New Orleans	46.0	35.1	77.1	9.9	40.8	21.7	13.3	5.7	95.6
Dallas	44.3	34.9	76.0	10.8	40.3	18.9	11.6	6.5	95.9
Philadelphia	46.1	36.0	77.2	11.3	39.2	23.2	15.0	6.7	96.2
Portland	45.1	35.6	76.6	11.7	41.7	20.9	12.1	6.0	96.3
Cleveland	45.5	35.7	74.8	9.9	40.4	21.0	12.8	6.8	96.7
Toronto	45.8	36.8	77.6	10.1	41.6	21.9	13.3	5.7	97.3
Orlando	44.6	35.8	75.4	11.0	41.7	21.5	12.7	7.1	99.0
Washington	46.1	38.6	75.4	11.0	41.2	23.9	13.4	6.5	99.2
Utah	46.1	35.7	74.9	10.3	37.8	19.9	15.4	7.5	99.3
Miami	46.8	36.9	75.5	11.2	43.1	22.1	13.5	7.7	100.0
Atlanta	46.3	36.2	75.2	11.8	40.9	22.3	13.2	7.5	100.0
Chicago	45.3	37.5	76.6	11.1	42.6	21.9	14.6	7.9	100.4
New Jersey	45.6	36.9	76.8	10.9	41.6	22.1	12.8	8.1	100.9
LA Clippers	46.7	34.9	75.1	11.2	43.6	22.4	13.2	7.2	101.1
LA Lakers	44.5	36.2	75.2	12.0	42.8	21.9	13.7	7.7	101.3
Charlotte	46.6	35.5	74.7	12.2	43.7	21.8	13.8	7.6	101.4
Minnesota	47.2	35.7	76.9	10.6	41.7	23.2	13.0	7.4	102.4
New York	47.4	36.9	73.9	11.3	42.6	21.6	12.3	7.6	103.5
Milwaukee	48.0	38.4	76.6	10.6	40.7	23.3	13.2	7.9	103.9
Sacramento	46.6	37.3	75.3	11.8	41.9	22.9	14.7	8.1	104.8
Phoenix	45.6	35.3	74.9	13.4	43.9	19.6	12.8	7.3	105.0
Indiana	45.4	38.6	75.7	11.3	45.5	22.2	15.0	8.1	105.4
Seattle	46.1	38.5	74.9	11.7	44.1	24.4	12.6	8.6	106.3
Memphis	48.0	36.4	77.4	11.4	44.5	23.9	12.9	8.7	106.9
Denver	45.7	36.3	73.0	12.7	45.4	25.7	15.6	7.9	107.0
Golden State	46.8	36.8	75.9	12.8	47.0	23.6	16.2	6.9	108.9

NBA Team-by-Team Statistical Leaders

Atlanta Hawks

			Field Goals			Rebounds								
Player	**GP**	**MPG**	**FG%**	**3Pt%**	**FT%**	**OFF**	**DEF**	**Total**	**APG**	**SPG**	**BPG**	**TO**	**PF**	**PPG**
Joe Johnson	82	40.8	43.2	38.1	83.4	1.0	3.5	4.5	5.8	1.0	0.2	2.7	2.0	21.7
Josh Smith	81	35.5	45.7	25.3	71.0	2.0	6.2	8.2	3.4	1.5	2.8	3.0	3.3	17.2
Marvin Williams	80	34.6	46.2	10.0	82.2	1.5	4.2	5.7	1.7	1.0	0.4	1.6	2.8	14.8
*Mike Bibby	33	33.3	41.4	36.9	79.7	0.2	3.0	3.2	6.5	1.1	0.1	2.5	1.9	14.1
Josh Childress	76	29.9	57.1	36.7	80.7	2.3	2.6	4.9	1.5	0.9	0.6	1.3	1.7	11.8
Al Horford	81	31.4	49.9	0.0	73.1	3.1	6.6	9.7	1.5	0.7	0.9	1.7	3.3	10.1
Tyronn Lue	33	17.2	43.9	43.5	85.7	0.3	1.0	1.2	1.8	0.3	0.0	0.7	1.2	6.8
Anthony Johnson	42	26.7	43.1	42.9	81.3	0.4	1.9	2.3	4.8	1.0	0.2	1.2	2.0	6.7
Salim Stoudamire	35	11.5	36.1	34.1	82.0	0.1	0.6	0.7	0.8	0.2	0.1	0.6	1.0	5.7
Zaza Pachulia	62	15.2	43.7	0.0	70.6	1.4	2.6	4.0	0.6	0.4	0.2	1.1	2.3	5.2
Acie Law	56	15.4	40.1	20.6	79.2	0.2	0.8	1.0	2.0	0.5	0.0	1.0	1.3	4.2
Shelden Williams	36	11.5	37.0	0.0	68.6	0.9	2.0	3.0	0.3	0.4	0.3	0.4	1.7	3.0
*Jeremy Richardson	19	4.6	41.9	41.7	0.0	0.1	0.3	0.4	0.0	0.1	0.0	0.3	0.3	1.6
Solomon Jones	35	4.1	40.0	0.0	55.0	0.5	0.7	1.2	0.0	0.1	0.1	0.3	0.8	1.0
Hawks	**82**	**242.1**	**44.4**	**35.6**	**77.2**	**12.3**	**29.9**	**42.2**	**22.0**	**7.3**	**5.5**	**14.9**	**20.4**	**98.2**
Opponents	**82**	**242.1**	**46.6**	**36.2**	**75.2**	**11.8**	**29.1**	**40.9**	**22.3**	**7.5**	**5.1**	**13.7**	**21.9**	**100.0**

Boston Celtics

			Field Goals			Rebounds								
Player	**GP**	**MPG**	**FG%**	**3Pt%**	**FT%**	**OFF**	**DEF**	**Total**	**APG**	**SPG**	**BPG**	**TO**	**PF**	**PPG**
Paul Pierce	80	35.9	46.4	39.2	84.3	0.7	4.5	5.1	4.5	1.3	0.4	2.8	2.5	19.6
Kevin Garnett	71	32.8	53.9	0.0	80.1	1.9	7.3	9.2	3.4	1.4	1.3	1.9	2.3	18.8
Ray Allen	73	35.9	44.5	39.8	90.7	1.0	2.6	3.7	3.1	0.9	0.2	1.7	2.0	17.4
Rajon Rondo	77	29.9	49.2	26.3	61.1	1.0	3.2	4.2	5.1	1.7	0.2	1.9	2.4	10.6
Leon Powe	56	14.4	57.2	0.0	71.0	1.7	2.4	4.1	0.3	0.3	0.3	0.8	2.3	7.9
*Sam Cassell	17	17.6	38.5	40.9	84.0	0.3	1.5	1.8	2.1	0.5	0.2	1.1	1.7	7.6
Eddie House	78	19.0	40.9	39.3	91.7	0.2	1.9	2.1	1.9	0.8	0.1	1.0	1.5	7.5
James Posey	74	24.6	41.8	38.0	80.9	0.4	3.9	4.4	1.5	1.0	0.3	0.9	2.5	7.4
Kendrick Perkins	78	24.5	61.5	0.0	62.3	1.9	4.2	6.1	1.1	0.4	1.5	1.6	3.1	6.9
Tony Allen	75	18.3	43.4	31.6	76.2	0.5	1.8	2.2	1.5	0.8	0.3	1.5	2.2	6.6
Glen Davis	69	13.6	48.4	0.0	66.0	1.4	1.6	3.0	0.4	0.5	0.3	0.9	2.3	4.5
P.J. Brown	18	11.6	34.1	0.0	68.8	1.6	2.2	3.8	0.6	0.3	0.4	0.6	1.6	2.2
Gabe Pruitt	15	6.3	35.9	25.0	50.0	0.1	0.5	0.5	0.9	0.3	0.0	0.3	0.7	2.1
Scot Pollard	22	7.9	52.2	0.0	68.2	0.6	1.0	1.7	0.1	0.1	0.3	0.2	2.0	1.8
Brian Scalabrine	48	10.7	30.9	32.6	75.0	0.5	1.2	1.6	0.8	0.2	0.2	0.5	1.3	1.8
Celtics	**82**	**240.9**	**47.5**	**38.1**	**77.1**	**10.1**	**31.9**	**42.0**	**22.4**	**8.5**	**4.6**	**15.2**	**22.7**	**100.5**
Opponents	**82**	**240.9**	**41.9**	**31.6**	**74.3**	**11.0**	**27.9**	**38.9**	**18.8**	**7.2**	**4.7**	**16.0**	**22.2**	**90.3**

Charlotte Bobcats

			Field Goals			Rebounds								
Player	**GP**	**MPG**	**FG%**	**3Pt%**	**FT%**	**OFF**	**DEF**	**Total**	**APG**	**SPG**	**BPG**	**TO**	**PF**	**PPG**
Jason Richardson	82	38.4	44.1	40.6	75.2	1.0	4.4	5.4	3.1	1.4	0.7	2.0	2.9	21.8
Gerald Wallace	62	38.3	44.9	32.1	73.1	0.9	5.1	6.0	3.5	2.1	0.9	2.9	3.0	19.4
Raymond Felton	79	37.6	41.3	2.80	80.0	0.5	2.5	3.0	7.4	1.2	0.2	2.7	2.3	14.4
Emeka Okafor	82	33.1	53.5	0.0	57.0	3.1	7.6	10.7	0.9	0.8	1.7	2.0	2.9	13.8
*Nazr Mohammed	61	23.3	52.0	0.0	61.7	2.7	4.2	6.9	1.1	0.6	0.9	1.5	3.2	9.3
Matt Carroll	80	25.2	42.8	43.6	80.4	0.4	2.4	2.8	0.9	0.6	0.2	0.7	2.3	9.0
Jared Dudley	73	19.0	46.8	22.0	73.7	1.7	2.3	3.9	1.1	0.8	0.1	0.7	1.8	5.8
Earl Boykins	36	16.0	35.5	31.8	83.1	0.3	0.7	0.9	2.7	0.4	0.0	1.1	0.6	5.1
Derek Anderson	28	14.1	37.6	36.5	73.7	0.3	1.5	1.9	1.6	0.4	0.0	0.9	1.8	5.0
Walter Hermann	17	10.4	38.5	34.6	90.0	0.6	1.5	2.1	0.2	0.2	0.0	0.1	0.7	4.0
Jeff McInnis	54	26.1	43.4	15.8	76.7	0.3	1.5	1.8	4.1	0.4	0.1	1.4	2.2	4.5
Jermareo Davidson	38	8.5	40.8	0.0	64.3	0.6	1.1	1.6	0.3	0.2	0.4	0.5	1.2	3.2
Ryan Hollins	60	8.9	48.9	0.0	67.1	0.9	0.9	1.8	0.2	0.2	0.5	0.4	1.6	2.5
Othella Harrington	22	7.6	42.9	0.0	62.5	0.5	1.4	1.9	0.2	0.1	0.2	0.5	1.5	2.1
Bobcats	**82**	**242.4**	**45.2**	**36.7**	**71.4**	**10.9**	**29.8**	**40.6**	**21.3**	**7.5**	**4.9**	**14.7**	**21.7**	**97.1**
Opponents	**82**	**242.4**	**46.6**	**35.5**	**74.7**	**12.2**	**31.6**	**43.7**	**21.8**	**7.6**	**5.8**	**14.4**	**21.0**	**101.4**

Chicago Bulls

			Field Goals			Rebounds								
Player	**GP**	**MPG**	**FG%**	**3Pt%**	**FT%**	**OFF**	**DEF**	**Total**	**APG**	**SPG**	**BPG**	**TO**	**PF**	**PPG**
Ben Gordon	72	31.8	43.4	41.0	90.8	0.6	2.5	3.1	3.0	0.8	0.1	2.1	2.4	18.6
Luol Deng	63	33.8	47.9	36.4	77.0	2.2	4.1	6.3	2.5	0.9	0.5	1.9	1.9	17.0
*Drew Gooden	18	31.0	46.1	0.0	81.3	3.2	6.1	9.3	1.7	0.7	1.3	1.7	3.3	14.0

* mid-season trade

Chicago Bulls *(Cont.)*

Player	GP	MPG	FG%	3Pt%	FT%	OFF	DEF	Total	APG	SPG	BPG	TO	PF	PPG
			Field Goals			Rebounds								
Andres Nocioni	82	24.6	43.2	36.4	80.7	0.6	3.6	4.2	1.2	0.3	0.5	1.6	3.0	13.2
*Larry Hughes	28	28.9	38.7	35.3	77.5	0.4	2.7	3.1	3.1	1.4	0.2	1.6	1.7	12.0
Kirk Hinrich	75	31.7	41.4	35.0	83.1	0.4	2.9	3.3	6.0	1.2	0.3	2.1	3.0	11.5
Joe Smith	50	22.9	46.6	0.0	80.7	2.2	3.1	5.3	0.9	0.5	0.6	1.0	2.3	11.2
Tyrus Thomas	74	18.0	42.3	16.7	74.1	1.4	3.2	4.6	1.2	0.7	1.0	1.0	2.3	6.8
Thabo Sefolosha	69	20.8	42.8	33.0	72.1	0.7	3.0	3.7	1.9	0.9	0.4	1.4	1.9	6.7
Joakim Noah	74	20.7	48.2	0.0	69.1	2.4	3.3	5.6	1.1	0.9	0.9	1.2	2.3	6.6
Chris Duhon	66	22.6	38.7	34.8	81.3	0.3	1.5	1.8	4.0	0.7	0.0	1.1	1.4	5.8
Thomas Gardner	4	11.3	39.1	25.0	0.0	0.8	0.3	1.0	0.3	0.0	0.0	1.0	1.0	5.3
Ben Wallace	50	32.5	37.3	0.0	42.4	3.5	5.3	8.8	1.8	1.4	1.6	1.0	1.7	5.1
Aaron Gray	61	10.0	50.5	0.0	56.6	1.1	1.6	2.8	0.7	0.3	0.3	0.9	1.9	4.3
Viktor Khryapa	9	11.7	38.7	0.0	57.1	0.7	1.6	2.2	0.9	0.7	0.0	0.7	1.2	3.6
Adrian Griffin	22	10.0	40.0	0.0	42.9	0.9	0.8	1.7	1.0	0.6	0.1	0.7	0.9	2.3
*Shannon Brown	6	3.7	20.0	0.0	50.0	0.2	0.2	0.3	0.0	0.2	0.3	0.8	0.3	1.5
*Demetris Nichols	11	2.7	33.3	30.0	0.0	0.0	0.4	0.4	0.1	0.0	0.3	0.2	0.4	1.2
Bulls	**82**	**241.5**	**43.5**	**36.3**	**75.6**	**12.8**	**30.2**	**43.0**	**22.1**	**7.7**	**5.2**	**14.6**	**21.8**	**97.3**
Opponents	**82**	**241.5**	**45.3**	**37.5**	**76.6**	**11.1**	**31.5**	**42.6**	**21.9**	**7.9**	**5.7**	**15.3**	**21.3**	**100.4**

Cleveland Cavaliers

Player	GP	MPG	FG%	3Pt%	FT%	OFF	DEF	Total	APG	SPG	BPG	TO	PF	PPG
			Field Goals			Rebounds								
LeBron James	75	40.4	48.4	31.5	71.2	1.8	6.1	7.9	7.2	1.8	1.1	3.4	2.2	30.0
Zydrunas Ilgauskas	73	30.4	47.4	0.0	80.2	3.6	5.7	9.3	1.4	0.5	1.6	1.8	3.4	14.1
*Larry Hughes	40	30.3	37.7	34.1	81.5	0.7	2.9	3.6	2.4	1.5	0.3	1.8	2.3	12.3
*Drew Gooden	51	30.7	44.4	0.0	72.8	2.3	6.0	8.3	1.0	0.7	0.6	1.8	2.8	11.3
Daniel Gibson	58	30.4	43.2	44.0	81.0	0.5	1.8	2.3	2.5	0.8	0.2	1.3	2.8	10.4
*Delonte West	26	31.0	44.0	36.7	78.8	0.7	3.0	3.7	4.5	1.1	0.7	2.0	2.3	10.3
*Wally Szczerbiak	25	22.3	35.9	36.5	87.8	0.7	2.5	3.2	1.4	0.4	0.3	0.8	1.4	8.2
*Joe Smith	27	21.4	51.2	0.0	65.2	2.0	3.0	5.0	0.7	0.3	0.6	0.8	2.7	8.1
Devin Brown	78	22.6	40.9	30.8	75.4	0.8	2.5	3.4	2.2	0.7	0.1	1.3	1.8	7.5
Sasha Pavlovic	51	23.3	36.2	29.8	68.8	0.7	1.8	2.5	1.6	0.6	0.1	1.1	2.3	7.4
*Shannon Brown	15	14.5	36.9	31.0	60.9	0.3	0.9	1.2	1.1	0.7	0.1	1.3	1.8	7.0
Anderson Varejao	48	27.5	46.1	0.0	59.8	2.8	5.5	8.3	1.1	0.8	0.5	1.2	2.8	6.7
Damon Jones	67	19.9	41.6	41.7	71.4	0.1	1.0	1.1	1.9	0.3	0.0	0.5	1.0	6.5
*Ira Newble	41	16.0	44.9	33.3	76.9	1.0	1.8	2.8	0.3	0.7	0.2	0.8	1.6	4.3
*Ben Wallace	22	26.3	45.7	0.0	43.2	2.7	4.7	7.4	0.6	0.9	1.7	0.8	1.6	4.2
*Donyell Marshall	11	14.3	29.5	34.8	77.8	0.8	1.9	2.7	0.5	0.2	0.8	0.5	1.5	3.7
*Billy Thomas	7	4.9	28.6	30.8	0.0	0.0	0.3	0.3	0.0	0.1	0.0	0.4	0.6	1.7
Dwayne Jones	56	8.4	53.2	0.0	48.3	1.2	1.3	2.5	0.2	0.2	0.5	0.3	1.6	1.4
Cavaliers	**82**	**242.1**	**43.9**	**35.8**	**71.7**	**13.3**	**31.3**	**44.6**	**20.0**	**7.1**	**5.2**	**14.0**	**20.9**	**96.4**
Opponents	**82**	**242.1**	**45.5**	**35.7**	**74.8**	**9.9**	**30.5**	**40.4**	**21.0**	**6.8**	**4.7**	**13.3**	**20.3**	**96.7**

Dallas Mavericks

Player	GP	MPG	FG%	3Pt%	FT%	OFF	DEF	Total	APG	SPG	BPG	TO	PF	PPG
			Field Goals			Rebounds								
Dirk Nowitzki	77	36.0	47.9	35.9	87.9	1.2	7.3	8.6	3.5	0.7	0.9	2.1	2.6	23.6
Josh Howard	76	36.3	45.5	31.9	81.3	1.6	5.4	7.0	2.2	0.8	0.4	1.5	2.7	19.9
Jason Terry	82	31.5	46.7	37.5	85.7	0.4	2.2	2.5	3.2	1.1	0.2	1.1	2.1	15.5
*Devin Harris	39	30.4	48.3	35.7	82.1	0.4	1.9	2.3	5.3	1.4	0.1	2.4	3.3	14.4
Jerry Stackhouse	58	24.3	40.5	32.6	89.2	0.6	1.7	2.3	2.5	0.5	0.2	1.5	1.4	10.7
*Jason Kidd	29	34.9	42.6	46.1	81.5	1.2	5.2	6.5	9.5	2.1	0.4	2.8	2.6	9.9
Brandon Bass	79	19.7	49.9	0.0	82.2	1.5	2.9	4.4	0.7	0.3	0.6	1.0	1.9	8.3
Erick Dampier	72	24.4	64.3	0.0	57.5	2.9	4.6	7.5	0.9	0.3	1.4	1.1	3.1	6.1
Jose Barea	44	10.5	41.8	38.9	80.0	0.1	1.0	1.1	1.3	0.3	0.0	0.8	1.1	4.3
*Tyronn Lue	17	10.1	47.4	52.9	25.0	0.0	0.8	0.8	0.9	0.0	0.1	0.3	1.6	3.8
Eddie Jones	47	19.6	36.7	29.3	71.4	0.4	2.4	2.8	1.5	0.6	0.2	0.6	1.5	3.7
Devean George	53	15.5	35.7	32.4	70.6	0.5	2.1	2.6	0.7	0.4	0.3	0.5	1.7	3.7
*Antoine Wright	15	11.7	50.0	55.6	55.6	0.3	1.1	1.5	0.9	0.1	0.3	0.7	1.5	3.5
*Malik Allen	25	13.3	50.0	0.0	91.7	1.0	1.8	2.7	0.6	0.2	0.4	0.5	2.4	3.1
*DeSagana Diop	52	17.3	58.3	0.0	60.0	2.1	3.1	5.2	0.5	0.4	1.2	0.8	1.9	3.0
*Trenton Hassell	37	12.6	46.3	25.0	50.0	0.3	0.9	1.2	0.7	0.2	0.0	0.4	1.5	2.1
*Jamaal Magloire	7	3.9	50.0	0.0	46.2	0.1	1.0	1.1	0.0	0.1	0.0	1.0	1.1	1.7
Mavericks	**82**	**240.6**	**46.4**	**35.2**	**81.4**	**10.8**	**32.2**	**43.0**	**21.0**	**6.0**	**4.9**	**12.6**	**21.8**	**100.4**
Opponents	**82**	**240.6**	**44.3**	**34.9**	**76.0**	**10.8**	**29.5**	**40.3**	**18.9**	**6.5**	**4.4**	**12.2**	**21.2**	**95.9**

* mid-season trade

Denver Nuggets

Player	GP	MPG	Field Goals FG%	3Pt%	FT%	Rebounds OFF	DEF	Total	APG	SPG	BPG	TO	PF	PPG
Allen Iverson	82	41.8	45.8	34.5	80.9	0.6	2.4	3.0	7.1	2.0	0.2	3.0	1.3	26.4
Carmelo Anthony	77	36.4	49.2	35.4	78.6	2.3	5.1	7.4	3.4	1.3	0.5	3.3	3.3	25.7
Kenyon Martin	71	30.4	53.8	18.2	58.0	1.5	5.0	6.5	1.3	1.2	1.2	1.3	3.3	12.4
J.R. Smith	74	19.2	46.1	40.3	71.9	0.6	1.5	2.1	1.7	0.8	0.2	1.5	1.9	12.3
Linas Kleiza	79	23.9	47.2	33.9	77.0	1.2	3.1	4.2	1.2	0.6	0.2	1.1	2.3	11.1
Marcus Camby	79	34.9	45.0	30.0	70.8	2.9	10.2	13.1	3.3	1.1	3.6	1.5	2.7	9.1
Anthony Carter	70	28.0	45.8	34.9	75.3	0.4	2.5	2.9	5.5	1.5	0.4	1.8	2.5	7.8
Eduardo Najera	78	21.3	473.	36.1	70.8	1.4	2.9	4.3	1.2	0.9	0.5	0.8	2.6	5.9
Nene	16	16.6	40.8	0.0	55.1	1.9	3.6	5.4	0.9	0.6	0.9	1.3	2.9	5.3
Chucky Atkins	24	14.7	34.4	31.6	44.4	0.1	1.2	1.3	2.0	0.4	0.0	0.4	1.1	4.7
*Bobby Jones	25	8.9	40.6	39.1	82.1	0.4	1.1	1.5	0.4	0.2	0.0	0.6	1.8	3.4
Yakhouba Diawara	54	10.0	41.0	31.8	71.0	0.4	0.7	1.1	0.7	0.2	0.1	0.3	1.1	2.8
Steven Hunter	19	6.3	53.6	0.0	45.0	0.5	1.0	1.5	0.0	0.0	0.3	0.4	1.1	2.1
*Von Wafer	21	4.3	26.3	6.7	75.0	0.0	0.4	0.5	0.2	0.1	0.1	0.5	0.5	1.3
*Taurean Green	9	3.3	33.3	33.3	75.0	0.0	0.7	0.7	0.3	0.1	0.0	0.2	0.2	1.1
Nuggets	**82**	**242.1**	**47.0**	**35.5**	**75.1**	**11.2**	**32.9**	**44.1**	**24.7**	**9.2**	**6.7**	**14.7**	**21.1**	**110.7**
Opponets	**82**	**242.1**	**45.7**	**36.3**	**73.0**	**12.7**	**32.7**	**45.4**	**25.7**	**7.8**	**4.8**	**16.4**	**23.8**	**107.0**

Detroit Pistons

Player	GP	MPG	Field Goals FG%	3Pt%	FT%	Rebounds OFF	DEF	Total	APG	SPG	BPG	TO	PF	PPG
Richard Hamilton	72	33.7	48.4	44.0	83.3	1.0	2.2	3.3	4.2	1.0	0.1	1.8	2.4	17.3
Chauncey Billups	78	32.3	44.8	40.1	91.8	0.5	2.2	2.7	6.8	1.3	0.2	2.1	1.7	17.0
Tayshaun Prince	82	32.9	44.8	36.3	76.8	1.3	3.5	4.9	3.3	0.5	0.4	1.1	1.1	13.2
Rasheed Wallace	77	30.5	43.2	35.6	76.7	1.1	5.5	6.6	1.8	1.2	1.7	1.1	2.8	12.7
Antonio McDyess	78	29.3	48.8	0.0	62.2	2.6	5.9	8.5	1.1	0.8	0.7	1.0	3.2	8.8
Jason Maxiell	82	21.6	53.8	0.0	63.3	2.2	3.1	5.3	0.6	0.3	1.2	0.9	2.2	7.9
Rodney Stuckey	57	19.0	40.1	18.8	81.4	0.6	1.7	2.3	2.8	0.9	0.1	1.4	2.0	7.6
Ronald Murray	19	18.2	41.0	22.2	59.5	0.7	1.2	1.9	3.4	0.7	0.1	1.6	1.0	7.5
Jarvis Hayes	82	15.7	43.1	37.6	75.0	0.4	1.7	2.2	0.8	0.6	0.1	0.6	1.7	6.7
Juan Dixon	17	14.4	48.0	39.4	42.9	0.4	1.3	1.6	1.9	0.0	0.0	1.1	1.4	6.5
Arron Afflalo	75	12.9	41.1	20.8	78.2	0.5	1.3	1.8	0.7	0.4	0.1	0.5	1.1	3.7
Amir Johnson	62	12.3	55.8	0.0	67.3	1.4	2.4	3.8	0.5	0.4	1.3	0.6	2.3	3.6
*Nazr Mohammed	21	10.9	47.5	0.0	43.3	1.4	2.1	3.5	0.3	0.3	0.4	0.5	1.7	3.3
Theo Ratliff	16	13.9	45.0	0.0	66.7	1.2	1.9	3.1	0.4	0.3	1.2	0.6	1.8	3.0
Walter Hermann	28	7.1	39.2	28.9	80.0	0.4	0.9	1.3	0.5	0.1	0.0	0.3	0.4	3.0
Lindsey Hunter	24	9.0	34.4	26.9	77.8	0.2	0.4	0.5	1.4	0.5	0.1	0.5	1.3	2.4
Pistons	**82**	**240.6**	**45.8**	**36.6**	**76.7**	**11.9**	**29.5**	**41.4**	**22.3**	**7.1**	**5.8**	**11.7**	**20.6**	**97.5**
Opponents	**82**	**240.6**	**43.7**	**33.2**	**74.4**	**10.5**	**28.6**	**39.1**	**19.1**	**5.8**	**3.9**	**13.5**	**19.7**	**90.1**

Golden State Warriors

Player	GP	MPG	Field Goals FG%	3Pt%	FT%	Rebounds OFF	DEF	Total	APG	SPG	BPG	TO	PF	PPG
Baron Davis	82	39.0	42.6	33.0	75.0	1.2	3.5	4.7	7.6	2.3	0.5	2.8	3.0	21.8
Monta Ellis	81	37.9	53.1	23.1	76.7	1.6	3.3	5.0	3.9	1.5	0.3	2.1	2.4	20.2
Stephen Jackson	73	39.1	40.5	36.3	83.2	0.9	3.4	4.4	4.1	1.3	0.4	2.7	2.3	20.1
Al Harrington	81	27.0	43.4	37.5	77.4	1.3	4.1	5.4	1.6	0.9	0.2	1.1	3.3	13.6
Andris Biedrins	76	27.3	62.6	0.0	62.0	3.4	6.4	9.8	1.0	0.7	1.2	1.1	3.4	10.5
Kelenna Azubuike	81	21.4	44.5	36.4	71.7	1.3	2.7	4.0	0.9	0.6	0.4	0.7	2.0	8.5
Mickael Pietrus	66	19.9	43.9	36.1	67.3	1.0	2.7	3.7	0.7	1.0	0.7	0.7	3.0	7.2
Matt Barnes	73	19.4	42.3	29.3	74.7	1.3	3.2	4.4	1.9	0.7	0.5	1.2	2.2	6.7
Brandan Wright	38	9.9	55.4	0.0	67.5	1.0	1.6	2.6	0.2	0.2	0.6	0.3	0.9	4.0
Chris Webber	9	14.0	48.4	0.0	41.7	0.2	3.3	3.6	2.0	0.4	0.7	1.2	1.9	3.9
Austin Croshere	44	10.4	44.5	36.1	90.6	0.8	1.6	2.4	0.7	0.2	0.1	0.5	1.4	3.9
C.J. Watson	32	11.5	42.6	34.6	79.3	0.4	0.6	1.0	1.1	0.5	0.1	0.6	0.6	3.7
Troy Hudson	9	10.3	29.0	33.3	100.0	0.0	0.8	0.8	1.0	0.3	0.0	0.8	0.4	3.1
Marco Belinelli	33	7.3	38.7	39.0	77.8	0.1	0.3	0.4	0.5	0.2	0.0	0.4	0.5	2.9
Patrick O'Bryant	24	4.1	55.2	0.0	60.0	0.4	0.8	1.2	0.2	0.2	0.4	0.3	1.1	1.5
Kosta Perovic	7	5.4	30.0	0.0	66.7	0.9	1.0	1.9	0.1	0.0	0.3	0.1	0.9	1.4
Warriors	**82**	**241.2**	**45.9**	**34.8**	**75.2**	**12.7**	**30.4**	**43.2**	**22.4**	**9.1**	**4.6**	**13.2**	**22.9**	**111.0**
Opponents	**82**	**241.2**	**46.8**	**36.8**	**75.9**	**12.8**	**34.2**	**47.0**	**23.6**	**6.9**	**5.0**	**16.9**	**21.2**	**108.8**

* mid-season trade

NBA Team-by-Team Statistical Leaders *(Cont.)*

Houston Rockets

			Field Goals			Rebounds								
Player	**GP**	**MPG**	**FG%**	**3Pt%**	**FT%**	**OFF**	**DEF**	**Total**	**APG**	**SPG**	**BPG**	**TO**	**PF**	**PPG**
Yao Ming	55	37.2	50.7	0.0	85.0	3.1	7.7	10.8	2.3	0.5	2.0	3.3	3.1	22.0
Tracy McGrady	66	37.0	41.9	29.2	68.4	0.6	4.5	5.1	5.9	1.0	0.5	2.4	1.4	21.6
Rafer Alston	74	34.1	39.4	35.1	71.5	0.4	3.1	3.5	5.3	1.3	0.2	2.2	1.9	13.1
Luis Scola	82	24.7	51.5	0.0	66.8	2.1	4.3	6.4	1.3	0.7	0.2	1.3	2.9	10.3
Shane Battier	80	36.3	42.8	37.7	74.3	1.6	3.5	5.1	1.9	1.0	1.1	1.0	2.5	9.3
*Bonzi Wells	51	22.1	42.5	21.1	63.8	1.2	3.9	5.1	1.6	1.0	0.5	1.5	2.2	9.2
*Bobby Jackson	26	19.2	41.9	34.1	75.0	0.4	2.3	2.7	2.4	0.5	0.1	1.1	1.4	8.8
Carl Landry	42	16.9	61.6	0.0	66.1	2.3	2.6	4.9	0.5	0.4	0.2	0.6	2.3	8.1
Luther Head	73	18.9	43.2	35.1	81.5	0.2	1.6	1.8	1.9	0.6	0.1	1.0	1.0	7.6
*Mike James	33	16.3	35.0	32.4	78.6	0.3	1.2	1.6	1.6	0.5	0.1	0.9	1.4	6.5
Steve Francis	10	19.9	33.3	23.5	56.5	0.8	1.5	2.3	3.0	0.9	0.5	1.4	2.5	5.5
Aaron Brooks	51	11.9	41.3	33.0	85.7	0.3	0.8	1.1	1.7	0.3	0.1	0.9	1.4	5.2
Steve Novak	35	7.5	48.0	47.9	75.0	0.1	0.9	1.0	0.2	0.1	0.1	0.1	0.5	3.9
*Kirk Snyder	9	8.9	46.4	22.2	54.5	0.6	0.8	1.3	0.9	0.1	0.1	0.4	0.7	3.8
Mike Harris	17	9.4	50.0	0.0	61.5	1.4	1.8	3.2	0.2	0.4	0.2	0.5	0.9	3.6
Chuck Hayes	79	19.9	51.1	0.0	45.8	1.7	3.7	5.4	1.2	1.1	0.5	0.8	2.7	3.0
Dikembe Mutombo	39	15.9	53.8	0.0	71.1	1.7	3.4	5.1	0.1	0.3	1.2	0.4	1.4	3.0
Rockets	**82**	**240.6**	**44.8**	**34.2**	**72.6**	**12.2**	**32.4**	**44.6**	**21.4**	**7.3**	**5.1**	**13.7**	**19.6**	**96.7**
Opponents	**82**	**240.6**	**43.3**	**36.5**	**73.7**	**10.9**	**29.8**	**40.7**	**18.9**	**7.6**	**4.6**	**13.3**	**19.7**	**92.0**

Indiana Pacers

			Field Goals			Rebounds								
Player	**GP**	**MPG**	**FG%**	**3Pt%**	**FT%**	**OFF**	**DEF**	**Total**	**APG**	**SPG**	**BPG**	**TO**	**PF**	**PPG**
Danny Granger	80	36.0	44.6	40.4	85.2	1.2	4.9	6.1	2.1	1.2	1.1	2.1	3.6	19.6
Mike Dunleavy	82	36.0	47.6	42.4	83.4	0.7	4.5	5.2	3.5	1.1	0.4	2.3	2.5	19.1
Jermaine O'Neal	42	28.7	43.9	0.0	74.2	2.0	4.8	6.7	2.2	0.5	2.1	2.5	3.1	13.6
Troy Murphy	75	28.1	45.5	39.8	79.7	1.4	5.8	7.2	2.2	0.7	0.4	1.3	2.9	12.2
Jamaal Tinsley	39	33.2	38.0	28.4	72.0	0.6	3.0	3.6	8.4	1.7	0.3	3.3	2.5	11.9
*Ronald Murray	23	22.9	42.5	38.9	75.4	0.4	1.6	2.0	3.5	1.1	0.1	2.3	1.3	11.0
Kareem Rush	71	21.2	40.1	38.9	71.4	0.3	2.1	2.4	1.3	0.6	0.3	0.9	1.5	8.3
Marquis Daniels	74	20.9	43.0	26.5	69.8	0.9	2.0	2.9	1.9	1.1	0.2	1.5	1.6	8.2
Travis Diener	66	20.5	37.0	31.8	90.1	0.4	1.3	1.7	3.8	0.5	0.1	0.8	1.6	6.9
Shawne Williams	65	14.9	42.7	31.4	71.7	0.8	1.9	2.7	0.9	0.4	0.4	0.9	2.0	6.7
Jeff Foster	77	24.5	55.0	0.0	59.3	3.4	5.2	8.7	1.7	0.7	0.4	0.8	2.9	6.4
Ike Diogu	30	10.2	47.8	0.0	85.1	1.3	1.6	2.8	0.3	0.2	0.1	0.7	1.4	5.6
David Harrison	55	12.8	52.9	0.0	51.0	0.8	1.4	2.1	0.3	0.4	1.1	1.1	3.0	4.2
Andre Owens	31	12.6	37.4	45.0	73.5	0.4	1.1	1.5	1.5	0.4	0.1	0.8	1.2	4.0
Stephen Graham	22	5.8	58.6	50.0	75.0	0.2	0.8	1.0	0.4	0.2	0.1	0.5	0.6	4.0
Pacers	**82**	**240.9**	**44.4**	**37.4**	**76.8**	**11.0**	**32.1**	**43.1**	**22.7**	**7.6**	**5.0**	**15.1**	**23.4**	**104.0**
Opponents	**82**	**240.9**	**45.4**	**38.6**	**75.7**	**11.3**	**34.1**	**45.5**	**22.2**	**8.1**	**5.1**	**15.8**	**21.7**	**105.4**

Los Angeles Clippers

			Field Goals			Rebounds								
Player	**GP**	**MPG**	**FG%**	**3Pt%**	**FT%**	**OFF**	**DEF**	**Total**	**APG**	**SPG**	**BPG**	**TO**	**PF**	**PPG**
Corey Maggette	70	35.7	45.8	38.4	81.2	1.1	4.5	5.6	2.7	1.0	0.1	2.8	3.0	22.1
Elton Brand	8	34.3	45.6	0.0	78.7	2.6	5.4	8.0	2.0	0.4	1.9	2.1	2.6	17.6
Chris Kaman	56	37.2	48.3	0.0	76.2	3.1	9.6	12.7	1.9	0.6	2.8	2.9	3.2	15.7
*Sam Cassell	38	25.7	45.5	25.9	89.1	0.3	2.4	2.8	4.7	0.7	0.1	2.1	1.8	12.8
Cuttino Mobley	77	35.1	43.3	34.9	81.9	0.6	2.9	3.6	2.6	1.0	0.4	1.6	2.0	12.8
Al Thornton	79	27.3	42.9	33.1	74.3	1.2	3.3	4.5	1.2	0.6	0.5	1.6	2.5	12.7
Tim Thomas	63	30.8	41.3	30.6	75.2	1.0	4.1	5.1	2.7	0.6	0.5	1.6	3.0	12.4
*Smush Parker	19	21.5	36.2	22.2	66.7	0.1	1.6	1.7	3.6	1.0	0.2	1.9	2.5	6.4
Josh Powell	64	19.2	46.0	0.0	72.4	1.8	3.4	5.2	0.7	0.2	0.4	1.0	2.0	5.5
Dan Dickau	67	15.5	41.9	33.3	82.9	0.2	1.3	1.4	2.6	0.5	0.0	0.8	1.6	5.3
Ruben Patterson	20	16.4	45.3	0.0	55.8	1.2	2.0	3.2	0.9	1.1	0.4	1.4	1.9	5.1
*Nick Fazekas	22	11.8	57.1	0.0	68.2	1.5	2.4	3.9	0.5	0.4	0.5	0.6	1.1	4.7
Richie Frahm	10	16.3	37.0	28.0	0.0	0.4	1.0	1.4	0.8	0.2	0.0	0.6	0.7	4.7
Brevin Knight	74	22.6	40.4	0.0	87.3	0.2	1.7	1.9	4.4	1.4	0.2	1.0	2.2	4.6
Quinton Ross	76	19.8	39.1	42.9	66.7	0.7	1.6	2.3	1.2	0.6	0.4	0.4	1.7	4.1
Paul Davis	22	8.8	36.9	0.0	60.0	1.1	1.0	2.1	0.5	0.3	0.3	0.4	1.5	2.5
Aaron Williams	30	9.9	49.1	0.0	77.8	0.5	1.5	2.0	0.3	0.4	0.5	0.4	1.5	2.3
Andre Barrett	4	6.3	40.0	33.3	50.0	0.0	0.3	0.3	1.8	0.0	0.0	0.3	0.3	1.5
*Marcus Williams	10	3.4	26.3	0.0	0.0	0.4	0.8	1.2	0.3	0.1	0.0	0.0	0.3	1.0
Clippers	**82**	**241.5**	**43.8**	**32.4**	**78.1**	**9.8**	**30.4**	**40.1**	**21.1**	**6.8**	**4.8**	**14.4**	**21.3**	**93.8**
Opponents	**82**	**241.5**	**46.7**	**34.9**	**75.1**	**11.2**	**32.4**	**43.6**	**22.4**	**7.2**	**4.7**	**13.6**	**21.6**	**101.1**

* mid-season trade

NBA Team-by-Team Statistical Leaders *(Cont.)*

Los Angeles Lakers

Player	GP	MPG	Field Goals FG%	3Pt%	FT%	Rebounds OFF	DEF	Total	APG	SPG	BPG	TO	PF	PPG
Kobe Bryant	82	38.9	45.9	36.1	84.0	1.1	5.2	6.3	5.4	1.8	0.5	3.1	2.8	28.3
*Pau Gasol	27	34.0	58.9	0.0	78.9	2.3	5.6	7.8	3.5	0.5	1.6	1.6	2.0	18.8
Lamar Odom	77	37.9	52.5	27.4	69.8	2.6	8.1	10.6	3.5	1.0	0.9	2.0	2.9	14.2
Andrew Bynum	35	28.8	63.6	0.0	69.5	3.0	7.2	10.2	1.7	0.3	2.1	1.5	2.8	13.1
Derek Fisher	82	27.4	43.6	40.6	88.3	0.3	1.8	2.1	2.9	1.1	0.0	1.1	2.3	11.7
Jordan Farmar	82	20.6	46.1	37.1	67.9	0.5	1.8	2.2	2.7	0.9	0.1	1.3	1.3	9.1
Sasha Vujacic	72	17.8	45.4	43.7	83.5	0.3	1.9	2.1	1.0	0.5	0.1	0.7	1.5	8.8
V. Radmanovic	65	22.8	45.3	40.6	80.0	0.9	2.4	3.3	1.9	0.7	0.1	1.1	2.3	8.4
Luke Walton	74	23.4	45.0	33.3	70.6	1.1	2.8	3.9	2.9	0.8	0.2	1.4	1.8	7.2
Ronny Turiaf	78	18.7	47.4	0.0	75.3	1.2	2.7	3.9	1.6	0.4	1.4	0.9	2.6	6.6
*Trevor Ariza	24	18.0	52.4	33.3	68.3	1.0	2.5	3.5	1.5	1.1	0.3	0.8	1.5	6.5
*Kwame Brown	23	22.2	51.5	0.0	40.6	1.3	4.3	5.7	1.2	0.7	0.8	1.6	2.5	5.7
*Maurice Evans	7	13.6	32.1	14.3	80.0	0.6	0.7	1.3	1.7	0.7	0.1	0.0	1.4	4.4
Chris Mihm	23	12.1	33.7	0.0	66.7	1.2	2.1	3.3	0.6	0.2	0.6	0.7	1.8	3.6
*Javaris Crittenton	22	7.9	49.1	33.3	67.9	0.3	0.6	1.0	0.8	0.3	0.0	1.0	0.5	3.3
*D.J. Mbenga	26	7.5	49.2	0.0	40.0	0.6	1.0	1.6	0.2	0.2	0.6	0.3	1.5	2.5
Lakers	**82**	**241.2**	**47.6**	**37.8**	**76.9**	**11.0**	**33.2**	**44.1**	**24.4**	**8.0**	**5.3**	**14.1**	**20.6**	**108.6**
Opponents	**82**	**241.2**	**44.5**	**36.2**	**75.2**	**12.0**	**30.7**	**42.8**	**21.9**	**7.7**	**4.5**	**14.2**	**22.6**	**101.3**

Memphis Grizzlies

Player	GP	MPG	Field Goals FG%	3Pt%	FT%	Rebounds OFF	DEF	Total	APG	SPG	BPG	TO	PF	PPG
Rudy Gay	81	37.0	46.2	34.6	78.5	1.7	4.4	6.2	2.0	1.4	1.0	2.4	2.8	20.1
*Pau Gasol	39	36.8	50.1	26.7	81.9	2.4	6.4	8.8	3.0	0.4	1.4	2.1	2.2	18.9
Mike Miller	70	35.3	50.2	43.2	77.4	0.7	5.9	6.7	3.4	0.5	0.2	2.6	2.1	16.4
Hakim Warrick	75	23.4	50.2	27.1	70.4	1.6	3.1	4.7	0.7	0.5	0.4	1.1	2.1	11.4
J. Carlos Navarro	82	25.8	40.2	36.1	84.9	0.4	2.1	2.6	2.2	0.6	0.0	1.6	1.1	10.9
Kyle Lowry	82	25.5	43.2	25.7	69.8	0.5	2.5	3.0	3.6	1.1	0.3	1.6	2.3	9.6
Mike Conley	53	26.1	42.8	33.0	73.2	0.4	2.2	2.6	4.2	0.8	0.0	1.7	1.6	9.4
*Javaris Crittenton	28	18.1	40.0	26.5	69.7	0.7	2.5	3.2	1.2	0.4	0.1	1.2	1.3	7.4
*Damon Stoudamire	29	21.6	39.7	38.3	80.8	0.5	2.0	2.4	3.9	0.6	0.0	1.7	1.6	7.3
Darko Milicic	70	23.8	43.8	0.0	55.4	1.8	4.2	6.1	0.8	0.5	1.6	1.4	2.6	7.2
*Stromile Swift	35	15.7	52.5	0.0	64.2	1.3	2.4	3.7	0.6	0.3	1.0	1.1	2.1	6.8
*Bobby Jones	9	15.3	38.9	23.1	90.0	1.1	1.9	3.0	1.2	0.6	0.2	0.6	1.9	4.4
Tarence Kinsey	11	8.7	42.1	42.9	83.3	0.3	0.8	1.1	0.2	0.3	0.0	0.3	1.0	3.6
*Kwame Brown	15	13.6	48.7	0.0	41.2	1.3	2.5	3.8	1.1	0.4	0.3	0.9	1.6	3.5
Brian Cardinal	37	11.9	34.1	30.9	68.4	0.7	1.9	2.6	0.6	0.3	0.1	0.6	1.7	3.4
Andre Brown	33	8.7	50.0	0.0	44.9	1.1	1.7	2.8	0.2	0.2	0.1	0.4	1.2	3.0
*Jason Collins	31	15.7	50.8	0.0	52.6	0.9	1.9	2.9	0.2	0.4	0.6	0.8	2.7	2.6
Grizzlies	**82**	**241.5**	**45.4**	**34.9**	**72.3**	**10.3**	**31.3**	**41.6**	**19.2**	**6.1**	**4.7**	**15.3**	**19.4**	**100.7**
Opponents	**82**	**241.5**	**48.0**	**36.4**	**77.4**	**11.4**	**33.2**	**44.5**	**23.9**	**8.7**	**4.9**	**13.4**	**22.5**	**106.9**

Miami Heat

Player	GP	MPG	Field Goals FG%	3Pt%	FT%	Rebounds OFF	DEF	Total	APG	SPG	BPG	TO	PF	PPG
Dwyane Wade	51	38.3	46.9	28.6	75.8	0.9	3.3	4.2	6.9	1.7	0.7	4.4	2.7	24.6
*Shawn Marion	16	37.6	45.9	25.8	69.0	3.1	8.1	11.2	2.5	1.9	0.9	2.3	2.1	14.3
*Shaquille O'Neal	33	28.7	58.1	0.0	49.4	3.0	4.8	7.8	1.4	0.6	1.6	3.0	4.1	14.2
Ricky Davis	82	36.1	43.3	40.5	78.7	0.7	3.6	4.3	3.4	1.1	0.2	2.3	2.3	13.8
Udonis Haslem	49	36.8	46.7	0.0	81.0	2.2	6.9	9.0	1.4	0.8	0.4	1.4	3.0	12.0
*Marcus Banks	12	21.6	51.2	40.5	78.9	0.1	2.0	2.1	3.0	0.5	0.4	1.8	2.3	9.5
Daequan Cook	59	24.4	38.1	33.2	82.5	0.3	2.7	3.0	1.3	0.4	0.2	1.1	2.7	8.8
Jason Williams	67	28.1	38.4	35.3	86.3	0.2	1.8	1.9	4.6	1.2	0.1	1.4	1.4	8.8
Mark Blount	69	22.3	46.2	38.6	63.8	1.0	2.8	3.8	0.6	0.5	0.5	1.0	1.9	8.4
*Bobby Jones	6	23.8	53.1	40.0	61.5	1.3	2.7	4.0	0.8	0.3	0.0	1.2	3.0	8.0
Dorell Wright	44	25.1	48.8	36.4	82.6	1.1	3.9	5.0	1.4	0.7	0.9	0.7	1.8	7.9
Chris Quinn	60	22.3	42.4	40.3	86.7	0.2	1.8	2.0	3.0	0.8	0.1	0.9	1.5	7.8
Kasib Powell	11	27.6	36.8	24.2	66.7	0.7	3.3	4.0	1.6	0.8	0.2	0.5	1.6	7.6
Earl Barron	46	19.3	40.4	7.7	70.1	1.5	2.8	4.3	0.6	0.4	0.2	1.0	2.5	7.1
Alonzo Mourning	25	15.6	54.7	0.0	59.2	1.4	2.4	3.7	0.3	0.2	1.7	1.0	2.2	6.0
Blake Ahearn	12	14.8	26.3	29.4	96.8	0.1	1.5	1.6	1.6	0.5	0.0	1.3	1.7	5.8
Luke Jackson	14	16.3	32.5	36.7	69.6	0.5	1.9	2.4	1.2	0.6	0.0	0.6	1.6	5.6
*Stephane Lasme	15	20.2	45.1	0.0	59.4	1.7	1.8	3.5	0.2	0.9	1.5	1.0	2.3	5.5
*Smush Parker	9	20.4	31.5	25.0	75.0	0.2	1.9	2.1	1.7	0.6	0.3	0.9	1.4	4.8
Alexander Johnson	43	12.8	48.8	0.0	68.7	0.7	1.4	2.2	0.3	0.3	0.2	1.0	1.9	4.2
A. Hardaway	16	20.3	36.7	42.1	88.9	0.2	2.0	2.2	2.2	1.2	0.1	0.8	1.5	3.8
Heat	**82**	**241.8**	**44.3**	**35.8**	**72.7**	**9.1**	**28.6**	**37.6**	**20.0**	**7.2**	**4.3**	**14.7**	**20.4**	**91.4**
Opponents	**82**	**241.8**	**46.8**	**36.9**	**75.5**	**11.2**	**31.9**	**43.1**	**22.2**	**7.7**	**4.2**	**14.2**	**20.1**	**100.0**

NBA Team-by-Team Statistical Leaders *(Cont.)*

Milwaukee Bucks

			Field Goals				Rebounds							
Player	**GP**	**MPG**	**FG%**	**3Pt%**	**FT%**	**OFF**	**DEF**	**Total**	**APG**	**SPG**	**BPG**	**TO**	**PF**	**PPG**
Michael Redd	72	37.5	44.2	36.2	82.0	1.2	3.1	4.3	3.4	0.9	0.2	2.5	1.7	22.7
Maurice Williams	66	36.5	48.0	38.5	85.6	0.6	2.9	3.5	6.3	1.2	0.2	2.8	2.8	17.2
Andrew Bogut	78	34.9	51.1	0.0	58.7	3.1	6.6	9.8	2.6	0.8	1.7	2.2	3.3	14.3
Charlie Villanueva	76	24.1	43.5	29.7	78.3	1.9	4.2	6.1	1.0	0.4	0.5	1.4	2.3	11.7
Desmond Mason	59	28.9	48.2	0.0	65.9	1.3	3.1	4.3	2.1	0.7	0.5	1.4	1.8	9.7
Yi Jianlin	66	25.0	42.1	28.6	84.1	1.6	3.6	5.2	0.8	0.6	0.9	1.4	2.3	8.6
Ramon Sessions	17	26.4	43.6	42.9	78.0	0.5	2.9	3.4	7.5	1.0	0.2	2.1	1.5	8.1
Charlie Bell	68	23.9	38.1	34.1	80.5	0.5	2.0	2.5	3.1	0.8	0.0	1.1	1.8	7.6
Bobby Simmons	70	21.7	42.1	35.1	75.7	1.0	2.3	3.2	1.1	0.1	0.7	1.1	2.0	7.6
Royal Ivey	75	19.1	39.4	32.7	72.6	0.5	1.1	1.6	2.1	0.6	0.1	1.0	2.2	5.6
Awvee Storey	26	10.0	43.8	0.0	48.3	1.2	0.9	2.1	0.6	0.3	0.0	0.4	1.6	3.5
Dan Gadzuric	51	10.5	41.6	0.0	52.4	1.3	1.5	2.8	0.2	0.4	0.5	0.7	1.6	3.2
Jake Voskuhl	44	8.8	46.3	0.0	82.8	0.7	1.5	2.2	0.3	0.2	0.5	0.7	1.9	2.2
Michael Ruffin	46	13.8	53.2	0.0	39.7	2.0	2.1	4.0	0.5	0.7	0.4	0.4	2.0	2.0
Bucks	**82**	**242.1**	**44.9**	**34.4**	**73.3**	**12.9**	**28.8**	**41.7**	**21.5**	**6.6**	**4.4**	**14.8**	**21.3**	**97.0**
Opponents	**82**	**242.1**	**48.0**	**38.4**	**76.6**	**10.6**	**30.0**	**40.7**	**23.3**	**7.9**	**4.9**	**13.7**	**21.1**	**103.9**

Minnesota Timberwolves

			Field Goals				Rebounds							
Player	**GP**	**MPG**	**FG%**	**3Pt%**	**FT%**	**OFF**	**DEF**	**Total**	**APG**	**SPG**	**BPG**	**TO**	**PF**	**PPG**
Al Jefferson	82	35.6	50.0	0.0	72.1	3.8	7.4	11.1	1.4	0.9	1.5	2.0	2.7	21.0
Rashad McCants	75	26.9	45.3	40.7	74.8	0.7	2.1	2.7	2.2	0.9	0.2	2.3	3.1	14.9
Randy Foye	39	32.3	42.9	41.2	81.5	0.3	2.9	3.3	4.2	0.9	0.1	2.0	2.6	13.1
Ryan Gomes	82	29.7	45.7	33.0	83.0	1.6	4.2	5.8	1.8	0.8	0.1	1.2	1.9	12.6
Craig Smith	77	20.1	56.3	0.0	66.5	1.6	3.0	4.6	0.8	0.5	0.2	1.2	2.8	9.4
Sebastian Telfair	60	32.2	40.1	28.1	74.3	0.3	2.0	2.3	5.9	1.0	0.2	1.9	2.9	9.3
*Kirk Snyder	27	25.2	51.6	21.4	75.3	0.9	3.3	4.2	2.1	0.7	0.5	1.8	1.8	8.4
Marko Jaric	75	29.2	43.0	36.2	74.2	0.5	2.5	3.0	4.1	1.3	0.4	1.7	2.4	8.3
Antoine Walker	46	19.4	36.3	32.4	53.0	1.2	2.4	3.7	1.0	0.7	0.2	1.0	1.7	8.0
*Theo Ratliff	10	21.3	51.1	0.0	68.0	1.3	2.6	3.9	0.7	0.3	1.9	1.2	3.0	6.3
Corey Brewer	79	22.8	37.4	19.4	80.0	1.0	2.7	3.7	1.4	1.0	0.3	1.1	2.4	5.8
Greg Buckner	31	16.8	38.5	30.0	86.4	0.3	1.8	2.1	1.3	0.7	0.1	0.9	2.0	4.0
Michael Doleac	24	10.7	44.4	0.0	50.0	0.7	1.4	2.0	0.3	0.4	0.4	0.5	1.8	2.4
Chris Richard	52	10.7	47.1	0.0	59.3	1.0	1.6	2.6	0.3	0.2	0.2	0.5	1.6	1.9
Mark Madsen	20	7.6	15.8	0.0	25.0	0.9	1.0	1.9	0.2	0.2	0.1	0.5	1.3	0.5
Timberwolves	**82**	**240.6**	**45.1**	**35.0**	**73.6**	**11.8**	**29.6**	**41.4**	**19.9**	**7.5**	**3.7**	**14.5**	**23.0**	**95.6**
Opponents	**82**	**240.6**	**47.2**	**35.7**	**76.9**	**10.6**	**31.0**	**41.7**	**23.2**	**7.4**	**5.7**	**13.4**	**17.5**	**102.4**

New Jersey Nets

			Field Goals				Rebounds							
Player	**GP**	**MPG**	**FG%**	**3Pt%**	**FT%**	**OFF**	**DEF**	**Total**	**APG**	**SPG**	**BPG**	**TO**	**PF**	**PPG**
Richard Jefferson	82	39.0	46.6	36.2	79.8	1.1	3.0	4.2	3.1	0.9	0.3	2.4	2.7	22.6
Vince Carter	76	38.9	45.6	35.9	81.6	1.5	4.5	6.0	5.1	1.2	0.4	2.4	3.2	21.3
*Devin Harris	25	33.5	43.8	32.0	82.9	0.4	2.8	3.3	6.5	1.4	0.3	2.7	2.5	15.4
*Jason Kidd	51	37.2	36.6	35.6	82.0	1.1	6.9	8.1	10.4	1.5	0.3	3.6	1.8	11.3
Bostjan Nachbar	75	22.1	40.2	35.9	78.6	0.7	2.7	3.5	1.2	0.6	0.3	1.1	2.4	9.8
Josh Boone	70	25.3	54.8	0.0	45.6	2.7	4.5	7.3	0.8	0.5	0.9	1.0	2.2	8.2
*Antoine Wright	41	25.8	40.1	26.7	70.7	0.9	2.2	3.0	1.6	0.6	0.4	1.0	2.6	7.3
Nenad Krstic	45	18.0	41.0	0.0	75.4	0.8	3.7	4.4	0.6	0.2	0.4	0.9	2.5	6.6
Marcus Williams	53	16.1	37.9	38.0	78.7	0.3	1.6	1.9	2.6	0.5	0.1	1.4	1.0	5.9
Sean Williams	73	17.5	53.8	0.0	60.9	1.6	2.8	4.4	0.4	0.4	1.5	1.0	2.6	5.6
*Malik Allen	48	15.9	47.5	50.0	92.3	0.9	1.8	2.7	0.6	0.3	0.4	0.7	1.9	5.4
*Stromile Swift	21	14.0	47.7	0.0	75.0	0.9	2.5	3.3	0.2	0.2	0.9	0.6	1.9	5.0
*Maurice Ager	14	6.3	42.1	27.3	16.7	0.2	0.4	0.6	0.3	0.0	0.0	0.2	0.4	2.6
*DeSagana Diop	27	14.9	41.5	0.0	46.7	1.8	2.7	4.5	0.5	0.2	0.9	0.6	1.7	2.5
Darrell Armstrong	50	11.0	36.4	33.3	66.7	0.3	1.0	1.3	1.5	0.6	0.0	0.8	1.1	2.5
*Jamaal Magloire	24	10.8	30.6	0.0	45.2	0.8	2.6	3.4	0.3	0.0	0.4	1.0	1.8	1.8
Trenton Hassell	26	11.9	36.4	20.0	75.0	0.3	1.2	1.5	0.6	0.2	0.1	0.3	1.3	1.8
*Jason Collins	43	25.9	42.6	0.0	38.9	0.8	1.3	2.1	0.4	0.3	0.2	0.5	2.6	1.4
Nets	**82**	**241.8**	**44.3**	**34.8**	**73.6**	**11.1**	**30.7**	**41.9**	**23.5**	**6.4**	**4.8**	**15.0**	**22.6**	**95.8**
Opponents	**82**	**241.8**	**45.6**	**36.9**	**76.8**	**10.9**	**30.7**	**41.6**	**22.1**	**8.1**	**4.4**	**13.4**	**22.4**	**100.9**

* mid-season trade

NBA Team-by-Team Statistical Leaders *(Cont.)*

New Orleans Hornets

Player	GP	MPG	Field Goals FG%	3Pt%	FT%	Rebounds OFF	DEF	Total	APG	SPG	BPG	TO	PF	PPG
Chris Paul	80	37.6	48.8	36.9	85.1	0.8	3.2	4.0	11.6	2.7	0.1	2.5	2.3	21.1
David West	76	37.8	48.2	24.0	85.0	2.4	6.5	8.9	2.3	0.8	1.3	2.2	2.7	20.6
Peja Stojakovic	77	35.2	44.0	44.1	92.9	0.8	3.5	4.3	1.2	0.7	0.1	0.8	1.6	16.4
Tyson Chandler	79	35.2	62.3	0.0	59.3	4.1	7.7	11.7	1.0	0.6	1.1	1.7	3.1	11.8
*Bonzi Wells	22	19.9	49.0	33.3	66.0	1.0	2.3	3.2	0.8	1.1	0.4	1.2	2.0	8.8
Jannero Pargo	80	18.7	39.0	34.9	87.7	0.3	1.3	1.6	2.4	0.6	0.1	1.2	1.5	8.1
Morris Peterson	76	23.6	41.7	39.4	76.5	0.5	2.2	2.7	0.9	0.6	0.1	0.5	1.6	8.0
*Bobby Jackson	46	19.3	39.2	36.8	81.6	0.5	1.9	2.4	1.7	0.7	0.1	0.7	1.3	7.1
Rasual Butler	51	17.2	35.0	33.1	83.9	0.3	1.6	2.0	0.7	0.3	0.4	0.2	1.3	4.9
Melvin Ely	52	11.9	47.2	0.0	55..2	0.5	2.3	2.8	0.4	0.1	0.4	0.8	1.5	3.9
Julian Wright	57	11.2	53.3	41.7	63.5	0.6	1.5	2.1	0.7	0.5	0.2	0.6	0.8	3.9
*Mike James	21	8.7	34.4	30.4	100.0	0.1	0.7	0.8	0.3	0.2	0.0	0.3	0.6	2.7
Hilton Armstrong	65	11.3	45.3	0.0	62.9	1.0	1.5	2.5	0.4	0.2	0.5	0.9	2.0	2.7
Ryan Bowen	53	12.5	49.0	0.0	55.2	1.0	0.8	1.9	0.5	0.6	0.2	0.3	1.5	2.2
Chris Andersen	5	6.8	28.6	0.0	50.0	0.4	1.4	1.8	0.0	0.0	0.5	0.2	1.2	1.2
Hornets	**82**	**241.5**	**46.6**	**38.9**	**76.9**	**11.4**	**30.4**	**41.8**	**21.8**	**7.8**	**3.9**	**11.9**	**18.7**	**100.9**
Opponents	**82**	**241.5**	**46.0**	**35.1**	**77.1**	**9.9**	**30.9**	**40.8**	**21.7**	**5.7**	**4.0**	**13.8**	**19.2**	**95.6**

New York Knicks

Player	GP	MPG	Field Goals FG%	3Pt%	FT%	Rebounds OFF	DEF	Total	APG	SPG	BPG	TO	PF	PPG
Jamal Crawford	80	39.9	41.0	35.6	86.4	0.5	2.1	2.6	5.0	1.0	0.2	2.4	1.8	20.6
Zach Randolph	69	32.5	45.9	27.5	77.2	2.7	7.6	10.3	2.0	0.9	0.2	2.7	2.8	17.6
Stephon Marbury	24	33.5	41.9	37.8	71.6	0.7	1.8	2.5	4.7	0.9	0.1	2.0	2.4	13.9
Eddy Curry	59	25.9	54.6	0.0	62.3	1.9	2.8	4.7	0.5	0.2	0.5	2.1	2.7	13.2
Nate Robinson	72	26.2	42.3	33.2	78.6	0.7	2.4	3.1	2.9	0.8	0.0	1.4	2.6	12.7
David Lee	81	29.1	55.2	0.0	81.9	3.0	6.0	8.9	1.2	0.7	0.4	1.2	2.6	10.8
Quentin Richardson	65	28.3	35.9	32.2	68.2	0.9	4.0	4.8	1.8	0.7	0.2	1.1	2.4	8.1
Fred Jones	70	25.1	42.1	38.5	74.6	0.4	2.0	2.4	2.4	0.7	0.3	1.1	2.0	7.6
Wilson Chandler	35	19.6	43.8	30.0	63.0	1.1	2.5	3.6	0.9	0.4	0.5	0.8	2.4	7.3
Jared Jeffries	73	18.2	40.0	16.0	52.7	1.6	1.7	3.3	0.9	0.5	0.3	0.8	1.8	3.7
Malik Rose	49	10.1	36.7	28.6	72.5	0.6	1.5	2.1	0.6	0.3	0.1	0.8	1.6	3.5
Renaldo Balkman	65	14.6	48.9	8.3	43.2	1.3	2.0	3.3	0.6	0.7	0.5	0.6	2.0	3.4
Mardy Collins	46	13.8	32.6	25.0	60.5	0.4	1.2	1.6	1.9	0.5	0.2	1.2	1.2	3.2
Randolph Morris	18	10.1	36.2	0.0	48.3	0.7	1.4	2.1	0.1	0.2	0.1	0.5	2.1	3.1
Jerome James	2	2.5	100.0	0.0	100.0	0.0	1.5	1.5	0.0	0.0	0.0	0.0	0.0	2.0
Knicks	**82**	**242.4**	**43.9**	**33.7**	**72.7**	**12.5**	**30.0**	**42.5**	**18.7**	**6.4**	**2.6**	**14.5**	**21.5**	**96.9**
Opponents	**82**	**242.4**	**47.4**	**36.9**	**73.9**	**11.3**	**31.4**	**42.6**	**21.6**	**7.6**	**5.2**	**12.8**	**20.3**	**103.5**

Orlando Magic

Player	GP	MPG	Field Goals FG%	3Pt%	FT%	Rebounds OFF	DEF	Total	APG	SPG	BPG	TO	PF	PPG
Dwight Howard	82	37.7	59.9	0.0	59.0	3.4	10.8	14.2	1.3	0.9	2.1	3.2	3.3	20.7
Hedo Turkoglu	82	36.9	45.6	40.0	82.9	1.0	4.7	5.7	5.0	0.9	0.3	3.0	3.0	19.5
Rashard Lewis	81	38.0	45.5	40.9	83.8	1.2	4.2	5.4	2.4	1.2	0.5	1.7	2.6	18.2
Jameer Nelson	69	28.4	46.9	41.6	82.8	0.4	3.1	3.5	5.6	0.9	0.1	2.0	2.4	10.9
*Maurice Evans	68	23.9	48.9	39.6	69.1	1.3	1.8	3.1	1.0	0.6	0.1	0.6	1.9	9.3
Keith Bogans	82	26.8	41.0	36.2	73.6	0.5	2.7	3.2	1.3	0.7	0.1	0.7	2.0	8.7
Keyon Dooling	72	18.5	46.8	33.8	84.5	0.1	1.3	1.4	1.8	0.5	0.1	0.9	1.8	8.1
Carlos Arroyo	62	20.5	45.1	34.5	85.3	0.2	1.7	1.8	3.5	0.4	0.0	1.2	1.4	6.9
*Brian Cook	45	12.4	39.4	39.0	88.2	0.5	1.7	2.2	0.5	0.2	0.3	0.8	1.9	5.0
J.J. Redick	34	8.1	44.4	39.5	79.4	0.0	0.6	0.7	0.5	0.1	0.0	0.4	0.9	4.1
*Trevor Ariza	11	10.5	45.2	0.0	53.3	0.5	1.7	2.2	0.7	0.5	0.3	0.5	0.8	3.3
Marcin Gortat	6	6.8	47.1	0.0	66.7	1.3	1.3	2.7	0.3	0.2	0.2	0.3	0.7	3.0
Pat Garrity	31	9.2	33.8	21.6	80.0	0.3	1.1	1.4	0.4	0.2	0.0	0.6	1.1	2.1
Bo Outlaw	2	3.5	66.7	0.0	0.0	0.0	0.0	0.0	0.0	0.0	0.0	0.5	0.5	2.0
Adonal Foyle	82	9.4	45.8	0.0	47.1	0.9	1.7	2.5	0.2	0.2	0.6	0.4	1.1	1.9
James Augustine	25	6.0	52.9	0.0	50.0	0.6	0.6	1.2	0.1	0.2	0.1	0.2	0.7	1.6
Magic	**82**	**241.2**	**47.4**	**38.6**	**72.1**	**9.4**	**32.6**	**42.0**	**20.8**	**6.3**	**4.1**	**14.3**	**20.6**	**104.5**
Opponents	**82**	**241.2**	**44.6**	**35.8**	**75.4**	**11.0**	**30.7**	**41.7**	**21.5**	**7.1**	**4.2**	**13.2**	**23.1**	**99.0**

* mid-season trade

Philadelphia 76ers

			Field Goals			Rebounds								
Player	**GP**	**MPG**	**FG%**	**3Pt%**	**FT%**	**OFF**	**DEF**	**Total**	**APG**	**SPG**	**BPG**	**TO**	**PF**	**PPG**
Andre Iguodala	82	39.5	45.6	32.9	72.1	1.0	4.4	5.4	4.8	2.1	0.6	2.6	2.3	19.9
Andre Miller	82	36.8	49.2	8.8	77.2	1.2	2.8	4.0	6.9	1.3	0.1	2.5	2.2	17.0
Willie Green	74	26.6	43.6	28.5	75.7	0.4	2.0	2.5	2.0	0.7	0.3	1.5	1.6	12.4
Louis Williams	80	23.3	42.4	35.9	78.3	0.5	1.6	2.1	3.2	1.0	0.2	1.6	1.6	11.5
Samuel Dalembert	82	33.2	51.3	0.0	70.7	3.7	6.6	10.4	0.5	0.5	2.3	1.9	3.3	10.5
*Kyle Korver	25	26.4	39.6	35.2	91.2	0.5	2.4	2.9	1.3	0.8	0.2	1.1	2.7	10.0
Thaddeus Young	74	21.0	53.9	31.6	73.8	1.6	2.6	4.2	0.8	1.0	0.1	0.9	1.7	8.2
Rodney Carney	70	14.8	40.3	31.7	67.9	0.7	1.4	2.1	0.5	0.6	0.3	0.5	1.4	5.8
Reggie Evans	81	23.2	43.9	100.0	46.7	2.8	4.8	7.5	0.8	1.1	0.1	1.3	2.6	5.2
Jason Smith	76	14.6	45.5	28.6	65.9	1.0	2.0	3.0	0.3	0.3	0.7	0.6	1.9	4.5
*Gordon Giricek	12	9.2	31.7	33.3	75.0	0.1	1.1	1.2	0.9	0.3	0.1	0.7	0.8	3.1
Kevin Ollie	40	7.5	42.0	0.0	80.0	0.1	0.4	0.5	1.0	0.3	0.0	0.1	0.7	1.8
Louis Amundson	16	4.0	50.0	0.0	28.6	0.4	0.3	0.8	0.0	0.1	0.1	0.1	0.8	1.1
Shavlik Randolph	9	3.0	28.6	0.0	0.0	1.0	0.2	1.2	0.3	0.1	0.3	0.2	0.6	0.9
Calvin Booth	31	6.6	33.3	0.0	60.0	0.2	1.0	1.2	0.3	0.2	0.6	0.1	1.1	0.8
76ers	**82**	**240.9**	**46.0**	**31.7**	**70.6**	**13.0**	**28.9**	**41.9**	**20.4**	**8.7**	**4.9**	**14.3**	**19.8**	**96.6**
Opponents	**82**	**240.9**	**46.1**	**36.0**	**77.2**	**11.3**	**28.0**	**39.2**	**23.2**	**6.7**	**5.1**	**15.7**	**20.8**	**96.2**

Phoenix Suns

			Field Goals			Rebounds								
Player	**GP**	**MPG**	**FG%**	**3Pt%**	**FT%**	**OFF**	**DEF**	**Total**	**APG**	**SPG**	**BPG**	**TO**	**PF**	**PPG**
Amare Stoudemire	79	33.9	59.0	16.1	80.5	2.3	6.8	9.1	1.5	0.8	2.1	2.2	3.7	25.2
Steve Nash	81	34.3	50.4	47.0	90.6	0.3	3.1	3.5	11.1	0.7	0.1	3.6	1.4	16.9
*Shawn Marion	47	36.4	52.6	34.7	71.3	1.8	8.0	9.9	2.1	2.0	1.5	1.0	2.5	15.8
Leandro Barbosa	82	29.5	46.2	38.9	82.2	0.5	2.3	2.8	2.6	0.9	0.2	1.4	2.4	15.6
Grant Hill	70	31.7	50.3	31.7	86.7	1.1	4.0	5.0	2.9	0.9	0.8	1.4	2.2	13.1
*Shaquille O'Neal	28	28.7	61.1	0.0	51.3	2.4	8.2	10.6	1.7	0.5	1.2	3.0	3.4	12.9
Raja Bell	75	35.3	42.1	40.1	86.8	0.6	3.0	3.7	2.2	0.7	0.4	0.9	2.9	11.9
Boris Diaw	82	28.1	47.7	31.7	74.4	1.2	3.4	4.6	3.9	0.7	0.5	1.9	2.0	8.8
*Gordon Giricek	22	20.1	49.7	38.0	94.1	0.4	1.9	2.3	1.6	0.4	0.1	1.1	2.2	8.8
*Marcus Banks	24	12.8	40.4	38.5	75.0	0.1	0.7	0.8	1.0	0.3	0.3	0.7	1.6	5.2
Alando Tucker	6	8.0	36.4	25.0	83.3	0.7	0.7	1.3	0.0	0.0	0.2	0.0	0.3	3.7
Brian Skinner	66	12.8	46.5	66.7	52.4	1.0	2.7	3.6	0.2	0.3	1.2	0.6	1.7	3.3
Sean Marks	19	6.8	53.5	25.0	63.2	0.5	1.4	1.9	0.2	0.2	0.5	0.4	1.2	3.1
*Linton Johnson	6	8.8	50.0	50.0	0.0	0.8	1.3	2.2	0.5	0.0	0.2	0.3	1.7	2.5
Eric Piatkowski	16	7.1	42.3	42.3	100.0	0.1	0.7	0.8	0.6	0.0	0.1	0.4	0.7	2.4
D.J. Strawberry	33	8.2	31.5	24.0	47.4	0.3	0.6	0.8	0.9	0.4	0.2	0.3	1.1	2.2
Suns	**82**	**241.2**	**50.0**	**39.3**	**78.3**	**8.8**	**32.7**	**41.5**	**26.7**	**6.5**	**6.3**	**14.4**	**19.9**	**110.1**
Opponents	**82**	**241.2**	**45.6**	**35.3**	**74.9**	**13.4**	**30.5**	**43.9**	**19.6**	**7.3**	**3.8**	**13.4**	**21.1**	**105.0**

Portland Trail Blazers

			Field Goals			Rebounds								
Player	**GP**	**MPG**	**FG%**	**3Pt%**	**FT%**	**OFF**	**DEF**	**Total**	**APG**	**SPG**	**BPG**	**TO**	**PF**	**PPG**
Brandon Roy	74	37.7	45.4	34.0	75.3	1.1	3.6	4.7	5.8	1.1	0.2	1.8	2.0	19.1
LaMarcus Aldridge	76	34.9	48.4	14.3	76.2	2.9	4.7	7.6	1.6	0.7	1.2	1.7	3.2	17.8
Travis Outlaw	82	26.7	43.3	39.6	74.1	1.2	3.4	4.6	1.3	0.7	0.8	1.3	2.1	13.3
Martell Webster	75	28.4	42.2	38.8	73.5	0.7	3.2	3.9	1.2	0.6	0.4	1.1	2.1	10.7
Jarrett Jack	82	27.2	43.1	34.2	86.7	0.4	2.5	2.9	3.8	0.7	0.0	2.2	1.6	9.9
Steve Blake	81	29.9	40.8	40.6	76.6	0.4	2.0	2.4	5.1	0.7	0.1	1.4	1.6	8.5
James Jones	58	22.0	43.7	44.4	87.8	0.7	2.0	2.8	0.6	0.4	0.3	0.5	1.7	8.0
Channing Frye	78	17.2	48.8	30.0	78.0	1.4	3.2	4.5	0.7	0.4	0.4	0.7	2.7	6.8
Joel Przybilla	77	23.6	57.6	0.0	68.0	2.5	5.9	8.4	0.4	0.2	1.2	1.2	3.0	4.8
Sergio Rodriguez	72	8.7	35.2	29.3	65.8	0.2	0.6	0.8	1.7	0.3	0.0	0.7	0.8	2.5
*Von Wafer	8	8.0	30.4	27.3	50.0	0.0	1.1	1.1	0.3	0.0	0.3	0.3	0.4	2.4
*Taurean Green	8	5.5	25.0	12.5	100.0	0.0	0.5	0.5	1.0	0.1	0.0	0.9	0.4	2.1
Raef LaFrentz	39	7.5	44.3	0.0	57.9	0.7	1.0	1.7	0.2	0.3	0.4	0.3	1.5	1.7
Josh McRoberts	8	3.5	60.0	0.0	0.0	0.3	1.0	1.3	0.3	0.1	0.0	0.3	0.1	1.5
Trail Blazers	**82**	**242.7**	**44.8**	**37.7**	**76.7**	**11.0**	**29.7**	**40.7**	**21.1**	**5.6**	**4.4**	**12.9**	**20.0**	**95.4**
Opponents	**82**	**242.7**	**45.1**	**35.6**	**76.6**	**11.7**	**30.1**	**41.7**	**20.9**	**6.0**	**3.7**	**12.5**	**20.2**	**96.3**

NBA Team-by-Team Statistical Leaders *(Cont.)*

Sacramento Kings

			Field Goals			Rebounds								
Player	**GP**	**MPG**	**FG%**	**3Pt%**	**FT%**	**OFF**	**DEF**	**Total**	**APG**	**SPG**	**BPG**	**TO**	**PF**	**PPG**
Kevin Martin	61	36.3	45.6	40.2	86.9	0.8	3.7	4.5	2.1	1.0	0.1	2.1	2.5	23.7
Ron Artest	57	38.1	45.3	38.0	71.9	1.8	4.0	5.8	3.5	2.3	0.7	2.6	2.8	20.5
*Mike Bibby	15	31.4	40.6	39.3	74.2	0.7	3.0	3.7	5.0	1.3	01	2.5	2.3	13.5
Brad Miller	72	34.9	46.3	31.1	84.8	2.3	7.1	9.5	3.7	1.0	1.0	2.3	3.4	13.4
Beno Udrih	65	32.0	46.4	38.7	85.0	0.5	2.8	3.3	4.3	0.9	0.2	2.3	2.1	12.8
John Salmons	81	31.1	47.7	32.5	82.3	0.9	3.4	4.3	2.6	1.2	0.4	2.1	2.1	12.5
Francisco Garcia	79	26.5	46.2	39.1	77.9	0.7	2.7	3.3	1.6	1.2	0.6	1.6	2.9	12.3
Mikki Moore	82	29.1	57.7	0.0	73.6	2.0	4.1	6.0	1.0	0.4	0.6	1.3	3.8	8.5
*Shelden Williams	28	12.9	49.1	0.0	66.7	1.2	2.3	3.5	0.3	0.3	0.4	0.8	1.8	5.2
Quincy Douby	74	11.8	39.4	34.4	92.3	0.2	0.9	1.1	0.7	0.4	0.2	0.8	1.1	4.8
Spencer Hawes	71	13.1	45.9	19.0	65.5	1.0	2.3	3.2	0.6	0.2	0.6	0.8	1.8	4.7
*Anthony Johnson	27	15.2	45.5	50.0	81.8	0.2	1.3	1.4	2.2	0.4	0.0	1.3	1.1	3.9
Dahntay Jones	25	8.2	43.4	16.7	66.7	0.3	1.1	1.4	0.5	0.3	0.2	0.4	1.1	3.2
S. Abdur-Rahim	6	8.5	21.4	0.0	100.0	1.0	0.7	1.7	0.7	0.2	0.0	0.2	1.5	1.7
Kenny Thomas	23	12.2	42.1	0.0	0.0	0.8	1.9	2.7	0.6	0.3	0.0	0.9	1.7	1.4
Darryl Watkins	9	7.9	33.3	0.0	40.0	0.6	0.8	1.3	0.0	0.2	0.2	0.8	0.9	1.3
Kings	**82**	**241.8**	**46.4**	**37.3**	**79.8**	**10.1**	**30.0**	**40.1**	**19.1**	**7.9**	**4.1**	**16.1**	**22.4**	**102.5**
Opponents	**82**	**241.8**	**46.6**	**37.3**	**75.3**	**11.8**	**30.1**	**41.9**	**22.9**	**8.1**	**5.5**	**15.2**	**23.1**	**104.8**

San Antonio Spurs

			Field Goals			Rebounds								
Player	**GP**	**MPG**	**FG%**	**3Pt%**	**FT%**	**OFF**	**DEF**	**Total**	**APG**	**SPG**	**BPG**	**TO**	**PF**	**PPG**
Manu Ginobili	74	31.0	46.0	40.1	86.0	0.9	3.9	4.8	4.5	1.5	0.5	2.7	2.3	19.5
Tim Duncan	78	34.0	49.7	0.0	73.0	3.0	8.3	11.3	2.8	0.7	2.0	2.3	2.4	19.3
Tony Parker	69	33.5	49.4	25.8	71.5	0.4	2.8	3.2	6.0	0.8	0.1	2.4	1.3	18.8
Michael Finley	82	26.9	41.4	37.0	80.0	0.3	2.8	3.1	1.4	0.4	0.1	0.7	1.1	10.1
Brent Barry	31	17.9	48.1	42.9	95.0	0.4	1.4	1.8	1.7	0.6	0.1	0.6	1.4	7.1
Bruce Bowen	81	30.2	40.7	41.9	65.2	0.4	2.5	2.9	1.1	0.7	0.3	0.6	2.2	6.0
Ime Udoka	73	18.0	42.4	37.0	75.9	0.5	2.6	3.1	0.9	0.8	0.2	0.8	1.7	5.8
Matt Bonner	68	12.5	41.6	33.6	86.4	0.8	2.0	2.8	0.5	0.2	0.3	0.6	1.6	4.8
Fabricio Oberto	82	20.1	60.8	0.0	60.7	1.9	3.4	5.2	1.2	0.5	0.2	0.6	2.5	4.8
*Kurt Thomas	28	18.7	44.8	0.0	58.3	1.3	3.6	4.9	0.5	0.8	0.5	0.6	2.0	4.5
Jacque Vaughn	74	15.4	42.8	30.0	76.3	0.2	0.8	1.0	2.1	0.3	0.0	0.7	1.3	4.1
*Francisco Elson	41	13.1	41.9	0.0	83.3	0.8	2.5	3.3	0.4	0.2	0.3	0.7	1.5	3.5
Ian Mahinmi	6	3.8	50.0	0.0	100.0	0.0	0.8	0.8	0.2	0.0	0.7	0.3	0.7	3.5
DerMarr Johnson	5	5.6	50.0	33.3	0.0	0.0	0.2	0.2	0.2	0.2	0.0	0.0	0.8	3.4
*Damon Stoudamire	31	13.3	30.1	25.5	75.0	0.2	1.3	1.5	1.7	0.4	0.1	1.0	1.0	3.4
Darius Washington	18	8.1	43.8	33.3	53.8	0.2	0.9	1.1	0.8	0.3	0.0	0.8	0.9	2.9
Robert Horry	45	13.0	31.9	25.7	64.3	0.8	1.6	2.4	1.0	0.5	0.4	0.5	1.2	2.5
Spurs	**82**	**240.6**	**45.7**	**36.9**	**76.1**	**9.4**	**31.9**	**41.3**	**21.0**	**6.4**	**4.1**	**12.6**	**18.7**	**95.4**
Opponents	**82**	**240.6**	**44.4**	**34.2**	**75.6**	**9.5**	**30.8**	**40.3**	**18.2**	**6.9**	**4.4**	**12.9**	**19.8**	**90.6**

Seattle SuperSonics

			Field Goals			Rebounds								
Player	**GP**	**MPG**	**FG%**	**3Pt%**	**FT%**	**OFF**	**DEF**	**Total**	**APG**	**SPG**	**BPG**	**TO**	**PF**	**PPG**
Kevin Durant	80	34.6	43.0	28.8	87.3	0.9	3.5	4.4	2.4	1.0	0.9	2.9	1.5	20.3
Chris Wilcox	62	28.0	52.4	0.0	64.5	2.0	5.0	7.0	1.2	0.7	0.6	1.7	2.8	13.4
*Wally Szczerbiak	50	23.6	46.0	42.8	84.3	0.3	2.4	2.7	1.4	0.3	0.1	1.1	1.3	13.1
Earl Watson	78	29.1	45.4	37.1	76.6	0.6	2.3	2.9	6.8	0.9	0.1	2.2	2.0	10.7
Jeff Green	80	28.2	42.7	27.6	74.4	1.3	3.5	4.7	1.5	0.6	0.6	2.0	2.5	10.5
Nick Collison	78	28.5	50.2	0.0	73.7	3.3	6.1	9.4	1.4	0.6	0.8	1.5	3.2	9.8
Damien Wilkins	76	24.3	40.3	32.3	73.6	0.9	2.3	3.2	2.0	0.8	0.3	1.2	1.7	9.2
*Kurt Thomas	42	25.2	51.3	0.0	69.6	2.2	6.5	8.8	1.3	0.8	1.0	0.7	3.1	7.5
*Delonte West	35	20.7	38.8	33.9	66.7	0.4	2.4	2.7	3.2	0.9	0.3	1.9	1.3	6.8
Luke Ridnour	61	20.0	39.9	29.6	85.7	0.2	1.3	1.5	4.0	0.6	0.2	1.3	2.0	6.4
Johan Petro	72	18.2	41.9	0.0	73.6	1.4	3.8	5.1	0.4	0.5	0.6	1.0	2.4	6.0
Mickael Gelabale	39	11.9	43.9	43.2	77.8	0.4	1.1	1.5	0.8	0.3	0.2	0.7	0.8	4.3
Mike Wilks	3	7.3	55.6	0.0	100.0	0.0	0.3	0.3	1.7	0.3	0.0	1.0	0.7	4.0
*Donyell Marshall	15	12.3	35.2	23.3	92.3	1.0	2.1	3.1	0.3	0.3	0.5	0.6	1.0	3.8
*Francisco Elson	22	12.7	34.1	0.0	46.2	0.8	2.2	3.0	0.4	0.3	0.3	0.8	1.5	3.0
Mouhamed Sene	13	4.8	45.8	0.0	47.1	0.5	0.7	1.2	0.1	0.0	0.5	0.0	0.7	2.3
Robert Swift	8	12.3	35.3	0.0	100.0	0.8	1.5	2.3	0.1	0.6	0.8	1.3	2.0	1.8
*Adrian Griffin	13	6.5	37.5	0.0	100.0	0.7	1.0	1.7	0.4	0.4	0.1	0.4	0.6	1.1
*Ronald Dupree	4	4.5	33.3	0.0	100.0	0.3	1.8	2.0	0.3	0.3	0.0	0.0	0.0	1.0
Sonics	**82**	**241.8**	**44.4**	**33.3**	**77.0**	**11.8**	**32.8**	**44.6**	**21.3**	**6.5**	**4.9**	**16.0**	**20.5**	**97.5**
Opponents	**82**	**241.8**	**46.1**	**38.5**	**74.9**	**11.7**	**32.4**	**44.1**	**24.4**	**8.6**	**5.4**	**13.2**	**19.6**	**106.3**

NBA Team-by-Team Statistical Leaders *(Cont.)*

Toronto Raptors

			Field Goals			Rebounds								
Player	**GP**	**MPG**	**FG%**	**3Pt%**	**FT%**	**OFF**	**DEF**	**Total**	**APG**	**SPG**	**BPG**	**TO**	**PF**	**PPG**
Chris Bosh	67	36.2	49.4	40.0	84.4	2.6	6.1	8.7	2.6	0.9	1.0	2.3	2.3	22.3
Anthony Parker	82	32.1	47.6	43.8	81.6	0.6	3.5	4.1	2.2	1.0	0.2	1.1	1.9	12.5
T.J. Ford	51	23.5	46.9	29.4	88.0	0.5	1.5	2.0	6.1	1.1	0.0	2.0	1.8	12.1
Jose Calderon	82	30.3	51.9	42.9	90.8	0.4	2.5	2.9	8.3	1.1	0.1	1.5	1.6	11.2
Andrea Bargnani	78	23.9	38.6	34.5	84.0	0.6	3.1	3.7	1.1	0.3	0.5	1.1	2.7	10.2
Carlos Delfino	82	23.5	39.7	38.2	74.4	0.8	3.6	4.4	1.8	0.8	0.1	0.9	2.2	9.0
Jamario Moon	78	27.8	48.5	32.8	74.1	1.2	5.0	6.2	1.2	1.0	1.4	0.7	1.9	8.5
Rasho Nesterovic	71	20.9	55.0	33.3	75.5	1.8	3.0	4.8	1.2	0.3	0.7	0.9	1.9	7.8
Jason Kapono	81	18.9	48.8	48.3	86.0	0.4	1.1	1.5	0.8	0.4	0.0	0.7	1.6	7.2
Kris Humphries	70	13.2	48.3	0.0	60.5	1.3	2.4	3.7	0.4	0.4	0.4	0.7	1.5	5.7
*Juan Dixon	36	11.8	36.9	43.6	94.7	0.3	1.1	1.3	1.8	0.6	0.1	1.0	1.1	4.3
*Primoz Brezec	13	8.5	44.7	0.0	66.7	0.7	0.7	1.4	0.1	0.1	0.2	0.3	1.9	3.7
Joey Graham	38	8.7	43.4	66.7	84.4	0.5	1.3	1.8	0.4	0.1	0.0	0.6	1.2	3.6
Jorge Garbajosa	7	10.6	32.0	37.5	0.0	0.3	1.9	2.1	0.4	0.4	0.0	0.1	0.3	3.1
*Linton Johnson	2	5.0	40.0	0.0	100.0	0.0	0.5	0.5	0.5	0.0	0.0	1.5	0.5	3.0
Maceo Baston	15	6.9	68.0	0.0	70.0	0.6	1.1	1.7	0.2	0.1	0.3	0.3	1.3	2.7
Darrick Martin	17	8.3	23.3	12.5	83.3	0.2	0.2	0.4	1.2	0.4	0.0	0.1	0.7	1.6
Raptors	**82**	**241.8**	**46.8**	**39.2**	**81.2**	**9.6**	**30.4**	**40.1**	**23.8**	**7.0**	**4.1**	**11.7**	**19.5**	**100.2**
Opponets	**82**	**241.8**	**45.8**	**36.8**	**77.6**	**10.1**	**31.5**	**41.6**	**21.9**	**5.7**	**4.1**	**14.0**	**18.4**	**97.3**

Utah Jazz

			Field Goals			Rebounds								
Player	**GP**	**MPG**	**FG%**	**3Pt%**	**FT%**	**OFF**	**DEF**	**Total**	**APG**	**SPG**	**BPG**	**TO**	**PF**	**PPG**
Carlos Boozer	81	34.9	54.7	0.0	73.8	2.4	8.0	10.4	2.9	1.2	0.5	2.6	3.6	21.1
Deron Williams	82	37.3	50.7	39.5	80.3	0.4	2.5	3.0	10.5	1.1	0.3	3.4	2.4	18.8
Mehmet Okur	72	33.2	44.5	38.8	80.4	1.8	5.9	7.7	2.0	0.8	0.4	1.4	3.3	14.5
Ronnie Brewer	76	27.5	55.8	22.0	75.9	1.3	1.6	2.9	1.8	1.7	0.3	0.9	1.4	12.0
Andrei Kirilenko	72	30.8	50.6	37.9	77.0	1.7	3.0	4.7	4.0	1.2	1.5	1.9	2.3	11.0
*Kyle Korver	50	21.5	47.4	38.8	91.7	0.2	1.8	2.0	1.4	0.4	0.5	0.9	2.5	9.8
Matt Harpring	76	18.1	50.0	20.0	71.2	1.3	1.9	3.2	1.1	0.6	0.2	1.3	2.1	8.2
Paul Millsap	82	20.8	50.4	0.0	67.7	2.0	3.6	5.6	1.0	0.9	0.9	1.1	3.3	8.1
C.J. Miles	60	11.5	47.9	39.0	78.8	0.3	1.0	1.3	0.9	0.5	0.1	0.5	1.6	5.0
*Gordan Giricek	22	12.6	40.2	35.3	100.0	0.3	1.1	1.4	0.7	0.6	0.1	1.0	1.1	4.3
Ronnie Price	61	9.6	43.1	34.7	68.4	0.1	0.6	0.8	1.3	0.5	0.1	0.5	1.4	3.7
Jason Hart	57	10.6	32.2	35.5	84.4	0.1	0.9	1.0	1.5	0.5	0.1	0.5	1.3	2.9
Jarron Collins	70	10.0	43.9	0.0	62.2	0.6	1.1	1.7	0.5	0.1	0.1	0.3	1.5	1.7
Kyrylo Fesenko	9	7.8	37.5	0.0	50.0	1.6	1.2	2.8	0.2	0.0	0.3	0.9	2.1	1.6
Morris Almond	9	4.3	26.7	25.0	66.7	0.0	0.2	0.2	0.3	0.1	0.0	0.2	0.6	1.4
Jazz	**82**	**240.3**	**49.7**	**37.2**	**75.9**	**11.5**	**29.4**	**40.9**	**26.4**	**8.7**	**4.3**	**14.6**	**24.0**	**106.2**
Opponents	**82**	**240.3**	**46.1**	**35.7**	**74.9**	**10.3**	**27.5**	**37.8**	**19.9**	**7.6**	**5.1**	**15.9**	**23.1**	**99.3**

Washington Wizards

			Field Goals			Rebounds								
Player	**GP**	**MPG**	**FG%**	**3Pt%**	**FT%**	**OFF**	**DEF**	**Total**	**APG**	**SPG**	**BPG**	**TO**	**PF**	**PPG**
Antawn Jamison	79	38.7	43.6	33.9	76.0	2.7	7.5	10.2	1.5	1.3	0.4	1.4	2.5	21.4
Caron Butler	58	39.9	46.6	35.7	90.1	1.6	5.1	6.7	4.9	2.2	0.3	2.6	2.8	20.3
Gilbert Arenas	13	32.7	39.8	28.2	77.1	0.5	3.5	3.9	5.1	1.8	0.1	3.8	2.3	19.4
DeShawn Stevenson	82	31.3	38.6	38.3	79.7	0.5	2.4	2.9	3.1	0.8	0.2	1.2	1.3	11.2
Brendan Haywood	80	27.9	52.8	0.0	73.5	3.4	3.8	7.2	0.9	0.4	1.7	1.4	2.7	10.6
Roger Mason	80	21.4	44.3	39.8	87.3	0.2	1.4	1.6	1.7	0.5	0.2	0.9	1.8	9.1
Antonio Daniels	71	30.4	45.9	23.0	77.6	0.3	2.5	2.9	4.8	1.0	0.0	1.3	1.1	8.4
Nick Young	75	15.4	43.9	40.0	81.5	0.3	1.2	1.5	0.8	0.5	0.1	1.3	1.7	7.5
Andray Blatche	82	20.4	47.4	23.1	69.5	2.0	3.2	5.2	1.1	0.7	1.4	1.4	3.1	7.5
Darius Songaila	80	19.4	45.8	0.0	91.8	1.0	2.4	3.4	1.7	0.7	0.2	1.1	2.3	6.2
Oleksiy Pecherov	35	9.1	35.2	28.3	64.5	0.6	1.3	1.9	0.2	0.2	0.1	0.5	0.9	3.6
Dominic McGuire	70	9.9	37.9	16.7	43.8	0.8	1.2	2.0	0.6	0.3	0.4	0.6	1.1	1.3
Wizards	**82**	**242.7**	**44.6**	**35.6**	**78.2**	**12.3**	**29.3**	**41.6**	**19.6**	**7.7**	**4.8**	**13.2**	**19.6**	**98.8**
Opponents	**82**	**242.7**	**46.1**	**38.6**	**75.4**	**11.0**	**30.2**	**41.2**	**23.9**	**6.4**	**4.4**	**14.0**	**20.2**	**99.2**

* mid-season trade

2008 NBA Draft

The 2008 NBA Draft was held on June 26, 2008 in New York City.

First Round

1. Derrick Rose, Chicago
2. Michael Beasley, Miami
3. O.J. Mayo, Minnesota (Mayo traded to Memphis)
4. Russell Westbrook, Seattle
5. Kevin Love, Memphis (Love traded to Minnesota)
6. Danilo Gallinari, New York
7. Eric Gordon, LA Clippers
8. Joe Alexander, Milwaukee
9. D.J. Augustin, Charlotte
10. Brook Lopez, New Jersey
11. Jerryd Bayless, Indiana (Bayless traded to Portland)
12. Jason Thompson, Sacramento
13. Brandon Rush, Portland (Rush traded to Indiana)
14. Anthony Randolph, Golden State
15. Robin Lopez, Phoenix (from Atlanta)
16. Marreese Speights, Philadelphia
17. Roy Hibbert, Toronto (Hibbert traded to Indiana)
18. JaVale McGee, Washington
19. J.J. Hickson, Cleveland
20. Alexis Ajinca, Chrlotte (from Denver)
21. Ryan Anderson, New Jersey (from Dallas)
22. Courtney Lee, Orlando
23. Kosta Koufos, Utah
24. Serge Ibaka, Seattle (from Phoenix)
25. Nicolas Batum, Houston (Batum traded to Portland)
26. George Hill, San Antonio
27. Darrell Arthur, New Orleans (Arthur traded to Memphis from Houston/Portland)
28. Donte Green, Memphis (from LA Lakers)
29. D.J. White, Detroit (White traded to Seattle)
30. J.R. Giddens, Boston

Second Round

31. Nikola Pekovic, Minnesota (from Miami through Boston)
32. Walter Sharpe, Seattle (Sharpe traded to Detroit)
33. Joey Dorsey, Portland (from Memphis)
34. Mario Chalmers, Minnesota (Chalmers traded to Miami)
35. DeAndre Jordan, LA Clippers
36. Omer Asik, Portland (from NY, traded to Chi.)
37. L.R. Mbah a Moute, Milwaukee
38. Kyle Weaver, Charlotte
39. Sonny Weems, Chicago
40. Chris Douglas-Roberts, NJ
41. Nathan Jawai, Indiana
42. Sean Singletary, Sacramento (from Atlanta)
43. Patrick Ewing Jr., Sacramento
44. Ante Tomic, Utah (from Philadelphia)
45. Goran Dragic, San Antonio (from Toronto, traded to Pho.)
46. Trent Plaisted, Seattle (from Portland through Boston, traded to Detroit)
47. Bill Walker, Washington (Walker traded to Boston)
48. Malik Hairston, Phoenix (from Cleveland, traded to SA)
49. Richard Hendrix, Golden State
50. Devon Hardin (from Denver)
51. Shan Foster, Dallas
52. Darnell Jackson, Miami (from Orlando)
53. Tadija Dragicevic, Utah
54. Maarty Leunen, Houston
55. Mike Taylor, Portland (from Phoenix through Indiana, traded to LA Clippers)
56. Sasha Kaun, Seattle (from NO through Houston)
57. James Gist, San Antonio
58. Joe Crawford, LA Lakers
59. Deron Washington, Detroit
60. Semih Erden, Boston

Women's National Basketball Association

2008 Final Standings

EASTERN CONFERENCE

Team	W	L	Pct	GB
†Detroit	22	12	.647	—
*Connecticut	21	13	.618	1.0
*New York	18	15	.559	3.0
*Indiana	17	17	.500	5.0
Chicago	12	22	.353	10.0
Washington	10	24	.294	12.0
Atlanta	4	30	.118	18.0

WESTERN CONFERENCE

Team	W	L	Pct	GB
†San Antonio	24	10	.706	—
*Seattle	22	12	.647	2.0
*Los Angeles	20	14	.588	4.0
*Sacramento	18	16	.529	6.0
Houston	17	17	.500	7.0
Phoenix	16	18	.471	8.0
Minnesota	16	18	.471	8.0

†Clinched conference title. *Clinched playoff berth.

2008 Playoffs

FIRST ROUND

EASTERN CONFERENCE

Game 1......Detroit 81 at Indiana 72
Game 2......Indiana 89 at Detroit 82 (OT)
Game 3......Indiana 61 at Detroit 80

Detroit won series 2–1.

Game 1......Connecticut 63 at New York 72
Game 2......New York 70 at Connecticut 73
Game 2......New York 66 at Connecticut 62

New York won series 2–1.

WESTERN CONFERENCE

Game 1......San Antonio 85 at Sacramento 78
Game 2......Sacramento 84 at San Antonio 67
Game 3......Sacramento 81 at San Antonio 86

San Antonio won series 2–1.

Game 1......Seattle 69 at Los Angeles 77
Game 2......Los Angeles 50 at Seattle 64
Game 3......Los Angeles 71 at Seattle 64

Los Angeles won series 2–1.

EASTERN CONFERENCE FINALS

Game 1......Detroit 56 at New York 60
Game 2......New York 55 at Detroit 64
Game 3......New York 73 at Detroit 75

Detroit won series 2–1.

WESTERN CONFERENCE FINALS

Game 1......San Antonio 70 at Los Angeles 85
Game 2......Los Angeles 66 at San Antonio 67
Game 3......Los Angeles 72 at San Antonio 76

San Antonio won series 2–1.

WNBA FINALS

Game 1..........Detroit 77 at San Antonio 69
Game 2..........Detroit 69 at San Antonio 61
Game 3..........San Antonio 60 at Detroit 76

Detroit won series 3–0.

FOR THE RECORD • Year by Year

NBA Champions

Season	Winner	Series	Runner-Up	Winning Coach	Finals MVP
1946–47	Philadelphia	4–1	Chicago	Eddie Gottlieb	—
1947–48	Baltimore	4–2	Philadelphia	Buddy Jeannette	—
1948–49	Minneapolis	4–2	Washington	John Kundla	—
1949–50	Minneapolis	4–2	Syracuse	John Kundla	—
1950–51	Rochester	4–3	New York	Les Harrison	—
1951–52	Minneapolis	4–3	New York	John Kundla	—
1952–53	Minneapolis	4–1	New York	John Kundla	—
1953–54	Minneapolis	4–3	Syracuse	John Kundla	—
1954–55	Syracuse	4–3	Ft Wayne	Al Cervi	—
1955–56	Philadelphia	4–1	Ft Wayne	George Senesky	—
1956–57	Boston	4–3	St Louis	Red Auerbach	—
1957–58	St Louis	4–2	Boston	Alex Hannum	—
1958–59	Boston	4–0	Minneapolis	Red Auerbach	—
1959–60	Boston	4–3	St Louis	Red Auerbach	—
1960–61	Boston	4–1	St Louis	Red Auerbach	—
1961–62	Boston	4–3	LA Lakers	Red Auerbach	—
1962–63	Boston	4–2	LA Lakers	Red Auerbach	—
1963–64	Boston	4–1	San Francisco	Red Auerbach	—
1964–65	Boston	4–1	LA Lakers	Red Auerbach	—
1965–66	Boston	4–3	LA Lakers	Red Auerbach	—
1966–67	Philadelphia	4–2	San Francisco	Alex Hannum	—
1967–68	Boston	4–2	LA Lakers	Bill Russell	—
1968–69	Boston	4–3	LA Lakers	Bill Russell	Jerry West, LA
1969–70	New York	4–3	LA Lakers	Red Holzman	Willis Reed, NY
1970–71	Milwaukee	4–0	Baltimore	Larry Costello	Kareem Abdul-Jabbar, Mil
1971–72	LA Lakers	4–1	New York	Bill Sharman	Wilt Chamberlain, LA
1972–73	New York	4–1	LA Lakers	Red Holzman	Willis Reed, NY
1973–74	Boston	4–3	Milwaukee	Tommy Heinsohn	John Havlicek, Bos
1974–75	Golden State	4–0	Washington	Al Attles	Rick Barry, GS
1975–76	Boston	4–2	Phoenix	Tommy Heinsohn	JoJo White, Bos
1976–77	Portland	4–2	Philadelphia	Jack Ramsay	Bill Walton, Port
1977–78	Washington	4–3	Seattle	Dick Motta	Wes Unseld, Wash
1978–79	Seattle	4–1	Washington	Lenny Wilkens	Dennis Johnson, Sea
1979–80	LA Lakers	4–2	Philadelphia	Paul Westhead	Magic Johnson, LA
1980–81	Boston	4–2	Houston	Bill Fitch	Cedric Maxwell, Bos
1981–82	LA Lakers	4–2	Philadelphia	Pat Riley	Magic Johnson, LA
1982–83	Philadelphia	4–0	LA Lakers	Billy Cunningham	Moses Malone, Phil
1983–84	Boston	4–3	LA Lakers	K.C. Jones	Larry Bird, Bos
1984–85	LA Lakers	4–2	Boston	Pat Riley	Kareem Abdul-Jabbar, LA
1985–86	Boston	4–2	Houston	K.C. Jones	Larry Bird, Bos
1986–87	LA Lakers	4–2	Boston	Pat Riley	Magic Johnson, LA
1987–88	LA Lakers	4–3	Detroit	Pat Riley	James Worthy, LA
1988–89	Detroit	4–0	LA Lakers	Chuck Daly	Joe Dumars, Det
1989–90	Detroit	4–1	Portland	Chuck Daly	Isiah Thomas, Det
1990–91	Chicago	4–1	LA Lakers	Phil Jackson	Michael Jordan, Chi
1991–92	Chicago	4–2	Portland	Phil Jackson	Michael Jordan, Chi
1992–93	Chicago	4–2	Phoenix	Phil Jackson	Michael Jordan, Chi
1993–94	Houston	4–3	New York	Rudy Tomjanovich	Hakeem Olajuwon, Hou
1994–95	Houston	4–0	Orlando	Rudy Tomjanovich	Hakeem Olajuwon, Hou
1995–96	Chicago	4–2	Seattle	Phil Jackson	Michael Jordan, Chi
1996–97	Chicago	4–2	Utah	Phil Jackson	Michael Jordan, Chi
1997–98	Chicago	4–2	Utah	Phil Jackson	Michael Jordan, Chi
1998–99	San Antonio	4–1	New York	Gregg Popovich	Tim Duncan, SA
1999–00	LA Lakers	4–2	Indiana	Phil Jackson	Shaquille O'Neal, LA
2000–01	LA Lakers	4–1	Philadelphia	Phil Jackson	Shaquille O'Neal, LA
2001–02	LA Lakers	4–0	New Jersey	Phil Jackson	Shaquille O'Neal, LA
2002–03	San Antonio	4–2	New Jersey	Gregg Popovich	Tim Duncan, SA
2003–04	Detroit	4–1	LA Lakers	Larry Brown	Chauncey Billups, Det
2004–05	San Antonio	4–3	Detroit	Gregg Popovich	Tim Duncan, SA
2005–06	Miami	4–2	Dallas	Pat Riley	Dwyane Wade, Mia
2006–07	San Antonio	4–0	Cleveland	Gregg Popovich	Tony Parker, SA
2007–08	Boston	4–2	LA Lakers	Doc Rivers	Paul Pierce, Bos

Most Valuable Player: Maurice Podoloff Trophy

			Field Goals		3-Pt FG		Free Throws		Rebounds					
Season	Player, Team	GP	FGM	Pct	FGM	Pct	FTM	Pct	Off	Total	A	Stl	BS	Avg
1955–56	Bob Pettit, StL	72	646	42.9	–	–	557	73.6	–	1,164	189	–	–	25.7
1956–57	Bob Cousy, Bos	64	478	37.8	–	–	363	82.1	–	309	478	–	–	20.6
1957–58	Bill Russell, Bos	69	456	44.2	–	–	230	51.9	–	1,564	202	–	–	16.6
1958–59	Bob Pettit, StL	72	719	43.8	–	–	667	75.9	–	1,182	221	–	–	29.2
1959–60	Wilt Chamberlain, Phil	72	1,065	46.1	–	–	577	58.2	–	1,941	168	–	–	37.6
1960–61	Bill Russell, Bos	78	532	42.6	–	–	258	55.0	–	1,868	264	–	–	16.9
1961–62	Bill Russell, Bos	76	575	45.7	–	–	286	59.5	–	1,891	341	–	–	18.9
1962–63	Bill Russell, Bos	78	511	43.2	–	–	287	55.5	–	1,843	348	–	–	16.8
1963–64	Oscar Robertson, Cin	79	840	48.3	–	–	800	85.3	–	783	868	–	–	31.4
1964–65	Bill Russell, Bos	78	429	43.8	–	–	244	57.3	–	1,878	410	–	–	14.1
1965–66	Wilt Chamberlain, Phil	79	1,074	54.0	–	–	501	51.3	–	1,943	414	–	–	33.5
1966–67	Wilt Chamberlain, Phil	81	785	68.3	–	–	386	44.1	–	1,957	630	–	–	24.1
1967–68	Wilt Chamberlain, Phil	82	819	59.5	–	–	354	38.0	–	1,952	702	–	–	24.3
1968–69	Wes Unseld, Balt	82	427	47.6	–	–	277	60.5	–	1,491	213	–	–	13.8
1969–70	Willis Reed, NY	81	702	50.7	–	–	351	75.6	–	1,126	161	–	–	21.7
1970–71	Lew Alcindor*, Mil	82	1,063	57.7	–	–	470	69.0	–	1,311	272	–	–	31.7
1971–72	Kareem Abdul-Jabbar, Mil	81	1,159	57.4	–	–	504	68.9	–	1,346	370	–	–	34.8
1972–73	Dave Cowens, Bos	82	740	45.2	–	–	204	77.9	–	1,329	333	–	–	20.5
1973–74	Kareem Abdul-Jabbar, Mil	81	948	53.9	–	–	295	70.2	287	1,178	386	112	283	27.0
1974–75	Bob McAdoo, Buff	82	1,095	51.2	–	–	641	80.5	307	1,155	179	92	174	34.5
1975–76	Kareem Abdul-Jabbar, LAL	82	914	52.9	–	–	447	70.3	272	1,383	413	119	338	37.7
1976–77	Kareem Abdul-Jabbar, LAL	82	888	57.9	–	–	376	70.1	266	1,090	319	101	261	26.2
1977–78	Bill Walton, Port	58	460	52.2	–	–	177	72.0	118	766	291	60	146	18.9
1978–79	Moses Malone, Hou	82	716	54.0	–	–	599	73.9	587	1,444	147	79	119	24.8
1979–80	Kareem Abdul-Jabbar, LAL	82	835	60.4	0	00.0	364	76.5	190	886	371	81	280	24.8
1980–81	Julius Erving, Phil	82	794	52.1	4	22.2	422	78.7	244	657	364	173	147	24.6
1981–82	Moses Malone, Hou	81	945	51.9	0	00.0	630	76.2	558	1,188	142	76	125	31.1
1982–83	Moses Malone, Phil	78	654	50.1	0	00.0	600	76.1	445	1,194	101	89	157	24.5
1983–84	Larry Bird, Bos	79	758	49.2	18	24.7	374	88.8	181	796	520	144	69	24.2
1984–85	Larry Bird, Bos	80	918	52.2	56	42.7	403	88.2	164	842	531	129	98	28.7
1985–86	Larry Bird, Bos	82	796	49.6	82	42.3	441	89.6	190	805	557	166	51	25.8
1986–87	Magic Johnson, LAL	80	683	52.2	8	20.5	535	84.8	122	504	977	138	36	23.9
1987–88	Michael Jordan, Chi	82	1,069	53.5	7	13.2	723	84.1	139	449	485	259	131	35.0
1988–89	Magic Johnson, LAL	77	579	50.9	59	31.4	513	91.1	111	607	988	138	22	22.5
1989–90	Magic Johnson, LAL	79	546	48.0	106	38.4	567	89.0	128	522	907	132	34	22.3
1990–91	Michael Jordan, Chi	82	990	53.9	29	31.2	571	85.1	118	492	453	223	83	31.5
1991–92	Michael Jordan, Chi	80	943	51.9	27	27.0	491	83.2	91	511	489	182	75	30.1
1992–93	Charles Barkley, Phx	76	716	52.0	67	30.5	445	76.5	237	928	385	119	74	25.6
1993–94	Hakeem Olajuwon, Hou	80	894	52.8	8	42.1	388	71.6	229	955	287	128	297	27.3
1994–95	David Robinson, SA	81	788	53.0	6	30.0	656	77.4	234	877	236	134	262	27.6
1995–96	Michael Jordan, Chi	82	916	49.5	111	42.7	548	83.4	148	543	352	180	42	30.4
1996–97	Karl Malone, Utah	82	864	55.0	0	00.0	521	75.5	193	809	368	113	48	27.4
1997–98	Michael Jordan, Chi	82	881	46.5	30	23.8	565	78.4	130	475	283	141	45	28.7
1998–99	Karl Malone, Utah	49	393	49.3	0	00.0	378	78.8	107	463	201	62	28	23.8
1999–00	Shaquille O'Neal, LAL	79	956	57.4	0	00.0	432	52.4	336	1078	299	36	239	29.7
2000–01	Allen Iverson, Phil	71	762	42.0	98	32.0	585	81.4	50	273	325	78	20	31.1
2001–02	Tim Duncan, SA	82	764	50.8	1	10.0	560	79.9	268	1042	307	61	203	25.5
2002–03	Tim Duncan, SA	81	714	51.3	6	27.3	450	71.0	260	1045	316	55	237	23.3
2003–04	Kevin Garnett, Minn	82	804	49.9	11	25.6	368	79.1	245	1139	409	120	178	24.2
2004–05	Steve Nash, Phx	75	430	50.2	94	43.1	211	88.7	80	330	861	74	6	26.0
2005–06	Steve Nash, Phx	79	541	51.2	150	43.9	257	92.1	47	333	826	61	12	18.8
2006–07	Dirk Nowitzki, Dal	78	673	50.2	72	41.6	498	90.4	122	693	263	52	62	24.6
2007–08	Kobe Bryant, LAL	82	775	45.9	150	36.1	623	84.0	94	517	441	151	40	28.3

*Alcindor changed his name to Kareem Abdul-Jabbar after the 1970–71 season.

Coach of the Year: Arnold (Red) Auerbach Trophy

1962–63...Harry Gallatin, StL
1963–64...Alex Hannum, SF
1964–65...Red Auerbach, Bos
1965–66...Dolph Schayes, Phil
1966–67...Johnny Kerr, Chi
1967–68...Richie Guerin, StL
1968–69...Gene Shue, Balt
1969–70...Red Holzman, NY
1970–71...Dick Motta, Chi
1971–72...Bill Sharman, LA
1972–73...Tom Heinsohn, Bos
1973–74...Ray Scott, Det
1974–75...Phil Johnson, KC-Oma
1975–76...Bill Fitch, Clev
1976–77...Tom Nissalke, Hou
1977–78...Hubie Brown, Atl
1978–79...Cotton Fitzsimmons, KC
1979–80...Bill Fitch, Bos
1980–81...Jack McKinney, Ind
1981–82...Gene Shue, Wash
1982–83...Don Nelson, Mil
1983–84...Frank Layden, Utah
1984–85...Don Nelson, Mil
1985–86...Mike Fratello, Atl
1986–87...Mike Schuler, Port
1987–88...Doug Moe, Den
1988–89...Cotton Fitzsimmons, Phx
1989–90...Pat Riley, LAL
1990–91...Don Chaney, Hou
1991–92...Don Nelson, GS
1992–93...Pat Riley, NY
1993–94...Lenny Wilkens, Atl
1994–95...Del Harris, LAL
1995–96...Phil Jackson, Chi
1996–97...Pat Riley, Mia
1997–98...Larry Bird, Ind
1998–99...Mike Dunleavy, Port
1999–00...Glenn (Doc) Rivers, Orl
2000–01...Larry Brown, Phil
2001–02...Rick Carlisle, Det
2002–03...Gregg Popovich, SA
2003–04...Hubie Brown, Mem
2004–05...Mike D'Antoni, Phx
2005–06...Avery Johnson, Dal
2006–07...Sam Mitchell, Tor
2007–08...Byron Scott, NO

Note: Award named after Auerbach in 1986.

Rookie of the Year: Eddie Gottlieb Trophy

1952–53...Don Meineke, FW
1953–54...Ray Felix, Balt
1954–55...Bob Pettit, Mil
1955–56...Maurice Stokes, Roch
1956–57...Tom Heinsohn, Bos
1957–58...Woody Sauldsberry, Phil
1958–59...Elgin Baylor, Minn
1959–60...Wilt Chamberlain, Phil
1960–61...Oscar Robertson, Cin
1961–62...Walt Bellamy, Chi
1962–63...Terry Dischinger, Chi
1963–64...Jerry Lucas, Cin
1964–65...Willis Reed, NY
1965–66...Rick Barry, SF
1966–67...Dave Bing, Det
1967–68...Earl Monroe, Balt
1968–69...Wes Unseld, Balt
1969–70...K. Abdul-Jabbar, Mil
1970–71...Dave Cowens, Bos
Geoff Petrie, Port
1971–72...Sidney Wicks, Port
1972–73...Bob McAdoo, Buff
1973–74...Ernie DiGregorio, Buf
1974–75...Keith Wilkes, GS
1975–76...Alvan Adams, Phx
1976–77...Adrian Dantley, Buf
1977–78...Walter Davis, Phx
1978–79...Phil Ford, KC
1979–80...Larry Bird, Bos
1980–81...Darrell Griffith, Utah
1981–82...Buck Williams, NJ
1982–83...Terry Cummings, SD
1983–84...Ralph Sampson, Hou
1984–85...Michael Jordan, Chi
1985–86...Patrick Ewing, NY
1986–87...Chuck Person, Ind
1987–88...Mark Jackson, NY
1988–89...Mitch Richmond, GS
1989–90...David Robinson, SA
1990–91...Derrick Coleman, NJ
1991–92...Larry Johnson, Cha
1992–93...Shaquille O'Neal, Orl
1993–94...Chris Webber, GS
1994–95...J. Kidd, Dal/G. Hill, Det
1995–96...Damon Stoudamire, Tor
1996–97...Allen Iverson, Phil
1997–98...Tim Duncan, SA
1998–99...Vince Carter, Tor
1999–00..Steve Francis, Hou
Elton Brand, Chi
2000–01..Mike Miller, Orl
2001–02..Pau Gasol, Mem
2002–03..Amare Stoudemire, Phx
2003–04..LeBron James, Clev
2004–05..Emeka Okafor, Cha
2005–06...Chris Paul, NO
2006–07...Brandon Roy, Port
2007–08...Kevin Durant, Sea

Defensive Player of the Year

1982–83...Sidney Moncrief, Mil
1983–84...Sidney Moncrief, Mil
1984–85...Mark Eaton, Utah
1985–86...Alvin Robertson, SA
1986–87...Michael Cooper, LAL
1987–88...Michael Jordan, Chi
1988–89...Mark Eaton, Utah
1989–90...Dennis Rodman, Det
1990–91...Dennis Rodman, Det
1991–92...David Robinson, SA
1992–93...Hakeem Olajuwon, Hou
1993–94...Hakeem Olajuwon, Hou
1994–95...Dikembe Mutombo, Den
1995–96...Gary Payton, Sea
1996–97...Dikembe Mutombo, Atl
1997–98...Dikembe Mutombo, Atl
1998–99...Alonzo Mourning, Mia
1999–00...Alonzo Mourning, Mia
2000–01...Dikembe Mutombo, Phil/Atl
2001–02...Ben Wallace, Det
2002–03...Ben Wallace, Det
2003–04...Ron Artest, Ind
2004–05...Ben Wallace, Det
2005–06...Ben Wallace, Det
2006–07...Marcus Camby, Den
2007–08...Kevin Garnett, Bos

Sixth Man Award

1982–83...Bobby Jones, Phil
1983–84...Kevin McHale, Bos
1984–85...Kevin McHale, Bos
1985–86...Bill Walton, Bos
1986–87...Ricky Pierce, Mil
1987–88...Roy Tarpley, Dal
1988–89...Eddie Johnson, Phx
1989–90...Ricky Pierce, Mil
1990–91...Detlef Schrempf, Ind
1991–92...Detlef Schrempf, Ind
1992–93...Cliff Robinson, Port
1993–94...Dell Curry, Cha
1994–95...Anthony Mason, NY
1995–96...Toni Kukoc, Chi
1996–97...John Starks, NY
1997–98...Danny Manning, Phx
1998–99...Darrell Armstrong, Orl
1999–00...Rodney Rogers, Phx
2000–01...Aaron McKie, Phil
2001–02...Corliss Williamson, Det
2002–03...Bobby Jackson, Sac
2003–04...Antawn Jamison, Dal
2004–05...Ben Gordon, Chi
2005–06...Mike Miller, Mem
2006–07...Leandro Barbosa, Phx
2007–08...Manu Ginobli, SA

NBA Awards (Cont.)

J. Walter Kennedy Citizenship Award

1974–75...Wes Unseld, Wash
1975–76...Slick Watts, Sea
1976–77...Dave Bing, Wash
1977–78...Bob Lanier, Det
1978–79...Calvin Murphy, Hou
1979–80...Austin Carr, Cle
1980–81...Mike Glenn, NY
1981–82...Kent Benson, Det
1982–83...Julius Erving, Phil
1983–84...Frank Layden, Utah
1984–85...Dan Issel, Den
1985–86...Michael Cooper, LAL
Rory Sparrow, NY
1986–87...Isiah Thomas, Det
1987–88...Alex English, Den
1988–89...Thurl Bailey, Utah
1989–90...Glenn (Doc) Rivers, Atl
1990–91...Kevin Johnson, Phx
1991–92...Magic Johnson, LAL
1992–93...Terry Porter, Port
1993–94...Joe Dumars, Det
1994–95...Joe O'Toole, Atl
1995–96...Chris Dudley, Port
1996–97...P.J. Brown, Mia
1997–98...Steve Smith, Atl
1998–99...Brian Grant, Port
1999–00...Vlade Divac, Sac
2000–01...Dikembe Mutombo, Phil
2001–02...Alonzo Mourning, Mia
2002–03...David Robinson, SA
2003–04...Reggie Miller, Ind
2004–05...Eric Snow, Clev
2005–06...Kevin Garnett, Min
2006–07...Luol Deng, Chi
2007–08...Grant Hill, Phx

Most Improved Player

1985–86...Alvin Robertson, SA
1986–87...Dale Ellis, Sea
1987–88...Kevin Duckworth, Port
1988–89...Kevin Johnson, Phx
1989–90...Rony Seikaly, Mia
1990–91...Scott Skiles, Orl
1991–92...Pervis Ellison, Wash
1992–93...Mahmoud Abdul-Rauf, Den
1993–94...Don MacLean, Wash
1994–95...Dana Barros, Phil
1995–96.....Gheorghe Muresan, Wash
1996–97...Isaac Austin, Mia
1997–98...Alan Henderson, Atl
1998–99...Darrell Armstrong, Orl
1999–00...Jalen Rose, Ind
2000–01...Tracy McGrady, Orl
2001–02...Jermaine O'Neal, Ind
2002–03...Gilbert Arenas, GS
2003–04...Zach Randolph, Port
2004–05...Bobby Simmons, LAC
2005–06...Boris Diaw, Phx
2006–07...Monta Ellis, GS
2007–08...Hedo Turkoglu, Orl

Executive of the Year

1972–73...Joe Axelson, KC-Oma
1973–74...Eddie Donovan, Buf
1974–75...Dick Vertlieb, GS
1975–76...Jerry Colangelo, Phx
1976–77...Ray Patterson, Hou
1977–78...Angelo Drossos, SA
1978–79...Bob Ferry, Wash
1979–80...Red Auerbach, Bos
1980–81...Jerry Colangelo, Phx
1981–82...Bob Ferry, Wash
1982–83...Zollie Volchok, Sea
1983–84...Frank Layden, Utah
1984–85...Vince Boryla, Den
1985–86...Stan Kasten, Atl
1986–87...Stan Kasten, Atl
1987–88...Jerry Krause, Chi
1988–89...Jerry Colangelo, Phx
1989–90...Bob Bass, SA
1990–91...Bucky Buckwalter, Port
1991–92...Wayne Embry, Clev
1992–93...Jerry Colangelo, Phx
1993–94...Bob Whitsitt, Sea
1994–95...Jerry West, LAL
1995–96...Jerry Krause, Chi
1996–97...Bob Bass, Cha
1997–98...Wayne Embry, Clev
1998–99...Geoff Petrie, Sac
1999–00...John Gabriel, Orl
2000–01...Geoff Petrie, Sac
2001–02...Rod Thorn, NJ
2002–03...Joe Dumars, Det
2003–04...Jerry West, Mem
2004–05...Bryan Colangelo, Phx
2005–06...Elgin Baylor, LAC
2006–07...Bryan Colangelo, Tor
2007–08...Danny Ainge, Bos

NBA Alltime Individual Leaders

Scoring

MOST POINTS, CAREER

	Pts	Avg
Kareem Abdul-Jabbar	38,387	24.6
Karl Malone	36,928	25.0
Michael Jordan	32,292	30.1
Wilt Chamberlain	31,419	30.1
Moses Malone	27,409	20.6
Elvin Hayes	27,313	21.0
Hakeem Olajuwon	26,946	21.8
Oscar Robertson	26,710	25.7
Dominique Wilkins	26,668	24.8
John Havlicek	26,395	20.8

MOST POINTS, SEASON

Wilt Chamberlain, Phil	4,029	1961–62
Wilt Chamberlain, SF	3,586	1962–63
Michael Jordan, Chi	3,041	1986–87
Wilt Chamberlain, Phil	3,033	1960–61
Wilt Chamberlain, SF	2,948	1963–64
Michael Jordan, Chi	2,868	1987–88
Kobe Bryant, LA	2,832	2005–06
Bob McAdoo, Buff	2,831	1974–75
Rick Barry, SF	2,775	1966–67
Michael Jordan, Chi	2,753	1989–90

HIGHEST SCORING AVERAGE, CAREER

Michael Jordan	30.1	1,072 games
Wilt Chamberlain	30.1	1,045 games
*Allen Iverson	27.7	829 games
Elgin Baylor	27.4	846 games
Jerry West	27.0	932 games
Bob Pettit	26.4	792 games
George Gervin	26.2	791 games
Oscar Robertson	25.7	1,040 games
*Shaquille O'Neal	25.2	1,042 games
Karl Malone	25.0	1,476 games
*Kobe Bryant	25.0	866 games

*Acitve in 2007–08. Note: Minimum 400 games.

HIGHEST SCORING AVERAGE, SEASON

Wilt Chamberlain, Phil	50.4	1961–62
Wilt Chamberlain, SF	44.8	1962–63
Wilt Chamberlain, Phil	38.4	1960–61
Wilt Chamberlain, Phil	37.6	1959–60
Michael Jordan, Chi	37.1	1986–87
Wilt Chamberlain, SF	36.9	1963–64
Rick Barry, SF	35.6	1966–67
Kobe Bryant, LA	35.4	2005–06
Michael Jordan, Chi	35.0	1987–88
Elgin Baylor, LA	34.8	1960–61

Note: Minimum 70 games.

Scoring (Cont.)

MOST POINTS, SINGLE GAME

	Player, Team	Opp	Date
100	Wilt Chamberlain, Phil	NY	3/2/62
81	Kobe Bryant, LAL	Tor	1/22/06
78	Wilt Chamberlain, Phil	LAL	12/8/61
73	Wilt Chamberlain, Phil	Chi	1/13/62
73	Wilt Chamberlain, SF	NY	11/16/62
73	David Thompson, Den	Det	4/9/78
72	Wilt Chamberlain, SF	LAL	11/3/62
71	David Robinson, SA	LAC	4/24/94
71	Elgin Baylor, LAL	NY	11/15/60
70	Wilt Chamberlain, SF	Syr	3/10/63

Field-Goal Percentage

Highest FG Percentage, Career: .599—Artis Gilmore

Highest FG Percentage, Season: .727—Wilt Chamberlain, LA Lakers, 1972–73 (426/586)

Free Throws

HIGHEST FREE-THROW PERCENTAGE, CAREER

Mark Price	.904
Rick Barry	.900
*Steve Nash	.897
*Peja Stojakovic	.894
Calvin Murphy	.892

Note: Minimum 1200 free throws made. *Active 2007–08.

HIGHEST FREE-THROW PERCENTAGE, SEASON

Calvin Murphy, Hou	.958	1980–81
Mahmoud Abdul-Rauf, Den	.956	1993–94
Jeff Hornacek, Utah	.950	1999–00
Mark Price, Clev	.948	1992–93
Mark Price, Clev	.947	1991–92
Rick Barry, Hou	.947	1978–79

MOST FREE THROWS MADE, CAREER

	No.	Yrs	Pct
Karl Malone	9,787	19	.742
Moses Malone	8,531	19	.769
Oscar Robertson	7,694	14	.838
Michael Jordan	7,327	15	.835
Jerry West	7,160	14	.814

Three-Point Field Goals

Most Three-Point Field-Goals, Career: 2,560—Reggie Miller

Highest Three-Point Field-Goal Percentage, Career: .464—Jason Kapono*

Most Three-Point Field Goals, Season: 269—Ray Allen, Sea, 2005–06

Highest Three-Point Field-Goal Percentage, Season: .524—Steve Kerr, Chi, 1994–95

Most Three-Point Field Goals, Game: 12—Kobe Bryant, LA Lakers vs Seattle, 1/7/03; Donyell Marshall, Toronto vs. Philadelphia, 3/13/05

Note: First season of three-point field goal: 1979–80. *Active 2007–08.

Steals

Most Steals, Career: 3,265—John Stockton

Most Steals, Season: 301—Alvin Robertson, San Antonio, 1985–86

Most Steals, Game: 11—Kendall Gill, New Jersey vs Miami, 4/3/99; Larry Kenon, San Antonio vs Kansas City, 12/26/76

Rebounds

MOST REBOUNDS, CAREER

	No.	Yrs	Avg
Wilt Chamberlain	23,924	14	22.9
Bill Russell	21,620	13	22.5
Kareem Abdul-Jabbar	17,440	20	11.2
Elvin Hayes	16,279	16	12.5
Moses Malone	16,212	19	12.2
Karl Malone	14,968	19	10.1
Robert Parish	14,715	21	9.1
Nate Thurmond	14,464	14	15.0
Walt Bellamy	14,241	14	13.7
Wes Unseld	13,769	13	14.0

MOST REBOUNDS, SEASON

Wilt Chamberlain, Phil	2,149	1960–61
Wilt Chamberlain, Phil	2,052	1961–62
Wilt Chamberlain, Phil	1,957	1966–67
Wilt Chamberlain, Phil	1,952	1967–68
Wilt Chamberlain, SF	1,946	1962–63
Wilt Chamberlain, Phil	1,943	1965–66
Wilt Chamberlain, Phil	1,941	1959–60
Bill Russell, Bos	1,930	1963–64
Bill Russell, Bos	1,878	1964–65
Bill Russell, Bos	1,868	1960–61

MOST REBOUNDS, GAME

	Player, Team	Opp	Date
55	Wilt Chamberlain, Phil	Bos	11/24/60
51	Bill Russell, Bos	Syr	02/05/60
49	Bill Russell, Bos	Phil	11/16/57
49	Bill Russell, Bos	Det	03/11/65
45	Wilt Chamberlain, Phil	Syr	02/06/60
45	Wilt Chamberlain, Phil	LA	01/21/61

Assists

MOST ASSISTS, CAREER

John Stockton	15,806
Mark Jackson	10,334
Magic Johnson	10,141
Oscar Robertson	9,887
Isiah Thomas	9,061

MOST ASSISTS, SEASON

John Stockton, Utah	1,164	1990–91
John Stockton, Utah	1,134	1989–90
John Stockton, Utah	1,128	1987–88
John Stockton, Utah	1,126	1991–92
Isiah Thomas, Det	1,123	1984–85

MOST ASSISTS, GAME: 30—Scott Skiles, Orlando vs Denver, 12/30/90

Blocked Shots

MOST BLOCKED SHOTS, CAREER

Hakeem Olajuwon	3,830
Dikembe Mutombo	3,230
Kareem Abdul-Jabbar	3,189
Mark Eaton	3,064
David Robinson	2,954

MOST BLOCKED SHOTS, SEASON

Mark Eaton, Utah	456	1984–85
Manute Bol, Wash	397	1985–86
Elmore Smith, LA	393	1973–74

MOST BLOCKED SHOTS, GAME: 17—Elmore Smith, LA Lakers vs Portland, 10/28/73

NBA Alltime Playoff Leaders

Scoring

MOST POINTS, CAREER

	Pts	App.	Avg
Michael Jordan	5,987	13	33.4
Kareem Abdul-Jabbar	5,762	18	24.3
*Shaquille O'Neal	5,121	15	25.2
Karl Malone	4,761	19	24.7
Jerry West	4,457	13	29.1
Larry Bird	3,897	12	23.8
John Havlicek	3,776	13	22.0
Hakeem Olajuwon	3,755	15	25.9
Magic Johnson	3,701	13	19.5
*Kobe Bryant	3,686	11	24.3

*Active 2007–08.

†HIGHEST SCORING AVERAGE, CAREER

	Avg	Games
Michael Jordan	33.4	179
*Allen Iverson	29.7	71
Jerry West	29.1	153
*Tracy McGrady	28.5	38
*LeBron James	27.5	46
Elgin Baylor	27.0	134
George Gervin	27.0	59
Hakeem Olajuwon	25.9	145
*Vince Carter	25.9	42
Bob Pettit	25.5	88
Dominique Wilkins	25.4	55
*Dirk Nowitzki	25.3	87
*Dwyane Wade	25.3	54
*Shaquille O'Neal	25.2	203
*Amare Stoudemire	25.1	36

†Minimum of 25 games. *Active 2007–08.

MOST POINTS, GAME

	Player, Team	Opp	Date
†63	Michael Jordan, Chi	Bos	4/20/86
61	Elgin Baylor, LA	Bos	4/14/62
56	Wilt Chamberlain, Phil	Syr	3/22/62
56	Michael Jordan, Chi	Mia	4/29/92
56	Charles Barkley, Phx	GS	5/4/94
55	Rick Barry, SF	Phil	4/18/67
55	Michael Jordan, Chi	Cle	5/1/88
55	Michael Jordan, Chi	Phx	4/16/95
55	Michael Jordan, Chi	Wash	4/27/97

†Double overtime game.

Rebounds

MOST REBOUNDS, CAREER

	No.	App.	Avg
Bill Russell	4,104	13	24.9
Wilt Chamberlain	3,913	13	24.5
Kareem Abdul-Jabbar	2,481	18	10.5
Shaquille O'Neal	2,447	15	12.1
Karl Malone	2,062	19	10.7
*Tim Duncan	1,975	10	12.7

*Active 2007–08.

MOST REBOUNDS, GAME

	Player, Team	Opp	Date
41	Wilt Chamberlain, Phil	Bos	4/5/67
40	Bill Russell, Bos	Phil	3/23/58
40	Bill Russell, Bos	StL	3/29/60
†40	Bill Russell, Bos	LA	4/18/62

†Overtime game. Three tied at 39.

Assists

MOST ASSISTS, CAREER

	No.	Games
Magic Johnson	2,346	190
John Stockton	1,839	182
Larry Bird	1,062	164
Scottie Pippen	1,048	208
Michael Jordan	1,022	179

MOST ASSISTS, GAME

	Player, Team	Opp	Date
24	Magic Johnson, LAL	Phx	5/15/84
24	John Stockton, Utah	LAL	5/17/88
23	Magic Johnson, LAL	Port	5/3/85
23	John Stockton, Utah	Port	4/25/96
23	Steve Nash, Phx	LAL	4/24/07

Games played

*Robert Horry	244
Kareem Abdul-Jabbar	237
Scottie Pippen	208
*Shaquille O'Neal	203
Danny Ainge	193
Karl Malone	193
Magic Johnson	190
Robert Parish	184
Byron Scott	183
John Stockton	182

Appearances

John Stockton	19
Karl Malone	19
Kareem Abdul-Jabbar	18
*Robert Horry	16
Robert Parish	16
Scottie Pippen	16
Terry Porter	16
Dolph Schayes	15
Clyde Drexler	15
Jerome Kersey	15
Hakeem Olajuwon	15
*Shaquille O'Neal	15
Tree Rollins	15

*Active 2007–08.

NBA Season Leaders

Scoring

Season	Player	Total
1946–47	Joe Fulks, Phil	1389
1947–48	Max Zaslofsky, Chi	1007
1948–49	George Mikan, Min	1698
1949–50	George Mikan, Min	1865
1950–51	George Mikan, Min	1932
1951–52	Paul Arizin, Phil	1674
1952–53	Neil Johnston, Phil	1564
1953–54	Neil Johnston, Phil	1759
1954–55	Neil Johnston, Phil	1631
1955–56	Bob Pettit, StL	1849
1956–57	Paul Arizin, Phil	1817
1957–58	George Yardley, Det	2001
1958–59	Bob Pettit, StL	2105
1959–60	Wilt Chamberlain, Phil	2707
1960–61	Wilt Chamberlain, Phil	3033
1961–62	Wilt Chamberlain, Phil	4029
1962–63	Wilt Chamberlain, SF	3586
1963–64	Wilt Chamberlain, SF	2948
1964–65	Wilt Chamberlain, SF-Phil	2534
1965–66	Wilt Chamberlain, Phil	2649
1966–67	Rick Barry, SF	2775
1967–68	Dave Bing, Det	2142
1968–69	Elvin Hayes, SD	2327
1969–70	Jerry West, LA	*31.2
1970–71	Kareem Abdul-Jabbar, Mil	31.7
1971–72	Kareem Abdul-Jabbar, Mil	34.8
1972–73	Nate Archibald, KC-Oma	34.0
1973–74	Bob McAdoo, Buff	30.6
1974–75	Bob McAdoo, Buff	34.5
1975–76	Bob McAdoo, Buff	31.1
1976–77	Pete Maravich, NO	31.1
1977–78	George Gervin, SA	27.2
1978–79	George Gervin, SA	29.6
1979–80	George Gervin, SA	33.1
1980–81	Adrian Dantley, Utah	30.7
1981–82	George Gervin, SA	32.3
1982–83	Alex English, Den	28.4
1983–84	Adrian Dantley, Utah	30.6
1984–85	Bernard King, NY	32.9
1985–86	Dominique Wilkins, Atl	30.3
1986–87	Michael Jordan, Chi	37.1
1987–88	Michael Jordan, Chi	35.0
1988–89	Michael Jordan, Chi	32.5
1989–90	Michael Jordan, Chi	33.6
1990–91	Michael Jordan, Chi	31.5
1991–92	Michael Jordan, Chi	30.1
1992–93	Michael Jordan, Chi	32.6
1993–94	David Robinson, SA	29.8
1994–95	Shaquille O'Neal, Orl	29.3
1995–96	Michael Jordan, Chi	30.4
1996–97	Michael Jordan, Chi	29.6
1997–98	Michael Jordan, Chi	28.7
1998–99	Allen Iverson, Phil	26.8
1999–00	Shaquille O'Neal, LA Lakers	29.7
2000–01	Allen Iverson, Phil	31.1
2001–02	Allen Iverson, Phil	31.4
2002–03	Tracy McGrady, Orl	32.1
2003–04	Tracy McGrady, Orl	28.0
2004–05	Allen Iverson, Phil	30.7
2005–06	Kobe Bryant, LA Lakers	35.4
2006–07	Kobe Bryant, LA Lakers	31.6
2007–08	LeBron James, Cle	30.0

*Based on per game average since 1969–70.

Rebounding

Season	Player	Total
1950–51	Dolph Schayes, Syr	1080
1951–52	Larry Foust, FW	880
	Mel Hutchins, Mil	880
1952–53	George Mikan, Min	1007
1953–54	Harry Gallatin, NY	1098
1954–55	Neil Johnston, Phil	1085
1955–56	Bob Pettit, StL	1164
1956–57	Maurice Stokes, Roch	1256
1957–58	Bill Russell, Bos	1564
1958–59	Bill Russell, Bos	1612
1959–60	Wilt Chamberlain, Phil	1941
1960–61	Wilt Chamberlain, Phil	2149
1961–62	Wilt Chamberlain, Phil	2052
1962–63	Wilt Chamberlain, SF	1946
1963–64	Bill Russell, Bos	1930
1964–65	Bill Russell, Bos	1878
1965–66	Wilt Chamberlain, Phil	1943
1966–67	Wilt Chamberlain, Phil	1957
1967–68	Wilt Chamberlain, Phil	1952
1968–69	Wilt Chamberlain, LA	1712
1969–70	Elvin Hayes, SD	*16.9
1970–71	Wilt Chamberlain, LA	18.2
1971–72	Wilt Chamberlain, LA	19.2
1972–73	Wilt Chamberlain, LA	18.6
1973–74	Elvin Hayes, Capital (Wash)	18.1
1974–75	Wes Unseld, Wash	14.8
1975–76	Kareem Abdul-Jabbar, LA	16.9
1976–77	Bill Walton, Port	14.4
1977–78	Len Robinson, NO	15.7
1978–79	Moses Malone, Hou	17.6
1979–80	Swen Nater, SD	15.0
1980–81	Moses Malone, Hou	14.8
1981–82	Moses Malone, Hou	14.7
1982–83	Moses Malone, Phil	15.3
1983–84	Moses Malone, Phil	13.4
1984–85	Moses Malone, Phil	13.1
1985–86	Bill Laimbeer, Det	13.1
1986–87	Charles Barkley, Phil	14.6
1987–88	Michael Cage, LAC	13.0
1988–89	Hakeem Olajuwon, Hou	13.5
1989–90	Hakeem Olajuwon, Hou	14.0
1990–91	David Robinson, SA	13.0
1991–92	Dennis Rodman, Det	18.7
1992–93	Dennis Rodman, Det	18.3
1993–94	Dennis Rodman, SA	17.3
1994–95	Dennis Rodman, SA	16.8
1995–96	Dennis Rodman, Chi	14.9
1996–97	Dennis Rodman, Chi	16.1
1997–98	Dennis Rodman, Chi	15.0
1998–99	Chris Webber, Sac	13.0
1999–00	Dikembe Mutombo, Atl	14.1
2000–01	Dikembe Mutombo, Atl	13.5
2001–02	Ben Wallace, Det	13.0
2002–03	Ben Wallace, Det	15.4
2003–04	Kevin Garnett, Min	13.9
2004–05	Kevin Garnett, Min	13.5
2005–06	Kevin Garnett, Min	12.7
2006–07	Kevin Garnett, Min	12.8
2007–08	Dwight Howard, Orl	14.2

*Based on per game average since 1969–70.

NBA Season Leaders *(Cont.)*

Assists

Season	Player	Total
1946–47	Ernie Calverly, Prov	202
1947–48	Howie Dallmar, Phil	120
1948–49	Bob Davies, Roch	321
1949–50	Dick McGuire, NY	386
1950–51	Andy Phillip, Phil	414
1951–52	Andy Phillip, Phil	539
1952–53	Bob Cousy, Bos	547
1953–54	Bob Cousy, Bos	518
1954–55	Bob Cousy, Bos	557
1955–56	Bob Cousy, Bos	642
1956–57	Bob Cousy, Bos	478
1957–58	Bob Cousy, Bos	463
1958–59	Bob Cousy, Bos	557
1959–60	Bob Cousy, Bos	715
1960–61	Oscar Robertson, Cin	690
1961–62	Oscar Robertson, Cin	899
1962–63	Guy Rodgers, SF	825
1963–64	Oscar Robertson, Cin	868
1964–65	Oscar Robertson, Cin	861
1965–66	Oscar Robertson, Cin	847
1966–67	Guy Rodgers, Chi	908
1967–68	Wilt Chamberlain, Phil	702
1968–69	Oscar Robertson, Cin	772
1969–70	Lenny Wilkens, Sea	*9.1
1970–71	Norm Van Lier, Cin	10.1
1971–72	Jerry West, LA	9.7
1972–73	Nate Archibald, KC-Oma	11.4
1973–74	Ernie DiGregorio, Buf	8.2
1974–75	Kevin Porter, Wash	8.0
1975–76	Don Watts, Sea	8.1
1976–77	Don Buse, Ind	8.5
1977–78	Kevin Porter, NJ-Det	10.2
1978–79	Kevin Porter, Det	13.4
1979–80	Micheal Ray Richardson, NY	10.1
1980–81	Kevin Porter, Wash	9.1
1981–82	Johnny Moore, SA	9.6
1982–83	Magic Johnson, LA	10.5
1983–84	Magic Johnson, LA	13.1
1984–85	Isiah Thomas, Det	13.9
1985–86	Magic Johnson, LA Lakers	12.6
1986–87	Magic Johnson, LA Lakers	12.2
1987–88	John Stockton, Utah	13.8
1988–89	John Stockton, Utah	13.6
1989–90	John Stockton, Utah	14.5
1990–91	John Stockton, Utah	14.2
1991–92	John Stockton, Utah	13.7
1992–93	John Stockton, Utah	12.0
1993–94	John Stockton, Utah	12.6
1994–95	John Stockton, Utah	12.3
1995–96	John Stockton, Utah	11.2
1996–97	Mark Jackson, Ind	11.4
1997–98	Rod Strickland, Wash	10.5
1998–99	Jason Kidd, Phx	10.8
1999–00	Jason Kidd, Phx	10.1
2000–01	Jason Kidd, Phx	9.8
2001–02	Andre Miller, Cle	10.9
2002–03	Jason Kidd, NJ	8.9
2003–04	Jason Kidd, NJ	9.2
2004–05	Steve Nash, Phx	11.5
2005–06	Steve Nash, Phx	10.5
2006–07	Steve Nash, Phx	11.6
2007–08	Chris Paul, NO	11.6

*Based on per game average since 1969–70.

Field-Goal Percentage

Season	Player	Pct
1946–47	Bob Feerick, Wash	40.1
1947–48	Bob Feerick, Wash	34.0
1948–49	Arnie Risen, Roch	42.3
1949–50	Alex Groza, Ind	47.8
1950–51	Alex Groza, Ind	47.0
1951–52	Paul Arizin, Phil	44.8
1952–53	Neil Johnston, Phil	45.2
1953–54	Ed Macauley, Bos	48.6
1954–55	Larry Foust, FW	48.7
1955–56	Neil Johnston, Phil	45.7
1956–57	Neil Johnston, Phil	44.7
1957–58	Jack Twyman, Cin	45.2
1958–59	Ken Sears, NY	49.0
1959–60	Ken Sears, NY	47.7
1960–61	Wilt Chamberlain, Phil	50.9
1961–62	Walt Bellamy, Chi	51.9
1962–63	Wilt Chamberlain, SF	52.8
1963–64	Jerry Lucas, Cin	52.7
1964–65	Wilt Chamberlain, SF-Phil	51.0
1965–66	Wilt Chamberlain, Phil	54.0
1966–67	Wilt Chamberlain, Phil	68.3
1967–68	Wilt Chamberlain, Phil	59.5
1968–69	Wilt Chamberlain, LAL	58.3
1969–70	Johnny Green, Cin	55.9
1970–71	Johnny Green, Cin	58.7
1971–72	Wilt Chamberlain, LAL	64.9
1972–73	Wilt Chamberlain, LAL	72.7
1973–74	Bob McAdoo, Buf	54.7
1974–75	Don Nelson, Bos	53.9
1975–76	Wes Unseld, Wash	56.1
1976–77	Kareem Abdul-Jabbar, LAL	57.9
1977–78	Bobby Jones, Den	57.8
1978–79	Cedric Maxwell, Bos	58.4
1979–80	Cedric Maxwell, Bos	60.9
1980–81	Artis Gilmore, Chi	67.0
1981–82	Artis Gilmore, Chi	65.2
1982–83	Artis Gilmore, SA	62.6
1983–84	Artis Gilmore, SA	63.1
1984–85	James Donaldson, LAC	63.7
1985–86	Steve Johnson, SA	63.2
1986–87	Kevin McHale, Bos	60.4
1987–88	Kevin McHale, Bos	60.4
1988–89	Dennis Rodman, Det	59.5
1989–90	Mark West, Phx	62.5
1990–91	Buck Williams, Port	60.2
1991–92	Buck Williams, Port	60.4
1992–93	Cedric Ceballos, Phx	57.6
1993–94	Shaquille O'Neal, Orl	59.9
1994–95	Chris Gatling, GS	63.3
1995–96	Gheorghe Muresan, Wash	58.4
1996–97	Gheorghe Muresan, Wash	60.4
1997–98	Shaquille O'Neal, LAL	58.4
1998–99	Shaquille O'Neal, LAL	57.6
1999–00	Shaquille O'Neal, LAL	57.4
2000–01	Shaquille O'Neal, LAL	57.2
2001–02	Shaquille O'Neal, LAL	57.9
2002–03	Eddy Curry, Chi	58.5
2003–04	Shaquille O'Neal, LAL	58.4
2004–05	Shaquille O'Neal, Mia	60.1
2005–06	Shaquille O'Neal, Mia	60.0
2006–07	Mikki Moore, NJ	60.9
2007–08	Andris Biedrins, GS	62.6

NBA Season Leaders *(Cont.)*

Free-Throw Percentage

Season	Player	Pct
1946–47	Fred Scolari, Wash	81.1
1947–48	Bob Feerick, Wash	78.8
1948–49	Bob Feerick, Wash	85.9
1949–50	Max Zaslofsky, Chi	84.3
1950–51	Joe Fulks, Phil	85.5
1951–52	Bob Wanzer, Roch	90.4
1952–53	Bill Sharman, Bos	85.0
1953–54	Bill Sharman, Bos	84.4
1954–55	Bill Sharman, Bos	89.7
1955–56	Bill Sharman, Bos	86.7
1956–57	Bill Sharman, Bos	90.5
1957–58	Dolph Schayes, Syr	90.4
1958–59	Bill Sharman, Bos	93.2
1959–60	Dolph Schayes, Syr	89.3
1960–61	Bill Sharman, Bos	92.1
1961–62	Dolph Schayes, Syr	89.7
1962–63	Larry Costello, Syr	88.1
1963–64	Oscar Robertson, Cin	85.3
1964–65	Larry Costello, Phil	87.7
1965–66	Larry Siegfried, Bos	88.1
1966–67	Adrian Smith, Cin	90.3
1967–68	Oscar Robertson, Cin	87.3
1968–69	Larry Siegfried, Bos	86.4
1969–70	Flynn Robinson, Mil	89.8
1970–71	Chet Walker, Chi	85.9
1971–72	Jack Marin, Balt	89.4
1972–73	Rick Barry, GS	90.2
1973–74	Ernie DiGregorio, Buf	90.2
1974–75	Rick Barry, GS	90.4
1975–76	Rick Barry, GS	92.3
1976–77	Ernie DiGregorio, Buf	94.5
1977–78	Rick Barry, GS	92.4
1978–79	Rick Barry, Hou	94.7
1979–80	Rick Barry, Hou	93.5
1980–81	Calvin Murphy, Hou	95.8
1981–82	Kyle Macy, Phx	89.9
1982–83	Calvin Murphy, Hou	92.0
1983–84	Larry Bird, Bos	88.8
1984–85	Kyle Macy, Phx	90.7
1985–86	Larry Bird, Bos	89.6
1986–87	Larry Bird, Bos	91.0
1987–88	Jack Sikma, Mil	92.2
1988–89	Magic Johnson, LAL	91.1
1989–90	Larry Bird, Bos	93.0
1990–91	Reggie Miller, Ind	91.8
1991–92	Mark Price, Clev	94.7
1992–93	Mark Price, Clev	94.8
1993–94	Mahmoud Abdul-Rauf, Den	95.6
1994–95	Spud Webb, Sac	93.4
1995–96	Mahmoud Abdul-Rauf, Den	93.0
1996–97	Mark Price, GS	90.6
1997–98	Chris Mullin, Ind	93.9
1998–99	Reggie Miller, Ind	91.5
1999–00	Jeff Hornacek, Utah	95.0
2000–01	Reggie Miller, Ind	92.8
2001–02	Reggie Miller, Ind	91.1
2002–03	Allan Houston, NY	91.9
2003–04	Peja Stojakovic, Sac	92.7
2004–05	Reggie Miller, Ind	93.3
2005–06	Steve Nash, Phx	92.1
2006–07	Kyle Korver, Phil	91.4
2007–08	Peja Stojakovic, NO	92.9

Three-Point Field-Goal Percentage

Season	Player	Pct
1979–80	Fred Brown, Sea	44.3
1980–81	Brian Taylor, SD	38.3
1981–82	Campy Russell, NY	43.9
1982–83	Mike Dunleavy, SA	34.5
1983–84	Darrell Griffith, Utah	36.1
1984–85	Byron Scott, LAL	43.3
1985–86	Craig Hodges, Mil	45.1
1986–87	Kiki Vandeweghe, Por	48.1
1987–88	Craig Hodges, Mil-Phx	49.1
1988–89	Jon Sundvold, Mia	52.2
1989–90	Steve Kerr, Clev	50.7
1990–91	Jim Les, Sac	46.1
1991–92	Dana Barros, Sea	44.6
1992–93	Chris Mullin, GS	45.1
1993–94	Tracy Murray, Por	45.9
1994–95	Steve Kerr, Chi	52.4
1995–96	Tim Legler, Wash	52.2
1996–97	Glen Rice, Cha	47.0
1997–98	Dale Ellis, Sea	46.0
1998–99	Dell Curry, Cha	47.6
1999–00	Hubert Davis, Dal	49.1
2000–01	Brent Barry, Sea	47.6
2001–02	Steve Smith, SA	47.2
2002–03	Bruce Bowen, SA	44.1
2003–04	Anthony Peeler, Sac	48.2
2004–05	Fred Hoiberg, Min	48.3
2005–06	Richard Hamilton, Det	45.8
2006–07	Jason Kapono, Mia	51.4
2007–08	Jason Kapono, Tor	48.3

Steals

Season	Player	Avg
1973–74	Larry Steele, Por	2.68
1974–75	Rick Barry, GS	2.85
1975–76	Don Watts, Sea	3.18
1976–77	Don Buse, Ind	3.47
1977–78	Ron Lee, Phx	2.74
1978–79	M.L. Carr, Det	2.46
1979–80	Micheal Ray Richardson, NY	3.23
1980–81	Magic Johnson, LAL	3.43
1981–82	Magic Johnson, LAL	2.67
1982–83	Micheal Ray Richardson, GS-NJ	2.84
1983–84	Rickey Green, Utah	2.65
1984–85	Micheal Ray Richardson, NJ	2.96
1985–86	Alvin Robertson, SA	3.67
1986–87	Alvin Robertson, SA	3.21
1987–88	Michael Jordan, Chi	3.16
1988–89	John Stockton, Utah	3.21
1989–90	Michael Jordan, Chi	2.77
1990–91	Alvin Robertson, Mil	3.04
1991–92	John Stockton, Utah	2.98
1992–93	Michael Jordan, Chi	2.83
1993–94	Nate McMillan, Sea	2.96
1994–95	Scottie Pippen, Chi	2.94
1995–96	Gary Payton, Sea	2.85
1996–97	Mookie Blaylock, Atl	2.72
1997–98	Mookie Blaylock, Atl	2.61
1998–99	Kendall Gill, NJ	2.68
1999–00	Eddie Jones, Cha	2.67
2000–01	Allen Iverson, Phil	2.51
2001–02	Allen Iverson, Phil	2.80
2002–03	Allen Iverson, Phil	2.74
2003–04	Baron Davis, NO	2.36
2004–05	Larry Hughes, Wash	2.89
2005–06	Gerald Wallace, Cha	2.51
2006–07	Baron Davis, GS	2.14
2007–08	Chris Paul, NO	2.71

NBA Season Leaders *(Cont.)*

Blocked Shots

Season	Player	Avg
1973–74	Elmore Smith, LAL	4.85
1974–75	Kareem Abdul-Jabbar, Mil	3.26
1975–76	Kareem Abdul-Jabbar, LAL	4.12
1976–77	Bill Walton, Port	3.25
1977–78	George Johnson, NJ	3.38
1978–79	Kareem Abdul-Jabbar, LAL	3.95
1979–80	Kareem Abdul-Jabbar, LAL	3.41
1980–81	George Johnson, SA	3.39
1981–82	George Johnson, SA	3.12
1982–83	Wayne Rollins, Atl	4.29
1983–84	Mark Eaton, Utah	4.28
1984–85	Mark Eaton, Utah	5.56
1985–86	Manute Bol, Wash	4.96
1986–87	Mark Eaton, Utah	4.06
1987–88	Mark Eaton, Utah	3.71
1988–89	Manute Bol, GS	4.31
1989–90	Hakeem Olajuwon, Hou	4.59
1990–91	Hakeem Olajuwon, Hou	3.95
1991–92	David Robinson, SA	4.49
1992–93	Hakeem Olajuwon, Hou	4.17
1993–94	Dikembe Mutombo, Den	4.10
1994–95	Dikembe Mutombo, Den	3.91
1995–96	Dikembe Mutombo, Den	4.49
1996–97	Shawn Bradley, NJ	3.40
1997–98	Marcus Camby, Tor	3.65
1998–99	Alonzo Mourning, Mia	3.91
1999–00	Alonzo Mourning, Mia	3.72
2000–01	Theo Ratliff, Phil/Atl	3.74
2001–02	Ben Wallace, Det	3.48
2002–03	Theo Ratliff, Atl	3.23
2003–04	Theo Ratliff, Port	3.61
2004–05	Andrei Kirilenko, Utah	3.32
2005–06	Marcus Camby, Den	3.29
2006–07	Marcus Camby, Den	3.30
2007–08	Marcus Camby, Den	3.61

NBA All-Star Game Results

Year	Result	Site	Winning Coach	Most Valuable Player
1951	East 111, West 94	Boston	Joe Lapchick	Ed Macauley, Bos
1952	East 108, West 91	Boston	Al Cervi	Paul Arizin, Phil
1953	West 79, East 75	Ft Wayne	John Kundla	George Mikan, Min
1954	East 98, West 93 (OT)	New York	Joe Lapchick	Bob Cousy, Bos
1955	East 100, West 91	New York	Al Cervi	Bill Sharman, Bos
1956	West 108, East 94	Rochester	Charley Eckman	Bob Pettit, StL
1957	East 109, West 97	Boston	Red Auerbach	Bob Cousy, Bos
1958	East 130, West 118	St Louis	Red Auerbach	Bob Pettit, StL
1959	West 124, East 108	Detroit	Ed Macauley	B. Pettit, StL/ E. Baylor, Min
1960	East 125, West 115	Philadelphia	Red Auerbach	Wilt Chamberlain, Phil
1961	West 153, East 131	Syracuse	Paul Seymour	Oscar Robertson, Cin
1962	West 150, East 130	St Louis	Fred Schaus	Bob Pettit, StL
1963	East 115, West 108	Los Angeles	Red Auerbach	Bill Russell, Bos
1964	East 111, West 107	Boston	Red Auerbach	Oscar Robertson, Cin
1965	East 124, West 123	St Louis	Red Auerbach	Jerry Lucas, Cin
1966	East 137, West 94	Cincinnati	Red Auerbach	Adrian Smith, Cin
1967	West 135, East 120	San Francisco	Fred Schaus	Rick Barry, SF
1968	East 144, West 124	New York	Alex Hannum	Hal Greer, Phil
1969	East 123, West 112	Baltimore	Gene Shue	Oscar Robertson, Cin
1970	East 142, West 135	Philadelphia	Red Holzman	Willis Reed, NY
1971	West 108, East 107	San Diego	Larry Costello	Lenny Wilkens, Sea
1972	West 112, East 110	Los Angeles	Bill Sharman	Jerry West, LA
1973	East 104, West 84	Chicago	Tom Heinsohn	Dave Cowens, Bos
1974	West 134, East 123	Seattle	Larry Costello	Bob Lanier, Det
1975	East 108, West 102	Phxnix	K.C. Jones	Walt Frazier, NY
1976	East 123, West 109	Philadelphia	Tom Heinsohn	Dave Bing, Wash
1977	West 125, East 124	Milwaukee	Larry Brown	Julius Erving, Phil
1978	East 133, West 125	Atlanta	Billy Cunningham	Randy Smith, Buff
1979	West 134, East 129	Detroit	Lenny Wilkens	David Thompson, Den
1980	East 144, West 135 (OT)	Washington	Billy Cunningham	George Gervin, SA
1981	East 123, West 120	Cleveland	Billy Cunningham	Nate Archibald, Bos
1982	East 120, West 118	New Jersey	Bill Fitch	Larry Bird, Bos
1983	East 132, West 123	Los Angeles	Billy Cunningham	Julius Erving, Phil
1984	East 154, West 145 (OT)	Denver	K.C. Jones	Isiah Thomas, Det
1985	West 140, East 129	Indiana	Pat Riley	Ralph Sampson, Hou
1986	East 139, West 132	Dallas	K.C. Jones	Isiah Thomas, Det
1987	West 154, East 149 (OT)	Seattle	Pat Riley	Tom Chambers, Sea
1988	East 138, West 133	Chicago	Mike Fratello	Michael Jordan, Chi
1989	West 143, East 134	Houston	Pat Riley	Karl Malone, Utah
1990	East 130, West 113	Miami	Chuck Daly	Magic Johnson, LAL
1991	East 116, West 114	Charlotte	Chris Ford	Charles Barkley, Phil
1992	West 153, East 113	Orlando	Don Nelson	Magic Johnson, LAL
1993	West 135, East 132	Salt Lake City	Paul Westphal	K. Malone/J. Stockton, Utah
1994	East 127, West 118	Minneapolis	Lenny Wilkens	Scottie Pippen, Chi

NBA All-Star Game Results *(Cont.)*

Year	Result	Site	Winning Coach	Most Valuable Player
1995	West 139, East 112	Phoenix	Paul Westphal	Mitch Richmond, Sac
1996	East 129, West 118	San Antonio	Phil Jackson	Michael Jordan, Chi
1997	East 132, West 120	Cleveland	Doug Collins	Glen Rice, Cha
1998	East 135, West 114	New York	Larry Bird	Michael Jordan, Chi
1999	Cancelled due to lockout.			
2000	West 137, East 126	Oakland	Phil Jackson	S. O'Neal, LAL/T. Duncan, SA
2001	East 111, West 110	Washington	Larry Brown	Allen Iverson, Phill
2002	West 135, East 120	Philadelphia	Don Nelson	Kobe Bryant, LAL
2003	West 155, East 145 (2OT)	Atlanta	Rick Adelman	Kevin Garnett, Min
2004	West 136, East 132	Los Angeles	Flip Saunders	Shaquille O'Neal, LAL
2005	East 125, West 115	Denver	Stan Van Gundy	Allen Iverson, Phil
2006	East 122, West 120	Houston	Flip Saunders	LeBron James, Cle
2007	West 153, East 132	Las Vegas	Mike D'Antoni	Kobe Bryant, LAL
2008	East 134, West 128	New Orleans	Doc Rivers	LeBron James, Cle

Members of the Basketball Hall of Fame

Contributors

Senda Abbott (1984)
Clair F. Bee (1967)
Danny Biasone (2000)
Hubie Brown (2005)
Walter A. Brown (1965)
John W. Bunn (1964)
Jerry Colangelo (2004)
William Davidson (2008)
Bob Douglas (1971)
Al Duer (1981)
Wayne Embry (1999)
Clifford Fagan (1983)
Harry A. Fisher (1973)
Larry Fleisher (1991)
Dave Gavitt (2006)
Edward Gottlieb (1971)
Luther H. Gulick (1959)
Lester Harrison (1979)
Chick Hearn (2003)
Ferenc Hepp (1980)
Edward J. Hickox (1959)
Paul D. (Tony) Hinkle (1965)
Ned Irish (1964)
R. William Jones (1964)
J. Walter Kennedy (1980)
Meadowlark Lemon (2003)
Emil S. Liston (1974)
Earl Lloyd (2003)
Bill Mokray (1965)
Ralph Morgan (1959)
Frank Morgenweck (1962)
James Naismith (1959)
C.M. Newton (2000)
John J. O'Brien (1961)
Larry O'Brien (1991)
Harold G. Olsen (1959)
Maurice Podoloff (1973)
H. V. Porter (1960)
William A. Reid (1963)
Elmer Ripley (1972)
Lynn W. St. John (1962)
Abe Saperstein (1970)
Arthur A. Schabinger (1961)
Amos Alonzo Stagg (1959)
Boris Stankovic (1991)
Edward Steitz (1983)
Chuck Taylor (1968)
Bertha F. Teague (1984)
Oswald Tower (1959)
Arthur L. Trester (1961)
Dick Vitale (2008)
Clifford Wells (1971)
Lou Wilke (1982)
Fred Zollner (1999)

Players

Kareem Abdul-Jabbar (1995)
Nate (Tiny) Archibald (1991)
Paul J. Arizin (1977)
Charles Barkley (2006)
Thomas B. Barlow (1980)
Rick Barry (1987)
Elgin Baylor (1976)
John Beckman (1972)
Walt Bellamy (1993)
Sergei Belov (1992)
Dave Bing (1990)
Larry Bird (1998)
Carol Blazejowski (1994)
Bennie Borgmann (1961)
Bill Bradley (1982)
Joseph Brennan (1974)
Al Cervi (1984)
Wilt Chamberlain (1978)
Charles (Tarzan) Cooper (1976)
Kresimir Cosic (1996)
Bob Cousy (1970)
Dave Cowens (1991)
Joan Crawford (1997)
Billy Cunningham (1986)
Denise Curry (1997)
Drazen Dalipagic (2004)
Adrian Dantley (2008)
Bob Davies (1969)
Forrest S. DeBernardi (1961)
Dave DeBusschere (1982)
H.G. (Dutch) Dehnert (1968)
Anne Donovan (1995)
Clyde Drexler (2004)
Joe Dumars (2006)
Paul Endacott (1971)
Alex English (1997)
Julius Erving (1993)
Patrick Ewing (2008)
Harold (Bud) Foster (1964)
Walter (Clyde) Frazier (1987)
Max (Marty) Friedman (1971)
Joe Fulks (1977)
Lauren (Laddie) Gale (1976)
Harry (the Horse) Gallatin (1991)
William Gates (1989)
George Gervin (1996)
Tom Gola (1975)
Gail Goodrich (1996)
Hal Greer (1981)
Robert (Ace) Gruenig (1963)
Clifford O. Hagan (1977)
Victor Hanson (1960)
Lusia Harris-Stewart (1992)
John Havlicek (1983)
Connie Hawkins (1992)
Elvin Hayes (1990)
Marques Haynes (1998)
Tom Heinsohn (1986)
Nat Holman (1964)
Robert J. Houbregs (1987)
Bailey Howell (1997)
Chuck Hyatt (1959)
Dan Issel (1993)
Harry (Buddy) Jeannette (1994)
Earvin (Magic) Johnson (2002)
William C. Johnson (1976)
D. Neil Johnston (1990)
K.C. Jones (1989)
Sam Jones (1983)
Edward (Moose) Krause (1975)
Bob Kurland (1961)
Bob Lanier (1992)

Members of the Basketball Hall of Fame *(Cont.)*

Players (*Cont.*)

Joe Lapchick (1966)
Nancy Lieberman-Cline (1996)
Clyde Lovellette (1988)
Jerry Lucas (1979)
Angelo (Hank) Luisetti (1959)
C. Edward Macauley (1960)
Moses Malone (2001)
Peter P. Maravich (1987)
Hortencia Marcari (2005)
Slater Martin (1981)
Bob McAdoo (2000)
Branch McCracken (1960)
Jack McCracken (1962)
Bobby McDermott (1988)
Dick McGuire (1993)
Kevin McHale (1999)
Dino Meneghin (2003)
Ann Meyers (1993)
George L. Mikan (1959)
Vern Mikkelsen (1995)
Cheryl Miller (1995)
Earl Monroe (1990)
Calvin Murphy (1993)
Charles (Stretch) Murphy (1960)
Hakeem Olajuwon (2008)
H. O. (Pat) Page (1962)
Robert Parish (2003)
Drazen Petrovic (2002)
Bob Pettit (1970)
Andy Phillip (1961)
Jim Pollard (1977)
Frank Ramsey (1981)
Willis Reed (1981)
Arnie Risen (1998)
Oscar Robertson (1979)
John S. Roosma (1961)
Bill Russell (1974)
John (Honey) Russell (1964)
Adolph Schayes (1972)
Ernest J. Schmidt (1973)
John J. Schommer (1959)
Barney Sedran (1962)
Uljana Semjonova (1993)
Bill Sharman (1975)
Christian Steinmetz (1961)
Lusia Harris Stewart (1992)
Maurice Stokes (2004)
Isiah Thomas (2000)
David Thompson (1996)
John A. (Cat) Thompson (1962)
Nate Thurmond (1984)
Jack Twyman (1982)
Wes Unseld (1988)
Robert (Fuzzy) Vandivier (1974)
Edward A. Wachter (1961)
Bill Walton (1993)
Robert F. Wanzer (1987)
Jerry West (1979)
Nera White (1992)
Lenny Wilkens (1989)
Dominique Wilkins (2006)
Lynette Woodard (2004)
John R. Wooden (1960)
James Worthy (2003)
George (Bird) Yardley (1996)

Coaches

Forest C. (Phog) Allen (1959)
Harold Anderson (1984)
Red Auerbach (1968)
Geno Auriemma (2006)
Leon Barmore (2003)
Sam Barry (1978)
Ernest A. Blood (1960)
Jim Boeheim (2005)
Larry Brown (2002)
Jim Calhoun (2005)
Howard G. Cann (1967)
H. Clifford Carlson (1959)
Lou Carnesecca (1992)
Ben Carnevale (1969)
Pete Carril (1997)
Everett Case (1981)
Van Chancellor (2007)
John Chaney (2001)
Jody Conradt (1998)
Denny Crum (1994)
Chuck Daly (1994)
Everett S. Dean (1966)
Antonio Diaz-Miguel (1997)
Edgar A. Diddle (1971)
Bruce Drake (1972)
Pedro Ferrandiz (2007)
Sandro Gamba (2006)
Clarence Gaines (1981)
Jack Gardner (1983)
Amory T. (Slats) Gill (1967)
Aleksandr Gomelsky (1995)
Sue Gunter (2005)
Alex Hannum (1998)
Marv Harshman (1984)
Don Haskins (1997)
Edgar S. Hickey (1978)
Howard A. Hobson (1965)
Red Holzman (1986)
Hank Iba (1968)
Phil Jackson (2007)
Alvin F. (Doggie) Julian (1967)
Frank W. Keaney (1960)
George E. Keogan (1961)
Bob Knight (1991)
Mike Krzyzewski (2001)
John Kundla (1995)
Ward L. Lambert (1960)
Harry Litwack (1975)
Kenneth D. Loeffler (1964)
A.C. (Dutch) Lonborg (1972)
John B. McLendon (1978)
Arad A. McCutchan (1980)
Al McGuire (1992)
Frank McGuire (1976)
Walter E. Meanwell (1959)
Raymond J. Meyer (1978)
Ralph Miller (1988)
Billie Moore (1999)
Peter F. Newell (1978)
Aleksandar Nikolic (1998)
Mirko Novosel (2007)
Lute Olson (2002)
Jack Ramsay (1992)
Pat Riley (2008)
Cesare Rubini (1994)
Adolph F. Rupp (1968)
Cathy Rush (2008)
Leonard D. Sachs (1961)
Bill Sharman (2004)
Everett F. Shelton (1979)
Dean Smith (1982)
Pat Summitt (2000)
Fred R. Taylor (1985)
John Thompson (1999)
Margaret Wade (1984)
Stanley H. Watts (1985)
Lenny Wilkens (1998)
Roy Williams (2007)
John R. Wooden (1972)
Morgan Wooten (2000)
Phil Woolpert (1992)
Kay Yow (2002)

Referees

James E. Enright (1978)
George T. Hepbron (1960)
George Hoyt (1961)
Matthew P. Kennedy (1959)
Lloyd Leith (1982)
Zigmund J. Mihalik (1985)
John P. Nucatola (1977)
Ernest C. Quigley (1961)
Marvin Rudolph (2007)
J. Dallas Shirley (1979)
Earl Strom (1995)
David Tobey (1961)
David H. Walsh (1961)

Teams

Buffalo Germans (1961)
First Team (1959)
Harlem Globetrotters (2002)
Original Celtics (1959)
Renaissance (1963)
1966 Texas Western (2007)

Note: Year of election in parentheses.

American Basketball Association

Champions

Year	Champion	Series	Runner-up	Winning Coach
1968	Pittsburgh Pipers	4–3	New Orleans Bucs	Vince Cazetta
1969	Oakland Oaks	4–1	Indiana Pacers	Alex Hannum
1970	Indiana Pacers	4–2	Los Angeles Stars	Bob Leonard
1971	Utah Stars	4–3	Kentucky Colonels	Bill Sharman
1972	Indiana Pacers	4–2	New York Nets	Bob Leonard
1973	Indiana Pacers	4–3	Kentucky Colonels	Bob Leonard
1974	New York Nets	4–1	Utah Stars	Kevin Loughery
1975	Kentucky Colonels	4–1	Indiana Pacers	Hubie Brown
1976	New York Nets	4–2	Denver Nuggets	Kevin Loughery

ABA Postseason Awards

Most Valuable Player

1967–68................Connie Hawkins, Pitt
1968–69................Mel Daniels, Ind
1969–70................Spencer Haywood, Den
1970–71................Mel Daniels, Ind
1971–72................Artis Gilmore, Ken
1972–73................Billy Cunningham, Car
1973–74................Julius Erving, NY
1974–75................Julius Erving, NY
George McGinnis, Ind
1975–76................Julius Erving, NY

Rookie of the Year

1967–68................Mel Daniels, Minn
1968–69................Warren Armstrong, Oak
1969–70................Spencer Haywood, Den
1970–71................Charlie Scott, Vir
Dan Issel, Ken
1971–72................Artis Gilmore, Ken
1972–73................Brian Taylor, NY
1973–74................Swen Nater, SA
1974–75................Marvin Barnes, StL
1975–76................David Thompson, Den

Coach of the Year

1967–68................Vince Cazetta, Pitt
1968–69................Alex Hannum, Oak
1969–70................Bill Sharman, LA
Joe Belmont, Den
1970–71................Al Bianchi, Vir
1971–72................Tom Nissalke, Dal
1972–73................Larry Brown, Car
1973–74................Babe McCarthy, Ken
Joe Mullaney, Utah
1974–75................Larry Brown, Den
1975–76................Larry Brown, Den

ABA Season Leaders

Scoring

		GP	Pts	Avg
1967–68	Connie Hawkins, Pitt	70	1875	26.8
1968–69	Rick Barry, Oak	35	1190	34.0
1969–70	Spencer Haywood, Den	84	2519	30.0
1970–71	Dan Issel, Ken	83	2480	29.9
1971–72	Charlie Scott, Vir	79	2637	33.4
1972–73	Julius Erving, Vir	71	2268	31.9
1973–74	Julius Erving, NY	84	2299	27.4
1974–75	George McGinnis, Ind	79	2353	29.8
1975–76	Julius Erving, NY	84	2462	29.3

Rebounds

1967–68	Mel Daniels, Minn	15.6
1968–69	Mel Daniels, Ind	16.5
1969–70	Spencer Haywood, Den	19.5
1970–71	Mel Daniels, Ind	18.0
1971–72	Artis Gilmore, Ken	17.8
1972–73	Artis Gilmore, Ken	17.6
1973–74	Artis Gilmore, Ken	18.3
1974–75	Swen Nater, SA	16.4
1975–76	Artis Gilmore, Ken	15.5

Assists

1967–68	Larry Brown, NO	6.5
1968–69	Larry Brown, Oak	7.1
1969–70	Larry Brown, Wash	7.1
1970–71	Bill Melchionni, NY	8.3
1971–72	Bill Melchionni, NY	8.4
1972–73	Bill Melchionni, NY	7.4
1973–74	Al Smith, Den	8.2
1974–75	Mack Calvin, Den	7.7
1975–76	Don Buse, Ind	8.2

Steals

1973–74	Ted McClain, Car	2.98
1974–75	Brian Taylor, NY	2.80
1975–76	Don Buse, Ind	4.12

Blocked Shots

1973–74	Caldwell Jones, SD	4.00
1974–75	Caldwell Jones, SD	3.24
1975–76	Billy Paultz, SA	3.05

World Championship of Basketball

Year	Winner	Runner-Up	Score	Site
1950	Argentina	United States	†	Buenos Aires
1954	United States	Brazil	†	Rio de Janeiro
1959	Brazil	United States	†	Santiago, Chile
1963	Brazil	Yugoslavia	†	Rio de Janeiro
1967	Soviet Union	Yugoslavia	†	Montevideo, Uruguay
1970	Yugoslavia	Brazil	†	Ljubljana, Yugoslavia
1974	Soviet Union	Yugoslavia	†	San Juan
1978	Yugoslavia	Soviet Union	82–81 (OT)	Manila
1982	Soviet Union	United States	95–94	Cali, Colombia
1986	United States	Soviet Union	87–85	Madrid
1990	Yugoslavia	Soviet Union	92–75	Buenos Aires
*1994	United States	Russia	137–91	Toronto
†1998	Yugoslavia	Russia	64–62	Athens
2002	Yugoslavia	Argentina	84–77 (OT)	Indianapolis
2006	Spain	Greece	70–47	Saitama, Japan

*U.S. professionals began competing in 1994.†In 1998, a labor dispute resulted in a boycott of the World Championship by NBA stars; the U.S. roster was filled by members of the CBA and European professional leagues and college players.
†Result determined by overall record in final round of competition.

College Basketball

Mario Chalmers' thrilling, last-second shot helped the Kansas Jayhawks to a national title

JOHN BIEVER

Top of the Tops

Led by a coach long overdue for a title and heading into the most elite Final Four in history, unheralded Kansas rode to victory on an improbable last-minute comeback

BY B.J. SCHECTER

WHEN THE BALL LEFT HIS hand it was the sweetest feeling in the world. With Kansas trailing Memphis 63–60 in the closing seconds of the national title game, the Jayhawks' Mario Chalmers had just released a three-pointer over the outstretched arms of Memphis sensational freshman Derrick Rose, and as the ball hung in the air for a second, Chalmers knew it was good. There are few sure things in sports (fewer in college basketball), but with the game on the line Mario is money; his shot was true and the championship game was headed to overtime. "It will probably be," said Jayhawks coach Bill Self, "the biggest shot ever made in Kansas history."

The extra time was a fitting conclusion for a heavyweight Final Four, in which four No. 1 seeds made it for the first time in history. There were three blue bloods—North Carolina, Kansas and UCLA (which was making its third straight Final Four appearance)—and Memphis, the gritty newcomer but perhaps the most talented team in the field. The Tigers, coached by the combative John Calipari, were on the verge of a national title, up by nine points with just over two minutes remaining before Kansas stormed back by going after Memphis' Achilles heel.

Talented as the Tigers were, spotty free-throw shooting had been an issue all season long and Memphis entered the tournament shooting just over 61 percent as a team from the line. Entering the Kansas game, Memphis claimed that free throw shooting wasn't a problem. The Tigers had shot well from the line all tournament, including 87 percent in the national semifinal win over UCLA, prompting Calipari to say: "We make them when they matter."

But Memphis didn't make them when they mattered the most, even with its two best free throw shooters on the line. Chris Douglas-Roberts hit just one of five down the stretch and when Rose hit just one of two in the closing seconds, it opened up the door for Chalmers' heroics. "It definitely came back to haunt us," Tigers forward Robert Dozier said. "But even with those [missed] free throws, we were still up three."

When the game went into overtime Memphis was deflated and Kansas dominated the extra period en route to a 75–68 victory. As confetti rained down on the court and the Jayhawks jumped around in jubilation, Memphis was left to wonder what happened. "When you're up nine [with two minutes left] you're supposed to win," said Calipari. "Being so close to a national title, to not have it, I feel bad for our city and our players, because we had it. We collectively let it slip out of our hands."

A key lapse in strategy made the defeat harder to swallow. After Rose hit a free throw to put Memphis up three with 12 seconds left in regulation, most coaches agree that the smart strategy is to foul and not let the opponent get off a three-point attempt. But Kansas' Sherron Collins raced upcourt past Rose and dished to Chalmers. Calipari said the plan was to foul, but if that was the case why didn't he call a timeout so there was no confusion? And after Chalmers hit the shot, why didn't he call a timeout to set up a final shot?

Instead, it was Kansas celebrating on the court, taking in "One Shining Moment" as Jayhawks assistant Danny Manning cut down a piece of the net 20 years after he led Kansas to an even more improbable championship. The title was a defining moment for Self, who entered the tournament with the label as the best coach never to have made a Final Four. It was unfair, to be sure, but following in the footsteps of Roy Williams—who went to four Final Fours with the Jayhawks—and coming to Lawrence a year before Illinois went to the title game (with Self's players), Self was tired of hearing the critics say he couldn't win the big one.

In 2008, Candace Parker was once again named Most Outstanding Player of the Final Four, while guiding the Lady Vols to a second straight title.

"I was happy that Illinois was there, but I was also, to be quite candid, jealous," said Self of the 2005 title game between Illinois and North Carolina. "Because those were the guys my staff had put together. Then you had the Kansas contingent that was jealous because Roy was playing and we were not. It was the most frustrating time for me as a coach that didn't have anything to do with winning or losing."

Winning and losing is everything to the North Carolina faithful. With coach Roy Williams back in Tar Heel blue, the program is on steady ground. After a collapse against Georgetown in the 2007 Elite Eight, the Tar Heels came into the season hungry and determined. Led by Player of the Year Tyler Hansbrough, affectionately known as "Psycho T" for his intensity, North Carolina began the season at No. 1 and entered the tournament as the No. 1-overall seed.

A mid-season ankle injury that sidelined star point guard Tywon Lawson turned out to be a blessing in disguise as the Tar Heels gelled as a team and developed even more weapons off the bench. Carolina cruised into the Final Four, where Williams met his nightmare scenario: a date with Kansas.

Having coached 15 years in Lawrence, Williams vowed never to schedule the Jayhawks and said the only way he'd play them was in the NCAA tournament. Under the bright lights of the Final Four, it played out worse than Williams could have imagined as Kansas dominated from the opening tip,

JOHN BIEVER

Memphis point guard Derrick Rose didn't win an NCAA tile in 2008, but he did become the No. 1-overall pick at the NBA Draft.

jumping out to a 40–12 lead. North Carolina made a run in the second half to cut the lead to four, but Kansas answered and cruised to a comfortable 84–66 victory.

"No matter how much I said there was no pressure [last week], the players felt it," said Self. "I knew if we got here [to the Final Four], the pressure would subside and our guys would go play."

Self and the Jayhawks knew that pressure all too well in the Elite Eight. With the Final Four carrot dangling in front of them, Kansas faced red-hot Davidson and tournament darling Stephen Curry, the son of former NBA player Dell Curry. In his first three NCAA games (wins over Gonzaga, Georgetown and Wisconsin), the sharpshooting Curry was all but unstoppable, scoring 40, 30 and 33 points. LeBron James, in town for a game against the Pistons, made an appearance at one Davidson game and was seen gasping "Wow!" after a Curry three-point play.

Kansas played him well in the regional final, but Davidson still had a shot to win or tie, down 59-57 with the ball in the closing seconds. Curry (who finished with 25 points) got the ball on a clearout and Kansas rotated defenders on him so that he would have a clear shot. Curry held the ball a little too long and dished to point guard Jason Richardson, who clanked a long shot off the backboard as time expired.

Kneeling on the sideline as the play unfolded, Self dropped his head when the buzzer sounded and breathed a huge sigh of relief. The monkey was finally off his back.

The 2007–08 season became known for the young and the old, the youngsters who came in and continued to transcend the game and the coaches who made history on and off the court. Another group of one-and-doners made their mark on the college game before heading off to the NBA. In addition to Rose, Michael Beasley and O.J. Mayo led Kansas State and USC, respectively, back to the NCAA tournament. And Kevin Love (UCLA) and Eric Gordon (Indiana) immediately became the go-to guys at already strong programs.

The winningest (and perhaps most controversial) coach of alltime, Bob Knight, stepped down at Texas Tech with 10 games remaining and turned the reins over to his son, Pat. Eddie Sutton came out of retirement to reach 800 wins then retired after he reached the milestone—barely. His son Sean, who was forced to resign at the end of the season, didn't fare much better at Oklahoma State. And then there was Kelvin Sampson, who stepped down at Indiana after being charged with major recruiting violations for the second time in his career.

After Kansas won the title, there was a strong push among Oklahoma State's boosters (led by billionaire T. Boone Pickens) to lure Self back to his alma mater. But in the end, the history and tradition of Kansas kept Self in Lawrence. After watching his team overcome a seemingly insurmountable deficit in the national title game, Self knew that, in Kansas, there's no place like home.

NCAA Men's Championship Game Box Score

Kansas 75

	Min	FG M–A	FT M–A	Reb O–T	A	PF	TP
D. Arthur	35	9–13	2–2	5–10	1	3	20
D. Jackson	29	3–4	2–2	1–8	1	1	8
R. Robinson	20	1–1	0–0	0–4	1	3	2
M. Chalmers	40	5–13	6–6	1–3	3	3	18
B. Rush	42	5–9	2–3	1–6	2	3	12
S. Collins	34	4–10	2–2	0–4	6	3	11
S. Kaun	21	2–5	0–0	1–2	0	2	4
C. Aldrich	4	0–0	0–0	0–0	0	0	0
Totals		29–55	14–15	9–37	14	18	75

Percentages: FG-.527, FT-.933. 3-Point Goals: 3–12, .250 (B. Rush 0–2, M. Chalmers 2–6, S. Collins 1–4). Team Rebounds: 2. Blocked Shots: 1 (B. Rush 1). Turnovers: 17 (B. Rush 3, M. Chalmers 3, S. Collins 4, R. Robinson 3, S. Kaun 1, D. Arthur 3). Steals: 11 (B. Rush 1, M. Chalmers 4, D. Jackson 1, S. Collins 3, D. Arthur 1, R. Robinson 1).
Halftime: Kansas 33, Memphis 28.
Final (Regulation): Kansas 63, Memphis 63.

Officials: John Cahill, Ed Hightower, Ed Corbett.
A: 43,257.

Memphis 68 (OT)

	Min	FG M–A	FT M–A	Reb O–T	A	PF	TP
R. Dozier	39	4–11	2–3	5–10	3	2	11
J. Dorsey	26	3–3	0–0	1–2	1	5	6
A. Anderson	42	3–9	1–3	1–5	1	3	9
C. D-Roberts	42	7–16	6–9	0–1	1	4	22
D. Rose	45	7–17	3–4	2–6	8	1	18
S. Taggart	24	1–5	0–0	2–3	0	2	2
W. Kemp	4	0–0	0–0	0–0	0	0	0
P. Niles	1	0–0	0–0	0–0	0	0	0
D. Mack	2	0–1	0–0	0–0	0	0	0
Totals		25–62	12–19	11–27	14	17	68

Percentages: FG-.403, FT-.632. 3-Point Goals: 6–22, .273 (D. Rose 1–6, A. Anderson 2–7, S. Taggart 0–1, C. Douglas-Roberts 2–5, R. Dozier 1–2, D. Mack 0–1). Team Rebounds: 1. Blocked Shots: 3 (J. Dorsey 2, R. Dozier 1). Turnovers: 13 (D. Rose 5, A. Anderson 2, S. Taggart 1, J. Dorsey 1, C. Douglas-Roberts 2, R. Dozier 1, W. Kemp 1). Steals: 11 (A. Anderson 4, D. Rose 2, S. Taggart 1, J. Dorsey 1, C. Douglas-Roberts 1, R. Dozier 1, W. Kemp 1).

Final ESPN/*USA Today* Top 25 Poll

1. Kansas (31) 37–3
2. Memphis 38–2
3. North Carolina 36–3
4. UCLA 35–4
5. Texas 31–7
6. Louisville 27–9
7. Tennessee 31–5
8. Xavier 30–7
9. Davidson 29–7
10. Wisconsin 31–5
11. Stanford 28–8
12. Georgetown 28–6
13. Michigan St 27–9
14. Butler 30–4
15. Washington St 26–9
16. Duke 28–6
17. West Virginia 26–11
18. Pittsburgh 27–10
19. Notre Dame 25–8
20. Purdue 25–9
21. Marquette 25–10
22. Western Kentucky 29–7
23. Drake 28–5
24. Villanova 22–13
25. Vanderbilt 26–8

National Invitation Tournament Scores

First round: Ohio St 84, UNC-Asheville 66; Massachusetts 80, Stephen F. Austin 60; Syracuse 87, Robert Morris 81; Akron 65, Florida St 60; Southern Illinois 69, Oklahoma St 53; Maryland 68, Minnesota 58; Creighton 74, Rhode Island 73; Arizona St 64, Alabama St 53; Virginia Tech 94, Morgan St 62; Dayton 66, Cleveland St 57; Mississippi 83, UC-Santa Barbara 68; Nebraska 67, Charlotte 48; UAB 80, VCU 77; Florida 73, San Diego St 49; Illinois State 61, Utah St 57; California 68, New Mexico 66.
Second round: Ohio St 73, California 56; Mississippi 85, Nebraska 75; Dayton 55, Illinois St 48; Virginia Tech 75, UAB 49; Massachusetts 68, Akron 63; Florida 82, Creighton 54; Arizona St 65, Southern Illinois 51; Syracuse 88, Maryland 72.
Quarterfinals: Ohio St 74, Dayton 63; Mississippi 81, Virginia Tech 72; Massachusetts 81, Syracuse 77; Florida 70, Arizona St 57.
Semifinals: Ohio St 81, Mississippi 69; Massachusetts 78, Florida 66.
Championship Game: Ohio St 92, Massachusetts 85.

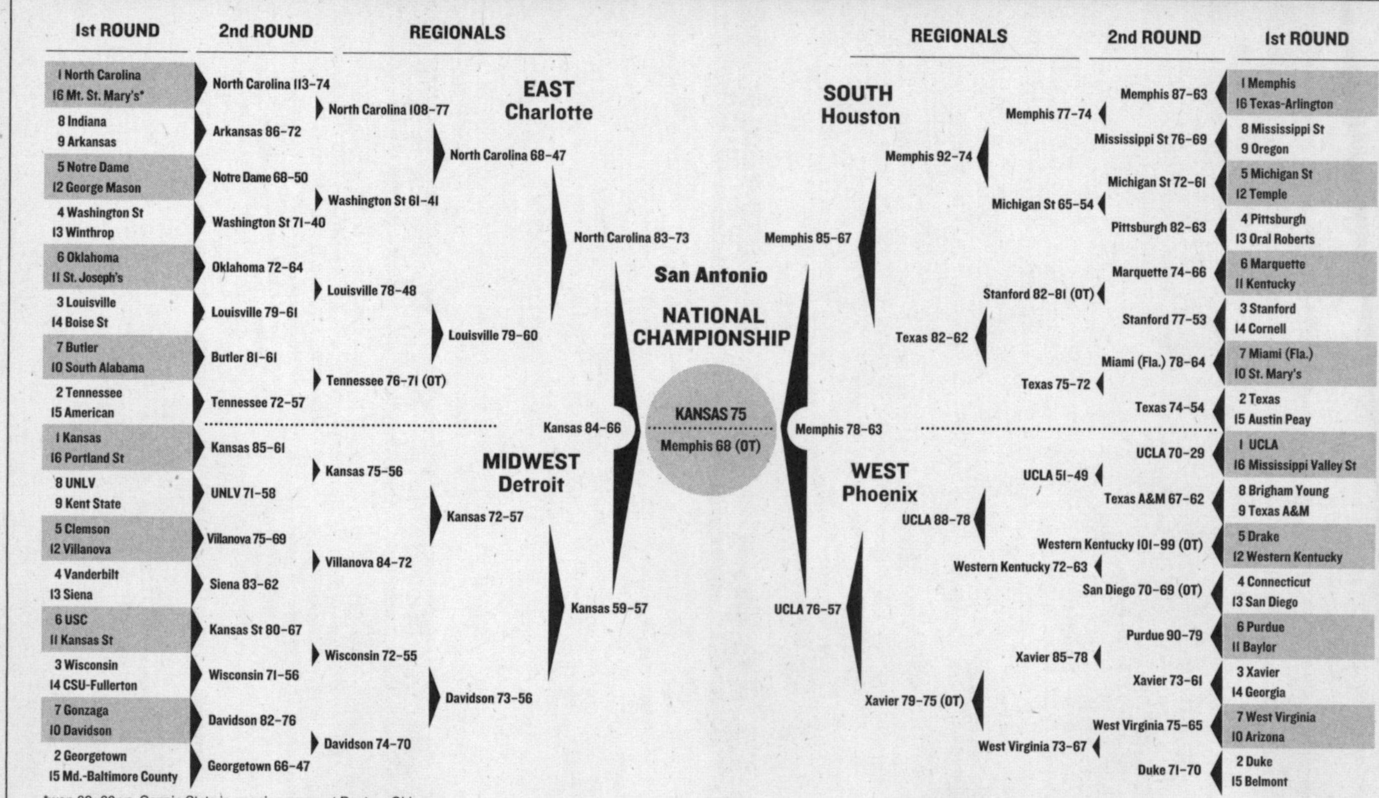
2008 NCAA Basketball Men's Division I Tournament
1st ROUND
2nd ROUND
REGIONALS
REGIONALS
2nd ROUND
1st ROUND
1 North Carolina
16 Mt. St. Mary's*
8 Indiana
9 Arkansas
5 Notre Dame
12 George Mason
4 Washington St
13 Winthrop
6 Oklahoma
11 St. Joseph's
3 Louisville
14 Boise St
7 Butler
10 South Alabama
2 Tennessee
15 American
1 Kansas
16 Portland St
8 UNLV
9 Kent State
5 Clemson
12 Villanova
4 Vanderbilt
13 Siena
6 USC
11 Kansas St
3 Wisconsin
14 CSU-Fullerton
7 Gonzaga
10 Davidson
2 Georgetown
15 Md.-Baltimore County
North Carolina 113–74
Arkansas 86–72
Notre Dame 68–50
Washington St 71–40
Oklahoma 72–64
Louisville 79–61
Butler 81–61
Tennessee 72–57
Kansas 85–61
UNLV 71–58
Villanova 75–69
Siena 83–62
Kansas St 80–67
Wisconsin 71–56
Davidson 82–76
Georgetown 66–47
North Carolina 108–77
Washington St 61–41
Louisville 78–48
Tennessee 76–71 (OT)
Kansas 75–56
Villanova 84–72
Wisconsin 72–55
Davidson 74–70
North Carolina 68–47
Louisville 79–60
Kansas 72–57
Davidson 73–56
EAST
Charlotte
MIDWEST
Detroit
North Carolina 83–73
Kansas 59–57
Kansas 84–66
San Antonio
NATIONAL CHAMPIONSHIP
KANSAS 75
Memphis 68 (OT)
Memphis 78–63
SOUTH
Houston
WEST
Phoenix
Memphis 85–67
UCLA 76–57
Memphis 92–74
Texas 82–62
UCLA 88–78
Xavier 79–75 (OT)
Memphis 77–74
Michigan St 65–54
Stanford 82–81 (OT)
Texas 75–72
UCLA 51–49
Western Kentucky 72–63
Xavier 85–78
West Virginia 73–67
Memphis 87–63
Mississippi St 76–69
Michigan St 72–61
Pittsburgh 82–63
Marquette 74–66
Stanford 77–53
Miami (Fla.) 78–64
Texas 74–54
UCLA 70–29
Texas A&M 67–62
Western Kentucky 101–99 (OT)
San Diego 70–69 (OT)
Purdue 90–79
Xavier 73–61
West Virginia 75–65
Duke 71–70
1 Memphis
16 Texas-Arlington
8 Mississippi St
9 Oregon
5 Michigan St
12 Temple
4 Pittsburgh
13 Oral Roberts
6 Marquette
11 Kentucky
3 Stanford
14 Cornell
7 Miami (Fla.)
10 St. Mary's
2 Texas
15 Austin Peay
1 UCLA
16 Mississippi Valley St
8 Brigham Young
9 Texas A&M
5 Drake
12 Western Kentucky
4 Connecticut
13 San Diego
6 Purdue
11 Baylor
3 Xavier
14 Georgia
7 West Virginia
10 Arizona
2 Duke
15 Belmont

*won 69–60 vs. Coppin State in opening game at Dayton, Ohio.

NCAA Men's Division I Conference Standings

America East

	Conference W	L	Pct	All Games W	L	Pct
*Md.-Baltimore Cty.	13	3	.813	24	9	.826
Hartford	10	6	.625	18	16	.529
Albany	10	6	.625	15	15	.500
Vermont	9	7	.563	16	15	.516
Binghamton	9	7	.563	14	16	.467
Boston Univ.	9	7	.563	14	17	.452
New Hampshire	6	10	.375	9	20	.310
Stony Brook	3	13	.188	7	23	.233
Maine	3	13	.188	7	23	.233

Atlantic Coast

	Conference W	L	Pct	All Games W	L	Pct
*North Carolina	14	2	.875	36	3	.923
Duke	13	3	.813	28	6	.824
Clemson	10	6	.625	24	10	.706
Virginia Tech	9	7	.563	21	14	.600
Miami (Fla.)	8	8	.500	23	11	.676
Maryland	8	8	.500	19	15	.559
Wake Forest	7	9	.438	17	13	.567
Florida St	7	9	.438	19	15	.559
Georgia Tech	7	9	.438	15	17	.469
Virginia	5	11	.313	17	16	.515
North Carolina St	4	12	.250	15	16	.484
Boston College	4	12	.250	14	17	.452

Atlantic Sun

	Conference W	L	Pct	All Games W	L	Pct
*Belmont	14	2	.875	25	9	.735
Jacksonville	12	4	.750	18	13	.581
East Tennnessee St	11	5	.688	19	13	.594
Stetson	11	5	.688	16	16	.500
Gardner–Webb	9	7	.563	16	16	.500
Lipscomb	9	7	.563	15	16	.484
Kennesaw St.	7	9	.438	10	20	.333
Mercer	6	10	.375	11	19	.367
Florida Gulf Coast	6	10	.375	10	21	.326
Campbell	5	11	.313	10	20	.333
S.C.-Upstate	5	11	.313	7	23	.233
North Florida	1	15	.063	3	26	.103

Atlantic 10

	Conference W	L	Pct	All Games W	L	Pct
Xavier	14	2	.875	30	7	.811
*Temple	11	5	.688	21	13	.618
Massachusetts	10	6	.625	25	11	.694
St. Joseph's	9	7	.563	21	13	.618
Charlotte	9	7	.563	20	14	.588
Richmond	9	7	.563	16	15	.516
Dayton	8	8	.500	23	11	.676
La Salle	8	8	.500	15	17	.469
Rhode Island	7	9	.438	21	12	.636
Duquesne	7	9	.438	17	13	.567
St. Louis	7	9	.438	16	15	.516
Fordham	6	10	.375	12	17	.414
George Washington	5	11	.313	9	17	.346
St. Bonaventure	2	14	.125	8	22	.267

Big East

	Conference W	L	Pct	All Games W	L	Pct
Georgetown	15	3	.833	28	6	.824
Notre Dame	14	4	.777	25	8	.758
Louisville	14	4	.777	27	9	.750
Connecticut	13	5	.722	24	9	.727
Marquette	11	7	.611	25	10	.714
West Virginia	11	7	.611	26	11	.703
*Pittsburgh	10	8	.555	27	10	.730
Villanova	9	9	.500	22	13	.629
Syracuse	9	9	.500	21	14	.600
Cincinnati	8	10	.444	13	19	.406
Seton Hall	7	11	.389	17	15	.531
Providence	6	12	.333	15	16	.484
DePaul	6	12	.333	11	19	.367
St. John's	5	13	.278	11	19	.367
South Florida	3	15	.167	12	19	.387
Rutgers	3	15	.167	11	20	.355

Big Sky

	Conference W	L	Pct	All Games W	L	Pct
*Portland St	14	2	.875	23	10	.697
Northern Arizona	11	5	.688	21	11	.656
Weber St	10	6	.625	16	14	.533
Montana	8	8	.500	14	16	.467
Idaho St	8	8	.500	12	19	.387
Montana St	7	9	.438	15	15	.500
Northern Colorado	6	10	.375	13	16	.448
Eastern Washington	6	10	.375	11	19	.367
Sacramento St	2	14	.125	4	24	.143

Big South

	Conference W	L	Pct	All Games W	L	Pct
UNC-Asheville	10	4	.714	23	10	.697
*Winthrop	10	4	.714	22	12	.647
High Point	8	6	.571	17	14	.548
Liberty	7	7	.500	16	16	.500
Virginia Military Inst.	6	8	.429	14	15	.483
Coastal Carolina	6	8	.429	13	15	.464
Radford	5	9	.357	10	20	.333
Charleston Southern	4	10	.286	10	20	.333

Big 10

	Conference W	L	Pct	All Games W	L	Pct
*Wisconsin	16	2	.889	31	5	.861
Purdue	15	3	.833	25	9	.735
Indiana	14	4	.778	25	8	.758
Michigan St	12	6	.667	27	9	.750
Ohio St	10	8	.556	24	13	.686
Minnesota	8	10	.444	20	14	.588
Penn St	7	11	.389	15	16	.484
Iowa	6	12	.333	13	19	.406
Illinois	5	13	.278	16	19	.457
Michigan	5	13	.278	10	22	.313
Northwestern	1	17	.055	8	22	.267

Note: Standings based on regular-season conference play only; overall records include all tournament play.
*Conference tournament winner.

Big 12

	Conference			All Games		
	W	L	Pct	W	L	Pct
*Kansas	13	3	.813	37	3	.925
Texas	13	3	.813	31	7	.816
Kansas St	10	6	.625	21	12	.636
Oklahoma	9	7	.563	23	12	.657
Baylor	9	7	.563	21	11	.656
Texas A&M	8	8	.500	25	11	.694
Nebraska	7	9	.438	20	13	.606
Texas Tech	7	9	.438	16	15	.516
Oklahoma St	7	9	.438	17	16	.515
Missouri	6	10	.375	16	16	.500
Iowa St	4	12	.250	14	18	.438
Colorado	3	13	.188	12	20	.375

Big West

	Conference			All Games		
	W	L	Pct	W	L	Pct
*CSU-Fullerton	12	4	.750	24	9	.727
UC-Santa Barbara	12	4	.750	23	9	.719
CSU-Northridge	12	4	.750	20	10	.667
Pacific	11	5	.688	21	10	.677
UC-Irvine	9	7	.563	18	16	.529
Cal Poly	7	9	.438	12	18	.400
UC-Riverside	4	12	.250	9	21	.300
Long Beach St	3	13	.188	6	25	.193
UC-Davis	2	14	.125	9	22	.290

Colonial

	Conference			All Games		
	W	L	Pct	W	L	Pct
VCU	15	3	.833	24	8	.750
*George Mason	12	6	.667	23	11	.676
UNC-Wilmingto	12	6	.667	20	13	.606
Old Dominion	11	7	.611	18	16	.529
William & Mary	10	8	.556	17	16	.515
Delaware	9	9	.500	14	17	.452
Northeastern	9	9	.500	14	17	.452
Hofstra	8	10	.444	12	18	.400
Towson	7	11	.389	13	18	.419
James Madison	5	13	.278	13	17	.433
Drexel	5	13	.278	12	20	.375
Georgia St	5	13	.278	9	21	.300

Conference USA

	Conference			All Games		
	W	L	Pct	W	L	Pct
*Memphis	16	0	1.000	38	2	.950
UAB	12	4	.750	23	11	.676
Houston	11	5	.688	24	10	.706
Southern Miss	9	7	.563	19	14	.576
Central Florida	9	7	.563	16	15	.516
Tulsa	8	8	.500	25	14	.641
UTEP	8	8	.500	19	14	.576
Marshall	8	8	.500	16	14	.533
Tulane	6	10	.375	17	15	.531
East Carolina	5	11	.313	11	19	.367
SMU	4	12	.250	10	20	.333
Rice	0	16	.000	3	27	.100

Horizon League

	Conference			All Games		
	W	L	Pct	W	L	Pct
*Butler	16	2	.889	30	4	.882
Wright St	12	6	.667	21	10	.677
Cleveland St	12	6	.667	21	13	.618
Valparaiso	9	9	.500	22	14	.611
Ill.-Chicago	9	9	.500	18	15	.545
UW-Green Bay	9	9	.500	15	15	.500
UW-Milwaukee	9	9	.500	14	16	.467
Loyola (Ill.)	6	12	.333	12	19	.387
Youngstown St	5	13	.278	9	21	.300
Detroit	3	15	.167	7	23	.233

Ivy League†

	Conference			All Games		
	W	L	Pct	W	L	Pct
Cornell	14	0	1.000	22	6	.786
Brown	11	3	.786	19	10	.655
Pennsylvania	8	6	.571	13	18	.419
Columbia	7	7	.500	14	15	.483
Yale	7	7	.500	13	15	.464
Dartmouth	3	11	.214	10	18	.357
Harvard	3	11	.214	8	22	.267
Princeton	3	11	.214	6	23	.207

Metro Atlantic

	Conference			All Games		
	W	L	Pct	W	L	Pct
*Siena	13	5	.722	23	11	.676
Rider	13	5	.722	23	11	.676
Niagara	12	6	.667	19	10	.655
Loyola (Md.)	12	6	.677	19	14	.576
Marist	11	7	.611	18	14	.563
Fairfield	11	7	.611	14	16	.467
Iona	8	10	.444	12	20	.375
Manhattan	5	13	.278	12	19	.387
St. Peter's	3	15	.167	6	24	.200
Canisius	2	16	.111	6	25	.194

Mid-American

	Conference			All Games		
EAST	W	L	Pct	W	L	Pct
*Kent St	13	3	.813	28	7	.800
Akron	11	5	.688	24	11	.686
Ohio	9	7	.563	20	13	.606
Miami (Ohio)	9	7	.563	17	16	.515
Bowling Green	7	9	.438	13	17	.433
Buffalo	3	13	.188	10	20	.333
WEST						
Western Michigan	12	4	.750	20	12	.625
Eastern Michigan	8	8	.500	14	17	.452
Central Michigan	8	8	.500	14	17	.452
Toledo	7	8	.467	11	19	.367
Ball St	5	11	.313	6	24	.200
Northern Illinois	3	12	.200	6	22	.214

*Conference tournament winner.
†Does not hold conference tournament.

NCAA Men's Division I Conference Standings *(Cont.)*

Summit

	Conference W	L	Pct	All Games W	L	Pct
*Oral Roberts	16	2	.889	24	9	.727
IUPUI	15	3	.833	26	7	.788
Oakland	11	7	.611	17	14	.548
North Dakota St	10	8	.625	16	13	.552
IPFW	9	9	.500	13	18	.419
Southern Utah	9	9	.500	11	19	.367
Western Illinois	7	11	.389	12	18	.400
Mo.-Kansas City	6	12	.333	11	21	.344
Centenary	4	14	.222	10	21	.323
South Dakota St	3	15	.167	8	21	.276

Mid-Eastern Athletic

	Conference W	L	Pct	All Games W	L	Pct
Morgan St	14	2	.875	22	11	.667
Hampton	11	5	.688	18	12	.600
Norfolk St	11	5	.688	16	15	.516
Delaware St	10	6	.625	14	16	.467
North Carolina A&T	9	7	.563	15	16	.484
Florida A&M	9	7	.563	15	17	.469
*Coppin St	7	9	.438	16	21	.432
South Carolina St	7	9	.438	13	20	.394
Bethune-Cookman	5	11	.313	11	21	.344
Howard	3	13	.188	6	26	.188
Md.-Eastern Shore	2	14	.125	4	28	.125

Missouri Valley

	Conference W	L	Pct	All Games W	L	Pct
*Drake	15	3	.833	28	5	.848
Illinois St	13	5	.722	25	10	.714
Southern Illinois	11	7	.611	18	15	.545
Creighton	10	8	.555	22	11	.667
Northern Iowa	9	9	.500	18	14	.563
Bradley	9	9	.500	21	17	.553
Missouri St	8	10	.444	17	16	.515
Indiana St	8	10	.444	15	16	.484
Wichita St	4	14	.222	11	20	.355
Evansville	3	15	.167	9	21	.300

Mountain West

	Conference W	L	Pct	All Games W	L	Pct
Brigham Young	14	2	.875	27	8	.771
*UNLV	12	4	.750	27	8	.771
New Mexico	11	5	.688	24	9	.727
San Diego St	9	7	.563	20	13	.606
Air Force	8	8	.500	16	14	.533
Utah	7	9	.438	18	15	.545
TCU	6	10	.375	14	16	.467
Wyoming	5	11	.313	12	18	.400
Colorado St	0	16	.000	7	25	.219

Northeast

	Conference W	L	Pct	All Games W	L	Pct
Robert Morris	16	2	.889	26	8	.765
Wagner	15	3	.833	23	8	.742
Sacred Heart	13	5	.722	18	14	.563
*Mount St. Mary's	11	7	.611	19	15	.559
Quinnipiac	11	7	.611	15	15	.500
Central Conn. St	10	8	.555	14	16	.467
Long Island	7	11	.389	15	15	.500
Fairleigh Dickinson	4	14	.222	8	20	.286
St. Francis (N.Y.)	4	14	.222	7	22	.241
Monmouth	4	14	.222	7	24	.226
St. Francis (Pa.)	4	14	.222	6	23	.207

Ohio Valley

	Conference W	L	Pct	All Games W	L	Pct
*Austin Peay	16	4	.800	24	11	.686
Murray St	13	7	.650	18	13	.581
Morehead St	12	8	.600	15	15	.500
Tenn.-Martin	11	9	.550	17	16	.515
Tennessee St	10	10	.500	15	17	.469
Eastern Kentucky	10	10	.500	14	16	.467
Samford	10	10	.500	14	16	.467
Tennessee Tech	10	10	.500	13	19	.406
SE Missouri St	7	13	.350	12	19	.387
Eastern Illinois	6	14	.300	7	22	.241
Jacksonville St	5	15	.250	7	22	.241

Pac 10

	Conference W	L	Pct	All Games W	L	Pct
*UCLA	16	2	.889	35	4	.897
Stanford	13	5	.722	28	8	.778
Washington St	11	7	.611	26	9	.743
USC	11	7	.611	21	12	.636
Arizona St	9	9	.500	21	13	.618
Oregon	9	9	.500	18	14	.563
Arizona	8	10	.444	19	15	.543
Washington	7	11	.389	16	17	.485
California	6	12	.333	17	16	.515
Oregon St	0	18	.000	6	25	.194

Patriot League

	Conference W	L	Pct	All Games W	L	Pct
*American	10	4	.714	21	12	.636
Navy	9	5	.643	16	14	.533
Colgate	7	7	.500	18	14	.563
Lehigh	7	7	.500	14	15	.483
Lafayette	6	8	.429	15	15	.500
Army	6	8	.429	14	16	.467
Bucknell	6	8	.429	12	19	.387
Holy Cross	5	9	.357	15	14	.517

*Conference tournament winner.

NCAA Men's Division I Conference Standings *(Cont.)*

Southeastern

EAST	Conference W	L	Pct	All Games W	L	Pct
Tennessee	14	2	.875	31	5	.861
Kentucky	12	4	.750	18	13	.581
Vanderbilt	10	6	.625	26	8	.765
Florida	8	8	.500	24	12	.667
South Carolina	5	11	.313	14	18	.438
*Georgia	4	12	.250	17	17	.500
WEST						
Mississippi St	12	4	.750	23	11	.676
Arkansas	9	7	.563	23	12	.657
Mississippi	7	9	.438	24	11	.686
LSU	6	10	.375	13	18	.419
Alabama	5	11	.313	17	16	.515
Auburn	4	12	.250	14	16	.467

Southern

NORTH	Conference W	L	Pct	All Games W	L	Pct
Appalachian St	13	7	.650	18	13	.581
Chattanooga	13	7	.650	18	13	.581
UNC-Greensboro	12	8	.600	19	12	.613
Elon	9	11	.450	14	19	.424
Western Carolina	6	14	.300	10	21	.323
SOUTH						
*Davidson	20	0	1.000	29	7	.806
Georgia Southern	13	7	.650	20	12	.625
Coll. of Charleston	9	11	.450	16	17	.485
Wofford	8	12	.400	16	16	.500
Furman	6	14	.300	7	23	.233
Citadel	1	19	.050	6	24	.200

Southland

EAST	Conference W	L	Pct	All Games W	L	Pct
Lamar	13	3	.813	19	11	.633
SE Louisiana	9	7	.563	17	13	.567
Northwestern St	9	7	.563	15	18	.455
McNeese St	7	9	.438	13	16	.448
Nicholls St	5	11	.313	10	21	.323
Central Arkansas	4	12	.250	14	16	.467
WEST						
Stephen F. Austin	13	3	.813	26	6	.813
Sam Houston St	10	6	.625	23	8	.742
*Tex.-Arlington	7	9	.438	21	12	.636
Tex.-San Antonio	7	9	.438	13	17	.433
Texas St	6	10	.375	13	16	.448
Tex. A&M-Corp. Chrs.	6	10	.375	9	20	.310

Southwestern Athletic

	Conference W	L	Pct	All Games W	L	Pct
Alabama St	15	3	.833	20	11	.645
*Mississippi Valley St	12	6	.667	17	16	.515
Alabama A&M	11	7	.611	14	15	.483
Jackson St	10	8	.555	14	20	.412
Southern Univ.	9	9	.500	11	19	.367
Ark.-Pine Bluff	8	10	.444	13	18	.419
Grambling St	7	11	.389	7	19	.269
Prairie View A&M	6	12	.333	8	22	.267
Alcorn St	6	12	.333	7	24	.226
Texas Southern	6	12	.333	7	25	.219

Sun Belt

EAST	Conference W	L	Pct	All Games W	L	Pct
*Western Kentucky	16	2	.889	29	7	.806
South Alabama	16	2	.889	26	7	.788
Mid. Tennessee St	11	7	.611	17	15	.531
Florida Atlantic	8	10	.444	15	18	.455
Florida Int'l	6	12	.333	9	20	.310
Troy	4	14	.222	12	19	.387
WEST						
Ark.-Little Rock	11	7	.611	20	11	.645
La.-Lafayette	11	7	.611	15	15	.500
North Texas	10	8	.556	20	11	.645
New Orleans	8	10	.444	19	13	.594
Denver	7	11	.389	11	19	.367
Arkansas St	5	13	.278	10	20	.333
La.-Monroe	4	14	.222	10	21	.323

West Coast

	Conference W	L	Pct	All Games W	L	Pct
Gonzaga	13	1	.929	25	8	.758
St. Mary's (Ca.)	12	2	.857	25	7	.781
*San Diego	11	3	.786	22	14	.611
Santa Clara	6	8	.429	15	16	.484
San Francisco	5	9	.357	10	21	.323
Pepperdine	4	10	.286	11	21	.344
Portland	3	11	.214	9	22	.290
Loyola-Marymount	2	12	.143	5	26	.161

Western Athletic

	Conference W	L	Pct	All Games W	L	Pct
*Boise St	12	4	.750	25	9	.735
Utah St	12	4	.750	24	11	.686
Nevada	12	4	.750	21	12	.636
New Mexico St	12	4	.750	21	14	.600
Hawaii	7	9	.563	11	19	.367
Fresno St	5	11	.313	13	19	.406
Idaho	5	11	.313	8	21	.276
San Jose St	4	12	.250	13	19	.406
Louisiana Tech	3	13	.188	6	24	.200

Independents

	All Games W	L	Pct
Tex.-Pan American	18	13	.581
Utah Valley St	15	14	.517
Savannah St	13	18	.419
Winston-Salem	12	18	.400
Chicago St	11	17	.393
Longwood	9	22	.290
CSU-Bakersfield	8	21	.276
Presbyterian	5	25	.167
North Carolina Central	4	26	.133
New Jersey Inst. of Tech.	0	29	.000

*Conference tournament winner.

NCAA Men's Division I Individual Leaders*

Scoring

	Class	GP	FG	3FG	FT	Pts	Avg
Reggie Williams, Virginia Military Inst.	Sr.	25	269	43	114	695	27.8
Charron Fisher, Niagara	Sr.	29	256	69	219	800	27.6
Michael Beasley, Kansas St	Fr.	33	307	36	216	866	26.2
Stephen Curry, Davidson	So.	36	317	162	135	931	25.9
Lester Hudson, Tenn.-Martin	Jr.	33	291	124	141	847	25.7
Arizona Reid, High Point	Sr.	31	304	34	100	742	23.9
Stefon Jackson, UTEP	Jr.	33	261	35	221	778	23.6
Robert McIver, Houston	Sr.	34	233	145	190	801	23.6
Bo McCalebb, New Orleans	Sr.	32	261	47	173	742	23.2
David Holston, Chicago St	Jr.	28	202	130	112	646	23.1
Antoine Agudio, Hofstra	Sr.	27	207	84	114	612	22.7
Tyler Hansbrough, North Carolina	Jr.	39	289	0	304	882	22.6
Jaycee Carroll, Utah St	Sr.	35	267	114	137	785	22.4
Greg Sprink, Navy	Sr.	30	189	76	199	653	21.8
DeMario Anderson, Quinnipiac	Sr.	28	220	35	132	607	21.7
George Hill, IUPUI	Jr.	32	220	49	199	688	21.5
Donovan Morris, Long Beach St	Jr.	31	202	75	177	656	21.2
Ryan Anderson, Califorina	So.	33	230	64	173	697	21.1
Robert Vaden, UAB	Jr.	33	220	142	113	695	21.1
Tyrese Rice, Boston College	Jr.	30	200	64	165	629	21.0
Eric Gordon, Indiana	Fr.	32	184	70	231	669	20.9
Jonathan Rodriguez, Campbell	So.	30	202	14	208	626	20.9
Jermaine Taylor, Central Florida	Jr.	31	231	79	105	646	20.8
Manny Ubilla, Farleigh Dickinson	Sr.	28	178	93	133	582	20.8
O.J. Mayo, USC	Fr.	33	237	88	122	684	20.7

FIELD-GOAL PERCENTAGE

	Class	GP	FG	FGA	Pct
Kenny George, UNC-Asheville	Jr.	28	151	217	69.6
Vladimir Kuljanin, UNC-Wilmington	Sr.	33	188	282	66.7
Matt Nelson, Boise St	Sr.	33	202	312	64.7
Ahmad Nivins, St. Joseph's	Jr.	33	165	255	64.7
Will Thomas, George Mason	Sr.	34	208	324	64.2
Andrew Strait, Montana	Sr.	30	166	260	63.8
Dwayne Curtis, Mississippi	Sr.	35	212	335	63.3
Arinze Onuaku, Syracuse	Jr.	35	186	296	62.8
Marreese Speights, Florida	So.	36	216	346	62.4
Jordan Hill, Arizona	So.	34	184	297	62.0

Note: Minimum 5 made per game.

REBOUNDS

	Class	GP	Reb	Avg
Michael Beasley, Kansas St	Fr.	33	408	12.4
Jason Thompson, Rider	Sr.	34	412	12.1
Jon Brockman, Washington	Jr.	32	370	11.6
Durell Vinson, Wagner	Sr.	31	358	11.5
Marqus Blakely, Vermont	So.	29	320	11.0
Arizona Reid, High Point	Sr.	31	342	11.0
Boubacar Coly, Morgan St	Sr.	33	361	10.9
Ryan Bright, Sam Houston St	Sr.	31	337	10.9
Kentrell Gransberry, South Florida	Sr.	30	325	10.8
Thomas Sanders, Gardner-Webb	Sr.	32	346	10.8

FREE-THROW PERCENTAGE

	Class	GP	FT	FTA	Pct
Tyler Relph, St. Bonaventure	Sr.	29	75	80	93.8
Jaycee Carroll, Utah St	Sr.	35	137	149	91.9
Jack McClinton, Miami (Fla.)	Jr.	32	114	124	91.9
Justin Hare, Belmont	Sr.	33	112	122	91.8
Julio Anthony, Eastern Illinois	Sr.	27	75	82	91.5
Mike Schachtner, UW-Green Bay	Jr.	30	104	115	90.4
Josn Akognon, CSU-Fullerton	Jr.	32	107	119	89.9
Louis Dale, Cornell	So.	28	96	107	89.7
Stephen Curry, Davidson	So.	36	135	151	89.4
Deven Mitchell, Missouri St	Sr.	33	159	178	89.3

Note: Minimum 2.5 made per game.

ASSISTS

	Class	GP	A	Avg
Jason Richards, Davidson	Sr.	36	293	8.1
Teejay Bannister, Liberty	Sr.	31	224	7.2
Paul Stoll, Tex.-Pan American	Sr.	31	224	7.2
Jay Greene, Md.-Baltimore County	Jr.	33	236	7.2
Mike Jefferson, High Point	Sr.	31	216	7.0
Nikola Stojakovic, Morehead St	Sr.	30	204	6.8
Greivis Vasquez, Maryland	So.	34	231	6.8
Adam Emmenecker, Drake	Sr.	33	213	6.5
Kris Clark, Utah St	Sr.	35	224	6.4
Tony Lee, Robert Morris	Sr.	34	217	6.4
DeAndre Bray, Jacksonville St	Jr.	29	185	6.4
Josh Jenkins, CSU-Northridge	Jr.	30	191	6.4

*Includes games played in tournaments.

NCAA Men's Division I Individual Leaders *(Cont.)*

THREE-POINT FIELD-GOAL PERCENTAGE

	Class	GP	FG	FGA	Avg
Jaycee Carroll, Utah St	Sr.	35	114	229	49.8
Chad Toppert, New Mexico	Jr.	33	85	177	48.0
Shawn Huff, Valparaiso	Sr.	36	91	190	47.9
Darnelle Harris, LaSalle	Sr.	32	123	257	47.9
Henry Salter, TCU	Jr.	24	62	130	47.7
Paul Stoll, Tex.-Pan American	Sr.	31	86	181	47.5
Josh Mayo, Ill.-Chicago	Jr.	33	94	200	47.0
Shan Foster, Vanderbilt	Sr.	34	134	286	46.9
Ryan Whitman, Cornell	So.	28	78	170	45.9
Pete Campbell, Butler	Sr.	31	102	223	45.7

Note: Minimum 2.5 made per game.

BLOCKED SHOTS

	Class	GP	BS	Avg
Jarvis Varnado, Mississippi St	So.	34	157	4.6
Mickell Gladness, Alabama A&M	Sr.	29	131	4.5
Hasheem Thabeet, Connecticut	So.	33	147	4.5
Kleon Penn, McNeese St	Sr.	29	117	4.0
Shawn James, Duquesne	Jr.	28	111	4.0
Jerome Jordan, Tulsa	So.	39	143	3.7
Tyrelle Blair, Boston College	Sr.	31	105	3.4
Kenny George, UNC-Asheville	Jr.	28	93	3.3
Kyle Hines, UNC-Greensboro	Sr.	31	95	3.1
Hamady N'Diaye, Rutgers	So.	31	93	3.0

THREE-POINT FIELD GOALS MADE PER GAME

	Class	GP	3FG	Avg
David Holston, Chicago St	Jr.	28	130	4.6
Stephen Curry, Davidson	So.	36	162	4.5
Robert Vaden, UAB	Jr.	33	142	4.3
Robert McKiver, Houston	Sr.	34	145	4.3
Garrison Carr, American	Jr.	33	135	4.1
Jack Leasure, Coastal Carolina	Sr.	28	111	4.0
Shan Foster, Vanderbilt	Sr.	34	134	3.9
Darnelle Harris, LaSalle	Sr.	32	123	3.8
Leemire Goldwire, Charlotte	Sr.	34	128	3.8
Lester Hudson, Tenn. Martin	Jr.	33	124	3.8

STEALS

	Class	GP	S	Avg
Devin Gibson, Tex.-San Antonio	Fr.	28	93	3.3
Devan Downey, South Carolina	So.	32	103	3.2
Chris Gaynor, Winthrop	Sr.	34	97	2.9
Lester Hudson, Tenn.-Martin	Jr.	33	94	2.8
Tony Lee, Robert Morris	Sr.	34	95	2.8
Brandon Johnson, Old Dominion	Sr.	34	91	2.7
Toney Douglas, Florida St	Jr.	34	90	2.6
Jonathan Amos, Toledo	Jr.	30	78	2.6
Cedric Jackson, Cleveland St	Jr.	34	88	2.6
Paul Stoll, Tex.-Pan American	Sr.	31	79	2.5
Derek Wright, Austin Peay	Sr.	35	89	2.5
Jeremy Chappell, Robert Morris	Jr.	32	80	2.5
Mario Chalmers, Kansas	Jr.	39	97	2.5

Single-Game Highs

POINTS

52.........Robert McKiver, Houston, February 27, 2008 (vs. Southern Miss)
46.........Tyrese Rice, Boston College, March 1, 2008 (vs. North Carolina)
45.........Charron Fisher, Niagara, February 10, 2008 (vs. Loyola (Md.))
44.........Michael Beasley, Kansas St, February 23, 2008 (vs. Baylor)
44.........Justin Jonas, Troy, November 14, 2007 (vs. Paul Quinn)

REBOUNDS

24.........Jason Thompson, Rider, February 10, 2008 (vs. Siena)
24.........Michael Beasley, Kansas St, November 9, 2007 (vs. Sacramento St)
23.........J.J. Hickson, North Carolina St, February 16, 2008 (vs. Clemson)
23.........Richard Hendrix, Alabama, November 9, 2007 (vs. Troy)
Six tied with 22.

ASSISTS

20.........Brandon Brooks, Alabama St, March 8, 2008 (vs. Jackson St)
16.........Mitch Johnson, Stanford, March 22, 2008 (vs. Marquette)
Three tied with15.

THREE POINT FIELD GOALS

11.........Gary Patterson, IUPUI, January 31, 2008 (vs. Southern Utah)
10.........Justin Jonas, Troy, February 10, 2008 (vs. South Alabama)
10.........Andre Smith, George Mason, January 19, 2008 (vs. James Madison)
10.........Samuel Haanpaa, Valparaiso, December 15, 2007 (vs. Chicago St)
10.........Steven Rush, North Carolina A&T, November 24, 2007 (vs. DePaul)

STEALS

10.........Lester Hudson, Tenn.-Martin, November 13, 2007 (vs. Central Baptist)
9..........Jerome Dyson, Connecticut, January 8, 2008 (vs. St. John's (N.Y.))
Eight tied with 8.

BLOCKED SHOTS

12.........Shawn James, Duquesne, November 20, 2007 (vs. Oakland)
11.........Tyrelle Blair, Boston College, December 9, 2007 (vs. Maryland)
Six tied with 10.

NCAA Men's Division I Team Leaders

SCORING OFFENSE

	GP	W	L	Pts	Avg
Virginia Military Institute	29	14	15	2649	91.3
North Carolina	39	36	3	3454	88.6
Texas St	29	13	16	2423	83.6
Duke	34	28	6	2830	83.2
Duquesne	30	17	13	2470	82.3
Tennessee	36	31	5	2946	81.8
CSU-Fullerton	33	24	9	2700	81.8
Massachusetts	36	25	11	2934	81.5
Lamar	30	19	11	2445	81.5
Boise St	34	25	9	2767	81.4

SCORING DEFENSE

	GP	W	L	Pts	Avg
Wisconsin	36	31	5	1958	54.4
Stephen F. Austin	32	26	6	1805	56.4
Washington St	35	26	9	1975	56.4
Air Force	30	16	14	1715	57.2
Iowa	32	13	19	1857	58.0
Georgetown	34	28	6	1976	58.1
Butler	34	30	4	1985	58.4
Winthrop	34	22	12	1990	58.5
VCU	32	24	8	1881	58.8
UCLA	39	35	4	2300	59.0

SCORING MARGIN

	Off	Def	Mar
Kansas	80.5	61.5	19.0
Memphis	79.9	61.9	18.0
North Carolina	88.6	72.5	16.1
Davidson	77.9	63.2	14.7
UCLA	73.5	59.0	14.5
Duke	83.2	69.4	13.8
Wisconsin	67.3	54.4	12.9
Gonzaga	76.5	63.8	12.7
St. Mary's (Ca.)	75.7	63.7	12.0
Tennessee	81.8	70.0	11.9

FIELD-GOAL PERCENTAGE

	FG	FGA	Pct
Utah St	923	1797	51.4
Kansas	1176	2314	50.8
Boise St	994	1956	50.8
IUPUI	883	1754	50.3
Pacific	772	1569	49.2
Georgetown	855	1744	49.0
Murray St	812	1659	48.9
Florida	1029	2108	48.8
UNC-Asheville	901	1846	48.8
North Carolina	1250	2564	48.8

FIELD-GOAL PERCENTAGE DEFENSE

	Opp FG	Opp FGA	Opp Pct
Georgetown	669	1827	36.6
Mississippi St	790	2137	37.0
Kansas	853	2249	37.9
VCU	647	1698	38.1
Wisconsin	719	1879	38.3
Connecticut	839	2170	38.7
Sam Houston St	668	1727	38.7
Louisville	774	1997	38.8
Texas	861	2214	38.9
Ohio St	846	2175	38.9
BYU	792	2035	38.9

FREE-THROW PERCENTAGE

	FT	FTA	Pct
Utah St	532	672	79.2
UC-Davis	401	515	77.9
California	533	687	77.6
IUPUI	498	642	77.6
Florida St	529	684	77.3
Houston	552	717	77.0
Loyola (Md.)	541	704	76.8
Denver	373	489	76.3
Cornell	392	515	76.1
Indiana	577	760	75.9
Drake	498	656	75.9

THREE-POINT FIELD GOALS MADE PER GAME

	GP	3FG	Avg
Virginia Military Institute	29	336	11.6
Houston	34	375	11.0
Troy	31	335	10.8
Belmont	34	357	10.5
Lafayette	30	299	10.0
Navy	30	288	9.6
New Hampshire	29	275	9.5
Citadel	30	283	9.4
Drake	33	310	9.4
Butler	34	319	9.4
Tenn.-Martin	33	309	9.4

REBOUNDING MARGIN

	GP	REB	Opp REB	Margin Avg
North Carolina	39	1695	1266	11.0
New Mexico St	35	1461	1149	8.9
Kansas St	33	1362	1086	8.4
UCLA	39	1432	1111	8.2
Kansas	40	1547	1233	7.9
Stanford	36	1409	1129	7.8
Albany	30	1124	905	7.3
Texas A&M	36	1402	1148	7.1
Michigan St	36	1330	1087	6.8
Sam Houston St	31	1278	1069	6.7

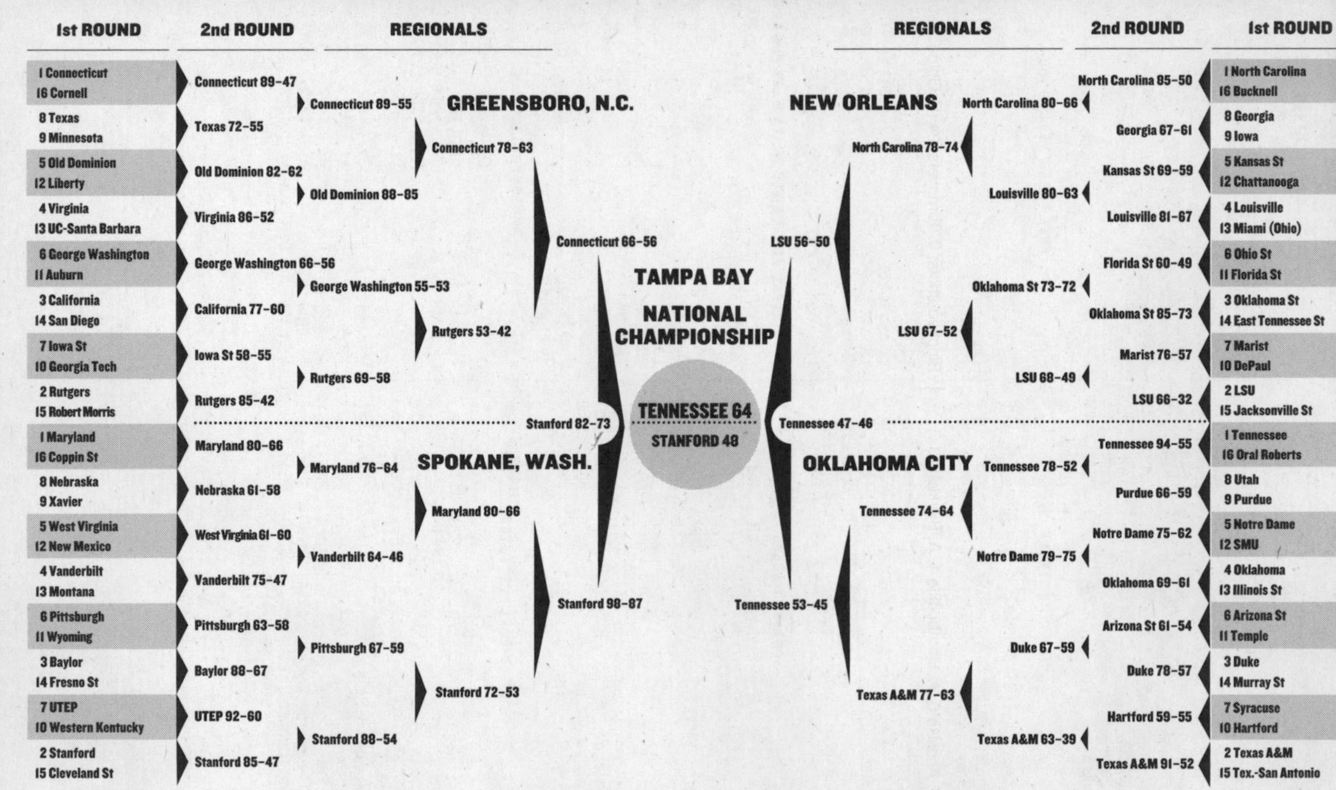

2008 NCAA Basketball Women's Division I Tournament
1st ROUND
2nd ROUND
REGIONALS
REGIONALS
2nd ROUND
1st ROUND
1 Connecticut
16 Cornell
8 Texas
9 Minnesota
5 Old Dominion
12 Liberty
4 Virginia
13 UC-Santa Barbara
6 George Washington
11 Auburn
3 California
14 San Diego
7 Iowa St
10 Georgia Tech
2 Rutgers
15 Robert Morris
1 Maryland
16 Coppin St
8 Nebraska
9 Xavier
5 West Virginia
12 New Mexico
4 Vanderbilt
13 Montana
6 Pittsburgh
11 Wyoming
3 Baylor
14 Fresno St
7 UTEP
10 Western Kentucky
2 Stanford
15 Cleveland St
Connecticut 89–47
Texas 72–55
Old Dominion 82–62
Virginia 86–52
George Washington 66–56
California 77–60
Iowa St 58–55
Rutgers 85–42
Maryland 80–66
Nebraska 61–58
West Virginia 61–60
Vanderbilt 75–47
Pittsburgh 63–58
Baylor 88–67
UTEP 92–60
Stanford 85–47
Connecticut 89–55
Old Dominion 88–85
George Washington 55–53
Rutgers 69–58
Maryland 76–64
Vanderbilt 64–46
Pittsburgh 67–59
Stanford 88–54
GREENSBORO, N.C.
Connecticut 78–63
Rutgers 53–42
Connecticut 66–56
SPOKANE, WASH.
Maryland 80–66
Stanford 72–53
Stanford 98–87
Stanford 82–73
TAMPA BAY
NATIONAL CHAMPIONSHIP
TENNESSEE 64
STANFORD 48
Tennessee 47–46
LSU 56–50
Tennessee 53–45
NEW ORLEANS
North Carolina 78–74
LSU 67–52
OKLAHOMA CITY
Tennessee 74–64
Texas A&M 77–63
North Carolina 80–66
Louisville 80–63
Oklahoma St 73–72
LSU 68–49
Tennessee 78–52
Notre Dame 79–75
Duke 67–59
Texas A&M 63–39
North Carolina 85–50
Georgia 67–61
Kansas St 69–59
Louisville 81–67
Florida St 60–49
Oklahoma St 85–73
Marist 76–57
LSU 66–32
Tennessee 94–55
Purdue 66–59
Notre Dame 75–62
Oklahoma 69–61
Arizona St 61–54
Duke 78–57
Hartford 59–55
Texas A&M 91–52
1 North Carolina
16 Bucknell
8 Georgia
9 Iowa
5 Kansas St
12 Chattanooga
4 Louisville
13 Miami (Ohio)
6 Ohio St
11 Florida St
3 Oklahoma St
14 East Tennessee St
7 Marist
10 DePaul
2 LSU
15 Jacksonville St
1 Tennessee
16 Oral Roberts
8 Utah
9 Purdue
5 Notre Dame
12 SMU
4 Oklahoma
13 Illinois St
6 Arizona St
11 Temple
3 Duke
14 Murray St
7 Syracuse
10 Hartford
2 Texas A&M
15 Tex.-San Antonio

NCAA Women's Championship Game Box Score

Tennessee 64

	Min	FG M-A	FT M-A	Reb O-T	A	PF	TP
C. Parker	37	5–10	7–11	1–9	1	2	17
A. Auguste	39	3–7	1–2	3–7	2	4	7
N. Anosike	29	6–11	0–1	3–8	0	3	12
S. Bobbitt	37	4–12	2–2	0–0	0	0	13
A. Hornbuckle	28	1–7	4–5	0–1	3	3	6
A. Bjorklund	15	0–5	0–0	1–1	0	0	0
S. Smallbone	1	0–0	1–2	0–1	0	0	1
V. Baugh	13	3–4	2–2	3–4	0	2	8
A. Fuller	1	0–0	0–0	0–0	0	0	0
Totals		22–56	17–25	11–31	6	14	64

Percentages: FG-.393, FT-.680, 3-pt goals: 3–9, .333 (S. Bobbitt 3–8, A. Bjorklund 0–1). Team rebounds: 7. Blocked shots: 2 (N. Anosike 1, C. Parker1). Turnovers: 14 (S. Bobbitt 3, N. Anosike 2, C. Parker 4, A. Hornbuckle 2, A. Auguste 3). Steals: 13 (C. Parker 4, N. Anosike 6, A. Hornbuckle 1, A. Bjorklund 1, A. Auguste 1).

Halftime: Tennessee 37, Stanford 29
Final Four Most Outstanding Player: Candace Parker
A: 21,655.

Stanford 48

	Min	FG M-A	FT M-A	Reb O-T	A	PF	TP
K. Pedersen	37	2–7	3–4	2–10	0	4	7
J. Appel	36	6–13	4–10	3–5	3	5	16
J. Hones	34	2–5	0–0	0–2	3	2	5
C. Wiggins	39	6–16	0–0	1–4	1	3	14
R. G-Onwude	16	1–2	0–0	0–3	0	2	2
C. Pierce	1	0–0	0–0	0–0	0	0	0
H. Donaghe	1	0–0	0–0	0–0	0	0	0
J. Pohlen	10	0–2	0–0	0–1	0	1	0
A. Cimino	1	0–0	0–0	0–0	0	0	0
M. Clyburn	1	0–1	0–0	0–0	0	0	0
J. Harmon	24	2–3	0–0	2–4	1	4	4
Totals		19–49	7–14	8–29	8	21	48

Percentages: FG-.388, FT-.500, 3-pt goals: 3-11, .273 (J. Hones 1–2, J. Pohlen 0–1, K. Pedersen 0–2, C. Wiggins 2–5, M. Clyburn 0–1). Team rebounds: 7. Blocked shots: 0. Turnovers: 24 (R. Gold-Onwude 4, J. Hones 4, J. Pohlen 1, J. Harmon 3, C. Wiggins 6, K. Pedersen 2, J. Appel 4). Steals: 7 (C. Wiggins 4, J. Harmon 1, R. Gold-Onwude 1, J. Appel 1).

Officials: Eric Brewton, D. Brooks-Clauser, Dee Kantner.

NCAA Women's Division I Individual Leaders

SCORING

Player and Team	Class	GP	TFG	3FG	FT	Pts	Avg
Amber Holt, Middle Tennessee St	Sr.	34	352	20	206	930	27.4
Natalie Doma, Idaho St	Sr.	30	272	25	173	742	24.7
Sade Logan, Robert Morris	Jr.	33	305	126	79	815	24.7
Angel McCoughtry, Louisville	Jr.	36	321	50	166	858	23.8
Andrea Riley, Oklahoma St	So.	35	268	70	201	807	23.1
Crystal Kelly, Western Kentucky	Sr.	34	251	5	260	767	22.6
Amanda Jackson, Miami (Ohio)	Sr.	33	239	59	175	712	21.6
Candace Parker, Tennessee	Jr.	38	300	8	201	809	21.3
Traci Edwards, UW-Milwaukee	Jr.	31	201	20	217	639	20.6
Valerie Nainima, Long Island	So.	32	216	86	135	653	20.4
Tamera Young, James Madison	Sr.	34	259	14	161	693	20.4
Candice Wiggins, Stanford	Sr.	39	258	87	184	787	20.2
Heather Bowman, Gonzaga	So.	29	217	0	150	584	20.1
Jolene Anderson, Wisconsin	Sr.	30	232	57	77	598	19.9
Kailey Klein, Cleveland St	So.	33	199	45	211	654	19.8
Daphanie Kennedy, Pepperdine	Sr.	28	198	46	107	549	19.6
Johnna Lewis-Carlisle, IPFW	Sr.	30	208	47	121	584	19.5
Krystal Ellis, Marquette	Jr.	31	212	67	110	601	19.4
Allie Quigley, DePaul	Sr.	32	224	57	115	620	19.4
Shantia Grace, South Florida	Jr.	31	183	75	152	593	19.1
Laura Menty, Siena	Sr.	29	193	0	167	553	19.1
Gabriela Marginean, Drexel	So.	30	213	26	118	570	19.0
Katherine Plummer, Nicholls St	Sr.	27	172	26	140	510	18.9
Jackie McFarland, Colorado	Sr.	34	209	16	203	637	18.7
Joyce Ekworomadu, Texas St	Sr.	32	201	82	113	597	18.7

NCAA Women's Division I Individual Leaders *(Cont.)*

FIELD-GOAL PERCENTAGE

Player and Team	Class	GP	FG	FGA	Pct
Crystal Langhorne, Maryland	Sr.	31	211	326	64.7
Crystal Kelly, Western Ky	Sr.	34	251	390	64.4
Carolyn Swords, Boston College	Fr.	33	192	299	64.2
Tina Charles, Connecticut	So.	38	220	364	60.4
Sarah Acker, St. Joseph's	Fr.	31	155	260	59.6
Ta'Shia Phillips, Xavier	Fr.	33	192	323	59.4
Olayinka Sanni, West Virginia	Sr.	33	227	386	58.8
Jayne Appel, Stanford	So.	39	251	427	58.8
Shawntawnee Collins, Alcorn St.	Sr.	30	162	276	58.7
Sylvia Fowles, LSU	Sr.	35	239	409	58.4

Note: Minimum 5 FG per game.

REBOUNDS

Player and Team	Class	GP	Reb	Avg
Courtney Paris, Oklahoma	Jr.	31	466	15.0
Natalie Doma, Idaho St	Sr.	30	371	12.4
Tanya Smith, Hawaii	Sr.	30	353	11.8
Khadijah Whittington, N.C. St.	Sr.	34	398	11.7
Tia Lewis, Central Florida	Fr.	30	345	11.5
Ta'Shia Phillips, Xavier	Fr.	33	371	11.2
Laura Markwood, Miami (Ohio)	Sr.	34	359	10.6
Crystal Kelly, Western Kentucky	Sr	34	357	10.5
Noteisha Womack, Seton Hall	Jr.	21	220	10.5
Tamera Young, James Madison	Sr.	34	352	10.4

FREE-THROW PERCENTAGE

Player and Team	Class	GP	FT	FTA	Pct
Gabriela Marginean, Drexel	So.	30	118	129	91.5
Laiken Dollente, Portland St.	So.	30	139	152	91.4
Crystal Jones, Eastern Kentucky	Sr.	28	88	97	90.7
Andrea Lightfoot, Idaho St	Sr.	30	145	161	90.1
Jacqui Kalin, Northern Iowa	Fr.	31	89	99	89.9
Amber Guffey, Murray St	Jr.	32	179	201	89.1
Jessica Campbell, UC-Davis	Sr.	31	104	117	88.9
Sara Tuomi, Weber St	Sr.	27	127	143	88.8
Lauren Kohn, Ohio	Sr.	33	104	118	88.1
Megan Frazee, Liberty	Jr.	32	151	172	87.8

Note: Minimum 2.5 made per game.

ASSISTS

Player and Team	Class	GP	A	Avg
Claire Faucher, Portland St	So.	31	274	8.8
Amanda Rego, San Diego	Sr.	32	272	8.5
Tiera DeLaHoussaye, W. Michigan	Jr.	32	251	7.8
Leilani Mitchell, Utah	Sr.	32	240	7.5
Kristi Toliver, Maryland	Jr.	37	275	7.4
Patrika Barlow, Louisville	Sr.	36	251	7.0
Kate Archer, Bowling Green	Sr.	34	234	6.9
Christine Kinneary, Boston Univ.	Jr.	32	214	6.7
Shantae Robinson, Alabama St	Sr.	29	193	6.7
Sharneé Zoll, Virginia	Sr.	34	216	6.4

THREE-POINT FIELD-GOAL PERCENTAGE

	Class	GP	3FG	3FGA	Pct
Sonya Rogers, Montana	Jr.	32	72	148	48.6
Whitney Lewis, Wright St	Sr.	29	58	122	47.5
Wendy Ausdemore, Iowa	Jr.	32	78	171	45.6
Meg Bulger, West Virginia	Sr.	30	83	187	44.4
Audrey McDonald, Ball St	So.	30	81	184	44.0
Amber Guffey, Murray St	Jr.	32	72	165	43.6
Joyce Ekworomadu, Texas St	Sr.	32	82	188	43.6
Gretchen Gregg, Cornell	Sr.	29	59	136	43.4
Gabrielle Cottrell, Manhattan	Sr.	30	74	171	43.3
Jordan Zuppe, IPFW	Fr.	30	74	171	43.3

Note: Minimum 2.0 made per game.

BLOCKED SHOTS

	Class	GP	BS	Avg
Louella Tomlinson, St. Mary's (Ca.)	Fr.	32	156	4.9
Brittany Pittman, Morehead St	So.	30	123	4.1
Allyssa DeHaan, Michigan St	So.	37	150	4.1
Courtney Paris, Oklahoma	Jr.	31	108	3.5
Kaitlin Sowinski, Sacred Heart	Jr.	30	101	3.4
Ashley Ingle, Northern Arizona	Jr.	30	99	3.3
Julia Whitted, IUPUI	So.	33	105	3.2
Tina Huff, Alcorn St	Sr.	26	82	3.2
Crystal Hahs, CSU-Northridge	Jr.	27	76	2.8
Kelli Darden, Radford	Sr.	35	98	2.8
Amber Harris, Xavier	So.	33	92	2.8

NCAA Men's Division II Individual Leaders

SCORING

Player and Team	Class	GP	TFG	3FG	FT	Pts	Avg
Michael Sturns, Holy Family	Sr.	31	292	56	184	824	26.6
Chris Commons, S.C.-Aiken	Jr.	31	258	48	111	675	21.8
Chris Banal, West Liberty St	Sr.	29	233	44	113	623	21.5
Jelani Jackson, Davis & Elkins	Sr.	28	222	25	132	601	21.5
Thad McFadden, Fairmont St	Jr.	29	206	110	99	621	21.4
Chris LeBorious, Ohio Valley	Sr.	23	184	16	105	489	21.3
Sean Barnette, Wingate	Sr.	31	245	46	121	657	21.2
Brian Stamer, Colorado Christian	Sr.	31	245	9	151	650	21.0
Matt Hall, Harding	Sr.	31	199	53	192	643	20.7
Kyle Pape, Colorado Mines	Jr.	29	196	54	155	601	20.7
Scooby Johnson, Texas A&M-Commerce	Sr.	30	232	15	142	621	20.7
Will Stephensen, Oklahoma Panhandle	Sr.	26	205	31	97	538	20.7
Austin Randel, North Greenville	So.	27	185	83	105	558	20.7
Billy Arre, Lock Haven	Jr.	26	190	66	90	536	20.6
Drake Beranek, Neb.-Kearney	So.	29	209	67	110	595	20.5

NCAA Men's Division II Individual Leaders *(Cont.)*

REBOUNDS

Player and Team	Class	GP	Reb	Avg
Vincent Falzone, Molloy	Sr.	27	334	12.4
Jeff Fahnbulleh, Kentucky Wesleyan	Sr.	29	350	12.1
Mike Zuiderveen, Saginaw Valley	Sr.	26	313	12.0
Anthony Hilliard, Elizabeth City St	Jr.	27	308	11.4
Jeremy Black, Tampa	Sr.	30	331	11.0
Nick Kohs, Christian Brothers	Jr.	32	348	10.9
Leslie Malone, Cameron	Jr.	27	289	10.7
Norman Plummer, Southern Indiana	Sr.	27	289	10.7
Atila Santos, Minn. St-Mankato	Sr.	29	308	10.6
Stephan Bolt, Lewis	Sr.	31	328	10.6

ASSISTS

Player and Team	Class	GP	A	Avg
Luke Cooper, Ak.-Anchorage	Sr.	35	310	8.9
Ronnie Means, Fairmont St	Sr.	29	238	8.2
Ryan Ballard, Florida Tech	Jr.	28	210	7.5
William Kane, Armstrong Atlantic	Sr.	28	207	7.4
Jonny Reibel, Rollins	Sr.	28	202	7.2
Darren Duncan, Merrimack	So.	29	208	7.2
T. J. Smith, Kentucky Wesleyan	Jr.	32	222	6.9
Timmy Crowell, Fort Lewis	Sr.	30	206	6.9
Dusty Wabiszewski, St. Cloud St	Sr.	28	189	6.8
Jerod Haynes, Angelo St	Sr.	27	182	6.7
Hayden Heiber, Chaminade	Sr.	29	193	6.7

FIELD-GOAL PERCENTAGE

Player and Team	Class	GP	FG	FGA	Pct
Garret Siler, Augusta St	Jr.	34	211	277	76.2
Dzaflo Larkai, Bellarmine	Sr.	28	192	281	68.3
Brandon Streeter, Mt. Olive	Sr.	29	184	272	67.6
Kenny Jones, Kentucky St	Sr.	28	188	280	67.1
Kyle Goldcamp, Gannon	Jr.	31	187	281	66.5
Willie Shaw, District of Columbia	Sr.	19	131	198	66.2
Bryan Grier, Wingate	Sr.	29	153	232	65.9
Rece Hampton, Adams St	Sr.	27	181	278	65.1
Kenney Boyd, Morehouse	Jr.	25	169	260	65.0
Ben Mohr, Colorado Mines	Sr.	24	132	205	64.4

Note: Minimum 5 made per game.

FREE-THROW PERCENTAGE

Player and Team	Class	GP	FT	FTA	Pct
Jake Linton, St. Martin's	Jr.	27	162	168	96.4
Rory Morgan, Colorado Christian	Sr.	31	85	90	94.4
Darroll Phillips, CSU-Chico	Jr.	27	83	88	94.3
Chris Diasparra, Adelphi	Jr.	30	75	81	92.6
Chris Vetrano, St. Anselm	Sr.	27	87	97	89.7
Rodney Edgerson, Ky. Wesleyan	Sr.	29	124	139	89.2
Kyle Pape, Colorado Mines	Jr.	29	155	174	89.1
Steve Dagostino, St. Rose	Sr.	31	191	215	88.8
Brett Barlett, Ashland	Sr.	27	79	89	88.8
Pierce Caldwell, Incarnate Word	So.	28	91	104	87.5
A. Tsagarakis, Cal Poly-Pomona	Sr.	28	84	96	87.5
Andray Glenn, Grand Canyon	Jr.	26	70	80	87.5

Note: Minimum 2.5 made per game.

NCAA Women's Division II Individual Leaders

SCORING

Player and Team	Class	GP	TFG	3FG	FT	Pts	Avg
Katie Cezat, Hillsdale	Jr.	28	266	0	141	673	24.0
Celeste Trahan, Elizabeth City St	Sr.	24	198	2	171	569	23.7
Johannah Leedham, Franklin Pierce	So.	33	262	54	180	758	23.0
Lauren Beckley, Shippensburg	So.	28	217	55	135	624	22.3
Georgia Mueller, Truman	Jr.	29	250	10	128	638	22.0
Kate Lynch, Southern Connecticut St	Sr.	29	213	37	169	632	21.8
Emily Brister, West Texas A&M	Jr.	31	219	39	198	675	21.8
Michelle Stueve, Emporia St	Sr.	31	213	102	146	674	21.7
Toni Jones, Goldey-Beacom	Sr.	27	231	12	107	581	21.5
Amber Shelton, SIU-Edwardsville	Sr.	28	218	19	147	602	21.5
Lacey Goldwire, East Central	Sr.	25	172	26	157	527	21.1
Syretha Marble, North Georgia	Jr.	29	222	21	132	597	20.6
Jessica Keller, Quincy	Jr.	30	207	30	172	616	20.5
Sarah Van Horn, West Virginia Wesleyan	Jr.	30	218	3	167	606	20.2
Shantrell Moss, Clark Atlanta	Fr.	21	136	16	134	422	20.1

REBOUNDS

Player and Team	Class	GP	Reb	Avg
Celeste Trahan, Elizabeth City St	Sr.	24	382	15.9
Vanessa Wilt, CSU-San Bernardino	Sr.	29	388	13.4
Katie Cezat, Hillsdale	Jr.	28	353	12.6
Bianca Burton, Stillman	Sr.	30	369	12.3
Delmara Reece, Mercy	Fr.	27	332	12.3
Karina Kendrick, Glenville St	Sr.	30	358	11.9
Stephany Neptune, Tusculum	Jr.	31	351	11.3
Brooke Burgess, Palm Beach Atl.	So.	27	304	11.3
Lauren Beckley, Shippensburg	So.	28	310	11.1
Nikki Anthony, Anderson (S.C.)	Sr.	32	349	10.9
Michelle Osier, UC-San Diego	Jr.	35	380	10.9
Jennifer Robbins, Queens (N.Y.)	So.	28	304	10.9

ASSISTS

Player and Team	Class	GP	A	Avg
Lisa Perry, West Liberty St	Sr.	30	290	9.7
Katie LaViolette, Concordia-St. Paul	Sr.	31	262	8.5
Anna Atikinson, Wingate	Jr.	34	281	8.3
Erika Stupinski, Stonehill	Sr.	31	244	7.9
Jamie Cluesman, Concord	Sr.	29	211	7.3
Lynne-Ann Kokosi, Bryant	Sr.	32	213	6.7
Amy Lawson, Bemidji St	Sr.	28	186	6.6
Tricia Everett, Saginaw Valley	Jr.	27	174	6.4
Breanne Burley, Regis (Colo.)	Sr.	26	167	6.4
Ashley Grimm, Clarion	Sr.	27	171	6.3
Catherine Rottier, Michigan Tech	Sr.	30	189	6.3

NCAA Women's Division II Individual Leaders (Cont.)

FIELD-GOAL PERCENTAGE

Player and Team	Class	GP	FG	FGA	Pct
Allison Rosel, Fort Lewis	So.	30	169	247	68.4
Andi Winney, Lincoln Memorial	So.	28	155	235	66.0
Jessica Fesenmaier, MSU-M'rhead	Sr.	29	185	293	63.1
Shannon Malone, Bridgeport	So.	28	192	328	58.5
Amy Achesinski, Mercyhurst	Fr.	27	156	267	58.4
Katie Cezat, Hillsdale	Jr.	28	266	457	58.2
Mattie Jones, Kentucky St.	Jr.	31	160	277	57.8
Brittany Wells, Findlay	Jr.	26	134	232	57.8
Kierah Kimbrough, North Dakota	Jr.	31	223	387	57.6
NeKeithia Howard, Catawba	Sr.	28	161	282	57.1

Note: Minimum 5 FG per game.

FREE-THROW PERCENTAGE

Player and Team	Class	GP	FT	FTA	Pct
Amber Rutherford, N. Alabama	Jr.	28	132	141	93.6
Lindsey Maple, Central Missouri	Sr.	28	146	161	90.7
Brittany Brooks, Ohio Valley	Jr.	21	85	94	90.4
Jamey Gelhar, St. Martin's	So.	28	72	80	90.0
Emily Jones, Charleston (W.V.)	Sr.	28	80	89	89.9
Amy Mathis, Neb.-Kearney	Sr.	34	132	147	89.8
Lindsay Cale, Pitt.-Johnstown	Jr.	28	87	97	89.7
Cayla Hargrove, Neb.-Omaha	Jr.	29	77	86	89.5
Katrina Greer, Clarion	Jr.	27	127	142	89.4
Jenny Steffen, Winona St.	Fr.	30	84	94	89.4

Note: Minimum 2.5 made per game.

NCAA Men's Division III Individual Leaders

SCORING

Player and Team	Class	GP	TFG	3FG	FT	Pts	Avg
John Grotberg, Grinnell	Jr.	24	212	140	111	675	28.1
Jake Baldwin, Piedmont	Sr.	26	270	30	134	704	27.1
Nick Harrington, Southern Vermont	Sr.	24	247	1	152	647	27.0
Ben Strong, Guilford	Sr.	29	289	1	168	747	25.8
Kent Raymond, Wheaton (Ill.)	Jr.	30	237	75	185	734	24.5
Ryan Jaziri, New England	Sr.	25	215	56	121	607	24.3
Anthony Williams, Plattsburgh St.	Sr.	30	236	84	171	727	24.2
Jimmy Bartolotta, MIT	Jr.	24	208	59	99	574	23.9
Dante Blanton-Holcombe, Lincoln (Pa.)	Jr.	26	201	86	126	614	23.6
Chad McGowan, York (Pa.)	Sr.	24	211	5	134	561	23.4
Douglas Hammond, Green Mountain	Sr.	25	242	1	99	584	23.4
Tom Conboy, Macalester	Sr.	25	229	29	84	581	23.2
Steve Djurickovic, Carthage	Fr.	25	189	16	186	580	23.2
Richard Jean-Baptiste, Brooklyn	So.	27	222	60	111	615	22.8
Wes Ladwig, Carroll (Wisc.)	Jr.	24	174	41	153	542	22.6

REBOUNDS

Player and Team	Class	GP	Reb	Avg
Nick Harrington, S. Vermont	Sr.	24	369	15.4
Douglas Hammond, Green Mtn.	Sr.	25	367	14.7
Daniel Waajid, Pitt.-Greensburg	Jr.	23	270	11.7
Jose Guitian, Lasell	Jr.	29	340	11.7
Jeff Bostic, Ithaca	Jr.	24	279	11.6
Ryan Phillip, City Tech	Jr.	27	305	11.3
Tom Bicknell, Scranton	Sr.	28	316	11.3
Drew Baker, Centenary	Jr.	24	270	11.3
Travis Gorham, Plattsburgh St	Sr.	30	336	11.2
Jeremiah Lawrence, Shenandoah	Sr.	26	290	11.2

FIELD-GOAL PERCENTAGE

Player and Team	Class	GP	FG	FGA	Pct
Keith Pedersen, Central (Ia.)	Sr.	24	124	178	69.7
Kyle Meyer, Ohio Northern	So.	27	136	209	65.1
Jeff Skemp, UW-Platteville	Jr.	26	163	252	64.7
Marty Young, Franklin	Sr.	28	157	248	63.3
Femi Solaja, Augsburg	Sr.	25	149	238	62.6
Jake Baldwin, Piedmont	Sr.	26	270	432	62.5
Phil Stricker, DeSales	Sr.	27	152	245	62.0
Mark Carson, Rochester Inst. Tech.	Jr.	25	162	262	61.8
Brent Ruch, Elmhurst	Jr.	26	173	280	61.8
Christopher Orr, Maryville (Tenn.)	So.	27	137	222	61.7

Note: Minimum 5 made per game.

ASSISTS

Player and Team	Class	GP	A	Avg
David Arseneault, Grinnell	Jr.	21	219	10.4
Corey McAdam, Nazareth	So.	28	244	8.7
Reece Freeman, Mass.-Dartmouth	Jr.	29	222	7.7
Adam Fisher, Green Mountain	Sr.	25	190	7.6
Eddie Ohlson, DeSales	Sr.	27	199	7.4
Andrew Olson, Amherst	Sr.	31	223	7.2
Davon Barton, Chris. Newport	Jr.	26	187	7.2
Ajani Edwards, SUNY-IT	Jr.	25	174	7.0
Mike Moore, DePauw	Jr.	26	168	6.5
Jason Seipt, Delaware Valley	Jr.	24	155	6.5

FREE-THROW PERCENTAGE

Player and Team	Class	GP	FT	FTA	Pct
Ryan Junghans, Hood	Jr.	26	118	123	95.9
Ryan Miller, Moravian	Sr.	25	64	68	94.1
Kris Saiberlich, Lakeland	Sr.	28	89	95	93.7
Aaron Regal, Lakeland	Sr.	28	98	107	91.6
Sherrod Harris, Brockport St	Sr.	24	94	103	91.3
Michael Tierney, Cornell Coll.	Jr.	21	61	67	91.0
Kevin Herring, Case Reserve	Fr.	25	76	84	90.5
Brandon Fortes, Worcester St.	So.	25	72	80	90.0
Ben Huntington, Plymouth St.	Jr.	26	72	80	90.0
Kyle Opitz, Juniata	Sr.	28	116	129	89.9

Note: Minimum 2.5 made per game.

NCAA Women's Division III Individual Leaders

SCORING

Player and Team	Class	GP	TFG	3FG	FT	Pts	Avg
Lindsay Ippel, Millikin	Sr.	27	248	3	180	679	25.1
Pamela Robinson, SUNY-Old Westbury	So.	26	203	20	191	617	23.7
Emilee Ackerman, Westminster (Pa.)	Sr.	26	194	5	218	611	23.5
Shadae Swan, Goucher	Sr.	24	197	33	111	538	22.4
Megan Scheele, Edgewood	Jr.	28	243	1	124	611	21.8
Chelsie Schweers, Christopher Newport	Fr.	28	217	80	90	604	21.6
Jessica Carter, Mary Baldwin	Sr.	25	192	66	76	526	21.0
Alison Kessler, St. Mary's (Ind.)	Sr.	26	161	53	169	544	20.9
Juliana Eagles, Anna Maria	So.	25	166	79	109	520	20.8
Jessica McEntee, New York Univ.	Jr.	25	152	20	196	520	20.8
Erica Eneks, Ozarks (Ark.)	Sr.	25	170	61	109	510	20.4
Colleen Feeney, Bridgewater St	Sr.	27	194	0	160	548	20.3
Julia Fagan, Southern Vermont	Fr.	22	169	18	89	445	20.2
Hannah Wolf, Grinnell	Sr.	23	166	69	64	465	20.2
Dione Eccles, Greensboro	Fr.	23	150	62	102	464	20.2

REBOUNDS

Player and Team	Class	GP	Reb	Avg
Ruchelle Austin, New Rochelle	Sr.	16	287	17.9
Nikki McClease, Albertus Magnus	Fr.	25	359	14.4
Chari' Cooper, Kean	Sr.	32	450	14.1
Kathryn Stockbower, Swarthmore	Fr.	24	335	14.0
Nicole Fisher, Eureka	Sr.	25	336	13.4
Colleen Feeney, Bridgewater St	Sr.	27	354	13.1
Tempestt Casey, City Tech	So.	26	327	12.6
Jacque Calandriello, Polytechnic (N.Y.)	Sr.	24	301	12.5
Allison Moen, Salve Regina	Sr.	23	283	12.3
Kelly Oakes, Cedar Crest	So.	25	305	12.2

ASSISTS

Player and Team	Class	GP	A	Avg
Dani Dudek, Stevens Inst.	Jr.	30	222	7.4
Melanie Auguste, Colorado Coll.	Jr.	26	192	7.4
Sarah Barton, Bates	Sr.	25	177	7.1
Nicole Hall, Meredith	Sr.	24	165	6.9
Chelsea Slater, Rockford	Sr.	25	158	6.6
Ebony Jackson, Kean	Jr.	32	199	6.2
Dankery Perez, SUNY-Farmingdale	Sr.	26	161	6.2
Courtney Musser, Dubuque	Sr.	27	166	6.1
Lindsey Shiomi, La Verne	Jr.	27	166	6.1
Marisa Vespa, William Smith	Sr.	29	177	6.1

FIELD-GOAL PERCENTAGE

Player and Team	Class	GP	FG	FGA	Pct
Julia Hirssig, UW-Stout	So.	27	175	270	64.8
Hilary Klimowicz, TCNJ	Jr.	29	206	320	64.4
Dana Alexander, East Tex. Baptist	So.	24	133	208	63.9
Jessica Salinas, Dominican (Ill.)	So.	25	191	299	63.9
Jessica Mckenzie, Muskingum	Jr.	25	171	268	63.8
Colandra Rollins, Chris. Newport	Sr.	28	187	308	60.7
Lindsay Ippel, Millikin	Sr.	27	248	411	60.3
Christine Halter, D'Youville	Jr.	28	179	297	60.3
Ashley Stanfill, Westminster (Mo.)	Jr.	24	120	202	59.4
Tamika Curtis, Benedictine (Ill.)	Sr.	26	194	328	59.1

Note: Minimum 5 made per game.

FREE-THROW PERCENTAGE

Player and Team	Class	GP	FT	FTA	Pct
Kim Rarick, DeSales	Jr.	30	146	157	93.0
Katie Streck, Wilmington (Ohio)	Sr.	29	94	102	92.2
Mary Padden, Pomona-Pitzer	Fr.	25	105	114	92.1
Kirsty Stearns, Moravian	So.	26	82	90	91.1
Kennan Killeen, Wash. & Jeff	So.	28	102	113	90.3
Holly Stein, Defiance	Fr.	24	84	94	89.4
Jessica Foran, Moravian	So.	22	106	119	89.1
Lindsey Geissler, UW-Stout	Sr.	27	70	79	88.6
Brianne Parra, North Central (Ill.)	Jr.	19	83	95	87.4
Jennifer Dabrowski, W. New England	Sr.	29	116	133	87.2

Note: Minimum 2.5 made per game.

NCAA Men's Division I Championship Results

NCAA Final Four Results

Year	Winner	Score	Runner-up	Third Place	Fourth Place	Winning Coach
1939	Oregon	46–33	Ohio St	*Oklahoma	*Villanova	Howard Hobson
1940	Indiana	60–42	Kansas	*Duquesne	*USC	Branch McCracken
1941	Wisconsin	39–34	Washington St	*Pittsburgh	*Arkansas	Harold Foster
1942	Stanford	53–38	Dartmouth	*Colorado	*Kentucky	Everett Dean
1943	Wyoming	46–34	Georgetown	*Texas	*DePaul	Everett Shelton
1944	Utah	42–40 (OT)	Dartmouth	*Iowa St	*Ohio St	Vadal Peterson
1945	Oklahoma St	49–45	NYU	*Arkansas	*Ohio St	Hank Iba
1946	Oklahoma St	43–40	North Carolina	Ohio St	California	Hank Iba
1947	Holy Cross	58–47	Oklahoma	Texas	CCNY	Alvin Julian
1948	Kentucky	58–42	Baylor	Holy Cross	Kansas St	Adolph Rupp
1949	Kentucky	46–36	Oklahoma St	Illinois	Oregon St	Adolph Rupp
1950	CCNY	71–68	Bradley	North Carolina St	Baylor	Nat Holman
1951	Kentucky	68–58	Kansas St	Illinois	Oklahoma St	Adolph Rupp
1952	Kansas	80–63	St. John's (N.Y.)	Illinois	Santa Clara	Forrest Allen
1953	Indiana	69–68	Kansas	Washington	LSU	Branch McCracken
1954	La Salle	92–76	Bradley	Penn St	USC	Kenneth Loeffler
1955	San Francisco	77–63	La Salle	Colorado	Iowa	Phil Woolpert
1956	San Francisco	83–71	Iowa	Temple	SMU	Phil Woolpert
1957	North Carolina	54–53 (3OT)	Kansas	San Francisco	Michigan St	Frank McGuire
1958	Kentucky	84–72	Seattle	Temple	Kansas St	Adolph Rupp
1959	California	71–70	West Virginia	Cincinnati	Louisville	Pete Newell
1960	Ohio St	75–55	California	Cincinnati	NYU	Fred Taylor
1961	Cincinnati	70–65 (OT)	Ohio St	Vacated‡	Utah	Edwin Jucker
1962	Cincinnati	71–59	Ohio St	Wake Forest	UCLA	Edwin Jucker
1963	Loyola (Ill.)	60–58 (OT)	Cincinnati	Duke	Oregon St	George Ireland
1964	UCLA	98–83	Duke	Michigan	Kansas St	John Wooden
1965	UCLA	91–80	Michigan	Princeton	Wichita St	John Wooden
1966	UTEP	72–65	Kentucky	Duke	Utah	Don Haskins
1967	UCLA	79–64	Dayton	Houston	North Carolina	John Wooden
1968	UCLA	78–55	North Carolina	Ohio St	Houston	John Wooden
1969	UCLA	92–72	Purdue	Drake	North Carolina	John Wooden
1970	UCLA	80–69	Jacksonville	New Mexico St	St. Bonaventure	John Wooden
1971	UCLA	68–62	Vacated‡	Vacated‡	Kansas	John Wooden
1972	UCLA	81–76	Florida St	North Carolina	Louisville	John Wooden
1973	UCLA	87–66	Memphis St	Indiana	Providence	John Wooden
1974	North Carolina St	76–64	Marquette	UCLA	Kansas	Norm Sloan
1975	UCLA	92–85	Kentucky	Louisville	Syracuse	John Wooden
1976	Indiana	86–68	Michigan	UCLA	Rutgers	Bob Knight
1977	Marquette	67–59	North Carolina	UNLV	UNC-Charlotte	Al McGuire
1978	Kentucky	94–88	Duke	Arkansas	Notre Dame	Joe Hall
1979	Michigan St	75–64	Indiana St	DePaul	Penn	Jud Heathcote
1980	Louisville	59–54	Vacated‡	Purdue	Iowa	Denny Crum
1981	Indiana	63–50	North Carolina	Virginia	LSU	Bob Knight
1982	North Carolina	63–62	Georgetown	*Houston	*Louisville	Dean Smith
1983	North Carolina St	54–52	Houston	*Georgia	*Louisville	Jim Valvano
1984	Georgetown	84–75	Houston	*Kentucky	*Virginia	John Thompson
1985	Villanova	66–64	Georgetown	St. John's (N.Y.)	Vacated‡	Rollie Massimino
1986	Louisville	72–69	Duke	*Kansas	*LSU	Denny Crum
1987	Indiana	74–73	Syracuse	*UNLV	*Providence	Bob Knight
1988	Kansas	83–79	Oklahoma	*Arizona	*Duke	Larry Brown
1989	Michigan	80–79 (OT)	Seton Hall	*Duke	*Illinois	Steve Fisher
1990	UNLV	103–73	Duke	*Arkansas	*Georgia Tech	Jerry Tarkanian
1991	Duke	72–65	Kansas	*UNLV	*North Carolina	Mike Krzyzewski
1992	Duke	71–51	Michigan	*Cincinnati	*Indiana	Mike Krzyzewski
1993	North Carolina	77–71	Michigan	*Kansas	*Kentucky	Dean Smith
1994	Arkansas	76–72	Duke	*Arizona	*Florida	Nolan Richardson
1995	UCLA	89–78	Arkansas	*North Carolina	*Oklahoma St	Jim Harrick
1996	Kentucky	76–67	Syracuse	Vacated‡	Mississippi St	Rick Pitino
1997	Arizona	84–79 (OT)	Kentucky	*Minnesota	*North Carolina	Lute Olson
1998	Kentucky	78–69	Utah	*Stanford	*North Carolina	Tubby Smith
1999	Connecticut	77–74	Duke	*Michigan St	*Ohio St	Jim Calhoun
2000	Michigan St	89–76	Florida	*Wisconsin	*North Carolina	Tom Izzo
2001	Duke	82–72	Arizona	*Maryland	*Michigan St	Mike Krzyzewski

NCAA Men's Division I Championship Results (Cont.)

NCAA Final Four Results (Cont.)

Year	Winner	Score	Runner-up	Third Place	Fourth Place	Winning Coach
2002	Maryland	64–52	Indiana	*Kansas	*Oklahoma	Gary Williams
2003	Syracuse	81–78	Kansas	*Marquette	*Texas	Jim Boeheim
2004	Connecticut	82–73	Georgia Tech	*Oklahoma St	*Duke	Jim Calhoun
2005	North Carolina	75-70	Illinois	*Louisville	*Michigan St	Roy Williams
2006	Florida	73–57	UCLA	*George Mason	*LSU	Billy Donovan
2007	Florida	84–75	Ohio St	*UCLA	*Georgetown	Billy Donovan
2008	Kansas	75–68 (OT)	Memphis	*UCLA	*North Carolina	Bill Self

*Tied for third place. ‡Student-athletes representing St. Joseph's (Pa.) in 1961, Villanova in 1971, Western Kentucky in 1971, UCLA in 1980, Memphis State in 1985 and Massachusetts in 1996 were declared ineligible subsequent to the tournament. Under NCAA rules, the teams' and ineligible student-athletes' records were deleted, and the teams' places in the standings were vacated.

NCAA Final Four Most Outstanding Players

			Field Goals		3-Pt FG		Free Throws						
Year	Winner, School	GP	FGM	Pct	FGA	FGM	FTM	Pct	Reb	Asst	Stl	BS	Avg
1939	None selected												
1940	Marv Huffman, Indiana	2	7	—	—	—	4	—	—	—	—	—	9.0
1941	John Kotz, Wisconsin	2	8	—	—	—	6	—	—	—	—	—	11.0
1942	Howard Dallmar, Stanford	2	8	—	—	—	4	66.7	—	—	—	—	10.0
1943	Ken Sailors, Wyoming	2	10	—	—	—	8	72.7	—	—	—	—	14.0
1944	Arnie Ferrin, Utah	2	11	—	—	—	6	—	—	—	—	—	14.0
1945	Bob Kurland, Oklahoma St	2	16	—	—	—	5	—	—	—	—	—	18.5
1946	Bob Kurland, Oklahoma St	2	21	—	—	—	10	66.7	—	—	—	—	26.0
1947	George Kaftan, Holy Cross	2	18	—	—	—	12	70.6	—	—	—	—	24.0
1948	Alex Groza, Kentucky	2	16	—	—	—	5	—	—	—	—	—	18.5
1949	Alex Groza, Kentucky	2	19	—	—	—	14	—	—	—	—	—	26.0
1950	Irwin Dambrot, CCNY	2	12	42.9	—	—	4	50.0	—	—	—	—	14.0
1951	None selected												
1952	Clyde Lovellette, Kansas	2	24	—	—	—	18	—	—	—	—	—	33.0
1953	*B.H. Horn, Kansas	2	17	—	—	—	17	—	—	—	—	—	25.5
1954	Tom Gola, La Salle	2	12	—	—	—	14	—	—	—	—	—	19.0
1955	Bill Russell, San Francisco	2	19	—	—	—	9	—	—	—	—	—	23.5
1956	*Hal Lear, Temple	2	32	—	—	—	16	—	—	—	—	—	40.0
1957	*Wilt Chamberlain, Kansas	2	18	51.4	—	—	19	70.4	25	—	—	—	32.5
1958	*Elgin Baylor, Seattle	2	18	34.0	—	—	12	75.0	41	—	—	—	24.0
1959	*Jerry West, West Virginia	2	22	66.7	—	—	22	68.8	25	—	—	—	33.0
1960	Jerry Lucas, Ohio St	2	16	66.7	—	—	3	100.0	23	—	—	—	17.5
1961	*Jerry Lucas, Ohio St	2	20	71.4	—	—	16	94.1	25	—	—	—	28.0
1962	Paul Hogue, Cincinnati	2	23	63.9	—	—	12	63.2	38	—	—	—	29.0
1963	Art Heyman, Duke	2	18	41.0	—	—	15	68.2	19	—	—	—	25.5
1964	Walt Hazzard, UCLA	2	11	55.0	—	—	8	66.7	10	—	—	—	15.0
1965	*Bill Bradley, Princeton	2	34	63.0	—	—	19	95.0	24	—	—	—	43.5
1966	*Jerry Chambers, Utah	2	25	53.2	—	—	20	83.3	35	—	—	—	35.0
1967	Lew Alcindor, UCLA	2	14	60.9	—	—	11	45.8	38	—	—	—	19.5
1968	Lew Alcindor, UCLA	2	22	62.9	—	—	9	90.0	34	—	—	—	26.5
1969	Lew Alcindor, UCLA	2	23	67.7	—	—	16	64.0	41	—	—	—	31.0
1970	Sidney Wicks, UCLA	2	15	71.4	—	—	9	60.0	34	—	—	—	19.5
1971	*†Howard Porter, Villanova	2	20	48.8	—	—	7	77.8	24	—	—	—	23.5
1972	Bill Walton, UCLA	2	20	69.0	—	—	17	73.9	41	—	—	—	28.5
1973	Bill Walton, UCLA	2	28	82.4	—	—	2	40.0	30	—	—	—	29.0
1974	David Thompson, N.C. St	2	19	51.4	—	—	11	78.6	17	—	—	—	24.5
1975	Richard Washington, UCLA	2	23	54.8	—	—	8	72.7	20	—	—	—	27.0
1976	Kent Benson, Indiana	2	17	50.0	—	—	7	63.6	18	—	—	—	20.5
1977	Butch Lee, Marquette	2	11	34.4	—	—	8	100.0	6	2	1	1	15.0
1978	Jack Givens, Kentucky	2	28	65.1	—	—	8	66.7	17	4	1	3	32.0
1979	Earvin Johnson, Michigan St	2	17	68.0	—	—	19	86.4	17	3	0	2	26.5
1980	Darrell Griffith, Louisville	2	23	62.2	—	—	11	68.8	7	15	0	2	28.5
1981	Isiah Thomas, Indiana	2	14	56.0	—	—	9	81.8	4	9	3	4	18.5
1982	James Worthy, North Carolina	2	20	74.1	—	—	2	28.6	8	9	0	4	21.0
1983	*Akeem Olajuwon, Houston	2	16	55.2	—	—	9	64.3	40	3	2	5	20.5
1984	Patrick Ewing, Georgetown	2	8	57.1	—	—	2	100.0	18	1	1	15	9.0
1985	Ed Pinckney, Villanova	2	8	57.1	—	—	12	75.0	15	6	3	0	14.0
1986	Pervis Ellison, Louisville	2	15	60.0	—	—	6	75.0	24	2	3	1	18.0
1987	Keith Smart, Indiana	2	14	63.6	1	0	7	77.8	7	7	0	2	17.5
1988	Danny Manning, Kansas	2	25	55.6	1	0	6	66.7	17	4	8	9	28.0

*Not a member of the championship-winning team. †Record later vacated.

NCAA Final Four MOPs (Cont.)

Year	Winner, School	GP	Field Goals FGM	Field Goals Pct	3-Pt FG FGA	3-Pt FG FGM	Free Throws FTM	Free Throws Pct	Reb	Asst	Stl	BS	Avg
1989	Glen Rice, Michigan	2	24	49.0	16	7	4	100.0	16	1	0	3	29.5
1990	Anderson Hunt, UNLV	2	19	61.3	16	9	2	50.0	4	9	1	1	24.5
1991	Christian Laettner, Duke	2	12	54.5	1	1	21	91.3	17	2	1	2	23.0
1992	Bobby Hurley, Duke	2	10	41.7	12	7	8	80.0	3	11	0	3	17.5
1993	Donald Williams, North Carolina	2	15	65.2	14	10	10	100.0	4	2	2	0	25.0
1994	Corliss Williamson, Arkansas	2	21	50.0	0	0	10	71.4	21	8	4	3	26.0
1995	Ed O'Bannon, UCLA	2	16	45.7	8	3	10	76.9	25	3	7	1	22.5
1996	Tony Delk, Kentucky	2	15	41.7	16	8	6	54.6	9	2	3	2	22.0
1997	Miles Simon, Arizona	2	17	45.9	10	3	17	77.3	8	6	0	1	27.0
1998	Jeff Sheppard, Kentucky	2	16	55.2	10	4	7	77.8	10	7	4	0	21.5
1999	Richard Hamilton, Connecticut	2	20	51.3	7	3	8	72.7	12	4	2	1	25.5
2000	Mateen Cleaves, Michigan St	2	8	44.4	4	3	10	83.3	6	5	2	0	14.5
2001	Shane Battier, Duke	2	13	50.0	12	5	12	70.6	19	8	2	6	21.5
2002	Juan Dixon, Maryland	2	16	59.3	15	7	12	80.0	8	5	7	0	25.5
2003	Carmelo Anthony, Syracuse	2	19	54.3	6	9	9	81.1	24	8	4	0	26.5
2004	Emeka Okafor, Connecticut	2	17	65.4	0	0	8	53.3	22	2	1	4	21.0
2005	Sean May, North Carolina	2	19	65.5	0	0	10	71.4	17	5	1	2	24.0
2006	Joakim Noah, Florida	2	12	60.0	1	0	4	100.0	17	5	2	10	14.0
2007	Corey Brewer, Florida	2	9	47.3	13	7	7	87.5	10	2	3	5	16.0
2008	Mario Chalmers, Kansas	2	10	43.5	9	3	6	75.0	7	6	7	0	14.5

Best NCAA Tournament Single-Game Scoring Performances

Player and Team	Year	Round	FG	3FG	FT	TP
Austin Carr, Notre Dame vs Ohio	1970	1st	25	—	11	61
Bill Bradley, Princeton vs Wichita St	1965	C*	22	—	14	58
Oscar Robertson, Cincinnati vs Arkansas	1958	C	21	—	14	56
Austin Carr, Notre Dame vs Kentucky	1970	2nd	22	—	8	52
Austin Carr, Notre Dame vs TCU	1971	1st	20	—	12	52
David Robinson, Navy vs Michigan	1987	1st	22	0	6	50
Elvin Hayes, Houston vs Loyola (Ill.)	1968	1st	20	—	9	49
Hal Lear, Temple vs SMU	1956	C*	17	—	14	48
Austin Carr, Notre Dame vs Houston	1971	C	17	—	13	47
Dave Corzine, DePaul vs Louisville	1978	2nd	18	—	10	46

C=regional third place; C*=third-place game.

NIT Championship Results

Year	Winner	Score	Runner-up
1938	Temple	60–36	Colorado
1939	Long Island U.	44–32	Loyola (Ill.)
1940	Colorado	51–40	Duquesne
1941	Long Island U.	56–42	Ohio U
1942	West Virginia	47–45	W. Kentucky
1943	St. John's (N.Y.)	48–27	Toledo
1944	St. John's (N.Y.)	47–39	DePaul
1945	DePaul	71–54	Bowling Green
1946	Kentucky	46–45	Rhode Island
1947	Utah	49–45	Kentucky
1948	St. Louis	65–52	NYU
1949	San Francisco	48–47	Loyola (Ill.)
1950	CCNY	69–61	Bradley
1951	BYU	62–43	Dayton
1952	La Salle	75–64	Dayton
1953	Seton Hall	58–46	St. John's (N.Y.)
1954	Holy Cross	71–62	Duquesne
1955	Duquesne	70–58	Dayton
1956	Louisville	93–80	Dayton
1957	Bradley	84–83	Memphis St
1958	Xavier (Ohio)	78–74 (OT)	Dayton
1959	St. John's (N.Y.)	76–71 (OT)	Bradley
1960	Bradley	88–72	Providence
1961	Providence	62–59	St. Louis
1962	Dayton	73–67	St. John's (N.Y.)
1963	Providence	81–66	Canisius
1964	Bradley	86–54	New Mexico
1965	St. John's (N.Y.)	55–51	Villanova
1966	BYU	97–84	NYU
1967	Southern Illinois	71–56	Marquette
1968	Dayton	61–48	Kansas
1969	Temple	89–76	Boston College
1970	Marquette	65–53	St. John's (N.Y.)
1971	North Carolina	84–66	Georgia Tech
1972	Maryland	100–69	Niagara
1973	Virginia Tech	92–91 (OT)	Notre Dame
1974	Purdue	97–81	Utah
1975	Princeton	80–69	Providence
1976	Kentucky	71–67	UNC-Charlotte
1977	St. Bonaventure	94–91	Houston
1978	Texas	101–93	North Carolina St
1979	Indiana	53–52	Purdue
1980	Virginia	58–55	Minnesota
1981	Tulsa	86–84 (OT)	Syracuse
1982	Bradley	67–58	Purdue
1983	Fresno St	69–60	DePaul
1984	Michigan	83–63	Notre Dame
1985	UCLA	65–62	Indiana
1986	Ohio St	73–63	Wyoming
1987	Southern Miss	84–80	La Salle
1988	Connecticut	72–67	Ohio St
1989	St. John's (N.Y.)	73–65	St. Louis
1990	Vanderbilt	74–72	St. Louis
1991	Stanford	78–72	Oklahoma

NCAA Men's Division I Championship Results (Cont.)

NIT Championship Results (Cont.)

Year	Winner	Score	Runner-up	Year	Winner	Score	Runner-up
1992	Virginia	81–76	Notre Dame	2001	Tulsa	79–60	Alabama
1993	Minnesota	62–61	Georgetown	2002	Memphis	72–62	South Carolina
1994	Villanova	80–73	Vanderbilt	2003	St. John's	70–67	Georgetown
1995	Virginia Tech	65–64 (OT)	Marquette	2004	Michigan	62–55	Rutgers
1996	Nebraska	60–56	St. Joseph's	2005	South Carolina	60–57	Saint Joseph's
1997	Michigan	82–73	Florida St	2006	South Carolina	76–64	Michigan
1998	Minnesota	79–72	Penn St	2007	West Virginia	78–73	Clemson
1999	California	61–60	Clemson	2008	Ohio St	92–85	Massachusetts
2000	Wake Forest	71–61	Notre Dame				

NCAA Men's Division I Season Leaders

Scoring Average

Year	Player and Team	Ht	Class	GP	FG	3FG	FT	Pts	Avg
1948	Murray Wier, Iowa	5-9	Sr.	19	152	—	95	399	21.0
1949	Tony Lavelli, Yale	6-3	Sr.	30	228	—	215	671	22.4
1950	Paul Arizin, Villanova	6-3	Sr.	29	260	—	215	735	25.3
1951	Bill Mlkvy, Temple	6-4	Sr.	25	303	—	125	731	29.2
1952	Clyde Lovellette, Kansas	6-9	Sr.	28	315	—	165	795	28.4
1953	Frank Selvy, Furman	6-3	Jr.	25	272	—	194	738	29.5
1954	Frank Selvy, Furman	6-3	Sr.	29	427	—	355	1209	41.7
1955	Darrell Floyd, Furman	6-1	Jr.	25	344	—	209	897	35.9
1956	Darrell Floyd, Furman	6-1	Sr.	28	339	—	268	946	33.8
1957	Grady Wallace, South Carolina	6-4	Sr.	29	336	—	234	906	31.2
1958	Oscar Robertson, Cincinnati	6-5	So.	28	352	—	280	984	35.1
1959	Oscar Robertson, Cincinnati	6-5	Jr.	30	331	—	316	978	32.6
1960	Oscar Robertson, Cincinnati	6-5	Sr.	30	369	—	273	1011	33.7
1961	Frank Burgess, Gonzaga	6-1	Sr.	26	304	—	234	842	32.4
1962	Billy McGill, Utah	6-9	Sr.	26	394	—	221	1009	38.8
1963	Nick Werkman, Seton Hall	6-3	Jr.	22	221	—	208	650	29.5
1964	Howard Komives, Bowling Green	6-1	Sr.	23	292	—	260	844	36.7
1965	Rick Barry, Miami (Fla.)	6-7	Sr.	26	340	—	293	973	37.4
1966	Dave Schellhase, Purdue	6-4	Sr.	24	284	—	213	781	32.5
1967	Jim Walker, Providence	6-3	Sr.	28	323	—	205	851	30.4
1968	Pete Maravich, LSU	6-5	So.	26	432	—	274	1138	43.8
1969	Pete Maravich, LSU	6-5	Jr.	26	433	—	282	1148	44.2
1970	Pete Maravich, LSU	6-5	Sr.	31	522	—	337	1381	44.5
1971	Johnny Neumann, Mississippi	6-6	So.	23	366	—	191	923	40.1
1972	Dwight Lamar, SW Louisiana	6-1	Jr.	29	429	—	196	1054	36.3
1973	William Averitt, Pepperdine	6-1	Sr.	25	352	—	144	848	33.9
1974	Larry Fogle, Canisius	6-5	So.	25	326	—	183	835	33.4
1975	Bob McCurdy, Richmond	6-7	Sr.	26	321	—	213	855	32.9
1976	Marshall Rodgers, Tex.-Pan American	6-2	Sr.	25	361	—	197	919	36.8
1977	Freeman Williams, Portland St	6-4	Jr.	26	417	—	176	1010	38.8
1978	Freeman Williams, Portland St	6-4	Sr.	27	410	—	149	969	35.9
1979	Lawrence Butler, Idaho St	6-3	Sr.	27	310	—	192	812	30.1
1980	Tony Murphy, Southern-Birmingham	6-3	Sr.	29	377	—	178	932	32.1
1981	Zam Fredrick, South Carolina	6-2	Sr.	27	300	—	181	781	28.9
1982	Harry Kelly, Texas Southern	6-7	Jr.	29	336	—	190	862	29.7
1983	Harry Kelly, Texas Southern	6-7	Sr.	29	333	—	169	835	28.8
1984	Joe Jakubick, Akron	6-5	Sr.	27	304	—	206	814	30.1
1985	Xavier McDaniel, Wichita St	6-8	Sr.	31	351	—	142	844	27.2
1986	Terrance Bailey, Wagner	6-2	Jr.	29	321	—	212	854	29.4
1987	Kevin Houston, Army	5-11	Sr.	29	311	63	268	953	32.9
1988	Hersey Hawkins, Bradley	6-3	Sr.	31	377	87	284	1125	36.3
1989	Hank Gathers, Loyola Marymount	6-7	Jr.	31	419	0	177	1015	32.7
1990	Bo Kimble, Loyola Marymount	6-5	Sr.	32	404	92	231	1131	35.3
1991	Kevin Bradshaw, U.S. Int'l	6-6	Sr.	28	358	60	278	1054	37.6
1992	Brett Roberts, Morehead St	6-8	Sr.	29	278	66	193	815	28.1
1993	Greg Guy, Tex.-Pan American	6-1	Jr.	19	189	67	111	556	29.3
1994	Glenn Robinson, Purdue	6-8	Jr.	34	368	79	215	1030	30.3
1995	Kurt Thomas, TCU	6-9	Sr.	27	288	3	202	781	28.9
1996	Kevin Granger, Texas Southern	6-3	Sr.	24	194	30	230	648	27.0
1997	Charles Jones, LIU-Brooklyn	6-3	Jr.	30	338	109	118	903	30.1
1998	Charles Jones, LIU-Brooklyn	6-3	Sr.	30	326	116	101	869	29.0
1999	Alvin Young, Niagara	6-3	Sr.	29	253	65	157	728	25.1

NCAA Men's Division I Season Leaders (Cont.)

Scoring Average (Cont.)

Year	Player and Team	Ht	Class	GP	FG	3FG	FT	Pts	Avg
2000	....Courtney Alexander, Fresno St	6-6	Sr.	27	252	58	107	669	24.8
2001	....Ronnie McCollum, Centenary	6-4	Sr.	27	244	85	214	787	29.1
2002	....Jason Conley, Virginia Military	6-5	Fr.	28	285	79	171	820	29.3
2003	....Ruben Douglas, New Mexico	6-5	Sr.	28	218	94	253	783	28.0
2004	....Keydren Clark, St. Peter's	5-8	So.	29	233	112	197	775	26.7
2005	....Keydren Clark, St. Peter's	5-9	Jr.	28	230	109	152	721	25.8
2006	....Adam Morrison, Gonzaga	6-8	Jr.	33	306	74	240	926	28.1
2007	....Reggie Williams, Virginia Military Institute	6-5	Jr.	33	338	76	176	928	28.1

Rebounds

Year	Player and Team	Ht	Class	GP	Reb	Avg
1951	..............Ernie Beck, Pennsylvania	6-4	So.	27	556	20.6
1952	..............Bill Hannon, Army	6-3	So.	17	355	20.9
1953	..............Ed Conlin, Fordham	6-5	So.	26	612	23.5
1954	..............Art Quimby, Connecticut	6-5	Jr.	26	588	22.6
1955	..............Charlie Slack, Marshall	6-5	Jr.	21	538	25.6
1956	..............Joe Holup, George Washington	6-6	Sr.	26	604	†.256
1957	..............Elgin Baylor, Seattle	6-6	Jr.	25	508	†.235
1958	..............Alex Ellis, Niagara	6-5	Sr.	25	536	†.262
1959	..............Leroy Wright, Pacific	6-8	Jr.	26	652	†.238
1960	..............Leroy Wright, Pacific	6-8	Sr.	17	380	†.234
1961	..............Jerry Lucas, Ohio St	6-8	Jr.	27	470	†.198
1962	..............Jerry Lucas, Ohio St	6-8	Sr.	28	499	†.211
1963	..............Paul Silas, Creighton	6-7	Sr.	27	557	20.6
1964	..............Bob Pelkington, Xavier (Ohio)	6-7	Sr.	26	567	21.8
1965	..............Toby Kimball, Connecticut	6-8	Sr.	23	483	21.0
1966	..............Jim Ware, Oklahoma City	6-8	Sr.	29	607	20.9
1967	..............Dick Cunningham, Murray St	6-10	Jr.	22	479	21.8
1968	..............Neal Walk, Florida	6-10	Jr.	25	494	19.8
1969	..............Spencer Haywood, Detroit	6-8	So.	22	472	21.5
1970	..............Artis Gilmore, Jacksonville	7-2	Jr.	28	621	22.2
1971	..............Artis Gilmore, Jacksonville	7-2	Sr.	26	603	23.2
1972	..............Kermit Washington, American	6-8	Jr.	23	455	19.8
1973	..............Kermit Washington, American	6-8	Sr.	22	439	20.0
1974	..............Marvin Barnes, Providence	6-9	Sr.	32	597	18.7
1975	..............John Irving, Hofstra	6-9	So.	21	323	15.4
1976	..............Sam Pellom, Buffalo	6-8	So.	26	420	16.2
1977	..............Glenn Mosley, Seton Hall	6-8	Sr.	29	473	16.3
1978	..............Ken Williams, North Texas St	6-7	Sr.	28	411	14.7
1979	..............Monti Davis, Tennessee St	6-7	Jr.	26	421	16.2
1980	..............Larry Smith, Alcorn St	6-8	Sr.	26	392	15.1
1981	..............Darryl Watson, Miss. Valley St	6-7	Sr.	27	379	14.0
1982	..............LaSalle Thompson, Texas	6-10	Jr.	27	365	13.5
1983	..............Xavier McDaniel, Wichita St	6-7	So.	28	403	14.4
1984	..............Akeem Olajuwon, Houston	7-0	Jr.	37	500	13.5
1985	..............Xavier McDaniel, Wichita St	6-8	Sr	31	460	14.8
1986	..............David Robinson, Navy	6-11	Jr.	35	455	13.0
1987	..............Jerome Lane, Pittsburgh	6-6	So.	33	444	13.5
1988	..............Kenny Miller, Loyola (Ill.)	6-9	Fr.	29	395	13.6
1989	..............Hank Gathers, Loyola (Calif.)	6-7	Jr.	31	426	13.7
1990	..............Anthony Bonner, St. Louis	6-8	Sr.	33	456	13.8
1991	..............Shaquille O'Neal, LSU	7-1	So.	28	411	14.7
1992	..............Popeye Jones, Murray St	6-8	Sr.	30	431	14.4
1993	..............Warren Kidd, Middle Tenn. St	6-9	Sr.	26	386	14.8
1994	..............Jerome Lambert, Baylor	6-8	Jr.	24	355	14.8
1995	..............Kurt Thomas, TCU	6-9	Sr.	27	393	14.6
1996	..............Marcus Mann, Miss. Valley St	6-8	Sr.	29	394	13.6
1997	..............Tim Duncan, Wake Forest	6-11	Sr.	31	457	14.7
1998	..............Ryan Perryman, Dayton	6-7	Sr.	33	412	12.5
1999	..............Ian McGinnis, Dartmouth	6-8	So.	26	317	12.2
2000	..............Darren Phillips, Fairfield	6-7	Sr.	29	405	14.0
2001	..............Chris Marcus, Western Kentucky	7-1	Jr.	31	374	12.1
2002	..............Jeremy Bishop, Quinnipiac	6-6	J..	29	347	12.0

†From 1956–1962, title was based on highest individual recoveries out of total by both teams in all games.

NCAA Men's Division I Season Leaders (Cont.)

Rebounds (Cont.)

Year	Player and Team	Ht	Class	GP	Reb	Avg
2003	Brandon Hunter, Ohio	6-7	Sr.	30	378	12.6
2004	Paul Millsap, Louisiana Tech	6-7	Fr.	30	374	12.5
2005	Paul Millsap, Louisiana Tech	6-8	So.	29	360	12.4
2006	Paul Millsap, Louisiana Tech	6-8	Jr.	33	438	13.3
2007	Rashad Jones-Jennings, Ark.-Little Rock	6-8	Sr.	30	392	13.3

Assists

Year	Player and Team	Class	GP	Ast	Avg
1984	Craig Lathen, Ill.-Chicago	Jr.	29	274	9.45
1985	Rob Weingard, Hofstra	Sr.	24	228	9.50
1986	Mark Jackson, St. John's (N.Y.)	Jr.	36	328	9.11
1987	Avery Johnson, Southern-Birm.	Jr.	31	333	10.74
1988	Avery Johnson, Southern-Birm.	Sr.	30	399	13.30
1989	Glenn Williams, Holy Cross	Sr.	28	278	9.93
1990	Todd Lehmann, Drexel	Sr.	28	260	9.29
1991	Chris Corchiani, North Carolina St	Sr.	31	299	9.65
1992	Van Usher, Tennessee Tech	Sr.	29	254	8.76
1993	Sam Crawford, New Mex. St	Sr.	34	310	9.12
1994	Jason Kidd, California	So.	30	272	9.06
1995	Nelson Haggerty, Baylor	Sr.	28	284	10.10
1996	Raimonds Miglinieks, UC-Irvine	Sr.	27	230	8.52
1997	Kenny Mitchell, Dartmouth	Sr.	26	203	7.81
1998	Ahlon Lewis, Arizona St	Sr.	32	294	9.19
1999	Doug Gottlieb, Oklahoma St	Jr.	34	299	8.79
2000	Mark Dickel, UNLV	Sr.	31	280	9.03
2001	Markus Carr, CSU–Northridge	Jr.	32	286	8.94
2002	T.J. Ford, Texas	Fr.	33	273	8.27
2003	Martell Bailey, Ill.-Chicago	Jr.	30	244	8.13
2004	Greg Davis, Troy St	Sr.	31	256	8.26
2005	Damitrius Coleman, Mercer	Jr.	28	224	8.00
	Will Funn, Portland St	Sr.	28	224	8.00
2006	Jared Jordan, Marist	Jr.	29	247	8.52
2007	Jared Jordan, Marist	Sr.	31	274	8.83

Blocked Shots

Year	Player and Team	Class	GP	BS	Avg
1986	David Robinson, Navy	Jr.	35	207	5.91
1987	David Robinson, Navy	Sr.	32	144	4.50
1988	Rodney Blake, St. Joseph's (Pa.)	Sr.	29	116	4.00
1989	Alonzo Mourning, Georgetown	Fr.	34	169	4.97
1990	Kenny Green, Rhode Island	Sr.	26	124	4.77
1991	Shawn Bradley, BYU	Fr.	34	177	5.21
1992	Shaquille O'Neal, LSU	Jr.	30	157	5.23
1993	Theo Ratliff, Wyoming	Jr.	28	124	4.43
1994	Grady Livingston, Howard	Jr.	26	115	4.42
1995	Keith Closs, Central Conn. St	Fr.	26	139	5.35
1996	Keith Closs, Central Conn. St	So.	28	178	6.36
1997	Adonal Foyle, Colgate	Jr.	28	180	6.43
1998	Jerome James, Florida A&M	Sr.	27	125	4.63
1999	Tarvis Williams, Hampton	Jr.	27	135	5.00
2000	Ken Johnson, Ohio St	Sr.	30	161	5.37
2001	Tarvis Williams, Hampton	Sr	32	147	4.59
2002	Wojciech Myrda, La.-Monroe	Sr.	32	172	5.38
2003	Emeka Okafor, Connecticut	So.	33	156	4.73
2004	Anwar Ferguson, Houston	Sr.	27	111	4.11
2005	Deng Gai, Fairfield	Sr.	30	165	5.50
2006	Shawn James, Northeastern	So.	30	196	6.53
2007	Mickell Gladness, Ala.-A&M	Jr.	30	188	6.26

Steals

Year	Player and Team	Class	GP	Stl	Avg
1986	Darron Brittman, Chicago St	Sr.	28	139	4.96
1987	Tony Fairley, Charleston South.	Sr.	28	114	4.07
1988	Aldwin Ware, Florida A&M	Sr.	29	142	4.90
1989	Kenny Robertson, Cleveland St	Jr.	28	111	3.96
1990	Ronn McMahon, E. Washington	Sr.	29	130	4.48
1991	Van Usher, Tennessee Tech	Jr.	28	104	3.71

NCAA Men's Division I Season Leaders (Cont.)

Steals (Cont.)

Year	Player and Team	Class	GP	Stl	Avg
1992	Victor Snipes, NE Illinois	So.	25	86	3.44
1993	Jason Kidd, California	Fr.	29	110	3.80
1994	Shawn Griggs, SW Louisiana	Sr.	30	120	4.00
1995	Roderick Anderson, Texas	Sr.	30	101	3.37
1996	Pointer Williams, McNeese St	Sr.	27	118	4.37
1997	Joel Hoover, Md.-Eastern Shore	Fr.	28	90	3.21
1998	Bonzi Wells, Ball St	Sr.	29	103	3.55
1999	Shawnta Rogers, George Wash.	Sr.	29	103	3.55
2000	Carl Williams, Liberty	Sr.	28	107	3.82
2001	Greedy Daniels, TCU	Jr.	25	108	4.32
2002	Desmond Cambridge, Ala. A&M	Sr.	29	160	5.52
2003	Alexis McMillan, Stetson	Sr.	22	87	3.95
2004	Marques Green, St. Bonaventure	Sr.	27	107	3.96
2005	Obie Trotter, Alabama A&M	Jr.	32	125	3.91
2006	Tim Smith, East Tennessee St	Sr.	28	95	3.39
2007	Travis Holmes, Virginia Military Inst.	So..	33	111	3.36

NCAA Men's Division I Alltime Individual Leaders

Single Game Records

SCORING HIGHS VS DIVISION I OPPONENT

Pts	Player and Team vs Opponent	Date
72	Kevin Bradshaw, U.S. Int'l vs Loyola Marymount	1-5-91
69	Pete Maravich, LSU vs Alabama	2-7-70
68	Calvin Murphy, Niagara vs Syracuse	12-7-68
66	Jay Handlan, Washington & Lee vs Furman	2-17-51
66	Pete Maravich, LSU vs Tulane	2-10-69
66	Anthony Roberts, Oral Roberts vs North Carolina A&T	2-19-77
65	Anthony Roberts, Oral Roberts vs Oregon	3-9-77
65	Scott Haffner, Evansville vs Dayton	2-18-89
64	Pete Maravich, LSU vs Kentucky	2-21-70
63	Johnny Neumann, Mississippi vs LSU	1-30-71
63	Hersey Hawkins, Bradley vs Detroit	2-22-88

SCORING HIGHS VS NON-DIVISION I OPPONENT

Pts	Player and Team vs Opponent	Date
100	Frank Selvy, Furman vs Newberry	2-13-54
85	Paul Arizin, Villanova vs Philadelphia NAMC	2-12-49
81	Freeman Williams, Portland St vs Rocky Mountain	2-3-78
73	Bill Mlkvy, Temple vs Wilkes	3-3-51
71	Freeman Williams, Portland St vs S. Oregon	2-9-77

REBOUNDING HIGHS ALL-TIME

Reb	Player and Team vs Opponent	Date
51	Bill Chambers, William & Mary vs Virginia	2-14-53
43	Charlie Slack, Marshall vs Morris Harvey	1-12-54
42	Tom Heinsohn, Holy Cross vs Boston College	3-1-55
40	Art Quimby, Connecticut vs Boston University	1-11-55
39	Maurice Stokes, St. Francis (Pa.) vs John Carroll	1-28-55
39	Dave DeBusschere, Detroit vs C. Michigan	1-30-60
39	Keith Swagerty, Pacific vs UC-Santa Barbara	3-5-65

REBOUNDING HIGHS SINCE 1973*

Reb	Player and Team vs Opponent	Date
35	Larry Abney, Fresno St vs SMU	2-17-00
34	David Vaughn, Oral Roberts vs Brandeis	1-8-73
32	Jervaughn Scales, Southern-Birm. vs Grambling	2-7-94
32	Durand Macklin, LSU vs Tulane	11-26-76
31	Jim Bradley, Northern Illinois vs UW-Milwaukee	2-19-73
31	Calvin Natt, NE Louisiana vs Georgia Southern	12-29-76

ASSISTS

Asst	Player and Team vs Opponent	Date
22	Tony Fairley, Baptist vs Armstrong St	2-9-87
22	Avery Johnson, Southern-Birm. vs Texas Southern	1-25-88
22	Sherman Douglas, Syracuse vs Providence	1-28-89
21	Kelvin Scarborough, New Mexico vs Hawaii	2-13-87

*Freshmen became eligible for varsity play in 1973

NCAA Men's Division I Alltime Individual Leaders (Cont.)

Single Game Records (Cont.)

ASSISTS

Asst	Player and Team vs Opponent	Date
21	Anthony Manuel, Bradley vs UC-Irvine	12-19-87
21	Avery Johnson, Southern-Birm. vs Alabama St	1-16-88

STEALS

Stl	Player and Team vs Opponent	Date
13	Mookie Blaylock, Oklahoma vs Centenary	12-12-87
13	Mookie Blaylock, Oklahoma vs Loyola Marymount	12-17-88
12	Kenny Robertson, Cleveland St vs Wagner	12-3-88
12	Terry Evans, Oklahoma vs Florida A&M	1-27-93
12	Richard Duncan, Middle Tenn. St vs Eastern Kentucky	2-20-99
12	Greedy Daniels, Texas Christian vs Ark.–Pine Bluff	12-30-00
12	Jehiel Lewis, Navy vs Bucknell	1-12-02
12	Carldell Johnson, Ala.-Birmingham vs. South Carolina St	11-27-05

BLOCKED SHOTS

BS	Player and Team vs Opponent	Date
16	Mickell Gladness, Alabama A&M vs Texas Southern	2-24-07
14	David Robinson, Navy vs UNC–Wilmington	1-4-86
14	Shawn Bradley, BYU vs Eastern Kentucky	12-7-90
14	Roy Rogers, Alabama vs Georgia	2-10-96
14	Loren Woods, Arizona vs Oregon	2-3-00

Ten tied with 13

Single Season Records

POINTS

Player and Team	Year	GP	FG	3FG	FT	Pts
Pete Maravich, LSU	1970	31	522	—	337	1381
Elvin Hayes, Houston	1968	33	519	—	176	1214
Frank Selvy, Furman	1954	29	427	—	355	1209
Pete Maravich, LSU	1969	26	433	—	282	1148
Pete Maravich, LSU	1968	26	432	—	274	1138
Bo Kimble, Loyola Marymount	1990	32	404	92	231	1131
Hersey Hawkins, Bradley	1988	31	377	87	284	1125
Austin Carr, Notre Dame	1970	29	444	—	218	1106
Austin Carr, Notre Dame	1971	29	430	—	241	1101
Otis Birdsong, Houston	1977	36	452	—	186	1090

SCORING AVERAGE

Player and Team	Year	GP	FG	3FG	FT	Pts
Pete Maravich, LSU	1970	31	522	337	1381	44.5
Pete Maravich, LSU	1969	26	433	282	1148	44.2
Pete Maravich, LSU	1968	26	432	274	1138	43.8
Frank Selvy, Furman	1954	29	427	355	1209	41.7
Johnny Neumann, Mississippi	1971	23	366	191	923	40.1
Freeman Williams, Portland St	1977	26	417	176	1010	38.8
Billy McGill, Utah	1962	26	394	221	1009	38.8
Calvin Murphy, Niagara	1968	24	337	242	916	38.2
Austin Carr, Notre Dame	1970	29	444	218	1106	38.1
Austin Carr, Notre Dame	1971	29	430	241	1101	38.0

REBOUNDS

Player and Team	Year	GP	Reb
Walt Dukes, Seton Hall	1953	33	734
Leroy Wright, Pacific	1959	26	652
Tom Gola, La Salle	1954	30	652
Charlie Tyra, Louisville	1956	29	645
Paul Silas, Creighton	1964	29	631
Elvin Hayes, Houston	1968	33	624

Player and Team	Year	GP	Reb
Artis Gilmore, Jacksonville	1970	28	621
Tom Gola, La Salle	1955	31	618
Ed Conlin, Fordham	1953	26	612
Art Quimby, Connecticut	1955	25	611
Bill Russell, San Francisco	1956	29	609
Jim Ware, Oklahoma City	1966	29	607

REBOUND AVERAGE ALL-TIME

Player and Team	Year	GP	Reb	Avg
Charlie Slack, Marshall	1955	21	538	25.6
Leroy Wright, Pacific	1959	26	652	25.1
Art Quimby, Connecticut	1955	25	611	24.4
Charlie Slack, Marshall	1956	22	520	23.6
Ed Conlin, Fordham	1953	26	612	23.5

REBOUND AVERAGE SINCE 1973*

Player and Team	Year	GP	Reb	Avg
Kermit Washington, American	1973	22	439	20.0
Marvin Barnes, Providence	1973	30	571	19.0
Marvin Barnes, Providence	1974	32	597	18.7
Pete Padgett, Nev.-Reno	1973	26	462	17.8
Jim Bradley, Northern Illinois	1973	24	426	17.8

NCAA Men's Division I Alltime Individual Leaders (Cont.)

Single Season Records (Cont.)

ASSISTS

Player and Team	Year	GP	Asst
Mark Wade, UNLV	1987	38	406
Avery Johnson, Southern-Birm.	1988	30	399
Anthony Manuel, Bradley	1988	31	373
Avery Johnson, Southern-Birm.	1987	31	333
Mark Jackson, St. John's (N.Y.)	1986	32	328
Sherman Douglas, Syracuse	1989	38	326
Sam Crawford, New Mex. St	1993	34	310
Greg Anthony, UNLV	1991	35	310
Reid Gettys, Houston	1984	37	309
Carl Golston, Loyola (Ill.)	1985	33	305

ASSIST AVERAGE

Player and Team	Year	GP	Asst	Avg
Avery Johnson, Southern-Birm.	1988	30	399	13.3
Anthony Manuel, Bradley	1988	31	373	12.0
Avery Johnson, Southern-Birm.	1987	31	333	10.7
Mark Wade, UNLV	1987	38	406	10.7
Nelson Haggerty, Baylor	1995	28	284	10.1
Glenn Williams, Holy Cross	1989	28	278	9.9
Chris Corchiani, North Carolina St.	1991	31	299	9.6
Tony Fairley, Charleston South.*	1987	28	270	9.6
Tyrone Bogues, Wake Forest	1987	29	276	9.5
Ron Weingard, Hofstra	1985	24	228	9.5
Craig Neal, Georgia Tech	1988	32	303	9.5

FIELD-GOAL PERCENTAGE

Player and Team	Year	GP	FG	FGA	Pct
Steve Johnson, Oregon St	1981	28	235	315	74.6
Dwayne Davis, Florida	1989	33	179	248	72.2
Keith Walker, Utica	1985	27	154	216	71.3
Steve Johnson, Oregon St	1980	30	211	297	71.0
Adam Mark, Belmont	2002	26	150	212	70.8
Oliver Miller, Arkansas	1991	38	254	361	70.4
Alan Williams, Princeton	1987	25	163	232	70.3
Mark McNamara, California	1982	27	231	329	70.2
Warren Kidd, Middle Tennessee St	1991	30	173	247	70.0
Pete Freeman, Akron	1991	28	175	250	70.0

Based on qualifiers for annual championship.

FREE-THROW PERCENTAGE

Player and Team	Year	GP	FT	FTA	Pct
Blake Ahearn SW Missouri St†	2004	33	117	120	97.5
Ryan Toolson, Utah Valley St	2006	29	96	99	97.0
Derek Raivio, Gonzaga	2006	33	146	152	96.1
Craig Collins, Penn St	1985	27	94	98	95.9
A.J. Graves, Butler	2006	32	137	143	95.8
J.J. Redick, Duke	2004	37	143	150	95.3
Steve Drabyn, Belmont	2003	29	78	82	95.1
Rod Foster, UCLA	1982	27	95	100	95.0
Clay McKnight, Pacific	2000	24	74	78	94.9
Matt Logie, Lehigh	2003	28	91	96	94.8
Blake Ahearn, Missouri State	2005	32	90	95	94.7

THREE-POINT FIELD-GOAL PERCENTAGE

Player and Team	Year	GP	3FG	3FGA	Pct
Glenn Tropf, Holy Cross	1988	29	52	82	63.4
Sean Wightman, Western Michigan	1992	30	48	76	63.2
Keith Jennings, East Tennessee St	1991	33	84	142	59.2
Dave Calloway, Monmouth (N.J.)	1989	28	48	82	58.5
Steve Kerr, Arizona	1988	38	114	199	57.3
Reginald Jones, Prairie View	1987	28	64	112	57.1
Jim Cantamessa, Siena	1998	29	66	117	56.4
Joel Tribelhorn, Colorado St	1989	33	76	135	56.3
Mike Joseph, Bucknell	1988	28	65	116	56.0
Brian Jackson, Evansville	1995	27	53	95	55.8

Based on qualifiers for annual championship.

*Formerly Baptist

†Southwest Missouri State changed name to Missouri State after 2004–05 season

Based on qualifiers for annual championship.

NCAA Men's Division I Alltime Individual Leaders (Cont.)

Single Season Records (Cont.)

STEALS

Player and Team	Year	GP	Stl
Desmond Cambridge, Alabama A&M	2002	29	160
Mookie Blaylock, Oklahoma	1988	39	150
Aldwin Ware, Florida A&M	1988	29	142
Darron Brittman, Chicago St	1986	28	139
John Linehan, Providence	2002	31	139

BLOCKED SHOTS

Player and Team	Year	GP	BS
David Robinson, Navy	1986	35	207
Shawn James, Northeastern	2005	30	196
Mickell Gladness, Alabama A&M	2006	30	188
Adonal Foyle, Colgate	1997	28	180
Keith Closs, Central Conn. St	1996	28	178

STEAL AVERAGE

Player and Team	Year	GP	Stl	Avg
D. Cambridge, Alabama A&M	2002	29	160	5.52
Darron Brittman, Chicago St	1986	28	139	4.96
Aldwin Ware, Florida A&M	1988	29	142	4.90
John Linehan, Providence	2002	31	139	4.48
Ronn McMahon, E. Washington	1990	29	130	4.48

BLOCKED-SHOT AVERAGE

Player and Team	Year	GP	BS	Avg
Shawn James, Northeastern	2005	30	196	6.53
Adonal Foyle, Colgate	1997	28	180	6.43
Keith Closs, Central Conn. St	1996	28	178	6.36
Mickell Gladness, Alabama A&M	2006	30	188	6.26
David Robinson, Navy	1986	35	207	5.91

Career Records

POINTS

Player and Team	Ht	Final Year	GP	FG	3FG*	FT	Pts
Pete Maravich, LSU	6-5	1970	83	1387	—	893	3667
Freeman Williams, Portland St	6-4	1978	106	1369	—	511	3249
Lionel Simmons, La Salle	6-7	1990	131	1244	56	673	3217
Alphonso Ford, Mississippi Valley St	6-2	1993	109	1121	333	590	3165
Harry Kelly, Texas Southern	6-7	1983	110	1234	—	598	3066
Keydren Clark, St. Peter's	5-9	2006	118	967	435	689	3058
Hersey Hawkins, Bradley	6-3	1988	125	1100	118	690	3008
Oscar Robertson, Cincinnati	6-5	1960	88	1052	—	869	2973
Danny Manning, Kansas	6-10	1988	147	1216	10	509	2951
Alfredrick Hughes, Loyola (Ill.)	6-5	1985	120	1226	—	462	2914
Elvin Hayes, Houston	6-8	1968	93	1215	—	454	2884
Larry Bird, Indiana St	6-9	1979	94	1154	—	542	2850
Otis Birdsong, Houston	6-4	1977	116	1176	—	480	2832
Kevin Bradshaw, Bethune-Cookman, U.S. Int'l	6-6	1991	111	1027	132	618	2804
Allan Houston, Tennessee	6-6	1993	128	902	346	651	2801
J.J. Redick, Duke	6-4	2006	139	825	457	662	2769
Hank Gathers, USC, Loyola Marymount	6-7	1990	117	1127	0	469	2723
Reggie Lewis, Northeastern	6-7	1987	122	1043	30 (1)	592	2708
Daren Queenan, Lehigh	6-5	1988	118	1024	29	626	2703
Byron Larkin, Xavier (Ohio)	6-3	1988	121	1022	51	601	2696
Bo McCalebb, New Orleans	6-0	2008	128	977	115	610	2679

*Listed is the number of three-pointers scored since it became the national rule in 1987; the number in the parentheses is number scored prior to 1987—these counted as three points in the game but counted as two-pointers in the national rankings. The three-pointers in the parentheses are not included in total points.

SCORING AVERAGE

Player and Team	Final Year	GP	FG	FT	Pts	Avg
Pete Maravich, LSU	1968	83	1387	893	3667	44.2
Austin Carr, Notre Dame	1971	74	1017	526	2560	34.6
Oscar Robertson, Cincinnati	1960	88	1052	869	2973	33.8
Calvin Murphy, Niagara	1970	77	947	654	2548	33.1
Dwight Lamar, SW Louisiana	1973	57	768	326	1862	32.7
Frank Selvy, Furman	1954	78	922	694	2538	32.5
Rick Mount, Purdue	1970	72	910	503	2323	32.3
Darrell Floyd, Furman	1956	71	868	545	2281	32.1
Nick Werkman, Seton Hall	1964	71	812	649	2273	32.0
Willie Humes, Idaho St	1971	48	565	380	1510	31.5
William Averitt, Pepperdine	1973	49	615	311	1541	31.4
Elgin Baylor, Coll. of Idaho, Seattle	1958	80	956	588	2500	31.3
Elvin Hayes, Houston	1968	93	1215	454	2884	31.0
Freeman Williams, Portland St	1978	106	1369	511	3249	30.7
Larry Bird, Indiana St	1979	94	1154	542	2850	30.3

Career Records (Cont.)

REBOUNDS ALL-TIME

Player and Team	Final Year	GP	Reb
Tom Gola, La Salle	1955	118	2201
Joe Holup, George Washington	1956	104	2030
Charlie Slack, Marshall	1956	88	1916
Ed Conlin, Fordham	1955	102	1884
Dickie Hemric, Wake Forest	1955	104	1802

REBOUNDS SINCE 1973*

Player and Team	Final Year	GP	Reb
Tim Duncan, Wake Forest	1997	128	1570
Derrick Coleman, Syracuse	1990	143	1537
Malik Rose, Drexel	1996	120	1514
Ralph Sampson, Virginia	1983	132	1511
Pete Padgett, Nev.-Reno	1976	104	1464

ASSISTS

Player and Team	Final Year	GP	Asst
Bobby Hurley, Duke	1993	140	1076
Chris Corchiani, North Carolina St	1991	124	1038
Ed Cota, North Carolina	2000	138	1030
Keith Jennings, East Tennessee St	1991	127	983
Steve Blake, Maryland	2003	138	972

FIELD-GOAL PERCENTAGE

Player and Team	Final Year	FG	FGA	Pct
Steve Johnson, Oregon St	1981	828	1222	67.8
Michael Bradley, Kentucky/Villanova	2001	441	651	67.7
Murray Brown, Florida St	1980	566	847	66.8
Lee Campbell, SW Missouri St	1990	411	618	66.5
Warren Kidd, Middle Tennessee St	1993	496	747	66.4

Note: Minimum 400 field goals and 4 FG made per game.

FREE-THROW PERCENTAGE

Player and Team	Final Year	FT	FTA	Pct
Blake Ahearn, Missouri St	2007	435	460	94.6
Derek Raivio, Gonzaga	2007	343	370	92.7
Gary Buchanan, Villanova	2003	324	355	91.3
J.J. Redick, Duke	2006	662	726	91.2
Greg Starrick, Kentucky/Southern Illinois	1972	341	375	90.9

Note: Minimum 300 free throws made.
*Freshmen became eligible for varsity play in 1973.

THREE-POINT FIELD GOALS MADE

Player and Team	Final Year	GP	3FG
J.J. Redick, Duke	2006	139	457
Keydren Clark, St. Peter's	2006	118	435
Chris Lofton, Tennessee	2008	128	431
Curtis Staples, Virginia	1998	122	413
Jack Leasure, Coastal Carolina	2008	117	411

THREE-POINT FIELD-GOAL PERCENTAGE

Player and Team	Final Year	3FG	3FGA	Pct
Tony Bennett, UW–Green Bay	1992	290	584	49.7
Stephen Sir, San Diego St/Northern Ariz	2007	323	689	46.9
David Olson, Eastern Illinois	1992	262	562	46.6
Jaycee Carroll, Utah St	2008	369	793	46.5
Ross Land, Northern Arizona	2000	308	664	46.4

Note: Minimum 200 3-point field goals and 2.0 3FG/G.

NCAA Men's Division I Alltime Individual Leaders (Cont.)

Career Records (Cont.)

STEALS

Player and Team	Final Year	GP	Stl
John Linehan, Providence	2002	122	385
Eric Murdock, Providence	1991	117	376
Pepe Sanchez, Temple	2000	116	365
Cookie Belcher, Nebraska	2001	131	353
Kevin Braswell, Georgetown	2002	128	349

BLOCKED SHOTS

Player and Team	Final Year	GP	BS
Wojciech Myrda, La.-Monroe	2002	115	535
Adonal Foyle, Colgate	1997	87	492
Tim Duncan, Wake Forest	1997	128	481
Alonzo Mourning, Georgetown	1992	120	453
Tarvis Williams, Hampton	2001	114	452

NCAA Men's Division I Team Leaders

Division I Team Alltime Wins

Team	First Year	Yrs	W	L	T
Kentucky	1903	105	1966	621	1
North Carolina	1911	98	1950	699	0
Kansas	1899	110	1943	785	0
Duke	1906	103	1846	808	0
Syracuse	1901	107	1725	796	0
Temple	1895	112	1689	948	0
St. John's (N.Y.)	1908	101	1670	850	0
Pennsylvania	1897	108	1647	931	2
UCLA	1920	89	1646	717	0
Indiana	1901	108	1635	884	0
Notre Dame	1898	103	1630	893	1
Utah	1909	100	1613	848	0
Illinois	1906	103	1585	843	0
Western Kentucky	1915	89	1577	771	0
Oregon St	1902	107	1576	1162	0

Division I Alltime Winning Percentage

Team	First Year	Yrs	W	L	T	Pct
Kentucky	1903	105	1966	621	1	.760
North Carolina	1911	98	1950	699	0	.736
UNLV	1959	50	1037	418	0	.713
Kansas	1899	110	1943	785	0	.712
UCLA	1920	90	1646	717	0	.697
Duke	1906	103	1846	808	0	.696
Syracuse	1901	107	1725	796	0	.684
Western Kentucky	1915	89	1577	771	0	.672
St. John's (N.Y.)	1908	101	1670	850	0	.663
Utah	1909	100	1613	848	0	.655
Louisville	1912	94	1556	825	0	.654
Illinois	1906	103	1585	843	0	.653
Indiana	1901	108	1635	884	0	.649
Arizona	1905	103	1547	844	1	.647
Missouri St	1909	96	1487	813	0	.647

Note: Minimum of 25 years in Division I.

NCAA Men's Division I Winning Streaks

Longest—Full Season

Team	Games	Years	Ended by
UCLA	88	1971–74	Notre Dame (71–70)
San Francisco	60	1955–57	Illinois (62–33)
UCLA	47	1966–68	Houston (71–69)
UNLV	45	1990–91	Duke (79–77)
Texas	44	1913–17	Rice (24–18)
Seton Hall	43	1939–41	LIU-Brooklyn (49–26)
LIU-Brooklyn	43	1935–37	Stanford (45–31)
UCLA	41	1968–69	USC (46–44)
Marquette	39	1970–71	Ohio St (60–59)
Cincinnati	37	1962–63	Wichita St (65–64)
North Carolina	37	1957–58	W Virginia (75–64)

Longest—Regular Season

Team	Games	Years	Ended by
UCLA	76	1971–74	Notre Dame (71–70)
Indiana	57	1975–77	Toledo (59–57)
Marquette	56	1970–72	Detroit (70–49)
Kentucky	54	1952–55	Georgia Tech (59–58)
San Francisco	51	1955–57	Illinois (62–33)
Pennsylvania	48	1970–72	Temple (57–52)
Ohio State	47	1960–62	Wisconsin (86–67)
Texas	44	1913–17	Rice (24–18)
UCLA	43	1966–68	Houston (71–69)
LIU-Brooklyn	43	1935–37	Stanford (45–31)
Seton Hall	42	1939–41	LIU-Brooklyn (49–26)

NCAA Men's Division I Winning Streaks (Cont.)

Longest—Home Court

Team	Games	Years
Kentucky	129	1943–55
St. Bonaventure	99	1948–61
UCLA	98	1970–76
Cincinnati	86	1957–64
Marquette	81	1967–73
Arizona	81	1945–51
Lamar	80	1978–84
Long Beach St	75	1968–74
UNLV	72	1974–78
Arizona	71	1987–92
Cincinnati	68	1972–78
Western Kentucky	67	1949–55

NCAA Men's Division I Winningest Coaches

Active Coaches*

WINS

Coach and Team	W
Mike Krzyzewski, Duke	803
Lute Olson, Arizona	780
Jim Calhoun, Connecticut	774
Jim Boeheim, Syracuse	771
Bob Huggins, West Virginia	616
Tom Penders, Houston	608
Gary Williams, Maryland	604
Homer Drew, Valparaiso	593
Roy Williams, North Carolina	560
Bo Bryan, Wisconsin	556
Ben Braun, Rice	556

Note: Minimum 5 years as a Division I head coach; includes record at 4-year colleges only.

WINNING PERCENTAGE

Coach and Team	Yrs	W	L	Pct
Roy Williams, North Carolina	20	560	134	.807
Mark Few, Gonzaga	9	236	60	.797
Bruce Pearl, Tennessee	16	394	108	.785
Bo Ryan, Wisconsin	24	556	163	.773
Jamie Dixon, Pittsburgh	5	132	40	.767
Thad Matta, Ohio St	8	207	66	.758
John Calipari, Memphis	16	408	135	.751
Mike Krzyzewski, Duke	33	803	267	.750
Lute Olson, Arizona	34	780	280	.736
Bob Huggins, West Virginia	26	616	222	.735

Note: Minimum 5 years as a Division I head coach; includes record at 4-year colleges only.

Alltime Winningest Men's Division I Coaches

	W
Bob Knight (Army, Indiana, Texas Tech)	902
Dean Smith (North Carolina)	879
Adolph Rupp (Kentucky)	876
Jim Phelan (Mt. St. Mary's)	830
Eddie Sutton (Creighton, Arkansas, Kentucky, Oklahoma St)	804
*Mike Krzyzewski (Army, Duke)	803
Lefty Driesell (Davidson, Maryland, James Madison, Georgia St)	786
*Lute Olson (Long Beach St, Iowa, Arizona)	780
Lou Henson (Hardin-Simmons, New Mexico St, Illinois, New Mexico St)	779
*Jim Calhoun (Northeastern, Connecticut)	774
*Jim Boeheim (Syracuse)	771
Henry Iba (NW Missouri St, Colorado, Oklahoma St)	764
Ed Diddle (Western Kentucky)	759
Phog Allen (Baker, Kansas, Haskell, Central Missouri St, Kansas)	746
John Chaney (Cheyney St, Temple)	741
Jerry Tarkanian (Long Beach St, UNLV, Fresno St)	729
Norm Stewart (Northern Iowa, Missouri)	728
Ray Meyer (DePaul)	724
Don Haskins (Oklahoma St, UTEP)	719
Denny Crum (UCLA, Louisville)	675
John Wooden (Purdue, Indiana St, UCLA)	664
Ralph Miller (Wichita St, Iowa, Oregon St)	657
Gene Bartow (C. Missouri St, Valparaiso, Memphis, Illinois, UCLA, UAB)	647
Billy Tubbs (Lamar, Southwestern [Tex.], Oklahoma, TCU)	641
Marv Harshman (Pacific Lutheran, Washington St, Washington)	637

Note: Minimum 10 head coaching seasons in Division I.

*Active in 2007–08.

Alltime Winningest Men's Division I Coaches (Cont.)

WINNING PERCENTAGE

Coach (Team, Years)	Yrs	W	L	Pct
Clair Bee (Rider 1929–31, LIU-Brooklyn 1932–45, 1946–51)	21	412	87	.826
Adolph Rupp (Kentucky 1931–72)	41	876	190	.822
*Roy Williams (Kansas 1989–2003, North Carolina 2003–)	20	560	134	.807
John Wooden (Indiana St 1947–48, UCLA 1949–75)	29	664	162	.804
John Kresse (College of Charleston 1980–2002)	23	560	143	.797
Jerry Tarkanian (Long Beach St 1969–73, UNLV 1974–92, Fresno St 1995–2002)	31	729	201	.784
Francis Schmidt (Tulsa 1916–17, Arkansas 1924–29, TCU 1930–34)	17	258	72	.782
Dean Smith (North Carolina 1962–97)	36	879	254	.776
Jack Ramsay (St. Joseph's [Pa.] 1956–66)	11	231	71	.765
Frank Keaney (Rhode Island 1921–48)	28	401	124	.764
George Keogan (St. Louis 1916, Allegheny 1919, Valparaiso 1920–21, Notre Dame 1924–43)	27	414	127	.764
Vic Bubas (Duke 1960–69)	10	213	67	.761
Harry Fisher (Columbia 1907–16, Army 1922–23, 1925)	16	189	60	.759
*John Calipari (Massachusetts 1989–96, Memphis 2001–)	16	408	135	.751
*Mike Krzyzewski (Army 1976–80, Duke 1981–)	33	803	267	.750
Fred Bennion (Brigham Young 1909–10, Utah 1911-14, Montana St 1915-19)	11	95	32	.748
Charles (Chick) Davies (Duquesne 1925–43, 1947–48)	21	314	106	.748
Ray Mears (Wittenberg 1957–62, Tennessee 1963–77)	21	399	135	.747
Edward McNichol (Penn 1921-30)	10	186	63	.747
Al McGuire (Belmont Abbey 1958–64, Marquette 1965–77)	20	406	142	.741
Phog Allen (Baker 1906–08, Haskell 1909, C. Mo. St 1913–19, Kansas 1908–09, 1920–56)	50	746	264	.739
Everett Case (North Carolina St 1947–65)	19	377	134	.738
*Lute Olson (Long Beach St 1973–74, Iowa 1974–83, Arizona 1983–)	34	780	280	.736
Arthur Schabinger (Ottawa 1917–20, Emporia St 1921–22, Creighton 1924–25)	19	245	88	.736
*Bob Huggins (Walsh 1980–83, Akron 1984–89, Cinn. 1989–2005, Kan. St 2006–07, W.V. 2007–)	26	616	222	.735

Note: Minimum 10 head coaching seasons in Division I.

*Active in 2007–08.

Alltime Winningest Women's Division I Coaches

WINNING PERCENTAGE

Coach (Team, Years)	Yrs	W	L	Pct
Leon Barmore (Louisiana Tech 1983–02)	20	576	87	.869
*Pat Summitt (Tennessee 1975–)	34	983	182	.844
*Geno Auriemma (Connecticut 1986–)	23	657	122	.843
*Tara VanDerveer (Idaho 1979-80, Ohio St 1981–85, Stanford 1986–95, 97–)	29	724	188	.794
*Gail Goestenkors (Duke 1993–07, Texas 2007–)	16	418	112	.789
*Wes Moore (Maryville 1988–93, Francis Marion 1996–98, Chattanooga 1999–)	19	444	122	.785
Bill Sheahan (Mt. St. Mary's 1982–98)	17	372	104	.782
*Robin Selvig (Montana 1979–)	30	697	199	.778
*Andy Landers (Georgia 1980–)	29	707	225	.759
Marsha Sharp (Texas Tech 1983–06)	24	571	189	.751

Note: Minimum 10 head coaching seasons in Division I.

*Active in 2007–08.

Alltime Winningest Women's Division I Coaches

	W
*Pat Summitt (Tennessee)	983
Jody Conradt (Sam Houston St, Tex.-Arlington, Texas)	900
*C. Vivian Stringer (Cheyney St, Iowa, Rutgers)	804
*Sylvia Rhyne Hatchell (Francis Marison, North Carolina)	784
*Kay Yow (Elon, North Carolina St)	729
*Tara VanDerveer (Idaho, Ohio St, Stanford)	724
Sue Gunter (Stephen F. Austin, LSU)	708
*Andy Landers (Georgia)	707
*Robin Selvig (Montana)	697
Rene Portland (St. Joseph's, Colorado, Penn St)	693

Note: Minimum 10 head coaching seasons in Division I.

*Active in 2007–08.

NCAA Women's Division I Championship Results

Year	Winner	Score	Runner-up	Winning Coach
1982	Louisiana Tech	76–62	Cheyney	Sonja Hogg/Leon Barmore
1983	USC	69–67	Louisiana Tech	Linda Sharp
1984	USC	72–61	Tennessee	Linda Sharp
1985	Old Dominion	70–65	Georgia	Marianne Stanley
1986	Texas	97–81	USC	Jody Conradt
1987	Tennessee	67–44	Louisiana Tech	Pat Summitt
1988	Louisiana Tech	56–54	Auburn	Leon Barmore
1989	Tennessee	76–60	Auburn	Pat Summitt
1990	Stanford	88–81	Auburn	Tara VanDerveer
1991	Tennessee	70–67 (OT)	Virginia	Pat Summitt
1992	Stanford	78–62	Western Kentucky	Tara VanDerveer
1993	Texas Tech	84–82	Ohio State	Marsha Sharp
1994	North Carolina	60–59	Louisiana Tech	Sylvia Hatchell
1995	Connecticut	70–64	Tennessee	Geno Auriemma
1996	Tennessee	83–65	Georgia	Pat Summitt
1997	Tennessee	68–59	Old Dominion	Pat Summitt
1998	Tennessee	93–75	Louisiana Tech	Pat Summitt
1999	Purdue	62–45	Duke	Carolyn Peck
2000	Connecticut	71–52	Tennessee	Geno Auriemma
2001	Notre Dame	68–66	Purdue	Muffet McGraw
2002	Connecticut	82–70	Oklahoma	Geno Auriemma
2003	Connecticut	73–68	Tennessee	Geno Auriemma
2004	Connecticut	70–61	Tennessee	Geno Auriemma
2005	Baylor	84–62	Michigan St	Kim Mulkey-Robinson
2006	Maryland	78–75	Duke	Brenda Frese
2007	Tennessee	59–46	Rutgers	Pat Summitt
2008	Tennessee	64–48	Stanford	Pat Summitt

NCAA Women's Division I Alltime Individual Leaders

Single-Game Records

SCORING HIGHS

Pts	Player and Team vs Opponent	Year
60	Cindy Brown, Long Beach St vs San Jose St	1987
58	Kim Perrot, SW Louisiana vs SE Louisiana	1990
58	Lorri Bauman, Drake vs SW Missouri St*	1984
56	Jackie Stiles, SW Missouri St vs Evansville	2000
55	Patricia Hoskins, Mississippi Valley St vs Southern-Birm.	1989
55	Patricia Hoskins, Mississippi Valley St vs Alabama St	1989
54	Anjinea Hopson, Grambling vs Jackson St	1994
54	Mary Lowry, Baylor vs Texas	1994
54	Wanda Ford, Drake vs SW Missouri St*	1986

Three tied with 53.

REBOUNDS

Reb	Player and Team vs Opponent	Year
40	Deborah Temple, Delta St vs UAB	1983
37	Rosina Pearson, Bethune-Cookman vs Florida Memorial	1985
33	Maureen Formico, Pepperdine vs Loyola (Calif.)	1985
32	Lachelle Lyles, Southeast Mo. St. vs Tennessee St.	2006
31	Darlene Beale, Howard vs South Carolina St	1987
30	Cindy Bonforte, Wagner vs Queens (N.Y.)	1983
30	Kayone Hankins, New Orleans vs. Nicholls St	1994
30	Wanda Ford, Drake vs Eastern Illinois	1985
30	Jennifer Butler, Massachusetts vs Florida	2003

Three tied with 29.

ASSISTS

Asst	Player and Team vs Opponent	Year
23	Michelle Burden, Kent St vs Ball St	1991
22	Shawn Monday, Tennessee Tech vs Morehead St	1988
22	Veronica Pettry, Loyola (Ill.) vs Detroit	1989
22	Tine Freil, Pacific vs Wichita St	1991
21	Tine Freil, Pacific vs Fresno St	1992
21	Amy Bauer, Wisconsin vs Detroit	1989
21	Neacole Hall, Alabama St vs Southern-Birm.	1989

Six tied with 20.

*school changed name to Missouri State after 2004–05 season

Single Season Records

POINTS

Player and Team	Year	GP	FG	3FG	FT	Pts
Jackie Stiles, SW Missouri St*	2001	35	365	65	267	1062
Cindy Brown, Long Beach St	1987	35	362	—	250	974
Genia Miller, CSU-Fullerton	1991	33	376	0	217	969
Sheryl Swoopes, Texas Tech	1993	34	356	32	211	955
Andrea Congreaves, Mercer	1992	28	353	77	142	925
Wanda Ford, Drake	1986	30	390	—	139	919
Chamique Holdsclaw, Tennessee	1998	39	370	9	166	915
Barbara Kennedy, Clemson	1982	31	392	—	124	908
Patricia Hoskins, Mississippi Valley St	1989	27	345	13	205	908
LaTaunya Pollard, Long Beach St	1983	31	376	—	155	907

SEASON SCORING AVERAGE

Player and Team	Year	GP	FG	3FG	FT	Pts	Avg
Patricia Hoskins, Mississippi Valley St	1989	27	345	13	205	908	33.6
Andrea Congreaves, Mercer	1992	28	353	77	142	925	33.0
Deborah Temple, Delta St	1984	28	373	—	127	873	31.2
Andrea Congreaves, Mercer	1993	26	302	51	150	805	31.0
Wanda Ford, Drake	1986	30	390	—	139	919	30.6
Anucha Browne, Northwestern	1985	28	341	—	173	855	30.5
LeChandra LeDay, Grambling	1988	28	334	36	146	850	30.4
Jackie Stiles, SW MIssouri St*	2001	35	365	65	267	1062	30.3
Kim Perrot, SW Louisiana	1990	28	308	95	128	839	30.0
Tina Hutchinson, San Diego St	1984	30	383	—	132	898	29.9
Jan Jensen, Drake	1991	30	358	6	166	888	29.6
Genia Miller, CSU-Fullerton	1991	33	376	0	217	969	29.4
Barbara Kennedy, Clemson	1982	31	392	—	124	908	29.3
LaTaunya Pollard, Long Beach St	1983	31	376	—	155	907	29.3
Lisa McMullen, Alabama St	1991	28	285	126	119	815	29.1

REBOUNDS

Player and Team	Year	GP	Reb	Player and Team	Year	GP	Reb
Courtney Paris, Oklahoma	2006	36	539	Darlene Jones, Miss Valley St	1983	31	487
Wanda Ford, Drake	1985	30	534	Melanie Simpson, Okla. City	1982	37	481
Lachelle Lyles, SE Missouri St.	2006	30	517	R. Pearson, Beth.-Cookman	1985	26	480
Wanda Ford, Drake	1986	30	506	Patricia Hoskins, Miss. Valley St	1987	28	476
Anne Donovan, Old Dominion	1983	35	504	Cheryl Miller, USC	1985	30	474

REBOUND AVERAGE

Player and Team	Year	GP	Reb	Avg
Rosina Pearson, Bethune-Cookman	1985	26	480	18.5
Wanda Ford, Drake	1985	30	534	17.8
Katie Beck, East Tennessee St	1988	25	441	17.6
DeShawne Blocker, East Tennessee St	1994	26	450	17.3
Lachelle Lyles, SE Missouri St.	2006	30	517	17.2
Patricia Hoskins, Mississippi Valley St	1987	28	476	17.0
Wanda Ford, Drake	1986	30	506	16.9
Patricia Hoskins, Mississippi Valley St	1989	27	440	16.3
Joy Kellogg, Oklahoma City	1984	23	373	16.2
Courtney Paris, Oklahoma	2006	30	485	16.2
Deborah Mitchell, Mississippi Coll.	1983	28	447	16.0
Cheryl Miller, USC	1985	30	474	15.8

*school changed name to Missouri State after 2004–05 season

Single Season Records (Cont.)

FIELD-GOAL PERCENTAGE

Player and Team	Year	GP	FG	FGA	Pct
Myndee Larsen, Southern Utah	1998	28	249	344	72.4
Chantelle Anderson, Vanderbilt	2001	34	292	404	72.3
Deneka Knowles, SE Louisiana	1996	26	199	276	72.1
Crystal Langhorne, Maryland	2006	32	202	280	72.1
Barbara Farris, Tulane	1998	27	151	210	71.9
Renay Adams, Tennessee Tech	1991	30	185	258	71.7
Regina Days, Georgia Southern	1986	27	234	332	70.5
Kim Wood, UW-Green Bay	1994	27	188	271	69.4
Kelly Lyons, Old Dominion	1990	31	308	444	69.4
Alisha Hill, Howard	1995	28	194	281	69.0

Based on qualifiers for annual championship.

FREE-THROW PERCENTAGE

Player and Team	Year	GP	FT	FTA	Pct
Adrienne Squire, Penn St	2006	29	80	83	96.4
Shanna Zolman, Tennessee	2004	35	88	92	95.7
Ginny Doyle, Richmond	1992	29	96	101	95.0
Jill Marano, La Salle	2003	29	88	93	94.6
Sue Bird, Connecticut	2002	39	98	104	94.2
Paula Corder-King, SE Missouri St	1999	28	111	118	94.1
Kandi Brown, Morehead St	2003	28	104	111	93.7
Linda Cyborski, Delaware	1991	29	74	79	93.7
Kandi Brown, Morehead St	2002	29	74	79	93.7
Kristin Iwanaga, California	2005	29	85	91	93.4

Based on qualifiers for annual championship.

Career Records

POINTS

Player and Team	Yrs	GP	Pts
Jackie Stiles, SW Missouri St*	1997–01	129	3393
Patricia Hoskins, Mississippi Valley St	1985–89	110	3122
Lorri Bauman, Drake	1981–84	120	3115
Chamique Holdsclaw, Tennessee	1995–99	148	3025
Cheryl Miller, USC	1983–86	128	3018
Cindy Blodgett, Maine	1994–98	118	3005
LaToya Thomas, Mississippi St	1999–2003	125	2981
Valorie Whiteside, Appalachian St	1984–88	116	2944
Kelly Mazzante, Penn St	2000–04	133	2919
Joyce Walker, LSU	1981–84	117	2906

SCORING AVERAGE

Player and Team	Yrs	GP	FG	3FG	FT	Pts	Avg
Patricia Hoskins, Mississippi Valley St	1985–89	110	1196	24	706	3122	28.4
Sandra Hodge, New Orleans	1981–84	107	1194	—	472	2860	26.7
Jackie Stiles, SW Missouri St*	1997–01	129	1160	221	852	3393	26.3
Lorri Bauman, Drake	1981–84	120	1104	—	907	3115	26.0
Andrea Congreaves, Mercer	1989–93	108	1107	153	429	2796	25.9
Cindy Blodgett, Maine	1994–98	118	1055	219	676	3005	25.5
Valorie Whiteside, Appalachian St	1984–88	116	1153	0	638	2944	25.4
Joyce Walker, LSU	1981–84	117	1259	—	388	2906	24.8
Tarcha Hollis, Grambling	1989–91	84	891	3	246	2031	24.2
Korie Hlede, Duquesne	1994–98	109	1045	162	379	2631	24.1
Karen Pelphrey, Marshall	1983–86	114	1175	—	396	2746	24.1

*school changed name to Missouri State after 2004–05 season

NCAA Men's Division II Championship Results

Year	Winner	Score	Runner-up	Third Place	Fourth Place
1957	Wheaton (Ill.)	89–65	Kentucky Wesleyan	Mt. St. Mary's (Md.)	CSU-Los Angeles
1958	South Dakota	75–53	St. Michael's	Evansville	Wheaton (Ill.)
1959	Evansville	83–67	SW Missouri St	North Carolina A&T	CSU-Los Angeles
1960	Evansville	90–69	Chapman	Kentucky Wesleyan	Cornell College
1961	Wittenberg	42–38	SE Missouri St	South Dakota St	Mt. St. Mary's (Md.)
1962	Mt. St. Mary's (Md.)	58–57 (OT)	CSU-Sacramento	Southern Illinois	Nebraska Wesleyan
1963	South Dakota St	44–42	Wittenberg	Oglethorpe	Southern Illinois
1964	Evansville	72–59	Akron	North Carolina A&T	Northern Iowa
1965	Evansville	85–82 (OT)	Southern Illinois	North Dakota	St. Michael's
1966	Kentucky Wesleyan	54–51	Southern Illinois	Akron	North Dakota
1967	Winston-Salem	77–74	SW Missouri St	Kentucky Wesleyan	Illinois St
1968	Kentucky Wesleyan	63–52	Indiana St	Trinity (Tex.)	Ashland
1969	Kentucky Wesleyan	75–71	SW Missouri St	†Vacated	Ashland
1970	Philadelphia Textile	76–65	Tennessee St	UC-Riverside	Buffalo St
1971	Evansville	97–82	Old Dominion	†Vacated	Kentucky Wesleyan
1972	Roanoke	84–72	Akron	Tennessee St	Eastern Mich
1973	Kentucky Wesleyan	78–76 (OT)	Tennessee St	Assumption	Brockport St
1974	Morgan St	67–52	SW Missouri St	Assumption	New Orleans
1975	Old Dominion	76–74	New Orleans	Assumption	Tenn.-Chattanooga
1976	Puget Sound	83–74	Tenn.-Chattanooga	Eastern Illinois	Old Dominion
1977	Tenn.-Chattanooga	71–62	Randolph-Macon	North Alabama	Sacred Heart
1978	Cheyney	47–40	UW-Green Bay	Eastern Illinois	Central Florida
1979	North Alabama	64–50	UW-Green Bay	Cheyney	Bridgeport
1980	Virginia Union	80–74	New York Tech	Florida Southern	North Alabama
1981	Florida Southern	73–68	Mt. St. Mary's (Md.)	Cal Poly-SLO	UW-Green Bay
1982	District of Columbia	73–63	Florida Southern	Kentucky Wesleyan	CSU-Bakersfield
1983	Wright St	92–73	District of Columbia	*CSU-Bakersfield	*Morningside
1984	Central Missouri St	81–77	St. Augustine's	*Kentucky Wesleyan	*N Alabama
1985	Jacksonville St	74–73	South Dakota St	*Kentucky Wesleyan	*Mt. St. Mary's (Md.)
1986	Sacred Heart	93–87	SE Missouri St	*Cheyney	*Florida Southern
1987	Kentucky Wesleyan	92–74	Gannon	*Delta St	*Eastern Montana
1988	Lowell	75–72	Ak.-Anchorage	Florida Southern	Troy St
1989	North Carolina Central	73–46	SE Missouri St	UC-Riverside	Jacksonville St
1990	Kentucky Wesleyan	93–79	CSU-Bakersfield	North Dakota	Morehouse
1991	North Alabama	79–72	Bridgeport (Conn.)	*CSU-Bakersfield	*Virginia Union
1992	Virginia Union	100–75	Bridgeport (Conn.)	*CSU-Bakersfield	*California (Pa.)
1993	CSU-Bakersfield	85–72	Troy St (Ala.)	*New Hampshire Coll	*Wayne St (Mich.)
1994	CSU-Bakersfield	92–86	Southern Indiana	*New Hampshire Coll	*Washburn
1995	Southern Indiana	71–63	UC–Riverside	*Norfolk St	*Indiana (Pa.)
1996	Fort Hays St	70–63	Northern Kentucky	*California (Pa.)	*Virginia Union
1997	CSU-Bakersfield	57–56	Northern Kentucky	*Lynn	*Salem-Teikyo
1998	UC-Davis	83–77	Kentucky Wesleyan	*St. Rose	*Virginia Union
1999	Kentucky Wesleyan	75–60	Metropolitan St	*Truman St	*Florida Southern
2000	Metropolitan St	97–79	Kentucky Wesleyan	*Missouri Southern	*Seattle Pacific
2001	Kentucky Wesleyan	72–63	Washburn	*Western Washington	*Tampa
2002	Metropolitan St	80–72	Kentucky Wesleyan	*Shaw	*Indiana (Pa.)
2003	Northeastern St (Okla.)	75–64	†Vacated	*Bowie St	*Queens (N.Y.)
2004	Kennesaw St	84–59	Southern Indiana	*Humboldt St	*Metropolitan St
2005	Virginia Union	63–58	Bryant	*Lynn	*Tarleton St
2006	Winona St (Minn.)	73–61	Virginia Union	*Seattle Pacific	*Stonehill
2007	Barton	77–75	Winona St (Minn.)	*CSU-San Bernardino	*Central Missouri
2008	Winona St (Minn.)	87–76	Augusta St	*Bentley	*Ak.-Anchorage

*tied for third place

*Indicates tied for third. †Student-athletes representing American International in 1969, Southwestern Louisiana in 1971, and Kentucky Wesleyan in 2003 were declared ineligible subsequent to the tournament. Under NCAA rules, the teams' and ineligible student-athletes' records were deleted, and the teams' places in the final standings were vacated.

NCAA Men's Division II Alltime Individual Leaders

SINGLE-GAME SCORING HIGHS

Pts	Player and Team vs Opponent	Date
113	Bevo Francis, Rio Grande vs Hillsdale	1954
84	Bevo Francis, Rio Grande vs Alliance	1954
82	Bevo Francis, Rio Grande vs Bluffton	1954
80	Paul Crissman, USC vs Pacific Christian	1966
77	William English, Winston-Salem vs Fayetteville St	1968

Single Season Records

SCORING AVERAGE

Player and Team	Year	GP	FG	FT	Pts	Avg
Bevo Francis, Rio Grande	1954	27	444	367	1255	46.5
Earl Glass, Mississippi Industrial	1963	19	322	171	815	42.9
Earl Monroe, Winston-Salem	1967	32	509	311	1329	41.5
John Rinka, Kenyon	1970	23	354	234	942	41.0
Willie Shaw, Lane	1964	18	303	121	727	40.4

REBOUND AVERAGE

Player and Team	Year	GP	Reb	Avg
Tom Hart, Middlebury	1956	21	620	29.5
Tom Hart, Middlebury	1955	22	649	29.5
Frank Stronczek, American Int'l	1966	26	717	27.6
R.C. Owens, College of Idaho	1954	25	677	27.1
Maurice Stokes, St. Francis (Pa.)	1954	26	689	26.5

ASSISTS

Player and Team	Year	GP	Asst
Steve Ray, Bridgeport	1989	32	400
Steve Ray, Bridgeport	1990	33	385
Tony Smith, Pfeiffer	1992	35	349
Jim Ferrer, Bentley	1989	31	309
Rob Paternostro, New Hamp. Coll	1995	33	309

ASSIST AVERAGE

Player and Team	Year	GP	Asst	Avg
Steve Ray, Bridgeport	1989	32	400	12.5
Steve Ray, Bridgeport	1990	33	385	11.7
Demetri Beekman, Assumption	1993	23	264	11.5
Ernest Jenkins, N.M.-Highlands	1995	27	291	10.8
Brian Gregory, Oakland	1989	28	300	10.7

FIELD-GOAL PERCENTAGE

Player and Team	Year	Pct
Todd Linder, Tampa	1987	75.2
Maurice Stafford, North Alabama	1984	75.0
Matthew Cornegay, Tuskegee	1982	74.8
Callistus Eziukwu, Grand Valley St	2005	73.7
Brian Moten, W. Georgia	1992	73.4

FREE-THROW PERCENTAGE

Player and Team	Year	Pct
Paul Cluxton, Northern Kentucky	1997	100.0
Tomas Rimkus, Pace	1997	95.6
C.J. Cowgill, Chaminade	2001	95.0
Billy Newton, Morgan St	1976	94.4
Kent Andrews, McNeese St	1968	94.4

Career Records

POINTS

Player and Team	Yrs	Pts
Travis Grant, Kentucky St	1969–72	4045
Bob Hopkins, Grambling	1953–56	3759
Tony Smith, Pfeiffer	1989–92	3350
Earnest Lee, Clark Atlanta	1984–87	3298
Joe Miller, Alderson-Broaddus	1954–57	3294

CAREER SCORING AVERAGE

Player and Team	Yrs	GP	Pts	Avg
Travis Grant, Kentucky St	1969–72	121	4045	33.4
John Rinka, Kenyon	1967–70	99	3251	32.8
Florindo Vieira, Quinnipiac	1954–57	69	2263	32.8
Willie Shaw, Lane	1961–64	76	2379	31.3
Mike Davis, Virginia Union	1966–69	89	2758	31.0

REBOUND AVERAGE

Player and Team	Yrs	GP	Reb	Avg
Tom Hart, Middlebury	1953, 55–56	63	1738	27.6
Maurice Stokes, St. Francis (Pa.)	1953–55	72	1812	25.2
Frank Stronczek, American Int'l	1965–67	62	1549	25.0
Bill Thieben, Hofstra	1954–56	76	1837	24.2
Hank Brown, Lowell Tech	1965–67	49	1129	23.0

NCAA Men's Division II Alltime Individual Leaders (Cont.)

Career Records (Cont.)

ASSISTS

Player and Team	Yrs	Asst
Demetri Beekman, Assumption	1990–93	1044
Adam Kaufman, Edinboro	1998–01	936
Rob Paternostro, New Hamp. Coll.	1992–95	919
Luke Cooper, Alaska-Anchorage	2005–08	880
Tony Smith, Pfeiffer	1989–92	828

ASSIST AVERAGE

Player and Team	Yrs	GP	Asst	Avg
Steve Ray, Bridgeport	1989-90	65	785	12.1
Demetri Beekman, Assumption	1990-93	119	1044	8.8
Ernest Jenkins, N.M.-Highlands	1992-95	84	699	8.3
Zack Whiting, Chaminade	2004–07	86	703	8.2
Adam Kaufman, Edinboro	1998-01	116	936	8.1

Note: Minimum 550 Assists.

FIELD-GOAL PERCENTAGE

Player and Team	Yrs	Pct
Todd Linder, Tampa	1984–87	70.8
Tom Schurfranz, Bellarmine	1989–92	70.2
Chad Scott, California (Pa.)	1991–94	70.0
Ed Phillips, Alabama A&M	1968–71	68.9
Ulysses Hackett, SC-Spartanburg	1990–92	67.9

Note: Minimum 400 FGM.

FREE-THROW PERCENTAGE

Player and Team	Yrs	Pct
Paul Cluxton, Northern Kentucky	1994-97	93.5
Kent Andrews, McNeese St	1967-69	91.6
Chris Brunson, Souther Ind.	2002–05	90.1
Jon Hagen, Minnesota St–Mankato	1963-65	90.0
Drew Carlson, Minn. St–Mankato	2000–03	89.5

Note: Minimum 250 FTM.

NCAA Men's Division III Championship Results

Year	Winner	Score	Runner-up	Third Place	Fourth Place
1975	LeMoyne-Owen	57–54	Glassboro St	Augustana (Ill.)	Brockport St
1976	Scranton	60–57	Wittenberg	Augustana (Ill.)	Plattsburgh St
1977	Wittenberg	79–66	Oneonta St	Scranton	Hamline
1978	North Park	69–57	Widener	Albion	Stony Brook
1979	North Park	66–62	Potsdam St	Franklin & Marshall	Centre
1980	North Park	83–76	Upsala	Wittenberg	Longwood
1981	Potsdam St	67–65 (OT)	Augustana (Ill.)	Ursinus	Otterbein
1982	Wabash	83–62	Potsdam St	Brooklyn	CSU-Stanislaus
1983	Scranton	64–63	Wittenberg	Roanoke	UW–Whitewater
1984	UW–Whitewater	103–86	Clark (Mass.)	DePauw	Upsala
1985	North Park	72–71	Potsdam St	Nebraska Wesleyan	Widener
1986	Potsdam St	76–73	LeMoyne-Owen	Nebraska Wesleyan	Jersey City St
1987	North Park	106–100	Clark (Mass.)	Wittenberg	Stockton St
1988	Ohio Wesleyan	92–70	Scranton	Nebraska Wesleyan	Hartwick
1989	UW–Whitewater	94–86	Trenton St	Southern Maine	Centre
1990	Rochester	43–42	DePauw	Washington (Md.)	Calvin
1991	UW–Platteville	81–74	Franklin & Marshall	Otterbein	Ramapo (N.J.)
1992	Calvin	62–49	Rochester	UW–Platteville	Jersey City St
1993	Ohio Northern	71–68	Augustana	Mass.–Dartmouth	Rowan
1994	Lebanon Valley Coll	66–59 (OT)	NYU	Wittenberg	St Thomas (Minn.)
1995	UW–Platteville	69-55	Manchester	Rowan	Trinity (Conn.)
1996	Rowan	100–93	Hope (Mich.)	Illinois Wesleyan	Franklin & Marshall
1997	Illinois Wesleyan	89–86	Nebraska Wesleyan	Williams	Alvernia
1998	UW–Platteville	69–56	Hope (Mich.)	Williams	Wilkes
1999	UW–Platteville	76–75 (2 OT)	Hampden-Sydney	William Paterson	Connecticut Coll.
2000	Calvin	79–74	UW-Eau Claire	Salem St	Franklin & Marshall
2001	Catholic	76–62	William Paterson	Illinois Wesleyan	Ohio Northern
2002	Otterbein	102–83	Elizabethtown	Carthage	Rochester
2003	Williams	67–65	Gustavus Adolphus	Wooster	Hampden Sydney
2004	UW–Stevens Point	84–82	Williams	John Carroll	Amherst
2005	UW–Stevens Point	73–49	Rochester	Calvin	York
2006	Virginia Wesleyan	59–56	Wittenberg	Illinois Wesleyan	Amherst
2007	Amherst	80–67	Virginia Wesleyan	Washington (Mo.)	Wooster
2008	Washington-St. Louis	90–860	Amherst	Hope	Ursinus

NCAA Men's Division III Alltime Individual Leaders

SINGLE-GAME SCORING HIGHS

Pts	Player and Team vs Opponent	Year
77	Jeff Clement, Grinnell vs Illinois College	1998
69	Steve Diekmann, Grinnell vs Simpson	1995
64	Tim Russell, Albertus Magnus	2005
63	Ryan Hodges, Cal-Lutheran	2005
63	Joe DeRoche, Thomas vs St. Joseph's (Me.)	1988
62	Kyle Myrick, Lincoln (Pa.) vs. Penn St.-Abington	2006
62	Nick Pelotte, Plymouth St	2005
62	Shannon Lilly, Bishop vs Southwest Assembly of God	1983
61	Steve Honderd, Calvin vs Kalamazoo	1993
61	Dana Wilson, Husson vs Ricker	1974

Single Season Records

SCORING AVERAGE

Player and Team	Year	GP	FG	FT	Pts	Avg
Steve Diekmann, Grinnell	1995	20	223	162	745	37.3
Rickey Sutton, Lyndon St	1976	14	207	93	507	36.2
Shannon Lilly, Bishop	1983	26	345	218	908	34.9
Dana Wilson, Husson	1974	20	288	122	698	34.9
Rickey Sutton, Lyndon St	1977	16	223	112	558	34.9

REBOUND AVERAGE

Player and Team	Year	GP	Reb	Avg
Joe Manley, Bowie St	1976	29	579	20.0
Fred Petty, New Hampshire Coll.	1974	22	436	19.8
Larry Williams, Pratt	1977	24	457	19.0
Charles Greer, Thomas	1977	17	318	18.7
Larry Parker, Plattsburgh St	1975	23	430	18.7

ASSISTS

Player and Team	Year	GP	Asst
Robert James, Kean	1989	29	391
Tennyson Whitted, Ramapo	2002	29	319
Ricky Spicer, UW-Whitewater	1989	31	295
Joe Marcotte, New Jersey Tech	1995	30	292
Andre Bolton, Chris. Newport	1996	30	289

ASSIST AVERAGE

Player and Team	Year	GP	Asst	Avg
Robert James, Kean	1989	29	391	13.5
Albert Kirchner, Mt. St. Vincent	1990	24	267	11.1
Tennyson Whitted, Ramapo	2002	29	319	11.0
Ron Torgalski, Hamilton	1989	26	275	10.6
Louis Adams, Rust	1989	22	227	10.3

FIELD-GOAL PERCENTAGE

Player and Team	Year	Pct
Travis Weiss, St. John's (Minn.)	1994	76.6
Brian Schmitting, Ripon	2006	76.3
Pete Metzelaars, Wabash	1982	75.3
Tony Rychlec, Mass. Maritime	1981	74.9
Tony Rychlec, Mass. Maritime	1982	73.1

FREE-THROW PERCENTAGE

Player and Team	Year	Pct
Korey Coon, Illinois Wesleyan	2000	96.3
Chanse Young, Manchester	1998	95.6
Andy Enfield, Johns Hopkins	1991	95.3
Nick Wilkins, Coe	2003	95.7
Chris Carideo, Widener	1992	95.2

Career Records

POINTS

Player and Team	Yrs	Pts
Andre Foreman, Salisbury St	1989–92	2940
Willie Chandler, Misericordia	2000–03	2898
Lamont Strothers, Chris. Newport	1988–91	2709
Matt Hancock, Colby	1987–90	2678
Scott Fitch, Geneseo St	1990–94	2634

SCORING AVERAGE

Player and Team	Yrs	GP	Avg
Dwain Govan, Bishop	1974–75	55	32.8
Dave Russell, Shepherd	1974–75	60	30.6
Kyle Myrick, Lincoln (Pa.)	2005–06	57	30.2
Rickey Sutton, Lyndon St	1976–79	80	29.7
John Atkins, Knoxville	1976–78	70	28.7

REBOUND AVERAGE

Player and Team	Yrs	GP	Reb	Avg
Larry Parker, Plattsburgh St	1975–78	85	1482	17.4
Charles Greer, Thomas	1975–77	58	926	16.0
Willie Parr, LeMoyne-Owen	1974–76	76	1182	15.6
Michael Smith, Hamilton	1989–92	107	1632	15.2
Dave Kufeld, Yeshiva	1977–80	81	1222	15.1

ASSIST AVERAGE

Player and Team	Yrs	Avg
Phil Dixon, Shenandoah	1993–96	8.6
Tennyson Whitted, Ramapo	2000–03	8.5
Steve Artis, Chris. Newport	1990–93	8.1
David Genovese, Mt. St. Vincent	1992–95	7.5
Kevin Root, Eureka	1989–91	7.1

Hockey

Goalie Chris Osgood led the Detroit Red Wings to the Stanley Cup

DAVID E. KLUTHO/SPORTS ILLUSTRATED

Return of Hockeytown

One veteran franchise and a few young guns gave the NHL a much-needed—and well-deserved—boost in 2008

BY B.J. SCHECTER

THE POST-LOCKOUT NHL HAS largely been an afterthought in U.S. sports, overtaken as the fourth major professional league by NASCAR and the ever growing mixed martial arts (part wrestling, part boxing, part mortal combat). Much of the hockey on national television has been banished to the strangely named Versus network and most of the league's stars could walk through the streets of any U.S. city unnoticed. Even Detroit, known for years as Hockeytown USA, experienced a temporary blip as there were thousands of empty seats at Joe Louis Arena during the 2007 playoffs. Overall the game is better and the league is more financially sound, but to the general public it's still the same old NHL. That's too bad because the new-age NHL is exciting, intense and entertaining.

Despite some compelling storylines during the regular season—the fantastic season by the Captials' Alex Ovechkin, an outdoor game in Buffalo and several historic milestones—there was little buzz as the league skated along, but that all changed with a fantastic postseason that featured the return of a dominant franchise, the coming of age of a young star and a Pennsylvania showdown in the Eastern Conference final. Most importantly, it was the return of Hockeytown. A gripping playoffs and compelling finals played well not only in Detroit—where the Red Wings went head-to-head with the Pistons and won—but also the nation, as television ratings were up significantly. If only the NHL had shortened the season and gone right to the postseason.

In the end, the grit and experience of Detroit was enough to overcome Sidney Crosby and the emerging Pittsburgh Penguins in six games as the Red Wings won their 11th Stanley Cup, but Crosby & Co. put up quite a fight. After falling behind three games to one, the Penguins pulled out a thrilling 4–3, triple-overtime victory in Game 5, the fifth longest game in Cup history. Pittsburgh wouldn't go quietly and nearly forced a Game 7 before falling 3–2 in Game 6. Sports fans across the nation took notice as 6.8 million—including 45 percent of all television viewers in Detroit—tuned into the clincher, making it the most-watched Game 6 in 13 years.

The championship was a crowning achievement for Detroit's Nicklas Lidstrom, Hendrik Zetterberg and Pavel Datsyuk, a trio who dispelled the notion that Europeans were soft and couldn't lead a team to the Cup in the modern NHL. "Why do people still think we're a soft team?" asked Red Wings GM Ken Holland. "Because of our passports, right?"

BRUCE BENNETT/GETTY IMAGES

Detroit was far from soft and won its fourth Stanley Cup in 11 years because it had the best players and the best team, regardless of nationality. Take it from former captain Steve Yzerman, now the team's vice president. "Our top players are Europeans—and they're also our top competitors," he said. "Good players come from all over."

These weren't the Wings of old, to be sure. Before the salary cap was introduced post-lockout, Detroit would simply outspend everyone with the exception of the New York Rangers. Now, the Red Wings mix seasoned pros with an array of up-and-coming young players. As veteran *Sports Illustrated* hockey writer Michael Farber wrote: "The Red Wings used to be the New York Yankees. Now they are Moneyball."

If the Red Wings are hockey's version of Moneyball, the Penguins are back in the money after a well-publicized fall from the highlife. After the Mario Lemieux era, the franchise filed for bankruptcy, was nearly relocated to Kansas City, endured years of losing and saw its average game attendance dwindle to 11,877. Then the Penguins won the lottery—literally—and selected Sidney Crosby with the No. 1 pick in the 2005 Draft. Pittsburgh's fortunes changed immediately.

In addition to leading the NHL in goals (65) and points (112), Washington Capitals winger Alexander Ovechkin collected the Hart, Pearson and Art Ross trophies.

In just his third year, Crosby overcame a mid-season ankle injury which sidelined him for 29 games and carried the Penguins to the Stanley Cup finals before his 21st birthday. By comparison, Wayne Gretzky took four years to reach the finals and it took Lemieux seven. It wasn't all Crosby, however. He had a terrific supporting cast in Evgeni Malkin, Jordan Staal and newly invigorated goalie Marc-Andre Fleury. "If you go to the bottom and stay there a couple of years good things [can] happen," said

LOU CAPOZZOLA

Crosby scored 24 goals and had 48 assists in the '07–08 regular season, despite missing 29 games to injury.

Penguins CEO Ken Sawyer.

Crosby had a marvelous postseason, proving his star power when it mattered with a playoff-best 27 points. And though Crosby failed to bring the Stanley Cup back to Pittsburgh, he gave notice that the Penguins would be a factor for years to come. "We showed we were a complete team," said Crosby. "Every game is not going to be your team's strength. We have to be patient sometimes, and we proved we could play that way. And if you want to skate up and down with us, yeah, we can do that too."

Not many players could skate with the Captials' Ovechkin, who led the league with 65 goals and 112 points, propelling Washington to a stunning mid-season turnaround. Ovechkin went on to win the Hart, Pearson and Ross trophies. There were a couple of other notable milestones reached in the 2007–08 season. Dallas forward Mike Modano became the all-time leading scorer among U.S.-born players with his 1,233rd point, and erstwhile Devils netminder Martin Brodeur became the first goalie to record 10 consecutive 30-win seasons.

However, the biggest buzz of the regular season was generated with a New Year's Day outdoor game at Buffalo's Ralph Wilson Stadium between the Sabres and the Penguins. More than 71,000 fans braved the snow and frigid cold and watched Sidney Crosby (who else?) beat Buffalo 2–1 with a shootout goal. The event was such a hit that the league decided to do it again with the Blackhawks set to host the Red Wings on New Year's Day 2009 at Wrigley Field.

That game will generate plenty of good publicity, something the league sorely needs after the botched sale of the Nashville Predators. The team was bought by Canadian investor William Del Biaggio and shortly thereafter reports about Del Biaggio's questionable business dealings surfaced along with questions about whether the NHL did its due diligence in checking Del Biaggo (a charge the league denied). The saga stretched into the 2008–09 season with no resolution.

The offseason drama couldn't overshadow the glow of the finals, though. Having the Red Wings as champion is good for the league; marketing the game around a 21-year-old star who isn't yet approaching his prime is even better. And given Detroit's new strategy of developing young talent to complement its stars, it's conceivable that Detroit-Pittsburgh could be a budding rivalry. For now, though, the Red Wings are a step above the rest.

"This group has three more years [as an elite team]," said Detroit assistant GM Jim Nill, "then we've got a lot of guys who are 27, 28, or 29, so they have five years left. And our kids are getting better. There's a definite chain of command here."

FOR THE RECORD•2007–2008

2007–08 NHL Final Regular Season Standings

Western Conference

CENTRAL DIVISION

	GP	W	L	OTL	Pts	GF	GA
†Detroit	82	54	21	7	115	252	179
*Nashville	82	41	32	9	91	227	224
Chicago	82	40	34	8	88	234	231
Columbus	82	34	36	12	80	190	210
St. Louis	82	33	36	13	79	202	232

NORTHWEST DIVISION

	GP	W	L	OTL	Pts	GF	GA
†Minnesota	82	44	28	10	98	220	210
*Colorado	82	44	31	7	95	224	216
*Calgary	82	42	30	10	94	226	224
Edmonton	82	41	35	6	88	220	247
Vancouver	82	39	33	10	88	207	206

PACIFIC DIVISION

	GP	W	L	OTL	Pts	GF	GA
†San Jose	82	49	23	10	108	216	187
*Anaheim	82	47	27	8	102	197	184
*Dallas	82	45	30	7	97	237	204
Phoenix	82	38	37	7	83	209	225
Los Angeles	82	32	43	7	71	226	263

OTL=overtime loss; worth 1 pt.

Eastern Conference

NORTHEAST DIVISION

	GP	W	L	OTL	Pts	GF	GA
†Montreal	82	47	25	10	104	257	216
*Ottawa	82	43	31	8	94	258	242
*Boston	82	41	29	12	94	206	215
Buffalo	82	39	31	12	90	251	233
Toronto	82	36	35	11	83	228	256

ATLANTIC DIVISION

	GP	W	L	OTL	Pts	GF	GA
†Pittsburgh	82	47	27	8	102	240	212
*New Jersey	82	46	29	7	99	198	193
*NY Rangers	82	42	27	13	97	205	190
*Philadelphia	82	42	29	11	95	245	227
NY Islanders	82	35	38	9	79	189	240

SOUTHEAST DIVISION

	GP	W	L	OTL	Pts	GF	GA
†Washington	82	43	31	8	94	238	227
Carolina	82	43	33	6	92	250	246
Florida	82	38	35	9	85	211	220
Atlanta	82	34	40	8	76	207	266
Tampa Bay	82	31	42	9	71	221	266

†Division winner. *Playoff team.

2008 Stanley Cup Playoffs

Stanley Cup Playoff Results

Conference Quarterfinals

EASTERN CONFERENCE

Date	Team	Score	Opponent	Score
April 9	NY Rangers	4	at New Jersey	1
April 11	NY Rangers	2	at New Jersey	1
April 13	New Jersey	4	at NY Rangers	3*
April 16	New Jersey	3	at NY Rangers	5
April 18	NY Rangers	5	at New Jersey	3

*Overtime game.

NY Rangers won series 4–1.

Stanley Cup Playoff Results *(Cont.)*

Conference Quarterfinals *(Cont.)*

EASTERN CONFERENCE *(CONT.)*

Date	Visitor	Score	Home	Score
April 10	Boston	1	at Montreal	4
April 12	Boston	2	at Montreal	3*
April 13	Montreal	1	at Boston	2*
April 15	Montreal	1	at Boston	0
April 17	Boston	5	at Montreal	1
April 19	Montreal	4	at Boston	5
April 21	Boston	0	at Montreal	5

Montreal won series 4–3.

Date	Visitor	Score	Home	Score
April 9	Ottawa	0	at Pittsburgh	4
April 11	Ottawa	3	at Pittsburgh	5
April 14	Pittsburgh	4	at Ottawa	1
April 16	Pittsburgh	3	at Ottawa	1

Pittsburgh won series 4–0.

Date	Visitor	Score	Home	Score
April 11	Philadelphia	4	at Washington	5
April 13	Philadelphia	2	at Washington	0
April 15	Washington	3	at Philadelphia	6
April 17	Washington	3	at Philadelphia	4†
April 19	Philadelphia	2	at Washington	3
April 21	Washington	4	at Philadelphia	2
April 22	Philadelphia	3	at Washington	2*

Philadelphia won series 4–3.

WESTERN CONFERENCE

Date	Visitor	Score	Home	Score
April 10	Nashville	1	at Detroit	3
April 12	Nashville	2	at Detroit	4
April 14	Detroit	3	at Nashville	5
April 16	Detroit	2	at Nashville	3
April 18	Nashville	1	at Detroit	2*
April 20	Detroit	3	at Nashville	0

Detroit won series 4–2.

Date	Visitor	Score	Home	Score
April 9	Colorado	3	at Minnesota	2*
April 11	Colorado	2	at Minnesota	3*
April 14	Minnesota	3	at Colorado	2*
April 15	Minnesota	1	at Colorado	5
April 17	Colorado	3	at Minnesota	2
April 19	Minnesota	1	at Colorado	2

Colorado won series 4–2.

Date	Visitor	Score	Home	Score
April 10	Dallas	4	at Anaheim	0
April 12	Dallas	5	at Anaheim	2
April 15	Anaheim	4	at Dallas	2
April 17	Anaheim	1	at Dallas	3
April 18	Dallas	2	at Anaheim	5
April 20	Anaheim	1	at Dallas	4

Dallas won series 4–2.

Date	Visitor	Score	Home	Score
April 9	Calgary	3	at San Jose	2
April 10	Calgary	0	at San Jose	2
April 13	San Jose	3	at Calgary	4
April 15	San Jose	3	at Calgary	2
April 17	Calgary	3	at San Jose	4
April 20	San Jose	0	at Calgary	2
April 22	Calgary	3	at San Jose	5

San Jose won series 4–3.

Conference Semifinals

EASTERN CONFERENCE

Date	Visitor	Score	Home	Score
April 25	NY Rangers	4	at Pittsburgh	5
April 27	NY Rangers	0	at Pittsburgh	2
April 29	Pittsburgh	5	at NY Rangers	3
May 1	Pittsburgh	0	at NY Rangers	3
May 4	NY Rangers	2	at Pittsburgh	3*

Pittsburgh won series 4–1.

Date	Visitor	Score	Home	Score
April 24	Philadelphia	3	at Montreal	4*
April 26	Philadelphia	4	at Montreal	2
April 28	Montreal	2	at Philadelphia	3
April 30	Montreal	2	at Philadelphia	4
May 3	Philadelphia	6	at Montreal	4

Philadelphia won series 4–1.

WESTERN CONFERENCE

Date	Visitor	Score	Home	Score
April 24	Colorado	3	at Detroit	4
April 26	Colorado	1	at Detroit	5
April 29	Detroit	4	at Colorado	3
May 1	Detroit	8	at Colorado	2

Detroit won series 4–0.

Date	Visitor	Score	Home	Score
April 25	Dallas	3	at San Jose	2*
April 27	Dallas	5	at San Jose	2
April 29	San Jose	1	at Dallas	2*
April 30	San Jose	2	at Dallas	1
May 2	Dallas	2	at San Jose	3*
May 4	San Jose	1	at Dallas	2‡

Dallas won series 4–2.

Eastern Conference Finals

Date	Visitor	Score	Home	Score
May 9	Philadelphia	2	at Pittsburgh	4
May 11	Philadelphia	2	at Pittsburgh	4
May 13	Pittsburgh	4	at Philadelphia	1
May 15	Pittsburgh	2	at Philadelphia	4
May 18	Philadelphia	0	at Pittsburgh	6

Pittsburgh won series 4–1.

Western Conference Finals

Date	Visitor	Score	Home	Score
May 8	Dallas	1	at Detroit	4
May 10	Dallas	1	at Detroit	2
May 12	Detroit	5	at Dallas	2
May 14	Detroit	1	at Dallas	3
May 17	Dallas	2	at Detroit	1
May 19	Detroit	4	at Dallas	1

Detroit won series 4–2.

Stanley Cup Finals

Date	Visitor	Score	Home	Score
May 24	Pittsburgh	0	at Detroit	4
May 26	Pittsburgh	0	at Detroit	3
May 28	Detroit	2	at Pittsburgh	3
May 31	Detroit	2	at Pittsburgh	1
June 2	Pittsburgh	4	at Detroit	3**
June 4	Detroit	3	at Pittsburgh	2

Detroit won series 4–2.

*Overtime game. †Double overtime game. **Triple overtime game. ‡Quadruple overtime game.

Stanley Cup Final Box Scores

Game 1

Pittsburgh	0	0	0—0
Detroit	0	1	3—4

FIRST PERIOD

Scoring: None. Penalties: K Leating, Pitt (interference), 3:51; T Holmstrom, Det (high-sticking), 4:02; N Lidstrom, Det (hooking), 10:15; D Helm (tripping), 12:38; T Holmstrom, Det (goalie interference), 15:20; H Gill, Pitt (high-sticking), 19:00.

SECOND PERIOD

Scoring: 1, Detroit, M Samuelsson (unassisted), 13:01. Penalties: S Crosby, Pitt (slashing), 1:55; R Whitney, Pitt (holding), 13:13; E Malkin (tripping), 19:28.

THIRD PERIOD

Scoring: 3, Detroit, M Samuelsson (unassisted), 2:16; D Cleary (SH–B Stuart), 17:18; H Zetterberg (PP–T Holmstrom, N Lidstrom), 19:47. Penalties: N Lidstrom, Det (interference), 15:27; J Ruutu, Pitt (slashing), 18:08;

Shots on goal: DET 11-16-9—36; PIT 12-4-3—19.

Power-play opportunities: DET 1-6, PIT 0-5.

Goalies: Det, C Osgood (19 shots, 19 saves). Pitt, M. Fleury (36 shots, 32 saves).

Referees: Devorski, O'Halloran. Linesmen: Sharrers, Heyer.

A: 20,066.

Game 2

Pittsburgh	0	0	0—0
Detroit	2	0	1—3

FIRST PERIOD

Scoring: 2, Detroit, B Stuart (V Filppula), 6:55; T Homstrom (H Zetterberg), 11:18. Penalties: B Stuart, Det (tripping), 11:33; R Malone, Pitt (interference), 15:14; D Cleary, Det (hooking), 17:49; G Roberts, Pitt (roughing), 19:46.

SECOND PERIOD

Scoring: None. Penalties: B Orpik, Pitt (roughing), 11:17; T Holmstrom, Det (slashing), 11:17; R Malone, Det (slashing), 17:30.

THIRD PERIOD

Scoring: 1, Detroit, V Filppula, Det (J Franzen, B Stuart), 8:48. Penalties: M Hossa, Pitt (holding), 0:22; R Malone, Pitt (roughing), 3:42; P Datsyuk, Det

THIRD PERIOD (Cont.)

(roughing), 3:42; D Drake, Det (tripping), 7:49; R Malone, Pitt (goalie interference), 8:04; M Talbot, Pitt (roughing, served by T Kennedy), 11:51; J Franzen, Det (roughing), 11:51; M Talbot, Pitt (roughing), 11:51; R Whitney, Pitt (roughing), 16:08; G Roberts, Pitt (roughing), 18:52; P Sykora, Pitt (goalie interference), 18:52; E Malkin, Pitt (roughing), 18:52; A Lilja, Det (roughing), 18:52; J Franzen, Det (roughing), 18:52; G Roberts, Pitt (misconduct), 18:52; M Talbot, Pitt (misconduct), 20:00.

Shots on goal: DET 12-11-11—34; PIT 6-6-10—22.

Power-play opportunities: DET 0-8, PIT 0-3.

Goalies: Det, C Osgood (22 shots, 22 saves). Pitt, M Fleury (34 shots, 31 saves).

Referees: Joannette, Watson. Linesmen: Racicot, Morin. A: 20,066.

Game 3

Detroit	0	1	1—2
Pittsburgh	1	1	1—3

FIRST PERIOD

Scoring: 1, Pittsburgh, S Crosby (M Hossa), 17:25. Penalties: J Franzen, Det (holding), 1:04; J Staal, Pitt, (holding), 3:05; S Gonchar, Pitt (hooking), 12:07; B Rafalski, Det (tripping), 19:19.

SECOND PERIOD

Scoring: 1, Pittsburgh, S Crosby (PP–M Hossa, R Malone), 2:34; Detroit 1, J Franzen (PP–N Lidstrom, N Kronwall), 14:48. Penalties: N Kronwall, Det (hooking), 2:02; H Gill, Pitt (cross-checking), 8:54; H Gill, Pitt (cross-checking), 12:57.

THIRD PERIOD

Scoring: 1, Pittsburgh, A Hall (M Talbot, G Roberts), 7:18; 1, Detroit, M Samuelsson (B Stuart, V Filppula), 13:37. Penalties: E Malkin, Pitt (hooking), 15:42.

Shots on goal: DET 9-9-16—34; PIT 6-13-5—24.

Power-play opportunities: DET 1-5, PIT 1-3.

Goalies: Det, C Osgood (24 shots, 21 saves). Pitt, M Fleury (34 shots, 32 saves).

Referees: Devorski, O'Halloran. Linesmen: Sharrers, Heyer.

A: 17,132.

Game 4

Detroit	1	0	1—2
Pittsburgh	1	0	0—1

FIRST PERIOD

Scoring: 1, Pittsburgh, M Hossa (PP–S Gonchar, S Crosby), 2:51. 1, Detroit, N Lidstrom (B Rafalski, P Datsyuk), 7:06. Penalties: D Drake, Det (roughing), 2:11; P Dupuis, Pitt (cross-checking), 5:04; B Rafalski, Det (roughing), 9:03; K Draper, Det (holding), 14:28; B Lebda, Det (cross-checking),16:59; M Talbot, Pitt (diving), 16:59; J Franzen, Det (elbowing), 17:55; B Orpik, Pitt (roughing), 17:55.

SECOND PERIOD

Scoring: None. Penalties: J Staal, Pitt (interference), 3:44; B Rafalski, Det (holding), 16:04.

THIRD PERIOD

Scoring: 1, Detroit, J Hudler (D Helm, B Stuart). Penalties: M Fleury, Pitt (delay, served by M Hossa), 4:08; K Maltby, Det (hooking), 9:36; A Lilja, Det (interference), 10:10.

Shots on goal: DET 14-7-9—30; PIT 9-8-6—23.

Power-play opportunities: DET 0-3, PIT 1-5.

Goalies: Det, C Osgood (23 shots, 22 saves). Pitt, M Fleury (30 shots, 28 saves).

Referees: Joannette, Watson. Linesmen: Racicot, Morin.

A: 17,132.

Game 5

Pittsburgh	**2**	**0**	**1**	**0**	**0**	**1—4**
Detroit	**0**	**1**	**2**	**0**	**0**	**0—3**

FIRST PERIOD

Scoring: 2, Pittsburgh, M Hossa (S Crosby, P Dupuis), 8:37; A Hall (unassisted), 14:41. Penalties: B Orpik, PItt (hooking), 2:06; bench penalty, Pitt (too many men on ice, served by T Kennedy), 4:15; P Datsyuk, Det (tripping), 5:24; M Talbot, Pitt (roughing), 10:50; K Maltby, Det (roughing), 10:50.

SECOND PERIOD

Scoring: 1, Detroit, D Helm (K Maltby), 2:54. Penalties: K Maltby, Det (interference), 5:48; S Crosby, Pitt (high-sticking), 10:18.

THIRD PERIOD

Scoring: 2, Detroit, P Datsyuk (PP–H Zetterberg, B Rafalski), 6:43; B Rafalski (J Franzen, H Zetterberg), 9:23; 1, Pittsburgh, M Talbot (M Hossa, S Crosby), 19:25. Penalties: T Kennedy, Pitt (hooking), 6:21.

FIRST OVERTIME PERIOD

Scoring: None. Penalties: H Zetterberg, Det (goalie interference), 17:25.

SECOND OVERTIME PERIOD

Scoring: None. Penalties: D Cleary, Det (goalie interference), 3:41. P Sykora, Pitt (hooking), 17:44.

THIRD OVERTIME PERIOD

Scoring: 1, Pittsburgh, P Sykora (PP–E Malkin, S Gonchar), 9:57. Penalties: J Hudler, Det (high-sticking), 9:21.

Shots on goal: DET 8-12-14-13-7-4—58; PIT 7-7-4-2-8-4–32.

Power-play Opportunities: DET 1-5, PIT 1-5.

Goalies : Det, C Osgood (32 shots, 28 saves). Pitt, M Fleury (58 shots, 55 saves).

Referees: Devorksi, O'Halloran. Linesmen: Sharrers, Heyer.

A: 20,066.

Game 6

Detroit	**1**	**1**	**1—3**
Pittsburgh	**0**	**1**	**1—2**

FIRST PERIOD

Scoring: 1, Detroit, B Rafalski (PP–H Zetterberg, P Datsyuk), 5:03. Penalties: D Sydor, Pitt (interference), 4:17; D Drake, Det (charging), 8:28; K Draper, Det (roughing),8:55; A Hall, Pitt (high-sticking), 11:15.

SECOND PERIOD

Scoring: 1, Detroit, V Filppula (M Samuelsson, N Kronwall), 8:07; 1, Pittsburgh, E Malkin (PP–S Crosby, M Hossa), 15:26. Penalties: A Lilja, Det (slashing), 2:06; P Datsyuk, Det (interference), 14:22; G Roberts, Pitt (high-sticking), 16:13; J Franzen, Det (roughing), 17:58; B Orpik, Pitt (roughing), 17:58.

THIRD PERIOD

Scoring: 1, Detroit, H Zetterberg (P Datsyuk, N Kronwall), 7:36; 1, Pittsburgh, M Hossa (PP–S Gonchar, E Malkin), 18:33. Penalties: J Hudler, Det, (hooking), 18:13.

Shots on goal: DET 9-9-12—30; PIT 8-8-6—22.

Power-play Opportunities: DET 1-3, PIT 2-4.

Goalies : Det, C Osgood (22 shots, 20 saves). Pitt, M Fleury (30 shots, 27 saves).

Referees: Watson, Joannette. Linesmen: Racicot, Morin.

A: 17,132.

Individual Playoff Leaders

Scoring

POINTS

Player and Team	GP	G	A	Pts	+/-	PM
Henrik Zetterberg, Det	22	13	14	27	16	16
Sidney Crosby, Pitt	20	6	21	27	7	12
Marian Hossa, Pitt	20	12	14	26	8	12
Pavel Datsyuk, Det	22	10	13	23	13	6
Evgeni Malkin, Pitt	20	10	12	22	3	24
Johan Franzen, Det	16	13	5	18	13	14
Mike Ribeiro, Dal	18	3	14	17	0	16
Daniel Briere, Phil	17	9	7	16	-3	20
Ryan Malone, Pitt	20	6	10	16	4	25
R.J. Umberger, Phil	17	10	5	15	7	10
Brenden Morrow, Dal	18	9	6	15	0	22
Jaromir Jagr, NYR	10	5	10	15	3	12
Brad Richards, Dal	18	3	12	15	1	8
Niklas Kronwall, Det	22	0	15	15	16	18
Mike Richards, Phil	17	7	7	14	0	10
Jiri Hudler, Det	22	5	9	14	-1	14
Brian Rafalski, Det	22	4	10	14	6	12
Sergei Gonchar, Pitt	20	1	13	14	0	8
Mikael Samuelsson, Det	22	5	8	13	8	8
Nicklas Lidstrom, Det	22	3	10	13	8	14
Vaclav Prospal, Phil	17	3	10	13	-3	6
Mike Modano, Dal	18	5	7	12	-3	22
Tomas Holmstrom, Det	21	4	8	12	4	26

Four others at 11 points.

GOALS

Player and Team	GP	G
Henrik Zetterberg, Det	22	13
Johan Franzen, Det	16	13
Marian Hossa, Pitt	20	12
Pavel Datsyuk, Det	22	10
Evgeni Malkin, Pitt	20	10
R.J. Umberger, Phil	17	10

SHORT-HANDED GOALS

Player and Team	GP	SH
Mike Richards, Phil	17	2
Patrick Marleau, SJ	13	2
Henrik Zetterberg, Det	22	2
Johan Franzen, Det	16	2

POWER PLAY GOALS

Player and Team	GP	PP
Johan Franzen, Det	16	6
Daniel Briere, Phil	17	6
Marian Hossa, Pitt	20	5
Evgeni Malkin, Pitt	20	5
Mike Modano, Dal	18	5

ASSISTS

Player and Team	GP	A
Sidney Crosby, Pitt	20	21
Niklas Kronwall, Det	22	15
Henrik Zetterberg, Det	22	14
Marian Hossa, Pitt	20	14
Mike Ribeiro, Dal	18	14

PLUS/MINUS

Player and Team	GP	+/-
Henrik Zetterberg, Det	22	16
Niklas Kronwall, Det	22	16
Brad Stuart, Det	21	15
Pavel Datsyuk, Det	22	13
Johan Franzen, Det	16	13
Nicklas Lidstrom, Det	22	8
Marian Hossa, Pitt	20	8
Mikael Samuelsson, Det	22	8
Ryan Whitney, Pitt	20	8
Valtteri Filppula, Det	22	7
Sidney Crosby, Pitt	20	7
R.J. Umberger, Phil	17	7

Goaltending*

GOALS AGAINST AVERAGE

Player and Team	GP	W-L	Avg
Chris Osgood, Det	19	14–4	1.55
Marc-Andre Fleury, Pitt	20	14–6	1.97
Marty Turco, Dal	18	10–8	2.08
Evgeni Nabokov, SJ	13	6–7	2.18
Henrik Lundqvist, NYR	10	5–5	2.57
Tim Thomas, Bos	7	3–4	2.65

*minimum of 420 minutes

SAVE PERCENTAGE

Player and Team	GP	W-L	GAA	GA	SV	SV%	SA
M-Andre Fleury, Pitt	20	14–6	1.97	41	569	.933	610
Chris Osgood, Det	19	14–4	1.55	30	400	.930	430
Marty Turco, Dal	18	10–8	2.08	40	471	.922	511
Tim Thomas, Bos	7	3–4	2.65	19	202	.914	221
H. Ludqvist, NYR	10	5–5	2.57	26	261	.909	287
Cristobal Huet, Wsh	7	3–4	2.93	22	220	.909	242

NHL Awards

Award	Player and Team
Hart Trophy (MVP)	Alexander Ovechkin, Wsh
Calder Trophy (top rookie)	Patrick Kane, Chi
Vezina Trophy (top goaltender)	Martin Brodeur, NJ
Norris Trophy (top defenseman)	Nicklas Lidstrom, Det
Lady Byng Trophy (for gentlemanly play)	Pavel Datsyuk, Det
Adams Award (top coach)	Bruce Boudreau, Wsh
Selke Trophy (top defensive forward)	Pavel Datsyuk, Det
Jennings Trophy (goaltender on club allowing fewest goals)	Chris Osgood/ Dominik Hasek, Det
Conn Smythe Trophy (playoff MVP)	Henrik Zetterberg, Det

Individual Regular Season Leaders

Scoring

POINTS

Player and Team	GP	G	A	Pts	+/-	PM
A. Ovechkin, Wsh	82	65	47	112	28	40
Evgeni Malkin, Pitt	82	47	59	106	16	78
Jarome Iginla, Cgy	82	50	48	98	27	83
Pavel Datsyuk, Det	82	31	66	97	41	20
Joe Thornton, SJ	82	29	67	96	18	59
Henrik Zetterberg, Det	75	43	49	92	30	34
Vincent Lecavalier, TB	81	40	52	92	-17	89
Jason Spezza, Ott	76	34	58	92	26	66
Daniel Alfredsson, Ott	70	40	49	89	15	34
Ilya Kovalchuk, Atl	79	52	35	87	-12	52
Alexei Kovalev, Mtl	82	35	49	84	18	70
Marian Gaborik, Min	77	42	41	83	17	63
Mike Ribeiro, Dal	76	27	56	83	21	46
Martin St. Louis, TB	82	25	58	83	-23	26
Dany Heatley, Ott	71	41	41	82	33	76
Eric Staal, Car	82	38	44	82	-2	50
Ryan Getzlaf, Ana	77	24	58	82	32	94
Derek Roy, Buf	78	32	49	81	13	46

Individual Regular Season Leaders (*Cont.*)

Scoring (*Cont.*)

GOALS

Player and Team	GP	G
A. Ovechkin, Wsh	82	65
Ilya Kovalchuk, Atl	79	52
Jarome Iginla, Cgy	82	50
Evgeni Malkin, Pitt	82	47
H. Zetterberg, Det	75	43
Brad Boyes, StL	82	43
Marian Gaborik, Min	77	42
Dany Heatley, Ott	71	41
V. Lecavalier, TB	81	40
D. Alfredsson, Ott	70	40

POWER PLAY GOALS

Player and Team	GP	PP
A. Ovechkin, Wsh	82	22
Thomas Vanek, Buf	82	19
Olli Jokinen, Fla	82	18
Evgeni Malkin, Pitt	82	17
Alexei Kovalev, Mtl	82	17

ASSISTS

Player and Team	GP	A
Joe Thornton, SJ	82	67
Pavel Datsyuk, Det	82	66
Marc Savard, Bos	74	63
Henrik Sedin, Van	82	61
Nicklas Lidstrom, Det	76	60
Evgeni Malkin, Pitt	82	59

Three tied with 58.

SHORT-HANDED GOALS

Player and Team	GP	SHG
D. Alfredsson, Ott	70	7
Patrick Sharp, Chi	80	7
Mike Richards, Phil	73	5
Rene Bourque, Chi	62	5

Three tied with 4.

GAME-WINNING GOALS

Player and Team	GP	GW
A. Ovechkin, Wsh	82	11
Jeremy Roenick, SJ	69	10
Jarome Iginla, Cgy	82	9
Thomas Vanek, Buf	82	9
Brad Boyes, Stl	82	9

Nine tied with 8.

PLUS/MINUS

Player and Team	GP	+/-
Pavel Datsyuk, Det	82	41
Nicklas Lidstrom, Det	76	40
Dany Heatley, Ott	71	33
Ryan Getzlaf, Ana	77	32
Duncan Keith, Chi	82	30
Henrik Zetterberg, Det	75	30
Viktor Kozlov, Wsh	81	28
A. Ovechkin, Wsh	82	28

Three tied with 27.

Goaltending (Minimum 25 games)

GOALS AGAINST AVERAGE

Player and Team	GP	W-L	GAA	GA
Chris Osgood, Det	43	27–9	2.09	84
J. Giguere, Ana	58	35–17	2.12	117
Evgeni Nabokov, SJ	77	46–21	2.14	163
Dominik Hasek, Det	41	27–10	2.14	84
Martin Brodeur, NJ	77	44–27	2.17	168
H. Lundqvist, NYR	72	37–24	2.23	160
Pascal Leclaire, CBJ	54	24–17	2.25	112

WINS

Player and Team	GP	GAA	W	L
Evgeny Nabokov, SJ	77	2.14	46	21
Martin Brodeur, NJ	77	2.17	44	27
Miikka Kiprusoff, Cgy	76	2.69	39	26
Henrik Lundqvist, NYR	72	2.23	37	24
Cam Ward, Car	69	2.75	37	25

SAVE PERCENTAGE

Player and Team	GP	W-L	GA	SV	Pct
Dan Ellis, Nsh	44	23–10	87	1060	.924
Ty Conklin, Pitt	33	18–8	78	935	.923
J. Giguere, Ana	58	35–17	117	1391	.922
Tim Thomas, Bos	57	28–19	136	1595	.921
M. Fleury, Pitt	35	19–10	72	837	.921

Five tied at .920.

SHUTOUTS

Player and Team	GP	W	L	SO
Henrik Lundqvist, NYR	77	37	24	10
Pascal Leclaire, CBJ	54	24	17	9
Evgeni Nabokov, SJ	77	46	21	6
Roberto Luongo, Van	73	35	29	6
Dan Ellis, Nsh	44	23	10	6

NHL Team-by-Team Statistical Leaders

Anaheim Ducks

SCORING

Player	GP	G	A	Pts	+/-	PM
Ryan Getzlaf, C	77	24	58	82	32	94
Corey Perry, RW	70	29	25	54	12	108
Chris Kunitz, LW	82	21	29	50	8	80
Chris Pronger, D	72	12	31	43	-1	128
Todd Bertuzzi, LW	68	14	26	40	8	97
Mathieu Schneider, D	65	12	27	39	22	50
Scott Niedermayer, D	48	8	17	25	-2	16
Teemu Selanne, RW	26	12	11	23	5	8
F. Beauchemin, D	82	2	19	21	-9	59
Kent Huskins, D	76	4	15	19	23	59
Todd Marchant, C	75	9	7	16	-3	48
Andy McDonald, C	33	4	12	16	-4	30
Rob Niedermayer, C	78	8	8	16	1	54
Samuel Pahlsson, C	56	6	9	15	-2	34
Doug Weight, C	38	6	8	14	E	20
Bobby Ryan, RW	23	5	5	10	-1	6

SCORING (*CONT.*)

Player	GP	G	A	Pts	+/-	PM
Sean O'Donnell, D	82	2	7	9	9	84
Travis Moen, LW	77	3	5	8	-10	81
Ryan Carter, C	34	4	4	8	-2	36
Joe DiPenta, D	23	1	4	5	3	16
George Parros, RW	69	1	4	5	3	183
Drew Miller, LW	26	2	3	5	-1	6
Brad May, LW	61	3	1	4	2	53
B. Bochenski, RW	12	2	2	4	2	6
Shane Hnidy, D	33	1	2	3	2	30
Mark Mowers, RW	17	1	0	1	E	8
Brian Sutherby, C	45	0	1	1	-2	57

GOALTENDING

Player	GP	Mins	W	L	TGA	GAA	SO
J. Giguere	58	3310	35	17	117	2.12	4
Jonas Hiller	23	1223	10	7	42	2.06	0
Ilya Bryzgalov	9	447	2	3	19	2.55	0

NHL Team-by-Team Statistical Leaders

Atlanta Thrashers

SCORING

Player	GP	G	A	Pts	+/-	PM
Ilya Kovalchuk, LW	79	52	35	87	-12	52
Marian Hossa, RW	60	26	30	56	-14	30
Eric Perrin, C	81	12	33	45	-5	26
Slava Kozlov, LW	82	17	24	41	-10	26
Mark Recchi, RW	53	12	28	40	-16	20
Tobias Enstrom, D	82	5	33	38	-5	42
Todd White, C	74	14	23	37	-12	36
Bobby Holik, C	82	15	19	34	-14	90
Chris Thorburn, RW	73	5	13	18	-4	92
Bryan Little, C	48	6	10	16	-2	18
Pascal Dupuis, LW	62	10	5	15	-4	24
Niclas Havelid, D	81	1	13	14	2	42
Jim Slater, C	69	8	5	13	-10	41
Colby Armstrong, RW	18	4	7	11	-2	6
Ken Klee, D	72	1	9	10	-5	60
Eric Boulton, LW	74	4	5	9	-10	127
Alexei Zhitnik, D	65	3	5	8	-8	58
Darren Haydar, RW	16	1	7	8	4	2
Steve McCarthy, D	55	1	6	7	-23	48
Garnet Exelby, D	79	2	5	7	-21	85
Joel Kwiatkowski, D	18	0	5	5	-5	20
Colin Stuart, LW	18	3	2	5	2	6
Brad Larsen, LW	62	1	3	4	-17	12
Erik Christensen, C	10	2	2	4	-7	2
Brett Sterling, LW	13	1	2	3	-2	14
Mark Popovic, D	33	0	2	2	-4	10
Jordan LaVallee, LW	2	1	1	2	2	0
Kevin Doell, C	8	0	1	1	-2	4

GOALTENDING

Player	GP	Mins	W	L	TGA	GAA	SO
Kari Lehtonen	48	2707	17	22	131	2.90	4
Johan Hedberg	36	1927	14	15	111	3.46	1
Ondrej Pavelec	7	347	3	3	18	3.11	0

Boston Bruins

SCORING

Player	GP	G	A	Pts	+/-	PM
Marc Savard, C	74	15	63	78	3	66
Marco Sturm, LW	80	27	29	56	11	40
Zdeno Chara, D	77	17	34	51	14	114
Chuck Kobasew, RW	73	22	17	39	6	29
Phil Kessel, RW	82	19	18	37	-6	28
Dennis Wideman, D	81	13	23	36	11	70
Glen Metropolit, C	82	11	22	33	-3	36
Glen Murray, RW	63	17	13	30	-4	50
P.J. Axelsson, LW	75	13	16	29	11	15
David Krejci, C	56	6	21	27	-3	20
Milan Lucic, LW	77	8	19	27	-2	89
Peter Schaefer, LW	63	9	17	26	4	18
Andrew Ference, D	59	1	14	15	-14	50
Aaron Ward, D	65	5	8	13	9	54
Petteri Nokelainen, C	57	7	3	10	E	19
Mark Stuart, D	82	4	4	8	2	81
Shawn Thornton, LW	58	4	3	7	-1	74
Patrice Bergeron, C	10	3	4	7	2	2
Vladimir Sobotka, C	48	1	6	7	1	24
B. Bochenski, RW	20	0	6	6	2	6
Shane Hnidy, D	43	1	4	5	-4	41
Matt Lashoff, D	18	1	4	5	-2	0
Jeremy Reich, LW	58	2	2	4	-5	78
Andrew Alberts, D	35	0	2	2	4	39
Matt Hunwick, D	13	0	1	1	-1	4

GOALTENDING

Player	GP	Mins	W	L	TGA	GAA	SO
Tim Thomas	57	3342	28	19	136	2.44	3
Alex Auld	23	1213	9	7	47	2.32	2
Manny Fernandez	4	244	2	2	16	3.93	1
Tuuka Rask	4	184	2	1	10	3.25	0

Buffalo Sabres

SCORING

Player	GP	G	A	Pts	+/-	PM
Derek Roy, C	78	32	49	81	13	46
Jason Pominville, RW	82	27	53	80	16	20
Thomas Vanek, LW	82	36	28	64	-5	64
Jochen Hecht, C	75	22	27	49	1	38
Brian Campbell, D	63	5	38	43	-1	12
Ales Kotalik, RW	79	23	20	43	-5	58
Tim Connolly, C	48	7	33	40	4	8
Drew Stafford, RW	64	16	22	38	3	51
Paul Gaustad, C	82	10	26	36	-4	85
Daniel Paille, LW	77	19	16	35	9	14
Jaroslav Spacek, D	60	9	23	32	7	42
M. Afinogenov, RW	56	10	18	28	-16	42
Toni Lydman, D	82	4	22	26	1	74
Henrik Tallinder, D	71	1	17	18	5	48
Adam Mair, C	72	5	12	17	-2	66
Clarke MacArthur, LW	37	8	7	15	3	20

SCORING *(CONT.)*

Player	GP	G	A	Pts	+/-	PM
Nathan Paetsch, D	59	2	7	9	3	27
Steve Bernier, RW	17	3	6	9	1	2
Dmitry Kalinin, D	46	1	7	8	-7	32
Michael Ryan, C	46	4	4	8	-4	30
Andrej Sekera, D	37	2	6	8	5	16
Nolan Pratt, D	55	1	6	7	1	30
Patricka Kaleta, RW	40	3	2	5	1	41
Mike Weber, D	16	0	3	3	12	14
Andrew Peters, LW	44	1	1	2	-4	100

GOALTENDING

Player	GP	Mins	W	L	TGA	GAA	SO
Ryan Miller	76	4474	36	27	197	2.64	3
Jocelyn Thibault	12	507	3	4	28	3.31	2

NHL Team-by-Team Statistical Leaders *(Cont.)*

Calgary Flames

SCORING

Player	GP	G	A	Pts	+/-	PM
Jarome Iginla, RW	82	50	48	98	27	83
Kristian Huselius, LW	81	25	41	66	10	40
Daymond Langkow, C	80	30	35	65	16	19
Dion Phaneuf, D	82	17	43	60	12	182
Alex Tanguay, LW	78	18	40	58	11	48
Matthew Lombardi, C	82	14	22	36	-6	67
Adrian Aucoin, D	76	10	25	35	13	37
Craig Conroy, C	79	12	22	34	6	71
Owen Nolan, RW	77	16	16	32	6	71
Robyn Regehr, D	82	5	15	20	11	79
Anders Eriksson, D	61	1	17	18	-5	36
Stephane Yelle, C	74	3	9	12	-4	20
Dustin Boyd, C	48	7	5	12	-11	6
David Moss, RW	41	4	7	11	-4	10
Wayne Primeau, C	43	3	7	10	-3	26
Eric Nystrom, LW	44	3	7	10	-5	48
Cory Sarich, D	80	2	5	7	2	135
Marcus Nilson, LW	47	3	2	5	2	4
Mark Smith, C	54	1	3	4	-6	59
Rhett Warrener, D	31	1	3	4	-2	21
Eric Godard, RW	74	1	1	2	-8	171
Jim Vandermeer, D	21	0	2	2	4	39
David Hale, D	58	0	2	2	E	46

GOALTENDING

Player	GP	Mins	W	L	TGA	GAA	SO
Miikka Kiprusoff	76	4398	39	26	197	2.69	2
Curtis Jospeh	9	400	3	2	17	2.55	0
Curtis McElhinney	5	150	0	2	5	2.00	0

Carolina Hurricanes

SCORING

Player	GP	G	A	Pts	+/-	PM
Eric Staal, C	82	38	44	82	-2	50
Ray Whitney, LW	66	25	36	61	-6	30
Rod Brind'Amour, C	59	19	32	51	E	38
Erik Cole, RW	73	22	29	51	5	76
Matt Cullen, C	59	13	36	49	2	32
Cory Stillman, LW	55	21	25	46	-7	14
Sergei Samsonov, LW	38	14	18	32	6	10
Scott Walker, RW	58	14	18	32	-3	115
Justin Williams, RW	37	9	21	30	2	43
Jeff Hamilton, RW	58	9	15	24	-8	10
Chad LaRose, LW	58	11	12	23	6	46
Frantisek Kaberle, D	80	0	22	22	-4	30
Joe Corvo, D	23	7	14	21	4	8
Tim Gleason, D	80	3	16	19	5	84
Trevor Letowski, RW	75	9	9	18	-10	30
Andrew Ladd, LW	43	9	9	18	9	31
Bret Hedican, D	66	2	15	17	17	70
Dennis Seidenberg, D	47	0	15	15	6	18
Keith Aucoin, RW	38	5	8	13	3	10
Mike Commodore, D	41	3	9	12	2	74
Tuomo Ruutu, LW	17	4	7	11	1	16
Niclas Wallin, D	66	2	6	8	-18	54
Glen Wesley, D	78	1	7	8	-3	52
Ryan Bayda, LW	31	3	3	6	-2	28
Craig Adams, RW	40	2	3	5	-8	34
Patrick Eaves, RW	11	1	4	5	-2	4
Tim Conboy, D	19	0	5	5	1	60
David Tanabe, D	18	1	2	3	2	8
Casey Borer, D	11	1	2	3	-3	4
Wade Brookbank, LW	32	1	1	2	4	76

GOALTENDING

Player	GP	Mins	W	L	TGA	GAA	SO
Cam Ward	69	3930	37	25	180	2.75	4
John Grahame	17	848	5	7	53	3.75	0
Michael Leighton	3	158	1	1	7	2.66	0

Chicago Blackhawks

SCORING

Player	GP	G	A	Pts	+/-	PM
Patrick Kane, RW	82	21	51	72	-5	52
Patrick Sharp, LW	80	36	26	62	23	55
Robert Lang, C	76	21	33	54	9	50
Jonathan Toews, C	64	24	30	54	11	44
Jason Williams, RW	43	13	23	36	-2	22
Dustin Byfuglien, D	67	19	17	36	-7	59
Duncan Keith, D	82	12	20	32	30	56
Brent Seabrook, D	82	9	23	32	13	90
Martin Havlat, RW	35	10	17	27	4	22
James Wisniewski, D	68	7	19	26	12	103
Rene Bourque, LW	62	10	14	24	6	42
Tuomo Ruutu, LW	60	6	15	21	3	75
Brent Sopel, D	58	1	19	20	9	28
Cam Barker, D	45	6	12	18	-3	52
Dave Bolland, C	39	4	13	17	6	28
Yanic Perreault, C	53	9	5	14	-1	24
Andrew Ladd, LW	20	5	7	12	4	4
Jim Vandermeer, D	26	2	7	9	3	44
Adam Burish, RW	81	4	4	8	-13	214

SCORING *(CONT.)*

Player	GP	G	A	Pts	+/-	PM
Martin Lapointe, RW	52	3	4	7	-3	47
Craig Adams, RW	35	2	4	6	-8	24
Andrei Zyuzin, D	32	2	3	5	-11	38
Jack Skille, RW	16	3	2	5	1	0
Petri Kontiola, C	12	0	5	5	5	6
Sergei Samsonov, LW	23	0	4	4	-7	6
Kris Versteeg, RW	13	2	2	4	-1	6
Jordan Hendry, D	40	1	3	4	E	22
Magnus Johansson, D	18	0	4	4	-5	4
Jacob Dowell, C	19	2	1	3	1	10
Kevyn Adams, C	27	0	2	2	-7	13
Ben Eager, LW	9	0	2	2	-1	27

GOALTENDING

Player	GP	Mins	W	L	TGA	GAA	SO
Nikolai Khabibulin	50	2892	23	20	127	2.63	2
Patrick Lalime	32	1828	16	12	86	2.82	1
Corey Crawford	5	224	1	2	8	2.14	1

NHL Team-by-Team Statistical Leaders (*Cont.*)

Colorado Avalanche

SCORING

Player	GP	G	A	Pts	+/-	PM
Paul Stastny, C	66	24	47	71	22	24
Andrew Brunette, LW	82	19	40	59	5	14
Milan Hejduk, RW	77	29	25	54	8	36
Wojtek Wolski, LW	77	18	30	48	10	14
Joe Sakic, C	44	13	27	40	-4	20
Ryan Smyth, LW	55	14	23	37	-4	50
Marek Svatos, RW	62	26	11	37	13	32
John-Michael Liles, D	81	6	26	32	2	26
Tyler Arnason, C	70	10	21	31	-1	16
Jaroslav Hlinka, LW	63	8	20	28	6	16
Ben Guite, RW	79	11	11	22	1	47
Brett Clark, D	57	5	16	21	5	33
Scott Hannan, D	82	2	19	21	-5	55
Ian Laperriere, RW	70	4	15	19	-5	140
Jeff Finger, D	72	8	11	19	12	40
Peter Forsberg, C	9	1	13	14	7	8
Jordan Leopold, D	43	5	8	13	5	20
T.J. Hensick, C	31	6	5	11	-4	2
Cody McLoed, LW	49	4	5	9	-6	120
Ruslan Salei, D	17	3	4	7	1	23
Kurt Sauer, D	54	1	5	6	17	41
David Jones, RW	27	2	4	6	-5	8
Brad Richardson, RW	22	2	3	5	-3	8
Kyle Cumiskey, D	38	0	5	5	-3	16
Karlis Skrastins, D	43	1	3	4	-2	20
Cody McCormick, C	40	2	2	4	5	50
Wyatt Smith, C	25	0	3	3	-4	8

GOALTENDING

Player	GP	Mins	W	L	TGA	GAA	SO
Jose Theodore	53	3028	28	21	123	2.44	3
Peter Budaj	35	1912	16	10	82	2.57	0

Dallas Stars

SCORING

Player	GP	G	A	Pts	+/-	PM
Mike Ribeiro, C	76	27	56	83	21	46
Brenden Morrow, LW	82	32	42	74	23	105
Mike Modano, C	82	21	36	57	-11	48
Niklas Hagman, LW	82	27	14	41	4	51
Jere Lehtinen, RW	48	15	22	37	9	14
Sergei Zubov, D	46	4	31	35	6	12
Antti Miettinen, RW	69	15	19	34	4	34
Loui Eriksson, LW	69	14	17	31	5	28
Jussi Jokinen, LW	52	14	14	28	2	14
Stephane Robidas, D	82	9	17	26	E	85
Matt Niskanen, D	78	7	19	26	22	36
Jeff Halpern, C	64	10	14	24	-2	40
Trevor Daley, D	82	5	19	24	-1	85
Stu Barnes, C	79	12	11	23	-3	26
Steve Ott, C	73	11	11	22	2	147
Philippe Boucher, D	38	2	12	14	3	26
Joel Lundqvist, C	55	3	11	14	-3	22
Mattias Nordstrom, D	66	2	11	13	3	40
Brad Richards, C	12	2	9	11	-2	0
Nicklas Grossman, D	62	0	7	7	10	22
Chris Conner, RW	22	3	2	5	E	6
Toby Petersen, C	8	0	3	3	E	4
Krys Barch, RW	48	1	2	3	-3	105
Brad Winchester, LW	41	1	2	3	-9	46

GOALTENDING

Player	GP	Mins	W	L	TGA	GAA	SO
Marty Turco	62	3628	32	21	140	2.32	3
Mike Smith	21	1172	12	9	48	2.46	2
Johan Holmqvist	2	80	1	0	5	3.75	0

Columbus Blue Jackets

SCORING

Player	GP	G	A	Pts	+/-	PM
Rick Nash, LW	80	38	31	69	3	95
Nikolai Zherdev, RW	82	26	35	61	-9	34
Michael Peca, C	65	8	26	34	-1	64
Ron Hainsey, D	78	8	24	32	-7	25
Jason Chimera, LW	81	14	17	31	-5	98
Manny Malhotra, C	71	11	18	29	-2	34
David Vyborny, RW	66	7	19	26	-8	34
Jiri Novotny, C	65	8	14	22	-10	24
Dan Fritsche, C	69	10	12	22	2	22
Rostislav Klesla, D	82	6	12	18	7	60
Sergei Fedorov, C	18	2	11	13	-2	8
Curtis Glencross, LW	26	9	4	13	5	28
Jan Hejda, D	81	0	13	13	20	61
Fredrik Modin, LW	23	6	6	12	1	20
Andrew Murray, C	39	6	4	10	-1	12
Kris Russell, D	67	2	8	10	-12	14
Jared Boll, RW	75	5	5	10	-4	226
Kris Beech, C	16	5	4	9	3	2
Gilbert Brule, C	61	1	8	9	-4	24
Joakim Lindstrom, C	25	3	4	7	E	14
Dick Tarnstrom, C	29	1	4	5	-6	40
Duvie Westcott, D	23	1	3	4	-10	30
Ole-Kristian Tollefsen, D	51	2	2	4	-3	111
Derek McKenzie, C	17	2	0	2	-2	8
Aaron Rome, D	17	1	1	2	-4	33
Clay Wilson, D	7	1	1	2	3	2

GOALTENDING

Player	GP	Mins	W	L	TGA	GAA	SO
Pascal Leclaire	54	2986	24	17	112	2.25	9
Fredrik Norrena	37	2000	10	19	89	2.73	2

Detroit Red Wings

SCORING

Player	GP	G	A	Pts	+/-	PM
Pavel Datsyuk, C	82	31	66	97	41	20
Henrik Zetterberg, LW	75	43	49	92	30	34
Nicklas Lidstrom, D	76	10	60	70	40	40
Brian Rafalski, D	73	13	42	55	27	34
Daniel Cleary, RW	63	20	22	42	21	33
Jiri Hudler, RW	81	13	29	42	11	26
T. Holmstrom, RW	59	20	20	40	9	58
Mikael Samuelsson, RW	73	11	29	40	21	26
Johan Franzen, C	72	27	11	38	12	51
Valtteri Filppula, C	78	19	17	36	16	28
Niklas Kronwall, C	65	7	28	35	25	44
Kris Draper, C	65	9	8	17	-2	68
Brett Lebda, D	78	3	11	14	-1	48
Chris Chelios, D	69	3	9	12	11	36
Andreas Lilja, D	79	2	10	12	-2	93
Tomas Kopecky, RW	77	5	7	12	2	43
Kirk Maltby, LW	61	6	4	10	-8	32
Dallas Drake, RW	65	3	3	6	-12	41
Matt Ellis, LW	35	2	4	6	1	12
Mark Hartigan, C	23	3	1	4	-2	16
Aaron Downey, RW	56	0	3	3	E	116
Derek Meech, D	32	0	3	3	-5	6
Brad Stuart, D	9	1	1	2	6	2

GOALTENDING

Player	GP	Mins	W	L	TGA	GAA	SO
Chris Osgood	43	2409	27	9	84	2.09	4
Dominik Hasek	41	2350	27	10	84	2.14	5

NHL Team-by-Team Statistical Leaders *(Cont.)*

Edmonton Oilers

SCORING

Player	GP	G	A	Pts	+/-	PM
Ales Hemsky, RW	74	20	51	71	-9	34
Shawn Horcoff, C	53	21	29	50	1	30
Sam Gagner, C	79	13	36	49	-21	23
Dustin Penner, LW	82	23	24	47	-12	45
Andrew Cogliano, C	82	18	27	45	1	20
Robert Nilsson, LW	71	10	31	41	8	22
Jarret Stoll, C	81	14	22	36	-23	74
Tom Gilbert, D	82	13	20	33	-6	20
Kyle Brodziak, C	80	14	17	31	-6	33
Joni Pitkanen, D	63	8	18	26	-5	56
Marty Reasoner, C	82	11	14	25	-17	50
Fernando Pisani, RW	56	13	9	22	-5	28
Denis Grebeshkov, D	71	3	15	18	2	22
Steve Staios, D	82	7	9	16	-14	121
Geoff Sanderson, LW	41	3	10	13	-7	16
Curtis Glencross, LW	26	9	4	13	5	28
Zack Stortini, RW	66	3	9	12	3	201
Raffi Torres, LW	32	5	6	11	-4	36
Sheldon Souray, D	26	3	7	10	-7	36
Ethan Moreau, LW	25	5	4	9	-4	39
Marc Pouliot, C	24	1	6	7	-1	12
Dick Tarnstrom, D	29	1	4	5	-6	40
Ladislav Smid, D	65	0	4	4	-15	58
Patrick Thoresen, LW	17	2	1	3	-4	6
Mathieu Roy, D	13	0	1	1	E	27
Matt Greene, D	46	0	1	1	-3	53

GOALTENDING

Player	GP	Mins	W	L	TGA	GAA	SO
Mathieu Garon	47	2658	26	18	118	2.66	4
Dwayne Roloson	43	2340	15	17	119	3.05	0

Florida Panthers

SCORING

Player	GP	G	A	Pts	+/-	PM
Olli Jokinen, C	82	34	37	71	-19	67
Nathan Horton, RW	82	27	35	62	15	85
Stephen Weiss, C	74	13	29	42	14	40
David Booth, LW	73	22	18	40	13	26
Brett McLean, C	67	14	23	37	-5	34
Jay Bouwmeester, D	82	15	22	37	-5	72
Richard Zednik, LW	54	15	11	26	-5	43
Rostislav Olesz, LW	56	14	12	26	3	16
Kamil Kreps, C	76	8	17	25	10	29
Steve Montador, D	73	8	15	23	1	73
Ruslan Salei, D	65	3	20	23	-5	75
Ville Peltonen, LW	56	5	15	20	-2	20
Jozef Stumpel, RW	52	7	13	20	-11	10
Gregory Campbell, C	81	5	13	18	-12	72
Radek Dvorak, RW	67	8	9	17	-1	16
Cory Murphy, D	47	2	15	17	E	22
Bryan Allen, D	73	2	14	16	5	67
Jassen Cullimore, D	65	3	10	13	21	38
Magnus Johansson, D	27	0	10	10	E	14
Branislav Mezei, D	57	2	2	4	-13	64
Mike Van Ryn, D	20	0	2	2	-2	14
Shawn Matthias, C	4	2	0	2	-2	2
Tanner Glass, LW	41	1	1	2	-5	39
Karlis Skrastins, D	17	1	0	1	-9	12
Anthony Stewart, C	26	0	1	1	-1	0
Drew Larman, C	6	0	1	1	1	2
David Brine, C	9	0	1	1	-1	4

GOALTENDING

Player	GP	Mins	W	L	TGA	GAA	SO
Tomas Vokoun	69	4031	30	29	180	2.68	4
Craig Anderson	17	935	8	6	35	2.25	2

Los Angeles Kings

SCORING

Player	GP	G	A	Pts	+/-	PM
Anze Kopitar, C	82	32	45	77	-15	22
Alexander Frolov, LW	71	23	44	67	1	22
Dustin Brown, RW	78	33	27	60	-13	55
Patrick O'Sullivan, C	82	22	31	53	-8	36
M. Cammalleri, LW	63	19	28	47	-16	30
Lubomir Visnovsky, D	82	8	33	41	-18	34
Derek Armstrong, C	77	8	27	35	4	63
Rob Blake, D	71	9	22	31	-19	98
Ladislav Nagy, LW	38	9	17	26	-2	18
Tom Preissing, D	77	8	16	24	-6	16
Michal Handzus, C	82	7	14	21	-21	45
Brad Stuart, D	63	5	16	21	-16	67
Kyle Calder, LW	65	7	13	20	-11	18
Brian Willsie, RW	53	4	8	12	-8	30
Jack Johnson, D	74	3	8	11	-19	76
Matt Moulson, LW	22	5	4	9	2	4
Scott Thornton, LW	47	5	3	8	1	39
Raitis Ivanans, LW	73	6	2	8	-10	134
Kevin Dallman, D	34	3	4	7	4	4

SCORING *(CONT.)*

Player	GP	G	A	Pts	+/-	PM
Jaroslav Modry, D	61	1	5	6	2	42
Jeff Giuliano, LW	53	0	6	6	-9	14
Peter Harrold, D	25	2	3	5	3	2
Brian Boyle, C	8	4	1	5	4	4
Teddy Purcell, RW	10	1	2	3	2	0
Matt Ellis, LW	19	1	1	2	2	14
John Zeiler, RW	36	0	1	1	-6	23

GOALTENDING

Player	GP	Mins	W	L	TGA	GAA	SO
Jason LaBarbera	45	2421	17	23	121	3.00	1
J. Aubin	19	828	5	6	44	3.19	0
Erik Ersberg	14	799	6	5	33	2.48	2
Dan Cloutier	9	489	2	4	28	3.43	0

NHL Team-by-Team Statistical Leaders (*Cont.*)

Minnesota Wild

SCORING

Player	GP	G	A	Pts	+/-	PM
Marian Gaborik, RW	77	42	41	83	17	63
P. Bouchard, RW	81	13	50	63	11	34
Brian Rolston, LW	81	31	28	59	-1	53
Pavol Demitra, LW	68	15	39	54	9	24
Brent Burns, D	82	15	28	43	12	80
Mikko Koivu, C	57	11	31	42	13	42
Eric Belanger, C	75	13	24	37	-6	30
Mark Parrish, RW	66	16	14	30	2	16
Kim Johnsson, D	80	4	23	27	-4	42
Kurtis Foster, D	56	7	12	19	E	37
James Sheppard, C	78	4	15	19	E	29
Stephane Veilleux, LW	77	11	7	18	-13	61
B. Radivojevic, RW	73	7	10	17	-14	48
Nick Schultz, D	81	2	13	15	9	42
Aaron Voros, LW	55	7	7	14	-7	141
Keith Carney, D	61	1	10	11	8	42
Todd Fedoruk, LW	58	6	5	11	E	106
Martin Skoula, D	80	3	8	11	-16	26
Sean Hill, D	35	2	7	9	-16	32
Petteri Nummelin, D	27	2	7	9	-2	2
Matt Foy, RW	28	4	4	8	-1	28
Wes Walz, C	11	1	3	4	-5	6
Dominic Moore, C	30	1	2	3	-11	10
Benoit Pouliot, LW	11	2	1	3	-1	0

GOALTENDING

Player	GP	Mins	W	L	TGA	GAA	SO
Niklas Backstrom	58	3409	33	13	131	2.31	4
Josh Harding	29	1571	11	15	77	2.94	1

Nashville Predators

SCORING

Player	GP	G	A	Pts	+/-	PM
Jason Arnott, C	79	28	44	72	19	54
J.P. Dumont, RW	80	29	43	72	5	34
A. Radulov, RW	81	26	32	58	7	44
Martin Erat, RW	76	23	34	57	-3	40
David Legwand, C	65	15	29	44	-4	38
Marek Zidlicky, D	79	5	38	43	-5	63
Vernon Fiddler, LW	79	11	21	32	-4	47
Ryan Suter, D	76	7	24	31	3	71
Radek Bonk, C	79	14	15	29	-31	40
Dan Hamhuis, D	80	4	23	27	-4	66
Martin Gelinas, LW	57	9	11	20	5	20
Shea Weber, D	54	6	14	20	-6	49
Scott Nichol, C	73	10	8	18	12	72
Jordin Tootoo, RW	63	11	7	18	-8	100
Ville Koistinen, D	48	4	13	17	13	18
Jerred Smithson, C	81	7	9	16	-9	50
Greg de Vries, D	77	4	11	15	7	71
Jan Hlavac, LW	18	3	10	13	9	8
Rich Peverley, C	33	5	5	10	4	8
Jed Ortmeyer, RW	51	4	4	8	-8	32
Greg Zanon, D	78	0	5	5	-5	24
Darcy Hordichuk, LW	45	1	2	3	-1	60
B. Bochenski, RW	8	1	2	3	2	0
Kevin Klein, D	13	0	2	2	-3	6

GOALTENDING

Player	GP	Mins	W	L	TGA	GAA	SO
Chris Mason	51	2692	18	22	130	2.90	4
Dan Ellis	44	2229	23	10	87	2.34	6

Montreal Canadiens

SCORING

Player	GP	G	A	Pts	+/-	PM
Alexei Kovalev, RW	82	35	49	84	18	70
Tomas Plekanec, C	81	29	40	69	15	42
Mark Streit, D	81	13	49	62	-6	28
Andrei Markov, D	82	16	42	58	1	63
Saku Koivu, C	77	16	40	56	-4	93
Andrei Kostitsyn, LW	78	26	27	53	15	29
C. Higgins, LW	82	27	25	52	E	22
Michael Ryder, RW	70	14	17	31	-4	30
G. Latendresse, RW	73	16	11	27	-2	41
Sergei Kostitsyn, LW	52	9	18	27	9	51
Roman Hamrlik, D	77	5	21	26	7	38
Bryan Smolinski, C	64	8	17	25	-6	20
Maxim Lapierre, C	53	7	11	18	5	60
Mike Komisarek, D	75	4	13	17	9	101
M. Dandenault, RW	61	9	5	14	-11	34
Tom Kostopoulos, RW	67	7	6	13	-3	113
Patrice Brisebois, D	43	3	8	11	-2	26
Kyle Chipchura, C	36	4	7	11	-1	10
Josh Gorges, D	62	0	9	9	E	32
Mikhail Grabovski, C	24	3	6	9	-4	8
Steve Begin, LW	44	3	5	8	E	48
Francis Bouillon, D	74	2	6	8	9	61
Ryan O'Byrne, D	33	1	6	7	7	45

GOALTENDING

Player	GP	Mins	W	L	TGA	GAA	SO
Carey Price	41	2413	24	12	103	2.56	3
Cristobal Huet	39	2277	21	12	97	2.56	2
Jaroslav Halak	6	285	2	1	10	2.11	1

New Jersey Devils

SCORING

Player	GP	G	A	Pts	+/-	PM
Zach Parise, LW	81	32	33	65	13	25
Patrik Elias, LW	74	20	35	55	10	38
Brian Gionta, RW	82	22	31	53	1	46
John Madden, C	80	20	23	43	1	26
J. Langenbrunner, RW	64	13	28	41	-1	30
Dainius Zubrus, C	82	13	25	38	2	38
Travis Zajac, C	82	14	20	34	-11	31
Paul Martin, D	73	5	27	32	20	22
Johnny Oduya, D	75	6	20	26	27	46
Jay Pandolfo, LW	54	12	12	24	10	22
David Clarkson, RW	81	9	13	22	1	183
Mike Mottau, D	76	4	13	17	-11	48
Sergei Brylin, C	82	6	10	16	-5	20
Karel Rachunek, D	47	4	9	13	3	40
Arron Asham, RW	77	6	4	10	-6	84
Colin White, D	57	2	8	10	-5	26
Andy Greene, D	59	2	8	10	E	22
Michael Rupp, C	64	3	6	9	-8	58
S. Brookbank, D	44	0	8	8	E	63
Vitaly Vishnevski, D	69	2	5	7	-12	50
Rod Pelley, C	58	2	4	6	-3	19

GOALTENDING

Player	GP	Mins	W	L	TGA	GAA	SO
Martin Brodeur	77	4635	44	27	168	2.17	4
Kevin Weekes	9	343	2	2	17	2.97	0

NHL Team-by-Team Statistical Leaders (Cont.)

New York Islanders

SCORING

Player	GP	G	A	Pts	+/-	PM
Mike Comrie, C	76	21	28	49	-21	87
Bill Guerin, RW	81	23	21	44	-15	65
Miroslav Satan, RW	80	16	25	41	-11	39
Trent Hunter, RW	82	12	29	41	-17	43
Josef Vasicek, C	81	16	19	35	1	53
Ruslan Fedotenko, LW	67	16	17	33	-9	40
Richard Park, RW	82	12	20	32	-4	20
Mike Sillinger, C	52	14	12	26	-10	28
Bryan Berard, D	54	5	17	22	-17	48
Sean Bergenheim, LW	78	10	12	22	-3	62
M. Bergeron, D	46	9	9	18	-14	16
Chris Campoli, D	46	4	14	18	-1	16
Andy Hilbert, C	70	8	8	16	2	18
Radek Martinek, D	69	0	15	15	-9	40
Blake Comeau, LW	51	8	7	15	1	22
Bruno Gervais, D	60	0	13	13	-5	34
Freddy Meyer, D	52	3	9	12	6	22
Andy Sutton, D	58	1	7	8	-6	86
Brendan Witt, D	59	2	5	7	-8	51
Kyle Okposo, RW	9	2	3	5	3	2
Tim Jackman, RW	36	1	3	4	-3	57
Jeff Tambellini, LW	31	1	3	4	-9	8
Chris Simon, LW	28	1	2	3	-1	43
Frans Nielsen, C	16	2	1	3	1	0
Aaron Johnson, D	30	0	2	2	2	30
Rob Davison, D	19	1	1	2	-3	32

GOALTENDING

Player	GP	Mins	W	L	TGA	GAA	SO
Rick DiPietro	63	3707	26	28	174	2.82	3
W. Dubielewicz	20	1132	9	9	51	2.70	0
Joey McDonald	2	120	0	1	6	2.99	0

Ottawa Senators

SCORING

Player	GP	G	A	Pts	+/-	PM
Jason Spezza, C	76	34	58	92	26	66
Daniel Alfredsson, RW	70	40	49	89	15	34
Dany Heatley, LW	71	41	41	82	33	76
Antoine Vermette, LW	81	24	29	53	3	51
Mike Fisher, C	79	23	24	47	-10	82
Wade Redden, D	80	6	32	38	11	60
Andrej Meszaros, D	82	9	27	36	5	50
Chris Kelly, C	75	11	19	30	3	30
Randy Robitaille, C	68	10	19	29	4	18
Joe Corvo, D	51	6	21	27	13	18
C. Schubert, D	82	8	16	24	7	64
D. McAmmond, LW	68	9	13	22	1	12
Chris Neil, RW	68	6	14	20	-3	199
Cory Stillman, LW	24	3	16	19	-8	10
Chris Phillips, D	81	5	13	18	15	56
Anton Volchenkov, D	67	1	14	15	14	55
Shean Donovan, RW	82	5	7	12	-3	73
Patrick Eaves, RW	26	4	6	10	E	6
Luke Richardson, D	76	2	7	9	1	41
Nick Foligno, LW	45	6	3	9	E	20
Martin Lapointe, RW	18	3	3	6	-2	23
Cody Bass, C	21	2	2	4	-1	19
Brian McGrattan, RW	38	0	3	3	E	46
Mike Commodore, D	26	0	2	2	-9	26

GOALTENDING

Player	GP	Mins	W	L	TGA	GAA	SO
Martin Gerber	57	3197	30	18	145	2.72	2
Ray Emery	31	1689	12	13	88	3.13	0
Brian Elliott	1	60	1	0	1	1.01	0

New York Rangers

SCORING

Player	GP	G	A	Pts	+/-	PM
Jaromir Jagr, RW	82	25	46	71	8	58
Scott Gomez, C	81	16	54	70	3	36
Chris Drury, C	82	25	33	58	-3	45
Brendan Shanahan, LW	73	23	23	46	-2	35
Martin Straka, LW	65	14	27	41	5	22
Brandon Dubinsky, C	82	14	26	40	8	79
Michal Rozsival, LW	80	13	25	38	E	80
Sean Avery, LW	57	15	18	33	6	154
Nigel Dawes, LW	61	14	15	29	11	10
Daniel Girardi, D	82	10	18	28	E	14
Fedor Tyutin, D	82	5	15	20	5	43
Paul Mara, D	61	1	16	17	1	52
Petr Prucha, LW	62	7	10	17	3	22
Ryan Callahan, RW	52	8	5	13	7	31
Marek Malik, D	42	2	8	10	7	48
Marc Staal, D	80	2	8	10	2	42
Marcel Hossa, LW	36	1	7	8	8	24
Christian Backman, D	18	2	6	8	2	20
Blair Betts, C	75	2	5	7	-4	20
Ryan Hollweg, LW	70	2	2	4	-12	96
Jason Strudwick, D	52	1	1	2	E	40
Fredrik Sjostrom, RW	18	2	0	2	E	8
Colton Orr, RW	74	1	1	2	-13	159

GOALTENDING

Player	GP	Mins	W	L	TGA	GAA	SO
Henrik Lundqvist	72	4305	37	24	160	2.23	10
S. Valiquette	15	686	5	3	25	2.19	2

Philadelphia Flyers

SCORING

Player	GP	G	A	Pts	+/-	PM
Mike Richards, C	73	28	47	75	14	76
Daniel Briere, C	79	31	41	72	-22	68
Mike Knuble, RW	82	29	26	55	-3	72
Jeff Carter, C	82	29	24	53	6	55
R.J. Umberger, C	74	13	37	50	E	19
Joffrey Lupul, RW	56	20	26	46	2	35
Kimmo Timonen, D	80	8	36	44	E	50
Scott Hartnell, LW	80	24	19	43	2	159
Braydon Coburn, D	78	9	27	36	17	74
Randy Jones, D	71	5	26	31	8	58
Scottie Upshall, RW	61	14	16	30	2	74
Simon Gagne, LW	25	7	11	18	-8	4
Vaclav Prospal, LW	18	4	10	14	7	6
Steve Downie, RW	32	6	6	12	2	73
Jim Dowd, C	73	5	5	10	E	41
Jason Smith, D	77	1	9	10	-4	86
Sami Kapanen, RW	74	5	3	8	-12	16
Derian Hatcher, D	44	2	5	7	4	33
Jim Vandermeer, D	28	1	5	6	-1	27
Denis Tolpeko, C	26	1	5	6	-4	24
Lasse Kukkonen, D	53	1	4	5	3	38
Patrick Thoreses, LW	21	0	5	5	-6	8
Riley Cote, LW	70	1	3	4	2	202

GOALTENDING

Player	GP	Mins	W	L	TGA	GAA	SO
Martin Biron	62	3539	30	20	153	2.59	5
Antero Niittymaki	28	1424	12	9	69	2.91	1

Phoenix Coyotes

SCORING

Player	GP	G	A	Pts	+/-	PM
Shane Doan, RW	80	28	50	78	4	59
Radim Vrbata, RW	76	27	29	56	6	14
Peter Mueller, C	81	22	32	54	-13	32
Ed Jovanowski, D	80	12	39	51	-13	73
Steve Reinprecht, C	81	16	30	46	-3	26
Martin Hanzal, C	72	8	27	35	-7	28
Niko Kapanen, C	79	10	18	28	-1	34
Daniel Winnik, C	79	11	15	26	-3	25
Derek Morris, D	82	8	17	25	8	83
Daniel Carcillo, LW	57	13	11	24	1	324
Keith Ballard, D	82	6	15	21	7	85
Fredrik Sjostrom, RW	51	10	9	19	-2	14
Zbynek Michalek, D	75	4	13	17	9	34
Joel Perrault, C	49	7	10	17	-11	48
Mike York, LW	63	6	8	14	-8	4
Nick Boynton, D	79	3	9	12	-9	125
Freddy Meyer, D	52	3	9	12	6	22
Keith Yandle, D	43	5	7	12	-12	14
Craig Weller, RW	59	3	8	11	-7	80
M. Tjarnqvist, LW	78	4	7	11	-1	34
Enver Lisin, RW	13	4	1	5	-5	6
Mike Zigomanis, C	33	2	1	3	-7	6
Matt Jones, D	45	0	2	2	-13	10
Matt Murley, LW	3	0	1	1	1	0
Kyle Turris, C	3	0	1	1	-5	2

GOALTENDING

Player	GP	Mins	W	L	TGA	GAA	SO
Ilya Bryzgalov	55	3167	26	22	128	2.42	3
Mikael Tellqvist	22	1224	9	8	56	2.74	2
Alex Auld	9	509	3	6	30	3.54	1

Pittsburgh Penguins

SCORING

Player	GP	G	A	Pts	+/-	PM
Evgeni Malkin, C	82	47	59	106	16	78
Sidney Crosby, C	53	24	48	72	18	39
Sergei Gonchar, D	78	12	53	65	13	66
Petr Sykora, RW	81	28	35	63	1	41
Ryan Malone, LW	77	27	24	51	14	103
Ryan Whitney, D	76	12	28	40	-2	45
Jordan Staal, C	82	12	16	28	-5	55
Max Talbot, C	63	12	14	26	8	53
Colby Armstrong, RW	54	9	15	24	6	50
Erik Christensen, C	49	9	11	20	-3	28
Tyler Kennedy, C	55	10	9	19	2	35
Kris Letang, D	63	6	11	17	-1	23
Jarkko Ruutu, LW	71	6	10	16	3	138
Gary Roberts, LW	38	3	12	15	-3	40
Georges Laraque, RW	71	4	9	13	E	141
Darryl Sydor, D	74	1	12	13	1	26
Pascal Dupuis, LW	16	2	10	12	4	8
Jeff Taffe, LW	45	5	7	12	2	8
Brooks Orpik, D	78	1	10	11	11	57
Marian Hossa, RW	12	3	7	10	E	6
Mark Recchi, RW	19	2	6	8	-2	12
Adam Hall, RW	46	2	4	6	-2	24
Robert Scuderi, D	71	0	5	5	3	26
Hal Gill, D	18	1	3	4	6	16
Mark Eaton, D	36	0	3	3	6	4

GOALTENDING

Player	GP	Mins	W	L	TGA	GAA	SO
Marc-Andre Fleury	35	1857	19	10	72	2.33	4
Ty Conklin	33	1866	18	8	78	2.51	2
Dany Sabourin	24	1242	10	9	57	2.75	2

San Jose Sharks

SCORING

Player	GP	G	A	Pts	+/-	PM
Joe Thornton, C	82	29	67	96	18	59
Milan Michalek, LW	79	24	31	55	19	47
Patrick Marleau, C	78	19	29	48	-19	33
Joe Pavelski, C	82	19	21	40	1	28
Jonathan Cheechoo, RW	69	23	14	37	11	46
Craig Rivet, D	74	5	30	35	3	104
Jeremy Roenick, C	69	14	19	33	-8	26
Steve Bernier, RW	59	13	10	23	-2	62
Mike Grier, RW	78	9	13	22	-8	24
Christian Ehrhoff, D	77	1	21	22	9	72
Torrey Mitchell, C	82	10	10	20	-3	50
Brian Campbell, D	20	3	16	19	9	8
Patrick Rissmiller, LW	79	8	9	17	-8	30
Devin Setoguchi, RW	44	11	6	17	6	8
Sandis Ozolinsh, D	39	3	13	16	-11	24
Matt Carle, D	62	2	13	15	-8	26

SCORING *(CONT.)*

Player	GP	G	A	Pts	+/-	PM
Marc-Eduoard Vlasic, D	82	2	12	14	-12	24
Kyle McLaren, D	61	3	8	11	3	84
Douglas Murray, D	66	1	9	10	20	98
Curtis Brown, C	33	5	4	9	4	10
Marcel Goc, C	51	5	3	8	-15	12
Ryane Clowe, LW	15	3	5	8	-1	22
Jody Shelley, LW	31	1	6	7	-2	91
Alexei Semenov, D	22	1	3	4	-8	36
Tomas Plihal, C	22	2	1	3	4	4

GOALTENDING

Player	GP	Mins	W	L	TGA	GAA	SO
Evgeni Nabokov	77	4561	46	21	163	2.14	6
Brian Boucher	5	238	3	1	7	1.76	1
Thomas Greiss	3	129	0	1	7	3.26	0

NHL Team-by-Team Statistical Leaders *(Cont.)*

St. Louis Blues

SCORING

Player	GP	G	A	Pts	+/-	PM
Paul Kariya, LW	82	16	49	65	-10	50
Brad Boyes, RW	82	43	22	65	1	20
Keith Tkachuk, C	79	27	31	58	-2	69
Lee Stempniak, RW	80	13	25	38	E	40
Andy McDonald, C	49	14	22	36	-17	32
Erik Johnson, D	69	5	28	33	-9	28
David Backes, RW	72	13	18	31	-11	99
Jamal Mayers, RW	80	12	15	27	-19	91
David Perron, LW	62	13	14	27	16	38
Eric Brewer, D	77	1	21	22	-18	91
Jay McClement, C	81	9	13	22	-17	26
Ryan Johnson, C	79	5	13	18	-2	22
Martin Rucinsky, LW	40	5	11	16	-9	40
Barret Jackman, D	78	2	14	16	-12	93
Bryce Salvador, D	56	1	10	11	12	43
Doug Weight, C	29	4	7	11	4	12
Dan Hinote, RW	58	5	5	10	-3	42
Christian Backman, D	45	1	9	10	-4	30
Jay McKee, D	66	2	7	9	2	42
Jeff Woywitka, D	27	2	6	8	2	12
Steve Wagner, D	24	2	6	8	-4	8
D.J. King, LW	61	3	3	6	-4	100
Mike Johnson, RW	21	2	3	5	-4	8
Matt Walker, D	43	1	1	2	-3	61
Yan Stastny, C	12	1	1	2	E	9

GOALTENDING

Player	GP	Mins	W	L	TGA	GAA	SO
Manny Legace	66	3666	27	25	147	2.41	5
Hannu Toivonen	23	1202	6	10	69	3.44	0
Marek Schwarz	2	50	0	1	6	7.25	0

Tampa Bay Lightning

SCORING

Player	GP	G	A	Pts	+/-	PM
Vincent Lecavalier, C	81	40	52	92	-17	89
Martin St. Louis, RW	82	25	58	83	-23	26
Vaclav Prospal, LW	62	29	28	57	-7	39
Brad Richards, C	62	18	33	51	-25	15
Michel Ouellet, RW	64	17	19	36	11	12
Filip Kuba, D	75	6	25	31	-8	40
Paul Ranger, D	72	10	21	31	-13	56
Dan Boyle, D	37	4	21	25	-29	57
Jan Hlavac, LW	62	9	13	22	-10	32
Mathieu Darche, LW	73	7	15	22	-14	20
Chris Gratton, C	60	10	11	21	-7	77
Shane O'Brien, D	77	4	17	21	-2	154
Jeff Halpern, C	19	10	8	18	2	14
Jason Ward, RW	79	8	6	14	-18	42
Jussi Jokinen, LW	20	2	12	14	-16	4
Craig MacDonald, C	65	2	9	11	-10	16
Nick Tarnasky, C	80	6	4	10	-15	78
Brad Lukowich, D	59	1	6	7	-15	20
Andre Roy, RW	63	4	3	7	-1	108
Alexandre Picard, D	20	3	3	6	-9	8
Mike Lundin, D	81	0	6	6	3	16
Andreas Karlsson, C	58	2	2	4	-7	10
Doug Janik, D	61	1	3	4	-3	45
Ryan Craig, C	7	1	1	2	-1	0
Junior Lessard, RW	19	1	1	2	-5	9

GOALTENDING

Player	GP	Mins	W	L	TGA	GAA	SO
Johan Holmqvist	45	2469	20	16	124	3.01	2
Karri Ramo	22	1269	7	11	64	3.03	0
Mike Smith	13	774	3	10	36	2.79	1
Marc Denis	10	415	1	5	28	4.05	0

Toronto Maple Leafs

SCORING

Player	GP	G	A	Pts	+/-	PM
Mats Sundin, C	74	32	46	78	17	76
Nik Antropov, C	72	26	30	56	10	92
Tomas Kaberle, D	82	8	45	53	-8	22
Jason Blake, LW	82	15	37	52	-4	28
Alexander Steen, LW	76	15	27	42	E	32
Pavel Kubina, D	72	11	29	40	5	116
A. Ponikarovsky, LW	66	18	17	35	3	36
Darcy Tucker, RW	74	18	16	34	-8	100
Matt Stajan, C	82	16	17	33	-11	47
Bryan McCabe, D	54	5	18	23	-2	81
Kyle Wellwood, C	59	8	13	21	-12	0
Ian White, D	81	5	16	21	-9	44
Hal Gill, D	63	2	18	20	E	52
Boyd Devereaux, C	62	7	11	18	-6	24
Chad Kilger, LW	53	10	7	17	1	18
Jiri Tlusty, C	58	10	6	16	-12	14

SCORING *(CONT.)*

Player	GP	G	A	Pts	+/-	PM
Dominic Moore, C	38	4	10	14	7	14
Mark Bell, LW	35	4	6	10	-2	60
Andy Wozniewski, D	48	2	7	9	5	54
Anton Stralman, D	50	3	6	9	-10	18
Carlo Colaiacovo, D	28	2	4	6	-4	10
Johnny Pohl, C	33	1	4	5	-4	10
Simon Gamache, LW	11	2	2	4	-1	6
Kris Newbury, C	28	1	1	2	-7	32
Jeremy Williams, RW	18	2	0	2	-3	4

GOALTENDING

Player	GP	Mins	W	L	TGA	GAA	SO
Vesa Toskala	66	3837	33	25	175	2.74	3
Andrew Raycroft	19	965	2	9	63	3.92	1
Scott Clemmensen	3	154	1	1	10	3.89	0

NHL Team-by-Team Statistical Leaders *(Cont.)*

Vancouver Canucks

SCORING

Player	GP	G	A	Pts	+/-	PM
Henrik Sedin, C	82	15	61	76	6	56
Daniel Sedin, LW	82	29	45	74	6	50
Markus Naslund, LW	82	25	30	55	-7	46
Taylor Pyatt, LW	79	16	21	37	9	60
Ryan Kesler, C	80	21	16	37	1	79
Alex Burrows, LW	82	12	19	31	11	179
Brendan Morrison, C	39	9	16	25	-3	18
Sami Salo, D	63	8	17	25	8	38
Mattias Ohlund, D	53	9	15	24	-1	79
Mason Raymond, LW	49	9	12	21	1	2
Alexander Edler, D	75	8	12	20	6	42
Matt Cooke, LW	61	7	9	16	-4	64
Ryan Shannon, RW	27	5	8	13	-1	24
Trevor Linden, C	59	7	5	12	E	15
Willie Mitchell, D	72	2	10	12	6	81
Kevin Bieska, D	34	2	10	12	-11	90

SCORING

Player	GP	G	A	Pts	+/-	PM
Brad Isbister, LW	55	6	5	11	-4	38
Byron Ritchie, C	71	3	8	11	-10	80
Lukas Krajicek, D	39	2	9	11	-3	36
Aaron Miller, D	57	1	8	9	-1	32
Matt Pettinger, LW	20	4	2	6	E	11
Jason Jaffray, RW	19	2	4	6	4	19
Rick Rypien, C	22	1	2	3	-5	41
Kris Beech, C	4	1	1	2	1	0
Luc Bourdon, D	27	2	0	2	7	20
Jeff Cowan, LW	46	0	1	1	-5	110

GOALTENDING

Player	GP	Mins	W	L	TGA	GAA	SO
Roberto Luongo	73	4233	35	29	168	2.38	6
Curtis Sanford	16	679	4	3	32	2.83	0
Drew MacIntyre	2	61	0	1	3	2.95	0

Washington Capitals

SCORING

Player	GP	G	A	Pts	+/-	PM
Alexander Ovechkin, LW	82	65	47	112	28	40
Nicklas Backstrom, C	82	14	55	69	13	24
Mike Green, D	82	18	38	56	6	62
Viktor Kozlov, C	81	16	38	54	28	18
Alexander Semin, LW	63	26	16	42	-18	54
Michael Nylander, C	40	11	26	37	-19	24
Brooks Laich, C	82	21	16	37	-3	35
T. Fleischmann, RW	75	10	20	30	-7	18
Tom Poti, D	71	2	27	29	9	46
Matt Bradley, RW	77	7	11	18	1	74
Jeff Schultz, D	72	5	13	18	12	28
Boyd Gordon, C	67	7	9	16	5	12
Brian Pothier, D	38	5	9	14	5	20
Sergei Fedorov, C	18	2	11	13	-2	8
Dave Steckel, C	67	5	7	12	1	34
Shaone Morrisonn, D	76	1	9	10	4	63

SCORING

Player	GP	G	A	Pts	+/-	PM
Chris Clark, RW	18	5	4	9	E	43
John Erksine, D	51	2	7	9	1	96
Milan Jurcina, D	75	1	8	9	4	30
Donald Brashear, LW	80	5	3	8	-7	119
Matt Cooke, LW	17	3	4	7	5	27
Matt Pettinger, LW	56	2	5	7	-11	25
Quintin Laing, LW	39	1	5	6	4	10
Eric Fehr, RW	23	1	5	6	4	6
Joe Motzko, RW	8	2	2	4	1	0
Steve Eminger, D	20	0	2	2	-4	8

GOALTENDING

Player	GP	Mins	W	L	TGA	GAA	SO
Olaf Kolzig	54	3154	25	21	153	2.91	1
Brent Johnson	19	1032	7	8	46	2.67	0
Cristobal Huet	13	771	11	2	21	1.63	2

2008 NHL Draft

First Round

The opening round of the 2008 NHL draft was held on June 20 in Ottawa, Ontario, Canada.

	Team	Selection	Position
1	Tampa Bay	Steve Stamkos	C
2	Los Angeles	Drew Doughty	D
3	Atlanta	Zach Bogosian	D
4	St. Louis	Alex Pietrangelo	D
5	Toronto	Luke Schenn	D
6	Columbus	Nikita Filatov	LW
7	Nashville	Colin Wilson	C
8	Phoenix	Mikkel Boedker	LW
9	NY Islanders	Joshua Bailey	C
10	Vancouver	Cody Hodgson	C
11	Chicago	Kyle Beach	C
12	Buffalo	Tyler Myers	D
13	Los Angeles	Colten Teubert	D
14	Carolina	Zach Boychuk	C
15	Ottawa	Erik Karlsson	D
16	Boston	Joe Colborne	LW
17	Anaheim	Jake Gardiner	D
18	Nashville	Chet Pickard	G
19	Philadelphia	Luca Sbisa	D
20	NY Rangers	Michael DelZotto	D
21	Washington	Anton Gustafsson	C
22	Edmonton	Jordan Eberle	C
23	Minnesota	Tyler Cuma	D
24	New Jersey	Mattias Tedenby	LW
25	Calgary	Greg Nemisz	C
26	Buffalo	Tyler Ennis	C
27	Washington	John Carlson	D
28	Phoenix	Viktor Tikhonov	LW
29	Atlanta	Daultan Leveille	C
30	Detroit	Thomas McCollum	G

FOR THE RECORD • Year by Year

The Stanley Cup

Awarded annually to the team that wins the NHL's best-of-seven final-round playoffs. The Stanley Cup is the oldest trophy competed for by professional athletes in North America. It was donated in 1893 by Frederick Arthur, Lord Stanley of Preston.

Results

1892–93.............Montreal A.A.
1893–94.............Montreal A.A.
1894–95.............Montreal Victorias
1895–96.............Winnipeg Victorias (Feb)
1895–96.............Montreal Victorias (Dec)
1896–97.............Montreal Victorias
1897–98.............Montreal Victorias
1898–99.............Montreal Victorias (Feb)
1898–99.............Montreal Shamrocks (Mar)
1899–1900..........Montreal Shamrocks
1900–01.............Winnipeg Victorias
1901–02.............Winnipeg Victorias (Jan)
1901–02.............Montreal A.A.A. (Mar)
1902–03.............Montreal A.A.A. (Feb)
1902–03.............Ottawa Silver Seven (Mar)
1903–04.............Ottawa Silver Seven
1904–05.............Ottawa Silver Seven
1905–06.............Ottawa Silver Seven (Feb)
1905–06.............Montreal Wanderers (Mar)
1906–07.............Kenora Thistles (Jan)
1906–07.............Montreal Wanderers (Mar)
1907–08.............Montreal Wanderers
1908–09.............Ottawa Senators
1909–10.............Montreal Wanderers
1910–11.............Ottawa Senators
1911–12.............Quebec Bulldogs
1912–13.............Quebec Bulldogs
1913–14.............Toronto Blueshirts
1914–15.............Vancouver Millionaires
1915–16.............Montreal Canadiens
1916–17.............Seattle Metropolitans

NHL WINNERS AND FINALISTS

Season	Champion	Finalist	GP in Final
1917–18	Toronto Arenas	Vancouver Millionaires	5
1918–19	No decision*	No decision*	5
1919–20	Ottawa Senators	Seattle Metropolitans	5
1920–21	Ottawa Senators	Vancouver Millionaires	5
1921–22	Toronto St. Pats	Vancouver Millionaires	5
1922–23	Ottawa Senators	Vancouver Maroons, Edmonton Eskimos	2, 4
1923–24	Montreal Canadiens	Vancouver Maroons, Calgary Tigers	2, 2
1924–25	Victoria Cougars	Montreal Canadiens	4
1925–26	Montreal Maroons	Victoria Cougars	4
1926–27	Ottawa Senators	Boston Bruins	4
1927–28	New York Rangers	Montreal Maroons	5
1928–29	Boston Bruins	New York Rangers	2
1929–30	Montreal Canadiens	Boston Bruins	2
1930–31	Montreal Canadiens	Chicago Black Hawks	5
1931–32	Toronto Maple Leafs	New York Rangers	3
1932–33	New York Rangers	Toronto Maple Leafs	4
1933–34	Chicago Black Hawks	Detroit Red Wings	4
1934–35	Montreal Maroons	Toronto Maple Leafs	3
1935–36	Detroit Red Wings	Toronto Maple Leafs	4
1936–37	Detroit Red Wings	New York Rangers	5
1937–38	Chicago Black Hawks	Toronto Maple Leafs	4
1938–39	Boston Bruins	Toronto Maple Leafs	5
1939–40	New York Rangers	Toronto Maple Leafs	6
1940–41	Boston Bruins	Detroit Red Wings	4
1941–42	Toronto Maple Leafs	Detroit Red Wings	7
1942–43	Detroit Red Wings	Boston Bruins	4
1943–44	Montreal Canadiens	Chicago Black Hawks	4
1944–45	Toronto Maple Leafs	Detroit Red Wings	7
1945–46	Montreal Canadiens	Boston Bruins	5
1946–47	Toronto Maple Leafs	Montreal Canadiens	6
1947–48	Toronto Maple Leafs	Detroit Red Wings	4
1948–49	Toronto Maple Leafs	Detroit Red Wings	4
1949–50	Detroit Red Wings	New York Rangers	7
1950–51	Toronto Maple Leafs	Montreal Canadiens	5
1951–52	Detroit Red Wings	Montreal Canadiens	4
1952–53	Montreal Canadiens	Boston Bruins	5
1953–54	Detroit Red Wings	Montreal Canadiens	7
1954–55	Detroit Red Wings	Montreal Canadiens	7

NHL WINNERS AND FINALISTS

Season	Champion	Finalist	GP in Final
1955–56	Montreal Canadiens	Detroit Red Wings	5
1956–57	Montreal Canadiens	Boston Bruins	5
1957–58	Montreal Canadiens	Boston Bruins	6
1958–59	Montreal Canadiens	Toronto Maple Leafs	5
1959–60	Montreal Canadiens	Toronto Maple Leafs	4
1960–61	Chicago Blackhawks	Detroit Red Wings	6
1961–62	Toronto Maple Leafs	Chicago Blackhawks	6
1962–63	Toronto Maple Leafs	Detroit Red Wings	5
1963–64	Toronto Maple Leafs	Detroit Red Wings	7
1964–65	Montreal Canadiens	Chicago Blackhawks	7
1965–66	Montreal Canadiens	Detroit Red Wings	6
1966–67	Toronto Maple Leafs	Montreal Canadiens	6
1967–68	Montreal Canadiens	St. Louis Blues	4
1968–69	Montreal Canadiens	St. Louis Blues	4
1969–70	Boston Bruins	St. Louis Blues	4
1970–71	Montreal Canadiens	Chicago Blackhawks	7
1971–72	Boston Bruins	New York Rangers	6
1972–73	Montreal Canadiens	Chicago Blackhawks	6
1973–74	Philadelphia Flyers	Boston Bruins	6
1974–75	Philadelphia Flyers	Buffalo Sabres	6
1975–76	Montreal Canadiens	Philadelphia Flyers	4
1976–77	Montreal Canadiens	Boston Bruins	4
1977–78	Montreal Canadiens	Boston Bruins	6
1978–79	Montreal Canadiens	New York Rangers	5
1979–80	New York Islanders	Philadelphia Flyers	6
1980–81	New York Islanders	Minnesota North Stars	5
1981–82	New York Islanders	Vancouver Canucks	4
1982–83	New York Islanders	Edmonton Oilers	4
1983–84	Edmonton Oilers	New York Islanders	5
1984–85	Edmonton Oilers	Philadelphia Flyers	5
1985–86	Montreal Canadiens	Calgary Flames	5
1986–87	Edmonton Oilers	Philadelphia Flyers	7
1987–88	Edmonton Oilers	Boston Bruins	4
1988–89	Calgary Flames	Montreal Canadiens	6
1989–90	Edmonton Oilers	Boston Bruins	5
1990–91	Pittsburgh Penguins	Minnesota North Stars	6
1991–92	Pittsburgh Penguins	Chicago Blackhawks	4
1992–93	Montreal Canadiens	Los Angeles Kings	5
1993–94	New York Rangers	Vancouver Canucks	7
1994–95	New Jersey Devils	Detroit Red Wings	4
1995–96	Colorado Avalanche	Florida Panthers	4
1996–97	Detroit Red Wings	Philadelphia Flyers	4
1997–98	Detroit Red Wings	Washington Capitals	4
1998–99	Dallas Stars	Buffalo Sabres	6
1999–2000	New Jersey Devils	Dallas Stars	6
2000–01	Colorado Avalanche	New Jersey Devils	7
2001–02	Detroit Red Wings	Carolina Hurricanes	5
2002–03	New Jersey Devils	Anaheim Mighty Ducks	7
2003–04	Tampa Bay Lightning	Calgary Flames	7
2004–05	No Stanley Cup due to season lockout		
2005–06	Carolina Hurricanes	Edmonton Oilers	7
2006–07	Anaheim Ducks	Ottawa Senators	5
2007–08	Detroit Red Wings	Pittsburgh Penguins	6

*In 1919 the Montreal Canadiens traveled to meet Seattle, the PCHL champions. After five games had been played—the teams were tied at two wins and one tie—the series was called off by the local Department of Health because of the influenza epidemic and the death of Canadiens defenseman Joe Hall from influenza.

Conn Smythe Trophy

Awarded to the Most Valuable Player of the Stanley Cup playoffs, as selected by the Professional Hockey Writers Association. The trophy is named after the former coach, general manager, president and owner of the Toronto Maple Leafs.

1965	Jean Beliveau, Mtl
1966	Roger Crozier, Det
1967	Dave Keon, Tor
1968	Glenn Hall, StL
1969	Serge Savard, Mtl
1970	Bobby Orr, Bos
1971	Ken Dryden, Mtl
1972	Bobby Orr, Bos
1973	Yvan Cournoyer, Mtl
1974	Bernie Parent, Phil
1975	Bernie Parent, Phil
1976	Reggie Leach, Phil
1977	Guy Lafleur, Mtl
1978	Larry Robinson, Mtl
1979	Bob Gainey, Mtl
1980	Bryan Trottier, NYI
1981	Butch Goring, NYI
1982	Mike Bossy, NYI
1983	Bill Smith, NYI
1984	Mark Messier, Edm
1985	Wayne Gretzky, Edm
1986	Patrick Roy, Mtl
1987	Ron Hextall, Phil
1988	Wayne Gretzky, Edm
1989	Al MacInnis, Cgy
1990	Bill Ranford, Edm
1991	Mario Lemieux, Pitt
1992	Mario Lemieux, Pitt
1993	Patrick Roy, Mtl
1994	Brian Leetch, NYR
1995	Claude Lemieux, NJ
1996	Joe Sakic, Col
1997	Mike Vernon, Det
1998	Steve Yzerman, Det
1999	Joe Nieuwendyk, Dall
2000	Scott Stevens, NJ
2001	Patrick Roy, Col
2002	Nicklas Lidstrom, Det
2003	J.-S. Giguere, Ana
2004	Brad Richards, TB
2005	No Award–No Season
2006	Cam Ward, Car
2007	Scott Niedermayer, Ana
2008	Henrik Zetterberg, Det

Alltime Stanley Cup Playoff Leaders

Points

	Yrs	GP	G	A	Pts
Wayne Gretzky, four teams	16	208	122	260	382
Mark Messier, Edm, Van, NYR	18	236	109	186	295
Jari Kurri, four teams	15	200	106	127	233
Glenn Anderson, four teams	15	225	93	121	214
Paul Coffey, six teams	16	194	59	137	196
Brett Hull, four teams	19	202	103	87	190
Doug Gilmour, seven teams	18	182	60	128	188
*Joe Sakic, Que, Col	13	172	84	104	188
Steve Yzerman, Det	20	196	70	115	185
Bryan Trottier, NYI, Pitt	17	221	71	113	184
*Jaromir Jagr, Pitt, Wsh, NYR	15	169	77	104	181
Ray Bourque, Bos, Col	21	214	41	139	180
Jean Beliveau, Mtl	17	162	79	97	176
Denis Savard, Chi, Mtl	16	169	66	109	175
Mario Lemieux, Pitt	8	107	76	96	172
*Peter Forsberg, Que, Col, Phil	13	151	64	107	171
*Sergei Fedorov, Det, Ana	14	169	51	117	168
Denis Potvin, NYI	14	185	56	108	164
Mike Bossy, NYI	10	129	85	75	160
Gordie Howe, Det, Hart	20	157	68	92	160
Bobby Smith, Minn, Mtl	13	184	64	96	160
Al MacInnis, Cgy, StL	19	177	39	121	160

*Active in 2007–08.

Goals

	Yrs	GP	G
Wayne Gretzky, four teams	16	208	122
Mark Messier, Edm, NYR	18	236	109
Jari Kurri, five teams	15	200	106
Brett Hull, Cgy, StL, Dall, Det	19	202	103
Glenn Anderson, four teams	15	225	93
Mike Bossy, NYI	10	129	85
*Joe Sakic, Que, Col	13	172	84
Maurice Richard, Mtl	15	133	82
Claude Lemieux, six teams	17	233	80
Jean Beliveau, Mtl	17	162	79
*Jaromir Jagr, Pitt, Wsh, NYR	15	169	77
Mario Lemieux, Pitt	8	107	76
Dino Ciccarelli, Minn, Wsh, Det	14	141	73
Esa Tikkanen, five teams	13	186	72
Bryan Trottier, NYI, Pitt	17	221	71

*Active in 2007–08.

Assists

	Yrs	GP	A
Wayne Gretzky, four teams	16	208	260
Mark Messier, Edm, NYR	18	236	186
Ray Bourque, Bos, Col	21	214	139
Paul Coffey, six teams	16	194	137
Doug Gilmour, seven teams	18	182	128
Jari Kurri, five teams	15	200	127
Glenn Anderson, four teams	15	225	121
Al MacInnis, Cgy, StL	19	177	121
*Sergei Fedorov, Det, Wsh	14	169	117
Larry Robinson, Mtl, LA	20	227	116
Steve Yzerman, Det	20	196	115
Lawrence Murphy, six teams	20	215	115
Adam Oates, six teams	15	163	114
Bryan Trottier, NYI, Pitt	17	221	113
*Chris Chelios, Mtl, Chi, Det	23	260	113

*Active in 2007–08.

Alltime Stanley Cup Playoff Goaltending Leaders

WINS	W	L	Pct
Patrick Roy, Mtl, Col	151	94	.616
*Martin Brodeur, NJ	95	74	.562
Grant Fuhr, five teams	92	50	.648
Billy Smith, LA, NYI	88	36	.710
Ed Belfour, four teams	88	68	.564
Ken Dryden, Mtl	80	32	.714
Mike Vernon, four teams	77	56	.579
Jacques Plante, five teams	71	36	.663
Andy Moog, four teams	68	57	.544
*Dominik Hasek, Chi, Buff, Det	65	49	.570
*Curtis Joseph, four teams	63	66	.488
Tom Barrasso, Buff, Pitt, Ott	61	54	.530
Turk Broda, Tor	60	39	.606
*Chris Osgood, NYI, StL, Det	59	41	.590

*Active in 2007–08.

SHUTOUTS	GP	W	SO
Patrick Roy, Mtl, Col	247	151	23
*Martin Brodeur, NJ	169	95	22
*Curtis Joseph, four teams	133	63	16

Four tied with 14 shutouts.

GOALS AGAINST AVG	Avg
George Hainsworth, Mtl, Tor	1.93
*Martin Brodeur, NJ	1.96
Turk Broda, Tor	1.98
*Dominik Hasek, Chi, Buff, Det	2.02
*Jean-Sebastien Giguere, Ana	2.10
*Chris Osgood, NYI, StL, Det	2.11

Note: At least 50 games played.
*Active in 2007–08.

Alltime Stanley Cup Playoff Wins

TEAM	W	L	Pct
Montreal	398	273	.593
Detroit	285	254	.529
Toronto	251	269	.483
Boston	245	268	.478
Pittsburgh	195	176	.526
NY Rangers	194	208	.483
Philadelphia	189	173	.522
Chicago	188	218	.463
Edmonton	152	99	.606
Dallas#	148	149	.498
St. Louis	138	165	.455
NY Islanders	131	102	.562
Colorado**	130	113	.535
Buffalo	119	124	.490
New Jersey†	118	100	.541
Calgary*	92	110	.455
Vancouver	71	96	.425
Washington	72	89	.447
Los Angeles	65	105	.382
Carolina§	51	58	.468
San Jose	57	62	.479
Ottawa	49	54	.476
Anaheim	46	33	.582
Phoenix††	29	63	.315
Tampa Bay	26	25	.551
Florida	13	18	.419
Minnesota	10	14	.417
Nashville	5	12	.294

*Atlanta Flames 1972–80. †Colorado Rockies 1976–82. #Minnesota North Stars 1967–93. **Quebec Nordiques 1979–95. ††Winnipeg Jets 1979–96. §Hartford Whalers 1979–97. Note: Teams ranked by playoff victories.

Stanley Cup Playoff Coaching Records

				Series			Games				
Coach	Team	Yrs	Series	W	L	Games	W	L	T	Cups	Pct
Glen Sather	Edm	10	27	21	6	†126	89	37	0	4	.706
Toe Blake	Mtl	13	23	18	5	119	82	37	0	8	.689
Scott Bowman	Five teams	28	68	49	19	353	223	130	0	9	.632
Hap Day	Tor	9	14	10	4	80	49	31	0	5	.613
Al Arbour	StL, NYI	16	42	30	12	209	123	86	0	4	.589
*Bob Hartley	Col, Atl	5	14	10	4	84	49	35	0	1	.583
Fred Shero	Phil, NYR	8	21	15	6	110	63	47	0	2	.573
*Ken Hitchcock	Dal, Phil	8	20	13	7	117	66	51	0	1	.564
*Mike Keenan	five teams	12	29	18	11	167	94	73	0	1	.563
*Jacques Lemaire	Mtl, NJ, Minn	9	20	12	8	112	60	54	0	1	.526

†Does not include suspended game, May 24, 1988. *Active in 2007–08.
Note: Coaches ranked by winning percentage. Minimum: 65 games.

The 10 Longest Overtime Games

Date	Result	OT	Scorer	Series	Series Winner
3-24-36	Det 1 vs Mtl M 0	116:30	Mud Bruneteau	SF	Det
4-3-33	Tor 1 vs Bos 0	104:46	Ken Doraty	SF	Tor
5-4-00	Phil 2 vs Pitt 1	92:01	Keith Primeau	CSF	Phil
4-24-03	Ana 4 vs Dall 3	80:48	Petr Sykora	CSF	Ana
4-24-96	Pitt 3 vs Wash 2	79:15	Petr Nedved	CQF	Pitt
3-23-43	Tor 3 vs Det 2	70:18	Jack McLean	SF	Det
3-28-30	Mtl 2 vs NYR 1	68:52	Gus Rivers	SF	Mtl
4-18-87	NYI 3 vs Wash 2	68:47	Pat LaFontaine	DSF	NYI
4-27-94	Buff 1 vs NJ 0	65:43	Dave Hannan	CQF	NJ
3-27-51	Mtl 3 vs Det 2	61:09	Maurice Richard	SF	Mtl

Hart Memorial Trophy

Awarded annually "to the player adjudged to be the most valuable to his team." The original trophy was donated by Dr. David A. Hart, father of Cecil Hart, former manager-coach of the Montreal Canadiens. In the 1980s Wayne Gretzky won the award nine times.

Year	Winner	Key Statistics	Runner-Up
1924	Frank Nighbor, Ott	10 goals, 3 assists in 20 games	Sprague Cleghorn, Mtl
1925	Billy Burch, Ham	20 goals, 4 assists in 27 games	Howie Morenz, Mtl
1926	Nels Stewart, Mtl M	42 points in 36 games	Sprague Cleghorn, Mtl
1927	Herb Gardiner, Mtl	12 points in 44 games as defenseman	Bill Cook, NYR
1928	Howie Morenz, Mtl	33 goals, 18 assists	Roy Worters, Pitt
1929	Roy Worters, NYA	1.21 goals against, 13 shutouts	Ace Bailey, Tor
1930	Nels Stewart, Mtl M	39 goals, 16 assists	Lionel Hitchman, Bos
1931	Howie Morenz, Mtl	28 goals, 23 assists	Eddie Shore, Bos
1932	Howie Morenz, Mtl	24 goals, 25 assists	Ching Johnson, NYR
1933	Eddie Shore, Bos	27 assists in 48 games as defenseman	Bill Cook, NYR
1934	Aurel Joliat, Mtl	27 points	Lionel Conacher, Chi
1935	Eddie Shore, Bos	26 assists in 48 games as defenseman	Charlie Conacher, Tor
1936	Eddie Shore, Bos	16 assists in 46 games as defenseman	Hooley Smith, Mtl M
1937	Babe Siebert, Mtl	28 points	Lionel Conacher, Mtl M
1938	Eddie Shore, Bos	17 points in 47 games as defenseman	Paul Thompson, Chi
1939	Toe Blake, Mtl	led NHL in points (47)	Syl Apps, Tor
1940	Ebbie Goodfellow, Det	28 points	Syl Apps, Tor
1941	Bill Cowley, Bos	led NHL in assists (45) and points (62)	Dit Clapper, Bos
1942	Tom Anderson, Bos	41 points	Syl Apps, Tor
1943	Bill Cowley, Bos	led NHL in assists (45)	Doug Bentley, Chi
1944	Babe Pratt, Tor	57 points in 50 games	Bill Cowley, Bos
1945	Elmer Lach, Mtl	led NHL in assists (54) and points (80)	Maurice Richard, Mtl
1946	Max Bentley, Chi	61 points in 47 games	Gaye Stewart, Tor
1947	Maurice Richard, Mtl	led NHL in goals (45); 26 assists	Milt Schmidt, Bos
1948	Buddy O'Connor, NYR	60 points in 60 games	Frank Brimsek, Bos
1949	Sid Abel, Det	28 goals, 26 assists	Bill Durnan, Mtl
1950	Charlie Rayner, NYR	6 shutouts	Ted Kennedy, Tor
1951	Milt Schmidt, Bos	61 points in 62 games	Maurice Richard, Mtl
1952	Gordie Howe, Det	led NHL in goals (47) and points (86)	Elmer Lach, Mtl
1953	Gordie Howe, Det	led NHL in goals (49) and points (95)	Al Rollins, Chi
1954	Al Rollins, Chi	5 shutouts	Red Kelly, Det
1955	Ted Kennedy, Tor	52 points	Harry Lumley, Tor
1956	Jean Beliveau, Mtl	led NHL in goals (47) and points (88)	Tod Sloan, Tor
1957	Gordie Howe, Det	led NHL in goals (44) and points (89)	Jean Beliveau, Mtl
1959	Andy Bathgate, NYR	74 points in 70 games	Gordie Howe, Det
1960	Gordie Howe, Det	45 assists, 73 points	Bobby Hull, Chi
1961	Bernie Geoffrion, Mtl	50 goals, 95 points	Johnny Bower, Tor
1962	Jacques Plante, Mtl	42 wins, 2.37 goals against avg.	Doug Harvey, NYR
1963	Gordie Howe, Det	47 assists, 73 points	Stan Mikita, Chi
1964	Jean Beliveau, Mtl	50 assists, 78 points	Bobby Hull, Chi
1965	Bobby Hull, Chi	39 goals, 32 assists	Norm Ullman, Det
1966	Bobby Hull, Chi	led NHL in goals (54) and points (97)	Jean Beliveau, Mtl
1967	Stan Mikita, Chi	led NHL in assists (62) and points (97)	Ed Giacomin, NYR
1968	Stan Mikita, Chi	40 goals, 47 assists	Jean Beliveau, Mtl
1969	Phil Esposito, Bos	led NHL in assists (77) and points (126)	Jean Beliveau, Mtl
1970	Bobby Orr, Bos	led NHL in assists (87) and points (120)	Tony Esposito, Chi
1971	Bobby Orr, Bos	102 assists, 139 points	Phil Esposito, Bos
1972	Bobby Orr, Bos	80 assists, 117 points	Ken Dryden, Mtl
1973	Bobby Clarke, Phil	67 assists, 104 points	Phil Esposito, Bos
1974	Phil Esposito, Bos	led NHL in goals (68) and points (145)	Bernie Parent, Phil
1975	Bobby Clarke, Phil	89 assists, 116 points	Rogatien Vachon, LA
1976	Bobby Clarke, Phil	89 assists, 119 points	Denis Potvin, NYI
1977	Guy Lafleur, Mtl	led NHL in assists (80) and points (136)	Bobby Clarke, Phil
1978	Guy Lafleur, Mtl	led NHL in goals (60) and points (132)	Bryan Trottier, NYI
1979	Bryan Trottier, NYI	led NHL in assists (87) and points (134)	Guy Lafleur, Mtl
1980	Wayne Gretzky, Edm	51 goals, 86 assists	Marcel Dionne, LA
1981	Wayne Gretzky, Edm	led NHL in assists (109) and points (164)	Mike Liut, StL
1982	Wayne Gretzky, Edm	NHL-record 92 goals and 212 points	Bryan Trottier, NYI
1983	Wayne Gretzky, Edm	led NHL in goals (71) and points (196)	Pete Peeters, Bos
1984	Wayne Gretzky, Edm	led NHL in goals (87) and points (205)	Rod Langway, Wash
1985	Wayne Gretzky, Edm	led NHL in goals (73) and points (208)	Dale Hawerchuk, Winn
1986	Wayne Gretzky, Edm	NHL-record 163 assists and 215 points	Mario Lemieux, Pitt
1987	Wayne Gretzky, Edm	led NHL in assists (121) and points (183)	Ray Bourque, Bos

Hart Memorial Trophy *(Cont.)*

Year	Winner	Key Statistics	Runner-Up
1988	Mario Lemieux, Pitt	led NHL in goals (70) and points (168)	Grant Fuhr, Edm
1989	Wayne Gretzky, LA	114 assists, 168 points	Mario Lemieux, Pitt
1990	Mark Messier, Edm	84 assists, 129 points	Ray Bourque, Bos
1991	Brett Hull, StL	led NHL in goals (86); 131 points	Wayne Gretzky, LA
1992	Mark Messier, NYR	72 assists, 107 points	Patrick Roy, Mtl
1993	Mario Lemieux, Pitt	69 goals, 91 assists in 60 games	Doug Gilmour, Tor
1994	Sergei Fedorov, Det	56 goals, 64 assists	Dominik Hasek, Buff
1995	Eric Lindros, Phil	29 goals, 41 assists in 46 games	Jaromir Jagr, Pitt
1996	Mario Lemieux, Pitt	led NHL in goals (69) and points (161)	Mark Messier, NYR
1997	Dominik Hasek, Buff	5 shutouts, 2.27 goals against avg.	Paul Kariya, Ana
1998	Dominik Hasek, Buff	13 shutouts, 2.09 goals against avg.	Jaromir Jagr, Pitt
1999	Jaromir Jagr, Pitt	44 goals, 127 points	Alexei Yashin, Ott
2000	Chris Pronger, StL	62 points, +52 plus/minus rating	Jaromir Jagr, Pitt
2001	Joe Sakic, Col	118 points, +45 plus/minus rating	Mario Lemieux, Pitt
2002	Jose Theodore, Mtl	2.11 goals against avg./7 shutouts	Jarome Iginla, Cal
2003	Peter Forsberg, Col	77 assists, +52 plus/minus rating	Markus Naslund, Van
2004	Martin St. Louis, TB	94 points, +35 plus/minus rating	Jarome Iginla, Cal
2005	No Award–No Season.		
2006	Joe Thornton, Bos/SJ	29 goals, 96 assists; 125 points	Jaromir Jagr, NYR
2007	Sidney Crosby, Pitt	36 goals, 84 assists; 120 points	Roberto Luongo, Van
2008	Alexander Ovechkin, Wsh	65 goals, 47 assists; 112 points	Evgeni Malkin, Pitt

Art Ross Trophy

Awarded annually "to the player who leads the league in scoring points at the end of the regular season." The trophy was presented to the NHL in 1947 by Arthur Howie Ross, former manager-coach of the Boston Bruins. The tie-breakers, in order, are as follows: (1) player with most goals, (2) player with fewer games played, (3) player scoring first goal of the season. Bobby Orr is the only defenseman in NHL history to win this trophy, and he won it twice (1970 and 1975).

Year	Winner	Pts
1919	Newsy Lalonde, Mtl	44
1920	Joe Malone, Que	30
1921	Newsy Lalonde, Mtl	48
1922	Punch Broadbent, Ott	41
1923	Babe Dye, Tor	46
1924	Cy Denneny, Ott	37
1925	Babe Dye, Tor	23
1926	Nels Stewart, Mtl M	44
1927	Bill Cook, NYR	42
1928	Howie Morenz, Mtl	37
1929	Ace Bailey, Tor	51
1930	Cooney Weiland, Bos	32
1931	Howie Morenz, Mtl	73
1932	Harvey Jackson, Tor	51
1933	Bill Cook, NYR	53
1934	Charlie Conacher, Tor	50
1935	Charlie Conacher, Tor	57
1936	Sweeney Schriner, NYA	45
1937	Sweeney Schriner, NYA	46
1938	Gordie Drillon, Tor	52
1939	Toe Blake, Mtl	47
1940	Milt Schmidt, Bos	52
1941	Bill Cowley, Bos	62
1942	Bryan Hextall, NYR	56
1943	Doug Bentley, Chi	73
1944	Herb Cain, Bos	82
1945	Elmer Lach, Mtl	80
1946	Max Bentley, Chi	61
1947	*Max Bentley, Chi	72
1948	Elmer Lach, Mtl	61
1949	Roy Conacher, Chi	68
1950	Ted Lindsay, Det	78
1951	Gordie Howe, Det	86
1952	Gordie Howe, Det	86
1953	Gordie Howe, Det	95
1954	Gordie Howe, Det	81
1955	Bernie Geoffrion, Mtl	75
1956	Jean Beliveau, Mtl	88
1957	Gordie Howe, Det	89
1958	Dickie Moore, Mtl	84
1959	Dickie Moore, Mtl	96
1960	Bobby Hull, Chi	81
1961	Bernie Geoffrion, Mtl	95
1962	Bobby Hull, Chi	84
1963	Gordie Howe, Det	86
1964	Stan Mikita, Chi	89
1965	Stan Mikita, Chi	87
1966	Bobby Hull, Chi	97
1967	Stan Mikita, Chi	97
1968	Stan Mikita, Chi	87
1969	Phil Esposito, Bos	126
1970	Bobby Orr, Bos	120
1971	Phil Esposito, Bos	152
1972	Phil Esposito, Bos	133
1973	Phil Esposito, Bos	130
1974	Phil Esposito, Bos	145
1975	Bobby Orr, Bos	135
1976	Guy Lafleur, Mtl	125
1977	Guy Lafleur, Mtl	136
1978	Guy Lafleur, Mtl	132
1979	Bryan Trottier, NYI	134
1980	Marcel Dionne, LA	137
1981	Wayne Gretzky, Edm	164
1982	Wayne Gretzky, Edm	212
1983	Wayne Gretzky, Edm	196
1984	Wayne Gretzky, Edm	205
1985	Wayne Gretzky, Edm	208
1986	Wayne Gretzky, Edm	215
1987	Wayne Gretzky, Edm	183
1988	Mario Lemieux, Pitt	168
1989	Mario Lemieux, Pitt	199
1990	Wayne Gretzky, LA	142
1991	Wayne Gretzky, LA	163
1992	Mario Lemieux, Pitt	131
1993	Mario Lemieux, Pitt	160
1994	Wayne Gretzky, LA	130
1995	Jaromir Jagr, Pitt	70
1996	Mario Lemieux, Pitt	161

NHL Awards *(Cont.)*

Art Ross Trophy *(Cont.)*

Year	Winner	Pts	Year	Winner	Pts
1997	Mario Lemieux, Pitt	122	2003	Peter Forsberg, Col	106
1998	Jaromir Jagr, Pitt	102	2004	Martin St. Louis, TB	94
1999	Jaromir Jagr, Pitt	127	2005	No Award	
2000	Jaromir Jagr, Pitt	96	2006	Joe Thornton, Bos/SJ	125
2001	Jaromir Jagr, Pitt	121	2007	Sidney Crosby, Pitt	120
2002	Jarome Iginla, Cgy	96	2008	Alexander Ovechkin, Wsh	112

Note: Listing includes scoring leaders prior to inception of Art Ross Trophy in 1947–48.

Lady Byng Memorial Trophy

Awarded annually "to the player adjudged to have exhibited the best type of sportsmanship and gentlemanly conduct combined with a high standard of playing ability." Lady Byng, who first presented the trophy in 1925, was the wife of Canada's Governor-General. She donated a second trophy in 1936 after the first was given permanently to Frank Boucher of the New York Rangers, who won it seven times in eight seasons. Stan Mikita, one of the league's most penalized players during his early years in the NHL, won the trophy twice late in his career (1967 and 1968).

1925..........Frank Nighbor, Ott
1926..........Frank Nighbor, Ott
1927..........Billy Burch, NYA
1928..........Frank Boucher, NYR
1929..........Frank Boucher, NYR
1930..........Frank Boucher, NYR
1931..........Frank Boucher, NYR
1932..........Joe Primeau, Tor
1933..........Frank Boucher, NYR
1934..........Frank Boucher, NYR
1935..........Frank Boucher, NYR
1936..........Doc Romnes, Chi
1937..........Marty Barry, Det
1938..........Gordie Drillon, Tor
1939..........Clint Smith, NYR
1940..........Bobby Bauer, Bos
1941..........Bobby Bauer, Bos
1942..........Syl Apps, Tor
1943..........Max Bentley, Chi
1944..........Clint Smith, Chi
1945..........Billy Mosienko, Chi
1946..........Toe Blake, Mtl
1947..........Bobby Bauer, Bos
1948..........Buddy O'Connor, NYR
1949..........Bill Quackenbush, Det
1950..........Edgar Laprade, NYR
1951..........Red Kelly, Det
1952..........Sid Smith, Tor
1953..........Red Kelly, Det
1954..........Red Kelly, Det
1955..........Sid Smith, Tor
1956..........Earl Reibel, Det
1957..........Andy Hebenton, NYR
1958..........Camille Henry, NYR
1959..........Alex Delvecchio, Det
1960..........Don McKenney, Bos
1961..........Red Kelly, Tor
1962..........Dave Keon, Tor
1963..........Dave Keon, Tor
1964..........Ken Wharram, Chi
1965..........Bobby Hull, Chi
1966..........Alex Delvecchio, Det
1967..........Stan Mikita, Chi
1968..........Stan Mikita, Chi
1969..........Alex Delvecchio, Det
1970..........Phil Goyette, StL
1971..........John Bucyk, Bos
1972..........Jean Ratelle, NYR
1973..........Gilbert Perreault, Buff
1974..........John Bucyk, Bos
1975..........Marcel Dionne, Det
1976..........Jean Ratelle, NYR-Bos
1977..........Marcel Dionne, LA
1978..........Butch Goring, LA
1979..........Bob MacMillan, Atl
1980..........Wayne Gretzky, Edm
1981..........Rick Kehoe, Pitt
1982..........Rick Middleton, Bos
1983..........Mike Bossy, NYI
1984..........Mike Bossy, NYI
1985..........Jari Kurri, Edm
1986..........Mike Bossy, NYI
1987..........Joe Mullen, Cgy
1988..........Mats Naslund, Mtl
1989..........Joe Mullen, Cgy
1990..........Brett Hull, StL
1991..........Wayne Gretzky, LA
1992..........Wayne Gretzky, LA
1993..........Pierre Turgeon, NYI
1994..........Wayne Gretzky, LA
1995..........Ron Francis, Pitt
1996..........Paul Kariya, Ana
1997..........Paul Kariya, Ana
1998..........Ron Francis, Pitt
1999..........Wayne Gretzky, NYR
2000..........Pavol Demitra, StL
2001..........Joe Sakic, Col
2002..........Ron Francis, Car
2003..........Alexander Mogilny, Det
2004..........Brad Richards, TB
2005..........No Award
2006..........Pavel Datsyuk, Det
2007..........Pavel Datsyuk, Det
2008..........Pavel Datsyuk, Det

James Norris Memorial Trophy

Awarded annually "to the defense player who demonstrates throughout the season the greatest all-around ability in the position." James Norris was the former owner-president of the Detroit Red Wings. Bobby Orr holds the record for most consecutive times winning the award (eight, 1968–1975).

1954 ....Red Kelly, Det
1955 ....Doug Harvey, Mtl
1956 ....Doug Harvey, Mtl
1957 ....Doug Harvey, Mtl
1958 ....Doug Harvey, Mtl
1959 ....Tom Johnson, Mtl
1960 ....Doug Harvey, Mtl
1961 ....Doug Harvey, Mtl
1962 ....Doug Harvey, NYR
1963 ....Pierre Pilote, Chi
1964 ....Pierre Pilote, Chi
1965 ....Pierre Pilote, Chi
1966 ....Jacques Laperriere, Mtl
1967 ....Harry Howell, NYR
1968 ....Bobby Orr, Bos
1969 ....Bobby Orr, Bos
1970 ....Bobby Orr, Bos
1971 ....Bobby Orr, Bos
1972 ....Bobby Orr, Bos
1973 ....Bobby Orr, Bos
1974 ....Bobby Orr, Bos
1975 ....Bobby Orr, Bos
1976 ....Denis Potvin, NYI
1977 ....Larry Robinson, Mtl
1978 ....Denis Potvin, NYI
1979 ....Denis Potvin, NYI
1980 ....Larry Robinson, Mtl
1981 ....Randy Carlyle, Pitt
1982 ....Doug Wilson, Chi
1983 ....Rod Langway, Wash
1984 ....Rod Langway, Wash
1985 ....Paul Coffey, Edm
1986 ....Paul Coffey, Edm
1987 ....Ray Bourque, Bos
1988 ....Ray Bourque, Bos
1989 ....Chris Chelios, Mtl
1990 ....Ray Bourque, Bos
1991 ....Ray Bourque, Bos
1992 ....Brian Leetch, NYR
1993 ....Chris Chelios, Chi
1994 ....Ray Bourque, Bos
1995 ....Paul Coffey, Det
1996 ....Chris Chelios, Chi
1997 ....Brian Leetch, NYR
1998 ....Rob Blake, LA
1999 ....Al MacInnis, StL
2000 ....Chris Pronger, StL
2001 ....Nicklas Lidstrom, Det
2002 ....Nicklas Lidstrom, Det
2003 ....Nicklas Lidstrom, Det
2004 ....Scott Niedermayer, NJ
2005 ....No Award
2006 ....Nicklas Lidstrom, Det
2007 ....Nicklas Lidstrom, Det
2008 ....Nicklas Lidstrom, Det

Calder Memorial Trophy

Awarded annually "to the player selected as the most proficient in his first year of competition in the National Hockey League." Frank Calder was a former NHL president. Sergei Makarov, who won the award in 1989–90, was the oldest recipient of the trophy, at 31. Players are no longer eligible for the award if they are 26 or older as of September 15th of the season in question.

1933.......Carl Voss, Det
1934.......Russ Blinko, Mtl M
1935.......Dave Schriner, NYA
1936.......Mike Karakas, Chi
1937.......Syl Apps, Tor
1938.......Cully Dahlstrom, Chi
1939.......Frank Brimsek, Bos
1940.......Kilby MacDonald, NYR
1941.......Johnny Quilty, Mtl
1942.......Grant Warwick, NYR
1943.......Gaye Stewart, Tor
1944.......Gus Bodnar, Tor
1945.......Frank McCool, Tor
1946.......Edgar Laprade, NYR
1947.......Howie Meeker, Tor
1948.......Jim McFadden, Det
1949.......Pentti Lund, NYR
1950.......Jack Gelineau, Bos
1951.......Terry Sawchuk, Det
1952.......Bernie Geoffrion, Mtl
1953.......Gump Worsley, NYR
1954.......Camille Henry, NYR
1955.......Ed Litzenberger, Chi
1956.......Glenn Hall, Det
1957.......Larry Regan, Bos
1958.......Frank Mahovlich, Tor
1959.......Ralph Backstrom, Mtl
1960.......Bill Hay, Chi
1961.......Dave Keon, Tor
1962.......Bobby Rousseau, Mtl
1963.......Kent Douglas, Tor
1964.......Jacques Laperriere, Mtl
1965.......Roger Crozier, Det
1966.......Brit Selby, Tor
1967.......Bobby Orr, Bos
1968.......Derek Sanderson, Bos
1969.......Danny Grant, Minn
1970.......Tony Esposito, Chi
1971.......Gilbert Perreault, Buff
1972.......Ken Dryden, Mtl
1973.......Steve Vickers, NYR
1974.......Denis Potvin, NYI
1975.......Eric Vail, Atl
1976.......Bryan Trottier, NYI
1977.......Willi Plett, Atl
1978.......Mike Bossy, NYI
1979.......Bobby Smith, Minn
1980.......Ray Bourque, Bos
1981.......Peter Stastny, Que
1982.......Dale Hawerchuk, Winn
1983.......Steve Larmer, Chi
1984.......Tom Barrasso, Buff
1985.......Mario Lemieux, Pitt
1986.......Gary Suter, Cgy
1987.......Luc Robitaille, LA
1988.......Joe Nieuwendyk, Cgy
1989.......Brian Leetch, NYR
1990.......Sergei Makarov, Cgy
1991.......Ed Belfour, Chi
1992.......Pavel Bure, Van
1993.......Teemu Selanne, Winn
1994.......Martin Brodeur, NJ
1995.......Peter Forsberg, Que
1996.......Daniel Alfredsson, Ott
1997.......Bryan Berard, NYI
1998.......Sergei Samsonov, Bos
1999.......Chris Drury, Col
2000.......Scott Gomez, NJ
2001.......Evgeni Nabokov, SJ
2002.......Dany Heatley, Atl
2003.......Barret Jackman, StL
2004.......Andrew Raycroft, Bos
2005.......No Award
2006.......Alexander Ovechkin, Wash
2007.......Evgeni Malkin, Pitt
2008.......Patrick Kane, Chi

Vezina Trophy

Awarded annually "to the goalkeeper adjudged to be the best at his position." The trophy is named after Georges Vezina, an outstanding goalie for the Montreal Canadiens who collapsed during a game on November 28, 1925, and died four months later of tuberculosis. The general managers of the NHL teams vote on the award.

1927.......George Hainsworth, Mtl
1928.......George Hainsworth, Mtl
1929.......George Hainsworth, Mtl
1930.......Tiny Thompson, Bos
1931.......Roy Worters, NYA
1932.......Charlie Gardiner, Chi
1933.......Tiny Thompson, Bos
1934.......Charlie Gardiner, Chi
1935.......Lorne Chabot, Chi
1936.......Tiny Thompson, Bos
1937.......Normie Smith, Det
1938.......Tiny Thompson, Bos
1939.......Frank Brimsek, Bos
1940.......Dave Kerr, NYR
1941.......Turk Broda, Tor
1942.......Frank Brimsek, Bos
1943.......Johnny Mowers, Det
1944.......Bill Durnan, Mtl
1945.......Bill Durnan, Mtl
1946.......Bill Durnan, Mtl
1947.......Bill Durnan, Mtl
1948.......Turk Broda, Tor
1949.......Bill Durnan, Mtl
1950.......Bill Durnan, Mtl
1951.......Al Rollins, Tor
1952.......Terry Sawchuk, Det
1953.......Terry Sawchuk, Det
1954.......Harry Lumley, Tor
1955.......Terry Sawchuk, Det
1956.......Jacques Plante, Mtl
1957.......Jacques Plante, Mtl
1958.......Jacques Plante, Mtl
1959.......Jacques Plante, Mtl
1960.......Jacques Plante, Mtl
1961.......Johnny Bower, Tor
1962.......Jacques Plante, Mtl
1963.......Glenn Hall, Chi
1964.......Charlie Hodge, Mtl
1965.......Terry Sawchuk, Tor
Johnny Bower, Tor
1966.......Gump Worsley, Mtl
Charlie Hodge, Mtl
1967.......Glenn Hall, Chi
Denis DeJordy, Chi
1968.......Lorne Worsley, Mtl
1969.......Jacques Plante, StL
Glenn Hall, StL
1970.......Tony Esposito, Chi
1971.......Ed Giacomin, NYR
Gilles Villemure, NYR
1972.......Tony Esposito, Chi
Gary Smith, Chi
1973.......Ken Dryden, Mtl
1974.......Bernie Parent, Phil
Tony Esposito, Chi
1975.......Bernie Parent, Phil
1976.......Ken Dryden, Mtl
1977.......Ken Dryden, Mtl
Michel Larocque, Mtl
1978.......Ken Dryden, Mtl
Michel Larocque, Mtl
1979.......Ken Dryden, Mtl
Michel Larocque, Mtl
1980.......Bob Sauve, Buff
Don Edwards, Buff
1981.......Richard Sevigny, Mtl
Michel Larocque, Mtl
1982.......Billy Smith, NYI
Denis Herron, Mtl
1983.......Pete Peeters, Bos
1984.......Tom Barrasso, Buff
1985.......Pelle Lindbergh, Phil
1986.......John Vanbiesbrouck, NYR
1987.......Ron Hextall, Phil
1988.......Grant Fuhr, Edm
1989.......Patrick Roy, Mtl
1990.......Patrick Roy, Mtl
1991.......Ed Belfour, Chi
1992.......Patrick Roy, Mtl
1993.......Ed Belfour, Chi
1994.......Dominik Hasek, Buff
1995.......Dominik Hasek, Buff
1996.......Jim Carey, Wash
1997.......Dominik Hasek, Buff
1998.......Dominik Hasek, Buff
1999.......Dominik Hasek, Buff
2000.......Olaf Kolzig, Wash
2001.......Dominik Hasek, Buff
2002.......Jose Theodore, Mtl
2003.......Martin Brodeur, NJ
2004.......Martin Brodeur, NJ
2005.......No Award
2006.......Miikka Kiprusoff, Cgy
2007.......Martin Brodeur, NJ
2008.......Martin Brodeur, NJ

NHL Awards (Cont.)

Selke Trophy

Awarded annually "to the forward who best excels in the defensive aspects of the game." The trophy is named after Frank J. Selke, the architect of the Montreal Canadians dynasty that won five consecutive Stanley Cups in the late '50s. The winner is selected by a vote of the Professional Hockey Writers Association.

1978........Bob Gainey, Mtl
1979........Bob Gainey, Mtl
1980........Bob Gainey, Mtl
1981........Bob Gainey, Mtl
1982........Steve Kasper, Bos
1983........Bobby Clarke, Phil
1984........Doug Jarvis, Wash
1985........Craig Ramsay, Buff
1986........Troy Murray, Chi
1987........Dave Poulin, Phil
1988........Guy Carbonneau, Mtl
1989........Guy Carbonneau, Mtl
1990........Rick Meagher, StL
1991........Dirk Graham, Chi
1992........Guy Carbonneau, Mtl
1993........Doug Gilmour, Tor
1994........Sergei Fedorov, Det
1995........Ron Francis, Pitt
1996........Sergei Fedorov, Det
1997........Michael Peca, Buff
1998........Jere Lehtinen, Dall
1999........Jere Lehtinen, Dall
2000........Steve Yzerman, Det
2001........John Madden, NJ
2002........Michael Peca, NYI
2003........Jere Lehtinen, Dall
2004........Kris Draper, Det
2005........No Award
2006........Rod Brind'Amour, Car
2007........Rod Brind'Amour, Car
2008........Pavel Datsyuk, Det

Adams Award

Awarded annually "to the NHL coach adjudged to have contributed the most to his team's success." The trophy is named in honor of Jack Adams, longtime coach and general manager of the Detroit Red Wings. The winner is selected by a vote of the National Hockey League Broadcasters' Association.

1974.....Fred Shero, Phil
1975.....Bob Pulford, LA
1976.....Don Cherry, Bos
1977.....Scott Bowman, Mtl
1978.....Bobby Kromm, Det
1979.....Al Arbour, NYI
1980.....Pat Quinn, Phil
1981.....Red Berenson, StL
1982.....Tom Watt, Winn
1983.....Orval Tessier, Chi
1984.....Bryan Murray, Wash
1985.....Mike Keenan, Phil
1986.....Glen Sather, Edm
1987.....Jacques Demers, Det
1988.....Jacques Demers, Det
1989.....Pat Burns, Mtl
1990.....Bob Murdoch, Winn
1991.....Brian Sutter, StL
1992.....Pat Quinn, Van
1993.....Pat Burns, Tor
1994.....Jacques Lemaire, NJ
1995.....Marc Crawford, Que
1996.....Scotty Bowman, Det
1997.....Ted Nolan, Buff
1998.....Pat Burns, Bos
1999.....Jacques Martin, Ott
2000.....Joel Quenneville, StL
2001.....Bill Barber, Phil
2002.....Bob Francis, Phoe
2003.....Jacques Lemaire, Minn
2004.....John Tortorella, TB
2005.....No Award
2006.....Lindy Ruff, Buff
2007.....Alain Vigneault, Van
2008.....Bruce Boudreau, Wsh

Career Records

Alltime Point Leaders

Player	Yrs	GP	G	A	Pts	Pts/game
Wayne Gretzky, Edm, LA, StL, NYR	20	1487	894	1963	2857	1.921
Mark Messier, Edm, NYR, Van	25	1756	694	1193	1887	1.074
Gordie Howe, Det, Hart	26	1767	801	1049	1850	1.047
Ron Francis, four teams	23	1731	549	1249	1798	1.039
Marcel Dionne, Det, LA, NYR	18	1348	731	1040	1771	1.314
Steve Yzerman, Det	22	1514	692	1063	1755	1.159
Mario Lemieux, Pitt	17	915	690	1033	1723	1.883
*Joe Sakic, Que, Col	19	1363	623	1006	1629	1.195
*Jaromir Jagr, Pitt, Wsh, NYR	17	1273	646	953	1599	1.256
Phil Esposito, Chi, Bos, NYR	18	1282	717	873	1590	1.240
Ray Bourque, Bos, Col	22	1612	410	1169	1579	.980
Paul Coffey, eight teams	21	1409	396	1135	1531	1.087
Stan Mikita, Chi	22	1394	541	926	1467	1.052
Bryan Trottier, NYI, Pitt	18	1279	524	901	1425	1.114
Adam Oates, seven teams	19	1337	341	1079	1420	1.062

Alltime Goal-Scoring Leaders

Player	Yrs	GP	G	G/game
Wayne Gretzky, Edm, LA, StL, NYR	20	1487	894	.601
Gordie Howe, Det, Hart	26	1767	801	.453
Brett Hull, Cgy, StL, Dall, Det	19	1269	741	.584
Marcel Dionne, Det, LA, NYR	18	1348	731	.542
Phil Esposito, Chi, Bos, NYR	18	1282	717	.559
Mike Gartner, Wash, Minn, NYR, Tor, Phoe	19	1432	708	.494
Mark Messier, Edm, NYR, Van	25	1756	694	.395
Steve Yzerman, Det.	22	1514	692	.457
Mario Lemieux, Pitt	17	915	690	.754
Luc Robitaille, LA, Pitt, NYR, Det	19	1431	668	.467
*Brendan Shanahan, NJ, Stl, Hfd, Det, NYR	20	1490	650	.436
*Jaromir Jagr, Pitt, Wsh, NYR	17	1273	646	.507

*Active in 2007–08.

Alltime Assist Leaders

Player	Yrs	GP	A	A/game
Wayne Gretzky, Edm, LA, StL, NYR	20	1487	1963	1.320
Ron Francis, Hart, Pitt, Car	23	1731	1249	.722
Mark Messier, Edm, NYR, Van	25	1756	1193	.679
Ray Bourque, Bos, Col	22	1612	1169	.725
Paul Coffey, eight teams	21	1409	1135	.806
Adam Oates, seven teams	22	1337	1079	.807
Steve Yzerman, Det	22	1514	1063	.702
Gordie Howe, Det, Hart	26	1767	1049	.594
Marcel Dionne, Det, LA, NYR	18	1348	1040	.772
Mario Lemieux, Pitt	17	915	1033	1.129

Alltime Penalty Minutes Leaders

Player	Yrs	GP	PIM	Min/game
Dave Williams, Tor, Van, Det, LA, Hart	14	962	3966	4.12
Dale Hunter, Que, Wash, Col	19	1407	3565	2.53
Tie Domi, Tor, NYR, Winn	16	1020	3515	3.45
Marty McSorley, Pitt, Edm, LA, NYR, SJ, Bos	17	961	3381	3.52
Bob Probert, Det, Chi	16	935	3300	3.53
Rob Ray, Buff, Ott	15	900	3207	3.56
Craig Berube, Phil, Tor, Cgy, Wash, NYI	17	1054	3149	2.99
Tim Hunter, Cgy, Que, Van, SJ	16	815	3146	3.86
Chris Nilan, Mtl, NYR, Bos	13	688	3043	4.42
Rick Tocchet, Phil, Pitt, LA, Bos, Wash, Phoe	18	1144	2972	2.60

Goaltending Records

ALLTIME GOALTENDING LEADERS, BY WINS

Goaltender	W	L	T/OTL	Pct
Patrick Roy, Mtl, Col	551	315	131	.618
*Martin Brodeur, NJ	538	290	118	.631
Ed Belfour, five teams	484	320	121	.590
*Curtis Joseph, five teams	449	343	92	.560
Terry Sawchuk, five teams	447	330	172	.562
Jacques Plante, five teams	437	246	145	.615
Tony Esposito, Mtl, Chi	423	306	151	.566
Glenn Hall, Det, Chi, StL	407	326	163	.545
Grant Fuhr, six teams	403	295	114	.567
*Dominik Hasek, Chi, Buff, Ott, Det	389	223	91	.618

*Active in 2007–08. OTL are counted from 2005 on.

ACTIVE GOALTENDING LEADERS, BY PERCENTAGE

Goaltender	W	L	T/OTL	Pct
Marty Turco, Dal	207	103	42	.648
Manny Legace, LA, Det, StL	164	83	34	.644
Martin Brodeur, NJ	538	290	118	.631
Chris Osgood, Det, NYI, StL	363	195	81	.631
Dominik Hasek, Chi, Buff, Det, Ott	389	223	91	.618
Miikka Kiprusoff, SJ, Cgy	159	101	37	.598
Evgeni Nabokov, SJ	208	150	48	.571
Curtis Joseph, five teams	449	343	95	.560
Patrick Lalime, Pitt, Ott, StL, Chi	191	148	43	.556
J. Giguere, Hfd, Cgy, Ana	191	151	50	.551

Note: Ranked by winning percentage; minimum 250 games played. All players active in 2007–08.

ALLTIME SHUTOUT LEADERS

Goaltender	Team	Yrs	GP	SO
Terry Sawchuk	Det, Bos, Tor, LA, NYR	21	971	103
*Martin Brodeur	NJ	15	968	96
George Hainsworth	Mtl, Tor	11	465	94
Glenn Hall	Det, Chi, StL	18	906	84
Jacques Plante	Mtl, NYR, StL, Tor, Bos	18	837	82
Tiny Thompson	Bos, Det	12	553	81
Alex Connell	Ott, Det, NYA, Mtl M	12	417	81
*Dominik Hasek	Chi, Buff, Ott, Det	16	735	81
Tony Esposito	Mtl, Chi	16	886	76
Ed Belfour	Chi, SJ, Dall, Tor	17	963	76

*Active in 2007–08.

ALLTIME GOALS AGAINST AVERAGE LEADERS (PRE-1950)

Goaltender	Team	Yrs	GP	GA	GAA
Alec Connell	Ott, Det, NYA, Mtl M	12	417	830	1.91
George Hainsworth	Mtl, Tor	11	465	937	1.93
Chuck Gardiner	Chi	7	316	664	2.02
Lorne Chabot	NYR, Tor, Mtl, Chi, Mtl M, NYA	11	411	860	2.04
Tiny Thompson	Bos, Det	12	553	1183	2.08

Career Records *(Cont.)*

ALLTIME GOALS AGAINST AVERAGE LEADERS (POST-1950)

Goaltender	Team	Yrs	GP	GA	GAA
*Marty Turco	Dal	7	382	775	2.15
*Martin Brodeur	NJ	15	968	2099	2.20
*Dominik Hasek	Chi, Buff, Det, Ott	16	735	1572	2.20
Ken Dryden	Mtl	8	397	870	2.24
Roman Turek	Dall, StL, Cgy	8	328	734	2.31
*Manny Legace	LA, Det, StL	9	308	663	2.31

*Active in 2007–08. Note: Minimum 250 games played. GAA equals goals against per 60 minutes played.

Alltime Coaching Leaders

Coach	Team	Seasons	W	L	T	OTL	Pct
Scotty Bowman	five teams	1967–87, 91–2002	1244	584	313	0	.654
Toe Blake	Mtl	1955–68	500	255	159	0	.634
Fred Shero	Phil, NYR	1971–81	390	225	119	0	.612
*Ken Hitchcock	Dall, Phil, CBJ	1995–	470	314	88	29	.599
Glen Sather	Edm, NYR	1979-89, 93-94, 2003-04	497	307	121	0	.598
Emile Francis	NYR, StL	1965–77, 81–83	388	273	117	0	.574
Billy Reay	Tor, Chi	1957–59, 63–77	542	385	175	0	.571
Pat Burns	Mtl, Tor, Bos, NJ	1988–2001, 2002–05	501	367	151	0	.566
Al Arbour	StL, NYI	1970–94	781	577	248	0	.564
Pat Quinn	Phil, LA, Van, Tor	1978–2006	657	499	154	8	.560
Dick Irvin	Chi, Tor, Mtl	1930–56	690	521	226	0	.559

*Active in 2007–08. Note: Minimum 600 regular-season games. Ranked by win percentage. Overtime losses up through 2004 are counted as losses. After 2004, ties were eliminated and overtime losses were awarded one point and so are listed in separate OTL column (and counted like ties).

Single-Season Records

Goals

Player	Season	GP	G
Wayne Gretzky, Edm	1981–82	80	92
Wayne Gretzky, Edm	1983–84	74	87
Brett Hull, StL	1990–91	78	86
Mario Lemieux, Pitt	1988–89	76	85
Alexander Mogilny, Buff	1992–93	77	76
Phil Esposito, Bos	1970–71	78	76
Teemu Selanne, Winn	1992–93	84	76
Wayne Gretzky, Edm	1984–85	80	73
Brett Hull, StL	1989–90	80	72
Jari Kurri, Edm	1984–85	73	71
Wayne Gretzky, Edm	1982–83	80	71
Brett Hull, StL	1991–92	73	70
Mario Lemieux, Pitt	1987–88	77	70
Bernie Nicholls, LA	1988–89	79	70
Mario Lemieux, Pitt	1992–93	60	69
Mario Lemieux, Pitt	1995–96	70	69
Mike Bossy, NYI	1978–79	80	69
Phil Esposito, Bos	1973–74	78	68
Jari Kurri, Edm	1985–86	78	68
Mike Bossy, NYI	1980–81	79	68

Assists

Player	Season	GP	Asst
Wayne Gretzky, Edm	1985–86	80	163
Wayne Gretzky, Edm	1984–85	80	135
Wayne Gretzky, Edm	1982–83	80	125
Wayne Gretzky, LA	1990–91	78	122
Wayne Gretzky, Edm	1986–87	79	121
Wayne Gretzky, Edm	1981–82	80	120
Wayne Gretzky, Edm	1983–84	74	118
Mario Lemieux, Pitt	1988–89	76	114
Wayne Gretzky, LA	1988–89	78	114
Wayne Gretzky, Edm	1987–88	64	109
Wayne Gretzky, Edm	1980–81	80	109
Wayne Gretzky, LA	1989–90	73	102
Bobby Orr, Bos	1970–71	78	102
Mario Lemieux, Pitt	1987–88	77	98
Adam Oates, Bos	1992–93	84	97
Joe Thornton, SJ	2005-06	81	96
Doug Gilmour, Tor	1992–93	83	95
Pat LaFontaine, Buff	1992–93	84	95
Mario Lemieux, Pitt	1985–86	79	93
Peter Stastny, Que	1981–82	80	93
Wayne Gretzky, LA	1993–94	81	92
Mario Lemieux, Pitt	1995–96	70	92
Ron Francis, Pitt	1995–96	77	92
Joe Thornton, SJ	2006-07	82	92

Points

Player	Season	G	Asst	Pts
Wayne Gretzky, Edm	1985–86	52	163	215
Wayne Gretzky, Edm	1981–82	92	120	212
Wayne Gretzky, Edm	1984–85	73	135	208
Wayne Gretzky, Edm	1983–84	87	118	205
Mario Lemieux, Pitt	1988–89	85	114	199
Wayne Gretzky, Edm	1982–83	71	125	196
Wayne Gretzky, Edm	1986–87	62	121	183
Mario Lemieux, Pitt	1987–88	70	98	168
Wayne Gretzky, LA	1988–89	54	114	168
Wayne Gretzky, Edm	1980–81	55	109	164
Wayne Gretzky, LA	1990–91	41	122	163
Mario Lemieux, Pitt	1995–96	69	92	161
Mario Lemieux, Pitt	1992–93	69	91	160
Steve Yzerman, Det	1988–89	65	90	155
Phil Esposito, Bos	1970–71	76	76	152
Bernie Nicholls, LA	1988–89	70	80	150
Wayne Gretzky, Edm	1987–88	40	109	149
Pat LaFontaine, Buff	1992–93	53	95	148
Mike Bossy, NYI	1981–82	64	83	147
Phil Esposito, Bos	1973–74	68	77	145

Points per Game

Player	Season	GP	Pts	Avg
Wayne Gretzky, Edm	1983–84	74	205	2.77
Wayne Gretzky, Edm	1985–86	80	215	2.69
Mario Lemieux, Pitt	1992–93	60	160	2.67
Wayne Gretzky, Edm	1981–82	80	212	2.65
Mario Lemieux, Pitt	1988–89	76	199	2.62
Wayne Gretzky, Edm	1984–85	80	208	2.60
Wayne Gretzky, Edm	1982–83	80	196	2.45
Wayne Gretzky, Edm	1987–88	64	149	2.33
Wayne Gretzky, Edm	1986–87	79	183	2.32
Mario Lemieux, Pitt	1995–96	70	161	2.30
Mario Lemieux, Pitt	1987–88	77	168	2.18
Wayne Gretzky, LA	1988–89	78	168	2.15
Wayne Gretzky, LA	1990–91	78	163	2.09
Mario Lemieux, Pitt	1989–90	59	123	2.08
Wayne Gretzky, Edm	1980–81	80	164	2.05
Mario Lemieux, Pitt	1991–92	64	131	2.05
Bill Cowley, Bos	1943–44	36	71	1.97
Phil Esposito, Bos	1970–71	78	152	1.95
Wayne Gretzky, LA	1989–90	73	142	1.95
Steve Yzerman, Det	1988–89	80	155	1.94

Note: Minimum 50 points in one season.

Goals per Game

Player	Season	GP	G	Avg
Joe Malone, Mtl	1917–18	20	44	2.20
Cy Denneny, Ott	1917–18	20	36	1.80
Newsy Lalonde, Mtl	1917–18	14	23	1.64
Joe Malone, Que	1919–20	24	39	1.63
Newsy Lalonde, Mtl	1919–20	23	36	1.57
Reg Noble, Tor	1917–18	20	30	1.50
Babe Dye, Ham-Tor	1920–21	24	35	1.46
Cy Denneny, Ott	1920–21	24	34	1.42
Joe Malone, Ham	1920–21	20	28	1.40
Newsy Lalonde, Mtl	1920–21	24	33	1.38

Note: Minimum 20 goals in one season.

Assists per Game

Player	Season	GP	Asst	Avg
Wayne Gretzky, Edm	1985–86	80	163	2.04
Wayne Gretzky, Edm	1987–88	64	109	1.70
Wayne Gretzky, Edm	1984–85	80	135	1.69
Wayne Gretzky, Edm	1983–84	74	118	1.59
Wayne Gretzky, Edm	1982–83	80	125	1.56
Wayne Gretzky, LA	1990–91	78	122	1.56
Wayne Gretzky, Edm	1986–87	79	121	1.53
Mario Lemieux, Pitt	1992–93	60	91	1.52
Wayne Gretzky, Edm	1981–82	80	120	1.50
Mario Lemieux, Pitt	1988–89	76	114	1.50

Note: Minimum 35 assists in one season.

Shutout Leaders

	Season	SO	Length of Schedule
George Hainsworth, Mtl	1928–29	22	44
Alec Connell, Ott	1925–26	15	36
Alec Connell, Ott	1927–28	15	44
Hal Winkler, Bos	1927–28	15	44
Tony Esposito, Chi	1969–70	15	76
George Hainsworth, Mtl	1926–27	14	44
Clint Benedict, Mtl M	1926–27	13	44
Alec Connell, Ott	1926–27	13	44
George Hainsworth, Mtl	1927–28	13	44
John Roach, NYR	1928–29	13	44
Roy Worters, NYA	1928–29	13	44
Harry Lumley, Tor	1953–54	13	70
Dominik Hasek, Buff	1997–98	13	82
Tiny Thompson, Bos	1928–29	12	44
Chuck Gardiner, Chi	1930–31	12	44
Terry Sawchuk, Det	1951–52	12	70
Terry Sawchuk, Det	1953–54	12	70
Terry Sawchuk, Det	1954–55	12	70
Glenn Hall, Det	1955–56	12	70
Bernie Parent, Phil	1973–74	12	78
Bernie Parent, Phil	1974–75	12	80
Martin Brodeur, NJ	2006-07	12	82
Lorne Chabot, NYR	1927–28	11	44
Harry Holmes, Det	1927–28	11	44
Roy Worters, Pitt Pirates	1927–28	11	44
Lorne Chabot, Tor	1928–29	11	44
Clint Benedict, Mtl M	1928–29	11	44
Joe Miller, Pitt Pirates	1928–29	11	44
Tiny Thompson, Bos	1932–33	11	48
Terry Sawchuck, Det	1950–51	11	70
Dominik Hasek, Buff	2000–01	11	82
Martin Brodeur, NJ	2003–04	11	82
Lorne Chabot, NYR	1926–27	10	44
Clarence Dolson, Det	1928–29	10	44
John Roach, Det	1932–33	10	48
Chuck Gardiner, Chi	1933–34	10	48
Tiny Thompson, Bos	1935–36	10	48
Frank Brimsek, Bos	1938–39	10	48
Bill Durnan, Mtl	1948–49	10	60
Gerry McNeil, Mtl	1952–53	10	70
Harry Lumley, Tor	1952–53	10	70
Tony Esposito, Chi	1973–74	10	78
Ken Dryden, Mtl	1976–77	10	80
Martin Brodeur, NJ	1996–97	10	82
Martin Brodeur, NJ	1997–98	10	82
Roman Cechmanek, Phil	2000–01	10	82
Byron Dafoe, Bos	1998–99	10	82
Ed Belfour, Tor	2003–04	10	82
Miikka Kiprusoff, Cgy	2005–06	10	82
Henrik Lundqvist, NYR	2007–08	10	82

Wins

	Season	Record*
Martin Brodeur, NJ	2006-07	48-23
Roberto Luongo, Van	2006-07	47-22
Bernie Parent, Phil	1973–74	47-13-12
Evgeni Nabokov, SJ	2007–08	46–21
Bernie Parent, Phil	1974–75	44-14-9
Terry Sawchuk, Det	1950–51	44-13-13
Terry Sawchuk, Det	1951–52	44-14-12
Martin Brodeur, NJ	2007–08	44–27
Tom Barrasso, Pitt	1992–93	43-14-5
Ed Belfour, Chi	1990–91	43-19-7
Martin Brodeur, NJ	1997–98	43-17-8
Martin Brodeur, NJ	1999–00	43-20-8
Martin Brodeur, NJ	2005–06	43-23
Jacques Plante, Mtl	1955–56	42-12-10
Jacques Plante, Mtl	1961–62	42-14-14
Ken Dryden, Mtl	1975–76	42-10-8
Mike Richter, NYR	1993–94	42-12-6
Roman Turek, StL	1999–00	42-15-9
Martin Brodeur, NJ	2000–01	42-17-11
Miikka Kiprusoff, Cgy	2005–06	42-20

*Starting in the 2005–06 season, ties were eliminated.

Single-Season Records (*Cont.*)

Goals Against Average

(PRE-1950)

	Season	GP	GAA
George Hainsworth, Mtl	1928–29	44	0.92
George Hainsworth, Mtl	1927–28	44	1.05
Alec Connell, Ott	1925–26	36	1.12
Tiny Thompson, Bos	1928–29	44	1.15
Roy Worters, NYA	1928–29	38	1.15

(POST-1950)

	Season	GP	GAA
Miika Kiprusoff, Cal	2003–04	38	1.69
Marty Turco, Dall	2002–03	55	1.73
Tony Esposito, Chi	1971–72	48	1.7698
Al Rollins, Tor	1950–51	40	1.7744
Ron Tugnutt, Ott	1998–99	43	1.79

Single-Game Records

Goals

	Date	G
Joe Malone, Que vs Tor	1-31-20	7
Newsy Lalonde, Mtl vs Tor	1-10-20	6
Joe Malone, Que vs Ott	3-10-20	6
Corb Denneny, Tor vs Ham	1-26-21	6
Cy Denneny, Ott vs Ham	3-7-21	6
Syd Howe, Det vs NYR	2-3-44	6
Red Berenson, StL vs Phil	11-7-68	6
Darryl Sittler, Tor vs Bos	2-7-76	6

Assists

	Date	A
Billy Taylor, Det vs Chi	3-16-47	7
Wayne Gretzky, Edm vs Wash	2-15-80	7
Wayne Gretzky, Edm vs Chi	12-11-85	7
Wayne Gretzky, Edm vs Que	2-14-86	7

Note: 24 tied with 6.

Points

	Date	G	A	Pts
Darryl Sittler, Tor vs Bos	2-7-76	6	4	10
Maurice Richard, Mtl vs Det	12-28-44	5	3	8
Bert Olmstead, Mtl vs Chi	1-9-54	4	4	8
Tom Bladon, Phil vs Clev	12-11-77	4	4	8
Bryan Trottier, NYI vs NYR	12-23-78	5	3	8
Peter Stastny, Que vs Wash	2-22-81	4	4	8
Anton Stastny, Que vs Wash	2-22-81	3	5	8
Wayne Gretzky, Edm vs NJ	11-19-83	3	5	8
Wayne Gretzky, Edm vs Minn	1-4-84	4	4	8
Paul Coffey, Edm vs Det	3-14-86	2	6	8
Mario Lemieux, Pitt vs StL	10-15-88	2	6	8
Bernie Nicholls, LA vs Tor	12-1-88	2	6	8
Mario Lemieux, Pitt vs NJ	12-31-88	5	3	8

NHL Season Leaders

Points

Season	Player and Club	Pts
1917–18	Joe Malone, Mtl	44
1918–19	Newsy Lalonde, Mtl	30
1919–20	Joe Malone, Que	48
1920–21	Newsy Lalonde, Mtl	41
1921–22	Punch Broadbent, Ott	46
1922–23	Babe Dye, Tor	37
1923–24	Cy Denneny, Ott	23
1924–25	Babe Dye, Tor	44
1925–26	Nels Stewart, Mtl M	42
1926–27	Bill Cook, NY	37
1927–28	Howie Morenz, Mtl	51
1928–29	Ace Bailey, Tor	32
1929–30	Cooney Weiland, Bos	73
1930–31	Howie Morenz, Mtl	51
1931–32	Harvey Jackson, Tor	53
1932–33	Bill Cook, NY	50
1933–34	Charlie Conacher, Tor	52
1934–35	Charlie Conacher, Tor	57
1935–36	Sweeney Schriner, NYA	45
1936–37	Sweeney Schriner, NYA	46
1937–38	Gord Drillon, Tor	52
1938–39	Hector Blake, Mtl	47
1939–40	Milt Schmidt, Bos	52
1940–41	Bill Cowley, Bos	62
1941–42	Bryan Hextall, NY	54
1942–43	Doug Bentley, Chi	73
1943–44	Herb Cain, Bos	82
1944–45	Elmer Lach, Mtl	80
1945–46	Max Bentley, Chi	61
1946–47	Max Bentley, Chi	72
1947–48	Elmer Lach, Mtl	61
1948–49	Roy Conacher, Chi	68
1949–50	Ted Lindsay, Det	78
1950–51	Gordie Howe, Det	86
1951–52	Gordie Howe, Det	86
1952–53	Gordie Howe, Det	95
1953–54	Gordie Howe, Det	81
1954–55	Bernie Geoffrion, Mtl	75
1955–56	Jean Beliveau, Mtl	88
1956–57	Gordie Howe, Det	89
1957–58	Dickie Moore, Mtl	84
1958–59	Dickie Moore, Mtl	96
1959–60	Bobby Hull, Chi	81
1960–61	Bernie Geoffrion, Mtl	95
1961–62	Andy Bathgate, NY	84
	Bobby Hull, Chi	84
1962–63	Gordie Howe, Det	86
1963–64	Stan Mikita, Chi	89
1964–65	Stan Mikita, Chi	87
1965–66	Bobby Hull, Chi	97
1966–67	Stan Mikita, Chi	97
1967–68	Stan Mikita, Chi	87
1968–69	Phil Esposito, Bos	126
1969–70	Bobby Orr, Bos	120
1970–71	Phil Esposito, Bos	152
1971–72	Phil Esposito, Bos	133
1972–73	Phil Esposito, Bos	130
1973–74	Phil Esposito, Bos	145
1974–75	Bobby Orr, Bos	135
1975–76	Guy Lafleur, Mtl	125
1976–77	Guy Lafleur, Mtl	136
1977–78	Guy Lafleur, Mtl	132
1978–79	Bryan Trottier, NYI	134
1979–80	Marcel Dionne, LA	137
	Wayne Gretzky, Edm	137
1980–81	Wayne Gretzky, Edm	164

NHL Season Leaders (Cont.)

Points (Cont.)

Season	Player and Club	Pts
1981–82	Wayne Gretzky, Edm	212
1982–83	Wayne Gretzky, Edm	196
1983–84	Wayne Gretzky, Edm	205
1984–85	Wayne Gretzky, Edm	208
1985–86	Wayne Gretzky, Edm	215
1986–87	Wayne Gretzky, Edm	183
1987–88	Mario Lemieux, Pitt	168
1988–89	Mario Lemieux, Pitt	199
1989–90	Wayne Gretzky, LA	142
1990–91	Wayne Gretzky, LA	163
1991–92	Mario Lemieux, Pitt	131
1992–93	Mario Lomieux, Pitt	160
1993–94	Wayne Gretzky, LA	130
1994–95	Jaromir Jagr, Pitt	70
1995–96	Mario Lemieux, Pitt	161
1996–97	Mario Lemieux, Pitt	122
1997–98	Jaromir Jagr, Pitt	102
1998–99	Jaromir Jagr, Pitt	127
1999–00	Jaromir Jagr, Pitt	96
2000–01	Jaromir Jagr, Pitt	121
2001–02	Jarome Iginla, Cgy	96
2002–03	Peter Forsberg, Col	106
2003–04	Martin St. Louis, TB	94
2004–05	No season	
2005–06	Joe Thornton, Bos/SJ	125
2006–07	Sidney Crosby, Pitt	120
2007–08	Alexander Ovechkin, Wsh	112

Goals

Season	Player and Club	G
1917–18	Joe Malone, Mtl	44
1918–19	Odie Cleghorn, Mtl	23
1919–20	Joe Malone, Que	39
1920–21	Babe Dye, Ham-Tor	35
1921–22	Punch Broadbent, Ott	32
1922–23	Babe Dye, Tor	26
1923–24	Cy Denneny, Ott	22
1924–25	Babe Dye, Tor	38
1925–26	Nels Stewart, Mtl	34
1926–27	Bill Cook, NY	33
1927–28	Howie Morenz, Mtl	33
1928–29	Ace Bailey, Tor	22
1929–30	Cooney Weiland, Bos	43
1930–31	Charlie Lonacher, Tor	31
1931–32	Charlie Conacher, Tor	34
	Bill Cook, NY	34
1932–33	Bill Cook, NY	28
1933–34	Charlie Conacher, Tor	32
1934–35	Charlie Conacher, Tor	36
1935–36	Charlie Conacher, Tor	23
	Bill Thoms, Tor	23
1936–37	Larry Aurie, Det	23
	Nels Stewart, Bos-NYA	23
1937–38	Gord Drillon, Tor	26
1938–39	Roy Conacher, Bos	26
1939–40	Bryan Hextall, NY	24
1940–41	Bryan Hextall, NY	26
1941–42	Lynn Patrick, NY	32
1942–43	Doug Bentley, Chi	33
1943–44	Doug Bentley, Chi	38
1944–45	Maurice Richard, Mtl	50
1945–46	Gaye Stewart, Tor	37
1946–47	Maurice Richard, Mtl	45
1947–48	Ted Lindsay, Det	33
1948–49	Sid Abel, Det	28
1949–50	Maurice Richard, Mtl	43
1950–51	Gordie Howe, Det	43
1951–52	Gordie Howe, Det	47
1952–53	Gordie Howe, Det	49
1953–54	Maurice Richard, Mtl	37
1954–55	Bernie Geoffrion, Mtl	38
	Maurice Richard, Mtl	38
1955–56	Jean Beliveau, Mtl	47
1956–57	Gordie Howe, Det	44
1957–58	Dickie Moore, Mtl	36
1958–59	Jean Beliveau, Mtl	45
1959–60	Bobby Hull, Chi	39
	Bronco Horvath, Bos	39
1960–61	Bernie Geoffrion, Mtl	50
1961–62	Bobby Hull, Chi	50
1962–63	Gordie Howe, Det	38
1963–64	Bobby Hull, Chi	43
1964–65	Norm Ullman, Det	42
1965–66	Bobby Hull, Chi	54
1966–67	Bobby Hull, Chi	52
1967–68	Bobby Hull, Chi	44
1968–69	Bobby Hull, Chi	58
1969–70	Phil Esposito, Bos	43
1970–71	Phil Esposito, Bos	76
1971–72	Phil Esposito, Bos	66
1972–73	Phil Esposito, Bos	55
1973–74	Phil Esposito, Bos	68
1974–75	Phil Esposito, Bos	61
1975–76	Guy Lafleur, Mtl	56
1976–77	Steve Shutt, Mtl	60
1977–78	Guy Lafleur, Mtl	60
1978–79	Mike Bossy, NYI	69
1979–80	Charlie Simmer, LA	56
	Blaine Stoughton, Hart	56
1980–81	Mike Bossy, NYI	68
1981–82	Wayne Gretzky, Edm	92
1982–83	Wayne Gretzky, Edm	71
1983–84	Wayne Gretzky, Edm	87
1984–85	Wayne Gretzky, Edm	73
1985–86	Jari Kurri, Edm	68
1986–87	Wayne Gretzky, Edm	62
1987–88	Mario Lemieux, Pitt	70
1988–89	Mario Lemieux, Pitt	85
1989–90	Brett Hull, StL	72
1990–91	Brett Hull, StL	86
1991–92	Brett Hull, StL	70
1992–93	Alexander Mogilny, Buff	76
	Teemu Selanne, Winn	76
1993–94	Pavel Bure, Van	60
1994–95	Peter Bondra, Wash	34
1995–96	Mario Lemieux, Pitt	69
1996–97	Keith Tkachuk, Phoe	52
1997–98	Teemu Selanne, Ana	52
	Peter Bondra, Wash	52
1998–99	Teemu Selanne, Ana	47
1999–00	Pavel Bure, Fla	58
2000–01	Pavel Bure, Fla	59
2001–02	Jarome Iginla, Cgy	52
2002–03	Milan Hejduk, Col	50
2003–04	Jarome Iginla, Cgy	41
	Rick Nash, Clb	41
	Ilya Kovalchuk, Atl	41
2004–05	No season	
2005–06	Jonathan Cheechoo, SJ	56
2006–07	Vincent Lecavalier, TB	52
2007–08	Alexander Ovechkin, Wsh	65

Assists

Season	Player and Club	Asst
1917–18	statistic not kept	
1918–19	Newsy Lalonde, Mtl	9
1919–20	Corbett Denneny, Tor	12
1920–21	Louis Berlinquette, Mtl	9
1921–22	Punch Broadbench, Ott	14
1922–23	Babe Dye, Tor	11
1923–24	Billy Boucher, Mtl	6
1924–25	Cy Denneny, Ott	15
1925–26	Frank Nighbor, Ott	13
1926–27	Dick Irvin, Chi	18
1927–28	Howie Morenz, Mtl	18
1928–29	Frank Boucher, NY	16
1929–30	Frank Boucher, NY	36
1930–31	Joe Primeau, Tor	32
1931–32	Joe Primeau, Tor	37
1932–33	Frank Boucher, NY	28
1933–34	Joe Primeau, Tor	32
1934–35	Art Chapman, NYA	34
1935–36	Art Chapman, NYA	28
1936–37	Syl Apps, Tor	29
1937–38	Syl Apps, Tor	29
1938–39	Bill Cowley, Bos	34
1939–40	Milt Schmidt, Bos	30
1940–41	Bill Cowley, Bos	45
1941–42	Phil Watson, NY	37
1942–43	Bill Cowley, Bos	45
1943–44	Clint Smith, Chi	49
1944–45	Elmer Lach, Mtl	54
1945–46	Elmer Lach, Mtl	34
1946–47	Billy Taylor, Det	46
1947–48	Doug Bentley, Chi	37
1948–49	Doug Bentley, Chi	43
1949–50	Ted Lindsay, Det	55
1950–51	Gordie Howe, Det	43
	Ted Kennedy, Tor	43
1951–52	Elmer Lach, Mtl	50
1952–53	Gordie Howe, Det	46
1953–54	Gordie Howe, Det	48
1954–55	Bert Olmstead, Mtl	48
1955–56	Bert Olmstead, Mtl	56
1956–57	Ted Lindsay, Det	55
1957–58	Henri Richard, Mtl	52
1958–59	Dickie Moore, Mtl	55
1959–60	Bobby Hull, Chi	42
1960–61	Jean Beliveau, Mtl	58
1961–62	Andy Bathgate, NY	56
1962–63	Henri Richard, Mtl	50
1963–64	Andy Bathgate, NY-Tor	58
1964–65	Stan Mikita, Chi	59
1965–66	Stan Mikita, Chi	48
	Bobby Rousseau, Mtl	48
	Jean Beliveau, Mtl	48
1966–67	Stan Mikita, Chi	62
1967–68	Phil Esposito, Bos	49
1968–69	Phil Esposito, Bos	77
1969–70	Bobby Orr, Bos	87
1970–71	Bobby Orr, Bos	102
1971–72	Bobby Orr, Bos	80
1972–73	Phil Esposito, Bos	75
1973–74	Bobby Orr, Bos	90
1974–75	Bobby Clarke, Phil	89
	Bobby Orr, Bos	89
1975–76	Bobby Clarke, Phil	89
1976–77	Guy Lafleur, Mtl	80
1977–78	Bryan Trottier, NYI	77
1978–79	Bryan Trottier, NYI	87
1979–80	Wayne Gretzky, Edm	86
1980–81	Wayne Gretzky, Edm	109
1981–82	Wayne Gretzky, Edm	120
1982–83	Wayne Gretzky, Edm	125
1983–84	Wayne Gretzky, Edm	118
1984–85	Wayne Gretzky, Edm	135
1985–86	Wayne Gretzky, Edm	163
1986–87	Wayne Gretzky, Edm	121
1987–88	Wayne Gretzky, Edm	109
1988–89	Wayne Gretzky, LA	114
	Mario Lemieux, Pitt	114
1989–90	Wayne Gretzky, LA	102
1990–91	Wayne Gretzky, LA	122
1991–92	Wayne Gretzky, LA	90
1992–93	Adam Oates, Bos	97
1993–94	Wayne Gretzky, LA	92
1994–95	Ron Francis, Pitt	48
1995–96	Mario Lemieux, Pitt	92
	Ron Francis, Pitt	92
1996–97	Mario Lemieux, Pitt	72
1997–98	Jaromir Jagr, Pitt	67
	Wayne Gretzky, NYR	67
1998–99	Jaromir Jagr, Pitt	83
1999–00	Mark Recchi, Phil	63
2000–01	Jaromir Jagr, Pitt	69
	Adam Oates, Wash	69
2001–02	Adam Oates, Wash	64
2002–03	Peter Forsberg, Col	77
2003–04	Scott Gomez, NJ	56
	Martin St. Louis, TB	56
2004–05	No season	
2005–06	Joe Thornton, Bos/SJ	96
2006–07	Joe Thornton, SJ	92
2007–08	Joe Thornton, SJ	67

Goals Against Average

Season	Goaltender and Club	GP	Min	GA	SO	Avg
1917–18	Georges Vezina, Mtl	21	1282	84	1	3.93
1918–19	Clint Benedict, Ott	18	1113	53	2	2.86
1919–20	Clint Benedict, Ott	24	1444	64	5	2.66
1920–21	Clint Benedict, Ott	24	1457	75	2	3.09
1921–22	Clint Benedict, Ott	24	1508	84	2	3.34
1922–23	Clint Benedict, Ott	24	1478	54	4	2.18
1923–24	Georges Vezina, Mtl	24	1459	48	3	1.97
1924–25	Georges Vezina, Mtl	30	1860	56	5	1.81
1925–26	Alec Connell, Ott	36	2251	42	15	1.12
1926–27	Clint Benedict, Mtl M	43	2748	65	13	1.42
1927–28	George Hainsworth, Mtl	44	2730	48	13	1.05
1928–29	George Hainsworth, Mtl	44	2800	43	22	0.92
1929–30	Tiny Thompson, Bos	44	2680	98	3	2.19

Goals Against Average (Cont.)

Season	Goaltender and Club	GP	Min	GA	SO	Avg
1930–31	Roy Worters, NYA	44	2760	74	8	1.61
1931–32	Chuck Gardiner, Chi	48	2989	92	4	1.85
1932–33	Tiny Thompson, Bos	48	3000	88	11	1.76
1933–34	Wilf Cude, Det-Mtl	30	1920	47	5	1.47
1934–35	Lorne Chabot, Chi	48	2940	88	8	1.80
1935–36	Tiny Thompson, Bos	48	2930	82	10	1.68
1936–37	Normie Smith, Det	48	2980	102	6	2.05
1937–38	Tiny Thompson, Bos	48	2970	89	7	1.80
1938–39	Frank Brimsek, Bos	43	2610	68	10	1.56
1939–40	Dave Kerr, NYR	48	3000	77	8	1.54
1940–41	Turk Broda, Tor	48	2970	99	5	2.00
1941–42	Frank Brimsek, Bos	47	2930	115	3	2.35
1942–43	Johnny Mowers, Det	50	3010	124	6	2.47
1943–44	Bill Durnan, Mtl	50	3000	109	2	2.18
1944–45	Bill Durnan, Mtl	50	3000	121	1	2.42
1945–46	Bill Durnan, Mtl	40	2400	104	4	2.60
1946–47	Bill Durnan, Mtl	60	3600	138	4	2.30
1947–48	Turk Broda, Tor	60	3600	143	5	2.38
1948–49	Bill Durnan, Mtl	60	3600	126	10	2.10
1949–50	Bill Durnan, Mtl	64	3840	141	8	2.20
1950–51	Al Rollins, Tor	40	2367	70	5	1.77
1951–52	Terry Sawchuk, Det	70	4200	133	12	1.90
1952–53	Terry Sawchuk, Det	63	3780	120	9	1.90
1953–54	Harry Lumley, Tor	69	4140	128	13	1.86
1954–55	Harry Lumley, Tor	69	4140	134	8	1.94
1955–56	Jacques Plante, Mtl	64	3840	119	7	1.86
1956–57	Jacques Plante, Mtl	61	3660	122	9	2.00
1957–58	Jacques Plante, Mtl	57	3386	119	9	2.11
1958–59	Jacques Plante, Mtl	67	4000	144	9	2.16
1959–60	Jacques Plante, Mtl	69	4140	175	3	2.54
1960–61	Charlie Hodge, Mtl	30	1800	74	4	2.47
1961–62	Jacques Plante, Mtl	70	4200	166	4	2.37
1962–63	Don Simmons, Tor	28	1680	69	1	2.46
1963–64	Johnny Bower, Tor	51	3009	106	5	2.11
1964–65	Johnny Bower, Tor	34	2040	81	3	2.38
1965–66	Johnny Bower, Tor	35	1998	75	3	2.25
1966–67	Glenn Hall, Chi	32	1664	66	2	2.38
1967–68	Gump Worsley, Mtl	40	2213	73	6	1.98
1968–69	Jacques Plante, StL	37	2139	70	5	1.96
1969–70	Ernie Wakely, StL	30	1651	58	4	2.11
1970–71	Jacques Plante, Tor	40	2329	73	4	1.88
1971–72	Tony Esposito, Chi	48	2780	82	9	1.77
1972–73	Ken Dryden, Mtl	54	3165	119	6	2.26
1973–74	Bernie Parent, Phil	73	4314	136	12	1.89
1974–75	Bernie Parent, Phil	68	4041	137	12	2.03
1975–76	Ken Dryden, Mtl	62	3580	121	8	2.03
1976–77	Michel Larocque, Mtl	26	1525	53	4	2.09
1977–78	Ken Dryden, Mtl	52	3071	105	5	2.05
1978–79	Ken Dryden, Mtl	47	2814	108	5	2.30
1979–80	Bob Sauve, Buff	32	1880	74	4	2.36
1980–81	Richard Sevigny, Mtl	33	1777	71	2	2.40
1981–82	Denis Herron, Mtl	27	1547	68	3	2.64
1982–83	Pete Peeters, Bos	62	3611	142	8	2.36
1983–84	Pat Riggin, Wash	41	2299	102	4	2.66
1984–85	Tom Barrasso, Buff	54	3248	144	5	2.66
1985–86	Bob Froese, Phil	51	2728	116	5	2.55
1986–87	Brian Hayward, Mtl	37	2178	102	1	2.81
1987–88	Pete Peeters, Wash	35	1896	88	2	2.78
1988–89	Patrick Roy, Mtl	48	2744	113	4	2.47
1989–90	Patrick Roy, Mtl	54	3173	134	3	2.53
	Mike Liut, Hart-Wash	37	2161	91	4	2.53
1990–91	Ed Belfour, Chi	74	4127	170	4	2.47
1991–92	Patrick Roy, Mtl	67	3935	155	5	2.36
1992–93	Felix Potvin, Tor	48	2781	116	2	2.50
1993–94	Dominik Hasek, Buff	58	3358	109	7	1.95
1994–95	Dominik Hasek, Buff	41	2416	85	5	2.11

Goals Against Average (Cont.)

Season	Goaltender and Club	GP	Min	GA	SO	Avg
1995–96	Ron Hextall, Phil	53	3102	112	4	2.17
	Chris Osgood, Det	50	2932	106	5	2.17
1996–97	Martin Brodeur, NJ	67	3838	120	10	1.88
1997–98	Ed Belfour, Dall	61	3581	112	9	1.88
1998–99	Ron Tugnutt, Ott	43	2508	75	3	1.79
1999–00	Brian Boucher, Phil	35	2038	65	4	1.91
2000–01	Marty Turco, Dall	26	1266	40	3	1.90
2001–02	Patrick Roy, Col	63	3773	122	9	1.94
2002–03	Marty Turco, Dall	55	3202	92	7	1.72
2003–04	Miikka Kiprusoff, Cgy	38	2301	65	4	1.69
2004–05	No season					
2005–06	Miikka Kiprusoff, Cgy	74	4379	151	10	2.07
2006–07	Niklas Backstrom, Minn	41	2226	73	5	1.97
2007–08	Chris Osgood, Det	43	2409	84	4	2.09

Penalty Minutes

Season	Player and Club	GP	PIM
1918–19	Joe Hall, Mtl	17	135
1919–20	Cully Wilson, Tor	23	79
1920–21	Bert Corbeau, Mtl	24	86
1921–22	Sprague Cleghorn, Mtl	24	63
1922–23	Billy Boucher, Mtl	24	55
1923–24	Bert Corbeau, Tor	24	55
1924–25	Billy Boucher, Mtl	30	92
1925–26	Bert Corbeau, Tor	36	121
1926–27	Nels Stewart, Mtl M	44	133
1927–28	Eddie Shore, Bos	44	165
1928–29	Red Dutton, Mtl M	44	139
1929–30	Joe Lamb, Ott	44	119
1930–31	Harvey Rockburn, Det	42	118
1931–32	Red Dutton, NYA	47	107
1932–33	Red Horner, Tor	48	144
1933–34	Red Horner, Tor	42	126
1934–35	Red Horner, Tor	46	125
1935–36	Red Horner, Tor	43	167
1936–37	Red Horner, Tor	48	124
1937–38	Red Horner, Tor	47	82
1938–39	Red Horner, Tor	48	85
1939–40	Red Horner, Tor	30	87
1940–41	Jimmy Orlando, Det	48	99
1941–42	Pat Egan, Bklyn	48	124
1942–43	Jimmy Orlando, Det	40	89
1943–44	Mike McMahon, Mtl	42	98
1944–45	Pat Egan, Bos	48	86
1945–46	Jack Stewart, Det	47	73
1946–47	Gus Mortson, Tor	60	133
1947–48	Bill Barilko, Tor	57	147
1948–49	Bill Ezinicki, Tor	52	145
1949–50	Bill Ezinicki, Tor	67	144
1950–51	Gus Mortson, Tor	60	142
1951–52	Gus Kyle, Bos	69	127
1952–53	Maurice Richard, Mtl	70	112
1953–54	Gus Mortson, Chi	68	132
1954–55	Fern Flaman, Bos	70	150
1955–56	Lou Fontinato, NYR	70	202
1956–57	Gus Mortson, Chi	70	147
1957–58	Lou Fontinato, NYR	70	152
1958–59	Ted Lindsay, Chi	70	184
1959–60	Carl Brewer, Tor	67	150
1960–61	Pierre Pilote, Chi	70	165
1961–62	Lou Fontinato, Mtl	54	167
1962–63	Howie Young, Det	64	273
1963–64	Vic Hadfield, NYR	69	151
1964–65	Carl Brewer, Tor	70	177
1965–66	Reggie Fleming, Bos-NYR	69	166
1966–67	John Ferguson, Mtl	67	177
1967–68	Barclay Plager, StL	49	153
1968–69	Forbes Kennedy, Phil-Tor	77	219
1969–70	Keith Magnuson, Chi	76	213
1970–71	Keith Magnuson, Chi	76	291
1971–72	Brian Watson, Pitt	75	212
1972–73	Dave Schultz, Phil	76	259
1973–74	Dave Schultz, Phil	73	348
1974–75	Dave Schultz, Phil	76	472
1975–76	Steve Durbano, Pitt-KC	69	370
1976–77	Dave Williams, Tor	77	338
1977–78	Dave Schultz, LA-Pitt	74	405
1978–79	Dave Williams, Tor	77	298
1979–80	Jimmy Mann, Winn	72	287
1980–81	Dave Williams, Van	77	343
1981–82	Paul Baxter, Pitt	76	409
1982–83	Randy Holt, Wash	70	275
1983–84	Chris Nilan, Mtl	76	338
1984–85	Chris Nilan, Mtl	77	358
1985–86	Joey Kocur, Det	59	377
1986–87	Tim Hunter, Cgy	73	361
1987–88	Bob Probert, Det	74	398
1988–89	Tim Hunter, Cgy	75	375
1989–90	Basil McRae, Minn	66	351
1990–91	Rob Ray, Buff	66	350
1991–92	Mike Peluso, Chi	63	408
1992–93	Marty McSorley, LA	81	399
1993–94	Tie Domi, Winn	81	347
1994–95	Enrico Ciccone, TB	41	225
1995–96	Matthew Barnaby, Buff	73	335
1996–97	Gino Odjick, Van	70	371
1997–98	Donald Brashear, Van	77	372
1998–99	Rob Ray, Buff	76	261
1999–00	Denny Lambert, Atl	73	219
2000–01	Matthew Barnaby, TB	76	265
2001–02	Peter Worrell, Fla	79	354
2002–03	Jody Shelley, Clb	68	249
2003–04	Sean Avery, LA	76	261
2004–05	No season		
2005–06	Sean Avery, LA	75	257
2006–07	Ben Eager, Phil	63	233
2007–08	Daniel Carcillo, Phx	57	324

NHL All-Star Game

First played in 1947, this game was scheduled before the start of the regular season and used to match the defending Stanley Cup champions against a squad made up of the league All-Stars from other teams. In 1966 the game was moved to midseason, although there was no game that year. The format changed to a conference versus conference showdown in 1969.

Results

Year	Site	Score	MVP	Attendance
1947	Toronto	All-Stars 4, Toronto 3	None named	14,169
1948	Chicago	All-Stars 3, Toronto 1	None named	12,794
1949	Toronto	All-Stars 3, Toronto 1	None named	13,541
1950	Detroit	Detroit 7, All-Stars 1	None named	9,166
1951	Toronto	1st team 2, 2nd team 2	None named	11,469
1952	Detroit	1st team 1, 2nd team 1	None named	10,680
1953	Montreal	All-Stars 3, Montreal 1	None named	14,153
1954	Detroit	All-Stars 2, Detroit 2	None named	10,689
1955	Detroit	Detroit 3, All-Stars 1	None named	10,111
1956	Montreal	All-Stars 1, Montreal 1	None named	13,095
1957	Montreal	All-Stars 5, Montreal 3	None named	13,003
1958	Montreal	Montreal 6, All-Stars 3	None named	13,989
1959	Montreal	Montreal 6, All-Stars 1	None named	13,818
1960	Montreal	All-Stars 2, Montreal 1	None named	13,949
1961	Chicago	All-Stars 3, Chicago 1	None named	14,534
1962	Toronto	Toronto 4, All-Stars 1	Eddie Shack, Tor	14,236
1963	Toronto	All-Stars 3, Toronto 3	Frank Mahovlich, Tor	14,034
1964	Toronto	All-Stars 3, Toronto 2	Jean Beliveau, Mtl	14,232
1965	Montreal	All-Stars 5, Montreal 2	Gordie Howe, Det	13,529
1967	Montreal	Montreal 3, All-Stars 0	Henri Richard, Mtl	14,284
1968	Toronto	Toronto 4, All-Stars 3	Bruce Gamble, Tor	15,753
1969	Montreal	East 3, West 3	Frank Mahovlich, Det	16,260
1970	St. Louis	East 4, West 1	Bobby Hull, Chi	16,587
1971	Boston	West 2, East 1	Bobby Hull, Chi	14,790
1972	Minnesota	East 3, West 2	Bobby Orr, Bos	15,423
1973	NY Rangers	East 5, West 4	Greg Polis, Pitt	16,986
1974	Chicago	West 6, East 4	Garry Unger, StL	16,426
1975	Montreal	Wales 7, Campbell 1	Syl Apps Jr, Pitt	16,080
1976	Philadelphia	Wales 7, Campbell 5	Pete Mahovlich, Mtl	16,436
1977	Vancouver	Wales 4, Campbell 3	Rick Martin, Buff	15,607
1978	Buffalo	Wales 3, Campbell 2 (OT)	Billy Smith, NYI	16,433
1980	Detroit	Wales 6, Campbell 3	Reg Leach, Phil	21,002
1981	Los Angeles	Campbell 4, Wales 1	Mike Liut, StL	15,761
1982	Washington	Wales 4, Campbell 2	Mike Bossy, NYI	18,130
1983	NY Islanders	Campbell 9, Wales 3	Wayne Gretzky, Edm	15,230
1984	New Jersey	Wales 7, Campbell 6	Don Maloney, NYR	18,939
1985	Calgary	Wales 6, Campbell 4	Mario Lemieux, Pitt	16,825
1986	Hartford	Wales 4, Campbell 3 (OT)	Grant Fuhr, Edm	15,100
1988	St. Louis	Wales 6, Campbell 5 (OT)	Mario Lemieux, Pitt	17,878
1989	Edmonton	Campbell 9, Wales 5	Wayne Gretzky, LA	17,503
1990	Pittsburgh	Wales 12, Campbell 7	Mario Lemieux, Pitt	16,236
1991	Chicago	Campbell 11, Wales 5	Vince Damphousse, Tor	18,472
1992	Philadelphia	Campbell 10, Wales 6	Brett Hull, StL	17,380
1993	Montreal	Wales 16, Campbell 6	Mike Gartner, NYR	17,137
1994	NY Rangers	East 9, West 8	Mike Richter, NYR	18,200
1996	Boston	East 5, West 4	Ray Bourque, Bos	17,565
1997	San Jose	East 11, West 7	Mark Recchi, Mtl	17,422
1998	Vancouver	N America 8, World 7	Teemu Selanne, Ana (World)	18,422
1999	Tampa Bay	N America 8, World 6	Wayne Gretzky, NYR (N America)	19,758
2000	Toronto	World 9, N America 4	Pavel Bure, Fla (World)	19,300
2001	Denver	N America 14, World 12	Bill Guerin, Bos (N America)	18,646
2002	Los Angeles	World 8, N America 5	Eric Daze, Chi (N America)	18,118
2003	Sunrise, Fla.	West 6, East 5 (shootout)	Dany Heatley, Atl (East)	19,250
2004	St. Paul, Minn.	East 6, West 4	Joe Sakic, Col (West)	19,434
2005	No game played			
2006	No game played due to Winter Olympics			
2007	Dallas	West 12, East 9	Daniel Briere, Buff (East)	18,532
2008	Atlanta	East 8, West 7	Eric Staal, Car (East)	18,644

Note: The Challenge Cup, a series between the NHL All-Stars and the Soviet Union, was played instead of the All-Star Game in 1979. Eight years later, Rendez-Vous '87, a two-game series matching the Soviet Union and the NHL All-Stars, replaced the All-Star Game. The 1995 NHL All-Star game was cancelled due to a labor dispute. The 1998 NHL All-Star game, billed as a preview to the 1998 Winter Olympics in Nagano, Japan, matched North Amercian–born All-Stars and All-Stars born elsewhere. In 2005, no game was played due to season-long lockout.

Hockey Hall of Fame

Located in Toronto, the Hockey Hall of Fame was officially opened on August 26, 1961. The current chairman is William C. Hay. There are, at present, 306 members of the Hockey Hall of Fame—209 players, 84 "builders," and 14 on-ice officials. (One member, Alan Eagleson, resigned from the Hall March 25, 1998.) To be eligible, player and referee/linesman candidates should have been out of the game for three years, but the Hall's Board of Directors can make exceptions.

Players

Sid Abel (1969)
Jack Adams (1959)
Glenn Anderson (2008)
Charles (Syl) Apps (1961)
George Armstrong (1975)
Irvine (Ace) Bailey (1975)
Donald H. (Dan) Bain (1945)
Hobey Baker (1945)
Bill Barber (1990)
Marty Barry (1965)
Andy Bathgate (1978)
Bobby Bauer (1996)
Jean Beliveau (1972)
Clint Benedict (1965)
Douglas Bentley (1964)
Max Bentley (1966)
Hector (Toe) Blake (1966)
Leo Boivin (1986)
Dickie Boon (1952)
Mike Bossy (1991)
Emile (Butch) Bouchard (1966)
Frank Boucher (1958)
George (Buck) Boucher (1960)
Ray Bourque (2004)
Johnny Bower (1976)
Russell Bowie (1945)
Frank Brimsek (1966)
Harry L. (Punch) Broadbent (1962)
Walter (Turk) Broda (1967)
John Bucyk (1981)
Billy Burch (1974)
Harry Cameron (1962)
Gerry Cheevers (1985)
Francis (King) Clancy (1958)
Aubrey (Dit) Clapper (1947)
Bobby Clarke (1987)
Sprague Cleghorn (1958)
Paul Coffey (2004)
Neil Colville (1967)
Charlie Conacher (1961)
Lionel Conacher (1994)
Roy Conacher (1998)
Alex Connell (1958)
Bill Cook (1952)
Fred (Bun) Cook (1995)
Arthur Coulter (1974)
Yvan Cournoyer (1982)
Bill Cowley (1968)
Samuel (Rusty) Crawford (1962)
Jack Darragh (1962)
Allan M. (Scotty) Davidson (1950)
Clarence (Hap) Day (1961)
Alex Delvecchio (1977)
Cy Denneny (1959)
Marcel Dionne (1992)
Gordie Drillon (1975)
Charles Drinkwater (1950)
Ken Dryden (1983)
Terrance (Dick) Duff (2006)
Woody Dumart (1992)
Thomas Dunderdale (1974)
Bill Durnan (1964)
Mervyn A. (Red) Dutton (1958)
Cecil (Babe) Dye (1970)
Phil Esposito (1984)
Tony Esposito (1988)
Arthur F. Farrell (1965)
Bernie Federko (2002)
Viacheslav Fetisov (2001)
Ferdinand (Fern) Flaman (1990)
Frank Foyston (1958)
Ron Francis (2007)
Frank Frederickson (1958)
Grant Fuhr (2003)
Bill Gadsby (1970)
Bob Gainey (1992)
Chuck Gardiner (1945)
Herb Gardiner (1958)
Jimmy Gardner (1962)
Mike Gartner (2001)
Bernie (Boom Boom) Geoffrion (1972)
Eddie Gerard (1945)
Ed Giacomin (1987)
Rod Gilbert (1982)
Clark Gillies (2002)
Hamilton (Billy) Gilmour (1962)
Frank (Moose) Goheen (1952)
Ebenezer R. (Ebbie) Goodfellow (1963)
Michel Goulet (1998)
Mike Grant (1950)
Wilfred (Shorty) Green (1962)
Jim Gregory (2007)
Wayne Gretzky (1999)
Si Griffis (1950)
George Hainsworth (1961)
Glenn Hall (1975)
Joe Hall (1961)
Doug Harvey (1973)
Dale Hawerchuk (2001)
George Hay (1958)
William (Riley) Hern (1962)
Bryan Hextall (1969)
Harry (Hap) Holmes (1972)
Tom Hooper (1962)
George (Red) Horner (1965)
Miles (Tim) Horton (1977)
Gordie Howe (1972)
Syd Howe (1965)
Harry Howell (1979)
Bobby Hull (1983)
John (Bouse) Hutton (1962)
Harry M. Hyland (1962)
James (Dick) Irvin (1958)
Harvey (Busher) Jackson (1971)
Ernest (Moose) Johnson (1952)
Ivan (Ching) Johnson (1958)

Hockey Hall of Fame *(Cont.)*

Players *(Cont.)*

Tom Johnson (1970)
Aurel Joliat (1947)
Gordon (Duke) Keats (1958)
Leonard (Red) Kelly (1969)
Ted (Teeder) Kennedy (1966)
Dave Keon (1986)
Valeri Kharlamov (2005)
Jari Kurri (2001)
Elmer Lach (1966)
Guy Lafleur (1988)
Pat LaFontaine (2003)
Edouard (Newsy) Lalonde (1950)
Rod Langway (2002)
Jacques Laperriere (1987)
Guy Lapointe (1993)
Edgar Laprade (1993)
Igor Larionov (2008)
Jean (Jack) Laviolette (1962)
Hugh Lehman (1958)
Jacques Lemaire (1984)
Mario Lemieux (1997)
Percy LeSueur (1961)
Herbert A. Lewis (1989)
Ted Lindsay (1966)
Harry Lumley (1980)
Lanny McDonald (1992)
Frank McGee (1945)
Billy McGimsie (1962)
George McNamara (1958)
Al MacInnis (2007)
Duncan (Mickey) MacKay (1952)
Frank Mahovlich (1981)
Joe Malone (1950)
Sylvio Mantha (1960)
Jack Marshall (1965)
Fred G. (Steamer) Maxwell (1962)
Mark Messier (2007)
Stan Mikita (1983)
Dicky Moore (1974)
Patrick (Paddy) Moran (1958)
Howie Morenz (1945)
Billy Mosienko (1965)
Joe Mullen (2000)
Larry Murphy (2004)
Cam Neely (2005)
Frank Nighbor (1947)
Reg Noble (1962)
Herbert (Buddy) O'Connor (1988)
Harry Oliver (1967)
Bert Olmstead (1985)
Bobby Orr (1979)
Bernie Parent (1984)
Brad Park (1988)
Lester Patrick (1947)
Lynn Patrick (1980)
Gilbert Perreault (1990)
Tommy Phillips (1945)
Pierre Pilote (1975)
Didier (Pit) Pitre (1962)
Jacques Plante (1978)
Denis Potvin (1991)
Walter (Babe) Pratt (1966)
Joe Primeau (1963)
Marcel Pronovost (1978)
Bob Pulford (1991)
Harvey Pulford (1945)
Hubert (Bill) Quackenbush (1976)
Frank Rankin (1961)
Jean Ratelle (1985)
Claude (Chuck) Rayner (1973)
Kenneth Reardon (1966)
Henri Richard (1979)
Maurice (Rocket) Richard (1961)
George Richardson (1950)
Gordon Roberts (1971)
Larry Robinson (1995)
Art Ross (1945)
Patrick Roy (2006)
Blair Russel (1965)
Ernest Russell (1965)
Jack Ruttan (1962)
Borje Salming (1996)
Denis Savard (2000)
Serge Savard (1986)
Terry Sawchuk (1971)
Fred Scanlan (1965)
Milt Schmidt (1961)
Dave (Sweeney) Schriner (1962)
Earl Seibert (1963)
Oliver Seibert (1961)
Eddie Shore (1947)
Steve Shutt (1993)
Albert C. (Babe) Siebert (1964)
Harold (Bullet Joe) Simpson (1962)
Daryl Sittler (1989)
Alfred E. Smith (1962)
Billy Smith (1993)
Clint Smith (1991)
Reginald (Hooley) Smith (1972)
Thomas Smith (1973)
Allan Stanley (1981)
Russell (Barney) Stanley (1962)
Peter Stastny (1998)
Scott Stevens (2007)
John (Black Jack) Stewart (1964)
Nels Stewart (1962)
Bruce Stuart (1961)
Hod Stuart (1945)
Frederic (Cyclone) (O.B.E.)
Taylor (1947)
Cecil R. (Tiny) Thompson (1959)
Vladislav Tretiak (1989)
Harry J. Trihey (1950)
Bryan Trottier (1997)
Norm Ullman (1982)
Georges Vezina (1945)
Jack Walker (1960)
Marty Walsh (1962)
Harry Watson (1994)
Harry E. Watson (1962)
Ralph (Cooney) Weiland (1971)
Harry Westwick (1962)
Fred Whitcroft (1962)
Gordon (Phat) Wilson (1962)
Lorne (Gump) Worsley (1980)
Roy Worters (1969)

Note: Year of election to the Hall of Fame is in parentheses after the member's name.

Builders

Charles Adams (1960)
Weston W. Adams (1972)
Thomas (Frank) Ahearn (1962)
John (Bunny) Ahearne (1977)
Montagu Allan (C.V.O.) (1945)
Keith Allen (1992)
Al Arbour (1996)
Harold Ballard (1977)
David Bauer (1989)
John Bickell (1978)
Scott Bowman (1991)
Herb Brooks (2006)
George V. Brown (1961)
Walter A. Brown (1962)
Frank Buckland (1975)
Walter L. Bush (2000)
Jack Butterfield (1980)
Frank Calder (1947)
Angus D. Campbell (1964)
Clarence Campbell (1966)
Joe Cattarinich (1977)
Ed Chynoweth (2008)
Bob Cole (1996, Media)
Murray Costello (2005)
Joseph (Leo) Dandurand (1963)
Francis Dilio (1964)
George S. Dudley (1958)
James A. Dunn (1968)
*Robert Alan Eagleson (1989–98)
Cliff Fletcher (2004)
Emile Francis (1982)
Jack Gibson (1976)
Tommy Gorman (1963)
Frank Griffiths (1993)
William Hanley (1986)
Charles Hay (1974)
James C. Hendy (1968)
Foster Hewitt (1965)
William Hewitt (1947)
Harley Hotchkiss (2006)
Fred J. Hume (1962)
Mike Ilitch (2003)
George (Punch) Imlach (1984)
Tommy Ivan (1974)
William M. Jennings (1975)
Bob Johnson (1992)
Gordon W. Juckes (1979)
John Kilpatrick (1960)
Brian Kilrea (2003)
Seymour Knox III (1993)
George Leader (1969)
Robert LeBel (1970)
Thomas F. Lockhart (1965)
Paul Loicq (1961)
Frederic McLaughlin (1963)
John Mariucci (1985)
Frank Mathers (1992)
John (Jake) Milford (1984)
Hartland Molson (1973)
Scotty Morrison (1999)
Mngr. Athol (Pere) Murray (1998)
Roger Neilson (2002)
Francis Nelson (1947)
Bruce A. Norris (1969)
James Norris, Sr. (1958)
James D. Norris (1962)
William M. Northey (1947)
John O'Brien (1962)
Brian O'Neill (1994)
Fred Page (1993)
Craig Patrick (1996)
Frank Patrick (1958)
Allan W. Pickard (1958)
Rudy Pilous (1985)
Norman (Bud) Poile (1990)
Samuel Pollock (1978)
Donat Raymond (1958)
John Robertson (1947)
Claude C. Robinson (1947)
Philip D. Ross (1976)
Gunther Sabetzki (1995)
Glen Sather (1997)
Frank J. Selke (1960)
Harry Sinden (1983)
Frank D. Smith (1962)
Conn Smythe (1958)
Edward M. Snider (1988)
Lord Stanley of Preston (1945)
James T. Sutherland (1947)
Anatoli V. Tarasov (1974)
Bill Torrey (1995)
Lloyd Turner (1958)
William Tutt (1978)
Carl Potter Voss (1974)
Fred C. Waghorn (1961)
Arthur Wirtz (1971)
Bill Wirtz (1976)
John A. Ziegler, Jr. (1987)

Referees/Linesmen

Neil Armstrong (1991)
John Ashley (1981)
William L. Chadwick (1964)
John D'Amico (1993)
Chaucer Elliott (1961)
George Hayes (1988)
Robert W. Hewitson (1963)
Fred J. (Mickey) Ion (1961)
Matt Pavelich (1987)
Mike Rodden (1962)
Ray Scapinello (2008)
J. Cooper Smeaton (1961)
Roy (Red) Storey (1967)
Frank Udvari (1973)
Andy Van Hellemond (1999)

*Eagleson resigned from Hall March 25, 1998.

Tennis

JULIAN FINNEY/GETTY IMAGES

Rafael Nadal (r.) ended Roger Federer's Wimbledon reign in a match many called the best ever.

And So We Meet Again

Rafael Nadal finally got the best of Roger Federer in 2008 while the Williams sisters got the best of each other

BY B.J. SCHECTER

ON ONE SIDE OF THE NET STOOD the man who many maintain is the greatest tennis player all time. On the other, the king of clay, desperately trying to prove that his game was complete, that he could etch his name among the game's greats by winning in tennis' grass court cathedral. Back and forth they went, trading ground strokes and displaying the highest level of tennis skills and intensity since McEnroe and Borg. As the final specks of daylight peered through the darkness on Centre Court at the All-England Club, Rafael Nadal collapsed to his knees after capitalizing on his fourth championship point. Nadal lay on the grass for a few seconds trying to comprehend what he had just done. Not only had he dethroned five-time defending champion Roger Federer with an astonishing 6–4, 6–4, 6–7, 6–7, 9–7 victory, he was also a part of the greatest match ever played.

"There is a new king tonight," declared a BBC announcer. "We may have to rethink tennis history."

Indeed, it was the first sign that the 22-year-old Nadal could beat Federer on grass and served notice that the Spaniard was ready to assume the world No. 1 ranking. It was also the latest sign of a dent in Federer's armor. After dominating the game by winning three of the four Grand Slams in each of the two previous years, Federer had enjoyed a Tiger Woods-like run. But Nadal proved to be as mentally tough as Federer and finally got over the hump by beating Federer on his best surface.

"You know how people say, 'It feels like a dream?'" Nadal told the Spanish media after the match. "A match like this? How could it not feel like a dream?"

In the end, it was a dream year for tennis with the best match in history, a thriving heavyweight rivalry in the men's game and the return of the Williams sisters on the women's side. It didn't start out well for the women as world No. 1 Justine Henin abruptly retired at the beginning of the year. But Venus and Serena Williams quickly reestablished that when they're on top of their game they're still the best, by winning Wimbledon and the U.S. Open, respectively. Venus beat her younger sister in the Wimbledon final. Serena got her older sis back in a pulsating U.S. Open quarterfinal.

After Nadal ended Federer's four-and-a-half-year run at No. 1, Federer proved at the U.S. Open that reports of his demise were greatly exaggerated. Entering the year's final Slam, Federer's confidence was clearly shaken, and many questioned his ability to get back to No. 1 given he hadn't won a major title entering the tournament. But critics were overlooking the difficult year Federer

Djokovic upset Federer in the Australian Open semifinals in straight sets and went on to win his first Grand Slam singles title at age 20.

had, which began with an illness that turned out to be mononucleosis at the Australian Open and continued with losses to Nadal in the French and Wimbledon *finals*—it's not like he was losing in the first round.

But he was losing. Coming into 2008, Federer was a remarkable 27–1 against Americans Andy Roddick, James Blake and Mardy Fish, his one loss coming to a hot-handed Roddick five years earlier. All three men, whose serve-centered games look all but rudimentary compared to top shelf Federer, beat the Swiss in 2008. He lost nine other matches between the Australian and US Open. Perhaps the top shelf was getting harder to reach.

When Federer came to Flushing Meadows after flaming out in the Olympics (he lost to Blake in the quarterfinals, though he did win the gold in doubles) there was blood in the water. Opponents no longer viewed Federer as unbeatable and some went so far as to see him as *vulnerable*. But a funny thing happened between Federer's Olympic flameout and his arrival in New York: he regained his mojo. Displaying emotion rarely seen during his reign, Federer marched through the U.S. Open draw and easily disposed of up-and-coming Brit Andy Murray 6–2, 7–5, 6–2 in the final. It was his fifth straight U.S. Open title and 13th major championship, leaving him one shy of Pete Sampras' all-time record.

"It felt great," said Federer, adding that he's not going to stop at 13 majors. "I felt like I was invincible for a while again."

Murray, who beat Nadal in four sets a round earlier, offered the following assessment of Federer: "[I] came up against, in my opinion, the best player ever to play. He definitely set the record straight today."

Though Nadal and Serbian world No. 3 Novak Djokovic (who knocked off Federer in the Australian Open semifinals) closed the gap on Federer, the unflappable Swiss star showed that, when he's healthy, he's still the man to beat. And on the women's side, Venus and Serena Williams again proved that, no matter their ranking, they're always a threat to win championships. How confident are the Williams sisters? "I just always assumed [Venus and I] would be the best," Serena says.

Spoken like a true champion.

2008 Grand Slam Champions

Australian Open

Men's Singles

	Winner	Runner-up	Score
Quarterfinals	Roger Federer	James Blake	7–5, 7–6 (7–5), 6–4
	Novak Djokovic	David Ferrer	6–0, 6–3, 7–5
	Jo-Wilfried Tsonga	Mikhail Youzhny	7–5, 6–0, 7–6 (7–6)
	Rafael Nadal	Jarkko Nieminen	7–5, 6–3, 6–1
Semifinals	Novak Djokovic	Roger Federer	7–5, 6–3, 7–6 (7–5)
	Jo-Wilfried Tsonga	Rafael Nadal	6–2, 6–3, 6–2
Final	Novak Djokovic	Jo-Wilfried Tsonga	4–6, 6–4, 6–3, 7–6 (7–5)

Women's Singles

	Winner	Runner-up	Score
Quarterfinals	Maria Sharapova	Justine Henin	6–4, 6–0
	Jelena Jankovic	Serena Williams	6–3, 6–4
	Ana Ivanovic	Venus Williams	7–6 (7–3), 6–4
	Daniela Hantuchova	Agnieszka Radwanska	6–2, 6–2
Semifinals	Maria Sharapova	Jelena Jankovic	6–3, 6–1
	Ana Ivanovic	Daniela Hantuchova	0–6, 6–3, 6–4
Final	Maria Sharapova	Ana Ivanovic	7–5, 6–3

Doubles

	Winner	Runner-up	Score
Men's Final	Jonathan Erlich/ Andy Ram	Arnaud Clement/ Michael Llodra	7–5, 7–6 (7–4)
Women's Final	Alona Bondarenko/ Kateryna Bondarenko	Victoria Azarenka/ Shahar Peer	2–6, 6–1, 6–4
Mixed Final	Tiantian Sun/ Nenad Zimonjic	Sania Mirza/ Mahesh Bhupathi	7–6 (7–4), 6–4

French Open

Men's Singles

	Winner	Runner-up	Score
Quarterfinals	Roger Federer	Fernando Gonzalez	2–6, 6–2, 6–3, 6–4
	Gael Monfils	David Ferrer	6–3, 3–6, 6–3, 6–1
	Novak Djokovic	Ernests Gulbis	7–5, 7–6 (6–3), 7–5
	Rafael Nadal	Nicolas Almagro	6–1, 6–1, 6–1
Semifinals	Roger Federer	Gael Monfils	6–2, 5–7, 6–3, 7–5
	Rafael Nadal	Novak Djokovic	6–4, 6–2, 7–6 (7–3)
Final	Rafael Nadal	Roger Federer	6–1, 6–3, 6–0

Women's Singles

	Winner	Runner-up	Score
Quarterfinals	Dinara Safina	Elena Dementieva	4–6, 7–6 (7–5), 6–0
	Svetlana Kuznetsova	Kaia Kanepi	7–5, 6–2
	Jelena Jankovic	Carla Suarez Navarro	6–3, 6–2
	Ana Ivanovic	Patty Schnyder	6–3, 6–2
Semifinals	Dinara Safina	Svetlana Kuznetsova	6–3, 6–2
	Ana Ivanovic	Jelena Jankovic	6–4, 3–6, 6–4
Final	Ana Ivanovic	Dinara Safina	6–4, 6–3

Doubles

	Winner	Runner-Up	Score
Men's Final	Pablo Cuevas/ Luis Horna	Daniel Nestor/ Nenad Zimonjic	6–2, 6–3
Women's Final	Anabel Medina Garrigues/ Virginia Ruano Pascual	Casey Dellacqua/ Francesca Schiavone	2–6, 7–5, 6–4
Mixed Final	Victoria Azarenka/ Bob Bryan	Katarina Srebotnik/ Nenad Zimonjic	6–2, 7–6 (7–4)

2008 Grand Slam Champions *(Cont.)*

Wimbledon

Men's Singles

	Winner	Runner-Up	Score
Quarterfinals	Roger Federer	Mario Ancic	6–1, 7–5, 6–4
	Marat Safin	Feliciano Lopez	3–6, 7–5, 7–6 (7–1), 6–3
	Rainer Schuettler	Arnaud Clement	6–3, 5–7, 7–6 (8–6), 6–7 (7–9), 8–6
	Rafael Nadal	Andy Murray	6–3, 6–2, 6–4
Semifinals	Roger Federer	Marat Safin	6–3, 7–6 (7–3), 6–4
	Rafael Nadal	Rainer Schuettler	6–1, 7–6 (7–3), 6–4
Final	Rafael Nadal	Roger Federer	6–4, 6–4, 6–7 (5–7), 6–7 (8–10), 9–7

Women's Singles

	Winner	Runner-Up	Score
Quarterfinals	Jie Zhang	Nicole Vaidisova	6–2, 5–7, 6–1
	Serena Williams	Agnieszka Radwanska	6–4, 6–0
	Elena Dementieva	Nadia Petrova	6–1, 6–7 (6–8), 6–3
	Venus Williams	Tamarine Tanasugarn	6–4, 6–3
Semifinals	Serena Williams	Jie Zheng	6–7, 7–6 (7–5)
	Venus Williams	Elena Dementieva	6–1, 7–6 (7–3)
Final	Venus Williams	Serena Williams	7–5, 6–4

Doubles

	Winner	Runner-Up	Score
Men's Final	Daniel Nestor/ Nenad Zimonjic	Jonas Bjorkman/ Kevin Ullyet	7–6(14–12),6–7(3–7),6–3,6–3
Women's Final	Serena Williams/ Venus Williams	Lisa Raymond/ Samantha Stosur	6–2, 6–2
Mixed Final	Samantha Stosur/ Bob Bryan	Katarina Srebotnik/ Mike Bryan	7–5, 6–4

U.S. Open

Men's Singles

	Winner	Runner-Up	Score
Quarterfinals	Rafael Nadal	Mardy Fish	3–6, 6–1, 6–4, 6–2
	Andy Murray	Juan Martin Del Potro	7–6 (7–2), 7–6 (7–1), 4–6, 7–5
	Roger Federer	Gilles Muler	7–6 (7–5), 6–4, 7–6 (7–5)
	Novak Djokovic	Andy Roddick	6–2, 6–3, 3–6, 7–6 (7–5)
Semifinals	Andy Murray	Rafael Nadal	6–2, 7–6 (7–5), 4–6, 6–4
	Roger Federer	Novak Djokovic	6–3, 5–7, 7–5, 6–2
Final	Roger Federer	Andy Murray	6–2, 7–5, 6–2

Women's Singles

	Winner	Runner-Up	Score
Quarterfinals	Dinara Safina	Flavia Pennetta	6–2, 6–3
	Serena Williams	Venus Williams	7–6 (8–6), 7–6 (9–7)
	Elena Dementieva	Patty Schnyder	6–2, 6–3
	Jelena Jankovic	Sybille Bammer	6–1, 6–4
Semifinals	Serena Williams	Dinara Safina	6–3, 6–2
	Jelena Jankovic	Elena Dementieva	6–4, 6–4
Final	Serena Williams	Jelena Jankovic	6–4, 7–5

Doubles

	Winner	Runner-Up	Score
Men's Final	Bob Bryan/ Mike Bryan	Lukas Dlouhy/ Leander Paes	7–6(7–5), 7–6(12–10)
Women's Final	Cara Black/ Liezel Huber	Lisa Raymond/ Samantha Stosur	6–3, 7–6 (8–6)
Mixed Final	Cara Black/ Leander Paes	Liezel Huber/ Jamie Murray	7–6 (8–6), 6–4

Major Tournament Results

Men's Tour (late 2007 through September 8, 2008)

Date	Tournament	Site	Singles Winner	Surface	Prize Money ($)
Sep 30	Thailand Open	Bangkok, Thailand	Dmitry Tursunov	Indoor Hard	94,000
Oct 7	AIG Open	Tokyo, Japan	David Ferrer	Outdoor Hard	135,000
Oct 14	Kremlin Cup	Moscow, Russia	Nikolay Davydenko	Indoor Hard	255,000
Oct 21	Madrid Masters	Madrid, Spain	David Nalbandian	Indoor Hard	675,000
Oct 28	Swiss Indoor	Basel, Switzerland	Roger Federer	Indoor Hard	220,000
Oct 28	Lyon Grand Prix	Lyon, France	Sebastien Grosjean	Indoor Carpet	170,000
Oct 28	St. Petersburg Open	St. Petersburg, Russia	Andy Murray	Indoor Carpet	255,000
Nov 4	Paris Masters	Paris, France	David Nalbandian	Indoor Hard	675,000
Nov 18	China Masters	Shanghai, China	Roger Federer	Indoor Hard	1,400,000
Jan 6	Qatar Open	Doha, Qatar	Andy Murray	Outdoor Hard	220,000
Jan 27	Australian Open	Melbourne, Australia	Novak Djokovic	Outdoor Hard	1,281,000
Feb 17	Marseille Open	Marseille, France	Andy Murray	Indoor Hard	125,650
Feb 24	ABM/Amro	Rotterdam, Netherlands	Michael Llodra	Indoor Hard	255,000
Mar 9	Dubai Open	Dubai, U.A.E.	Andy Roddick	Outdoor Hard	300,000
Mar 23	Pacific Life Open	Indian Wells, California	Novak Djokovic	Outdoor Hard	555,000
Apr 6	Sony Ericsson Open	Miami, Fla.	Nikolay Davydenko	Outdoor Hard	590,000
Apr 20	Open SEAT Godó	Barcelona, Spain	Rafael Nadal	Outdoor Clay	200,500
Apr 20	Estoril Open	Estoril, Portugal	Roger Federer	Outdoor Clay	89,100
Apr 27	Monte Carlo Masters	Monte Carlo, Monaco	Rafael Nadal	Outdoor Clay	540,000
May 4	BMW Open	Munich, Germany	Fernando Gonzalez	Outdoor Clay	89,150
May 18	Hamburg Masters	Hamburg, Germany	Rafael Nadal	Outdoor Clay	540,000
June 8	French Open	Paris, France	Rafael Nadal	Outdoor Clay	1,500,000
June 15	Gerry Weber Open	Halle, Germany	Roger Federer	Outdoor Grass	170,000
June 22	Ordina Open	Hertog'bosch, Netherlands	David Ferrer	Outdoor Grass	89,150
July 6	Wimbledon	Wimbledon, England	Rafael Nadal	Outdoor Grass	1,050,000
July 13	Allianz Suisse Open	Gstaad, Switzerland	Victor Hanescu	Outdoor Clay	97,000
July 20	Dutch Open	Amersfoort, Netherlands	Albert Montanes	Outdoor Clay	81,400
July 20	RCA Championship	Indianapolis, Indiana	Gilles Simon	Outdoor Hard	83,500
July 20	Austrian Open	Kitzbuhel, Austria	Juan Martin Del Potro	Outdoor Clay	180,000
July 27	Rogers Cup	Toronto, Canada	Rafael Nadal	Outdoor Hard	420,500
Aug 3	Western & Southern	Cincinnati, Ohio	Andy Murray	Outdoor Hard	420,000
Sep 8	U.S. Open	New York City	Roger Federer	Outdoor Hard	1,200,000

Major Tournament Results *(Cont.)*

Women's Tour (Late 2007 through September 7, 2008)

Date	Tournament	Site	Winner	Runner-Up	Score
Sept 30	Porsche Grand Prix	Stuttgart, Germany	Justine Henin	Tatiana Golovin	2-6, 6-2, 6-1
Oct 7	Ladies Kremlin Cup	Moscow, Russia	Elena Dementieva	Serena Williams	5-7, 6-1, 6-1
Oct 14	Zurich Open	Zurich, Switzerland	Justine Henin	Tatiana Golovin	6-4, 6-4
Oct 21	Generali Ladies Open	Linz, Austia	Daniela Hantuchova	Patty Schnyder	6-4, 6-2
Jan 13	Medibank Int'l	Sydney, Australia	Justine Henin	Svetlana Kuznetsova	4-6, 6-2 6-4
Jan 26	Australian Open	Melbourne	Maria Sharapova	Ana Ivanovic	7-5, 6-3
Feb 24	Qatar Open	Doha, Qatar	Maria Sharapova	Vera Zvonareva	6-1, 2-6, 6-0
Mar 23	Pacific Life Open	Indian Wells, California	Ana Ivanovic	Svetlana Kuznetsova	6-4, 6-3
Apr 6	Sony Ericsson Open	Key Biscayne, Florida	Serena Williams	Jelena Jankovic	6-1, 5-7, 6-3
Apr 13	Bausch & Lomb Championships	Amelia Island, Florida	Maria Sharapova	Dominika Cibulkova	7-6 (9-7), 6-3
Apr 20	Family Circle Cup	Charleston, South Carolina	Serena Williams	Vera Zvonareva	6-4, 3-6, 6-3
May 11	German Open	Berlin	Dinara Safina	Elena Dementieva	3-6, 6-2, 6-2
May 18	Italia Masters	Rome, Italy	Jelena Jankovic	Alize Conet	6-2, 6-2
May 25	Int'l de Strasbourg	Strasbourg, France	Anabel Medina Garrigues	Katarina Srebotnik	4-6, 7-6 97-4) 6-0
June 7	French Open	Paris	Ana Ivanovic	Dinara Safina	6-4, 6-3
June 15	DFS Classic	Birmingham, England	Kateryna Bondarenko	Yanina Wickmayer	7-6 (9-7), 3-6, 7-6 (7-4)
June 22	Hastings Direct Int'l Championships	Eastbourne, England	Agnieszka Radwanska	Nadia Petrova	6-4, 6-7 (11-13), 6-4
Jul 5	Wimbledon	Wimbledon, England	Venus Williams	Serena Williams	7-5, 6-4
July 13	Gaz de France Grand Prix	Budapest, Hungary	Alize Cornet	Andreja Klepac	7-6 (7-5), 6-3
July 20	Bank of the West	Stanford, California	Aleksandra Wozniak	Marion Bartoli	7-5, 6-3
July 27	East West Bank Classic	Los Angeles, California	Dinara Safina	Flavia Pennetta	6-4, 6-2
Aug 3	Rogers Cup	Montreal, Canada	Dinara Safina	Dominika Cibulkova	6-2, 6-1
Aug 24	Pilot Pen Int'l	New Haven, Connecticut	Caroline Wozniacki	Anna Chakvetadze	3-6, 6-4, 6-1
Sep 7	U.S. Open	New York City	Serena Williams	Jelena Jankovic	6-4, 7-5

2007 Final Singles Points Leaders

Men

Rank	Player	Country	Points	Events
1	Roger Federer	SUI	7180	16
2	Rafael Nadal	ESP	5735	19
3	Novak Djokovic	SRB	4470	20
4	Nikolay Davydenko	RUS	2825	26
5	David Ferrer	ESP	2640	23
6	Andy Rodick	USA	2530	20
7	Fernando Gonzalez	CHL	2005	19
8	Richard Gasquet	FRA	1930	23
9	David Nalbandian	ARG	1775	15
10	Tommy Robredo	ESP	1765	23

Note: Compiled by the ATP Tour, through the 2007 season.

Women

Rank	Player	Country	Points
1.	Justine Henin	BEL	6155
2.	Svetlana Kuznetsova	RUS	3725
3.	Jelena Jankovic	SRB	3475
4.	Ana Ivanovic	SRB	3461
5.	Maria Sharapova	RUS	2965
6.	Anna Chakvetadze	RUS	2935
7.	Serena Williams	USA	2802
8.	Venus Williams	USA	2470
9.	Daniela Hantuchova	SVK	2367
10.	Marion Bartoli	FRA	2191

Note: Compiled by the WTA, through the 2007 season.

FOR THE RECORD • Year by Year

Grand Slam Tournaments

MEN

Australian Championships

Year	Winner	Finalist	Score
1905	Rodney Heath	A. H. Curtis	4–6, 6–3, 6–4, 6–4
1906	Tony Wilding	H. A. Parker	6–0, 6–4, 6–4
1907	Horace M. Rice	H. A. Parker	6–3, 6–4, 6–4
1908	Fred Alexander	A. W. Dunlop	3–6, 3–6, 6–0, 6–2, 6–3
1909	Tony Wilding	E. F. Parker	6–1, 7–5, 6–2
1910	Rodney Heath	Horace M. Rice	6–4, 6–3, 6–2
1911	Norman Brookes	Horace M. Rice	6–1, 6–2, 6–3
1912	J. Cecil Parke	A. E. Beamish	3–6, 6–3, 1–6, 6–1, 7–5
1913	E. F. Parker	H. A. Parker	2–6, 6–1, 6–2, 6–3
1914	Pat O'Hara Wood	G. L. Patterson	6–4, 6–3, 5–7, 6–1
1915	Francis G. Lowe	Horace M. Rice	4–6, 6–1, 6–1, 6–4
1916–18	No tournament		
1919	A. R. F. Kingscote	E. O. Pockley	6–4, 6–0, 6–3
1920	Pat O'Hara Wood	Ron Thomas	6–3, 4–6, 6–8, 6–1, 6–3
1921	Rhys H. Gemmell	A. Hedeman	7–5, 6–1, 6–4
1922	Pat O'Hara Wood	Gerald Patterson	6–0, 3–6, 3–6, 6–3, 6–2
1923	Pat O'Hara Wood	C. B. St John	6–1, 6–1, 6–3
1924	James Anderson	R. E. Schlesinger	6–3, 6–4, 3–6, 5–7, 6–3
1925	James Anderson	Gerald Patterson	11–9, 2–6, 6–2, 6–3
1926	John Hawkes	J. Willard	6–1, 6–3, 6–1
1927	Gerald Patterson	John Hawkes	3–6, 6–4, 3–6, 18–16, 6–3
1928	Jean Borotra	R. O. Cummings	6–4, 6–1, 4–6, 5–7, 6–3
1929	John C. Gregory	R. E. Schlesinger	6–2, 6–2, 5–7, 7–5
1930	Gar Moon	Harry C. Hopman	6–3, 6–1, 6–3
1931	Jack Crawford	Harry C. Hopman	6–4, 6–2, 2–6, 6–1
1932	Jack Crawford	Harry C. Hopman	4–6, 6–3, 3–6, 6–3, 6–1
1933	Jack Crawford	Keith Gledhill	2–6, 7–5, 6–3, 6–2
1934	Fred Perry	Jack Crawford	6–3, 7–5, 6–1
1935	Jack Crawford	Fred Perry	2–6, 6–4, 6–4, 6–4
1936	Adrian Quist	Jack Crawford	6–2, 6–3, 4–6, 3–6, 9–7
1937	Vivian B. McGrath	John Bromwich	6–3, 1–6, 6–0, 2–6, 6–1
1938	Don Budge	John Bromwich	6–4, 6–2, 6–1
1939	John Bromwich	Adrian Quist	6–4, 6–1, 6–3
1940	Adrian Quist	Jack Crawford	6–3, 6–1, 6–2
1941–45	No tournament		
1946	John Bromwich	Dinny Pails	5–7, 6–3, 7–5, 3–6, 6–2
1947	Dinny Pails	John Bromwich	4–6, 6–4, 3–6, 7–5, 8–6
1948	Adrian Quist	John Bromwich	6–4, 3–6, 6–3, 2–6, 6–3
1949	Frank Sedgman	Ken McGregor	6–3, 6–3, 6–2
1950	Frank Sedgman	Ken McGregor	6–3, 6–4, 4–6, 6–1
1951	Richard Savitt	Ken McGregor	6–3, 2–6, 6–3, 6–1
1952	Ken McGregor	Frank Sedgman	7–5, 12–10, 2–6, 6–2
1953	Ken Rosewall	Mervyn Rose	6–0, 6–3, 6–4
1954	Mervyn Rose	Rex Hartwig	6–2, 0–6, 6–4, 6–2
1955	Ken Rosewall	Lew Hoad	9–7, 6–4, 6–4
1956	Lew Hoad	Ken Rosewall	6–4, 3–6, 6–4, 7–5
1957	Ashley Cooper	Neale Fraser	6–3, 9–11, 6–4, 6–2
1958	Ashley Cooper	Mal Anderson	7–5, 6–3, 6–4
1959	Alex Olmedo	Neale Fraser	6–1, 6–2, 3–6, 6–3
1960	Rod Laver	Neale Fraser	5–7, 3–6, 6–3, 8–6, 8–6
1961	Roy Emerson	Rod Laver	1–6, 6–3, 7–5, 6–4
1962	Rod Laver	Roy Emerson	8–6, 0–6, 6–4, 6–4
1963	Roy Emerson	Ken Fletcher	6–3, 6–3, 6–1
1964	Roy Emerson	Fred Stolle	6–3, 6–4, 6–2
1965	Roy Emerson	Fred Stolle	7–9, 2–6, 6–4, 7–5, 6–1
1966	Roy Emerson	Arthur Ashe	6–4, 6–8, 6–2, 6–3
1967	Roy Emerson	Arthur Ashe	6–4, 6–1, 6–1
1968	Bill Bowrey	Juan Gisbert	7–5, 2–6, 9–7, 6–4
1969*	Rod Laver	Andres Gimeno	6–3, 6–4, 7–5

*Became Open (amateur and professional) in 1969.

MEN (Cont.)

Australian Championships (Cont.)

Year	Winner	Finalist	Score
1970	Arthur Ashe	Dick Crealy	6–4, 9–7, 6–2
1971	Ken Rosewall	Arthur Ashe	6–1, 7–5, 6–3
1972	Ken Rosewall	Mal Anderson	7–6, 6–3, 7–5
1973	John Newcombe	Onny Parun	6–3, 6–7, 7–5, 6–1
1974	Jimmy Connors	Phil Dent	7–6, 6–4, 4–6, 6–3
1975	John Newcombe	Jimmy Connors	7–5, 3–6, 6–4, 7–5
1976	Mark Edmondson	John Newcombe	6–7, 6–3, 7–6, 6–1
1977 (Jan)	Roscoe Tanner	Guillermo Vilas	6–3, 6–3, 6–3
1977 (Dec)	Vitas Gerulaitis	John Lloyd	6–3, 7–6, 5–7, 3–6, 6–2
1978	Guillermo Vilas	John Marks	6–4, 6–4, 3–6, 6–3
1979	Guillermo Vilas	John Sadri	7–6, 6–3, 6–2
1980	Brian Teacher	Kim Warwick	7–5, 7–6, 6–3
1981	Johan Kriek	Steve Denton	6–2, 7–6, 6–7, 6–4
1982	Johan Kriek	Steve Denton	6–3, 6–3, 6–2
1983	Mats Wilander	Ivan Lendl	6–1, 6–4, 6–4
1984	Mats Wilander	Kevin Curren	6–7, 6–4, 7–6, 6–2
1985 (Dec)	Stefan Edberg	Mats Wilander	6–4, 6–3, 6–3
1987 (Jan)	Stefan Edberg	Pat Cash	6–3, 6–4, 3–6, 5–7, 6–3
1988	Mats Wilander	Pat Cash	6–3, 6–7, 3–6, 6–1, 8–6
1989	Ivan Lendl	Miloslav Mecir	6–2, 6–2, 6–2
1990	Ivan Lendl	Stefan Edberg	4–6, 7–6, 5–2, ret.
1991	Boris Becker	Ivan Lendl	1–6, 6–4, 6–4, 6–4
1992	Jim Courier	Stefan Edberg	6–3, 3–6, 6–4, 6–2
1993	Jim Courier	Stefan Edberg	6–2, 6–1, 2–6, 7–5
1994	Pete Sampras	Todd Martin	7–6, 6–4, 6–4
1995	Andre Agassi	Pete Sampras	4–6, 6–1, 7–6, 6–4
1996	Boris Becker	Michael Chang	6–2, 6–4, 2–6, 6–2
1997	Pete Sampras	Carlos Moya	6–2, 6–3, 6–3
1998	Petr Korda	Marcelo Ríos	6–2, 6–2, 6–2
1999	Yevgeny Kafelnikov	Thomas Enqvist	4–6, 6–0, 6–3, 7–6
2000	Andre Agassi	Yevgeny Kafelnikov	3–6, 6–3, 6–2, 6–4
2001	Andre Agassi	Arnaud Clement	6–4, 6–2, 6–2
2002	Thomas Johansson	Marat Safin	3–6, 6–4, 6–4, 7–6 (7-4)
2003	Andre Agassi	Rainer Schuettler	6–2, 6–2, 6–1
2004	Roger Federer	Marat Safin	7–6 (7–3), 6–4, 6–2
2005	Marat Safin	Lleyton Hewitt	1–6, 6–3, 6–4, 6–4
2006	Roger Federer	Marcos Baghdatis	5–7, 7–5, 6–0, 6–2
2007	Roger Federer	Fernando Gonzalez	7–6 (7–2), 6–4, 6–4
2008	Novak Djokovic	Jo-Wilfried Tsonga	4–6, 6–4, 6–3, 7–6 (7–2)

French Championships

Year	Winner	Finalist	Score
1925†	Rene Lacoste	Jean Borotra	7–5, 6–1, 6–4
1926	Henri Cochet	Rene Lacoste	6–2, 6–4, 6–3
1927	Rene Lacoste	Bill Tilden	6–4, 4–6, 5–7, 6–3, 11–9
1928	Henri Cochet	Rene Lacoste	5–7, 6–3, 6–1, 6–3
1929	Rene Lacoste	Jean Borotra	6–3, 2–6, 6–0, 2–6, 8–6
1930	Henri Cochet	Bill Tilden	3–6, 8–6, 6–3, 6–1
1931	Jean Borotra	Claude Boussus	2–6, 6–4, 7–5, 6–4
1932	Henri Cochet	Giorgio de Stefani	6–0, 6–4, 4–6, 6–3
1933	Jack Crawford	Henri Cochet	8–6, 6–1, 6–3
1934	Gottfried von Cramm	Jack Crawford	6–4, 7–9, 3–6, 7–5, 6–3
1935	Fred Perry	Gottfried von Cramm	6–3, 3–6, 6–1, 6–3
1936	Gottfried von Cramm	Fred Perry	6–0, 2–6, 6–2, 2–6, 6–0
1937	Henner Henkel	Henry Austin	6–1, 6–4, 6–3
1938	Don Budge	Roderick Menzel	6–3, 6–2, 6–4
1939	Don McNeill	Bobby Riggs	7–5, 6–0, 6–3
1940	No tournament		
1941‡	Bernard Destremau	n/a	n/a
1942‡	Bernard Destremau	n/a	n/a
1943‡	Yvon Petra	n/a	n/a
1944‡	Yvon Petra	n/a	n/a
1945‡	Yvon Petra	Bernard Destremau	7–5, 6–4, 6–2

†1925 was the first year that entries were accepted from all countries.
‡From 1941 to 1945 the event was called Tournoi de France and was closed to all foreigners.

Grand Slam Tournaments *(Cont.)*

MEN *(Cont.)*

French Championships *(Cont.)*

Year	Winner	Finalist	Score
1946	Marcel Bernard	Jaroslav Drobny	3–6, 2–6, 6–1, 6–4, 6–3
1947	Joseph Asboth	Eric Sturgess	8–6, 7–5, 6–4
1948	Frank Parker	Jaroslav Drobny	6–4, 7–5, 5–7, 8–6
1949	Frank Parker	Budge Patty	6–3, 1–6, 6–1, 6–4
1950	Budge Patty	Jaroslav Drobny	6–1, 6–2, 3–6, 5–7, 7–5
1951	Jaroslav Drobny	Eric Sturgess	6–3, 6–3, 6–3
1952	Jaroslav Drobny	Frank Sedgman	6–2, 6–0, 3–6, 6–4
1953	Ken Rosewall	Vic Seixas	6–3, 6–4, 1–6, 6–2
1954	Tony Trabert	Arthur Larsen	6–4, 7–5, 6–1
1955	Tony Trabert	Sven Davidson	2–6, 6–1, 6–4, 6–2
1956	Lew Hoad	Sven Davidson	6–4, 8–6, 6–3
1957	Sven Davidson	Herbie Flam	6–3, 6–4, 6–4
1958	Mervyn Rose	Luis Ayala	6–3, 6–4, 6–4
1959	Nicola Pietrangeli	Ian Vermaak	3–6, 6–3, 6–4, 6–1
1960	Nicola Pietrangeli	Luis Ayala	3–6, 6–3, 6–4, 4–6, 6–3
1961	Manuel Santana	Nicola Pietrangeli	4–6, 6–1, 3–6, 6–0, 6–2
1962	Rod Laver	Roy Emerson	3–6, 2–6, 6–3, 9–7, 6–2
1963	Roy Emerson	Pierre Darmon	3–6, 6–1, 6–4, 6–4
1964	Manuel Santana	Nicola Pietrangeli	6–3, 6–1, 4–6, 7–5
1965	Fred Stolle	Tony Roche	3–6, 6–0, 6–2, 6–3
1966	Tony Roche	Istvan Gulyas	6–1, 6–4, 7–5
1967	Roy Emerson	Tony Roche	6–1, 6–4, 2–6, 6–2
1968*	Ken Rosewall	Rod Laver	6–3, 6–1, 2–6, 6–2
1969	Rod Laver	Ken Rosewall	6–4, 6–3, 6–4
1970	Jan Kodes	Zeljko Franulovic	6–2, 6–4, 6–0
1971	Jan Kodes	Ilie Nastase	8–6, 6–2, 2–6, 7–5
1972	Andres Gimeno	Patrick Proisy	4–6, 6–3, 6–1, 6–1
1973	Ilie Nastase	Nikki Pilic	6–3, 6–3, 6–0
1974	Bjorn Borg	Manuel Orantes	6–7, 6–0, 6–1, 6–1
1975	Bjorn Borg	Guillermo Vilas	6–2, 6–3, 6–4
1976	Adriano Panatta	Harold Solomon	6–1, 6–4, 4–6, 7–6
1977	Guillermo Vilas	Brian Gottfried	6–0, 6–3, 6–0
1978	Bjorn Borg	Guillermo Vilas	6–1, 6–1, 6–3
1979	Bjorn Borg	Victor Pecci	6–3, 6–1, 6–7, 6–4
1980	Bjorn Borg	Vitas Gerulaitis	6–4, 6–1, 6–2
1981	Bjorn Borg	Ivan Lendl	6–1, 4–6, 6–2, 3–6, 6–1
1982	Mats Wilander	Guillermo Vilas	1–6, 7–6, 6–0, 6–4
1983	Yannick Noah	Mats Wilander	6–2, 7–5, 7–6
1984	Ivan Lendl	John McEnroe	3–6, 2–6, 6–4, 7–5, 7–5
1985	Mats Wilander	Ivan Lendl	3–6, 6–4, 6–2, 6–2
1986	Ivan Lendl	Mikael Pernfors	6–3, 6–2, 6–4
1987	Ivan Lendl	Mats Wilander	7–5, 6–2, 3–6, 7–6
1988	Mats Wilander	Henri Leconte	7–5, 6–2, 6–1
1989	Michael Chang	Stefan Edberg	6–1, 3–6, 4–6, 6–4, 6–2
1990	Andres Gomez	Andre Agassi	6–3, 2–6, 6–4, 6–4
1991	Jim Courier	Andre Agassi	3–6, 6–4, 2–6, 6–1, 6–4
1992	Jim Courier	Petr Korda	7–5, 6–2, 6–1
1993	Sergi Bruguera	Jim Courier	6–4, 2–6, 6–2, 3–6, 6–3
1994	Sergi Bruguera	Alberto Berasategui	6–3, 7–5, 2–6, 6–1
1995	Thomas Muster	Michael Chang	7–5, 6–2, 6–4
1996	Yevgeny Kafelnikov	Michael Stich	7–6, 7–5, 7–6
1997	Gustavo Kuerten	Sergi Bruguera	6–3, 6–4, 6–2
1998	Carlos Moya	Alex Corretja	6–3, 7–5, 6–3
1999	Andre Agassi	Andrei Medvedev	1–6, 2–6, 6–4, 6–3, 6–4
2000	Gustavo Kuerten	Magnus Norman	6–2, 6–3, 2–6, 7–6
2001	Gustavo Kuerten	Alex Corretja	6–7, 7–5, 6–2, 6–0
2002	Albert Costa	Juan Cárlos Ferrero	6-1, 6–0, 4–6, 6–3
2003	Juan Carlos Ferrero	Martin Verkerk	6–1, 6–3, 6–2
2004	Gaston Gaudio	Guillermo Coria	0–6, 3–6, 6–4, 6–1, 8–6
2005	Rafael Nadal	Mariano Puerta	6–7, 6–3, 6–1, 7–5
2006	Rafael Nadal	Roger Federer	1–6, 6–1, 6–4, 7–6
2007	Rafael Nadal	Roger Federer	6–3, 4–6, 6–3, 6–4
2008	Rafael Nadal	Roger Federer	6–1, 6–3, 6–0

*Became Open (amateur and professional) in 1968, but restricted to only contract professionals in 1972.

MEN (Cont.)

Wimbledon Championships

Year	Winner	Finalist	Score
1877	Spencer W. Gore	William C. Marshall	6–1, 6–2, 6–4
1878	P. Frank Hadow	Spencer W. Gore	7–5, 6–1, 9–7
1879	John T. Hartley	V. St Leger Gould	6–2, 6–4, 6–2
1880	John T. Hartley	Herbert F. Lawford	6–0, 6–2, 2–6, 6–3
1881	William Renshaw	John T. Hartley	6–0, 6–2, 6–1
1882	William Renshaw	Ernest Renshaw	6–1, 2–6, 4–6, 6–2, 6–2
1883	William Renshaw	Ernest Renshaw	2–6, 6–3, 6–3, 4–6, 6–3
1884	William Renshaw	Herbert F. Lawford	6–0, 6–4, 9–7
1885	William Renshaw	Herbert F. Lawford	7–5, 6–2, 4–6, 7–5
1886	William Renshaw	Herbert F. Lawford	6–0, 5–7, 6–3, 6–4
1887	Herbert F. Lawford	Ernest Renshaw	1–6, 6–3, 3–6, 6–4, 6–4
1888	Ernest Renshaw	Herbert F. Lawford	6–3, 7–5, 6–0
1889	William Renshaw	Ernest Renshaw	6–4, 6–1, 3–6, 6–0
1890	William J. Hamilton	William Renshaw	6–8, 6–2, 3–6, 6–1, 6–1
1891	Wilfred Baddeley	Joshua Pim	6–4, 1–6, 7–5, 6–0
1892	Wilfred Baddeley	Joshua Pim	4–6, 6–3, 6–3, 6–2
1893	Joshua Pim	Wilfred Baddeley	3–6, 6–1, 6–3, 6–2
1894	Joshua Pim	Wilfred Baddeley	10–8, 6–2, 8–6
1895	Wilfred Baddeley	Wilberforce V. Eaves	4–6, 2–6, 8–6, 6–2, 6–3
1896	Harold S. Mahoney	Wilfred Baddeley	6–2, 6–8, 5–7, 8–6, 6–3
1897	Reggie F. Doherty	Harold S. Mahoney	6–4, 6–4, 6–3
1898	Reggie F. Doherty	H. Laurie Doherty	6–3, 6–3, 2–6, 5–7, 6–1
1899	Reggie F. Doherty	Arthur W. Gore	1–6, 4–6, 6–2, 6–3, 6–3
1900	Reggie F. Doherty	Sidney H. Smith	6–8, 6–3, 6–1, 6–2
1901	Arthur W. Gore	Reggie F. Doherty	4–6, 7–5, 6–4, 6–4
1902	H. Laurie Doherty	Arthur W. Gore	6–4, 6–3, 3–6, 6–0
1903	H. Laurie Doherty	Frank L. Riseley	7–5, 6–3, 6–0
1904	H. Laurie Doherty	Frank L. Riseley	6–1, 7–5, 8–6
1905	H. Laurie Doherty	Norman E. Brookes	8–6, 6–2, 6–4
1906	H. Laurie Doherty	Frank L. Riseley	6–4, 4–6, 6–2, 6–3
1907	Norman E. Brookes	Arthur W. Gore	6–4, 6–2, 6–2
1908	Arthur W. Gore	H. Roper Barrett	6–3, 6–2, 4–6, 3–6, 6–4
1909	Arthur W. Gore	M. J. G. Ritchie	6–8, 1–6, 6–2, 6–2, 6–2
1910	Anthony F. Wilding	Arthur W. Gore	6–4, 7–5, 4–6, 6–2
1911	Anthony F. Wilding	H. Roper Barrett	6–4, 4–6, 2–6, 6–2, ret.
1912	Anthony F. Wilding	Arthur W. Gore	6–4, 6–4, 4–6, 6–4
1913	Anthony F. Wilding	Maurice E. McLoughlin	8–6, 6–3, 10–8
1914	Norman E. Brookes	Anthony F. Wilding	6–4, 6–4, 7–5
1915–18	No tournament		
1919	Gerald L. Patterson	Norman E. Brookes	6–3, 7–5, 6–2
1920	Bill Tilden	Gerald L. Patterson	2–6, 6–3, 6–2, 6–4
1921	Bill Tilden	Brian I. C. Norton	4–6, 2–6, 6–1, 6–0, 7–5
1922	Gerald L. Patterson	Randolph Lycett	6–3, 6–4, 6–2
1923	Bill Johnston	Francis T. Hunter	6–0, 6–3, 6–1
1924	Jean Borotra	Rene Lacoste	6–1, 3–6, 6–1, 3–6, 6–4
1925	Rene Lacoste	Jean Borotra	6–3, 6–3, 4–6, 8–6
1926	Jean Borotra	Howard Kinsey	8–6, 6–1, 6–3
1927	Henri Cochet	Jean Borotra	4–6, 4–6, 6–3, 6–4, 7–5
1928	Rene Lacoste	Henri Cochet	6–1, 4–6, 6–4, 6–2
1929	Henri Cochet	Jean Borotra	6–4, 6–3, 6–4
1930	Bill Tilden	Wilmer Allison	6–3, 9–7, 6–4
1931	Sidney B. Wood Jr	Francis X. Shields	walkover
1932	Ellsworth Vines	Henry Austin	6–4, 6–2, 6–0
1933	Jack Crawford	Ellsworth Vines	4–6, 11–9, 6–2, 2–6, 6–4
1934	Fred Perry	Jack Crawford	6–3, 6–0, 7–5
1935	Fred Perry	Gottfried von Cramm	6–2, 6–4, 6–4
1936	Fred Perry	Gottfried von Cramm	6–1, 6–1, 6–0
1937	Don Budge	Gottfried von Cramm	6–3, 6–4, 6–2
1938	Don Budge	Henry Austin	6–1, 6–0, 6–3
1939	Bobby Riggs	Elwood Cooke	2–6, 8–6, 3–6, 6–3, 6–2
1940–45	No tournament		
1946	Yvon Petra	Geoff E. Brown	6–2, 6–4, 6–7 (7–9), 5–7, 6–4
1947	Jack Kramer	Tom P. Brown	6–1, 6–3, 6–2
1948	Bob Falkenburg	John Bromwich	7–5, 0–6, 6–2, 3–6, 7–5
1949	Ted Schroeder	Jaroslav Drobny	3–6, 6–0, 6–3, 4–6, 6–4

Note: Prior to 1922 the tournament was run on a challenge-round system. The previous year's winner "stood out" of an All Comers event, which produced a challenger to play him for the title.

Grand Slam Tournaments *(Cont.)*

MEN *(Cont.)*

Wimbledon Championships *(Cont.)*

Year	Winner	Finalist	Score
1950	Budge Patty	Frank Sedgman	6–1, 6–7 (8–10), 6–2, 6–3
1951	Dick Savitt	Ken McGregor	6–4, 6–4, 6–4
1952	Frank Sedgman	Jaroslav Drobny	4–6, 6–3, 6–2, 6–3
1953	Vic Seixas	Kurt Nielsen	9–7, 6–3, 6–4
1954	Jaroslav Drobny	Ken Rosewall	13–11, 4–6, 6–2, 9–7
1955	Tony Trabert	Kurt Nielsen	6–3, 7–5, 6–1
1956	Lew Hoad	Ken Rosewall	6–2, 4–6, 7–5, 6–4
1957	Lew Hoad	Ashley Cooper	6–2, 6–1, 6–2
1958	Ashley Cooper	Neale Fraser	3–6, 6–3, 6–4, 13–11
1959	Alex Olmedo	Rod Laver	6–4, 6–3, 6–4
1960	Neale Fraser	Rod Laver	6–4, 3–6, 9–7, 7–5
1961	Rod Laver	Chuck McKinley	6–3, 6–1, 6–4
1962	Rod Laver	Martin Mulligan	6–2, 6–2, 6–1
1963	Chuck McKinley	Fred Stolle	9–7, 6–1, 6–4
1964	Roy Emerson	Fred Stolle	6–4, 12–10, 4–6, 6–3
1965	Roy Emerson	Fred Stolle	6–2, 6–4, 6–4
1966	Manuel Santana	Dennis Ralston	6–4, 11–9, 6–4
1967	John Newcombe	Wilhelm Bungert	6–3, 6–1, 6–1
1968*	Rod Laver	Tony Roche	6–3, 6–4, 6–2
1969	Rod Laver	John Newcombe	6–4, 5–7, 6–4, 6–4
1970	John Newcombe	Ken Rosewall	5–7, 6–3, 6–2, 3–6, 6–1
1971	John Newcombe	Stan Smith	6–3, 5–7, 2–6, 6–4, 6–4
1972	Stan Smith	Ilie Nastase	4–6, 6–3, 6–3, 4–6, 7–5
1973	Jan Kodes	Alex Metreveli	6–1, 9–8, 6–3
1974	Jimmy Connors	Ken Rosewall	6–1, 6–1, 6–4
1975	Arthur Ashe	Jimmy Connors	6–1, 6–1, 5–7, 6–4
1976	Bjorn Borg	Ilie Nastase	6–4, 6–2, 9–7
1977	Bjorn Borg	Jimmy Connors	3–6, 6–2, 6–1, 5–7, 6–4
1978	Bjorn Borg	Jimmy Connors	6–2, 6–2, 6–3
1979	Bjorn Borg	Roscoe Tanner	6–7, 6–1, 3–6, 6–3, 6–4
1980	Bjorn Borg	John McEnroe	1–6, 7–5, 6–3, 6–7, 8–6
1981	John McEnroe	Bjorn Borg	4–6, 7–6, 7–6, 6–4
1982	Jimmy Connors	John McEnroe	3–6, 6–3, 6–7, 7–6, 6–4
1983	John McEnroe	Chris Lewis	6–2, 6–2, 6–2
1984	John McEnroe	Jimmy Connors	6–1, 6–1, 6–2
1985	Boris Becker	Kevin Curren	6–3, 6–7, 7–6, 6–4
1986	Boris Becker	Ivan Lendl	6–4, 6–3, 7–5
1987	Pat Cash	Ivan Lendl	7–6, 6–2, 7–5
1988	Stefan Edberg	Boris Becker	4–6, 7–6, 6–4, 6–2
1989	Boris Becker	Stefan Edberg	6–0, 7–6, 6–4
1990	Stefan Edberg	Boris Becker	6–2, 6–2, 3–6, 3–6, 6–4
1991	Michael Stich	Boris Becker	6–4, 7–6, 6–4
1992	Andre Agassi	Goran Ivanisevic	6–7, 6–4, 6–4, 1–6, 6–4
1993	Pete Sampras	Jim Courier	7–6, 7–6, 3–6, 6–3
1994	Pete Sampras	Goran Ivanisevic	7–6, 7–6, 6–0
1995	Pete Sampras	Boris Becker	6–7, 6–2, 6–4, 6–2
1996	Richard Krajicek	MaliVai Washington	6–3, 6–4, 6–3
1997	Pete Sampras	Cedric Pioline	6–4, 6–2, 6–4
1998	Pete Sampras	Goran Ivanisevic	6–7, 7–6, 6–4, 3–6, 6–2
1999	Pete Sampras	Andre Agassi	6–3, 6–4, 7–5
2000	Pete Sampras	Patrick Rafter	6–7, 7–6, 6–4, 6–2
2001	Goran Ivanisevic	Patrick Rafter	6–3, 3–6, 6–3, 2–6, 9–7
2002	Lleyton Hewitt	David Nalbandian	6–1, 6–3, 6–2
2003	Roger Federer	Mark Philippoussis	7–6 (7-5), 6–2, 7–6 (7-3)
2004	Roger Federer	Andy Roddick	4–6, 7–5, 7–6 (7-3), 6–4
2005	Roger Federer	Andy Roddick	6–2, 7–6 (7–2), 6–4
2006	Roger Federer	Rafael Nadal	6–0, 7–6, (7–5), 6–7 (2–7), 6–3
2007	Roger Federer	Rafael Nadal	7–6 (9–7), 4–6, 7–6 (7–3), 2–6, 6–2
2008	Rafael Nadal	Roger Federer	6–4, 6–4, 6–7 (5–7), 6–7 (8–10) 9–7

*Became Open (amateur and professional) in 1968, but restricted to only contract professionals in 1972.

MEN (Cont.)

United States Championships

Year	Winner	Finalist	Score
1881	Richard D. Sears	W.E. Glyn	6–0, 6–3, 6–2
1882	Richard D. Sears	C.M. Clark	6–1, 6–4, 6–0
1883	Richard D. Sears	James Dwight	6–2, 6–0, 9–7
1884	Richard D. Sears	H.A. Taylor	6–0, 1–6, 6–0, 6–2
1885	Richard D. Sears	G.M. Brinley	6–3, 4–6, 6–0, 6–3
1886	Richard D. Sears	R.L. Beeckman	4–6, 6–1, 6–3, 6–4
1887	Richard D. Sears	H.W. Slocum Jr	6–1, 6–3, 6–2
1888†	H. W. Slocum Jr	H.A. Taylor	6–4, 6–1, 6–0
1889	H. W. Slocum Jr	Q.A. Shaw	6–3, 6–1, 4–6, 6–2
1890	Oliver S. Campbell	H.W. Slocum Jr	6–2, 4–6, 6–3, 6–1
1891	Oliver S. Campbell	Clarence Hobart	2–6, 7–5, 7–9, 6–1, 6–2
1892	Oliver S. Campbell	Frederick H. Hovey	7–5, 3–6, 6–3, 7–5
1893†	Robert D. Wrenn	Frederick H. Hovey	6–4, 3–6, 6–4, 6–4
1894	Robert D. Wrenn	M.F. Goodbody	6–8, 6–1, 6–4, 6–4
1895	Frederick H. Hovey	Robert D. Wrenn	6–3, 6–2, 6–4
1896	Robert D. Wrenn	Frederick H. Hovey	7–5, 3–6, 6–0, 1–6, 6–1
1897	Robert D. Wrenn	Wilberforce V. Eaves	4–6, 8–6, 6–3, 2–6, 6–2
1898†	Malcolm D. Whitman	Dwight F. Davis	3–6, 6–2, 6–2, 6–1
1899	Malcolm D. Whitman	J. Parmly Paret	6–1, 6–2, 3–6, 7–5
1900	Malcolm D. Whitman	William A. Larned	6–4, 1–6, 6–2, 6–2
1901†	William A. Larned	Beals C. Wright	6–2, 6–8, 6–4, 6–4
1902	William A. Larned	Reggie F. Doherty	4–6, 6–2, 6–4, 8–6
1903	H. Laurie Doherty	William A. Larned	6–0, 6–3, 10–8
1904†	Holcombe Ward	William J. Clothier	10–8, 6–4, 9–7
1905	Beals C. Wright	Holcombe Ward	6–2, 6–1, 11–9
1906	William J. Clothier	Beals C. Wright	6–3, 6–0, 6–4
1907†	William A. Larned	Robert LeRoy	6–2, 6–2, 6–4
1908	William A. Larned	Beals C. Wright	6–1, 6–2, 8–6
1909	William A. Larned	William J. Clothier	6–1, 6–2, 5–7, 1–6, 6–1
1910	William A. Larned	Thomas C. Bundy	6–1, 5–7, 6–0, 6–8, 6–1
1911	William A. Larned	Maurice E. McLoughlin	6–4, 6–4, 6–2
1912‡	Maurice E. McLoughlin	Bill Johnson	3–6, 2–6, 6–2, 6–4, 6–2
1913	Maurice E. McLoughlin	Richard N. Williams	6–4, 5–7, 6–3, 6–1
1914	Richard N. Williams	Maurice E. McLoughlin	6–3, 8–6, 10–8
1915	Bill Johnston	Maurice E. McLoughlin	1–6, 6–0, 7–5, 10–8
1916	Richard N. Williams	Bill Johnston	4–6, 6–4, 0–6, 6–2, 6–4
1917#	R.L. Murray	N. W. Niles	5–7, 8–6, 6–3, 6–3
1918	R.L. Murray	Bill Tilden	6–3, 6–1, 7–5
1919	Bill Johnston	Bill Tilden	6–4, 6–4, 6–3
1920	Bill Tilden	Bill Johnston	6–1, 1–6, 7–5, 5–7, 6–3
1921	Bill Tilden	Wallace F. Johnson	6–1, 6–3, 6–1
1922	Bill Tilden	Bill Johnston	4–6, 3–6, 6–2, 6–3, 6–4
1923	Bill Tilden	Bill Johnston	6–4, 6–1, 6–4
1924	Bill Tilden	Bill Johnston	6–1, 9–7, 6–2
1925	Bill Tilden	Bill Johnston	4–6, 11–9, 6–3, 4–6, 6–3
1926	Rene Lacoste	Jean Borotra	6–4, 6–0, 6–4
1927	Rene Lacoste	Bill Tilden	11–9, 6–3, 11–9
1928	Henri Cochet	Francis T. Hunter	4–6, 6–4, 3–6, 7–5, 6–3
1929	Bill Tilden	Francis T. Hunter	3–6, 6–3, 4–6, 6–2, 6–4
1930	John H. Doeg	Francis X. Shields	10–8, 1–6, 6–4, 16–14
1931	Ellsworth Vines	George M. Lott Jr	7–9, 6–3, 9–7, 7–5
1932	Ellsworth Vines	Henri Cochet	6–4, 6–4, 6–4
1933	Fred Perry	Jack Crawford	6–3, 11–13, 4–6, 6–0, 6–1
1934	Fred Perry	Wilmer L. Allison	6–4, 6–3, 1–6, 8–6
1935	Wilmer L. Allison	Sidney B. Wood Jr	6–2, 6–2, 6–3
1936	Fred Perry	Don Budge	2–6, 6–2, 8–6, 1–6, 10–8
1937	Don Budge	Gottfried von Cramm	6–1, 7–9, 6–1, 3–6, 6–1
1938	Don Budge	Gene Mako	6–3, 6–8, 6–2, 6–1
1939	Bobby Riggs	Welby Van Horn	6–4, 6–2, 6–4
1940	Don McNeill	Bobby Riggs	4–6, 6–8, 6–3, 6–3, 7–5
1941	Bobby Riggs	Francis Kovacs II	5–7, 6–1, 6–3, 6–3
1942	Ted Schroeder	Frank Parker	8–6, 7–5, 3–6, 4–6, 6–2
1943	Joseph R. Hunt	Jack Kramer	6–3, 6–8, 10–8, 6–0
1944	Frank Parker	William F. Talbert	6–4, 3–6, 6–3, 6–3

†No challenge round played. ‡Challenge round abolished. #National Patriotic Tournament.

MEN (Cont.)

United States Championships (Cont.)

Year	Winner	Finalist	Score
1945	Frank Parker	William F. Talbert	14–12, 6–1, 6–2
1946	Jack Kramer	Tom P. Brown	9–7, 6–3, 6–0
1947	Jack Kramer	Frank Parker	4–6, 2–6, 6–1, 6–0, 6–3
1948	Pancho Gonzales	Eric W. Sturgess	6–2, 6–3, 14–12
1949	Pancho Gonzales	Ted Schroeder	16–18, 2–6, 6–1, 6–2, 6–4
1950	Arthur Larsen	Herbie Flam	6–3, 4–6, 5–7, 6–4, 6–3
1951	Frank Sedgman	Vic Seixas	6–4, 6–1, 6–1
1952	Frank Sedgman	Gardnar Mulloy	6–1, 6–2, 6–3
1953	Tony Trabert	Vic Seixas	6–3, 6–2, 6–3
1954	Vic Seixas	Rex Hartwig	3–6, 6–2, 6–4, 6–4
1955	Tony Trabert	Ken Rosewall	9–7, 6–3, 6–3
1956	Ken Rosewall	Lew Hoad	4–6, 6–2, 6–3, 6–3
1957	Mal Anderson	Ashley J. Cooper	10–8, 7–5, 6–4
1958	Ashley J. Cooper	Mal Anderson	6–2, 3–6, 4–6, 10–8, 8–6
1959	Neale Fraser	Alex Olmedo	6–3, 5–7, 6–2, 6–4
1960	Neale Fraser	Rod Laver	6–4, 6–4, 9–7
1961	Roy Emerson	Rod Laver	7–5, 6–3, 6–2
1962	Rod Laver	Roy Emerson	6–2, 6–4, 5–7, 6–4
1963	Rafael Osuna	Frank Froehling III	7–5, 6–4, 6–2
1964	Roy Emerson	Fred Stolle	6–4, 6–2, 6–4
1965	Manuel Santana	Cliff Drysdale	6–2, 7–9, 7–5, 6–1
1966	Fred Stolle	John Newcombe	4–6, 12–10, 6–3, 6–4
1967	John Newcombe	Clark Graebner	6–4, 6–4, 8–6
1968*	Arthur Ashe	Tom Okker	14–12, 5–7, 6–3, 3–6, 6–3
1968**	Arthur Ashe	Bob Lutz	4–6, 6–3, 8–10, 6–0, 6–4
1969	Rod Laver	Tony Roche	7–9, 6–1, 6–3, 6–2
1969**	Stan Smith	Bob Lutz	9–7, 6–3, 6–1
1970	Ken Rosewall	Tony Roche	2–6, 6–4, 7–6, 6–3
1971	Stan Smith	Jan Kodes	3–6, 6–3, 6–2, 7–6
1972	Ilie Nastase	Arthur Ashe	3–6, 6–3, 6–7, 6–4, 6–3
1973	John Newcombe	Jan Kodes	6–4, 1–6, 4–6, 6–2, 6–3
1974	Jimmy Connors	Ken Rosewall	6–1, 6–0, 6–1
1975	Manuel Orantes	Jimmy Connors	6–4, 6–3, 6–3
1976	Jimmy Connors	Bjorn Borg	6–4, 3–6, 7–6, 6–4
1977	Guillermo Vilas	Jimmy Connors	2–6, 6–3, 7–6, 6–0
1978	Jimmy Connors	Bjorn Borg	6–4, 6–2, 6–2
1979	John McEnroe	Vitas Gerulaitis	7–5, 6–3, 6–3
1980	John McEnroe	Bjorn Borg	7–6, 6–1, 6–7, 5–7, 6–4
1981	John McEnroe	Bjorn Borg	4–6, 6–2, 6–4, 6–3
1982	Jimmy Connors	Ivan Lendl	6–3, 6–2, 4–6, 6–4
1983	Jimmy Connors	Ivan Lendl	6–3, 6–7, 7–5, 6–0
1984	John McEnroe	Ivan Lendl	6–3, 6–4, 6–1
1985	Ivan Lendl	John McEnroe	7–6, 6–3, 6–4
1986	Ivan Lendl	Miloslav Mecir	6–4, 6–2, 6–0
1987	Ivan Lendl	Mats Wilander	6–7, 6–0, 7–6, 6–4
1988	Mats Wilander	Ivan Lendl	6–4, 4–6, 6–3, 5–7, 6–4
1989	Boris Becker	Ivan Lendl	7–6, 1–6, 6–3, 7–6
1990	Pete Sampras	Andre Agassi	6–4, 6–3, 6–2
1991	Stefan Edberg	Jim Courier	6–2, 6–4, 6–0
1992	Stefan Edberg	Pete Sampras	3–6, 6–4, 7–6, 6–2
1993	Pete Sampras	Cedric Pioline	6–4, 6–4, 6–3
1994	Andre Agassi	Michael Stich	6–1, 7–6, 7–5
1995	Pete Sampras	Andre Agassi	6–4, 6–3, 4–6, 7–5
1996	Pete Sampras	Michael Chang	6–1, 6–4, 7–6
1997	Patrick Rafter	Greg Rusedski	6–3, 6–2, 4–6, 7–5
1998	Patrick Rafter	Mark Philippoussis	6–3, 3–6, 6–2, 6–0
1999	Andre Agassi	Todd Martin	6–4, 6–7, 6–7, 6–3, 6–2
2000	Marat Safin	Pete Sampras	6–4, 6–3, 6–3
2001	Lleyton Hewitt	Pete Sampras	7–6, 6–1, 6–1
2002	Pete Sampras	Andre Agassi	6–3, 6–4, 5–7, 6–4
2003	Andy Roddick	Juan Carlos Ferrero	6–3, 7–6 (7-2), 6–3
2004	Roger Federer	Lleyton Hewitt	6–0, 7–6 (7-3), 6–0
2005	Roger Federer	Andre Agassi	6–3, 2–6, 7–6 (7–1), 6–1
2006	Roger Federer	Andy Roddick	6–2, 4–6, 7–5, 6–1
2007	Roger Federer	Novak Djokovic	7–6 (7–4), 7–6 (7–2), 6–4
2008	Roger Federer	Andy Murray	6–2, 7–5, 6–2

*Became Open (amateur and professional) in 1968. **Amateur event held.

WOMEN

Australian Championships

Year	Winner	Finalist	Score
1922	Margaret Molesworth	Esna Boyd	6–3, 10–8
1923	Margaret Molesworth	Esna Boyd	6–1, 7–5
1924	Sylvia Lance	Esna Boyd	6–3, 3–6, 6–4
1925	Daphne Akhurst	Esna Boyd	1–6, 8–6, 6–4
1926	Daphne Akhurst	Esna Boyd	6–1, 6–3
1927	Esna Boyd	Sylvia Harper	5–7, 6–1, 6–2
1928	Daphne Akhurst	Esna Boyd	7–5, 6–2
1929	Daphne Akhurst	Louise Bickerton	6–1, 5–7, 6–2
1930	Daphne Akhurst	Sylvia Harper	10–8, 2–6, 7–5
1931	Coral Buttsworth	Margorie Crawford	1–6, 6–3, 6–4
1932	Coral Buttsworth	Kathrine Le Messurier	9–7, 6–4
1933	Joan Hartigan	Coral Buttsworth	6–4, 6–3
1934	Joan Hartigan	Margaret Molesworth	6–1, 6–4
1935	Dorothy Round	Nancye Wynne Bolton	1–6, 6–1, 6–3
1936	Joan Hartigan	Nancye Wynne Bolton	6–4, 6–4
1937	Nancye Wynne Bolton	Emily Westacott	6–3, 5–7, 6–4
1938	Dorothy Bundy	D. Stevenson	6–3, 6–2
1939	Emily Westacott	Nell Hopman	6–1, 6–2
1940	Nancye Wynne Bolton	Thelma Coyne	5–7, 6–4, 6–0
1941–45	No tournament		
1946	Nancye Wynne Bolton	Joyce Fitch	6–4, 6–4
1947	Nancye Wynne Bolton	Nell Hopman	6–3, 6–2
1948	Nancye Wynne Bolton	Marie Toomey	6–3, 6–1
1949	Doris Hart	Nancye Wynne Bolton	6–3, 6–4
1950	Louise Brough	Doris Hart	6–4, 3–6, 6–4
1951	Nancye Wynne Bolton	Thelma Long	6–1, 7–5
1952	Thelma Long	H. Angwin	6–2, 6–3
1953	Maureen Connolly	Julia Sampson	6–3, 6–2
1954	Thelma Long	J. Staley	6–3, 6–4
1955	Beryl Penrose	Thelma Long	6–4, 6–3
1956	Mary Carter	Thelma Long	3–6, 6–2, 9–7
1957	Shirley Fry	Althea Gibson	6–3, 6–4
1958	Angela Mortimer	Lorraine Coghlan	6–3, 6–4
1959	Mary Carter-Reitano	Renee Schuurman	6–2, 6–3
1960	Margaret Smith	Jan Lehane	7–5, 6–2
1961	Margaret Smith	Jan Lehane	6–1, 6–4
1962	Margaret Smith	Jan Lehane	6–0, 6–2
1963	Margaret Smith	Jan Lehane	6–2, 6–2
1964	Margaret Smith	Lesley Turner	6–3, 6–2
1965	Margaret Smith	Maria Bueno	5–7, 6–4, 5–2, ret.
1966	Margaret Smith	Nancy Richey	Default
1967	Nancy Richey	Lesley Turner	6–1, 6–4
1968	Billie Jean King	Margaret Smith	6–1, 6–2
1969*	Margaret Smith Court	Billie Jean King	6–4, 6–1
1970	Margaret Smith Court	Kerry Melville Reid	6–3, 6–1
1971	Margaret Smith Court	Evonne Goolagong	2–6, 7–6, 7–5
1972	Virginia Wade	Evonne Goolagong	6–4, 6–4
1973	Margaret Smith Court	Evonne Goolagong	6–4, 7–5
1974	Evonne Goolagong	Chris Evert	7–6, 4–6, 6–0
1975	Evonne Goolagong	Martina Navratilova	6–3, 6–2
1976	Evonne Goolagong Cawley	Renata Tomanova	6–2, 6–2
1977 (Jan)	Kerry Melville Reid	Dianne Balestrat	7–5, 6–2
1977 (Dec)	Evonne Goolagong Cawley	Helen Gourlay	6–3, 6–0
1978	Chris O'Neil	Betsy Nagelsen	6–3, 7–6
1979	Barbara Jordan	Sharon Walsh	6–3, 6–3
1980	Hana Mandlikova	Wendy Turnbull	6–0, 7–5
1981	Martina Navratilova	Chris Evert Lloyd	6–7, 6–4, 7–5
1982	Chris Evert Lloyd	Martina Navratilova	6–3, 2–6, 6–3
1983	Martina Navratilova	Kathy Jordan	6–2, 7–6
1984	Chris Evert Lloyd	Helena Sukova	6–7, 6–1, 6–3
1985 (Dec)	Martina Navratilova	Chris Evert Lloyd	6–2, 4–6, 6–2
1987 (Jan)	Hana Mandlikova	Martina Navratilova	7–5, 7–6
1988	Steffi Graf	Chris Evert	6–1, 7–6
1989	Steffi Graf	Helena Sukova	6–4, 6–4
1990	Steffi Graf	Mary Joe Fernandez	6–3, 6–4
1991	Monica Seles	Jana Novotna	5–7, 6–3, 6–1

*Became Open (amateur and professional) in 1969.

WOMEN *(Cont.)*

Australian Championships *(Cont.)*

Year	Winner	Finalist	Score
1992	Monica Seles	Mary Joe Fernandez	6–2, 6–3
1993	Monica Seles	Steffi Graf	4–6, 6–3, 6–2
1994	Steffi Graf	Arantxa Sánchez Vicario	6–0, 6–2
1995	Mary Pierce	Arantxa Sánchez Vicario	6–3, 6–2
1996	Monica Seles	Anke Huber	6–4, 6–1
1997	Martina Hingis	Mary Pierce	6–2, 6–2
1998	Martina Hingis	Conchita Martinez	6–3, 6–3
1999	Martina Hingis	Amelie Mauresmo	6–2, 6–3
2000	Lindsay Davenport	Martina Hingis	6–1, 7–5
2001	Jennifer Capriati	Martina Hingis	6–4, 6–3
2002	Jennifer Capriati	Martina Hingis	4–6, 7–6 (9–7), 6–2
2003	Serena Williams	Venus Williams	7–6 (7-4), 3–6, 6–4
2004	Justine Henin-Hardenne	Kim Clijsters	6–3, 4–6, 6–3
2005	Serena Williams	Lindsay Davenport	2–6, 6–3, 6–0
2006	Amelie Mauresmo	Justine Henin-Hardenne	6–1, 2–0, ret.
2007	Serena Williams	Maria Sharapova	6–1, 6–2
2008	Maria Sharapova	Ana Ivanovic	7–5, 6–3

French Championships

Year	Winner	Finalist	Score
1925†	Suzanne Lenglen	Kathleen McKane	6–1, 6–2
1926	Suzanne Lenglen	Mary K. Browne	6–1, 6–0
1927	Kea Bouman	Irene Peacock	6–2, 6–4
1928	Helen Wills	Eileen Bennett	6–1, 6–2
1929	Helen Wills	Simone Mathieu	6–3, 6–4
1930	Helen Wills Moody	Helen Jacobs	6–2, 6–1
1931	Cilly Aussem	Betty Nuthall	8–6, 6–1
1932	Helen Wills Moody	Simone Mathieu	7–5, 6–1
1933	Margaret Scriven	Simone Mathieu	6–2, 4–6, 6–4
1934	Margaret Scriven	Helen Jacobs	7–5, 4–6, 6–1
1935	Hilde Sperling	Simone Mathieu	6–2, 6–1
1936	Hilde Sperling	Simone Mathieu	6–3, 6–4
1937	Hilde Sperling	Simone Mathieu	6–2, 6–4
1938	Simone Mathieu	Nelly Landry	6–0, 6–3
1939	Simone Mathieu	Jadwiga Jedrzejowska	6–3, 8–6
1940–45	No tournament		
1946	Margaret Osborne	Pauline Betz	1–6, 8–6, 7–5
1947	Patricia Todd	Doris Hart	6–3, 3–6, 6–4
1948	Nelly Landry	Shirley Fry	6–2, 0–6, 6–0
1949	Margaret Osborne duPont	Nelly Adamson	7–5, 6–2
1950	Doris Hart	Patricia Todd	6–4, 4–6, 6–2
1951	Shirley Fry	Doris Hart	6–3, 3–6, 6–3
1952	Doris Hart	Shirley Fry	6–4, 6–4
1953	Maureen Connolly	Doris Hart	6–2, 6–4
1954	Maureen Connolly	Ginette Bucaille	6–4, 6–1
1955	Angela Mortimer	Dorothy Knode	2–6, 7–5, 10–8
1956	Althea Gibson	Angela Mortimer	6–0, 12–10
1957	Shirley Bloomer	Dorothy Knode	6–1, 6–3
1958	Zsuzsi Kormoczi	Shirley Bloomer	6–4, 1–6, 6–2
1959	Christine Truman	Zsuzsi Kormoczi	6–4, 7–5
1960	Darlene Hard	Yola Ramirez	6–3, 6–4
1961	Ann Haydon	Yola Ramirez	6–2, 6–1
1962	Margaret Smith	Lesley Turner	6–3, 3–6, 7–5
1963	Lesley Turner	Ann Haydon Jones	2–6, 6–3, 7–5
1964	Margaret Smith	Maria Bueno	5–7, 6–1, 6–2
1965	Lesley Turner	Margaret Smith	6–3, 6–4
1966	Ann Jones	Nancy Richey	6–3, 6–1
1967	Francoise Durr	Lesley Turner	4–6, 6–3, 6–4
1968*	Nancy Richey	Ann Jones	5–7, 6–4, 6–1
1969	Margaret Smith Court	Ann Jones	6–1, 4–6, 6–3
1970	Margaret Smith Court	Helga Niessen	6–2, 6–4

†1925 was the first year that entries were accepted from all countries. *Became Open (amateur and professional) in 1968, but restricted to only contract professionals in1972.

WOMEN (Cont.)

French Championships (Cont.)

Year	Winner	Finalist	Score
1971	Evonne Goolagong	Helen Gourlay	6–3, 7–5
1972	Billie Jean King	Evonne Goolagong	6–3, 6–3
1973	Margaret Smith Court	Chris Evert	6–7, 7–6, 6–4
1974	Chris Evert	Olga Morozova	6–1, 6–2
1975	Chris Evert	Martina Navratilova	2–6, 6–2, 6–1
1976	Sue Barker	Renata Tomanova	6–2, 0–6, 6–2
1977	Mima Jausovec	Florenza Mihai	6–2, 6–7, 6–1
1978	Virginia Ruzici	Mima Jausovec	6–2, 6–2
1979	Chris Evert Lloyd	Wendy Turnbull	6–2, 6–0
1980	Chris Evert Lloyd	Virginia Ruzici	6–0, 6–3
1981	Hana Mandlikova	Sylvia Hanika	6–2, 6–4
1982	Martina Navratilova	Andrea Jaeger	7–6, 6–1
1983	Chris Evert Lloyd	Mima Jausovec	6–1, 6–2
1984	Martina Navratilova	Chris Evert Lloyd	6–3, 6–1
1985	Chris Evert Lloyd	Martina Navratilova	6–3, 6–7, 7–5
1986	Chris Evert Lloyd	Martina Navratilova	2–6, 6–3, 6–3
1987	Steffi Graf	Martina Navratilova	6–4, 4–6, 8–6
1988	Steffi Graf	Natalia Zvereva	6–0, 6–0
1989	Arantxa Sánchez Vicario	Steffi Graf	7–6, 3–6, 7–5
1990	Monica Seles	Steffi Graf	7–6, 6–4
1991	Monica Seles	Arantxa Sánchez Vicario	6–3, 6–4
1992	Monica Seles	Steffi Graf	6–2, 3–6, 10–8
1993	Steffi Graf	Mary Joe Fernandez	4–6, 6–2, 6–4
1994	Arantxa Sánchez Vicario	Mary Pierce	6–4, 6–4
1995	Steffi Graf	Arantxa Sánchez Vicario	7–5, 4–6, 6–0
1996	Steffi Graf	Arantxa Sánchez Vicario	6–3, 6–7 (4–7), 10–8
1997	Iva Majoli	Martina Hingis	6–4, 6–2
1998	Arantxa Sánchez Vicario	Monica Seles	7–6 (7–5), 0–6, 6–2
1999	Steffi Graf	Martina Hingis	4–6, 7–5, 6–2
2000	Mary Pierce	Conchita Martinez	6–2, 7–5
2001	Jennifer Capriati	Kim Clijsters	1–6, 6–4, 12–10
2002	Serena Williams	Venus Williams	7–5, 6–3
2003	Justine Henin-Hardenne	Kim Clijsters	6–0, 6–4
2004	Anastasia Myskina	Elena Dementieva	6–1, 6–2
2005	Justine Henin-Hardenne	Mary Pierce	6–1, 6–1
2006	Justine Henin-Hardenne	Svetlana Kuznetsova	6–4, 6–4
2007	Justine Henin	Ana Ivanovic	6–1, 6–2
2008	Ana Ivanovic	Dinara Safina	6–4, 6–3

Wimbledon Championships

Year	Winner	Finalist	Score
1884	Maud Watson	Lilian Watson	6–8, 6–3, 6–3
1885	Maud Watson	Blanche Bingley	6–1, 7–5
1886	Blanche Bingley	Maud Watson	6–3, 6–3
1887	Charlotte Dod	Blanche Bingley	6–2, 6–0
1888	Charlotte Dod	Blanche Bingley Hillyard	6–3, 6–3
1889	Blanche Bingley Hillyard	n/a	n/a
1890	Lena Rice	n/a	n/a
1891	Charlotte Dod	n/a	n/a
1892	Charlotte Dod	Blanche Bingley Hillyard	6–1, 6–1
1893	Charlotte Dod	Blanche Bingley Hillyard	6–8, 6–1, 6–4
1894	Blanche Bingley Hillyard	n/a	n/a
1895	Charlotte Cooper	n/a	
1896	Charlotte Cooper	Mrs. W. H. Pickering	6–2, 6–3
1897	Blanche Bingley Hillyard	Charlotte Cooper	5–7, 7–5, 6–2
1898	Charlotte Cooper	n/a	n/a
1899	Blanche Bingley Hillyard	Charlotte Cooper	6–2, 6–3
1900	Blanche Bingley Hillyard	Charlotte Cooper	4–6, 6–4, 6–4
1901	Charlotte Cooper Sterry	Blanche Bingley Hillyard	6–2, 6–2
1902	Muriel Robb	Charlotte Cooper Sterry	7–5, 6–1
1903	Dorothea Douglass	n/a	n/a
1904	Dorothea Douglass	Charlotte Cooper Sterry	6–0, 6–3
1905	May Sutton	Dorothea Douglass	6–3, 6–4
1906	Dorothea Douglass	May Sutton	6–3, 9–7

Grand Slam Tournaments *(Cont.)*

WOMEN *(Cont.)*

Wimbledon Championships *(Cont.)*

Year	Winner	Finalist	Score
1907	May Sutton	Dorothea Douglass Lambert Chambers	6–1, 6–4
1908	Charlotte Cooper Sterry	n/a	n/a
1909	Dora Boothby	n/a	n/a
1910	Dorothea Douglass Lambert Chambers	Dora Boothby	6–2, 6–2
1911	Dorothea Douglass Lambert Chambers	Dora Boothby	6–0, 6–0
1912	Ethel Larcombe	n/a	n/a
1913	Dorothea Douglass Lambert Chambers		
1914	Dorothea Douglass Lambert Chambers	Ethel Larcombe	7–5, 6–4
1915–18	No tournament		
1919	Suzanne Lenglen	Dorothea Douglass Lambert Chambers	10–8, 4–6, 9–7
1920	Suzanne Lenglen	Dorothea Douglass Lambert Chambers	6–3, 6–0
1921	Suzanne Lenglen	Elizabeth Ryan	6–2, 6–0
1922	Suzanne Lenglen	Molla Mallory	6–2, 6–0
1923	Suzanne Lenglen	Kathleen McKane	6–2, 6–2
1924	Kathleen McKane	Helen Wills	4–6, 6–4, 6–2
1925	Suzanne Lenglen	Joan Fry	6–2, 6–0
1926	Kathleen McKane Godfree	Lili de Alvarez	6–2, 4–6, 6–3
1927	Helen Wills	Lili de Alvarez	6–2, 6–4
1928	Helen Wills	Lili de Alvarez	6–2, 6–3
1929	Helen Wills	Helen Jacobs	6–1, 6–2
1930	Helen Wills Moody	Elizabeth Ryan	6–2, 6–2
1931	Cilly Aussem	Hilde Kranwinkel	7–5, 7–5
1932	Helen Wills Moody	Helen Jacobs	6–3, 6–1
1933	Helen Wills Moody	Dorothy Round	6–4, 6–8, 6–3
1934	Dorothy Round	Helen Jacobs	6–2, 5–7, 6–3
1935	Helen Wills Moody	Helen Jacobs	6–3, 3–6, 7–5
1936	Helen Jacobs	Hilde Kranwinkel Sperling	6–2, 4–6, 7–5
1937	Dorothy Round	Jadwiga Jedrzejowska	6–2, 2–6, 7–5
1938	Helen Wills Moody	Helen Jacobs	6–4, 6–0
1939	Alice Marble	Kay Stammers	6–2, 6–0
1940–45	No tournament		
1946	Pauline Betz	Louise Brough	6–2, 6–4
1947	Margaret Osborne	Doris Hart	6–2, 6–4
1948	Louise Brough	Doris Hart	6–3, 8–6
1949	Louise Brough	Margaret Osborne duPont	10–8, 1–6, 10–8
1950	Louise Brough	Margaret Osborne duPont	6–1, 3–6, 6–1
1951	Doris Hart	Shirley Fry	6–1, 6–0
1952	Maureen Connolly	Louise Brough	6–4, 6–3
1953	Maureen Connolly	Doris Hart	8–6, 7–5
1954	Maureen Connolly	Louise Brough	6–2, 7–5
1955	Louise Brough	Beverly Fleitz	7–5, 8–6
1956	Shirley Fry	Angela Buxton	6–3, 6–1
1957	Althea Gibson	Darlene Hard	6–3, 6–2
1958	Althea Gibson	Angela Mortimer	8–6, 6–2
1959	Maria Bueno	Darlene Hard	6–4, 6–3
1960	Maria Bueno	Sandra Reynolds	8–6, 6–0
1961	Angela Mortimer	Christine Truman	4–6, 6–4, 7–5
1962	Karen Hantze Susman	Vera Sukova	6–4, 6–4
1963	Margaret Smith	Billie Jean Moffitt	6–3, 6–4
1964	Maria Bueno	Margaret Smith	6–4, 7–9, 6–3
1965	Margaret Smith	Maria Bueno	6–4, 7–5
1966	Billie Jean King	Maria Bueno	6–3, 3–6, 6–1
1967	Billie Jean King	Ann Haydon Jones	6–3, 6–4
1968*	Billie Jean King	Judy Tegart	9–7, 7–5
1969	Ann Haydon Jones	Billie Jean King	3–6, 6–3, 6–2

Note: Prior to 1922 the tournament was run on a challenge-round system. The previous year's winner "stood out" of an All-Comers event, which produced a challenger to play her for the title.

*Became Open (amateur and professional) in 1968, but restricted to only contract professionals in 1972.

WOMEN (Cont.)

Wimbledon Championships (Cont.)

Year	Winner	Finalist	Score
1970	Margaret Smith Court	Billie Jean King	14–12, 11–9
1971	Evonne Goolagong	Margaret Smith Court	6–4, 6–1
1972	Billie Jean King	Evonne Goolagong	6–3, 6–3
1973	Billie Jean King	Chris Evert	6–0, 7–5
1974	Chris Evert	Olga Morozova	6–0, 6–4
1975	Billie Jean King	Evonne Goolagong Cawley	6–0, 6–1
1976	Chris Evert	Evonne Goolagong Cawley	6–3, 4–6, 8–6
1977	Virginia Wade	Betty Stove	4–6, 6–3, 6–1
1978	Martina Navratilova	Chris Evert	2–6, 6–4, 7–5
1979	Martina Navratilova	Chris Evert Lloyd	6–4, 6–4
1980	Evonne Goolagong Cawley	Chris Evert Lloyd	6–1, 7–6
1981	Chris Evert Lloyd	Hana Mandlikova	6–2, 6–2
1982	Martina Navratilova	Chris Evert Lloyd	6–1, 3–6, 6–2
1983	Martina Navratilova	Andrea Jaeger	6–0, 6–3
1984	Martina Navratilova	Chris Evert Lloyd	7–6, 6–2
1985	Martina Navratilova	Chris Evert Lloyd	4–6, 6–3, 6–2
1986	Martina Navratilova	Hana Mandlikova	7–6, 6–3
1987	Martina Navratilova	Steffi Graf	7–5, 6–3
1988	Steffi Graf	Martina Navratilova	5–7, 6–2, 6–1
1989	Steffi Graf	Martina Navratilova	6–2, 6–7, 6–1
1990	Martina Navratilova	Zina Garrison	6–4, 6–1
1991	Steffi Graf	Gabriela Sabatini	6–4, 3–6, 8–6
1992	Steffi Graf	Monica Seles	6–2, 6–1
1993	Steffi Graf	Jana Novotna	7–6, 1–6, 6–4
1994	Conchita Martinez	Martina Navratilova	6–4, 3–6, 6–3
1995	Steffi Graf	Arantxa Sánchez Vicario	4–6, 6–1, 7–5
1996	Steffi Graf	Arantxa Sánchez Vicario	6–3, 7–5
1997	Martina Hingis	Jana Novotna	2–6, 6–3, 6–3
1998	Jana Novotna	Nathalie Tauziat	6–4, 7–6
1999	Lindsay Davenport	Steffi Graf	6–4, 7–5
2000	Venus Williams	Lindsay Davenport	6–3, 7–6
2001	Venus Williams	Justine Henin	6–1, 3–6, 6–0
2002	Serena Williams	Venus Williams	7–6 (7–4), 6–3
2003	Serena Williams	Venus Williams	4–6, 6–4, 6–2
2004	Maria Sharapova	Serena Williams	6–1, 6–4
2005	Venus Williams	Lindsay Davenport	4–6, 7–6 (7–4), 9–7
2006	Amelie Mauresmo	Justine Henin-Hardenne	2–6, 6–3, 6–4
2007	Venus Williams	Marion Bartoli	6–4, 6–1
2008	Venus Williams	Serena Williams	7–5, 6–4

United States Championships

Year	Winner	Finalist	Score
1887	Ellen Hansell	Laura Knight	6–1, 6–0
1888	Bertha L. Townsend	Ellen Hansell	6–3, 6–5
1889	Bertha L. Townsend	Louise Voorhes	7–5, 6–2
1890	Ellen C. Roosevelt	Bertha L. Townsend	6–2, 6–2
1891	Mabel Cahill	Ellen C. Roosevelt	6–4, 6–1, 4–6, 6–3
1892	Mabel Cahill	Elisabeth Moore	5–7, 6–3, 6–4, 4–6, 6–2
1893	Aline Terry	Alice Schultze	6–1, 6–3
1894	Helen Hellwig	Aline Terry	7–5, 3–6, 6–0, 3–6, 6–3
1895	Juliette Atkinson	Helen Hellwig	6–4, 6–2, 6–1
1896	Elisabeth Moore	Juliette Atkinson	6–4, 4–6, 6–2, 6–2
1897	Juliette Atkinson	Elisabeth Moore	6–3, 6–3, 4–6, 3–6, 6–3
1898	Juliette Atkinson	Marion Jones	6–3, 5–7, 6–4, 2–6, 7–5
1899	Marion Jones	Maud Banks	6–1, 6–1, 7–5
1900	Myrtle McAteer	Edith Parker	6–2, 6–2, 6–0
1901	Elisabeth Moore	Myrtle McAteer	6–4, 3–6, 7–5, 2–6, 6–2
1902*	Marion Jones	Elisabeth Moore	6–1, 1–0, ret.
1903	Elisabeth Moore	Marion Jones	7–5, 8–6
1904	May Sutton	Elisabeth Moore	6–1, 6–2
1905	Elisabeth Moore	Helen Homans	6–4, 5–7, 6–1
1906	Helen Homans	Maud Barger-Wallach	6–4, 6–3
1907	Evelyn Sears	Carrie Neely	6–3, 6–2
1908	Maud Barger-Wallach	Evelyn Sears	6–3, 1–6, 6–3
1909	Hazel Hotchkiss	Maud Barger-Wallach	6–0, 6–1

*Five-set final abolished;

WOMEN (Cont.)

United States Championships (Cont.)

Year	Winner	Finalist	Score
1910	Hazel Hotchkiss	Louise Hammond	6–4, 6–2
1911	Hazel Hotchkiss	Florence Sutton	8–10, 6–1, 9–7
1912†	Mary K. Browne	Eleanora Sears	6–4, 6–2
1913	Mary K. Browne	Dorothy Green	6–2, 7–5
1914	Mary K. Browne	Marie Wagner	6–2, 1–6, 6–1
1915	Molla Bjurstedt	Hazel Hotchkiss Wightman	4–6, 6–2, 6–0
1916	Molla Bjurstedt	Louise Hammond Raymond	6–0, 6–1
1917‡	Molla Bjurstedt	Marion Vanderhoef	4–6, 6–0, 6–2
1918	Molla Bjurstedt	Eleanor Goss	6–4, 6–3
1919	Hazel Hotchkiss Wightman	Marion Zinderstein	6–1, 6–2
1920	Molla Bjurstedt Mallory	Marion Zinderstein	6–3, 6–1
1921	Molla Bjurstedt Mallory	Mary K. Browne	4–6, 6–4, 6–2
1922	Molla Bjurstedt Mallory	Helen Wills	6–3, 6–1
1923	Helen Wills	Molla Bjurstedt Mallory	6–2, 6–1
1924	Helen Wills	Molla Bjurstedt Mallory	6–1, 6–3
1925	Helen Wills	Kathleen McKane	3–6, 6–0, 6–2
1926	Molla Bjurstedt Mallory	Elizabeth Ryan	4–6, 6–4, 9–7
1927	Helen Wills	Betty Nuthall	6–1, 6–4
1928	Helen Wills	Helen Jacobs	6–2, 6–1
1929	Helen Wills	Phoebe Holcroft Watson	6–4, 6–2
1930	Betty Nuthall	Anna McCune Harper	6–1, 6–4
1931	Helen Wills Moody	Eileen Whitingstall	6–4, 6–1
1932	Helen Jacobs	Carolin Babcock	6–2, 6–2
1933	Helen Jacobs	Helen Wills Moody	8–6, 3–6, 3–0, ret.
1934	Helen Jacobs	Sarah Palfrey	6–1, 6–4
1935	Helen Jacobs	Sarah Palfrey Fabyan	6–2, 6–4
1936	Alice Marble	Helen Jacobs	4–6, 6–3, 6–2
1937	Anita Lizane	Jadwiga Jedrzejowska	6–4, 6–2
1938	Alice Marble	Nancye Wynne	6–0, 6–3
1939	Alice Marble	Helen Jacobs	6–0, 8–10, 6–4
1940	Alice Marble	Helen Jacobs	6–2, 6–3
1941	Sarah Palfrey Cooke	Pauline Betz	7–5, 6–2
1942	Pauline Betz	Louise Brough	4–6, 6–1, 6–4
1943	Pauline Betz	Louise Brough	6–3, 5–7, 6–3
1944	Pauline Betz	Margaret Osborne	6–3, 8–6
1945	Sarah Palfrey Cooke	Pauline Betz	3–6, 8–6, 6–4
1946	Pauline Betz	Patricia Canning	11–9, 6–3
1947	Louise Brough	Margaret Osborne	8–6, 4–6, 6–1
1948	Margaret Osborne duPont	Louise Brough	4–6, 6–4, 15–13
1949	Margaret Osborne duPont	Doris Hart	6–4, 6–1
1950	Margaret Osborne duPont	Doris Hart	6–4, 6–3
1951	Maureen Connolly	Shirley Fry	6–3, 1–6, 6–4
1952	Maureen Connolly	Doris Hart	6–3, 7–5
1953	Maureen Connolly	Doris Hart	6–2, 6–4
1954	Doris Hart	Louise Brough	6–8, 6–1, 8–6
1955	Doris Hart	Patricia Ward	6–4, 6–2
1956	Shirley Fry	Althea Gibson	6–3, 6–4
1957	Althea Gibson	Louise Brough	6–3, 6–2
1958	Althea Gibson	Darlene Hard	3–6, 6–1, 6–2
1959	Maria Bueno	Christine Truman	6–1, 6–4
1960	Darlene Hard	Maria Bueno	6–4, 10–12, 6–4
1961	Darlene Hard	Ann Haydon	6–3, 6–4
1962	Margaret Smith	Darlene Hard	9–7, 6–4
1963	Maria Bueno	Margaret Smith	7–5, 6–4
1964	Maria Bueno	Carole Graebner	6–1, 6–0
1965	Margaret Smith	Billie Jean Moffitt	8–6, 7–5
1966	Maria Bueno	Nancy Richey	6–3, 6–1
1967	Billie Jean King	Ann Haydon Jones	11–9, 6–4
1968**	Virginia Wade	Billie Jean King	6–4, 6–4
1968#	Margaret Smith Court	Maria Bueno	6–2, 6–2
1969	Margaret Smith Court	Nancy Richey	6–2, 6–2
1969#	Margaret Smith Court	Virginia Wade	4–6, 6–3, 6–0

†Challenge round abolished. ‡National Patriotic Tournament.
**Became Open (amateur and professional) in 1968. #Amateur event held.

Grand Slam Tournaments *(Cont.)*

WOMEN *(Cont.)*

United States Championships *(Cont.)*

Year	Winner	Finalist	Score
1970	Margaret Smith Court	Rosie Casals	6–2, 2–6, 6–1
1971	Billie Jean King	Rosie Casals	6–4, 7–6
1972	Billie Jean King	Kerry Melville	6–3, 7–5
1973	Margaret Smith Court	Evonne Goolagong	7–6, 5–7, 6–2
1974	Billie Jean King	Evonne Goolagong	3–6, 6–3, 7–5
1975	Chris Evert	Evonne Goolagong Cawley	5–7, 6–4, 6–2
1976	Chris Evert	Evonne Goolagong Cawley	6–3, 6–0
1977	Chris Evert	Wendy Turnbull	7–6, 6–2
1978	Chris Evert	Pam Shriver	7–6, 6–4
1979	Tracy Austin	Chris Evert Lloyd	6–4, 6–3
1980	Chris Evert Lloyd	Hana Mandlikova	5–7, 6–1, 6–1
1981	Tracy Austin	Martina Navratilova	1–6, 7–6, 7–6
1982	Chris Evert Lloyd	Hana Mandlikova	6–3, 6–1
1983	Martina Navratilova	Chris Evert Lloyd	6–1, 6–3
1984	Martina Navratilova	Chris Evert Lloyd	4–6, 6–4, 6–4
1985	Hana Mandlikova	Martina Navratilova	7–6, 1–6, 7–6
1986	Martina Navratilova	Helena Sukova	6–3, 6–2
1987	Martina Navratilova	Steffi Graf	7–6, 6–1
1988	Steffi Graf	Gabriela Sabatini	6–3, 3–6, 6–1
1989	Steffi Graf	Martina Navratilova	3–6, 6–4, 6–2
1990	Gabriela Sabatini	Steffi Graf	6–2, 7–6
1991	Monica Seles	Martina Navratilova	7–6, 6–1
1992	Monica Seles	Arantxa Sánchez Vicario	6–3, 6–2
1993	Steffi Graf	Helena Sukova	6–3, 6–3
1994	Arantxa Sánchez Vicario	Steffi Graf	1–6, 7–6, 6–4
1995	Steffi Graf	Monica Seles	7–6, 0–6, 6–3
1996	Steffi Graf	Monica Seles	7–5, 7–4
1997	Martina Hingis	Venus Williams	6–0, 6–4
1998	Lindsay Davenport	Martina Hingis	6–3, 7–5
1999	Serena Williams	Martina Hingis	6–3, 7–6
2000	Venus Williams	Lindsay Davenport	6–4, 7–5
2001	Venus Williams	Serena Williams	6–2, 6–4
2002	Serena Williams	Venus Williams	6–4, 6–3
2003	Justine Henin-Hardenne	Kim Clijsters	7–5, 6–1
2004	Svetlana Kuznetsova	Elena Dementieva	6–3, 7–5
2005	Kim Clijsters	Mary Pierce	6–3, 6–1
2006	Maria Sharapova	Justine Henin-Hardenne	6–4, 6–4
2007	Justine Henin	Svetlana Kuznetsova	6–1, 6–3
2008	Serena Williams	Jelena Jankovic	6–4, 7–5

Single-Year Grand Slam Winners

Singles

Don Budge, 1938
Maureen Connolly, 1953
Rod Laver, 1962, 1969
Margaret Smith Court, 1970
Steffi Graf, 1988

Doubles

Frank Sedgman and Ken McGregor, 1951
Martina Navratilova and Pam Shriver, 1984
Maria Bueno and two partners, 1960
 Christine Truman (Australian),
 Darlene Hard (French, Wimbledon and U.S.)
Martina Hingis and two partners, 1998
 Mirjana Lucic (Australian),
 Jana Novotna (French, Wimbledon and U.S.)

Mixed Doubles

Margaret Smith and Ken Fletcher, 1963
Owen Davidson and two partners, 1967
 Lesley Turner (Australian),
 Billie Jean King (French, Wimbledon and U.S.)

Alltime Grand Slam Champions

Alltime Grand Slam Champions (Singles, Doubles, Mixed Doubles)

MEN

Player	Aus. S-D-M	French S-D-M	Wim. S-D-M	U.S. S-D-M	Total
Roy Emerson	6-3-0	2-6-0	2-3-0	2-4-0	28
John Newcombe	2-5-0	0-3-0	3-6-0	2-3-1	25
Frank Sedgman	2-2-2	0-3-2	1-2-2	2-2-2	22
Todd Woodbridge	0-3-1	0-1-1	0-9-1	0-3-3	22
Bill Tilden	†	0-0-1	3-1-0	7-5-4	21
Rod Laver	3-4-0	2-1-1	4-1-2	2-0-0	20
John Bromwich	2-8-1	0-0-0	0-2-2	0-3-1	19
Jean Borotra	1-1-1	1-5-2	2-3-1	0-0-1	18
Fred Stolle	0-3-1	1-2-0	0-2-3	1-3-2	18
Ken Rosewall	4-3-0	2-2-0	0-2-0	2-2-1	18
Neale Fraser	0-3-1	0-3-0	1-2-0	2-3-3	18
Adrian Quist	3-10-0	0-1-0	0-2-0	0-1-0	17
John McEnroe	0-0-0	0-0-1	3-4-0	4-5-0	17
Jack Crawford	4-4-3	1-1-1	1-1-1	0-0-0	17
Mark Woodforde	0-2-2	0-1-1	0-6-1	0-3-1	17

†Did not compete.

WOMEN

Player	Aus. S-D-M	French S-D-M	Wim. S-D-M	U.S. S-D-M	Total
Margaret Smith Court	11-8-2	5-4-4	3-2-5	5-5-8	62
Martina Navratilova	3-8-1	2-7-2	9-7-4	4-9-3	59
Billie Jean King	1-0-1	1-1-2	6-10-4	4-5-4	39
Doris Hart	1-1-2	2-5-3	1-4-5	2-4-5	35
Helen Wills Moody	†	4-2-0	8-3-1	7-4-2	31
Louise Brough	1-1-0	0-3-0	4-5-4	1-8-3	30**
Margaret Osborne duPont	†	2-3-0	1-5-1	3-8-6	29**
Elizabeth Ryan	†	0-4-0	0-12-7	0-1-2	26
Steffi Graf	4-0-0	6-0-0	7-1-0	5-0-0	23
Pam Shriver	0-7-0	0-4-1	0-5-0	0-5-0	22
Chris Evert	2-0-0	7-2-0	3-1-0	6-0-0	21
Darlene Hard	†	1-3-2	0-4-3	2-6-0	21
Suzanne Lenglen	†	2-2-2#	6-6-3	0-0-0	21
Nancye Wynne Bolton	6-10-4	0-0-0	0-0-0	0-0-0	20
Maria Bueno	0-1-0	0-1-1	3-5-0	4-4-0	19
Thelma Coyne Long	2-12-4	0-0-1	0-0-0	0-0-0	19

*Active player in 2008. †Did not compete. #Suzanne Lenglen also won four singles titles at the French Championships before 1925, when competition was first opened to entries from all nations.**From 1940–45, with competition in the U.S. Championships thinned due to wartime constraints, Louise Brough Clapp also won four doubles titles (1942–45) and one mixed doubles title (1942); and Margaret Osborne duPont won five doubles titles (1941–45) and three mixed doubles titles (1943–45).

Alltime Grand Slam Singles Champions

MEN

Player	Aus.	French	Wim.	U.S.	Total
Pete Sampras	2	0	7	5	14
*Roger Federer	3	0	5	5	13
Roy Emerson	6	2	2	2	12
Bjorn Borg	0	6	5	0	11
Rod Laver	3	2	4	2	11
Bill Tilden	†	0	3	7	10
Jimmy Connors	1	0	2	5	8
Ivan Lendl	2	3	0	3	8
Fred Perry	1	1	3	3	8
Ken Rosewall	4	2	0	2	8
Andre Agassi	4	1	1	2	8
Henri Cochet	†	4	2	1	7
Rene Lacoste	†	3	2	2	7
Bill Larned	†	†	0	7	7
John McEnroe	0	0	3	4	7
John Newcombe	2	0	3	2	7
Willie Renshaw	†	†	7	†	7
Dick Sears	†	†	0	7	7

WOMEN

Player	Aus.	French	Wim.	U.S.	Total
Margaret Smith Court	11	5	3	5	24
Steffi Graf	4	6	7	5	22
Helen Wills Moody	†	4	8	7	19
Chris Evert	2	7	3	6	18
Martina Navratilova	3	2	9	4	18
Billie Jean King	1	1	6	4	12
Maureen Connolly	1	2	3	3	9
Monica Seles	4	3	0	2	9
*Serena Williams	3	1	2	3	9
Suzanne Lenglen	†	2#	6	0	8
Molla Bjurstedt Mallory	†	†	0	8	8
Maria Bueno	0	0	3	4	7
Evonne Goolagong	4	1	2	0	7
Dorothea D.L. Chambers	†	†	7	0	7
*Justine Henin	1	4	0	2	7
*Venus Williams	0	0	5	2	7

*Active player in 2008. †Did not compete.
#Suzanne Lenglen also won four singles titles at the French Championships before 1925, when competition was first opened to entries from all nations.

Golf

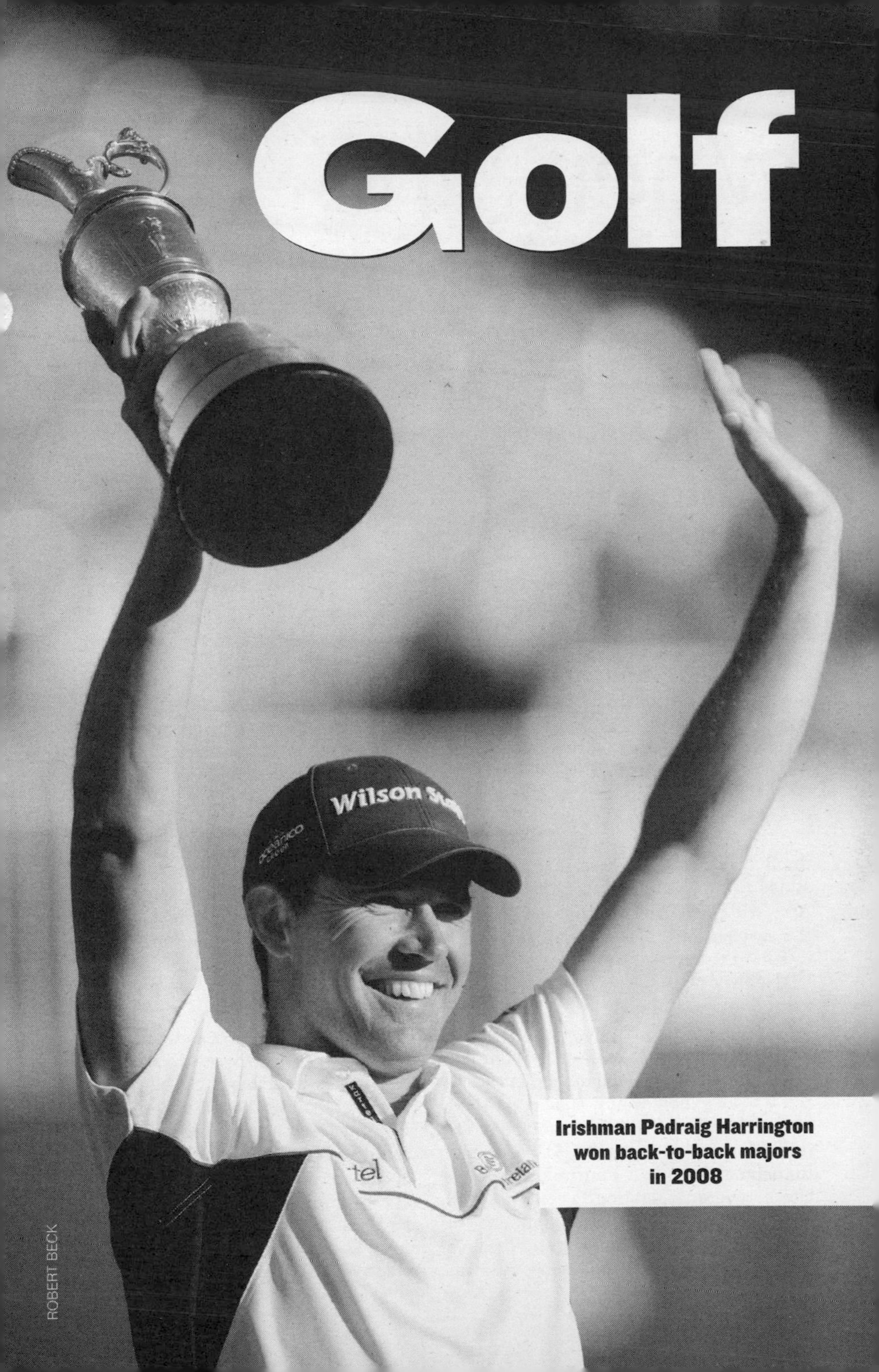

Irishman Padraig Harrington won back-to-back majors in 2008

ROBERT BECK

When The Cat's Away...

Tiger Woods and Lorena Ochoa began the season looking unbeatable, but injury and personal tragedy left the door open for the rest of the pack

BY MERRELL NODEN

AT THE START OF THE YEAR IT seemed possible that not one, but two golfers would win the elusive Grand Slam. Having won the final women's major of 2007, Lorena Ochoa looked even more dominant as the LPGA season got underway. She won five of her first six tournaments including the first major, the Kraft Nabisco Championship. The world's No. 1-ranked woman looked as capable of dominating her peers as Tiger Woods did his. Woods opened his season by winning the Buick Invitational by eight strokes. He added the Accenture Match Play and the Arnold Palmer Invitational. By the time the azaleas were blooming at Augusta, it was hard to see how anyone was going to beat either of these golfers in a tournament of consequence.

But the year did not go as expected. Woods played well at Augusta, but finished second to Trevor Immelman. Masters weekend was incredibly windy, making for some very high scores. On Sunday no one in the final 11 pairings managed to break par. Immelman, who just four months earlier had needed an operation to remove a golf ball-sized tumor from his diaphragm—it proved benign—shot three over for the final round. But under the conditions, that was enough to make him the first South African to win the Masters since Gary Player in 1978.

Two days later, Woods had surgery to repair torn cartilage in his left knee. Rehabbing it meant he could not play competitive golf until practice rounds for the U.S. Open began in mid-June, and even then he limited his play to just nine holes a day. If there were a way to compensate for his lack of practice, it was local knowledge. As kids, both Woods and world No. 2 Phil Mickelson played tons of golf at Torrey Pines, a muni set on the bluffs north of San Diego. At 7,643 yards it was easily the longest course ever to host a major. Mickelson was in it for only one round, finishing tied for 18th, leading many to question his decision to show up with no driver in his bag.

Replacing him as Tiger's foil was likeable Rocco Mediate, a garrulous, 45-year-old journeyman from Pennsylvania who has had his own share of injury woes. Eighteen months earlier, back trouble had put him in the Golf Channel broadcast booth. At Torrey Pines he clearly relished getting a second chance. He trailed Woods by two strokes going into Sunday's final round. But when Woods went three over for the first two holes, Mediate led the Open and never folded. Woods had to sink a 12-foot birdie putt on the 72nd hole to force a Monday playoff.

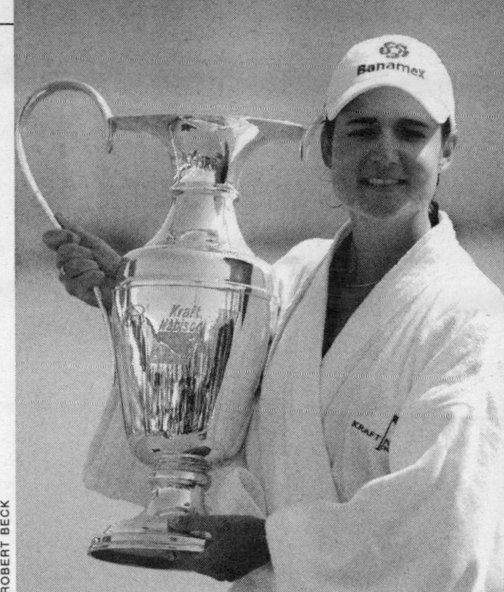

ROBERT BECK

Early in 2008, No. 1-ranked Lorena Ochoa won five of six tournaments and her second career major, at the Nabisco Championship.

He made it and the playoff was the most riveting 18 holes of golf all year. In the past, Tiger has won every which way, but that Monday playoff added "playing hurt" to the list. He grimaced, groaned, and hobbled off tees using his driver as a cane. Mediate birdied holes 13 through 15 to take a one-stroke lead, which he held to the 90th hole. Needing to sink another mid-length birdie putt to stay alive, Woods again produced magic. He beat Mediate on the 91st hole.

Two days later, Woods announced he'd been playing with a ruptured ACL and two stress fractures in his tibia. Opting for immediate reconstructive surgery, Woods said he would not compete, and perhaps not even swing a club, until 2009. Woods, of course, is famous for reinventing his swing several times in his career. But it was hard not to wonder whether he has one more reinvention in him, or whether he'll come back as a lesser player. After all, he's not Superman (is he?).

Ochoa, meanwhile, was having problems of her own. An uncle's death in May followed by her grandfather's death during the LPGA Championship left her devastated. Ochoa never looked like the dominating golfer she had been for most of the previous year. She led the LPGA at Bulle Rock after two rounds but finished tied for third (with Annika Sorenstam) behind 19-year-old Yani Tseng, who beat Maria Hjorth in a four-hole playoff. Ochoa would not win again until late September. Inbee Park won the U.S. Women's Open at Interlachen CC and Ji-Yai Shin won the British Women's Open at Sunningdale. Sorenstam, in what she says is her last competitive season, threatened at both the Nabisco and the LPGA. Reminding her fans of what they'll miss, she drilled a six iron 199 yards into the cup for an eagle on the final hole at Interlachen.

The men's British Open was held at Royal Birkdale. At 53, two-time champion Greg Norman played like his younger self, inspired, it seemed, by his recent marriage to Hall of Fame tennis star Chris Evert. Norman began the final round with a two stroke lead, which he frittered away with three opening bogeys before pulling himself together. After 65 holes, he shared the lead with defending champion Padraig Harrington, who had a sore wrist and had considered not playing at all. Good thing he chose to play: He shot a bogeyless 32 on the back nine, including two birdies and a spectacular eagle, to beat runnerup Ian Poulter by four. He became the first European to win consecutive British Opens. Norman finished tied for third, six strokes back.

Harrington was not finished. At the PGA at Oakland Hills poor Sergio Garcia, who had won the TPC and may yet break his winless streak at majors, was again Harrington's victim. He took the lead by holing a 10-foot putt for birdie on the 71st hole to win. That made three majors in 13 months for the likeable Irishman.

And it looks to be an intriguing 2009: Will Ochoa find her form again? Will Harrington extend his streak of majors? Will the rookies who helped guide the U.S. its first Ryder Cup in nine years make solo breakthroughs on the tour? And will Vijay Singh, who won the $10-million first prize in the FedEx Cup playoffs, return as Tiger's rival? Should be an interesting year.

FOR THE RECORD • 2007–2008

Men's Majors

The Masters

Augusta National GC (par 72; 7,445 yds); Augusta, Ga., April 3–6, 2008

Player	Score	Earnings ($)
Trevor Immelman	68-68-69-75--280	1,350,000
Tiger Woods	72-71-68-72--283	810,000
Brandt Snedeker	69-68-70-77--284	435,000
Stewart Cink	72-69-71-72--284	435,000
Padraig Harrington	74-71-69-72--286	273,750
Steve Flesch	72-67-69-78--286	273,750
Phil Mickelson	71-68-75-72--286	273,750
Miguel Angel Jimenez	77-70-72-68--287	217,500
Robert Karlsson	70-73-71-73--287	217,500
Andres Romero	72-72-70-73--287	217,500
Nick Watney	75-70-72-71--288	172,500
Paul Casey	71-69-69-79--288	172,500
Lee Westwood	69-73-73-73--288	172,500
Stuart Appleby	76-70-72-71--289	135,000
Sean O'Hair	72-71-71-75--289	135,000
Vijay Singh	72-71-72-74--289	135,000
Mike Weir	73-68-75-74--290	112,500
Henrik Stenson	74-72-72-72--290	112,500
Retief Goosen	71-71-72-76--290	112,500
Justin Leonard	72-74-72-73--291	84,300
Zach Johnson	70-76-68-77--291	84,300
Brian Bateman	69-76-72-74--291	84,300
Boo Weekley	72-74-68-77--291	84,300
Bubba Watson	74-71-73-73--291	84,300

U.S. Open

Torrey Pines GC (par 71; 7,643 yds); San Diego, Calif., June 12–15, 2008

Player	Score	Earnings ($)
*Tiger Woods	72-68-70-73-71--354	1,260,000
Rocco Mediate	69-71-72-71-71--354	730,667
Lee Westwood	70-71-70-73--284	491,995
Robert Karlsson	70-70-75-71--286	307,303
D.J. Trahan	72-69-73-72--286	307,303
Miguel Angel Jimenez	75-66-74-72--287	220,686
Carl Pettersson	71-71-77-68--287	220,686
John Merrick	73-72-71-71--287	220,686
Heath Slocum	75-74-74-65--288	160,769
Eric Axley	69-79-71-69--288	160,769
Geoff Ogilvy	69-73-72-74--288	160,769
Camilo Villegas	73-71-71-73--288	160,769
Brandt Snedeker	76-73-68-71--288	160,769
Rod Pampling	74-70-75-70--289	122,159
Stewart Cink	72-73-77-67--289	122,159
Retief Goosen	76-69-77-67--289	122,159
Ernie Els	70-72-74-73--289	122,159
Phil Mickelson	71-75-76-68--290	87,320
Ryuji Imada	74-75-70-71--290	87,320
Chad Campbell	77-72-71-70--290	87,320
Sergio Garcia	76-70-70-74--290	87,320
Mike Weir	73-74-69-74--290	87,320
Hunter Mahan	72-74-69-75--290	87,320
Robert Allenby	70-72-73-75--290	87,320
Brandt Jobe	73-75-69-73--290	87,320

*Won in first hole of sudden death after 18-hole playoff.

British Open

Royal Birkdale GC (par 72; 6,726 yds); Southport, England, July 17–20, 2008

Player	Score	Earnings ($)
Padraig Harrington	74-68-72-69--283	1,498,875
Ian Poulter	72-71-75-69–287	899,325
Greg Norman	70-70-72-77--289	509,618
Henrik Stenson	76-72-70-71--289	509,618
Jim Furyk	71-71-77-71--290	359,730
†Chris Wood	75-70-73-72--290	–
Ernie Els	80-69-74-69--292	193,743
David Howell	76-71-78-67--292	193,743
Ben Curtis	78-69-70-75--292	193,743
Paul Casey	78-71-73-70--292	193,743
Robert Karlsson	75-73-75-69--292	193,743
Steve Stricker	77-71-71-73--292	193,743
Robert Allenby	69-73-76-74--292	193,743
Anthony Kim	72-74-71-75--292	193,743
Stephen Ames	73-70-78-71--292	193,743
Justin Leonard	77-70-73-73--294	106,254
K.J. Choi	72-67-75-79--294	106,254
Adam Scott	70-74-77-72--294	106,254

PGA Championship

Oakland Hills CC (par 70; 7,395yds) Bloomfield Twp, Mich., August 4–10, 2008

Player	Score	Earnings ($)
Padraig Harrington	71-74-66-66--277	1,350,000
Sergio Garcia	69-73-69-68--279	660,000
Ben Curtis	73-67-68-71--279	660,000
Camilo Villegas	74-72-67-68--281	330,000
Henrik Stenson	71-70-68-72--281	330,000
Steve Flesch	73-70-70-69--282	270,000
Phil Mickelson	70-73-71-70--284	231,250
Andres Romero	69-78-65-72--284	231,250
Alastair Forsyth	73-72-70-70--285	176,725
Justin Rose	73-67-74-71--285	176,725
Jeev Milkha Singh	68-74-70-73--285	176,725
Charlie Wi	70-70-71-74--285	176,725
Ken Duke	69-73-73-71--286	137,250
Aaron Baddeley	71-71-71-73--286	137,250
Paul Casey	72-74-72-69--287	107,060
Stuart Appleby	76-70-69-72--287	107,060
Prayad Marksaeng	76-70-68-73--287	107,060
Graeme McDowell	74-72-68-73--287	107,060
David Toms	72-69-72-74--287	107,060
Brian Gay	70-74-72-72--288	78,900
Robert Karlsson	68-77-71-72--288	78,900
Angel Cabrera	70-72-72-74--288	78,900
Boo Weekley	72-71-79-66–288	78,900

† Amateur.

Men's Tour Results

Late 2007 PGA Tour Events

Tournament	Final Round	Winner	Score/ Under Par	Earnings ($)
*Valero Texas Open	Oct 7	Justin Leonard	261/-19	810,000
Frys.com Open	Oct 14	George McNeill	264/-23	720,000
Ginn sur Mer Classic	Oct 29	Daniel Chopra	273/-19	810,000
Children's Miracle Network Classic	Nov 4	Stephen Ames	271/-17	828,000

2008 PGA Tour Events

Tournament	Final Round	Winner	Score/ Under Par	Earnings ($)
*Mercedes-Benz Championship	Jan 6	Daniel Chopra	274/-18	1,100,000
Sony Open in Hawaii	Jan 13	K.J. Choi	266/-14	954,000
†Bob Hope Chrysler Classic	Jan 20	D.J. Trahan	334/-26	918,000
Buick Invitational	Jan 27	Tiger Woods	269/-19	936,000
*FBR Open	Feb 3	J.B. Holmes	270/-14	1,080,000
*AT&T Pebble Beach National Pro-Am	Feb 10	Steve Lowery	278/-10	1,080,000
Northern Trust Open	Feb 17	Phil Mickelson	272/-12	1,116,000
WGC Match Play Championship	Feb 24	Tiger Woods	2&1	1,350,000
Mayakoba Classic at Riviera Maya	Feb 24	Brian Gay	264/-16	630,000
Honda Classic	Mar 2	Ernie Els	274/-6	990,000
PODS Championship	Mar 9	Sean O'Hair	280/-4	954,000
Arnold Palmer Invitational	Mar 16	Tiger Woods	270/-10	1.044,000
Puerto Rico Open	Mar 23	Greg Kraft	274/-14	630,000
WGC-CA Championship	Mar 23	Geoff Ogilvy	271/-17	1,350,000
Zurich Classic	Mar 30	Andres Romero	275/-13	1,116,000
Shell Houston Open	Apr 6	Johnson Wagner	272/-16	1,008,000
The Masters	Apr 6	Trevor Immelman	280/-8	1,305,000
Verizon Heritage	Apr 20	Boo Weekley	269/-15	990,000
*EDS Byron Nelson Classic	Apr 27	Adam Scott	273/-7	1,152,000
Wachovia Championship	May 4	Anthony Kim	272/-16	1,152,000
*The Players Championship	May 11	Sergio Garcia	283/-5	1,710,000
*AT&T Classic	May 18	Ryuji Imada	273/-15	990,000
Crowne Plaza Invitational at Colonial	May 25	Phil Mickelson	266/-14	1,098,000
Memorial Tournament	June 1	Kenny Perry	280/-8	1,080,000
*St. Jude Championship	June 8	Justin Leonard	276/-4	1,080.000
*U.S. Open Championship	June 15	Tiger Woods	283/-1	1,350,000
Travelers Championship	June 22	Stewart Cink	262/-18	1,080,000
Buick Open	June 29	Kenny Perry	269/-19	900,000
AT&T National	July 6	Anthony Kim	268/-12	1,080,000
*John Deere Classic	July 13	Kenny Perry	268/-16	756,000
The Open Championship (British Open)	July 20	Padraig Harrington	283/+3	1,498,875
U.S. Bank Championship	July 20	Richard S. Johnson	264/-16	720,000
Canadian Open	July 27	Chez Reavie	267/-17	900,000
WGC Bridgestone Invitational	Aug 3	Vijay Singh	270/-10	1,350,000
Reno-Tahoe Open	Aug 3	Parker McLachlin	270/-18	540,000
PGA Championship	Aug 10	Padraig Harrington	277/-3	1,350,000
Wyndham Championship	Aug 17	Carl Pettersson	259/-21	918,000
*‡The Barclays	Aug 24	Vijay Singh	276/-8	1,260,000
‡Deutsche Bank Championship	Aug 31	Vijay Singh	262/-22	1,260,000
‡BMW Championship	Sept 7	Camilo Villegas	265/-15	1,260,000
Viking Classic	Sept 21	Will MacKenzie	269/-3	648,000
*‡TOUR Championship	Sept 28	Camilo Villegas	273/-7	1,260,000

* Won in playoff. † Five-round tournament. ‡Events part of four-tournament FedEx Cup, the PGA Tour's playoff format.

2008 FedEx Cup Playoff Results

Player	Points	Earnings ($)
1. Vijay Singh	125,101	10,000,000
2. Camilo Villegas	124,550	3,000,000
3. Sergio Garcia	119,400	2,000,000
4. Anthony Kim	114,419	1,500,000
5. Jim Furyk	113,180	1,000,000
6. Mike Weir	113,118	800,000
7. Phil Mickelson	112,201	700,000
8. Justin Leonard	111,638	600,000
9. Ben Curtis	110,702	550,000
10. K.J. Choi	110,646	500,000

Women's Majors

Kraft Nabisco Championship

Mission Hills CC; (par 72; 6,673 yds)
Rancho Mirage, Calif., April 3–6, 2008

Player	Score	Earnings ($)
Lorena Ochoa	68-71-71-67--277	300,000
Annika Sorenstam	71-70-73-68--282	160,369
Suzann Pettersen	74-75-65-68--282	160,369
Maria Hjorth	70-70-72-71--283	104,317
Seon Hwa Lee	73-71-68-72--284	83,963
Mi Hyun Kim	70-70-76-69--285	58,859
Na-Yeon Choi	74-72-69-70--285	58,859
Hee-Won Han	72-69-70-74--285	58,859
Inbee Park	73-70-70-73--286	45,289
Se Ri Pak	72-70-73-72--287	36,692
Heather Young	69-70-74-74--287	36,692
Karen Stupples	67-75-74-72--288	35,621
Natalie Gulbis	69-74-73-73--289	32,364
Karrie Webb	76-70-69-74--289	32,364
Angela Stanford	75-73-71-71--290	27,275
Meg Mallon	73-73-72-72--290	27,275
Diana D'Alessio	74-69-72-75--290	27,275
Liselotte Neumann	70-72-71-77--290	27,275
Janice Moodie	73-73-74-71--291	23,815
Sakura Yokomine	76-73-72-70--291	23,815
Helen Alfredsson	75-72-73-72--292	19,506
Jee Young Lee	73-71-75-73--292	19,506
Michele Redman	71-72-76-73--292	19,506
Angela Park	77-71-73-71--292	19,506
Paula Creamer	71-74-73-74--292	19,506
Yani Tseng	72-71-75-74--292	19,506
Brittany Lang	75-70-72-75--292	19,506
Candie Kung	73-74-75-70--292	19,506
Cristie Kerr	74-72-66-80--292	19,506

LPGA Championship

Bulle Rock GC; (par 72; 6,641 yds)
Havre de Grace, Md., June 5–8, 2008

Player	Score	Earnings ($)
*Yani Tseng	73-70-65-68--276	300,000
Maria Hjorth	68-72-65-71--276	180,180
Lorena Ochoa	69-65-72-71--277	115,911
Annika Sorenstam	70-68-68-71--277	115,911
Laura Diaz	71-68-69-70--278	81,385
Morgan Pressel	73-69-70-68--280	53,763
Shi Hyun Ahn	73-69-69-69--280	53,763
Kelli Kuehne	69-70-71-70--280	53,763
Irene Cho	72-68-69-71--280	53,763
Seon Hwa Lee	73-71-70-67--281	31,398
Mi Hyun Kim	72-70-71-68--281	31,398
Paula Creamer	71-70-71-69--281	31,398
Cristie Kerr	71-70-71-69--281	31,398
Candie Kung	70-72-70-69--281	31,398
Nicole Castrale	68-72-71-70--281	31,398
Giulia Sergas	71-71-69-70--281	31,398
Jimin Jeong	73-68-69-71--281	31,398
Jill McGill	72-70-72-68--282	21,929
Jeong Jang	72-72-68-70--282	21,929
Na-Yeon Choi	75-67-69-71--282	21,929
Marisa Baena	68-70-71-73--282	21,929
Brittany Lang	70-67-71-74--282	21,929
Lindsey Wright	67-68-73-74--282	21,929
Jee Young Lee	70-69-65-78--282	21,929
Kristy McPherson	73-70-72-68--283	17,806
Momoko Ueda	72-67-71-73--283	17,806
Jimin Kang	72-68-70-73--283	17,806
Angela Stanford	72-71-67-73--283	17,806

* Won in playoff.

U.S. Women's Open

Interlachen CC; (par 73; 6,789 yds)
Edina, Minn., June 23–29, 2008

Player	Score	Earnings ($)
Inbee Park	72-69-71-71--283	585,000
Helen Alfredsson	70-71-71-75--287	350,000
Angela Park	73-67-75-73--288	162,487
In-Kyung Kim	71-73-69-75--288	162,487
Stacy Lewis	73-70-67-78--288	162,487
Nicole Castrale	74-70-74-71--289	94,117
Giulia Sergas	73-74-72-70--289	94,117
Mi Hyun Kim	72-72-70-75--289	94,117
Paula Creamer	70-72-69-78--289	94,117
Teresa Lu	71-72-73-74--290	75,734
†Maria Jose Uribe	69-74-72-75--290	–
Stacy Prammanasudh	75-72-71-73--291	71,002
Suzann Pettersen	77-71-73-71--292	60,878
Jee Young Lee	71-75-74-72--292	60,878
Cristie Kerrr	72-70-75-75--292	60,878
Momoko Ueda	72-71-73-76--292	60,878
Morgan Pressel	74-74-72-73--293	51,380
Catriona Matthew	70-77-73-73--293	51,380
†Jessica Korda	72-78-75-69--294	–
Ji Yai Shin	69-74-79-72--294	43,376
Candie Kung	72-70-79-73--294	43,376
Na-Yeon Choi	76-71-71-76--294	43,376
Jeong Jang	73-69-74-78--294	43,376

Women's British Open

Sunningdale GC (par 72; 6,408 yds)
Berkshire, England, July 31–August 3, 2008

Player	Score	Earnings ($)
Ji-Yai Shin	66-68-70-66--270	314,464
Yani Tseng	70-69-68-66--273	196,540
Eun-Hee Ji	68-70-69-67--274	122,838
Yuri Fudoh	66-68-69-71--274	122,838
Ai Miyazato	68-69-68-70--275	88,443
Cristie Kerr	71-65-70-70--276	76,651
Lorena Ochoa	69-68-71-69--277	65,841
Momoko Ueda	66-72-70-69--277	65,841
In-Kyung Kim	71-68-72-67--278	47,563
Hee-Won Han	71-69-71-67--278	47,563
Paula Creamer	72-69-70-67--278	47,563
Karrie Webb	72-69-69-68--278	47,563
Natalie Gulbis	69-68-70-71--278	47,563
Seon Hwa Lee	71-68-70-70--279	33,739
Hee Young Park	69-71-69-70--279	33,739
Juli Inkster	65-70-71-73--279	33,739
Jee Young Lee	71-72-71-66--280	27,393
Minea Blomqvist	68-73-72-67--280	27,393
Shi Hyun Ahn	68-72-71-69--296	27,393
Ji Young Oh	66-73-71-70--296	27,393

† Amateur.

Women's Tour Results

Late 2007 LPGA Tour Events

Tournament	Final Round	Winner	Score/ Under Par	Earnings ($)
*Longs Drug Challenge	Oct 7	Suzann Pettersen	277/-11	160,000
Samsung World Championship	Oct 14	Lorena Ochoa	270/-18	250,000
Hana Bank Championship	Oct 21	Suzann Pettersen	141/(-3)	225,000
Honda LPGA Thailand	Oct 28	Suzann Pettersen	267/-21	195,000
Mizuno Classic	Nov 4	Momoko Ueda	203/-13	210,000
LPGA Tournament of Champions	Nov 11	Paula Creamer	268/-20	150,000
ADT Championship	Nov 18	Lorena Ochoa	272/-8	1,000,000

2008 LPGA Tour Events

Tournament	Final Round	Winner	Score/ Under Par	Earnings ($)
SBS Open	Feb 16	Annika Sorenstam	206/-10	165,000
Fields Open	Feb 23	Paula Creamer	200/-16	195,000
HSBC Championship	Mar 2	Lorena Ochoa	268/-20	300,000
MasterCard Classic	Mar 16	Louise Friberg	210/-6	195,000
Safeway International	Mar 30	Lorena Ochoa	266/-22	220,000
Kraft Nabisco Championship	Apr 6	Lorena Ochoa	277/-11	300,000
Corona Morelia Championship	Apr 13	Lorena Ochoa	267/-25	195,000
Ginn Open	Apr 20	Lorena Ochoa	269/-19	390,000
*Stanford International Pro Am	Apr 27	Annika Sorenstam	275/-8	300,000
*SemGroup Championship	May 4	Paula Creamer	282/-2	270,000
Michelob Ultra Open	May 11	Annika Sorenstam	265/-19	330,000
Sybase Classic	May 18	Lorena Ochoa	206/-10	300,000
*LPGA Corning Classic	May 25	Leta Lindley	277/-11	225,000
*GINN Tribute	June 1	Seon Hwa Lee	274/-14	390,000
*McDonald's LPGA Championship	June 8	Yani Tseng	276/-12	300,000
Wegman's Rochester LPGA	June 22	Eun-Hee Ji	272/-16	300,000
U.S. Women's Open	June 29	Inbee Park	283/-9	585,000
NW Arkansas Championship	July 6	Seon Hwa Lee	201/-15	255,000
Jamie Farr Owens Corning Classic	July 13	Paula Creamer	268/-16	195,000
*State Farm Classic	July 20	Ji Young Oh	270/-18	255,000
*Evian Masters	July 27	Helen Alfredsson	273/-15	487,500
Women's British Open	Aug 3	Ji-Yai Shin	270/-18	314,464
Canadian Women's Open	Aug 17	Katherine Hull	277/-11	337,500
Safeway Classic	Aug 24	Cristie Kerr	203/-13	255,000
Bell Micro Classic	Sept 14	Angela Stanford	273/-15	210,000
*Navistar Classic	Sept 28	Lorena Ochoa	273/-15	210,000

* Won in playoff.

Champions Tour Results

Late 2007 Champions Tour Events

Tournament	Final Round	Winner	Score/ Under Par	Earnings ($)
Administaff Small Business Classic	Oct 14	Bernhard Langer	191/-25	255,000
AT&T Championship	Oct 21	John Cook	198/-15	240,000
Charles Schwab Cup Championship	Oct 28	Jim Thorpe	268/-20	442,000

2008 Champions Tour Events

Tournament	Final Round	Winner	Score/ Under Par	Earnings ($)
MasterCard Championship	Jan 20	Fred Funk	195/-21	300,000
Turtle Bay Championship	Jan 27	Jerry Pate	211/-5	240,000
Allianz Championship	Feb 10	Scott Hoch	202/-14	247,500
*ACE Group Classic	Feb 17	Scott Hoch	202/-14	240,000
*Toshiba Senior Classic	Mar 9	Bernhard Langer	199/-14	255,000
*AT&T Champions Classic	Mar 16	Denis Watson	209/-7	128,000
Ginn Championship	Mar 30	Bernhard Langer	204/-12	375,000
Cap Cana Championship	April 6	Mark Wiebe	202/-14	300,000
Outback Steakhouse Pro-Am	April 20	Tom Watson	204/-9	255,000
FedEx Kinko's Classic	May 4	Denis Watson	206/-10	240,000
Regions Charity Classic	May 18	Andy Bean	203/-13	255,000
Senior PGA Championship	May 25	Jay Haas	287/+7	360,000
Principal Charity Classic	June 1	Jay Haas	203/-10	258,750
Bank of America Championship	June 22	Jeff Sluman	199/-17	247,500
Commerce Bank Championship	June 29	Loren Roberts	201/-12	240,000
Dick's Sporting Goods Open	July 6	Eduardo Romero	199/-17	240,000
3M Championship	July 20	R.W. Eaks	193/-23	262,500
*Senior Open Championship (British)	July 27	Bruce Vaughan	278/-6	315,600
US Senior Open	Aug 3	Eduardo Romero	274/-6	470,000
Jeld-Wen Tradition	Aug 17	Fred Funk	269/-19	392,000
The Boeing Championship	Aug 24	Tom Kite	202/-14	255,000
Wal-Mart First Tee Open	Aug 31	Jeff Sluman	202/-14	315,000
Greater Hickory Classic	Sep 14	R.W. Eaks	200/-16	255,000
SAS Championship	Sep 28	Eduardo Romero	201/-15	315,000

* Won in playoff

2008 U.S. Amateur Results*

Tournament	Final Round	Winner	Score	Runner-Up
Women's Amateur Public Links	June 21	Tiffany Joh	2 & 1	Jennifer Song
Men's Amateur Public Links	July 19	Jack Newman	5 & 3	John Chin
Girls' Junior Amateur	July 26	Alexis Thompson	5 & 4	Karen Chung
Boys' Junior Amateur	July 26	Cameron Peck	10 & 8	Evan Beck
Women's Amateur	Aug 10	Amanda Blumenherst	2 & 1	Azahara Munoz
Men's Amateur	Aug 24	Danny Lee	5 & 4	Drew Kittleson
Men's Mid-Amateur	Sep 11	Steve Wilson	5 & 4	Todd Mitchell

*Results through 10/01/08.

2008 International Results

Tournament	Final Round	Winner	Score	Runner-Up
Curtis Cup	June 1	United States	13–7	Great Britain/Ireland
Ryder Cup	Sept 21	United States	16½–11½	Europe

PGA Tour Final 2007 Money Leaders

Name	Events	Best Finish	Scoring Average*	Money ($)
Tiger Woods	16	1 (7)	66.12	10,867,052
Phil Mickelson	22	1 (3)	69.12	5,819,988
Vijay Singh	27	1 (2)	70.40	4,728,376
Steve Stricker	23	1 (1)	69.70	4,663,077
K.J. Choi	25	1 (2)	70.34	4,587,859
Rory Sabbatini	23	1 (1)	69.85	4,550,040
Jim Furyk	23	1 (1)	70.71	4,154,046
Zach Johnson	23	1 (2)	71.19	3,922,338
Sergio Garcia	19	2 (2)	69.48	3,721,185
Aaron Baddeley	23	1 (1)	70.09	3,441,119

*Adjusted for average score of field in each tournament entered.

LPGA Tour Final 2007 Money Leaders

Name	Events	Best Finish	Scoring Average	Money ($)
Lorena Ochoa	25	1 (8)	69.69	4,364,994
Suzann Pettersen	24	1 (5)	70.86	1,802,400
Paula Creamer	24	1 (2)	70.50	1,384,798
Mi Hyun Kim	27	1 (1)	71.36	1,273,848
Seon Hwa Lee	28	1 (1)	71.56	1,100,198
Cristie Kerr	22	1 (1)	71.88	1,098,921
Jeong Jang	27	2	71.52	1,038,598
Angela Park	28	2	71.54	983,922
Morgan Pressel	25	1 (1)	71.34	972,452
Jee Young Lee	24	2	71.66	966,256

Champions Tour Final 2007 Money Leaders

Name	Events	Best Finish	Scoring Average	Money ($)
Jay Haas	27	1 (4)	67.33	2,581,001
Loren Roberts	23	1 (2)	69.08	2,170,627
Brad Bryant	24	1 (2)	69.08	1,812,099
Denis Watson	25	1 (2)	71.00	1,636,123
D.A. Weibring	27	1 (1)	71.78	1,557,622
R.W. Eaks	26	1 (2)	71.08	1,534,098
Tom Kite	28	2 (3)	69.75	1,451,941
Tom Purtzer	27	1 (1)	70.17	1,382,436
Tom Watson	12	1 (2)	70.31	1,365,365
Hale Irwin	21	1 (1)	71.17	1,269,513

FOR THE RECORD • Year by Year

Men's Golf

THE MAJOR TOURNAMENTS

The Masters

Year	Winner	Score	Runner-Up
1934	...Horton Smith	284	Craig Wood
1935	Gene Sarazen* (144) (only 36-hole playoff)	282	Craig Wood (149)
1936	...Horton Smith	285	Harry Cooper
1937	...Byron Nelson	283	Ralph Guldahl
1938	...Henry Picard	285	Ralph Guldahl Harry Cooper
1939	...Ralph Guldahl	279	Sam Snead
1940	...Jimmy Demaret	280	Lloyd Mangrum
1941	...Craig Wood	280	Byron Nelson
1942	...Byron Nelson* (69)	280	Ben Hogan (70)
1943–45	No tournament		
1946	...Herman Keiser	282	Ben Hogan
1947	...Jimmy Demaret	281	Byron Nelson Frank Stranahan
1948	...Claude Harmon	279	Cary Middlecoff
1949	...Sam Snead	282	Johnny Bulla Lloyd Mangrum
1950	...Jimmy Demaret	283	Jim Ferrier
1951	...Ben Hogan	280	Skee Riegel
1952	...Sam Snead	286	Jack Burke Jr..
1953	...Ben Hogan	274	Ed Oliver Jr.
1954	...Sam Snead* (70)	289	Ben Hogan (71)
1955	...Cary Middlecoff	279	Ben Hogan
1956	...Jack Burke Jr.	289	Ken Venturi
1957	...Doug Ford	282	Sam Snead
1958	...Arnold Palmer	284	Doug Ford Fred Hawkins
1959	...Art Wall Jr.	284	Cary Middlecoff
1960	...Arnold Palmer	282	Ken Venturi
1961	...Gary Player	280	Charles R. Coe Arnold Palmer
1962	...Arnold Palmer* (68)	280	Gary Player (71) D. Finsterwald (77)
1963	...Jack Nicklaus	286	Tony Lema
1964	...Arnold Palmer	276	Dave Marr Jack Nicklaus
1965	...Jack Nicklaus	271	Arnold Palmer Gary Player
1966	...Jack Nicklaus* (70)	288	Tommy Jacobs (72) Gay Brewer Jr. (78)
1967	...Gay Brewer Jr.	280	Bobby Nichols
1968	...Bob Goalby	277	Roberto DeVicenzo
1969	...George Archer	281	Billy Casper George Knudson Tom Weiskopf
1970	...Billy Casper* (69)	279	Gene Littler (74)
1971	...Charles Coody	279	Johnny Miller Jack Nicklaus
1972	...Jack Nicklaus	286	Bruce Crampton Bobby Mitchell Tom Weiskopf
1973	...Tommy Aaron	283	J.C. Snead
1974	...Gary Player	278	Tom Weiskopf Dave Stockton
1975	...Jack Nicklaus	276	Johnny Miller Tom Weiskopf
1976	...Ray Floyd	271	Ben Crenshaw
1977	...Tom Watson	276	Jack Nicklaus
1978	...Gary Player	277	Hubert Green Rod Funseth Tom Watson
1979	...Fuzzy Zoeller* (4–3)†	280	Ed Sneed (4–4) Tom Watson (4–4)
1980	...Seve Ballesteros	275	Gibby Gilbert Jack Newton
1981	...Tom Watson	280	Johnny Miller Jack Nicklaus
1982	...Craig Stadler* (4)	284	Dan Pohl (5)
1983	...Seve Ballesteros	280	Ben Crenshaw Tom Kite
1984	...Ben Crenshaw	277	Tom Watson
1985	...Bernhard Langer	282	Curtis Strange Seve Ballesteros Ray Floyd
1986	...Jack Nicklaus	279	Greg Norman Tom Kite
1987	...Larry Mize* (4–3)	285	Seve Ballesteros (5) Greg Norman (4–4)
1988	...Sandy Lyle	281	Mark Calcavecchia
1989	...Nick Faldo* (5–3)	283	Scott Hoch (5–4)
1990	...Nick Faldo* (4–4)	278	Ray Floyd (4–x)
1991	Ian Woosnam	277	José María Olazábal
1992	...Fred Couples	275	Ray Floyd
1993	...Bernhard Langer	277	Chip Beck
1994	...José María Olazábal	279	Tom Lehman
1995	...Ben Crenshaw	274	Davis Love III
1996	...Nick Faldo	276	Greg Norman
1997	...Tiger Woods	270	Tom Kite
1998	...Mark O'Meara	279	David Duval Fred Couples
1999	...José María Olazábal	280	Davis Love III
2000	...Vijay Singh	278	Ernie Els
2001	...Tiger Woods	272	David Duval
2002	...Tiger Woods	276	Retief Goosen
2003	...Mike Weir	281	Len Mattiace
2004	...Phil Mickelson	279	Ernie Els
2005	...Tiger Woods	276	Chris DiMarco
2006	...Phil Mickelson	281	Tim Clark
2007	...Zach Johnson	289	Tiger Woods Retief Goosen Rory Sabbatini
2008	...Trevor Immelman	280	Tiger Woods

*Winner in playoff. Playoff scores are in parentheses. †Playoff cut from 18 holes to sudden death.
Note: Played at Augusta National Golf Club, Augusta, GA.

United States Open Championship

Year	Winner	Score	Runner-Up	Site
1895	Horace Rawlins	†173	Willie Dunn	Newport GC, Newport, RI
1896	James Foulis	†152	Horace Rawlins	Shinnecock Hills GC, Southampton, NY
1897	Joe Lloyd	†162	Willie Anderson	Chicago GC, Wheaton, IL
1898	Fred Herd	328	Alex Smith	Myopia Hunt Club, Hamilton, MA
1899	Willie Smith	315	George Low Val Fitzjohn W.H. Way	Baltimore CC, Baltimore, MD
1900	Harry Vardon	313	John H. Taylor	Chicago GC, Wheaton, IL
1901	Willie Anderson* (85)	331	Alex Smith (86)	Myopia Hunt Club, Hamilton, MA
1902	Laurie Auchterlonie	307	Stewart Gardner	Garden City GC, Garden City, NY
1903	Willie Anderson* (82)	307	David Brown (84)	Baltusrol GC, Springfield, NJ
1904	Willie Anderson	303	Gil Nicholls	Glen View Club, Golf, IL
1905	Willie Anderson	314	Alex Smith	Myopia Hunt Club, Hamilton, MA
1906	Alex Smith	295	Willie Smith	Onwentsia Club, Lake Forest, IL
1907	Alex Ross	302	Gil Nicholls	Philadelphia Cricket Club, Chestnut Hill, PA
1908	Fred McLeod* (77)	322	Willie Smith (83)	Myopia Hunt Club, Hamilton, MA
1909	George Sargent	290	Tom McNamara	Englewood GC, Englewood, NJ
1910	Alex Smith* (71)	298	John McDermott (75) Macdonald Smith (77)	Philadelphia Cricket Club, Chestnut Hill, PA
1911	John McDermott* (80)	307	Mike Brady (82) George Simpson (85)	Chicago GC, Wheaton, IL
1912	John McDermott	294	Tom McNamara	CC of Buffalo, Buffalo, NY
1913	Francis Ouimet* (72)	304	Harry Vardon (77) Edward Ray (78)	The Country Club, Brookline, MA
1914	Walter Hagen	290	Chick Evans	Midlothian CC, Blue Island, IL
1915	Jerry Travers	297	Tom McNamara	Baltusrol GC, Springfield, NJ
1916	Chick Evans	286	Jock Hutchison	Minikahda Club, Minneapolis. MN
1917–18	No tournament			
1919	Walter Hagen* (77)	301	Mike Brady (78)	Brae Burn CC, West Newton, MA
1920	Edward Ray	295	Harry Vardon Jack Burke Leo Diegel Jock Hutchison	Inverness CC, Toledo, OH
1921	Jim Barnes	289	Walter Hagen Fred McLeod	Columbia CC, Chevy Chase, MD
1922	Gene Sarazen	288	John L. Black Bobby Jones	Skokie CC, Glencoe, IL
1923	Bobby Jones* (76)	296	Bobby Cruickshank (78)	Inwood CC, Inwood, NY
1924	Cyril Walker	297	Bobby Jones	Oakland Hills CC, Birmingham, MI
1925	W. MacFarlane* (75–72)	291	Bobby Jones (75–73)	Worcester CC, Worcester, MA
1926	Bobby Jones	293	Joe Turnesa	Scioto CC, Columbus, OH
1927	Tommy Armour* (76)	301	Harry Cooper (79)	Oakmont CC, Oakmont, PA
1928	Johnny Farrell* (143)	294	Bobby Jones (144)	Olympia Fields CC, Matteson, IL
1929	Bobby Jones* (141)	294	Al Espinosa (164)	Winged Foot GC, Mamaroneck, NY
1930	Bobby Jones	287	Macdonald Smith	Interlachen CC, Hopkins, MN
1931	Billy Burke* (149–148)	292	George Von Elm (149–149)	Inverness Club, Toledo, OH
1932	Gene Sarazen	286	Phil Perkins Bobby Cruickshank	Fresh Meadows CC, Flushing, NY
1933	Johnny Goodman	287	Ralph Guldahl	North Shore CC, Glenview, IL
1934	Olin Dutra	293	Gene Sarazen	Merion Cricket Club, Ardmore, PA
1935	Sam Parks Jr.	299	Jimmy Thompson	Oakmont CC, Oakmont, PA
1936	Tony Manero	282	Harry Cooper	Baltusrol GC (Upper Course), Springfield, NJ
1937	Ralph Guldahl	281	Sam Snead	Oakland Hills CC, Birmingham, MI
1938	Ralph Guldahl	284	Dick Metz	Cherry Hills CC, Denver, CO
1939	Byron Nelson* (68–70)	284	Craig Wood (68–73) Denny Shute (76)	Philadelphia CC, Philadelphia, PA
1940	Lawson Little* (70)	287	Gene Sarazen (73)	Canterbury GC, Cleveland, OH
1941	Craig Wood	284	Denny Shute	Colonial Club, Fort Worth, TX
1942–45	No tournament			
1946	Lloyd Mangrum* (72–72)	284	Vic Ghezzi (72–73) Byron Nelson (72–73)	Canterbury GC, Cleveland, OH
1947	Lew Worsham* (69)	282	Sam Snead (70)	St. Louis CC, Clayton, MO
1948	Ben Hogan	276	Jimmy Demaret	Riviera CC, Los Angeles, CA
1949	Cary Middlecoff	286	Sam Snead Clayton Heafner	Medinah CC, Medinah, IL
1950	Ben Hogan* (69)	287	Lloyd Mangrum (73) George Fazio (75)	Merion GC, Ardmore, PA

United States Open Championship *(Cont.)*

Year	Winner	Score	Runner-Up	Site
1951	Ben Hogan	287	Clayton Heafner	Oakland Hills CC, Birmingham, MI
1952	Julius Boros	281	Ed Oliver	Northwood CC, Dallas, TX
1953	Ben Hogan	283	Sam Snead	Oakmont CC, Oakmont, PA
1954	Ed Furgol	284	Gene Littler	Baltusrol GC (Lower Course), Springfield, NJ
1955	Jack Fleck* (69)	287	Ben Hogan (72)	Olympic Club (Lake Course), San Fran., CA
1956	Cary Middlecoff	281	Ben Hogan Julius Boros	Oak Hill CC, Rochester, NY
1957	Dick Mayer* (72)	282	Cary Middlecoff (79)	Inverness Club, Toledo, OH
1958	Tommy Bolt	283	Gary Player	Southern Hills CC, Tulsa, OK
1959	Billy Casper	282	Bob Rosburg	Winged Foot GC, Mamaroneck, NY
1960	Arnold Palmer	280	Jack Nicklaus	Cherry Hills CC, Denver, CO
1961	Gene Littler	281	Bob Goalby Doug Sanders	Oakland Hills CC, Birmingham, MI
1962	Jack Nicklaus* (71)	283	Arnold Palmer (74)	Oakmont CC, Oakmont, PA
1963	Julius Boros* (70)	293	Jacky Cupit (73) Arnold Palmer (76)	The Country Club, Brookline, MA
1964	Ken Venturi	278	Tommy Jacobs	Congressional CC, Bethesda, MD
1965	Gary Player* (71)	282	Kel Nagle (74)	Bellerive CC, St. Louis, MO
1966	Billy Casper* (69)	278	Arnold Palmer (73)	Olympic Club (Lake Course), San Fran., CA
1967	Jack Nicklaus	275	Arnold Palmer	Baltusrol GC (Lower Course), Springfield, NJ
1968	Lee Trevino	275	Jack Nicklaus	Oak Hill CC, Rochester, NY
1969	Orville Moody	281	Deane Beman Al Geiberger Bob Rosburg	Champions GC (Cypress Creek Course), Houston, TX
1970	Tony Jacklin	281	Dave Hill	Hazeltine GC, Chaska, MN
1971	Lee Trevino* (68)	280	Jack Nicklaus (71)	Merion GC (East Course), Ardmore, PA
1972	Jack Nicklaus	290	Bruce Crampton	Pebble Beach GL, Pebble Beach, CA
1973	Johnny Miller	279	John Schlee	Oakmont CC, Oakmont, PA
1974	Hale Irwin	287	Forrest Fezler	Winged Foot GC, Mamaroneck, NY
1975	Lou Graham* (71)	287	John Mahaffey (73)	Medinah CC, Medinah, IL
1976	Jerry Pate	277	Tom Weiskopf Al Geiberger	Atlanta Athletic Club, Duluth, GA
1977	Hubert Green	278	Lou Graham	Southern Hills CC, Tulsa, OK
1978	Andy North	285	Dave Stockton J.C. Snead	Cherry Hills CC, Denver, CO
1979	Hale Irwin	284	Gary Player Jerry Pate	Inverness Club, Toledo, OH
1980	Jack Nicklaus	272	Isao Aoki	Baltusrol GC (Lower Course), Springfield, NJ
1981	David Graham	273	George Burns Bill Rogers	Merion GC, Ardmore, PA
1982	Tom Watson	282	Jack Nicklaus	Pebble Beach GL, Pebble Beach, CA
1983	Larry Nelson	280	Tom Watson	Oakmont CC, Oakmont, PA
1984	Fuzzy Zoeller* (67)	276	Greg Norman (75)	Winged Foot GC, Mamaroneck, NY
1985	Andy North	279	Dave Barr T.C. Chen Denis Watson	Oakland Hills CC, Birmingham, MI
1986	Ray Floyd	279	Lanny Wadkins Chip Beck	Shinnecock Hills GC, Southampton, NY
1987	Scott Simpson	277	Tom Watson	Olympic Club (Lake Course), San Fran., CA
1988	Curtis Strange* (71)	278	Nick Faldo (75)	The Country Club, Brookline, MA
1989	Curtis Strange	278	Chip Beck Mark McCumber Ian Woosnam	Oak Hill CC, Rochester, NY
1990	Hale Irwin* (74) (3)	280	Mike Donald (74) (4)	Medinah CC, Medinah, IL
1991	Payne Stewart* (75)	282	Scott Simpson (77)	Hazeltine GC, Chaska, MN
1992	Tom Kite	285	Jeff Sluman	Pebble Beach GL, Pebble Beach, CA
1993	Lee Janzen	272	Payne Stewart	Baltusrol GC, Springfield, NJ
1994	Ernie Els*	279	Loren Roberts Colin Montgomerie	Oakmont CC, Oakmont, PA
1995	Corey Pavin	280	Greg Norman	Shinnecock Hills GC, Southampton, NY
1996	Steve Jones	278	Davis Love III Tom Lehman	Oakland Hills CC, Birmingham, MI
1997	Ernie Els	276	Colin Montgomerie	Congressional CC, Bethesda, MD
1998	Lee Janzen	280	Payne Stewart	Olympic Club (Lake Course), San Fran., CA
1999	Payne Stewart	279	Phil Mickelson	Pinehurst Resort and CC, Pinehurst, NC
2000	Tiger Woods	272	Miguel Angel Jiménez Ernie Els	Pebble Beach GL, Pebble Beach, CA
2001	Retief Goosen* (70)	276	Mark Brooks (72)	Southern Hills CC, Tulsa, OK

Men's Golf *(Cont.)*

United States Open Championship *(Cont.)*

Year	Winner	Score	Runner-Up	Site
2002	Tiger Woods	277	Phil Mickelson	Bethpage GC (Black), Bethpage, NY
2003	Jim Furyk	272	Stephen Leaney	Olympia Fields CC, Olympia Fields, IL
2004	Retief Goosen	276	Phil Mickelson	Shinnecock Hills GC, Southampton, NY
2005	Michael Campbell	280	Tiger Woods	Pinehurst Resort and CC, Pinehurst, NC
2006	Geoff Ogilvy	285	Jim Furyk Colin Montgomerie Phil Mickelson	Winged Foot GC, Mamaroneck, NY
2007	Angel Cabrera	285	Jim Furyk Tiger Woods	Oakmont CC, Oakmont, PA
2008	Tiger Woods* (71) (4)	283	Rocco Mediate	Torrey Pines GC (South), San Diego, CA

*Winner in playoff. Playoff scores are in parentheses. The 1990 and 2008 playoffs went to one hole of sudden death after an 18-hole playoff. In the 1994 playoff, Montgomerie was eliminated after 18 playoff holes, and Els beat Roberts on the 20th.
†Before 1898, 36 holes. From 1898 on, 72 holes.

The Open Championship (British Open)

Year	Winner	Score	Runner-Up	Site
1860†	Willie Park	174	Tom Morris Sr.	Prestwick, Scotland
1861‡	Tom Morris Sr.	163	Willie Park	Prestwick, Scotland
1862	Tom Morris Sr.	163	Willie Park	Prestwick, Scotland
1863	Willie Park	168	Tom Morris Sr.	Prestwick, Scotland
1864	Tom Morris, Sr.	160	Andrew Strath	Prestwick, Scotland
1865	Andrew Strath	162	Willie Park	Prestwick, Scotland
1866	Willie Park	169	David Park	Prestwick, Scotland
1867	Tom Morris Sr.	170	Willie Park	Prestwick, Scotland
1868	Tom Morris Jr.	154	Tom Morris Sr.	Prestwick, Scotland
1869	Tom Morris Jr.	157	Tom Morris Sr.	Prestwick, Scotland
1870	Tom Morris Jr.	149	David Strath Bob Kirk	Prestwick, Scotland
1871	No tournament			
1872	Tom Morris Jr.	166	David Strath	Prestwick, Scotland
1873	Tom Kidd	179	Jamie Anderson	St. Andrews, Scotland
1874	Mungo Park	159	No record	Musselburgh, Scotland
1875	Willie Park	166	Bob Martin	Prestwick, Scotland
1876	Bob Martin#	176	David Strath	St. Andrews, Scotland
1877	Jamie Anderson	160	Bob Pringle	Musselburgh, Scotland
1878	Jamie Anderson	157	Robert Kirk	Prestwick, Scotland
1879	Jamie Anderson	169	Andrew Kirkaldy James Allan	St. Andrews, Scotland
1880	Robert Ferguson	162	No record	Musselburgh, Scotland
1881	Robert Ferguson	170	Jamie Anderson	Prestwick, Scotland
1882	Robert Ferguson	171	Willie Fernie	St. Andrews, Scotland
1883	Willie Fernie*	159	Robert Ferguson	Musselburgh, Scotland
1884	Jack Simpson	160	Douglas Rolland Willie Fernie	Prestwick, Scotland
1885	Bob Martin	171	Archie Simpson	St. Andrews, Scotland
1886	David Brown	157	Willie Campbell	Musselburgh, Scotland
1887	Willie Park Jr.	161	Bob Martin	Prestwick, Scotland
1888	Jack Burns	171	Bernard Sayers David Anderson	St. Andrews, Scotland
1889	Willie Park Jr.* (158)	155	Andrew Kirkaldy (163)	Musselburgh, Scotland
1890	John Ball	164	Willie Fernie	Prestwick, Scotland
1891	Hugh Kirkaldy	166	Andrew Kirkaldy Willie Fernie	St. Andrews, Scotland
1892	Harold Hilton	**305	John Ball Hugh Kirkaldy	Muirfield, Scotland
1893	William Auchterlonie	322	John E. Laidlay	Prestwick, Scotland
1894	John H. Taylor	326	Douglas Rolland	Royal St. George's, England
1895	John H. Taylor	322	Alexander Herd	St. Andrews, Scotland
1896	Harry Vardon* (157)	316	John H. Taylor (161)	Muirfield, Scotland
1897	Harold Hilton	314	James Braid	Royal Liverpool (Hoylake), England
1898	Harry Vardon	307	Willie Park Jr.	Prestwick, Scotland
1899	Harry Vardon	310	Jack White	Royal St. George's, England
1900	John H. Taylor	309	Harry Vardon	St. Andrews, Scotland
1901	James Braid	309	Harry Vardon	Muirfield, Scotland
1902	Alexander Herd	307	Harry Vardon	Royal Liverpool (Hoylake), England
1903	Harry Vardon	300	Tom Vardon	Prestwick, Scotland

The Open Championship (British Open) (Cont.)

Year	Winner	Score	Runner-Up	Site
1904	Jack White	296	John H. Taylor	Royal St. George's, England
1905	James Braid	318	John H. Taylor	St. Andrews, Scotland
			Rolland Jones	
1906	James Braid	300	John H. Taylor	Muirfield, Scotland
1907	Arnaud Massy	312	John H. Taylor	Royal Liverpool (Hoylake), England
1908	James Braid	291	Tom Ball	Prestwick, Scotland
1909	John H. Taylor	295	James Braid	Deal, England
			Tom Ball	
1910	James Braid	299	Alexander Herd	St. Andrews, Scotland
1911	Harry Vardon	303	Arnaud Massy	Royal St. George's, England
1912	Ted Ray	295	Harry Vardon	Muirfield, Scotland
1913	John H. Taylor	304	Ted Ray	Royal Liverpool (Hoylake), England
1914	Harry Vardon	306	John H. Taylor	Prestwick, Scotland
1915–19	No tournament			
1920	George Duncan	303	Alexander Herd	Deal, England
1921	Jock Hutchison* (150)	296	Roger Wethered (159)	St. Andrews, Scotland
1922	Walter Hagen	300	George Duncan	Royal St. George's, England
			Jim Barnes	
1923	Arthur G. Havers	295	Walter Hagen	Troon, Scotland
1924	Walter Hagen	301	Ernest Whitcombe	Royal Liverpool (Hoylake), England
1925	Jim Barnes	300	Archie Compston	Prestwick, Scotland
			Ted Ray	
1926	Bobby Jones	291	Al Watrous	Royal Lytham & St. Annes, England
1927	Bobby Jones	285	Aubrey Boomer	St. Andrews, Scotland
1928	Walter Hagen	292	Gene Sarazen	Royal St. George's, England
1929	Walter Hagen	292	Johnny Farrell	Muirfield, Scotland
1930	Bobby Jones	291	Macdonald Smith	Royal Liverpool (Hoylake), England
			Leo Diegel	
1931	Tommy Armour	296	Jose Jurado	Carnoustie, Scotland
1932	Gene Sarazen	283	Macdonald Smith	Prince's, England
1933	Denny Shute* (149)	292	Craig Wood (154)	St. Andrews, Scotland
1934	Henry Cotton	283	Sidney F. Brews	Royal St. George's, England
1935	Alfred Perry	283	Alfred Padgham	Muirfield, Scotland
1936	Alfred Padgham	287	James Adams	Royal Liverpool (Hoylake), England
1937	Henry Cotton	290	Reginald A. Whitcombe	Carnoustie, Scotland
1938	Reginald A. Whitcombe	295	James Adams	Royal St. George's, England
1939	Richard Burton	290	Johnny Bulla	St. Andrews, Scotland
1940–45	No tournament			
1946	Sam Snead	290	Bobby Locke	St. Andrews, Scotland
			Johnny Bulla	
1947	Fred Daly	293	Reginald W. Horne	Royal Liverpool (Hoylake), England
			Frank Stranahan	
1948	Henry Cotton	294	Fred Daly	Muirfield, Scotland
1949	Bobby Locke* (135)	283	Harry Bradshaw (147)	Royal St. George's, England
1950	Bobby Locke	279	Roberto DeVicenzo	Troon, Scotland
1951	Max Faulkner	285	Tony Cerda	Portrush, Ireland
1952	Bobby Locke	287	Peter Thomson	Royal Lytham & St. Annes, England
1953	Ben Hogan	282	Frank Stranahan	Carnoustie, Scotland
			Dai Rees	
			Peter Thomson	
			Tony Cerda	
1954	Peter Thomson	283	Sidney S. Scott	Royal Birkdale, Southport, England
			Dai Rees	
			Bobby Locke	
1955	Peter Thomson	281	John Fallon	St. Andrews, Scotland
1956	Peter Thomson	286	Flory Van Donck	Royal Liverpool (Hoylake), England
1957	Bobby Locke	279	Peter Thomson	St. Andrews, Scotland
1958	Peter Thomson* (139)	278	Dave Thomas (143)	Royal Lytham & St. Annes, England
1959	Gary Player	284	Fred Bullock	Muirfield, Scotland
			Flory Van Donck	
1960	Kel Nagle	278	Arnold Palmer	St. Andrews, Scotland
1961	Arnold Palmer	284	Dai Rees	Royal Birkdale, Southport, England
1962	Arnold Palmer	276	Kel Nagle	Troon, Scotland
1963	Bob Charles* (140)	277	Phil Rodgers (148)	Royal Lytham & St. Annes, England
1964	Tony Lema	279	Jack Nicklaus	St. Andrews, Scotland
1965	Peter Thomson	285	Brian Huggett	Royal Birkdale, Southport, England
			Christy O'Connor	

The Open Championship (British Open) *(Cont.)*

Year	Winner	Score	Runner-Up	Site
1966	Jack Nicklaus	282	Doug Sanders Dave Thomas	Muirfield, Scotland
1967	Robert DeVicenzo	278	Jack Nicklaus	Royal Liverpool (Hoylake), England
1968	Gary Player	289	Jack Nicklaus Bob Charles	Carnoustie, Scotland
1969	Tony Jacklin	280	Bob Charles	Royal Lytham & St. Annes, England
1970	Jack Nicklaus* (72)	283	Doug Sanders (73)	St. Andrews, Scotland
1971	Lee Trevino	278	Lu Liang Huan	Royal Birkdale, Southport, England
1972	Lee Trevino	278	Jack Nicklaus	Muirfield, Scotland
1973	Tom Weiskopf	276	Johnny Miller	Troon, Scotland
1974	Gary Player	282	Peter Oosterhuis	Royal Lytham & St. Annes, England
1975	Tom Watson* (71)	279	Jack Newton (72)	Carnoustie, Scotland
1976	Johnny Miller	279	Jack Nicklaus Seve Ballesteros	Royal Birkdale, Southport, England
1977	Tom Watson	268	Jack Nicklaus	Turnberry, Scotland
1978	Jack Nicklaus	281	Ben Crenshaw Tom Kite Ray Floyd Simon Owen	St. Andrews, Scotland
1979	Seve Ballesteros	283	Ben Crenshaw Jack Nicklaus	Royal Lytham & St. Annes, England
1980	Tom Watson	271	Lee Trevino	Muirfield, Scotland
1981	Bill Rogers	276	Bernhard Langer	Royal St. George's, England
1982	Tom Watson	284	Nick Price Peter Oosterhuis	Troon, Scotland
1983	Tom Watson	275	Andy Bean	Royal Birkdale, Southport, England
1984	Seve Ballesteros	276	Tom Watson Bernhard Langer	St. Andrews, Scotland
1985	Sandy Lyle	282	Payne Stewart	Royal St. George's, England
1986	Greg Norman	280	Gordon Brand	Turnberry, Scotland
1987	Nick Faldo	279	Paul Azinger Rodger Davis	Muirfield, Scotland
1988	Seve Ballesteros	273	Nick Price	Royal Lytham & St. Annes, England
1989††	Mark Calcavecchia* (4-3-3-3)	275	Wayne Grady (4-4-4-4) Greg Norman (3-3-4-x)	Troon, Scotland
1990	Nick Faldo	270	Payne Stewart Mark McNulty	St. Andrews, Scotland
1991	Ian Baker-Finch	272	Mike Harwood	Royal Birkdale, Southport, England
1992	Nick Faldo	272	John Cook	Muirfield, Scotland
1993	Greg Norman	267	Nick Faldo	Royal St. George's, England
1994	Nick Price	268	Jesper Parnevik	Turnberry, Scotland
1995	John Daly* (4-3-4-4)	282	C. Rocca (5-4-7-3)	St. Andrews, Scotland
1996	Tom Lehman	271	Mark McCumber Ernie Els	Royal Lytham & St. Annes, England
1997	Justin Leonard	272	Jesper Parnevik Darren Clarke	Troon, Scotland
1998	Mark O'Meara* (4-4-5-4)	280	Brian Watts (5-4-5-5)	Royal Birkdale, Southport, England
1999	Paul Lawrie* (5-4-3-3)	290	Jean Van de Velde (6-4-3-5) Justin Leonard (5-4-4-5)	Carnoustie, Scotland
2000	Tiger Woods	269	Thomas Bjorn Ernie Els	St. Andrews, Scotland
2001	David Duval	274	Niclas Fasth	Royal Lytham & St. Annes, England
2002	Ernie Els*	278	Stuart Appleby	Muirfield, Scotland
2003	Ben Curtis	283	Vijay Singh	Royal St. George's, England
2004	Todd Hamilton*	274	Ernie Els	Troon, Scotland
2005	Tiger Woods	274	Colin Montgomerie	St. Andrews, Scotland
2006	Tiger Woods	270	Chris DiMarco	Royal Liverpool (Hoylake), England
2007	Padraig Harrington*	277	Sergio Garcia	Carnoustie, Scotland
2008	Padraig Harrington	283	Ian Poulter	Royal Birkdale, Southport, England

*Winner in playoff. †The first event was open only to professional golfers.
‡The second annual open was open to amateurs and pros. #Tied, but refused playoff.
**Championship extended from 36 to 72 holes. ††Playoff cut from 18 holes to 4 holes.

PGA Championship

Year	Winner	Score	Runner-Up	Site
1916	Jim Barnes	1 up	Jock Hutchison	Siwanoy CC, Bronxville, NY
1917–18	No tournament			
1919	Jim Barnes	6 & 5	Fred McLeod	Engineers CC, Roslyn, NY
1920	Jock Hutchison	1 up	J. Douglas Edgar	Flossmoor CC, Flossmoor, IL
1921	Walter Hagen	3 & 2	Jim Barnes	Inwood CC, Far Rockaway, NY
1922	Gene Sarazen	4 & 3	Emmet French	Oakmont CC, Oakmont, PA
1923	Gene Sarazen	1 up 38 holes	Walter Hagen	Pelham CC, Pelham, NY
1924	Walter Hagen	2 up	Jim Barnes	French Lick CC, French Lick, IN
1925	Walter Hagen	6 & 5	William Mehlhorn	Olympia Fields CC, Olympia Fields, IL
1926	Walter Hagen	5 & 3	Leo Diegel	Salisbury GC, Westbury, NY
1927	Walter Hagen	1 up	Joe Turnesa	Cedar Crest CC, Dallas, TX
1928	Leo Diegel	6 & 5	Al Espinosa	Five Farms CC, Baltimore, MD
1929	Leo Diegel	6 & 4	Johnny Farrell	Hillcrest CC, Los Angeles, CA
1930	Tommy Armour	1 up	Gene Sarazen	Fresh Meadow CC, Flushing, NY
1931	Tom Creavy	2 & 1	Denny Shute	Wannamoisett CC, Rumford, RI
1932	Olin Dutra	4 & 3	Frank Walsh	Keller GC, St. Paul, MN
1933	Gene Sarazen	5 & 4	Willie Goggin	Blue Mound CC, Milwaukee, WI
1934	Paul Runyan	1 up	Craig Wood	Park CC, Williamsville, NY
1935	Johnny Revolta	5 & 4 38 holes	Tommy Armour	Twin Hills CC, Oklahoma City, OK
1936	Denny Shute	3 & 2	Jimmy Thomson	Pinehurst CC, Pinehurst, NC
1937	Denny Shute	1 up 37 holes	Harold McSpaden	Pittsburgh FC, Aspinwall, PA
1938	Paul Runyan	8 & 7	Sam Snead	Shawnee CC, Shawnee-on-Delaware, PA
1939	Henry Picard	1 up 37 holes	Byron Nelson	Pomonok CC, Flushing, NY
1940	Byron Nelson	1 up	Sam Snead	Hershey CC, Hershey, PA
1941	Vic Ghezzi	1 up 38 holes	Byron Nelson	Cherry Hills CC, Denver, CO
1942	Sam Snead	2 & 1	Jim Turnesa	Seaview CC, Atlantic City, NJ
1943	No tournament			
1944	Bob Hamilton	1 up	Byron Nelson	Manito G & CC, Spokane, WA
1945	Byron Nelson	4 & 3	Sam Byrd	Morraine CC, Dayton, OH
1946	Ben Hogan	6 & 4	Ed Oliver	Portland GC, Portland, OR
1947	Jim Ferrier	2 & 1	Chick Harbert	Plum Hollow CC, Detroit, MI
1948	Ben Hogan	7 & 6	Mike Turnesa	Norwood Hills CC, St. Louis, MO
1949	Sam Snead	3 & 2	Johnny Palmer	Hermitage CC, Richmond, VA
1950	Chandler Harper	4 & 3	Henry Williams Jr.	Scioto CC, Columbus, OH
1951	Sam Snead	7 & 6	Walter Burkemo	Oakmont CC, Oakmont, PA
1952	Jim Turnesa	1 up	Chick Harbert	Big Spring CC, Louisville, KY
1953	Walter Burkemo	2 & 1	Felice Torza	Birmingham CC, Birmingham, MI
1954	Chick Harbert	4 & 3	Walter Burkemo	Keller GC, St. Paul, MN
1955	Doug Ford	4 & 3	Cary Middlecoff	Meadowbrook CC, Detroit, MI
1956	Jack Burke	3 & 2	Ted Kroll	Blue Hill CC, Boston, MA
1957	Lionel Hebert	2 & 1	Dow Finsterwald	Miami Valley CC, Dayton, OH
1958	Dow Finsterwald	276	Billy Casper	Llanerch CC, Havertown, PA
1959	Bob Rosburg	277	Jerry Barber Doug Sanders	Minneapolis GC, St. Louis Park, MN
1960	Jay Hebert	281	Jim Ferrier	Firestone CC, Akron, OH
1961	Jerry Barber* (67)	277	Don January (68)	Olympia Fields CC, Olympia Fields, IL
1962	Gary Player	278	Bob Goalby	Aronimink GC, Newton Square, PA
1963	Jack Nicklaus	279	Dave Ragan Jr.	Dallas Athletic Club, Dallas, TX
1964	Bobby Nichols	271	Jack Nicklaus Arnold Palmer	Columbus CC, Columbus, OH
1965	Dave Marr	280	Billy Casper Jack Nicklaus	Laurel Valley CC, Ligonier, PA
1966	Al Geiberger	280	Dudley Wysong	Firestone CC, Akron, OH
1967	Don January* (69)	281	Don Massengale (71)	Columbine CC, Littleton, CO
1968	Julius Boros	281	Bob Charles Arnold Palmer	Pecan Valley CC, San Antonio, TX
1969	Ray Floyd	276	Gary Player	NCR CC, Dayton, OH
1970	Dave Stockton	279	Arnold Palmer Bob Murphy	Southern Hills CC, Tulsa, OK
1971	Jack Nicklaus	281	Billy Casper	PGA Nat'l GC, Palm Beach Gardens, FL

PGA Championship (Cont.)

Year	Winner	Score	Runner-Up	Site
1972	Gary Player	281	Tommy Aaron Jim Jamieson	Oakland Hills CC, Birmingham, MI
1973	Jack Nicklaus	277	Bruce Crampton	Canterbury GC, Cleveland, OH
1974	Lee Trevino	276	Jack Nicklaus	Tanglewood GC, Winston-Salem, NC
1975	Jack Nicklaus	276	Bruce Crampton	Firestone CC, Akron, OH
1976	Dave Stockton	281	Ray Floyd Don January	Congressional CC, Bethesda, MD
1977†	Lanny Wadkins* (4-4-4)	282	Gene Littler (4-4-5)	Pebble Beach GL, Pebble Beach, CA
1978	John Mahaffey* (4–3)	276	Jerry Pate (4–4) Tom Watson (4–5)	Oakmont CC, Oakmont, PA
1979	David Graham* (4-4-2)	272	Ben Crenshaw (4-4-4)	Oakland Hills CC, Birmingham, MI
1980	Jack Nicklaus	274	Andy Bean	Oak Hill CC, Rochester, NY
1981	Larry Nelson	273	Fuzzy Zoeller	Atlanta Athletic Club, Duluth, GA
1982	Raymond Floyd	272	Lanny Wadkins	Southern Hills CC, Tulsa, OK
1983	Hal Sutton	274	Jack Nicklaus	Riviera CC, Pacific Palisades, CA
1984	Lee Trevino	273	Gary Player Lanny Wadkins	Shoal Creek, Birmingham, AL
1985	Hubert Green	278	Lee Trevino	Cherry Hills CC, Denver, CO
1986	Bob Tway	276	Greg Norman	Inverness CC, Toledo, OH
1987	Larry Nelson* (4)	287	Lanny Wadkins (5)	PGA Natl GC, Palm Beach Gardens, FL
1988	Jeff Sluman	272	Paul Azinger	Oak Tree GC, Edmond, OK
1989	Payne Stewart	276	Mike Reid	Kemper Lakes GC, Hawthorn Woods, IL
1990	Wayne Grady	282	Fred Couples	Shoal Creek, Birmingham, AL
1991	John Daly	276	Bruce Lietzke	Crooked Stick GC, Carmel, IN
1992	Nick Price	278	Jim Gallagher Jr.	Bellerive CC, St. Louis, MO
1993	Paul Azinger* (4–4)	272	Greg Norman (4–5)	Inverness CC, Toledo, OH
1994	Nick Price	269	Corey Pavin	Southern Hills CC, Tulsa, OK
1995	Steve Elkington* (3)	267	Colin Montgomerie (4)	Riviera CC, Pacific Palisades, CA
1996	Mark Brooks* (3)	277	Kenny Perry (x)	Valhalla GC, Louisville, KY
1997	Davis Love III	269	Justin Leonard	Winged Foot GC, Mamaroneck, NY
1998	Vijay Singh	271	Steve Stricker	Sahalee CC, Redmond, WA
1999	Tiger Woods	277	Sergio Garcia	Medinah CC, Medinah, IL
2000	Tiger Woods* (3-4-5)	270	Bob May (4-4-x)	Valhalla GC, Louisville, KY
2001	David Toms	265	Phil Mickelson	Atlanta AC, Duluth, GA
2002	Rich Beem	278	Tiger Woods	Hazeltine National GC, Shaska, MN
2003	Shaun Micheel	276	Chad Campbell	Oak Hill CC, Rochester, NY
2004	Vijay Singh*	280	Chris DiMarco	Whistling Straits GC, Kohler, WI
2005	Phil Mickelson	276	Steve Elkington	Baltusrol GC, Springfield, NJ
2006	Tiger Woods	270	Shaun Micheel	Medinah CC, Medinah, IL
2007	Tiger Woods	272	Woody Austin	Southern Hills CC, Tulsa, OK
2008	Padraig Harrington	277	Sergio Garcia	Oakland Hills CC, Birmingham, MI

*Winner in playoff. †Playoff changed from 18 holes to sudden death.

Alltime Major Championship Winners

	Masters	U.S. Open	British Open	PGA Champ.	U.S. Amateur	British Amateur	Total
Jack Nicklaus	6	4	3	5	2	0	20
*Tiger Woods	4	3	3	4	3	0	17
Bobby Jones	0	4	3	0	5	1	13
Walter Hagen	0	2	4	5	0	0	11
Ben Hogan	2	4	1	2	0	0	9
Gary Player	3	1	3	2	0	0	9
John Ball	0	0	1	0	0	8	9
Arnold Palmer	4	1	2	0	1	0	8
Tom Watson	2	1	5	0	0	0	8
Harold Hilton	0	0	2	0	1	4	7
Gene Sarazen	1	2	1	3	0	0	7
Sam Snead	3	0	1	3	0	0	7
Harry Vardon	0	1	6	0	0	0	7

*Active PGA Tour player.

Alltime Multiple Professional Major Winners

MASTERS

Player	Wins
Jack Nicklaus	6
Arnold Palmer	4
*Tiger Woods	4
Jimmy Demaret	3
Nick Faldo	3
Gary Player	3
Sam Snead	3
Seve Ballesteros	2
Ben Crenshaw	2
Ben Hogan	2
*Bernhard Langer	2
*Phil Mickelson	2
Byron Nelson	2
*José María Olazábal	2
Horton Smith	2
Tom Watson	2

U.S. OPEN

Player	Wins
Willie Anderson	4
Ben Hogan	4
Bobby Jones	4
Jack Nicklaus	4
Hale Irwin	3
*Tiger Woods	3
Julius Boros	2
Billy Casper	2
*Ernie Els	2
*Retief Goosen	2
Ralph Guldahl	2
Walter Hagen	2
*Lee Janzen	2
John McDermott	2
Cary Middlecoff	2
Andy North	2
Gene Sarazen	2
Alex Smith	2
Payne Stewart	2
Curtis Strange	2
Lee Trevino	2

BRITISH OPEN

Player	Wins
Harry Vardon	6
James Braid	5
J.H. Taylor	5
Peter Thomson	5
Tom Watson	5
Walter Hagen	4
Bobby Locke	4
Tom Morris Sr.	4
Tom Morris Jr.	4
Willie Park	4
Jamie Anderson	3
Seve Ballesteros	3
Henry Cotton	3
Nick Faldo	3
Robert Ferguson	3
Bobby Jones	3
Jack Nicklaus	3
Gary Player	3
*Tiger Woods	3
*Padraig Harrington	2
Harold Hilton	2
Bob Martin	2
*Greg Norman	2
Arnold Palmer	2
Willie Park Jr.	2
Lee Trevino	2

PGA CHAMPIONSHIP

Player	Wins
Walter Hagen	5
Jack Nicklaus	5
*Tiger Woods	4
Gene Sarazen	3
Sam Snead	3
Jim Barnes	2
Leo Diegel	2
Raymond Floyd	2
Ben Hogan	2
Byron Nelson	2
Larry Nelson	2
Gary Player	2
Paul Runyan	2
Denny Shute	2
Dave Stockton	2
Lee Trevino	2
*Vijay Singh	2

* Active player.

THE PGA TOUR

Most Career Wins†

Player	Wins
Sam Snead	82
Jack Nicklaus	73
*Tiger Woods	65
Ben Hogan	64
Arnold Palmer	62
Byron Nelson	52
Billy Casper	51
Walter Hagen	44
Cary Middlecoff	40
Gene Sarazen	39
Tom Watson	39
Lloyd Mangrum	36
*Phil Mickelson	34
*Vijay Singh	34
Horton Smith	32
Harry Cooper	31
Jimmy Demaret	31
Leo Diegel	30

† Through 10/1/08. * Active player.

Season Money Leaders

Year	Player	Earnings ($)
1934	Paul Runyan	6,767.00
1935	Johnny Revolta	9,543.00
1936	Horton Smith	7,682.00
1937	Harry Cooper	14,138.69
1938	Sam Snead	19,534.49
1939	Henry Picard	10,303.00
1940	Ben Hogan	10,655.00
1941	Ben Hogan	18,358.00
1942	Ben Hogan	13,143.00
1943	No statistics compiled	
1944	Byron Nelson*	37,967.69
1945	Byron Nelson*	63,335.66
1946	Ben Hogan	42,556.16
1947	Jimmy Demaret	27,936.83
1948	Ben Hogan	32,112.00
1949	Sam Snead	31,593.83
1950	Sam Snead	35,758.83
1951	Lloyd Mangrum	26,088.83
1952	Julius Boros	37,032.97
1953	Lew Worsham	34,002.00
1954	Bob Toski	65,819.81
1955	Julius Boros	63,121.55
1956	Ted Kroll	72,835.83
1957	Dick Mayer	65,835.00
1958	Arnold Palmer	42,607.50
1959	Art Wall	53,167.60
1960	Arnold Palmer	75,262.85
1961	Gary Player	64,540.45
1962	Arnold Palmer	81,448.33
1963	Arnold Palmer	128,230.00
1964	Jack Nicklaus	113,284.50
1965	Jack Nicklaus	140,752.14
1966	Billy Casper	121,944.92
1967	Jack Nicklaus	188,998.08
1968	Billy Casper	205,168.67
1969	Frank Beard	164,707.11
1970	Lee Trevino	157,037.63
1971	Jack Nicklaus	244,490.50
1972	Jack Nicklaus	320,542.26
1973	Jack Nicklaus	308,362.10
1974	Johnny Miller	353,021.59
1975	Jack Nicklaus	298,149.17
1976	Jack Nicklaus	266,438.57
1977	Tom Watson	310,653.16
1978	Tom Watson	362,428.93
1979	Tom Watson	462,636.00
1980	Tom Watson	530,808.33
1981	Tom Kite	375,698.84
1982	Craig Stadler	446,462.00
1983	Hal Sutton	426,668.00
1984	Tom Watson	476,260.00
1985	Curtis Strange	542,321.00
1986	Greg Norman	653,296.00
1987	Curtis Strange	925,941.00
1988	Curtis Strange	1,147,644.00
1989	Tom Kite	1,395,278.00
1990	Greg Norman	1,165,477.00
1991	Corey Pavin	979,430.00
1992	Fred Couples	1,344,188.00
1993	Nick Price	1,478,557.00
1994	Nick Price	1,499,927.00
1995	Greg Norman	1,654,959.00
1996	Tom Lehman	1,780,159.00
1997	Tiger Woods	2,066,833.00
1998	David Duval	2,591,031.00
1999	Tiger Woods	6,616,585.00
2000	Tiger Woods	9,188,321.00
2001	Tiger Woods	5,687,777.00
2002	Tiger Woods	6,912,625.00
2003	Vijay Singh	7,573,907.00
2004	Vijay Singh	10,905,166.00
2005	Tiger Woods	10,628,024.00
2006	Tiger Woods	9,941,563.00
2007	Tiger Woods	10,867,052.00

* War bonds. Note: Total money listed from 1968 through 1974. Official money listed from 1975 on.

Year by Year Statistical Leaders

SCORING AVERAGE

Year	Player	Avg
1980	Lee Trevino	69.73
1981	Tom Kite	69.80
1982	Tom Kite	70.21
1983	Raymond Floyd	70.61
1984	Calvin Peete	70.56
1985	Don Pooley	70.36
1986	Scott Hoch	70.08
1987	David Frost	70.09
1988	Greg Norman	69.38
1989	Payne Stewart	69.485†
1990	Greg Norman	69.10
1991	Fred Couples	69.59
1992	Fred Couples	69.38
1993	Greg Norman	68.90
1994	Greg Norman	68.81
1995	Greg Norman	69.06
1996	Tom Lehman	69.32
1997	Nick Price	68.98
1998	David Duval	69.13
1999	Tiger Woods	68.43
2000	Tiger Woods	67.79
2001	Tiger Woods	68.81
2002	Tiger Woods	68.13
2003	Tiger Woods	68.41
2004	Vijay Singh	69.19
2005	Tiger Woods	68.66
2006	Tiger Woods	68.11
2007	Tiger Woods	67.79

Note: Scoring average per round, with adjustments made at each round for the field's course scoring average.

DRIVING DISTANCE

Year	Player	Yds
1980	Dan Pohl	274.3
1981	Dan Pohl	280.1
1982	Bill Calfee	275.3
1983	John McComish	277.4
1984	Bill Glasson	276.5
1985	Andy Bean	278.2
1986	Davis Love III	285.7
1987	John McComish	283.9
1988	Steve Thomas	284.6
1989	Ed Humenik	280.9
1990	Tom Purtzer	279.6
1991	John Daly	288.9
1992	John Daly	283.4
1993	John Daly	288.9
1994	Davis Love III	283.8
1995	John Daly	289.0
1996	John Daly	288.8
1997	John Daly	302.0
1998	John Daly	299.4
1999	John Daly	305.6
2000	John Daly	301.4
2001	John Daly	306.7
2002	John Daly	306.8
2003	Hank Kuehne	321.4
2004	Hank Kuehne	314.4
2005	Scott Hend	318.9
2006	Bubba Watson	319.6
2007	Bubba Watson	315.2

Note: Average computed by charting distance of two tee shots on a predetermined par-four or par-five hole (one on front nine, one on back nine).

DRIVING ACCURACY

Year	Player	Pct
1980	Mike Reid	79.5
1981	Calvin Peete	81.9
1982	Calvin Peete	84.6
1983	Calvin Peete	81.3
1984	Calvin Peete	77.5
1985	Calvin Peete	80.6
1986	Calvin Peete	81.7
1987	Calvin Peete	83.0
1988	Calvin Peete	82.5
1989	Calvin Peete	82.6
1990	Calvin Peete	83.7
1991	Hale Irwin	78.3
1992	Doug Tewell	82.3
1993	Doug Tewell	82.5
1994	David Edwards	81.6
1995	Fred Funk	81.3
1996	Fred Funk	78.7
1997	Allen Doyle	80.8
1998	Bruce Fleisher	81.4
1999	Fred Funk	80.2
2000	Fred Funk	79.7
2001	Joe Durant	81.1
2002	Fred Funk	81.2
2003	Fred Funk	77.9
2004	Fred Funk	77.2
2005	Jeff Hart	76.0
2006	Joe Durant	78.4
2007	Jose Coceres	75.5

Note: Percentage of fairways hit on number of par-four and par-five holes played; par-three holes excluded.

GREENS IN REGULATION

Year	Player	Pct
1980	Jack Nicklaus	72.1
1981	Calvin Peete	73.1
1982	Calvin Peete	72.4
1983	Calvin Peete	71.4
1984	Andy Bean	72.1
1985	John Mahaffey	71.9
1986	John Mahaffey	72.0
1987	Gil Morgan	73.3
1988	John Adams	73.9
1989	Bruce Lietzke	72.6
1990	Doug Tewell	70.9
1991	Bruce Lietzke	73.3
1992	Tim Simpson	74.0
1993	Fuzzy Zoeller	73.6
1994	Bill Glasson	73.0
1995	Lenny Clements	72.3
1996	Fred Couples	71.8
	Mark O'Meara	71.8
1997	Tom Lehman	72.7
1998	Hal Sutton	71.3
1999	Tiger Woods	71.4
2000	Tiger Woods	75.2
2001	Tom Lehman	74.5
2002	Tiger Woods	74.0
2003	Joe Durant	72.9
2004	Joe Durant	73.3
2005	Sergio Garcia	71.8

GREENS IN REGULATION *(Cont.)*

Year	Player	Pct
2006	Tiger Woods	74.2
2007	Tiger Woods	71.0

Note: Average of greens reached in regulation out of total holes played; hole is considered hit in regulation if any part of the ball rests on the putting surface in two shots less than the hole's par—a par-5 hit in two shots is one green in regulation.

PUTTING

Year	Player	Avg
1980	Jerry Pate	28.81
1981	Alan Tapie	28.70
1982	Ben Crenshaw	28.65
1983	Morris Hatalsky	27.96
1984	Gary McCord	28.57
1985	Craig Stadler	28.627†
1986	Greg Norman	1.736
1987	Ben Crenshaw	1.743
1988	Don Pooley	1.729
1989	Steve Jones	1.734
1990	Larry Rinker	1.7467†
1991	Jay Don Blake	1.7326†
1992	Mark O'Meara	1.731
1993	David Frost	1.739
1994	Loren Roberts	1.737
1995	Jim Furyk	1.708
1996	Brad Faxon	1.709
1997	Don Pooley	1.718
1998	Rick Fehr	1.722
1999	Brad Faxon	1.723
2000	Brad Faxon	1.704
2001	David Frost	1.708
2002	Bob Heintz	1.682
2003	John Huston	1.713
2004	Stewart Clink	1.723
2005	Arjun Atwal	1.710
2006	Daniel Chopra	1.712
2007	Tim Clark	1.727

Note: Average number of putts taken on greens reached in regulation; prior to 1986, based on average number of putts per 18 holes.

SAND SAVES

Year	Player	Pct
1980	Bob Eastwood	65.4
1981	Tom Watson	60.1
1982	Isao Aoki	60.2
1983	Isao Aoki	62.3
1984	Peter Oosterhuis	64.7
1985	Tom Purtzer	60.8
1986	Paul Azinger	63.8
1987	Paul Azinger	63.2
1988	Greg Powers	63.5
1989	Mike Sullivan	66.0
1990	Paul Azinger	67.2
1991	Ben Crenshaw	64.9
1992	Mitch Adcock	66.9
1993	Ken Green	64.4
1994	Corey Pavin	65.4
1995	Billy Mayfair	68.6
1996	Gary Rusnak	64.0
1997	Bob Estes	70.3
1998	Keith Fergus	71.0

† Number had to be carried to extra decimal place to determine winner.

Year by Year Statistical Leaders (*Cont.*)

SAND SAVES (*Cont.*)

1999	Jeff Sluman	67.3
2000	Fred Couples	67.0
2001	Franklin Langham	68.9
2002	J. Olazabal	64.9
2003	Stuart Appleby	62.1
2004	Dan Forsman	62.3
2005	Pat Perez	63.0
2006	Luke Donald	63.6
2007	Tim Clark	68.1

Note: Percentage of up-and-down efforts from greenside sand traps only—fairway bunkers excluded.

EAGLES

1980	Dave Eichelberger	16
1981	Bruce Lietzke	12
1982	Tom Weiskopf	10
	J.C. Snead	10
	Andy Bean	10
1983	Chip Beck	15
1984	Gary Hallberg	15
1985	Larry Rinker	14
1986	Joey Sindelar	16
1987	Phil Blackmar	20
1988	Ken Green	21
1989	Lon Hinkle	14
	Duffy Waldorf	14
1990	Paul Azinger	14
1991	Andy Bean	15
1992	Dan Forsman	18
1993	Davis Love III	15
1994	Davis Love III	18
1995	Kelly Gibson	16
1996	Tom Watson	97.2
1997	Tiger Woods	104.1
1998	Davis Love III	83.3
1999	Vijay Singh	104.8
2000	Tiger Woods	72.0

EAGLES (*Cont.*)

2001	Phil Mickelson	73.8
2002	John Daly	78.4
2003	Tiger Woods	76.5
2004	Nick Price	90.0
2005	Brenden Pappas	70.6
2006	J.B. Holmes	72.9
2007	Chris Tidland	88.5

Note: Total of eagles scored 1980–1995. Since 1996 winner determined by number of holes played per eagle.

BIRDIES

1980	Andy Bean	388
1981	Vance Heafner	388
1982	Andy Bean	392
1983	Hal Sutton	399
1984	Mark O'Meara	419
1985	Joey Sindelar	411
1986	Joey Sindelar	415
1987	Dan Forsman	409
1988	Dan Forsman	465
1989	Ted Schulz	415
1990	Mike Donald	401
1991	Scott Hoch	446
1992	Jeff Sluman	417
1993	John Huston	426
1994	Brad Bryant	397
1995	Steve Lowery	410
1996	Fred Couples	4.20
1997	Tiger Woods	4.25
1998	David Duval†	4.29
1999	Tiger Woods	4.46
2000	Tiger Woods	4.92
2001	Phil Mickelson	4.49
2002	Tiger Woods	4.47
2003	Vijay Singh	4.41
2004	Vijay Singh	4.40

BIRDIES (*Cont.*)

2005	Tiger Woods	4.57
2006	Tiger Woods	4.65
2007	Tiger Woods	4.03

Note: Total of birdies scored 1980–95. Since 1996, winner determined by average number of birdies per round.

ALL-AROUND

1987	Dan Pohl	170
1988	Payne Stewart	170
1989	Paul Azinger	250
1990	Paul Azinger	162
1991	Scott Hoch	283
1992	Fred Couples	256
1993	Gil Morgan	252
1994	Bob Estes	227
1995	Justin Leonard	323
1996	Fred Couples	214
1997	Bill Glasson	282
1998	John Huston	151
1999	Tiger Woods	120
2000	Tiger Woods	113
2001	Phil Mickelson	174
2002	Phil Mickelson	259
2003	Tiger Woods	206
2004	Jeff Ogilvy	268
2005	Tiger Woods	265
2006	Tiger Woods	216
2007	Tiger Woods	240

Note: Sum of the places of standing from the other statistical categories; the player with the number closest to zero leads.

† Number had to be carried to extra decimal place to determine winner.

PGA Player of the Year Award

1948	Ben Hogan
1949	Sam Snead
1950	Ben Hogan
1951	Ben Hogan
1952	Julius Boros
1953	Ben Hogan
1954	Ed Furgol
1955	Doug Ford
1956	Jack Burke
1957	Dick Mayer
1958	Dow Finsterwald
1959	Art Wall
1960	Arnold Palmer
1961	Jerry Barber
1962	Arnold Palmer
1963	Julius Boros
1964	Ken Venturi
1965	Dave Marr
1966	Billy Casper
1967	Jack Nicklaus
1968	Not awarded
1969	Orville Moody
1970	Billy Casper
1971	Lee Trevino
1972	Jack Nicklaus
1973	Jack Nicklaus
1974	Johnny Miller
1975	Jack Nicklaus
1976	Jack Nicklaus
1977	Tom Watson
1978	Tom Watson
1979	Tom Watson
1980	Tom Watson
1981	Bill Rogers
1982	Tom Watson
1983	Hal Sutton
1984	Tom Watson
1985	Lanny Wadkins
1986	Bob Tway
1987	Paul Azinger
1988	Curtis Strange
1989	Tom Kite
1990	Wayne Levi
1991	Fred Couples
1992	Fred Couples
1993	Nick Price
1994	Nick Price
1995	Greg Norman
1996	Tom Lehman
1997	Tiger Woods
1998	David Duval
1999	Tiger Woods
2000	Tiger Woods
2001	Tiger Woods
2002	Tiger Woods
2003	Tiger Woods
2004	Vijay Singh
2005	Tiger Woods
2006	Tiger Woods
2007	Tiger Woods

Men's Golf *(Cont.)*

Vardon Trophy: Scoring Average

Year	Winner	Avg	Year	Winner	Avg	Year	Winner	Avg
1937	Harry Cooper	*500	1964	Arnold Palmer	70.01	1987	Don Pohl	70.25
1938	Sam Snead	520	1965	Billy Casper	70.85	1988	Chip Beck	69.46
1939	Byron Nelson	473	1966	Billy Casper	70.27	1989	Greg Norman	69.49
1940	Ben Hogan	423	1967	Arnold Palmer	70.18	1990	Greg Norman	69.10
1941	Ben Hogan	494	1968	Billy Casper	69.82	1991	Fred Couples	69.59
1942–46	No award		1969	Dave Hill	70.34	1992	Fred Couples	69.38
1947	Jimmy Demaret	69.90	1970	Lee Trevino	70.64	1993	Nick Price	69.11
1948	Ben Hogan	69.30	1971	Lee Trevino	70.27	1994	Greg Norman	68.81
1949	Sam Snead	69.37	1972	Lee Trevino	70.89	1995	Steve Elkington	69.62
1950	Sam Snead	69.23	1973	Bruce Crampton	70.57	1996	Tom Lehman	69.32
1951	Lloyd Mangrum	70.05	1974	Lee Trevino	70.53	1997	Nick Price	68.98
1952	Jack Burke	70.54	1975	Bruce Crampton	70.51	1998	David Duval	69.13
1953	Lloyd Mangrum	70.22	1976	Don January	70.56	1999	Tiger Woods	68.43
1954	E.J. Harrison	70.41	1977	Tom Watson	70.32	2000	Tiger Woods	67.79
1955	Sam Snead	69.86	1978	Tom Watson	70.16	2001	Tiger Woods	68.81
1956	Cary Middlecoff	70.35	1979	Tom Watson	70.27	2002	Tiger Woods	68.13
1957	Dow Finsterwald	70.30	1980	Lee Trevino	69.73	2003	Tiger Woods	68.41
1958	Bob Rosburg	70.11	1981	Tom Kite	69.80	2004	Vijay Singh	68.84
1959	Art Wall	70.35	1982	Tom Kite	70.21	2005	Tiger Woods	68.66
1960	Billy Casper	69.95	1983	Raymond Floyd	70.61	2006	Jim Furyk	68.86
1961	Arnold Palmer	69.85	1984	Calvin Peete	70.56	2007	Tiger Woods	67.79
1962	Arnold Palmer	70.27	1985	Don Pooley	70.36			
1963	Billy Casper	70.58	1986	Scott Hoch	70.08			

*Point system used, 1937–41. NOTE: As of 1988, based on minimum of 60 rounds per year. Adjusted for average score of field in tournaments entered.

Women's Golf

THE MAJOR TOURNAMENTS

LPGA Championship

Year	Winner	Score	Runner-Up	Site
1955	Beverly Hanson† (4 & 3)	220	Louise Suggs	Orchard Ridge CC, Ft Wayne, IN
1956	Marlene Hagge*	291	Patty Berg	Forest Lake CC, Detroit, MI
1957	Louise Suggs	285	Wiffi Smith	Churchill Valley CC, Pittsburgh, PA
1958	Mickey Wright	288	Fay Crocker	Churchill Valley CC, Pittsburgh, PA
1959	Betsy Rawls	288	Patty Berg	Sheraton Hotel CC, French Lick, IN
1960	Mickey Wright	292	Louise Suggs	Sheraton Hotel CC, French Lick, IN
1961	Mickey Wright	287	Louise Suggs	Stardust CC, Las Vegas, NV
1962	Judy Kimball	282	Shirley Spork	Stardust CC, Las Vegas, NV
1963	Mickey Wright	294	Mary Lena Faulk Mary Mills Louise Suggs	Stardust CC, Las Vegas, NV
1964	Mary Mills	278	Mickey Wright	Stardust CC, Las Vegas, NV
1965	Sandra Haynie	279	Clifford A. Creed	Stardust CC, Las Vegas, NV
1966	Gloria Ehret	282	Mickey Wright	Stardust CC, Las Vegas, NV
1967	Kathy Whitworth	284	Shirley Englehorn	Pleasant Valley CC, Sutton, MA
1968	Sandra Post*	294	Kathy Whitworth (75)	Pleasant Valley CC, Sutton, MA
1969	Betsy Rawls	293	Susie Berning Carol Mann	Concord GC, Kiameshia Lake, NY
1970	Shirley Englehorn*	285	Kathy Whitworth (78)	Pleasant Valley CC, Sutton, MA
1971	Kathy Whitworth	288	Kathy Ahern	Pleasant Valley CC, Sutton, MA
1972	Kathy Ahern	293	Jane Blalock	Pleasant Valley CC, Sutton, MA
1973	Mary Mills	288	Betty Burfeindt	Pleasant Valley CC, Sutton, MA
1974	Sandra Haynie	288	JoAnne Carner	Pleasant Valley CC, Sutton, MA
1975	Kathy Whitworth	288	Sandra Haynie	Pine Ridge GC, Baltimore, MD
1976	Betty Burfeindt	287	Judy Rankin	Pine Ridge GC, Baltimore, MD
1977	Chako Higuchi	279	Pat Bradley Sandra Post Judy Rankin	Bay Tree Golf Plantation, N Myrtle Beach, SC
1978	Nancy Lopez	275	Amy Alcott	Jack Nicklaus GC, Kings Island, OH
1979	Donna Caponi	279	Jerilyn Britz	Jack Nicklaus GC, Kings Island, OH

LPGA Championship *(Cont.)*

Year	Winner	Score	Runner-Up	Site
1980	Sally Little	285	Jane Blalock	Jack Nicklaus GC, Kings Island, OH
1981	Donna Caponi	280	Jerilyn Britz Pat Meyers	Jack Nicklaus GC, Kings Island, OH
1982	Jan Stephenson	279	JoAnne Carner	Jack Nicklaus GC, Kings Island, OH
1983	Patty Sheehan	279	Sandra Haynie	Jack Nicklaus GC, Kings Island, OH
1984	Patty Sheehan	272	Beth Daniel Pat Bradley	Jack Nicklaus GC, Kings Island, OH
1985	Nancy Lopez	273	Alice Miller	Jack Nicklaus GC, Kings Island, OH
1986	Pat Bradley	277	Patty Sheehan	Jack Nicklaus GC, Kings Island, OH
1987	Jane Geddes	275	Betsy King	Jack Nicklaus GC, Kings Island, OH
1988	Sherri Turner	281	Amy Alcott	Jack Nicklaus GC, Kings Island, OH
1989	Nancy Lopez	274	Ayako Okamoto	Jack Nicklaus GC, Kings Island, OH
1990	Beth Daniel	280	Rosie Jones	Bethesda CC, Bethesda, MD
1991	Meg Mallon	274	Pat Bradley Ayako Okamoto	Bethesda CC, Bethesda, MD
1992	Betsy King	267	Karen Noble	Bethesda CC, Bethesda, MD
1993	Patty Sheehan	275	Lauri Merten	Bethesda CC, Bethesda, MD
1994	Laura Davies	279	Alice Ritzman	DuPont CC, Wilmington, DE
1995	Kelly Robbins	274	Laura Davies	DuPont CC, Wilmington, DE
1996	Laura Davies	213†	Julie Piers	DuPont CC, Wilmington, DE
1997	Chris Johnson*	281	Leta Lindley	DuPont CC, Wilmington, DE
1998	Se Ri Pak	273	Donna Andrews	DuPont CC, Wilmington, DE
1999	Juli Inkster	268	Liselotte Neumann	DuPont CC, Wilmington, DE
2000	Juli Inkster*	281	Stefania Croce	DuPont CC, Wilmington, DE
2001	Karrie Webb	270	Laura Diaz	DuPont CC, Wilmington, DE
2002	Se Ri Pak	279	Beth Daniel	DuPont CC, Wilmington, DE
2003	Annika Sorenstam*	278	Grace Park	DuPont CC, Wilmington, DE
2004	Annika Sorenstam	271	Shi Hyun Ahn	DuPont CC, Wilmington, DE
2005	Annika Sorenstam	277	Michelle Wie	Bulle Rock GC, Havre de Grace, MD
2006	Se Ri Pak*	280	Karrie Webb	Bulle Rock GC, Havre de Grace, MD
2007	Suzann Pettersen	274	Karrie Webb	Bulle Rock GC, Havre de Grace, MD
2008	Yani Tseng*	276	Maria Hjorth	Bulle Rock GC, Havre de Grace, MD

*Won playoff. †Won match-play final. #Shortened due to rain.

U.S. Women's Open

Year	Winner	Score	Runner-Up	Site
1946	Patty Berg	5 & 4	Betty Jameson	Spokane CC, Spokane, WA
1947	Betty Jameson	295	Sally Sessions Polly Riley	Starmount Forest CC, Greensboro, NC
1948	Babe Zaharias	300	Betty Hicks	Atlantic City CC, Northfield, NJ
1949	Louise Suggs	291	Babe Zaharias	Prince George's G & CC, Landover, MD
1950	Babe Zaharias	291	Betsy Rawls	Rolling Hills CC, Wichita, KS
1951	Betsy Rawls	293	Louise Suggs	Druid Hills GC, Atlanta, GA
1952	Louise Suggs	284	Marlene Bauer Betty Jameson	Bala GC, Philadelphia, PA
1953	Betsy Rawls* (71)	302	Jackie Pung (77)	CC of Rochester, Rochester, NY
1954	Babe Zaharias	291	Betty Hicks	Salem CC, Peabody, MA
1955	Fay Crocker	299	Mary Lena Faulk Louise Suggs	Wichita CC, Wichita, KS
1956	Kathy Cornelius* (75)	302	Barbara McIntire (82)	Northland CC, Duluth, MN
1957	Betsy Rawls	299	Patty Berg	Winged Foot GC, Mamaroneck, NY
1958	Mickey Wright	290	Louise Suggs	Forest Lake CC, Detroit, MI
1959	Mickey Wright	287	Louise Suggs	Churchill Valley CC, Pittsburgh
1960	Betsy Rawls	292	Joyce Ziske	Worcester CC, Worcester, MA
1961	Mickey Wright	293	Betsy Rawls	Baltusrol GC (Lower Course), Springfield, NJ
1962	Murle Breer	301	Jo Ann Prentice Ruth Jessen	Dunes GC, Myrtle Beach, SC
1963	Mary Mills	289	Sandra Haynie Louise Suggs	Kenwood CC, Cincinnati,OH
1964	Mickey Wright* (70)	290	Ruth Jessen (72)	San Diego CC, Chula Vista, CA
1965	Carol Mann	290	Kathy Cornelius	Atlantic City CC, Northfield, NJ
1966	Sandra Spuzich	297	Carol Mann	Hazeltine Natl GC, Chaska, MN
1967	Catherine LaCoste	294	Susie Berning Beth Stone	Hot Springs GC (Cascades Course), Hot Springs, VA
1968	Susie Berning	289	Mickey Wright	Moslem Springs GC, Fleetwood, PA

U.S. Women's Open *(Cont.)*

Year	Winner	Score	Runner-Up	Site
1969	Donna Caponi	294	Peggy Wilson	Scenic Hills CC, Pensacola, FL
1970	Donna Caponi	287	Sandra Haynie Sandra Spuzich	Muskogee CC, Muskogee, OK
1971	JoAnne Carner	288	Kathy Whitworth	Kahkwa CC, Erie, PA
1972	Susie Berning	299	Kathy Ahern Pam Barnett Judy Rankin	Winged Foot GC, Mamaroneck, NY
1973	Susie Berning	290	Gloria Ehret Shelley Hamlin	CC of Rochester, Rochester, NY
1974	Sandra Haynie	295	Carol Mann Beth Stone	La Grange CC, La Grange, IL
1975	Sandra Palmer	295	JoAnne Carner Sandra Post Nancy Lopez	Atlantic City CC, Northfield, NJ
1976	JoAnne Carner* (76)	292	Sandra Palmer (78)	Rolling Green CC, Springfield, PA
1977	Hollis Stacy	292	Nancy Lopez	Hazeltine Natl GC, Chaska, MN
1978	Hollis Stacy	289	JoAnne Carner Sally Little	CC of Indianapolis, Indianapolis, IN
1979	Jerilyn Britz	284	Debbie Massey Sandra Palmer	Brooklawn CC, Fairfield, CT
1980	Amy Alcott	280	Hollis Stacy	Richland CC, Nashville, TN
1981	Pat Bradley	279	Beth Daniel	La Grange CC, La Grange, IL
1982	Janet Anderson	283	Beth Daniel Sandra Haynie Donna White JoAnne Carner	Del Paso CC, Sacramento,CA
1983	Jan Stephenson	290	JoAnne Carner Patty Sheehan	Cedar Ridge CC, Tulsa, OK
1984	Hollis Stacy	290	Rosie Jones	Salem CC, Peabody, MA
1985	Kathy Baker	280	Judy Dickinson	Baltusrol GC (Upper Course), Springfield, NJ
1986	Jane Geddes* (71)	287	Sally Little (73)	NCR GC, Dayton, OH
1987	Laura Davies* (71)	285	Ayako Okamoto (73) JoAnne Carner (74)	Plainfield CC, Plainfield, NJ
1988	Liselotte Neumann	277	Patty Sheehan	Baltimore CC, Baltimore, MD
1989	Betsy King	278	Nancy Lopez	Indianwood G & CC, Lake Orion, MI
1990	Betsy King	284	Patty Sheehan	Atlanta Athletic Club, Duluth, GA
1991	Meg Mallon	283	Pat Bradley	Colonial Club, Fort Worth, TX
1992	Patty Sheehan* (72)	280	Juli Inkster	Oakmont CC, Oakmont, PA
1993	Lauri Merten	280	Donna Andrew Helen Alfredsson	Crooked Stick, Carmel, IN
1994	Patty Sheehan	277	Tammie Green	Indianwood G & CC, Lake Orion, MI
1995	Annika Sorenstam	278	Meg Mallon	The Broadmoor GC, Colorado Springs,CO
1996	Annika Sorenstam	272	Kris Tschetter	Pine Needles GC, Southern Pines, NC
1997	Alison Nicholas	274	Nancy Lopez	Pumpkin Ridge CC, North Plains, OR
1998	Se Ri Pak†	290	Jenny Chuasiriporn	Blackwolf Run Golf Resort, Kohler, WI
1999	Juli Inkster	272	Sherri Turner	Old Waverly GC, West Point, MS
2000	Karrie Webb	282	Cristie Kerr/ Meg Mallon	Merit GC, Libertyville, IL
2001	Karrie Webb	273	Se Ri Pak	Pine Needles GC, Southern Pines, NC
2002	Juli Inkster	276	Annika Sorenstam	Prairie Dunes CC, Hutchinson, KS
2003	Hilary Lunke*	283	Kelly Robbins	Pumpkin Ridge GC, North Plains, OR
2004	Meg Mallon	274	Annika Sorenstam	The Orchards GC, South Hadley, MA
2005	Birdie Kim	287	Brittany Lang Morgan Pressel	Cherry Hills CC, Cherry Hills Village, CO
2006	Annika Sorenstam*	284	Pat Hurst	Newport CC, Newport, RI
2007	Cristie Kerr	279	Angela Park Lorena Ochoa	Pine Needles GC, Southern Pines, NC
2008	Inbee Park	283	Helen Alfredsson	Interlachen CC, Edina, MN

* Winner in playoff. † Winner on second hole of sudden death after 18-hole playoff ended in a tie.

Nabisco Championship

Year	Winner	Score	Runner-Up
1972	Jane Blalock	213	Carol Mann
			Judy Rankin
1973	Mickey Wright	284	Joyce Kazmierski
1974	Jo Ann Prentice*	289	Jane Blalock
			Sandra Haynie
1975	Sandra Palmer	283	Kathy McMullen
1976	Judy Rankin	285	Betty Burfeindt
1977	Kathy Whitworth	289	JoAnne Carner
			Sally Little
1978	Sandra Post*	283	Penny Pulz
1979	Sandra Post	276	Nancy Lopez
1980	Donna Caponi	275	Amy Alcott
1981	Nancy Lopez	277	Carolyn Hill
1982	Sally Little	278	Hollis Stacy
			Sandra Haynie
1983	Amy Alcott	282	Beth Daniel
			Kathy Whitworth
1984	Juli Inkster*	280	Pat Bradley
1985	Alice Miller	275	Jan Stephenson
1986	Pat Bradley	280	Val Skinner
1987	Betsy King*	283	Patty Sheehan
1988	Amy Alcott	274	Colleen Walker
1989	Juli Inkster	279	Tammie Green
			JoAnne Carner
1990	Betsy King	283	Kathy Postlewait
			Shirley Furlong
1991	Amy Alcott	273	Dottie Mochrie
1992	Dottie Mochrie*	279	Juli Inkster
1993	Helen Alfredsson	284	Amy Benz
			Tina Barrett
			Betsy King
1994	Donna Andrews	276	Laura Davies
1995	Nanci Bowen	285	Susie Redman
1996	Patti Sheehan	281	Kelly Robbins
			Meg Mallon
			Annika Sorenstam
1997	Betsy King	276	Kris Tschetter
1998	Pat Hurst	281	Helen Dobson
1999	Dottie Pepper	269	Meg Mallon
2000	Karrie Webb	274	Dottie Pepper
2001	Annika Sorenstam	281	five players
2002	Annika Sorenstam	280	Liselotte Neumann
2003	P. Meunier-Lebouc	281	Annika Sorenstam
2004	Grace Park	277	Aree Song
2005	Anika Sorenstam	273	Rosie Jones
2006	Karrie Webb*	279	Lorena Ochoa
2007	Morgan Pressel	285	Catriona Matthew
			Brittany Lincicome
			Suzann Pettersen
2008	Lorena Ochoa	277	Annika Sorenstam

*Winner in sudden-death playoff. Note: Designated fourth major in 1983; played at Mission Hills CC, Rancho Mirage, CA.

du Maurier Classic

Year	Winner	Score	Runner-Up	Site
1973	Jocelyne Bourassa*	214	Sandra Haynie	Montreal GC, Montreal
			Judy Rankin	
1974	Carole Jo Callison	208	JoAnne Carner	Candiac GC, Montreal
1975	JoAnne Carner*	214	Carol Mann	St. George's CC, Toronto
1976	Donna Caponi*	212	Judy Rankin	Cedar Brae G & CC, Toronto
1977	Judy Rankin	214	Pat Meyers	Lachute G & CC, Montreal
			Sandra Palmer	
1978	JoAnne Carner	278	Hollis Stacy	St. George's CC, Toronto
1979	Amy Alcott	285	Nancy Lopez	Richelieu Valley CC, Montreal
1980	Pat Bradley	277	JoAnne Carner	St. George's CC, Toronto
1981	Jan Stephenson	278	Nancy Lopez	Summerlea CC, Dorion, Quebec
			Pat Bradley	
1982	Sandra Haynie	280	Beth Daniel	St. George's CC, Toronto
1983	Hollis Stacy	277	JoAnne Carner	Beaconsfield GC, Montreal
			Alice Miller	
1984	Juli Inkster	279	Ayako Okamoto	St. George's G & CC, Toronto
1985	Pat Bradley	278	Jane Geddes	Beaconsfield CC, Montreal
1986	Pat Bradley*	276	Ayako Okamoto	Board of Trade CC, Toronto
1987	Jody Rosenthal	272	Ayako Okamoto	Islesmere GC, Laval, Quebec
1988	Sally Little	279	Laura Davies	Vancouver GC, Coquitlam, British Columbia
1989	Tammie Green	279	Pat Bradley	Beaconsfield GC, Montreal
			Betsy King	
1990	Cathy Johnston	276	Patty Sheehan	Westmount G & CC, Kitchener, Ontario
1991	Nancy Scranton	279	Debbie Massey	Vancouver GC, Coquitlam, British Columbia
1992	Sherri Steinhauer	277	Judy Dickinson	St. Charles CC, Winnipeg, Manitoba
1993	Brandie Burton	277	Betsy King	London Hunt and CC, London, Ontario
1994	Martha Nause	279	Michelle McGann	Ottawa Hunt and GC, Ottawa, Ont.
1995	Jenny Lidback	280	Liselotte Neumann	Beaconsfield GC, Pointe-Claire, Quebec
1996	Laura Davies	277	Nancy Lopez	Edmonton CC, Edmonton, Alberta
			Karrie Webb	
1997	Colleen Walker	278	Liselotte Neumann	Glen Abbey GC, Oakville, Ontario
1998	Brandie Burton	270	Annika Sorenstam	Essex G & CC, Windsor, Ontario
1999	Karrie Webb	277	Laura Davies	Priddis Greens G & CC, Calgary, Alberta
2000	Meg Mallon	282	Rosie Jones	Royal Ottawa GC, Aylmer, Quebec

*Winner in sudden-death playoff. Note: Designated third major in 1979; discontinued in 2001.

Women's British Open

Year	Winner	Score	Runner-Up	Site
2001	Se Ri Pak	277	Mi Hyun Kim	Sunningdale GC, Berkshire, England
2002	Karrie Webb	273	Michelle Ellis Paula Marti	Turnberry GC, Ailsa, Scotland
2003	Annika Sorenstam	278	Se Ri Pak	Royal Lytham & St. Annes, England
2004	Karen Stupples	269	Rachel Teske	Sunningdale GC, Berklshire, England
2005	Jeong Jang	272	Sophie Gustafson	Royal Birkdale CC, Merseyside, England
2006	Sherri Steinhauer	281	Cristie Kerr	Royal Lytham & St. Anne's, England
2007	Lorena Ochoa	287	Jee Young Lee Maria Hjorth	Old Course, St. Andrew's, Scotland
2008	Ji-Yai Shin	270	Yani Tseng	Sunningdale GC, Berkshire, England

Note: Designated fourth major in 2001.

Alltime Major Championship Winners

	LPGA	U.S. Open	Nabisco	Brit. Open	‡du Maurier	#Titleholders	†Western	U.S. Am	Brit. Am	Total
Patty Berg	0	1	0	0	0	7	7	1	0	16
Mickey Wright	4	4	0	0	0	2	3	0	0	13
Louise Suggs	1	2	0	0	0	4	4	1	1	13
Babe Zaharias	0	3	0	0	0	3	4	1	1	12
*Juli Inkster	2	2	2	0	1	0	0	3	0	10
*Annika Sorenstam	3	3	3	1	0	0	0	0	0	10
Betsy Rawls	2	4	0	0	0	0	2	0	0	8
JoAnne Carner	0	2	0	0	0	0	0	5	0	7
*Karrie Webb	1	2	2	1	1	0	0	0	0	7
Kathy Whitworth	3	0	0	0	0	2	1	0	0	6
Pat Bradley	1	1	1	0	3	0	0	0	0	6
Patty Sheehan	3	2	1	0	0	0	0	0	0	6
Glenna Vare	0	0	0	0	0	0	0	6	0	6
Betsy King	1	2	3	0	0	0	0	0	0	6

*Active LPGA player.
#Major from 1937–1972. †Major from 1937–1967. ‡Major from 1979–2000.

Alltime Multiple Professional Major Winners

LPGA

Mickey Wright	4
Nancy Lopez	3
Se Ri Pak	3
Patty Sheehan	3
*Annika Sorenstam	3
Kathy Whitworth	3
Donna Caponi	2
Sandra Haynie	2
Mary Mills	2
Betsy Rawls	2
Laura Davies	2
*Juli Inkster	2

U.S. OPEN

Betsy Rawls	4
Mickey Wright	4
Susie Maxwell Berning	3
Hollis Stacy	3
Babe Zaharias	3
*Annika Sorenstam	3
JoAnne Carner	2
Donna Caponi	2
Betsy King	2
Meg Mallon	2
Patty Sheehan	2
Louise Suggs	2
Karrie Webb	2
*Juli Inkster	2

NABISCO/DINAH SHORE

*Amy Alcott	3
Betsy King	3
*Annika Sorenstam	3
*Juli Inkster	2
*Karrie Webb	2

TITLEHOLDERS

Patty Berg	7
Louise Suggs	4
Babe Zaharias	3
Dorothy Kirby	2
Marilynn Smith	2
Kathy Whitworth	2
Mickey Wright	2

WESTERN OPEN

Patty Berg	7
Louise Suggs	4
Babe Zaharias	4
Mickey Wright	3
June Beebe	2
Opal Hill	2
Betty Jameson	2
Betsy Rawls	2

DU MAURIER

Pat Bradley	3
Brandie Burton	2
JoAnne Carner	2

*Active player.

THE LPGA TOUR

Most Career Wins†

	Wins
Kathy Whitworth	88
Mickey Wright	82
*Annika Sorenstam	72
Patty Berg	60
Louise Suggs	58
Betsy Rawls	55
Nancy Lopez	48
JoAnne Carner	43
Sandra Haynie	42
Babe Zaharias	41
Carol Mann	38
Patty Sheehan	35
*Karrie Webb	35
Betsy King	34
*Beth Daniel	33
Pat Bradley	31
*Juli Inkster	31
*Amy Alcott	29
Jane Blalock	29
Judy Rankin	26
Marlene Hagge	26
*Lorena Ochoa	23

*Active player.

Season Money Leaders

Year	Player	Earnings ($)
1950	Babe Zaharias	14,800
1951	Babe Zaharias	15,087
1952	Betsy Rawls	14,505
1953	Louise Suggs	19,816
1954	Patty Berg	16,011
1955	Patty Berg	16,492
1956	Marlene Hagge	20,235
1957	Patty Berg	16,272
1958	Beverly Hanson	12,639
1959	Betsy Rawls	26,774
1960	Louise Suggs	16,892
1961	Mickey Wright	22,236
1962	Mickey Wright	21,641
1963	Mickey Wright	31,269
1964	Mickey Wright	29,800
1965	Kathy Whitworth	28,658
1966	Kathy Whitworth	33,517
1967	Kathy Whitworth	32,937
1968	Kathy Whitworth	48,379
1969	Carol Mann	49,152
1970	Kathy Whitworth	30,235
1971	Kathy Whitworth	41,181
1972	Kathy Whitworth	65,063
1973	Kathy Whitworth	82,864
1974	JoAnne Carner	87,094
1975	Sandra Palmer	76,374
1976	Judy Rankin	150,734
1977	Judy Rankin	122,890
1978	Nancy Lopez	189,814
1979	Nancy Lopez	197,489
1980	Beth Daniel	231,000
1981	Beth Daniel	206,998
1982	JoAnne Carner	310,400
1983	JoAnne Carner	291,404
1984	Betsy King	266,771
1985	Nancy Lopez	416,472
1986	Pat Bradley	492,021
1987	Ayako Okamoto	466,034
1988	Sherri Turner	350,851
1989	Betsy King	654,132
1990	Beth Daniel	863,578
1991	Pat Bradley	763,118
1992	Dottie Mochrie	693,335
1993	Betsy King	595,992
1994	Laura Davies	687,201
1995	Annika Sorenstam	666,533
1996	Karrie Webb	1,002,000
1997	Annika Sorenstam	1,236,789
1998	Annika Sorenstam	1,092,748
1999	Karrie Webb	1,591,959
2000	Karrie Webb	1,876,853
2001	Annika Sorenstam	2,105,868
2002	Annika Sorenstam	2,863.904
2003	Annika Sorenstam	2,029,506
2004	Annika Sorenstam	2,544,707
2005	Annika Sorenstam	2,588,240
2006	Lorena Ochoa	2,592,872
2007	Lorena Ochoa	4,364,994

LPGA Player of the Year

1966	Kathy Whitworth
1967	Kathy Whitworth
1968	Kathy Whitworth
1969	Kathy Whitworth
1970	Sandra Haynie
1971	Kathy Whitworth
1972	Kathy Whitworth
1973	Kathy Whitworth
1974	JoAnne Carner
1975	Sandra Palmer
1976	Judy Rankin
1977	Judy Rankin
1978	Nancy Lopez
1979	Nancy Lopez
1980	Beth Daniel
1981	JoAnne Carner
1982	JoAnne Carner
1983	Patty Sheehan
1984	Betsy King
1985	Nancy Lopez
1986	Pat Bradley
1987	Ayako Okamoto
1988	Nancy Lopez
1989	Betsy King
1990	Beth Daniel
1991	Pat Bradley
1992	Dottie Mochrie
1993	Betsy King
1994	Beth Daniel
1995	Annika Sorenstam
1996	Laura Davies
1997	Annika Sorenstam
1998	Annika Sorenstam
1999	Karrie Webb
2000	Karrie Webb
2001	Annika Sorenstam
2002	Annika Sorenstam
2003	Annika Sorenstam
2004	Annika Sorenstam
2005	Annika Sorenstam
2006	Lorena Ochoa
2007	Lorena Ochoa

†Through 10/1/08.

Vare Trophy: Best Scoring Average*

Year	Player	Avg
1953	Patty Berg	75.00
1954	Babe Zaharias	75.48
1955	Patty Berg	74.47
1956	Patty Berg	74.57
1957	Louise Suggs	74.64
1958	Beverly Hanson	74.92
1959	Betsy Rawls	74.03
1960	Mickey Wright	73.25
1961	Mickey Wright	73.55
1962	Mickey Wright	73.67
1963	Mickey Wright	72.81
1964	Mickey Wright	72.46
1965	Kathy Whitworth	72.61
1966	Kathy Whitworth	72.60
1967	Kathy Whitworth	72.74
1968	Carol Mann	72.04
1969	Kathy Whitworth	72.38
1970	Kathy Whitworth	72.26
1971	Kathy Whitworth	72.88
1972	Kathy Whitworth	72.38
1973	Judy Rankin	73.08
1974	JoAnne Carner	72.87
1975	JoAnne Carner	72.40
1976	Judy Rankin	72.25
1977	Judy Rankin	72.16
1978	Nancy Lopez	71.76
1979	Nancy Lopez	71.20
1980	Amy Alcott	71.51
1981	JoAnne Carner	71.75
1982	JoAnne Carner	71.49
1983	JoAnne Carner	71.41
1984	Patty Sheehan	71.40
1985	Nancy Lopez	70.73
1986	Pat Bradley	71.10
1987	Betsy King	71.14
1988	Colleen Walker	71.26
1989	Beth Daniel	70.38
1990	Beth Daniel	70.54
1991	Pat Bradley	70.76
1992	Dottie Mochrie	70.80
1993	Nancy Lopez	70.83
1994	Beth Daniel	70.90
1995	Annika Sorenstam	71.00
1996	Annika Sorenstam	70.47
1997	Karrie Webb	70.00
1998	Annika Sorenstam	69.99
1999	Karrie Webb	69.43
2000	Karrie Webb	70.05
2001	Annika Sorenstam	69.42
2002	Annika Sorenstam	68.70
2003	Se Ri Pak	70.03
2004	Grace Park	69.99
2005	Annika Sorenstam	69.33
2006	Lorena Ochoa	69.23
2007	Lorena Ochoa	69.69

*Must play 70 rounds or more to qualify; Annika Sorenstam compiled an average of 69.02 in 60 rounds in 2003.

Senior Golf

U.S. Senior Open

Year	Winner	Score	Runner-Up	Site
1980	Roberto DeVicenzo	285	William C. Campbell	Winged Foot GC, Mamaroneck, NY
1981	Arnold Palmer* (70)	289	Bob Stone (74) Billy Casper (77)	Oakland Hills CC, Birmingham, MI
1982	Miller Barber	282	Gene Littler, Dan Sikes, Jr.	Portland GC, Portland, OR
1983	Billy Casper* (75) (3)	288	Rod Funseth (75) (4)	Hazeltine GC, Chaska, MN
1984	Miller Barber	286	Arnold Palmer	Oak Hill CC, Rochester, NY
1985	Miller Barber	285	Roberto DeVicenzo	Edgewood Tahoe GC, Stateline, NV
1986	Dale Douglass	279	Gary Player	Scioto CC, Columbus, OH
1987	Gary Player	270	Doug Sanders	Brooklawn CC, Fairfield, CT
1988	Gary Player* (68)	288	Bob Charles (70)	Medinah CC, Medinah, IL
1989	Orville Moody	279	Frank Beard	Laurel Valley GC, Ligonier, PA
1990	Lee Trevino	275	Jack Nicklaus	Ridgewood CC, Paramus, NJ
1991	Jack Nicklaus* (65)	282	Chi Chi Rodriguez (69)	Oakland Hills CC, Birmingham, MI
1992	Larry Laoretti	275	Jim Colbert	Saucon Valley CC, Bethlehem, PA
1993	Jack Nicklaus	278	Tom Weiskopf	Cherry Hills CC, Englewood, CO
1994	Simon Hobday	274	Jim Albus	Pinehurst Resort & CC, Pinehurst, NC
1995	Tom Weiskopf	275	Jack Nicklaus	Congressional CC, Bethesda, MD
1996	Dave Stockton	277	Hale Irwin	Canterbury GC, Beachwood, OH
1997	Graham Marsh	280	Hale Irwin	Olympia Fields CC, Olympia Fields, IL
1998	Hale Irwin	285	Vicente Fernandez	Riviera CC, Pacific Palisades, CA
1999	Dave Eichelberger	281	Ed Dougherty	Des Moines G & CC, Des Moines, IA
2000	Hale Irwin	267	Bruce Fleisher	Saucon Valley CC, Bethlehem, PA
2001	Bruce Fleisher	280	Isao Aoki, Gil Morgan	Salem CC, Peabody, MA
2002	Don Pooley* (19) (5)	274	Tom Watson (18)	Caves Valley GC, Owings Mill, MD
2003	Bruce Lietzke	277	Tom Watson	Inverness GC, Toledo, OH
2004	Peter Jacobsen	272	Hale Irwin	Bellerive CC, St. Louis, MO
2005	Allen Doyle	274	D.A. Weibring Loren Roberts	NCR GC, Kettering, OH
2006	Allen Doyle	272	Tom Watson	Prairie Dunes CC, Hutchinson, KS
2007	Brad Bryant	282	Ben Crenshaw	Whistling Straits GC, Kohler, WI
2008	Eduardo Romero	274	Fred Funk	Broadmoor GC, Colorado Springs, CO

*Winner in playoff. Playoff scores are in parentheses. The 1983 playoff went to one hole of sudden death after an 18-hole playoff.

CHAMPIONS TOUR

Season Money Leaders

Year	Player	Earnings ($)
1980	Don January	44,100
1981	Miller Barber	83,136
1982	Miller Barber	106,890
1983	Don January	237,571
1984	Don January	328,597
1985	Peter Thomson	386,724
1986	Bruce Crampton	454,299
1987	Chi Chi Rodriguez	509,145
1988	Bob Charles	533,929
1989	Bob Charles	725,887
1990	Lee Trevino	1,190,518
1991	Mike Hill	1,065,657
1992	Lee Trevino	1,027,002
1993	Dave Stockton	1,175,944
1994	Dave Stockton	1,402,519
1995	Jim Colbert	1,444,386
1996	Jim Colbert	1,627,890
1997	Hale Irwin	2,449,420
1998	Hale Irwin	2,861,945
1999	Bruce Fleisher	2,515,705
2000	Larry Nelson	2,708,005
2001	Allen Doyle	2,553,582
2002	Hale Irwin	3,028,304
2003	Tom Watson	1,853,108
2004	Craig Stadler	2,306,066
2005	Dana Quigley	2,170,258
2006	Jay Haas	2,420,227
2007	Jay Haas	2,581,001

Most Career Wins†

Player	Wins
Hale Irwin	45
Lee Trevino	29
Gil Morgan	25
Miller Barber	24
Bob Charles	23
Don January	22
Chi Chi Rodriguez	22
Jim Colbert	20
Bruce Crampton	20
George Archer	19
Gary Player	19
Larry Nelson	19
Bruce Fleischer	18
Mike Hill	18

*Active player.

†Through 10/1/08.

International Golf

Ryder Cup Matches

Year	Results	Site
1927	United States 9½, Great Britain 2½	Worcester CC, Worcester, MA
1929	Great Britain 7, United States 5	Moortown GC, Leeds, England
1931	United States 9, Great Britain 3	Scioto CC, Columbus, OH
1933	Great Britain 6½, United States 5½	Southport and Ainsdale Courses, Southport, England
1935	United States 9, Great Britain 3	Ridgewood CC, Ridgewood, NJ
1937	United States 8, Great Britain 4	Southport and Ainsdale Courses, Southport, England
1939–1945	No tournament	
1947	United States 11, Great Britain 1	Portland GC, Portland, OR
1949	United States 7, Great Britain 5	Ganton GC, Scarborough, England
1951	United States 9½, Great Britain 2½	Pinehurst CC, Pinehurst, NC
1953	United States 6½, Great Britain 5½	Wentworth Club, Surrey, England
1955	United States 8, Great Britain 4	Thunderbird Ranch & CC, Palm Springs, CA
1957	Great Britain 7½, United States 4½	Lindrick GC, Yorkshire, England
1959	United States 8½, Great Britain 3½	Eldorado CC, Palm Desert, CA
1961	United States 14½, Great Britain 9½	Royal Lytham & St. Annes GC, St Anne's-on-the-Sea, England
1963	United States 23, Great Britain 9	East Lake CC, Atlanta
1965	United States 19½, Great Britain 12½	Royal Birkdale GC, Southport, England
1967	United States 23½, Great Britain 8½	Champions GC, Houston
1969	United States 16, Great Britain 16	Royal Birkdale GC, Southport, England
1971	United States 18½, Great Britain 13½	Old Warson CC, St. Louis
1973	United States 19, Great Britain 13	Hon Co of Edinburgh Golfers, Muirfield, Scotland
1975	United States 21, Great Britain 11	Laurel Valley GC, Ligonier, PA
1977	United States 12½, Great Britain 7½	Royal Lytham & St. Annes GC, St. Annes-on-the-Sea, Eng.
1979	United States 17, Europe 11	Greenbrier, White Sulphur Springs, WV
1981	United States 18½, Europe 9½	Walton Heath GC, Surrey, England
1983	United States 14½, Europe 13½	PGA National GC, Palm Beach Gardens, FL
1985	Europe 16½, United States 11½	Belfry GC, Sutton Coldfield, England
1987	Europe 15, United States 13	Muirfield GC, Dublin, OH
1989	Europe 14, United States 14	Belfry GC, Sutton Coldfield, England
1991	United States 14½, Europe 13½	Ocean Course, Kiawah Island, SC
1993	United States 15, Europe 13	Belfry GC, Sutton Coldfield, England
1995	Europe 14½, United States 13½	Oak Hill CC, Rochester, NY
1997	Europe 14½, United States 13½	Valderrama GC, Sotogrande, Spain
1999	United States 14½, Europe 13½	The Country Club, Brookline, MA
2002	Europe 15½, Unites States 12½	Belfry GC, Sutton Coldfield, England
2004	Europe 18½, United States 9½	Oakland Hills CC, Bloomfield Hills, MI
2006	Europe 18½, United States 9½	The K Club, County Kildare, Ireland
2008	United States 16½, Europe 11½	Valhalla GC, Louisville, KY

Team matches held every odd year between U.S. professionals and those of Great Britain/Europe. Team members selected on basis of finishes in PGA and European tour events. Match in 2001 canceled due to 9/11 terrorist attacks.

Walker Cup Matches

Year	Results	Site
1922	United States 8, Great Britain 4	Nat'l Golf Links of America, Southampton, NY
1923	United States 6, Great Britain 5	St. Andrews, Scotland
1924	United States 9, Great Britain 3	Garden City GC, Garden City, NY
1926	United States 6, Great Britain 5	St. Andrews, Scotland
1928	United States 11, Great Britain 1	Chicago GC, Wheaton, IL
1930	United States 10, Great Britain 2	Royal St. George GC, Sandwich, England
1932	United States 8, Great Britain 1	The Country Club, Brookline, MA
1934	United States 9, Great Britain 2	St. Andrews, Scotland
1936	United States 9, Great Britain 0	Pine Valley GC, Clementon, NJ
1938	Great Britain 7, United States 4	St. Andrews, Scotland
1940–46	No tournament	
1947	United States 8, Great Britain 4	St. Andrews, Scotland
1949	United States 10, Great Britain 2	Winged Foot GC, Mamaroneck, NY
1951	United States 6, Great Britain 3	Birkdale GC, Southport, England
1953	United States 9, Great Britain 3	The Kittansett Club, Marion, MA
1955	United States 10, Great Britain 2	St. Andrews, Scotland
1957	United States 8, Great Britain 3	Minikahda Club, Minneapolis
1959	United States 9, Great Britain 3	Muirfield, Scotland
1961	United States 11, Great Britain 1	Seattle GC, Seattle
1963	United States 12, Great Britain 8	Ailsa Course, Turnberry, Scotland
1965	Great Britain 11, United States 11	Baltimore CC, Five Farms, Baltimore, MD
1967	United States 13, Great Britain 7	Royal St. George's GC, Sandwich, England
1969	United States 10, Great Britain 8	Milwaukee CC, Milwaukee, WI
1971	Great Britain 13, United States 11	St. Andrews, Scotland
1973	United States 14, Great Britain 10	The Country Club, Brookline, MA
1975	United States 15½, Great Britain 8½	St. Andrews, Scotland
1977	United States 16, Great Britain 8	Shinnecock Hills GC, Southampton, NY
1979	United States 15½, Great Britain 8½	Muirfield, Scotland
1981	United States 15, Great Britain 9	Cypress Point Club, Pebble Beach, CA
1983	United States 13½, Great Britain 10½	Royal Liverpool GC, Hoylake, England
1985	United States 13, Great Britain 11	Pine Valley GC, Pine Valley, NJ
1987	United States 16½, Great Britain 7½	Sunningdale GC, Berkshire, England
1989	Great Britain 12½, United States 11½	Peachtree Golf Club, Atlanta
1991	United States 14, Great Britain 10	Portmarnock GC, Dublin, Ireland
1993	United States 19, Great Britain 5	Interlachen CC, Edina, MN
1995	Great Britain/Ireland 14, United States 10	Royal Porthcawl, Porthcawl, Wales
1997	United States 18, Great Britain/Ireland 6	Quaker Ridge GC, Scarsdale, NY
1999	Great Britain/Ireland 15, United States 9	Nairn GC, Nairn, Scotland
2001	Great Britain/Ireland 15, United States 9	Ocean Forest GC, Sea Island, GA
2003	Great Britain/Ireland 12½, United States 11½	Ganton GC, Ganton, England
2005	United States 12½, Great Britain/Ireland 11½	Chicago GC, Wheaton IL
2007	United States 12½, Great Britain/Ireland 11½	Royal County Down, Newcastle, N. Ireland

Men's amateur team competition every other year between United States and Great Britain/Ireland. U.S. team members selected by USGA.

Solheim Cup Matches

Year	Results	Site
1990	United States 11½, Europe 4½	Lake Nona GC, Orlando, FL
1992	Europe 11½, United States 6½	Dalmahoy Hotel GC, Edinburgh
1994	United States 13, Europe 7	The Greenbriar, White Sulpher Springs, WV
1996	United States 17, Europe 11	Marriot St Pierre Hotel & CC, Chepstow, Wales
1998	United States 16, Europe 12	Muirfield Village GC, Dublin, OH
2000	Europe 14½, United States, 11 ½	Loch Lomond GC, Luss, Scotand
2002	United States 15½, Europe 12 ½	Interlachen CC, Minneapolis, MN
2003	Europe 17½, United States 10 ½	Barseback G&CC, Malmo, Sweden
2005	United States 15½, Europe 12 ½	Crooked Stick GC, Carmel IN
2007	United States 16, Europe 12	Halmstad GC, Halmstad, Sweden

Women's team matches held every other year between U.S. professionals and those of Europe. Team members selected on the basis of finishes in LPGA and European tour events.

Curtis Cup Matches

Year	Results	Site
1932	United States 5½, British Isles 3½	Wentworth GC, Wentworth, England
1934	United States 6½, British Isles 2½	Chevy Chase Club, Chevy Chase, MD
1936	United States 4½ British Isles 4½	King's Course, Gleneagles, Scotland
1938	United States 5½, British Isles 3½	Essex CC, Manchester, MA
1940–46	No tournament	
1948	United States 6½, British Isles 2½	Birkdale GC, Southport, England
1950	United States 7½, British Isles 1½	CC of Buffalo, Williamsville, NY
1952	British Isles 5, United States 4	Muirfield, Scotland
1954	United States 6, British Isles 3	Merion GC, Ardmore, PA
1956	British Isles 5, United States 4	Prince's GC, Sandwich Bay, England
1958	British Isles 4½, United States 4½	Brae Burn CC, West Newton, Mass.
1960	United States 6½, British Isles 2½	Lindrick GC, Worksop, England
1962	United States 8, British Isles 1	Broadmoor CG, Colorado Springs,CO
1964	United States 10½, British Isles 7½	Royal Porthcawl GC, Porthcawl, South Wales
1966	United States 13, British Isles 5	Va. Hot Springs G & TC, Hot Springs, VA
1968	United States 10½, British Isles 7½	Royal County Down GC, Newcastle, N. Ire.
1970	United States 11½, British Isles 6½	Brae Burn CC, West Newton, MA
1972	United States 10, British Isles 8	Western Gailes, Ayrshire, Scotland
1974	United States 13, British Isles 5	San Francisco GC, San Francisco
1976	United States 11½, British Isles 6½	Royal Lytham & St. Annes GC, England
1978	United States 12, British Isles 6	Apawamis Club, Rye, NY
1980	United States 13, British Isles 5	St. Pierre G & CC, Chepstow, Wales
1982	United States 14½, British Isles 3½	Denver CC, Denver
1984	United States 9½ British Isles 8½	Muirfield, Scotland
1986	British Isles 13, United States 5	Prairie Dunes CC, Hutchinson, KS
1988	British Isles 11, United States 7	Royal St. George's GC, Sandwich, England
1990	United States 14, British Isles 4	Somerset Hills CC, Bernardsville, NJ
1992	Great Britain/Ireland 10, United States 8	Royal Liverpool GC, Hoylake, England
1994	Great Britain/Ireland 9, United States 9	The Honors Course, Ooltewah, TN
1996	Great Britain/Ireland 11½, United States 6½	Killarney Golf & Fishing Club, Killarney, Ireland
1998	United States 10, Great Britain/Ireland 8	The Minikahda Club, Minneapolis
2000	United States 10, Great Britain/Ireland 8	Ganton GC, North Yorkshire, England
2002	United States 11, Great Britain/Ireland 7	Fox Chapel GC, Pittsburgh, PA
2004	United States 10, Great Britain/Ireland 8	Formby GC, Merseyside, England
2006	United States 11½, Great Britain/Ireland 6½	Bandon Dunes GC, Bandon, OR
2008	United States 13, Great Britain/Ireland 7	Old Course, St. Andrews, Scotland

Women's amateur team competition every other year between the United States and Great Britain/Ireland. U.S. team members selected by USGA.

Presidents Cup Matches

Year	Results	Site
1994	United States 20, International 12	Robert Trent Jones GC, Lake Manassas, VA
1996	United States 16½, International 15½	Robert Trent Jones GC, Lake Manassas, VA
1998	International 20½ United States 11½	Royal Melbourne GC, Melbourne, Australia
2000	United States 21½, International 10½	Robert Trent Jones GC, Lake Manassas, VA
2003	International 17, United States 17	Fan Court Hotel CC, George, South Africa
2005	United States 18½, International 15½	Robert Trent Jones GC, Lake Manassas, VA
2007	United States 19½, International 14½	Royal Montreal Golf Club, Bizard, Quebec

A biennial event played in non-Ryder Cup years designed to provide non-European players with international team and match play.

Boxing

Kelly Pavlik claimed the WBC middleweight title in 2007

PHOTO: DAVID GARD

Middleweight Savior

Those looking to HBO or Pay-Per-View for the next great boxing sensation may have been out of luck, but the people of Youngstown, Ohio had a front row seat

BY CHRIS MANNIX

OUT WITH THE OLD, IN WITH the new. That was the theme for boxing in 2007, a year that ostensibly kicked off in May with one of the most anticipated fights in the sport's storied history: Oscar De La Hoya and Floyd Mayweather. For more than a year the two premier pugilists had been circling one another, De La Hoya the aging legend looking to cement his legacy with one final triumph and Mayweather the undefeated phenom seeking validation. It was billed as The Fight to Save Boxing: two superstars squaring off in an effort to regenerate interest in what was perceived to be a dying sport. The hype was unprecedented, including a nine-day, 11-city promotional press tour, a four-part reality series on HBO, a furious war of words between the two fighters ("Floyd is bad for boxing," said De La Hoya. "We don't need people like him in the sport."; countered Mayweather, "I'm bad for boxing? I think he has a grudge against black fighters. You ever hear him say anything negative about a Hispanic fighter? He doesn't like us because we speak our minds.") and the on-again, off-again involvement of former De La Hoya trainer/Mayweather patriarch Floyd Mayweather Sr. While the fight itself didn't remind anyone of Hagler-Hearns (the bigger De La Hoya won the early rounds before tiring and succumbing to the superior defense and hand speed of Mayweather), the numbers were staggering: the fight generated a record 2.4 million Pay Per View buys and $120 million in revenue. De La Hoya's cut was $52 million, the highest purse ever for one fighter.

With the boxing world buzzing for a rematch, a new star was emerging. Not many people outside of Youngstown, Ohio had heard of Kelly Pavlik before 2007 but Pavlik, a blue-collar middleweight bred in the shadows of Ray "Boom-Boom" Mancini, had quietly worked his way up the middleweight division, compiling an undefeated record that included several brutal knockouts. Pavlik finally burst onto the national scene two weeks after De La Hoya-Mayweather when he stopped highly touted Edison Miranda in the seventh round. That victory set Pavlik up for a middleweight title fight against Jermain Taylor, another young star who had established himself as the premiere middleweight with back-to-back wins over Bernard Hopkins. When an agreement was reached for the two to tangle in Octo-

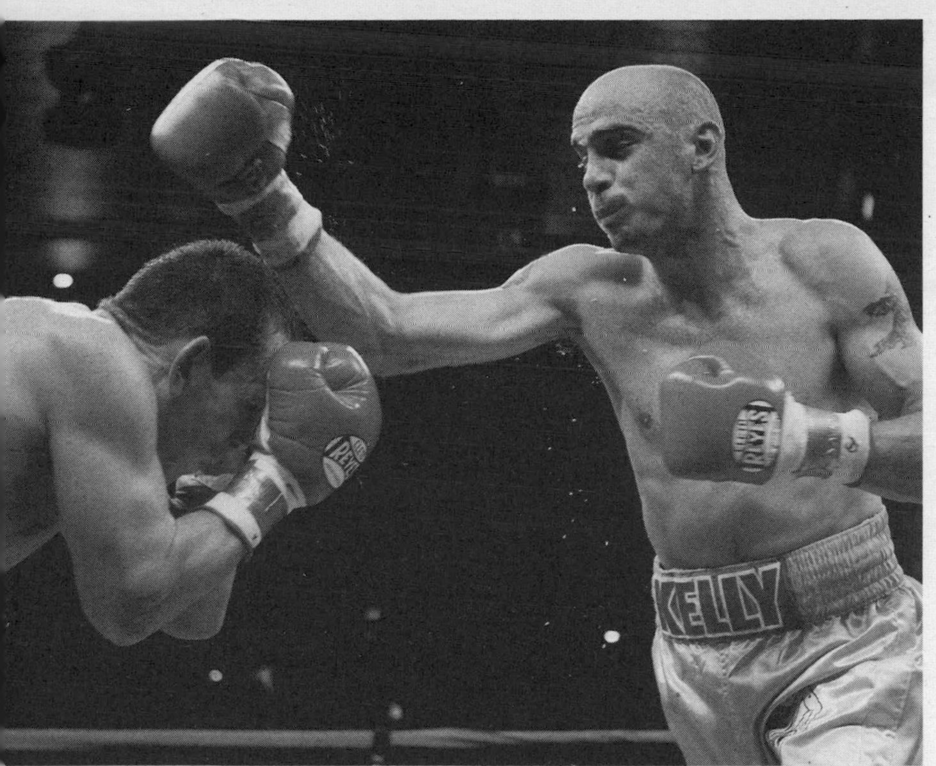

AP PHOTO/ DAVID GARD

ber, Taylor, a flashy prizefighter who was trained by the legendary Emmanual Steward, was a huge favorite over Pavlik, whose own trainer, Jack Loew, didn't have any other professional fighters in his stable.

From the opening bell it looked like the odds makers had forecast this one right. Utilizing a lightning quick jab and a potent right hand Taylor pressured Pavlik. In the second round a 15-punch onslaught from Taylor dropped Pavlik to the canvas and it looked to be the end of the night. But Pavlik gamely refused to stay down and quickly turned the tide against Taylor, who two rounds in, appeared to have punched himself out. Despite spending the entire fight leading with his chin, Pavlik continued to blast away at Taylor. By the seventh round, Taylor was beaten and a series of devastating right hands from Pavlik dropped Taylor to his knees in his corner. The referee waved off the fight, passing the crown to a new middleweight king.

Though an underdog, Pavlik won the title bout against Jermain Taylor with a TKO in the seventh round.

The attention of the sport had shifted to the future of Pavlik. First up, a February rematch with Taylor. While lacking the fireworks of their first encounter (neither Pavlik nor Taylor tasted the canvas in the rematch), it was nevertheless a dominant performance by Pavlik, who won on all three judges' scorecards to cement his status at the top of the division. Four months later Pavlik dropped Gary Lockett in the third round, punctuating his rise to the top. While Pavlik lost a light heavyweight nontitle fight to Bernard Hopkins in October, Hopkins put it best when he said that no one could beat Pavlik at 160 pounds.

A little over a year after boxing appeared to be on life support, a new American champion had emerged as a standard bearer for the sport. His name was Kelly Pavlik.

FOR THE RECORD • 2007—2008

Current Champions

Division	Weight Limit	WBA Champion	WBC Champion	IBF Champion
Heavyweight	None	Nikolay Valuev	Vitali Klitschko	Wladimir Klitschko
Cruiserweight	200	Firat Arslan	Vacant	Steve Cunningham
Light Heavyweight	175	Hugo Garay	Adrian Dianocu	Antonio Tarver
Super Middleweight	168	Mikkel Kessler	Vacant	Lucian Bute
Middleweight	160	Felix Sturm	Kelly Pavlik	Arthur Abraham
Super Welterweight	154	Daniel Santos	Vernon Forrest	Verno Phillips
Welterweight	147	Yuriy Nuzhenko	Andre Berto	Joshua Clottey
Super Lightweight	140	Andreas Kotelnik	Timothy Bradley	Paulie Malignaggi
Lightweight	135	Yusuke Kobori	Manny Pacquiao	Nate Campbell
Super Featherweight	130	Edwin Valero	Vacant	Cassius Baloyi
Featherweight	126	Chris John	Oscar Larios	Vacant
Super Bantamweight	122	Celestino Caballero	Israel Vazquez	Steve Molitor
Bantamweight	118	Anselmo Moreno	Hozumi Hasegawa	Joseph Agbeko
Super Flyweight	115	Nobuo Nashiro	Christian Mijares	Vic Darchinyan
Flyweight	112	Takefumi Sakata	Daisuke Naito	Nonito Donaire
Light Flyweight	108	Brahim Asloum	Edgar Sosa	Ulises Solis
Strawweight	105	Ramon Gonzalez	O. Sithsamerchai	Raul Garcia

Note: WBC=World Boxing Council; WBA=World Boxing Association; IBF=International Boxing Federation. Champions as of October 20, 2007.

Championship and Major Fights of 2007 and 2008

Abbreviations: WBC=World Boxing Council; WBA= World Boxing Association; IBF=International Boxing Federation; KO=knockout; TKO=technical knockout; UD=unanimous decision; SD=split decision; DQ=disqualification; MD=majority decision; TD=technical decision. Bouts from Sept. 1, 2005 to Sept. 1, 2006.

	Date	Winner	Loser	Result	Title/Org.	Site
HEAVYWEIGHT	Jan 19	Ruslan Chagaev	Matt Skelton	UD	WBA	Dusseldorf, Germany
	Mar 8	Samuel Peter	Oleg Maskaev	TKO 6	WBC	Cancun, Mexico
	July 12	Wladimir Klitschko	Tony Thompson	KO 11	IBF	Hamburg, Germany
	Aug 30	Nikolay Valuev	David Ruiz	UD	Interim WBA	Berlin, Germany
	Oct 11	Vitali Klitschko	Samuel Peter	TKO 8	WBC	Berlin, Germany
CRUISERWEIGHT	Nov 10	David Haye	Jean-Marc Mormeck	TKO 7	WBC/WBA	Paris
	Nov 24	Firat Arslan	Virgil Hill	UD	WBA	Dresden, Germany
	Dec 29	Steve Cunningham	Marco Huck	TKO 12	IBF	Bielefeld, Germany
	May 3	Firat Arsalan	Darnell Wilson	UD	WBA	Stuttgart, Germany
LIGHT HEAVYWEIGHT	April 12	Chad Dawson	Glen Johnson	UD	WBC	Tampa, Florida
	April 12	Antonio Tarver	Clinton Woods	UD	IBF	Tampa, Florida
	April 19	Adrian Dianocu	Chris Henry	UD	Interim WBC	Bucharest, Romania
	July 3	Hugo Garay	Yuri Barashian	UD	Vacant WBA	Buenos Aires
SUPER MIDDLEWEIGHT	Oct 19	Lucien Bute	Alejandro Berrio	TKO 11	IBF	Montreal, Canada
	Nov 3	Joe Calzaghe	Mikkel Kessler	UD	WBC/WBA	Cardiff, Wales
	Dec 10	Anthony Mundine	Jose Alberto Clavero	KO 4	WBA	Sydney, Australia
	June 21	Mikkel Kessler	Dimitri Sartison	KO 12	Vacant WBA	Copenhagen, Denmark
MIDDLEWEIGHT	Sept 29	Kelly Pavlik	Jermain Taylor	TKO 7	WBC	Atlantic City
	Feb 16	Kelly Pavlik	Jermain Taylor	UD	WBC	Las Vegas
	Mar 29	Arther Abraham	Elvin Ayala	KO 12	IBF	Kiel, Germany
	April 5	Felix Sturm	Jamie Pittman	TKO 7	WBA	Dusseldorf, Germany
	June 7	Kelly Pavlik	Gary Lockett	TKO 3	WBC	Atlantic City
	July 5	Felix Sturm	Randy Griffin	UD	WBA	Halle, Germany
JUNIOR MIDDLEWEIGHT (SUPER WELTERWEIGHT)	Mar 27	Verno Phillips	Cory Spinks	SD	IBF	St Louis
	June 7	Sergio Mora	Vernon Forrest	MD	WBC	Uncasville, Connecticut
	July 11	Daniel Santos	Jochim Alcine	KO 6	WBA	Montreal, Canada
	Sept 13	Vernon Forrest	Sergio Mora	UD	WBC	Las Vegas
WELTERWEIGHT	Dec 8	Yurify Nuzhnenko	Frederic Klose	UD	Vac. Int. WBA	Le Cannet, France
	April 12	Antonio Margarito	Kermit Cintron	KO 6	IBF	Atlantic City
	June 21	Andre Berto	Miguel Rodriguez	TKO 7	Vacant WBC	Memphis
	August 2	Joshua Clottey	Zab Judah	TD	Vacant IBF	Las Vegas

Championship and Major Fights of 2007 and 2008 *(Cont.)*

	Date	Winner	Loser	Result	Title/Org.	Site
SUPER LIGHTWEIGHT (JUNIOR WELTERWEIGHT)	Jan 5	Paulie Malignaggi	Herman Ngoudjo	UD	IBF	Atlantic City
	Mar 22	Andreas Kotelnik	Gavin Rees	TKO 12	WBA	Cardiff, Wales
	May 10	Timothy Bradley	Junior Witter	SD	WBC	Nottingham, England
	May 24	Paulie Malignaggi	Lovemore N'dou	SD	IBF	Manchester, England
LIGHTWEIGHT	Dec 29	Jose Alfaro	Prawet Singwancha	SD	Vacant WBA	Bielfeld, Germany
	Mar 8	Nate Campbell	Juan Diaz	SD	WBA/IBF	Cancun, Mexico
	May 19	Yusuke Kobori	Jose Alfaro	TKO 3	WBA	Tokyo
	June 28	Manny Pacquiao	David Diaz	TKO 9	WBC	Las Vegas
SUPER FEATHERWEIGHT (JUNIOR WELTERWEIGHT)	Mar 15	Manny Pacquiao	Juan Manuel Marquez	SD	WBC	Las Vegas
	April 12	Cassius Baloyi	Mzonke Fana	MD	IBF	Mafikeng, S. Africa
	June 12	Edwin Valero	Takehiro Shimada	TKO 7	WBA	Tokyo
	June 28	Francisco Lorenzo	Humberto Soto	DQ 4	Vacant Interim WBC	Las Vegas
FEATHERWEIGHT	Jan 26	Chris John	Roinet Caballero	TKO 7	WBA	Jakarta, Indonesia
	Feb 29	Roberto Guerrero	Jason Litzau	KO 8	IBF	Lemoore, California
	May 31	Oscar Larios	Fedor Viloria	TKO 5	WBC	Chetumal, Mexico
SUPER BANTAMWEIGHT (JUNIOR FEATHERWEIGHT)	Jan 19	Steve Molitor	Ricardo Castillo	UD	IBF	Orillia, Ontario, Canada
	Mar 1	Israel Vazquez	Rafael Marquez	SD	WBC	Carson, California
	June 7	Celestino Caballero	Lorenzo Parra	TKO 11	WBA	San Juan, Venezuela
BANTAMWEIGHT	Jan 10	Hozumi Hasegawa	Simone Maludrottu	UD	WBC	Osaka, Japan
	Jan 10	Wladimir Sidorenko	Nobuto Ikehara	UD	WBA	Osaka, Japan
	May 31	Anselmo Moreno	Wladimir Sidorenko	UD	WBA	Dusseldorf, Germany
	June 12	Hozumi Hasegawa	Cristian Faccio	TKO 2	WBC	Tokyo
SUPER FLYWEIGHT (JUNIOR BANTAMWEIGHT)	Jan 14	Alexander Munoz	Katsushige Kawashima	UD	WBA	Yokohama, Japan
	Feb 16	Cristian Mijares	Jorse Navarro	SD	WBC	Las Vegas
	Feb 28	Dimitri Kirilov	Cecilio Santos	Draw	IBF	New York City
	July 26	Rafael Concepcion	AJ Banal	KO 10	Vacant Interim WBA	Cebu City, Philippines
	Aug 2	Vic Darchinyan	Dimitri Kirilov	KO 5	IBF	Tacoma, Washington
	Sept 15	Nobuo Nashiro	Kohei Kono	SD	Vacant WBA	Yokohama, Japan
FLYWEIGHT	Dec 1	Nonito Donaire	Luis Maldonado	TKO 8	IBF	Mashantucket, Conn.
	Mar 8	Daisuke Naito	Pongsaklek Wonjongkam	SD	WBC	Tokyo
	Mar 29	Takefumi Sakata	Shingo Yamaguch	UD	WBA	Chiba City, Japan
	July 30	Daisuke Naito	Tomonobu Shimizu	KO 10	WBC	Tokyo
	July 30	Takefumi Sakata	Hiroyuki Hisataka	UD	WBA	Tokyo
LIGHT FLYWEIGHT (JUNIOR FLYWEIGHT)	Dec 8	Brahim Asloum	Juan Carlos Reveco	UD	WBA	Le Cannet, France
	Feb 9	Edgar Sosa	Jesus Iribe	UD	WBC	Leon, Mexico
	June 14	Edgar Sosa	Takashi Kunishige	TKO 8	WBC	Mexico City
	July 12	Ulises Solis	Glenn Donaire	UD	IBF	Hermosillo, Mexico
	July 26	Cesar Canchila	Giovanni Segura	UD	Vacant Interim WBA	Las Vegas
STRAWWEIGHT (MINI FLYWEIGHT) *MINIMUM WEIGHT*	Mar 1	Yutaka Niida	Jose Luis Varela	KO 6	WBA	Tokyo
	June 14	Raul Garcia	Florante Condes	SD	IBF	La Paz, Mexico
	June 18	Oleydong Sithsamerchai	Junichi Ebisuoka	TKO 9	WBC	Saphanhin, Thailand
	Aug 2	Juan Palacios	Omar Soto	KO 10	Vacant Interim WBC	Ponce, Puerto Rico
	Sept 15	Roman Gonzalez	Yitaka Niida	TKO 4	WBA	Yokohama, Japan

FOR THE RECORD • Year by Year

World Champions

Sanctioning bodies: the National Boxing Association (NBA), the New York State Athletic Commission (NY), the World Boxing Association (WBA), the World Boxing Council (WBC), and the International Boxing Federation (IBF).

Heavyweights (Weight: Unlimited)

Champion	Reign
John L. Sullivan*	1885–92
James J. Corbett*	1892–97
Bob Fitzsimmons*	1897–99
James J. Jeffries*	1899–05†
Marvin Hart*	1905–06
Tommy Burns*	1906–08
Jack Johnson*	1908–15
Jess Willard*	1915–19
Jack Dempsey*	1919–26
Gene Tunney*	1926–28†
Max Schmeling*	1930–32
Jack Sharkey*	1932–33
Primo Carnera*	1933–34
Max Baer*	1934–35
James J. Braddock*	1935–37
Joe Louis*	1937–49†
Ezzard Charles*	1949–51
Jersey Joe Walcott*	1951–52
Rocky Marciano*	1952–56†
Floyd Patterson*	1956–59
Ingemar Johansson*	1959–60
Floyd Patterson*	1960–62
Sonny Liston*	1962–64
Muhammad Ali*	1964–70†
Ernie Terrell WBA	1965–67
Joe Frazier* NY	1968–70
Jimmy Ellis WBA	1968–70
Joe Frazier*	1970–73
George Foreman*	1973–74
Muhammad Ali*	1974–78
Leon Spinks*	1978
Ken Norton WBC	1978
Larry Holmes WBC	1978–80
Muhammad Ali*	1978–79†
John Tate WBA	1979–80
Mike Weaver WBA	1980–82
Larry Holmes*	1980–85
Michael Dokes WBA	1982–83
Gerrie Coetzee WBA	1983–84
Tim Witherspoon WBC	1984
Pinklon Thomas WBC	1984–86
Greg Page WBA	1984–85
Michael Spinks*	1985–87
Tim Witherspoon WBA	1986
Trevor Berbick WBC	1986
Mike Tyson WBC	1986–87
James Smith WBA	1986–87
Tony Tucker IBF	1987
Mike Tyson*	1987–90
Buster Douglas*	1990
Evander Holyfield*	1990–92
Lennox Lewis WBC	1993–95
Riddick Bowe*	1992–93
Evander Holyfield*	1993–94
Michael Moorer*	1994
George Foreman*	1994–95
Oliver McCall WBC	1995
Frank Bruno WBC	1995–96
Bruce Seldon WBA	1995–96
Mike Tyson WBA	1996
Michael Moorer IBF	1996–97
Shannon Briggs*	1997–98
Lennox Lewis* WBC	1997–01
E. Holyfield WBA, IBF	1996–99
Lennox Lewis	1999–01
E. Holyfield WBA	2000–01
John Ruiz WBA	2001–03
Hasim Rahman* WBC, IBF	2001-05
Chris Byrd IBF	2002-06
Roy Jones Jr. WBA	2003-05
Lennox Lewis* WBC	2001–04
John Ruiz, WBA	2003–05
Vitali Klitschko WBC	2004–05
Hasim Rahman WBC	2005–06
Nikolay Valuev WBA	2005–07
Oleg Maskaev WBC	2006–08
Wladimir Klitschko IBF	2006–
Ruslan Chagaev WBA	2007–08
Samuel Peter WBC	2008
Nikolai Valuev WBA	2008–
Vitali Klitschko WBC	2008–

Cruiserweights (Weight Limit: 200 pounds)

Champion	Reign
Marvin Camel* WBC	1980
Carlos De Leon* WBC	1980–82
Ossie Ocasio WBA	1982–84
S.T. Gordon* WBC	1982–83
Carlos De Leon* WBC	1983–85
Marvin Camel IBF	1983–84
Lee Roy Murphy IBF	1984–86
Piet Crous WBA	1984–85
Alfonso Ratliff* WBC	1985
Dwight Braxton WBA	1985–86
Bernard Benton* WBC	1985–86
Carlos De Leon* WBC	1986–88
Evander Holyfield* WBA	1986–88
Ricky Parkey IBF	1986–87
E. Holyfield* WBA, IBF	1987–88
Evander Holyfield*	1988†
Toufik Belbouli WBA	1989
Robert Daniels WBA	1989–91
Carlos De Leon* WBC	1989–90
Glenn McCrory IBF	1989–90
Jeff Lampkin IBF	1990
M. Duran* WBC	1990–91
Bobby Czyz WBA	1991–92†
Anaclet Wamba* WBC	1991–95†
James Pritchard IBF	1991
James Warring IBF	1991–92
Alfred Cole IBF	1992–96
Orlin Norris WBA	1993–95
Nate Miller WBA	1995–97
M. Dominguez* WBC	1996–98
A. Washington IBF	1996–97
Uriah Grant IBF	1997
Imamu Mayfield IBF	1997–98
Fabrice Tiozzo WBA	1997–00
J.C. Gomez* WBC	1998–02†
Arthur Williams IBF	1998–99
Vassiliy Girov* IBF	1999–03
James Toney* IBF	2003
Virgil Hill WBA	2000–02
Wayne Braithwaite WBC	2002–05
J.M. Mormeck WBA	2002–06
J.M. Mormeck WBC	2005–06
Melvin Davis IBF	2004–05
O'Neil Bell IBF	2005–06
O'Neil Bell WBC/WBA	2006–07
Steve Cunningham IBF	2006–
J.M. Mormeck WBC/WBA	2007
David Haye WBC	2007–08
David Haye WBA	2007–

Light Heavyweights (Weight Limit: 175 pounds)

Champion	Reign
Jack Root*	1903
George Gardner*	1903
Bob Fitzsimmons*	1903–05
Jack O'Brien*	1905–12†
Jack Dillon*	1914–16
Battling Levinsky*	1916–20
Georges Carpentier*	1920–22
Battling Siki*	1922–23
Mike McTigue*	1923–25
Paul Berlenbach*	1925–26
Jack Delaney*	1926–27†
Jimmy Slattery NBA	1927
Tommy Loughran*	1927–29†
Maxie Rosenbloom*	1930–34
George Nichols NBA	1932
Bob Godwin NBA	1933
Bob Olin*	1934–35
John Henry Lewis*	1935–38†

*Lineal champion.
†Champion relinquished title to retire or switch weight classes, or had title stripped by boxing organization.

World Champions *(Cont.)*

Light Heavyweights *(Cont.)*

Champion	Reign
Melio Bettina	1939
Billy Conn*	1939–40†
Anton Christoforidis	1941
Gus Lesnevich*	1941–48
Freddie Mills*	1948–50
Joey Maxim*	1950–52
Archie Moore*	1952–62†
Harold Johnson NBA	1961
Harold Johnson*	1962–63
Willie Pastrano*	1963–65
Jose Torres*	1965–66
Dick Tiger*	1966–68
Bob Foster*	1968–74†
Vicente Rondon WBA	1971–72
John Conteh WBC	1974–77
Victor Galindez* WBA	1974–78
Miguel A. Cuello WBC	1977–78
Mate Parlov WBC	1978
Mike Rossman* WBA	1978–79
Victor Galindez* WBA	1979
Marvin Johnson* WBC	1978–79
M.S. Muhammad* WBC	1979–81
Marvin Johnson WBA	1979–80
E.M. Muhammad* WBA	1980–81
Michael Spinks* WBA	1981–83
Dwight Qawi WBC	1981–83
Michael Spinks*	1983–85†
J. B. Williamson WBC	1985–86
Slobodan Kacar IBF	1985–86
Marvin Johnson* WBA	1986–87
Dennis Andries WBC	1986–87
Bobby Czyz IBF	1986–87
Leslie Stewart WBA	1987
Virgil Hill* WBA	1987–91
Pr Charles Williams IBF	1987–93
Thomas Hearns WBC	1987†
Donny Lalonde WBC	1987–88
Sugar Ray Leonard WBC	1988
Dennis Andries WBC	1989
Jeff Harding WBC	1989–90
Dennis Andries WBC	1990–91
Thomas Hearns* WBA	1991–92
Jeff Harding WBC	1991–94
Iran Barkley* WBA	1992
Virgil Hill* WBA	1992–97
Henry Maske IBF	1993–96
Mike McCallum WBC	1994–95
Fabrice Tiozzo WBC	1995–96
D. Michalczewski* IBF	1997†
Roy Jones Jr. WBC, WBA	1997–03
William Guthrie IBF	1997–98
Reggie Johnson IBF	1998–99
Roy Jones Jr.*	1999–03
Bruno Girard WBA	2001–03
Mehdi Sahnoune WBA	2003
Silvio Branco WBA	2003–04
Antonio Tarver WBC, IBF	2003
Roy Jones Jr. WBC	2003
Glencoffe Johnson IBF	2004–05
Fabrice Tiozzo WBA	2004–5
Antonio Tarver* WBC	2004–05
Silvio Branco WBA	2005–07
Clinton Woods IBF	2005–08
Tomasz Adamek WBC	2005–07
Stipe Drews WBA	2007
Chad Dawson WBC	2007–08
Danny Green WBA	2007–
Antonio Tarver IBF	2008–
Adrian Diaconu WBC	2008–

Super Middleweights (Weight Limit: 168 pounds)

Champion	Reign
Murray Sutherland* IBF	1984
Chong-Pal Park* IBF	1984–87
Chong-Pal Park* WBA	1987–88
G. Rocchigiani IBF	1988–89
F. Obelmejias* WBA	1988–89
Sugar Ray Leonard WBC	1988–90†
In-Chul Baek* WBA	1989–90
Lindell Holmes IBF	1990–91
Chris Tiozzo* WBA	1990–91
Mauro Galvano WBC	1990–92
Victor Cordova* WBA	1991
Darrin Van Horn IBF	1991–92
Iran Barkley IBF	1992
Nigel Benn WBC	1992–96
James Toney IBF	1992–94
Michael Nunn* WBA	1992–94
Steve Little* WBA	1994
Frank Liles* WBA	1994–99
Roy Jones Jr. IBF	1994–96
Thulane Malinga WBC	1996
V. Nardiello WBC	1996
Robin Reid WBC	1996–97
Charles Brewer IBF	1997–98
Thulane Malinga WBC	1997–98
Richie Woodhall WBC	1998–99
Sven Ottke IBF	1998–03
Byron Mitchell* WBA	1999–00
Markus Beyer WBC	1999–00
Bruno Girard* WBA	2000–01†
Glenn Catley WBC	2000–01
Eric Lucas WBC	2000–03
Byron Mitchell WBA	2000–03
Sven Ottke WBA	2003†
Anthony Mundine WBA	2003
Markus Beyer WBC	2003–04
Sven Ottke, IBF	2003–05
Cristian Sanavia WBC	2004
Manny Siaca, WBA	2004
Mikel Kessler WBA	2004–07
Markus Beyer WBC	2004–06
Jeff Lacy IBF	2005
Joe Calzaghe IBF	2006–07
Mikkel Kessler WBC	2006–07
Robert Stieglitz IBF	2007
Alejandro Berrio IBF	2007
Joe Calzaghe, WBC	2007–08
Lucian Bute, IBF	2007–
Joe Calzaghe, WBA	2007–

Middleweights (Weight Limit: 160 pounds)

Champion	Reign
Jack Dempsey*	1884–91
Bob Fitzsimmons*	1891–97†
Kid McCoy	1897–98
Tommy Ryan*	1898–07†
Stanley Ketchel*	1908
Billy Papke*	1908
Stanley Ketchel*	1908–10†
Frank Klaus*	1913
George Chip*	1913–14
Al McCoy*	1914–17
Mike O'Dowd*	1917–20
Johnny Wilson*	1920–23
Harry Greb*	1923–26
Tiger Flowers*	1926
Mickey Walker*	1926–31†
Gorilla Jones*	1931–32
Marcel Thil*	1932–37
Fred Apostoli*	1937–39
Al Hostak NBA	1938
Solly Krieger NBA	1938–39
Al Hostak NBA	1939–40
Ceferino Garcia*	1939–40
Ken Overlin*	1940–41
Tony Zale NBA	1940–41
Billy Soose*	1941
Tony Zale*	1941–47
Rocky Graziano*	1947–48
Tony Zale*	1948
Marcel Cerdan*	1948–49
Jake La Motta*	1949–51
Sugar Ray Robinson*	1951
Randy Turpin*	1951
Sugar Ray Robinson*	1951–52†
Bobo Olson*	1953–55
Sugar Ray Robinson*	1955–57
Gene Fullmer*	1957
Sugar Ray Robinson*	1957
Carmen Basilio*	1957–58
Sugar Ray Robinson*	1958–60
Gene Fullmer NBA	1959–62
Paul Pender*	1960–61
Terry Downes*	1961–62
Paul Pender*	1962–63†
Dick Tiger WBA	1962–63
Dick Tiger*	1963
Joey Giardello*	1963–65
Dick Tiger*	1965–66
Emile Griffith*	1966–67
Nino Benvenuti*	1967
Emile Griffith*	1967–68
Nino Benvenuti*	1968–70
Carlos Monzon*	1970–77†
Rodrigo Valdez WBC	1974–76
Rodrigo Valdez*	1977–78
Hugo Corro*	1978–79
Vito Antuofermo*	1979–80
Alan Minter*	1980

*Lineal champion. †Champion retired or relinquished title.

World Champions *(Cont.)*

Middleweights *(Cont.)*

Champion	Reign
Marvin Hagler*	1980–87
Sugar Ray Leonard*	1987†
Frank Tate IBF	1987–88
Sumbu Kalambay WBA	1987–89
Thomas Hearns* WBC	1987–88
Iran Barkley* WBC	1988–89
Michael Nunn IBF	1988–91
Roberto Duran* WBC	1989–90†
Michael Nunn* IBF	1991
Mike McCallum WBA	1989–91
Julian Jackson WBC	1990–93
James Toney* IBF	1991–93†
Reggie Johnson WBA	1992–94
Roy Jones Jr.* IBF	1993–95†
G. McClellan WBC	1993–95†
Jorge Castro WBA	1994–95
Shinji Takehara WBA	1995–96
Jullian Jackson WBC	1995
Quincy Taylor WBC	1995–96
Bernard Hopkins* IBF	1994–
Keith Holmes WBC	1996–98
William Joppy WBA	1996–97
J.C. Green WBA	1997
William Joppy WBA	1998–01
Hassine Cherifi WBC	1998–99
Keith Holmes WBC	1999–00
Felix Trinidad WBA	2001
William Joppy WBA	2001–03
Bernard Hopkins* WBC/IBF	2001–05
Bernard Hopkins WBA	2003–05
Jermain Taylor IBF	2005
Jermain Taylor WBA	2005–06
Jermain Taylor WBC	2005–07
Arthur Abraham IBF	2005–
Felix Sturm WBA	2006
Javier Castillejo WBA	2006–07
Felix Sturm WBA	2007–
Kelly Pavlik WBC	2007–

Junior Middleweights (Weight Limit: 154 pounds)

Champion	Reign
Emile Griffith (EBU)	1962–63
Dennis Moyer*	1962–63
Ralph Dupas*	1963
Sandro Mazzinghi*	1963–65
Nino Benvenuti*	1965–66
Ki-Soo Kim*	1966–68
Sandro Mazzinghi*	1968
Freddie Little*	1969–70
Carmelo Bossi*	1970–71
Koichi Wajima*	1971–74
Oscar Albarado*	1974–75
Koichi Wajima*	1975
Miguel de Oliveira WBC	1975–76
Jae-Do Yuh*	1975–76
Elisha Obed WBC	1975–76
Koichi Wajima*	1976
Jose Duran*	1976
Eckhard Dagge WBC	1976–77
Miguel Angel Castellini*	1976–77
Eddie Gazo*	1977–78
Rocky Mattioli WBC	1977–79
Masashi Kudo*	1978–79
Maurice Hope WBC	1979–81
Ayub Kalule*	1979–81
Wilfred Benitez WBC	1981–82
Sugar Ray Leonard*	1981–82†
Tadashi Mihara WBA	1981–82
Davey Moore WBA	1982–83
Thomas Hearns* WBC	1982–84
Roberto Duran WBA	1983–84
Mark Medal IBF	1984
Thomas Hearns*	1984–86†
Mike McCallum* WBA	1984–87†
Carlos Santos IBF	1984–86
Buster Drayton IBF	1986–87
Duane Thomas WBC	1986–87
Matthew Hilton IBF	1987–88
Lupe Aquino WBC	1987
Gianfranco Rosi WBC	1987–88
Julian Jackson WBA	1987–90
Donald Curry WBC	1988–89
Robert Hines IBF	1988–89
Darrin Van Horn IBF	1989
Rene Jacquot WBC	1989
John Mugabi* WBC	1989–90
Gianfranco Rosi IBF	1989–94
Terry Norris* WBC	1990–93
Gilbert Dele WBA	1991
Vinny Pazienza WBA	1991–92
Julio C. Vasquez WBA	1992–95
Simon Brown* WBC	1993–94
Terry Norris* WBC	1994
Luis Santana* WBC	1995–95
Vincent Pettway IBF	1994–95
Paul Vaden IBF	1995
Carl Daniels WBA	1995
Terry Norris* WBC	1995–97
Terry Norris* IBF	1995–96†
L. Boudouani WBA	1996–99
Raul Marquez IBF	1997
Keith Mullings* WBC	1997–99
Yori Boy Campas IBF	1997–98
Fernando Vargas IBF	1998–00
F. Javier Castillejo* WBC	1999–01
David Reid WBA	1999–00
Felix Trinidad WBA	2000–01
Felix Trinidad WBA, IBF	2001†
Oscar De La Hoya* WBC	2001–03
Fernando Vargas WBA	2001–02
Ronald Wright IBF†	2001–04
Oscar De La Hoya* WBC/WBA	2002–03
Shane Mosley* WBC	2003–04
Alejandro Garcia WBA	2003–05
Ronald Wright WBA, WBC	2004–05
Verno Phillips IBF	2004–05
Ricardo Mayora WBC	2005–06
Alex T. Garcia WBA	2005–06
Roman Karmazin IBF	2005–06
Jose A. Rivera WBA	2006–07
Oscar De La Hoya WBC	2006–07
Cory Spinks IBF	2006–08
Travis Simms WBA	2007
F. Mayweather Jr. WBC	2007
Joachim Alcine WBA	2007–08
Vernon Forrest WBC	2007–08
Sergio Mora WBC	2008
Verno Phillips IBF	2008–
Daniel Santos WBA	2008–
Vernon Forrest WBC	2008–

Welterweights (Weight Limit: 147 pounds)

Champion	Reign
Paddy Duffy*	1888–90†
Mysterious Billy Smith*	1892–94
Tommy Ryan*	1894–98†
Mysterious Billy Smith*	1898–1900
Rube Ferns*	1900
Matty Matthews*	1900–01
Rube Ferns*	1901
Joe Walcott*	1901–04
The Dixie Kid*	1904–05†
Honey Mellody*	1906–07
Mike Sullivan*	1907–08†
Jimmy Gardner*	1908†
Jimmy Clabby*	1910–1†
Waldemar Holberg*	1914
Tom McCormick*	1914
Matt Wells*	1914–15
Mike Glover*	1915
Jack Britton*	1915
Ted "Kid" Lewis*	1915–16
Jack Britton*	1916–17
Ted "Kid" Lewis*	1917–19
Jack Britton*	1919–22
Mickey Walker*	1922–26
Pete Latzo*	1926–27
Joe Dundee*	1927–29
Jackie Fields*	1929–30
Young Jack Thompson*	1930
Tommy Freeman*	1930–31
Young Jack Thompson*	1931
Lou Brouillard*	1931–32
Jackie Fields*	1932–33
Young Corbett III*	1933
Jimmy McLarnin*	1933–34
Barney Ross*	1934
Jimmy McLarnin*	1934–35
Barney Ross*	1935–38
Henry Armstrong*	1938–40
Fritzie Zivic*	1940–41
Red Cochrane*	1941–46
Marty Servo*	1946
Sugar Ray Robinson*	1946–51†
Johnny Bratton	1951

*Lineal champion. †Champion relinquished title to retire or switch weight classes, or had title stripped by boxing organization.

World Champions *(Cont.)*

Welterweights *(Cont.)*

Champion	Reign
Kid Gavilan*	1951–54
Johnny Saxton*	1954–55
Tony DeMarco*	1955
Carmen Basilio*	1955–56
Johnny Saxton*	1956
Carmen Basilio*	1956–57†
Virgil Akins*	1958
Don Jordan*	1958–60
Kid Paret*	1960–61
Emile Griffith*	1961
Kid Paret*	1961–62
Emile Griffith*	1962–63
Luis Rodriguez*	1963
Emile Griffith*	1963–66†
Curtis Cokes*	1966–69
Jose Napoles*	1969–70
Billy Backus*	1970–71
Jose Napoles*	1971–75
Hedgemon Lewis NY	1972–73
Angel Espada WBA	1975–76
John H. Stracey*	1975–76
Carlos Palomino*	1976–79
Pipino Cuevas WBA	1976–80
Wilfredo Benitez*	1979
Sugar Ray Leonard*	1979–80
Roberto Duran*	1980
Thomas Hearns WBA	1980–81
Sugar Ray Leonard*	1980–82†
Donald Curry* WBA	1983–85
Milton McCrory WBC	1983–85
Donald Curry*	1985–86
Lloyd Honeyghan*	1986–87
Jorge Vaca* WBC	1987–88
Lloyd Honeyghan* WBC	1988–89
Mark Breland WBA	1987
Marlon Starling WBA	1987–88
Tomas Molinares WBA	1988–89
Simon Brown IBF	1988–91
Mark Breland WBA	1989–90
Marlon Starling* WBC	1989–90
Aaron Davis WBA	1990–91
Maurice Blocker* WBC	1990–91
Meldrick Taylor WBA	1991–92
Simon Brown* WBC	1991
Buddy McGirt* WBC	1991–93
Felix Trinidad IBF	1993–00
Pernell Whitaker* WBC	1993–97
Crisanto Espana WBA	1992–94
Ike Quartey WBA	1994–97†
Oscar De La Hoya* WBC	1997–99
James Page WBA	1998–01
Felix Trinidad* IBF, WBC	1999–00†
Shane Mosley* WBC	2000–02
Andrew Lewis WBA	2001–02
Vernon Forrest IBF	2001
Vernon Forrest* WBC	2001–03
Ricardo Mayorga WBA	2002
Ricardo Mayorga* WBC	2003–05
Michele Piccirillo IBF	2002–03
Jose Rivera WBA	2003
Cory Spinks IBF, WBC, WBA	2003–05
Zab Judah WBA/WBC/IBF	2005–06
Luis Collazo WBA	2006
Ricky Hatton WBA	2006
Carlos Baldomir WBC	2006
F. Mayweather, Jr. IBF	2006
Miguel Cotto WBA	2006–08
F. Mayweather Jr. WBC	2006–08
Kermit Cintron IBF	2006–08
A. Margarito IBF	2008
Joshua Clottey IBF	2008–
A. Margarito WBA	2008–
Andre Berto WBC	2008–

Super Lightweights (Weight Limit: 140 pounds)

Champion	Reign
Pinkey Mitchell*	1922–25
Red Herring	1925
Mushy Callahan*	1926–30
Jack (Kid) Berg*	1930–31
Tony Canzoneri*	1931–32
Johnny Jadick*	1932–33
Sammy Fuller	1932–33
Battling Shaw*	1933
Tony Canzoneri*	1933
Barney Ross*	1933–35†
Tippy Larkin*	1946
Carlos Ortiz*	1959–60
Duilio Loi*	1960–62
Eddie Perkins*	1962
Duilio Loi*	1962–63†
Roberto Cruz WBA	1963
Eddie Perkins*	1963–65
Carlos Hernandez*	1965–66
Sandro Lopopolo*	1966–67
Paul Fujii*	1967–68
Nicolino Loche*	1968–72
Pedro Adigue WBC	1968–70
Bruno Arcari WBC	1970–74
Alfonso Frazer*	1972
Antonio Cervantes*	1972–76
Perico Fernandez WBC	1974–75
S. Muangsurin WBC	1975–76
Wilfred Benitez*	1976–79†
M. Velasquez WBC	1976
S. Muangsurin WBC	1976–78
A. Cervantes WBA	1977–80
Sang-Hyun Kim WBC	1978–80
Saoul Mamby WBC	1980–82
Aaron Pryor* WBA	1980–83
Leroy Haley WBC	1982–83
Aaron Pryor* IBF	1983–85†
Bruce Curry WBC	1983–84
Johnny Bumphus WBA	1984
Bill Costello WBC	1984–85
Gene Hatcher WBA	1984–85
Ubaldo Sacco WBA	1985–86
Lonnie Smith* WBC	1985–86
Patrizio Oliva WBA	1986–87
Gary Hinton IBF	1986
Rene Arredondo* WBC	1986
Tsuyoshi Hamada WBC	1986–87
Joe Louis Manley IBF	1986–87
Terry Marsh IBF	1987
Juan Coggi WBA	1987–90
Rene Arredondo WBC	1987
R. Mayweather* WBC	1987–89
James McGirt IBF	1988
Meldrick Taylor IBF	1988–90
Julio César Chávez* WBC	1989–94
Julio César Chávez* IBF	1990–91
Loreto Garza WBA	1990–91
Juan Coggi WBA	1991
Edwin Rosario WBA	1991–92
Rafael Pineda IBF	1991–92
Akinobu Hiranaka WBA	1992
Pernell Whitaker IBF	1992–93†
Charles Murray IBF	1993–94
Jake Rodriguez IBF	1994–95
Juan Coggi WBA	1993–94
Frankie Randall* WBC	1994
Frankie Randall WBA	1994–96
Juan Coggi WBA	1996
Julio César Chávez* WBC	1994–96
Kostya Tszyu IBF	1995–97
Frankie Randall WBA	1996–97
Oscar De La Hoya* WBC	1996–97†
Khalid Rahilou WBA	1997–98
Vincent Phillips* IBF	1997–99
Sharmba Mitchell WBA	1998–01
Kostya Tszyu WBC	1998–
Terronn Millett* IBF	1999–00
Zab Judah* IBF	2000–01
Kostya Tszyu*† WBA/C	2001–03
Kostya Tszyu* IBF	2003–05
Vivian Harris WBA	2003–05
Arturo Gatti WBC	2004–05
F. Mayweather Jr. WBC	2005–06
Carlos Maussa WBA	2005–06
Ricky Hatton IBF	2005–06
Souleymane M'baye WBA	2006–07
Juan Urango IBF	2006–07
Junior Witter WBC	2006–08
Gavin Rees WBA	2007–08
Ricky Hatton IBF	2007
Lovemore N'Dou IBF	2007
Paul Malignaggo IBF	2007–
Timothy Bradley WBC	2008–
Andreas Kotelnik WBA	2008–

Lightweights (Weight Limit: 135 pounds)

Champion	Reign
Jack McAuliffe*	1886–94†
Kid Lavigne*	1896–99
Frank Erne*	1899–1902
Joe Gans*	1902–04
Jimmy Britt*	1904–05
Battling Nelson*	1905–06
Joe Gans*	1906–08
Battling Nelson*	1908–10
Ad Wolgast*	1910–12
Willie Ritchie*	1912–14
Freddie Welsh*	1915–17
Benny Leonard*	1917–25†
Jimmy Goodrich*	1925
Rocky Kansas*	1925–26
Sammy Mandell*	1926–30
Al Singer*	1930
Tony Canzoneri*	1930–33
Barney Ross*	1933–35†

Lightweights (*Cont.*)

Champion	Reign
Tony Canzoneri*	1935–36
Lou Ambers*	1936–38
Henry Armstrong*	1938–39
Lou Ambers*	1939–40
Sammy Angott NBA	1940–41
Lew Jenkins*	1940–41
Sammy Angott*	1941–42†
Beau Jack* NY	1942–43
Bob Montgomery* NY	1943
Sammy Angott NBA	1943–44
Beau Jack* NY	1943–44
Bob Montgomery* NY	1944–47
Juan Zurita NBA	1944–45
Ike Williams*	1947–51
James Carter*	1951–52
Lauro Salas*	1952
James Carter*	1952–54
Paddy DeMarco*	1954
James Carter*	1954–55
Wallace Smith*	1955–56
Joe Brown*	1956–62
Carlos Ortiz*	1962–65
Ismael Laguna*	1965
Carlos Ortiz*	1965–68
Carlos Teo Cruz*	1968–69
Mando Ramos*	1969–70
Ismael Laguna*	1970
Ken Buchanan*	1970–72
Roberto Duran*	1972–79†
Chango Carmona WBC	1972
Rodolfo Gonzalez WBC	1972–74
Ishimatsu Suzuki WBC	1974–76
Estaban DeJesus WBC	1976–78
Jim Watt WBC*	1979–81
Ernesto Espana WBA	1979–80
Hilmer Kenty WBA	1980–81
Sean O'Grady WBA	1981
Claude Noel WBA	1981
Alexis Arguello* WBC	1981–82†
Arturo Frias WBA	1981–82
Ray Mancini* WBA	1982–84
Alexis Arguello	1982–83
Edwin Rosario WBC	1983–84
Choo Choo Brown IBF	1984
L. Bramble* WBA	1984–86
Jose Luis Ramirez WBC	1984–85
Harry Arroyo IBF	1984–85
Jimmy Paul IBF	1985–86
Hector Camacho WBC	1985–86
Greg Haugen IBF	1986–87
Edwin Rosario* WBA	1986–87
Julio César Chávez* WBA	1987–88
Jose Luis Ramirez WBC	1987–88
Julio César Chávez*	1988–89†
Vinny Pazienza IBF	1987–88
Greg Haugen IBF	1988–89
P. Whitaker* WBC, IBF	1989–90
Edwin Rosario WBA	1989–90
Juan Nazario WBA	1990
P. Whitaker* WBA, WBC	1990–92†
Pernell Whitaker* IBF	1991–92†
Julio César Chávez IBF	1990–91
Edwin Rosario WBA	1991–92
Julio César Chávez WBC	1990–92
Miguel Gonzalez WBC	1992–95
Joey Gamache WBA	1992–93
Dingaan Thobela WBA	1993
Fred Pendleton* IBF	1993–94
Orzubek Nazarov WBA	1993–98
Rafael Ruelas* IBF	1994–95
Oscar De La Hoya* IBF	1995†
Phillip Holiday IBF	1995–97
Jean B. Mendy* WBC	1996–97
Steve Johnston* WBC	1997–98
Shane Mosley IBF	1997–99†
Jean B. Mendy WBA	1998–99
Cesar Bazan* WBC	1998–99
Steve Johnston* WBC	1999–00
Julien Lorcy WBA	1999
Stefano Zoff WBA	1999
Paul Spadafora IBF	1999–03
Gilbert Serrano WBA	1999–00
T. Hatakeyama WBA	2000–01
Jose Luis Castillo* WBC	2000–02
Julien Lorcy WBA	2001
Raul Balbi WBA	2001
F. Mayweather* WBC	2002–03
Leonard Dorin WBA	2002–03
Javier Jauregui IBF	2003–04
Julio Diaz IBF	2004–05
Lakva Sim WBA	2004
Juan Diaz WBA	2004–08
Jose Luis Castillo WBC	2004–05
Diego Corrales WBC	2005–06
Jesus Chavez IBF	2005–07
Joel Casamayor WBC	2006–08
Julio Diaz IBF	2007
Juan Diaz	2007–08
David Diaz WBC	2008
Yusuke Kobori WBA	2008–
Nate Campbell IBF	2008–
Manny Pacquiao WBC	2008–

Super Featherweights (Weight Limit: 130 pounds)

Champion	Reign
Johnny Dundee*	1921–23
Jack Bernstein*	1923
Johnny Dundee*	1923–24
Steve (Kid) Sullivan*	1924–25
Mike Ballerino*	1925
Tod Morgan*	1925–29
Benny Bass*	1929–31
Kid Chocolate*	1931–33
Frankie Klick*	1933–34†
Sandy Saddler*	1949–50†
Harold Gomes*	1959–60
Gabriel (Flash) Elorde*	1960–67
Yoshiaki Numata*	1967
Hiroshi Kobayashi*	1967–71
Rene Barrientos WBC	1969–70
Yoshiaki Numata WBC	1970–71
Alfredo Marcano*	1971–72
R. Arredondo WBC	1971–74
Ben Villaflor*	1972–73
Kuniaki Shibata*	1973
Ben Villaflor*	1973–76
Kuniaki Shibata WBC	1974–75
Alfredo Escalera WBC	1975–78
Samuel Serrano*	1976–80
Alexis Arguello WBC	1978–80
Yasutsune Uehara*	1980–81
Rafael Limon WBC	1980–81
C. Boza-Edwards WBC	1981
Samuel Serrano*	1981–83
R. Navarrete WBC	1981–82
Rafael Limon WBC	1982
Bobby Chacon WBC	1982–83
Roger Mayweather*	1983–84
Hector Camacho WBC	1983–84
Rocky Lockridge*	1984–85
Hwan-Kil Yuh IBF	1984–85
Julio César Chávez WBC	1984–87
Lester Ellis IBF	1985
Wilfredo Gomez*	1985–86
Barry Michael IBF	1985–87
Alfredo Layne* WBA	1986
Brian Mitchell* WBA	1986–91†
Rocky Lockridge IBF	1987–88
Azumah Nelson* WBC	1988–94
Tony Lopez IBF	1988–89
Juan Molina IBF	1989–90
Tony Lopez IBF	1990–91
Joey Gamache WBA	1991
Brian Mitchell IBF	1991
Genaro Hernandez WBA	1991–95
James Leija* WBC	1994
Juan Molina IBF	1991–95
Gabriel Ruelas* WBC	1994–95
Eddie Hopson IBF	1995
Tracy Patterson IBF	1995
Azumah Nelson* WBC	1995–97
Choi Yong-Soo WBA	1995–98
Arturo Gatti IBF	1995–98†
Genaro Hernandez* WBC	1997–98
Roberto Garcia IBF	1998–99
Floyd Mayweather* WBC	1998–01†
T. Hatakeyama WBA	1998–99
Lakva Sim WBA	1999
Diego Corrales IBF	1999–01
Jong Kwon Baek WBA	1999–00
Joel Casamayor WBA	2000–02
Steve Forbes IBF	2000–02†
Acelino Freitas* WBA	2002–04
Y. Nantchachai WBA	2002–05
S. Singmanassak WBC	2002–03
Jesus Chavez WBC	2003–04
Carlos Hernandez IBF	2003–04
Erik Morales WBC/IBF	2004–05
Erik Morales IBF	2004–05
Marco A. Barrera WBC	2005–07
Vicente Mosquera WBA	2005–06
Robbie Peden, IBF	2005
Marco A. Barrera, IBF	2005–06
Cassius Baloyi, IBF	2006
Edwin Valero, WBA	2006–
Gairy St. Clair IBF	2006
Malcolm Klassen IBF	2006–07
Mzonke Fana IBF	2007–08
Juan Marquez WBC	2007–08
Manny Pacquiao WBC	2008
Cassius Baloyi IBF	2008–

World Champions *(Cont.)*

Featherweights (Weight Limit: 126 pounds)

Champion	Reign
Torpedo Billy Murphy*	1890
Young Griffo*	1890–92†
George Dixon*	1892–97
Solly Smith*	1897–98
Dave Sullivan*	1898
George Dixon*	1898–1900
Terry McGovern*	1900–01
Young Corbett II*	1901–03†
Abe Attell*	1903–04
Tommy Sullivan*	1904–05†
Abe Attell*	1906–12
Johnny Kilbane*	1912–23
Eugene Criqui*	1923
Johnny Dundee*	1923–24†
"Kid" Kaplan*	1925–26†
Tony Canzoneri*	1927–28
Andre Routis*	1928–29
Battling Battalino*	1929–32†
Tommy Paul NBA	1932–33
Kid Chocolate NY	1932–33†
Freddie Miller NBA	1933–36
Mike Beloise NY	1936–37
Petey Sarron NBA	1936–37
Maurice Holtzer	1937–38
Henry Armstrong*	1937–38†
Joey Archibald* NY	1938–39
Leo Rodak NBA	1938–39
Joey Archibald	1939–40
Petey Scalzo NBA	1940–41
Harry Jeffra*	1940–41
Joey Archibald*	1941
Richie Lamos NBA	1941
Chalky Wright*	1941–42
Jackie Wilson NBA	1941–43
Willie Pep*	1942–48
Jackie Callura NBA	1943
Phil Terranova NBA	1943–44
Sal Bartolo NBA	1944–46
Sandy Saddler*	1948–49
Willie Pep*	1949–50
Sandy Saddler*	1950–57†
Kid Bassey*	1957–59
Davey Moore*	1959–63
Sugar Ramos*	1963–64
Vicente Saldivar*	1964–67†
Paul Rojas WBA	1968
Jose Legra WBC	1968–69
Shozo Saijyo WBA	1968–71
J. Famechon* WBC	1969–70
Vicente Saldivar* WBC	1970
Kuniaki Shibata* WBC	1970–72
Antonio Gomez WBA	1971–72
C. Sanchez* WBC	1972
Ernesto Marcel WBA	1972–74
Jose Legra* WBC	1972–73
Eder Jofre* WBC	1973–74†
Ruben Olivares WBA	1974
Bobby Chacon WBC	1974–75
Alexis Arguello* WBA	1974–76†
Ruben Olivares WBC	1975
Poison Kotey WBC	1975–76
Danny Lopez* WBC	1976–80
Rafael Ortega WBA	1977
Cecilio Lastra WBA	1977–78
Eusebio Pedroza* WBA	1978–85
S. Sanchez* WBC	1980–82†
Juan LaPorte WBC	1982–84
Wilfredo Gomez WBC	1984
Min-Keun Oh IBF	1984–85
Azumah Nelson WBC	1984–88
Barry McGuigan* WBA	1985–86
Ki Young Chung IBF	1985–86
Steve Cruz* WBA	1986–87
Antonio Rivera IBF	1986–88
A. Esparragoza* WBA	1987–91
Calvin Grove IBF	1988
Jorge Paez IBF	1988–91
Jeff Fenech WBC	1988–90†
Marcos Villasana WBC	1990–91
Paul Hodkinson WBC	1991–93
Troy Dorsey IBF	1991
Manuel Medina IBF	1991–93
Yung Kyun Park* WBA	1991–93
Gregorio Vargas WBC	1993
Tom Johnson IBF	1993–97†
Eloy Rojas* WBA	1993–96
Kevin Kelley WBC	1993–95
A. Gonzalez WBC	1995
Manuel Medina WBC	1995–95
Luisito Espinosa WBC	1995–99
Wilfredo Vazquez* WBA	1996–98
Hector Lizarraga IBF	1997–98
Naseem Hamed* WBA	1998†
Naseem Hamed*	1998–01
Freddy Norwood WBA	1998
Manuel Medina IBF	1998–99
Antonio Cermeno WBA	1998–99
Cesar Soto WBC	1999
Freddy Norwood WBA	1999–00
Naseem Hamed* WBC	1999†
Paul Ingle IBF	1999–00
Guty Espadas WBC	2000–01
Erik Morales WBC	2000–02
Derrick Gainer WBA	2000–03
Mbulelo Botile IBF	2001
Frankie Toledo IBF	2001
Manuel Medina IBF	2001–02
Marco A. Barrera* WBA/WBC	2001–03
Johnny Tapia IBF	2002
Marco A. Barrera* WBC	2002†
Erik Morales WBC	2002–03
Juan Marquez IBF	2003–06
Chris John WBA	2003–
In Jin Chi WBC	2004–06
Valdemir Pereira, IBF	2006
Eric Aiken IBF	2006
T. Koshimoto, WBC	2006
Rudolfo Lopez WBC	2006
Robert Guerrero IBF	2006
Orlando Salido IBF	2006
In Jin Chi WBC	2006–07
Robert Guerrero IBF	2007
Jorge Linares WBC	2007–08
Oscar Larios WBC	2008–

Super Bantamweights (Weight Limit: 122 pounds)

Champion	Reign
Jack (Kid) Wolfe*	1922–23
Carl Duane*	1923–24
Rigoberto Riasco* WBC	1976
R. Kobayashi* WBC	1976
Dong-Kyun Yum* WBC	1976–77
Wilfredo Gomez* WBC	1977–83†
Soo-Hwan Hong WBA	1977–78
Ricardo Cardona WBA	1978–80
Leo Randolph WBA	1980
Sergio Palma WBA	1980–82
Leonardo Cruz WBA	1982–84
Jaime Garza* WBC	1983
Bobby Berna IBF	1983–84
Loris Stecca WBA	1984
Seung-Il Suh IBF	1984–85
Victor Callejas WBA	1984–86
Juan Meza* WBC	1984–85
Ji-Won Kim IBF	1985–86
Lupe Pintor* WBC	1985–86
S. Payakaroon* WBC	1986–87
Seung-Hoon Lee IBF	1987–88
Louie Espinoza WBA	1987
Jeff Fenech* WBC	1987†
Julio Gervacio WBA	1987–88
Daniel Zaragoza* WBC	1988–90
Jose Sanabria IBF	1988–89
B. Pinango WBA	1988
J.J. Estrada WBA	1988–89
Fabrice Benichou IBF	1989–90
Jesus Salud WBA	1989–90
Welcome Ncita IBF	1990–92
Paul Banke* WBC	1990
Luis Mendoza WBA	1990–91
Raul Perez WBA	1992
Pedro Decima* WBC	1990–91
K. Hatanaka* WBC	1991
Daniel Zaragoza* WBC	1991–92
Thiery Jacob* WBC	1992
Tracy Patterson* WBC	1992–94
Kennedy McKinney IBF	1993–94
Wilfredo Vasquez WBA	1992–95
Vuyani Bungu IBF	1994–99†
H. Acero* Sanchez WBC	1994–95
Antonio Cermeno WBA	1995–98†
Daniel Zaragoza* WBC	1995–97
Erik Morales* WBC	1997–00†
Enrique Sanchez WBA	1998
Nestor Garza WBA	1998–00
Benedict Ledwaba IBF	1999–01
Clarence Adams WBA	2000–01†
Willie Jorrin WBC	2000–02
Manny Pacquiao IBF	2001–04
Yober Ortega WBA	2001–02
Y. Sithyodthong WBA	2002
Osamu Sato WBA	2002
Salim Medjkoune WBA	2002–03
Mahyar Monshipour WBA	2003–06
Oscar Larios WBC	2002–05
Israel Vazquez IBF	2004–05
S. Sithchatchawal WBA	2006
Israel Vazquez WBC	2005–07
C. Caballero WBA	2006–
Michael Hunter IBF	2006
Steve Molitor IBF	2006–
Rafael Marquez WBC	2007
Israel Vazquez WBC	2007–

*Lineal champion. †Champion relinquished title to retire or switch weight classes, or had title stripped by boxing organization.

World Champions (*Cont.*)

Bantamweights (Weight Limit: 118 pounds)

Champion	Reign
Spider Kelly	1887
Hughey Boyle	1887–88
Spider Kelly	1889
Chappie Moran	1889–90
George Dixon	1890–91
Pedlar Palmer	1895–99
Terry McGovern*	1899–00†
Harry Harris	1901
Harry Forbes*	1901–03
Frankie Neil*	1903–04
Joe Bowker*	1904–05†
Jimmy Walsh*	1905–06†
Owen Moran	1907–08
Monte Attell	1909–10
Frankie Conley	1910–11
Johnny Coulon*	1910–14
Kid Williams*	1914–17
Kewpie Ertle	1915
Pete Herman*	1917–20
Joe Lynch*	1920–21
Pete Herman*	1921
Johnny Buff*	1921–22
Joe Lynch*	1922–24
Abe Goldstein*	1924
Cannonball Martin*	1924–25
Phil Rosenberg*	1925–27†
Bud Taylor NBA	1927–28
Bushy Graham NY	1928–29
Panama Al Brown*	1929–35
Sixto Escobar NBA	1934–35
Baltazar Sangchilli*	1935–36
Lou Salica NBA	1935
Sixto Escobar NBA	1935–36
Tony Marino*	1936
Sixto Escobar*	1936–37
Harry Jeffra*	1937–38
Sixto Escobar*	1938–39†
Georgie Pace NBA	1939–40
Lou Salica*	1940–42
Manuel Ortiz*	1942–47
Harold Dade*	1947
Manuel Ortiz*	1947–50
Vic Toweel*	1950–52
Jimmy Carruthers*	1952–54†
Robert Cohen*	1954–56
Paul Macias NBA	1955–57
Mario D'Agata*	1956–57
Alphonse Halimi*	1957–59
Joe Becerra*	1959–60†
Eder Jofre*	1961–65
Fighting Harada*	1965–68
Lionel Rose*	1968–69
Ruben Olivares*	1969–70
Chucho Castillo*	1970–71
Ruben Olivares*	1971–72
Rafael Herrera*	1972
Enrique Pinder*	1972–73
Romeo Anaya*	1973
Arnold Taylor*	1973–74
Rafael Herrera WBC	1973–74
Soo-Hwan Hong*	1974–75
Rodolfo Martinez WBC	1974–76
Alfonso Zamora*	1975–77
Carlos Zarate* WBC	1976–79
Jorge Lujan	1977–80
Lupe Pintor* WBC	1979–83†
Julian Solis	1980
Jeff Chandler*	1980–84
Albert Davila WBC	1983–85
Richard Sandoval*	1984–86
Satoshi Shingaki IBF	1984–85
Jeff Fenech IBF	1985
Daniel Zaragoza WBC	1985
Miguel Lora WBC	1985–88
Gaby Canizales*	1986
Bernardo Pinango*	1986–87†
W. Vasquez WBA	1987–88
Kevin Seabrooks* IBF	1987–88
Kaokor Galaxy WBA	1988
Moon Sung-Kil WBA	1988–89
Kaokor Galaxy WBA	1989
Raul Perez WBC	1988–91
O. Canizales* IBF	1988–95†
Luisito Espinosa WBA	1989–91
Israel Contreras WBA	1991–92
Eddie Cook WBA	1992–93
Greg Richardson WBC	1991
J. Tatsuyoshi, WBC	1991–92
Victor Rabanales WBC	1992–93
Jung-Il Byun WBC	1993
Jorge Julio WBA	1993
Yasuei Yakushiji WBC	1993–95
Junior Jones WBA	1994
John M. Johnson WBA	1994
D. Chuvatana WBA	1994–95
V. Sahaprom* WBA	1995–96
W. McCullough WBC	1995–96
Harold Mestre IBF	1995
Mbulelo Botile IBF	1995–97
Nana Konadu* WBA	1996–98
S. Singmanassak WBC	1996–97
Tim Austin IBF	1997–03
J.Tatsuyoshi WBC	1997–98
Johnny Tapia* WBA	1998–99
V. Sahaprom* WBC	1998–05
Paulie Ayala* WBA	1999–01†
Eidy Moya WBA	2001–02
Johnny Bredahl WBA	2002–05
Rafael Marquez IBF	2003–07
W. Sidorenko WBA	2005–08
H. Hasegawa WBC	2005–
Luis Perez IBF	2007
Joseph Agbeko IBF	2007–
Anselmo Moreno WBA	2008–

Super Flyweights (Weight Limit: 115 pounds)

Champion	Reign
Rafael Orono* WBC	1980–81
Chul-Ho Kim* WBC	1981–82
Gustavo Ballas WBA	1981
Rafael Pedroza WBA	1981–82
Jiro Watanabe WBA	1982–84
Rafael Orono* WBC	1982–83
Payao Poontarat* WBC	1983–84
Joo-Do Chun IBF	1983–85
Jiro Watanabe*	1984–86
Kaosai Galaxy WBA	1984
Ellyas Pica IBF	1985–86
Cesar Polanco IBF	1986
Gilberto Roman* WBC	1986–87
Ellyas Pical IBF	1986
Santos Laciar* WBC	1987
Tae-Il Chang IBF	1987
Sugar Rojas* WBC	1987–88
Ellyas Pical IBF	1987–89
Giberto Roman* WBC	1988–89
Juan Polo Perez IBF	1989–90
Nana Konadu* WBC	1989–90
Sung-Kil Moon* WBC	1990–93
Robert Quiroga IBF	1990–93
Julio Borboa IBF	1993–94
Katsuya Onizuka WBA	1993–94
Lee Hyung-Chul WBA	1994–95
Jose Luis Bueno* WBC	1993–94
H. Kawashima* WBC	1994–97
Harold Grey IBF	1994–95
Alimi Goitia WBA	1995–96
Yokthai Sith-Oar WBA	1996–97
Carlos Salazar IBF	1995–96
Harold Grey IBF	1996
Danny Romero IBF	1996–97
Gerry Penalosa* WBC	1997–98
Johnny Tapia IBF	1997–99†
Satoshi Iida WBA	1997–98
In-Joo Cho* WBC	1998–00
Jesus Rojas WBA	1998–99
Mark Johnson IBF	1999–00
Hideki Todaka WBA	1999–00
Felix Machado IBF	2000–03
M. Tokuyama* WBC	2000–04
Leo Gamez WBA	2000–01
Celes Kobayashi WBA	2001–02
Alexander Munoz WBA	2002–05
Luis Alberto Perez IBF	2003–06
Katsushige Kawashima WBC	2004–05
M. Tokuyama WBC	2005–06
Jose M. Castillo WBA	2005–06
Nobuo Nashiro WBA	2006–
Cristian Mijares WBC	2006–
Dmitri Kirilov IBF	2007–08
Vic Darchinyan IBF	2008–

*Lineal champion.

†Champion relinquished title to retire or switch weight classes, or had title stripped by boxing organization.

Flyweights (Weight Limit: 112 pounds)

Champion	Reign
Sid Smith*	1913
Bill Ladbury*	1913–14
Percy Jones*	1914†
Joe Symonds*	1914–16
Jimmy Wilde*	1916–23
Pancho Villa*	1923–25†
Fidel La Barba*	1925–27†
Frenchy Belanger* NBA	1927–28
Izzy Schwartz NY	1927–29
Frankie Genaro* NBA	1928–29
Spider Pladner* NBA	1929
Frankie Genaro* NBA	1929–31
Midget Wolgast NY	1930–35
Young Perez* NBA	1931–32
Jackie Brown* NBA	1932–35
Benny Lynch*	1935–38†
Small Montana NY	1935–37
Peter Kane*	1938–43
Little Dado NY	1938–40
Jackie Paterson*	1943–48
Rinty Monaghan*	1948–50†
Terry Allen*	1950
Dado Marino*	1950–52
Yoshio Shirai*	1952–54
Pascual Perez*	1954–60
Pone Kingpetch*	1960–62
Masahiko Harada*	1962–63
Pone Kingpetch*	1963
Hiroyuki Ebihara*	1963–64
Pone Kingpetch*	1964–65
Salvatore Burrini*	1965–66
H. Accavallo WBA	1966–68
Walter McGowan*	1966
Chartchai Chionoi*	1966–69
Efren Torres*	1969–70
Hiroyuki Ebihara WBA	1969
B. Villacampo WBA	1969–70
Chartchai Chionoi*	1970
B. Chartvanchai WBA	1970
Masao Ohba WBA	1970–73
Erbito Salavarria*	1970–73†
B. Gonzalez WBA	1972
V. Borkorsor WBC	1972–73†
Venice Borkorsor*	1973†
Chartchai Chionoi WBA	1973–74
B. Gonzalez* WBA	1973–74
Shoji Oguma* WBC	1974–75
S. Hanagata WBA	1974–75
Miguel Canto* WBC	1975–79
Erbito Salavarria WBA	1975–76
Alfonso Lopez WBA	1976
G. Espadas WBA	1976–78
B. Gonzalez WBA	1978–79
Chan-Hee Park* WBC	1979–80
Luis Ibarra WBA	1979–80
Tae-Shik Kim WBA	1980
Shoji Oguma* WBC	1980–81
Peter Mathebula WBA	1980–81
Santos Laciar WBA	1981
Antonio Avelar* WBC	1981–82
Luis Ibarra WBA	1981
Juan Herrera WBA	1981–82
P. Cardona* WBC	1982
Santos Laciar WBA	1982–85
Freddie Castillo* WBC	1982
E. Mercedes* WBC	1982–83
Charlie Magri* WBC	1983
Frank Cedeno* WBC	1983–84
Soon-Chun Kwon IBF	1983–85
Koji Kobayashi* WBC	1984
Gabriel Bernal* WBC	1984
Sot Chitalada* WBC	1984–88
Hilario Zapate WBA	1985–87
Chong-Kwan Chung IBF	1985–86
Bi-Won Chung IBF	1986
Hi-Sup Shin IBF	1986–87
Dodie Penalosa IBF	1987
Fidel Bassa WBA	1987–89
Choi-Chang Ho IBF	1987–88
Rolando Bohol IBF	1988
Yong-Kang Kim* WBC	1988–89
Duke McKenzie IBF	1988–89
Sot Chitalada* WBC	1989–91
Dave McAuley IBF	1989–92
Jesus Rojas WBA	1989–90
Yul-Woo Lee WBA	1990
L. Tamakuma WBA	1990–91
M. Kittikasem* WBC	1991–92
Yuri Arbachakov* WBC	1992–97
Yong Kang Kim WBA	1991–92
Rodolfo Blanco IBF	1992–93
P. Sithbangprachan IBF	1993–95
David Griman WBA	1992–94
S.S. Ploenchit WBA	1994–96
Francisco Tejedor IBF	1995
Danny Romero IBF	1995–96
Mark Johnson IBF	1996–99†
Jose Bonilla WBA	1996–98
Chatchai Sasakul* WBC	1997–98
Hugo Soto WBA	1998–99
Manny Pacquiao* WBC	1998–99
Leo Gamez WBA	1999
Irene Pacheco IBF	1999–05
S. Pisnurachan WBA	1999–00
M. Sinsurat* WBC	1999–00
Malcolm Tunacao* WBC	2000–01
Eric Morel WBA	2000–03
P. Wonjongkam* WBC	2001–07
Lorenzo Parra WBA	2003–07
Vic Darchinyan IBF	2005–07
Takefumi Sakata WBA	2007–
Daisuke Naito WBC	2007–
Nonito Donaire IBF	2007–

Light Flyweights (Weight Limit: 108 pounds)

Champion	Reign
Franco Udella WBC	1975
Jaime Rios WBA	1975–76
Luis Estaba* WBC	1975–78
Juan Guzman WBA	1976
Yoko Gushiken WBA	1976–81
Freddy Castillo* WBC	1978
Sor Vorasingh* WBC	1978
Sung-Jun Kim* WBC	1978–80
Shigeo Nakajima* WBC	1980
Hilario Zapata* WBC	1980–82
Pedro Flores WBA	1981
Hwan-Jin Kim WBA	1981
Katsuo Tokashiki WBA	1981–83
Amado Urzua* WBC	1982
Tadashi Tomori* WBC	1982
Hilario Zapata* WBC	1982–83
Jung-Koo Chang* WBC	1983–88†
Lupe Madera WBA	1983–84
Dodie Penalosa IBF	1983–86
Francisco Quiroz WBA	1984–85
Joey Olivo WBA	1985
Myung-Woo Yuh* WBA	1985–91
Jum-Hwan Choi IBF	1986–88
Tacy Macalos IBF	1988–89
German Torres WBC	1988–89
Yul-Woo Lee WBC	1989
M. Kittikasem IBF	1989–90
H. Gonzalez WBC	1989–90
Michael Carbajal IBF	1990–94
R. Pascua WBC	1990
M. C. Castro WBC	1991
H. Gonzalez WBC	1991–93
Hirokia Ioka* WBA	1991–92
Myung-Woo Yuh* WBA	1993†
Michael Carbajal* WBC	1993–94
Leo Gamez WBA	1993–95
H. Gonzalez* WBC, IBF	1994–95
Choi Hi-Yong WBA	1995–96
S. Sor Jaturong WBC, IBF	1995–96
Carlos Murillo WBA	1996
Keiji Yamaguchi WBA	1996
Michael Carbajal IBF	1996–97
Saman Jaturong* WBC	1995–99
Phichitchor Siriwat WBA	1996–00
Mauricio Pastrana IBF	1997–98†
Will Grigsby IBF	1998–99
Ricardo Lopez IBF	1999–02
Yo-Sam Choi* WBC	1999–02
Beibis Mendoza WBA	2000–01
Rosendo Alvarez WBA	2001–05
Jorge Arce* WBC	2002–05
Jose Burgos IBF	2003–05
Brian Viloria WBC	2005–06
R. Vasquez WBA	2005–06
Will Grigsby IBF	2005–06
Koki Kameda WBA	2006–07
Omar Nino Rivero WBC	2006–07
Ulises Solis IBF	2006–
J. C. Reveco WBA	2007
Edgar Sosa WBC	2007–
Brahim Asloum WBA	2007–

*Lineal champion.
†Champion relinquished title to retire or switch weight classes, or had title stripped by boxing organization.

World Champions *(Cont.)*

Strawweights (Weight Limit: 105 pounds)

Champion	Reign
Kyung-Yun Lee* IBF	1987
Hiroki Ioka* WBC	1987–88
Leo Gamez WBA	1988–89
S. Sithnaruepol IBF	1988–89
N. Kiatwanchai* WBC	1988–89
Bong-Jun Kim WBA	1989–91
Nico Thomas IBF	1989
Eric Chavez IBF	1989–90
Jum-Hwan Choi* WBC	1989–90
Hideyuki Ohashi* WBC	1990
F. Lookmingkwan IBF	1990–92
Ricardo Lopez* WBC	1990–98†
Hi-Yong Choi WBA	1991–92
Manny Melchor IBF	1992
Hideyuki Ohashi WBA	1992–93
R.S. Voraphin IBF	1992–96
Chana Porpaoin WBA	1993–95
Rosendo Alvarez WBA	1995–98
R. Sor Vorapin IBF	1996–97
Zolani Petelo* IBF	1997–00†
W. Chor Charoen WBC	1998–00
R. Lopez* WBA, WBC	1998–99†
Songkram Popaoin WBA	1999
Noel Arambulet WBA	1999–00
Jose Aguirre* WBC	2000–04
Joma Gamboa WBA	2000
Keitaro Hoshino WBA	2000–01
Chana Porpaoin WBA	2001
Roberto Leyva IBF	2001–02
Yutaka Niida WBA	2001†
Miguel Barrera IBF	2002–03
Edgar Cardenas IBF	2003
Noel Arambulet WBA	2002–04
Daniel Reyes IBF	2003–05
Eagle Junlaphan WBC	2004
Isaac Bustos WBC	2004–05
Yukata Niida WBA	2004–08
K. Takayama WBC	2005
Eagle Junlaphan WBC	2005–07
M. Rachman IBF	2005–07
Florante Condes IBF	2007–08
O. Sithsamerchai WBC	2007–
Roman Gonzalez WBA	2008–
Raul Garcia IBF	2008–

*Lineal champion. †Champion relinquished title to retire or switch weight classes, or had title stripped by boxing organization.

Lineal Heavyweight Champions

Champion	Reign	Age*	Career	W-L-D (KO)	SD
John L. Sullivan	1885–92	26	1878–92	38-1-3 (33)	0
James J. Corbett	1892–97	26	1884–03	11-4-2 (7)	1
Bob Fitzsimmons	1897–99	33	1880–16	74-8-3 (67)	0
James J. Jeffries†	1899–05	24	1896–10	18-1-2 (15)	7
Marvin Hart	1905–06	28	1899–10	28-7-4 (19)	0
Tommy Burns	1906–08	24	1900–20	46-5-8 (37)	11
Jack Johnson	1908–15	30	1894–28	77-13-14 (48)	9
Jess Willard	1915–19	33	1911–23	23-6-1 (20)	1
Jack Dempsey	1919–26	24	1914–27	60-6-8 (50)	5
Gene Tunney†	1926–28	29	1915–28	61-1-1 (45)	2
Max Schmeling	1930–32	24	1924–48	56-10-4 (39)	1
Jack Sharkey	1932–33	29	1924–36	38-13-3 (14)	0
Primo Carnera	1933–34	26	1928–37	88-14-0 (69)	2
Max Baer	1934–35	25	1929–41	72-12-0 (53)	0
James J. Braddock	1935–37	29	1926–38	51-26-7 (26)	0
Joe Louis†	1937–49	23	1934–51	68-3-0 (54)	25
Ezzard Charles	1949–51	27	1940–59	96-25-1 (59)	8
Jersey Joe Walcott	1951–52	37	1930–53	53-18-1 (33)	1
Rocky Marciano†	1952–56	29	1947–56	49-0-0 (43)	6
Floyd Patterson	1956–59	21	1952–72	55-8-1 (40)	4
Ingemar Johansson	1959–60	26	1952–63	26-2-0 (17)	0
Floyd Patterson	1960–62	25	1952–72	55-8-1 (40)	2
Sonny Liston	1962–64	30	1953–70	50-4-0 (39)	1
Muhammad Ali	1964–71	22	1960–81	56-5-0 (37)	9
Joe Frazier	1971–73	27	1965–81	32-4-1 (27)	2
George Foreman	1973–74	24	1969–97	76-5-0 (68)	2
Muhammad Ali	1974–78	32	1960–81	56-5-0 (37)	10
Leon Spinks	1978	24	1977–95	26-17-3 (14)	0
Muhammad Ali†	1978–79	36	1960–81	56-5-0 (37)	0
Larry Holmes	1980–85	29	1973–2002	69-6-0 (44)	20
Michael Spinks	1985–88	29	1977–88	32-1-0 (21)	3
Mike Tyson	1988–90	21	1985–2005	49-4-0 (43)	2
Buster Douglas	1990	29	1981–99	38-6-1 (25)	0
Evander Holyfield	1990–92	28	1984–	38-5-2 (26)	3
Riddick Bowe	1992–93	25	1989–96	40-1-0 (32)	2
Evander Holyfield	1993–94	31	1984–	38-5-2 (26)	0
Michael Moorer	1994	26	1988–97	39-2-0 (31)	0
George Foreman	1994–97	45	1969–97	76-5-0 (68)	3
Shannon Briggs	1997–98	25	1992–00	32-3-1 (25)	0
Lennox Lewis	1998–01	32	1989–2004	40-2-1 (31)	5
Hasim Rahman	2001	28	1994–	35-4-0 (29)	0
Lennox Lewis†	2001–04	36	1989–2004	41-2-1 (32)	2
Chris Byrd	2002–06	35	1993–	38-2-1 (20)	3
John Ruiz	2001–03	31	1992–	38-5-1 (28)	2
Roy Jones, Jr.	2003	34	1989–	49-3-0 (38)	0
John Ruiz	2003–05	33	1992–	41-6-1 (28)	2
Vitali Klitschko†	2004–05	34	1996–2005; 2007–	34-2-0 (33)	1
Hasim Rahman	2005-06	33	1994–	41-5-2 (33)	1
Oleg Maskaev	2006–08	37	1993–	32-5-0 (26)	0
Wladimir Klitschko	2006–	30	1996–	46-3-0 (41)	0
Nikolay Valuev	2005–07	32	1993–	44-0-0 (32)	1
Ruslan Chagaev	2007–08	28	2001	24-0-1 (17)	1
Samuel Peter	2008	28	2004–	30-2-0 (23)	0
Vitali Klitschko^	2008–	37	1996–2005; 2007–	36-2-0 (35)	0
Nikolay Valuev	2008–	35	1993–	49-1-0 (49)	0

*Age when boxer won world championship.
† Boxer retired or relinquished world title.
^ Boxer returned from retirement.

Horse Racing

2008 Kentucky Derby and Preakness winner Big Brown

BILL FRAKES

...And Yet So Far...

Big Brown came oh-so-close to the Triple Crown while another thoroughbred forever lost the chance to try

BY CHRIS MANNIX

GREAT THOROUGHBREDS ARE largely anonymous until the age of three, when they set their hardened hooves on the Kentucky Derby track for the first time. So despite his status as an undefeated 2–1 favorite, Big Brown was hardly a household name upon his arrival in Louisville. Purchased for $60,000 at a yearling sale in 2006, Big Brown was only valued at $190,000 one year before his first Derby, when trucking company owner Paul Pompa bought the horse, named him Big Brown (to honor his company's relationship with UPS) and sent him to race for trainer Patrick Reynolds in New York. In his first race as a two-year-old, Big Brown blew away the field, winning at the Saratoga Race Course by 11¼ lengths. In attendance that afternoon was Michael Iavarone, co-president of IAEH Stables, who immediately purchased a 75 percent stake in Big Brown for $3.5 million. "It was not ever a question that I wanted him," Iavarone said. "It was a question of what it would cost and whether he was for sale."

With three starts and three wins under his belt, Big Brown kept his unbeaten streak alive at the 134th Kentucky Derby. Bursting out of the gate and showcasing staggering breakaway speed down the stretch, Big Brown finished the Derby 4¾ lengths ahead of runner up Eight Belles. The victory would be overshadowed, however, when Eight Belles shattered both front ankles after crossing the finish line and had to be euthanized on the track.

Still, by the time the Preakness rolled around a few weeks later the buzz surrounding this powerful colt had grown. Entering the race a 2–5 favorite, Big Brown again stormed out of the gate and cruised to a 5¼-lengths victory over Macho Again, becoming just the fourth horse to win the Derby and the Preakness while remaining undefeated. "We just got beat by a monster," said Macho Again jockey Julien Leparoux. "I don't like to be second but it's not bad to be second to this horse."

The victory, however, did not come without consequence: A week after his dominating win, Big Brown developed a V-shaped crack in his left front hoof (called a "quarter crack" in racing parlance). Even with the shadow cast by the injury, the three weeks between the Preakness and the 1½ mile Belmont Stakes seemed like a prelude to a coronation. Big Brown's trainer, Rick Dutrow, called the outcome of the race "a foregone conclusion." Two days before the Belmont he said, "I know my horse; I know the other horses. I don't see any problem."

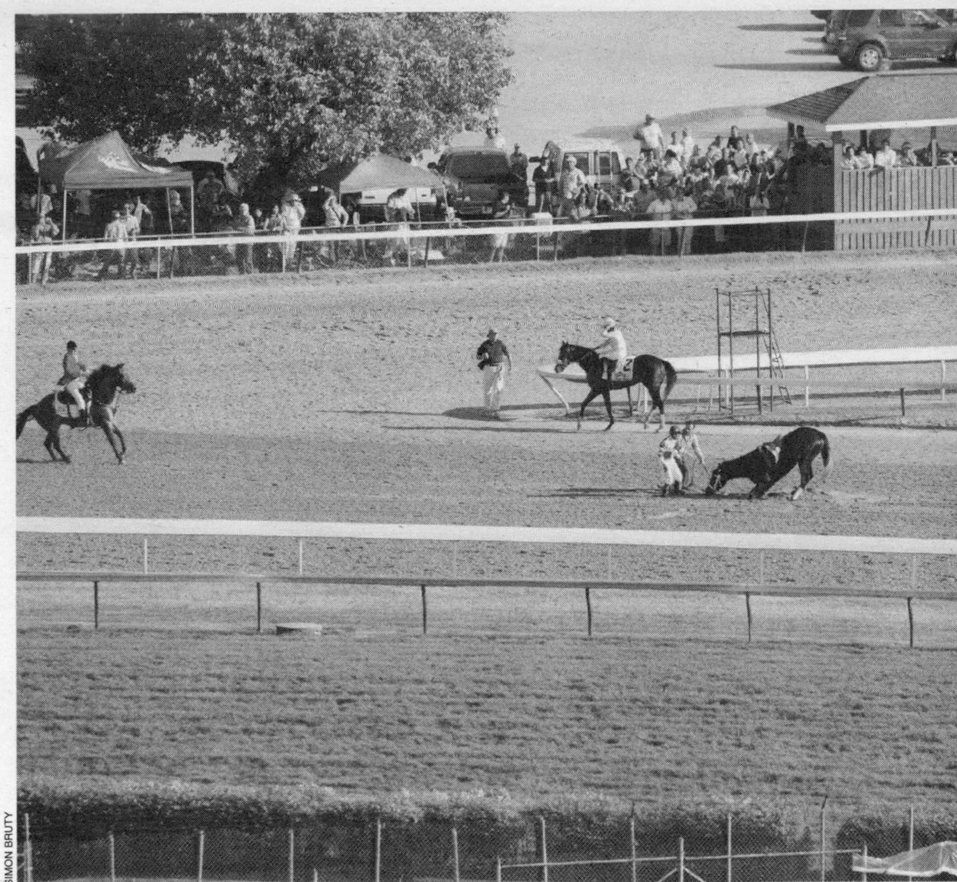
SIMON BRUTY

The quality of the competition was weakened by the race-day scratch of Casino Drive, the Japan-based half brother to the previous two Belmont winners Jazil and Rags to Riches.

With the fourth-largest crowd in Belmont history (94,476) looking on, the noise was deafening as the horses were loaded into the starting gate. But it was not a smooth race for the would-be king. Initially jockey Kent Desormeaux tried to hustle Big Brown into a gap between leader Da' Tara and Tale of Ekati. Forced to check for several jumps when the hole suddenly closed, Desormeaux then bulled Big Brown to the outside, bouncing off Anak Nakal.

Once in position on the backstretch Big Brown sauntered along in third place, but with more than a half mile to run, Desormeaux began urging a horse that, in his previous races, had rarely needed it. It was an ominous sign. In the middle of the second turn, just before the long run down the Belmont stretch, Big Brown abruptly stumbled from third place to last. Desormeaux positioned his prized horse outside in front of the grandstand and slowed him to a trot to the finish. For the seventh time in 12 years a horse had fallen short of greatness on the Belmont's daunting track. To be sure, Big Brown won't be the last.

In a tragic finish, Kentucky Derby runner-up Eight Belles became the first Derby entrant to be euthanized on the track after the race left the filly with two shattered ankles.

THOROUGHBRED RACING

The Triple Crown

134th Kentucky Derby

May 3, 2008. Grade I, 3-year-olds; 10th race, Churchill Downs, Louisville. All 126 lbs. Distance: 1¼ miles. Purse: $2,000,000 guaranteed. Track: Fast. Off: 6:15 p.m. Winner: Big Brown (By Boundary out of Mien by Nureyev); Times: 0:23.30, 0:47.04, 1:11.14, 1:36.56, 2:01.82. Won: Driving. Breeder: James B. Tafel

Horse	Finish-PP	Margin	Jockey/Trainer
Big Brown	1–20	4¾	Kent Desormeaux/Richard Dutrow, Jr.
Eight Belles	2–5	3½	Gabriel Saez/Larry Jones
Denis of Cork	3–16	2¾	Calvin Borel/David Carroll
Tale of Ekati	4–2	¾	Eibar Coa/Barclay Tagg
Recapturetheglory	5–18	2½	E.T. Baird/Louis J. Roussel III & Ronald Lamarque
Colonel John	6–10	¾	Corey Nakatani/Eoin Harty
Anak Nakal	7–3	nose	Rafael Bejarano/Nick Zito
Pyro	8–9	¾	Shaun Bridgmohan/Steve Asmussen
Cowboy Cal	9–17	3¾	John Velazquez/Todd Pletcher
Z Fortune	10–6	1½	Robby Albarado/Steve Asmussen
Smooth Air	11–12	1¾	Manoel Cruz/Bennie Stutts Jr.
Visionaire	12–8	1½	Jose Lezcano/Michael Matz
Court Vision	13–4	neck	Garrett Gomez/Bill Mott
Z Humor	14–11	7¼	Rene Douglas/Bill Mott
Cool Coal Man	15–1	neck	Julien Leparoux/Nick Zito
Bob Black Jack	16–13	4¾	Richard Migliore/William Kasparoff
Gayego	17–19	12	Mike Smith/Paulo Lobo
Big Truck	18–7	2	Javier Castellano/Barclay Tagg
Adriano	19–15	8¾	Edgar Prado/Graham Motion
Monba	20–14	—	Ramon Dominguez/Todd Pletcher

133rd Preakness Stakes

May 17, 2008. Grade I, 3-year-olds; 12th race, Pimlico Race Course, Baltimore. All 126 lbs. Distance: 1³⁄₁₆ miles; Stakes value: $1,000,000. Track: Fast. Off: 6:15 p.m. Winner: Big Brown (By Boundary out of Mien by Nureyev); Times: 0:23.59, 0:46.81, 1:10.48, 1:35.72, 1:54.80. Won: Driving. Breeder: James B. Tafel

Horse	Finish-PP	Margin	Jockey/Trainer
Big Brown	1-6	5¼	Kent Desormeaux/Richard Dutrow, Jr.
Macho Again	2–1	½	Julien Leparoux/Dallas Stewart
Icabad Crane	3–3	¾	Jeremy Rose/H. Graham Motion
Racecar Rhapsody	4–5	4¼	Robby Albarado/Kenneth McPeek
Stevil	5–8	3¾	John Velazquez/Nicholas Zito
Kentucky Bear	6–7	½	Jamie Theriot/Reade Baker
Hey Byrn	7–12	1¾	Charles Lopez/Edward Plesa, Jr.
Giant Moon	8–10	¾	Ramon Dominguez/Richard Schosberg
Tres Barrachos	9–2	1¼	Tyler Baze/C. Beau Greely
Yankee Bravo	10–4	7¼	Alex Solis/Patrick Gallagher
Gayego	11–11	neck	Mike Smith/Paulo Lobo
Riley Tucker	12–9	—	Edgar Prado/William Mott

140th Belmont Stakes

June 7, 2008. Grade I, 3-year-olds; 11th race, Belmont Park, Elmont, NY. All 126 lbs. Distance: 1½ miles. Stakes value: $1,000,000. Track: Fast. Off: 6:29 p.m. Winner: Da'Tara (By Tiznow out of Torchera by Cee's Tizzy); Times: 0:23.82, 48.30, 1:12.90, 1:37.96, 2:03.21, 2:29.65. Won: Driving. Breeder: WinStar Farm

Horse	Finish-PP	Margin	Jockey/Trainer
Da' Tara	1–5	5¼	Alan Garcia/Nick Zito
Denis of Cork	2–4	2¾	Robby Albarado/David Carroll
Ready's Echo	3–8	3	John Velazquez/Todd Pletcher
Anak Nakal	3–7	3	Julien Leparoux/Nick Zito
Macho Again	5–3	7¼	Garrett Gomez/Dallas Stewart
Tale of Ekati	6–6	6½	Eibar Coa/Barclay Tagg
Guadalcanal	7–2	½	Javier Castellano/Fred Seitz
Icabad Crane	9–9	—	Jeremy Rose/H. Graham Motion
Big Brown	10–1	—	Kent Desormeaux/Rick Dutrow

Major Stakes Races

Late 2007

Date	Race	Track	Distance	Winner	Trainer/Jockey	Purse ($)
Sept 1	Woodward Stakes	Saratoga	1⅛ miles	Lawyer Ron	T. Pletcher/ J. Velazquez	500,000
Sept 1	Kent Stakes	Delaware	1⅛ miles	Nobiz Like Showbiz	B. Tagg/ J. Castellano	501,200
Sept 2	Del Mar Derby	Del Mar	1⅛ miles	Medici Code	D. Vienna/ M. Pedroza	400,000
Sept 16	Woodbine Mile Stakes	Woodbine	1 mile	Shakespeare	W. Mott/ G. Gomez	973,892
Sept 22	Super Derby XXVII	Louisiana Downs	1⅛ miles	Going Ballistic	D.V. Hemel/ M. Berry	515,000
Sept 29	Hawthorne Gold Cup	Hawthorne	1¼ miles	Student Council	S. Asmussen/ R. Migliore	500,000
Sept 29	Yellow Ribbon Stakes	Santa Anita	1¼ miles	Nashoba's Key	C. Gaines/ J. Talamo	400,000
Sept 29	Flower Bowl Invitational	Belmont	1¼ miles	Lahudood	K. McLaughlin/ A. Garcia	600,000
Sept 29	Goodwood Stakes	Santa Anita	1⅛ miles	Tiago	J. Shirreffs/ M. Smith	520,000
Sept 30	Jockey Club Gold Cup	Belmont	1¼ miles	Curlin	S. Asmussen/ R. Albaradoo	765,000
Sept 30	Joe Hirsch Turf Classic Invitational	Belmont	1½ miles	English Channel	T. Pletcher/ J. Velazquez	612,000
Sept 30	Vosburgh Stakes	Belmont	6 furlongs	Fabulous Strike	T. Beattie/ R. Dominguez	416,000
Sept 30	Beldame Stakes	Belmont	1⅛ miles	Unbridled Belle	T. Pletcher/ R. Dominguez	612,000
Oct 6	Champagne Stakes	Belmont	1 mile	War Pass	N. Zito/ C. Velasquez	416,000
Oct 6	Shadwell Turf Mile	Keeneland	1 mile	Purim	T. Proctor/ J. Theriot	648,000
Oct 6	Indiana Derby	Hoosier	1¹⁄₁₆ miles	Zanjero	S. Asmussen/ R. Albarado	510,600
Oct 6	Lane's End B. Futurity	Keeneland	1¹⁄₁₆ miles	Wicked Style	G.R. Arnold/ R. Albarado	560,000
Oct 6.	Frizette Stakes	Belmont	1 mile	Indian Blessing	B. Baffert/ G. Gomez	400,000
Oct 6.	First Lady Stakes	Keeneland	1 mile	Vacare	C. Clement/ C. Nakatani	432,000
Oct 7	Juddmonte Spinster Stakes	Keeneland	1⅛ miles	Panty Raid	T. Pletcher/ G. Gomez	540,000
Oct 13	Queen Elizabeth II Challenge Cup	Keeneland	1⅛ miles	Bit of Whimsy	B. Tagg/ J. Castellano	500,000
Oct 21	E.P. Taylor Stakes	Woodbine	1¼ miles	Mrs. Lindsay	F. Rohaut/ J. Murtagh	1,000,000
Oct 21	Pattison Canadian International	Woodbine	1½ miles	Cloudy's Knight	F. Kirby/ R. Zimmerman	2,000,000
Oct 27	Breeders Cup Classic	Monmouth	1¼ mile	Curlin	S. Asmussen/ R. Albarado	4,580,000
Oct 27	Breeders Cup Turf	Monmouth	1½ miles	English Channel	T. Pletcher/ J. Velazquez	2,748,000
Oct 27	Breeders Cup Distaff	Monmouth	1⅛ mile	Ginger Punch	R. Frankel/ R. Bejarano	2,070,160
Oct 27	Breeders Cup Mile	Monmouth	1 mile	Kip Deville	R. Dutrow Jr./ C. Velasquez	2,409,080
Oct 27	Breeders Cup Juvenile	Monmouth	1¹⁄₁₆ miles	War Pass	N. Zito/ C. Velasquez	1,832,000
Oct 27	Breeders Cup Juvenile Fillies	Monmouth	1¹⁄₁₆ miles	Indian Blessing	B. Baffert/ G. Gomez	1,832,000
Oct 27	Breeders Cup F & M Turf	Monmouth	1⅜ miles	Lahudood	K. McLaughlin/ A. Garcia	1,951,080
Oct 27	Breeders Cup Sprint	Monmouth	6 furlongs	Mignight Lut	B. Baffert/ G. Gomez	1,832,000
Nov 23	Clark Handicap	Churchill Downs	1⅛ miles	A.P. Arrow	T. Pletcher/ R. Dominguez	554,000

Major Stakes Races *(Cont.)*

2008 (through September 20)

Date	Race	Track	Distance	Winner	Trainer/Jockey	Purse ($)
Jan 26	Sunshine Millions Classic	Santa Anita	1⅛ miles	Go Between	W. Mott/ G. Gomez	1,000,000
Jan 26	Sunshine Millions Turf	Gulfstream	1⅛ miles	War Monger	W. Mott/ K. Desormeaux	500,000
Jan 26	Sunshine Millions Distaff	Gulfstream	1$\frac{1}{16}$ miles	Ginger Punch	R. Frankel/ R. Bejarano	500,000
Jan 26	Sunshine Milions Sprint	Gulfstream	6 furlongs	Benny the Bull	R. Dutrow/ E. Prado	300,000
Jan 26	Sunshine Millions F&M Turf	Santa Anita	1⅛ miles	Quite A Bride	W. Mott/ G. Gomez	500,000
Feb 2	Donn Handicap	Gulfstream	1⅛ miles	Spring at Last	E. Coa/ D. O'Neill	500,000
Mar 1	Santa Anita Handicap	Santa Anita	1¼ miles	Heatseeker	J. Hollendorfer/ R. Bejarano	1,000,000
Mar 16	Winstar Derby	Sunland	1⅛ miles	Liberty Bull	T. Amoss/ G. Melancon	600,000
Mar 22	Lane's End Stakes	Turfway	1⅛ miles	Adriano	H.G. Motion/ E. Prado	500,000
Mar 29	Dubai World Cup	Nad al Sheba	1¼ miles	Curlin	S. Asmussen/ R. Albarado	6,000,000
Mar 29	Dubai Duty Free	Nad al Sheba	1⅛ miles	Jay Peg	H. Brown/ M. Anton	5,000,000
Mar 29	Dubai Golden Shaheen	Nad al Sheba	6 furlongs	Benny the Bull	R. Dutrow Jr./ E. Prado	2,000,000
Mar 29	UAE Derby	Nad al Sheba	1⅛ miles	Honour Devil	M. de Kock/ J. Murtagh/	2,000,000
Mar 29	Dubai Sheema Classic	Nad al Sheba	1½ miles	Sun Classique	M. de Cock/ K. Shea	5,000,000
Mar 29	Godolphin Mile	Nad al Sheba	1 mile	Diamond Stripes	R. Dutro Jr./ E. Prado	1,000,000
Mar 29	Florida Derby	Gulfstream	1⅛ miles	Big Brown	R. Dutrow Jr./ K. Desormeaux	1,000,000
Apr 5	Wood Memorial Stakes	Aqueduct	1⅛ miles	Tale of Ekati	B. Tagg/ E. Prado	750,000
Apr 5	Santa Anita Derby	Santa Anita	1⅛ miles	Colonel John	E. Harty/ C. Nakatani	750,000
Apr 5	Ashland Stakes	Keeneland	1$\frac{1}{16}$ miles	Little Belle	K. McLaughlin/ R. Maragh	500,000
Apr 5	Apple Blossom Handicap	Oaklawn	1$\frac{1}{16}$ miles	Zenyatta	J. Shirreffs/ M. Smith	500,000
Apr 5	Illinois Derby	Hawthorne	1⅛ miles	Recapture-theglory	L. Roussell III/ E.T. Baird	500,000
Apr 5	Oaklawn Handicap	Oaklawn	1⅛ miles	Tiago	J. Shirreffs/ M. Smith	500,000
Apr 14	Toyota Blue Grass Stakes	Keeneland	1⅛ miles	Monba	T. Pletcher/ E. Prado	750,000
Apr 14	Arkansas Derby	Oaklawn	1⅛ miles	Gayego	P. Lobo/ M. Smith	1,000,000
May 2	Kentucky Oaks	Churchill Downs	1$\frac{3}{16}$ miles	Proud Spell	L. Jones/ G. Saez	500,000
May 3	Kentucky Derby	Churchill Downs	1¼ miles	Big Brown	R. Dutrow Jr./ K. Desormeaux	2,211,800
May 3	Woodford Reserve Classic	Churchill Downs	1⅛ miles	Einstein	H. Pitts/ R. Albarado	500,000
May 17	Preakness Stakes	Pimlico	1$\frac{3}{16}$ miles	Big Brown	R. Dutrow Jr./ K. Desmoreaux	1,000,000
May 26	Metropolitan Handicap	Belmont	1 mile	Divine Park	K. McLaughlin/ A. Garcia	600,000
May 26	Lone Star Park Handicap	Lone Star	1$\frac{1}{16}$ miles	Giant Gizmo	B. Frankel/ G. Gomez	400,000
June 7	Belmont Stakes	Belmont	1½ miles	Da' Tara	N. Zito/ A. Garcia	1,000,000
June 7	Manhattan Handicap	Belmont	1¼ miles	Dancing Forever	S. McGaughey/ R. Douglas	400,000
June 14	Stephen Foster Handicap	Churchill Downs	1⅛ miles	Curlin	S. Asmussen/ R. Albarado	1,000,000

Major Stakes Races (*Cont.*)

2008 (through September 20) (*Cont.*)

Date	Race	Track	Distance	Winner	Trainer/Jockey	Purse ($)
June 22	Queen's Plate Stakes	Woodbine	1¼ miles	Not Bourbon	R. Attfield/ J. Jones	986,737
June 28	Suburban Handicap	Belmont	1¼ miles	Frost Giant	R. Dutrow Jr./ R. Rodriguez	400,000
June 28	Hollywood Gold Cup	Hollywood	1¼ miles	Mast Track	R. Frankel/ T. Baze	750,000
July 5	United Nations Stakes	Monmouth	1⅜ miles	Precious Passion	M. Hartmann E. Castro	750,000
July 5	American Oaks	Hollywood	1¼ miles	Pure Clan	B. Holthus/ J. Leparoux	750,000
July 5	Vanity Handicap	Hollywood	1⅛ miles	Zenyatta	J. Shirreffs/ M. Smith	300,000
July 5	Cashcall Mile	Hollywood	1 mile	Diamond Diva	J. Cassidy/ D. Flores	750,000
July 12	Dance Smartly Stakes	Woodbine	1⅛ miles	The Niagara Queen	S. Asmussen/ J. McAleney	333,205
July 12	Princess Rooney Handicap	Calder	6 furlongs	Mistical Plan	D. O'Neill/ C. Nakatani	400,000
July 12	Smile Sprint Handicap	Calder	6 furlongs	Benny the Bull	R. Dutrow Jr./ E. Prado	400,000
July 12	Delaware Oaks	Delaware	1¹⁄₁₆ miles	Proud Spell	L. Jones/ G. Saez	500,300
July 12	Man O'War Stakes	Belmont	1⅜ miles	Red Rocks	B. Meehan/ J. Castellano	500,000
July 13	Delaware Handicap	Delaware	1¼ miles	Hystericalady	J. Hollendorfer/ G. Gomez	1,000,900
July 19	Virginia Derby	Colonial Downs	1¼ miles	Gio Ponti	C. Clement/ G. Gomez	772,500
July 19	San Diego Handicap	Del Mar	1¹⁄₁₆ miles	Well Armed	E. Harty/ A. Gryder	300,000
July 20	Eddie Reade Handicap	Del Mar	1⅛ miles	Monzante	M. Mitchell/ R. Bejarano	400,000
July 26	Diana Stakes	Saratoga	1⅛ miles	Forever Together	J. Sheppard/ J. Leparoux	500,000
July 26	Whitney Handicap	Saratoga	1⅛ miles	Commentator	N. Zito/ J. Velazquez	750,000
July 29	Jim Dandy Stakes	Saratoga	1⅛ miles	Macho Again	D. Stewart/ J. Leparoux	500,000
Aug 2	West Virginia Derby	Mountaineer	1⅛ miles	Ready Set	M. Matz/ J. Leparoux	750,000
Aug 3	John C. Mabee Handicap	Del Mar	1⅛ miles	Black Mamba	J. Sadler/ G. Gomez	400,000
Aug 5	Haskell Stakes	Monmouth	1⅛ miles	Big Brown	R. Dutrow Jr./ K. Desormeaux	1,000,000
Aug 9	Arlington Million Stakes	Arlington	1¼ miles	Spirit One	P. Demercastel/ I. Mendizabal	1,000,000
Aug 9	Beverly D. Stakes	Arlington	¹³⁄₁₆ mile	Mauralakana	C. Clement/ K. Desormeaux	750,000
Aug 9	Secretariat Stakes	Arlington	1¼ miles	Winchester	D. Weld/ R. Douglas	400,000
Aug 16	Sword Dancer Invitational	Saratoga	1½ miles	Grand Couturier	R. Ribaudo/ A. Garcia	500,000
Aug 16	Alabama Stakes	Saratoga	1¼ miles	Proud Spell	L. Jones/ G. Saez	588,000
Aug 23	Travers Stakes	Saratoga	1¼ miles	Colonel John	E. Harty/ G. Gomez	1,000,000
Aug 24	Pacific Classic	Del Mar	1¼ miles	Go Between	W. Mot/ G. Gomez	1,000,000
Aug 30	Woodward Stakes	Saratoga	1⅛ miles	Curlin	S. Asmussen/ R. Albarado	500,000
Aug 31	Del Mar Derby	Del Mar	1⅛ miles	Madeo	J. Shireffs/ M. Smith	350,000
Sept 7	Woodbine Mile	Woodbine	1 mile	Rahy's Attorney	I. Black/ S. Callaghan	1,013,938
Sept 20	Super Derby XXVIII	Louisiana Downs	1⅛ miles	My Pal Charlie	A. Stall Jr./ C. Bourque	500,000

FOR THE RECORD • Year by Year

THOROUGHBRED RACING

Kentucky Derby

Run at Churchill Downs, Louisville, KY, on the first Saturday in May.

Year	Winner (Margin)	Jockey	Second	Third	Time
1875	Aristides (1)	Oliver Lewis	Volcano	Verdigris	2:37¾
1876	Vagrant (2)	Bobby Swim	Creedmoor	Harry Hill	2:38¼
1877	Baden-Baden (2)	William Walker	Leonard	King William	2:38
1878	Day Star (2)	Jimmie Carter	Himyar	Leveler	2:37¼
1879	Lord Murphy (1)	Charlie Shauer	Falsetto	Strathmore	2:37
1880	Fonso (1)	George Lewis	Kimball	Bancroft	2:37½
1881	Hindoo (4)	Jimmy McLaughin	Lelex	Alfambra	2:40
1882	Apollo (½)	Babe Hurd	Runnymede	Bengal	2:40¼
1883	Leonatus (3)	Billy Donohue	Drake Carter	Lord Raglan	2:43
1884	Buchanan (2)	Isaac Murphy	Loftin	Audrain	2:40¼
1885	Joe Cotton (Neck)	Erskine Henderson	Bersan	Ten Booker	2:37¼
1886	Ben Ali (½)	Paul Duffy	Blue Wing	Free Knight	2:36½
1887	Montrose (2)	Isaac Lewis	Jim Gore	Jacobin	2:39¼
1888	MacBeth II (1)	George Covington	Gallifet	White	2:38¼
1889	Spokane (Nose)	Thomas Kiley	Proctor Knott	Once Again	2:34½
1890	Riley (2)	Isaac Murphy	Bill Letcher	Robespierre	2:45
1891	Kingman (1)	Isaac Murphy	Balgowan	High Tariff	2:52¼
1892	Azra (Nose)	Alonzo Clayton	Huron	Phil Dwyer	2:41½
1893	Lookout (5)	Eddie Kunze	Plutus	Boundless	2:39¼
1894	Chant (2)	Frank Goodale	Pearl Song	Sigurd	2:41
1895	Halma (3)	Soup Perkins	Basso	Laureate	2:37½
1896	Ben Brush (Nose)	Willie Simms	Ben Eder	Semper Ego	2:07¼
1897	Typhoon II (Head)	Buttons Garner	Ornament	Dr. Catlett	2:12½
1898	Plaudit (Neck)	Willie Simms	Lieber Karl	Isabey	2:09
1899	Manuel (2)	Fred Taral	Corsini	Mazo	2:12
1900	Lieut. Gibson (4)	Jimmy Boland	Florizar	Thrive	2:06¼
1901	His Eminence (2)	Jimmy Winkfield	Sannazarro	Driscoll	2:07¾
1902	Alan-a-Dale (Nose)	Jimmy Winkfield	Inventor	The Rival	2:08¾
1903	Judge Himes (¾)	Hal Booker	Early	Bourbon	2:09
1904	Elwood (½)	Frankie Prior	Ed Tierney	Brancas	2:08½
1905	Agile (3)	Jack Martin	Ram's Horn	Layson	2:10¾
1906	Sir Huon (2)	Roscoe Troxler	Lady Navarre	James Reddick	2:08⅕
1907	Pink Star (2)	Andy Minder	Zal	Ovelando	2:12⅗
1908	Stone Street (1)	Arthur Pickens	Sir Cleges	Dunvegan	2:15⅕
1909	Wintergreen (4)	Vincent Powers	Miami	Dr. Barkley	2:08⅕
1910	Donau (½)	Fred Herbert	Joe Morris	Fighting Bob	2:06⅖
1911	Meridian (¾)	George Archibald	Governor Gray	Colston	2:05
1912	Worth (Neck)	Carroll H. Schilling	Duval	Flamma	2:09⅖
1913	Donerail (½)	Roscoe Goose	Ten Point	Gowell	2:04⅘
1914	Old Rosebud (8)	John McCabe	Hodge	Bronzewing	2:03⅖
1915	Regret (2)	Joe Notter	Pebbles	Sharpshooter	2:05⅖
1916	George Smith (Neck)	Johnny Loftus	Star Hawk	Franklin	2:04
1917	Omar Khayyam (2)	Charles Borel	Ticket	Midway	2:04⅗
1918	Exterminator (1)	William Knapp	Escoba	Viva America	2:10⅘
1919	Sir Barton (5)	Johnny Loftus	Billy Kelly	Under Fire	2:09⅘
1920	Paul Jones (Head)	Ted Rice	Upset	On Watch	2:09
1921	Behave Yourself (Head)	Charles Thompson	Black Servant	Prudery	2:04⅕
1922	Morvich (½)	Albert Johnson	Bet Mosie	John Finn	2:04⅗
1923	Zev (1½)	Earl Sande	Martingale	Vigil	2:05⅖
1924	Black Gold (½)	John Mooney	Chilhowee	Beau Butler	2:05⅕
1925	Flying Ebony (1½)	Earl Sande	Captain Hal	Son of John	2:07⅗
1926	Bubbling Over (5)	Albert Johnson	Bagenbaggage	Rock Man	2:03⅗
1927	Whiskery (Head)	Linus McAtee	Osmond	Jock	2:06
1928	Reigh Count (3)	Chick Lang	Misstep	Toro	2:10⅖
1929	Clyde Van Dusen (2)	Linus McAtee	Naishapur	Panchio	2:10⅘
1930	Gallant Fox (2)	Earl Sande	Gallant Knight	Ned O.	2:07⅗
1931	Twenty Grand (4)	Charles Kurtsinger	Sweep All	Mate	2:01⅘

Kentucky Derby *(Cont.)*

Year	Winner (Margin)	Jockey	Second	Third	Time
1932	Burgoo King (5)	Eugene James	Economic	Stepenfetchit	2:05⅕
1933	Brokers Tip (Nose)	Don Meade	Head Play	Charley O.	2:06⅘
1934	Cavalcade (2½)	Mack Garner	Discovery	Agrarian	2:04
1935	Omaha (1½)	Willie Saunders	Roman Soldier	Whiskolo	2:05
1936	Bold Venture (Head)	Ira Hanford	Brevity	Indian Broom	2:03⅗
1937	War Admiral (1¾)	Charles Kurtsinger	Pompoon	Reaping Reward	2:03⅕
1938	Lawrin (1)	Eddie Arcaro	Dauber	Can't Wait	2:04⅘
1939	Johnstown (8)	James Stout	Challedon	Heather Broom	2:03⅗
1940	Gallahadion (1½)	Carroll Bierman	Bimelech	Dit	2:05
1941	Whirlaway (8)	Eddie Arcaro	Staretor	Market Wise	2:01⅖
1942	Shut Out (2¼)	Wayne Wright	Alsab	Valdina Orphan	2:04⅖
1943	Count Fleet (3)	John Longden	Blue Swords	Slide Rule	2:04
1944	Pensive (4½)	Conn McCreary	Broadcloth	Stir Up	2:04⅕
1945	Hoop Jr. (6)	Eddie Arcaro	Pot o' Luck	Darby Dieppe	2:07
1946	Assault (8)	Warren Mehrtens	Spy Song	Hampden	2:06⅗
1947	Jet Pilot (Head)	Eric Guerin	Phalanx	Faultless	2:06⅘
1948	Citation (3½)	Eddie Arcaro	Coaltown	My Request	2:05⅖
1949	Ponder (3)	Steve Brooks	Capot	Palestinian	2:04⅕
1950	Middleground (1¼)	William Boland	Hill Prince	Mr. Trouble	2:01⅗
1951	Count Turf (4)	Conn McCreary	Royal Mustang	Ruhe	2:02⅗
1952	Hill Gail (2)	Eddie Arcaro	Sub Fleet	Blue Man	2:01⅗
1953	Dark Star (Head)	Hank Moreno	Native Dancer	Invigorator	2:02
1954	Determine (1½)	Ray York	Hasty Road	Hasseyampa	2:03
1955	Swaps (1½)	Bill Shoemaker	Nashua	Summer Tan	2:01⅘
1956	Needles (¾)	Dave Erb	Fabius	Come On Red	2:03⅖
1957	Iron Liege (Nose)	Bill Hartack	Gallant Man	Round Table	2:02⅕
1958	Tim Tam (½)	Ismael Valenzuela	Lincoln Road	Noureddin	2:05
1959	Tomy Lee (Nose)	Bill Shoemaker	Sword Dancer	First Landing	2:02⅕
1960	Venetian Way (3½)	Bill Hartack	Bally Ache	Victoria Park	2:02⅖
1961	Carry Back (¾)	John Sellers	Crozier	Bass Clef	2:04
1962	Decidedly (2¼)	Bill Hartack	Roman Line	Ridan	2:00⅖
1963	Chateaugay (1¼)	Braulio Baeza	Never Bend	Candy Spots	2:01⅘
1964	Northern Dancer (Neck)	Bill Hartack	Hill Rise	The Scoundrel	2:00
1965	Lucky Debonair (Neck)	Bill Shoemaker	Dapper Dan	Tom Rolfe	2:01⅕
1966	Kauai King (½)	Don Brumfield	Advocator	Blue Skyer	2:02
1967	Proud Clarion (1)	Bobby Ussery	Barbs Delight	Damascus	2:00⅗
1968	Forward Pass (Disq.)	Ismael Valenzuela	Francie's Hat	T.V. Commercial	2:02⅕
1969	Majestic Prince (Neck)	Bill Hartack	Arts and Letters	Dike	2:01⅘
1970	Dust Commander (5)	Mike Manganello	My Dad George	High Echelon	2:03⅖
1971	Canonero II (3¾)	Gustavo Avila	Jim French	Bold Reason	2:03⅕
1972	Riva Ridge (3¼)	Ron Turcotte	No Le Hace	Hold Your Peace	2:01⅘
1973	Secretariat (2½)	Ron Turcotte	Sham	Our Native	1:59⅖
1974	Cannonade (2¼)	Angel Cordero Jr.	Hudson County	Agitate	2:04
1975	Foolish Pleasure (1¾)	Jacinto Vasquez	Avatar	Diabolo	2:02
1976	Bold Forbes (1)	Angel Cordero Jr.	Honest Pleasure	Elocutionist	2:01⅗
1977	Seattle Slew (1¾)	Jean Cruguet	Run Dusty Run	Sanhedrin	2:02⅕
1978	Affirmed (1¼)	Steve Cauthen	Alydar	Believe It	2:01⅕
1979	Spectacular Bid (2¾)	Ronald J. Franklin	General Assembly	Golden Act	2:02⅖
1980	Genuine Risk (1)	Jacinto Vasquez	Rumbo	Jaklin Klugman	2:02
1981	Pleasant Colony (¾)	Jorge Velasquez	Woodchopper	Partez	2:02
1982	Gato Del Sol (2½)	Eddie Delahoussaye	Laser Light	Reinvested	2:02⅕
1983	Sunny's Halo (2)	Eddie Delahoussaye	Desert Wine	Caveat	2:02⅕
1984	Swale (3¼)	Laffit Pincay Jr.	Coax Me Chad	At the Threshold	2:02⅖
1985	Spend A Buck (5)	Angel Cordero Jr.	Stephan's Odyssey	Chief's Crown	2:00⅕
1986	Ferdinand (2¼)	Bill Shoemaker	Bold Arrangement	Broad Brush	2:02⅘
1987	Alysheba (¾)	Chris McCarron	Bet Twice	Avies Copy	2:03⅖
1988	Winning Colors (Neck)	Gary Stevens	Forty Niner	Risen Star	2:02⅕
1989	Sunday Silence (2½)	Pat Valenzuela	Easy Goer	Awe Inspiring	2:05
1990	Unbridled (3½)	Craig Perret	Summer Squall	Pleasant Tap	2:02
1991	Strike the Gold (1¾)	Chris Antley	Best Pal	Mane Minister	2:03
1992	Lil E. Tee (1)	Pat Day	Casual Lies	Dance Floor	2:03
1993	Sea Hero (2½)	Jerry Bailey	Prairie Bayou	Wild Gale	2:02⅖
1994	Go for Gin (2½)	Chris McCarron	Strodes Creek	Blumin Affair	2:03⅗
1995	Thunder Gulch (2¼)	Gary Stevens	Tejano Run	Timber Country	2:01⅕
1996	Grindstone (Nose)	Jerry Bailey	Cavonnier	Prince of Thieves	2:01
1997	Silver Charm (Head)	Gary Stevens	Captain Bodgit	Free House	2:02⅖

Kentucky Derby *(Cont.)*

Year	Winner (Margin)	Jockey	Second	Third	Time
1998	Real Quiet (½)	Kent Desormeaux	Victory Gallop	Indian Charlie	2:02⅒
1999	Charismatic (Neck)	Chris Antley	Menifee	Cat Thief	2:03⅕
2000	Fusaichi Pegasus (1½)	Kent Desormeaux	Aptitude	Impeachment	2:01.12
2001	Monarchos (4¾)	Jorge Chavez	Invisible Ink	Congaree	1:59.97
2002	War Emblem (4)	Victor Espinoza	Proud Citizen	Perfect Drift	2:01.13
2003	Funny Cide (1¾)	Jose Santos	Empire Maker	Peace Rules	2:01.19
2004	Smarty Jones (2¾)	Stewart Elliott	Lion Heart	Imperialism	2:04.06
2005	Giacomo (½)	Mike Smith	Closing Argument	Afleet Alex	2:02.75
2006	Barbaro (1½)	Edgar Prado	Bluegrass Cat	Steppenwolfer	2:01.36
2007	Street Sense (2¼)	Calvin Borel	Hard Spun	Curlin	2:02.17
2008	Big Brown (4¾)	Kent Desormeaux	Eight Belles	Denis of Cork	2:01.82

Note: Distance: 1½ miles (1875–95), 1¼ miles (1896–present).

Preakness

Run at Pimlico Race Course, Baltimore, Md., two weeks after the Kentucky Derby.

Year	Winner (Margin)	Jockey	Second	Third	Time
1873	Survivor (10)	G. Barbee	John Boulger	Artist	2:43
1874	Culpepper (¾)	W. Donohue	King Amadeus	Scratch	2:56½
1875	Tom Ochiltree (2)	L. Hughes	Viator	Bay Final	2:43½
1876	Shirley (4)	G. Barbee	Rappahannock	Algerine	2:44¾
1877	Cloverbrook (4)	C. Holloway	Bombast	Lucifer	2:45½
1878	Duke of Magenta (6)	C. Holloway	Bayard	Albert	2:41¾
1879	Harold (3)	L. Hughes	Jericho	Rochester	2:40½
1880	Grenada (¾)	L. Hughes	Oden	Emily F.	2:40½
1881	Saunterer (½)	T. Costello	Compensation	Baltic	2:40½
1882	Vanguard (Neck)	T. Costello	Heck	Col Watson	2:44½
1883*	Jacobus (4)	G. Barbee	Parnell		2:42½
1884*	Knight of Ellerslie (2)	S. Fisher	Welcher		2:39½
1885	Tecumseh (2)	Jim McLaughlin	Wickham	John C.	2:49
1886	The Bard (3)	S. Fisher	Eurus	Elkwood	2:45
1887	Dunboyne (1)	W. Donohue	Mahoney	Raymond	2:39½
1888	Refund (3)	F. Littlefield	Judge Murray	Glendale	2:49
1889*	Buddhist (8)	W. Anderson	Japhet	*	2:17½
1890*	Montague (3)	W. Martin	Philosophy	Barrister	2:36¾
1894	Assignee (3)	Fred Taral	Potentate	Ed Kearney	1:49¼
1895	Belmar (1)	Fred Taral	April Fool	Sue Kittie	1:50½
1896	Margrave (1)	H. Griffin	Hamilton II	Intermission	1:51
1897	Paul Kauvar (1½)	C. Thorpe	Elkins	On Deck	1:51¼
1898	Sly Fox (2)	C. W. Simms	The Huguenot	Nuto	1:49⅗
1899	Half Time (1)	R. Clawson	Filigrane	Lackland	1:47
1900	Hindus (Head)	H. Spencer	Sarmation	Ten Candles	1:48⅖
1901	The Parader (2)	F. Landry	Sadie S.	Dr. Barlow	1:47⅕
1902	Old England (Nose)	L. Jackson	Major Daingerfield	Namtor	1:45⅘
1903	Flocarline (½)	W. Gannon	Mackey Dwyer	Rightful	1:44⅘
1904	Bryn Mawr (1)	E. Hildebrand	Wotan	Dolly Spanker	1:44⅕
1905	Cairngorm (Head)	W. Davis	Kiamesha	Coy Maid	1:45⅘
1906	Whimsical (4)	Walter Miller	Content	Larabie	1:45
1907	Don Enrique (1)	G. Mountain	Ethon	Zambesi	1:45⅖
1908	Royal Tourist (4)	E. Dugan	Live Wire	Robert Cooper	1:46⅖
1909	Effendi (1)	Willie Doyle	Fashion Plate	Hilltop	1:39⅘
1910	Layminster (½)	R. Estep	Dalhousie	Sager	1:40⅗
1911	Watervale (1)	E. Dugan	Zeus	The Nigger	1:51
1912	Colonel Holloway (5)	C. Turner	Bwana Tumbo	Tipsand	1:56⅗
1913	Buskin (Neck)	J. Butwell	Kleburne	Barnegat	1:53⅖
1914	Holiday (¾)	A. Schuttinger	Brave Cunarder	Defendum	1:53⅘
1915	Rhine Maiden (1½)	Douglas Hoffman	Half Rock	Runes	1:58
1916	Damrosch (1½)	Linus McAtee	Greenwood	Achievement	1:54⅘
1917	Kalitan (2)	E. Haynes	Al M. Dick	Kentucky Boy	1:54⅖
1918*	War Cloud (¾)	Johnny Loftus	Sunny Slope	Lanius	1:53⅗
1918*	Jack Hare, Jr (2)	C. Peak	The Porter	Kate Bright	1:53⅖
1919	Sir Barton (4)	Johnny Loftus	Eternal	Sweep On	1:53
1920	Man o' War (1½)	Clarence Kummer	Upset	Wildair	1:51⅗

Preakness (*Cont.*)

Year	Winner (Margin)	Jockey	Second	Third	Time
1921	Broomspun (¾)	F. Coltiletti	Polly Ann	Jeg	1:54⅕
1922	Pillory (Head)	L. Morris	Hea	June Grass	1:51⅗
1923	Vigil (1¼)	B. Marinelli	General Thatcher	Rialto	1:53⅗
1924	Nellie Morse (1½)	J. Merimee	Transmute	Mad Play	1:57⅕
1925	Coventry (4)	Clarence Kummer	Backbone	Almadel	1:59
1926	Display (Head)	J. Maiben	Blondin	Mars	1:59⅘
1927	Bostonian (½)	A. Abel	Sir Harry	Whiskery	2:01⅗
1928	Victorian (Nose)	Sonny Workman	Toro	Solace	2:00⅕
1929	Dr. Freeland (1)	Louis Schaefer	Minotaur	African	2:01⅗
1930	Gallant Fox (¾)	Earl Sande	Crack Brigade	Snowflake	2:00⅗
1931	Mate (1½)	G. Ellis	Twenty Grand	Ladder	1:59
1932	Burgoo King (Head)	E. James	Tick On	Boatswain	1:59⅘
1933	Head Play (4)	Charles Kurtsinger	Ladysman	Utopian	2:02
1934	High Quest (Nose)	R. Jones	Cavalcade	Discovery	1:58⅕
1935	Omaha (6)	Willie Saunders	Firethorn	Psychic Bid	1:58⅖
1936	Bold Venture (Nose)	George Woolf	Granville	Jean Bart	1:59
1937	War Admiral (Head)	Charles Kurtsinger	Pompoon	Flying Scot	1:58⅖
1938	Dauber (7)	M. Peters	Cravat	Menow	1:59⅘
1939	Challedon (1¼)	George Seabo	Gilded Knight	Volitant	1:59⅘
1940	Bimelech (3)	F. A. Smith	Mioland	Gallahadion	1:58⅗
1941	Whirlaway (5½)	Eddie Arcaro	King Cole	Our Boots	1:58⅘
1942	Alsab (1)	B. James	Requested Sun Again	(dead heat for second)	1:57
1943	Count Fleet (8)	Johnny Longden	Blue Swords	Vincentive	1:57⅖
1944	Pensive (¾)	Conn McCreary	Platter	Stir Up	1:59⅕
1945	Polynesian (2½)	W. D. Wright	Hoop Jr.	Darby Dieppe	1:58⅘
1946	Assault (Neck)	Warren Mehrtens	Lord Boswell	Hampden	2:01⅖
1947	Faultless (1¼)	Doug Dodson	On Trust	Phalanx	1:59
1948	Citation (5½)	Eddie Arcaro	Vulcan's Forge	Boyard	2:02⅖
1949	Capot (Head)	Ted Atkinson	Palestinian	Noble Impulse	1:56
1950	Hill Prince (5)	Eddie Arcaro	Middleground	Dooley	1:59⅕
1951	Bold (7)	Eddie Arcaro	Counterpoint	Alerted	1:56⅖
1952	Blue Man (3½)	Conn McCreary	Jampol	One Count	1:57⅖
1953	Native Dancer (Neck)	Eric Guerin	Jamie K.	Royal Bay Gem	1:57⅘
1954	Hasty Road (Neck)	Johnny Adams	Correlation	Hasseyampa	1:57⅖
1955	Nashua (1)	Eddie Arcaro	Saratoga	Traffic Judge	1:54⅗
1956	Fabius (¾)	Bill Hartack	Needles	No Regrets	1:58⅖
1957	Bold Ruler (2)	Eddie Arcaro	Iron Liege	Inside Tract	1:56⅕
1958	Tim Tam (1½)	I. Valenzuela	Lincoln Road	Gone Fishin'	1:57⅕
1959	Royal Orbit (4)	William Harmatz	Sword Dancer	Dunce	1:57
1960	Bally Ache (4)	Bobby Ussery	Victoria Park	Celtic Ash	1:57⅗
1961	Carry Back (¾)	Johnny Sellers	Globemaster	Crozier	1:57⅗
1962	Greek Money (Nose)	John Rotz	Ridan	Roman Line	1:56⅕
1963	Candy Spots (3½)	Bill Shoemaker	Chateaugay	Never Bend	1:56⅕
1964	Northern Dancer (2¼)	Bill Hartack	The Scoundrel	Hill Rise	1:56⅘
1965	Tom Rolfe (Neck)	Ron Turcotte	Dapper Dan	Hail to All	1:56⅕
1966	Kauai King (1¾)	Don Brumfield	Stupendous	Amberoid	1:55⅖
1967	Damascus (2¼)	Bill Shoemaker	In Reality	Proud Clarion	1:55⅕
1968	Forward Pass (6)	I. Valenzuela	Out of the Way	Nodouble	1:56⅘
1969	Majestic Prince (Head)	Bill Hartack	Arts and Letters	Jay Ray	1:55⅗
1970	Personality (Neck)	Eddie Belmonte	My Dad George	Silent Screen	1:56⅕
1971	Canonero II (1½)	Gustavo Avila	Eastern Fleet	Jim French	1:54
1972	Bee Bee Bee (1¼)	Eldon Nelson	No Le Hace	Key to the Mint	1:55⅗
1973	Secretariat (2½)	Ron Turcotte	Sham	Our Native	1:54⅖
1974	Little Current (7)	Miguel Rivera	Neapolitan Way	Cannonade	1:54⅗
1975	Master Derby (1)	Darrel McHargue	Foolish Pleasure	Diabolo	1:56⅖
1976	Elocutionist (3)	John Lively	Play the Red	Bold Forbes	1:55
1977	Seattle Slew (1½)	Jean Cruguet	Iron Constitution	Run Dusty Run	1:54⅖
1978	Affirmed (Neck)	Steve Cauthen	Alydar	Believe It	1:54⅖
1979	Spectacular Bid (5½)	Ron Franklin	Golden Act	Screen King	1:54⅕
1980	Codex (4¾)	Angel Cordero Jr.	Genuine Risk	Colonel Moran	1:54⅕
1981	Pleasant Colony (1)	Jorge Velasquez	Bold Ego	Paristo	1:54⅗
1982	Aloma's Ruler (½)	Jack Kaenel	Linkage	Cut Away	1:55⅖
1983	Deputed Testamony (2¾)	Donald Miller Jr.	Desert Wine	High Honors	1:55⅖
1984	Gate Dancer (1½)	Angel Cordero Jr.	Play On	Fight Over	1:53⅗
1985	Tank's Prospect (Head)	Pat Day	Chief's Crown	Eternal Prince	1:53⅖
1986	Snow Chief (4)	Alex Solis	Ferdinand	Broad Brush	1:54⅘
1987	Alysheba (½)	Chris McCarron	Bet Twice	Cryptoclearance	1:55⅘

Preakness *(Cont.)*

Year	Winner (Margin)	Jockey	Second	Third	Time
1988	Risen Star (1¼)	E. Delahoussaye	Brian's Time	Winning Colors	1:56⅕
1989	Sunday Silence (Nose)	Pat Valenzuela	Easy Goer	Rock Point	1:53⅘
1990	Summer Squall (2¼)	Pat Day	Unbridled	Mister Frisky	1:53⅗
1991	Hansel (Head)	Jerry Bailey	Corporate Report	Mane Minister	1:54
1992	Pine Bluff (¾)	Chris McCarron	Alydeed	Casual Lies	1:55⅗
1993	Prairie Bayou (½)	Mike Smith	Cherokee Run	El Bakan	1:56⅗
1994	Tabasco Cat (¾)	Pat Day	Go For Gin	Concern	1:56⅖
1995	Timber Country (½)	Pat Day	Oliver's Twist	Thunder Gulch	1:54⅖
1996	Louis Quatorze (3¼)	Pat Day	Skip Away	Editor's Note	1:53⅖
1997	Silver Charm (Head)	Gary Stevens	Free House	Captain Bodgit	1:54⅖
1998	Real Quiet (2¼)	Kent Desormeaux	Victory Gallop	Classic Cat	1:54⅗
1999	Charismatic (1½)	Chris Antley	Menifee	Badge	1:55⅕
2000	Red Bullet (3¾)	Jerry Bailey	Fusaichi Pegasus	Impeachment	1:56.04
2001	Point Given (2¼)	Gary Stevens	A P Valentine	Congaree	1:55.51
2002	War Emblem (¾)	Victor Espinoza	Magic Weisner	Proud Citizen	1:56.36
2003	Funny Cide (9¾)	Jose Santos	Midway Road	Scrimshaw	1:55.61
2004	Smarty Jones (11½)	Stewart Elliott	Rock Hard Ten	Eddington	1:55.59
2005	Afleet Alex (7)	Jeremy Rose	Scrappy T	Giacomo	1:55.04
2006	Bernardini (5¼)	Javier Castellano	Sweetnorthernsaint	Hemingway's Key	1:54.65
2007	Curlin (Head)	Robby Albarado	Street Sense	Hard Spun	1:53.46
2008	Big Brown (5¼)	Kent Desormeaux	Macho Again	Icabad Crane	1:54.80

*Preakness was a two-horse race in 1883, '84 and '89. It was not run 1891–1893; and in 1918, it was run in two divisions.

Note: Distance: 1½ miles (1873–88), 1¼ miles (1889), 1½ miles (1890), 1 1/16 miles (1894–1900), 1 mile and 70 yards (1901–1907), 1 1/16 miles (1908), 1 mile (1909–10), 1⅛ miles (1911–24), 1 3/16 miles (1925–present).

Belmont

Run at Belmont Park, Elmont, NY, three weeks after the Preakness Stakes. Held previously at two locations in the Bronx (NY): Jerome Park (1867–1889) and Morris Park (1890–1904).

Year	Winner (Margin)	Jockey	Second	Third	Time
1867	Ruthless (Head)	J. Gilpatrick	De Courcy	Rivoli	3:05
1868	General Duke (2)	R. Swim	Northumberland	Fannie Ludlow	3:02
1869	Fenian (Unknown)	C. Miller	Glenelg	Invercauld	3:04¼
1870	Kingfisher (½)	E. Brown	Foster	Midday	2:59½
1871	Harry Bassett (3)	W. Miller	Stockwood	By-the-Sea	2:56
1872	Joe Daniels (¾)	James Rowe	Meteor	Shylock	2:58¼
1873	Springbok (4)	James Rowe	Count d'Orsay	Strachino	3:01¾
1874	Saxon (Neck)	G. Barbee	Grinstead	Aaron Pennington	2:39½
1875	Calvin (2)	R. Swim	Aristides	Milner	2:40¼
1876	Algerine (Head)	W. Donahue	Fiddlestick	Barricade	2:40½
1877	Cloverbrook (1)	C. Holloway	Loiterer	Baden-Baden	2:46
1878	Duke of Magenta (2)	L. Hughes	Bramble	Sparta	2:43½
1879	Spendthrift (5)	S. Evans	Monitor	Jericho	2:42¾
1880	Grenada (½)	L. Hughes	Ferncliffe	Turenne	2:47
1881	Saunterer (Neck)	T. Costello	Eole	Baltic	2:47
1882	Forester (5)	James McLaughlin	Babcock	Wyoming	2:43
1883	George Kinney (2)	James McLaughlin	Trombone	Renegade	2:42½
1884	Panique (½)	James McLaughlin	Knight of Ellerslie	Himalaya	2:42
1885	Tyrant (3½)	Paul Duffy	St. Augustine	Tecumseh	2:43
1886	Inspector B (1)	James McLaughlin	The Bard	Linden	2:41
1887*	Hanover (28-32)	James McLaughlin	Oneko		2:43½
1888*	Sir Dixon (12)	James McLaughlin	Prince Royal		2:40¼
1889	Eric (Head)	W. Hayward	Diable	Zephyrus	2:47
1890	Burlington (1)	S. Barnes	Devotee	Padishah	2:07¾
1891	Foxford (Neck)	E. Garrison	Montana	Laurestan	2:08¾
1892*	Patron (Unknown)	W. Hayward	Shellbark		2:17
1893	Comanche (Head)	Willie Simms	Dr. Rice	Rainbow	1:53¼
1894	Henry of Navarre (2-4)	Willie Simms	Prig	Assignee	1:56½
1895	Belmar (Head)	Fred Taral	Counter Tenor	Nanki Pooh	2:11½
1896	Hastings (Neck)	H. Griffin	Handspring	Hamilton II	2:24½
1897	Scottish Chieftain (1)	J. Scherrer	On Deck	Octagon	2:23¼
1898	Bowling Brook (8)	P. Littlefield	Previous	Hamburg	2:32
1899	Jean Bereaud (Head)	R. R. Clawson	Half Time	Glengar	2:23

Belmont (*Cont.*)

Year	Winner (Margin)	Jockey	Second	Third	Time
1900	Ildrim (Head)	N. Turner	Petrucio	Missionary	2:21½
1901	Commando (½)	H. Spencer	The Parader	All Green	2:21
1902	Masterman (2)	John Bullmann	Ranald	King Hanover	2:22½
1903	Africander (2)	John Bullmann	Whorler	Red Knight	2:23⅕
1904	Delhi (3½)	George Odom	Graziallo	Rapid Water	2:06⅗
1905	Tanya (1/2)	E. Hildebrand	Blandy	Hot Shot	2:08
1906	Burgomaster (4)	L. Lyne	The Quail	Accountant	2:20
1907	Peter Pan (1)	G. Mountain	Superman	Frank Gill	Unknown
1908	Colin (Head)	Joe Notter	Fair Play	King James	Unknown
1909	Joe Madden (8)	E. Dugan	Wise Mason	Donald MacDonald	2:21⅗
1910*	Sweep (6)	J. Butwell	Duke of Ormonde		2:22
1913	Prince Eugene (½)	Roscoe Troxler	Rock View	Flying Fairy	2:18
1914	Luke McLuke (8)	M. Buxton	Gainer	Charlestonian	2:20
1915	The Finn (4)	G. Byrne	Half Rock	Pebbles	2:18⅖
1916	Friar Rock (3)	E. Haynes	Spur	Churchill	2:22
1917	Hourless (10)	J. Butwell	Skeptic	Wonderful	2:17⅘
1918	Johren (2)	Frank Robinson	War Cloud	Cum Sah	2:20⅖
1919	Sir Barton (5)	Johnny Loftus	Sweep On	Natural Bridge	2:17⅖
1920*	Man o' War (20)	Clarence Kummer	Donnacona		2:14⅕
1921	Grey Lag (3)	Earl Sande	Sporting Blood	Leonardo II	2:16⅘
1922	Pillory (2)	C. H. Miller	Snob II	Hea	2:18⅘
1923	Zev (1½)	Earl Sande	Chickvale	Rialto	2:19
1924	Mad Play (2)	Earl Sande	Mr. Mutt	Modest	2:18⅘
1925	American Flag (8)	Albert Johnson	Dangerous	Swope	2:16⅘
1926	Crusader (1)	Albert Johnson	Espino	Haste	2:32⅕
1927	Chance Shot (1½)	Earl Sande	Bois de Rose	Flambino	2:32⅖
1928	Vito (3)	Clarence Kummer	Genie	Diavolo	2:33⅕
1929	Blue Larkspur (¾)	Mack Garner	African	Jack High	2:32⅘
1930	Gallant Fox (3)	Earl Sande	Whichone	Questionnaire	2:31⅗
1931	Twenty Grand (10)	Charles Kurtsinger	Sun Meadow	Jamestown	2:29⅗
1932	Faireno (1½)	T. Malley	Osculator	Flag Pole	2:32⅘
1933	Hurryoff (1½)	Mack Garner	Nimbus	Union	2:32⅗
1934	Peace Chance (6)	W. D. Wright	High Quest	Good Goods	2:29⅕
1935	Omaha (1½)	Willie Saunders	Firethorn	Rosemont	2:30⅗
1936	Granville (Nose)	James Stout	Mr. Bones	Hollyrood	2:30
1937	War Admiral (3)	Charles Kurtsinger	Sceneshifter	Vamoose	2:28⅗
1938	Pasteurized (Neck)	James Stout	Dauber	Cravat	2:29⅖
1939	Johnstown (5)	James Stout	Belay	Gilded Knight	2:29⅗
1940	Bimelech (¾)	F. A. Smith	Your Chance	Andy K	2:29⅗
1941	Whirlaway (2½)	Eddie Arcaro	Robert Morris	Yankee Chance	2:31
1942	Shut Out (2)	Eddie Arcaro	Alsab	Lochinvar	2:29⅕
1943	Count Fleet (25)	Johnny Longden	Fairy Manhurst	Deseronto	2:28⅕
1944	Bounding Home (½)	G. L. Smith	Pensive	Bull Dandy	2:32⅕
1945	Pavot (5)	Eddie Arcaro	Wildlife	Jeep	2:30⅕
1946	Assault (3)	Warren Mehrtens	Natchez	Cable	2:30⅘
1947	Phalanx (5)	R. Donoso	Tide Rips	Tailspin	2:29⅖
1948	Citation (8)	Eddie Arcaro	Better Self	Escadru	2:28⅕
1949	Capot (½)	Ted Atkinson	Ponder	Palestinian	2:30⅕
1950	Middleground (1)	William Boland	Lights Up	Mr. Trouble	2:28⅗
1951	Counterpoint (4)	D. Gorman	Battlefield	Battle Morn	2:29
1952	One Count (2½)	Eddie Arcaro	Blue Man	Armageddon	2:30⅕
1953	Native Dancer (Neck)	Eric Guerin	Jamie K.	Royal Bay Gem	2:38⅗
1954	High Gun (Neck)	Eric Guerin	Fisherman	Limelight	2:30⅘
1955	Nashua (9)	Eddie Arcaro	Blazing Count	Portersville	2:29
1956	Needles (Neck)	David Erb	Career Boy	Fabius	2:29⅘
1957	Gallant Man (8)	Bill Shoemaker	Inside Tract	Bold Ruler	2:26⅗
1958	Cavan (6)	Pete Anderson	Tim Tam	Flamingo	2:30⅕
1959	Sword Dancer (¾)	Bill Shoemaker	Bagdad	Royal Orbit	2:28⅖
1960	Celtic Ash (5½)	Bill Hartack	Venetian Way	Disperse	2:29⅗
1961	Sherluck (2¼)	Braulio Baeza	Globemaster	Guadalcanal	2:29⅕
1962	Jaipur (Nose)	Bill Shoemaker	Admiral's Voyage	Crimson Satan	2:28⅘
1963	Chateaugay (2½)	Braulio Baeza	Candy Spots	Choker	2:30⅕
1964	Quadrangle (2)	Manuel Ycaza	Roman Brother	Northern Dancer	2:28⅖
1965	Hail to All (Neck)	John Sellers	Tom Rolfe	First Family	2:28⅖
1966	Amberold (2½)	William Boland	Buffle	Advocator	2:29⅗
1967	Damascus (2½)	Bill Shoemaker	Cool Reception	Gentleman	2:28⅘

Belmont *(Cont.)*

Year	Winner (Margin)	Jockey	Second	Third	Time
1968	Stage Door Johnny (1¼)	Hellodoro Gustines	Forward Pass	James Call Me Prince	2:27⅕
1969	Arts and Letters (5½)	Braulio Baeza	Majestic Prince	Dike	2:28⅘
1970	High Echelon (¾)	John L. Rotz	Needles N Pins	Naskra	2:34
1971	Pass Catcher (¾)	Walter Blum	Jim French	Bold Reason	2:30⅖
1972	Riva Ridge (7)	Ron Turcotte	Ruritania	Cloudy Dawn	2:28
1973	Secretariat (31)	Ron Turcotte	Twice a Prince	My Gallant	2:24
1974	Little Current (7)	Miguel A. Rivera	Jolly Johu	Cannonade	2:29⅕
1975	Avatar (Neck)	Bill Shoemaker	Foolish Pleasure	Master Derby	2:28⅕
1976	Bold Forbes (Neck)	Angel Cordero Jr.	McKenzie Bridge	Great Contractor	2:29
1977	Seattle Slew (4)	Jean Cruguet	Run Dusty Run	Sanhedrin	2:29⅗
1978	Affirmed (Head)	Steve Cauthen	Alydar	Darby Creek Road	2:26⅘
1979	Coastal (3¼)	Ruben Hernandez	Golden Act	Spectacular Bid	2:28⅗
1980	Temperence Hill (2)	Eddie Maple	Genuine Risk	Rockhill Native	2:29⅘
1981	Summing (Neck)	George Martens	Highland Blade	Pleasant Colony	2:29
1982	Conquistador Cielo (14½)	Laffit Pincay, Jr.	Gato Del Sol	Illuminate	2:28⅕
1983	Caveat (3½)	Laffit Pincay Jr.	Slew o'Gold	Barberstown	2:27⅘
1984	Swale (4)	Laffit Pincay Jr.	Pine Circle	Morning Bob	2:27⅕
1985	Creme Fraiche (½)	Eddie Maple	Stephan's Odyssey	Chief's Crown	2:27
1986	Danzig Connection (1¼)	Chris McCarron	Johns Treasure	Ferdinand	2:29⅘
1987	Bet Twice (14)	Craig Perret	Cryptoclearance	Gulch	2:28⅕
1988	Risen Star (14¾)	Eddie Delahoussaye	Kingpost	Brian's Time	2:26⅖
1989	Easy Goer (8)	Pat Day	Sunday Silence	Le Voyageur	2:26
1990	Go and Go (8¼)	Michael Kinane	Thirty Six Red	Baron de Vaux	2:27⅕
1991	Hansel (Head)	Jerry Bailey	Strike the Gold	Mane Minister	2:28
1992	A.P. Indy (¾)	Eddie Delahoussaye	My Memoirs	Pine Bluff	2:26
1993	Colonial Affair (2¼)	Julie Krone	Kissin Kris	Wild Gale	2:29⅘
1994	Tabasco Cat (2)	Pat Day	Go For Gin	Strodes Creek	2:26⅘
1995	Thunder Gulch (2)	Gary Stevens	Star Standard	Citadeed	2:32
1996	Editor's Note (1)	Rene Douglas	Skip Away	My Flag	2:28⅘
1997	Touch Gold (¾)	Chris McCarron	Silver Charm	Free House	2:28⅘
1998	Victory Gallop (Nose)	Gary Stevens	Real Quiet	Thomas Jo	2:28⅘
1999	Lemon Drop Kid (Head)	Jose Santos	Vision and Verse	Charismatic	2:27⅘
2000	Commendable (1½)	Pat Day	Aptitude	Unshaded	2:31.19
2001	Point Given (12¾)	Gary Stevens	A P Valentine	Monarchos	2:26.56
2002	Sarava (½)	Edgar Prado	Medaglia d'Oro	Sunday Break	2:29.71
2003	Empire Maker (¾)	Jerry Bailey	Ten Most Wanted	Funny Cide	2:28.26
2004	Birdstone (1)	Edgar Prado	Smarty Jones	Royal Assault	2:27.59
2005	Afleet Alex(4¾)	Jeremy Rose	Andromeda's Hero	Nolan's Cat	2:28.75
2006	Jazil (1¼)	Fernando Jara	Bluegrass Cat	Sunriver	2:27.86
2007	Rags to Riches (Head)	John Velazquez	Curlin	Tiago	2:28.74
2008	Da' Tara (5¼)	Alan Garcia	Denis of Cork	Ready's Echo	2:29.65

*Belmont was a two-horse race in 1887, '88, '92, 1910 and '20; and was not held in 1911–1912.
Note: Distance: 1 mile 5 furlongs (1867–89), 1¼ miles (1890–1905), 1⅜ miles (1906–25), 1½ miles (1926–present).

Triple Crown Winners

Year	Horse	Jockey	Owner	Trainer
1919	Sir Barton	John Loftus	J. K. L. Ross	H. G. Bedwell
1930	Gallant Fox	Earle Sande	Belair Stud	James Fitzsimmons
1935	Omaha	William Saunders	Belair Stud	James Fitzsimmons
1937	War Admiral	Charles Kurtsinger	Samuel D. Riddle	George Conway
1941	Whirlaway	Eddie Arcaro	Calumet Farm	Ben Jones
1943	Count Fleet	John Longden	Mrs J. D. Hertz	Don Cameron
1946	Assault	Warren Mehrtens	King Ranch	Max Hirsch
1948	Citation	Eddie Arcaro	Calumet Farm	Jimmy Jones
1973	Secretariat	Ron Turcotte	Meadow Stable	Lucien Laurin
1977	Seattle Slew	Jean Cruguet	Karen L. Taylor	William H. Turner Jr.
1978	Affirmed	Steve Cauthen	Harbor View Farm	Laz Barrera

Motor Sports

JONATHAN FERREY/GETTY IMAGES

Danica Patrick won her maiden race at the 2008 Indy Japan 300

A Woman's Place? First.

The 2008 racing season was one for the books—complete with bad boys, big flame-outs and one amazing woman

BY BJ SCHECTER

When she led the 2005 Indy 500 for 19 laps and nearly won the race, Danica Patrick became an instant phenomenon. Women adored her, men were intrigued by her and the media couldn't get enough of her. And though it was clear she had considerable talent, for three years she struggled to win her first race and critics began to wonder if Patrick would turn out to be the Anna Kournikova of motor sports. On April 20 in Motegi, Japan, Patrick ended any doubts by winning the Indy Japan 300 in her 50th career start.

It was a crowing achievement for the 26-year-old driver, who became the first female winner in IndyCar history. But neither Patrick nor anyone else on the IndyCar circuit was surprised by Patrick's historic victory. "It's been a long time coming," said Patrick. "I'm glad it finally happened, but I'd be lying if I told you I didn't think it would be me...I've been asked so many times when and if I can win my first race. And, finally, no more questions."

Just as impressive as the victory itself was how Patrick won. She and her team used perfect fuel strategy (something that ultimately failed Patrick in the 2005 Indy 500) as Patrick passed Helio Castroneves on lap 198 of the 200-lap race. "I knew from the start of the last fuel load that I was going to have a chance," Patrick said. "I was saving fuel from the first lap, but it wasn't until I passed Helio that I knew I was going to win."

Patrick has earned the respect of other drivers on the Indy series and many praised her accomplishment, including the driver she passed to win the race. "When Danica passed me, I realized she was the leader," said Castroneves. "She did a great job, passed me fair and square, and that just shows you how competitive our series is."

Ever since Patrick was 9 years old and her father bought her a go-cart, she had been shooting for her first IndyCar victory. The media may have been infatuated with her because she's an attractive 5'2", 100-pound marketing dream, but on the track she quickly showed she belonged by keeping the pedal to the metal and never backing down. Prior to the 2007 season, Patrick signed on with Andretti Green racing, one of the premier teams in IndyCar, and had the full support of co-owner Michael Andretti.

Patrick entered the Indy 500 with a wave of momentum and one of the fastest cars on the track. But in the end she didn't come close to seeing the checkered flag as points

GEORGE TIEDEMANN/GT IMAGES

Despite stumbling in the Chase for the Cup, Kyle Busch dominated NASCAR for much of the year, winning eight races in 2008.

leader Scott Dixon won the race and Patrick lagged far behind, finishing a disappointing 22nd. Still, it was quite a year for Patrick. She entered October sixth in the IndyCar standings and established herself as a threat to win any race she entered.

During the NASCAR season, no driver was a bigger threat than Kyle Bush, who won eight races, finished in the top five 15 times, was atop the standings for 19 straight weeks and entered the Chase as the points leader. He did so while driving the new Car of Tomorrow, a taller, safer and more efficient vehicle NASCAR introduced to the circuit in 2007. Bush's talent is undeniable, but the 23-year-old, who ruffles many feathers and draws the most boos at just about every track, showed he still has something to learn before he's ready to win the Chase.

The odds-on favorite entering the 10-race Chase, Bush crashed and burned in the first three races, finishing 34th at New Hampshire, 43rd at Dover and 28th at Kansas City. That left him dead last in the Chase standings and virtually out of the running for the title.

After Bush's freefall, the Chase favorites became Carl Edwards, who came on strong at the end of the regular season and checked in with six wins and 19 top-10 finishes, and two-time defending champion Jimmie Johnson. The Chase wouldn't be the Chase without Johnson, who was shooting to become the first driver in 30 years (Cale Yarborough was the last to do it) to win the Chase three years in a row. Johnson's victory at Kansas City gave him the overall lead and put him in prime position to accomplish the feat.

Earlier in the season, Tony Stewart shook up NASCAR when he left Joe Gibbs Racing to start his own team (a year after Dale Earnhardt Jr. left DEI) and 18-year-old phenom Joey Logano made his Cup debut, finishing a respectable 32nd (ahead of Kyle Bush) at New Hampshire.

But the year belonged to Patrick, who not only broke down barriers, but also established herself as the biggest name in Indy and the future of open-wheel racing in the United States. "I'm thrilled for her that the monkey is finally off her back," said Michael Andretti after Patrick's victory in Japan. "We have all believed in her, and she proved that she is a winner. Frankly, I think this is the first of many."

Indy Racing League

Indianapolis 500

Results of the 92nd running of the Indianapolis 500 and sixth race of the 2008 Indy Racing League season. Held Sunday, May 25, 2008, at the 2.5-mile Indianapolis Motor Speedway in Indianapolis.
Distance, 500 miles; starters, 33; winning time of race, 3 hours, 28 mins., 57.6792 seconds; average speed, 143.567 mph; margin of victory, 1.7498 seconds; caution flags, 8 for 69 laps; lead, 18 among nine drivers.

TOP 10 FINISHERS

Pos.	Driver (start pos.)	C/E/T	Qual. Speed	Laps	Status
1	Scott Dixon (1)	D/H/F	226.366	200	running
2	Vitor Meira (8)	D/H/F	224.346	200	running
3	Marco Andretti (7)	D/H/F	224.417	200	running
4	Helio Castroneves (4)	D/H/F	225.733	200	running
5	Ed Carpenter (10)	D/H/F	223.835	200	running
6	†Ryan Hunter-Reay (20)	D/H/F	221.579	200	running
7	†Hideki Mutoh (9)	D/H/F	223.887	200	running
8	Buddy Rice (17)	D/H/F	222.101	200	running
9.	Darren Manning (14)	D/H/F	222.430	200	running
10	Townsend Bell (12)	D/H/F	222.539	200	running

†-Rookie driver.

2008 Indy Racing League Results

Date	Race	Winner (start pos.)	C/E/T	Qual. Speed
Mar 29	Miami 300	Scott Dixon (1)	D/H/F	213.341
Apr 6	Grand Prix of St. Petersburg	Graham Rahal (9)	D/H/F	103.165
Apr 19	Japan 300	Danica Patrick (6)	D/H/F	0.000†
Apr 20	Grand Prix of Long Beach^	Will Power (4)	D/H/F	105.421
Apr 27	Kansas 300	Dan Wheldon(2)	D/H/F	213.641
May 25	Indianapolis 500	Scott Dixon (1)	D/H/F	226.366
June 1	Milwaukee 225	Ryan Briscoe (11)	D/H/F	164.106
June 7	Texas 550	Scott Dixon (1)	D/H/F	214.878
June 22	Iowa 250	Dan Wheldon (3)	D/H/F	0.000†
June 28	Richmond 300*	Tony Kanaan (1)	D/H/F	167.876
July 6	Grand Prix of Watkins Glen	Ryan Hunter-Reay (3)	D/H/F	135.348
July 12	Nashville 200	Scott Dixon (5)	D/H/F	203.233
July 20	Mid-Ohio 200	Ryan Briscoe (2)	D/H/F	120.846
July 26	Edmonton 95*	Scott Dixon (4)	D/H/F	116.710
Aug 9	Kentucky 300	Scott Dixon (1)	D/H/F	218.968
Aug 24	Sonoma Grand Prix	Helio Castroneves (1)	D/H/F	107.809
Aug 31	Grand Prix of Belle Isle	Justin Wilson (4)	D/H/F	102.008
Sept 7	Chicago 300	Helio Castroneves (28)	D/H/F	215.553

Note: Distances are in miles unless followed by * (laps). †Qualification round rained out. ^Points earned in final Champ Car race before merger with IRL counted toward 2008 IRL standings.

2008 Final Championship Standings

Driver	Pts
Scott Dixon	646
Helio Castroneves	629
Tony Kanaan	513
Dan Wheldon	492
Ryan Briscoe	447
Danica Patrick	379
Marco Andretti	363
Ryan Hunter-Reay	360
Oriol Servia	358
Hideki Mutoh	346

Champ Car World Series

2007 Championship Standings

Driver	Points
Sebastian Bourdais	364
Justin Wilson	281
Robert Doornbos	268
Will Power	262
Graham Rahal	243
Oriol Servia	237
Bruno Junqueira	233
Simon Pagenaud	232
Neel Jani	231
Alex Tagliani	205

Note: On Februray 22, 2008, the Champ Car World Series merged with the Indy Racing League.

National Association for Stock Car Auto Racing

Daytona 500

Results of the 50th Daytona 500, the opening round of the 2008 Sprint Cup series. Held Sunday, February 17, 2008, at the 2.5-mile high-banked Daytona International Speedway.
Distance, 500 miles; starters, 43; winning time of race, 3:16:30; average speed, 152.672 mph; margin of victory, 0.092 seconds; caution flags, 7 for 23 laps; lead changes, 42.

TOP 10 FINISHERS

Pos.	Driver (start pos.)	Car	Laps	Winnings ($)
1	Ryan Newman (7)	Dodge	200	1,506,040
2	Kurt Busch (43)	Dodge	200	1,063,870
3	Tony Stewart (6)	Toyota	200	871,049
4	Kyle Busch (24)	Toyota	200	652,938
5	Reed Sorenson (5)	Dodge	200	545,959
6	Elliott Sadler (35)	Dodge	200	430,015
7	Kasey Kahne (10)	Dodge	200	389,204
8	Robby Gordon (26)	Dodge	200	352,921
9	Dale Earnhardt Jr. (3)	Chevrolet	200	352,920
10	Greg Biffle (18)	Ford	200	313,763

2007 Nextel Cup* Final Standings

Driver	Pts	Starts	Wins	Top 5	Top 10
Jimmie Johnson	6723	36	10	20	24
Jeff Gordon	6646	36	6	21	30
Clint Bowyer	6377	36	1	5	17
Matt Kenseth	6298	36	2	13	22
Kyle Busch.	6293	36	1	11	20
Tony Stewart	6242	36	3	11	23
Kurt Busch	6231	36	2	6	14
Jeff Burton	6231	36	1	9	18
Carl Edwards	6222	36	3	11	15
Kevin Harvick	6199	36	1	4	15

2007 Nextel Cup* Final Driver Winnings

Driver	Winnings ($)
Jimmie Johnson	7,646,420
Kevin Harvick	7,494,590
Jeff Gordon	7,148,620
Matt Kenseth	6,485,630
Tony Stewart	6,396,750
Jeff Burton	6,015,670
Kurt Busch.	5,287,850
Martin Truex Jr.	5,003,880
Denny Hamlin	4,943,810
Kyle Busch	4,685,520

*Series name changed from Winston Cup to Nextel Cup after 2003 season, then to Sprint Cup beginning in 2008.

Late 2007 Nextel Cup Series Results

Date	Track/Distance	Winner (start pos.)	Car	Laps	Winnings ($)
*Oct 13	Charlotte 500	Jeff Gordon (4)	Chevrolet	337	268,236
*Oct 21	Martinsville 500	Jimmie Johnson (4)	Chevrolet	506	244,486
*Oct 28	Atlanta 500	Jimmie Johnson (6)	Chevrolet	329	343,861
*Nov 4	Texas 500	Jimmie Johnson (8)	Chevrolet	334	486,211
*Nov 11	Phoenix 500	Jimmie Johnson (6)	Chevrolet	312	245,011
*Nov 18	Homestead/Miami 400	Matt Kenseth (4)	Ford	267	359,941

2008 Sprint Cup Series Results†

Date	Track/Distance	Winner (start pos.)	Car	Laps	Winnings ($)
Feb 17	Daytona 500	Ryan Newman (34)	Dodge	200	1,506,045
Feb 25	Fontana 500	Carl Edwards (9)	Ford	250	340,500
Mar 2	Las Vegas 400	Carl Edwards (2)	Ford	267	425,675
Mar 9	Atlanta 500	Kyle Busch (6)	Toyota	325	185,375
Mar 16	Bristol 500	Jeff Burton (8)	Chevrolet	506	209,558
Mar 30	Martinsville 500	Denny Hamlin (2)	Toyota	500	210,391
Apr 6	Texas 500	Carl Edwards (2)	Ford	339	541,150
Apr 12	Phoenix 500	Jimmie Johnson (7)	Chevrolet	312	262,111
Apr 27	Talladega 499	Kyle Busch (5)	Toyota	188	321,400
May 3	Richmond 400	Clint Bowyer (31)	Chevrolet	410	226,550
May 10	Darlington 500	Kyle Busch (6)	Toyota	367	313,700
May 25	Charlotte 600	Kasey Kahne (2)	Dodge	400	422,766
June 1	Dover 400	Kyle Busch (3)	Toyota	400	302,550
June 8	Pocono 500	Kasey Kahne (1)	Dodge	200	260,866
June 15	Michigan 400	Dale Earnhardt Jr. (3)	Chevrolet	203	173,550
June 22	Sonoma 350	Kyle Busch (30)	Toyota	112	309,925
June 29	New Hampshire 300	Kurt Busch (26)	Dodge	284	204,950
July 5	Daytona 400	Kyle Busch (9)	Toyota	162	315,950
July 12	Chicagoland 400	Kyle Busch (1)	Toyota	267	331,175
July 27	Brickyard 400	Jimmie Johnson (1)	Chevrolet	160	509,236
Aug 3	Pocono 500	Carl Edwards (15)	Ford	200	241,875
Aug 10	Watkins Glen 220	Kyle Busch (1)	Toyota	90	227,000
Aug 17	Michigan 400	Carl Edwards (27)	Ford	200	226,075
Aug 23	Bristol 500	Carl Edwards (1)	Ford	500	344,625
Aug 31	California 500	Jimmie Johnson (1)	Chevrolet	250	314,611
Sept 6	Richmond 400	Jimmie Johnson (3)	Chevrolet	400	256,836
*Sept 14	New Hampshire 300	Greg Biffle (9)	Ford	300	233,575
*Sept 21	Dover 400	Greg Biffle (5)	Ford	400	218,450
*Sept 28	Kansas 400	Jimmie Johnson (1)	Chevrolet	267	364,411
*Oct 5	Talladega 500	Tony Stewart	Toyota	190	270,136

† Through October 5, 2008.
* Part of 10-race Chase for the Cup

Formula One Grand Prix Racing

2008 Formula One Results†

Grand Prix	Date	Winner	Car	Laps	Time
Australia	Mar 16	Lewis Hamilton	McLaren-Mercecdes	58	1:34:50.616
Malaysia	Mar 23	Kimi Raikkonen	Ferrari	56	1:31:18.555
Bahrain	Apr 6	Felipe Massa	Ferrari	57	1:31:06.970
Spain	Apr 27	Kimi Raikkonen	Ferrari	66	1:38:19.051
Turkey	May 11	Felipe Massa	Ferrari	58	1:26:49:451
Monaco	May 25	Lewis Hamilton	McLaren-Mercedes	76	2:00:42.742
Canada	June 8	Robert Kubica	BMW Sauber	70	1:36:24.447
France	June 22	Felipe Massa	Ferrari	70	1:31:50.245
Britain	July 6	Lewis Hamilton	McLaren-Mercedes	60	1:39:09.440
Germany	July 20	Lewis Hamilton	McLaren-Mercedes	67	1:31:20.874
Hungary	Aug 3	Heikki Kovalainen	McLaren-Mercedes	70	1:37:27.067
Europe	Aug 24	Felipe Massa	Ferrari	57	1:35:32.339
Belgium	Sept 7	Felipe Massa	Ferrari	44	1:22:59.394
Italy	Sept 14	Sebastian Vettel	STR-Ferrari	53	1:26:47.494
Singapore	Sept 28	Fernando Alonso	Renault	61	1:57:16.304

† Through September 28, 2008.

2007 World Championship Final Standings

Drivers compete in Grand Prix races for the title of World Driving Champion. Below are the top 10 drivers from the 2007 season. Points are awarded for places 1–6 as follows: 10-6-4-3-2-1.

Driver	Country	Team	Pts
Kimi Raikkonen	Finland	Ferrari	110
Lewis Hamilton	Great Britain	McLaren-Mercedes	109
Fernando Alonso	Spain	McLaren-Mercedes	109
Felipe Massa	Brazil	Ferrari	94
Nick Heidfeld	Germany	BMW Sauber	61
Robert Kubica	Poland	BMW Sauber	39
Heikki Kovalainen	Finland	Renault	30
Giancarlo Fisichella	Italy	Renault	21
Nico Rosberg	Germany	Williams-Toyota	20
David Coulthard	Great Britain	Renault	14

Professional Sports Car Racing

The 24 Hours of Daytona

Held at the Daytona International Speedway on Jan 26–27, 2008, the 24 Hours of Daytona serves as the opening round of the Grand American Road Racing Association's season.

Place	Drivers	Car (Class)	Distance
1	S. Pruett, M. Rojas, J. Montoya, D. Franchitti	Lexus Riley	695 laps (103.057 mph)
2	J. Fogarty, A. Gurney, J. Vasser, J. Johnson	Pontiac Riley	693
3	R. Briscoe, H. Castroneves, K. Busch	Pontiac Riley	689
4	N. Jonsson, R. Zonta, D. Turner	Pontiac Riley	688
5	W. Taylor, M. Angelelli, M. Valiante, R. Taylor	Pontiac Riley	687

2008 American Le Mans Series—Prototype Class†

Date	Race	Winners	Car
Mar 15	12 Hours of Sebring	R. Capello, T. Kristensen, A. McNish	Audi R10 TDI
April 5	St. Petersburg Challenge	L. Luhr, M. Werner	Audi R10 TDI
April 19	Grand Prix of Long Beach	L. Luhr, M. Werner	Audi R10 TDI
May 18	Utah Grand Prix	L. Luhr, M. Werner	Audi R10 TDI
July 12	Northeast Grand Prix	L. Luhr, M. Werner	Audi R10 TDI
July 19	Mid Ohio	L. Luhr, M. Werner	Audi R10 TDI
Aug 9	Road America 500	L. Luhr, M. Werner	Audi R10 TDI
Aug 24	Grand Prix of Mosport	L. Luhr, M. Werner	Audi R10 TDI
Aug 30	Detroit Challenge	C. Field, J. Field, R. Berry	Lola B06/10
Oct 4	Petit Le Mans	D. Capello, A. McNish, E. Pirro	Audi R10 TDI

2007 American Le Mans Series—GTS Class†

Date	Race	Winners	Car
Mar 15	12 Hours of Sebring	J. O'Connell, J. Magnussen, R. Fellows	Corvette C6.R
April 5	St. Petersburg Challenge	O. Beretta, O. Gavin	Corvette C6.R
April 19	Grand Prix of Long Beach	J. O'Connell, J. Magnussen	Corvette C6.R

Professional Sports Car Racing *(Cont.)*

2008 American Le Mans Series—GTS Class *(Cont.)*

Date	Race	Winners	Car
May 18	Utah Grand Prix	J. O'Connell, J. Magnussen	Corvette C6.R
July 7	Northeast Grand Prix	J. O'Connell, J. Magnussen	Corvette C6.R
July 19	Mid Ohio	J. O'Connell, J. Magnussen	Corvette C6.R
Aug 9	Road America 500	J. O'Connell, J. Magnussen	Corvette C6.R
Aug 24	Grand Prix of Mosport	J. O'Connell, J. Magnussen	Corvette C6.R
Aug 30	Detroit Challenge	O. Beretta, O. Gavin	Corvette C6.R
Oct 4	Petit Le Mans	J. O'Connell, J. Magnussen	Corvette C6.R

2008 American Le Mans Series—GT Class†

Date	Race	Winners	Car
Mar 15	12 Hours of Sebring	J. Bergmeister, W. Henzler, M. Lieb	Porsche 911 GT3
April 5	St. Petersburg Challenge	D. Farnbacher, D. Muller, R. Bell	Ferrari F430GT
April 19	Grand Prix of Long Beach	D. Farnbacher, D. Muller	Ferrari F430GT
May 18	Utah Grand Prix	J. Bergmeister, W. Henzler	Porsche 911 GT3
July 12	Northeast Grand Prix	J. Bergmeister, W. Henzler	Porsche 911 GT3
July 19	Mid Ohio	D. Farnbacher, D. Muller	Ferrari F430GT
Aug 9	Road America 500	R. Westbrook, D. Werner, B. Miller	Porsche 911 GT3
Aug 24	Grand Prix of Mosport	M. Salo, J. Melo	Ferrari F430GT
Aug 30	Detroit Challenge	J. Bergmeister, W. Henzler	Porsche 911 GT3
Oct 4	Petit Le Mans	M. Salo, J. Melo	Ferrari F430GT

† Through October 4, 2008.

2007 American Le Mans Series Championship Final Standings

PROTOTYPE CLASS	Pts	GTS CLASS	Pts	GT CLASS	Pts
Rinaldo Capello	246	Oliver Gavin	246	Mika Salo	202
Allan McNish	246	Olivier Beretta	246	Jaime Melo	202
Marco Werner	210	Johnny O'Connell	184	Jorg Bergmeister	170
Emanuele Pirro	175	Jan Magnussen	184	Johannes Van Overbeek	170
Clint Field	95	Max Papis	52	Wolf Henzler	126
Chris McMurry	89	Fredy Lienhard	38	Tom Milner Jr.	107
Jon Field	82	Didier Theys	38	Ralf Kelleners	107

24 Hours of Le Mans

Held at Le Mans, France, on June 14–15, 2008, the 24 Hours of Le Mans is the most prestigious international event in endurance racing.

Place	Drivers	Car	Laps
1	R. Capello, T. Kristensen, A. McNish	Audi R10	381
2	M. Gene, N. Minassian, J. Villeneuve	Peugeot 908	381
3	F. Montagny, C. Klien, R. Zonta	Peugeot 908	379
4	L. Luhr, A. Premat, M. Rockenfeller	Audi R10	374
5	P. Lamy, S. Sarrazin, A. Wurz	Peugeot 908	368

FOR THE RECORD • Year by Year

Indianapolis 500

First held in 1911, the Indianapolis 500—200 laps of the 2.5-mile Indianapolis Motor Speedway Track (called the Brickyard in honor of its original pavement)—grew to become the most famous auto race in the world. Though the Memorial Day weekend event lost participants and prestige in the mid-1990s due to feuding in the world of U.S. open-wheel racing, it annually attracts crowds of over 100,000.

Year	Winner (start pos.)	Chassis-Engine	Avg Speed	Pole Winner	Speed
1911	Ray Harroun (28)	Marmon-Marmon	74.590	Lewis Strang	First entered
1912	Joe Dawson (7)	National-National	78.720	Gil Anderson	First entered
1913	Jules Goux (7)	Peugeot-Peugeot	75.930	Caleb Bragg	Drew pole
1914	Rene Thomas (15)	Delage-Delage	82.470	Jean Chassagne	Drew pole
1915	Ralph DePalma (2)	Mercedes-Mercedes	89.840	Howard Wilcox	98.90
1916	Dario Resta (4)	Peugeot-Peugeot	84.000	John Aitken	96.69
1917–18	No race				
1919	Howard Wilcox (2)	Peugeot-Peugeot	88.050	Rene Thomas	104.78
1920	Gaston Chevrolet (6)	Frontenac-Frontenac	88.620	Ralph DePalma	99.15
1921	Tommy Milton (20)	Frontenac-Frontenac	89.620	Ralph DePalma	100.75
1922	Jimmy Murphy (1)	Duesenberg-Miller	94.480	Jimmy Murphy	100.50
1923	Tommy Milton (1)	Miller-Miller	90.950	Tommy Milton	108.17
1924	L.L. Corum Joe Boyer (21)	Duesenberg-Duesenberg	98.230	Jimmy Murphy	108.037
1925	Peter DePaolo (2)	Duesenberg-Duesenberg	101.130	Leon Duray	113.196
1926	Frank Lockhart (20)	Miller-Miller	95.904	Earl Cooper	111.735
1927	George Souders (22)	Duesenberg-Duesenberg	97.545	Frank Lockhart	120.100
1928	Louis Meyer (13)	Miller-Miller	99.482	Leon Duray	122.391
1929	Ray Keech (6)	Miller-Miller	97.585	Cliff Woodbury	120.599
1930	Billy Arnold (1)	Summers-Miller	100.448	Billy Arnold	113.268
1931	Louis Schneider (13)	Stevens-Miller	96.629	Russ Snowberger	112.796
1932	Fred Frame (27)	Wetteroth-Miller	104.144	Lou Moore	117.363
1933	Louis Meyer (6)	Miller-Miller	104.162	Bill Cummings	118.524
1934	Bill Cummings (10)	Miller-Miller	104.863	Kelly Petillo	119.329
1935	Kelly Petillo (22)	Wetteroth-Offy	106.240	Rex Mays	120.736
1936	Louis Meyer (28)	Stevens-Miller	109.069	Rex Mays	119.664
1937	Wilbur Shaw (2)	Shaw-Offy	113.580	Bill Cummings	123.343
1938	Floyd Roberts (1)	Wetteroth-Miller	117.200	Floyd Roberts	125.681
1939	Wilbur Shaw (3)	Maserati-Maserati	115.035	Jimmy Snyder	130.138
1940	Wilbur Shaw (2)	Maserati-Maserati	114.277	Rex Mays	127.850
1941	Floyd Davis Mauri Rose (17)	Wetteroth-Offy	115.117	Mauri Rose	128.691
1942–45	No race				
1946	George Robson (15)	Adams-Sparks	114.820	Cliff Bergere	126.471
1947	Mauri Rose (3)	Deidt-Offy	116.338	Ted Horn	126.564
1948	Mauri Rose (3)	Deidt-Offy	119.814	Rex Mays	130.577
1949	Bill Holland (4)	Deidt-Offy	121.327	Duke Nalon	132.939
1950	Johnnie Parsons (5)	Kurtis-Offy	124.002	Walt Faulkner	134.343
1951	Lee Wallard (2)	Kurtis-Offy	126.244	Duke Nalon	136.498
1952	Troy Ruttman (7)	Kuzma-Offy	128.922	Fred Agabashian	138.010
1953	Bill Vukovich (1)	KK500A-Offy	128.740	Bill Vukovich	138.392
1954	Bill Vukovich (19)	KK500A-Offy	130.840	Jack McGrath	141.033
1955	Bob Sweikert (14)	KK500C-Offy	128.209	Jerry Hoyt	140.045
1956	Pat Flaherty (1)	Watson-Offy	128.490	Pat Flaherty	145.596
1957	Sam Hanks (13)	Salih-Offy	135.601	Pat O'Connor	143.948
1958	Jim Bryan (7)	Salih-Offy	133.791	Dick Rathmann	145.974
1959	Rodger Ward (6)	Watson-Offy	135.857	Johnny Thomson	145.908
1960	Jim Rathmann (2)	Watson-Offy	138.767	Eddie Sachs	146.592
1961	A.J. Foyt (7)	Trevis-Offy	139.130	Eddie Sachs	147.481
1962	Rodger Ward (2)	Watson-Offy	140.293	Parnelli Jones	150.370
1963	Parnelli Jones (1)	Watson-Offy	143.137	Parnelli Jones	151.153
1964	A.J. Foyt (5)	Watson-Offy	147.350	Jim Clark	158.828
1965	Jim Clark (2)	Lotus-Ford	150.686	A.J. Foyt	161.233
1966	Graham Hill (15)	Lola-Ford	144.317	Mario Andretti	165.899
1967	A.J. Foyt (4)	Coyote-Ford	151.207	Mario Andretti	168.982
1968	Bobby Unser (3)	Eagle-Offy	152.882	Joe Leonard	171.559
1969	Mario Andretti (2)	Hawk-Ford	156.867	A.J. Foyt	170.568
1970	Al Unser (1)	PJ Colt-Ford	155.749	Al Unser	170.221
1971	Al Unser (5)	PJ Colt-Ford	157.735	Peter Revson	178.696
1972	Mark Donohue (3)	McLaren-Offy	162.962	Bobby Unser	195.940

Indianapolis 500 *(Cont.)*

Year	Winner (start pos.)	Chassis-Engine	Avg speed	Pole Winner	Speed
1973	Gordon Johncock (11)	Eagle-Offy	159.036	Johnny Rutherford	198.413
1974	Johnny Rutherford (25)	McLaren-Offy	158.589	A.J. Foyt	191.632
1975	Bobby Unser (3)	Racers Eagle-Offy	149.213	A.J. Foyt	193.976
1976	Johnny Rutherford (1)	McLaren-Offy	148.725	Johnny Rutherford	188.957
1977	A.J. Foyt (4)	Coyote-Ford	161.331	Tom Sneva	198.884
1978	Al Unser (5)	Lola-Cosworth	161.361	Tom Sneva	202.156
1979	Rick Mears (1)	Penske-Cosworth	158.899	Rick Mears	193.736
1980	Johnny Rutherford (1)	Chaparral-Coswoth	142.862	Johnny Rutherford	192.256
1981	Bobby Unser (1)	Penske-Cosworth	139.084	Bobby Unser	200.546
1982	Gordon Johncock (5)	Wildcat-Cosworth	162.026	Rick Mears	207.004
1983	Tom Sneva (4)	March-Cosworth	162.117	Teo Fabi	207.395
1984	Rick Mears (3)	March-Cosworth	163.612	Tom Sneva	210.029
1985	Danny Sullivan (8)	March-Cosworth	152.982	Pancho Carter	212.583
1986	Bobby Rahal (4)	March-Cosworth	170.722	Rick Mears	216.828
1987	Al Unser (20)	March-Cosworth	162.175	Mario Andretti	215.390
1988	Rick Mears (1)	Penske-Chevrolet	144.809	Rick Mears	219.198
1989	Emerson Fittipaldi (3)	Penske-Chevrolet	167.581	Rick Mears	223.885
1990	Arie Luyendyk (3)	Lola-Chevrolet	185.981*	Emerson Fittipaldi	225.301
1991	Rick Mears (1)	Penske-Chevrolet	176.457	Rick Mears	224.113
1992	Al Unser Jr. (12)	Galmer-Chevrolet	134.477	Roberto Guerrero	232.482
1993	Emerson Fittipaldi (9)	Penske-Chevrolet	157.207	Arie Luyendyk	223.967
1994	Al Unser Jr. (1)	Penske-Mercedes	160.872	Al Unser Jr.	228.011
1995	Jacques Villeneuve (5)	Reynard-Ford	153.616	Scott Brayton	231.616
1996	Buddy Lazier (5)	Reynard-Ford	147.956	Tony Stewart	233.100†
1997	Arie Luyendyk (1)	G Force-Oldsmobile	145.827	Arie Luyendyk	231.468
1998	Eddie Cheever (17)	Dallara-Oldsmobile	145.155	Billy Boat	223.503
1999	Kenny Brack (8)	Dallara-Oldsmobile	153.176	Arie Luyendyk	225.179
2000	Juan Montoya (2)	G Force-Oldsmobile	167.607	Greg Ray	223.471
2001	Helio Castroneves (11)	Dallara-Oldsmobile	153.601	Scott Sharp	226.037
2002	Helio Castroneves (13)	Dallara-Chevrolet	166.499	Bruno Junqueira	231.342
2003	Gil de Ferran	Panoz-Toyota	156.291	Helio Castroneves	231.725
2004	Buddy Rice (1)	G Force-Honda	138.518	Buddy Rice	222.024
2005	Dan Wheldon	Dallara-Honda	157.603	Tony Kanaan	227.566
2006	Sam Hornish Jr.(1)	Dallara-Honda	157.085	Sam Hornish Jr.	228.985
2007	Dario Franchitti (3)	Dallara-Honda	151.744	Helio Castroneves	225.817
2008	Scott Dixon (1)	Dallara-Honda	143.567	Scott Dixon	226.366

*Track record, winning speed. †Track record, qualifying speed.

Indianapolis 500 Rookie of the Year Award

1952 ....Art Cross
1953 ....Jimmy Daywalt
1954 ....Larry Crockett
1955 ....Al Herman
1956 ....Bob Veith
1957 ....Don Edmunds
1958 ....George Amick
1959 ....Bobby Grim
1960 ....Jim Hurtubise
1961 ....Parnelli Jones*
Bobby Marshman
1962 ....Jimmy McElreath
1963 ....Jim Clark*
1964 ....Johnny White
1965 ....Mario Andretti*
1966 ....Jackie Stewart
1967 ....Denis Hulme
1968 ....Billy Vukovich
1969 ....Mark Donohue*
1970 ....Donnie Allison
1971 ....Denny Zimmerman
1972 ....Mike Hiss
1973 ....Graham McRae
1974 ....Pancho Carter
1975 ....Bill Puterbaugh
1976 ....Vern Schuppan
1977 ....Jerry Sneva
1978 ....Rick Mears*
Larry Rice
1979 ....Howdy Holmes
1980 ....Tim Richmond
1981 ....Josele Garza
1982 ....Jim Hickman
1983 ....Teo Fabi
1984 ....Michael Andretti
Roberto Guerrero
1985 ....Arie Luyendyk*
1986 ....Randy Lanier
1987 ....Fabrizio Barbazza
1988 ....Billy Vukovich III
1989 ....Bernard Jourdain
Scott Pruett
1990 ....Eddie Cheever*
1991 ....Jeff Andretti
1992 ....Lyn St. James
1993 ....Nigel Mansell
1994 ....Jacques Villeneuve*
1995 ....Gil de Ferran*
1996 ....Tony Stewart
1997 ....Jeff Ward
1998 ....Steve Knapp
1999 ....Robby McGehee
2000 ....Juan Montoya*
2001 ....Helio Castroneves*
2002 ....Alex Barron
Tomas Scheckter
2003 ....Tora Tagaki
2004 ....Kosuke Matsuura
2005 ....Danica Patrick
2006 ....Marco Andretti
2007 ....Phil Giebler
2008 ....Ryan Hunter-Reay

*Future winner of Indy 500.

Champ Car World Series

Champ Car World Series Champions

From 1909 to 1955, this championship was awarded by the American Automobile Association (AAA), and from 1956 to 1979 by the United States Auto Club (USAC). Since 1979, Championship Auto Racing Teams (CART) has conducted the championship. Known as PPG CART World Series until 1998. Series name changed to Champ Car World Series for 2005 racing season. On Februray 22, 2008, the Champ Car World Series merged with the Indy Racing League.

1909 ....George Robertson
1910 ....Ray Harroun
1911 ....Ralph Mulford
1912 ....Ralph DePalma
1913 ....Earl Cooper
1914 ....Ralph DePalma
1915 ....Earl Cooper
1916 ....Dario Resta
1917 ....Earl Cooper
1918 ....Ralph Mulford
1919 ....Howard Wilcox
1920 ....Tommy Milton
1921 ....Tommy Milton
1922 ....Jimmy Murphy
1923 ....Eddie Hearne
1924 ....Jimmy Murphy
1925 ....Peter DePaolo
1926 ....Harry Hartz
1927 ....Peter DePaolo
1928 ....Louis Meyer
1929 ....Louis Meyer
1930 ....Billy Arnold
1931 ....Louis Schneider
1932 ....Bob Carey
1933 ....Louis Meyer
1934 ....Bill Cummings
1935 ....Kelly Petillo
1936 ....Mauri Rose
1937 ....Wilbur Shaw
1938 ....Floyd Roberts
1939 ....Wilbur Shaw
1940 ....Rex Mays
1941 ....Rex Mays
1942–45 ....No racing
1946 ....Ted Horn
1947 ....Ted Horn
1948 ....Ted Horn
1949 ....Johnnie Parsons
1950 ....Henry Banks
1951 ....Tony Bettenhausen
1952 ....Chuck Stevenson
1953 ....Sam Hanks
1954 ....Jimmy Bryan
1955 ....Bob Sweikert
1956 ....Jimmy Bryan
1957 ....Jimmy Bryan
1958 ....Tony Bettenhausen
1959 ....Rodger Ward
1960 ............A.J. Foyt
1961 ............A.J. Foyt
1962 ....Rodger Ward
1963 ............A.J. Foyt
1964 ............A.J. Foyt
1965 ....Mario Andretti
1966 ....Mario Andretti
1967 ............A.J. Foyt
1968 ....Bobby Unser
1969 ....Mario Andretti
1970 ....Al Unser
1971 ....Joe Leonard
1972 ....Joe Leonard
1973 ....Roger McCluskey
1974 ....Bobby Unser
1975 ............A.J. Foyt
1976 ....Gordon Johncock
1977 ....Tom Sneva
1978 ....Tom Sneva
1979 ............A.J. Foyt
1979 ....Rick Mears
1980 ....Johnny Rutherford
1981 ....Rick Mears
1982 ....Rick Mears
1983 ....Al Unser
1984 ....Mario Andretti
1985 ....Al Unser
1986 ....Bobby Rahal
1987 ....Bobby Rahal
1988 ....Danny Sullivan
1989 ....Emerson Fittipaldi
1990 ....Al Unser Jr.
1991 ....Michael Andretti
1992 ....Bobby Rahal
1993 ....Nigel Mansell
1994 ....Al Unser Jr.
1995 ....Jacques Villeneuve
1996 ....Jimmy Vasser
1997 ....Alex Zanardi
1998 ....Alex Zanardi
1999 ....Juan Montoya
2000 ....Gil de Ferran
2001 ....Gil de Ferran
2002 ....Cristiano da Matta
2003 ....Paul Tracy
2004 ....Sebastian Bourdais
2005 ....Sebastian Bourdais
2006 ....Sebastian Bourdais
2007 ....Sebastian Bourdais

Alltime Champ Car* Leaders

WINS

A.J. Foyt 67
Mario Andretti 52
Michael Andretti....................42
Al Unser 39
Bobby Unser..........................35
Al Unser Jr 31
†Paul Tracy 31
Rick Mears.............................29
†Sebastian Bourdais.............29
Johnny Rutherford 27
Rodger Ward 26
Gordon Johncock 25
Bobby Rahal 24
Ralph DePalma.......................24
Tommy Milton........................23
Tony Bettenhausen 22
Emerson Fittipaldi 22
Earl Cooper............................20
Jimmy Bryan..........................19
Jimmy Murphy 19
Danny Sullivan 17
Ralph Mulford 17

POLE POSITIONS

Mario Andretti 67
A.J. Foyt 53
Bobby Unser..........................49
Rick Mears.............................40
Michael Andretti....................32
†Sebastian Bourdais.............28
Al Unser 27
†Paul Tracy 25
Johnny Rutherford 23
Gordon Johncock 20
Rex Mays 19
Danny Sullivan 19
Bobby Rahal 18
Emerson Fittipaldi 17
Gil de Ferran 16
Tony Bettenhausen 14
Juan Montoya 14
Don Branson 14
Tom Sneva 14
Parnelli Jones 12

*Series known as CART prior to 2003 season
†Active driver. Note: Leaders through September 2007.

Stock Car Racing's Major Events

In 1985, Winston began offering a $1 million bonus to any driver to win three of the top four NASCAR events in the same season. A fifth event, the Brickyard 400 (in Indianapolis) was added in 1994. As of 1998 the Winston million was awarded to any driver who won three of the five events. The other four races are the richest (Daytona 500), the fastest (Talladega 500), the longest (Charlotte 600) and the oldest (Southern 500 at Darlington). Only five drivers, Lee Roy Yarbrough (1969), David Pearson (1976), Bill Elliott (1985), Dale Jarrett (1996) and Jeff Gordon (1997, '98) have scored the three-track hat trick.

Daytona 500

Year	Winner (start pos.)	Chassis-Engine	Avg speed	Pole Winner	Qual. speed
1959	Lee Petty	Oldsmobile	135.520	Cotton Owens	143.198
1960	Junior Johnson	Chevrolet	124.740	Fireball Roberts	151.556
1961	Marvin Panch	Pontiac	149.601	Fireball Roberts	155.709
1962	Fireball Roberts	Pontiac	152.529	Fireball Roberts	156.995
1963	Tiny Lund	Ford	151.566	Johnny Rutherford	165.183
1964	Richard Petty	Plymouth	154.345	Paul Goldsmith	174.910
1965	Fred Lorenzen	Ford	141.539	Darel Dieringer	171.151
1966	Richard Petty	Plymouth	160.627	Richard Petty	175.165
1967	Mario Andretti	Ford	149.926	Curtis Turner	180.831
1968	Cale Yarborough	Mercury	143.251	Cale Yarborough	189.222
1969	Lee Roy Yarbrough	Ford	157.950	David Pearson	190.029
1970	Pete Hamilton	Plymouth	149.601	Cale Yarborough	194.015
1971	Richard Petty	Plymouth	144.462	A.J. Foyt	182.744
1972	A.J. Foyt	Mercury	161.550	Bobby Isaac	186.632
1973	Richard Petty	Dodge	157.205	Buddy Baker	185.662
1974	Richard Petty	Dodge	140.894	David Pearson	185.017
1975	Benny Parsons	Chevrolet	153.649	Donnie Allison	185.827
1976	David Pearson	Mercury	152.181	A.J. Foyt	185.943
1977	Cale Yarborough	Chevrolet	153.218	Donnie Allison	188.048
1978	Bobby Allison	Ford	159.730	Cale Yarborough	187.536
1979	Richard Petty	Oldsmobile	143.977	Buddy Baker	196.049
1980	Buddy Baker	Oldsmobile	177.602*	A.J. Foyt	195.020
1981	Richard Petty	Buick	169.651	Bobby Allison	194.624
1982	Bobby Allison	Buick	153.991	Benny Parsons	196.317
1983	Cale Yarborough	Pontiac	155.979	Ricky Rudd	198.864
1984	Cale Yarborough	Chevrolet	150.994	Cale Yarborough	201.848
1985	Bill Elliott	Ford	172.265	Bill Elliott	205.114
1986	Geoff Bodine	Chevrolet	148.124	Bill Elliott	205.039
1987	Bill Elliott	Ford	176.263	Bill Elliott	210.364†
1988	Bobby Allison	Buick	137.531	Ken Schrader	193.823
1989	Darrell Waltrip	Chevrolet	148.466	Ken Schrader	196.996
1990	Derrike Cope	Chevrolet	165.761	Ken Schrader	196.515
1991	Ernie Irvan	Chevrolet	148.148	Davey Allison	195.955
1992	Davey Allison	Ford	160.256	Sterling Marlin	192.213
1993	Dale Jarrett	Chevrolet	154.972	Kyle Petty	189.426
1994	Sterling Marlin	Chevrolet	156.931	Loy Allen Jr	190.158
1995	Sterling Marlin	Chevrolet	141.710	Dale Jarrett	193.498
1996	Dale Jarrett	Ford	154.308	Dale Earnhardt	189.510
1997	Jeff Gordon	Chevrolet	148.295	Mike Skinner	189.813
1998	Dale Earnhardt	Chevrolet	172.712	Bobby Labonte	192.415
1999	Jeff Gordon	Chevrolet	161.551	Jeff Gordon	195.067
2000	Dale Jarrett	Ford	155.669	Dale Jarrett	191.091
2001	Michael Waltrip	Chevrolet	161.783	Bill Elliott	183.570
2002	Ward Burton	Dodge	142.971	Jimmie Johnson	185.831
2003	Michael Waltrip	Chevrolet	133.870	Jeff Green	186.606
2004	Dale Earnhardt Jr.	Chevrolet	156.345	Greg Biffle	188.387
2005	Jeff Gordon	Chevrolet	135.173	Dale Jarrett	188.312
2006	Jimmie Johnson	Chevrolet	142.667	Jeff Burton	188.887
2007	Kevin Harvick	Chevrolet	149.335	David Gilliland	186.320
2008	Ryan Newman	Dodge	152.672	Jimmie Johnson	187.075

Note: The Daytona 500, held annually in February, now opens the NASCAR season with 200 laps around the 2.5-mile high-banked Daytona International Speedway. Starting in 1988, cars racing at Daytona have used restrictor plates that lower power and acceleration.

*Track record, winning speed. †Track record, qualifying speed.

Brickyard 400

Year	Winner	Car	Avg Speed	Pole Winner	Speed
1994	Jeff Gordon	Chevrolet	131.977	Rick Mast	172.414
1995	Dale Earnhardt	Chevrolet	155.206	Jeff Gordon	172.536
1996	Dale Jarrett	Ford	139.508	Jeff Gordon	176.419
1997	Ricky Rudd	Ford	130.814	Ernie Irvan	177.736
1998	Jeff Gordon	Chevrolet	126.772	Ernie Irvan	179.394
1999	Dale Jarrett	Ford	148.194	Jeff Gordon	179.612
2000	Bobby Labonte	Pontiac	155.912*	Ricky Rudd	181.068
2001	Jeff Gordon	Chevrolet	130.790	Jimmy Spencer	179.666
2002	Bill Elliott	Dodge	125.033	Tony Stewart	182.960
2003	Kevin Harvick	Chevrolet	134.554	Kevin Harvick	184.343
2004	Jeff Gordon	Chevrolet	115.037	Casey Mears	186.293†
2005	Tony Stewart	Chevrolet	148.782	Elliott Sadler	184.117
2006	Jimmie Johnson	Chevrolet	137.182	Jeff Burton	182.778
2007	Tony Stewart	Chevrolet	117.379	Reed Sorenson	184.207
2008	Jimmie Johnson	Chevrolet	115.117	Jimmie Johnson	181.763

Note: Held at the 2.5-mile Indianapolis Motor Speedway
*Track record, winning speed. †Track record, qualifying speed

Talladega 500

Year	Winner	Car	Avg Speed	Pole Winner	Speed
1970	Pete Hamilton	Plymouth	152.321	Bobby Isaac	199.658
1971	Donnie Allison	Mercury	147.419	Donnie Allison	185.869
1972	David Pearson	Mercury	134.400	Bobby Isaac	192.428
1973	David Pearson	Mercury	131.956	Buddy Baker	193.435
1974	David Pearson	Mercury	130.220	David Pearson	186.086
1975	Buddy Baker	Ford	144.94	Buddy Baker	189.947
1976	Buddy Baker	Ford	169.887	Dave Marcis	189.197
1977	Darrell Waltrip	Chevrolet	164.887	A.J. Foyt	192.424
1978	Cale Yarborough	Oldsmobile	155.699	Cale Yarborough	191.904
1979	Bobby Allison	Ford	154.770	Darrell Waltrip	195.644
1980	Buddy Baker	Oldsmobile	170.481	David Pearson	197.704
1981	Bobby Allison	Buick	149.376	Bobby Allison	195.864
1982	Darrell Waltrip	Buick	156.697	Benny Parsons	200.176
1983	Richard Petty	Pontiac	135.936	Cale Yarborough	202.650
1984	Cale Yarborough	Chevrolet	172.988	Cale Yarborough	202.692
1985	Bill Elliott	Ford	186.288	Bill Elliott	209.398
1986	Bobby Allison	Buick	157.698	Bill Elliott	212.229
1987	Davey Allison	Ford	154.228	Bill Elliott	221.809†
1988	Phil Parsons	Oldsmobile	156.547	Davey Allison	198.969
1989	Davey Allison	Ford	155.869	Mark Martin	193.061
1990	Dale Earnhardt	Chevrolet	159.571	Bill Elliott	199.388
1991	Harry Gant	Oldsmobile	165.620	Ernie Irvan	195.186
1992	Davey Allison	Ford	167.609	Ernie Irvan	192.831
1993	Ernie Irvan	Chevrolet	155.412	Dale Earnhardt	192.355
1994	Dale Earnhardt	Chevrolet	157.478	Ernie Irvan	193.298
1995	Mark Martin	Ford	178.902	Terry Labonte	196.532
1996	Sterling Marlin	Chevrolet	149.999	Ernie Irvan	192.855
1997	Mark Martin	Ford	188.354*	John Andretti	193.627
1998	Dale Jarrett	Ford	159.318	Ken Schrader	196.153
1999	Dale Earnhardt	Chevrolet	166.632	Joe Nemechek	198.331
2000	Dale Earnhardt	Chevrolet	165.681	Joe Nemechek	190.279
2001	Dale Earnhardt Jr.	Chevrolet	164.185	Stacy Compton	185.240
2002	Dale Earnhardt Jr.	Chevrolet	183.665	qualifying cancelled	—
2003	Michael Waltrip	Chevrolet	156.045	Elliott Sadler	189.943
2004	Jeff Gordon	Chevrolet	129.396	Ricky Rudd	191.180
2005	Dale Jarrett	Ford	143.818	Elliott Sadler	189.260
2006	Brian Vickers	Chevrolet	157.602	David Gilliland	191.712
2007	Jeff Gordon	Chevrolet	143.438	Michael Waltrip	189.070
2008	Kyle Busch	Toyota	157.409	Joe Nemechek	187.396

*Track record, winning speed. †Track record, qualifying speed.

Charlotte 600

Year	Winner	Car	Avg Speed	Pole Winner
1960	Joe Lee Johnson	Chevrolet	107.752	Joe Lee Johnson
1961	David Pearson	Pontiac	111.634	Richard Petty
1962	Nelson Stacy	Ford	125.552	Fireball Roberts
1963	Fred Lorenzen	Ford	132.418	Junior Johnson
1964	Jim Paschal	Plymouth	125.772	Junior Johnson
1965	Fred Lorenzen	Ford	121.772	Fred Lorenzon
1966	Marvin Panch	Plymouth	135.042	Paul Goldsmith
1967	Jim Paschal	Plymouth	135.832	Cale Yarborough
1968	Buddy Baker	Dodge	104.207	Donnie Allison
1969	Lee Roy Yarbrough	Mercury	134.631	Donnie Allison
1970	Donnie Allison	Ford	129.680	Bobby Isaac
1971	Bobby Allison	Mercury	140.442	Charlie Glotzbach
1972	Buddy Baker	Dodge	142.255	Bobby Allison
1973	Buddy Baker	Dodge	134.890	Buddy Baker
1974	David Pearson	Mercury	135.720	David Pearson
1975	Richard Petty	Dodge	145.327	David Pearson
1976	David Pearson	Mercury	137.352	David Pearson
1977	Richard Petty	Dodge	137.636	David Pearson
1978	Darrell Waltrip	Chevrolet	138.355	David Pearson
1979	Darrell Waltrip	Chevrolet	136.674	Neil Bonnet
1980	Benny Parsons	Chevrolet	119.265	Cale Yarborough
1981	Bobby Allison	Buick	129.326	Neil Bonnett
1982	Neil Bonnett	Ford	130.508	David Pearson
1983	Neil Bonnett	Chevrolet	140.406	Buddy Baker
1984	Bobby Allison	Buick	129.233	Harry Gant
1985	Darrell Waltrip	Chevrolet	141.807	Bill Elliott
1986	Dale Earnhardt	Chevrolet	140.406	Geoff Bodine
1987	Kyle Petty	Ford	131.483	Bill Elliott
1988	Darrell Waltrip	Chevrolet	124.460	Davey Allison
1989	Darrell Waltrip	Chevrolet	144.077	Alan Kulwicki
1990	Rusty Wallace	Pontiac	137.650	Ken Schrader
1991	Davey Allison	Ford	138.951	Mark Martin
1992	Dale Earnhardt	Chevrolet	132.980	Bill Elliott
1993	Dale Earnhardt	Chevrolet	145.504	Ken Schrader
1994	Jeff Gordon	Chevrolet	139.445	Jeff Gordon
1995	Bobby Labonte	Chevrolet	151.952*	Jeff Gordon
1996	Dale Jarrett	Ford	147.581	Jeff Gordon
1997	Jeff Gordon	Chevrolet	136.745	Jeff Gordon
1998	Jeff Gordon	Chevrolet	136.424	Jeff Gordon
1999	Jeff Burton	Ford	151.367	Bobby Labonte
2000	Matt Kenseth	Ford	142.640	Dale Earnhardt Jr
2001	Jeff Burton	Ford	138.107	Ryan Newman
2002	Mark Martin	Ford	137.729	Jimmie Johnson
2003	Jimmie Johnson	Chevrolet	126.198	Ryan Newman
2004	Jimmie Johnson	Chevrolet	142.763	Jimmie Johnson
2005	Jimmie Johnson	Chevrolet	114.698	Ryan Newman
2006	Kasey Kahne	Dodge	128.840	Scott Riggs
2007	Casey Mears	Chevrolet	130.222	Ryan Newman
2008	Kasey Kahne	Dodge	135.772	Kyle Busch

Note: Held at the 1.5 mile high-banked Lowe's Motor Speedway in Charlotte on Memorial Day weekend.

*Track record, winning speed.

Darlington 500

Note: Formerly the Winston 500, held at the 2.66-mile Talladega Superspeedway. Starting in 1988, cars racing at Talladega have used restrictor plates that lower power and acceleration.

Year	Winner	Car	Avg Speed	Pole Winner
1950	Johnny Mantz	Plymouth	76.260	Wally Campbell
1951	Herb Thomas	Hudson	76.900	Marshall Teague
1952	Fonty Flock	Oldsmobile	74.510	Dick Rathman
1953	Buck Baker	Oldsmobile	92.780	Fonty Flock
1954	Herb Thomas	Hudson	94.930	Buck Baker
1955	Herb Thomas	Chevrolet	92.281	Tim Flock
1956	Curtis Turner	Ford	95.067	Buck Baker
1957	Speedy Thompson	Chevrolet	100.100	Paul Goldsmith
1958	Fireball Roberts	Chevrolet	102.590	Fireball Roberts
1959	Jim Reed	Chevrolet	111.836	Fireball Roberts
1960	Buck Baker	Pontiac	105.901	Cotton Owens
1961	Nelson Stacy	Ford	117.880	Fireball Roberts
1962	Larry Frank	Ford	117.965	Fireball Roberts
1963	Fireball Roberts	Ford	129.784	Fireball Roberts
1964	Buck Baker	Dodge	117.757	Richard Petty
1965	Ned Jarrett	Ford	115.924	Junior Johnson
1966	Darel Dieringer	Mercury	114.830	Lee Yarborough
1967	Richard Petty	Plymouth	131.933	David Pearson
1968	Cale Yarborough	Mercury	126.132	Charlie Glotzbach
1969	Lee Roy Yarbrough	Ford	105.612	Cale Yarborough
1970	Buddy Baker	Dodge	128.817	David Pearson
1971	Bobby Allison	Mercury	131.398	Bobby Allison
1972	Bobby Allison	Chevrolet	128.124	David Pearson
1973	Cale Yarborough	Chevrolet	134.033	David Pearson
1974	Cale Yarborough	Chevrolet	111.075	Richard Petty
1975	Bobby Allison	Matador	116.825	David Pearson
1976	David Pearson	Mercury	120.534	David Pearson
1977	David Pearson	Mercury	106.797	Darrell Waltrip
1978	Cale Yarborough	Oldsmobile	116.828	David Pearson
1979	David Pearson	Chevrolet	126.259	Bobby Allison
1980	Terry Labonte	Chevrolet	115.210	Darrell Waltrip
1981	Neil Bonnett	Ford	126.410	Harry Gant
1982	Cale Yarborough	Buick	126.703	David Pearson
1983	Bobby Allison	Buick	123.343	Neil Bonnett
1984	Harry Gant	Chevrolet	128.270	Harry Gant
1985	Bill Elliott	Ford	121.254	Bill Elliott
1986	Tim Richmond	Chevrolet	121.068	Tim Richmond
1987	Dale Earnhardt	Chevrolet	115.520	Davey Allison
1988	Bill Elliott	Ford	128.297	Bill Elliott
1989	Dale Earnhardt	Chevrolet	135.462	Alan Kulwicki
1990	Dale Earnhardt	Chevrolet	123.141	Dale Earnhardt
1991	Harry Gant	Oldsmobile	133.508	Davey Allison
1992	Darrell Waltrip	Chevrolet	129.114	Sterling Marlin
1993	Mark Martin	Ford	137.932	Ken Schrader
1994	Bill Elliott	Ford	127.915	Geoff Bodine
1995	Jeff Gordon	Chevrolet	121.231	John Andretti
1996	Jeff Gordon	Chevrolet	135.757	Dale Jarrett
1997	Jeff Gordon	Chevrolet	121.149	Bobby Labonte
1998	Jeff Gordon	Chevrolet	139.031*	Dale Jarrett
1999	Jeff Burton	Ford	100.816	Kenny Irwin
2000	Bobby Labonte	Pontiac	108.275	Jeremy Mayfield
2001	Ward Burton	Dodge	122.773	Kurt Busch
2002	Jeff Gordon	Chevrolet	118.617	Sterling Marlin
2003	Terry Labonte	Chevrolet	120.744	Ryan Newman
2004	Jimmie Johnson	Chevrolet	125.044	Kurt Busch
2005	Greg Biffle	Ford	135.127	Kasey Kahne
2006	Greg Biffle	Ford	123.031	Kasey Kahne
2007	Jeff Gordon	Chevrolet	124.372	Clint Bowyer
2008	Kyle Busch	Toyota	140.350	Greg Biffle

Through 2004, results listed were for the Southern 500, traditionally the second race of the year at the 1.366-mile Darlington (S.C.) Raceway. Starting in 2005, Darlington only hosted one race a year, in May.

*Track record, winning speed.

Nextel Cup* NASCAR Champions

Year	Driver	Car	Wins	Poles	Winnings ($)
1949	Red Byron	Oldsmobile	2	1	5,800
1950	Bill Rexford	Oldsmobile	1	0	6,175
1951	Herb Thomas	Hudson	7	4	18,200
1952	Tim Flock	Hudson	8	4	20,210
1953	Herb Thomas	Hudson	11	10	27,300
1954	Lee Petty	Dodge	7	3	26,706
1955	Tim Flock	Chrysler	18	19	33,750
1956	Buck Baker	Chrysler	14	12	29,790
1957	Buck Baker	Chevrolet	10	5	24,712
1958	Lee Petty	Oldsmobile	7	4	20,600
1959	Lee Petty	Plymouth	10	2	45,570
1960	Rex White	Chevrolet	6	3	45,260
1961	Ned Jarrett	Chevrolet	1	4	27,285
1962	Joe Weatherly	Pontiac	9	6	56,110
1963	Joe Weatherly	Mercury	3	6	58,110
1964	Richard Petty	Plymouth	9	8	98,810
1965	Ned Jarrett	Ford	13	9	77,966
1966	David Pearson	Dodge	14	7	59,205
1967	Richard Petty	Plymouth	27	18	130,275
1968	David Pearson	Ford	16	12	118,824
1969	David Pearson	Ford	11	14	183,700
1970	Bobby Isaac	Dodge	11	13	121,470
1971	Richard Petty	Plymouth	21	9	309,225
1972	Richard Petty	Plymouth	8	3	227,015
1973	Benny Parsons	Chevrolet	1	0	114,345
1974	Richard Petty	Dodge	10	7	299,175
1975	Richard Petty	Dodge	13	3	378,865
1976	Cale Yarborough	Chevrolet	9	2	387,173
1977	Cale Yarborough	Chevrolet	9	3	477,499
1978	Cale Yarborough	Oldsmobile	10	8	530,751
1979	Richard Petty	Chevrolet	5	1	531,292
1980	Dale Earnhardt	Chevrolet	5	0	588,926
1981	Darrell Waltrip	Buick	12	11	693,342
1982	Darrell Waltrip	Buick	12	7	873,118
1983	Bobby Allison	Buick	6	0	828,355
1984	Terry Labonte	Chevrolet	2	2	713,010
1985	Darrell Waltrip	Chevrolet	3	4	1,318,735
1986	Dale Earnhardt	Chevrolet	5	1	1,783,880
1987	Dale Earnhardt	Chevrolet	11	1	2,099,243
1988	Bill Elliott	Ford	6	6	1,574,639
1989	Rusty Wallace	Pontiac	6	4	2,247,950
1990	Dale Earnhardt	Chevrolet	9	4	3,083,056
1991	Dale Earnhardt	Chevrolet	4	0	2,396,685
1992	Alan Kulwicki	Ford	2	6	2,322,561
1993	Dale Earnhardt	Chevrolet	6	2	3,353,789
1994	Dale Earnhardt	Chevrolet	4	2	3,400,733
1995	Jeff Gordon	Chevrolet	7	9	4,347,343
1996	Terry Labonte	Chevrolet	2	4	4,030,648
1997	Jeff Gordon	Chevrolet	10	1	4,201,227
1998	Jeff Gordon	Chevrolet	13	7	6,175,867
1999	Dale Jarrett	Ford	4	0	3,608,829
2000	Bobby Labonte	Pontiac	4	2	4,041,750
2001	Jeff Gordon	Chevrolet	6	8	6,649,076
2002	Tony Stewart	Pontiac	3	4	4,695,150
2003	Matt Kenseth	Ford	1	2	4,038,120
2004	Kurt Busch	Ford	3	1	4,200,330
2005	Tony Stewart	Chevrolet	5	3	6,987,530
2006	Jimmie Johnson	Chevrolet	5	1	8.909,140
2007	Jimmie Johnson	Chevrolet	10	4	7,646,420

*Series name changed from Winston Cup after 2003 season, then to Sprint Cup beginning in 2008.

NASCAR (Cont.)

Alltime NASCAR Leaders

	WINS		WINS
Richard Petty	200	Lee Petty	54
David Pearson	105	Ned Jarrett	50
Bobby Allison	84	Junior Johnson	50
Darrell Waltrip	84	Herb Thomas	48
Cale Yarborough	83	Buck Baker	46
*Jeff Gordon	81	Bill Elliott	44
Dale Earnhardt	76	Tim Flock	40
Rusty Wallace	55	*Jimmie Johnson	38

	POLE POSITIONS		POLE POSITIONS
Richard Petty	126	Junior Johnson	47
David Pearson	113	Buck Baker	44
Cale Yarborough	70	*Mark Martin	43
*Jeff Gordon	67	*Ryan Newman	42
Darrell Waltrip	59	Buddy Baker	40
Bobby Allison	57	Tim Flock	39
Bill Elliott	54	Herb Thomas	39
Bobby Isaac	51		

*Active drivers. Note: NASCAR wins leaders and pole position leaders through Oct 5, 2008.

Formula One Grand Prix Racing

World Driving Champions

Year	Winner	Car
1950	Guiseppe Farina, Italy	Alfa Romeo
1951	Juan-Manuel Fangio, Argentina	Alfa Romeo
1952	Alberto Ascari, Italy	Ferrari
1953	Alberto Ascari, Italy	Ferrari
1954	Juan-Manuel Fangio, Argentina	Maserati-Mercedes
1955	Juan-Manuel Fangio, Argentina	Mercedes
1956	Juan-Manuel Fangio, Argentina	Ferrari
1957	Juan-Manuel Fangio, Argentina	Maserati
1958	Mike Hawthorn, Grt Britain	Ferrari
1959	Jack Brabham, Australia	Cooper-Climax
1960	Jack Brabham, Australia	Cooper-Climax
1961	Phil Hill, U.S.	Ferrari
1962	Graham Hill, Grt Britain	BRM
1963	Jim Clark, Scotland	Lotus-Climax
1964	John Surtees, Grt Britain	Ferrari
1965	Jim Clark, Scotland	Lotus-Climax
1966	Jack Brabham, Australia	Brabham-Repco
1967	Denny Hulme, New Zealand	Brabham-Repco
1968	Graham Hill, Grt Britain	Lotus-Ford
1969	Jackie Stewart, Scotland	Matra-Ford
1970	Jochen Rindt, Austria*	Lotus-Ford
1971	Jackie Stewart, Scotland	Tyrell-Ford
1972	Emerson Fittipaldi, Brazil	Lotus-Ford
1973	Jackie Stewart, Scotland	Tyrell-Ford
1974	Emerson Fittipaldi, Brazil	McLaren-Ford
1975	Niki Lauda, Austria	Ferrari
1976	James Hunt, Grt Britain	McLaren-Ford
1977	Niki Lauda, Austria	Ferrari
1978	Mario Andretti, U.S.	Lotus-Ford
1979	Jody Scheckter, S Africa	Ferrari
1980	Alan Jones, Australia	Williams-Ford
1981	Nelson Piquet, Brazil	Brabham-Ford
1982	Keke Rosberg, Finland	Williams-Ford
1983	Nelson Piquet, Brazil	Brabham-BMW
1984	Niki Lauda, Austria	McLaren-Porsche
1985	Alain Prost, France	McLaren-Porsche
1986	Alain Prost, France	McLaren-Porsche
1987	Nelson Piquet, Brazil	Williams-Honda
1988	Ayrton Senna, Brazil	McLaren-Honda
1989	Alain Prost, France	McLaren-Honda
1990	Ayrton Senna, Brazil	McLaren-Honda
1991	Ayrton Senna, Brazil	McLaren-Honda
1992	Nigel Mansell, Grt Britain	Williams-Renault
1993	Alain Prost, France	Williams-Renault
1994	Michael Schumacher,Ger	Benetton-Ford
1995	Michael Schumacher,Ger	Benetton-Renault
1996	Damon Hill, Grt Britain	Williams-Renault
1997	Jacques Villeneuve, Can	Williams-Renault
1998	Mika Hakkinen, Finland	McLaren-Mercedes
1999	Mika Hakkinen, Finland	McLaren-Mercedes
2000	Michael Schumacher, Ger	Ferrari
2001	Michael Schumacher, Ger	Ferrari
2002	Michael Schumacher, Ger	Ferrari
2003	Michael Schumacher, Ger	Ferrari
2004	Michael Schumacher, Ger	Ferrari
2005	Fernando Alonso, Spain	Renault
2006	Fernando Alonso, Spain	Renault
2007	Kimi Raikkonen, Finland	Ferrari

*The championship was awarded posthumously, after Rindt was killed during practice for the Italian Grand Prix.

Alltime Grand Prix Winners

Driver	Wins
Michael Schumacher, Germany	91
Alain Prost, France	51
Ayrton Senna, Brazil	41
Nigel Mansell, Great Britain	31
Jackie Stewart, Great Britain	27
Jim Clark, Great Britain	25
Niki Lauda, Austria	25
Juan Manuel Fangio, Argentina	24
Nelson Piquet, Brazil	23
Damon Hill, Great Britain	22

Alltime Grand Prix Pole Winners

Driver	Poles
Michael Schumacher, Germany	68
Ayrton Senna, Brazil	65
Alain Prost, France	33
Jim Clark, Great Britain	33
Nigel Mansell, Great Britain	31
Juan Manuel Fangio, Argentina	29
Mika Hakkinen, Finland	26
Niki Lauda, Austria	24
Nelson Piquet, Brazil	24
Damon Hill, Great Britain	20
*Fernando Alonso	20

*Active driver in 2008. Note: Grand Prix winners through Oct 4, 2008.

Professional Sports Car Racing

The 24 Hours of Daytona

Year	Winner	Car	Avg Speed	Distance
1962	Dan Gurney	Lotus 19-Class SP11	104.101 mph	3 hrs (312.42 mi)
1963	Pedro Rodriguez	Ferrari-Class 12	102.074 mph	3 hrs (308.61 mi)
1964	Pedro Rodriguez/Phil Hill	Ferrari 250 LM	98.230 mph	2,000 km
1965	Ken Miles/Lloyd Ruby	Ford	99.944 mph	2,000 km
1966	Ken Miles/Lloyd Ruby	Ford Mark II	108.020 mph	24 hrs (2,570.63 mi)
1967	Lorenzo Bandini/Chris Amon	Ferrari 330 P4	105.688 mph	24 hrs (2,537.46 mi)
1968	Vic Elford/Jochen Neerpasch	Porsche 907	106.697 mph	24 hrs (2,565.69 mi)
1969	Mark Donohue/Chuck Parsons	Chevy Lola	99.268 mph	24 hrs (2,383.75 mi)
1970	Pedro Rodriguez/Leo Kinnunen	Porsche 917	114.866 mph	24 hrs (2,758.44 mi)
1971	Pedro Rodriguez/Jackie Oliver	Porsche 917K	109.203 mph	24 hrs (2,621.28 mi)
1972*	Mario Andretti/Jacky Ickx	Ferrari 312/P	122.573 mph	6 hrs (738.24 mi)
1973	Peter Gregg/Hurley Haywood	Porsche Carrera	106.225 mph	24 hrs (2,552.7 mi)
1974	(No race)			
1975	Peter Gregg/Hurley Haywood	Porsche Carrera	108.531 mph	24 hrs (2,606.04 mi)
1976†	Peter Gregg/Brian Redman/ John Fitzpatrick	BMW CSL	104.040 mph	24 hrs (2,092.8 mi)
1977	John Graves/Hurley Haywood/ Dave Helmick	Porsche Carrera	108.801 mph	24 hrs (2,615 mi)
1978	Rolf Stommelen/ Antoine Hezemans/Peter Gregg	Porsche Turbo	108.743 mph	24 hrs (2,611.2 mi)
1979	Ted Field/Danny Ongais/ Hurley Haywood	Porsche Turbo	109.249 mph	24 hrs (2,626.56 mi)
1980	Volkert Meri/Rolf Stommelen/ Reinhold Joest	Porsche Turbo	114.303 mph	24 hrs
1981	Bob Garretson/Bobby Rahal/ Brian Redman	Porsche Turbo	113.153 mph	24 hrs
1982	John Paul Jr/John Paul Sr/ Rolf Stommelen	Porsche Turbo	114.794 mph	24 hrs
1983	Preston Henn/Bob Wollek/ Claude Ballot-Lena/A.J. Foyt	Porsche Turbo	98.781 mph	24 hrs
1984	Sarel van der Merwe/ Graham Duxbury/Tony Martin	Porsche March	103.119 mph	24 hrs (2,476.8 mi)
1985	A.J. Foyt/Bob Wollek/ Al Unser/Thierry Boutsen	Porsche 962	104.162 mph	24 hrs (2,502.68 mi)
1986	Al Holbert/Derek Bell/Al Unser Jr.	Porsche 962	105.484 mph	24 hrs (2,534.72 mi)
1987	Chip Robinson/Derek Bell/ Al Holbert/Al Unser Jr.	Porsche 962	111.599 mph	24 hrs (2,680.68 mi)
1988	Martin Brundle/John Nielsen/ Raul Boesel	Jaguar XJR-9	107.943 mph	24 hrs (2,591.68 mi)
1989	John Andretti/Derek Bell/ Bob Wollek	Porsche 962	92.009 mph	24 hrs (2,210.76 mi)
1990	Davy Jones/ Jan Lammers/ Andy Wallace	Jaguar XJR-12	112.857 mph	24 hrs (2,709.16 mi)
1991	Hurley Haywood/ John Winter/ Frank Jelinski/ Henri Pescarolo/ Bob Wollek	Porsche 962C	106.633 mph	24 hrs (2,559.64 mi)
1992	Massahiro Hasemi/ Kazuoyshi Hoshino/ Toshio Suzuki/ Anders Olofsson	Nissan R91CP	112.987 mph	24 hrs (2,712.72 mi)
1993	P.J. Jones/Mark Dismore/ Rocky Moran	Toyota Eagle MK III	103.537 mph	24 hrs (2,484.88 mi)
1994	Paul Gentilozzi/ Scott Pruett/ Butch Leitzinger/ Steve Millen	Nissan 300 ZX	104.80 mph	24 hrs (2,693.67 mi)
1995	Jurgen Lassig/ Christophe Buochut/ Giovanni Lavaggi/ Marco Werner	Porsche Spyder K8	102.28 mph	690 laps (2,456.4 mi)
1996	Wayne Taylor/ Scott Sharp/ Jim Pace	Oldsmobile Mark III	103.32 mph	697 laps (2,481.32 mi)
1997	Elliot Forbes-Robinson/ John Schneider/Rob Dyson/ John Paul Jr/Butch Leitzinger/James Weaver/Andy Wallace	Ford R & S MK III	102.292 mph	690 laps (2,456.4 mi)
1998	Arie Luyendyk/Didier Theys/ Mauro Baldi	Ferrari 333 SP	105.565 mph	711 laps (2,531.16 mi)
1999	Elliott Forbes-Robinson/ Butch Leitzinger/ Andy Wallace	Ford R & S MK III	104.9 mph	708 laps (2,520.48 mi)
2000	Olivier Beretta/Karl Wendlinger/ Dominique Dupuy	Dodge Viper	107.207 mph	723 laps (2,573.88 m)

Professional Sports Car Racing *(Cont.)*

The 24 Hours of Daytona *(Cont.)*

2001	Ron Fellows/Chris Kneifel/Franck Freon/Johnny O'Connell	Corvette	97.293 mph	656 laps (2,335.360 mi)
2002	Didier Theys/Fredy Lienhard/ Max Papis/Mauro Baldi	Dallara-Judd (SRP)	106.143 mph	716 laps (2,548.96 mi)
2003	Kevin Buckler/Michael Schrom Timo Bernhard/Jorg Bergmeister	Porsche GT3 RS	114.068 mph‡	694 laps (2,470.64 mi)
2004	Forest Barber/Terry Borcheller Andy Pilgrim/Christian Fittipaldi	Pontiac Doran	117.651 mph	526 laps (1,872.56 mi)
2005	Wayne Taylor, Max Angelelli, Emmanuel Collard	Pontiac Riley	119.397 mph	710 laps (2,527.60 mi)
2006	Scott Dixon/Dan Wheldon Casey Mears	Lexus Riley	108.826 mph	734 laps (2,613.04 mi)
2007	Scott Pruett/Salvador Duran Juan Pablo Montoya	Lexus Riley	99.020 mph	668 laps (2,378.08 mi)
2008	Scott Pruett/Memo Rojas Juan Pablo Montoya Dario Franchitti	Lexus Riley	103.057 mph	695 laps (2,474.20 mi)

*Race shortened due to fuel crisis. †Course lengthened from 3.81 miles to 3.84 miles. ‡Top speed.

World SportsCar Champions*

Year	Winner	Car
1978	Peter Gregg	Porsche 935
1979	Peter Gregg	Porsche 935
1980	John Fitzpatrick	Porsche 935
1981	Brian Redman	Chevy Lola
1982	John Paul Jr	Chevy Lola
1983	Al Holbert	Chevy March
1984	Randy Lanier	Chevy March
1985	Al Holbert	Porsche 962
1986	Al Holbert	Porsche 962
1987	Chip Robinson	Porsche 962
1988	Geoff Brabham	Nissan GTP
1989	Geoff Brabham	Nissan GTP
1990	Geoff Brabham	Nissan GTP
1991	Geoff Brabham	Nissan NPT
1992	Juan Fangio II	Toyota EGL MKIII
1993	Juan Fangio II	Toyota EGL MKIII
1994	Wayne Taylor	Mazda Kudzu
1995	Fermin Velez	Ferrari 333 SP
1996	Wayne Taylor	Mazda Kudzu
1997	Butch Leitzinger	Ford R&S MKIII
1998	Butch Leitzinger	Ford R&S MKIII

Year	Prototype	GTS	GT
1999	Elliott Forbes-Robinson	Olivier Beretta	Cort Wagner
2000	Allan McNish	Olivier Beretta	Sascha Maassen
2001	Emanuele Pirro	Terry Borcheller	Jörg Müller
2002	Tom Kristensen	Ron Fellows	Lucas Luhr
2003	Frank Biela/Marco Werner	Ron Fellows/John O'Connell	Sascha Maassen/L. Luhr
2004	Frank Biela/Emanuele Pirro	Oliver Gavin/Olivier Beretta	Patrick Long/Jorg Bergmeister
2005	Frank Biela/Emanuele Pirro	Oliver Gavin/Olivier Beretta	Patrick Long/Jorg Bergmeister
2006	R. Capello/A. McNish	Oliver Gavin/Olivier Beretta	Johannes van Overbeek
2007	R. Capello/A. McNish	Oliver Gavin/Olivier Beretta	Mika Salo/Jaime Melo

*1978–93 champions raced in the GT series, which in 1994 was replaced by the World SportsCar series. Beginning in 1999, racing was reclassified according to the American Le Mans Series. The Series is comprised of two different types of race cars divided into two categories and five separate classes. The Prototype category features open-cockpit prototype as well as Grand Touring Prototype (GTP) class cars. The Grand Touring category features the Grand Touring S (GTS) class cars, formerly known as GT2, and Grand Touring (GT) cars, formerly known as GT3. Both classes feature purpose-built race cars with an emphasis on spectator car identification.

Alltime SportsCar Leaders

PROTOTYPE WINS

Driver	Wins
*Rinaldo Capello	32
*Allan McNish	25
*Marco Werner	24
*Frank Biela	22
J.J. Lehto	19
*Emanuele Pirro	18
James Weaver	16
*Butch Leitzinger	15

GTS AND GT WINS

Driver	Wins
Al Holbert	49
Peter Gregg	41
*Olivier Beretta	38
*Johnny O'Connell	34
Hurley Haywood	31
*Oliver Gavin	29
Geoff Brabham	26
Parker Johnstone	25
Ron Fellows	25

* Active driver in 2008. Note: Leaders through Oct 4, 2008.

24 Hours of Le Mans

Year	Winning Drivers	Car
1923	André Lagache/ René Léonard	Chenard & Walker
1924	John Duff/Francis Clement	Bentley
1925	Gérard de Courcelles/ André Rossignol	La Lorraine
1926	Robert Bloch/ André Rossignol	La Lorraine
1927	J. Dudley Benjafield/ Sammy Davis	Bentley
1928	Woolf Barnato/Bernard Rubin	Bentley
1929	Woolf Barnato/ Sir Henry Birkin	Bentley Speed 6
1930	Woolf Barnato/Glen Kidston	Bentley Speed 6
1931	Earl Howe/ Sir Henry Birkin	Alfa Romeo 8C-2300 sc
1932	Raymond Sommer/ Luigi Chinetti	Alfa Romeo 8C-2300 sc
1933	Raymond Sommer/ Tazio Nuvolari	Alfa Romeo 8C-2300 sc
1934	Luigi Chinetti/ Philippe Etancelin	Alfa Romeo 8C-2300 sc
1935	John Hindmarsh/Louis Fontés	Lagonda M45R
1936	RACE CANCELLED	
1937	Jean-Pierre Wimille/Robert Benoist	Bugatti 57G sc
1938	Eugene Chaboud/Jean Tremoulet	Delahaye 135M
1939	Jean-Pierre Wimille/Pierre Veyron	Bugatti 57G sc
1940–48	RACES CANCELLED	
1949	Luigi Chinetti/Lord Selsdon	Ferrari 166MM
1950	Louis Rosier/Jean-Louis Rosier	Talbot-Lago
1951	Peter Walker/Peter Whitehead	Jaguar C
1952	Hermann Lang/Fritz Reiss	Mercedes-Benz 300 SL
1953	Tony Rolt/Duncan Hamilton	Jaguar C
1954	Froilan Gonzales/ Maurice Trintignant	Ferrari 375
1955	Mike Hawthorn/Ivor Bueb	Jaguar D
1956	Ron Flockhart/Ninian Sanderson	Jaguar D
1957	Ron Flockhart/Ivor Bueb	Jaguar D
1958	Olivier Gendebien/Phil Hill	Ferrari 250 TR58
1959	Carroll Shelby/Roy Salvadori	Aston Martin DBR1
1960	Olivier Gendebien/Paul Frère	Ferrari 250 TR59/60
1961	Olivier Gendebien/Phil Hill	Ferrari 250 TR61
1962	Olivier Gendebien/Phil Hill	Ferrari 250P
1963	Lodovico Scarfiotti/ Lorenzo Bandini	Ferrari 250P
1964	Jean Guichel/ Nino Vaccarella	Ferrari 275P
1965	Jochen Rindt/Masten Gregory	Ferrari 250LM
1966	Chris Amon/Bruce McLaren	Ford Mk2
1967	Dan Gurney/A.J. Foyt	Ford Mk4
1968	Pedro Rodriguez/Lucien Bianchi	Ford GT40
1969	Jacky Ickx/Jackie Oliver	Ford GT40
1970	Hans Herrmann/ Richard Attwood	Porsche 917
1971	Helmut Marko/ Gijs van Lennep	Porsche 917
1972	Henri Pescarolo/Graham Hill	Matra-Simca MS670
1973	Henri Pescarolo/ Gérard Larrousse	Matra-Simca MS670B
1974	Henri Pescarolo/ Gérard Larrousse	Matra-Simca MS670B
1975	Jacky Ickx/Derek Bell	Mirage-Ford MB
1976	Jacky Ickx/Gijs van Lennep	Porsche 936
1977	Jacky Ickx/Jurgen Barth/ Hurley Haywood	Porsche 936
1978	Jean-Pierre Jaussaud/ Didier Pironi	Renault-Alpine A442
1979	Klaus Ludwig/ Bill Whittington/Don Whittington	Porsche 935
1980	Jean-Pierre Jaussaud/ Jean Rondeau	Rondeau-Ford M379B
1981	Jacky Ickx/Derek Bell	Porsche 936-81
1982	Jacky Ickx/Derek Bell	Porsche 956
1983	Vern Schuppan/ Hurley Haywood/Al Holbert	Porsche 956-83
1984	Klaus Ludwig/Henri Pescarolo	Porsche 956B
1985	Klaus Ludwig/ Paolo Barilla/John Winter	Porsche 956B
1986	Derek Bell/ Hans-Joachim Stuck/Al Holbert	Porsche 962C
1987	Derek Bell/ Hans-Joachim Stuck/Al Holbert	Porsche 962C
1988	Jan Lammers/ Johnny Dumfries/Andy Wallace	Jaguar XJR9LM
1989	Jochen Mass/ Manuel Reuter/Stanley Dickens	Sauber-Mercedes C9-88
1990	John Nielsen/ Price Cobb/Martin Brundle	TWR Jaguar XJR-12
1991	Volker Weidler/ Johnny Herbert/Bertrand Gachof	Mazda 787B
1992	Derek Warwick/ Yannick Dalmas/Mark Blundell	Peugeot 905B
1993	Geoff Brabham/ Christophe Bouchut/Eric Helary	Peugeot 905
1994	Yannick Dalmas/ Hurley Haywood/Mauro Baldi	Porsche 962
1995	Yannick Dalmas/ J.J. Lehto/Masanori Sekiya	McLaren BMW
1996	Manuel Reuter/ Davy Jones/Alexander Wurz	TWR Porsche
1997	Michele Alboreto/ Stefan Johansson/Tom Kristensen	TWR Porsche
1998	Allan McNish/ Laurent Aiello/Stephane Ortelli	Porsche GT One
1999	Yannick Dalmas/ Joachim Winkelhock/Pierluigi Martini	BMW V12 LMR
2000	Frank Biela/ Tom Kristensen/Emanuele Pirro	Audi R8
2001	Frank Biela/ Tom Kristensen/Emanuele Pirro	Audi R8
2002	Frank Biela/ /Tom Kristensen/Emanuele Pirro	Audi R8
2003	Rinaldo Capello/ Tom Kristensen/Guy Smith	Bentley EXP Speed 8
2004	Rinaldo Capello/ Seiji Ara/Tom Kristensen	Audi R8
2005	J.J. Lehto/ Marco Werner/Tom Kristensen	Audi R8
2006	Frank Biela/ Emanuele Pirro/Marco Werner	Audi R10
2007	Frank Biela/ Emanuele Pirro/Marco Werner	Audi R10
2008	Rinaldo Capello Tom Kristensen/Allan McNish	Audi R10

Soccer

After more than four decades of frustration, Spain found a way to win the Euro Cup title

PAUL ELLIS/AFP/GETTY IMAGES

Kicking It Old School

In 2008, the respective men's and women's national teams from Spain and the United States recaptured their former glory using equal parts hustle and hope

BY HANK HERSCH

IT FELT LIKE FOREVER—44 YEARS. Despite producing a raft of stars in leagues around the world, Spain had failed to win a major trophy since the 1964 European Championships, biannually reinforcing its reputation as the continent's leading choker. Perhaps the regional differences among the players undermined their unity of purpose; the divisions run so deep that the lyrics to the national anthem aren't even used. But in Euro '08, after steaming into the final unbeaten, Spain entered Ernst Happel Stadium in Vienna with a chance to remake its underachieving image by beating Germany.

It felt like forever—11 months. In the 2007 World Cup semifinal in China, U.S. goalkeeper Hope Solo had been famously benched by her coach, Greg Ryan, before a 4–0 loss to Brazil, then banished from the team for criticizing him as well as her replacement, Briana Scurry. But under a new coach, Pia Sundhage, and with the acceptance of her teammates (at least to varying degrees) the 27-year-old Solo had reestablished herself as the starter for the 2008 Olympic Games. In the gold-medal match she had a chance to redeem herself in China against the team she supposedly couldn't stop: Brazil.

Sometimes the perception of a team or a player, like a good free kick, is ultimately a matter of its spin. Throughout a scintillating three weeks of European Cup matches—including Turkey's breakout run to the semifinals, which ended in a 3–2 loss to Germany on a late goal from left back Philipp Lahm—Spain reached an unprecedented level of fluidity and consistency. Its cohesiveness was on full display during a 3–0 rout of Italy in the semis, but the victory came at a cost: a first-half injury to leading scorer David Villa.

In the past, that would have been enough to cause the Spanish to crumble. Yet with the three Barcelona-bred amigos—Xavi, Andres Iniesta and Cesc Fabregas—controlling the midfield, Michael Ballack and his counterparts could do little to ignite the German attack. In the 33rd minute Liverpool wunderkind Fernando Torres helped erase 44 years of frustration, outracing Lahm to Xavi's right-side through-ball and chipping a shot over onrushing keeper Jens Lehmann. The 1–0 victory culminated with cries of "Viva Espana!" "I hope this

SIMON BRUTY

Keeper Hope Solo (r.), whose controversial statements got her booted from the U.S. team in 2007, returned in 2008 to help lead the U.S. women to Olympic gold.

is good for football as well as for Spain," Torres said, "because the best team won."

Brazil was considered the best women's team in the Olympic field, an explosive outfit inspired by the brilliance of Marta, the two-time World Player of the Year. The U.S., meanwhile, had looked flat in its opener, a 2–0 loss to Norway in which Solo was less than solid, then needed overtime to defeat Canada 1–0 in the quarterfinals. The gold-medal match at Workers' Stadium in Beijing was scoreless in the 72nd minute, when the outcome appeared to be all but decided: Marta loaded up to shoot on Solo from the left side, eight yards out.

Once, in a club game in Sweden, Marta beat Solo four times. "I thought for sure it was a goal," Solo would say. "I wasn't coming out too hard, because if I bought her fake she would school me for sure." Solo stood tall and with a raised right forearm deflected the near-post blast, preserving the scoreless tie. It would remain that way until extra time, when midfielder Carli Lloyd's 21-yard strike propelled the U.S. to a 1–0 win. "I didn't think it was going to be this fairy-tale ending," Solo said. "I knew I needed to have a great last game for us to win, and it felt so good to be that impact player."

2007 Major League Soccer

2007 Final Standings

EASTERN CONFERENCE

Team	GP	W	L	T	Pts	GF	GA
†D.C. United	30	16	7	7	55	56	34
*New England	30	14	8	8	50	51	43
*New York	30	12	11	7	43	47	45
*Chicago	30	10	10	10	40	31	36
*Kansas City	30	11	12	7	40	45	45
Columbus	30	9	11	10	37	39	44
Toronto FC	30	6	17	7	25	25	49

WESTERN CONFERENCE

Team	GP	W	L	T	Pts	GF	GA
†Chivas USA	30	15	7	8	53	46	28
*Houston	30	15	8	7	52	43	23
*FC Dallas	30	13	12	5	44	37	44
Colorado	30	9	13	8	35	29	34
Los Angeles	30	9	14	7	34	38	48
Real Salt Lake	30	6	15	9	27	31	45

Note: Three points for a win. One point for a tie. †Conference champion. *Qualified for playoffs

SCORING LEADERS

Player, Team	GP	G	A	Pts
Juan Pablo Angel, NY	24	19	5	43
Luciano Emillio, DC	29	20	1	41
Eddie Johnson, KC	24	15	6	36
Taylor Twellman, NE	26	16	3	35
Ante Razov, CHV	26	11	8	30
Maykel Galindo, CHV	28	12	5	29
Christian Gomez, DC	27	10	9	29
Landon Donovan, LA	25	8	13	29
Jozy Altidore, NY	22	9	4	22
Fred, DC	26	7	8	22

ASSISTS LEADERS

Player, Team	GP	A
Steve Ralston, NE	26	14
Landon Donovan, LA	25	13
Sacha Kljestan, CHV	25	13
Guillermo Barros Schelotto, CLB	22	11
Davy Arnaud, KC	28	9
Christian Gomez, DC	27	9
Fred, DC	26	8
Ante Razov, CHV	26	8
Dave van den Bergh, NY	29	8

GOALS LEADERS

Player, Team	GP	G
Luciano Emilio, DC	29	20
Juan Pablo Angel, NY	24	19
Taylor Twellman, NE	26	16
Eddie Johnson, KC	24	15
Maykel Galindo, CHV	28	12
Ante Razov, CHV	26	11
Christian Gomez, DC	27	10
Jozy Altidore, NY	22	9

GOALS-AGAINST-AVERAGE LEADERS

Player, Team	GAA
Pat Onstad, Hou	0.82
Brad Guzan, CHV	0.93
Bouna Coundoul, Col	1.08
Jon Conway, NY	1.10
Troy Perkins, DC	1.10
Matt Pickens, Chi	1.15
Nick Rimando, RSL	1.37
Matt Reis, NE	1.43

Eastern Conference Playoffs

IST ROUND (TWO LEGS)

Chicago	**1**	**2—3**
D.C.	**0**	**2—2**
N.E.	**0**	**1—1**
N.Y.	**0**	**0—0**

CONF. CHAMPIONSHIP

Chicago	**0**
N.E.	**1**

Western Conference Playoffs

IST ROUND (TWO LEGS)

K.C.	**1**	**0—1**
Chivas	**0**	**0—0**
Houston	**0**	**4—4**
FC Dallas	**1**	**1—2**

CONF. CHAMPIONSHIP

Houston	**2**
Kansas City	**0**

2007 MLS CUP

Houston	**0**	**2 — 2**
New England	**1**	**0 — 1**

FIRST HALF: Scoring: 1, New England, Twellman (20).

SECOND HALF: Scoring: 2, Houston, Ngwenya (61); De Rosario (74).

Houston: Onstad, Barrett, Cochrane, Robinson, Waibel, Davis, De Rosario, Mullan, Mulrooney, Jaqua, Ngwenya (Holden 80).

New England: Reis, Heaps, John, Parkhurst, Joseph, Larentowicz, Ralston (Dorman 78), Smith, Thompson, Noonan, Twellman.

Attendance: 56,500.

Referee: Prus; Asst. Referees: Wienckowski, Fereday; Official: Hall.

MLS Cup MVP: Dwayne De Rosario.

Summer Olympics 2008

Women's Soccer Group Standings

GROUP E

Country	GP	W	L	T	GF	GA	Pts
*China	3	2	0	1	5	2	7
*Sweden	3	2	1	0	4	3	6
*Canada	3	1	1	1	4	4	4
Argentina	3	0	3	0	1	5	0

GROUP F

Country	GP	W	L	T	GF	GA	Pts
*Brazil	3	2	0	1	5	2	7
*Germany	3	2	0	1	2	0	7
North Korea	3	1	2	0	2	3	3
Nigeria	3	0	3	0	1	5	0

GROUP G

Country	GP	W	L	T	GF	GA	Pts
*United States	3	2	1	0	5	2	6
*Norway	3	2	1	0	4	5	6
*Japan	3	1	1	1	7	4	4
New Zealand	3	0	2	1	2	7	1

GROUP E

Canada 2, Argentina 1
Sweden 2, China 1
Sweden 1, Argentina 0
Canada 1, China 1
China 2, Argentina 0
Sweden 2, Canada 1

GROUP F

Germany 0, Brazil 0
North Korea 1, Nigeria 0
Germany 1, Nigeria 0
Brazil 2, North Korea 0
Germany 1, North Korea 0
Brazil 3, Nigeria 1

GROUP G

Japan 2, New Zealand 2
Norway 2, U.S. 0
U.S. 1, Japan 0
Norway 1, New Zealand 0
Japan 5, Norway 1
U.S. 4, New Zealand 0

QUARTERFINALS

Brazil 2, Norway 1
Germany 2, Sweden 0 (ot)

QUARTERFINALS

Japan 2, China 0
U.S. 2, Canada 1 (ot)

SEMIFINALS

Brazil 4, Germany 1
U.S. 4, Japan 2

MEDAL MATCHES

GOLD U.S. 1, Brazil 0 (ot)
BRONZE Germany 2, Japan 0

Men's Soccer Group Standings

GROUP A

Country	GP	W	L	T	GF	GA	Pts
*Argentina	3	3	0	0	5	1	9
*Cote D'Ivoire	3	2	1	0	6	4	6
Australia	3	0	2	1	1	3	1
Serbia	3	0	2	1	3	7	1

GROUP B

Country	GP	W	L	T	GF	GA	Pts
*Nigeria	3	2	0	1	4	2	7
*Netherlands	3	1	0	2	3	2	5
United States	3	1	1	1	4	4	4
Japan	3	0	3	0	1	4	0

GROUP C

Country	GP	W	L	T	GF	GA	Pts
*Brazil	3	3	0	0	9	0	9
*Belgium	3	2	1	0	3	1	6
China	3	0	2	1	1	6	1
New Zealand	3	0	2	1	1	7	1

GROUP D

Country	GP	W	L	T	GF	GA	Pts
*Italy	3	2	0	1	6	0	7
*Cameroon	3	1	0	2	2	1	5
South Korea	3	1	1	1	2	4	4
Honduras	3	0	3	0	0	5	0

GROUP A

Australia 1, Serbia 1
Argentina 2, Cote D'Ivoire 1
Argentina 1, Australia 0
Cote D'Ivoire 4, Serbia 2
Cote D'Ivoire 1, Australia 0
Argentina 2, Serbia 0

GROUP B

U.S. 1, Japan 0
Netherlands 0, Nigeria 0
Nigeria 2, Japan 1
U.S. 2, Netherlands 2
Netherlands 1, Japan 0
Nigeria 2, U.S. 1

GROUP C

Brazil 1, Belgium 0
China 1, New Zealand 1
Brazil 5, New Zealand 0
Belgium 2, China 0
Brazil 3, China 0
Belgium 1, New Zealand 0

GROUP D

Italy 3, Honduras 0
S. Korea 1, Cameroon 1
Cameroon 1, Honduras 0
Italy 3, S. Korea 0
S. Korea 1, Honduras 0
Cameroon 0, Italy 0

QUARTERFINALS

Nigeria 2, Cote D'Ivoire 0
Belgium 3, Italy 2

QUARTERFINALS

Argentina 2, Netherlands 1
Brazil 2, Cameroon 0

SEMIFINALS

Nigeria 4, Belgium 1
Argentina 3, Brazil 0

MEDAL MATCHES

GOLD Argentina 1, Nigeria 0
BRONZE Brazil 3, Belgium 0

*Advanced to quarterfinals. Note: In group play, teams are awarded three points for a victory, one for a tie.

International Club Competition

Date	Event	Winner	Runner-Up	Score	Site
Dec. 15, 2007	Club World Cup	Milan (Ita)	Boca Juniors (Arg)	4–2	Yokohama, Japan
May 14, 2008	UEFA Cup	Zenit St. Petersburg (Rus)	Rangers (Scot)	2–0	Manchester, Eng.
May 21, 2008	European Cup (Champions League)	Manchester United (Eng)	Chelsea (Eng)	1–1 (6–5 pk)	Moscow, Russia
June 25, 2008	Libertadores Cup (1st leg)	LDU Quito (Ecu)	Fluminense (Brz)	5–5 (tot.)	Quito, Ecuador
July 2, 2008	Libertadores Cup (2nd leg)			(3–1 pk)	Rio de Jan'ro, Brazil

The World Cup

Results—Men

Year	Champion	Score	Runner-Up	Winning Coach
1930	Uruguay	4–2	Argentina	Alberto Supicci
1934	Italy	2–1	Czechoslovakia	Vittorio Pozzo
1938	Italy	4–2	Hungary	Vittorio Pozzo
1950	Uruguay	2–1	Brazil	Juan Lopez
1954	W Germany	3–2	Hungary	Sepp Herberger
1958	Brazil	5–2	Sweden	Vicente Feola
1962	Brazil	3–1	Czechoslovakia	Aymore Moreira
1966	England	4–2	W Germany	Alf Ramsey
1970	Brazil	4–1	Italy	Mario Zagalo
1974	W Germany	2–1	Netherlands	Helmut Schoen
1978	Argentina	3–1	Netherlands	César Menotti
1982	Italy	3–1	W Germany	Enzo Bearzot
1986	Argentina	3–2	W Germany	Carlos Bilardo
1990	W Germany	1–0	Argentina	Franz Beckenbauer
1994	Brazil	0–0 (3–2)	Italy	Carlos Alberto Parreira
1998	France	3–0	Brazil	Aime Jacquet
2002	Brazil	2–0	Germany	Luis Felipe Scolari
2006	Italy	1–1 (5–3)	France	Marcello Lippi

Alltime World Cup Participation

Nation	Matches	W	T	L	Goals For	Goals Against
Brazil	92	64	14	14	201	84
*Germany	92	55	19	18	190	112
Italy	77	44	19	14	122	69
Argentina	65	33	13	19	113	73
England	55	25	17	13	74	47
France	51	25	10	16	95	64
Spain	49	22	12	15	80	60
†Russia	37	17	6	14	64	44
Yugoslavia	37	17	6	14	60	46
Netherlands	35	16	10	9	58	36
Poland	31	15	5	11	44	40
Hungary	32	15	3	14	87	57
Uruguay	40	15	10	15	65	57
Sweden	45	15	11	19	70	69
Austria	29	12	4	13	42	48
Czech Republic	33	12	5	16	47	49
Portugal	19	11	1	7	32	21
Mexico	45	11	12	22	48	84
Belgium	36	10	9	17	46	63
Romania	21	8	5	8	30	32
Switzerland	26	8	5	13	37	51
Denmark	13	7	2	4	24	18
Chile	25	7	6	12	31	40
Paraguay	22	6	7	9	27	36
United States	25	6	3	16	27	51
Turkey	10	5	1	4	20	17
Croatia	12	5	2	5	13	10
Nigeria	11	4	1	6	14	16
Cameroon	17	4	7	6	16	28
Peru	15	4	3	8	19	31
Scotland	23	4	7	12	25	41
S. Korea	24	4	7	13	21	53
Ecuador	7	3	0	4	7	8
Northern Ireland	13	3	5	5	13	23
Costa Rica	10	3	1	6	12	21
Colombia	13	3	2	8	14	23
Bulgaria	25	3	8	14	22	49
Wales	5	2	6	1	10	7
Senegal	5	2	2	1	7	6
Ukraine	5	2	1	1	5	7
E Germany	6	2	2	2	5	5
Ghana	4	2	0	2	4	6
Norway	8	2	3	3	7	8
Algeria	6	2	1	3	6	10
Morocco	10	2	4	4	10	13
Japan	10	2	2	6	8	14
Saudi Arabia	13	2	2	9	9	32
Cuba	3	1	1	1	5	12
S Africa	6	1	3	2	8	11
N Korea	4	1	1	2	5	9
Ivory Coast	3	1	0	2	5	6
Jamaica	3	1	0	2	3	9
Israel	3	1	0	2	1	3
Republic of Ireland	13	2	7	4	10	10
Australia	7	1	2	4	5	11
Iran	9	1	2	6	6	18
Tunisia	12	1	4	7	8	17
Honduras	3	0	2	1	2	3
Angola	3	0	2	1	1	2
Dutch East Indies	1	0	0	1	0	6
Egypt	4	0	2	2	3	6
Kuwait	3	0	1	2	2	6
Trinidad and Tobago	3	0	1	2	0	4
Slovenia	3	0	0	3	2	7
Serbia & Montenegro	3	0	0	3	2	10
United Arab Emirates	3	0	0	3	2	11
New Zealand	3	0	0	3	2	12
Haiti	3	0	0	3	2	14
Iraq	3	0	0	3	1	4
Togo	3	0	0	3	1	6
Canada	3	0	0	3	0	5
Greece	3	0	0	3	0	8
China	3	0	0	3	0	9
Zaire	3	0	0	3	0	14
Bolivia	6	0	1	5	1	20
El Salvador	6	0	0	6	1	22

*Includes West Germany 1950–90. †Includes USSR 1930–1990.
Note: Matches decided by penalty kicks are shown as drawn games.

World Cup Final Box Scores (*Cont.*)

URUGUAY 1930

Uruguay	1	3	—4
Argentina	2	0	—2

FIRST HALF: Scoring: 1, Uruguay, Dorado (12); 2, Argentina, Peucelle (20); 3, Argentina, Stabile (37).

SECOND HALF: Scoring: 4, Uruguay, Cea (57); 5, Uruguay, Iriarte (68); 6, Uruguay, Castro (89).

Argentina: Botosso, Della Toree, Paternoster, J. Evaristo, Monti, Suarez, Peucelle, Varallo, Stabile, Ferreira, M. Evaristo.

Uruguay: Ballesteros, Nasazzi, Mascheroni, Andrade, Fernandez, Gestido, Dorado, Scarone, Castro, Cea, Iriarte.

Referee: Langenus (Belgium).

ITALY 1934

Italy	0	1	1—2
Czechoslovakia	0	1	0—1

SECOND HALF: Scoring: 1, Czech., Puc (70); 2, Italy, Orsi (80).

OVERTIME: Scoring: 3, Italy, Schiavio (95).

Italy: Combi, Monzeglio, Allemandi, Ferraris Monti, Monti, Bertolini, Guaita, Meazza, Schiavio, Ferrari, Orsi.

Czechoslovakia: Planicka, Zenisek, Ctyroky, Kostalek, Cambal, Cambal, Krcil, Junek, Svoboda, Sobotka, Nejedly, Puc.

Referee: Eklind (Sweden).

FRANCE 1938

Italy	3	1	—4
Hungary	1	1	—2

FIRST HALF: Scoring: 1, Italy, Colaussi (5); 2, Hungary, Titkos (7); 3, Italy, Piola (16); 4, Italy, Piola (35).

SECOND HALF: Scoring: 5, Hungary, Sarosi (70); 6, Italy, Colaussi (82).

Italy: Olivieri, Foni, Rava, Serantoni, Andreolo, Locatelli, Biavati, Meazza, Piola, Ferrari, Colaussi.

Hungary: Szabo, Polger, Biro, Szalay, Szucs, Lazar, Sas, Vincze, Sarosi, Zsengeller, Titkos.

Referee: Capdeville (France).

BRAZIL 1950

Uruguay	0	2	—2
Brazil	0	1	—1

SECOND HALF: Scoring: 1, Brazil, Friaca (47); 2, Uruguay, Schiaffino (66); 3, Uruguay, Ghiggia (79).

Uruguay: Maspoli, Gonzales, Tejera, Gambretta, Varela, Andrade, Ghiggia, Perez, Miguez, Schiffiano, Moran.

Brazil: Barbosa, Augusto, Juvenal, Bauer, Banilo, Bigode, Friaca, Zizinho, Ademir, Jair, Chico.

Referee: Reader (England).

SWITZERLAND 1954

W Germany	2	1	—3
Hungary	2	0	—2

FIRST HALF: Scoring: 1, Hungary, Puskas (6); 2, Hungary, Czibor (8); 3, W Germ., Morlock (10); 4, W Germ., Rahn (18).

SECOND HALF: Scoring: 5, W Germany, Rahn (84).

W Germany: Turek, Posipal, Kohlmeyer, Eckel, Liebrich, Mai, Rahn, Morlock, O.Walter, F. Walter, Schaefer.

Hungary: Grosics, Buzansky, Lantos, Bozsik, Lorant, Zakarias, Czibor, Kocsis, Hidegkuti, Puskas, Toth.

Referee: Ling (England).

SWEDEN 1958

Brazil	2	3	—5
Sweden	1	1	—2

FIRST HALF: Scoring:1, Sweden, Liedholm (3); 2, Brazil, Vava (9); 3, Brazil, Vava (32).

SECOND HALF: Scoring: 4, Brazil, Pelé (55); 5, Brazil, Zagalo (68); 6, Sweden Simonsson (80); 7, Brazil, Pelé (90).

Brazil: Glymar, D. Santos, N. Santos, Zito, Bellini, Orlando, Garrincha, Didi, Vava, Pelé, Zagalo.

Sweden: Svensson, Bergmark, Axbom, Boerjesson, Gustavsson, Parling, Hamrin, Gren, Simonsson, Liedholm, Skoglund.

Referee: Guigue (France).

CHILE 1962

Brazil	1	2	—3
Czechoslovakia	1	0	—1

FIRST HALF: Scoring: 1, Czech., Masopust (15); 2, Brazil, Amarildo (17).

SECOND HALF: Scoring: 3, Brazil, Zito (68); 4, Brazil, Vava (77).

Brazil: Glymar, D. Santos, N. Santos, Zito, Mauro, Zozimo, Garrincha, Didi, Vava, Amarildo, Zagalo.

Czechoslovakia: Schroiff, Tichy, Novak, Pluskal, Popluhar, Masopust, Pospichal, Scherer, Kvasnak, Kadraba, Jelinek.

Referee: Latychev (USSR).

ENGLAND 1966

England	1	1	2—4
W Germany	1	1	0—2

FIRST HALF: Scoring: 1, W Germany, Haller (12); 2, England, Hurst (18).

SECOND HALF: Scoring: 3, England, Peters (78); 4, W. Germany, Weber (90).

OVERTIME: Scoring: 5, England, Hurst (101); 6, England, Hurst (120).

England: Banks, Cohen, Wilson, Stiles, J. Charlton, Moore, Ball, Hurst, Hunt, R. Charlton, Peters.

W Germany: Tilkowski, Hottges, Schmellinger, Beckenbauer, Schulz, Weber, Held, Haller, Seeler, Overath, Emmerich.

Referee: Dienst (Switzerland).

MEXICO 1970

Brazil	1	3	—4
Italy	1	0	—1

FIRST HALF: Scoring: 1, Brazil, Pelé (18); 2, Italy, Boninsegna (32).

SECOND HALF: Scoring: 3, Brazil, Gerson (65); 4, Brazil, Jairzinho (70); 5, Brazil, Alberto (86).

Brazil: Feliz, Alberto, Brito, Wilson, Piazza, Everaldo, Clodoaldo, Gerson, Jairzinho, Tostao, Pelé, Rivelino.

Italy: Albertosi, Burgnich, Cera, Rosato, Facchetti, Bertini (Juliano), Mazzola, De Sisti, Domenghini, Boninsegna (Rivera), Riva.

Referee: Glockner (E Germany).

W GERMANY 1974

W Germany	2	0	—2
Netherlands	1	0	—1

FIRST HALF: Scoring: 1, Netherlands, Neeskens, PK (1); 2, W Germany, Breitner, PK (26); 3, W Germany, Müller (44).

The World Cup *(Cont.)*

World Cup Final Box Scores *(Cont.)*

W GERMANY 1974 *(CONT.)*

W Germany: Maier, Vogts, Beckenbauer, Schwarzenbeck, Breitner, Hoeness, Bonhof, Overath, Grabowski, Müller, Holzenbein.

Netherlands: Jongbloed, Suurbier, Rijsbergen (de Jong), Haan, Krol, Jansen, Neeskens, van Hanagem, Cruyff, Rensenbrink (van der Kerkhof).

Referee: Taylor (England).

ARGENTINA 1978

Argentina	**1**	**0**	**2—3**
Netherlands	**0**	**1**	**0—1**

FIRST HALF: Scoring: 1, Argentina, Kempes (38).

SECOND HALF: Scoring: 2, Netherlands, Nanninga (81).

OVERTIME: Scoring: 3, Arg., Kempes (104); 4, Arg., Bertoni (114).

ARGENTINA 1978 *(Cont.)*

Argentina: Fillol, Olguin, Galvan, Passarella, Tarantini, Ardiles (Larrosa), Gallego, Kempes, Bertoni, Luque, Ortiz (Houseman).

Netherlands: Jongbloed, Jansen (Suurbier), Krol, Brandts, Poortvliet, Neeskens, Haan, W. van der Kerkhoff, R. van der Kerkhoff, Rep (Nanninga), Rensenbrink.

Referee: Gonella (Italy).

ITALY 1982

Italy	**0**	**3—3**
W Germany	**0**	**1—1**

SECOND HALF: Scoring: 1, Italy, Rossi (57); 2, Italy, Tardelli (68); 3, Italy, Altobelli (81); 4, W Germany, Breitner (83).

Italy: Zoff, Bergomi, Scirea, Collovati, Cabrini, Oriali, Gentile, Tardelli, Conti, Rossi, Graziani (Altobelli, Causio).

W Germany: Schumacher, Kaltz, Stielike, K. Foerster, B. Foerster, Dremmler (Hrubesch), Breitner, Briegel, Rummenigge (Müller), Fishcher (Littbarski).

Referee: Coelho (Brazil).

MEXICO 1986

Argentina	**1**	**2—3**
W Germany	**0**	**2—2**

FIRST HALF: Scoring: 1, Argentina, Brown (22).

SECOND HALF: Scoring: 2, Arg., Valdano (55); 3, W Germ., Rummenigge (73); 4, W Germ., Voller (81); 5, Arg., Burruchaga (83).

Argentina: Pumpido, Brown, Cuciuffo, Ruggeri, Olarticoecha, Bastista, Giusti, Burruchaga (Trobbiani 90), Enrique, Maradona, Valdona.

W Germany: Schumacher, Jakobs, Forster, Eder, Brehme, Matthaus, Berthold, Magath (Hoeness 62), Briegel, Rummenigge, Allofs (Voller 46).
Referee: Filho (Brazil).

ITALY 1990

W Germany	**0**	**1—1**
Argentina	**0**	**0—0**

SECOND HALF: Scoring: 1, W Germany, Brehme, PK (84).
W Germany: Illgner, Brehme, Kohler, Augenthaler, Buchwald, Berthold (Reuter), Littbarski, Haessler, Mattaeus, Voeller, Klinsmann.

Argentina: Goychoechea, Lorenzo, Serrizuela, Sensini, Ruggeri (Monzon), Simon, Basualdo, Burruchag (Calderon), Maradona, Troglio, Dezottir.

Referee: Coelho (Brazil).

UNITED STATES 1994

Italy	**0**	**0**	**0—0**
Brazil	**0**	**0**	**0—0**

Scoring: None. Shootout goals: Italy—2: Albertini, Evani; Brazil—3: Romario, Branco, Dunga.

Italy: Pagliuca, Benarrivo, Maldini, Baresi, Mussi

UNITED STATES 1994 *(Cont.)*

(Apolloni 35), Albertini, D. Baggio (Evani 95), Berti, Donadoni, Baggio, Massaro.

Brazil: Taffarel, Jorginho (Cafu 21), Branco, Aldair, Santos, Silva, Dunga, Zinho (Viola 106), Mazinho, Bebeto, Romario.

Referee: Puhl (Hungary).

FRANCE 1998

Brazil	**0**	**0—0**
France	**2**	**1—3**

FIRST HALF: Scoring: 1, France, Zidane (27); 2, France, Zidane (45).

SECOND HALF: Scoring: 3, France, Petit (90).

Brazil: Taffarel, Cafu, Aldair, Baiano, Carlos, Sampaio (Edmundo 74), Dunga, Rivaldo, Leonardo, (Denilson 46), Bebeto, Ronaldo.

France: Barthez, Lizarazu, Desailly, Thuram, Leboeuf, Djorkaeff (Vieira 75) Deschamps, Zidane, Petit, Karembeu (Boghossian 57), Guivarc'h (Dugarry 66).

Referee: Belqola (Morocco).

KOREA/JAPAN 2002

Brazil	**0**	**2—2**
Germany	**0**	**0—0**

SECOND HALF: Scoring: 1, Brazil, Ronaldo (67); 2, Brazil, Ronaldo (79).

Brazil: Marcos, Cafu, Lucio, Roque Junior, Edmilson, Carlos, Silva, Ronaldo (Denilson, 90), Rivaldo, Ronaldinho (Juninho, 85), Kleberson.

Germany: Kahn, Linke, Ramelow, Neuville, Hamann, Klose (Bierhoff, 74), Jeremies (Asamoah, 77), Bode (Ziege, 84), Schneider, Metzelder, Frings.

Referee: Collina (Italy).

GERMANY 2006

Italy	**1**	**0**	**0—1**
France	**1**	**0**	**0—1**

Italy won on penalty kicks, 5-3.

FIRST HALF: Scoring: 1, France, Zidane (7); 1, Italy, Materazzi (19).

SHOOTOUT GOALS: Italy—Pirlo, Materazzi, De Rossi, Del Piero, Grosso; France—Wiltord, Abidal, Sagnol.

Italy: Buffon, Zambrotta, Cannavaro, Materazzi, Grosso, Camoranesi (Del Piero 86), Pirlo, Gattuso, Perrotta (Iaquinta 61), Totti (De Rossi 61), Toni.
France: Barthez, Sagnol, Thuram, Gallas, Abidal, Ribery (Trezeguet 100), Vieira (Diarra 56), Makelele, Zidane, Malouda, Henry (Wiltord 107).

Referee: Elizondo (Argentina).

The World Cup *(Cont.)*

Alltime Leaders

GOALS

Player, Nation	Tournaments	Goals
Ronaldo, Brazil	1998, 2002, '04, '06	15
Gerd Müller, W Germany	1970, '74	14
Just Fontaine, France	1958	13
Pelé, Brazil	1958, '62, '66, '70	12
Sandor Kocsis, Hungary	1954	11
Teofilo Cubillas, Peru	1970, '78	10
Gregorz Lato, Poland	1974, '78, '82	10
Helmut Rahn, W Germany	1954, '58	10
Gary Lineker, England	1986, '90	10
Miroslav Klose, Germany	2002, '04	10
Ademir, Brazil	1950	9
Eusebio, Portugal	1966	9
Jairzinho, Brazil	1970, '74	9
Paolo Rossi, Italy	1982, '86	9
K.H. Rummenigge, W Germany	1978, '82, '86	9
Uwe Seeler, W Germany	1958, '62, '66, '70	9
Vava, Brazil	1958, '62	9

LEADING SCORER, CUP BY CUP

Year	Player, Nation	Goals
1930	Guillermo Stabile, Argentina	8
1934	Oldrich Nejedly, Czechoslovakia	5
1938	Leonidas da Silva, Brazil	8
1950	Ademir de Menenzes, Brazil	9
1954	Sandor Kocsis, Hungary	11
1958	Just Fontaine, France	13
1962	Florian Albert, Hungary Valentin Ivanov, USSR, Garrincha, Brazil, Vava, Brazil, Drazan Jerkovic, Yugoslavia Leonel Sanchez, Chile	4
1966	Eusebio Ferreira, Portugal	9
1970	Gerd Müller, W Germany	10
1974	Gregorz Lato, Poland	7
1978	Mario Kempes, Argentina	6
1982	Paolo Rossi, Italy	6
1986	Gary Lineker, England	6
1990	Salvatore Schillaci, Italy	6
1994	Hristo Stoichkov, Bulgaria Oleg Salenko, Russia	6
1998	Davor Suker, Croatia	6
2002	Ronaldo, Brazil	8
2006	Miroslav Klose, Germany	5

Most Goals, Individual, One Game

Goals	Player, Nation	Score	Date
5	Oleg Salenko, Russia	Russia–Cameroon, 6–1	6-28-94
4	Leonidas, Brazil	Brazil–Poland, 6–5	6-5-38
4	Ernest Willimowski, Poland	Brazil–Poland, 6–5	6-5-38
4	Gustav Wetterstrîm, Sweden	Sweden–Cuba, 8–0	6-12-38
4	Juan Alberto Schiaffino, Uruguay	Uruguay–Bolivia, 8–0	7-2-50
4	Ademir, Brazil	Brazil–Sweden, 7–1	7-9-50

The World Cup *(Cont.)*

Most Goals, Individual, One Game *(Cont.)*

Goals	Player, Nation	Score	Date
4	Sandor Kocsis, Hungary	Hungary–W Germany, 8–3	6-20-54
4	Just Fontaine, France	France–W Germany, 6–3	6-28-58
4	Eusebio, Portugal	Portugal–N Korea, 5–3	7-23-66
4	Emilio Butragueño, Spain	Spain–Denmark, 5–1	6-18-86

Note: 31 players have scored 32 World Cup hat tricks. Gerd Müller of West Germany is the only man to have two World Cup hat tricks, both in 1970. The last hat tricks were 6-1-02, Miroslav Klose (Ger) vs. Saudi Arabia; 6-21-98, Gabriel Batistuta (Arg) vs. Jamaica; 6-23-90, Tomas Skuhravy (Czech) vs. Costa Rica; and 6-17-90, Michel (Spain) vs. S Korea.

Attendance and Goal Scoring, Year by Year

Year	Site	No. of Games	Goals	Goals/Game	Attendance	Avg Att
1930	Uruguay	18	70	3.89	434,500	24,139
1934	Italy	17	70	4.12	395,000	23,235
1938	France	18	84	4.67	483,000	26,833
1950	Brazil	22	88	4.00	1,337,000	60,773
1954	Switzerland	26	140	5.38	943,000	36,269
1958	Sweden	35	126	3.60	868,000	24,800
1962	Chile	32	89	2.78	776,000	24,250
1966	England	32	89	2.78	1,614,677	50,459
1970	Mexico	32	95	2.97	1,673,975	52,312
1974	W Germany	38	97	2.55	1,774,022	46,685
1978	Argentina	38	102	2.68	1,610,215	42,374
1982	Spain	52	146	2.80	1,856,277	35,698
1986	Mexico	52	132	2.54	2,441,731	46,956
1990	Italy	52	115	2.21	2,514,443	48,354
1994	United States	52	140	2.69	3,567,415	68,604
1998	France	64	171	2.67	2,775,400	43,366
2002	Korea/Japan	64	161	2.52	2,705,216	42,269
2006	Germany	64	147	2.23	3,353,655	52,40
Totals		644	1,901	2.95	28,418,310	44,128

The World Cup *(Cont.)*

Results—Women's World Cup

Year	Champion	Score	Runner-Up	Third Place	Fourth Place
1991	United States	2–1	Norway	Sweden	Germany
1995	Norway	2–0	Germany	United States	China
1999	United States	0–0 (5–4 pk)	China	Brazil	Norway
2003	Germany	2–1	Sweden	United States	Canada
2007	Germany	2–0	Brazil	United States	Norway

Major League Soccer Finals

MLS Cup Results

Year	Champion	Score	Runner-up	Regular Season MVP
1996	D.C. United	3–2 (ot)	Los Angeles	Carlos Valderrama, TB
1997	D.C. United	2–1	Colorado	Preki, Kansas City
1998	Chicago	2–0	D.C. United	Marco Etcheverry, D.C.
1999	D.C. United	2–0	Los Angeles	Jason Kreis, Dallas
2000	Kansas City	1–0	Chicago	Tony Meola, Kansas City
2001	San Jose	2–1 (ot)	Los Angeles	Alex Pineda Chacon, Miami
2002	Los Angeles	1–0 (ot)	New England	Carlos Ruiz, Los Angeles
2003	San Jose	4–2	Chicago	Preki, Kansas City
2004	D.C. United	3–2	Kansas City	Amado Guevara, MetroStars
2005	Los Angeles	1–0 (ot)	New England	Taylor Twellman, NE
2006	Houston	1–1 (ot, 4-3 PKs)	New England	Christian Gomez, D.C.
2007	Houston	2–1	New England	Luciano Emilio, D.C.

United Soccer League Finals

Year	Champion	Score	Runner-Up	Regular Season MVP
1991	San Francisco	1–3, 2–0 (1–0 on PKs)	Albany	Jean Harbor, Maryland
1992	Colorado	1–0	Tampa Bay	Taifour Diane, Colorado
1993	Colorado	3–1 (OT)	Los Angeles	Taifour Diane, Colorado
1994	Montreal	1–0	Colorado	Paulinho, Los Angeles
1995	Seattle	1–2 (SO), 3–0, 2–1 (SO)	Atlanta	Peter Hattrup, Seattle
1996	Seattle	2–0	Rochester	Wolde Harris, Colorado
1997	Milwaukee	2–1 (SO)	Carolina	Doug Miller, Rochester
1998	Rochester	3–1	Minnesota	Mark Baena, Seattle
1999	Minnesota	2–1	Rochester	John Swallen, Minnesota
2000	Rochester	3–1	Minnesota	Vitalis Takawira, Mil
2001	Rochester	2–0	Vancouver	Paul Conway, Charleston
2002	Milwaukee	2–1 (2 OT)	Richmond	Leighton O'Brien, Seattle
2003	Charleston	3–0	Minnesota	Thiago Martins, Pittsburgh
2004	Montreal	2–0	Seattle	Greg Sutton, Montreal
2005	Seattle	1–1 (4–3 on PKs)	Richmond	Jason Jordan, Vancouver
2006	Vancouver	3–0	Rochester	Joey Gjertsen, Vancouver
2007	Seattle	4–0	Atlanta	Sebastien Le Toux, Seattle
2008	Vancouver	2–1	Puerto Rico	Jonathan Steele, Puerto Rico

NCAA Sports

Steve Detwiler of the College World Series national champion Fresno State Bulllldogs

DOUGLAS JONES/ICON SMI

Wonderdog Stories

The NCAA championships gave us three compelling reasons to believe in the little guys

BY HANK HERSCH

YOU CAN'T GO HOME AGAIN. SIZE matters. Success breeds success. All are phrases that have the ring of truth—or at least they did, until the 2007–08 NCAA champions were decided.

MEN'S SOCCER

Wake Forest forward Marcus Tracy raced up the field, drawing a pair of defenders before slotting the ball through to sophomore Zack Schilawski in front of the Ohio State goal. Schilawski had been in this position before. He was raised in Cary, N.C., five minutes from SAS Soccer Park, the site of the 2007 College Cup. Day after day he came to the complex and banged balls into the nets.

Which is what Schilawski did with this one. The forward's 10-yard strike in the 86th minute lifted the Demon Deacons to a 2–1 victory and their first national championship. "Luckily Marcus did the work and the ball bounced my way," Schiwalski said. "I saw the keeper coming after the ball a little bit and I knocked it in."

Entering the final on a 15–game win streak, Ohio State had stormed to a 1–0 lead, outshooting the Demon Deacons 12–3 in the first half. But the Buckeyes didn't muster a shot after intermission. Tracy, who was named the tournament's Most Outstanding Player, erased the deficit in the 66th minute before setting up the game-winner.

"Growing up here, I've seen a lot of great games on that field," said Schilawski afterward. "It's just a thrill to be part of a game like that, much less to win it. It was perfect."

MEN'S HOCKEY

Nathan Gerbe grew up in Oxford, Mich., although he stopped growing when he was around 14. All of 5'5" and 165 pounds, he decided to attend Boston College in part because of the school's history in developing small players. "Brian Gionta, Ryan Shannon—they made the footsteps for me to follow," Gerbe says.

As a junior left wing, Gerbe laid down some huge tracks of his own: Combining exceptional stick-handling and skating ability with an acute understanding of the game, he led the nation in scoring with 35 goals and 32 assists and was one of three finalists for the Hobey Baker Award. Gerbe also led the Eagles to their third straight title match—only unlike the previous two heartbreakers, he made certain they wouldn't lose.

At the Pepsi Center in Denver, Gerbe gave BC a 1–0 lead over Notre Dame in the second period with a one-timer from the lower left circle. His second goal, on a power play, typified his skill and his spirit: After forward Ben Smith's shot bounced off the backboards Gerbe scooped up the ricochet and, while sliding chest-first on the

DOUG PENSINGER/GETTY IMAGES

ice, knocked the puck inside the near post. And when the Irish cut the lead to 3–1 in the third period, Gerbe whipped a blind pass to Smith, whose slap shot widened the gap to three.

Thanks to Gerbe and the Eagles' penalty killers—the Irish were 0-for-8 on the power play, with just five shots—BC avenged title-game losses to Wisconsin in 2006 and Michigan State in '07 with a 5–2 victory. Said Notre Dame coach Jeff Jackson of Gerbe, whose seven goals tied the tournament record, "He was tremendous on the biggest stage. God bless the small guy, because he is fearless."

BASEBALL

Entering the decisive Game 3 in Omaha, Fresno State sophomore right fielder Steve Detwiler was hitting .231 in the College World Series. He was playing despite a torn ligament in his left thumb that would require surgery. Asked to lay down a sacrifice bunt in one game, he'd failed. And because Georgia would be starting a lefthander Detwiler, normally the No. 8 hitter, would have to bat sixth.

If not much was expected of Detwiler, even less had been expected of the Bulldogs, who lost 12 of their first 20 games, went

Diminutive left winger Gerbe scored two goals and added an assist to help the Eagles defeat the Irish and avenge their two previous title games losses in '06 and '07.

16–16 in non-conference play and had to win the WAC tournament to qualify for the post-season field of 64. After winning Game 1, Georgia had a 5–0 lead in Game 2 before Fresno State stormed back for a 19–10 victory. With that victory more T-shirts bearing the team's slogan could be seen in the Rosenblatt Stadium stands: UNDERDOGS TO WONDERDOGS.

In Game 3 the wonder of it all was Detwiler. He hit a two-run homer in the second inning, had an RBI double in the fourth and mashed a three-run shot deep into the left field stand in the sixth. In other words, he drove in all six runs in the Bulldogs' 6–1 victory, which clinched the school's second NCAA title. (It won the women's softball championship in 1998). No previous CWS champion had more losses than the Bulldogs (47–31).

Georgia's final out, fittingly, fell into the glove that encased Detwiler's injured thumb. "It's mind over matter," Detwiler said. "It's just a little pain. The pain is temporary. Pride is forever."

FOR THE RECORD • 2007—2008

NCAA Team Champions

Fall 2007

			Champion	Runner-Up
Cross-Country	MEN	Division I:	Oregon	Iona
		Division II:	Abilene Christian	Western St
		Division III:	NYU	Haverford
	WOMEN	Division I:	Stanford	Oregon
		Division II:	Adams St	Seattle Pacific
		Division III:	Amherst	Plattsburgh St
Field Hockey	WOMEN	Division I:	North Carolina	Penn State
		Division II	Bloomsburg	UMass-Lowell
		Division III:	Bowdoin	Middlebury
Football	MEN	FCS (I-AA):	Appalachian St	Delaware
		Division II:	Valdosta State	NW Missouri St
		Division III:	UW-Whitewater	Mount Union
Soccer	MEN	Division I:	Wake Forest	Ohio St
		Division II:	Franklin Pierce	Lincoln Memorial
		Division III:	Middlebury	Trinity
	WOMEN	Division I:	USC	Florida St
		Division II:	Tampa	Franklin Pierce
		Division III:	Wheaton (Ill.)	Messiah
Volleyball	WOMEN	Division I:	Penn St	Stanford
		Division II:	Concordia-St. Paul	Western Washington
		Division III:	Washington-St. Louis	UW-Whitewater
Water Polo	MEN		California	USC

Winter 2007-2008

			Champion	Runner-Up
Basketball	MEN	Division I:	Kansas	Memphis
		Division II:	Winona St	Augusta
		Division III:	Washington-St. Louis	Amherst
	WOMEN	Division I:	Tennessee	Stanford
		Division II:	Northern Kentucky	South Dakota
		Division III:	Howard Payne (Tex.)	Messiah Collage (Pa.)
Fencing			Ohio St	Notre Dame
Gymnastics	MEN		Oklahoma	Stanford
	WOMEN		Georgia	Utah
Ice Hockey	MEN	Division I:	Boston College	Notre Dame
		Division III:	St. Norbert	Plattsburgh St
	WOMEN	Division I:	Minn.-Duluth	Wisconsin
		Division III:	Plattsburgh St	Manhattanville
Rifle			Ak.-Fairbanks	Army
Skiing			Denver	Colorado
Swimming and Diving	MEN	Division I:	Arizona	Texas
		Division II:	Drury	Missouri S&T
		Division III:	Kenyon	Johns Hopkins
	WOMEN	Division I:	Arizona	Auburn
		Division II:	Truman St	Drury
		Division III:	Kenyon	Denison
Wrestling	MEN	Division I:	Iowa	Ohio St
		Division II:	Neb.-Kearney	Minn.St.-Mankato
		Division III:	Wartburg	UW-La Crosee

NCAA Team Champions *(Cont.)*

Winter 2007-2008 *(Cont.)*

			Champion	Runner-Up
Indoor Track and Field	MEN	Division I:	Arizona St	Florida St
		Division II:	St. Augustine's	Abilene Christian
		Division III:	UW-La Crosse	Monmouth (Ill.)
	WOMEN	Division I:	Arizona St	LSU
		Division II:	Adams St	St. Augustine's
		Division III:	Illinois Wesleyan	Wartburg

Spring 2008

			Champion	Runner-Up
Baseball		Division I:	Fresno St	Georgia
		Division II:	Mount Olive	Ouachita Baptist
		Division III:	Trinity (Conn.)	Johns Hopkins
Golf	MEN	Division I:	UCLA	Stanford
		Division II:	West Florida	North Alabama/ St. Edward's
		Division III:	St. John's (Minn.)	Redlands
	WOMEN	Division I:	USC	UCLA
		Division II:	Rollins	Nova Sou'eastern
		Division III	Methodist	DePauw
Lacrosse	MEN	Division I:	Syracuse	Johns Hopkins
		Division II:	NYIT	LeMoyne
		Division III:	Salisbury	Cortland St
	WOMEN	Division I:	Northwestern	Penn
		Division II	West Chester	LIU-C.W. Post
		Division III:	Hamilton	Franklin & Marshall
Rowing	WOMEN	Division I:	Brown	Washington
		Division II	Western Washington	UC-San Diego
		Division III:	Williams	Trinity (Conn.)
Softball		Division I:	Arizona St	Texas A&M
		Division II:	Humboldt St	Emporia St
		Division III:	UW-Eau Claire	UW-Whitewater
Tennis	MEN	Division I:	Georgia	Texas
		Division II:	Armstrong Atlantic St	Barry
		Division III:	Washington-St. Louis	Emory
	WOMEN	Division I:	UCLA	California
		Division II:	Armstrong Atlantic St	Lynn
		Division III:	Williams	Washington & Lee
Outdoor Track and Field	MEN	Division I:	Florida St	LSU/Auburn
		Division II:	Abilene Christian	St. Augustine's
		Division III:	McMurry	Cortland St
	WOMEN	Division I:	LSU	Arizona St
		Division II:	Abilene Christian	Adams St
		Division III:	UW-River Falls/Wesleyan	Wartburg
Volleyball	MEN		Penn St	Pepperdine
Water Polo	WOMEN		UCLA	USC
Bowling	WOMEN		Md.-Eastern Shore	Arkansas St

NCAA Division I Individual Champions

Fall 2007

Cross Country

	Champion	Runner-Up
MEN	Josh McDougal, Liberty	Galen Rupp, Oregon
WOMEN	Sally Kipyego, Texas Tech	Jenny Barringer, Colorado

NCAA Division I Individual Champions

Winter 2007–2008

Gymnastics

	Event	Champion	Runner-Up
MEN	All-around	Casey Sandy, Penn St	Jonathan Horton, Oklahoma
	Vault	Steven Legendre, Oklahoma	David Sender, Stanford
	Parallel bars	Tim McNeill, California	Casey Sandy, Penn St
	Horizontal bar	Paul Ruggeri, Illinois	Cole Storer, Minnesota
	Floor exercise	Steve Legendre, Oklahoma	Jimmy Wickham, Ohio St/ Casey Sandy, Penn St
	Pommel horse	Timothy McNeill, California	Casey Sandy, Penn St
	Rings	Jonathan Horton, Oklahoma	David Sender, Stanford
WOMEN	All-around	Tasha Schwikert, UCLA	Ashley Postell, Georgia
	Balance beam	Grace Taylor, Georgia	Emily Parsons. Nebraska/ Ashley Postell, Georgia
	Uneven bars	Tasha Schwikert, UCLA	Kristina Comforte, UCLA/ Katie Herring, Georgia
	Floor exercise	Courtney McCool, Georgia	Tasha Schwikert, UCLA
	Vault	Susan Jackson, LSU	Julie Dwyer, Auburn/ Kristina Baskett, Utah

Skiing

	Event	Champion	Runner-Up
MEN	Slalom	John Buchar, Denver	Seppi Stiegler, Denver
	Giant slalom	John Buchar, Denver	Greg Hardy, Vermont
	10-kilometer free	Glenn Randall, Dartmouth	Marius Korthauer, Ak.-Fairbanks
	20-kilometer classic	Marius Korthauer, Ak.-Fairbanks	Kit Richmond, Colorado
WOMEN	Slalom	Lucie Zikova, Colorado	Eva Huckova, Utah
	Giant slalom	Lucie Zikova, Colorado	Eva Huckova, Utah
	5-kilometer free	Maria Moe Grevsgaard, Colorado	Lenka Palanova, Colorado
	15-kilometer classic	Maria Moe Grevsgaard, Colorado	Polina Ermoshina, Northern Mich.

Wrestling

Weight	Champion	Runner-Up
125 lb	Angel Escobedo, Indiana	Jayson Ness, Minnesota
133 lb	Coleman Scott, Oklahoma	Joey Slaton, Iowa
141 lb	J Jaggers, Ohio St	Chad Mendes, Cal Poly
149 lb	Brent Metcalf, Iowa	Bubba Jenkins, Penn St
157 lb	Jordan Leen, Cornell	Michael Poeta, Illinois
165 lb	Mark Perry, Iowa	Eric Tannenbaum, Michigan
174 lb	Keith Gavin, Pittsburgh	Steve Luke, Michigan
184 lb	Mike Pucillo, Ohio St	Jake Varner, Iowa St
197 lb	Phil Davis, Penn St	Wynn Michalak, Central Mich.
285 lb	Dustin Fox, Northwestern	J.D. Bergman, Ohio St

Swimming and Diving — Men

Event	Champion	Time	Runner-Up	Time
50-yd freestyle	Cesar Cielo, Auburn	18.52*	Alex Righi, Yale	19.08
100-yd freestyle	Cesar Cielo, Auburn	40.92*	Alex Righi, Yale	42.13
200-yd freestyle	Dave Walters, Texas	1:32.56	Darian Townsend, Arizona	1:32.85
500-yd freestyle	Sebastien Rouault, Georgia	4:09.48	Michael Klueh, Texas	4:10.00
1650-yd freestyle	Sebastien Rouault, Georgia	14:26.86	Troy Prinsloo, Georgia	14:28.06
100-yd backstroke	Ben Hesen, Indiana	44.72	Albert Subirats, Arizona	45.40
200-yd backstroke	Patrick Schirk, Penn St	1:40.22	Cory Chitwood, Arizona	1:41.20
100-yd breaststroke	Paul Kornfeld, Stanford	52.03	Marcus Titus, Arizona	52.61
200-yd breaststroke	Paul Kornfeld, Stanford	1:53.11	Scott Spann, Michigan	1:54.16
100-yd butterfly	Albert Subirats, Arizona	45.07	Alexei Puninski, Auburn	45.51
200-yd butterfly	Gil Stovall, Georgia	1:41.33*	Mark Dylla, Georgia	1:42.08
200-yd IM	Darian Townsend, Arizona	1:42.72	Ricky Berens, Texas	1:43.25
400-yd IM	Alex Vanderkaay, Michigan	3:41.58	Sebastien Rouault, Georgia	3:42.25
200-yd free relay	Auburn	1:15.66	Arizona	1:16.55
400-yd free relay	Arizona	2:49.01	Auburn	2:49.48
800-yd free relay	Arizona	6:12.85	Texas	6:16.54
200-yd medley relay	Auburn	1:23.24*	Arizona	1:24.08
400-yd free relay	Arizona	3:04.43	California	3:05.38
1-meter diving	Chris Colwill, Georgia	407.25	Magnus Frick, Hawaii	399.70
3-meter diving	Reuben Ross, Miami	466.80	Chris Colwill, Georgia	460.55
Platform	Sean Moore, Ohio St	478.20	Chris Colwill, Georgia	460.60

*NCAA record.

NCAA Division I Individual Champions *(Cont.)*

Swimming and Diving — Women

	Champion	Time/Pts	Runner-Up	Time/Pts
50-yd freestyle	Lara Jackson, Arizona	21.69	Michele King, Tennessee	21.86
100-yd freestyle	Lacey Nymeyer, Arizona	47.50	Julia Wilkinson, Texas A&M	47.56
200-yd freestyle	Caroline Burckle, Florida	1:43.10	Lacey Nymeyer, Arizona	1:43.33
500-yd freestyle	Caroline Burckle, Florida	4:33.60*	Maggie Bird, Auburn	4:39.51
1650-yd freestyle	Emily Brunemann, Michigan	15:53.69	Whitney Sprague, N. Carolina	15:57.77
100-yd backstroke	Gemma Spofforth, Florida	51.78	Hailey Degolia, Arizona	51.89
200-yd backstroke	Gemma Spofforth, Florida	1:50.70	Kateryna Zubkova, Indiana	1:53.17
100-yd breaststroke	Rebecca Soni, USC	59.19	Jillian Tyler, Minnesota	59.87
200 yd breaststroke	Rebecca Soni, USC	2:06.32	Elizabeth Smith, Stanford	2:08.73
100-yd butterfly	Christine Magnuson, Tenn.	50.70	Dana Vollmer, California	51.32
200-yd butterfly	Saori Haruguchi, Oregon St	1:52.39	Elaine Breeden, Stanford	1:53.27
200-yd IM	Ava Ohlgren, Auburn	1:53.94	Ariana Kukors, Washington	1:55.26
400-yd IM	Julia Smit, Stanford	4:02.41	Ava Ohlgren, Auburn	4:04.07
200-yd free relay	Arizona	1:26.90*	California	1:27.52
400-yd free relay	Arizona	3:11.34	California	3:13.03
800-yd free relay	Arizona	6:58.69	Texas	6:59.50
200-yd medley relay	Arizona	1:35.29*	Stanford	1:37.63
400-yd medley relay	Arizona	3:26.06*	Auburn	3:32.84
1-meter diving	Emma Friesen, Hawaii	336.20	Mary Yarrison, Texas	331.60
3-meter diving	Chelsea Davis, Ohio St	365.85	Bianca Alvarez, Ohio St	354.50
Platform	Brittany Viola, Miami	362.60	Margaret Hostage, Stanford	347.20

Indoor Track and Field — Men

	Champion	Time/Mark	Runner-Up	Time/Mark
60-meter dash	Richard Thompson, LSU	6.51	Trindon Holliday, LSU	6.54
60-meter hurdles	Drew Brunson, Florida St	7.53	Jason Richardson, South Carolina	7.53
200-meter dash	Rubin Williams, Tennessee	20.36	Charles Clark, Florida St	20.50
400-meter dash	Andretti Bain, Oral Roberts	46.19	Joel Phillip, Arizona St	46.27
800-meter run	Tyler Mulder, Iowa	1:49.20	Elkana Kosgei, LSU	1:49.47
4x400-meter relay	Florida St	3:07.47	Western Kentucky	3:08.16
Mile run	Leonel Manzano, Texas	4:04.45	Jake Morse, Texas	4:04.88
3,000-meter run	Kyle Alcorn, Arizona St	8:00.82	Andrew Bumbalough, G'getown	8:02.22
5,000-meter run	Shadrack Songok, Tex A&M-CC	13:51.26	Jacob Korir, Eastern Kentucky	13:52.91
Distance medley	Texas	9:32.04	Arizona St	9:32.49
High jump	Dusty Jonas, Nebraska	2.31m	Scott Sellers, Kansas St	2.25m
Pole Vault	Rory Quiller, Binghamton	5.50m	Mitch Greeley, Clemson	5.40m
Long jump	Reindell Cole, CSU-Northridge	8.12m	Norris Frederick, Washington	7.99m
Triple jump	Nkosinza Balumbu, Arkansas	16.54m	Tydree Lewis, Oklahoma	16.52m
Shot put	Ryan Whiting, Arizona St	21.73m	Russ Winger, Idaho	21.29m
35-pound wt throw	Egor Agafonov, Kansas	22.71m	Jake Dunkleberger, Auburn	22.24m
Heptathlon	Gonzalo Barroilhet, Florida St	5,951 pts	Josh Hustedt, Stanford	5,836 pts

Indoor Track and Field — Women

	Champion	Time/Mark	Runner-Up	Time/Mark
60-meter dash	Kelly-Ann Baptiste, LSU	7.163	Alexandria Anderson, Texas	7.169
60-meter hurdles	Tiffany Ofili, Michigan	7.94	Kristi Castlin, Virgina Tech	8.02
200-meter dash	Bianca Knight, Texas	22.40	Nickesha Anderson, Kansas	22.62
400-meter dash	Krista Simkins, Miami	52.16	Trish Bartholomew, Alabama	52.37
800-meter run	Latavia Thomas, LSU	2:05.07	Heather Dorniden, Minnesota	2:05:45
4x400-meter relay	Arizona St	3:33.63	Texas	3:33.69
Mile run	Hannah England, Florida St	4:35.30	Nicole Edwards, Michigan	4:35.74
3,000-meter run	Susan Kuijken, Florida St	8:58.14	Brie Felnagle, North Carolina	9.00.31
5,000-meter run	Sally Kipyego, Texas Tech	15:31.91	Lisa Koll, Iowa St	15:54.90
Distance medley	Tennessee	11:01.97	Michigan	11:02.22
High jump	Ebba Jungmark, Washington St	1.89m	Sharon Day, Cal Poly-SLO	1.86m
Pole vault	Elouise Rudy, Montana St	4.30m	April Kubishta, Arizona St	4.30m
Long jump	Brittany Resse, Mississippi	6.76m	Blessing Okagbare, UTEP	6.68m
Triple jump	Erica McLain, Stanford	14.20m	Kimberly Williams, Florida St	13.82m
Shot Put	Miriam Kevkhishvili, Florida St	17.83m	Sarah Stevens, Arizona St	17.64m
20-pound wt throw	Brittany Riley, Southern Illinois	25.34m	Jessica Pressley, Arizona St	22.04m
Pentathlon	Jacquelyn Johnson, Arizona St	4,496 pts*	Bettie Wade, Michigan	4,366 pts

Rifle

	Champion	Pts	Runner-Up	Pts
Smallbore	Chris Abalo, Army	87.6	Brian Kern, Army	81.6
Air rifle	Patrick Sartz, Ak.-Fairbanks	96.4	Joshua Albright, Navy	93.9

*NCAA record.

NCAA Division I Individual Champions *(Cont.)*

Spring 2008

Golf

	Champion	Score	Runners-Up	Score
MEN	Kevin Chappell. UCLA	286	Nick Taylor, Washington/	289
			Jorge Campillo, Indiana	289
WOMEN	Azahara Munoz, Arizona St	287	Tiffany Joh, UCLA	289 (Munoz won playoff)

Outdoor Track and Field

MEN

	Champion	Mark	Runner-Up	Mark
100-meter dash	Richard Thompson, LSU	10.12	Travis Padgett, Clemson	10.16
200-meter dash	Walter Dix, Florida St	20.40	Richard Thompson, LSU	20.44
400-meter dash	Andretti Bain, Oral Roberts	44.62	Lionel Larry, USC	44.63
4x100-meter relay	LSU	38.42	Texas A&M	38.58
800-meter run	Jacob Hernandez, Texas	1:45.31	Andrew Wheating, Oregon	1:45.32
1,500-meter run	Leonel Manzano, Texas	3:41.25	Dorian Ulrey, Northern Iowa	3:42.56
4x400-meter relay	Baylor	3:00.22	Texas A&M	3:01.78
5,000-meter run	Robert Curtis, Villanova	13:33.93	Stephen Pifer, Colorado	13:39.34
10,000-meter run	Shadrack Songok, Texas A&M-CC	28:46.69	Shawn Forrest, Arkansas	28:47.08
110-meter hurdles	Jason Richardson, South Carolina	13.40	Ty Akins, Auburn	13.46
400-meter hurdles	Jeshua Anderson, Washington St	48.69	Reuben McCoy, Auburn	48.71
3,000-meter steeple	Kyle Alcorn, Arizona St	8:28.26	Billy Nelson, Colorado	8:28.85
High jump	Mickael Hanany, UTEP	2.32m	Dusty Jonas, Nebraska	2.26m
Pole vault	Maston Wallace, Texas	5.35m	Yavgeniy Olhovsky, Virginia Tech	5.25m
Long jump	Ngonidzashe Makusha, Florida St	8.30m	Matt Turner, Arizona St	8.01m
Triple jump	Muhammad Halim, Cornell	16.66m	Andre Black, Louisville	16.65m
Shot put	Cory Martin, Auburn	20.35m	Ryan Whiting, Arizona St	20.24m
Discus throw	Rashaud Scott, Kentucky	60.87m	Yemi Ayeni, Virginia	59.50m
Hammer throw	Cory Martin, Auburn	74.13m	Jake Dunkleberger, Auburn	72.98m
Javelin throw	Chris Hill, Georgia	78.41m	Corey White, USC	77.79m
Decathlon	Ashton Eaton, Oregon	8,055 pts	Jangy Addy, Tennessee	7,916 pts

WOMEN

	Champion	Mark	Runner-Up	Mark
100-meter dash	Kelly-Ann Baptiste, LSU	11.20	Simone Facey, Texas A&M	11.27
200-meter dash	Simone Facey, Texas A&M	22.63	Porscha Lucas, Texas A&M	22.67
400-meter dash	Shana Cox, Penn St	50.97	Trish Bartholomew, Alabama	51.29
4x100-meter relay	Texas A&M	42.59	LSU	42.85
800-meter run	Geena Gall, Michigan	2:03.91	Latavia Thomas, LSU	2:04.38
1,500-meter run	Hannah England, Florida St	4:06.19*	Sally Kipyego, Texas Tech	4:06.67
4x400-meter relay	Penn St	3:27.69	LSU	3:28.33
5,000-meter run	Sally Kipyego, Texas Tech	15:15.08*	Angela Bizzarri, Illinois	15:46.08
10,000-meter run	Lisa Koll, Iowa St	32:44.95	Danette Doetzel, Providence	33:44.23
100-meter hurdles	Tiffany Ofili, Michigan	12.84	Nikiesha Wilson, LSU	13.00
400-meter hurdles	Nicole Leach, UCLA	54.32	Nickiesha Wilson, LSU	55.68
3,000-meter steeple	Jenny Barringer, Colorado	9:29.20*	Silje Fjortoft, SMU	9:55.54
High jump	Elizabeth Patterson, Arizona	1.86m	Sharon Day, Cal Poly-SLO	1.86m
Pole vault	Katie Morgan, California	4.20m	Stephanie Bagan, San Diego St	4.20m
Long jump	Brittney Reese, Mississippi	6.93m	Natasha Harvey, Jacksonville	6.65m
Triple jump	Erica McLain, Stanford	14.60m	Blessing Okagbare, UTEP	14.01m
Shot put	Jessica Pressley, Arizona St	18.13m	Susan King, Memphis	17.68m
Discus throw	Sarah Stevens, Arizona St	56.14m	Tai Battle, Arizona St	55.69m
Hammer throw	Eva Orban, USC	68.71m	Brittany Riley, Southern Illinois	67.44m
Javelin throw	Rachel Yurkovich, Oregon	56.58m	Katie Coronado, New Mexico	54.71m
Heptathlon	Jacquelyn Johnson, Arizona St	5,984 pts	Liz Roehrig, Minnesota	5,811 pts

Tennis

		Champion	Score	Runner-Up
MEN	Singles	Somdev Devvarman, Virginia	6–3, 6–2	J.P. Smith, Tennessee
	Doubles	R. Farah/K. Van't Hof, USC	7–6 (10),7–6 (6)	J. Berg/E. Tveit, Mississippi
WOMEN	Singles	Audra Cohen, Miami (Fla.)	7-5, 6-2	Lindsey Nelson, USC
	Doubles	Sara Anundsen/Jenna Long North Carolina	1-6, 6-2, 6-2	Megan Moulton-Levy/Katarina Zoricic William & Mary

*NCAA meet record.

CHAMPIONSHIP RESULTS

Baseball

DIVISION I

Year	Champion	Coach	Score	Runner-Up	Most Outstanding Player
1947	California*	Clint Evans	8–7	Yale	No award
1948	USC	Sam Barry	9–2	Yale	No award
1949	Texas*	Bibb Falk	10–3	Wake Forest	Charles Teague, Wake Forest, 2B
1950	Texas	Bibb Falk	3–0	Washington St	Ray VanCleef, Rutgers, CF
1951	Oklahoma*	Jack Baer	3–2	Tennessee	Sidney Hatfield, Tennessee, P-1B
1952	Holy Cross	Jack Barry	8–4	Missouri	James O'Neill, Holy Cross, P
1953	Michigan	Ray Fisher	7–5	Texas	J.L. Smith, Texas, P
1954	Missouri	John (Hi) Simmons	4–1	Rollins	Tom Yewcic, Michigan St, C
1955	Wake Forest	Taylor Sanford	7–6	Western Michigan	Tom Borland, Oklahoma St, P
1956	Minnesota	Dick Siebert	12–1	Arizona	Jerry Thomas, Minnesota, P
1957	California*	George Wolfman	1–0	Penn St	Cal Emery, Penn St, P-1B
1958	USC	Rod Dedeaux	8–7†	Missouri	Bill Thom, USC, P
1959	Oklahoma St	Toby Greene	5–3	Arizona	Jim Dobson, Oklahoma St, 3B
1960	Minnesota	Dick Siebert	2–1‡	USC	John Erickson, Minnesota, 2B
1961	USC*	Rod Dedeaux	1–0	Oklahoma St	Littleton Fowler, Oklahoma St, P
1962	Michigan	Don Lund	5–4	Santa Clara	Bob Garibaldi, Santa Clara, P
1963	USC	Rod Dedeaux	5–2	Arizona	Bud Hollowell, USC, C
1964	Minnesota	Dick Siebert	5–1	Missouri	Joe Ferris, Maine, P
1965	Arizona St	Bobby Winkles	2–1#	Ohio St	Sal Bando, Arizona St, 3B
1966	Ohio St	Marty Karow	8–2	Oklahoma St	Steve Arlin, Ohio St, P
1967	Arizona St	Bobby Winkles	11–2	Houston	Ron Davini, Arizona St, C
1968	USC*	Rod Dedeaux	4–3	Southern Illinois	Bill Seinsoth, USC, 1B
1969	Arizona St	Bobby Winkles	10–1	Tulsa	John Dolinsek, Arizona St, LF
1970	USC	Rod Dedeaux	2–1	Florida St	Gene Ammann, Florida St, P
1971	USC	Rod Dedeaux	7–2	Southern Illinois	Jerry Tabb, Tulsa, 1B
1972	USC	Rod Dedeaux	1–0	Arizona St	Russ McQueen, USC, P
1973	USC*	Rod Dedeaux	4–3	Arizona St	Dave Winfield, Minnesota, P-OF
1974	USC	Rod Dedeaux	7–3	Miami (Fla.)	George Milke, USC, P
1975	Texas	Cliff Gustafson	5–1	S Carolina	Mickey Reichenbach, Texas, 1B
1976	Arizona	Jerry Kindall	7–1	Eastern Michigan	Steve Powers, Arizona, P-DH
1977	Arizona St	Jim Brock	2–1	S Carolina	Bob Horner, Arizona St, 3B
1978	USC*	Rod Dedeaux	10–3	Arizona St	Rod Boxberger, USC, P
1979	CSU–Fullerton	Augie Garrido	2–1	Arkansas	Tony Hudson, CSU–Fullerton, P
1980	Arizona	Jerry Kindall	5–3	Hawaii	Terry Francona, Arizona, LF
1981	Arizona St	Jim Brock	7–4	Oklahoma St	Stan Holmes, Arizona St, LF
1982	Miami (Fla.)*	Ron Fraser	9–3	Wichita St	Dan Smith, Miami (Fla.), P
1983	Texas*	Cliff Gustafson	4–3	Alabama	Calvin Schiraldi, Texas, P
1984	CSU–Fullerton	Augie Garrido	3–1	Texas	John Fishel, CSU–Fullerton, LF
1985	Miami (Fla.)	Ron Fraser	10–6	Texas	Greg Ellena, Miami (Fla.), DH
1986	Arizona	Jerry Kindall	10–2	Florida St	Mike Senne, Arizona, LF
1987	Stanford	Mark Marquess	9–5	Oklahoma St	Paul Carey, Stanford, RF
1988	Stanford	Mark Marquess	9–4	Arizona St	Lee Plemel, Stanford, P
1989	Wichita St	Gene Stephenson	5–3	Texas	Greg Brummett, Wichita St, P
1990	Georgia	Steve Webber	2–1	Oklahoma St	Mike Rebhan, Georgia, P
1991	LSU	Skip Bertman	6–3	Wichita St	Gary Hymel, LSU, C
1992	Pepperdine	Andy Lopez	3–2	CSU–Fullerton	Phil Nevin, CSU–Fullerton, 3B
1993	LSU	Skip Bertman	8–0	Wichita St	Todd Walker, LSU, 2B
1994	Oklahoma	Larry Cochell	13–5	Georgia Tech	Chip Glass, Oklahoma, CF
1995	CSU–Fullerton*	Augie Garrido	11–5	USC	Mark Kotsay, CSU–Fullerton, CF-P
1996	LSU*	Skip Bertman	9–8	Miami (Fla.)	Pat Burrell, Miami (Fla.), 3B
1997	LSU*	Skip Bertman	13–6	Alabama	Brandon Larson, LSU, SS
1998	USC	Mike Gillespie	21–14	Arizona St	Wes Rachels, USC, 2B
1999	Miami (Fla.)	Jim Morris	6–5	Florida St	Marshall McDougall, FSU 3B/2B
2000	LSU*	Skip Bertman	6–5	Stanford	Trey Hodges, LSU, P
2001	Miami (Fla.)*	Jim Morris	12–1	Stanford	Charlton Jimerson, Miami (Fla.), OF
2002	Texas	Augie Garrido	12–6	South Carolina	Huston Street, Texas, P
2003	Rice	Wayne Graham	14–2^	Stanford	John Hudgins, Stanford, P
2004	CSU–Fullerton	George Horton	3–2^	Texas	Jason Windsor, CSU–Fullerton

*Undefeated teams in College World Series play.
†12 innings. ‡10 innings. #15 innings. ^Score of decisive game of best-of-three series.

Baseball *(Cont.)*

DIVISION I *(CONT.)*

Year	Champion	Coach	Score	Runner-Up	Most Outstanding Player
2005	Texas	Augie Garrido	6–2^	Florida	David Maroul, Texas
2006	Oregon St	Pat Casey	3–2^	North Carolina	Jonah Nickerson, Oregon St, P
2007	Oregon St	Pat Casey	9–3^	North Carolina	Jorge Reyes, Oregon St, P
2008	Fresno St	Mike Batesole	6–1	Georgia	Tommy Mendonca. Fresno St, 3B

*Undefeated teams in College World Series play.
†12 innings. ‡10 innings. #15 innings. ^Score of decisive game of best-of-three series.

DIVISION II

Year	Champion
1968	Chapman*
1969	Illinois St*
1970	CSU-Northridge
1971	Florida Southern
1972	Florida Southern
1973	UC–Irvine*
1974	UC–Irvine
1975	Florida Southern
1976	Cal Poly–Pomona
1977	UC–Riverside
1978	Florida Southern
1979	Valdosta St
1980	Cal Poly–Pomona*
1981	Florida Southern*
1982	UC–Riverside*
1983	Cal Poly–Pomona*
1984	CSU–Northridge
1985	Florida Southern*
1986	Troy St
1987	Troy St*
1988	Florida Southern*
1989	Cal Poly–SLO
1990	Jacksonville St
1991	Jacksonville St
1992	Tampa*
1993	Tampa
1994	Central Missouri St
1995	Florida Southern*
1996	Kennesaw St*
1997	CSU–Chico*
1998	Tampa*
1999	CSU–Chico
2000	SE Oklahoma St
2001	St. Mary's (Tex.)
2002	Columbus St
2003	Central Missouri St
2004	Kennesaw St
2005	Florida Southern
2006	Tampa
2007	Tampa
2008	Mount Olive

DIVISION III

Year	Champion
1976	CSU-Stanislaus
1977	CSU-Stanislaus
1978	Glassboro St
1979	Glassboro St
1980	Ithaca
1981	Marietta
1982	Eastern Connecticut St
1983	Marietta
1984	Ramapo
1985	UW-Oshkosh
1986	Marietta
1987	Montclair St
1988	Ithaca
1989	N. Carolina Wesleyan
1990	Eastern Connecticut St
1991	Southern Maine
1992	William Paterson
1993	Montclair St
1994	UW-Oshkosh
1995	La Verne
1996	William Paterson
1997	Southern Maine
1998	Eastern Connecticut St
1999	N.Carolina Wesleyan
2000	Montclair St
2001	St. Thomas (Minn.)
2002	Eastern Connecticut St
2003	Chapman
2004	UW-Stevens Pt
2005	Wisconsin
2006	Marietta
2007	Kean
2008	Trinity (Conn.)

*Undefeated teams in final series.

Ice Hockey

Men

DIVISION I

Year	Champion	Coach	Score	Runner-Up	Most Outstanding Player
1948	Michigan	Vic Heyliger	8–4	Dartmouth	Joe Riley, Dartmouth, F
1949	Boston College	John Kelley	4–3	Dartmouth	Dick Desmond, Dartmouth, G
1950	Colorado College	Cheddy Thompson	13–4	Boston University	Ralph Bevins, Boston University, G
1951	Michigan	Vic Heyliger	7–1	Brown	Ed Whiston, Brown, G
1952	Michigan	Vic Heyliger	4–1	Colorado College	Kenneth Kinsley, Colorado Coll, G
1953	Michigan	Vic Heyliger	7–3	Minnesota	John Matchefts, Michigan, F
1954	Rensselaer	Ned Harkness	5–4 (OT)	Minnesota	Abbie Moore, Rensselaer, F
1955	Michigan	Vic Heyliger	5–3	Colorado College	Philip Hilton, Colorado College, D
1956	Michigan	Vic Heyliger	7–5	Michigan Tech	Lorne Howes, Michigan, G
1957	Colorado College	Thomas Bedecki	13–6	Michigan	Bob McCusker, Colorado Coll, F
1958	Denver	Murray Armstrong	6–2	North Dakota	Murray Massier, Denver, F
1959	North Dakota	Bob May	4–3 (OT)	Michigan St	Reg Morelli, North Dakota, F
1960	Denver	Murray Armstrong	5–3	Michigan Tech	Bob Marquis, Boston University, F
1961	Denver	Murray Armstrong	12–2	St. Lawrence	Barry Urbanski, Boston Univ, G
1962	Michigan Tech	John MacInnes	7–1	Clarkson	Louis Angotti, Michigan Tech, F
1963	North Dakota	Barney Thorndycraft	6–5	Denver	Al McLean, North Dakota, F
1964	Micbigan	Allen Renfrew	6–3	Denver	Bob Gray, Michigan, G
1965	Michigan Tech	John MacInnes	8–2	Boston College	Gary Milroy, Michigan Tech, F
1966	Michigan St	Amo Bessone	6–1	Clarkson	Gaye Cooley, Michigan St, G
1967	Cornell	Ned Harkness	4–1	Boston University	Walt Stanowski, Cornell, D

Men *(Cont.)*

DIVISION I *(CONT.)*

Year	Champion	Coach	Score	Runner-Up	Most Outstanding Player
1968	Denver	Murray Armstrong	4–0	North Dakota	Gerry Powers, Denver, G
1969	Denver	Murray Armstrong	4–3	Cornell	Keith Magnuson, Denver, D
1970	Cornell	Ned Harkness	6–4	Clarkson	Daniel Lodboa, Cornell, D
1971	Boston University	Jack Kelley	4–2	Minnesota	Dan Brady, Boston University, G
1972	Boston University	Jack Kelley	4–0	Cornell	Tim Regan, Boston University, G
1973	Wisconsin	Bob Johnson	4–2	Vacated	Dean Talafous, Wisconsin, F
1974	Minnesota	Herb Brooks	4–2	Michigan Tech	Brad Shelstad, Minnesota, G
1975	Michigan Tech	John MacInnes	6–1	Minnesota	Jim Warden, Michigan Tech, G
1976	Minnesota	Herb Brooks	6–4	Michigan Tech	Tom Vanelli, Minnesota, F
1977	Wisconsin	Bob Johnson	6–5 (OT)	Michigan	Julian Baretta, Wisconsin, G
1978	Boston University	Jack Parker	5–3	Boston College	Jack O'Callahan, Boston Univ, D
1979	Minnesota	Herb Brooks	4–3	North Dakota	Steve Janaszak, Minnesota, G
1980	North Dakota	John Gasparini	5–2	Northern Michigan	Doug Smail, North Dakota, F
1981	Wisconsin	Bob Johnson	6–3	Minnesota	Marc Behrend, Wisconsin, G
1982	North Dakota	John Gasparini	5–2	Wisconsin	Phil Sykes, North Dakota, F
1983	Wisconsin	Jeff Sauer	6–2	Harvard	Marc Behrend, Wisconsin, G
1984	Bowling Green	Jerry York	5–4 (OT)	Minn.–Duluth	Gary Kruzich, Bowling Green, G
1985	Rensselaer	Mike Addesa	2–1	Providence	Chris Terreri, Providence, G
1986	Michigan St	Ron Mason	6–5	Harvard	Mike Donnelly, Michigan St, F
1987	North Dakota	John Gasparini	5–3	Michigan St	Tony Hrkac, North Dakota, F
1988	Lake Superior St	Frank Anzalone	4–3 (OT)	St. Lawrence	Bruce Hoffort, Lake Superior St, G
1989	Harvard	Bill Cleary	4–3 (OT)	Minnesota	Ted Donato, Harvard, F
1990	Wisconsin	Jeff Sauer	7–3	Colgate	Chris Tancill, Wisconsin, F
1991	Northern Michigan	Rick Comley	8–7 (3OT)	Boston University	Scott Beattie, Northern Michigan, F
1992	Lake Superior St	Jeff Jackson	4–2	Wisconsin	Paul Constantin, Lake Superior St, F
1993	Maine	Shawn Walsh	5–4	Lake Superior St	Jim Montgomery, Maine, F
1994	Lake Superior St	Jeff Jackson	9–1	Boston University	Sean Tallaire, Lake Superior St, F
1995	Boston University	Jack Parker	6–2	Maine	Chris O'Sullivan, Boston Univ, F
1996	Michigan	Red Berenson	3–2 (OT)	Colorado College	Brendan Morrison, Michigan, F
1997	North Dakota	Dean Blais	6–4	Boston University	Matt Henderson, North Dakota, F
1998	Michigan	Red Berenson	3–2 (OT)	Boston College	Marty Turco, Michigan, G
1999	Maine	Shawn Walsh	3–2 (OT)	New Hampshire	Alfie Michaud, Maine, G
2000	North Dakota	Dean Blais	4–2	Boston College	Lee Goren, North Dakota, F
2001	Boston College	Jerry York	3–2 (OT)	North Dakota	Chuck Kobasew, Boston Coll, F
2002	Minnesota	Don Lucia	4–3 (OT)	Maine	Grant Potulny, Minnesota, F
2003	Minnesota	Don Lucia	5–1	New Hampshire	Thomas Vanek, Minnesota, F
2004	Denver	George Gwozdecky	1–0	Maine	Adam Berkhoel, Denver, G
2005	Denver	George Gwozdecky	4–1	North Dakota	Peter Mannino, Denver
2006	Wisconsin	Mike Eaves	2–1	Boston College	Robbie Earl, Wisconsin, F
2007	Michigan St	Rick Comley	3–1	Boston College	Justin Abdelkader, Michigan St, F
2008	Boston College	Jerry York	4–1	Notre Dame	Nathan Gerbe, Boston Coll, F

DIVISION II *(Discontinued)*

Year	Champion	Coach	Score	Runner-Up
1978	Merrimack	Thom Lawler	12–2	Lake Forest
1979	Lowell	Bill Riley Jr	6–4	Mankato St
1980	Mankato St	Don Brose	5–2	Elmira
1981	Lowell	Bill Riley Jr	5–4	Plattsburgh St
1982	Lowell	Bill Riley Jr	6–1	Plattsburgh St
1983	RIT	Brian Mason	4–2	Bemidji St
1984	Bemidji St	R.H. (Bob) Peters	14–4*	Merrimack
1993	Bemidji St	R.H. (Bob) Peters	15–6*	Mercyhurst
1994	Bemidji St	R.H. (Bob) Peters	7–6*	Ala.–Huntsville
1995	Bemidji St	R.H. (Bob) Peters	11–6*	Mercyhurst
1996	Ala.–Huntsville	Doug Ross	10–1*	Bemidji St
1997	Bemidji St	R.H. (Bob) Peters	7–4*	Ala.–Huntsville
1998	Ala.–Huntsville	Doug Ross	11–4*	Bemidji St
1999	St. Michael's (Vt.)	Lou DiMasi	12–9*	New Hamp. Coll

*Two-game, total-goal series.

Ice Hockey *(Cont.)*

Men *(Cont.)*

DIVISION III

Year	Champion	Coach	Score	Runner-Up
1984	Babson	Bob Riley	8–0	Union (N.Y.)
1985	RIT	Bruce Delventhal	5–1	Bemidji St
1986	Bemidji St	R.H. (Bob) Peters	8–5	Vacated
1987	Vacated			Oswego St
1988	UW-River Falls	Rick Kozuback	7–1, 3–5, 3–0	Elmira
1989	UW-Stevens Point	Mark Mazzoleni	3–3, 3–2	RIT
1990	UW-Stevens Point	Mark Mazzoleni	10–1, 3–6, 1–0	Plattsburgh St
1991	UW-Stevens Point	Mark Mazzoleni	6–2	Mankato St
1992	Plattsburgh St	Bob Emery	7–3	UW-Stevens Point
1993	UW-Stevens Point	Joe Baldarotta	4–3	UW-River Falls
1994	UW-River Falls	Dean Talafous	6–4	UW-Superior
1995	Middlebury	Bill Beaney	1–0	Fredonia St
1996	Middlebury	Bill Beaney	3–2	RIT
1997	Middlebury	Bill Beaney	3–2	UW-Superior
1998	Middlebury	Bill Beaney	2–1	UW-Stevens Point
1999	Middlebury	Bill Beaney	5–0	UW-Superior
2000	Norwich	Michael McShane	2–1	St. Thomas (Minn.)
2001	Plattsburgh	Bob Emery	6–2	RIT
2002	UW-Superior	Dan Stauber	3–2	Norwich
2003	Norwich	Michael McShane	2–1	Oswego St
2004	Middlebury	Bill Beaney	1–0	St. Norbert
2005	Middlebury	Bill Beaney	5–0	St. Thomas (Minn.)
2006	Middlebury	Bill Beaney	3–0	St. Norbert
2007	Oswego	Ed Gosek	4–3	Middlebury
2008	St. Norbert	Tim Coghlin	2–0	Plattsburgh St

Women - DIVISION I

Year	Champion	Coach	Score	Runner-Up
2001	Minn.-Duluth	Shannon Miller	4–2	St. Lawrence
2002	Minn.-Duluth	Shannon Miller	3–2	Brown
2003	Minn.-Duluth	Shannon Miller	4–3 (2 OT)	Harvard
2004	Minnesota	Laura Holldorson	6–2	Harvard
2005	Minnesota	Laura Holldorson	4–3	Harvard
2006	Wisconsin	Mark Johnson	3–0	Minnesota
2007	Wisconsin	Mark Johnson	4–1	Minnesota
2008	Minn.-Duluth	Shannon Miller	4–0	Wisconsin

Soccer

Men - DIVISION I

Year	Champion	Coach	Score	Runner-Up
1959	St. Louis	Bob Guelker	5–2	Bridgeport
1960	St. Louis	Bob Guelker	3–2	Maryland
1961	West Chester	Mel Lorback	2–0	St. Louis
1962	St. Louis	Bob Guelker	4–3	Maryland
1963	St. Louis	Bob Guelker	3–0	Navy
1964	Navy	F.H. Warner	1–0	Michigan St
1965	St. Louis	Bob Guelker	1–0	Michigan St
1966	San Francisco	Steve Negoesco	5–2	LIU–Brooklyn
1967	Michigan St St. Louis	Gene Kenney Harry Keough	0–0	Game called due to inclement weather
1968	Maryland Michigan St	Doyle Royal Gene Kenney	2–2 (2 OT)	
1969	St. Louis	Harry Keough	4–0	San Francisco
1970	St. Louis	Harry Keough	1–0	UCLA
1971	Vacated		3–2	St. Louis
1972	St. Louis	Harry Keough	4–2	UCLA
1973	St. Louis	Harry Keough	2–1 (OT)	UCLA
1974	Howard	Lincoln Phillips	2–1 (4 OT)	St. Louis
1975	San Francisco	Steve Negoesco	4–0	SIU–Edwardsville
1976	San Francisco	Steve Negoesco	1–0	Indiana
1977	Hartwick	Jim Lennox	2–1	San Francisco
1978	Vacated		2–0	Indiana

Soccer

Men - DIVISION I *(CONT.)*

Year	Champion	Coach	Score	Runner-Up
1979	SIU–Edwardsville	Bob Guelker	3–2	Clemson
1980	San Francisco	Steve Negoesco	4–3 (OT)	Indiana
1981	Connecticut	Joe Morrone	2–1 (OT)	Alabama A&M
1982	Indiana	Jerry Yeagley	2–1 (8 OT)	Duke
1983	Indiana	Jerry Yeagley	1–0 (2 OT)	Columbia
1984	Clemson	I.M. Ibrahim	2–1	Indiana
1985	UCLA	Sigi Schmid	1–0 (8 OT)	American
1986	Duke	John Rennie	1–0	Akron
1987	Clemson	I.M. Ibrahim	2–0	San Diego St
1988	Indiana	Jerry Yeagley	1–0	Howard
1989	Santa Clara	Steve Sampson	1–1 (2 OT)	
	Virginia	Bruce Arena		
1990	UCLA	Sigi Schmid	1–0 (OT)	Rutgers
1991	Virginia	Bruce Arena	0–0*	Santa Clara
1992	Virginia	Bruce Arena	2–0	San Diego
1993	Virginia	Bruce Arena	2–0	South Carolina
1994	Virginia	Bruce Arena	1–0	Indiana
1995	Wisconsin	Jim Launder	2–0	Duke
1996	St. John's (N.Y.)	Dave Masur	4–1	Florida International
1997	UCLA	Sigi Schmid	2–1	Virginia
1998	Indiana	Jerry Yeagley	3–1	Stanford
1999	Indiana	Jerry Yeagley	1–0	Santa Clara
2000	Connecticut	Ray Reid	2–0	Creighton
2001	N.Carolina	Elmar Bolowich	2–0	Indiana
2002	UCLA	Tom Fitzgerald	1–0	Stanford
2003	Indiana	Jerry Yeagley	2–1	St. John's (N.Y.)
2004	Indiana	Jerry Yeagley	1–1 (2 OT 3-2)	UC–Santa Barbara
2005	Maryland	Sasho Cirovski	1–0	New Mexico
2006	UC-Santa Barbara	Tim Vom Steeg	2–1	UCLA
2007	Wake Forest	Tony da Luz	2–0	Ohio St

*Under a rule passed in 1991, the NCAA determined that when a score is tied after regulation and overtime, and the championship is determined by penalty kicks, the official score will be 0–0.

Men - DIVISION II

Year	Champion
1972	SIU–Edwardsville
1973	Missouri–St. Louis
1974	Adelphi
1975	Baltimore
1976	Loyola (Md.)
1977	Alabama A&M
1978	Seattle Pacific
1979	Alabama A&M
1980	Lock Haven
1981	Tampa
1982	Florida International
1983	Seattle Pacific
1984	Florida International
1985	Seattle Pacific
1986	Seattle Pacific
1987	Southern Conn St
1988	Florida Tech
1989	New Hampshire College
1990	Southern Conn St
1991	Florida Tech
1992	Southern Conn St
1993	Seattle Pacific
1994	Tampa
1995	Southern Conn St
1996	Grand Canyon
1997	CSU-Bakersfield
1998	Southern Conn St
1999	Southern Conn St
2000	CSU–Dominguez Hills
2001	Tampa
2002	Sonoma St
2003	Lynn
2004	Seattle
2005	Fort Lewis
2006	Dowling (N.Y.)
2007	Franklin Pierce

Men - DIVISION III

Year	Champion
1974	Brockport St
1975	Babson
1976	Brandeis
1977	Lock Haven
1978	Lock Haven
1979	Babson
1980	Babson
1981	Glassboro St
1982	NC–Greensboro
1983	NC–Greensboro
1984	Wheaton (Ill.)
1985	NC–Greensboro
1986	NC–Greensboro
1987	NC–Greensboro
1988	UC–San Diego
1989	Elizabethtown
1990	Glassboro St
1991	UC–San Diego
1992	Kean
1993	UC–San Diego
1994	Bethany (W.V.)
1995	Williams
1996	College of New Jersey*
1997	Wheaton (Ill.)
1998	Ohio Wesleyan
1999	St. Lawrence
2000	Messiah
2001	Richard Stockton
2002	Messiah
2003	Trinity (Tex.)
2004	Messiah
2005	Messiah
2006	Messiah
2007	Middlebury

*Formerly Trenton St

Women

DIVISION I

Year	Champion	Coach	Score	Runner-Up
1982	North Carolina	Anson Dorrance	2–0	Central Florida
1983	North Carolina	Anson Dorrance	4–0	George Mason
1984	North Carolina	Anson Dorrance	2–0	Connecticut
1985	George Mason	Hank Leung	2–0	North Carolina
1986	North Carolina	Anson Dorrance	2–0	Colorado College
1987	North Carolina	Anson Dorrance	1–0	Massachusetts
1988	North Carolina	Anson Dorrance	4–1	North Carolina St
1989	North Carolina	Anson Dorrance	2–0	Colorado College
1990	North Carolina	Anson Dorrance	6–0	Connecticut
1991	North Carolina	Anson Dorrance	3–1	Wisconsin
1992	North Carolina	Anson Dorrance	9–1	Duke
1993	North Carolina	Anson Dorrance	6–0	George Mason
1994	North Carolina	Anson Dorrance	5–0	Notre Dame
1995	Notre Dame	Chris Petrucelli	1–0	Portland
1996	North Carolina	Anson Dorrance	1–0	Notre Dame
1997	North Carolina	Anson Dorrance	2–0	Connecticut
1998	Florida	Becky Burleigh	1–0	North Carolina
1999	North Carolina	Anson Dorrance	2–0	Notre Dame
2000	North Carolina	Anson Dorrance	2–1	UCLA
2001	Santa Clara	Jerry Smith	1–0	North Carolina
2002	Portland	Clive Charles	2–1	Santa Clara
2003	North Carolina	Anson Dorrance	6–0	Connecticut
2004	Norte Dame	Randy Waldrum	1–1 (OT 4–3)	UCLA
2005	Portland	Garrett Smith	4–0	UCLA
2006	North Carolina	Anson Dorrance	2–1	Notre Dame
2007	USC	Ali Khosroshahin	2–0	Florida St

DIVISION II

Year	Champion
1988	CSU–Hayward
1989	Barry
1990	Sonoma St
1991	CSU–Dominguez Hills
1992	Barry
1993	Barry
1994	Franklin Pierce
1995	Franklin Pierce
1996	Franklin Pierce
1997	Franklin Pierce
1998	Lynn
1999	Franklin Pierce
2000	UC-San Diego
2001	UC-San Diego
2002	Christian Brothers
2003	Kennesaw St
2004	Metro St
2005	Nebraska-Omaha
2006	Metro St
2007	Tampa

DIVISION III

Year	Champion
1986	Rochester
1987	Rochester
1988	William Smith
1989	UC–San Diego
1990	Ithaca
1991	Ithaca
1992	Cortland St
1993	Trenton St
1994	Trenton St
1995	UC–San Diego
1996	UC–San Diego
1997	UC–San Diego
1998	Macalester
1999	UC–San Diego
2000	College of New Jersey*
2001	Ohio Wesleyan
2002	Ohio Wesleyan
2003	Oneonta St
2004	Wheaton College
2005	Messiah
2006	Wheaton (Ill.)
2007	Wheaton (Ill.)

Olympics

SIMON BRUTY

Michael Phelps won eight gold medals and set seven world records in Beijing.

Welcome To The Future

Fear and controversy surrounded the 2008 Summer Olympics in Beijing, but neither was as gripping as the competition

BY MERRELL NODEN

THAT LOUD EXHALATION YOU heard on August 24th, the night of the Closing Ceremony at the Beijing Olympics? It wasn't Michael Phelps heaving a sigh of relief at pulling off his audacious goal of going eight-for-eight in gold medal swims. No, what you heard was the members of the International Olympic Committee exhaling in unison as they watched the Olympic torch being passed from Beijing to London. The 2008 Games were over, and not one of their quite reasonable fears—deadly pollution, terrorist attacks, televised scenes of brutal repression—had come to pass.

Not that the Chinese authorities had entirely kept their promise to respect human rights as practiced in the democratic, 21st-century world they aspire to join. They hadn't: Journalists found that certain "controversial" websites, like Amnesty International's, were being blocked, while protest zones set up by the government were never occupied because police arrested anyone who got near them. Even the Opening Ceremony, which was rumored to cost $300 million and universally acclaimed to be the most spectacular we have ever seen—and ever will see—put one uncomfortably in mind of a totalitarian rally, as a sea of drummers—2,008 to be exact—pounded in unison and some 22,000 human cogs enacted scenes from Chinese history illuminated by flashes from 43,000 fireworks. The overall effect was breathtaking, but only if you could overlook the strict regimentation that made it possible.

But whatever the methods of their leaders, the Chinese people were magnificent hosts, bursting with pride to be hosting such an important event. The facilities, from the "Bird's Nest" main stadium to the "Water Cube" natatorium and a road cycling course that passed the Great Wall, were breathtaking. Once the Games had begun, the athletes, as always, performed so magnificently it was hard to take your eyes off them.

Who were the big winners in Beijing? Phelps, for sure. His big toothy grin was everywhere, even though there was real drama in only two of his swims. In the 400-meter freestyle relay, anchor Jason Lezak turned a body length behind world record holder Alain Bernard and swam him down in the final 50 to keep Phelps on track. And in Phelps's only other close call, the 100 fly, he somehow managed to out-touch Milorad Cavic of Serbia, whose fingers were only inches from the wall when Phelps's were

JOHN W. MCDONOUGH

Led by coach Mike Krzyzewski (front row, 3rd from right), the U.S. men's basketball team defeated Spain to win gold at Beijing.

still down near his hips. It sure looked as if Cavic had won, and the Serbs filed a protest before being satisfied by slow-motion replay that Phelps had indeed won. The eight gold medals Phelps won in Beijing surpassed Mark Spitz's record for a single Games, and his career total of 14 beat the former record of ten held by Olympian Ray Ewry. The Beijing Games will always be remembered as Phelps's, just as the 1936 Games belonged to Jesse Owens.

But just as exhilarating—and far more unexpected—was the performance of Jamaican sprinter Usain Bolt. Taller than any top sprinter before him and far more extroverted than the rest of that stone-faced brotherhood, Bolt became the first person to set world records while winning both the 100 (9.69) and 200 (19.30) and anchoring the relay (37.10). But it was not Bolt's speed that awed us, it was the ease with which he ran, easing up and gesturing to the fans some 20 meters before the 100's finish.

There were allegations—later dispelled—that the Chinese lied about the age of some of their gymnasts, using several who were younger than the permitted 16 years old. Whatever the age of the competition, it didn't stop American Nastia Liukin, the willowy 19-year-old daughter of a Soviet gold medalist, from winning the all-round and four other medals. And Liukin's teammate Shawn Johnson, who had been favored in the all-round, also won four medals, including gold in the balance beam.

Those were the individual stars of the Games but some U.S. teams did well, too. The so-called "Redeem Team" of NBA stars beat everyone in sight to avenge their predecessor's weak bronze showing in Athens, and the U.S. women won gold too. Teams in two sports being removed from the Games didn't fare so well. The U.S. baseball team got a disappointing bronze

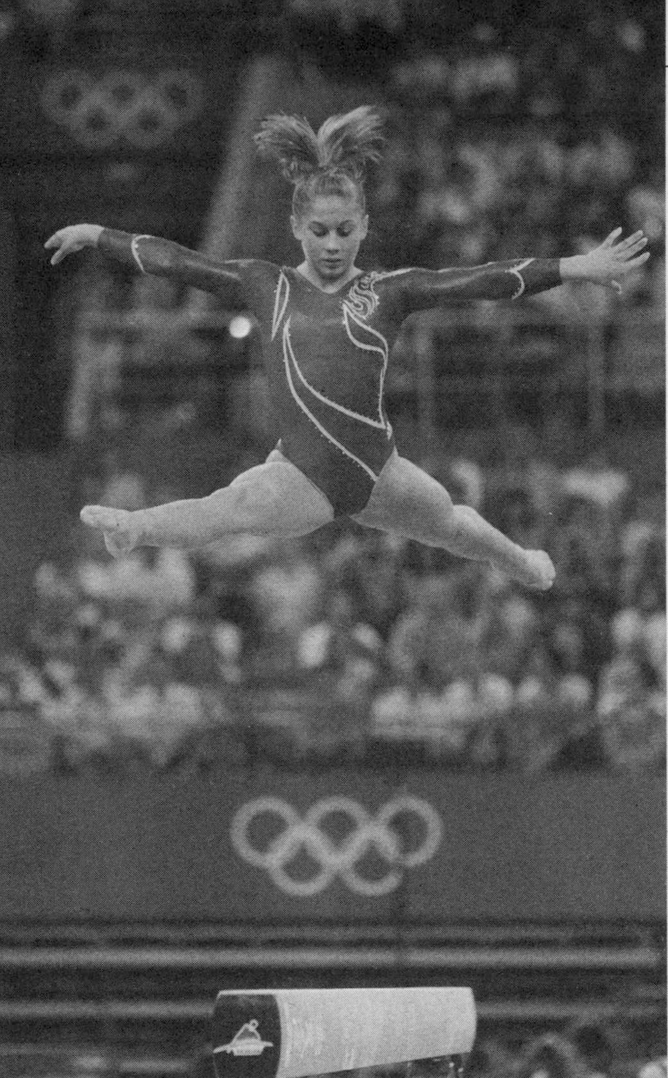

PETER READ MILLER

Among Johnson's four medals at the 2008 Summer Games was a gold in the balance beam.

Todd Bachman, father-in-law of assistant coach Hugh McCutcheon, was murdered, and his wife critically injured, in a random non-political stabbing while visiting Beijing's Drum Tower.

In the end, the U.S. took home the most medals but did not come close to China in golds (earning 36 to China's 51). Chinese athletes fared especially well in diving, winning nine of 10 possible golds, as well as weightlifting; badminton; table tennis; and gymnastics, where Wei Yang won the men's all-around title.

And so it's on to London, where organizers have already acknowledged that they have neither the funds nor the control over their citizenry to dream of outdoing the Chinese effort. One suspects that things won't run quite so perfectly in jolly old London as in Beijing, but that may well be a good thing. As IOC head Jacques Rogge said of the Beijing Games, "The IOC and the Olympic Games cannot force changes on sovereign nations or solve all the ills of the world. But we can, and we do, contribute to positive change through sport."

That's a pretty fair summary of what we can expect of our modern Olympic Games. The Beijing Olympics may yet produce the "positive change" Rogge hopes for. When, exactly, that might happen is another question.

medal, while Japan beat the U.S. women for gold in softball. Even more disappointing was the U.S. boxing team: Only two of its members made the quarterfinals and only one got a medal, Deontay Wilder's bronze at 91 kg.

NBC favorites Misty May-Trainor and Kerry Walsh defended the gold they'd won in Athens. But the more compelling story was the U.S. men's volleyball team's upset of Brazil, three games to one. This was perhaps the most emotional win of the Games. Two weeks before the gold medal match,

2008 Summer Games

TRACK AND FIELD

Men

100 METERS

1. ...Usain Bolt Jamaica 9.69 WR
2. ...Richard Thompson, Trinidad 9.89
3. ...Walter Dix, United States 9.91

200 METERS

1. ...Usain Bolt, Jamaica 19.30 WR
2. ...Shawn Crawford, United States 19.96
3. ...Walter Dix, United States 19.98

400 METERS

1. ...Lashawn Merritt, United States 43.75
2. ...Jeremy Wariner, United States 44.74
3. ...David Neville, United States 44.80

800 METERS

1. ...Wilfred Kipkemboi Bungei, Kenya 1:44.65
2. ...Ismail Ahmed Ismail, Sudan 1:44.70
3. ...Alfred Kirwa Yego, Kenya 1:44.82

1,500 METERS

1. ...Rasheed Ramzi, Bahrain 3:32.94
2. ...Asbel Kipruto Kiprop, Kenya 3:33.11
3. ...Nick Willis, New Zealand 3:34.16

5,000 METERS

1. ...Kenenisa Bekele, Ethiopia 12:57.82 OR
2. ...Eliud Kipchoge, Kenya 13:02.80
3. ...Edwin Cheruiyot Soi , Kenya 13:06.22

10,000 METERS

1. ...Kenenisa Bekele, Ethiopia 27:01.17 OR
2. ...Sileshi Sihine, Ethiopia 27:02.77
3. ...Micah Kikemboi Kogo, Kenya 27:04.11

MARATHON

1. ...Samuel Kamau, Kenya 2:06:32 OR
2. ...Jaouad Gharib, Morocco 2:07:16
3. ...Tsegay Kebede, Ethiopia 2:!0:00

110-METER HURDLES

1. ...Dayron Robles, Cuba 12.93
2. ....David Payne, United States 13.17
3. ....David Oliver, United States 13.18

400-METER HURDLES

1. ...Angelo Taylor, United States 47.25
2. ...Kerron Clement, United States 47.98
3. ...Bershawn Jackson, United States 48.06

3,000-METER STEEPLECHASE

1. ...Brimin Kipruto, Kenya 8:10.34
2. ...Mahiedine Mekissi-Banabbad, France 8:10.49
3. ...Richard Kipkemboi Mateelong, Kenya 8:11.01

4 X 100-METER RELAY

1. ...Jamaica (A. Powell, M. Frater Usain Bolt, N. Carter) 37.10 WR
2. ...Trinidad & Tobago 38.06
3. ...Japan 38.15

4 X 400-METER RELAY

1. ...United States: (A. Taylor J. Wariner, L. Merritt, D. Neville) 2.55.39 OR
2. ...Bahamas 2.58.03
3. ...Russia 2.58.06

20-KILOMETER WALK

1. ...Valeriy Borchin, Russia 1:19.01
2. ...Jefferson Perez, Ecuador 1:19.15
3. ...Jared Tallent, Australia 1:19.42

50-KILOMETER WALK

1. ...Alex Schwazer, Italy 3:37.09 OR
2. ...Jared Tallent, Australia 3:39.27
3. ...Denis Nizhegorodov, Russia 3:40.14

HIGH JUMP

1. ...Andrey Silnov, Russia 7 ft 9 in
2. ...Germaine Mason, Great Britian 7 ft 8 in
3. ...Yaroslav Rybakov, Russia 7 ft 8 in

POLE VAULT

1. ...Steve Hooker, Australia 19 ft 6½ in OR
2. ...Eugeny Lukyanenko, Russia 19 ft 2¼ in
3. ...Denys Yurchenko, Ukraine 18 ft 8½ in

LONG JUMP

1. ...Irving Jahir Saladino, Panama 27 ft 4¼ in
2. ...Godfrey Khotso Mokoena, S. Africa 27 ft ½ in
3. ...Ibrahim Camejo, Cuba 26 ft 10¾ in

TRIPLE JUMP

1. ...Nelson Evora, Portugal 57 ft 11½ in
2. ...Phillips Idowa, Great Britian 57 ft 9¾ in
3. ...Leevan Sands, Bahamas 57 ft 8½ in

SHOT PUT

1. ...Tomasz Majewski, Poland 70 ft 6¾ in
2. ...Christian Cantwell, United States 69 ft 2¼ in
3. ...Andrei Mikhnevich, Belarus 69 ft ¾ in

DISCUS THROW

1. ...Gerd Kanter, Estonia 225 ft 9½ in
2. ...Piotr Malachowski, Poland 222 ft 6 in
3. ...Virgilijus Alekna, Lithuania 222 ft 4¾ in

HAMMER THROW

1. ...Primoz Kozmus, Slovenia 269 ft 1 in
2. ...Vadim Devyaovskiy, Belarus 267 ft 9 in
3. ...Ivan Tsikhan, Belarus 267 ft 5 in

JAVELIN

1. ...Andreas Thorkildsen, Norway 297 ft 1¾ in OR
2. ...Ainars Kovals, Latvia 284 ft 3 in
3. ...Tero Pitkamaki, Finland 282 ft 8 in

DECATHLON

Pts

1. ...Bryan Clay, United States 8791
2. ...Andrei Krauchanka,Belarus 8551
3. ...Leonel Suarez, Cuba 8527

TRACK AND FIELD

Women

100 METERS

1. ...Shelly-Ann Fraser, Jamaica 10.78
2. ...Sherone Simpson, Jamaica 10.98
2. ...Kerron Stewart, Jamaica 10.98

200 METERS

1. ...Veronica Campbell-Brown, Jamaica 21.74
2. ...Allyson Felix, United States 21.93
3. ...Kerron Stewart, Jamaica 22.00

Note: OR=Olympic Record. WR=World Record. EOR=Equals Olympic Record. EWR=Equals World Record.

TRACK AND FIELD (CONT.)

Women *(Cont.)*

400 METERS

1. ...Christine Ohuruogo, Great Britain 49.62
2. ...Shericka Williams, Jamaica 49.69
3. ...Sanya Richards, United States 49.93

800 METERS

1. ...Pamela Jelimo, Kenya 1:54.87
2. ...J. Jepkosgei Busienei, Kenya 1:56.07
3. ...Hasna Benhassi, Morocco 1:56.73

1,500 METERS

1. ...Nancy Jebet Lagat, Kenya 4:00.23
2. ...Iryna Lishchynska, Ukraine 4:01.63
3. ...Nataliya Tobias, Ukraine 4:01.78

5,000 METERS

1. ...Tirunesh Dibaba Kenene, Ethiopia 15:41.40
2. ...Elvan Abeylegesse, Turkey 15:42.74
3. ...Meseret Defar Tola, Ethiopia 15:44.96

10,000 METERS

1. ...Tirunesh Dibaba Kenene, Ethiopia 29:54.66 OR
2. ...Elvan Abeylegesse, Turkey 29:56.34
3. ...Shalane Flanagan, United States 30:22.22

MARATHON

1. ...Constantina Tomescu Dita, Romania 2:26:44
2. ...Nyambura Wincatherine, Kenya 2:27:06
3. ...Zhou Chunxiu, China 2:27:07

100-METER HURDLES

1. ...Dawn Harper, United States 12.54
2. ...Sally McLellan, Australia 12.64
3. ...Priscilla Lopes-Schliep, Canada 12.64

400-METER HURDLES

1. ...Melaine Walker, Jamaica 52.64 OR
2. ...Sheena Tosta, United States 53.70
3. ...Tasha Danvers, Great Britain 53.84

3,000-METER STEEPLECHASE

1. ...Gulnara Samitova-Galkina, Russia 8:58.81 WR
2. ...Eunice Jepkorir, Kenya 9:07.41
3. ...Yekaterina Volkova, Russia 9:07.64

4 X 100-METER RELAY

1. ...Russia (Y. Chermoshanskaya, Y. Gushchina, E. Polyakova, A. Fedoriva) 42.31
2. ...Belgium 42.54
3. ...Nigeria 43.04

4 X 400-METER RELAY

1. ...United States (A. Felix, S. Richards, M. Henderson, M. Wineberg) 3:18.54
2. ...Russia 3:18.82
3. ...Jamaica 3:20.40

20-KILOMETER WALK

1. ...Olga Kaniskina, Russia 1:26:31 OR
2. ...Kjersti Tysse Platzer, Norway 1:27:07
3. ...Elisa Rigaudo, Italy 1:27:12

HIGH JUMP

1. ...Tia Hellebaut, Belgium 6 ft 8¾ in
2. ...Blanka Vlasic, Croatia 6 ft 8¾ in
3. ...Anna Chicherova, Russia 6 ft 8 in

POLE VAULT

1. ...Yelena Isinbayeva, Russia 16 ft 6¾ in WR
2. ...Jennifer Stuczynski, United States 15 ft 9 in
3. ...Svetlana Feofanova, Russia 15 ft 7 in

LONG JUMP

1. ...Maurren Higa Maggi, Brazil 23 ft 1 in
2. ...Tatiana Lebedeva, Russia 23 ft
3. ...Blessing Okhagbare, Nigeria 22 ft 8 in

TRIPLE JUMP

1. ...Francoise Mbango Etone, Cameroon 50 ft 5 in
2. ...Tatiana Lebdeva, Russia 50 ft 3 in
3. ...Hrysopiyi Devetzi, Greece 49 ft 11½ in

SHOT PUT

1. ...Valerie Vili, New Zealand 67 ft 5½ in
2. ...Natallia Mikhnevich, Belarus 66 ft 6½ in
3. ...Nadzeya Ostapchuk, Belarus 65 ft 2 in

DISCUS THROW

1. ...Stephanie Brown-Trafton, United States 212 ft 4¾ in
2. ...Yarelys Barrios, Cuba 208 ft 9½ in
3. ...Olena Antonova, Ukraine 205 ft 4 in

JAVELIN

1. ...Barbora Spotakova, Czech Republic 234 ft 3¾ in
2. ...Maria Abakumova, Russia 232 ft 2½ in
3. ...Christina Obergfoll, Germany 216 ft 11½ in

HEPTATHLON **Pts**

1. ...Natalia Dobrynska, Ukraine 6733
2. ...Hyleas Fountain, United States 6619
3. ...Tatiana Chernova, Russia 6591

HAMMER THROW

1. ...Aksana Miankova, Belarus 250 ft 5½ in OR
2. ...Yipsi Moreno, Cuba 246 ft 8½ in
3. ...Zhang Wenxiu, China 243 ft 10 in

INDIVIDUAL ARCHERY

Men

1. ...Viktor Ruban, Ukraine
2. ...Kyung-Mo Park, South Korea
3. ...Bair Badenov, Russia

Women

1. ...Zhang Juan Juan, China
2. ...Sung-Hyun Park, South Korea
3. ...Ok-Hee Yun, South Korea

TEAM ARCHERY

Men

1. ....South Korea
2. ....Italy
3. ....China

Women

1. ....South Korea
2. ....China
3. .... France

Note: OR=Olympic Record. WR=World Record. EOR=Equals Olympic Record. EWR=Equals World Record.

BADMINTON

Men

SINGLES

1. ....Lin Dan, China
2. ....Chong,Wei Lee, Malaysia
3. ....Chen Jin, China

DOUBLES

1. ....M.Kido/H. Setiawan, Indonesia
2. ....H. Fu/Y. Yun, China
3. ....L.Jaejin/H. Jiman, South Korea

Women

SINGLES

1. .... Zhang Ning, China
2. ....Xingfang Xie, China
3. ....Maria Kristin Yulianti, Indonesia

DOUBLES

1. .....D. Jing/Yu Yang, China
2. ....H. Lee/K. Lee, South Korea
3. ....Y. Wei/Y. Zhang, China

MIXED DOUBLES

1. Y. Lee/H. Lee, South Korea
2. N. Widianto/ L. Natsir, Indonesia
3. He Hanbin/ Yu Yang, China

BMX

Men

1. ....Maris Strombergs, Latvia
2. ....Mike Day, United States
3. ....Donny Robinson, United States

Women

1. ....Anne-Caroline Chausson, France
2. ....Laetitia le Corquille, France
3. ....Jill Kintner, United States

BASEBALL

1. .....South Korea
2. .....Cuba
3. .....United States

BASKETBALL

Men

Final: United States 118, Spain 107
Argentina (3rd)
United States: Carmelo Anthony, Carlos Boozer, Chris Bosh, Kobe Bryant, Dwight Howard, LeBron James, Jason Kidd, Chris Paul, Tayshaun Prince, Michael Redd, Dwyane Wade, Deron Williams

Women

Final: United States 92, Australia 65
Russia (3rd)
United States: Seimone Augustus, Sue Bird, Sylvia Fowles, Lisa Leslie, DeLisha Milton-Jones, Candace Parker, Cappie Pondexter, Tamika Catchings, Tina Thompson, Diana Taurasi, Katie Smith

BOXING

LIGHT FLYWEIGHT (106 LB)

1. ......Zou Shiming, China
2. ......Serdamba Pureydori, Mongolia
3. ......Paddy Barnes, Ireland
3. ......Yampier Hernandez, Cuba

FLYWEIGHT (112 LB)

1. ......Somit Jongjohor, Thailand
2. ......Andris Laffita Hernandez, Cuba
3. ......Vincenzo Picardi, Italy
3. ......Georgy Balakshin, Russia

BANTAMWEIGHT (119 LB)

1. ......Badar-Uugan Enkhbat, Mongolia
2. ......Yankiel Leon Alarcon, Cuba
3. ......Veaceslav Gojan, Moldova
3. ......Bruno Julie, Mauritius

FEATHERWEIGHT (125 LB)

1. ......Vasyl Lomachenko, Ukraine
2. ......Khedafi Djelkhir, France
3. ......Shahin Imranov, Azerbaijan
3. ......Yakup Kilic, Turkey

LIGHTWEIGHT (132 LB)

1. ......Alexey Tishchenko, Russia
2. ......Daouda Sow, France
3. ......Hrachik Javakhyan, Armenia
3. ......Yordenis Ugas, Cuba

LIGHT WELTERWEIGHT (139 LB)

1. ......Felix Diaz, Dominican Republic
2. ......Manus Boonjumnong, Thailand
3. ......Alexis Vastine, France
3. ......Roniel Iglesias Sotolongo, Cuba

WELTERWEIGHT (147 LB)

1. ......Bakhyt Sarsekbayev, Kazakhstan
2. ......Carlos Banteaux Suarez, Cuba
3. ......Hanati Silamu, China
3. ......Kim Jungjoo, South Korea

MIDDLEWEIGHT (165 LB)

1. ......James Degale, Great Britain
2. ......Emilio Correa Bayeaux, Cuba
3. ......Vjender, India
3. ......Darren John Sutherland, Ireland

LIGHT HEAVYWEIGHT (178 LB)

1. ......Zhang Xiaoping, China
2. ......Kenny Egan, Ireland
3. ......Tony Jeffries, Great Britain
3. ......Yerkebulan Shynaliyev, Kazakhstan

HEAVYWEIGHT (201 LB)

1. ......Rakhim Chakhkiev, Russia
2. ....Clemente Russo, Italy
3. ......Deontay Wilder, United States
3. ......Osmai Acosta Duarte, Cuba

SUPERHEAVYWEIGHT (201+ LB)

1. ......Roberto Cammarelle, Italy
2. ......Zhang Zhilei, China
3. ......David Price, Great Britain
3. ......Vyacheslav Glazkov, Ukraine

CANOE/KAYAK

Men

C-1 FLATWATER 500 METERS

1....Maxim Opalev, Russia	1:47.140
2....David Cal, Spain	1:48.397
3....Iurli Cheban, Ukraine	1:48.766

C-1 FLATWATER 1,000 METERS

1....Attila Sandor Vajda, Hungary	3:50.467
2....David Cal, Spain	3:52.751
3....Thomas Hall, Canada	3:53.653

C-2 FLATWATER 500 METERS

1....M. Guanliang/Y. Wenjun, China	1:41.025
2....A. Kostogold/S. Ulegin, Russia	1:41.282
3....C. Gille/T. Wylenzek, Germany	1:41.964

C-2 FLATWATER 1,000 METERS

1....Aliaksandr/Andrei Bahdanovich, Belarus	3:36.365
2....C. Gille/T. Wylenzek, Germany	3:36.588
3....G. Kozmann/T. Kiss, Hungary	3:40.258

C-1 WHITEWATER SLALOM

	Pts
1....Michal Martikan, Slovakia	176.65
2....David Florence, Great Britain	178.61
3....Robin Bell, Australia	180.59

C-2 WHITEWATER SLALOM

	Pts
1....Pavel/Peter Hochschorner, Slovakia	190.82
2....J. Volf/O. Stepanek, Czech Republic	192.89
3....M. Kuznetsov/D. Larionov, Russia	197.37

CANOE/KAYAK

Men (*Cont.*)

K-1 FLATWATER 500 METERS

1. ...Ken Wallace, Australia 1:37.252
2. ...Adam van Koeverden, Canada 1:37.630
3. ...Tim Brabants, Great Britain 1:37.671

K-1 FLATWATER 1,000 METERS

1. ...Tim Brabants, Great Britain 3:26.323
2. ...Erik Veraas Larsen, Norway 3:27.342
3. ...Ken Wallace, Australia 3:27.485

K-2 FLATWATER 1,000 METERS

1. ...A. Ihle/M. Hollstein, Germany 3:11.809
2. ...K. Knudsen/R. Poulsen, Denmark 3:13.580
3. ...A. Facchin/A. Scaduto, Italy 3:14.750

K-2 FLATWATER 5000 METERS

1. ...S. Cravlotto/C. Perez, Spain 1:28.736
2. ...R. Rauhe/T. Wieskotler, Germany 1:28.827
3. ...P. Piatrushenka/V. Makehneu, Belarus 1:30.005

K-4 FLATWATER 1,000 METERS

1. ...Belarus 2:55.714
2. ...Slovakia 2:56.593
3. ...Germany 2:56.676

Women

K-1 FLATWATER 500 METERS

1. ...Inna Osypenko-Radomska, Ukraine 1:50.673
2. ...Josefa Idem, Italy 1:50.677
3. ...Katrin Wagner-Augustin, Germany 1:51.022

K-2 FLATWATER 500 METERS

1. ...K. Kovacs/N. Janic, Hungary 1:41.308
2. ...A. Konieczna/B. Mikolajczyk, Poland 1:42.092
3. ...M. Delattre/A. Viard, France 1:42.128

K-4 FLATWATER 500 METERS

1. ...Germany 1:32.231
2. ...Hungary 1:32.971
3. ...Australia 1:34.704

K-1 WHITEWATER SLALOM Pts

1. ...Elena Kaliska, Slovakia 192.64
2. ...Jacqueline Lawrence, Australia 206.94
3. ...Violetta Oblinger Peters, Austria 214.77

CYCLING–Men

ROAD RACE

1. ...Samuel Sanchez, Spain 6:23:49
2. ...David Rebellin, Italy 6:23:49
3. ...Fabian Cancellara, Switzerland 6:23:49

INDIVIDUAL TIME TRIAL

1. ...Fabian Cancellara, Switzerland 1:02:11.43
2. ...Gustav Larsson, Sweden 1:02:44.79
3. ...Levi Leipheimer, United States 1:03:21.11

4,000-METER INDIVIDUAL PURSUIT

1. ...Bradley Wiggins, Great Britain 4:16.977
2. ...Hayden Roulston, New Zealand 4:19.611
3. ...Steven Burke, Great Britain 4:20.947

4,000-METER TEAM PURSUIT

1. ...Great Britain (Ed Clancy, Paul Manning, Geraint Thomas, Bradley WIggins) 3:53.314 WR
2. ...Denmark 4:00.040
3. ...New Zealand 3:57.776

SPRINT

1. ...Chris Hoy, Great Britain 9.815 OR
2. ...Jason Kenny, Great Britain 9.857
3. ...Stefan Nimke, Germany 10.064

POINTS RACE

1. ...Juan Llaneras, Spain 60,2
2. ...Roger Kluge, Germany 58,2
3. ...Chris Newton, Great Britain 56,2

KIERIN

1. ...Chris Hoy, Great Britain
2. ...Ross Edgar, Great Britain
3. ...Kiyofumi Nagai, Japan

MADISON

1. ...J. Curuchet/W. Perez, Argentina 8,0
2. ...J. Llaneras/A. Tauler, Spain 7,0
3. ...M. Ignatyev/A. Markov, Russia 6,0

OLYMPIC SPRINT

1. ...Great Britain 43.128
2. ...France 43.651
3. ...Germany 44.014

CROSS COUNTRY

1. ...Julien Absalon, France 1:55.59
2. ...Jean-Christophe Peraud, France 1:57.06
3. ...Nino Schwurter, Switzerland 1:57.52

Women

POINTS RACE

1. ...Marianne Vos, Netherlands 30,1
2. ...Yoanka Gonzalez, Cuba 18,0
3. ...Leire Olaverria, Spain 13,0

INDIVIDUAL TIME TRIAL

1. ...Kristin Armstrong, United States 34:51.72
2. ...Emma Pooley, Great Britain 35:16.01
3. ...Karin Thurig, Switzerland 35:50.99

3,000-METER INDIVIDUAL PURSUIT

1. ...Rebecca Romero, Great Britain 3:28.321
2. ...Wendy Houvenaghel, Great Britain 3:30.395
3. ...Lesya Kalitovska, Ukraine 3:31.413

SPRINT

1. ...Victoria Pendleton, Great Britain 11.118
2. ...Anna Meares, Australia —
3. ...Shuang Guo, China 11.617

ROAD RACE

1. ...Nicole Cooke, Great Britain 3:32:24
2. ...Emma Johansson, Sweden 3:32:24
3. ...Tatiana Guderzo, Italy 3:32:24

CROSS COUNTRY

1. ...Sabine Spitz, Germany 1:45.11
2. ...Maja Wloszczowska, Poland 1:45.52
3. ...Irina Kalentyeva, Russia 1:46.28

DIVING

Men

SPRINGBOARD

	Pts
1.....Chong He, China	572.90
2.....Alexandre Despatie, Canada	536.65
3.....Kai Oin, China	530.10

PLATFORM

	Pts
1.....Matthew Mitcham, Australia	537.95
2.....Luxin Zhou, China	533.15
3.....Gleb Galperin, Russia	525.80

Women

SPRINGBOARD

	Pts
1.....Jingjing Guo, China	415.35
2.....Julia Pakhalina, Russia	398.60
3.....Minxia Wu, China	389.85

PLATFORM

	Pts
1.....Ruoulin Chen, China	447.70
2.....Emilie Heymans, Canada	437.05
3.....Xin Wang, China	429.90

EQUESTRIAN

TEAM EVENTING

1. ......Germany
2. ......Australia
3. ......Great Britain

INDIVIDUAL EVENTING

	Pts
1. ......Hinrich Romeike, Germany	54.20
2. ......Gina Miles, United States	56.10
3. ......Kristina Cook, Great Britain	57.40

TEAM DRESSAGE

1. ......Germany
2. ......Netherlands
3. ......Denmark

INDIVIDUAL DRESSAGE

	Pts
1. ......Anky van Grunsven, Netherlands	82.400
2. ......Isabell Werth, Germany	78.100
3. ......Heike Kemmer, Germany	75.950

TEAM JUMPING

1. ......United States
2. ......Canada
3. ......Norway

INDIVIDUAL JUMPING

	Pen. Pts
1. ......Eric Lamaze, Canada	0.00
2. ......Rolf-Goran Bengtsson, Sweden	0.00
3. ......Beezie Madden, United States	4.00

FENCING

Men

FOIL

1. ......Benjamin Kleibrink, Germany
2. ......Yuki Ota, Japan
3. ......Salvatore Sanzo, Italy

SABRE

1. ......Man Zhong, China
2. ......Nicolas Lopez, France
3. ......Mihai Covaliu, Romania

ÉPÉE

1. ......Matteo Tagliariol, Italy
2. ......Fabrice Jeannet, France
3. ......Jose Luis Abajo, Spain

TEAM SABRE

1. ......France
2. ......United States
3. ......Italy

TEAM ÉPÉE

1. ......France
2. ......Poland
3. ......Italy

Women

FOIL

1. ......Maria Valentina Vezzali, Italy
2. ......Hyunhee Nam, South Korea
3. ......Margherita Granbassi, Italy

SABRE

1. ......Mariel Zagunis, United States
2. ......Sada Jacobson, United States
3. ......Becca Ward, United States

ÉPÉE

1. ......Britta Heidemann, Germany
2. ......Ana Maria Branza, Romania
3. ......I. Mincza-Nebald, Hungary

TEAM SABRE

1. ....Ukraine
2. ....China
3. ....United States

TEAM FOIL

1. ....Russia
2. ....United States
3. ....Italy

FIELD HOCKEY

Men

1. Germany
2. Spain
3. Australia

Women

1. Netherlands
2. China
3. Argentina

GYMNASTICS

Men

ALL-AROUND

	Pts
1. ....Yang Wei, China	94.575
2. ....Kohei Uchimura, Japan	91.975
3. ....Benoit Caranobe, France	91.925

HORIZONTAL BAR

	Pts
1. ....Zou Kai, China	16.200
2. ....Jonathan Horton, United States	16.175
3. ....Fabian Hambuchen, Germany	15.875

PARALLEL BARS

	Pts
1. ....Li Xiaopeng, China	16.450
2. ....Yoo Wonchul, South Korea	16.250
3. ....Anton Fokin, Uzbekistan	16.200

VAULT

	Pts
1. ....Leszek Blanik, Poland	16.537
2. ....Thomas Bouhail, France	16.537
3. ....Anton Golotsutskov, Russia	16.475

GYMNASTICS *(Cont.)*

Men

POMMEL HORSE

		Pts
1.	Xiao Oin, China	15.875
2.	Filip Ude, Croatia	15.725
3.	Louis Smith, Great Britain	15.725

RINGS

		Pts
1.	Chen Yibing, China	16.600
2.	Wei Yang, China	16.425
3.	Oleksandr Vorobiov, Ukraine	16.325

FLOOR EXERCISE

		Pts
1.	Zou Kai, China	16.050
2.	Gervasio Deferr, Spain	15.775
3.	Anton Golotsutskov, Russia	15.725

TEAM COMBINED EXERCISES

1. ....China
2. ....Japan
3. ....United States

Women

ALL-AROUND

		Pts
1.	Nastia Liukin, United States	63.325
2.	Shawn Johnson, United States	62.725
3.	Yang Yilin, China	62.650

VAULT

		Pts
1.	Un Jong Hong, North Korea	15.650
2.	Oksana Chusovitina, Germany	15.575
3.	Cheng Fei, China	15.562

UNEVEN BARS

		Pts
1.	He Kexin, China	16.725
2.	Nastia Liukin, United States	16.725
3.	Yang Yilin, China	16.650

BALANCE BEAM

		Pts
1.	Shawn Johnson, United States	16.225
2.	Nastia Liukin, United States	16.025
3.	Cheng Fei, China	15.950

FLOOR EXERCISE

		Pts
1.	Sandra Izbasa, Romania	15.650
2.	Shawn Johnson, United States	15.500
3.	Nastia Liukin, United States	15.425

TEAM COMBINED EXERCISES

1. ....China
2. ....United States
3. ....Romania

JUDO

Men

EXTRA-LIGHTWEIGHT

1. ....Minho Choi, South Korea
2. ....Ludwig Paischer, Austria
3. ....Rishod Sobirov, Uzbekistan
3. ....Ruben Houkes, Netherlands

HALF-LIGHTWEIGHT

1. ....Masato Uchishiba, Japan
2. ....Benjamin Darbelet, France
3. ....Yordanis Arencibia, Cuba
3. ....Choi Min Pak, North Korea

LIGHTWEIGHT

1. ....Elnur Mammadli, Azerbaijan
2. ....Kichyn Wang, South Korea
3. ....Rasul Booiev, Tajikistan
3. ....Leandro Guilhero, Brazil

HALF-MIDDLEWEIGHT

1. ....Ole Bischof, Germany
2. ....Jaebum Kim, South Korea
3. ....Tiago Camilo, Brazil
3. ....Roman Gontiuk, Ukraine

MIDDLEWEIGHT

1. ....Irakli Tsirekidze, Georgia
2. ....Amar Benikhlef, Algeria
3. ....Hesham Mesbah, Egypt
3. ....Sergei Aschwanden, Switzerland

HALF-HEAVYWEIGHT

1. ....Tuyshinbayar Naidan, Mongolia
2. ....Askhat Zhitkeyev, Kazakhstan
3. ....Movlud Miraliyev, Azerbaijan
3. ....Henk Grol, Netherlands

HEAVYWEIGHT

1. ....Satoshi Ishii, Japan
2. ....Abdullo Tangriev, Uzbekistan
3. ....Oscar Brayson, Cuba
3. ....Teddy Riner, France

Women

EXTRA-LIGHTWEIGHT

1. ....Alina Alexandra Dumitru, Romania
2. ....Yanet Bermoy, Cuba
3. ....Paula Belen Pareto, Argentina
3. ....Ryoko Tani, Japan

HALF-LIGHTWEIGHT

1. ....Dongmei Xien, China
2. ....Ae Kum An, North Korea
3. ....Soraya Haddad, Algeria
3. ....Misato Nakamura, Japan

LIGHTWEIGHT

1. ....Giulia Quintavalle, Italy
2. ....Deborah Gravenstijn, Netherlands
3. ....Ketleyn Quadros, Brazil
3. ....Yan Xu, China

HALF-MIDDLEWEIGHT

1. ....Ayumi Tanimoto, Japan
2. ....Lucie Decosse, France
3. ....Elisabeth Willeboordse, Netherlands
3. ....Ok Im Won, North Korea

MIDDLEWEIGHT

1. ....Masae Ueno, Japan
2. ....Anaysi Hernandez, Cuba
3. ....Ronda Rousey, United States
3. ....Edith Bosch, Netherlands

HALF-HEAVYWEIGHT

1. ....Yang Xiuli, China
2. ....Yalennis Castillo, Cuba
3. ....Gyeongmi Jeong, South Korea
3. ....Stephanie Possamai, France

HEAVYWEIGHT

1. ....Tong Wen, China
2. ....Maki Tsukada, Japan
3. ....Lucija Polavder, Slovenia
3. ....Idalys Ortiz, Cuba

MODERN PENTATHLON

Men

1. ......Andrev Moiseev, Russia
2. ......Edvinas Krungolcas, Lituania
3. ......Andreius Zadneprovskis, Lithuania

Women

1. ......Lena Schoneborn, Germany
2. ......Heather Fell, Great Britain
3. ......Victoria Tereshuk, Ukraine

MOUNTAIN BIKING

Men

1. ......Julien Absalon, France	1:55.59
2. ......Jean-Christophe Peraud, France	1:57.06
3. ......Nino Schurter, Switzerland	1:57.52

Women

1. ......Sabine Spitz, Germany	1:45.11
2. ......Maia Wloszczowska, Poland	1:45.52
3. ......Irina Kalentyeva, Russia	1:46.28

ROWING

Men

SINGLE SCULLS

1. ...Olaf Tufte, Norway	6:59.83
2. ...Ondrej Synek, Estonia	7:00.63
3. ...Mahe Drysdale, New Zealand	7:01.56

DOUBLE SCULLS

1. ...D. Crawshay/S. Brennan, Australia	6:27.77
2. ...T. Endrekson/J. Jaanson, Estonia	6:29.05
3. ...M. Wells/S. Rowbotham, Great Britain	6:29.10

LIGHTWEIGHT DOUBLE SCULLS

1. ...Z. Purchase/M. Hunter, Great Britain	6:10.99
2. ...D. Mougios/V. Polymeros, Greece	6:11.72
3. ...M. Rasmussen/R. Hansen, Denmark	6:12.45

QUADRUPLE SCULLS

1. ...Poland	5:41.33
2. ...Italy	5:43.57
3. ...France	5:44.34

COXLESS PAIR

1. ...D. Ginn/D. Free, Australia	6:37.44
2. ...D. Calder/S. Frandsen, Canada	6:39.55
3. ...N. Twaddle/G. Bridgewater, New Zealand	6:44.19

COXLESS FOUR

1. ...Great Britain	6:06.57
2. ...Australia	6:07.85
3. ...France	6:09.31

LIGHTWEIGHT COXLESS FOUR

1. ...Denmark	5:47.76
2. ...Poland	5:49.39
3. ...Canada	5:50.09

EIGHT-OARS

1. ...Canada	5:23.89
2. ...Great Britain	5:25.11
3. ...United States	5:25.34

Women

SINGLE SCULLS

1. ...Rumyana Neykova, Bulgaria	7:22.34
2. ...Michelle Guerette, United States	7:22.78
3. ...Ekaterina Karsten, Belarus	7:23.98

DOUBLE SCULLS

1. ...Caroline/Georgina Evers-Swindell, N.Z.	7:07.32
2. ...A. Thiele/C. Huth, Germany	7:07.33
3. ...E. Laverick/A. Bebington, Great Britain	7:07.55

LIGHTWEIGHT DOUBLE SCULLS

1. ...K. van der Kolk/M. van Eupen, Neth	6:54.74
2. ...S. Stern/M. Nieminen, Finland	6:56.03
3. ...M. Kok/T. Cameron, Canada	6:56.68

QUADRUPLE SCULLS

1. ...China	6:16.06
2. ...Great Britain	6:17.37
3. ...Germany	6:19.56

COXLESS PAIR

1. ...G. Andrunache/V. Susanu, Romania	7:20.60
2. ...W. You/G. Youlan, China	7:22.28
3. ...Y. Bichyk/N. Helakh, Belarus	7:22.91

EIGHT-OARS

1. ...United States	6:05.34
2. ...Netherlands	6:07.22
3. ...Romania	6:07.25

SHOOTING- Men

RAPID-FIRE PISTOL	Pts
1. ....Oleksandr Petriy, Ukraine	780.2
2. ....Ralf Schumann, Germany	779.5
3. ....Christian Rietz, Germany	779.3

FREE PISTOL	Pts
1. ....Jin Jongoh, South Korea	660.4
2. ....Zongliang Tan, China	659.5
3. ....Vladimir Isakov, Russia	658.9

AIR PISTOL	Pts
1. ....Pang Wei, China	688.2
2. ....Jin Jongoh, South Korea	684.5
3. ....Jason Turner, United States	682.0

SMALL-BORE RIFLE, THREE-POSITION	Pts
1. ....Oiu Jian, China	1272.5
2. ....Yuriy Sukhorukov, Ukraine	1272.4
3. ....Raimond Debevec, Slovenia	1271.7

SMALL-BORE RIFLE, PRONE	Pts
1. ....Artur Ayvazyan, Ukraine	702.7
2. ....Matt Emmons, United States	701.7
3. ....Warren Potent, Australia	700.5

AIR RIFLE	Pts
1. ....Abhinav Bindra, India	700.5
2. ....Zhu Oinan, China	699.7
3. ....Henri Hakkinen, Finland	699.4

2008 Summer Games (*Cont.*)

TRAP Pts
1. ....David Kostelecky, Czech Republic 146.0
2. ....Giovanni Pellielo, Italy 143.0
3. ....Aleksey Alipov, Russia 142.0

DOUBLE TRAP Pts
1. ....Walton Eller, United States 190.0
2. ....Francesco D'aniello, Italy 187.0
3. ....Hu Binyuan, China 184.0

SKEET Pts
1. ....Vincent Hancock, United States 145.0
2. ....Tore Brovold, Norway 145.0
3. ....Anthony Terras, France 144.0

SHOOTING - Women

SPORT PISTOL Pts
1. ......Ying Chen, China 793.4
2. ......Gundegmaa Otryad, Mongolia 792.2
3. ......Munkhbayar Dorisuren, Germany 789.2

AIR PISTOL Pts
1. ......Wenjun Guo, China 492.3 OR
2. ......Natalia Paderina, Russia 489.1
3. ......Nino Salukvadze, Georgia 487.4

SMALL-BORE RIFLE, THREE-POSITION Pts
1. ......Du Li, China 690.3
2. ......Katerina Emmons, Czech Republic 687.7
3. ......Eglys Cruz, Cuba 687.6

AIR RIFLE Pts
1. ......Katerina Emmons, Czech Republic 503.5
2. ......Lyoubov Galkina, Russia 502.1
3. ......Snjezana Pejic, Croatia 500.9

TRAP Pts
1. ......Satu Makela-Nummela, Finland 91.0
2. ......Zuzana Stefecekova, Slovakia 89.0
3. ......Corey Cogdell, United States 86.0

SKEET Pts
1. ......Chiara Cainero, Italy 93.0
2. ......Kimberly Rhode, United States 93.0
3. ......Christine Brinker, Germany 93.0

SOCCER

Men
1. ....Argentina
2. ....Nigeria
3. ....Brazil

Women
1. ....United States
2. ....Brazil
3. ....Germany

SOFTBALL

1. ......Japan
2. ......United States
3. ......Australia

SWIMMING - Men

50-METER FREESTYLE
1. ...Cesar Cielo Filho, Brazil 21.30 OR
2. ...Amaury Leveaux, France 21.45
3. ...Alain Bernard, France 21.49

100-METER FREESTYLE
1. ...Alain Bernard, France 47.21
2. ...Eamon Sullivan, Australia 47.32
3. ...Cesar Cielo Filho, Brazil 47.67
3. ...Jason Lezak, United States 47.67

200-METER FREESTYLE
1. ...Michael Phelps, United States 1:42.96 WR
2. ...Park Taehwan, South Korea 1:44.85
3. ...Peter Vanderkaay, United States 1:45.14

400-METER FREESTYLE
1. ...Park Taehwan, South Korea 3:41.86
2. ...Zhang Lin, China 3:42.44
3. ...Larsen Jensen, United States 3:42.78

1,500-METER FREESTYLE
1. ...Oussama Mellouli, Tunisia 14:40.84
2. ...Grant Hackett, Australia 14:41.53
3. ...Ryan Cochrane, Canada 14:42.69

100-METER BACKSTROKE
1. ...Aaron Peirsol, United States 52.54 WR
2. ...Matt Greyers, United States 53.11
3. ...Hayden Stoeckel, Australia 53.18
3. ...Arkady Vyatchanin, Russia 53.18

200-METER BACKSTROKE
1. ...Ryan Lochte, United States 1:53.94 WR
2. ...Aaron Peirsol, United States 1:54.33
3. ...Arkady Vyatchanin, Russia 1:54.93

100-METER BREASTSTROKE
1. ...Kosuke Kitajima, Japan 58.91 WR
2. ...Alexander Dale Oen, Norway 59.20
3. ...Hugues Duboscq, France 59.37

200-METER BREASTSTROKE
1. ...Kosuke Kitajima, Japan 2:07.64 OR
2. ...Brenton Rickard, Australia 2:08.88
3. ...Hugues Duboscq, France 2:08.94

100-METER BUTTERFLY
1. ...Michael Phelps, United States 50.58 OR
2. ...Milorad Cavic, Serbia 50.59
3. ...Andrew Lauterstein, Australia 51.12

200-METER BUTTERFLY
1. ...Michael Phelps, United States 1:52.03 WR
2. ...Laszlo Cseh, Hungary 1:52.70
3. ...Takeshi Matsuda, Japan 1:52.97

200-METER INDIVIDUAL MEDLEY
1. ...Michael Phelps, United States 1:54.23 WR
2. ...Laszlo Cseh, Hungary 1:56.52
3. ...Ryan Lochte, United States 1:56.53

400-METER INDIVIDUAL MEDLEY
1. ...Michael Phelps, United States 4:03.84 WR
2. ...Laszlo Cseh, Hungary 4:06.16
3. ...Ryan Lochte, United States 4:08.09

4 X 100-METER MEDLEY RELAY
1. ...United States (Peirsol, Hansen, Lezak, Phelps) 3:29.34 WR
2. ...Australia 3:30.04
3. ...Japan 3:31.18

4 X 100-METER FREESTYLE RELAY
1. ...United States (Lezak, Phelps, Weber-Gale, Jones) 3:08.24 WR
2. ...France 3:08.32
3. ...Australia 3:09.91

2008 Summer Games (*Cont.*)

SWIMMING - Men (*Cont.*)

4 X 200-METER FREESTYLE RELAY

1. ...United States (Lochte, Phelps Vanderkaay, Berens) 6:58.56 WR
2. ...Russia 7:03.70
3. ...Australia 7:04.98

10 KM MARATHON

1. ...Maarten van der Weijden, Netherlands 1:51:51.60
2. ...David Davies, Great Britain 1:51:53.10
3. ...Thomas Lurz, Germany 1:51:53.60

SWIMMING - Women

50-METER FREESTYLE

1. ...Britta Steffen, Germany 24.06 OR
2. ...Dara Torres, United States 24.07
3. ...Cate Campbell, Australia 24.17

100-METER FREESTYLE

1. ...Britta Steffen, Germany 53.12 OR
2. ...Lisbeth Trickett, Australia 53.16
3. ...Natalie Coughlin, United States 53.39

200-METER FREESTYLE

1. ...Frederica Pellegrini, Italy 1:54.82 WR
2. ...Sara Isakovic, Slovenia 1:54.97
3. ...Jiaying Pang, China 1:55.05

400-METER FREESTYLE

1. ...Rebecca Adlington, Great Britain 4:03.22
2. ...Katie Hoff, United States 4:03.29
3. ...Joanne Jackson, Great Britain 4:03.52

800-METER FREESTYLE

1. ...Rebecca Adlington, Great Britain 8:14.10 WR
2. ...Alessia Filippi, Italy 8:20.23
3. ...Lotte Friis, Denmark 8:23.03

100-METER BACKSTROKE

1. ...Natalie Coughlin, United States 58.96
2. ...Kirsty Coventry, Zimbabwe 59.19
3. ...Margaret Hoelzer, United States 59.34

200-METER BACKSTROKE

1. ...Kirsty Coventry, Zimbabwe 2:05.24 WR
2. ...Margaret Hoelzer, United States 2:06.23
3. ...Reiko Nakamura, Japan 2:07.13

100-METER BREASTSTROKE

1. ...Leisel Jones, Australia 1:05.17 WR
2. ...Rebecca Soni, United States 1:06.73
3. ...Mirna Jukic, Austria 1:07.34

200-METER BREASTSTROKE

1. ...Rebecca Soni, United States 2:20.22 WR
2. ...Leisel Jones, Australia 2:22.05
3. ...Sara Nordenstam, Norway 2:23.02

100-METER BUTTERFLY

1. ...Lisbeth Trickett, Australia 56.73
2. ...Christine Magnuson, United States 57.10
3. ...Jessicah Schipper, Australia 57.25

200-METER BUTTERFLY

1. ...Liu Zige, China 2:04.18 WR
2. ...Jiao Liuyang, China 2:04.72
3. ...Jessicah Schipper, Australia 2:06.26

200-METER INDIVIDUAL MEDLEY

1. ...Stephanie Rice, Australia 2:08.45 WR
2. ...Kirsty Coventry, Zimbabwe 2:08.59
3. ...Natalie Coughlin, United States 2:10.34

400-METER INDIVIDUAL MEDLEY

1. ...Stephanie Rice, Australia 4:29.45 WR
2. ...Kirsty Coventry, Zimbabwe 4:29.89
3. ...Katie Hoff, United States 4:31.71

4 X 100-METER MEDLEY RELAY

1. ...Australia (Jones, Schipper, Seebohm, Trickett) 3:52.69 WR
2. ...United States 3:53.30
3. ...China 3:56.11

4 X 100-METER FREESTYLE RELAY

1. ...Netherlands (Dekker, Veldhuis, Heemserk, Kromowidjojo) 3:33.76 OR
2. ...United States 3:34.33
3. ...Australia 3:35.05

4 X 200-METER FREESTYLE RELAY

1. ...Australia (Mackenzie, Rice, Barratt, Palmer) 7:44.31 WR
2. ...China 7:45.93
3. ...United States 7:46.33

10-KM MARATHON

1. ...Larisa Ilchenko, Russia 1:59.27.70
2. ...Keri-Anne Payne, Great Britain 1:59.29.20
3. ...Cassandra Patten, Great Britain 1:59.31.00

SYNCHRONIZED DIVING

Men

3M SPRINGBOARD

		Pts
1.	W. Feng/K. Qin, China	469.08
2.	D. Sautin/Y. Kunakov, Russia	421.98
3.	I. Kvasha/O. Prygorov, Ukraine	415.05

10M PLATFORM

		Pts
1.	Y. Lin/L. Huo, China	468.18
2.	P. Hausding/S. Klein, Germany	450.42
3.	G. Galperin/D. Dobroskok, Russia	445.26

Women

3M SPRINGBOARD

		Pts
1.	J. Guo/M. Wu, China	343.50
2.	J. Pakhalina/A. Pozdnyakova, Russia	323.61
3.	D. Kotzian/H. Fischer, Germany	318.90

10M PLATFORM

		Pts
1.	X. Wang/R. Chen, China	363.54
2.	B. Cole/M. Wu, Australia	335.16
3.	P. Espinosa/T. Ortiz, Mexico	330.06

Note: OR=Olympic record. WR=world record. EOR=equals Olympic record. EWR=equals world record.

SYNCHRONIZED SWIMMING

DUET

1. ....Russia
2. ....Spain
3. ....Japan

TEAM

1. ....Russia
2. ....Spain
3. ....China

TABLE TENNIS

Men

SINGLES

1. ....Ma Lin, China
2. ....Hao Wang, China
3. ....Ligin Wang, China

DOUBLES

1. ....H. Wang/L. Wang, China
2. ....C. Suss/T. Boll, Germany
3. ....J. Yoon/S. Oh, South Korea

Women

SINGLES

1. ....Zhang Yining, China
2. ....Nan Wang, China
3. ....Guo Yue, China

DOUBLES

1. ....G. Yue/Z. Yining, China
2. ....Y. Wang/J. Li, Singapore
3. ....M. Park/K. Kim, South Korea

TAEKWONDO

Men

FLYWEIGHT

1. ....Guillermo Perez, Mexico
2. ....Yulis Gabriel Mercedes, Dom. Republic
3. ....Chu Mu-Yen, Taiwan
3. ....Rohulla Nikpai, Afghanistan

FEATHERWEIGHT

1. ....Son Taejin, South Korea
2. ....Mark Lopez, United States
3. ....Sung Yu-Chi, Taiwan
3. ....Servet Tazegul, Turkey

WELTERWEIGHT

1. ....Hadi Saei, Iran
2. ....Mauro Sarmiento, Italy
3. ....Zhu Guo, China
3 ....Steven Lopez, United States

HEAVYWEIGHT

1. ....Cha Dongmin, South Korea
2. ....Alexandros Nikolaidis, Greece
3. ....Arman Chilmanov, Kazakhstan
3. ....Chika Yagazie Chukwumerije, Nigeria

Women

FLYWEIGHT

1. ....Wu Jingyu, China
2. ....Buttree Puedpong, Thailand
3. ....Dalia Contreras Rivero, Venezuela
3. ....Daynellis Montejo, Cuba

FEATHERWEIGHT

1. ....Lim Sujeong, South Korea
2. ....Azize Tanrikulu, Turkey
3. ....Martina Zubcic, Croatia
3 ....Diana Lopez, United States

WELTERWEIGHT

1. ....Hwang Kyungseon, South Korea
2. ....Karine Sergerie, Canada
3. ....Sandra Saric, Croatia
3 ....Gwladys Patience Epangue, France

HEAVYWEIGHT

1. ....Maria del Rosario Espinoza, Mexico
2. ....Nina Solheim, Norway
3. ....Natalia Falavigna, Brazil
3. ....Sarah Stevenson, Great Britain

TEAM HANDBALL

Men

1. ....France
2. ....Iceland
3. ....Spain

Women

1. ....Norway
2. ....Russia
3. ....South Korea

TENNIS

Men

SINGLES

1. ....Rafael Nadal, Spain
2. ....Fernando Gonzalez, Chile
3. ....Novak Djokovic, Serbia

DOUBLES

1. ....Roger Federer/Stanislas Wawrinka, Switzerland
2. ....Thomas Johansson/Simon Aspelin, Sweden
3. ....Bob Bryan/Mike Bryan, United States

Women

SINGLES

1. ....Elena Dementieva, Russia
2. ....Dinara Safina, Russia
3. ....Vera Zvonareva, Russia

DOUBLES

1. ....Serena Willams/Venus Williams, United States
2. ....Virginia Ruano/Anabel Medina, Spain
3. ....Yan Zi/Zheng Jie, China

TRAMPOLINE

Men

1.	Lu Chunlong, China	41.00
2.	Jason Burnett, Canada	40.70
3.	Dong Dong, China	40.60

Women

1.	Ha Wenna, China	37.80
2.	Karen Cockburn, Canada	37.00
3.	Ekaterina Khilko, Uzbekistan	36.90

TRIATHLON

Men

1..........Jan Frodeno, Germany 1:48:53
2..........Simon Whitfield, Canada 1:48:58
3..........Bevan Docherty, New Zealand 1:49:05

Women

1..........Emma Snowsill, Australia 1:58:27
2..........Vanessa Fernandes, Portugal 1:59:34
3..........Emma Moffatt, Australia 1:59:55

VOLLEYBALL

Men

1..........United States
2..........Brazil
3..........Russia

Women

1..........Brazil
2..........United States
3..........China

BEACH VOLLEYBALL

Men

1..........Phil Dalhausser/Todd Rogers, United States
2..........Marcio Araujo/Fabio Magalhaes, Brazil
3..........Emanuel Rego/Ricardo Santos, Brazil

Women

1..........Misty May-Treanor/Kerri Walsh, United States
2..........Tian Jia/Wang Jie, China
3..........Zhang Xi/Xue Chen, China

WATER POLO

Men

1..........Hungary
2..........United States
3..........Serbia

Women

1..........Netherlands
2..........United States
3..........Australia

WEIGHTLIFTING - Men

123 POUNDS

1. ....Long Oingguan, China 644 lb
2. ....Anh Tuan Hoang, Vietnam 639 lb
3. ....Eko Yuli Irawan, Indonesia 635 lb

137 POUNDS

1. ....Zhang Xiangxiang, China 703 lb
2. ....Diego Salazar, Colombia 672 lb
3. ....Triyatno, Indonesia 657 lb

152 POUNDS

1. ....Liao Hui, China 767 lb
2. ....Vancelas Dabaya-Tientcheu, France 745 lb
3. ....Tigran G. Martirosyan, Armenia 745 lb

170 POUNDS

1. ....Sa Jaehyouk, South Korea 807 lb
2. ....Li Hongli, China 807 lb
3. ....Geyorg Davtyan, Armenia 793.5 lb

187 POUNDS

1. ....Lu Yong, China 868.5 lb WR
2. ....Andrei Rybakou, Belarus 868.5 lb
3. ....Tigran V. Martirosyan, Armenia 838 lb

207 POUNDS

1. ....Ilya Ilin, Kazakhstan 895 lb
2. ....Szymon Kolecki, Poland 888.5 lb
3. ....Khadzhimurat Akkaev, Russia 886 lb

231 POUNDS

1. ....Andrei Aramnau, Belarus 961 lb WR
2. ....Dmitriy Klokov, Russia 932.5 lb
3. ....Dmitry Lapikov, Russia 926 lb

231+ POUNDS

1. ....Matthias Steiner, Germany 1016 lb
2. ....Evgeny Chigishev, Russia 1014 lb
3. ....Viktors Scerbatihs, Latvia 987 lb

WEIGHTLIFTING - Women

106 POUNDS

1. ....Chen Xiexia, China 467 lb OR
2. ....Sibel Özkan, Turkey 439 lb
3. ....Chen Wei-Ling, Taiwan 432 lb

117 POUNDS

1. ....P. Jaroenrattanatarakoon, Thailand 487 lb
2. ....Yoon Jinhee, South Korea 469.5 lb
3. ....Natassia Novikava, Belarus 469.5 lb

128 POUNDS

1. ....Chen Yanging, China 538 lb OR
2. ....Marina Shainova, Russia 500.5 lb
3. ....O Jong Ae, North Korea 498 lb

139 POUNDS

1. ....Pak Hyon Suk, North Korea 531.5 lb
2. ....Irina Nekrassova, Kazakhstan 529 lb
3. ....Lu Ying-Chi, Taiwan 509 lb

152 POUNDS

1. ....Liu Chunhong, China 630.5 lb WR
2. ....Oxana Silvenko, Russia 562 lb
3. ....Natalya Davydova, Ukraine 551 lb

165 POUNDS

1. ....Cao Lei, China 622 lb OR
2. ....Alla Vazhenina, Kazakhstan 586.5 lb
3. ....Nadezda Evstyukhina, Russia 582 lb

165+ POUNDS

1. ....Jang Miran, South Korea 719 lb WR
2. ....Olha Korobka, Ukraine 611 lb
3. ....Mariya Grabovetskaya, Kazakhstan 595 lb

Note: OR=Olympic Record. WR=World Record. EOR=Equals Olympic Record. EWR=Equals World Record.

FREESTYLE WRESTLING

121 POUNDS

1. ....Henry Cejudo, United States
2. ....Tomohiro Matsunaga, Japan
3. ....Radoslav Velikov, Bulgaria
3. ....Besik Kudukhov, Russia

132 POUNDS

1. ....Mavlet Batirov, Russia
2. ....Vasyl Fedoryshyn, Ukraine
3. ....Seyedmorad Mohammadi, Iran
3. ....Kenichi Yumoto, Japan

145.5 POUNDS

1. ....Ramazan Sahin, Turkey
2. ....Andriy Stadnik, Ukraine
3. ....Otar Tushishvili, Georgia
3. ....Sushil Kumar, India

163 POUNDS

1. ....Buvaysa Saytive, Russia
2. ....Soslan Tigiev, Uzbekistan
3. ....Murad Gaidarov, Belarus
3. ....Kiril Terziev, Bulgaria

185 POUNDS

1. ....Revazi Mindorashvili, Georgia
2. ....Yusup Abdusalomov, Tajikistan
3. ....Georgy Ketoev, Russia
3. ....Taras Danko, Ukraine

211.5 POUNDS

1. ....Shirvani Muradov, Russia
2. ....Taimuraz Tigiyev, Kazakhstan
3. ....Khetag Gazyumov, Azerbaijan
3. ....George Gogshelidze, Georgia

264.5 POUNDS

1. ....Artur Taymazov, Uzbekistan
2. ....Bakhtivar Akhmedov, Russia
3. ....Marid Mutalimov, Kazakhstan
3. ....David Musulbes, Slovakia

GRECO-ROMAN WRESTLING

121 POUNDS

1. ....Islam-Beka Albiev, Russia
2. ....Vitaliy Rahimov, Azerbaijan
3. ....Nurbakyt Tengizbayev, Kazakhstan
3. ....Ruslan Tiumenbaev, Kyrgyzstan

132 POUNDS

1. ....Nazyr Mankiev, Russia
2. ....Royshan Bayramov, Azerbaijan
3. ....Roman Amoyan, Armenia
3. ....Park Eunchol, South Korea

145.5 POUNDS

1. ....Steeve Guenot, France
2. ....Kanatbek Begaliev, Kyrgyzstan
3. ....Mikhail Siamionau, Belarus
3. ....Armen Varandyan, Ukraine

163 POUNDS

1. ....Manuchar Kyirkelia, Georgia
2. ....Chang Yongxiang, China
3. ....Yavor Yanakiev, Bulgaria
3. ....Christophe Guenot, France

185 POUNDS

1. ....Andrea Minguzzi, Italy
2. ....Zoltan Fodor, Hungary
3. ....Nazmi Avluca, Turkey

211.5 POUNDS

1. ....Aslanbek Khushtov, Russia
2. ....Mirko Englich, Germany
3. ....Asset Mambetov, Kazakhstan
3. ....Adam Wheeler, United States

264.5 POUNDS

1. ....Mijain Lopez, Cuba
2. ....Khasan Baroev, Russia
3. ....Yuri Patrikeev, Armenia
3. ....Mindaugas Mizgaitis, Lithuania

YACHTING

Men

DINGHY 470

1. ....Australia
2. ....Great Britain
3. ....France

FINN

1. ....Great Britain
2. ....Denmark
3. ....Spain

DINGHY

1. ....Paul Goodison, G.B.
2. ....Vasilji Zbogar, Slvn.
3. ....Diego Romero, Ita.

TORNADO

1. ....Spain
2. ....Australia
3. ....Argentina

LASER

1. ....New Zealand
2. ....Slovenia
3. ....Argentina

49ER

1. ....Denmark
2. ....Spain
3. ....Germany

STAR

1. ....Great Britain
2. ....Brazil
3. ....Sweden

MISTRAL

1. ....Tom Ashley, N.Z.
2. ....J. Bontemps, Fra.
3. ....Shaher Zubari, Isr.

HW DINGHY

1. ....Ben Ainslie, G.B.
2. ....Zach Railey, U.S.
3. ....G. Florent, France

Women

MISTRAL

1. ....Yin Jian, China
2. ....Alessandra Sensini, Italy
3. ....Bryonny Shaw, Great Britain

470

1. ....Australia
2. ....Netherlands
3. ....Brazil

EUROPE

1. ....Anna Tunnicliffe, United States
2. ....Gintare Volungeviciute, Lithuania
3. ....Xin Lijia, China

KEEL

1. ....Great Britain
2. ....Netherlands
3. ....Greece

Note: OR=Olympic Record. WR=World Record. EOR=Equals Olympic Record. EWR=Equals World Record.

FOR THE RECORD • Year by Year

Summer Olympic Games Locations and Dates

	Year	Site	Dates	COMPETITORS Men	Women	Nations	Most Medals	US Medals
I	1896	Athens, Greece	Apr 6–15	311	0	13	Greece (10-19-18—47)	11-6-2—19 (2nd)
II	1900	Paris, France	May 20–Oct 28	1319	11	22	France (29-41-32—102)	20-14-19—53 (2nd)
III	1904	St Louis, United States	July 1–Nov 23	681	6	12	United States (80-86-72—238)	
—	1906	Athens, Greece	Apr 22–May 28	77	7	20	France (15-9-16—40)	12-6-5—23 (4th)
IV	1908	London, Great Britain	Apr 27–Oct 31	1999	36	23	Britain (56-50-39—145)	23-12-12—47 (2nd)
V	1912	Stockholm, Sweden	May 5–July 22	2490	57	28	Sweden (24-24-17—65)	23-19-19—61 (2nd)
VI	1916	Berlin, Germany	Canceled because of war					
VII	1920	Antwerp, Belgium	Apr 20–Sep 12	2543	64	29	United States (41-27-28—96)	
VIII	1924	Paris, France	May 4–July 27	2956	136	44	United States (45-27-27—99)	
IX	1928	Amsterdam, Netherlands	May 17–Aug 12	2724	290	46	United States (22-18-16—56)	
X	1932	Los Angeles, United States	July 30–Aug 14	1281	127	37	United States (41-32-31—104)	
XI	1936	Berlin, Germany	Aug 1–16	3738	328	49	Germany (33-26-30—89)	24-20-12—56 (2nd)
XII	1940	Tokyo, Japan	CANCELED BECAUSE OF WAR					
XIII	1944	London, Great Britain	CANCELED BECAUSE OF WAR					
XIV	1948	London, Great Britain	July 29–Aug 14	3714	385	59	United States (38-27-19—84)	
XV	1952	Helsinki, Finland	July 19–Aug 3	4407	518	69	United States (40-19-17—76)	
XVI	1956	Melbourne, Australia*	Nov 22–Dec 8	2958	384	67	USSR (37-29-32—98)	32-25-17—74 (2nd)
XVII	1960	Rome, Italy	Aug 25–Sep 11	4738	610	83	USSR (43-29-31—103)	34-21-16—71 (2nd)
XVIII	1964	Tokyo, Japan	Oct 10–24	4457	683	93	United States (36-26-28—90)	
XIX	1968	Mexico City, Mexico	Oct 12–27	4750	781	112	United States (45-28-34—107)	
XX	1972	Munich, W Germany	Aug 26–Sep 10	5848	1299	122	USSR (50-27-22—99)	33-31-30—94 (2nd)
XXI	1976	Montreal, Canada	July 17–Aug 1	4834	1251	92†	USSR (49-41-35—125)	34-35-25—94 (3rd)
XXII	1980	Moscow, USSR	July 19–Aug 3	4265	1088	81‡	USSR (80-69-46—195)	Did not compete
XXIII	1984	Los Angeles, United States	July 28–Aug 12	5458	1620	141#	United States (83-61-30—174)	
XXIV	1988	Seoul, S Korea	Sep 17–Oct 2	7105	2476	160	USSR (55-31-46—132)	36-31-27—94 (3rd)
XXV	1992	Barcelona, Spain	July 25–Aug. 9	7555	3008	172	Unified Team (45-38-29—112)	37-34-37—108 (2nd)
XXVI	1996	Atlanta, United States	July 19–Aug 4	6984	3766	197	United States (44-32-25—101)	
XXVII	2000	Sydney, Australia	Sept 15–Oct 1	6862	4254	199	United States (39-25-33—97)	
XXVIII	2004	Athens, Greece	Aug 11–Aug 29	11099 total		202	United States (35-39-29—103)	

Summer Olympic Games Locations and Dates *(Cont.)*

	Year	Site	Dates	Competitors: Men	Women	Nations	Most Medals	US Medal
XXIX	2008	Beijing, China	Aug 8–Aug 24	11028 total		204	United States (36-38-36—110)	

*The equestrian events were held in Stockholm, Sweden, June 10–17, 1956.

†This figure includes Cameroon, Egypt, Morocco, and Tunisia, countries that boycotted the 1976 Olympics after some of their athletes had already competed.

‡The U.S. was among 65 countries that did not participate in the 1980 Summer Games in Moscow.

#The USSR, East Germany, and 14 other countries did not participate in the 1984 Summer Games in Los Angeles.

Alltime Olympic Medal Winners

Summer

NATIONS

Nation	Gold	Silver	Bronze	Total
United States	930	730	638	2298
USSR (1952–88)	395	319	296	1010
Great Britain	207	255	253	715
France	191	212	233	636
Germany (1896–1936, 1992–)	163	163	203	529
Italy	190	158	174	522
Sweden	142	160	173	475
Hungary	159	140	159	458
East Germany (1956–88)	159	150	136	445
Australia	131	137	164	432
China	163	117	106	386
Japan	123	112	125	360
Russia	108	97	110	315
West Germany (1952–88)	77	104	120	301
Finland	101	83	115	299
Romania	86	89	116	291
Poland	62	80	119	261
Canada	58	94	108	260
The Netherlands	71	79	96	246
Bulgaria	51	84	77	212
Cuba	67	64	63	194
Switzerland	45	70	65	180
Denmark	41	63	66	170

INDIVIDUALS – OVERALL

Men

Athlete, Nation	Sport	G	S	B	Tot
Michael Phelps, United States	Swim	14	0	2	16
Nikolai Andrianov, USSR	Gym	7	5	3	15
Boris Shakhlin, USSR	Gym	7	4	2	13
Edoardo Mangiarotti, Italy	Fen	6	5	2	13
Takashi Ono, Japan	Gym	5	4	4	13
Paavo Nurmi, Finland	Track	9	3	0	12
Sawao Kato, Japan	Gym	8	3	1	12
Alexei Nemov, Russia	Gym	4	2	6	12
Mark Spitz, United States	Swim	9	1	1	11
Matt Biondi, United States	Swim	8	2	1	11
Viktor Chukarin, USSR	Gym	7	3	1	11
Carl Osburn, United States	Shoot	5	4	2	11
Ray Ewry, United States	Track	10	0	0	10
Carl Lewis, United States	Track	9	1	0	10
Aladár Gerevich, Hungary	Fen	7	1	2	10
Akinori Nakayama, Japan	Gym	6	2	2	10
Vitaly Scherbo, UT/Belarus	Gym	6	0	4	10
Aleksandr Dityatin, USSR	Gym	3	6	1	10

Women

Athlete, Nation	Sport	G	S	B	Tot
Larissa Latynina, USSR	Gym	9	5	4	18
Jenny Thompson, United States	Swim	8	3	1	12
Vera Cáslavská, Czech	Gym	7	4	0	11
Agnes Keleti, Hungary	Gym	5	3	2	10
Polina Astaknova, USSR	Gym	5	2	3	10
Dara Torres, United States	Swim	4	1	4	9
Nadia Comaneci, Romania	Gym	5	3	1	9
Lyudmila Tourischeva, USSR	Gym	4	3	2	9
Kornelia Ender, E Germany	Swim	4	4	0	8
Dawn Fraser, Australia	Swim	4	4	0	8
Shirley Babashoff, United States	Swim	2	6	0	8
Sofia Muratova, USSR	Gym	2	2	4	8
Inge de Bruijn, Netherlands	Swim	4	2	2	8

Eight tied with seven.

INDIVIDUALS – GOLD

Men

Micheal Phelps, United States	14
Ray Ewry, United States	10
Paavo Nurmi, Finland	9
Carl Lewis, United States	9
Mark Spitz, United States	9
Sawao Kato, Japan	8
Matt Biondi, United States	8
Nikolai Andrianov, USSR	7
Boris Shakhlin, USSR	7
Viktor Chukarin, USSR	7
Aladár Gerevich, Hungary	7

Women

Larissa Latynina, USSR	9
Jenny Thompson, U.S.	8
Vera Cáslavská, Czech	7
Kristin Otto, E Germany	6
Agnes Keleti, Hungary	5
Nadia Comaneci, Romania	5
Polina Astaknova, USSR	5
Krisztina Egerszegi, Hungary	5
Kornelia Ender, E Germany	4
Dawn Fraser, Australia	4
Lyudmila Tourischeva, USSR	4
Evelyn Ashford, United States	4
Janet Evans, United States	4
Fanny Blankers-Koen, Neth	4
Betty Cuthbert, Australia	4
Pat McCormick, United States	4
Bärbel Eckert Wöckel, E Ger	4
Amy Van Dyken, United States	4
Inge de Bruijn, Netherlands	4
Yana Klochkova, Ukraine	4
Dara Torres, United States	4

Summer Games Champions

TRACK AND FIELD — Men

100 METERS

Year	Champion	Time
1896	Thomas Burke, United States	12.0
1900	Frank Jarvis, United States	11.0
1904	Archie Hahn, United States	11.0
1906	Archie Hahn, United States	11.2
1908	Reginald Walker, S Africa	10.8 OR
1912	Ralph Craig, United States	10.8
1920	Charles Paddock, United States	10.8
1924	Harold Abrahams, Great Britain	10.6 OR
1928	Percy Williams, Canada	10.8
1932	Eddie Tolan, United States	10.3 OR
1936	Jesse Owens, United States	10.3
1948	Harrison Dillard, United States	10.3
1952	Lindy Remigino, United States	10.4
1956	Bobby Morrow, United States	10.5
1960	Armin Hary, W Germany	10.2 OR
1964	Bob Hayes, United States	10.0 EWR
1968	Jim Hines, United States	9.95 WR
1972	Valery Borzov, USSR	10.14
1976	Hasely Crawford, Trinidad	10.06
1980	Allan Wells, Great Britain	10.25
1984	Carl Lewis, United States	9.99
1988	Carl Lewis, United States*	9.92 WR
1992	Linford Christie, Great Britain	9.96
1996	Donovan Bailey, Canada	9.84 WR
2000	Maurice Greene, United States	9.87
2004	Justin Gatlin, United States	9.85
2008	Usain Bolt, Jamaica	9.69 WR

*Ben Johnson, Canada, disqualified.

200 METERS

Year	Champion	Time
1900	John Walter Tewksbury, United States	22.2
1904	Archie Hahn, United States	21.6 OR
1906	Not held	
1908	Robert Kerr, Canada	22.6
1912	Ralph Craig, United States	21.7
1920	Allen Woodring, United States	22.0
1924	Jackson Scholz, United States	21.6
1928	Percy Williams, Canada	21.8
1932	Eddie Tolan, United States	21.2 OR
1936	Jesse Owens, United States	20.7 OR
1948	Mel Patton, United States	21.1
1952	Andrew Stanfield, United States	20.7
1956	Bobby Morrow, United States	20.6 OR
1960	Livio Berruti, Italy	20.5 EWR
1964	Henry Carr, United States	20.3 OR
1968	Tommie Smith, United States	19.83 WR
1972	Valery Borzov, USSR	20.00
1976	Donald Quarrie, Jamaica	20.23
1980	Pietro Mennea, Italy	20.19
1984	Carl Lewis, United States	19.80 OR
1988	Joe DeLoach, United States	19.75 OR
1992	Mike Marsh, United States	20.01
1996	Michael Johnson, United States	19.32 WR
2000	Konstadinos Kederis, Greece	20.09
2004	Shawn Crawford, United States	19.79
2008	Usain Bolt, Jamaica	19.30 WR

400 METERS

Year	Champion	Time
1896	Thomas Burke, United States	54.2
1900	Maxey Long, United States	49.4 OR
1904	Harry Hillman, United States	49.2 OR
1906	Paul Pilgrim, United States	53.2
1908	Wyndham Halswelle, Great Britain	50.0
1912	Charles Reidpath, United States	48.2 OR
1920	Bevil Rudd, South Africa	49.6
1924	Eric Liddell, Great Britain	47.6 OR
1928	Ray Barbuti, United States	47.8
1932	William Carr, United States	46.2 WR
1936	Archie Williams, United States	46.5
1948	Arthur Wint, Jamaica	46.2

400 METERS *(Cont.)*

Year	Champion	Time
1952	George Rhoden, Jamaica	45.9
1956	Charles Jenkins, United States	46.7
1960	Otis Davis, United States	44.9 WR
1964	Michael Larrabee, United States	45.1
1968	Lee Evans, United States	43.86 WR
1972	Vincent Matthews, United States	44.66
1976	Alberto Juantorena, Cuba	44.26
1980	Viktor Markin, USSR	44.60
1984	Alonzo Babers, United States	44.27
1988	Steve Lewis, United States	43.87
1992	Quincy Watts, United States	43.50 OR
1996	Michael Johnson, United States	43.49 OR
2000	Michael Johnson, United States	43.84
2004	Jeremy Wariner, United States	44.00
2008	Lashawn Merritt, United States	43.75

800 METERS

Year	Champion	Time
1896	Edwin Flack, Australia	2:11
1900	Alfred Tysoe, Great Britain	2:01.2
1904	James Lightbody, United States	1:56 OR
1906	Paul Pilgrim, United States	2:01.5
1908	Mel Sheppard, United States	1:52.8 WR
1912	James Meredith, United States	1:51.9 WR
1920	Albert Hill, Great Britain	1:53.4
1924	Douglas Lowe, Great Britain	1:52.4
1928	Douglas Lowe, Great Britain	1:51.8 OR
1932	Thomas Hampson, Great Britain	1:49.8 WR
1936	John Woodruff, United States	1:52.9
1948	Mal Whitfield, United States	1:49.2 OR
1952	Mal Whitfield, United States	1:49.2 EOR
1956	Thomas Courtney, United States	1:47.7 OR
1960	Peter Snell, New Zealand	1:46.3 OR
1964	Peter Snell, New Zealand	1:45.1 OR
1968	Ralph Doubell, Australia	1:44.3 EWR
1972	Dave Wottle, United States	1:45.9
1976	Alberto Juantorena, Cuba	1:43.50 WR
1980	Steve Ovett, Great Britain	1:45.40
1984	Joaquim Cruz, Brazil	1:43.00 OR
1988	Paul Ereng, Kenya	1:43.45
1992	William Tanui, Kenya	1:43.66
1996	Vebjoern Rodal, Norway	1:42.58 OR
2000	Nils Schumann, Germany	1:45.08
2004	Yuriy Borzakovskiy, Russia	1:44.45
2008	Wilfred Kipkemboi Bungei, Kenya	1:44.65

1,500 METERS

Year	Champion	Time
1896	Edwin Flack, Australia	4:33.2
1900	Charles Bennett, Great Britain	4:06.2 WR
1904	James Lightbody, United States	4:05.4 WR
1906	James Lightbody, United States	4:12.0
1908	Mel Sheppard, United States	4:03.4 OR
1912	Arnold Jackson, Great Britain	3:56.8 OR
1920	Albert Hill, Great Britain	4:01.8
1924	Paavo Nurmi, Finland	3:53.6 OR
1928	Harry Larva, Finland	3:53.2 OR
1932	Luigi Beccali, Italy	3:51.2 OR
1936	Jack Lovelock, New Zealand	3:47.8 WR
1948	Henri Eriksson, Sweden	3:49.8
1952	Josef Barthel, Luxemburg	3:45.1 OR
1956	Ron Delany, Ireland	3:41.2 OR
1960	Herb Elliott, Australia	3:35.6 WR
1964	Peter Snell, New Zealand	3:38.1
1968	Kipchoge Keino, Kenya	3:34.9 OR
1972	Pekkha Vasala, Finland	3:36.3
1976	John Walker, New Zealand	3:39.17
1980	Sebastian Coe, Great Britain	3:38.4
1984	Sebastian Coe, Great Britain	3:32.53 OR
1988	Peter Rono, Kenya	3:35.96
1992	Fermin Cacho, Spain	3:40.12
1996	Noureddine Morceli, Algeria	3:35.78
2000	Noah Ngeni, Kenya	3:32.07 OR

Note: OR=Olympic Record. WR=World Record. EOR=Equals Olympic Record. EWR=Equals World Record. WB=World Best.

TRACK AND FIELD — Men *(Cont.)*

1,500 METERS *(Cont.)*

2004....Hicham El Guerrouj, Morocco 3:34.18
2008....Rasheed Ramzi, Bahrain 3:32.94

5,000 METERS

1912....Hannes Kolehmainen, Finland 14:36.6 WR
1920....Joseph Guillemot, France 14:55.6
1924....Paavo Nurmi, Finland 14:31.2 OR
1928....Villie Ritola, Finland 14:38
1932....Lauri Lehtinen, Finland 14:30 OR
1936....Gunnar Hîckert, Finland 14:22.2 OR
1948....Gaston Reiff, Belgium 14:17.6 OR
1952....Emil Zatopek, Czechoslovakia 14:06.6 OR
1956....Vladimir Kuts, USSR 13:39.6 OR
1960....Murray Halberg, New Zealand 13:43.4
1964....Bob Schul, United States 13:48.8
1968....Mohamed Gammoudi, Tunisia 14:05.0
1972....Lasse Viren, Finland 13:26.4 OR
1976....Lasse Viren, Finland 13:24.76
1980....Miruts Yifter, Ethiopia 13:21.0
1984....Said Aouita, Morocco 13:05.59 OR
1988....John Ngugi, Kenya 13:11.70
1992....Dieter Baumann, Germany 13:12.52
1996....Venuste Niyongabo, Burundi 13:07.96
2000....Millon Wolde, Ethiopia 13:35.49
2004....Hicham El Guerrouj, Morocco 13:14.39
2008....Kenenisa Bekele, Ethiopia 12:57.82OR

10,000 METERS

1912....Hannes Kolehmainen, Finland 31:20.8
1920....Paavo Nurmi, Finland 31:45.8
1924....Vilho (Ville) Ritola, Finland 30:23.2 WR
1928....Paavo Nurmi, Finland 30:18.8 OR
1932....Janusz Kusocinski, Poland 30:11.4 OR
1936....Ilmari Salminen, Finland 30:15.4
1948....Emil Zatopek, Czechoslovakia 29:59.6 OR
1952....Emil Zatopek, Czechoslovakia 29:17.0 OR
1956....Vladimir Kuts, USSR 28:45.6 OR
1960....Pyotr Bolotnikov, USSR 28:32.2 OR
1964....Billy Mills, United States 28:24.4 OR
1968....Naftali Temu, Kenya 29:27.4
1972....Lasse Viren, Finland 27:38.4 WR
1976....Lasse Viren, Finland 27:40.38
1980....Miruts Yifter, Ethiopia 27:42.7
1984....Alberto Cova, Italy 27:47.54
1988....Brahim Boutaib, Morocco 27:21.46 OR
1992....Khalid Skah, Morocco 27:46.70
1996....Haile Gebrselassie, Ethiopia 27:07.34 OR
2000....Haile Gebrselassie, Ethiopia 27:18.20
2004....Kenenisa Bekele, Ethiopia 27:05.10 OR
2008....Kenenisa Bekele, Ethiopia 27:01.17 OR

MARATHON

1896....Spiridon Louis, Greece 2:58:50
1900....Michel Theato, France 2:59:45
1904....Thomas Hicks, United States 3:28:53
1906....William Sherring, Canada 2:51:23.6
1908....John Hayes, United States 2:55:18.4 OR
1912....Kenneth McArthur, S Africa 2:36:54.8
1920....Hannes Kolehmainen, Finland 2:32:35.8 WB
1924....Albin Stenroos, Finland 2:41:22.6
1928....Boughera El Ouafi, France 2:32:57
1932....Juan Zabala, Argentina 2:31:36 OR
1936....Kijung Son, Japan (Korea) 2:29:19.2 OR
1948....Delfo Cabrera, Argentina 2:34:51.6
1952....Emil Zatopek, Czechoslovakia 2:23:03.2 OR
1956....Alain Mimoun O'Kacha, France 2:25:00.0
1960....Abebe Bikila, Ethiopia 2:15:16.2 WB
1964....Abebe Bikila, Ethiopia 2:12:11.2 WB
1968....Mamo Wolde, Ethiopia 2:20:26.4
1972....Frank Shorter, United States 2:12:19.8
1976....Waldemar Cierpinski, E Germ. 2:09:55 OR
1980....Waldemar Cierpinski, E Germ. 2:11:03.0
1984....Carlos Lopes, Portugal 2:09:21.0 OR
1988....Gelindo Bordin, Italy 2:10:32

MARATHON *(Cont.)*

1992....Hwang Young-Cho, S Korea 2:13:23
1996....Josia Thugwane, S Africa 2:12:36
2000....Gezahgne Abera, Ethiopia 2:10:11
2004....Stefano Baldini, Italy 2:10:55
2008....Samuel Kamau, Kenya 2:06:32 OR

110-METER HURDLES

1896....Thomas Curtis, United States 17.6
1900....Alvin Kraenzlein, United States 15.4 OR
1904....Frederick Schule, United States 16.0
1906....Robert Leavitt, United States 16.2
1908....Forrest Smithson, United States 15.0 WR
1912....Frederick Kelly, United States 15.1
1920....Earl Thomson, Canada 14.8 WR
1924....Daniel Kinsey, United States 15.0
1928....Sydney Atkinson, S Africa 14.8
1932....George Saling, United States 14.6
1936....Forrest Towns, United States 14.2
1948....William Porter, United States 13.9 OR
1952....Harrison Dillard, United States 13.7 OR
1956....Lee Calhoun, United States 13.5 OR
1960....Lee Calhoun, United States 13.8
1964....Hayes Jones, United States 13.6
1968....Willie Davenport, United States 13.3 OR
1972....Rod Milburn, United States 13.24 EWR
1976....Guy Drut, France 13.30
1980....Thomas Munkelt, E Germany 13.39
1984....Roger Kingdom, United States 13.20 OR
1988....Roger Kingdom, United States 12.98 OR
1992....Mark McKoy, Canada 13.12
1996....Allen Johnson, United States 12.95 OR
2000....Anier Garcia, Cuba 13.00
2004....Xiang Liu, China 12.91 EWR
2008....Dayron Robles, Cuba 12.93

400-METER HURDLES

1900....John Walter Tewksbury, U.S. 57.6
1904....Harry Hillman, United States 53.0
1906....Not held
1908....Charles Bacon, United States 55.0 WR
1912....Not held
1920....Frank Loomis, United States 54.0 WR
1924....F. Morgan Taylor, United States 52.6
1928....David Burghley, Great Britain 53.4 OR
1932....Robert Tisdall, Ireland 51.7
1936....Glenn Hardin, United States 52.4
1948....Roy Cochran, United States 51.1 OR
1952....Charles Moore, United States 50.8 OR
1956....Glenn Davis, United States 50.1 EOR
1960....Glenn Davis, United States 49.3 EOR
1964....Rex Cawley, United States 49.6
1968....Dave Hemery, Great Britain 48.12 WR
1972....John Akii-Bua, Uganda 47.82 WR
1976....Edwin Moses, United States 47.64 WR
1980....Volker Beck, E Germany 48.70
1984....Edwin Moses, United States 47.75
1988....Andre Phillips, United States 47.19 OR
1992....Kevin Young, United States 46.78 WR
1996....Derrick Adkins, United States 47.54
2000....Angelo Taylor, United States 47.50
2004....Felix Sanchez, Dominican Rep 47.63
2008....Angelo Taylor, United States 47.25

3,000-METER STEEPLECHASE

1920....Percy Hodge, Great Britain 10:00.4 OR
1924....Vilho (Ville) Ritola, Finland 9:33.6 OR
1928....Toivo Loukola, Finland 9:21.8 WR
1932....Volmari Iso-Hollo, Finland 10:33.4*
1936....Volmari Iso-Hollo, Finland 9:03.8 WR
1948....Thore Sjöstrand, Sweden 9:04.6
1952....Horace Ashenfelter, U.S. 8:45.4 WR
1956....Chris Brasher, Great Britain 8:41.2 OR
1960....Zdzislaw Krzyszkowiak, Poland 8:34.2 OR
1964....Gaston Roelants, Belgium 8:30.8 OR

TRACK AND FIELD — Men (Cont.)

3,000-METER STEEPLECHASE (Cont.)

1968....Amos Biwott, Kenya 8:51
1972....Kipchoge Keino, Kenya 8:23.6 OR
1976....Anders Gärderud, Sweden 8:08.2 WR
1980....Bronislaw Malinowski, Poland 8:09.7
1984....Julius Korir, Kenya 8:11.8
1988....Julius Kariuki, Kenya 8:05.51 OR
1992....Matthew Birir, Kenya 8:08.84
1996....Joseph Keter, Kenya 8:07.12
2000....Reuben Kosgei, Kenya 8:21.43
2004....Ezekiel Kemboi, Kenya 8:05.81
2008....Brimin Kipruto, Kenya 8:10.34

*About 3,450 meters; extra lap by error.

4 X 100-METER RELAY

1912 ....Great Britain 42.4 OR
1920 ....United States 42.2 WR
1924 ....United States 41.0 EWR
1928 ....United States 41.0 EWR
1932 ....United States 40.0 EWR
1936 ....United States 39.8 WR
1948 ....United States 40.6
1952 ....United States 40.1
1956 ....United States 39.5 WR
1960 ....W Germany 39.5 EWR
1964 ....United States 39.0 WR
1968 ....United States 38.2 WR
1972 ....United States 38.19 EWR
1976 ....United States 38.33
1980 ....USSR 38.26
1984 ....United States 37.83 WR
1988 ....USSR 38.19
1992 ....United States 37.40 WR
1996 ....Canada 37.69
2000 ....United States 37.61
2004 ....Great Britain 38.07
2008 ....Jamaica 37.10 WR

4 X 400-METER RELAY

1908 ....United States 3:29.4
1912 ....United States 3:16.6 WR
1920 ....Great Britain 3:22.2
1924 ....United States 3:16.0 WR
1928 ....United States 3:14.2 WR
1932 ....United States 3:08.2 WR
1936 ....Great Britain 3:09.0
1948 ....United States 3:10.4 WR
1952 ....Jamaica 3:03.9 WR
1956 ....United States 3:04.8
1960 ....United States 3:02.2 WR
1964 ....United States 3:00.7 WR
1968 ....United States 2:56.16 WR
1972 ....Kenya 2:59.8
1976 ....United States 2:58.65
1980 ....USSR 3:01.1
1984 ....United States 2:57.91
1988..................United States 2:56.16 EWR
1992 ....United States 2:55.74 WR
1996 ....United States 2:55.99
2000 ....United States 2:56.35
2004 ....United States 2:55.91
2008 ....United States 2:55.39 OR

20-KILOMETER WALK

1956....Leonid Spirin, USSR 1:31:27.4
1960....Vladimir Golubnichiy, USSR 1:33:07.2
1964....Kenneth Mathews, Great Britain 1:29:34.0 OR
1968....Vladimir Golubnichiy, USSR 1:33:58.4
1972....Peter Frenkel, E Germany 1:26:42.4 OR
1976....Daniel Bautista, Mexico 1:24:40.6 OR
1980....Maurizio Damilano, Italy 1:23:35.5 OR
1984....Ernesto Canto, Mexico 1:23:13.0 OR

20-KILOMETER WALK (Cont.)

1988....Jozef Pribilinec, Czechoslovakia 1:19:57.0 OR
1992....Daniel Plaza, Spain 1:21:45.0
1996....Jefferson Pérez, Ecuador 1:20:07
2000....Robert Korzeniowski, Poland 1:18:59 OR
2004....Ivano Brugnetti, Italy 1:19:40
2008....Valeriy Borchin, Russia 1:19:01

50-KILOMETER WALK

1932....Thomas Green, Great Britain 4:50:10
1936....Harold Whitlock, Great Britain 4:30:41.4 OR
1948....John Ljunggren, Sweden 4:41:52
1952....Giuseppe Dordoni, Italy 4:28:07.8 OR
1956....Norman Read, New Zealand 4:30:42.8
1960....Donald Thompson, Great Britain 4:25:30 OR
1964....Abdon Parnich, Italy 4:11:12.4 OR
1968....Christoph Höhne, E Germany 4:20:13.6
1972....Bernd Kannenberg, W Germany 3:56:11.6 OR
1980....Hartwig Gauder, E Germany 3:49:24.0 OR
1984....Raul Gonzalez, Mexico 3:47:26.0 OR
1988....Viacheslav Ivanenko, USSR 3:38:29.0 OR
1992....Andrey Perlov, Unified Team 3:50:13
1996....Robert Korzeniowski, Poland 3:43:30
2000....Robert Korzeniowski, Poland 3:42:22 OR
2004....Robert Korzeniowski, Poland 3:38:46
2008....Alex Schwazer, Italy 3:37:09 OR

HIGH JUMP

1896...Ellery Clark, United States 5 ft 11¼ in
1900...Irving Baxter, United States 6 ft 2¾ in OR
1904...Samuel Jones, United States 5 ft 11 in
1906...Cornelius Leahy, Great Britain/Ireland 5 ft 10 in
1908...Harry Porter, United States 6 ft 3 in OR
1912...Alma Richards, United States 6 ft 4 in OR
1920...Richmond Landon, United States 6 ft 4 in OR
1924...Harold Osborn, United States 6 ft 6 in OR
1928...Robert W. King, United States 6 ft 4½ in
1932...Duncan McNaughton, Canada 6 ft 5½ in
1936...Cornelius Johnson, United States 6 ft 8 in OR
1948...John L. Winter, Australia 6 ft 6 in
1952...Walter Davis, United States 6 ft 8½ in OR
1956...Charles Dumas, United States 6 ft 11½ in OR
1960...Robert Shavlakadze, USSR 7 ft 1 in OR
1964...Valery Brumel, USSR 7 ft 1¾ in OR
1968...Dick Fosbury, United States 7 ft 4¼ in OR
1972...Yuri Tarmak, USSR 7 ft 3¾ in
1976...Jacek Wszola, Poland 7 ft 4½ in OR
1980...Gerd Wessig, E Germany 7 ft 8¾ in WR
1984...Dietmar Mögenburg, W Ger 7 ft 8½ in
1988...Gennadiy Avdeyenko, USSR 7 ft 9¾ in OR
1992...Javier Sotomayor, Cuba 7 ft 8 in.
1996...Charles Austin, United States 7 ft 10 in OR
2000...Sergey Kliugin, Russia 7 ft 8¼ in
2004...Stefan Holm, Sweden 7 ft 8¾ in
2008...Andrey Silnov, Russia 7 ft 9 in

POLE VAULT

1896...William Hoyt, United States 10 ft 10 in
1900...Irving Baxter, United States 10 ft 10 in
1904...Charles Dvorak, United States 11 ft 5¾ in
1906...Fernand Gonder, France 11 ft 5¾ in
1908...Alfred Gilbert, United States 12 ft 2 in OR
Edward Cooke Jr., United States
1912...Harry Babcock, United States 12 ft 11½ in OR
1920...Frank Foss, United States 13 ft 5 in WR
1924...Lee Barnes, United States 12 ft 11½ in
1928...Sabin Carr, United States 13 ft 9¼ in OR
1932...William Miller, United States 14 ft 1¾ in OR

Note: OR=Olympic Record. WR=World Record. EOR=Equals Olympic Record. EWR=Equals World Record. WB=World Best.

TRACK AND FIELD — Men (Cont.)

POLE VAULT (Cont.)

1936...Earle Meadows, United States 14 ft 3¼ in OR
1948...Guinn Smith, United States 14 ft 1¼ in
1952...Robert Richards, United States 14 ft 11 in OR
1956...Robert Richards, United States 14 ft 11½ in OR
1960...Don Bragg, United States 15 ft 5 in OR
1964...Fred Hansen, United States 16 ft 8¾ in OR
1968...Bob Seagren, United States 17 ft 8½ in OR
1972...Wolfgang Nordwig, E Germany 18 ft ½ in OR
1976...Tadeusz Slusarski, Poland 18 ft ½ in EOR
1980...Wladyslaw Kozakiewicz, Pol 18 ft 11½ in WR
1984...Pierre Quinon, France 18 ft 10¼ in
1988...Sergei Bubka, USSR 19 ft 4¼ in OR
1992...Maksim Tarasov, Unified Team 19 ft ¼ in
1996...Jean Galfione, France 19 ft 5 ¼ in OR
2000...Nick Hysong, United States 19 ft 4¼ in
2004...Timothy Mack, United States 19 ft 6¼ in
2008...Steve Hooker, Australia 19 ft 6½ in OR

LONG JUMP

1896...Ellery Clark, United States 20 ft 10 in
1900...Alvin Kraenzlein, United States 23 ft 6¾ in OR
1904...Meyer Prinstein, United States 24 ft 1 in OR
1906...Meyer Prinstein, United States 23 ft 7½ in
1908...Frank Irons, United States 24 ft 6½ in OR
1912...Albert Gutterson, United States 24 ft 11¼ in OR
1920...William Peterssen, Sweden 23 ft 5½ in
1924...DeHart Hubbard, United States 24 ft 5 in
1928...Edward B. Hamm, United States 25 ft 4½ in OR
1932...Edward Gordon, United States 25 ft ¾ in
1936...Jesse Owens, United States 26 ft 5½ in OR
1948...William Steele, United States 25 ft 8 in
1952...Jerome Biffle, United States 24 ft 10 in
1956...Gregory Bell, United States 25 ft 8¼ in
1960...Ralph Boston, United States 26 ft 7¾ in OR
1964...Lynn Davies, Great Britain 26 ft 5¾ in
1968...Bob Beamon, United States 29 ft 2½ in WR
1972...Randy Williams, United States 27 ft ½ in
1976...Arnie Robinson, United States 27 ft 4¾ in
1980...Lutz Dombrowski, E Germany 28 ft ¼ in
1984...Carl Lewis, United States 28 ft ¼ in
1988...Carl Lewis, United States 28 ft 7½ in
1992...Carl Lewis, United States 28 ft 5½ in
1996...Carl Lewis, United States 27 ft 10¾ in
2000...Ivan Pedrosa, Cuba 28 ft ¾ in
2004...Dwight Phillips, United States 28 ft 2¼ in
2008...Irving Jahir Saladino, Panama 27 ft 4¼ in

TRIPLE JUMP

1896...James Connolly, United States 44 ft 11¾ in
1900...Meyer Prinstein, United States 47 ft 5¾ in OR
1904...Meyer Prinstein, United States 47 ft 1 in
1906...Peter O'Connor, GB/ Ire 46 ft 2¼ in
1908...Timothy Ahearne, GB/ Ire 48 ft 11¼ in OR
1912...Gustaf Lindblom, Sweden 48 ft 5¼ in
1920...Vilho Tuulos, Finland 47 ft 7 in
1924...Anthony Winter, Australia 50 ft 11¼ in WR
1928...Mikio Oda, Japan 49 ft 11 in
1932...Chuhei Nambu, Japan 51 ft 7 in WR
1936...Naoto Tajima, Japan 52 ft 6 in WR
1948...Arne Ahman, Sweden 50 ft 6¼ in
1952...Adhemar da Silva, Brazil 53 ft 2¾ in WR
1956...Adhemar da Silva, Brazil 53 ft 7¾ in OR
1960...Jozef Schmidt, Poland 55 ft 2 in
1964...Jozef Schmidt, Poland 55 ft 3½ in OR
1968...Viktor Saneyev, USSR 57 ft ¾ in WR
1972...Viktor Saneyev, USSR 56 ft 11¾ in
1976...Viktor Saneyev, USSR 56 ft 8¾ in
1980...Jaak Uudmae, USSR 56 ft 11¼ in
1984...Al Joyner, United States 56 ft 7½ in

TRIPLE JUMP (Cont.)

1988...Khristo Markov, Bulgaria 57 ft 9½ in OR
1992...Mike Conley, United States 59 ft 7½ in (w)
1996...Kenny Harrison, United States 59 ft 4¼ in OR
2000...Jonathon Edwards, G. Britain 58 ft 1¼ in
2004...Christian Olsson, Sweden 58 ft 4½ in
2008...Nelson Evora, Portugal 57 ft 11½ in

SHOT PUT

1896...Robert Garrett, United States 36 ft 9¾ in
1900...Richard Sheldon, United States 46 ft 3¼ in OR
1904...Ralph Rose, United States 48 ft 7 in WR
1906...Martin Sheridan, United States 40 ft 5¼ in
1908...Ralph Rose, United States 46 ft 7½ in
1912...Pat McDonald, United States 50 ft 4 in OR
1920...Ville Porhola, Finland 48 ft 7¼ in
1924...Clarence Houser, United States 49 ft 2¼ in
1928...John Kuck, United States 52 ft ¾ in WR
1932...Leo Sexton, United States 52 ft 6 in OR
1936...Hans Woellke, Germany 53 ft 1¾ in OR
1948...Wilbur Thompson, United States 56 ft 2 in OR
1952...Parry O'Brien, United States 57 ft ½ in OR
1956...Parry O'Brien, United States 60 ft 11¼ in OR
1960...William Nieder, United States 64 ft 6¾ in OR
1964...Dallas Long, United States 66 ft 8½ in OR
1968...Randy Matson, United States 67 ft 4¾ in
1972...Wladyslaw Komar, Poland 69 ft 6 in OR
1976...Udo Beyer, E Germany 69 ft ¾ in
1980...Vladimir Kiselyov, USSR 70 ft ½ in OR
1984...Alessandro Andrei, Italy 69 ft 9 in
1988...Ulf Timmermann, E Germany 73 ft 8¾ in OR
1992...Mike Stulce, United States 71 ft 2½ in
1996...Randy Barnes, United States 70 ft 11 in
2000...Arsi Harju, Finland 69 ft 10¼ in
2004...Yuriy Bilonog, Ukraine 69 ft 5¼ in
2008...Tomasz Majewski, Poland 70 ft 6¾ in

DISCUS THROW

1896...Robert Garrett, United States 95 ft 7½ in
1900...Rudolf Bauer, Hungary 118 ft 3 in OR
1904....Martin Sheridan, United States 128 ft 10½ in OR
1906...Martin Sheridan, United States 136 ft
1908...Martin Sheridan, United States 134 ft 2 in OR
1912...Armas Taipele, Finland 148 ft 3 in OR
1920...Elmer Niklander, Finland 146 ft 7 in
1924...Clarence Houser, United States 151 ft 4 in OR
1928...Clarence Houser, United States 155 ft 3 in OR
1932...John Anderson, United States 162 ft 4 in OR
1936...Ken Carpenter, United States 165 ft 7 in OR
1948...Adolfo Consolini, Italy 173 ft 2 in OR
1952...Sim Iness, United States 180 ft 6 in OR
1956...Al Oerter, United States 184 ft 11 in OR
1960...Al Oerter, United States 194 ft 2 in OR
1964...Al Oerter, United States 200 ft 1 in OR
1968...Al Oerter, United States 212 ft 6 in OR
1972...Ludvik Danek, Czechoslovakia 211 ft 3 in
1976...Mac Wilkins, United States 221 ft 5 in OR
1980...Viktor Rashchupkin, USSR 218 ft 8 in
1984...Rolf Dannenberg, W Ger 218 ft 6 in
1988...Jürgen Schult, E Germany 225 ft 9 in OR
1992...Romas Ubartas, Lithuania 213 ft 8 in
1996...Lars Riedel, Germany 227 ft 8 in OR
2000...Virgilijus Alekna, Lithuania 227 ft 4 in
2004...Virgilijus Alekna, Lithuania 229 ft 3 in
2008...Gerd Kanter, Estonia 225 ft 9½ in

HAMMER THROW

1900...John Flanagan, United States 163 ft 1 in
1904...John Flanagan, United States 168 ft 1 in OR
1906...Not held
1908...John Flanagan, United States 170 ft 4 in OR
1912...Matt McGrath, United States 179 ft 7 in OR

(w)-wind aided

TRACK AND FIELD — Men (Cont.)

HAMMER THROW (Cont.)

1920...Pat Ryan, United States 173 ft 5 in
1924...Fred Tootell, United States 174 ft 10 in
1928...Patrick O'Callaghan, Ireland 168 ft 7 in
1932...Patrick O'Callaghan, Ireland 176 ft 11 in
1936...Karl Hein, Germany 185 ft 4 in OR
1948...Imre Nemeth, Hungary 183 ft 11 in
1952...Jozsef Csermak, Hungary 197 ft 11 in WR
1956...Harold Connolly, United States 207 ft 3 in OR
1960...Vasily Rudenkov, USSR 220 ft 2 in OR
1964...Romuald Klim, USSR 228 ft 10 in OR
1968...Gyula Zsivotsky, Hungary 240 ft 8 in OR
1972...Anatoli Bondarchuk, USSR 247 ft 8 in OR
1976...Yuri Sedykh, USSR 254 ft 4 in OR
1980...Yuri Sedykh, USSR 268 ft 4 in WR
1984...Juha Tiainen, Finland 256 ft 2 in
1988...Sergei Litvinov, USSR 278 ft 2 in OR
1992...Andrey Abduvaliyev, Unified T 270 ft 9 in
1996...Balazs Kiss, Hungary 266 ft 6 in
2000...Szymon Ziolkowski, Poland 262 ft 6 in
2004...Adrian Zsolt, Hungary 272 fr 11 in
2008...Primoz Kozmus, Slovenia 269 ft 1 in

JAVELIN

1908...Erik Lemming, Sweden 179 ft 10 in
1912...Erik Lemming, Sweden 198 ft 11 in WR
1920...Jonni Myyrä, Finland 215 ft 10 in OR
1924...Jonni Myyrä, Finland 206 ft 6 in
1928...Eric Lundkvist, Sweden 218 ft 6 in OR
1932...Matti Jarvinen, Finland 238 ft 6 in OR
1936...Gerhard Stöck, Germany 235 ft 8 in
1948...Kai Rautavaara, Finland 228 ft 10½ in
1952...Cy Young, United States 242 ft 1 in OR
1956...Egil Danielson, Norway 281 ft 2¼ in WR
1960...Viktor Tsibulenko, USSR 277 ft 8 in
1964...Pauli Nevala, Finland 271 ft 2 in
1968...Janis Lusis, USSR 295 ft 7 in OR
1972...Klaus Wolfermann, W Germany 296 ft 10 in OR

JAVELIN (Cont.)

1976...Miklos Nemeth, Hungary 310 ft 4 in WR
1980...Dainis Kuta, USSR 299 ft 2⅜ in
1984...Arto Härkönen, Finland 284 ft 8 in
1988...Tapio Korjus, Finland 276 ft 6 in
1992...Jan Zelezny, Czechoslovakia 294 ft 2 in OR
1996...Jan Zelezny, Czech Republic 289 ft 3 in
2000...Jan Zelezny, Czech Republic 295 ft 9½ in OR
2004...Andreas Thorkildsen, Norway 283 ft 9 in
2008...Andreas Thorkildsen, Norway 297 ft 1¾ in OR

DECATHLON

	Pts
1904 ...Thomas Kiely, Ireland	6036
1912 ...Jim Thorpe, United States*	8412 WR
1920 ...Helge Lövland, Norway	6803
1924 ...Harold Osborn, United States	7711 WR
1928 ...Paavo Yrjölä, Finland	8053.29 WR
1932 ...James Bausch, United States	8462 WR
1936 ...Glenn Morris, United States	7900 WR
1948 ...Robert Mathias, United States	7139
1952 ...Robert Mathias, United States	7887 WR
1956 ...Milton Campbell, United States	7937 OR
1960 ...Rafer Johnson, United States	8392 OR
1964 ...Willi Holdorf, W Germany	7887
1968 ...Bill Toomey, United States	8193 OR
1972 ...Nikolai Avilov, USSR	8454 WR
1976 ...Bruce Jenner, United States	8617 WR
1980 ...Daley Thompson, Great Britain	8495
1984 ...Daley Thompson, Great Britain	8798 EWR
1988 ...Christian Schenk, E Germany	8488
1992 ...Robert Zmelik, Czechoslovakia	8611
1996 ...Dan O'Brien, United States	8824 OR
2000 ...Erki Nool, Estonia	8641
2004 ...Roman Seberle, Czech Rep	8893 OR
2008 ...Bryan Clay, United States	8791

*In 1913, Thorpe was disqualified for having played professional baseball in 1910. His record was restored in 1982.

TRACK AND FIELD — Women

100 METERS

1928....Elizabeth Robinson, US 12.2 EWR
1932....Stella Walsh, Poland 11.9 EWR
1936....Helen Stephens, United States 11.5
1948....Francina Blankers-Koen, Neth 11.9
1952....Marjorie Jackson, Australia 11.5 EWR
1956....Betty Cuthbert, Australia 11.5 EWR
1960....Wilma Rudolph, United States 11.0
1964....Wyomia Tyus, United States 11.4
1968....Wyomia Tyus, United States 11.0 WR
1972....Renate Stecher, E Germany 11.07
1976....Annegret Richter, W Germany 11.08
1980....Lyudmila Kondratyeva, USSR 11.06
1984....Evelyn Ashford, United States 10.97 OR
1988....Florence Griffith Joyner, United States 10.54 WR
1992....Gail Devers, United States 10.82
1996....Gail Devers, United States 10.94
2000....Vacant*
2004....Yuliya Nesterenko, Belarus 10.93
2008....Shelly-Ann Fraser, Jamaica 10.78

200 METERS

1948....Francina Blankers-Koen, Neth 24.4
1952....Marjorie Jackson, Australia 23.7
1956....Betty Cuthbert, Australia 23.4 EOR
1960....Wilma Rudolph, United States 24.0

200 METERS (Cont.)

1964....Edith McGuire, United States 23.0 OR
1968....Irena Szewinska, Poland 22.5 WR
1972....Renate Stecher, E Germany 22.40 EWR
1976....Bärbel Eckert, E Germany 22.37 OR
1980....Bärbel Wöckel (Eckert), E Germ. 22.03 OR
1984....Valerie Brisco-Hooks, U.S. 21.81 OR
1988....Florence Griffith Joyner, U.S. 21.34 WR
1992....Gwen Torrence, United States 21.81
1996....Marie-José Pérec, France 22.12
2000....Vacant*
2004....Veronica Campbell, Jamaica 22.05
2008....Veronica Campbell-Brown, Jamaica 21.74

400 METERS

1964....Betty Cuthbert, Australia 52.0 OR
1968....Colette Besson, France 52.0 EOR
1972....Monika Zehrt, E Germany 51.08 OR
1976....Irena Szewinska, Poland 49.29 WR
1980....Marita Koch, E Germany 48.88 OR
1984....Valerie Brisco-Hooks, U.S. 48.83 OR
1988....Olga Bryzgina, USSR 48.65 OR
1992....Marie-José Pérec, France 48.83
1996....Marie-José Pérec, France 48.25 OR
2000....Cathy Freeman, Australia 49.11
2004....T. Williams-Darling, Bahamas 49.41
2004....T. Williams-Darling, Bahamas 49.41

Note: OR=Olympic Record. WR=World Record. EOR=Equals Olympic Record. EWR=Equals World Record. WB=World Best.

*Marion Jones was stripped of her medals from the 2000 Olympics, no decision on replacing her victories has been made.

TRACK AND FIELD — Women *(Cont.)*

800 METERS

1928....Lina Radke, Germany 2:16.8 WR
1932-56..Not held
1960....Lyudmila Shevtsova, USSR 2:04.3 EWR
1964....Ann Packer, Great Britain 2:01.1 OR
1968....Madeline Manning, United States 2:00.9 OR
1972....Hildegard Falck, W Germany 1:58.55 OR
1976....Tatyana Kazankina, USSR 1:54.94 WR
1980....Nadezhda Olizarenko, USSR 1:53.42 WR
1984....Doina Melinte, Romania 1:57.6
1988....Sigrun Wodars, E Germany 1:56.10
1992....Ellen Van Langen, Netherlands 1:55.54
1996....Svetlana Masterkova, Russia 1:57.73
2000....Maria Mutola, Mozambique 1:56.15
2004....Kelly Holmes, Great Britain 1:56.38
2008....Pamela Jelimo, Kenya 1:54.87

1,500 METERS

1972....Lyudmila Bragina, USSR 4:01.4 WR
1976....Tatyana Kazankina, USSR 4:05.48
1980....Tatyana Kazankina, USSR 3:56.6 OR
1984....Gabriella Dorio, Italy 4:03.25
1988....Paula Ivan, Romania 3:53.96 OR
1992....Hassiba Boulmerka, Algeria 3:55.30
1996....Svetlana Masterkova, Russia 4:00.83
2000....Nouria Merah-Benida, Algeria 4:05.10
2004....Kelly Holmes, Great Britain 3:57.90
2008....Nancy Jebet Lagat, Kenya 4:00.23

3,000 METERS

1984....Maricica Puica, Romania 8:35.96 OR
1988....Tatyana Samolenko, USSR 8:26.53 OR
1992....Elena Romanova, Unified Team 8:46.04

5,000 METERS

1996....Wang Junxia, China 14:57.88
2000....Gabriela Szabo, Romania 14:40.79 OR
2004.....Meseret Defar, Ethiopia 14:45.65
2008.....Tirunesh Dibaba Kenene, Ethiopia 15:41.40

10,000 METERS

1988....Olga Bondarenko, USSR 31:05.21 OR
1992....Derartu Tulu, Ethiopia 31:06.02
1996....Fernanda Ribeiro, Portugal 31:01.63 OR
2000....Derartu Tulu, Ethiopia 30:17.49 OR
2004....Huina Xing, China 30:24.36
2008....Tirunesh Dibaba Kenene, Ethiopia 29:54.66 OR

MARATHON

1984....Joan Benoit, United States 2:24:52 OR
1988....Rosa Mota, Portugal 2:25:40
1992....Valentin Yegorova, Unified Team 2:32:41
1996....Fatuma Roba, Ethiopia 2:26:05
2000....Naoko Takahashi, Japan 2:23:14 OR
2004....Noguchi Mizuki, Japan 2:26:20
2008....Constantina Tomescu Dita, Romania 2:26:44

80-METER HURDLES

1932....Babe Didrikson, United States 11.7 WR
1936....Trebisonda Valla, Italy 11.7
1948....Francina Blankers-Koen, Neth 11.2 OR
1952....Shirley Strickland, Australia 10.9 WR
1956....Shirley Strickland, Australia 10.7 OR
1960....Irina Press, USSR 10.8
1964....Karin Balzer, E Germany 10.5
1968....Maureen Caird, Australia 10.3 OR

100-METER HURDLES

1972....Annelie Ehrhardt, E Germany 12.59 WR
1976....Johanna Schaller, E Germany 12.77

100-METER HURDLES *(Cont.)*

1980....Vera Komisova, USSR 12.56 OR
1984....Benita Fitzgerald-Brown, U.S. 12.84
1988....Yordanka Donkova, Bulgaria 12.38 OR
1992....Paraskevi Patoulidou, Greece 12.64
1996....Lyudmila Engqvist, Sweden 12.58
2000....Olga Shishigina, Kazakhstan 12.65
2004....Joanna Hayes, United States 12.37 OR
2008....Dawn Harper, United States 12.54

400-METER HURDLES

1984....Nawal el Moutawakel, Morocco 54.61 OR
1988....Debra Flintoff-King, Australia 53.17 OR
1992....Sally Gunnell, Great Britain 53.23
1996....Deon Hemmings, Jamaica 52.82 OR
2000....Irina Privalova, Russia 53.02
2004....Faní Halkiá, Greece 52.82
2008....Melaine Walker, Jamaica 52.64

4 X 100-METER RELAY

1928 ....Canada 48.4 WR
1932 ....United States 46.9 WR
1936 ....United States 46.9
1948 ....Netherlands 47.5
1952 ....United States 45.9 WR
1956 ....Australia 44.5 WR
1960 ....United States 44.5
1964 ....Poland 43.6
1968 ....United States 42.8 WR
1972 ....W Germany 42.81 EWR
1976 ....E Germany 42.55 OR
1980 ....E Germany 41.60 WR
1984 ....United States 41.65
1988 ....United States 41.98
1992 ....United States 42.11
1996 ....United States 41.95
2000 ....Bahamas 41.95
2004 ....Jamaica 41.73
2008 ....Russia 42.31

4 X 400-METER RELAY

1972 ....E Germany 3:23 WR
1976 ....E Germany 3:19.23 WR
1980 ....USSR 3:20.02
1984 ....United States 3:18.29 OR
1988 ....USSR 3:15.18 WR
1992 ....Unified Team 3:20.20
1996 ....United States 3:20.91
2000 ....Vacant†
2004 ....United States 3:19.01
2008 ....United States 3:18.54

10-KILOMETER WALK

1992....Chen Yueling, China 44:32
1996....Elena Nikolayeva, Russia 41:49 OR

20-KILOMETER WALK

2000....Liping Wang, China 1:29:05
2004....Athanasía Tsouméléka, Greece 1:29:12
2008....Olga Kaniskina, Russia 1:26:31 OR

HIGH JUMP

1928...Ethel Catherwood, Canada 5 ft 2½ in
1932...Jean Shiley, United States 5 ft 5¼ in WR
1936...Ibolya Csak, Hungary 5 ft 3 in
1948...Alice Coachman, United States 5 ft 6 in OR
1952...Esther Brand, South Africa 5 ft 5¾ in
1956...Mildred L. McDaniel, U.S. 5 ft 9¼ in WR
1960...Iolanda Balas, Romania 6 ft ¾ in OR
1964...Iolanda Balas, Romania 6 ft 2¾ in OR

Note: OR=Olympic Record; WR=World Record; EOR=Equals Olympic Record; EWR=Equals World Record; WB=World Best.
†Marion Jones was stripped of her medals from the 2000 Olympics, no decision on replacing her victories has been made.

TRACK AND FIELD — Women (Cont.)

HIGH JUMP (Cont.)

1968...Miloslava Reskova, Czech. 5 ft 11½ in
1972...Ulrike Meyfarth, W. Germany 6 ft 3½ in EWR
1976...Rosemarie Ackermann, E Germ 6 ft 4 in OR
1980...Sara Simeoni, Italy 6 ft 5½ in OR
1984...Ulrike Meyfarth, W Germany 6 ft 7½ in OR
1988...Louise Ritter, United States 6 ft 8 in OR
1992...Heike Henkel, Germany 6 ft 7½ in
1996...Stefka Kostadinova, Bulgaria 6 ft 8¾ in OR
2000...Yelena Yelesina, Russia 6 ft 7 in
2004...Yelena Slesarenko, Russia 6 ft 9 in
2008...Tia Hellebaut, Belgium 6 ft 8¾ in

POLE VAULT

2000....Stacy Dragila, United States 15 ft 1 in OR
2004....Yelena Isinbayeva, Russia 16 ft 1¼ in WR
2008....Yelena Isinbayeva, Russia 16 ft 6¾ in WR

LONG JUMP

1948...Olga Gyarmati, Hungary 18 ft 8¼ in
1952...Yvette Williams, New Zealand 20 ft 5¾ in OR
1956...Elzbieta Krzeskinska, Poland 20 ft 10 in EWR
1960...Vyera Krepkina, USSR 20 ft 10¾ in OR
1964...Mary Rand, Great Britain 22 ft 2¼ in WR
1968...Viorica Viscopoleanu, Rom 22 ft 4½ in WR
1972...Heidemarie Rosendahl, W Ger 22 ft 3 in
1976...Angela Voigt, E Germany 22 ft ¾ in
1980...Tatyana Kolpakova, USSR 23 ft 2 in OR
1984...Anisoara Stanciu, Romania 22 ft 10 in
1988...Jackie Joyner-Kersee, U.S. 24 ft 3½ in OR
1992...Heike Drechsler, Germany 23 ft 5¼ in
1996...Chioma Ajunwa, Nigeria 23 ft 4½ in
2000...Heike Drechsler, Germany 22 ft 11¼ in
2004...Tatyana Lebedeva, Russia 23 ft 2½ in
2008...Maurren Higa Maggi, Brazil 23 ft 1 in

TRIPLE JUMP

1996...Inessa Kravets, Ukraine 50 ft 3½ in
2000...Tereza Marinova, Bulgaria 49 ft 10½ in
2004...Francoise M. Etone, Cameroon 50 ft 2½ in
2008...Francoise M. Etone, Cameroon 50 ft 5 in

SHOT PUT

1948...Micheline Ostermeyer, France 45 ft 1½ in
1952...Galina Zybina, USSR 50 ft 1¾ in WR
1956...Tamara Tyshkevich, USSR 54 ft 5 in OR
1960...Tamara Press, USSR 56 ft 10 in OR
1964...Tamara Press, USSR 59 ft 6¼ in OR
1968...Margitta Gummel, E Germany 64 ft 4 in WR
1972...Nadezhda Chizhova, USSR 69 ft WR
1976...Ivanka Hristova, Bulgaria 69 ft 5¼ in OR
1980...Ilona Slupianek, E Germany 73 ft 6¼ in
1984...Claudia Losch, W Germany 67 ft 2¼ in
1988...Natalya Lisovskaya, USSR 72 ft 11¾ in
1992...Svetlana Kriveleva, Unified Team 69 ft 1¼ in
1996...Astrid Kumbernuss, Germany 67 ft 5½ in
2000...Yanina Korolchik, Belarus 67 ft 5½ in
2004...Yumileidi Cumba Jay, Cuba 64 ft 3¼ in
2008...Valerie Vili, New Zealand 67 ft 5½ in

DISCUS THROW

1928...Helena Konopacka, Poland 129 ft 11¾ in WR
1932...Lillian Copeland, United States 133 ft 2 in OR
1936...Gisela Mauermayer, Germany 156 ft 3 in OR
1948...Micheline Ostermeyer, France 137 ft 6 in
1952...Nina Romaschkova, USSR 168 ft 8 in OR
1956...Olga Fikotova, Czechoslovakia 176 ft 1 in OR
1960...Nina Ponomaryeva, USSR 180 ft 9 in OR
1964...Tamara Press, USSR 187 ft 10 in OR
1968...Lia Manoliu, Romania 191 ft 2 in OR
1972...Faina Melnik, USSR 218 ft 7 in OR
1976...Evelin Schlaak, E Germany 226 ft 4 in OR
1980...Evelin Jahl (Schlaak), E Germ. 229 ft 6 in OR
1984...Ria Stalman, Netherlands 214 ft 5 in
1988...Martina Hellmann, E Germany 237 ft 2 in OR
1992...Maritza Martén, Cuba 229 ft 10 in
1996...Ilke Wyludda, Germany 228 ft 6 in
2000...Ellina Zvereva, Belarus 224 ft 5 in
2004...Natalya Sadova, Russia 219 ft 10 in
2008...S. Brown-Trafton, United States 212 ft 4¾ in

HAMMER THROW

2000...Kamila Skolimowska, Russia 233 ft 5 in OR
2004...Olga Kuzenkova, Russia 246 ft 1½ in OR
2008...Aksana Miankova, Belarus 250 ft 5½ in OR

JAVELIN THROW

1932...Babe Didrikson, United States 143 ft 4 in OR
1936...Tilly Fleischer, Germany 148 ft 3 in OR
1948...Herma Bauma, Austria 149 ft 6 in
1952...Dana Zatopkova, Czechoslovakia 165 ft 7 in
1956...Inese Jaunzeme, USSR 176 ft 8 in
1960...Elvira Ozolina, USSR 183 ft 8 in OR
1964...Mihaela Penes, Romania 198 ft 7 in
1968...Angela Nemeth, Hungary 198 ft
1972...Ruth Fuchs, E Germany 209 ft 7 in OR
1976...Ruth Fuchs, E Germany 216 ft 4 in OR
1980...Maria Colon, Cuba 224 ft 5 in OR
1984...Tessa Sanderson, Great Britain 228 ft 2 in OR
1988...Petra Felke, E Germany 245 ft OR
1992...Silke Renk, Germany 224 ft 2 in
1996...Heli Rantanen, Finland 222 ft 11 in
2000...Trine Hattestad, Norway 226 ft ½ in OR
2004...Osleidys Menendez, Cuba 234 ft 8 in OR
2008...B. Spotakova, Czech Republic 234 ft 3¾ in

PENTATHLON — Pts

1964...Irina Press, USSR 5246 WR
1968...Ingrid Becker, W Germany 5098
1972...Mary Peters, Great Britain 4801 WR
1976...Siegrun Siegl, E Germany 4745
1980...Nadezhda Tkachenko, USSR 5083 WR

HEPTATHLON — Pts

1984...Glynis Nunn, Australia 6390 OR
1988...Jackie Joyner-Kersee, U.S. 7291 WR
1992...Jackie Joyner-Kersee, U.S. 7044
1996...Ghada Shouaa, Syria 6780
2000...Denise Lewis, Great Britain 6584
2004...Carolina Kluft, Sweden 6952
2008...Natalia Dobrynska, Ukraine 6733

BASKETBALL — Men *(Cont.)*

1936

Final: United States 19, Canada 8
United States: Ralph Bishop, Joe Fortenberry, Carl Knowles, Jack Ragland, Carl Shy, William Wheatley, Francis Johnson, Samuel Balter, John Gibbons, Frank Lubin, Arthur Mollner, Donald Piper, Duane Swanson, Willard Schmidt

1948

Final: United States 65, France 21
United States: Cliff Barker, Don Barksdale, Ralph Beard, Lewis Beck, Vince Boryla, Gordon Carpenter, Alex Groza, Wallace Jones, Bob Kurland, Ray Lumpp, Robert Pitts, Jesse Renick, Bob Robinson, Ken Rollins

1952

Final: United States 36, USSR 25
United States: Charles Hoag, Bill Hougland, Melvin Dean Kelley, Bob Kenney, Clyde Lovellette, Marcus Freiberger, Victor Wayne Glasgow, Frank McCabe, Daniel Pippen, Howard Williams, Ronald Bontemps, Bob Kurland, William Lienhard, John Keller

1956

Final: United States 89, USSR 55
United States: Carl Cain, Bill Hougland, K.C. Jones, Bill Russell, James Walsh, William Evans, Burdette Haldorson, Ron Tomsic, Dick Boushka, Gilbert Ford, Bob Jeangerard, Charles Darling

1960

Final: United States 90, Brazil 63
United States: Jay Arnette, Walt Bellamy, Bob Boozer, Terry Dischinger, Jerry Lucas, Oscar Robertson, Adrian Smith, Burdette Haldorson, Darrall Imhoff, Allen Kelley, Lester Lane, Jerry West

1964

Final: United States 73, USSR 59
United States: Jim Barnes, Bill Bradley, Larry Brown, Joe Caldwell, Mel Counts, Richard Davies, Walt Hazzard, Lucius Jackson, John McCaffrey, Jeff Mullins, Jerry Shipp, George Wilson

1968

Final: United States 65, Yugoslavia 50
United States: John Clawson, Ken Spain, Jo-Jo White, Michael Barrett, Spencer Haywood, Charles Scott, William Hosket, Calvin Fowler, Michael Silliman, Glynn Saulters, James King, Donald Dee

1972

Final: USSR 51, United States 50
United States: Kenneth Davis, Doug Collins, Thomas Henderson, Mike Bantom, Bobby Jones, Dwight Jones, James Forbes, James Brewer, Tom Burleson, Tom McMillen, Kevin Joyce, Ed Ratleff

1976

Final: United States 95, Yugoslavia 74
United States: Phil Ford, Steve Sheppard, Adrian Dantley, Walter Davis, Quinn Buckner, Ernie Grunfield, Kenny Carr, Scott May, Michel Armstrong, Tom La Garde, Phil Hubbard, Mitch Kupchak

1980

Final: Yugoslavia 86, Italy 77
U.S. participated in boycott.

1984

Final: United States 96, Spain 65
United States: Steve Alford, Leon Wood, Patrick Ewing, Vern Fleming, Alvin Robertson, Michael Jordan, Joe Kleine, Jon Koncak, Wayman Tisdale, Chris Mullin, Sam Perkins, Jeff Turner

1988

Final: USSR 76, Yugoslavia 63
U.S. (3rd): Mitch Richmond, Charles E. Smith IV, Vernell Coles, Hersey Hawkins, Jeff Grayer, Charles D. Smith, Willie Anderson, Stacey Augmon, Dan Majerle, Danny Manning, J.R. Reid, David Robinson

1992

Final: United States 117, Croatia 85
United States: David Robinson, Christian Laettner, Patrick Ewing, Larry Bird, Scottie Pippen, Michael Jordan, Clyde Drexler, Karl Malone, John Stockton, Chris Mullin, Charles Barkley, Earvin Johnson

1996

Final: United States 95, Yugoslavia 69
United States: Charles Barkley, Anfernee Hardaway, Grant Hill, Karl Malone, Reggie Miller, Hakeem Olajuwon, Shaquille O'Neal, Scottie Pippen, Mitch Richmond, John Stockton, David Robinson, Gary Payton

2000

Final: United States 85, France 75
United States: Shareef Abdur-Rahim, Ray Allen, Vin Baker, Vince Carter, Kevin Garnett, Tim Hardaway, Allan Houston, Jason Kidd, Antonio McDyess, Alonzo Mourning, Gary Payton, Steve Smith

2004

Final: Argentina 84, Italy 69
U.S. (3rd): Allen Iverson, LeBron James, Tim Duncan, Carmelo Anthony, Dwyane Wade, Richard Jefferson, Lamar Odom, Stephon Marbury, Carlos Boozer, Emeka Okafor, Amare Stoudemire, Shawn Marion

2008

Final: United States 118, Spain 107
U.S.: Carmelo Anthony, Carlos Boozer, Chris Bosh, Kobe Bryant, Dwight Howard, LeBron James, Jason Kidd, Chirs Paul, Tayshaun Prince, Michael Redd, Dwyane Wade, Deron Williams

BASKETBALL — Women

1976

Gold, USSR; Silver, United States*
United States: Cindy Brogdon, Susan Rojcewicz, Ann Meyers, Lusia Harris, Nancy Dunkle, Charlotte Lewis, Nancy Lieberman, Gail Marquis, Patricia Roberts, Mary Anne O'Connor, Patricia Head, Julienne Simpson

*In 1976 the women played a round-robin tournament, with the gold medal going to the team with the best record. The USSR won with a 5–0 record, and the USA, with a 3–2 record, was given the silver by virtue of a 95–79 victory over Bulgaria, which was also 3–2.

1980

Final: USSR 104, Bulgaria 73
U.S. participated in boycott.

1984

Final: United States 85, Korea 55
United States: Teresa Edwards, Lea Henry, Lynette Woodard, Anne Donovan, Cathy Boswell, Cheryl Miller, Janice Lawrence, Cindy Noble, Kim Mulkey, Denise Curry, Pamela McGee, Carol Menken-Schaudt

1988

Final: United States 77, Yugoslavia 70
United States: Teresa Edwards, Mary Ethridge, Cynthia Brown, Anne Donovan, Teresa Weatherspoon, Bridgette Gordon, Victoria Bullett, Andrea Lloyd, Katrina McClain, Jennifer Gillom, Cynthia Cooper, Suzanne McConnell

1992

Final: Unified Team 76, China 66
United States (3rd): Teresa Edwards, Teresa Weatherspoon, Victoria Bullett, Katrina McClain, Cynthia Cooper, Suzanne McConnell, Daedra Charles, Clarissa Davis, Tammy Jackson, Vickie Orr, Carolyn Jones, Medina Dixon

1996

Final: United States 111, Brazil 87
United States: Jennifer Azzi, Ruthie Bolton, Teresa Edwards, Lisa Leslie, Rebecca Lobo, Katrina McClain, Nikki McCray, Carla McGhee, Dawn Staley, Katy Steding, Sheryl Swoopes, Venus Lacey

2000

Final: United States 76, Australia 54
United States: Ruthie Bolton-Holifield, Teresa Edwards, Yolanda Griffith, Chamique Holdsclaw, Lisa Leslie, Nikki McCray, Delisha Milton, Katie Smith, Dawn Staley, Sheryl Swoopes, Natalie Williams, Kara Wolters

2004

Final: United States 74, Australia 63
United States: Dawn Staley, Diana Taurasi, Lisa Leslie, Sheryl Swoopes, Tamika Catchings, Sue Bird, Ruth Riley, Shannon Johnson, Katie Smith, Yolanda Griffith, Swintayla Cash, Tina Thompson

2008

Final: United States 92, Australia 65
United States: Seimone Augustus, Sue Bird, Sylvia Fowles, Lisa Leslie, DeLisha Milton-Jones, Candace Parker, Cappie Pondexter, Tamika Catchings, Tina Thompson, Diana Taurasi, Katie Smith

BOXING

LIGHT FLYWEIGHT (106 LB)

1968 ....Francisco Rodriguez, Venezuela
1972 ....Gyorgy Gedo, Hungary
1976 ....Jorge Hernandez, Cuba
1980 ....Shamil Sabyrov, USSR
1984 ....Paul Gonzalez, United States
1988 ....Ivailo Hristov, Bulgaria
1992 ....Rogelio Marcelo, Cuba
1996 ....Daniel Petrov, Bulgaria
2000 ....Brahim Asloum, France
2004 ....Yan Bhartelemy Varela, Cuba
2008 ....Zou Shiming, China

FLYWEIGHT (112 LB)

1904 ....George Finnegan, United States
1920 ....Frank Di Gennara, United States
1924 ....Fidel LaBarba, United States
1928 ....Antal Kocsis, Hungary
1932 ....Istvan Enekes, Hungary
1936 ....Willi Kaiser, Germany
1948 ....Pascual Perez, Argentina
1952 ....Nathan Brooks, United States
1956 ....Terence Spinks, Great Britain
1960 ....Gyula Torok, Hungary
1964 ....Fernando Atzori, Italy
1968 ....Ricardo Delgado, Mexico
1972 ....Georgi Kostadinov, Bulgaria
1976 ....Leo Randolph, United States
1980 ....Peter Lessov, Bulgaria
1984 ....Steve McCrory, United States
1988 ....Kim Kwang Sun, S Korea
1992 ....Su Choi Chol, N Korea
1996 ....Maikro Romero, Cuba

FLYWEIGHT (112 LB) *(Cont.)*

2000 ....Wijan Ponlid, Thailand
2004 ....Yuriokis Toledano, Cuba
2008 ....Sumit Jongjohor, Thailand

BANTAMWEIGHT (119 LB)

1904 ....Oliver Kirk, United States
1908 ....A. Henry Thomas, Great Britain
1920 ....Clarence Walker, S Africa
1924 ....William Smith, S Africa
1928 ....Vittorio Tamagnini, Italy
1932 ....Horace Gwynne, Canada
1936 ....Ulderico Sergo, Italy
1948 ....Tibor Csik, Hungary
1952 ....Pentti Hamalainen, Finland
1956 ....Wolfgang Behrendt, E Germany
1960 ....Oleg Grigoryev, USSR
1964 ....Takao Sakurai, Japan
1968 ....Valery Sokolov, USSR
1972 ....Orlando Martinez, Cuba
1976 ....Yong Jo Gu, N Korea
1980 ....Juan Hernandez, Cuba
1984 ....Maurizio Stecca, Italy
1988 ....Kennedy McKinney, United States
1992 ....Joel Casamayor, Cuba
1996 ....István Kovács, Hungary
2000 ....Guillermo Ortiz, Cuba
2004 ....Guillermo Ortiz, Cuba
2008 ....Badar-Uugan Enkhbat, Mongolia

FEATHERWEIGHT (125 LB)

1904 ....Oliver Kirk, United States
1908 ....Richard Gunn, Great Britain
1920 ....Paul Fritsch, France

BOXING (Cont.)

FEATHERWEIGHT (125 LB) (Cont.)

1924 ....John Fields, United States
1928 ....Lambertus van Klaveren, Netherlands
1932 ....Carmelo Robledo, Argentina
1936 ....Oscar Casanovas, Argentina
1948 ....Ernesto Formenti, Italy
1952 ....Jan Zachara, Czechoslovakia
1956 ....Vladimir Safronov, USSR
1960 ....Francesco Musso, Italy
1964 ....Stanislav Stephashkin, USSR
1968 ....Antonio Roldan, Mexico
1972 ....Boris Kousnetsov, USSR
1976 ....Angel Herrera, Cuba
1980 ....Rudi Fink, E Germany
1984 ....Meldrick Taylor, United States
1988 ....Giovanni Parisi, Italy
1992 ....Andreas Tews, Germany
1996 ....Somluck Kamsing, Thailand
2000 ....Bekzat Sattarkhanox, Kazakhsta
2004 ....Alexei Tichtchenko, Russia
2008 ....Vasyl Lomachenko, Ukraine

LIGHTWEIGHT (132 LB)

1904 ....Harry Spanger, United States
1908 ....Frederick Grace, Great Britain
1920 ....Samuel Mosberg, United States
1924 ....Hans Nielsen, Denmark
1928 ....Carlo Orlandi, Italy
1932 ....Lawrence Stevens, S Africa
1936 ....Imre Harangi, Hungary
1948 ....Gerald Dreyer, S Africa
1952 ....Aureliano Bolognesi, Italy
1956 Richard McTaggart, Great Britain
1960 ....Kazimierz Pazdzior, Poland
1964 ....Jozef Grudzien, Poland
1968 ....Ronald Harris, United States
1972 ....Jan Szczepanski, Poland
1976 ....Howard Davis, United States
1980 ....Angel Herrera, Cuba
1984 ....Pernell Whitaker, United States
1988 ....Andreas Zuelow, E Germany
1992 ....Oscar De La Hoya, United States
1996 ....Hocine Soltani, Algeria
2000 ....Mario Mesa, Cuba
2004 ....Mario Mesa, Cuba
2008 ....Alexey Tishchenko, Russia

LIGHT WELTERWEIGHT (139 LB)

1952 ....Charles Adkins, United States
1956 ....Vladimir Yengibaryan, USSR
1960 ....Bohumil Nemecek, Czechoslovakia
1964 ....Jerzy Kulej, Poland
1968 ....Jerzy Kulej, Poland
1972 ....Ray Seales, United States
1976 ....Ray Leonard, United States
1980 ....Patrizio Oliva, Italy
1984 ....Jerry Page, United States
1988 ....Viatcheslav Janovski, USSR
1992 ....Hector Vinent, Cuba
1996 ....Hector Vinent, Cuba
2000 ....Mahamadkadyz Abdullaev, Uzbekistan
2004 ....Manus Boonjumnong, Thailand
2008 ....Felix Diaz, Dominican Rebublic

WELTERWEIGHT (147 LB)

1904 ....Albert Young, United States
1920 ....Albert Schneider, Canada
1924 ....Jean Delarge, Belgium
1928 ....Edward Morgan, New Zealand
1932 ....Edward Flynn, United States
1936 ....Sten Suvio, Finland
1948 ....Julius Torma, Czechoslovakia

WELTERWEIGHT (147 LB)

1952 ....Zygmunt Chychla, Poland
1956 ....Nicolae Linca, Romania
1960 ....Giovanni Benvenuti, Italy
1964 ....Marian Kasprzyk, Poland
1968 ....Manfred Wolke, E Germany
1972 ....Emilio Correa, Cuba
1976 ....Jochen Bachfeld, E Germany
1980 ....Andres Aldama, Cuba
1984 ....Mark Breland, United States
1988 ....Robert Wangila, Kenya
1992 ....Michael Carruth, Ireland
1996 ....Oleg Saitov, Russia
2000 ....Oleg Saitov, Russia
2004 ....Bakhtiyar Artayev, Kazakhstan
2008 ....Bakhyt Sarsekbayev, Kazakhstan

LIGHT MIDDLEWEIGHT (156 LB)

1952 ....Laszlo Papp, Hungary
1956 ....Laszlo Papp, Hungary
1960 ....Wilbert McClure, United States
1964 ....Boris Lagutin, USSR
1968 ....Boris Lagutin, USSR
1972 ....Dieter Kottysch, W Germany
1976 ....Jerzy Rybicki, Poland
1980 ....Armando Martinez, Cuba
1984 ....Frank Tate, United States
1988 ....Park Si-Hun, S Korea
1992 ....Juan Lemus, Cuba
1996 ....David Reid, United States
2000 ....Yermakhan Ibraimov, Kazakhstan

MIDDLEWEIGHT (165 LB)

1904 ....Charles Mayer, United States
1908 ....John Douglas, Great Britain
1920 ....Harry Mallin, Great Britain
1924 ....Harry Mallin, Great Britain
1928 ....Piero Toscani, Italy
1932 ....Carmen Barth, United States
1936 ....Jean Despeaux, France
1948 ....Laszlo Papp, Hungary
1952 ....Floyd Patterson, United States
1956 ....Gennady Schatkov, USSR
1960 ....Edward Crook, United States
1964 ....Valery Popenchenko, USSR
1968 ....Christopher Finnegan, Great Britain
1972 ....Vyacheslav Lemechev, USSR
1976 ....Michael Spinks, United States
1980 ....Jose Gomez, Cuba
1984 ....Shin Joon Sup, S Korea
1988 ....Henry Maske, E Germany
1992 ....Ariel Hernandez, Cuba
1996 ....Ariel Hernandez, Cuba
2000 ....Jorge Gutierrez, Cuba
2004 ....Gaydarbek Gaydarbekov, Russia
2008 ....James Degale, Great Britain

LIGHT HEAVYWEIGHT (178 LB)

1920 ....Edward Eagan, United States
1924 ....Harry Mitchell, Great Britain
1928 ....Victor Avendano, Argentina
1932 ....David Carstens, S Africa
1936 ....Roger Michelot, France
1948 ....George Hunter, S Africa
1952 ....Norvel Lee, United States
1956 ....James Boyd, United States
1960 ....Cassius Clay, United States
1964 ....Cosimo Pinto, Italy
1968 ....Dan Poznyak, USSR
1972 ....Mate Parlov, Yugoslavia

Summer Games Champions *(Cont.)*

BOXING *(Cont.)*

LIGHT HEAVYWEIGHT (178 LB) *(Cont.)*

1976 ....Leon Spinks, United States
1980 ....Slobodan Kacer, Yugoslavia
1984 ....Anton Josipovic, Yugoslavia
1988 ....Andrew Maynard, United States
1992 ....Torsten May, Germany
1996 ....Vassili Jirov, Kazakhstan
2000 ....Alexander Lebziak, Russia
2004 ....Andre Ward, United States
2008 ....Zhang Xiaoping, China

HEAVYWEIGHT (OVER 201 LB)

1904 ....Samuel Berger, United States
1908 ....Albert Oldham, Great Britain
1920 ....Ronald Rawson, Great Britain
1924 ....Otto von Porat, Norway
1928 ....Arturo Rodriguez Jurado, Argentina
1932 ....Santiago Lovell, Argentina
1936 ....Herbert Runge, Germany
1948 ....Rafael Inglesias, Argentina
1952 ....H. Edward Sanders, United States
1956 ....T. Peter Rademacher, United States
1960 ....Franco De Piccoli, Italy
1964 ....Joe Frazier, United States
1968 ....George Foreman, United States

HEAVYWEIGHT (201* LB) *(Cont.)*

1972 ....Teofilo Stevenson, Cuba
1976 ....Teofilo Stevenson, Cuba
1980 ....Teofilo Stevenson, Cuba
1984 ....Henry Tillman, United States
1988 ....Ray Mercer, United States
1992 ....Félix Sávon, Cuba
1996 ....Félix Sávon, Cuba
2000 ....Félix Sávon, Cuba
2004 ....Odlanier Fonte, Cuba
2008 ....Rakhim Chakhiev, China

SUPERHEAVYWEIGHT (UNLIMITED)

1984 ....Tyrell Biggs, United States
1988 ....Lennox Lewic, Canada
1992 ....Roberto Balado, Cuba
1996 ....Vladimir Klitchko, Ukraine
2000 ....Audley Harrison, Great Britain
2004 ....Alexander Povetkin, Russia
2008 ....Roberto Cammarelle, Italy

*Until 1984 the heavyweight division was unlimited. With the addition of the super heavyweight division, a limit of 201 pounds was imposed.

SWIMMING—Men

50-METER FREESTYLE

Year	Champion	Time
1904	Zoltan Halmay, Hungary (50 yds)	28.0
1988	Matt Biondi, United States	22.14 WR
1992	Aleksandr Popov, Unified Team	22.30
1996	Aleksandr Popov, Russia	22.13
2000	Anthony Ervin, United States	21.98
	Gary Hall Jr, United States	21.98
2004	Gary Hall Jr, United States	21.93
2008	Cesar Cielo Filho, Brazil	21.30 OR

100-METER FREESTLYE

Year	Champion	Time
1896	Alfred Hajos, Hungary	1:22.2 OR
1904	Zoltan Halmay, Hungary (100 yds)	1:02.8
1906	Charles Daniels, United States	1:13.4
1908	Charles Daniels, United States	1:05.6 WR
1912	Duke Kahanamoku, United States	1:03.4
1920	Duke Kahanamoku, United States	1:00.4 WR
1924	John Weissmuller, United States	59.0 OR
1928	John Weissmuller, United States	58.6 OR
1932	Yasuji Miyazaki, Japan	58.2
1936	Ferenc Csik, Hungary	57.6
1948	Wally Ris, United States	57.3 OR
1952	Clarke Scholes, United States	57.4
1956	Jon Henricks, Australia	55.4 OR
1960	John Devitt, Australia	55.2 OR
1964	Don Schollander, United States	53.4 OR
1968	Mike Wenden, Australia	52.2 WR
1972	Mark Spitz, United States	51.22 WR
1976	Jim Montgomery, United States	49.99 WR
1980	Jörg Woithe, E Germany	50.40
1984	Rowdy Gaines, United States	49.80 OR
1988	Matt Biondi, United States	48.63 OR
1992	Aleksandr Popov, Unified Team	49.02
1996	Aleksandr Popov, Russia	48.74
2000	P. van den Hoogenband, Neth	48.30
2004	P. van den Hoogenband, Neth	48.17
2008	Alain Bernard France, Neth	47.21

200-METER FREESTYLE

Year	Champion	Time
1900	Frederick Lane, Australia	2:25.2 OR
1904	Charles Daniels, United States	2:44.2
1968	Michael Wenden, Australia	1:55.2 OR
1972	Mark Spitz, United States	1:52.78 WR

200-METER FREESTLYE *(CONT.)*

Year	Champion	Time
1976	Bruce Furniss, United States	1:50.29 WR
1980	Sergei Kopliakov, USSR	1:49.81 OR
1984	Michael Gross, W Germany	1:47.44 WR
1988	Duncan Armstrong, Australia	1:47.25 WR
1992	Evgueni Sadovyi, Unified Team	1:46.70 OR
1996	Danyon Loader, New Zealand	1:47.63
2000	Pieter van den Hoogenband, Neth	1:45.35 EWR
2004	Ian Thorpe, Australia	1:44.71 OR
2008	Michael Phelps, United States	1:42.96 WR

400-METER FREESTYLE

Year	Champion	Time
1896	Paul Neumann, Austria (500 yds)	8:12.6
1904	Charles Daniels, U.S. (440 yds)	6:16.2
1906	Otto Scheff, Austria (440 yds)	6:23.8
1908	Henry Taylor, Great Britain	5:36.8
1912	George Hodgson, Canada	5:24.4
1920	Norman Ross, United States	5:26.8
1924	John Weissmuller, United States	5:04.2 OR
1928	Albert Zorilla, Argentina	5:01.6 OR
1932	Buster Crabbe, United States	4:48.4 OR
1936	Jack Medica, United States	4:44.5 OR
1948	William Smith, United States	4:41.0 OR
1952	Jean Boiteux, France	4:30.7 OR
1956	Murray Rose, Australia	4:27.3 OR
1960	Murray Rose, Australia	4:18.3 OR
1964	Don Schollander, United States	4:12.2 WR
1968	Mike Burton, United States	4:09.0 OR
1972	Brad Cooper, Australia	4:00.27 OR
1976	Brian Goodell, United States	3:51.93 WR
1980	Vladimir Salnikov, USSR	3:51.31 OR
1984	George DiCarlo, United States	3:51.23 OR
1988	Uwe Dassler, E Germany	3:46.95 WR
1992	Evgueni Sadovyi, Unified Team	3:45.00 WR
1996	Danyon Loader, New Zealand	3:47.97
2000	Ian Thorpe, Australia	3:40.59 WR
2004	Ian Thorpe, Australia	3:43.10
2008	Park Taehwan, S Korea	3:41.86

1,500-METER FREESTYLE

Year	Champion	Time
1908	Henry Taylor, Great Britain	22:48.4 WR
1912	George Hodgson, Canada	22:00.0 WR
1920	Norman Ross, United States	22:23.2

SWIMMING— Men *(Cont.)*

1,500-METER FREESTLYE *(CONT.)*

1924	Andrew Charlton, Australia	20:06.6 WR
1928	Arne Borg, Sweden	19:51.8 OR
1932	Kusuo Kitamura, Japan	19:12.4 OR
1936	Noboru Terada, Japan	19:13.7
1948	James McLane, United States	19:18.5
1952	Ford Konno, United States	18:30.3 OR
1956	Murray Rose, Australia	17:58.9
1960	John Konrads, Australia	17:19.6 OR
1964	Robert Windle, Australia	17:01.7 OR
1968	Mike Burton, United States	16:38.9 OR
1972	Mike Burton, United States	15:52.58 OR
1976	Brian Goodell, United States	15:02.40 WR
1980	Vladimir Salnikov, USSR	14:58.27 WR
1984	Michael O'Brien, United States	15:05.20
1988	Vladimir Salnikov, USSR	15:00.40
1992	Kieren Perkins, Australia	14:43.48 WR
1996	Kieren Perkins, Australia	14:56.40
2000	Grant Hackett, Australia	14:48.33
2004	Grant Hackett, Australia	14:43.40 OR
2008	Ousama Mellouli, Tunisia	14:40.84

100-METER BACKSTROKE

1904	Walter Brack, Germany (100 yds)	1:16.8
1908	Arno Bieberstein, Germany	1:24.6 WR
1912	Harry Hebner, United States	1:21.2
1920	Warren Kealoha, United States	1:15.2
1924	Warren Kealoha, United States	1:13.2 OR
1928	George Kojac, United States	1:08.2 WR
1932	Masaji Kiyokawa, Japan	1:08.6
1936	Adolph Kiefer, United States	1:05.9 OR
1948	Allen Stack, United States	1:06.4
1952	Yoshi Oyakawa, United States	1:05.4 OR
1956	David Thiele, Australia	1:02.2 OR
1960	David Thiele, Australia	1:01.9 OR
1968	Roland Matthes, E Germany	58.7 OR
1972	Roland Matthes, E Germany	56.58 OR
1976	John Naber, United States	55.49 WR
1980	Bengt Baron, Sweden	56.33
1984	Rick Carey, United States	55.79
1988	Daichi Suzuki, Japan	55.05
1992	Mark Tewksbury, Canada	53.98 WR
1996	Jeff Rouse, United States	54.10
2000	Lenny Krayzelburg, United States	53.72 OR
2004	Aaron Peirsol, United States	54.06
2008	Aaron Peirsol, United States	52.54 WR

200-METER BACKSTROKE

1900	Ernst Hoppenberg, Germany	2:47.0
1964	Jed Graef, United States	2:10.3 WR
1968	Roland Matthes, E Germany	2:09.6 OR
1972	Roland Matthes, E Germany	2:02.82 EWR
1976	John Naber, United States	1:59.19 WR
1980	Sandor Wladar, Hungary	2:01.93
1984	Rick Carey, United States	2:00.23
1988	Igor Polianski, USSR	1:59.37
1992	Martin Lopez-Zubero, Spain	1:58.47 OR
1996	Brad Bridgewater, United States	1:58.54
2000	Lenny Krayzelburg, United States	1:56.76 OR
2004	Aaron Peirsol, United States	1:54.95 OR
2008	Ryan Lochte, United States	1:53.94 WR

100-METER BREASTSTROKE

1968	Don McKenzie, United States	1:07.7 OR
1972	Nobutaka Taguchi, Japan	1:04.94 WR
1976	John Hencken, United States	1:03.11 WR
1980	Duncan Goodhew, Great Britain	1:03.44
1984	Steve Lundquist, United States	1:01.65 WR
1988	Adrian Moorhouse, Great Britain	1:02.04

100-METER BREASTROKE *(CONT.)*

1992	Nelson Diebel, United States	1:01.50 OR
1996	Fred DeBurghgraeve, Belgium	1:00.65
2000	Domenico Fioravanti, Italy	1:00.46 OR
2004	Kosuke Kitajima, Japan	1:00.08
2008	Kosuke Kitajima, Japan	58.91 WR

200-METER BREASTSTROKE

1908	Frederick Holman, Great Britain	3:09.2 WR
1912	Walter Bathe, Germany	3:01.8 OR
1920	Haken Malmroth, Sweden	3:04.4
1924	Robert Skelton, United States	2:56.6
1928	Yoshiyuki Tsuruta, Japan	2:48.8 OR
1932	Yoshiyuki Tsuruta, Japan	2:45.4
1936	Tetsuo Hamuro, Japan	2:41.5 OR
1948	Joseph Verdeur, United States	2:39.3 OR
1952	John Davies, Australia	2:34.4 OR
1956	Masura Furukawa, Japan	2:34.7 OR
1960	William Mulliken, United States	2:37.4
1964	Ian O'Brien, Australia	2:27.8 WR
1968	Felipe Munoz, Mexico	2:28.7
1972	John Hencken, United States	2:21.55 WR
1976	David Wilkie, Great Britain	2:15.11 WR
1980	Robertas Zhulpa, USSR	2:15.85
1984	Victor Davis, Canada	2:13.34 WR
1988	Jozsef Szabo, Hungary	2:13.52
1992	Mike Barrowman, United States	2:10.16 WR
1996	Norbert Rózsa, Hungary	2:12.57
2000	Domenico Fioravanti, Italy	2:10.87
2004	Kosuke Kitajima, Japan	2:09.44 OR
2008	Kosuke Kitajima, Japan	2:07.64 OR

100-METER BUTTERFLY

1968	Doug Russell, United States	55.9 OR
1972	Mark Spitz, United States	54.27 WR
1976	Matt Vogel, United States	54.35
1980	Pär Arvidsson, Sweden	54.92
1984	Michael Gross, W Germany	53.08 WR
1988	Anthony Nesty, Suriname	53.00 OR
1992	Pablo Morales, United States	53.32
1996	Denis Pankratov, Russia	52.27 WR
2000	Lars Froelander, Sweden	52.00
2004	Michael Phelps, United States	51.25 OR
2008	Michael Phelps, United States	50.58 OR

200-METER BUTTERFLY

1956	William Yorzyk, United States	2:19.3 OR
1960	Michael Troy, United States	2:12.8 WR
1964	Kevin Berry, Australia	2:06.6 WR
1968	Carl Robie, United States	2:08.7
1972	Mark Spitz, United States	2:00.70 WR
1976	Mike Bruner, United States	1:59.23 WR
1980	Sergei Fesenko, USSR	1:59.76
1984	Jon Sieben, Australia	1:57.04 WR
1988	Michael Gross, W Germany	1:56.94 OR
1992	Melvin Stewart, United States	1:56.26 OR
1996	Denis Pankratov, Russia	1:56.51
2000	Tom Malchow, United States	1:55.35 OR
2004	Michael Phelps, United States	1:54.04 OR
2008	Michael Phelps, United States	1:52.03 WR

200-METER INDIVIDUAL MEDLEY

1968	Charles Hickcox, United States	2:12.0 OR
1972	Gunnar Larsson, Sweden	2:07.17 WR
1984	Alex Baumann, Canada	2:01.42 WR
1988	Tamas Darnyi, Hungary	2:00.17 WR
1992	Tamas Darnyi, Hungary	2:00.76
1996	Attila Czene, Hungary	1:59.91 OR
2000	Massimiliano Rosolino, Italy	1:58.98 OR
2004	Michael Phelps, United States	1:57.14 OR

Note: OR=Olympic Record. WR=World Record. EOR=Equals Olympic Record. EWR=Equals World Record. WB=World Best.

SWIMMING — Men (Cont.)

200-METER INDIVIDUAL MEDLEY (Cont.)

2008....Michael Phelps, United States 1:54.23 WR

400-METER INDIVIDUAL MEDLEY

1964....Richard Roth, United States 4:45.4 WR
1968....Charles Hickcox, United States 4:48.4
1972....Gunnar Larsson, Sweden 4:31.98 OR
1976....Rod Strachan, United States 4:23.68 WR
1980....Aleksandr Sidorenko, USSR 4:22.89 OR
1984....Alex Baumann, Canada 4:17.41 WR
1988....Tamas Darnyi, Hungary 4:14.75 WR
1992....Tamas Darnyi, Hungary 4:14.23 OR
1996....Tom Dolan United States 4:14.90
2000....Tom Dolan, United States 4:11.76 WR
2004....Michael Phelps, United States 4:08.26 WR
2008....Michael Phelps, United States 4:03.84 WR

4 X 100-METER MEDLEY RELAY

1960 ....United States 4:05.4 WR
1964 ....United States 3:58.4 WR
1968 ....United States 3:54.9 WR
1972 ....United States 3:48.16 WR
1976 ....United States 3:42.22 WR
1980 ....Australia 3:45.70
1984 ....United States 3:39.30 WR
1988 ....United States 3:36.93 WR
1992 ....United States 3:36.93 EWR
1996 ....United States 3:34.84 WR
2000 ....United States 3:33.73 WR
2004 ....United States 3:30.68 WR
2008 ....United States 3:29.34 WR

4 X 100-METER FREESTYLE RELAY

1964 ....United States 3:32.2 WR
1968 ....United States 3:31.7 WR
1972 ....United States 3:26.42 WR
1984 ....United States 3:19.03 WR

4 X 100-METER FREESTYLE RELAY (Cont.)

1988 ....United States 3:16.53 WR
1992 ....United States 3:16.74
1996 ....United States 3:15.41 OR
2000 ....Australia 3:13.67 WR
2004 ....S Africa 3:13.17 WR
2008 ....United States 3:08.24 WR

4 X 200-METER FREESTYLE RELAY

1906 ....Hungary (1,000 m) 16:52.4
1908 ....Great Britain 10:55.6
1912 ....Australia/New Zealand 10:11.6 WR
1920 ....United States 10:04.4 WR
1924 ....United States 9:53.4 WR
1928 ....United States 9:36.2 WR
1932 ....Japan 8:58.4 WR
1936 ....Japan 8:51.5 WR
1948 ....United States 8:46.0 WR
1952 ....United States 8:31.1 OR
1956 ....Australia 8:23.6 WR
1960 ....United States 8:10.2 WR
1964 ....United States 7:52.1 WR
1968 ....United States 7:52.33
1972 ....United States 7:35.78 WR
1976 ....United States 7:23.22 WR
1980 ....USSR 7:23.50
1984 ....United States 7:15.69 WR
1988 ....United States 7:12.51 WR
1992 ....Unified Team 7:11.95 WR
1996 ....United States 7:14.84
2000 ....Australia 7:07.05 WR
2004 ....United States 7:07.33
2008 ....United States 6:58.56

SWIMMING — Women

50-METER FREESTYLE

1988....Kristin Otto, E Germany 25.49 OR
1992....Yang Wenyi, China 24.79 WR
1996....Amy Van Dyken, United States 24.87
2000....Inge de Bruijn, Netherlands 24.32 WR
2004....Inge de Bruijn, Netherlands 24.58
2008....Britta Stefan, Germany 24.06 OR

100-METER FREESTYLE

1912....Fanny Durack, Australia 1:22.2
1920....Ethelda Bleibtrey, United States 1:13.6 WR
1924....Ethel Lackie, United States 1:12.4
1928....Albina Osipowich, United States 1:11.0 OR
1932....Helene Madison, United States 1:06.8 OR
1936....Hendrika Mastenbroek, Neth 1:05.9 OR
1948....Greta Andersen, Denmark 1:06.3
1952....Katalin Szöke, Hungary 1:06.8
1956....Dawn Fraser, Australia 1:02.0 WR
1960....Dawn Fraser, Australia 1:01.2 OR
1964....Dawn Fraser, Australia 59.5 OR
1968....Jan Henne, United States 1:00.0
1972....Sandra Neilson, United States 58.59 OR
1976....Kornelia Ender, E Germany 55.65 WR
1980....Barbara Krause, E Germany 54.79 WR
1984....Carrie Steinseifer, United States 55.92
Nancy Hogshead, United States 55.92
1988....Kristin Otto, E Germany 54.93
1992....Zhuang Yong, China 54.64 OR

100-METER FREESTYLE (CONT.)

1996....Le Jingyi, China 54.50 OR
2000....Inge de Bruijn, Netherlands 53.83 OR
2004....Jodie Henry, Australia 53.84
2008....Britta Stefan, Germany 53.12 OR

200-METER FREESTYLE

1968....Debbie Meyer, United States 2:10.5 OR
1972....Shane Gould, Australia 2:03.56 WR
1976....Kornelia Ender, E Germany 1:59.26 WR
1980....Barbara Krause, E Germany 1:58.33 OR
1984....Mary Wayte, United States 1:59.23
1988....Heike Friedrich, E Germany 1:57.65 OR
1992....Nicole Haislett, United States 1:57.90
1996....Claudia Poll, Costa Rica 1:58.16
2000....Susie O'Neill, Australia 1:58.24
2004....Camelia Potec, Romania 1:58.03
2008....Frederica Pellegrini, Italy 1:54.82 WR

400-METER FREESTYLE

1924....Martha Norelius, United States 6:02.2 OR
1928....Martha Norelius, United States 5:42.8 WR
1932....Helene Madison, United States 5:28.5 WR
1936....Hendrika Mastenbroek, Neth 5:26.4 OR
1948....Ann Curtis, United States 5:17.8 OR
1952....Valeria Gyenge, Hungary 5:12.1 OR
1956....Lorraine Crapp, Australia 4:54.6 OR
1960....Chris von Saltza, United States 4:50.6 OR
1964....Virginia Duenkel, United States 4:43.3 OR

Note: OR=Olympic Record. WR=World Record. EOR=Equals Olympic Record. EWR=Equals World Record. WB=World Best.

SWIMMING — Women (Cont.)

400-METER FREESTYLE (CONT.)

1968....Debbie Meyer, United States 4:31.8 OR
1972....Shane Gould, Australia 4:19.44 WR
1976....Petra Thümer, E Germany 4:09.89 WR
1980....Ines Diers, E Germany 4:08.76 WR
1984....Tiffany Cohen, United States 4:07.10 OR
1988....Janet Evans, United States 4:03.85 WR
1992....Dagmar Hase, Germany 4:07.18
1996....Michelle Smith, Ireland 4:07.25
2000....Brooke Bennett, United States 4:05.80
2004....Laure Manaudou, France 4:05.34
2008....Rebecca Adlington, Great Britain 4:03.22

800-METER FREESTYLE

1968....Debbie Meyer, United States 9:24.0 OR
1972....Keena Rothhammer, United States 8:53.68 WR
1976....Petra Thümer, E Germany 8:37.14 WR
1980....Michelle Ford, Australia 8:28.90 OR
1984....Tiffany Cohen, United States 8:24.95 OR
1988....Janet Evans, United States 8:20.20 OR
1992....Janet Evans, United States 8:25.52
1996....Brooke Bennett, United States 8:27.89
2000....Brooke Bennett, United States 8:19.67 OR
2004....Ai Shibata, Japan 8:24.54
2008....Rebecca Adlington, Great Britain 8:14.10 WR

100-METER BACKSTROKE

1924....Sybil Bauer, United States 1:23.2 OR
1928....Marie Braun, Netherlands 1:22.0
1932....Eleanor Holm, United States 1:19.4
1936....Dina Senff, Netherlands 1:18.9
1948....Karen Harup, Denmark 1:14.4 OR
1952....Joan Harrison, South Africa 1:14.3
1956....Judy Grinham, Great Britain 1:12.9 OR
1960....Lynn Burke, United States 1:09.3 OR
1964....Cathy Ferguson, United States 1:07.7 WR
1968....Kaye Hall, United States 1:06.2 WR
1972....Melissa Belote, United States 1:05.78 OR
1976....Ulrike Richter, E Germany 1:01.83 OR
1980....Rica Reinisch, E Germany 1:00.86 WR
1984....Theresa Andrews, United States 1:02.55
1988....Kristin Otto, E Germany 1:00.89
1992....Krisztina Egerszegi, Hungary 1:00.68 OR
1996....Beth Botsford, United States 1:01.19
2000....Diana Iuliana Mocanu, Romania 1:00.21 OR
2004....Natalie Coughlin, United States 1:00.37
2008....Natalie Coughlin, United States 58.96

200-METER BACKSTROKE

1968....Pokey Watson, United States 2:24.8 OR
1972....Melissa Belote, United States 2:19.19 WR
1976....Ulrike Richter, E Germany 2:13.43 OR
1980....Rica Reinisch, E Germany 2:11.77 WR
1984....Jolanda De Rover, Netherlands 2:12.38
1988....Krisztina Egerszegi, Hungary 2:09.29 OR
1992....Krisztina Egerszegi, Hungary 2:07.06 OR
1996....Krisztina Egerszegi, Hungary 2:07.83
2000....Diana Iuliana Mocanu, Romania 2:08.16
2004....Kirsty Coventry, Zimbabwe 2:09.19
2008....Kirsty Coventry, Zimbabwe 2:05.24 WR

100-METER BREASTSTROKE

1968....Djurdjica Bjedov, Yugoslavia 1:15.8 OR
1972....Catherine Carr, United States 1:13.58 WR
1976....Hannelore Anke, E Germany 1:11.16
1980....Ute Geweniger, E Germany 1:10.22
1984....Petra Van Staveren, Netherlands 1:09.88 OR
1988....Tania Dangalakova, Bulgaria 1:07.95 OR
1992....Elena Roudkovskaia, Unified Team 1:08.00
1996....Penelope Heyns, S Africa 1:07.73
2000....Megan Quann, United States 1:07.05

100-METER BREASTSTROKE (CONT.)

2004....Xue Juan Luo, China 1:06.64
2008....Liesel Jones, Australia 1:05.17 WR

200-METER BREASTSTROKE

1924....Lucy Morton, Great Britain 3:33.2 OR
1928....Hilde Schrader, Germany 3:12.6
1932....Clare Dennis, Australia 3:06.3 OR
1936....Hideko Maehata, Japan 3:03.6
1948....Petronella Van Vliet, Netherlands 2:57.2
1952....Eva Szekely, Hungary 2:51.7 OR
1956....Ursula Happe, W Germany 2:53.1 OR
1960....Anita Lonsbrough, Great Britain 2:49.5 WR
1964....Galina Prozumenshikova, USSR 2:46.4 OR
1968....Sharon Wichman, United States 2:44.4 OR
1972....Beverly Whitfield, Australia 2:41.71 OR
1976....Marina Koshevaia, USSR 2:33.35 WR
1980....Lina Kaciusyte, USSR 2:29.54 OR
1984....Anne Ottenbrite, Canada 2:30.38
1988....Silke Hoerner, E Germany 2:26.71 WR
1992....Kyoko Iwasaki, Japan 2:26.65 OR
1996....Penelope Heyns, S Africa 2:25.41 OR
2000....Agnes Kovacs, Hungary 2:24.35 OR
2004....Amanda Beard, United States 2:23.37 OR
2008....Rebecca Soni, United States 2:20.22 WR

100-METER BUTTERFLY

1956....Shelley Mann, United States 1:11.0 OR
1960....Carolyn Schuler, United States 1:09.5 OR
1964....Sharon Stouder, United States 1:04.7 WR
1968....Lynn McClements, Australia 1:05.5
1972....Mayumi Aoki, Japan 1:03.34 WR
1976....Kornelia Ender, E Germany 1:00.13 EWR
1980....Caren Metschuck, E Germany 1:00.42
1984....Mary T. Meagher, United States 59.26
1988....Kristin Otto, E Germany 59.00 OR
1992....Qian Hong, China 58.62 OR
1996....Amy Van Dyken, United States 59.13
2000....Inge de Bruijn, Netherlands 56.61 WR
2004....Petria Thomas, Australia 57.72
2008....Lisbeth Trickett, Australia 56.73

200-METER BUTTERFLY

1968....Ada Kok, Netherlands 2:24.7 OR
1972....Karen Moe, United States 2:15.57 WR
1976....Andrea Pollack, E Germany 2:11.41 OR
1980....Ines Geissler, E Germany 2:10.44 OR
1984....Mary T. Meagher, United States 2:06.90 OR
1988....Kathleen Nord, E Germany 2:09.51
1992....Summer Sanders, United States 2:08.67
1996....Susan O'Neill, Australia 2:07.76
2000....Misty Hyman, United States 2:05.88 OR
2004....Otylia Jedrzegczak, Poland 2:06.05
2008....Zige Lie, China 2:04.18 WR

200-METER INDIVIDUAL MEDLEY

1968....Claudia Kolb, United States 2:24.7 OR
1972....Shane Gould, Australia 2:23.07 WR
1984....Tracy Caulkins, United States 2:12.64 OR
1988....Daniela Hunger, E Germany 2:12.59 OR
1992....Lin Li, China 2:11.65 WR
1996....Michelle Smith, Ireland 2:13.93
2000....Yana Klochkova, Ukraine 2:10.68 OR
2004....Yana Klochkova, Ukraine 2:11.14
2008....Stephanie Rice, Australia 2:08.45 WR

400-METER INDIVIDUAL MEDLEY

1964....Donna de Varona, United States 5:18.7 OR
1968....Claudia Kolb, United States 5:08.5 OR
1972....Gail Neall, Australia 5:02.97 WR
1976....Ulrike Tauber, E Germany 4:42.77 WR

Note: OR=Olympic Record. WR=World Record. EOR=Equals Olympic Record. EWR=Equals World Record. WB=World Best.

SWIMMING — Women (Cont.)

400-METER INDIVIDUAL MEDLEY (CONT.)

1980	Petra Schneider, E Germany	4:36.29 WR
1984	Tracy Caulkins, United States	4:39.24
1988	Janet Evans, United States	4:37.76
1992	Krisztina Egerszegi, Hungary	4:36.54
1996	Michelle Smith, Ireland	4:39.18
2000	Yana Klochkova, Ukraine	4:33.59 WR
2004	Yana Klochkova, Ukraine	4:34.83
2008	Stephanie Rice, Australia	4:29.45 WR

4 X 100-METER MEDLEY RELAY

1960	United States	4:41.1 WR
1964	United States	4:33.9 WR
1968	United States	4:28.3 OR
1972	United States	4:20.75 WR
1976	E Germany	4:07.95 WR
1980	E Germany	4:06.67 WR
1984	United States	4:08.34
1988	E Germany	4:03.74 OR
1992	United States	4:02.54 WR
1996	United States	4:02.88
2000	United States	3:58:30 WR
2004	Australia	3:57.32 WR
2008	Australia	3:52.69 WR

4 X 100-METER FREESTYLE RELAY

1912	Great Britain	5:52.8 WR
1920	United States	5:11.6 WR

4 X 100-METER FREESTYLE RELAY (CONT.)

1924	United States	4:58.8 WR
1928	United States	4:47.6 WR
1932	United States	4:38.0 WR
1936	Netherlands	4:36.0 OR
1948	United States	4:29.2 OR
1952	Hungary	4:24.4 WR
1956	Australia	4:17.1 WR
1960	United States	4:08.9 WR
1964	United States	4:03.8 WR
1968	United States	4:02.5 OR
1972	United States	3:55.19 WR
1976	United States	3:44.82 WR
1980	E Germany	3:42.71 WR
1984	United States	3:43.43
1988	E Germany	3:40.63 OR
1992	United States	3:39.46 WR
1996	United States	3:39.29 OR
2000	United States	3:36.61 WR
2004	Australia	3:35.94 WR
2008	Netherlands	3:33.76 OR

4 X 200-METER FREESTYLE RELAY

1996	United States	7:59.87
2000	United States	7:57.80 OR
2004	United States	7:53.42 WR
2008	Australia	7:44.31 WR

DIVING — Men

SPRINGBOARD

		Pts
1908	Albert Zürner, Germany	85.5
1912	Paul Günther, Germany	79.23
1920	Louis Kuehn, United States	675.40
1924	Albert White, United States	97.46
1928	Pete DesJardins, United States	185.04
1932	Michael Galitzen, United States	161.38
1936	Richard Degener, United States	163.57
1948	Bruce Harlan, United States	163.64
1952	David Browning, United States	205.29
1956	Robert Clotworthy, United States	159.56
1960	Gary Tobian, United States	170.00
1964	Kenneth Sitzberger, United States	159.90
1968	Bernie Wrightson, United States	170.15
1972	Vladimir Vasin, USSR	594.09
1976	Phil Boggs, United States	619.05
1980	Aleksandr Portnov, USSR	905.02
1984	Greg Louganis, United States	754.41
1988	Greg Louganis, United States	730.80
1992	Mark Lenzi, United States	676.53
1996	Xiong Ni, China	701.46
2000	Xiong Ni, China	708.72
2004	Bo Peng, China	787.38
2008	He Chong, China	572.90

PLATFORM

		Pts
1904	George Sheldon, United States	12.66
1906	Gottlob Walz, Germany	156.0
1908	Hjalmar Johansson, Sweden	83.75
1912	Erik Adlerz, Sweden	73.94
1920	Clarence Pinkston, United States	100.67
1924	Albert White, United States	97.46
1928	Pete DesJardins, United States	98.74
1932	Harold Smith, United States	124.80
1936	Marshall Wayne, United States	113.58
1948	Sammy Lee, United States	130.05
1952	Sammy Lee, United States	156.28
1956	Joaquin Capilla, Mexico	152.44
1960	Robert Webster, United States	165.56
1964	Robert Webster, United States	148.58
1968	Klaus Dibiasi, Italy	164.18
1972	Klaus Dibiasi, Italy	504.12
1976	Klaus Dibiasi, Italy	600.51
1980	Falk Hoffmann, E Germany	835.65
1984	Greg Louganis, United States	710.91
1988	Greg Louganis, United States	638.61
1992	Sun Shuwei, China	677.31
1996	Dmitri Sautin, Russia	692.34
2000	Tian Liang, China	724.53
2004	Jia Hu, China	748.08
2008	Matthew Mitcham, Australia	537.95

DIVING — Women

SPRINGBOARD

Year	Champion	Pts
1920	Aileen Riggin, United States	539.90
1924	Elizabeth Becker, United States	474.50
1928	Helen Meany, United States	78.62
1932	Georgia Coleman, United States	87.52
1936	Marjorie Gestring, United States	89.27
1948	Victoria Draves, United States	108.74
1952	Patricia McCormick, United States	147.30
1956	Patricia McCormick, United States	142.36
1960	Ingrid Krämer, E Germany	155.81
1964	Ingrid Engel Krämer, E Germany	145.00
1968	Sue Gossick, United States	150.77
1972	Micki King, United States	450.03
1976	Jennifer Chandler, United States	506.19
1980	Irina Kalinina, USSR	725.91
1984	Sylvie Bernier, Canada	530.70
1988	Gao Min, China	580.23
1992	Gao Min, China	572.40
1996	Fu Mingxia, China	547.68
2000	Fu Mingxia, China	609.42
2004	Guo Jingjing, China	633.15
2008	Guo Jingjing, China	415.35

PLATFORM

Year	Champion	Pts
1912	Greta Johansson, Sweden	39.90
1920	Stefani Fryland-Clausen, Denmark	34.60
1924	Caroline Smith, United States	33.20
1928	Elizabeth B. Pinkston, United States	31.60
1932	Dorothy Poynton, United States	40.26
1936	Dorothy Poynton Hill, United States	33.93
1948	Victoria Draves, United States	68.87
1952	Patricia McCormick, United States	79.37
1956	Patricia McCormick, United States	84.85
1960	Ingrid Krämer, E Germany	91.28
1964	Lesley Bush, United States	99.80
1968	Milena Duchkova, Czechoslovakia	109.59
1972	Ulrika Knape, Sweden	390.00
1976	Elena Vaytsekhovskaya, USSR	406.59
1980	Martina Jäschke, E Germany	596.25
1984	Zhou Jihong, China	435.51
1988	Xu Yanmei, China	445.20
1992	Mingxia Fu, China	461.43
1996	Mingxia Fu, China	521.58
2000	Laura Wilkinson, United States	543.75
2004	Chantelle Newbery, Australia	590.31
2008	Chen Ruoulin, China	447.70

GYMNASTICS — Men

ALL-AROUND

Year	Champion	Pts
1900	Gustave Sandras, France	302
1904	Julius Lenhart, Austria	69.80
1906	Pierre Paysse, France	97
1908	Alberto Braglia, Italy	317.0
1912	Alberto Braglia, Italy	135.0
1920	Giorgio Zampori, Italy	88.35
1924	Leon Stukelj, Yugoslavia	110.340
1928	Georges Miez, Switzerland	247.500
1932	Romeo Neri, Italy	140.625
1936	Alfred Schwarzmann, Germany	113.100
1948	Veikko Huhtanen, Finland	229.70
1952	Viktor Chukarin, USSR	115.70
1956	Viktor Chukarin, USSR	114.25
1960	Boris Shakhlin, USSR	115.95
1964	Yukio Endo, Japan	115.95
1968	Sawao Kato, Japan	115.90
1972	Sawao Kato, Japan	114.65
1976	Nikolai Andrianov, USSR	116.65
1980	Aleksandr Dityatin, USSR	118.65
1984	Koji Gushiken, Japan	118.70
1988	Vladimir Artemov, USSR	119.125
1992	Vitaly Scherbo, Unified Team	59.025
1996	Li Xiaoshuang, China	58.423
2000	Alexei Nemov, Russia	58.474
2004	Paul Hamm, United States	57.823
2008	Yang Wei, China	94.575

HORIZONTAL BAR

Year	Champion	Pts
1896	Hermann Weingärtner, Germany	—
1904	Anton Heida, United States	40
1924	Leon Stukelj, Yugoslavia	19.73
1928	Georges Miez, Switzerland	19.17
1932	Dallas Bixler, United States	18.33
1936	Aleksanteri Saarvala, Finland	19.367
1948	Josef Stafler, Switzerland	19.85
1952	Jack Günthard, Switzerland	19.55
1956	Takashi Ono, Japan	19.60

HORIZONTAL BAR *(CONT)*

Year	Champion	Pts
1960	Takashi Ono, Japan	19.60
1964	Boris Shakhlin, USSR	19.625
1968	Akinori Nakayama, Japan	19.55
1972	Mitsuo Tsukahara, Japan	19.725
1976	Mitsuo Tsukahara, Japan	19.675
1980	Stoyan Deltchev, Bulgaria	19.825
1984	Shinji Morisue, Japan	20.00
1988	Vladimir Artemov, USSR	19.90
1992	Trent Dimas, United States	9.875
1996	Andreas Wecker, Germany	9.850
2000	Alexei Nemov, Russia	9.787
2004	Igor Cassina, Italy	9.812
2008	Zou Kai, China	16.200

PARALLEL BARS

Year	Champion	Pts
1896	Alfred Flatow, Germany	—
1904	George Eyser, United States	44
1924	August Güttinger, Switzerland	21.63
1928	Ladislav Vacha, Czechoslovakia	18.83
1932	Romeo Neri, Italy	18.97
1936	Konrad Frey, Germany	19.067
1948	Michael Reusch, Switzerland	19.75
1952	Hans Eugster, Switzerland	19.65
1956	Viktor Chukarin, USSR	19.20
1960	Boris Shakhlin, USSR	19.40
1964	Yukio Endo, Japan	19.675
1968	Akinori Nakayama, Japan	19.475
1972	Sawao Kato, Japan	19.475
1976	Sawao Kato, Japan	19.675
1980	Aleksandr Tkachyov, USSR	19.775
1984	Bart Conner, United States	19.95
1988	Vladimir Artemov, USSR	19.925
1992	Vitaly Scherbo, Unified Team	9.900
1996	Rustan Sharipov, Ukraine	9.837
2000	Li Xiaopeng, China	9.825
2004	Valeri Goncharov, Ukraine	9.787
2008	Li Xiaopeng, China	16.450

GYMNASTICS — Men (*Cont.*)

VAULT

Year	Champion	Pts
1896	Karl Schumann, Germany	—
1904	George Eyser, United States	36
1924	Frank Kriz, United States	9.98
1928	Eugen Mack, Switzerland	9.58
1932	Savino Guglielmetti, Italy	18.03
1936	Alfred Schwarzmann, Germany	19.20
1948	Paavo Aaltonen, Finland	19.55
1952	Viktor Chukarin, USSR	19.20
1956	Helmut Bantz, Germany	18.85
1960	Takashi Ono, Japan	19.35
1964	Haruhiro Yamashita, Japan	19.60
1968	Mikhail Voronin, USSR	19.00
1972	Klaus Köste, E Germany	18.85
1976	Nikolai Andrianov, USSR	19.45
1980	Nikolai Andrianov, USSR	19.825
1984	Lou Yun, China	19.95
1988	Lou Yun, China	19.875
1992	Vitaly Scherbo, Unified Team	9.856
1996	Alexei Nemov, Russia	9.787
2000	Gervasio Deferr, Spain	9.712
2004	Gervasio Deferr, Spain	9.737
2008	Leszek Blanik, Poland	16.537

POMMEL HORSE

Year	Champion	Pts
1896	Louis Zutter, Switzerland	—
1904	Anton Heida, United States	42
1924	Josef Wilhelm, Switzerland	21.23
1928	Hermann Hänggi, Switzerland	19.75
1932	Istvan Pelle, Hungary	19.07
1936	Konrad Frey, Germany	19.333
1948	Paavo Aaltonen, Finland	19.35
1952	Viktor Chukarin, USSR	19.50
1956	Boris Shakhlin, USSR	19.25
1960	Eugen Ekman, Finland	19.375
1964	Miroslav Cerar, Yugoslavia	19.525
1968	Miroslav Cerar, Yugoslavia	19.325
1972	Viktor Klimenko, USSR	19.125
1976	Zoltan Magyar, Hungary	19.70
1980	Zoltan Magyar, Hungary	19.925
1984	Li Ning, China	19.95
1988	Dmitri Bilozerchev, USSR	19.95
1992	Vitaly Scherbo, Unified Team	9.925
1996	Donghua Li, Switzerland	9.875
2000	Marius Urzica, Romania	9.862
2004	Haibin Teng, China	9.837
2008	Xiao Oin, China	15.875

RINGS

Year	Champion	Pts
1896	Ioannis Mitropoulos, Greece	—
1904	Hermann Glass, United States	45
1924	Francesco Martino, Italy	21.553
1928	Leon Stukelj, Yugoslavia	19.25
1932	George Gulack, United States	18.97
1936	Alois Hudec, Czechoslovakia	19.433
1948	Karl Frei, Switzerland	19.80
1952	Grant Shaginyan, USSR	19.75
1956	Albert Azaryan, USSR	19.35
1960	Albert Azaryan, USSR	19.725
1964	Takuji Haytta, Japan	19.475

RINGS (*CONT.*)

Year	Champion	Pts
1968	Akinori Nakayama, Japan	19.45
1972	Akinori Nakayama, Japan	19.35
1976	Nikolai Andrianov, USSR	19.65
1980	Aleksandr Dityatin, USSR	19.875
1984	Koji Gushiken, Japan	19.85
1988	Holger Behrendt, E Germany	19.925
1992	Vitaly Scherbo, Unified Team	9.937
1996	Yuri Chechi, Italy	9.887
2000	Szilveszter Csollany, Hungary	9.862
2004	Dimosthenis Tampakos, Greece	9.862
2008	Chen Yibing, China	16.600

FLOOR EXERCISE

Year	Champion	Pts
1932	Istvan Pelle, Hungary	9.60
1936	Georges Miez, Switzerland	18.666
1948	Ferenc Pataki, Hungary	19.35
1952	K. William Thoresson, Sweden	19.25
1956	Valentin Muratov, USSR	19.20
1960	Nobuyuki Aihara, Japan	19.45
1964	Franco Menichelli, Italy	19.45
1968	Sawao Kato, Japan	19.475
1972	Nikolai Andrianov, USSR	19.175
1976	Nikolai Andrianov, USSR	19.45
1980	Roland Brückner, E Germany	19.75
1984	Li Ning, China	19.925
1988	Sergei Kharkov, USSR	19.925
1992	Li Xiaoshuang, China	9.925
1996	Ioannis Melissanidis, Greece	9.850
2000	Igors Vihrovs, Latvia	9.812
2004	Kyle Shewfelt, Canada	9.787
2008	Zou Kai, China	16.050

TEAM COMBINED EXERCISES

Year	Champion	Pts
1904	Turngemeinde Philadelphia	374.43
1906	Norway	19.00
1908	Sweden	438
1912	Italy	265.75
1920	Italy	359.855
1924	Italy	839.058
1928	Switzerland	1718.625
1932	Italy	541.850
1936	Germany	657.430
1948	Finland	1358.30
1952	USSR	574.40
1956	USSR	568.25
1960	Japan	575.20
1964	Japan	577.95
1968	Japan	575.90
1972	Japan	571.25
1976	Japan	576.85
1980	USSR	598.60
1984	United States	591.40
1988	USSR	593.35
1992	Unified Team	585.45
1996	Russia	576.778
2000	China	231.919
2004	Japan	173.821
2008	China	286.125

GYMNASTICS — Women

ALL-AROUND

Year	Champion	Pts
1952	Maria Gorokhovskaya, USSR	76.78
1956	Larissa Latynina, USSR	74.933
1960	Larissa Latynina, USSR	77.031
1964	Vera Caslavska, Czechoslovakia	77.564
1968	Vera Caslavska, Czechoslovakia	78.25
1972	Lyudmila Tousischeva, USSR	77.025
1976	Nadia Comaneci, Romania	79.275
1980	Yelena Davydova, USSR	79.15
1984	Mary Lou Retton, United States	79.175
1988	Yelena Shushunova, USSR	79.662
1992	Tatiana Gutsu, Unified Team	39.737
1996	Lilia Podkopayeva, Ukraine	39.255
2000	Simona Amanar, Romania	38.642
2004	Carly Patterson, United States	38.387
2008	Nastia Liukin, United States	63.325

GYMNASTICS - Women (Cont.)

VAULT

Year	Champion	Pts
1952	Yekaterina Kalinchuk, USSR	19.20
1956	Larissa Latynina, USSR	18.833
1960	Margarita Nikolayeva, USSR	19.316
1964	Vera Caslavska, Czechoslovakia	19.483
1968	Vera Caslavska, Czechoslovakia	19.775
1972	Karin Janz, E Germany	19.525
1976	Nelli Kim, USSR	19.80
1980	Natalya Shaposhnikova, USSR	19.725
1984	Ecaterina Szabo, Romania	19.875
1988	Svetlana Boginskaya, USSR	19.905
1992	Henrietta Onodi, Hungary	9.925
	Lavinia Milosovici, Romania	9.925
1996	Simona Amanar, Romania	9.825
2000	Yelena Zamolodtchikova, Russia	9.731
2004	Monica Rosu, Romania	9.656
2008	Un Jong Hong, N Korea	15.650

UNEVEN BARS

Year	Champion	Pts
1952	Margit Korondi, Hungary	19.40
1956	Agnes Keleti, Hungary	18.966
1960	Polina Astakhova, USSR	19.616
1964	Polina Astakhova, USSR	19.332
1968	Vera Caslavska, Czechoslovakia	19.65
1972	Karin Janz, E Germany	19.675
1976	Nadia Comaneci, Romania	20.00
1980	Maxi Gnauck, E Germany	19.875
1984	Ma Yanhong, China	19.95
1988	Daniela Silivas, Romania	20.00
1992	Lu Li, China	10.00
1996	Svetlana Khorkina, Russia	9.850
2000	Svetlana Khorkina, Russia	9.862
2004	Emilie Lepennec, France	9.687
2008	He Kexin, China	16.725

BALANCE BEAM

Year	Champion	Pts
1952	Nina Bocharova, USSR	19.22
1956	Agnes Keleti, Hungary	18.80
1960	Eva Bosakova, Czechoslovakia	19.283
1964	Vera Caslavska, Czechoslovakia	19.449
1968	Natalya Kuchinskaya, USSR	19.65
1972	Olga Korbut, USSR	19.40
1976	Nadia Comaneci, Romania	19.95
1980	Nadia Comaneci, Romania	19.80
1984	Simona Pauca, Romania	19.80
1988	Daniela Silivas, Romania	19.924
1992	Tatiana Lisenko, Unified Team	9.975
1996	Shannon Miller, United States	9.862
2000	Xuan Li, China	9.825
2004	Catalina Ponor, Romania	9.787
2008	Shawn Johnson, United States	16.225

FLOOR EXERCISE

Year	Champion	Pts
1952	Agnes Keleti, Hungary	19.36
1956	Agnes Keleti, Hungary	18.733
1960	Larissa Latynina, USSR	19.583
1964	Larissa Latynina, USSR	19.599
1968	Vera Caslavska, Czechoslovakia	19.675
1972	Olga Korbut, USSR	19.575
1976	Nelli Kim, USSR	19.85
1980	Nadia Comaneci, Romania	19.875
1984	Ecaterina Szabo, Romania	19.975
1988	Daniela Silivas, Romania	19.937
1992	Lavinia Milosovici, Romania	10.00
1996	Lilia Podkopayeva, Ukraine	9.887
2000	Yelena Zamolodtchikova, Russia	9.850
2004	Catalina Ponor, Romania	9.750
2008	Sandra Izbasa, Romania	15.650

TEAM COMBINED EXERCISES

Year	Champion	Pts
1928	The Netherlands	316.75
1932	Not held	
1936	Germany	506.50
1948	Czechoslovakia	445.45
1952	USSR	527.03
1956	USSR	444.800
1960	USSR	382.320
1964	USSR	280.890
1968	USSR	382.85
1972	USSR	380.50
1976	USSR	466.00
1980	USSR	394.90
1984	Romania	392.02
1988	USSR	395.475
1992	Unified Team	395.666
1996	United States	389.225
2000	Romania	154.608
2004	Romania	114.283
2004	China	188.900

RHYTHMIC ALL-AROUND

Year	Champion	Pts
1984	Lori Fung, Canada	57.95
1988	Marina Lobach, USSR	60.00
1992	A. Timoshenko, Unified Team	59.037
1996	E. Serebrianskaya, Ukraine	39.683
2000	Yulia Barsukova, Russia	39.632
2004	Alina Kabaeva, Russia	108.400
2008	Evgeniya Kanaeva, Russia	75.500

RHYTHMIC TEAM COMBINED EXERCISES

Year	Champion	Pts
1996	Spain	38.933
2000	Russia	39.500
2004	China	249.750
2008	Russia	35.550

SOCCER

Men

1900 .....Great Britain
1904 .....Canada
1908 .....Great Britain
1912 .....Great Britain
1920 .....Belgium
1924 .....Uruguay
1928 .....Uruguay
1936 .....Italy
1948 .....Sweden
1952 .....Hungary
1956 .....USSR
1960 .....Yugoslavia
1964 .....Hungary
1968 .....Hungary
1972 .....Poland
1976 .....E Germany
1980 .....Czechoslovakia
1984 .....France
1988 .....USSR
1992 .....Spain
1996 .....Nigeria
2000 .....Cameroon
2004 .....Argentina
2008 .....Argentina

Women

1996 ....United States
2000 ....Norway
2004 ....United States
2008 ....United States

Track & Field

Jamaican sprinter Usain Bolt (r.) blew by the field at Beijing to take the 100-meter gold

JOHN BIEVER

TRACK & FIELD

Bolt from the Blue

Breakout star Usain Bolt rocked Beijing, leaving no doubt that the world's best sprinters hail from the Caribbean

BY MERRELL NODEN

AN AMAZING YEAR FOR TRACK and field began at the New York Games on May 31. There, on a wet track under the lights, Usain Bolt ran 100 meters in 9.72 seconds, breaking Asafa Powell's world record and beating world champion Tyson Gay by more than a meter. That was big news, of course, but the 21-year-old Jamaican was not quite an unknown: ever since he won the world junior 200 at the age of 15, the tall, lanky sprinter had been touted as an extraordinary talent waiting to blossom. This year, in finally doing so, he looked so impressive—so utterly unlike past sprinters in size and gait and demeanor—that track fans were left wondering if what they were seeing was not just the future of sprinting but a new prototype.

Bolt was clearly the big track and field star of the Beijing Olympics, winning three gold medals, all in world-record time. He also faced the usual slew of questions about drugs, and no wonder. Among the athletes missing from the Olympics was Justin Gatlin, the defending champion in both sprints, whose appeal to be allowed to compete following a drug positive was turned down. Marion Jones, who won five medals at the Sydney Olympics eight years ago, was disgraced. She served most of a six-month term for lying to a grand jury investigating the BALCO drug case.

The U.S. Olympic Trials, held in Eugene, Oregon, offered its usual mix of heartbreak and stirring performances. Returned to form, Gay looked capable of giving Bolt a race in Beijing, setting an American record (9.78) in the quarterfinals of the 100, then coming back to win the final in a wind-aided 9.68. But the effort left Gay sore and tight and, in the quarterfinals of the 200, he tumbled to the track with what turned out to be a muscle strain in his left hamstring. He would not fully recover all season.

This was disappointing but nothing compared to what the poor Chinese would suffer. High hurdler Liu Xiang, who surprised most everyone by winning the 110-meter hurdles in Athens, had spent the last four years as the host nation's greatest hope for Olympic glory. Xiang pulled out of the New York Games with a sore foot and, despite assurances that he would be healthy in time for the Olympics, he was not. In Beijing he climbed into the blocks for the first round of the hurdles but after a few steps pulled up and walked off the track. All over China his countrymen wept inconsolably. The gold medal they so fervently hoped would be his went to Dayron Robles of Cuba, who on June 12 had broken Xiang's world record by running 12.87.

As great as Robles was, the top athlete in the weeks leading up to the Games was pole vaulter Yelena Isinbayeva. The 26-year-old Russian had set 21 world records and her outdoor record had stood since 2005. But with American Jennifer Stuczynski inching closer to her at the U.S. Trials with a U.S. record 16'1¾", Isinbayeva found new inspi-

BOB MARTIN

Jamaica's dominance continued in the women's events as Fraser, Simpson and Stewart (l. to r.) swept the medals in the 100.

ration. In Rome, late on the night of July 11, she cleared 16'6" and went to Beijing as the clear favorite.

Isinbayeva set another world record in winning in Beijing. But she and everyone else—even the magnificent Ethiopian pair of Kenenisa Bekele and Tirunesh Dibaba, each of whom won both the 5,000 and 10,000—were overshadowed by Bolt, who seemed a breed apart almost from the moment he walked out on the track. Unlike his stone-faced brethren, Bolt mugs and preens for the camera, mimicking shooting an arrow—or perhaps it's a bolt—into the sky. His quarter-final race was mind-blowing, not so much for the time—a by now ho-hum 9.92—but for the way he ran it. Bolt was already easing up some 30 yards from the finish, spreading his arms wide as if to embrace the greater glories still to come. In the final he simply ran away from the field, clocking a 9.69 that could have been much faster had Bolt not—yet again—eased up before the finish but still winning by two full meters.

That only heightened anticipation for Bolt's preferred race, the 200. For many, Michael Johnson's 200 world record of 19.32 was the greatest run in recent memory, the sprint equivalent of Bob Beamon's historic long jump. In the longer sprint Bolt ran hard all the way and dipped at the finish, clocking 19.30, .02 seconds faster than Johnson. He won his third gold medal in anchoring the Jamaican 400 relay team to a world record 37.10.

Bolt's Jamaican teammates also had an awesome Games, claiming a total of six gold medals. Shelly-Ann Fraser (gold), Sherone Simpson (silver) and Kerron Stewart (bronze) helped Jamaica sweep the women's 100, Veronica Campbell-Brown won the 200, and Melaine Walker won the women's 400 hurdles. The women's 4x100 relay seemed sure to be a showdown between the Jamaicans and the revenge-hungry Americans. But both teams dropped the baton—as did the U.S. men in their relay—leaving the door open for Russia to claim gold. The U.S. would win both the men's and women's 4x400 relays, but that hardly made up for the dropped batons. It felt strange watching another country dominate the sprints. And given the fast times both Bolt and Powell continued to run in post-Olympic meets, there should be more to come from the Amazin' Jamaicans and their Lightning Bolt.

2008 U.S. Olympic Trials

Eugene, Oregon, June 27–July 6, 2008

Men

100 METERS
1. ....Tyson Gay, adidas 9.68
2. ....Walter Dix, Florida St 9.80
3. ....Darvis Patton, adidas 9.84

200 METERS
1......Walter Dix, Florida St 19.852
2......Shawn Crawford, Nike 19.857
3......Wallace Spearmon, Nike 19.90

400 METERS
1. ....LaShawn Merritt, Nike 44.00
2. ....Jeremy Wariner, adidas 44.20
3. ....David Neville, Nike 44.61

800 METERS
1. ....Nicholas Symmonds, OTC/Nike 1:44.10
2. ....Andrew Wheating, Oregon TC 1:45.03
3. ....Christian Smith, OTC/Nike 1:45.47

1,500 METERS
1. ....Bernard Lagat, Nike 3:40.37
2. ....Leonel Manzano, Nike 3:40.90
3. ....Lopez Lomong, Nike 3:41.00

3,000 M STEEPLECHASE
1. ....Anthony Famiglietti, adidas 8:20.24
2. ....William Nelson, Colorado 8:211.47
3. ....Joshua McAdams, New Balance 8:21.99

5,000 METERS
1. ....Bernard Lagat, Nike 13:27.47
2. ....Matt Tegenkamp, Nike 13:29.68
3. ....Ian Dobson, adidas 13:29.76

10,000 METERS
1. ....Abdi Abdirahman, Nike 27:41.89
2. ....Galen Rupp, unattached 27:43.11
3. ....Jorge Torres, Reebok 27:46.33

110-METER HURDLES
1. ....David Oliver, Nike 12.95
2. ....Terrence Trammell, Mizuno 13.00
3. ....David Payne, Nike 13.25

400-METER HURDLES
1. ....Bershawn Jackson, Nike 48.17
2. ....Kerron Clement, Nike 48.36
3. ....Angelo Taylor, Nike 48.42

20-KILOMETER RACE WALK
1. ....Kevin Eastler, U.S. Air Force 1:27.08
2. ....Matthew Boyles, Miami Valley TC1:28.20
3. ....Patrick Stroupe, unattached 1:29.17

HIGH JUMP
1. ....Jesse Williams, Nike 7'6½"
2. ....Jamie Nieto, Nike 7'5¼"
3. ....Andra Manson, Nike §7'5¼"

POLE VAULT
1. ....Derek Miles, Nike 19'½"
2. ....Jeff Hartwig, unattached 18'8¼"
3. ....Brad Walker, Nike 18'6½"

LONG JUMP
1. ....Miguel Pate, Nike 27'½"
2. ....JaRod Tobler, unattached 26'9¼"
3. ....Brian Johnson, Nike 26'6½"

TRIPLE JUMP
1. ....Aarik Wilson, Nike 57'2¼"
2. ....Kenta Bell, Mizuno 56'6½"
3. ....Rafeeq Curry, Shore AC 56'5¾"

SHOT PUT
1. ....Reese Hoffa, New York AC 72'6¼"
2. ....Christian Cantwell, Nike 71'2¾"
3. ....Adam Nelson, Nike 68'6½"

DISCUS THROW
1. ....Ian Waltz, Nike 216'1"
2. ....Michael Robertson, Nike 209'1"
3. ....Casey Malone, Nike 205'7"

HAMMER THROW
1. ....A.G. Kruger, Nike 248'9"
2. ....Kevin McMahon, unattached 244'5"
3. ....Thomas Freeman, unattached 241'5"

JAVELIN THROW
1. ....Bobby Smith, Monmouth TC 249'6"
2. ....Mike Hazle, Nike 248'7"
3. ....Brian Chaput, Javelin USA 248'1"

DECATHLON
1. ....Bryan Clay, Nike 8832
2. ....Trey Hardee, Nike 8534
3. ....Tom Pappas, Nike 8511

MARATHON*
1. ....Brian Sell 2:09.02
2. ....Ryan Hall 2:11.06
3. ....Dathan Ritzenheim 2:11.40

*Held November 7, 2007 in New York City.
§ Final place in high jump and pole vault decided by number of successful clearances at final height.

2008 U.S. Olympic Trials *(Cont.)*

Women

100 METERS
1. ....Muna Lee, Nike 10.85
2. ....Torri Edwards, Nike 10.894
3. ....Lauryn Williams, Nike 10.897

200 METERS
1. ....Allyson Felix, adidas 21.82
2. ....Muna Lee, Nike 21.99
3. ......Marshveet Hooker, adidas 22.20

400 METERS
1. ....Sanya Richards, Nike 49.89
2. ....Mary Wineberg, Nike 50.85
3. ....Dee Dee Trotter, adidas 50.88

800 METERS
1. ....Hazel Clark, Nike 1:59.82
2. ....Alice Schmidt, adidas 2:00.46
3. ....Kameisha Bennett, Nike 2:01.20

1,500 METERS
1. ....Shannon Rowbury, Nike 4:05.48
3. ....Erin Donohue, Nike 4:08.20
2. ....Christin Wurth, Nike 4:08.48

3,000 M STEEPLECHASE
1. ....Anna Willard, Nike 9:27.59
2. ....Lindsey Anderson, Nike 9:30.75
3. ....Jennifer Barringer, Colorado 9:33.11

5,000 METERS
1. ....Kara Goucher, Nike 15:01.02
2. ....Jennifer Rhines, adidas 15:02.02
3. ....Shalane Flanagan, Nike 15:02.81

10,000 METERS
1. ....Shalane Flanagan, Nike 31:34.81
2. ....Kara Goucher, Nike 31:37.72
3. ....Amy Begley, Nike 31:43.60

20-KILOMETER RACE WALK
1. ....Joanne Dow, adidas 1:35.11
2. ....Teresa Vaill, Walk USA 1:36.35
3. ....Susan Armenta, unattached 1:42.12

100-METER HURDLES
1. ....Lolo Jones, Asics 12.29
2. ....Damu Cherry, Nike 12.58
3. ....Dawn Harper, unattached 12.62

400-METER HURDLES
1. ....Tiffany Ross-Williams, Reebok 54.03
2. ....Queen Harrison, Virginia Tech 54.60
3. ....Sheena Tosta, Nike 54.62

HIGH JUMP
1. ....Chaunte Howard, Nike 6'5½"
2. ....Amy Acuff, Tri-Valley Asics 6'4"
3. ....Sharon Day, Asics §6'3¼"

POLE VAULT
1. ....Jennifer Stuczynski, adidas 16'1¾"
2. ....April Benne, adidas 15'1"
3. ....Erica Bartolina, unattached 14'11"

LONG JUMP
1. ....Brittney Reese, Nike 22'9¾"
2. ....Grace Upshaw, Nike 22'7"
3. ....Funmi Jimoh, Nike 22'¼"

TRIPLE JUMP
1. ....Shani Marks, Nike 47'2¼"
2. ....Shakeema Welsch, unattached 46'10"
3. ....Erica McLain, Nike 45'9¾"

SHOT PUT
1. ....Michelle Carter, unattached 61'10¼"
2. ....Kristin Heaston, Nike 60'2"
3. ....Jillian Camarena, New York AC 59'5½"

DISCUS THROW
1. ....Aretha Thurmond, Nike 213'11"
2. ....S. Powell-Roos, Tri-Valley Asics 206'5"
3. ....Stephanie Brown-Trafton, Nike 205'6"

HAMMER THROW
1. ....Jessica Cosby, Nike 232'
2. ....Amber Campbell, Mjolnir Throws 227'2"
3. ....Sarah Veress, unattached 225'1"

JAVELIN THROW
1. ....Kara Patterson, Purdue 191'9"
2. ....Dana Pounds, U.S. Air Force 189'9"
3. ....Rachel Yurkovich, Oregon 185'1"

HEPTATHLON
1. ....Hyleas Fountain, Nike 6667
2. ....Jacquelyn Johnson, Nike 6347
3. ....Diana Pickler, Asics 6257

MARATHON*
1. ....Deena Kastor 2:29.35
2. ....Magdalena Boulet 2:30.19
3. ....Blake Russell 2:32.40

*Held April 25 in Boston, Massachusetts.
§ Final place in high jump and pole vault decided by number of successful clearances at final height.

FOR THE RECORD • Year by Year

TRACK AND FIELD

World Records

As of October 1, 2008. World outdoor records are recognized by the International Amateur Athletics Federation (IAAF).

Men

Event	Mark	Record Holder	Date	Site
100 meters	9.69	Usain Bolt, Jamaica	8-16-08	Beijing
200 meters	19.30	Usain Bolt, Jamaica	8-20-08	Beijing
400 meters	43.18	Michael Johnson, United States	8-26-99	Seville, Spain
800 meters	1:41.11	Wilson Kipketer, Denmark	8-24-97	Cologne
1,000 meters	2:11.96	Noah Ngeny, Kenya	9-5-99	Rieti, Italy
1,500 meters	3:26.00	Hicham El Guerrouj, Morocco	7-14-98	Rome
Mile	3:43.13	Hicham El Guerrouj, Morocco	7-7-99	Rome
2,000 meters	4:44.79	Hicham El Guerrouj, Morocco	9-7-99	Berlin
3,000 meters	7:20.67	Daniel Komen, Kenya	9-1-96	Rieti, Italy
Steeplechase	7:53.63	Saif Saaeed Shaheen, Qatar	9-3-04	Brussels
5,000 meters	12:37.35	Kenenisa Bekele, Ethiopia	5-31-04	Hengelo, Netherlands
10,000 meters	26:17.53	Kenenisa Bekele, Ehtiopia	8-26-05	Brussels
20,000 meters	56:25.98	Haile Gebrselassie, Ethiopia	6-27-07	Ostrava, Czech Republic
Hour	21,285 meters	Haile Gebrselassie, Ethiopia	6-27-07	Ostrava, Czech Republic
25,000 meters	1:13:55.8	Toshihiko Seko, Japan	3-22-81	Christchurch, New Zealand
30,000 meters	1:29:18.8	Toshihiko Seko, Japan	3-22-81	Christchurch, New Zealand
Marathon	2:04:55	Paul Tergat, Kenya	9-28-03	Berlin
110-meter hurdles	12.87	Dayron Robles, Cuba	6-12-08	Ostrava, Czech Republic
400-meter hurdles	46.78	Kevin Young, United States	8-6-92	Barcelona
20-kilometer walk	1:17.16	Vladimir Kanaykin, Russia	9-29-07	Saransk, Russia
30-kilometer walk	2:01:44.1	Maurizio Damilano, Italy	10-3-92	Cuneo, Italy
50-kilometer walk	3:35:47	Nathan Deakes, Australia	12-2-06	Geelong, Austalia
4 x 100-meter relay	37.10	Jamaica (Nesta Carter, Michael Prater, Usain Bolt, Asafa Powell)	8-22-08	Beijing
4 x 200-meter relay	1:18.68	Santa Monica TC (Mike Marsh, Leroy Burrell, Floyd Heard, Carl Lewis)	4-17-94	Walnut, Calif.
4 x 400-meter relay	2:54.29	United States (Andrew Valmon, Quincy Watts, Harry Reynolds, Michael Johnson)	8-22-93	Stuttgart, Germany
4 x 800-meter relay	7:02.43	Kenya (Wilfred Bungei, William Yiampoy, Joseph Mutua, Ismael Kombich)	8-25-06	Brussels
4 x 1,500-meter relay	14:38.8	W Germany (Thomas Wessinghage, Harald Hudak, Michael Lederer, Karl Fleschen)	8-17-77	Cologne, Germany
High jump	2.45m	Javier Sotomayor, Cuba	7-27-93	Salamanca, Spain
Pole vault	6.14m	Sergei Bubka, Ukraine	7-31-94	Sestriere, Italy
Long jump	8.95m	Mike Powell, United States	8-30-91	Tokyo
Triple jump	18.29m	Jonathan Edwards, Great Britain	8-7-95	Göteborg, Sweden
Shot put	23.12m	Randy Barnes, United States	5-20-90	Westwood, Calif.
Discus throw	74.08m	Jürgen Schult, E Germany	6-6-86	Neubrandenburg, Germany
Hammer throw	86.74m	Yuri Syedykh, USSR	8-30-86	Stuttgart, Germany
Javelin throw	98.48m	Jan Zelezny, Czech Republic	5-25-96	Jena, Germany
Decathlon	9026 pts	Roman Sebrle, Czech Republic	5-27-01	Götzis, Austria

Note: The decathlon consists of 10 events: the 100 meters, long jump, shot put, high jump and 400 meters on the first day; the 110-meter hurdles, discus, pole vault, javelin and 1,500 meters on the second.

Event	Mark	Record Holder	Date	Site

Women

Event	Mark	Record Holder	Date	Site
100 meters	10.49	Florence Griffith Joyner, United States	7-16-88	Indianapolis
200 meters	21.34	Florence Griffith Joyner, United States	9-29-88	Seoul

World Records *(Cont.)*

Women

Event	Mark	Record Holder	Date	Site
800 meters	1:53.28	Jarmila Kratochvílová, Czechoslovakia	7-26-83	Munich
1,000 meters	2:28.98	Svetlana Masterkova, Russia	8-23-96	Brussels
1,500 meters	3:50.46	Yunxia Qu, China	9-11-93	Beijing
Mile	4:12.56	Svetlana Masterkova, Russia	8-14-96	Zurich
2,000 meters	5:25.36	Sonia O'Sullivan, Ireland	7-8-94	Edinburgh
3,000 meters	8:06.11	Junxia Wang, China	9-13-93	Beijing
Steeplechase	8:58.81	Gulnara Samitova-Galkina, Russia	8-17-08	Beijing
5,000 meters	14:11.15	Tirunesh Dibaba, Ethiopia	6-6-08	Oslo
10,000 meters	29:31.78	Junxia Wang, China	9-8-93	Beijing
Hour	18,517 meters	Dire Tune, Ethiopia	6-12-08	Ostrava, Czech Republic
20,000 meters	1:05:26.6	Tegla Loroupe, Kenya	9-3-00	Borgholzhausen, Germany
25,000 meters	1:27:05.9	Tegla Loroupe, Kenya	9-21-02	Mengerskirchen, Germany
30,000 meters	1:45:50	Tegla Loroupe, Kenya	6-6-03	Warstein, Germany
Marathon	2:15:25	Paula Radcliffe, Great Britain	4-13-03	London
100-meter hurdles	12.21	Yordanka Donkova, Bulgaria	8-20-88	Stara Zagora, Bulgaria
400-meter hurdles	52.34	Yuliya Nosova, Russia	8-8-03	Tula, Russia
5-kilometer walk	20:02.60	Gillian O'Sullivan, Ireland	7-13-02	Dublin
10-kilometer walk	41:56.23	Nadezhda Ryashkina, URS	7-24-90	Seattle
4 x 100-meter relay	41.37	East Germany (Silke Gladisch, Sabine Reiger, Ingrid Auerswald, Marlies Göhr)	10-6-85	Canberra, Australia
4 x 200-meter relay	1:27.46	United States (LaTasha Jenkins, LaTasha Colander-Richardson, Nanceen Perry, Marion Jones)	4-29-00	Philadelphia
4 x 400-meter relay	3:15.17	USSR (Tatyana Ledovskaya, Olga Nazarova, Maria Pinigina, Olga Bryzgina)	10-1-88	Seoul
4 x 800-meter relay	7:50.17	USSR (Nadezhda Olizarenko, Lyubov Gurina, Lyudmila Borisova, Irina Podyalovskaya)	8-5-84	Moscow
High jump	2.09m	Stefka Kostadinova, Bulgaria	8-30-87	Rome
Pole vault	5.05m	Yelena Isinbayeva, Russia	8-18-08	Beijing
Long jump	7.52m	Galina Chistyakova, USSR	6-11-88	Leningrad
Triple jump	15.50m	Inessa Kravets, Ukraine	8-10-95	Gothenburg, Sweden
Shot put	22.63m	Natalya Lisovskaya, USSR	6-7-87	Moscow
Discus throw	76.80m	Gabriele Reinsch, E Germany	7-9-88	Neubrandenburg, Germany
Hammer throw	77.80m	Tatyana Lysenko, Russia	8-15-06	Tallinn, Estonia
Javelin throw	71.70m	Osleidys Menéndez, Cuba	8-14-05	Helsinki
Heptathlon	7291 pts	Jackie Joyner-Kersee, United States	9-24-88	Seoul

Note: The heptathlon consists of 7 events: the 100-meter hurdles, high jump, shot put and 200 meters on the first day; the long jump, javelin and 800 meters on the second.

†Pending ratification.

World and American Indoor Records

As of September 15, 2004. American indoor records are recognized by USA Track and Field. World Indoor records are recognized by the International Amateur Athletics Federation (IAAF). (A) represents an American record, (W) represents a World record.

Men

Event	Mark	Record Holder	Date	Site
50 meters	5.56	Donovan Bailey, Canada (W)	2-9-96	Reno, Nev.
	5.56	Maurice Greene (A)	2-13-99	Los Angeles
55 meters*	5.99	Obadele Thompson, Barbados (W)	2-22-97	Colorado Springs
	6.00	Lee McRae (A)	3-14-86	Oklahoma City
60 meters	6.39	Maurice Greene (W, A)	3-1-98	Madrid
	6.39	Maurice Greene (W, A)	3-3-01	Atlanta
200 meters	19.92	Frankie Fredericks, Namibia (W)	2-18-96	Liévin, France
	20.10	Wallace Spearmon(A)	3-11-05	Fayetteville, Ark.
400 meters	44.57	Kerron Clement (A, W)	3-12-05	Fayetteville, Ark.
800 meters	1:42.67	Wilson Kipketer, Denmark (W)	3-9-97	Paris
	1:45.00	Johnny Gray (A)	3-8-92	Sindelfingen, Germany

World and American Indoor Records *(Cont.)*

Men *(Cont.)*

Event	Mark	Record Holder	Date	Site
1,000 meters	2:14.96	Wilson Kipketer, Denmark (W)	2-20-00	Birmingham, England
	2:17.86	David Krummenacker (A)	1-27-02	Boston
1,500 meters	3:31.18	Hicham El Guerrouj, Morocco (W)	2-02-97	Stuttgart, Germany
	3:35.23	Bernard Lagat (A)	2-16-08	Birmingham, England
Mile	3:48.45	Hicham El Guerrouj, Morocco (W)	2-12-97	Ghent, Belgium
	3:49.89	Bernard Lagat (A)	2-11-05	Fayetteville, Ark.
3,000 meters	7:24.90	Daniel Komen, Kenya (W)	2-6-98	Budapest, Hungary
	7:32.43	Bernard Lagat (A)	2-17-07	Birmingham, England
5,000 meters	12:49.60	Kenenisa Bekele, Ethiopia (W)	2-20-04	Birmingham, England
	13:20.55	Doug Padilla (A)	2-12-82	New York City
50-meter hurdles	6.25	Mark McKoy, Canada (W)	3-5-86	Kobe, Japan
	6.35	Greg Foster (A)	1-27-85	Rosemont, Illinois
55-meter hurdles*	6.89	Renaldo Nehemiah (A)	1-20-79	New York City
60-meter hurdles	7.30	Colin Jackson, Great Britain (W)	3-6-94	Sindelfingen, Germany
	7.36	Greg Foster (A)	1-16-87	Los Angeles
	7.36	Allen Johnson (A)	3-6-04	Budapest, Hungary
5,000-meter walk	18:07.08	Mikhail Shchennikov, Russia (W)	2-14-95	Moscow
	19:15.88	Tim Seaman (A)	3-7-87	Indianapolis
4 x 200-meter relay	1:22.11	Great Britain (W) (Linford Christie, Darren Braithwaite, Ade Mafe, John Regis)	3-3-91	Glasgow
	1:22.71	National Team (A) (Thomas Jefferson, Raymond Pierre, Antonio McKay Kevin Little)	3-3-91	Glasgow
4 x 400-meter relay	3:02.83	United States (W, A) (Andre Morris, Dameon Johnson, Deon Minor, Milton Campbell	3-7-99	Maebashi, Japan
4 x 800-meter relay	7:13.94	Global Athletics & Marketing (W, A) (Rich Kenah, Joel Woody, Karl Paranya, David Krummenacker)	2-6-00	Boston
High jump	2.43m	Javier Sotomayor, Cuba (W)	3-4-89	Budapest, Hungary
	2.40m	Hollis Conway (A)	3-10-91	Seville
Pole vault	6.15m	Sergei Bubka, Ukraine (W)	2-21-93	Donetsk, Ukraine
	6.02m	Jeff Hartwig (A)	3-10-02	Sindelfingen, Germany
Long jump	8.79m	Carl Lewis (W, A)	1-27-84	New York City
Triple jump	17.83m	Alicier Urrutia, Cuba (W)	3-1-97	Sindelfingen, Germany
	17.83m	Christian Olsson, Sweden (W)	3-7-04	Budapest, Hungary
	17.76m	Mike Conley (A)	2-27-87	New York City
Shot put	22.66m	Randy Barnes (W, A)	1-20-89	Los Angeles
Weight throw*	25.86m	Lance Deal (W, A)	3-4-95	Atlanta
Pentathlon*	4478 pts	Steve Fritz, (W, A)	1-14-95	Lawrence, Kan.
Heptathlon	6476 pts	Dan O'Brien (W, A)	3-13/14-93	Toronto

*No recognized world record.

Women

Event	Mark	Record Holder	Date	Site
50 meters	5.96	Irina Privolova, Russia (W)	2-9-95	Madrid
	6.02	Gail Devers (A)	2-21-99	Liévin, France
55 meters*	6.56	Gwen Torrence (A)	3-14-87	Oklahoma City, Okla.
60 meters	6.92	Irina Privalova, Russia (W)	2-11-93	Madrid
	6.92	Irina Privalova, Russia (W)	2-9-95	Madrid
	6.95	Gail Devers (A)	3-12-93	Toronto
	6.95	Marion Jones (A)	3-7-98	Maebashi, Japan
200 meters	21.87	Merlene Ottey, Jamaica (W)	2-13-93	Liévin, France
	22.18	Michelle Collins (A)	3-15-03	Birmingham, England
400 meters	49.59	Jarmila Kratochvilová, Czech. (W)	3-7-82	Milan
	50.64	Diane Dixon (A)	3-10-91	Seville
800 meters	1:55.82	Jolanda Ceplak, Slovenia (W)	3-3-02	Vienna
	1:58.71	Nicole Teter (A)	3-2-02	New York
1,000 meters	2:30.94	Maria Mutola, Mozambique (W)	2-25-99	Stockholm
	2:34.19	Jennifer Toomey (A)	2-20-04	Birmingham, England
1,500 meters	3:57.71	Yelena Soboleva, Russia (W)	3-9-08	Valencia, Spain
	3:59.98	Regina Jacobs, United States (A)	2-1-03	Boston
Mile	4:17.14	Doina Melinte, Romania (W)	2-9-90	East Rutherford, N.J.
	4:20.50	Mary Slaney (A)	2-19-82	San Diego
3,000 meters	8:23.72	Meseret Defar, Ethiopia (W)	2-3-07	Stuttgart
	8:33.25	Shalane Flanagan (A)	1-27-07	Boston

World and American Indoor Records (*Cont.*)

Women (*cont.*)

Event	Mark	Record Holder	Date	Site
5,000 meters	14:27.42	Tirunesh Dibaba, Ethiopia (W)	1-27-07	Boston
	15:07.33	Marla Runyan (A)	2-18-01	New York
50-meter hurdles	6.58	Cornelia Oschkenat, E Germany (W)	2-20-88	Berlin
	6.67	Jackie Joyner-Kersee (A)	2-10-95	Reno, Nev.
55-meter hurdles*	7.37	Jackie Joyner-Kersee (A)	2-3-89	New York
60-meter hurdles	7.69	Susanna Kallur, Sweden (W)	2-10-08	Karlsruhe, Germany
	7.74	Gail Devers (A)	3-1-03	Boston
3,000-meter walk	11:40.33	Claudia Stef, Romania	1-30-99	Bucharest, Romania
	12:20.79	Debbi Lawrence (A)	3-12-93	Toronto
4 x 200-meter relay	1:32.41	Russia (Y, Kondratyeva, I. Khabarova, Y.Pechonkina, Y. Gushchina) (W)	1-29-05	Glasgow
	1:33.24	National Team (A) (Flirtisha Harris, Chryste Gaines, Terri Dendy, Michele Collins)	2-12-94	Glasgow
4 x 400-meter relay	3:23.37	Russia (W)	1-28-06	Glasgow
	3:27.59	National Team (A) (Michelle Collins, Monique Hennagan, Zundra Feagin-Alexander, Shanelle Porter)	3-7-99	Maebashi, Japan
4 x 800-meter relay	8:18.54	Moskovskaya Region, Russia, (W) (Anna Balakshina,Nataliya Panteleeva, Anna Yemashova, Olesya Chumakova)	2-11-07	Volgograd, Russia
	8:25.65	Villanova Univ. (A) (Gina Procaccio, Celeste Halliday, Michelle Di Muro-Ave, Grant)	2-11-87	Gainesville, Florida
High jump	2.08m	Kajsa Bergqvist, Sweden (W)	2-4-06	Arnstadt, Germany
	2.01m	Tisha Waller (A)	2-28-98	Atlanta
Pole vault	4.95m	Yelena Isinbaeva, Russia (W)	2-16-08	Donetsk, Ukraine
	4.81m	Stacy Dragila (A)	3-6-04	Budapest, Hungary
Long jump	7.37m	Heike Drechsler, E Germany (W)	2-13-88	Vienna
	7.13m	Jackie Joyner-Kersee (A)	3-5-94	Atlanta
Triple jump	15.36m	Tatyana Lebedeva, Russia (W)	3-6-04	Budapest, Hungary
	14.23m	Sheila Hudson-Strudwick (A)	3-4-95	Atlanta
Shot put	22.50m	Helena Fibingerová, Czech. (W)	2-19-77	Jablonec, Czech.
	19.83m	Ramona Pagel (A)	2-20-87	Inglewood, Calif.
Weight throw*	24.57m†	Brittany Riley (A)	1-27-07	Bloomington, Ind.
Pentathlon	4991 pts	Irina Byelova, CIS (W)	2-14/15-92	Berlin
	4753 pts	Le Shundra Nathan (A)	3-4/5-99	Maebashi, Japan

*No recognized world record. †Pending ratification.

World Track and Field Championships

Men

100 METERS

Year	Winner	Time
1983	Carl Lewis, United States	10.07
1987*	Carl Lewis, United States	9.93 WR
1991	Carl Lewis, United States	9.86 WR
1993	Linford Christie, Great Britain	9.87
1995	Donovan Bailey, Canada	9.97
1997	Maurice Greene, United States	9.86
1999	Maurice Greene, United States	9.80
2001	Maurice Greene, United States	9.82
2003	Kim Collins, St. Kitts & Nevis	10.07
2005	Justin Gatlin, United States	9.88
2007	Tyson Gay, United States	9.85

200 METERS

Year	Winner	Time
1983	Calvin Smith, United States	20.14
1987	Calvin Smith, United States	20.16
1991	Michael Johnson, United States	20.01
1993	Frank Fredericks, Namibia	19.85
1995	Michael Johnson, United States	19.79
1997	Ato Boldon, Trinidad and Tobago	20.04
1999	Maurice Greene, United States	19.90
2001	Konstadínos Kedéris, Greece	20.04
2003	John Capel, United States	20.30
2005	Justin Gatlin, United States	20.04
2007	Tyson Gay, United States	19.76

400 METERS

Year	Winner	Time
1983	Bert Cameron, Jamaica	45.05
1987	Thomas Schoenlebe, E Germany	44.33
1991	Antonio Pettigrew, United States	44.57
1993	Michael Johnson, United States	43.65
1995	Michael Johnson, United States	43.39
1997	Michael Johnson, United States	44.12
1999	Michael Johnson, United States	43.18 WR
2001	Avard Moncur, Bahamas	44.64
2003	Jerome Young, United States	44.50
2005	Jeremy Wariner, United States	43.93
2007	Jeremy Wariner, United States	43.45

WR=World record. *Ben Johnson, Canada, disqualified.

Men (Cont.)

800 METERS

1983..............Willi Wulbeck, W Germany 1:43.65
1987..............Billy Konchellah, Kenya 1:43.06
1991..............Billy Konchellah, Kenya 1:43.99
1993..............Paul Ruto, Kenya 1:44.71
1995..............Wilson Kipketer, Denmark 1:45.08
1997..............Wilson Kipketer, Denmark 1:43.38
1999..............Wilson Kipketer, Denmark 1:43.30
2001..............André Bucher, Switzerland 1:43.70
2003..............Djabir Saïd-Guerni, Algeria 1:44.81
2005..............Rashid Ramzi, Brunei 1:44.24
2007..............Alfred Kirwa Yego 1:47.09

1,500 METERS

1983..............Steve Cram, Great Britain 3:41.59
1987..............Abdi Bile, Somalia 3:36.80
1991..............Noureddine Morceli, Algeria 3:32.84
1993..............Noureddine Morceli, Algeria 3:34.24
1995..............Noureddine Morceli, Algeria 3:33.73
1997..............Hicham El Guerrouj, Morocco 3:35.83
1999..............Hicham El Guerrouj, Morocco 3:27.65
2001..............Hicham El Guerrouj, Morocco 3:30.68
2003..............Hicham El Guerrouj, Morocco 3:31.77
2005..............Rashid Ramzi, Brunei 3:37.88
2007..............Bernard Lagat, United States 3:34.77

STEEPLECHASE

1983..............Patriz Ilg, W Germany 8:15.06
1987..............Francesco Panetta, Italy 8:08.57
1991..............Moses Kiptanui, Kenya 8:12.59
1993..............Moses Kiptanui, Kenya 8:06.36
1995..............Moses Kiptanui, Kenya 8:04.16
1997..............Wilson Boit Kipketer, Kenya 8:05.84
1999..............Christopher Koskei, Kenya 8:11.76
2001..............Reuben Kosgei, Kenya 8:15.16
2003..............Saif Saaeed Shaheen, Qatar 8:04.39
2005..............Saif Saaeed Shaheen, Qatar 8:13.31
2007..............Brimin Kipruto, Kenya 8:13.82

5,000 METERS

1983..............Eamonn Coghlan, Ireland 13:28.53
1987..............Said Aouita, Morocco 13:26.44
1991..............Yobes Ondieki, Kenya 13:14.45
1993..............Ismael Kirui, Kenya 13:02.75
1995..............Ismael Kirui, Kenya 13:16.77
1997..............Daniel Komen, Kenya 13:07.38
1999..............Salah Hissou, Morocco 12:58.13
2001..............Richard Limo, Kenya 13:00.77
2003..............Eliud Kipchoge, Kenya 12:52.79
2005..............Benjamin Limo, Kenya 13:32.55
2007..............Bernard Lagat, United States 13:45.87

10,000 METERS

1983..............Alberto Cova, Italy 28:01.04
1987..............Paul Kipkoech, Kenya 27:38.63
1991..............Moses Tanui, Kenya 27:38.74
1993..............Haile Gebrselassie, Ethiopia 27:46.02
1995..............Haile Gebrselassie, Ethiopia 27:12.95
1997..............Haile Gebrselassie, Ethiopia 27:24.58
1999..............Haile Gebrselassie, Ethiopia 27:57.27
2001..............Charles Kamathi, Kenya 27:53.25
2003..............Kenenisa Bekele, Ethiopia 26:49.57
2005..............Kenenisa Bekele, Ethiopia 27:08.33
2007..............Kenenisa Bekele, Ethiopia 27:05.90

MARATHON

1983..............Rob de Castella, Australia 2:10:03
1987..............Douglas Wakiihuri, Kenya 2:11:48
1991..............Hiromi Taniguchi, Japan 2:14:57
1993..............Mark Plaatjes, United States 2:13:57
1995..............Martín Fiz, Spain 2:11:41
1997..............Abel Anton, Spain 2:13:16
1999..............Abel Anton, Spain 2:13:36
2001..............Gezahegne Abera, Ethiopia 2:12:42
2003..............Jaouad Gharib, Morocco 2:08.31
2005..............Jaouad Gharib, Morocco 2:10:10
2007..............Luke Kibet, Kenya 2:15:59

110-METER HURDLES

1983..............Greg Foster, United States 13.42
1987..............Greg Foster, United States 13.21
1991..............Greg Foster, United States 13.06
1993..............Colin Jackson, Great Britain 12.91 WR
1995..............Allen Johnson, United States 13.00
1997..............Allen Johnson, United States 12.93
1999..............Colin Jackson, Great Britain 13.04
2001..............Allen Johnson, United States 13.04
2003..............Allen Johnson, United States 13.12
2005..............Ladji Doucoure, France 13:07
2007..............Liu Xiang, China 12.95

400-METER HURDLES

1983..............Edwin Moses, United States 47.50
1987..............Edwin Moses, United States 47.46
1991..............Samuel Matete, Zambia 47.64
1993..............Kevin Young, United States 47.18
1995..............Derrick Adkins, United States 47.98
1997..............Stéphane Diagana, France 47.70
1999..............Fabrizio Mori, Italy 47.72
2001..............Felix Sánchez, Dominican Rep. 47.49
2003..............Felix Sánchez, Dominican Rep. 47.25
2005..............Bershawn Jackson, United States47.30
2007..............Kerron Clement, United States 47.61

20-KILOMETER WALK

1983..............Ernesto Canto, Mexico 1:20:49
1987..............Maurizio Damilano, Italy 1:20:45
1991..............Maurizio Damilano, Italy 1:19:37
1993..............Valentin Massana, Spain 1:22:31
1995..............Michele Didoni, Italy 1:19:59
1997..............Daniel Garcia, Mexico 1:21:43
1999..............Ilya Markov, Russia 1:23:34
2001..............Roman Rasskazov, Russia 1:20:31
2003..............Jefferson Pérez, Ecuador 1:17.21 WR
2005..............Jefferson Pérez, Ecuador 1:18:35
2007..............Jefferson Pérez, Ecuador 1:22:20

50-KILOMETER WALK

1983..............Ronald Weigel, East Germany 3:43:08
1987..............Hartwig Gauder, East Germany3:40:53
1991..............Aleksandr Potashov, USSR 3:53:09
1993..............Jesus Angel Garcia, Spain 3:41:41
1995..............Valentin Kononen, Finland 3:43:42
1997..............Robert Korzeniowski, Poland 3:44:46
1999..............German Skurygin, Russia 3:44:23
2001..............Robert Korzeniowski, Poland 3:42:08
2003..............R. Korzeniowski, Poland 3:36:03 WR
2005..............S. Kirdyapkin, Russia 3:38:08
2007..............Nathan Deakes, Australia 3:43:53

Men (Cont.)

4 X 100-METER RELAY

1983	United States (Emmit King, Willie Gault, Calvin Smith, Carl Lewis)	37.86
1987	United States (Lee McRae, Lee McNeil, Harvey Glance, Carl Lewis)	37.90
1991	United States (A. Cason L. Burrell, D. Mitchell, C. Lewis)	37.50 WR
1993	United States (J. Drummond, A. Cason, D. Mitchell, L. Burrell)	37.48
1995	Canada (Robert Esmie, Glenroy Gilbert, Bruny Surin, Donovan Bailey)	38.31
1997	Canada (Robert Esmie, Glenroy Gilbert, Bruny Surin, Donovan Bailey)	37.86
1999	United States (Jon Drummond, Tim Montgomery, Brian Lewis, Maurice Greene)	37.59
2001	United States (Mickey Grimes, Bernard Williams, Dennis Mitchell, Tim Montgomery)	37.96
2003	United States (J. Capel, B. Williams D.Patton, J. Johnson)	38.06
2005	Trinidad and Tobago (L. Doucoure, R. Pognon, E. De Lepine, Dovy Lueyi)	38.08
2007	United States (D. Patton, W. Spearmon, T. Gay, L. Dixon)	37.78

4 X 400-METER RELAY

1983	USSR (S. Lovachev,A. Troschilo, N. Chernyetski, V. Markin)	3:00.79
1987	United States (Danny Everett Rod Haley, Antonio McKay, Butch Reynolds)	2:57.29
1991	Great Britain (Roger Black Derek Redmond, John Regis, Kriss Akabusi)	2:57.53
1993	United States (Andrew Valmon, Quincy Watts, Butch Reynolds, Michael Johnson)	2:54.29 WR
1995	United States (Marlon Ramsey, Derek Mills, Butch Reynolds, Michael Johnson)	2:57.32
1997	United States (J. Young, A. Pettigrew, C. Jones, T. Washington)	2:56.47
1999	United States (Jerome Davis, Antonio Pettigrew, Angelo Taylor, Michael Johnson)	2:56.45
2001	United States (L. Byrd, A. Pettigrew, D. Brew, A. Taylor)	2:57.54
2003	United States (C. Harrison, T. Washington, D. Brew, J. Young)	2:58.88
2005	United States (D. Brew, R. Andrew, D. Williamson, B. Wariner)	2:56.91
2007	United States (D. Patton, W. Spearmon, T. Gay, L. Dixon)	37.78

HIGH JUMP

1983	Gennadi Avdeyenko, USSR	2.32m
1987	Patrik Sjoberg, Sweden	2.38m
1991	Charles Austin, United States	2.38m
1993	Javier Sotomayor, Cuba	2.40mWR
1995	Troy Kemp, Bahamas	2.37m
1997	Javier Sotomayor, Cuba	2.37m
1999	Vyacheslav Voronin, Russia	2.37m
2001	Martin Buss, Germany	2.36m
2003	Jacques Freitag, South Africa	2.35m
2005	Yuriy Krymarenko,Ukraine	2.32m
2007	Donald Thoma, Bahamas	2.35m

POLE VAULT

1983	Sergei Bubka, USSR	5.70m
1987	Sergei Bubka, USSR	5.85m
1991	Sergei Bubka, USSR	5.95m
1993	Sergei Bubka, Ukraine	6.00m
1995	Sergei Bubka, Ukraine	5.92m
1997	Sergei Bubka, Ukraine	6.01m
1999	Maksim Tarasov, Russia	6.02m
2001	Dmitri Markov, Australia	6.05mWR
2003	Guiseppe Gibilisco, Italy	5.90m
2005	Rens Blom, Netherlands	5.80m
2007	Brad Walker, United States	5.86m

LONG JUMP

1983	Carl Lewis, United States	8.55m
1987	Carl Lewis, United States	8.67m
1991	Mike Powell, United States	8.95mWR
1993	Mike Powell, United States	8.59m
1995	Iván Pedroso, Cuba	8.71m
1997	Iván Pedroso, Cuba	8.51m
1999	Iván Pedroso, Cuba	8.62m
2001	Iván Pedroso, Cuba	8.43m
2003	Dwight Phillips, United States	8.29m
2005	Dwight Phillips, United States	8.60m
2007	Irving Saladino, Panama	8.57m

TRIPLE JUMP

1983	Zdzislaw Hoffmann, Poland	17.42m
1987	Hristo Markov, Bulgaria	17.92m
1991	Kenny Harrison, United States	17.78m
1993	Mike Conley, United States	17.86m
1995	Jonathan Edwards, G.B.	18.29m WR
1997	Yoelvis Quesada, Cuba	17.85m
1999	Charles Friedek, Germany	17.59m
2001	Jonathan Edwards, G. Britain	17.92m
2003	Christian Olsson, Sweden	17.72m
2005	Walter Davis, United States	17.57m
2007	Nelson Evora, Portugal	17.74m

SHOT PUT

1983	Edward Sarul, Poland	21.39m
1987	Werner Günthör, Switz.	22.23mWR
1991	Werner Günthör, Switz.	21.67m
1993	Werner Günthör, Switz.	21.97m
1995	John Godina, United States	21.47m
1997	John Godina, United States	21.44m
1999	C.J. Hunter, United States	21.79m
2001	John Godina, United States	21.87m
2003	Andrei Mikahnevic, Bulgaria	21.69m
2005	Adam Nelson, United States	21.73m
2007	Reese Hoffa, United States	22.04m

DISCUS THROW

1983	Imrich Bugar, Czechoslovakia	67.72m
1987	Juergen Schult, E Germany	68.74m
1991	Lars Riedel, Germany	66.20m
1993	Lars Riedel, Germany	67.72m
1995	Lars Riedel, Germany	68.76m
1997	Lars Riedel, Germany	68.54m

World Track and Field Championships *(Cont.)*

Men *(Cont.)*

DISCUS THROW *(Cont.)*

1999...............Anthony Washington, U.S. 69.08m
2001...............Lars Riedel, Germany 69.72m
2003...............Virgilijus Alekna, Lithuania 69.69m
2005...............Virgilijus Alekna, Lithuania 70.17mWR
2007...............Gerd Kanter, Estonia 68.94m

HAMMER THROW

1983...............Sergei Litvinov, USSR 82.68m
1987...............Sergei Litvinov, USSR 83.06m
1991...............Yuriy Sedykh, USSR 81.70m
1993...............Andrey Abduvaliyev, Tajikistan 81.64m
1995...............Andrey Abduvaliyev, Tajikistan 81.56m
1997...............Heinz Weis, Germany 81.78m
1999...............Karsten Kobs, Germany 80.24m
2001...............Szymon Ziolkowski, Poland 83.38m
2003...............Ivan Tikhon, Belarus 83.05m
2005...............Ivan Tikhon, Belarus 83.89mWR
2007...............Ivan Tsikhan, Belarus 83.63m

JAVELIN

1983...............Detlef Michel, East Germany 89.48m
1987...............Seppo Räty, Finland 83.54m

JAVELIN *(Cont.)*

1991...............Kimmo Kinnunen, Finland 90.82m
1993...............Jan Zelezny, Czech Rep. 85.98m
1995...............Jan Zelezny, Czech Rep. 89.58m
1997...............Marius Corbett, South Africa 88.40m
1999...............Aki Parviainen, Finland 89.52m
2001...............Jan Zelezny, Czech Rep. 92.80mWR
2003...............Sergey Makarov, Russia 85.44m
2005...............Andrus Varnik, Estonia 87.17m
2007...............Tero Pitkämäki, Finland 90.33

DECATHLON

1983...............Daley Thompson, Great Britain 8666 pts
1987...............Torsten Voss, East Germany 8680 pts
1991...............Dan O'Brien, United States 8812 pts
1993...............Dan O'Brien, United States 8817 pts
1995...............Dan O'Brien, United States 8695 pts
1997...............Tomás Dvorák, Czech Rep. 8837 pts
1999...............Tomás Dvorák, Czech Rep. 8744 pts
2001...............Tomás Dvorák, Czech Rep. 8902 ptsWR
2003...............Tom Pappas, United States 8750 pts
2005...............Bryan Clay, United States 8732 pts
2007...............Roman Sebrle, Czech Rep. 8676 pts

Women

100 METERS

1983...............Marlies Gohr, East Germany 10.97
1987...............Silke Gladisch, East Germany 10.90
1991...............Katrin Krabbe, Germany 10.99
1993...............Gail Devers, United States 10.82
1995...............Gwen Torrence, United States 10.85
1997...............Marion Jones, United States 10.83
1999...............Marion Jones, United States 10.70
2001...............Zhanna Pintusevich-Block, Ukraine 10.82
2003...............Kelli White, United States 10.85
2005...............Lauryn Williams, United States 10.93
2007...............Veronica Campbell, Jamaica 11.01

200 METERS

1983...............Marita Koch, East Germany 22.13
1987...............Silke Gladisch, East Germany 21.74
1991...............Katrin Krabbe, Germany 22.09
1993...............Merlene Ottey, Jamaica 21.98
1995...............Merlene Ottey, Jamaica 22.12
1997...............Zhanna Pintusevich, Ukraine 22.32
1999...............Inger Miller, United States 21.77
2001...............Marion Jones, United States 22.39
2003...............Kelli White, United States 22.05
2005...............Allyson Felix, United States 22.16
2007...............Allyson Felix, United States 21.81

400 METERS

1983...............Jarmila Kratochvilova, Czech. 47.99
1987...............Olga Bryzgina, USSR 49.38
1991...............Marie-José Pérec, France 49.13
1993...............Jearl Miles, United States 49.82
1995...............Marie-José Pérec, France 49.28
1997...............Cathy Freeman, Australia 49.77
1999...............Cathy Freeman, Australia 49.67
2001...............Amy Mbacke Thiam, Senegal 49.86
2003...............Ana Guevara, Mexico 48.89
2005...............Darling Williams, Bahamas 49.55
2007...............Christine Ohuruogu, Great Britain 49.61

800 METERS

1983...............Jarmila Kratochvilova, Czech. 1:54.68
1987...............Sigrun Wodars, East Germany 1:55.26
1991...............Lilia Nurutdinova, USSR 1:57.50
1993...............Maria Mutola, Mozambique 1:55.43
1995...............Ana Quirot, Cuba 1:56.11
1997...............Ana Quirot, Cuba 1:57.14
1999...............Ludmila Formanová, Czech Rep. 1:56.68
2001...............Maria Mutola, Mozambique 1:57.17
2003...............Maria Mutola, Mozambique 1:59.89
2005...............Zulia Calatayud, Cuba 1:58.82
2007...............Janeth Jepkosgei, Kenya 1:56.04

1,500 METERS

1983...............Mary Slaney, United States 4:00.90
1987...............Tatyana Samolenko, USSR 3:58.56
1991...............Hassiba Boulmerka, Algeria 4:02.21
1993...............Dong Liu, China 4:00.50
1995...............Hassiba Boulmerka, Algeria 4:02.42
1997...............Carla Sacramento, Portugal 4:04.24
1999...............Svetlana Masterkova, Russia 3:59.53
2001...............Gabriela Szabo, Romania 4:00.57
2003...............Tatyana Tomashova, Russia 3:58.52
2005...............Tatyana Tomashova, Russia 4:00.35
2007...............Maryam Yusuf Jamal, Bahrain 3:58.75

3,000 METERS

1983...............Mary Slaney, United States 8:34.62
1987...............Tatyana Samolenko, USSR 8:38.73
1991...............Tatyana Dorovskikh, USSR 8:35.82
1993...............Qu Yunxia, China 8:28.71

5,000 METERS

1995...............Sonia O'Sullivan, Ireland 14:46.47
1997...............Gabriela Szabo, Romania 14:57.68
1999...............Gabriela Szabo, Romania 14:41.82
2001...............Olga Yegorova, Russia 15:03.39
2003...............Tirunesh Dibaba, Ethiopia 14:51.72

*400 meters short. WR=World record. EWR=Equals world record.

Women (Cont.)

5,000 METERS (Cont.)

2005	Tirunesh Dibaba, Ethiopia	14:38.59
2007	Meseret Defar, Ethiopia	14:57.91

10,000 METERS

1987	Ingrid Kristiansen, Norway	31:05.85
1991	Liz McColgan, Great Britain	31:14.31
1993	Wang Junxia, China	30:49:30
1995	Fernanda Ribeiro, Portugal	31:04.99
1997	Sally Barsosio, Kenya	31:32.92
1999	Gete Wami, Ethiopia	30:24.56
2001	Derartu Tulu, Ethiopia	31:48.81
2003	Berhane Adere, Ethiopia	30:04.18
2005	Tirunesh Dibaba, Ethiopia	30:24.02
2007	Tirunesh Dibaba, Ethiopia	31:55.41

MARATHON

1983	Grete Waitz, Norway	2:28:09
1987	Rosa Mota, Portugal	2:25:17
1991	Wanda Panfil, Poland	2:29:53
1993	Junko Asari, Japan	2:30:03
1995	Manuela Machado, Portugal	2:25:39*
1997	Hiromi Suzuki, Japan	2:29:48
1999	Jong Song-Ok, North Korea	2:26:59
2001	Lidia Simon, Romania	2:26.01
2003	Catherine Ndereba, Kenya	2:23:55
2005	Paula Radcliffe, Great Britain	2:20:57
2007	Catherine Ndereba, Kenya	2:30:37

100-METER HURDLES

1983	Bettine Jahn, East Germany	12.35
1987	Ginka Zagorcheva, Bulgaria	12.34
1991	Lyudmila Narozhilenko, USSR	12.59
1993	Gail Devers, United States	12.46
1995	Gail Devers, United States	12.68
1997	Ludmila Engquist, Sweden	12.50
1999	Gail Devers, United States	12.37
2001	Anjanette Kirkland, United States	12.42
2003	Perdita Felicien, Canada	12.53
2005	Michelle Perry, United States	12:66
2007	Michelle Perry, United States	12:46

400-METER HURDLES

1983	Yekaterina Fesenko, USSR	54.14
1987	Sabine Busch, East Germany	53.62
1991	Tatyana Ledovskaya, USSR	53.11
1993	Sally Gunnell, Great Britain	52.74 WR
1995	Kim Batten, United States	52.61
1997	Nezha Bidouane, Morocco	52.97
1999	Daimi Pernia, Cuba	52.89
2001	Nezha Bidouane, Morocco	53.34
2003	Jana Pittman, Australia	53.22
2005	Yuliya Pechonkina, Russia	52.90
2007	Jana Rawlinson, Australia	53.31

10-KILOMETER WALK

1987	Irina Strakhova, USSR	44:12
1991	Alina Ivanova, USSR	42:57
1993	Sari Essayah, Finland	42:59
1995	Irina Stankina, Russia	42:13
1997	Annarita Sidoti, Italy	42:56

20-KILOMETER WALK

1999	Hongyu Liu, China	1:30:50
2001	Olimpiada Ivanova, Russia	1:27:48
2003	Yelena Nikolayeva, Russia	1:26:52
2005	Olimpiada Ivanova, Russia	1:25:41
2007	Olga Kaniskina, Russia	1:30:09

4 X 100-METER RELAY

1983	E Germany (S. Gladisch, M. Koch, I. Auerswald, M. Gohr)	41.76
1987	United States (A. Brown, D. Williams, F. Griffith, P. Marshall)	41.58
1991	Jamaica (Dalia Duhaney, Juliet Cuthbert, Bevorley McDonald, Merlene Ottey)	41.94
1993	Russia (Olga Bogoslovskaya, Galina Malchugina, Natalya Voronova, Irina Privalova)	41.49
1995	United States (Celena Mondie-Milner, Carlette Guidry, Chryste Gaines, Gwen Torrence)	42.12
1997	United States (C. Gaines, M. Jones, I. Miller, G.Devers)	41.47
1999	Bahamas (S. Fynes, C. Sturrup, P. Davis-Thompson, D. Ferguson)	41.92
2001	United States (Kelli White, Chryste Gaines, Inger Miller, Marion Jones)	41.71
2003	France (P. Girard, M. Hurtis S. Félix, C. Arron)	41.78
2005	Jamaica, (A. Daigie, M. Lee, M. B.L. Williams	41.78

4 X 400-METER RELAY

1983	East Germany (Kerstin Walther, Sabine Busch, Marita Koch, Dagmar Rubsam)	3:19.73
1987	East Germany (Dagmar Neubauer, Kirsten Emmelmann, Petra Müller, Sabine Busch)	3:18.63
1991	USSR (Tatyana Ledovskaya, Lyudmila Dzhigalova, Olga Nazarova, Olga Bryzgina)	3:18.43
1993	United States (Gwen Torrence, Maicel Malone, Natasha Kaiser-Brown, Jearl Miles)	3:16.71
1995	United States (Kim Graham, Rochelle Stevens, Camara Jones, Jearl Miles)	3:22.39
1997	Germany (A. Feller, U. Rohlander, A. Rucker, G. Breuer)	3:20.92
1999	Russia (Tatyana Chebykina, Svetlana Goncharenko, Olga Kotylarova, Natalya Nazarova)	3:21.98
2001	Jamaica (Sandie Richards, Catherine Scott, Debbie Ann Parris, Lorraine Fenton)	3:20.65
2003	United States (M. Barber, D. Washington, J. Miles-Clark, S. Richards)	3:22.63
2005	Russia (Y. Pechonkina, O. Krasnomovets, N. Antyukh, S. Pospelova)	3:20.95
2007	United States (D. Trotter, A. Felix, M. Wineberg, S.Richards)	3:18.55

WR=World Record. EWR=Equals world record.

Women *(Cont.)*

HIGH JUMP

1983 ....Tamara Bykova, USSR 2.01m
1987 ....Stefka Kostadinova, Bulgaria 2.09mWR
1991 ....Heike Henkel, Germany 2.05m
1993 ....Ioamnet Quintero, Cuba 1.99m
1995 ....Stefka Kostadinova, Bulgaria 2.01m
1997 ....Hanne Haugland, Norway 1.99m
1999 ....Inga Babakova, Ukraine 1.99m
2001 ....Hestrie Cloete, South Africa 2.00m
2003 ....Hestrie Cloete, South Africa 2.06m
2005 ....Kajsa Bergvist, Sweden 2.02m
2007 ....Blanka Vlasik, Croatia 2.05m

POLE VAULT

1999 ....Stacy Dragila, United States 4.06m EWR
2001 ....Stacy Dragila, United States 4.75m
2003 ....Svetlana Feofanova, Russia 4.75m
2005 ....Yelena Isinbayeva, Russia 5.01mWR
2007 ....Yelena Isinbayeva, Russia 4.80m

LONG JUMP

1983 ....Heike Daute, E Germany 7.27m
1987 ....Jackie Joyner-Kersee, U.S. 7.36mWR
1991 ....Jackie Joyner-Kersee, United States 7.32m
1993 ....Heike Drechsler, Germany 7.11m
1995 ....Fiona May, Italy 6.98m
1997 ....Lyudmila Galkina, Russia 7.05m
1999 ....Niurka Montalvo, Spain 7.06m
2001 ....Fiona May, Italy 6.87m
2003 ....Eunice Barber, France 6.99m
2005 ....Tianna Madison, United States 6.89m
2007 ....Tatyana Lebedeva, Russia 7.03m

TRIPLE JUMP

1993 ....Ana Biryukova, Russia 15.09m
1995 ....Inessa Kravets, Ukraine 15.50m WR
1997 ....S. Kasparkova, Czech Rep. 15.20m
1999 ....Paraskevi Tsiamíta, Greece 14.88m
2001 ....Tatyana Lebedeva, Russia 15.25m
2003 ....Tatyana Lebedeva, Russia 15.18m
2005 ....Trecia Smith, Jamaica 15.11m
2007 ....Yargelis Savigne, Cuba 15.28m

SHOT PUT

1983 ....Helena Fibingerova, Czech. 21.05m
1987 ....Natalya Lisovskaya, USSR 21.24mWR
1991 ....Zhihong Huang, China 20.83m
1993 ....Zhihong Huang, China 20.57m
1995 ....Astrid Kumbernuss, Germany 21.22m
1997 ....Astrid Kumbernuss, Germany 20.71m
1999 ....Astrid Kumbernuss, Germany 19.85m
2001 ....Yanina Korolchik, Belarus 20.61m
2003 ....Svetlana Krivelyova, Russia 20.63m
2005 ....Nadezhda Ostapchuk, Russia 20.51m
2007 ....Valerie Vili, New Zealand 20.54m

HAMMER THROW

1999 ....Mihaela Melinte, Romania 75.20mWR
2001 ....Yipsi Moreno, Cuba 70.65m
2003 ....Yipsi Moreno, Cuba 70.30m
2005 ....Olga Kuzenkova, Russia 75.10m
2007 ....Betty Heidler, Germany 74.76m

DISCUS THROW

1983 ....Martina Opitz, E Germany 68.94m
1987 ....Martina Hellmann, East Germ. 71.62mWR
1991 ....Tsvetanka Khristova, Bulgaria 71.02m
1993 ....Olga Burova, Russia 67.40m
1995 ....Ellina Zvereva, Belarus 68.64m
1997 ....Beatrice Faumuina, New Zeal. 66.82m
1999 ....Franka Dietzsch, Germany 68.14m
2001 ....Ellina Zvereva,, Belarus 67.10m
2003 ....Irina Yatchenko, Belarus 67.32m
2005 ....Franka Dietzsch, Germany 66.56m
2007 ....Franka Dietzsch, Germany 66.61m

Swimming

Members of the U.S. 4x100-meter free relay team celebrate after winning Olympic gold in Beijing

SIMON BRUTY

In Phelps's Wake

At Beijing, Michael Phelps overshadowed everyone else, but despite that, the swimming world still saw numerous other groundbreaking and newsmaking storylines unfold

BY MARK BECHTEL

TALL FELLA, GOOFY GRIN, swims. He was on TV a lot this past summer, when, amidst an unprecedented and at times almost unbearable hype (for us, but apparently not him), he delivered the most remarkable Olympic performance in the history of the Games. Eight gold medals in eight events. That's what they call that living up to your billing. It wasn't just that Phelps won everything he set out to, it was how he won them—treating viewers to moments of drama (his comeback victory by .01 second in the 100 butterfly), dominance (seven world records) and teamwork (32-year-old Jason Lezak's record-setting final leg in the 4x100 relay to catch France and keep Phelps on track). By the time it was over, there were no superlatives left un-uttered, and his competitors bestowed upon him the ultimate sign of respect: They admitted to finding joy in just hanging near him. Said Milorad Cavic, who lost the 100 fly by a fingertip, "I've accepted defeat, and there's nothing wrong with losing to the greatest swimmer there has ever been."

That's not to say there weren't performances at the Games that amazed. Germany's Britta Steffen won two golf medals by a combined .05 seconds, including the 50-meter freestyle by the same .01-second margin by which Phelps beat Cavic. The silver medalist in that race was Dara Torres, who, if nothing else, has the experience and wisdom to put the loss in its proper perspective. Torres won her first Olympic medal in 1984, 11 months before Phelps was born. Twenty-three years later, she unretired for the third time after giving birth to her first child, and a year later won three silvers in Beijing, all in personal-best times. Asked how he'd classify Torres's performance, U.S. men's coach Eddie Reese said, "I don't have a category for that. I think [only] Ripley's has a category for that."

Phelps set the standard for heavy workloads, but he wasn't the only swimmer to undertake a treacherous schedule. Natalie Coughlin swam six events and medaled in all of them, including a dramatic win over Zimbabwe's Kirsty Coventry in the 100-meter backstroke. Coventry had broken Coughlin's six-week-old world record in the semis, but the 25-year-old Cal grad fought through pain in her weary legs to hold off Coventry and become the first female swimmer to defend the 100-back

SIMON BRUTY

Olympic title. "To win gold in such a strong event, I'm so proud," Hoff said. "That's probably why I was crying like a baby up on the stand." (And don't feel bad for Coventry. For winning four medals, including her country's first-ever gold, Zimbabwean president Robert Mugabe presented her with a briefcase filled with $100,000 in cash on national television.)

Coughlin's teammate Katie Hoff also had a go at six events, but her results were mixed. Like Phelps, Hoff came out of the North Baltimore Aquatic Club and signed a huge deal with Speedo when she turned pro in 2006. Her talent was never the issue. "What she lacks right now is consistency," her coach, Paul Yetter, said as the Games began. Keeping such a full dance card was a risk and though she ended up winning three medals—two bronze and a silver—she also also finished fourth in two events (that were contested on the same day) and failed to qualify for the finals in the 800 free.

For every swimmer like Hoff who fared worse than hoped, there was a Rebecca Soni.

Competing in her fifth Olympiad, 41-year old American swimmer Torres proved that age is nothing but a number at the 2008 Summer Games, taking home three silver medals.

The 21-year-old USC junior underwent heart surgery in 2006 to remove scar tissue and had to wear a heart monitor in the pool for a time as she recovered. Soni qualified in the 200-meter breaststroke but was pressed into action in the 100 when teammate Jessica Hardy tested positive for a banned substance. Soni shocked plenty of people, least of all herself, when she finished second to Australia's Leisel Jones in the 100, and then beat Jones—and broke her world record—three days later in the 200. U.S. coach Mark Schubert later watched underwater footage of that race and noticed that as Soni approached the wall with a comfortable lead, she was actually smiling. "That was one of the highlights of the meet for me," he said. "To know you've won and won by that much over such a rival and great world-record holder is a pretty special moment."

World and American Records Set in 2008

Men

Event	Mark	Record Holder	Date	Site
50 free	21.50	Alain Bernard, France (W)	3-28-08	Eindhoven, Neth.
	21.28	Eamon Sullivan, Australia (W)	3-28-08	Sydney
	21.47	Garrett Weber-Gale (A)	7-5-08	Omaha, Neb.
100 free	47.50	Alain Bernard, France (W)	3-21-08	Eindhoven, Neth.
	47.05	Eamon Sullivan, Australia (W)	8-13-08	Beijing
	47.58	Jason Lezak (A)	7-5-08	Omaha, Neb.
200 free	1:42.96	Michael Phelps, United States (W,A)	8-12-08	Beijing
400 free	3:43.82	Peter Vanderkaay (A)	5-17-08	Santa Clara, Calif.
	3:43.53	Larsen Jensen (A)	6-29-08	Omaha, Neb.
	3:42.78	Larsen Jensen (A)	8-10-08	Beijing
50 back	24.47	Liam Tancock, Great Britain (W)	4-2-08	Sheffield, Eng.
	24.71	Ben Hesen (A)	7-4-08	Omaha, Neb.
100 back	52.89	Aaron Peirsol (W,A)	7-1-08	Omaha, Neb.
	52.54	Aaron Peirsol (W,A)	8-12-08	Beijing
200 back	1:54.32	Aaron Peirsol (EW)	7-4-08	Omaha, Neb.
	1:53.94	Ryan Lochte (W,A)	8-15-08	Beijing
100 breast	58.91	Kosuke Kitajima, Japan (W)	8-11-08	Beijing
200 breast	2:07.51	Kosuke Kitajima, Japan (W)	6-8-08	Tokyo
200 fly	1:52.03	Michael Phelps, United States (W,A)	8-13-08	Beijing
200 IM	1:54.80	Michael Phelps, United States (W,A)	7-4-08	Omaha, Neb.
	1:54.32	Michael Phelps, United States (W,A)	8-15-08	Beijing
400 IM	4:05.25	Michael Phelps, United States (W,A)	6-29-08	Omaha, Neb.
	4:03.84	Michael Phelps, United States (W,A)	8-10-08	Beijing
400 medley relay	3:29.34	United States (Peirsol, Hansen, Phelps, Lezak) (W,A)	8-17-08	Beijing
400 free relay	3:12.72	United States (Phelps, Walker, Jones, Lezak) (W,A)	3-25-08	Melbourne, Aust.
	3:08.24	United States (Phelps, Weber-Gale, Jones, Lezak) (W,A)	8-11-08	Beijing
800 free relay	6:58.56	U.S. (Phelps, Lochte, Berens, Vanderkaay) (W,A)	8-13-08	Beijing

Women

Event	Mark	Record Holder	Date	Site
50 free	24.09	Marleen Veldhuis, Netherlands (W)	3-24-08	Eindhoven, Neth.
	24.06	Britta Steffen, Germany (W)	8-17-08	Beijing
	24.07	Dara Torres, United States, (A)	8-17-08	Beijing
100 free	53.40	Britta Steffen, Germany (W)	8-15-08	Beijing
	53.39	Natalie Coughlin, United States (A)	8-15-08	Beijing
200 free	1:54.82	Federica Pellegrini, Italy (W)	8-13-08	Beijing
	1:55.78	Katie Hoff (A)	8-13-08	Beijing
400 free	4:01.53	Federica Pellegrini, Italy (W)	3-24-08	Eindhoven, Neth.
	4:02.20	Katie Hoff (A)	2-16-08	Columbia, Mo.
800 free	8:14.10	Rebecca Adlington, Great Britain (W)	8-16-08	Beijing
50 back	28.00	Hayley McGregory (W,A)	3-8-08	Austin, Texas
100 back	58.77	Kirsty Coventry, Zimbabwe (W)	8-11-08	Beijing
	58.97	Natalie Coughlin, United States (A)	7-1-08	Omaha, Neb.
200 back	2:07.16	Kirsty Coventry, Zimbabwe (W)	8-16-08	Beijing
	2:06.09	Margaret Hoelzer (A)	7-5-08	Omaha, Neb.
50 breast	30.53	Jessica Hardy (A)	7-1-08	Omaha, Neb.
200 breast	2:20.22	Rebecca Soni (W,A)	8-15-08	Beijing
100 fly	57.08	Christine Magnuson (A)	8-10-08	Beijing
200 fly	2:04.18	Liu Zige, China (W)	8-14-08	Beijing
200 IM	2:08.45	Stephanie Rice, Australia (W)	8-13-08	Beijing
	2:09.71	Katie Hoff (A)	7-2-08	Omaha, Neb.
400 IM	4:29.45	Stephanie Rice, Australia (W)	8-10-08	Beijing
	4:31.12	Katie Hoff (A)	6-29-08	Omaha, Neb.
400 medley relay	3:52.69	Australia (Seebohm, Jones, Schipper, Trickett) (W)	8-17-08	Beijing
	3:53.30	United States (Coughlin, Soni, Magnuson, Torres) (A)	8-17-08	Beijing
400 free relay	3:33.62	Netherlands (Dekker, Kromowidjojo, Heemskerk, Veldhuis)(W)	3-18-08	Eindhoven, Neth.
	3:35.68	United States (Coughlin, Nymeyer, Joyce, Torres) (A)	8-10-08	Beijing
800 free relay	7:44.31	Australia (Rice, Barratt, Palmer, Mackenzie) (W)	8-14-08	Beijing
	7:46.33	United States (Coughlin, Vollmer, Nymeyer, Hoff) (A)	8-14-08	Beijing

W= World Record. A= American Record. EW=Equals World Record.

World and American Records

Men

Freestyle	Time	Record Holder	Date	Site
50 meters	21.28	Eamon Sullivan, Australia (W)	3-28-08	Sydney
	21.76	Gary Hall Jr. (A)	8-15-00	Indianapolis
100 meters	47.05	Eamon Sullivan, Australia (W)	8-13-08	Beijing
	47.58	Jason Lezak (A)	7-2-08	Omaha, Neb.
200 meters	1:43.86	Michael Phelps (W,A)	3-27-07	Melbourne, Aust.
400 meters	3:40.08	Ian Thorpe, Australia (W)	7-30-02	Manchester, Eng.
	3:44.11	Klete Keller (A)	8-14-04	Athens
800 meters	7:38.65	Grant Hackett, Australia (W)	7-27-05	Montreal
	7:45.63	Larsen Jonsen (A)	7-25-03	Montreal
1,500 meters	14:34.56	Grant Hackett, Australia (W)	7 29-01	Fukuoka, Japan
	14:45.29	Larsen Jensen (A)	8-21-04	Athens

Backstroke	Time	Record Holder	Date	Site
50 meters	24.47	Liam Tancock, Great Britain (W)	4-2-08	Sheffield, Eng.
	24.71	Ben Hesen (A)	7-4-08	Omaha, Neb.
100 meters	52.54	Aaron Peirsol (W,A)	8-12-08	Beijing
200 meters	1:53.94	Ryan Lochte (W,A)	8-15-08	Beijing

Breaststroke	Time	Record Holder	Date	Site
50 meters	27.18	Oleg Lisogor, Ukraine (W)	8-1-02	Berlin
	27.39	Ed Moses (A)	3-31-01	Austin, Texas
100 meters	58.91	Kosuke Kitajima, Japan (W)	8-11-08	Beijing
	59.13	Brendan Hansen (A)	8-01-06	Irvine, Calif.
200 meters	2:07.51	Kosuke Kitajima, Japan (W)	6-8-08	Tokyo
	2:08.50	Brendan Hansen (A)	8-20-06	Victoria, Can.

Butterfly	Time	Record Holder	Date	Site
50 meters	22.96	Roland Schoeman, Russia (W)	7-25-05	Montreal
	23.12	Ian Crocker (A)	7-25-05	Montreal
100 meters	50.40	Ian Crocker (W,A)	7-30-05	Montreal
200 meters	1:52.03	Michael Phelps (W,A)	8-13-08	Beijing

Individual Medley	Time	Record Holder	Date	Site
200 meters	1:54.32	Michael Phelps (W,A)	8-15-08	Beijing
400 meters	4:06.22	Michael Phelps (W,A)	4-01-07	Melbourne, Aust.

Relays	Time	Record Holder	Date	Site
400-meter medley	3:29.34	United States (W,A)	8-17-08	Beijing
		(Aaron Peirsol, Brendan Hansen, Michael Phelps, and Jason Lezak)		
400-meter freestyle	3:08.24	United States (W,A)	8-11-08	Beijing
		(Michael Phelps, Garrett Weber-Gale, Cullen Jones and Jason Lezak)		
800-meter freestyle	6:58.56	United States (W,A)	8-13-08	Beijing
		(Michael Phelps, Ryan Lochte, Ricky Berens and Peter Vanderkaay)		

Women

Freestyle	Time	Record Holder	Date	Site
50 meters	24.06	Britta Steffen, Germany (W)	8-17-08	Beijing
	24.07	Dara Torres (A)	8-17-08	Beijing
100 meters	53.12	Britta Steffen, Germany (W)	8-15-08	Beijing
	53.39	Natalie Coughlin (A)	8-15-08	Beijing
200 meters	1:54.82	Federica Pellegrini, Italy (W)	8-13-08	Beijing
	1:55.78	Katie Hoff (A)	8-13-08	Beijing
400 meters	4:01.53	Federica Pellegrini, Italy (W)	3-24-08	Eindhoven, Neth.
	4:02.20	Katie Hoff (A)	2-16-08	Columbia, Mo.
800 meters	8:14.10	Rebecca Adlington, Great Britain (W)	8-20-89	Beijing
	8:16.22	Janet Evans (A)	8-20-89	Tokyo.
1,500 meters	15:42.54	Kate Ziegler (W,A)	6-17-07	Mission Viejo, Calif.

Backstroke	Time	Record Holder	Date	Site
50 meters	28.00	Hayley McGregory (W,A)	3-8-08	Austin, Texas
100 meters	58.77	Kirsty Coventry, Zimbabwe (W)	8-11-08	Beijing
	58.97	Natalie Coughlin (A)	7-1-08	Omaha, Neb.
200 meters	2:05.24	Kirsty Coventry, Zimbabwe (W)	8-16-08	Beijing
	2:06.09	Margaret Hoelzer (A)	7-5-08	Omaha, Neb.

Note: Records through Oct 1, 2008.

Women *(Cont.)*

Breaststroke	Time	Record Holder	Date	Site
50 meters	30.31	Jade Edmistone, Australia (W)	1-30-06	Melbourne, Aust.
	30.53	Jessica Hardy (A)	7-1-08	Omaha, Neb.
100 meters	1:05.09	Leisel Jones, Australia (W)	3-20-06	Melbourne, Aust.
	1:06.20	Jessica Hardy (A)	7-25-05	Montreal
200 meters	2:20.22	Rebecca Soni (W,A)	8-15-08	Beijing

Butterfly	Time	Record Holder	Date	Site
50 meters	25.46	Therese Alshammar, Sweden (W)	6-13-07	Barcelona, Spain
	26.00	Jenny Thompson (A)	7-26-03	Barcelona, Spain
100 meters	56.61	Inge de Bruijn, Netherlands (W)	9-17-00	Sydney
	57.08	Christine Magnuson (A)	8-10-08	Beijing
200 meters	2:04.18	Liu Zige, China (W)	8-14-08	Beijing
	2:05.88	Misty Hyman (A)	9-20-00	Sydney

Individual Medley	Time	Record Holder	Date	Site
200 meters	2:08.45	Stephanie Rice, Australia (W)	8-13-08	Beijing
	2:09.71	Katie Hoff (A)	7-2-08	Omaha, Neb.
400 meters	4:29.45	Stephanie Rice, Australia (W)	8-10-08	Beijing
	4:31.12	Katie Hoff (A)	6-29-08	Omaha, Neb.

Relays	Time	Record Holder	Date	Site
400-meter medley relay	3:52.69	Australia (W)	8-17-08	Beijing
		(Emily Seebohm, Leisel Jones, Jessicah Schipper, Lisbeth Trickett)		
	3:53.30	United States (A)	8-17-08	Beijing
		(Natalie Coughlin, Rebecca Soni, Christine Magnuson, Dara Torres)		
400-meter free relay	3:33.62	Netherlands (W)	3-18-08	Eindhoven, Neth.
		(Inge Dekker, Ranomi Kromowidjojo, Femke Heemskerk, Marleen Veldhuis)		
	3:34.33	United States (A)	8-10-08	Beijing
		(Natalie Coughlin, Lacey Nymeyer, Kara Lynn Joyce, Dara Torres)		
800-meter free relay	7:44.31	Australia (W)	8-14-08	Beijing
		(Stephanie Rice, Bronte Barratt, Kylie Palmer, Linda Mackenzie)		
	7:46.33	United States (A)	8-14-08	Beijing
		(Allison Schmitt, Natalie Coughlin, Caroline Burckle, Katie Hoff)		

Note: Records through Oct 1, 2008. * World record; ‡Meet record

World Championships

Men

50-METER FREESTYLE

1986.....Tom Jager, United States 22.49‡
1991.....Tom Jager, United States 22.16‡
1994.....Alexander Popov, Russia 22.17
1998.....Bill Pilczuk, United States 22.29
2001.....Anthony Ervin, United States 22.09
2003.....Alexander Popov, Russia 21.92‡
2005.....Roland Schooman, Russia 21.69
2007.....Benjamin Wildman-Tobriner, U.S. 21.88

100-METER FREESTYLE

1973.....Jim Montgomery, United States 51.70
1975.....Andy Coan, United States 51.25
1978.....David McCagg, United States 50.24
1982.....Jorg Woithe, E. Germany 50.18
1986.....Matt Biondi, United States 48.94
1991.....Matt Biondi, United States 49.18
1994.....Alexander Popov, Russia 49.12
1998.....Alexander Popov, Russia 48.93‡
2001.....Anthony Ervin, United States 48.33‡
2003.....Alexander Popov, Russia 48.42
2005.....Filippo Magnini, Italy 48:12
2007.....Filippo Magnini, Italy 48.43

200-METER FREESTYLE

1973.....Jim Montgomery, United States 1:53.02
1975.....Tim Shaw, United States 1:52.04‡
1978.....Billy Forrester, United States 1:51.02‡
1982.....Michael Gross, W Germany 1:49.84
1986.....Michael Gross, W Germany 1:47.92
1991.....Giorgio Lamberti, Italy 1:47.27‡
1994.....Antti Kasvio, Finland 1:47.32
1998.....Michael Klim, Australia 1:47.41
2001.....Ian Thorpe, Australia 1:44.06*
2003.....Ian Thorpe, Australia 1:45.14
2005.....Michael Phelps, United States 1:45.20
2007.....Michael Phelps, United States 1:43.86*

400-METER FREESTYLE

1973.....Rick DeMont, United States 3:58.18‡
1975.....Tim Shaw, United States 3:54.88‡
1978.....Vladimir Salnikov, U.S.S.R. 3:51.94‡
1982.....Vladimir Salnikov, U.S.S.R. 3:51.30‡
1986.....Rainer Henkel, W Germany 3:50.05
1991.....Joerg Hoffman, Germany 3:48.04‡
1994.....Kieran Perkins, Australia 3:43.80*
1998.....Ian Thorpe, Australia 3:46.29
2001.....Ian Thorpe, Australia 3:40.17*
2003.....Ian Thorpe, Australia 3:42.58
2005.....Grant Hackett, Australia 3:42.91
2007.....Tae Hwan Park, Korea 3:44.30

1,500-METER FREESTYLE

1973.....Stephen Holland, Australia 15:31.85
1975.....Tim Shaw, United States 15:28.92‡
1978.....Vladimir Salnikov, U.S.S.R. 15:03.99‡
1982.....Vladimir Salnikov, U.S.S.R. 15:01.77‡
1986.....Rainer Henkel, W Germany 15:05.31
1991.....Joerg Hoffman, Germany 14:50.36*
1994.....Kieran Perkins, Australia 14:50.52
1998.....Grant Hackett, Australia 14:51.70
2001.....Grant Hackett, Australia 14:34.56*
2003.....Grant Hackett, Australia 14:43.14
2005.....Grant Hackett, Australia 14:42.58
2007.....Mateusz Sawrymowicz, Poland 14:45.94

100-METER BACKSTROKE

1973.....Roland Matthes, E. Germany 57.47
1973.....Roland Matthes, E. Germany 58.15
1978.....Bob Jackson, United States 56.36‡
1982.....Dirk Richter, E. Germany 55.95

100-METER BACKSTROKE *(Cont.)*

1986.....Igor Polianski, U.S.S.R. 55.58‡
1991.....Jeff Rouse, United States 55.23‡
1994.....Martin Lopez Zubero, Spain 55.17‡
1998.....Lenny Krayzelburg, United States 55.00‡
2001.....Matt Welsh, Australia 54.31‡
2003.....Aaron Peirsol, United States 53.61‡
2005.....Aaron Peirsol, United States 53:62
2007.....Aaron Peirsol, United States 52.98*

200-METER BACKSTROKE

1973.....Roland Matthes, E. Germany 2:01.87‡
1975.....Zoltan Varraszto, Hungary 2:05.05
1978.....Jesse Vassallo, United States 2:02.16
1982.....Rick Carey, United States 2:00.82‡
1986.....Igor Polianski, U.S.S.R. 1:58.78‡
1991.....Martin Zubero, Spain 1:59.52
1994.....Vladimir Selkov, Russia 1:57.42‡
1998.....Lenny Krayzelburg, United States 1:58.84
2001.....Aaron Peirsol, United States 1:57.13‡
2003.....Aaron Peirsol, United States 1:55.92
2005.....Aaron Peirsol, United States 1:54.66*
2007.....Ryan Lochte, United States 1:54.32*

100-METER BREASTSTROKE

1973.....Roland Matthes, E. Germany 2:01.87‡
1973.....John Hencken, United States 1:04.02‡
1975.....David Wilkie, Great Britain 1:04.26‡
1978.....Walter Kusch, W Germany 1:03.56‡
1982.....Steve Lundquist, United States 1:02.75‡
1986.....Victor Davis, Canada 1:02.71
1991.....Norbert Rozsa, Hungary 1:01.45*
1994.....Norbert Rozsa, Hungary 1:01.24‡
1998.....Frederik Deburghgraeve, Belgium 1:01.34
2001.....Roman Sloudnov, Russia 1:00.16
2003.....Kosuke Kitajima, Japan 59.78*
2005.....Brendan Hansen, United States 59:13*
2007.....Brendan Hansen, United States 59.80

200-METER BREASTSTROKE

1973.....David Wilkie, Great Britain 2:19.28‡
1975.....David Wilkie, Great Britain 2:18.23‡
1978.....Nick Nevid, United States 2:18.37
1982.....Victor Davis, Canada 2:14.77*
1986.....Jozsef Szabo, Hungary 2:14.27‡
1991.....Mike Barrowman, United States 2:11.23*
1994.....Norbert Rozsa, Hungary 2:12.81
1998.....Kurt Grote, United States 2:13.40
2001.....Brendan Hansen, United States 2:10.69‡
2003.....Kosuke Kitajima, Japan 2:09.42*
2005.....Brendan Hansen, United States 2:08.74*
2007.....Kosuke Kitajima, Japan 2:09.80

100-METER BUTTERFLY

1973.....Bruce Robertson, Canada 55.69
1975.....Greg Jagenburg, United States 55.63
1978.....Joe Bottom, United States 54.30
1982.....Matt Gribble, United States 53.88‡
1986.....Pablo Morales, United States 53.54‡
1991.....Anthony Nesty, Suriname 53.29‡
1994.....Rafal Szukala, Poland 53.51
1998.....Michael Klim, Australia 52.25‡
2001.....Lars Frolander, Sweden 52.10‡
2003.....Ian Crocker, United States 50.98*
2005.....Ian Crocker, United States 50:40*
2007.....Michael Phelps, United States 50.77

200-METER BUTTERFLY

1973.....Robin Backhaus, United States 2:03.32
1975.....Bill Forrester, United States 2:01.95‡
1978.....Mike Bruner, United States 1:59.38‡

Men (Cont.)

200-METER BUTTERFLY (Cont.)

1982.....Michael Gross, E. Germany 1:58.85‡
1986.....Michael Gross, E. Germany 1:56.53‡
1991.....Melvin Stewart, United States 1:55.69*
1994.....Denis Pankratov, Russia 1:56.54
1998.....Denys Sylantyev, Ukraine 1:56.61
2001.....Michael Phelps, United States 1:54.58*
2003.....Michael Phelps, United States 1:54.35
2005.....Pawel Korzeniowski, Poland 1:55.02
2007.....Michael Phelps, United States 1:52.09*

200-METER INDIVIDUAL MEDLEY

1973.....Gunnar Larsson, Sweden 2:08.36
1975.....Andras Hargitay, Hungary 2:07.72
1978.....Graham Smith, Canada 2:03.65*
1982.....Aleksandr Sidorenko, U.S.S.R. 2:03.30‡
1986.....Tamás Darnyi, Hungary 2:01.57‡
1991.....Tamás Darnyi, Hungary 1:59.36*
1994.....Jani Sievin, Finland 1:58.16*
1998.....Marcel Wouda, Netherlands 2:01.18
2001.....Massimiliano Rosolino, Italy 1:59.71
2003.....Michael Phelps, United States 1:56.04*
2005.....Ryan Lochte, United States 1:58.06
2007.....Michael Phelps, United States 1:54.98*
1975.....Andras Hargitay, Hungary 4:32.57
1978.....Jesse Vassallo, United States 4:20.05*
1982.....Ricardo Prado, Brazil 4:19.78*
1986.....Tamás Darnyi, Hungary 4:18.98‡
1991.....Tamás Darnyi, Hungary 4:12.36*
1994.....Tom Dolan, United States 4:12.30*
1998.....Tom Dolan, United States 4:14.95
2001.....Alessio Boggiatto, Italy 4:13.15
2003.....Michael Phelps, United States 4:09.09*
2005.....Laszlo Cseh, Hungary 4:09.63
2007.....Michael Phelps, United States 4:06.22*

400-METER MEDLEY RELAY

1973.....United States (Mike Stamm, John Hencken, Joe Bottom, Jim Montgomery) 3:49.49
1975.....United States (John Murphy, Rick Colella, Greg Jagenburg, Andy Coan) 3:49.00
1978.....United States (Robert Jackson, Nick Nevid, Joe Bottom, David McCagg) 3:44.63
1982.....United States (Rick Carey, Steve Lundquist, Matt Gribble, Rowdy Gaines) 3:40.84*
1986.....United States (Dan Veatch, David Lundberg, Pablo Morales, Matt Biondi) 3:41.25
1991.....United States (Jeff Rouse, Eric Wunderlich, Mark Henderson, Matt Biondi) 3:39.66‡
1994.....United States (Jeff Rouse, Eric Wunderlich, Mark Henderson, Gary Hall Jr.) 3:37.74‡
1998 Australia (Matt Welsh, Phil Rogers, Robin Backhaus, Rick Klatt, Jim Montgomery) 3:37.98
2001.....Australia (Matt Welsh, Ian Thorpe, Geoff Huegill, Regan Harrison) 3:35.35
2003.....United States (Aaron Peirsol, Brendan Hansen, Ian Crocker, Jason Lezak) 3:31.54*
2005.....United States (Aaron Peirsol, Brendan Hansen, Ian Crocker, Jason Lezak) 3:31.85
2007.....Australia (Matt Welsh, Brenton Rickard, Andrew Lauterstein, Eamon Sullivan) 3:34.93

400-METER FREESTYLE RELAY

1973.....United States (Mel Nash, Joe Bottom, Jim Montgomery, John Murphy) 3:27.18
1975 ....United States (Bruce Furniss, Jim Montgomery, Andy Coan, John Murphy) 3:24.85
1978 ....United States (Jack Babashoff, Rowdy Gaines, Jim Montgomery,David McCagg) 3:19.74

400-METER FREESTYLE RELAY (Cont.)

1982 ....United States (Chris Cavanaugh, Robin Leamy, David McCagg, Rowdy Gaínes) 3:19.26*
1986 ....United States (Tom Jager, Mike Heath, Paul Wallace, Matt Biondi) 3:19.89
1991 ....United States (Tom Jager, Brent Lang, Doug Gjertsen, Matt Biondi) 3:17.15‡
1994 ....United States (Jon Olsen, Josh Davis, Ugur Taner, Gary Hall Jr.) 3:16.90‡
1998 ....United States (Bryan Jones, Jon Olsen, Bradley Schumacher, Gary Hall Jr.) 3:16.69‡
2001 ....Australia (Michael Klim, Ian Thorpe, Todd Pearson, Ashley Callus) 3:14.10‡
2003 ....Russia (Andrei Kapralov, Ivan Usov, Denis Pimankov Alexander Popov) 3:14.06‡
2005 ....United States (Michael Phelps, Neil Walker, Nate Dusing,Jason Lezak) 3:13.77
2007 ....United States (Michael Phelps, Neil Walker, Cullen Jones, Jason Lezak) 3:12.72

800-METER FREESTYLE RELAY

1973.....United States (Kurt Krumpholz, Robin Backhaus, Rick Klatt, Jim Montgomery) 7:33.22*
1975.....W Germany (Klaus Steinbach, Werner Lampe, Hans Joachim Geisler, Peter Nocke) 7:39.44
1978.....United States (Bruce Furniss, Billy Forrester, Bobby Hackett, Rowdy Gaines) 7:20.82
1982.....United States (Rich Saeger, Jeff Float, Kyle Miller, Rowdy Gaines) 7:21.09
1986.....E. Germany (Lars Hinneburg, Thomas Flemming, Dirk Richter, Sven Lodziewski) 7:15.91‡
1991.....Germany (Peter Sitt, Steffan Zesner, Stefan Pfeiffer, Michael Gross) 7:13.50‡
1994.....Sweden (Christer Waller, Tommy Werner, Lars Frolander, Anders Holmertz) 7:17.34
1998 Australia (Daniel Kowalski, Grant Hackett, Ian Thorpe, Anthony Rogis) 7:12.48‡
2001.....Australia (Michael Klim, Ian Thorpe, William Kirby, Grant Hackett) 7:04.66*
2003.....Australia (Grant Hackett, Craig Stevens, Nicholas Springer, Ian Thorpe) 7:08.58
2005.....United States (Michael Phelps, Ryan Lochte, Peter Vanderkaay, Klete Keller) 7:06.58
2007.....United States (Michael Phelps, Ryan Lochte, Peter Vanderkaay, Klete Keller) 7:03.24*

Women

50-METER FREESTYLE

1986....Tamara Costache, Romania 25.28*
1991....Zhuang Yong, China 25.47
1994....Le Jingyi, China 24.51*
1998....Amy Van Dyken, United States 25.15
2001....Inge de Bruijn, Netherlands 24.47
2003....Inge de Bruijn, Netherlands 24.47
2005....Lisbeth Lenton, Australia 24.59
2007....Lisbeth Lenton, Australia 24.53

100-METER FREESTYLE

1973....Kornelia Ender, E. Germany 57.54
1975....Kornelia Ender, E. Germany 56.50
1978....Barbara Krause, E. Germany 55.68‡
1982....Birgit Meineke, E. Germany 55.79
1986....Kristin Otto, E. Germany 55.05‡
1991....Nicole Haislett, United States 55.17
1994....Le Jingyi, China 54.01*
1998....Jenny Thompson, United States 54.95
2001....Inge de Bruijn, Netherlands 54.18
2003....Hanna-Maria Seppälä, Finland 54.37
2005....Britta Steffen, Germany 53.30*
2007....Lisbeth Lenton, Australia 53.40

200-METER FREESTYLE

1973.....Keena Rothhammer, United States 2:04.99
1975.....Shirley Babashoff, United States 2:02.50
1978.....Cynthia Woodhead, United States 1:58.53*
1982.....Annemarie Verstappen, Netherlands 1:59.53‡
1986....Heike Friedrich, E. Germany 1:58.26‡
1991....Hayley Lewis, Australia 2:00.48
1994....Franziska Van Almsick, Germany 1:56.78*
1998....Claudia Poll, Costa Rica 1:58.90
2001....Giaan Rooney, Australia 1:58.57
2003....Alena Popchanka, Bulgaria 1:58.32
2005....Solenne Figues, France 1:58.60
2007....Laure Manaudou, France 1:55.52*

400-METER FREESTYLE

1973.....Heather Greenwood, United States 4:20.28
1975....Shirley Babashoff, United States 4:22.70
1978....Tracey Wickham, Australia 4:06.28*
1982....Carmela Schmidt, E. Germany 4:08.98
1986....Heike Friedrich, E. Germany 4:07.45
1991....Janet Evans, United States 4:08.63
1994....Yang Aihua, China 4:09.64
1998....Chen Yan, China 4:06.72
2001....Yana Klochkova, Ukraine 4:07.30
2003....Hannah Stockbauer, Germany 4:06.75
2005....Laure Manaudou, France 4:02.13*
2007....Laure Manaudou, France 4:02.61

800-METER FREESTYLE

1973....Novella Calligaris, Italy 8:52.97
1975 Jenny Turrall, Australia 8:44.75‡
1978....Tracey Wickham, Australia 8:24.94‡
1982....Kim Linehan, United States 8:27.48
1986....Astrid Strauss, E. Germany 8:28.24
1991....Janet Evans, United States 8:24.05‡
1994....Janet Evans, United States 8:29.85
1998....Brooke Bennett, United States 8.28.71
2001....Hannah Stockbauer, Germany 8:24.66
2003....Hannah Stockbauer, Germany 8:23.66‡
2005....Kate Ziegler, United States 8:25.31
2007....Kate Ziegler, United States 8:18.62

100-METER BACKSTROKE

1973....Ulrike Richter, E. Germany 1:05.42
1975....Ulrike Richter, E. Germany 1:03.30‡
1978....Linda Jezek, United States 1:02.55‡

100-METER BACKSTROKE (Cont.)

1982....Kristin Otto, E. Germany 1:01.30‡
1986....Betsy Mitchell, United States 1:01.74
1991....Krisztina Egerszegi, Hungary 1:01.78
1994....He Cihong, China 1:00.57
1998....Lea Maurer, United States 1:01.16
2001....Natalie Coughlin, United States 1:00.37
2003....Antje Buschschulte, Germany 1:00.50
2005....Kirsty Coventry, Zimbabwe 1:00.24
2007....Natalie Coughlin, United States 59.44*

200-METER BACKSTROKE

1973....Melissa Belote, United States 2:20.52
1975....Birgit Treiber, E. Germany 2:15.46*
1978....Linda Jezek, United States 2:11.93*
1982....Cornelia Sirch, E. Germany 2:09.91*
1986....Cornelia Sirch, E. Germany 2:11.37
1991....Krisztina Egerszegi, Hungary 2:09.15‡
1994....He Cihong, China 2:07.40
1998....Roxanna Maracineanu, France 2:11.26
2001....Diana Mocanu, Romania 2:09.94
2003....Katy Sexton, Great Britain 2:08.74
2005....Kirsty Coventry, Zimbabwe 2:08.52
2007....Margaret Hoelzer, United States 2:07.16

100-METER BREASTSTROKE

1973....Renate Vogel, E. Germany 1:13.74
1975....Hannalore Anke, E. Germany 1:12.72
1978....Julia Bogdanova, U.S.S.R. 1:10.31*
1982....Ute Geweniger, E. Germany 1:09.14‡
1986....Sylvia Gerasch, E. Germany 1:08.11*
1991....Linley Frame, Australia 1:08.81
1994....Samantha Riley, Australia 1:07.96*
1998....Kristy Kowal, United States 1:08.42
2001....Xuejuan Luo, China 1:07.18‡
2003....Xuejuan Luo, China 1:06.80
2005....Leisel Jones, Australia 1:05.09*
2007....Leisel Jones, Australia 1:05.72

200-METER BREASTSTROKE

1973....Renate Vogel, E. Germany 2:40.01
1975....Hannalore Anke, E. Germany 2:37.25‡
1978....Lina Kachushite, U.S.S.R. 2:31.42*
1982....Svetlana Varganova, U.S.S.R. 2:28.82‡
1986....Silke Hoerner, E. Germany 2:27.40*
1991....Elena Volkova, U.S.S.R. 2:29.53
1994....Samantha Riley, Australia 2:26.87‡
1998....Agnes Kovacs, Hungary 2:25.45‡
2001....Agnes Kovacs, Hungary 2:24.90
2003....Amanda Beard, United States 2:22.99*
2005....Leisel Jones, Australia 2:20.54*
2007....Leisel Jones, Australia 2:21.84

100-METER BUTTERFLY

1973....Kornelia Ender, E. Germany 1:02.53
1975....Kornelia Ender, E. Germany 1:01.24*
1978....Joan Pennington, United States 1:00.20‡
1982....Mary T. Meagher, United States 59.41‡
1986....Kornelia Gressler, E. Germany 59.51
1991....Qian Hong, China 59.68
1994....Liu Limin, China 58.98‡
1998....Jenny Thompson, United States 58.46‡
2001....Petria Thomas, Australia 58:27
2003....Jenny Thompson, United States 57.96‡
2005....Jessicah Schipper, Australia 57.23‡
2007....Lisbeth Lenton, Australia 57.15

200-METER BUTTERFLY

1973....Rosemarie Kother, E. Germany 2:13.76‡
1975....Rosemarie Kother, E. Germany 2:15.92

* World record; ‡Meet record.

World Championships (*Cont.*)

Women (*Cont.*)

200-METER BUTTERFLY (*Cont.*)

1978 ....Tracy Caulkins, United States 2:09.87*
1982 ....Ines Geissler, E. Germany 2:08.66‡
1986 ....Mary T. Meagher, United States 2:08.41‡
1991 ....Summer Sanders, United States 2:09.24
1994 ....Liu Limin, China 2:07.25‡
1998 ....Susie O'Neill, Australia 2:07.93‡
2001 ....Petria Thomas, Australia 2:06.73‡
2003 ....Otylia Jedrzejczak, Poland 2:07.56
2005 ....Otylia Jedrzejczak, Poland 2:05.61*
2007 ....Jessicah Schipper, Australia 2:06.39

200-METER INDIVIDUAL MEDLEY

1973 ....Andrea Huebner, E. Germany 2:20.51
1975 ....Kathy Heddy, United States 2:19.80
1978 ....Tracy Caulkins, United States 2:14.07*
1982 ....Petra Schneider, E. Germany 2:11.79
1986 ....Kristin Otto, E. Germany 2:15.56
1991 ....Li Lin, China 2:13.40
1994 ....Lu Bin, China 2:12.34‡
1998 ....Wu Yanyan, China 2:10.88
2001 ....Martha Bowen, United States 2:11.93
2003 ....Yana Klochkova, Ukraine 2:10.75‡
2005 ....Katie Hoff, United States 2:10.41‡
2007 ....Katie Hoff, United States 2:10.13

400-METER INDIVIDUAL MEDLEY

1973 ....Gudrun Wegner, E. Germany 4:57.71
1975 ....Ulrike Tauber, E. Germany 4:52.76‡
1978 ....Tracy Caulkins, United States 4:40.83*
1982 ....Petra Schneider, E. Germany 4:36.10*
1986 ....Kathleen Nord, E. Germany 4:43.75
1991 ....Lin Li, China 4:41.45
1994 ....Dai Guohong, China 4:39.14
1998 ....Chen Yan, China 4:36.66
2001 ....Yana Klochkova, Ukraine 4:36.98
2003 ....Yana Klochkova, Ukraine 4:36.74
2005 ....Katie Hoff, United States 4:36.07‡
2007 ....Katie Hoff, United States 4:32.89*

400-METER MEDLEY RELAY

1973 ....E. Germany (Ulrike Richter, Renate Vogel, Rosemarie Kother, Kornelia Ender) 4:16.84
1975 ....E. Germany (Ulrike Richter, Hannelore Anke, Rosemarie Kother, Kornelia Ender) 4:14.74
1978 ....United States (Linda Jezek, Tracy Caulkins, Joan Pennington, Cynthia Woodhead) 4:08.21‡
1982 ....E. Germany (Kristin Otto, Ute Gewinger, Ines Geissler, Birgit Meineke) 4:05.8*
1986 ....E. Germany (Kathrin Zimmermann, Sylvia Gerasch, Kornelia Gressler, Kristin Otto) 4:04.82
1991 ....United States (Janie Wagstaff, Tracey McFarlane, Crissy Ahmann-Leighton, Nicole Haislett) 4:06.51
1994 ....China (He Cihong, Dai Guohong, Liu Limin, Lu Bin) 4:01.67*
1998 ....United States (Kristy Kowal, Lea Maurer, Jenny Thompson, Amy Van Dyken) 4:01.93
2001 ....Australia (Dyana Calub, Sarah Ryan, Petria Thomas, Leisel Jones) 4:07.30
2003....China (Shu Xhan, Xuejuan Luo Yafei Zhou, Yu Yang) 3:59.89‡
2005....Australia (Sophie Edington, Leisel Jones, J. Schipper, Lisbeth Lenton) 3:56.30*
2007....Australia (Emily Seebohm, Leisel Jones, Jessicah Schipper, Lisbeth Lenton) 3:55.74*

400-METER FREESTYLE RELAY

1973....E. Germany (Kornelia Ender, Andrea Eife, Andrea Huebner, Sylvia Eichner) 3:52.45
1975....E. Germany (Kornelia Ender, Barbara Krause, Claudia Hempel, Ute Bruckner) 3:49.37
1978....United States (Tracy Caulkins, Stephanie Elkins, Joan Pennington, Cynthia Woodhead) 3:43.43*
1982....E. Germany (Birgit Meineke, Susanne Link, Kristin Otto, Caren Metschuk) 3:43.97
1986....E. Germany (Kristin Otto, Manuela Stellmach, Sabine Schulze, Heike Friedrich) 3:40.57*
1991....United States (Nicole Haislett, Julie Cooper, Whitney Hedgepeth, Jenny Thompson) 3:43.26
1994....China (Le Jingyi, Ying Shan, Le Ying, Lu Bin) 3:37.91*
1998 .....United States (Catherine Fox, Lindsey Farella, Melanie Valerio, B.J. Bedford) 3:42.11
2001....Germany (Petra Dallman, Antje Buschschulte, Katrin Meissner, Sandra Volkner) 3:39.58
2003....United States (Natalie Coughlin, Lindsay Benko, Rhiannon Jeffrey, Jenny Thompson) 3:38.09
2005....Germany (Petra Dallman, Daniela Goetz, Britta Steffen, Annika Liebs) 3:35.22*
2007....Australia (Lisbeth Lenton, Melanie Schlanger, Shayne Reese, Jodie Henry) 3:35.48

800-METER FREESTYLE RELAY

1986....E. Germany (Manuela Stellmach, Astrid Strauss, Nadja Bergknecht, Heike Friedrich) 7:59.33*
1991....Germany (Kerstin Kielgass, Manuela Stellmach, Dagmar Hase, Stephanie Ortwig) 8:02.56
1994 China (Le Ying, Yang Alhua, Zhou Guabin, Lu Bin) 7:57.96
1998....Germany (Silvia Szalai, Antje Buschschulte, Janina Goetz, Franziska Van Almsick) 8:02.56
2001....Great Britain (Nicola Jackson, Janine Belton, Karen Legg,Karen Pickering) 7:58.69
2003....United States (Lindsay Benko, Rachel Komisarz, Rhiannon Jeffrey, Diana Munz) 7:55.70‡
2005....Germany (Petra Dallman, Daniela Samulski, Britta Steffen, Annika Liebs) 7:50.82*
2007....United States (Natalie Coughlin, Dana Vollmer, Lacey Nymeyer, Katie Hoff) 7:50.09*

* World record; ‡Meet record.

Miscellaneous Sports

American Lindsey Vonn won the overall skiing World Cup title in 2008

CHRISTOPHE SIMON/AFP/GETTY IMAGES

Downs and Ups

U.S. skiers soared while American figure skaters stumbled and nobody quite knew what to make of the Tour de France

BY MERRELL NODEN

IT WAS A TIME OF SURPRISES AND disappointments in 2008 with some rising stars and veteran competitors living up to their billing while others took an unfortunate step backward.

FIGURE SKATING

For the first time in years, the U.S. did not go to the world championships with a credible medal threat among the ladies. This was partly due to the fact that Kimmie Meissner, who showed such promise in winning the 2006 world championship at age 16, struggled mightily all season. But it was also due to the fact that neither U.S. champion Mirai Nagasu nor runner-up Rachael Flatt was old enough to compete at the worlds (skaters must be 15 by the previous July 1).

How their presence might have changed things, we'll never know. At the world championships in Gothenburg, Sweden, the winner was Mao Asada, a 17-year-old from Nagoya, Japan. Asada was sure she'd blown her chances when, on the opening triple Axel of her long program, she fell and went skidding into the boards. Meissner finished seventh and teammate Beatrisa Liang 10th. Their combined placing did not equal the 13 or lower the U.S. needed from its top two in order to send the full complement of three skaters to the 2010 Winter Olympics. And that's a shame because the U.S. has some fantastic young skaters coming up. At the world junior championships, Flatt led a U.S. sweep of the medals, with Caroline Zhang second and Nagasu third. Their teammate Adam Rippon won the boys title.

Jeffrey Buttle of Canada was a somewhat surprising winner of the men's title in Gothenburg. Buttle had been having a rough season that saw him fail to reach the Grand Prix final and finish second in the Canadian championships. Johnny Weir of the U.S. took the bronze medal. With U.S. ice dance partners Tanith Belbin and Benjamin Agosto suffering an uncharacteristic fall in the compulsory dance and finishing fourth, Weir's bronze was the sole medal won by the U.S. in Gothenburg.

SKIING

Most skiers go only one way—down. But over his long career Bode Miller has treated us to many ups and downs. Two years ago he turned in a maddening, medal-less performance at the Turin Olympics. Since then, Miller quit the U.S. Ski Team in response to its "Bode Rules" of conduct and struck out on his own. Judging by his performance this season, it was a smart move. In a banner season for U.S. skiing—only the second time in which American skiers claimed both the men's and women's world cup titles—Miller added a second overall world cup title to the one he'd won back in 2005. He also claimed the world cup title in the combined event and, with 31 career world cup wins, earned comparisons to Phil Mahre, who in the early 80s won three straight overall titles.

Miller's heroics were matched by Lindsey

In what was a tough year overall for U.S. figure skating, ice dancers Ben Agosto and Tanith Belbin didn't medal at the 2008 Worlds.

FRANCOIS MORI/AP PHOTO

Vonn, née Kildow. Still only 23, Vonn has been a highly decorated skier since 2002, when she capped a stellar junior career by finishing sixth in the combined at the Salt Lake City Olympics. This was the season she justified all the breathless expectation. Vonn won a U.S.-record five downhill World Cup races and added the overall title. The rare skier who's a threat in all four disciplines, Vonn attributed her success this year to her marriage to former Olympic skier Thomas Vonn and his companionship on the world cup circuit.

Looking ahead to 2010 Olympics, Miller and Vonn give the U.S. a great one-two punch. Add Julia Mancuso, who is as close a rival as Vonn is likely to have, and Ted Ligety, who won the world cup title in the giant slalom, and U.S. may have a better shot at medals than ever before.

CYCLING

At this year's Tour de France no one showed more dogged determination than race director Christian Prudhomme, who proclaimed, again and again, that this year's race marked a real turning point in the sport's battle against performance-enhancing drugs. "The difference between those who cheat and those who chase after them has narrowed considerably," declared Prudhomme, asking us to believe that the bad news—four positive tests for doping—was really good news and proof that the system was working.

And for once, it might be. But since cyclists are nothing if not experts at spinning, Prudhomme will have to forgive us if we require a few more years of proof. It didn't help that on June 30th, less than a week before the Tour began, we were given a strong reminder of cycling's sordid recent history when the Switzerland-based Court of Arbitration for Sport rejected Floyd Landis's appeal of his doping case from the 2006 Tour. The most prominent cyclist to be nailed in this year's Tour was Riccardo Ricco, an Italian who won two stages before testing positive for the blood-booster EPO. Ricco's Saunier Duval-Scott team withdrew from the Tour. Perhaps embarrassed sponsors will elicit the changes that tarnished honor cannot.

From this mixture of good and bad news emerged this year's winner, Carlos Sastre, a 33-year-old who became the third straight Spaniard to win cycling's greatest race. Sastre took the yellow jersey with a fierce attack on Stage 17, at the base of Alpe d'Huez. He went on to hold off the Australian rider Cadel Evans in the final time trial, losing just 29 seconds to Evans, who was widely considered to be his superior. The top American finisher was Christian Vandevelde, in fifth.

Sastre's winning margin over Evans was an exciting 58 seconds, but what's most worth celebrating is the possibility that Sastre may actually have been clean. His CSC-Saxo Bank team was one of three—the other two were the American teams, Columbia and Garmin-Chipotle—to pay a considerable amount of money for independent, third-party drug testing. Perhaps Prudhomme is right. The cycling world must hope he is.

FOR THE RECORD • 2007—2008

Miscellaneous Sport Champions

Archery	U.S. Outdoor Championships	**Winner (Recurve)**	**Winner (Compound)**
	MEN	Brady Ellison	Dave Cousins
	WOMEN	Jennifer Nichols	Kelly Ward
Bowling	Professional Bowling Association	**Money Winner ($)**	**Highest Average (pts.)**
	TOUR LEADERS	Norm Duke ($176,855)	Walter Williams Jr. (228.34)
	Senior Professional Bowling Association	**Money Winner ($)**	**Highest Average (pts.)**
	TOUR LEADERS	Wayne Webb ($30,575)	Wayne Webb (224.08)
Curling	World Championships	**Country**	**Skip**
	MEN	Canada	Kevin Martin
	WOMEN	Canada	Jennifer Jones
	U.S. Championships	**Club**	**Skip**
	MEN	Madison, Wisc.	Craig Brown
	WOMEN	Rio, Wisc.	Debbie McCormick
Cycling		**Winner**	**Time**
	ROAD RACE WORLD CHAMPIONSHIP	Alessandro Ballan, Italy	6:37:30
	TOUR DE FRANCE	Carlos Sastre, Spain	87:52:52
Sled Dog Racing		**Winner**	**Time**
	IDITAROD	Lance Mackey	9 days, 11:46:48
Figure Skating	World Championships	**Winner**	**Country**
	MEN	Jeremy Buttle	Canada
	WOMEN	Mao Asada	Japan
	PAIRS	Aliona Savchenko/ Robin Szolkowy	Germany
	ICE DANCING	Isabelle Delobel/ Olivier Schoenfelder	France
	U.S. Championships	**Winner**	**Club**
	MEN	Evan Lysacek	DuPage FSC
	WOMEN	Mirai Nagasu	Pasadena FSC
	PAIRS	Keauna McLaughlin/ Rockne Brubaker	Los Angeles FSC/ Broadmoor SC
	ICE DANCING	Tanith Belbin/ Ben Agosto	Arctic FSC
Handball	U.S.One-Wall Championships	**Winner**	
	MEN	Cesar Sala	
	WOMEN	Tracy Davis	
	U.S.Three-Wall Championships	**Winner**	
	MEN	Sean Lenning	
	WOMEN	Megan Mehilos	
Lacrosse	League	**Winner (Score)**	**Runner-up**
	AMERICAN LACROSSE LEAGUE	New York A.C. (14–12)	Capital
	NATIONAL LACROSSE LEAGUE	Buffalo Bandits (14–13)	Portland LumberJax
	MAJOR LEAGUE LACROSSE	Rochester Rattlers (16–6)	Denver Outlaws
Little League Baseball		**Winner**	**Runner-up** / **Score**
	WORLD SERIES CHAMPION	Waipio, Hawaii	Matamoros, Mex. 12–3
Motor Boat Racing	American Boat Racing Association	**Boat**	
	GOLD CUP CHAMPION	None (event cancelled because of bad weather)	
		Winner	**Wins**
	ABRA DRIVER OF THE YEAR	Steve David (U-6)	1
	ABRA BOAT OF THE YEAR	U-6 Oh Boy! Oberto	1
Polo	United States Polo Association	**Winner (Score)**	**Runner-up**
	U.S. OPEN	Crab Orchard (15–12)	Las Monjitas

Miscellaneous Sport Champions

Rodeo

PRCA World Champions	Winner(s)
ALL-AROUND	Trevor Brazile
SADDLE BRONC RIDING	Taos Muncy
BAREBACK RIDING	Bobby Mote
BULL RIDING	Wesley Silcox
STEER WRESTLING	Jason Miller
STEER ROPING	Trevor Brazile
CALF TIE-DOWN ROPING	Trevor Brazile
TEAM ROPING	Chad Masters, Walt Woodard

Rowing

Intercollegiate (Club) Rowing Association	Winner	Runner-Up
MEN	Wisconsin	Washington

Rugby

Rugby Union	Winner	Runner-Up
MEN'S CLUB	Life	Glendale Raptors
MEN'S COLLEGIATE	California	BYU

American National Rugby League	Winner	Runner-Up
U.S. CHAMPION	New Haven Warriors	Aston Bulls

Skiing

FIS World Champion	Men's Winner (Season)	Women's Winner (Season)
OVERALL	Bode Miller (USA)	Lindsey Vonn (USA)
DOWNHILL	Didier Cuche (SUI)	Lindsey Vonn (USA)
SLALOM	Manfred Moelgg (ITA)	Marlies Schild (AUT)
GIANT SLALOM	Ted Ligety (USA)	Denise Karbon (ITA)
SUPER G	Hannes Reichelt (AUT)	Maria Riesch (GER)
COMBINED	Bode Miller (USA)	Maria Riesch (GER)

Softball

U.S. ASA Championship	Major Fast Pitch Winner	Major Slow Pitch Winner
MEN	Patsy's	Flashback
WOMEN	So.Cal. Hurricanes	Hawks/Miss Kitty

Speed Skating

All-Around World Champion	Winner
MEN	Sven Kramer (NET)
WOMEN	Paulien von Deutekom (NET)

Squash

U.S. Championship	Hard Ball Winner	Soft Ball Winner
MEN	Eric Pearson	Julian Illingworth
WOMEN	N/A	Natalie Grainger

Triathlon

Ironman World Championship	Winner	Time
MEN	Chris McCormack (AUS)	8:15:34
WOMEN	Christine Wellington (UK)	9:10:00

U.S. Championship	Winner	Time
MEN	Matty Reed	1:54:29
WOMEN	Julie Ertel	2:05:46

Volleyball

U.S. Championship (Open Division)	Winner	Runner-Up
MEN	Paul Mitchell	TPC Beavers
WOMEN	USA A2 Red	Huskies VBC

Wrestling

U.S. Championship	Freestyle	Greco-Roman
121 LBS.	Matt Azevedo*	Spencer Mango*
132 LBS.	Shawn Bunch	Jim Gruenwald
145.5 LBS.	Doub Schwab	Mark Rial
163 LBS.	Ben Askren	T.C. Dantzler
185 LBS.	Mo Lawal	Brad Ahearn
211.5 LBS.	Daniel Cormier	Justin Ruiz
264.5 LBS.	Tommy Rowlands	Dremiel Byers
TEAM	Sunkist Kids	U.S. Army

*Most Outstanding Wrestler

Bowling

PBA TOUR RESULTS

2007–08 Tour

Date	Event	Winner	Earnings ($)	Runner-Up
Sept 18–23	Dydo Japan Cup	Mika Koivuniemi	50,000	Mike Wolfe
Oct. 21–28	USBC Masters	Sean Rash	100,000	Steve Jaros
Oct 31–Nov. 4	Motor City Classic	Walter Ray Williams Jr.	25,000	Eugene McCune
Nov 7–11	Etonic Championship	Mike Wolfe	25,111	Walter Ray Williams, Jr.
Nov 14–18	Lake County Indiana Classic	Michael Haugen Jr.	25,000	Wes Malott
Nov 21–25	Windy City Classic	Robert Smith	25,000	Brad Angelo
Nov 28–Dec 2	Great Lakes Classic	Walter Ray Williams Jr.	25,100	Chris Loschetter
Dec 5–9	Lumber Liquidators Championship	Patrick Allen	25,000	Wes Malott
Dec 12–16	Spartanburg Classic	Parker Bohn III	25,100	Rhino Page
Jan 2–6	ConstructionJobs.com Championship	Tommy Jones	25,000	Patrick Allen
Jan 9–13	Earl Anthony Medford Classic	Wes Malott	25,000	Rhino Page
Jan 15–20	Dick Weber Open	Mike Scroggins	25,000	Chris Barnes
Jan 20–22	Doubles Classic	Wiseman & Fagan	20,000	Russell & Ciccone
Jan 23–27	PBA Tournament of Champions	Michael Haugen Jr.	50,000	Chris Barnes
Feb 6–10	Bayer Classic	Chris Barnes	25,000	Tommy Jones
Feb 13–17	Pepsi Championship	Mike Scroggins	25,000	Walter Ray Williams, Jr.
Feb. 18–24	PBA World Championship	Norm Duke	50,000	Ryan Shafer
Feb 26–March 2	Buckeye State Classic	Chris Barnes	25,000	Ken Simard
March 5–9	Go RVing Classic	Rhino Page	25,000	Jack Jurek
March 19–23	GEICO Classic	Tommy Jones	25,000	Pete Weber
March 23–30	65th U.S. Open	Norm Duke	100,000	Mika Koivuniemi
Apr 7–8	Motel 6 Roll to Riches	Parker Bohn III	150,000*	Norm Duke

*not counted in tour's season earnings

TOUR LEADERS - PBA: 2007–08

MONEY LEADERS	Events	Earnings ($)
Norm Duke	15	175,855
Mika Koivuniemi	21	159,580
Sean Rash	21	151,500
Walter Ray Williams Jr.	21	144,220
Chris Barnes	21	142,410

AVERAGE	Events	Average
Walter Ray Williams Jr.	21	228.34
Chris Barnes	21	225.18
Wes Malott	18	223.77
Rhino Page	19	223.42
Patrick Allen	20	222.19

PBA Career Statistics

CAREER EARNINGS	
Walter Ray Williams Jr.	$3,817,722
Pete Weber	$3,040,948
Parker Bohn III	$2,552,074
Norm Duke	$2,541,466
Brian Voss	$2,336,642

Note: Career leaders through Sept. 1, 2008

CAREER TITLES	
Walter Ray Williams Jr.	44
Earl Anthony	41
Mark Roth	34
Pete Weber	34
Parker Bohn III	31

Cycling

Tour de France Winners

Year	Winner	Time
1903	Maurice Garin, France	94 hrs, 33 min
1904	Henry Cornet, France	96 hrs, 5 min, 56 sec
1905	Louis Trousselier, France	110 hrs, 26 min, 58 sec
1906	Rene Pottier, France	Not available
1907	Lucien Petit-Breton, France	158 hrs, 54 min, 5 sec
1908	Lucien Petit-Breton, France	Not available
1909	Francois Faber, Luxembourg	157 hrs, 1 min, 22 sec
1910	Octave Lapize, France	162 hrs, 41 min, 30 sec
1911	Gustave Garrigou, France	195 hrs, 37 min
1912	Odile Defraye, Belgium	190 hrs, 30 min, 28 sec
1913	Philippe Thys, Belgium	197 hrs, 54 min
1914	Philippe Thys, Belgium	200 hrs, 28 min, 48 sec
1915–18	NO RACE	
1919	Firmin Lambot, Belgium	231 hrs, 7 min, 15 sec
1920	Philippe Thys, Belgium	228 hrs, 36 min, 13 sec
1921	Leon Scieur, Belgium	221 hrs, 50 min, 26 sec
1922	Firmin Lambot, Belgium	222 hrs, 8 min, 6 sec
1923	Henri Pelissier, France	222 hrs, 15 min, 30 sec
1924	Ottavio Bottechia, Italy	226 hrs, 18 min, 21 sec
1925	Ottavio Bottechia, Italy	219 hrs, 10 min, 18 sec
1926	Lucien Buysse, Belgium	238 hrs, 44 min, 25 sec
1927	Nicolas Frantz, Luxembourg	198 hrs, 16 min, 42 sec
1928	Nicolas Frantz, Luxembourg	192 hrs, 48 min, 58 sec
1929	Maurice Dewaele, Belgium	186 hrs, 39 min, 16 sec
1930	Andre Leducq, France	172 hrs, 12 min, 16 sec
1931	Antonin Magne, France	177 hrs, 10 min, 3 sec
1932	Andre Leducq, France	154 hrs, 12 min, 49 sec
1933	Georges Speicher, France	147 hrs, 51 min, 37 sec
1934	Antonin Magne, France	147 hrs, 13 min, 58 sec
1935	Romain Maes, Belgium	141 hrs, 32 min
1936	Sylvere Maes, Belgium	142 hrs, 47 min, 32 sec
1937	Roger Lapebie, France	138 hrs, 58 min, 31 sec
1938	Gino Bartali, Italy	148 hrs, 29 min, 12 sec
1939	Sylvere Maes, Belgium	132 hrs, 3 min, 17 sec

Cycling (Cont.)

Tour de France Winners (Cont.)

Year	Winner	Time
1940–46	NO RACE	
1947	Jean Robic, France	148 hrs, 11 min, 25 sec
1948	Gino Bartali, Italy	147 hrs, 10 min, 36 sec
1949	Fausto Coppi, Italy	149 hrs, 40 min, 49 sec
1950	Ferdi Kubler, Switzerland	145 hrs, 36 min, 56 sec
1951	Hugo Koblet, Switzerland	142 hrs, 20 min, 14 sec
1952	Fausto Coppi, Italy	151 hrs, 57 min, 20 sec
1953	Louison Bobet, France	129 hrs, 23 min, 25 sec
1954	Louison Bobet, France	140 hrs, 6 min, 5 sec
1955	Louison Bobet, France	130 hrs, 29 min, 26 sec
1956	Roger Walkowiak, France	124 hrs, 1 min, 16 sec
1957	Jacques Anquetil, France	129 hrs, 46 min, 11 sec
1958	Charly Gaul, Luxembourg	116 hrs, 59 min, 5 sec
1959	Federico Bahamontes, Spain	123 hrs, 46 min, 45 sec
1960	Gastone Nencini, Italy	112 hrs, 8 min, 42 sec
1961	Jacques Anquetil, France	122 hrs, 1 min, 33 sec
1962	Jacques Anquetil, France	114 hrs, 31 min, 54 sec
1963	Jacques Anquetil, France	113 hrs, 30 min, 5 sec
1964	Jacques Anquetil, France	127 hrs, 9 min, 44 sec
1965	Felice Gimondi, Italy	116 hrs, 42 min, 6 sec
1966	Lucien Aimar, France	117 hrs, 34 min, 21 sec
1967	Roger Pingeon, France	136 hrs, 53 min, 50 sec
1968	Jan Janssen, Netherlands	133 hrs, 49 min, 32 sec
1969	Eddy Merckx, Belgium	116 hrs, 16 min, 2 sec
1970	Eddy Merckx, Belgium	119 hrs, 31 min, 49 sec
1971	Eddy Merckx, Belgium	96 hrs, 45 min, 14 sec
1972	Eddy Merckx, Belgium	108 hrs, 17 min, 18 sec
1973	Luis Ocana, Spain	122 hrs, 25 min, 34 sec
1974	Eddy Merckx, Belgium	116 hrs, 16 min, 58 sec
1975	Bernard Thevenet, France	114 hrs, 35 min, 31 sec
1976	Lucien Van Impe, Belgium	116 hrs, 22 min, 23 sec
1977	Bernard Thevenet, France	115 hrs, 38 min, 30 sec
1978	Bernard Hinault, France	108 hrs, 18 min
1979	Bernard Hinault, France	103 hrs, 6 min, 50 sec
1980	Joop Zoetemelk, Netherlands	109 hrs, 19 min, 14 sec
1981	Bernard Hinault, France	96 hrs, 19 min, 38 sec
1982	Bernard Hinault, France	92 hrs, 8 min, 46 sec
1983	Laurent Fignon, France	105 hrs, 7 min, 52 sec
1984	Laurent Fignon, France	112 hrs, 3 min, 40 sec
1985	Bernard Hinault, France	113 hrs, 24 min, 23 sec
1986	Greg LeMond, United States	110 hrs, 35 min, 19 sec
1987	Stephen Roche, Ireland	115 hrs, 27 min, 42 sec
1988	Pedro Delgado, Spain	84 hrs, 27 min, 53 sec
1989	Greg LeMond, United States	87 hrs, 38 min, 35 sec
1990	Greg LeMond, United States	90 hrs, 43 min, 20 sec
1991	Miguel Induráin, Spain	101 hrs, 1 min, 20 sec
1992	Miguel Induráin, Spain	100 hrs, 49 min, 30 sec
1993	Miguel Induráin, Spain	95 hrs, 57 min, 9 sec
1994	Miguel Induráin, Spain	103 hrs, 38 min, 38 sec
1995	Miguel Induráin, Spain	92 hrs, 44 min, 59 sec
1996	Bjarne Riis, Denmark	95 hrs, 57 min, 16 sec
1997	Jan Ullrich, Germany	100 hrs, 30 min, 35 sec
1998	Marco Pantani, Italy	92 hrs, 49 min, 46 sec
1999	Lance Armstrong, United States	91 hrs, 32 min, 16 sec
2000	Lance Armstrong, United States	92 hrs, 33 min, 8 sec
2001	Lance Armstrong, United States	86 hrs, 17 min, 28 sec
2002	Lance Armstrong, United States	82 hrs, 5 min, 12 sec
2003	Lance Armstrong, United States	83 hrs, 41 min, 12 sec
2004	Lance Armstrong, United States	83 hrs, 36 min, 2 sec
2005	Lance Armstrong, United States	82 hrs, 34 min, 5 sec
2006	Oscar Pereiro, Spain†	82 hrs, 48 min, 30 sec
2007	Alberto Contador, Spain	91 hrs, 26 sec
2008	Carlos Sastre, Spain	87 hrs, 52 min, 52 sec

†Floyd Landis, the initial winner, was officially stripped of his title on Sept. 20, 2007 by the ICU after a hearing affirmed that he had tested positive for using banned substances during Stage 17 of the 2006 Tour.

Figure Skating

WORLD CHAMPIONS

Women

1906.....Madge Sayers-Cave, Great Britain
1907.....Madge Sayers-Cave, Great Britain
1908.....Lily Kronberger, Hungary
1909.....Lily Kronberger, Hungary
1910.....Lily Kronberger, Hungary
1911.....Lily Kronberger, Hungary
1912.....Opika von Meray Horvath, Hungary
1913.....Opika von Meray Horvath, Hungary
1914.....Opika von Meray Horvath, Hungary
1915–21 NO COMPETITION
1922.....Herma Plank-Szabo, Austria
1923.....Herma Plank-Szabo, Austria
1924.....Herma Plank-Szabo, Austria
1925.....Herma Jaross-Szabo, Austria
1926.....Herma Jaross-Szabo, Austria
1927.....Sonja Henie, Norway
1928.....Sonja Henie, Norway
1929.....Sonja Henie, Norway
1930.....Sonja Henie, Norway
1931.....Sonja Henie, Norway
1932.....Sonja Henie, Norway
1933.....Sonja Henie, Norway
1934.....Sonja Henie, Norway
1935.....Sonja Henie, Norway
1936.....Sonja Henie, Norway
1937.....Cecilia Colledge, Great Britain
1938.....Megan Taylor, Great Britain
1939.....Megan Taylor, Great Britain
1940–46 NO COMPETITION
1947.....Barbara Ann Scott, Canada
1948.....Barbara Ann Scott, Canada
1949.....Alena Vrzanova, Czechoslovakia
1950.....Alena Vrzanova, Czechoslovakia
1951.....Jeannette Altwegg, Great Britain
1952.....Jacqueline duBief, France
1953.....Tenley Albright, United States
1954.....Gundi Busch, W. Germany
1955.....Tenley Albright, United States
1956.....Carol Heiss, United States
1957.....Carol Heiss, United States
1958.....Carol Heiss, United States
1959.....Carol Heiss, United States
1960.....Carol Heiss, United States
1961 NO COMPETITION
1962.....Sjoukje Dijkstra, Netherlands
1963.....Sjoukje Dijkstra, Netherlands
1964.....Sjoukje Dijkstra, Netherlands
1965.....Petra Burka, Canada
1966.....Peggy Fleming, United States
1967.....Peggy Fleming, United States
1968.....Peggy Fleming, United States
1969.....Gabriele Seyfert, E. Germany
1970.....Gabriele Seyfert, E. Germany
1971.....Beatrix Schuba, Austria
1972.....Beatrix Schuba, Austria
1973.....Karen Magnussen, Canada
1974.....Christine Errath, E. Germany
1975.....Dianne DeLeeuw, Netherlands
1976.....Dorothy Hamill, United States
1977.....Linda Fratianne, United States
1978.....Annett Poetzsch, E. Germany
1979.....Linda Fratianne, United States
1980.....Annett Poetzsch, E. Germany
1981.....Denise Biellmann, Switzerland
1982.....Elaine Zayak, United States
1983.....Rosalynn Sumners, United States
1984.....Katarina Witt, E. Germany
1985.....Katarina Witt, E. Germany
1986.....Debi Thomas, United States
1987.....Katarina Witt, E. Germany
1988.....Katarina Witt, E. Germany
1989.....Midori Ito, Japan
1990.....Jill Trenary, United States
1991.....Kristi Yamaguchi, United States
1992.....Kristi Yamaguchi, United States
1993.....Oksana Baiul, Ukraine
1994.....Yuka Sato, Japan
1995.....Chen Lu, China

WORLD CHAMPIONS (Cont.)

Women (Cont.)

1996.....Michelle Kwan, United States
1997.....Tara Lipinski, United States
1998.....Michelle Kwan, United States
1999.....Maria Butyrskaya, Russia
2000.....Michelle Kwan, United States
2001.....Michelle Kwan, United States
2002.....Irina Slutskaya, Russia
2003.....Michelle Kwan, United States
2004.....Shizuka Arakawa, Japan
2005.....Irina Slutskaya, Russia
2006.....Kimmie Meissner, United States
2007.....Miki Ando, Japan
2008.....Mao Asada, Japan

Men

1896.....Gilbert Fuchs, Germany
1897.....Gustav Hugel, Austria
1898.....Henning Grenander, Sweden
1899.....Gustav Hugel, Austria
1900.....Gustav Hugel, Austria
1901.....Ulrich Salchow, Sweden
1902.....Ulrich Salchow, Sweden
1903.....Ulrich Salchow, Sweden
1904.....Ulrich Salchow, Sweden
1905.....Ulrich Salchow, Sweden
1906.....Gilbert Fuchs, Germany
1907.....Ulrich Salchow, Sweden
1908.....Ulrich Salchow, Sweden
1909.....Ulrich Salchow, Sweden
1910.....Ulrich Salchow, Sweden
1911.....Ulrich Salchow, Sweden
1912.....Fritz Kachler, Austria
1913.....Fritz Kachler, Austria
1914.....Gosta Sandhal, Sweden
1915–21 NO COMPETITION
1922.....Gillis Grafstrom, Sweden
1923.....Fritz Kachler, Austria
1924.....Gillis Grafstrom, Sweden
1925.....Willy Bockl, Austria
1926.....Willy Bockl, Austria
1927.....Willy Bockl, Austria
1928.....Willy Bockl, Austria
1929.....Gillis Grafstrom, Sweden
1930.....Karl Schafer, Austria
1931.....Karl Schafer, Austria
1932.....Karl Schafer, Austria
1933.....Karl Schafer, Austria
1934.....Karl Schafer, Austria
1935.....Karl Schafer, Austria
1936.....Karl Schafer, Austria
1937.....Felix Kaspar, Austria
1938.....Felix Kaspar, Austria
1939.....Graham Sharp, Great Britain
1940–46 NO COMPETITION
1947.....Hans Gerschwiler, Switzerland
1948.....Dick Button, United States
1949.....Dick Button, United States
1950.....Dick Button, United States
1951.....Dick Button, United States
1952.....Dick Button, United States
1953.....Hayes Alan Jenkins, United States
1954.....Hayes Alan Jenkins, United States
1955.....Hayes Alan Jenkins, United States
1956.....Hayes Alan Jenkins, United States
1957.....David W. Jenkins, United States
1958.....David W. Jenkins, United States
1959.....David W. Jenkins, United States
1960.....Alan Giletti, France
1961.....No competition
1962.....Donald Jackson, Canada
1963.....Donald McPherson, Canada
1964.....Manfred Schneldorfer, W. Germany
1965.....Alain Calmat, France
1966.....Emmerich Danzer, Austria
1967.....Emmerich Danzer, Austria
1968.....Emmerich Danzer, Austria
1969.....Tim Wood, United States
1970.....Tim Wood, United States
1971.....Andrej Nepela, Czechoslovakia
1972.....Andrej Nepela, Czechoslovakia
1973.....Andrej Nepela, Czechoslovakia
1974.....Jan Hoffmann, E. Germany
1975.....Sergei Volkov, USSR
1976.....John Curry, Great Britain
1977.....Vladimir Kovalev, USSR
1978.....Charles Tickner, United States
1979.....Vladimir Kovalev, USSR
1980.....Jan Hoffmann, E. Germany
1981.....Scott Hamilton, United States
1982.....Scott Hamilton, United States
1983.....Scott Hamilton, United States
1984.....Scott Hamilton, United States
1985.....Aleksandr Fadeev, USSR
1986.....Brian Boitano, United States
1987.....Brian Orser, Canada
1988.....Brian Boitano, United States
1989.....Kurt Browning, Canada
1990.....Kurt Browning, Canada
1991.....Kurt Browning, Canada
1992.....Viktor Petrenko, CIS
1993.....Kurt Browning, Canada
1994.....Elvis Stojko, Canada
1995.....Elvis Stojko, Canada
1996.....Todd Eldredge, United States
1997.....Elvis Stojko, Canada
1998.....Alexei Yagudin, Russia
1999.....Alexei Yagudin, Russia
2000.....Alexei Yagudin, Russia
2001.....Evgeni Plushenko, Russia
2002.....Alexei Yagudin, Russia
2003.....Evgeni Plushenko, Russia
2004.....Evgeni Plushenko, Russia
2005.....Stephane Lambiel, Switzerland
2006.....Stephane Lambiel, Switzerland
2007.....Brian Joubert, France
2008.....Jeffrey Buttle, Canada

Pairs

1908.....Anna Hubler, Heinrich Burger, Germany
1909.....Phyllis Johnson, James H. Johnson, Great Britain
1910.....Anna Hubler, Heinrich Burger, Germany
1911.....Ludowika Eilers, Walter Jakobsson, Germany/Finland
1912.....Phyllis Johnson, James H. Johnson, Great Britain
1913.....Helene Engelmann, Karl Majstrik, Germany
1914.....Ludowika Jakobsson-Eilers, Walter Jakobsson-Eilers, Finland
1915–21 NO COMPETITION
1922.....Helene Engelmann, Alfred Berger, Germany
1923.....Ludowika Jakobsson-Eilers, Walter Jakobsson-Eilers, Finland
1924.....Helene Engelmann, Alfred Berger, Germany
1925.....Herma Jaross-Szabo, Ludwig Wrede, Austria
1926.....Andree Joly, Pierre Brunet, France
1927.....Herma Jaross-Szabo, Ludwig Wrede, Austria
1928.....Andree Joly, Pierre Brunet, France
1929.....Lilly Scholz, Otto Kaiser, Austria
1930.....Andree Brunet-Joly, Pierre Brunet-Joly, France
1931.....Emilie Rotter, Laszlo Szollas, Hungary
1932.....Andree Brunet-Joly, Pierre Brunet-Joly, France
1933.....Emilie Rotter, Laszlo Szollas, Hungary
1934.....Emilie Rotter, Laszlo Szollas, Hungary
1935.....Emilie Rotter, Laszlo Szollas, Hungary
1936.....Maxi Herber, Ernst Bajer, Germany
1937.....Maxi Herber, Ernst Bajer, Germany
1938.....Maxi Herber, Ernst Bajer, Germany
1939.....Maxi Herber, Ernst Bajer, Germany
1940–46 NO COMPETITION
1947.....Micheline Lannoy, Pierre Baugniet, Belgium
1948.....Micheline Lannoy, Pierre Baugniet, Belgium
1949.....Andrea Kekessy, Ede Kiraly, Hungary
1950.....Karol Kennedy, Peter Kennedy, United States
1951.....Ria Baran, Paul Falk, W. Germany
1952.....Ria Baran Falk, Paul Falk, W. Germany
1953.....Jennifer Nicks, John Nicks, Great Britain
1954.....Frances Dafoe, Norris Bowden, Canada
1955.....Frances Dafoe, Norris Bowden, Canada
1956.....Sissy Schwarz, Kurt Oppelt, Austria
1957.....Barbara Wagner, Robert Paul, Canada
1958.....Barbara Wagner, Robert Paul, Canada
1959.....Barbara Wagner, Robert Paul, Canada

Figure Skating

WORLD CHAMPIONS

Pairs

1960.....Barbara Wagner, Robert Paul, Canada
1961.....NO COMPETITION
1962.....Maria Jelinek, Otto Jelinek, Canada
1963.....Marika Kilius, Hans-Jurgen Baumler, W Germany
1964.....Marika Kilius, Hans-Jurgen Baumler, W Germany
1965.....Ljudmila Protopopov, Oleg Protopopov, USSR
1966.....Ljudmila Protopopov, Oleg Protopopov, USSR
1967.....Ljudmila Protopopov, Oleg Protopopov, USSR
1968.....Ljudmila Protopopov, Oleg Protopopov, USSR
1969.....Irina Rodnina, Aleksey Ulanov, USSR
1970.....Irina Rodnina, Aleksey Ulanov, USSR
1971.....Irina Rodnina, Aleksey Ulanov, USSR
1972.....Irina Rodnina, Aleksey Ulanov, USSR
1973.....Irina Rodnina, Aleksandr Zaytsev, USSR
1974.....Irina Rodnina, Aleksandr Zaytsev, USSR
1975.....Irina Rodnina, Aleksandr Zaytsev, USSR
1976.....Irina Rodnina, Aleksandr Zaytsev, USSR
1977.....Irina Rodnina, Aleksandr Zaytsev, USSR
1978.....Irina Rodnina, Aleksandr Zaytsev, USSR
1979.....Tai Babilonia, Randy Gardner, United States
1980.....Maria Cherkasova, Sergei Shakhrai, USSR
1981.....Irina Vorobieva, Igor Lisovsky, USSR
1982.....Sabine Baess, Tassilio Thierbach, E. Germany
1983.....Elena Valova, Oleg Vasiliev, USSR
1984.....Barbara Underhill, Paul Martini, Canada
1985.....Elena Valova, Oleg Vasiliev, USSR
1986.....Ekaterina Gordeeva, Sergei Grinkov, USSR
1987.....Ekaterina Gordeeva, Sergei Grinkov, USSR
1988.....Elena Valova, Oleg Vasiliev, USSR
1989.....Ekaterina Gordeeva, Sergei Grinkov, USSR
1990.....Ekaterina Gordeeva, Sergei Grinkov, USSR
1991.....Natalia Mishkutienok, Artur Dmitriev, USSR
1992.....Natalia Mishkutienok, Artur Dmitriev, CIS
1993.....Isabelle Brasseur, Lloyd Eisler, Canada
1994.....Evgenia Shishkova, Vadim Naumov, Russia
1995.....Radka Kovarikova, Rene Novotny, Czech Republic
1996.....Marina Eltsova, Andrey Buskhov, Russia
1997.....Mandy Wötzel, Ingo Steuer, Germany
1998.....Jenni Meno, Todd Sand, United States
1999.....Elena Berezhnaya, Anton Sikharulidze, Russia
2000.....Maria Petrova, Aleksei Tikhonov, Russia
2001.....Jamie Salé, David Pelletier, Canada
2002.....Xue Shen, Hongbo Zhao, China
2003.....Xue Shen, Hongbo Zhao, China
2004.....Tatiana Totmianina, Maxim Marinin, Russia
2005.....Tatiana Totmianina, Maxim Marinin, Russia
2006.....Qing Pang, Jian Tong, China
2007.....Shen Xue, Zhao Hongbo, China
2008.....Aliona Savchenko, Robin Szolkowy, Germany

Dance

1950....Lois Waring, Michael McGean, United States
1951....Jean Westwood, Lawrence Demmy, Great Britain
1952....Jean Westwood, Lawrence Demmy, Great Britain
1953....Jean Westwood, Lawrence Demmy, Great Britain
1954....Jean Westwood, Lawrence Demmy, Great Britain
1955....Jean Westwood, Lawrence Demmy, Great Britain
1956....Pamela Wieght, Paul Thomas, Great Britain
1957....June Markham, Courtney Jones, Great Britain
1958....June Markham, Courtney Jones, Doreen D. Denny, Courtney Jones, Great Britain
1960....Doreen D. Denny, Courtney Jones, Great Britain
1961....NO COMPETITION
1962....Eva Romanova, Pavel Roman, Czechoslovakia
1963....Eva Romanova, Pavel Roman, Czechoslovakia
1964....Eva Romanova, Pavel Roman, Czechoslovakia
1965....Eva Romanova, Pavel Roman, Czechoslovakia
1966....Diane Towler, Bernard Ford, Great Britain
1967....Diane Towler, Bernard Ford, Great Britain
1968....Diane Towler, Bernard Ford, Great Britain
1969....Diane Towler, Bernard Ford, Great Britain
1970....Ljudmila Pakhomova, Aleksandr Gorshkov, USSR
1971....Ljudmila Pakhomova, Aleksandr Gorshkov USSR
1972....Ljudmila Pakhomova, Aleksandr Gorshkov USSR
1973....Ljudmila Pakhomova, Aleksandr Gorshkov USSR
1974....Ljudmila Pakhomova, Aleksandr Gorshkov USSR
1975....Irina Moiseeva, Andreij Minenkov, USSR
1976....Ljudmila Pakhomova, Aleksandr Gorshkov USSR
1977....Irina Moiseeva, Andreij Minenkov, USSR
1978....Natalia Linichuk, Gennadi Karponosov, USSR
1979....Natalia Linichuk, Gennadi Karponosov, USSR
1980....Krisztina Regoeczy, Andras Sallai, Hungary
1981....Jayne Torvill, Christopher Dean, Great Britain
1982....Jayne Torvill, Christopher Dean, Great Britain
1983....Jayne Torvill, Christopher Dean, Great Britain
1984....Jayne Torvill, Christopher Dean, Great Britain
1985....Natalia Bestemianova, Andrei Bukin, USSR
1986....Natalia Bestemianova, Andrei Bukin, USSR
1987....Natalia Bestemianova, Andrei Bukin, USSR
1988....Natalia Bestemianova, Andrei Bukin, USSR
1989....Marina Klimova, Sergei Ponomarenko, USSR
1990....Marina Klimova, Sergei Ponomarenko, USSR
1991....Isabelle Duchesnay, Paul Duchesnay, France
1992....Marina Klimova, Sergei Ponomarenko, CIS
1993....Renee Roca, Gorsha Sur, United States
1994....Oksana Grishuk, Evgeny Platov, Russia
1995....Oksana Grishuk, Evgeny Platov, Russia
1996....Oksana Grishuk, Evgeny Platov, Russia
1997....Oksana Grishuk, Evgeny Platov, Russia
1998....Anjelika Krylova, Oleg Ovsyannikov, Russia
1999....Anjelika Krylova, Oleg Ovsyannikov, Russia
2000....Marina Anissina, Gwendal Peizerat, France
2001....Barbara Fusar Poli, Maurizio Margaglio, Italy
2002....Irina Lobacheva, Ilia Averbukh, Russia
2003....Shae-Lynn Bourne, Victor Kraatz, Canada
2004....Tatiana Navka, Roman Kostomarov, Russia
2005....Tatiana Navka, Roman Kostomarov, Russia
2006....Albena Denkova, Maxim Staviski, Bulgaria
2007....Albena Denkova ,Maxim Staviski, Bulgaria
2008....Isabelle Delobel, Olivier Schoenfelder, France

CHAMPIONS OF THE UNITED STATES

The championships held in 1914, 1918, 1920 and 1921 under the auspices of the International Skating Union of America were open to Canadians, although the competitions were considered to be United States championships. Beginning in 1922, the championships have been held under the auspices of the United States Figure Skating Association.

Women

1914....Theresa Weld, SC of Boston
1915–17 NO COMPETITION
1918....Rosemary S. Beresford, New York SC
1919 NO COMPETITION
1920....Theresa Weld, SC of Boston
1921....Theresa Weld Blanchard, SC of Boston
1922....Theresa Weld Blanchard, SC of Boston
1923....Theresa Weld Blanchard, SC of Boston
1924....Theresa Weld Blanchard, SC of Boston
1925....Beatrix Loughran, New York SC
1926....Beatrix Loughran, New York SC
1927....Beatrix Loughran, New York SC
1928....Maribel Y. Vinson, SC of Boston
1929....Maribel Y. Vinson, SC of Boston
1930....Maribel Y. Vinson, SC of Boston
1931....Maribel Y. Vinson, SC of Boston
1932....Maribel Y. Vinson, SC of Boston
1933....Maribel Y. Vinson, SC of Boston
1934....Suzanne Davis, SC of Boston
1935....Maribel Y. Vinson, SC of Boston
1936....Maribel Y. Vinson, SC of Boston
1937....Maribel Y. Vinson, SC of Boston
1938....Joan Tozzer, SC of Boston
1939....Joan Tozzer, SC of Boston
1940....Joan Tozzer, SC of Boston
1941....Jane Vaughn, Philadelphia SC & HS
1942....Jane Vaughn Sullivan, Philadelphia SC & HS
1943....Gretchen Van Zandt Merrill, SC of Boston
1944....Gretchen Van Zandt Merrill, SC of Boston
1945....Gretchen Van Zandt Merrill, SC of Boston
1946....Gretchen Van Zandt Merrill, SC of Boston
1947....Gretchen Van Zandt Merrill, SC of Boston
1948....Gretchen Van Zandt Merrill, SC of Boston
1949....Yvonne Claire Sherman, SC of New York
1950....Yvonne Claire Sherman, SC of New York
1951....Sonya Klopfer, Junior SC of New York
1952....Tenley E. Albright, SC of Boston
1953....Tenley E. Albright, SC of Boston
1954....Tenley E. Albright, SC of Boston
1955....Tenley E. Albright, SC of Boston
1956....Tenley E. Albright, SC of Boston
1957....Carol E. Heiss, SC of New York
1958....Carol E. Heiss, SC of New York
1959....Carol E. Heiss, SC of New York
1960....Carol E. Heiss, SC of New York
1961....Laurence R. Owen, SC of Boston
1962....Barbara Roles Pursley, Arctic Blades FSC
1963....Lorraine G. Hanlon, SC of Boston
1964....Peggy Fleming, Arctic Blades FSC
1965....Peggy Fleming, Arctic Blades FSC
1966....Peggy Fleming, City of Colorado Springs
1967....Peggy Fleming, Broadmoor SC
1968....Peggy Fleming, Broadmoor SC
1969....Janet Lynn, Wagon Wheel FSC
1970....Janet Lynn, Wagon Wheel FSC
1971....Janet Lynn, Wagon Wheel FSC
1972....Janet Lynn, Wagon Wheel FSC
1973....Janet Lynn, Wagon Wheel FSC
1974....Dorothy Hamill, SC of New York
1975....Dorothy Hamill, SC of New York
1976....Dorothy Hamill, SC of New York
1977....Linda Fratianne, Los Angeles FSC
1978....Linda Fratianne, Los Angeles FSC
1979....Linda Fratianne, Los Angeles FSC
1980....Linda Fratianne, Los Angeles FSC
1981....Elaine Zayak, SC of New York
1982....Rosalynn Sumners, Seattle SC
1983....Rosalynn Sumners, Seattle SC
1984....Rosalynn Sumners, Seattle SC
1985....Tiffany Chin, San Diego FSC
1986....Debi Thomas, Los Angeles FSC
1987....Jill Trenary, Broadmoor SC
1988....Debi Thomas, Los Angeles FSC
1989....Jill Trenary, Broadmoor SC
1990....Jill Trenary, Broadmoor SC
1991....Tonya Harding, Carousel FSC
1992....Kristi Yamaguchi, St Moritz ISC
1993....Nancy Kerrigan, Colonial FSC
1994....Tonya Harding, Portland FSC
1995....Nicole Bobek, Los Angeles FSC
1996....Michelle Kwan, Los Angeles FSC
1997....Tara Lipinski, Detroit SC
1998....Michelle Kwan, Los Angeles FSC
1999....Michelle Kwan, Los Angeles FSC
2000....Michelle Kwan, Los Angeles FSC
2001....Michelle Kwan, Los Angeles FSC
2002....Michelle Kwan, Los Angeles FSC
2003....Michelle Kwan, Los Angeles FSC
2004....Michelle Kwan, Los Angeles FSC
2005....Michelle Kwan, Los Angeles FSC
2006....Sasha Cohen, Orange County FSC
2007....Kimmie Meissner, Univ. of Delaware FSC
2008....Mirai Nagasu, Pasadena FSC

Men

1914 Norman M. Scott, WC of Montreal
1915–17 NO COMPETITION
1918....Nathaniel W. Niles, SC of Boston
1919 NO COMPETITION
1920....Sherwin C. Badger, SC of Boston
1921....Sherwin C. Badger, SC of Boston
1922....Sherwin C. Badger, SC of Boston
1923....Sherwin C. Badger, SC of Boston
1924....Sherwin C. Badger, SC of Boston
1925....Nathaniel W. Niles, SC of Boston
1926 Chris I. Christenson, Twin City FSC
1927....Nathaniel W. Niles, SC of Boston
1928....Roger F. Turner, SC of Boston
1929....Roger F. Turner, SC of Boston
1930....Roger F. Turner, SC of Boston
1931....Roger F. Turner, SC of Boston
1932....Roger F. Turner, SC of Boston
1933....Roger F. Turner, SC of Boston
1934....Roger F. Turner, SC of Boston
1935....Robin H. Lee, SC of New York
1936....Robin H. Lee, SC of New York
1937....Robin H. Lee, SC of New York
1938....Robin H. Lee, Chicago FSC
1939....Robin H. Lee, St Paul FSC
1940....Eugene Turner, Los Angeles FSC
1941....Eugene Turner, Los Angeles FSC
1942....Robert Specht, Chicago FSC
1943 Arthur R. Vaughn Jr., Phila. SC & HS
1944–45 NO COMPETITION
1946 Dick Button, Philadelphia SC & HS
1947....Dick Button, Philadelphia SC & HS
1948....Dick Button, Philadelphia SC & HS
1949....Dick Button, Philadelphia SC & HS
1950....Dick Button, SC of Boston
1951....Dick Button, SC of Boston
1952....Dick Button, SC of Boston
1953....Hayes Alan Jenkins, Cleveland SC
1954....Hayes Alan Jenkins, Broadmoor SC
1955....Hayes Alan Jenkins, Broadmoor SC
1956....Hayes Alan Jenkins, Broadmoor SC

CHAMPIONS OF THE UNITED STATES (Cont.)

Men (Cont.)

1957....David Jenkins, Broadmoor SC
1958....David Jenkins, Broadmoor SC
1959....David Jenkins, Broadmoor SC
1960....David Jenkins, Broadmoor SC
1961....Bradley R. Lord, SC of Boston
1962....Monty Hoyt, Broadmoor SC
1963....Thomas Litz, Hershey FSC
1964....Scott Ethan Allen, SC of New York
1965....Gary C. Visconti, Detroit SC
1966....Scott Ethan Allen, SC of New York
1967....Gary C. Visconti, Detroit SC
1968....Tim Wood, Detroit SC
1969....Tim Wood, Detroit SC
1970....Tim Wood, City of Colorado Springs
1971....John Misha Petkevich, Great Falls FSC
1972....Kenneth Shelley, Arctic Blades FSC
1973....Gordon McKellen Jr., SC of Lake Placid
1974....Gordon McKellen Jr., SC of Lake Placid
1975....Gordon McKellen Jr., SC of Lake Placid
1976....Terry Kubicka, Arctic Blades FSC
1977....Charles Tickner, Denver FSC
1978....Charles Tickner, Denver FSC
1979....Charles Tickner, Denver FSC
1980....Charles Tickner, Denver FSC
1981....Scott Hamilton, Philadelphia SC & HS
1982....Scott Hamilton, Philadelphia SC & HS
1983....Scott Hamilton, Philadelphia SC & HS
1984....Scott Hamilton, Philadelphia SC & HS
1985....Brian Boitano, Peninsula FSC
1986....Brian Boitano, Peninsula FSC
1987....Brian Boitano, Peninsula FSC
1988....Brian Boitano, Peninsula FSC
1989....Christopher Bowman, Los Angeles FSC
1990....Todd Eldredge, Los Angeles FSC
1991....Todd Eldredge, Los Angeles FSC
1992....Christopher Bowman, Los Angeles FSC
1993....Scott Davis, Broadmoor SC
1994....Scott Davis, Broadmoor SC
1995....Todd Eldredge, Detroit SC
1996....Rudy Galindo, St Moritz ISC
1997....Todd Eldredge, Detroit SC
1998....Todd Eldredge, Detroit SC
1999....Michael Weiss, Washington FSC
2000....Michael Weiss, Washington FSC
2001....Timothy Goebel, Winterhurst FSC
2002....Todd Eldredge, Los Angeles FSC
2003....Michael Weiss, Washington FSC
2004....Johnny Weir, SC of New York
2005....Johnny Weir, SC of New York
2006....Johnny Weir, SC of New York
2007....Evan Lysacek, DuPage FSC
2008....Evan Lysacek, DuPage FSC

Pairs

1914 Jeanne Chevalier, Norman M. Scott, WC of Montreal
1915–17 NO COMPETITION
1918 Theresa Weld, Nathaniel W. Niles, SC of Boston
1919 No competition
1920 Theresa Weld, Nathaniel W. Niles, SC of Boston
1921 Theresa Weld Blanchard, Nathaniel W. Niles, SC of Boston
1922 Theresa Weld Blanchard, Nathaniel W. Niles, SC of Boston
1923 Theresa Weld Blanchard, Nathaniel W. Niles, SC of Boston
1924 Theresa Weld Blanchard, Nathaniel W. Niles, SC of Boston
1925 Theresa Weld Blanchard, Nathaniel W. Niles, SC of Boston
1926 Theresa Weld Blanchard, Nathaniel W. Niles, SC of Boston
1927 Theresa Weld Blanchard, Nathaniel W. Niles, SC of Boston
1928 Maribel Y. Vinson, Thornton L. Coolidge, SC of Boston
1929 Maribel Y. Vinson, Thornton L. Coolidge, SC of Boston
1930 Beatrix Loughran, Sherwin C. Badger, SC of New York
1931 Beatrix Loughran, Sherwin C. Badger, SC of New York
1932 Beatrix Loughran, Sherwin C. Badger, SC of New York
1933 Maribel Y. Vinson, George E. B. Hill, SC of SC of Boston
1936 Maribel Y. Vinson, George E. B. Hill, SC of Boston
1937 Maribel Y. Vinson, George E. B. Hill, SC of Boston
1938 Joan Tozzer, M. Bernard Fox, SC of Boston
1939 Joan Tozzer, M. Bernard Fox, SC of Boston
1940 Joan Tozzer, M. Bernard Fox, SC of Boston
1941 Donna Atwood, Eugene Turner, Mercury FSC/Los Angeles FSC
1942 Doris Schubach, Walter Noffke, Springfield Ice Birds
1943 Doris Schubach, Walter Noffke, Springfield Ice Birds
1944 Doris Schubach, Walter Noffke, Springfield Ice Birds
1945 Donna Jeanne Pospisil, Jean-Pierre Brunet, SC of New York
1946 Donna Jeanne Pospisil, Jean-Pierre Brunet, SC of New York
1947 Yvonne Claire Sherman, Robert J. Swenning, SC of New York
1948 Karol Kennedy, Peter Kennedy, Seattle SC
1949 Karol Kennedy, Peter Kennedy, Seattle SC
1950 Karol Kennedy, Peter Kennedy, Broadmoor SC
1951 Karol Kennedy, Peter Kennedy, Broadmoor SC
1952 Karol Kennedy, Peter Kennedy, Broadmoor SC
1953 Carole Ann Ormaca, Robin Greiner, SC of Fresno
1954 Carole Ann Ormaca, Robin Greiner, SC of Fresno
1955 Carole Ann Ormaca, Robin Greiner, St Moritz ISC
1956 Carole Ann Ormaca, Robin Greiner, St Moritz ISC
1957 Nancy Rouillard Ludington, Ronald Ludington, Commonwealth FSC/SC of Boston
1958 Nancy Rouillard Ludington, Ronald Ludington, Commonwealth FSC/SC of Boston
1959 Nancy Rouillard Ludington, Ronald Ludington, Commonwealth FSC
1960 Nancy Rouillard Ludington, Ronald Ludington, Commonwealth FSC
1961 Maribel Y. Owen, Dudley S. Richards, SC of Boston
1962 Dorothyann Nelson, Pieter Kollen, Village of Lake Placid
1963 Judianne Fotheringill, Jerry J. Fotheringill, Broadmoor SC
1964 Judianne Fotheringill, Jerry J. Fotheringill, Broadmoor SC
1965 Vivian Joseph, Ronald Joseph, Chicago FSC
1966 Cynthia Kauffman, Ronald Kauffman, Seattle SC
1967 Cynthia Kauffman, Ronald Kauffman, Seattle SC
1968 Cynthia Kauffman, Ronald Kauffman, Seattle SC
1969 Cynthia Kauffman, Ronald Kauffman, Seattle SC
1970 Jo Jo Starbuck, Kenneth Shelley, Arctic Blades FSC
1971 Jo Jo Starbuck, Kenneth Shelley, Arctic Blades FSC
1972 Jo Jo Starbuck, Kenneth Shelley, Arctic Blades FSC
1973 Melissa Militano, Mark Militano, SC of New York

CHAMPIONS OF THE UNITED STATES (CONT.)

Pairs (Cont.)

1974 Melissa Militano, Johnny Johns, SC of New York/Detroit SC
1975 Melissa Militano, Johnny Johns, SC of New York/Detroit SC
1976 Tai Babilonia, Randy Gardner, LA FSC
1977 Tai Babilonia, Randy Gardner, LA FSC
1978 Tai Babilonia, Randy Gardner, Los Angeles FSC/ Santa Monica FSC
1979 Tai Babilonia, Randy Gardner, Los Angeles FSC/ Santa Monica FSC
1980 Tai Babilonia, Randy Gardner, Los Angeles FSC/ Santa Monica FSC
1981 Caitlin Carruthers, Peter Carruthers, SC of Wilmington
1982 Caitlin Carruthers, Peter Carruthers, SC of Wilmington
1983 Caitlin Carruthers, Peter Carruthers, SC of Wilmington
1984 Caitlin Carruthers, Peter Carruthers, SC of Wilmington
1985 Jill Watson, Peter Oppegard, LA FSC
1986 Gillian Wachsman, Todd Waggoner, SC of Wilmington
1987 Jill Watson, Peter Oppegard, LA FSC
1988 Jill Watson, Peter Oppegard, LA FSC
1989 Kristi Yamaguchi, Rudy Galindo, St Mortiz ISC
1990 Kristi Yamaguchi, Rudy Galindo, St Mortiz ISC
1991 Natasha Kuchiki, Todd Sand, LA FSC
1992 Calla Urbanski, Rocky Marval, U of Delaware FSC/ SC of New York
1993 Calla Urbanski, Rocky Marval, U of Delaware FSC/ SC of New York
1994 Jenni Meno, Todd Sand, Winterhurst FSC/ Los Angeles FSC
1995 Jenni Meno, Todd Sand, Winterhurst FSC/ Los Angeles FSC
1996 Jenni Meno, Todd Sand, Winterhurst FSC/ Los Angeles FSC
1997 Kyoko Ina, Jason Dungjen, SC of New York
1998 Kyoko Ina, Jason Dungjen, SC of New York
1999 Danielle Hartsell, Steve Hartsell, Detroit SC
2000 Kyoko Ina, John Zimmerman, SC of New York/Birmingham FSC
2001 Kyoko Ina, John Zimmerman, SC of New York/Birmingham FSC
2002 Kyoko Ina, John Zimmerman, SC of New York/Birmingham FSC
2003 Tiffany Scott, Philip Dulebohn, Colonial FSC/ Univ of Delaware FSC
2004 Rena Inoue, John Baldwin, All Year FSC
2005 Kathryn Orscher, Garrett Lucash, Charter Oak FSC
2006 Rena Inoue, John Baldwin, All Year FSC
2007 Brooke Castile, Benjamin Okolski, Arctic FSC
2008 Keauna McLaughlin, Rockne Brubaker Los Angeles FSC/Broadmoor SC

Dance

1914 Waltz: Theresa Weld, Nathaniel W. Niles, SC of Boston
1915–19 NO COMPETITION
1920 Waltz: Theresa Weld, Nathaniel W. Niles, SC of Boston
Fourteenstep: Gertrude Cheever Porter, Irving Brokaw, New York SC
1921 Waltz and Fourteenstep: Theresa Weld Blanchard, Nathaniel W. Niles, SC of Boston
1922 Waltz: Beatrix Loughran, Edward M. Howland, New York SC/ SC of Boston
Fourteenstep: Theresa Weld Blanchard, Nathaniel W. Niles, SC of Boston
1923 Waltz: Mr. & Mrs. Henry W. Howe, New York SC
Fourteenstep: Sydney Goode, James B. Greene, New York SC
1924 Waltz: Rosaline Dunn, Frederick Gabel, New York SC
Fourteenstep: Sydney Goode, James B. Greene, New York SC
1925 Waltz and Fourteenstep: Virginia Slattery, Ferrier T. Martin, New York SC
1926 Waltz: Rosaline Dunn, Joseph K. Savage, New York SC
Fourteenstep: Sydney Goode, James B.Greene, New York SC
1927 Waltz and Fourteenstep: Rosaline Dunn, Joseph K. Savage, New York SC
1928 Waltz: Rosaline Dunn, Joseph K. Savage, New York SC
Fourteenstep: Ada Bauman Kelly, George T. Braakman, New York SC
1929 Waltz and Original Dance combined: Edith C. Secord, Joseph K. Savage, SC of New York
1930 Waltz: Edith C. Secord, Joseph K. Savage, SC of New York
Original: Clara Rotch Frothingham, George E. B. Hill, SC of Boston
1931 Waltz: Edith C. Secord, Ferrier T. Martin, SC of New York
Original: Theresa Weld Blanchard, Nathaniel W. Niles, SC of Boston
1932 Waltz: Edith C. Secord, Joseph K. Savage, SC of New York
Original: Clara Rotch Frothingham, George E. B. Hill, SC of Boston
1933 Waltz: Ilse Twaroschk, Frederick F. Fleishmann, Brooklyn FSC
Original: Suzanne Davis, Frederick Goodridge, SC of Boston
1934 Waltz: Nettie C. Prantel, Roy Hunt, SC of New York
Original: Suzanne Davis, Frederick Goodridge, SC of Boston
1935 Waltz: Nettie C. Prantel, Roy Hunt, SC of New York
1936 Marjorie Parker, Joseph K. Savage, SC of New York
1937 Nettie C. Prantel, Harold Hartshorne, SC of New York
1938 Nettie C. Prantel, Harold Hartshorne, SC of New York
1939 Sandy Macdonald, Harold Hartshorne,SC of New York
1940 Sandy Macdonald, Harold Hartshorne, SC of New York
1941 Sandy Macdonald, Harold Hartshorne, SCNY
1942 Edith B. Whetstone, Alfred N. Richards, Jr, Philadelphia SC & HS
1943 Marcella May, James Lochead Jr., Skate & Ski Club
1944 Marcella May, James Lochead Jr., Skate & Ski Club
1945 Kathe Mehl Williams, Robert J. Swenning,SC of New York
1946 Anne Davies, Carleton C. Hoffner Jr., Washington FSC
1947 Lois Waring, Walter H. Bainbridge Jr., Baltimore FSC/Washigton FSC
1948 Lois Waring, Walter H. Bainbridge Jr.,Baltimore FSC/Washington FSC
1949 Lois Waring, Walter H. Bainbridge Jr.,Baltimore FSC/Washington FSC
1950 Lois Waring, Michael McGean, Baltimore FSC
1951 Carmel Bodel, Edward L. Bodel, St. Moritz ISC
1952 Lois Waring, Michael McGean, Baltimore FSC
1953 Carol Ann Peters, Daniel C. Ryan, Washington FSC
1954 Carmel Bodel, Edward L. Bodel, St Moritz ISC
1955 Carmel Bodel, Edward L. Bodel, St Moritz ISC

CHAMPIONS OF THE UNITED STATES (CONT.)

Dance (Cont.)

1956 Joan Zamboni, Roland Junso, Arctic Blades FSC
1957 Sharon McKenzie, Bert Wright, Los Angeles FSC
1958 Andree Anderson, Donald Jacoby, Buffalo SC
1959 Andree Anderson Jacoby, Donald Jacoby, Buffalo SC
1960 Margie Ackles, Charles W. Phillips Jr., Los Angeles FSC/Arctic Blades FSC
1961 Diane C. Sherbloom, Larry Pierce, Los Angeles FSC/ WC of Indianapolis
1962 Yvonne N. Littlefield, Peter F. Betts, Arctic Blades FSC/ Paramount, CA
1963 Sally Schantz, Stanley Urban, SC of Boston/Buffalo SC
1964 Darlene Streich, Charles D. Fetter Jr., WC of Indianapolis
1965 Kristin Fortune, Dennis Sveum, Los Angeles FSC
1966 Kristin Fortune, Dennis Sveum, Los Angeles FSC
1967 Lorna Dyer, John Carrell, Broadmoor SC
1968 Judy Schwomeyer, James Sladky, WC of Indianapolis/Genesee FSC
1969 Judy Schwomeyer, James Sladky, WC of Indianapolis/Genesee FSC
1970 Judy Schwomeyer, James Sladky, WC of Indianapolis/Genesee FSC
1971 Judy Schwomeyer, James Sladky, WC of Indianapolis/Genesee FSC
1972 Judy Schwomeyer, James Sladky, WC of Indianapolis/Genesee FSC
1973 Mary Karen Campbell, Johnny Johns, Lansing SC/Detroit SC
1974 Colleen O'Connor, Jim Millns, Broadmoor SC/ City of Colorado Springs
1975 Colleen O'Connor, Jim Millns, Broadmoor SC
1976 Colleen O'Connor, Jim Millns, Broadmoor SC
1977 Judy Genovesi, Kent Weigle, SC of Hartford/Charter Oak FSC
1978 Stacey Smith, John Summers, SC of Wilmington
1979 Stacey Smith, John Summers, SC of Wilmington
1980 Stacey Smith, John Summers, SC of Wilmington
1981 Judy Blumberg, Michael Seibert, Broadmoor SC/ISC of Indianapolis
1982 Judy Blumberg, Michael Seibert, Broadmoor SC/ISC of Indianapolis
1983 Judy Blumberg, Michael Seibert, Pittsburgh FSC
1984 Judy Blumberg, Michael Seibert, Pittsburgh FSC
1985 Judy Blumberg, Michael Seibert, Pittsburgh FSC
1986 Renee Roca, Donald Adair, Genesee FSC/Academy FSC
1987 Suzanne Semanick, Scott Gregory, U of Delaware SC
1988 Suzanne Semanick, Scott Gregory, U of Delaware SC
1989 Susan Wynne, Joseph Druar, Broadmoor SC/Seattle SC
1990 Susan Wynne, Joseph Druar, Broadmoor SC/Seattle SC
1991 Elizabeth Punsalan, Jerod Swallow, Broadmoor SC
1992 April Sargent, Russ Witherby, Ogdensburg FSC/ U of Delaware FSC
1993 Renee Roca, Gorsha Sur, Broadmoor SC
1994 Elizabeth Punsalan, Jerod Swallow, Broadmoor SC/Detroit SC
1995 Renee Roca, Gorsha Sur, Broadmoor SC
1996 Elizabeth Punsalan, Jerod Swallow, Detroit SC
1997 Elizabeth Punsalan, Jerod Swallow, Detroit SC
1998 Elizabeth Punsalan, Jerod Swallow, Detroit SC
1999 Naomi Lang, Peter Tchernyshev, Detroit SC
2000 Naomi Lang, Peter Tchernyshev, Detroit SC
2001 Naomi Lang, Peter Tchernyshev, Detroit SC
2002 Naomi Lang, Peter Tchernyshev, American Academy FSC
2003 Naomi Lang, Peter Tchernyshev, American Academy FSC
2004 Tanith Belbin, Ben Agosto, Detroit SC
2005 Tanith Belbin, Ben Agosto, Detroit SC
2006 Tanith Belbin, Ben Agosto, Arctic FSC
2007 Tanith Belbin, Ben Agosto, Arctic FSC
2008 Tanith Belbin, Ben Agosto, Arctic FSC

Gymnastics

World Champions — Men

All-Around

Year	Champion, Nation
1903	Joseph Martinez, France
1905	Marcel Lalue, France
1907	Joseph Czada, Czechoslovakia
1909	Marcos Torres, France
1911	Ferdinand Steiner, Czechoslovakia
1913	Marcos Torres, France
1922	Peter Sumi, Yugoslavia F. Pechacek, Czechoslovakia
1926	Peter Sumi, Yugoslavia
1930	Josip Primozic, Yugoslavia
1934	Eugene Mack, Switzerland
1938	Jan Gajdos, Czechoslovakia
1950	Walter Lehmann, Switzerland
1954	Valentin Mouratov, USSR Victor Chukarin, USSR
1958	Boris Shaklin, USSR
1962	Yuri Titov, USSR
1966	Mikhail Voronin, USSR
1970	Eizo Kenmotsu, Japan
1974	Shigeru Kasamatsu, Japan
1978	Nikolai Andrianov, USSR

All-Around (Cont.)

Year	Champion, Nation
1979	Alexander Ditiatin, USSR
1981	Yuri Korolev, USSR
1983	Dimitri Bilozertchev, USSR
1985	Yuri Korolev, USSR
1987	Dimitri Bilozertchev, USSR
1989	Igor Korobchinsky, USSR
1991	Grigori Misutin, CIS
1993	Vitaly Scherbo, Belarus
1994	Ivan Ivankov, Belarus
1995	Li Xiaoshuang, China
1997	Ivan Ivankov, Belarus
1999	Nicolae Krukov, Russia
2001	Feng Jing, China
2003	Paul Hamm, United States
2005	Hiroyuki Tomita, Japan
2007	Yang Wei, China

Pommel Horse

Year	Champion, Nation
1930	Josip Primozic, Yugoslavia
1934	Eugene Mack, Switzerland

Pommel Horse (Cont.)

Year	Champion, Nation
1938	Michael Reusch, Switzerland
1950	Josef Stalder, Switzerland
1954	Grant Chaguinjan, USSR
1958	Boris Shaklin, USSR
1962	Miroslav Cerar, Yugoslavia
1966	Miroslav Cerar, Yugoslavia
1970	Miroslav Cerar, Yugoslavia
1974	Zoltan Magyar, Hungary
1978	Zoltan Magyar, Hungary
1979	Zoltan Magyar, Hungary
1981	Michael Mikolai, East Germany
1983	Dmitri Bilozertchev, USSR
1985	Valentin Moguilny, USSR
1987	Zsolt Borkai, Hungary Dmitri Bilozertchev, USSR
1989	Valentin Moguilny, USSR
1991	Valeri Belenki, USSR
1992	Pae Gil Su, North Korea Vitaly Scherbo, CIS Li Jing, China

Gymnastics

World Champions — Men

Pommel Horse *(Cont.)*

Year	Champion, Nation
1993	Pae Gil Su, North Korea
1994	Marius Urzica, Romania
1995	Li Donghua, Switzerland
1996	Pae Gil Su, North Korea
1997	Valeri Belenki, Germany
1999	Alexei Nemov, Russia
2001	Marius Urzica, Romania
2003	Teng Haibin, China Takehiro Kashima, Japan
2005	Qin Xiao, China
2007	Qin Xiao, China

Floor Exercise

Year	Champion, Nation
1930	Josip Primozic, Yugoslavia
1934	Georges Miesz, Switzerland
1938	Jan Gajdos, Czechoslovakia
1950	Josef Stalder, Switzerland
1954	Valentin Mouratov, USSR Masao Takemoto, Japan
1958	Masao Takemoto, Japan
1962	Nobuyuki Aihara, Japan Yukio Endo, Japan
1966	Akinori Nakayama, Japan
1970	Akinori Nakayama, Japan
1974	Shigeru Kasamatsu, Japan
1978	Kurt Thomas, United States
1979	Kurt Thomas, United States Roland Brucker, East Germ.
1981	Yuri Korolev, USSR, Li Yuejui, China
1983	Tong Fei, China
1985	Tong Fei, China
1987	Lou Yun, China
1989	Igor Korobchinsky, USSR
1991	Igor Korobchinsky, USSR
1993	Grigori Misutin, Ukraine
1994	Vitaly Scherbo, Belarus
1995	Vitaly Scherbo, Belarus
1996	Vitaly Scherbo, Belarus
1997	Alexei Nemov, Russia
1999	Alexei Nemov, Russia
2001	Marian Dragulescu, Romania
2003	Paul Hamm, United States Jordan Jovtchev, Bulgaria
2005	Diego Hypolito, Brazil
2007	Zou Kai, China

Rings

Year	Champion, Nation
1930	Emanuel Loffler, Czechoslovakia
1934	Alois Hudec, Czechoslovakia
1938	Alois Hudec, Czechoslovakia
1950	Walter Lehmann, Switzerland
1954	Albert Azarian, USSR
1958	Albert Azarian, USSR
1962	Yuri Titov, USSR
1966	Mikhail Voronin, USSR
1970	Akinori Nakayama, Japan
1974	N. Andrianov, USSR D. Grecu, Rom.
1978	Nikolai Andrianov, USSR
1979	Alexander Ditiatin, USSR
1981	Alexander Ditiatin, USSR
1983	Dimitri Bilozertchev, USSR
1985	Li Ning, China, Yuri Korolev, USSR

Rings *(Cont.)*

Year	Champion, Nation
1987	Yuri Korolev, USSR
1989	Andreas Aguilar, West Germ.
1991	Grigory Misutin, USSR
1992	Vitaly Scherbo, CIS
1993	Yuri Chechi, Italy
1994	Yuri Chechi, Italy
1995	Yuri Chechi, Italy
1996	Yuri Chechi, Italy
1997	Yuri Chechi, Italy
1999	Zhen Dong, China
2001	Jordan Jovtchev, Bulgaria
2003	Jordan Jovtchev, Bulgaria Dimosthenis Tampakos, Greece
2005	Yuri Van Gelder, Netherlands
2007	Diego Hypolito, Brazil

Parallel Bars

Year	Champion, Nation
1930	Josip Primozic, Yugoslavia
1934	Eugene Mack, Switzerland
1938	Michael Reusch, Switzerland
1950	Hans Eugster, Switzerland
1954	Victor Chukarin, USSR
1958	Boris Shaklin, USSR
1962	Miroslav Cerar, Yugoslavia
1966	Sergei Diamidov, USSR
1970	Akinori Nakayama, Japan
1974	Eizo Kenmotsu, Japan
1978	Eizo Kenmotsu, Japan
1979	Bart Conner, United States
1981	Koji Gushiken, Japan Alexandr Ditiatin, USSR
1983	Vladimir Artemov, USSR Lou Yun, China
1985	Sylvio Kroll, East Germany Valentin Moguilny, USSR
1987	Vladimir Artemov, USSR
1989	Li Jing, China Vladimir Artemov, USSR
1991	Li Jing, China
1992	Li Jin, China, Alexei Voropaev, CIS
1993	Vitaly Scherbo, Belarus
1994	Huang Liping, China
1995	Vitaly Scherbo, Belarus
1996	Rustam Sharipov, Ukraine
1997	Zhang Jinjing, China
1999	Joo-Hyung Lee, South Korea
2001	Sean Townsend, U.S.
2003	Li Xiao-Peng, China
2005	Mitja Petkovsek, Slovenia
2007	Mitja Petkovsek, Slovenia

High Bar

Year	Champion, Nation
1930	Istvan Pelle, Hungary
1934	Ernst Winter, Germany
1938	Michael Reusch, Switzerland
1950	Paavo Aaltonen, Finland
1954	Valentin Mouratov, USSR
1958	Boris Shaklin, USSR
1962	Takashi Ono, Japan
1966	Akinori Nakayama, Japan
1970	Eizo Kenmotsu, Japan
1974	Eberhard Gienger, W Germany

High Bar *(Cont.)*

Year	Champion, Nation
1978	Shigeru Kasamatsu, Japan
1979	Kurt Thomas, United States
1981	Alexander Takchev, USSR
1983	Dimitri Bilozertchev, USSR
1985	Tong Fei, China
1987	Dimitri Bilozertchev, USSR
1989	Li Chunyang, China
1991	Li Chunyang, China R. Buechner, Germ
1992	Grigori Misutin, CIS
1993	Sergei Kharkov, Russia
1994	Vitaly Scherbo, Belarus
1995	Andreas Wecker, Germany
1996	Jesús Carballo, Spain
1997	Jani Tanskanen, Finland
1999	Jesus Carballo, Spain
2001	Vlasios Maras, Greece
2003	Takehiro Kashima, Japan
2005	Vlasios Maras, Greece
2007	Fabian Hambuechen, Germ.

Vault

Year	Champion, Nation
1934	Eugene Mack, Switzerland
1938	Eugene Mack, Switzerland
1950	Ernst Gebendinger, Switzerland
1954	Leo Sotornik, Czechoslovakia
1958	Yuri Titov, USSR
1962	Premysel Krbec, Czechoslovakia
1966	Haruhiro Yamashita, Japan
1970	Mitsuo Tsukahara, Japan
1974	Shigeru Kasamatsu, Japan
1978	Junichi Shimizu, Japan
1979	Alexander Ditiatin, USSR
1981	Ralf-Peter Hemmann, East Germany
1983	Arthur Akopian, USSR
1985	Yuri Korolev, USSR
1987	Lou Yun, China Sylvio Kroll, East Germany
1989	Joreg Behrend, East Germany
1991	Yoo Ok Youl, South Korea
1992	Yoo Ok Youl, South Korea
1993	Vitaly Scherbo, Belarus
1994	Vitaly Scherbo, Belarus
1995	G. Misutin, Ukraine A. Nemov, Russia
1996	Alexei Nemov, Russia
1997	Sergei Fedorchenko, Kazakhstan
1999	Li Xiao-Peng, China
2001	Marian Dragulescu, Romania
2003	Li Xiao-Peng, China
2005	Eichi Sekiguchi, Japan
2007	Leszek Blanik, Poland

World Champions — Women

All-Around

Year	Champion, Nation
1934	Vlasta Dekanova, Czechoslovakia
1938	Vlasta Dekanova, Czechoslovakia
1950	Helena Rakoczy, Poland
1954	Galina Roudiko, USSR
1958	Larissa Latynina, USSR
1962	Larissa Latynina, USSR
1966	Vera Caslavska, Czechoslovakia
1970	Ludmilla Tourischeva, USSR
1974	Ludmilla Tourischeva, USSR
1978	Elena Mukhina, USSR
1979	Nelli Kim, USSR
1981	Olga Bicherova, USSR
1983	Natalia Yurchenko, USSR
1985	Elena Shoushounova, USSR Oksana Omeliantchik, USSR
1987	Aurelia Dobre, Romania
1989	Svetlana Bouguinskaia, USSR
1991	Kim Zmeskal, United States
1993	Shannon Miller, United States
1994	Shannon Miller, United States
1995	Lilia Podkopayeva, Ukraine
1997	Svetlana Khorkina, Russia
1999	Maria Olaru, Romania
2001	Svetlana Khorkina, Russia
2003	Svetlana Khorkina, Russia
2005	Chellsie Memmel, United States
2007	Shawn Johnson, United States

Floor Exercise

Year	Champion, Nation
1950	Helena Rakoczy, Poland
1954	Tamara Manina, USSR
1958	Eva Bosakava, Czechoslovakia
1962	Larissa Latynina, USSR
1966	Natalia Kuchinskaya, USSR
1970	Ludmilla Tourischeva, USSR
1974	Ludmilla Tourischeva, USSR
1978	Nelli Kim, USSR Elena Mukhina, USSR
1979	Emilia Eberle, Romania
1981	Natalia Ilenko, USSR
1983	Ecaterina Szabo, Romania
1985	Oksana Omeliantchik, USSR
1987	Elena Shoushounova, USSR Daniela Silivas, Romania
1989	Svetlana Bouguinskaia, USSR Daniela Silivas, Romania
1991	Cristina Bontas, Romania Oksana Tchusovitina, USSR
1992	Kim Zmeskal, United States
1993	Shannon Miller, United States
1994	Dina Kochetkova, Russia

Floor Exercise (*Cont.*)

Year	Champion, Nation
1995	Gina Gogean, Romania
1996	Gina Gogean, Romania
1997	Gina Gogean, Romania
1999	Andreea Raducan, Romania
2001	Andreea Raducan, Romania
2003	Daiane Dos Santos, Brazil
2005	Nastia Liukin, United States
2007	Shawn Johnson, United States

Uneven Bars

Year	Champion, Nation
1950	Gertchen Kolar, Austria Anna Pettersson, Sweden
1954	Agnes Keleti, Hungary
1958	Larissa Latynina, USSR
1962	Irina Pervuschina, USSR
1966	Natalia Kuchinskaya, USSR
1970	Karin Janz, East Germany
1974	Annelore Zinke, East Germany
1978	Marcia Frederick, United States
1979	Ma Yanhong, China Maxi Gnauck, East Germany
1981	Maxi Gnauck, East Germany
1983	Maxi Gnauck, East Germany
1985	Gabriele Fahnrich, East Germany
1987	Daniela Silivas, Romania Doerte Thuemmler, East Germany
1989	Fan Di, China Daniela Silivas, Romania
1991	Gwang Suk Kim, North Korea
1992	Lavinia Milosivici, Romania
1993	Shannon Miller, United States
1994	Luo Li, China
1995	Svetlana Khorkina, Russia
1996	Svetlana Khorkina, Russia
1997	Svetlana Khorkina, Russia
1999	Svetlana Khorkina, Russia
2001	Svetlana Khorkina, Russia
2003	Chellsie Memmel, U.S. Hollie Vise, United States
2005	Nastia Liukin, United States
2007	Ksenia Semenov, Russia

Balance Beam

Year	Champion, Nation
1950	Helena Rakoczy, Poland
1954	Keiko Tanaka, Japan
1958	Larissa Latynina, USSR
1962	Eva Bosakova, Czech.
1966	Natalia Kuchinskaya, USSR
1970	Erika Zuchold, East Germany

Balance Beam (*Cont.*)

Year	Champion, Nation
1974	Ludmilla Tourischeva, USSR
1978	Nadia Comaneci, Romania
1979	Vera Cerna, Czechoslovakia
1981	Maxi Gnauck, East Germany
1983	Olga Mostepanova, USSR
1985	Daniela Silivas, Romania
1987	Aurelia Dobre, Romania
1989	Daniela Silivas, Romania
1991	Svetlana Boguinskaia, USSR
1992	Kim Zmeskal, United States
1993	Lavinia Milosovici, Romania
1994	Shannon Miller, United States
1995	Mo Huilan, China
1996	Dina Kochetkova, Russia
1997	Gina Gogean, Romania
1999	E. Zamolodchikova, Russia
2001	Andreea Raducan, Romania
2003	Fan Ye, China
2005	Nan Zhang, China
2007	Nastia Liukin, United States

Vault

Year	Champion, Nation
1950	Helena Rakoczy, Poland
1954	T. Manina, USSR Anna Pettersson, Sweden
1958	Larissa Latynina, USSR
1962	Vera Caslavska, Czech.
1966	Vera Caslavska, Czech.
1970	Erika Zuchold, East Germany
1974	Olga Korbut, USSR
1978	Nelli Kim, USSR
1979	Dumitrita Turner, Romania
1981	Maxi Gnauck, East Germany
1983	Boriana Stoyanova, Bulgaria
1985	Elena Shoushounova, USSR
1987	Elena Shoushounova, USSR
1989	Olesia Durnik, USSR
1991	Lavinia Milosovici, Romania
1992	Henrietta Onodi, Hungary
1993	Elena Piskun, Belarus
1994	Gina Gogean, Romania
1995	L. Podkopayeva, Ukraine Simona Amanar, Rom.
1996	Gina Gogean, Romania
1997	Simona Amanar, Romania
1999	Jie Ling, China
2001	Svetlana Khorkina, Russia
2003	Oksana Chusovitina, Uzbekistan
2005	Fei Cheng, China
2007	Fei Cheng, China

National Champions — Men

All-Around

Year	Champion
1963	Art Shurlock
1964	Rusty Mitchell
1965	Rusty Mitchell
1966	Rusty Mitchell
1967	Katsuzoki Kanzaki
1968	Yoshi Hayasaki
1969	Steve Hug
1970	Makoto Sakamoto, Mas Watanabe
1971	Yoshi Takei
1972	Yoshi Takei
1973	Marshall Avener
1974	John Crosby
1975	Tom Beach, Bart Conner
1976	Kurt Thomas
1977	Kurt Thomas
1978	Kurt Thomas
1979	Bart Conner
1980	Peter Vidmar
1981	Jim Hartung
1982	Peter Vidmar
1983	Mitch Gaylord
1984	Mitch Gaylord
1985	Brian Babcock
1986	Tim Daggett
1987	Scott Johnson

National Champions — Men (Cont.)

All-Around (Cont.)

Year	Champion
1988	Dan Hayden
1989	Tim Ryan
1990	John Roethlisberger
1991	Chris Waller
1992	John Roethlisberger
1993	John Roethlisberger
1994	Scott Keswick
1995	John Roethlisberger
1996	Blaine Wilson
1997	Blaine Wilson
1998	Blaine Wilson
1999	Blaine Wilson
2000	Blaine Wilson
2001	Sean Townsend
2002	Paul Hamm
2003	Paul Hamm
2004	Paul Hamm
2005	Todd Thornton
2006	Alexander Artemev
2007	David Durante
2008	David Sender

Floor Exercise

Year	Champion
1963	Tom Seward
1964	Rusty Mitchell
1965	Rusty Mitchell
1966	Dan Millman
1967	Katsuzoki Kanzaki Ron Aure
1968	Katsuzoki Kanzaki
1969	Steve Hug, Dave Thor
1970	Makoto Sakamoto
1971	John Crosby
1972	Yoshi Takei
1973	John Crosby
1974	John Crosby
1975	Peter Korman
1977	Ron Galimore
1978	Kurt Thomas
1979	Ron Galimore
1980	Ron Galimore
1981	Jim Hartung
1982	Jim Hartung
1983	Mitch Gaylord
1984	Peter Vidmar
1985	Mark Oates
1986	Robert Sundstrom
1987	John Sweeney
1988	Mark Oates Charles Lakes
1989	Mike Racanelli
1990	Bob Stelter
1991	Mike Racanelli
1992	Gregg Curtis
1993	Kerry Huston
1994	Jeremy Killen
1995	Daniel Stover
1996	Jay Thornton
1997	Jason Gatson
1998	Jason Gatson
1999	Jason Gatson
2000	Blaine Wilson
2001	Sean Townsend
2002	Morgan Hamm

Floor Exercise (Cont.)

Year	Champion
2003	Morgan Hamm
2004	Paul Hamm
2005	Guillermo Alvarez
2006	Jonathan Horton
2007	Paul Hamm
2008	Morgan Hamm

Pommel Horse

Year	Champion
1963	Larry Spiegel
1964	Sam Bailie
1965	Jack Ryan
1966	Jack Ryan
1967	Paul Mayer/Dave Doty
1968	Katsuoki Kanzaki
1969	Dave Thor
1970	Mas Watanabe
1971	Leonard Caling
1972	Sadao Hamada
1973	Marshall Avener
1974	Marshall Avener
1975	Bart Conner
1977	Gene Whelan
1978	Jim Hartung
1979	Bart Conner
1980	Jim Hartung
1981	Jim Hartung
1982	Jim Hartung
1983	Bart Conner
1984	Tim Daggett
1985	Phil Cahoy
1986	Phil Cahoy
1987	Tim Daggett
1988	Kevin Davis
1989	Kevin Davis
1990	Patrick Kirksey
1991	Chris Waller
1992	Chris Waller
1993	Chris Waller
1994	Mihai Begiu
1995	Mark Sohn
1996	Josh Stein
1997	John Roethlisberger
1998	John Roethlisberger
1999	John Roethlisberger
2000	John Roethlisberger
2001	Brett McClure
2002	Paul Hamm
2003	Paul Hamm
2004	Brett McClure
2005	Yewki Tomita
2006	Alexander Artemev
2007	Alexander Artemev
2008	Yewki Tomita

Rings

Year	Champion
1963	Art Shurlock
1964	Glen Gailis
1965	Glen Gailis
1966	Glen Gailis
1967	Fred Dennis, Don Hatch
1968	Yoshi Hayasaki
1969	Fred Dennis, Bob Emery
1970	Makoto Sakamoto

Rings (Cont.)

Year	Champion
1971	Yoshi Takei
1972	Yoshi Takei
1973	Jim Ivicek
1974	Tom Weeder
1975	Tom Beach
1977	Kurt Thomas
1978	Mike Silverstein
1979	Bart Conner
1980	Jim Hartung
1981	Jim Hartung
1982	Jim Hartung Peter Vidmar
1983	Mitch Gaylord
1984	Jim Hartung
1985	Dan Hayden
1986	Dan Hayden
1987	Scott Johnson
1988	Dan Hayden
1989	Scott Keswick
1990	Scott Keswick
1991	Scott Keswick
1992	Tim Ryan
1993	John Roethlisberger
1994	Scott Keswick
1995	Paul O'Neill
1996	Kip Simons
1997	Blaine Wilson
1998	Jeff Johnson
1999	Blaine Wilson
2000	Blaine Wilson
2001	Sean Townsend
2002	Blaine Wilson
2003	Blaine Wilson
2004	Raj Bhavsar
2005	Sean Golden
2006	Kevin Tan
2007	Kevin Tan
2008	Kevin Tan

Vault

Year	Champion
1963	Art Shurlock
1964	Gary Hery
1965	Brent Williams
1966	Dan Millman
1967	Jack Kenan, Sid Jensen
1968	Rich Scorza
1969	Dave Butzman
1970	Makoto Sakamoto
1971	Gary Morava
1972	Mike Kelley
1973	Gary Morava
1974	John Crosby
1975	Tom Beach
1977	Ron Galimore
1978	Jim Hartung
1979	Ron Galimore
1980	Ron Galimore
1981	Ron Galimore
1982	Jim Hartung/Jim Mikus
1983	Chris Reigel
1984	Chris Reigel
1985	Scott Johnson Mark Oates
1986	Scott Wilbanks
1987	John Sweeney

Vault (Cont.)

Year	Champion
1988	John Sweeney/Bill Paul
1989	Bill Roth
1990	Lance Ringnald
1991	Scott Keswick
1992	Trent Dimas
1993	Bill Roth
1994	Keith Wiley
1995	David St. Pierre
1996	Blaine Wilson
1997	Blaine Wilson
1998	Brent Klaus
1999	Guard Young
2000	Blaine Wilson
2001	Jason Furr
2002	Paul Hamm
2003	Raj Bhavsar
2004	David Sender
2005	Sean Golden
2006	David Sender
2007	Sean Golden
2008	David Sender

Parallel Bars

Year	Champion
1963	Tom Seward
1964	Rusty Mitchell
1965	Glen Gailis
1966	Ray Hadley
1967	Katsuzoki Kanzaki Tom Goldsborough
1968	Yoshi Hayasaki
1969	Steve Hug
1970	Makoto Sakamoto
1971	Brent Simmons
1972	Yoshi Takei
1973	Marshall Avener
1974	Jim Ivicek
1975	Bart Conner
1977	Kurt Thomas
1978	Bart Conner
1979	Bart Conner
1980	Phil Cahoy/Larry Gerard
1981	Bart Conner
1982	Peter Vidmar
1983	Mitch Gaylord
1984	Peter Vidmar, Mitch Gaylord, Tim Daggett
1985	Tim Daggett
1986	Tim Daggett
1987	Scott Johnson
1988	D. Hayden/K. Davis
1989	Conrad Voorsanger
1990	Trent Dimas
1991	Scott Keswick
1992	Jair Lynch
1993	Chainey Umphrey
1994	Steve McCain
1995	John Roethlisberger
1996	Jair Lynch
1997	Blaine Wilson
1998	Blaine Wilson
1999	Jason Gatson
2000	Trent Wells
2001	Sean Townsend
2002	Sean Townsend
2003	Jason Gatson

National Champions — Men (Cont.)

Parallel Bars (Cont.)

Year	Champion
2004	Alexander Artemev
2005	D.J. Bucher
2006	Alexander Artemev
2007	David Durante
2008	Justin Spring

High Bars

Year	Champion
1963	Art Shurlock
1964	Glen Gailis
1965	Rusty Mitchell
1966	Katsuzoki Kanzaki
1967	Katsuzoki Kanzaki
	Jerry Fontana
1968	Yoshi Hayasaki
1969	Rich Grisby
1970	Makoto Sakamoto
1971	Yoshi Takei
1972	Tom Lindner
1973	John Crosby
1974	Brent Simmons
1975	Tom Beach
1977	Kurt Thomas
1978	Kurt Thomas
1979	Yoichi Tomita
1980	Jim Hartung
1981	Bart Conner
1982	Mitch Gaylord
1983	Mario McCutcheon
1983	Mario McCutcheon
1984	Peter Vidmar
	Tim Daggett
	Mitch Gaylord
1985	Dan Hayden
1986	D. Hayden/D. Moriel
1987	David Moriel
1988	Dan Hayden
1989	Tim Ryan
1990	Trent Dimas
	Lance Ringnald
1991	Lance Ringnald
1992	Jair Lynch
1993	Steve McCain
1994	Scott Keswick
1995	John Roethlisberger
1996	Bill Roth
1997	Douglas Stibel
1998	Jason Gatson
1999	Jamie Natalie
2000	Trent Wells
	Jamie Natalie
2001	Daniel Diaz-Luong
2002	Blaine Wilson
2003	Paul Hamm
2004	Paul Hamm
2005	D.J. Bucher
2006	Chris Brooks
2007	Justin Spring
2008	Joseph Hagerty

National Champions — Women

All-Around

Year	Champion
1963	Donna Schanezer
1965	Gail Daley
1966	Donna Schanezer
1968	Linda Scott
1969	Joyce Tanac Schroeder
1970	Cathy Rigby
1971	Joan Moore Gnat
	Linda Metheny Mulvihill
1972	Joan Moore Gnat
	Cathy Rigby
1973	Joan Moore Gnat
1974	Joan Moore Gnat
1975	Tammy Manville
1976	Denise Cheshire
1977	Donna Turnbow
1978	Kathy Johnson
1979	Leslie Pyfer
1980	Julianne McNamara
1981	Tracee Talavera
1982	Tracee Talavera
1983	Dianne Durham
1984	Mary Lou Retton
1985	Sabrina Mar
1986	Jennifer Sey
1987	Kristie Phillips
1988	Phoebe Mills
1989	Brandy Johnson
1990	Kim Zmeskal
1991	Kim Zmeskal
1992	Kim Zmeskal
1993	Shannon Miller
1994	Dominique Dawes
1995	Dominique Moceanu
1996	Shannon Miller
1997	V. Adler/ K. Powell
1998	Kristen Maloney
1999	Kristen Maloney
2000	Elise Ray
2001	Tasha Schwikert
2002	Tasha Schwikert
2003	Courtney Kupets
2004	Courtney Kupets/Carly Patterson
2005	Nastia Liukin
2006	Nastia Liukin
2007	Shawn Johnson
2008	Shawn Johnson

Vault

Year	Champion
1963	Donna Schanezer
1965	Gail Daley
1966	Donna Schanezer
1968	Terry Spencer
1969	Joyce Tanac Schroeder
	Cleo Carver
1970	Cathy Rigby
1971	Joan Moore Gnat/Adele Gleaves
1972	Cindy Eastwood
1973	Roxanne Pierce Mancha
1974	Dianne Dunbar
1975	Kolleen Casey
1976	Debbie Wilcox
1977	Lisa Cawthron
1978	Rhonda Schwandt/Sharon Shapiro
1979	Christa Canary
1980	J. McNamara/B. Kline
1981	Kim Neal
1982	Yumi Mordre
1983	Dianne Durham
1984	Mary Lou Retton
1985	Yolanda Mavity
1986	Joyce Wilborn
1987	Rhonda Faehn
1988	Rhonda Faehn
1989	Brandy Johnson
1990	Brandy Johnson
1991	Kerri Strug
1992	Kerri Strug
1993	Dominique Dawes
1994	Dominique Dawes
1995	Shannon Miller
1996	Dominique Dawes
1997	Vanessa Atler
1998	Dominique Moceanu
1999	Vanessa Atler
2000	Kristen Maloney
2001	Mohini Bhardwaj
2002	Elizabeth Tricase
2003	Annia Hatch
2004	Liz Tricase
2005	Alicia Sacramone
2006	Alicia Sacramone
2007	Alicia Sacramone
2008	Alicia Sacramone

Uneven Bars

Year	Champion
1963	Donna Schanezer
1965	Irene Haworth
1966	Donna Schanezer
1968	Linda Scott
1969	Joyce Tanac Schroeder
	Lisa Nelson
1970	Roxanne Pierce Mancha
1971	Joan Moore Gnat
1972	Cathy Rigby
1973	Roxanne Pierce Mancha
1974	Diane Dunbar
1975	Leslie Wolfsberger
1976	Leslie Wolfsberger
1977	Donna Turnbow
1978	Marcia Frederick
1979	Marcia Frederick
1980	Marcia Frederick
1981	Julianne McNamara
1982	Marie Roethlisberger
1983	Julianne McNamara
1984	Julianne McNamara
1985	Sabrina Mar
1986	Marie Roethlisberger
1987	Melissa Marlowe
1988	Chelle Stack
1989	Chelle Stack
1990	Sandy Woolsey
1991	Elisabeth Crandall
1992	Dominique Dawes
1993	Shannon Miller
1994	Dominique Dawes
1995	Dominique Dawes
1996	Dominique Dawes
1997	Kristy Powell
1998	Elise Ray

Gymnastics (Cont.)

National Champions — Women

Uneven Bars (Cont.)

Year	Champion
1999	Jamie Dantzscher Jennie Thompson
2000	Elise Ray
2001	Katie Heenan
2002	Tasha Schwikert
2003	Katie Heenan
2004	Courtney Kupets
2005	Nastia Liukin
2006	Nastia Liukin
2007	Nastia Liukin
2008	Nastia Liukin

Balance Beam

Year	Champion
1963	Leissa Krol
1965	Gail Daley
1966	Irene Haworth Linda Scott
1968	Linda Scott
1969	Lonna Woodward
1970	Joyce Tanac Schroeder
1971	Linda Metheny Mulvihill
1972	Kim Chace
1973	Nancy Thies Marshall
1974	Joan Moore Gnat
1975	Kyle Gayner
1976	Carrie Englert
1977	Donna Turnbow
1978	Christa Canary
1979	Heidi Anderson
1980	Kelly Garrison-Steves
1981	Tracee Talavera
1982	Julianne McNamara
1983	Dianne Durham
1984	Pam Bileck Tracee Talavera
1986	Angie Denkins

Balance Beam (Cont.)

Year	Champion
1987	Kristie Phillips
1985	Kelly Garrison-Steves
1988	Kelly Garrison-Steves
1989	Brandy Johnson
1990	Betty Okino
1991	Shannon Miller
1992	Kerri Strug Kim Zmeskal
1993	Dominique Dawes
1994	Dominique Dawes
1995	Doni Thompson Monica Flammer
1996	Dominique Dawes
1997	Kendall Beck
1998	Dominique Moceanu
1999	Vanessa Atler
2000	Alyssa Beckerman Amy Chow
2001	Tasha Schwikert
2002	Tasha Schwikert
2003	Hollie Vise
2004	Courtney Kupets
2005	Nastia Liukin
2006	Nastia Liukin
2007	Shawn Johnson
2008	Nastia Liukin

Floor Exercise

Year	Champion
1963	Donna Schanezer
1965	Gail Daley
1966	Donna Schanezer
1968	Linda Scott
1970	Cathy Rigby
1971	Joan Moore Gnat Linda Metheny Mulvihill
1972	Joan Moore Gnat

Floor Exercise (Cont.)

Year	Champion
1973	Joan Moore Gnat
1974	Joan Moore Gnat
1975	Kathy Howard
1976	Carrie Englert
1977	Kathy Johnson
1978	Kathy Johnson
1979	Heidi Anderson
1980	Beth Kline
1981	Michelle Goodwin
1982	Amy Koopman
1983	Dianne Durham
1984	Mary Lou Retton
1985	Sabrina Mar
1986	Yolanda Mavity
1987	Kristie Phillips
1988	Phoebe Mills
1989	Brandy Johnson
1990	Brandy Johnson
1991	Kim Zmeskal Dominique Dawes
1992	Kim Zmeskal
1993	Shannon Miller
1994	Dominique Dawes
1995	Dominique Dawes
1996	Dominique Dawes
1997	Lindsay Wing
1998	Vanessa Atler
1999	Elise Ray
2000	Kristen Maloney
2001	Tabitha Yim
2002	Tasha Schwikert
2003	Ashley Postell
2004	Carly Patterson
2005	Alicia Sacramone
2006	Alicia Sacramone Randi Stageberg
2007	Shawn Johnson
2008	Shawn Johnson

Skiing

2008 World Cup Alpine Final Season Standings

Men

		Pts
OVERALL	Aksel Lund Svindal, Norway	1268
DOWNHILL	Didier Cuche, Swiss	652
SLALOM	Benjamin Raich, Austria	605
GIANT SLALOM	Aksel Lund Svindal, Norway	416
SUPER G	Bode Miller, USA	304
COMBINED	Aksel Lund Svindal, Norway	232

Women

		Pts
OVERALL	Nicole Hosp, Austria	1572
DOWNHILL	Renate Gotschl, Austria	705
SLALOM	Marlies Schild, Austria	760
GIANT SLALOM	Nicole Hosp, Austria	490
SUPER G	Renate Gotschl, Austria	540
COMBINED	Marlies Schild, Austria	220

World Cup Season Title Holders

Men – OVERALL

1967	Jean-Claude Killy, France
1968	Jean-Claude Killy, France
1969	Karl Schranz, Austria
1970	Karl Schranz, Austria
1971	Gustavo Thoeni, Italy
1972	Gustavo Thoeni, Italy
1973	Gustavo Thoeni, Italy
1974	Piero Gros, Italy
1975	Gustavo Thoeni, Italy
1976	Ingemar Stenmark, Sweden
1977	Ingemar Stenmark, Sweden
1978	Ingemar Stenmark, Sweden
1979	Peter Lüscher, Switzerland
1980	Andreas Wenzel, Liechtenstein

World Cup Season Title Holders

Men – OVERALL *(Cont.)*

1981 ....Phil Mahre, United States
1982 ....Phil Mahre, United States
1983 ....Phil Mahre, United States
1984 ....Pirmin Zurbriggen, Switzerland
1985 ....Marc Girardelli, Luxembourg
1986 ....Marc Girardelli, Luxembourg
1987 ....Pirmin Zurbriggen, Switzerland
1988 ....Pirmin Zurbriggen, Switzerland
1989 ....Marc Girardelli, Luxembourg
1990 ....Pirmin Zurbriggen, Switzerland
1991 ....Marc Girardelli, Luxembourg
1992 ....Paul Accola, Switzerland
1993 ....Marc Girardelli, Luxembourg
1994 ....Kjetil André Aamodt, Norway
1995 ....Alberto Tomba, Italy
1996 ....Lasse Kjus, Norway
1997 ....Luc Alphand, France
1998 ....Hermann Maier, Austria
1999 ....Lasse Kjus, Norway
2000 ....Hermann Maier, Austria
2001 ....Hermann Maier, Austria
2002 ....Stephan Eberharter, Austria
2003 ....Stephan Eberharter, Austria
2004 ....Hermann Maier, Austria
2005 ....Bode Miller, United States
2006 ....Benjamin Raich, Austria
2007 ....Akcel Lund Svindal, Norway
2008 ....Bode Miller, United States

Women – OVERALL

1967 ....Nancy Greene, Canada
1968 ....Nancy Greene, Canada
1969 ....Gertrud Gabl, Austria
1970 ....Michèle Jacot, France
1971 ....Annemarie Pröll, Austria
1972 ....Annemarie Pröll, Austria
1973 ....Annemarie Pröll, Austria
1974 ....Annemarie Moser-Proell, Austria
1975 ....Annemarie Moser-Proell, Austria
1976 ....Rosi Mitermaier, W Germany
1977 ....Lise-Marie Morerod, Switzerland
1978 ....Hanni Wenzel, Liechtenstein
1979 ....Annemarie Moser-Proell, Austria
1980 ....Hanni Wenzel, Liechtenstein
1981 ....Marie-Thérèse Nadig, Switzerland
1982 ....Erika Hess, Switzerland
1983 ....Tamara McKinney, United States
1984 ....Erika Hess, Switzerland
1985 ....Michela Figini, Switzerland
1986 ....Maria Walliser, Switzerland
1987 ....Maria Walliser, Switzerland
1988 ....Michela Figini, Switzerland
1989 ....Vreni Schneider, Switzerland
1990 ....Petra Kronberger, Austria
1991 ....Petra Kronberger, Austria
1992 ....Petra Kronberger, Austria
1993 ....Anita Wachter, Austria
1994 ....Vreni Schneider, Switzerland
1995 ....Vreni Schneider, Switzerland
1996 ....Katja Seizinger, Germany
1997 ....Pernilla Wiberg, Sweden
1998 ....Katja Seizinger, Germany
1999 ....Alexandra Meissnitzer, Austria
2000 ....Renate Goetschl, Austria
2001 ....Janica Kostelic, Croatia
2002 ....Michaela Dorfmeister, Austria
2003 ....Janica Kostelic, Austria
2004 ....Anja Paerson, Sweden
2005 ....Anja Paerson, Sweden
2006 ....Janica Kostelic, Croatia
2007 ....Nicole Hosp, Austria
2008 ....Lindsey Vonn, United States

Wrestling

United States National Champions

1983

FREESTYLE

105.5 ....Rich Salamone
114.5 ....Joe Gonzales
125.5 ....Joe Corso
136.5 ....Rich Dellagatta*
149.5 ....Bill Hugent
163 ....Lee Kemp
180.5 ....Chris Campbell
198 ....Pete Bush
220 ....Greg Gibson
Hvy ....Bruce Baumgartner
Team........Sunkist Kids

GRECO-ROMAN

105.5 .......T.J. Jones
114.5 ....Mark Fuller
125.5 ....Rob Hermann
136.5 ....Dan Mello
149.5 ....Jim Martinez
163 ....James Andre
180.5 ....Steve Goss
198 ....Steve Fraser*
220 ....Dennis Koslowski
Hvy ....No champion
Team........Minn. Wrestling Club

1984

FREESTYLE

105.5 ....Rich Salamone
114.5 ....Charlie Heard
125.5 ....Joe Corso
136.5 ....Rich Dellagatta*
149.5 ....Andre Metzger
163 ....Dave Schultz*
180.5 ....Mark Schultz
198 ....Steve Fraser
220 ....Harold Smith
Hvy ....Bruce Baumgartner
Team........Sunkist Kids

GRECO-ROMAN

105.5 .......T.J. Jones
114.5 ....Mark Fuller
136.5 ....Dan Mello
149.5 ....Jim Martinez*
163 ....John Matthews
180.5 ....Tom Press
198 ....Mike Houck
220 ....No champion
Hvy ....No champion
Team........Adirondack 3-Style, Wash.

1985

FREESTYLE

105.5 ....Tim Vanni
114.5 ....Jim Martin
125.5 ....Charlie Heard
136.5 ....Darryl Burley
149.5 ....Bill Nugent*
163 ....Kenny Monday
180.5 ....Mike Sheets
198 ....Mark Schultz
220 ....Greg Gibson
286 ....Bruce Baumgartner
Team........Sunkist Kids

GRECO-ROMAN

105.5 .......T.J. Jones
114.5 ....Mark Fuller
125.5 ....Eric Seward*
136.5 ....Buddy Lee
149.5 ....Jim Martinez
163 ....David Butler
180.5 ....Chris Catallo
198 ....Mike Houck
220 ....Greg Gibson
286 ....Dennis Koslowski
Team........U.S. Marine Corps

United States National Champions

1986

FREESTYLE

105.5 ....Rich Salamone
114.5 ....Joe Gonzales
125.5 ....Kevin Darkus
136.5 ....John Smith
149.5 ....Andre Metzger*
163 ....Dave Schultz
180.5 ....Mark Schultz
198 ....Jim Scherr
220 ....Dan Severn
286 ....Bruce Baumgartner
Team........Sunkist Kids (Div. I)
Hawkeye Wrestling Club (Div. II)

GRECO-ROMAN

105.5 ....Eric Wetzel
114.5 ....Shawn Sheldon
125.5 ....Anthony Amado
136.5 ....Frank Famiano
149.5 ....Jim Martinez
163 ....David Butler*
180.5 ....Darryl Gholar
198 ....Derrick Waldroup
220 ....Dennis Koslowski
286 ....Duane Koslowski
Team........U.S. Marine Corps (Div. I)
U.S. Navy (Div. II)

1987

FREESTYLE

105.5 ....Takashi Irie
114.5 ....Mitsuru Sato
125.5 ....Barry Davis
136.5 ....Takumi Adachi
149.5 ....Andre Metzger
163 ....Dave Schultz*
180.5 ....Mark Schultz
198 ....Jim Scherr
220 ....Bill Scherr
286 ....Bruce Baumgartner
Team........Sunkist Kids (Div. I)
Team Foxcatcher (Div. II)

GRECO-ROMAN

105.5 ....Eric Wetzel
114.5 ....Shawn Sheldon
125.5 ....Eric Seward
136.5 ....Frank Famiano
149.5 ....Jim Martinez
163 ....David Butler
180.5 ....Chris Catallo
198 ....Derrick Waldroup*
220 ....Dennis Koslowski
286 ....Duane Koslowski
Team........U.S. Marine Corp (Div. I)
U.S. Army (Div. II)

1988

FREESTYLE

105.5 ....Tim Vanni
114.5 ....Joe Gonzales
125.5 ....Kevin Darkus
136.5 ....John Smith*
149.5 ....Nate Carr
163 ....Kenny Monday
180.5 ....Dave Schultz
198 ....Melvin Douglas III
220 ....Bill Scherr
286 ....Bruce Baumgartner

1988 *(Cont.)*

FREESTYLE *(CONT)*

Team........Sunkist Kids (Div. I)
Team Foxcatcher (Div. II)

GRECO-ROMAN

105.5 .......T.J. Jones
114.5 ....Shawn Sheldon
125.5 ....Gogi Parseghian*
136.5 ....Dalen Wasmund
149.5 ....Craig Pollard
163 ....Tony Thomas
180.5 ....Darryl Gholar
198 ....Mike Carolan
220 ....Dennis Koslowski
286 ....Duane Koslowski
Team........U.S. Marine Corps (Div. I)
Sunkist Kids (Div. II)

1989

FREESTYLE

105.5 ....Tim Vanni
114.5 ....Zeke Jones
125.5 ....Brad Penrith
136.5 ....John Smith
149.5 ....Nate Carr
163 ....Rob Koll
180.5 ....Rico Chiapparelli
198 ....Jim Scherr*
220 ....Bill Scherr
286 ....Bruce Baumgartner
Team........Sunkist Kids (Div. I)
Team Foxcatcher (Div. II)

GRECO-ROMAN

105.5 ....Lew Dorrance
114.5 ....Mark Fuller
125.5 ....Gogi Parseghian
136.5 ....Isaac Anderson
149.5 ....Andy Seras*
163 ....David Butler
180.5 ....John Morgan
198 ....Michial Foy
220 ....Steve Lawson
286 ....Craig Pittman
Team........USMC (I) Jets USA (II)

1990

FREESTYLE

105.5 ....Rob Eiter
114.5 ....Zeke Jones
125,5 ....Joe Melchiore
136.5 ....John Smith
149.5 ....Nate Carr
163 ....Rob Koll
180.5 ....Royce Alger
198 ....Chris Campbell*
220 ....Bill Scherr
286 ....Bruce Baumgartner
Team........Sunkist Kids (Div. I)
Team Foxcatcher (Div. II)

GRECO-ROMAN

105.5 ....Lew Dorrance
114.5 ....Sam Henson
125.5 ....Mark Pustelnik
136.5 ....Isaac Anderson
149.5 ....Andy Seras
163 ....David Butler
180.5 ....Derrick Waldroup
198 ....Randy Couture*

1990 *(Cont.)*

GRECO-ROMAN *(CONT)*

220 ....Chris Tironi
286 ....Matt Ghaffari
Team........Jets USA (Div. I)
California Jets (Div. II)

1991

FREESTYLE

105.5 ....Tim Vanni
114.5 ....Zeke Jones
125.5 ....Brad Penrith
136.5 ....John Smith*
149.5 ....Townsend Saunders
163 ....Kenny Monday
180.5 ....Kevin Jackson
198 ....Chris Campbell
220 ....Mark Coleman
286 ....Bruce Baumgartner
Team........Sunkist Kids (Div. I)
Jets USA (Div. II)

GRECO-ROMAN

105.5 ....Eric Wetzel
114.5 ....Shawn Sheldon
125.5 ....Frank Famiano
136.5 ....Buddy Lee
149.5 ....Andy Seras
163 ....Gordy Morgan
180.5 ....John Morgan*
198 ....Michial Foy
220 ....Dennis Koslowski
286 ....Craig Pittman
Team........Jets USA (Div. I)
Sunkist Kids (Div. II)

1992

FREESTYLE

105.5 ....Rob Eiter
114.5 ....Jack Griffin
125.5 ....Kendall Cross*
136.5 ....John Fisher
149.5 ....Matt Demaray
163 ....Greg Elinsky
180.5 ....Royce Alger
198 ....Dan Chaid
220 ....Bill Scherr
286 ....Bruce Baumgartner
Team........Sunkist Kids (Div. I)
Team Foxcatcher (Div. II)

GRECO-ROMAN

105.5 ....Eric Wetzel
114.5 ....Mark Fuller
125.5 ....Dennis Hall
136.5 ....Buddy Lee*
149.5 ....Rodney Smith
163 ....Travis West
180.5 ....John Morgan
198 ....Michial Foy
220 ....Dennis Koslowski
286 ....Matt Ghaffari
Team........N.Y. Athletic Club (Div. I)
Sunkist Kids (Div. II)

1993

FREESTYLE

105.5 ....Rob Eiter
114.5 ....Zeke Jones
125.5 ....Brad Penrith
136.5 ....Tom Brands

*Outstanding wrestler.

United States National Champions

1993 (Cont.)

FREESTYLE

149.5 ....Matt Demaray
163 ....Dave Schultz*
180.5 ....Kevin Jackson
198 ....Melvin Douglas
220 ....Kirk Trost
286 ....Bruce Baumgartner
Team........Sunkist Kids (Div. I)
Team Foxcatcher (Div. II)

GRECO-ROMAN

105.5 ....Eric Wetzel
114.5 ....Shawn Sheldon
125.5 ....Dennis Hall*
136.5 ....Shon Lewis
149.5 ....Andy Seras
163 ....Gordy Morgan
180.5 ....Dan Henderson
198 ....Randy Couture
220 ....James Johnson
286 ....Matt Ghaffari
Team........N.Y. Athletic Club (Div. I)
Sunkist Kids (Div. II)

1994

FREESTYLE

105.5 ....Tim Vanni
114.5 ....Zeke Jones
125.5 ....Terry Brands
136.5 ....Tom Brands
149.5 ....Matt Demaray
163 ....Dave Schultz
180.5 ....Royce Alger
198 ....Melvin Douglas
220 ....Mark Kerr
286 ....Bruce Baumgartner*
Team........Sunkist Kids (Div. I)
Team Foxcatcher (Div. II)

GRECO-ROMAN

105.5 ....Isaac Ramaswamy
114.5 ....Shawn Sheldon
125.5 ....Dennis Hall
136.5 ....Shon Lewis
149.5 ....Andy Seras*
163 ....Gordy Morgan
180.5 ....Dan Henderson
198 ....Derrick Waldroup
220 ....James Johnson
286 ....Matt Ghaffari
Team........Armed Forces (Div. I)
N.Y. Athletic Club (Div. II)

1995

FREESTYLE

105.5 ....Tim Vanni
114.5 ....Zeke Jones
125.5 ....Terry Brands
136.5 ....Tom Brands
149.5 ....Matt Demaray
163 ....Dave Schultz
180.5 ....Royce Alger
198 ....Melvin Douglas
220 ....Mark Kerr
286 ....Bruce Baumgartner*
Team........Sunkist Kids (Div. I)
Team Foxcatcher (Div. II)

GRECO-ROMAN

105.5 ....Isaac Ramaswamy

1995 (Cont.)

GRECO-ROMAN (CONT)

114.5 ....Shawn Sheldon
125.5 ....Dennis Hall
136.5 ....Shon Lewis
149.5 ....Andy Seras*
163 ....Gordy Morgan
180.5 ....Dan Henderson
198 ....Derrick Waldroup
220 ....James Johnson
286 ....Matt Ghaffari
Team........Armed Forces (Div. I)
N.Y. Athletic Club (Div. II)

1996

FREESTYLE

105.5 ....Rob Eiter
114.5 ....Lou Rosselli
125.5 ....Kendall Cross*
136.5 ....Tom Brands
149.5 ....Matt Demaray
163 ....Dave Schultz
180.5 ....Kevin Jackson
198 ....Melvin Douglas
220 ....Kurt Angle
286 ....Bruce Baumgartner
Team........Sunkist Kids (Div. I)
Team Foxcatcher (Div. II)

GRECO-ROMAN

105.5 ....Isaac Ramaswamy
114.5 ....Shawn Sheldon
125.5 ....Dennis Hall*
136.5 ....Van Fronhofer
149.5 ....Heath Sims
163 ....Matt Lindland
180.5 ....Marty Morgan
198 ....Michial Foy
220 ....James Johnson
286 ....Rulon Gardner
Team........Armed Forces (Div. I)
Sunkist Kids (Div. II)

1997

FREESTYLE

110 ....Kanamti Soloman
119 ....Zeke Jones
127.75 .....Terry Brands
138.75 .....Carl Kolat
152 ....Lincoln McIlravy*
167.5 ....Dan St. John
187.25 .....Les Gutches
213.75 .....Melvin Douglas
275.5 ....Tom Erikson
Team........Sunkist Kids (Div. I)
N.Y. Athletic Club (Div. II)

GRECO-ROMAN

110 ....Mark Yanagihara
119 ....Broderick Lee
127.75 .....Dennis Hall
138.75 .....Kevin Bracken
152 ....Chris Saba
167.5 ....Miguel Spencer
187.25 .....Dan Henderson
213.75 .....Randy Couture*
275.5 ....Rulon Gardner
Team........Armed Forces (Div. I)
N.Y. Athletic Club (Div. II)

1998

FREESTYLE

119 ....Sam Henson
127.75 .....Tony Purler
138.75 .....Shawn Charles
152 ....Lincoln McIlravy
167.5 ....Steve Marianetti
187.25 .....Les Gutches*
213.75 .....Melvin Douglas
286 ....Tolly Thompson
Team........Sunkist Kids (Div. I)
N.Y. Athletic Club (Div. II)

GRECO-ROMAN

119 ....Shawn Sheldon
127.75 .....Dennis Hall
138.75 .....Shon Lewis
152 ....Chris Saba
167.5 ....Matt Lindland
187.25 .....Dan Niebuhr*
213.75 .....Jason Klohs
286 ....Matt Ghaffari
Team........Armed Forces (Div. I)
Sunkist Kids (Div. II)

1999

FREESTYLE

119 ....Lou Rosselli
127.75 .....Terry Brands
138.75 .....Cary Kolat
152 ....Lincoln McIlravy
167.5 ....Joe Williams
187.25 .....Les Gutches
213.75 .....Dominic Black
286 ....Stephen Neal*
Team........Sunkist Kids (Div. I)
N.Y. Athletic Club (Div. II)

1999 (Cont.)

GRECO-ROMAN

119 ....Steven Mays
127.75 .....Dennis Hall
138.75 .....Glen Nieradka
152 ....David Zuniga
167.5 ....Matt Lindland
187.25 .....Quincey Clark
213.75 .....Randy Couture
286 ....Dremiel Byers*
Team........Minnesota Storm (Div. I)
Sunkist Kids (Div. II)

2000

FREESTYLE

119 ....Sammie Henson
127.75 .....Keyy Boumans
138.75 .....Cary Kolat
152 ....Lincoln McIlravy
167.5 ....Brandon Slay*
187.25 .....Les Gutches
213.75 .....Melvin Douglas
286 ....Kerry McCoy
Team........Sunkist Kids (Div. I)
N.Y. Athletic Club (Div. II)

GRECO-ROMAN

119 ....Brandon Paulson
127.75 .....Dennis Hall
138.75 .....Kevin Bracken
152 ....Heath Sims
167.5 ....Matt Lindland
187.25 .....Quincey Clark*

United States National Champions

2000 (Cont.)

GRECO-ROMAN (CONT.)

213.75.....Jason Gleasman
286..........Rulon Gardner
Team........Armed Forces (Div. I)
Sunkist Kids (Div. II)

2001

FREESTYLE

119..........Eric Akin
127.75.....Eric Guerrero
138.75.....Bill Zadick
152..........Ramico Blackmon
167.5........Joe Williams
187.25.....Cael Sanderson*
213.75.....Dominic Black
286..........Kerry McCoy
Team........Sunkist Kids (Div. I)
New York A.C. (Div. II)

GRECO-ROMAN

119..........Jeff Cervone
127.75.....Dennis Hall
138.75.....Kevin Bracken
152..........Marcel Cooper
167.5........Keith Sieracki
187.25.....Matt Lindland*
213.75.....Garrett Lowney
286..........Rulon Gardner
Team........U.S. Army (Div. I)
Sunkist Kids (Div. II)

2002

FREESTYLE

121..........Teague Moore
132..........Eric Guerrero
145.5........Bill Zadick
163..........Joe Williams*
185..........Cael Sanderson
211.5........Tim Hartung
264.5........Kerry McCoy
Team........Sunkist Kids (Div. I)
New York A.C. (Div. II)

GRECO-ROMAN

121..........Brandon Paulson
132..........Glenn Nieradka*
145.5........Kevin Bracken
163..........Keith Sieracki
185..........Ethan Bosch
211.75.....Garrett Lowney
264.5........Dremiel Byers
Team........U.S. Army (Div. I)
New York A.C. (Div. II)

2003

FREESTYLE

121..........Stephen Abas
132..........Eric Guerrero*
145.5........Chris Bono
163..........Joe Williams
185..........Cael Sanderson
211.5........Daniel Cormier
264.5........Kerry McCoy
Team........Sunkist Kids (Div. I)
Gator WC (Div. II)

GRECO-ROMAN

121..........Brandon Paulson
132..........James Gruenwald*
145.5........Kevin Bracken

2003 (Cont.)

GRECO-ROMAN (CONT.)

163..........Keith Sieracki
185..........Brad Vering
211.5........Garrett Lowney
264.5........Dremiel Byers
Team........U.S. Army (Div. I)
Air Force (Div. II)

2004

FREESTYLE

121..........Stephen Abbas
132..........Eric Guerrero
145.5........Jamill Kelly
163..........Joe Williams
185..........Lee Fullhart*
211.5........Daniel Cormier
264.5........Kerry McCoy
Team........Sunkist Kids (Div. I)
Gator WC (Div. II)

GRECO-ROMAN

121..........Brandon Paulson
132..........James Gruenwald
145.5........Faruk Sahin
163..........Darryl Christian
185..........Brad Vering
211.5........Justin Ruiz
264.5........Dremiel Byers*
Team........New York A.C. (Div. I)
Air Force (Div. II)

2005

FREESTYLE

121..........Sam Henson
132..........Michael Lightner*
145.5........Chris Bono
163..........Joe Williams
185..........Mo Lawal
211.5........Daniel Cormier
264.5........Tolly Thompson
Team........Sunkist Kids (Div. I)
Gator WC (Div. II)

GRECO-ROMAN

121..........Sam Hazewinkel
132..........Joseph Warren
145.5........Harry Lester
163..........Darryl Christian
185..........Brad Vering
211.5........Justin Ruiz
264.5........Dremiel Byers*
Team........New York A.C. (Div.I)
Air Force (Div. II)

2006

FREESTYLE

121..........Henry Cejudo
132..........Zach Roberson
145.5........Chris Bono
163..........Donny Pritzlaff*
185..........Mo Lawal
211.5........Daniel Cormier
264.5........Tolly Thompson
Team........Sunkist Kids (Div. I)
Gator WC (Div. II)

GRECO-ROMAN

121..........Lindsey Durlacher
132..........Joseph Warren
145.5........Marcel Cooper

2006 (Cont.)

GRECO-ROMAN (CONT.)

163..........T.C. Dantzler
185..........Jacob Clark*
211.5........Justin Ruiz
264.5........Dremiel Byers
Team........U.S. Army (Div. I)
New York A.C. (Div. II)

2007

FREESTYLE

121..........Henry Cejudo
132..........Nate Gallick*
145.5........Chris Bono
163..........Joe Heskett
185..........Joe Williams
211.5........Daniel Cormier
264.5........Tommy Rowlands
Team........Sunkist Kids (Div. I)
Gator WC (Div. II)

GRECO-ROMAN

121..........Sam Hazewinkel*
132..........Joseph Warren
145.5........Glenn Garrison
163..........T.C. Dantzler
185..........Brad Vering
211.5........Justin Ruiz
264.5........Russ Davie
Team........U.S. Army (Div. I)
New York A.C. (Div. II)

2008

FREESTYLE

121..........Matt Azevedo*
132..........Shawn Bunch
145.5........Doug Schwab
163..........Ben Askren
185..........Mo Lawal
211.5........Daniel Cormier
264.5........Tommy Rowlands
Team........Sunkist Kids (Div. I)
New York A.C. (Div. II)

GRECO-ROMAN

121..........Spencer Mango*
132..........Jim Gruenwald
145.5........Mark Rial
163..........T.C. Dantzler
185..........Brad Ahearn
211.5........Justin Ruiz
264.5........Dremiel Byers
Team........U.S. Army (Div. I)
New York A.C. (Div. II)

*Outstanding wrestler.

Awards

WALTER IOOSS JR.

A CARDIAC THREAT TO YOUNG ATHLETES P. 90 • THE MESSAGE OF SEAN TAYLOR P. 70

Sports Illustrated

www.SI.com

Sportsman Of the Year

Brett Favre

Sports Illustrated's **2007 Sportsman of the Year Brett Favre**

Athlete Awards

Sports Illustrated Sportsman of the Year

1954	Roger Bannister, Track and Field
1955	Johnny Podres, Baseball
1956	Bobby Morrow, Track and Field
1957	Stan Musial, Baseball
1958	Rafer Johnson, Track and Field
1959	Ingemar Johansson, Boxing
1960	Arnold Palmer, Golf
1961	Jerry Lucas, Basketball
1962	Terry Baker, Football
1963	Pete Rozelle, Pro Football
1964	Ken Venturi, Golf
1965	Sandy Koufax, Baseball
1966	Jim Ryun, Track and Field
1967	Carl Yastrzemski, Baseball
1968	Bill Russell, Pro Basketball
1969	Tom Seaver, Baseball
1970	Bobby Orr, Hockey
1971	Lee Trevino, Golf
1972	B.J. King, Tennis/ J. Wooden, Bask
1973	Jackie Stewart, Auto Racing
1974	Muhammad Ali, Boxing
1975	Pete Rose, Baseball
1976	Chris Evert, Tennis
1977	Steve Cauthen, Horse Racing
1978	Jack Nicklaus, Golf
1979	Terry Bradshaw, Pro Football Willie Stargell, Baseball
1980	U.S. Olympic Hockey Team
1981	Sugar Ray Leonard, Boxing
1982	Wayne Gretzky, Hockey
1983	Mary Decker, Track and Field
1984	Mary Lou Retton, Gymnastics Edwin Moses, Track and Field
1985	Kareem Abdul-Jabbar, Pro Basketball
1986	Joe Paterno, Football
1987	Athletes Who Care: Bob Bourne, Hockey Kip Keino, Track and Field Judi Brown King, Track and Field Dale Murphy, Baseball Chip Rives, Football Patty Sheehan, Golf Rory Sparrow, Pro Basketball Reggie Williams, Pro Football
1988	Orel Hershiser, Baseball
1989	Greg LeMond, Cycling
1990	Joe Montana, Pro Football
1991	Michael Jordan, Pro Basketball
1992	Arthur Ashe, Tennis
1993	Don Shula, Pro Football
1994	Bonnie Blair, Speed Skating Johann Olav Koss, Speed Skating
1995	Cal Ripken Jr, Baseball
1996	Tiger Woods, Golf
1997	Dean Smith, College Basketball
1998	Mark McGwire, Sammy Sosa, Baseball
1999	U.S. Women's Soccer Team
2000	Tiger Woods, Golf
2001	C. Schilling/ R. Johnson, Baseball
2002	Lance Armstrong, Cycling
2003	Tim Duncan/David Robinson, Basketball
2004	Boston Red Sox, Baseball
2005	Tom Brady, Pro Football
2006	Dwyane Wade, Pro Basketball
2007	Brett Favre, Pro Football

Associated Press Athletes of the Year

Year	MEN	WOMEN
1931	Pepper Martin, Baseball	Helene Madison, Swimming
1932	Gene Sarazen, Golf	Babe Didrikson, Track and Field
1933	Carl Hubbell, Baseball	Helen Jacobs, Tennis
1934	Dizzy Dean, Baseball	Virginia Van Wie, Golf
1935	Joe Louis, Boxing	Helen Wills Moody, Tennis
1936	Jesse Owens, Track and Field	Helen Stephens, Track and Field
1937	Don Budge, Tennis	Katherine Rawls, Swimming
1938	Don Budge, Tennis	Patty Berg, Golf
1939	Nile Kinnick, Football	Alice Marble, Tennis
1940	Tom Harmon, Football	Alice Marble, Tennis
1941	Joe DiMaggio, Baseball	Betty Hicks Newell, Golf
1942	Frank Sinkwich, Football	Gloria Callen, Swimming
1943	Gunder Haegg, Track and Field	Patty Berg, Golf
1944	Byron Nelson, Golf	Ann Curtis, Swimming
1945	Bryon Nelson, Golf	Babe Didrikson Zaharias, Golf
1946	Glenn Davis, Football	Babe Didrikson Zaharias, Golf
1947	Johnny Lujack, Football	Babe Didrikson Zaharias, Golf
1948	Lou Boudreau, Baseball	Fanny Blankers-Koen, Track and Field
1949	Leon Hart, Football	Marlene Bauer, Golf
1950	Jim Konstanty, Baseball	Babe Didrikson Zaharias, Golf
1951	Dick Kazmaier, Football	Maureen Connolly, Tennis
1952	Bob Mathias, Track and Field	Maureen Connolly, Tennis
1953	Ben Hogan, Golf	Maureen Connolly, Tennis
1954	Willie Mays, Baseball	Babe Didrikson Zaharias, Golf
1955	Hopalong Cassidy, Football	Patty Berg, Golf
1956	Mickey Mantle, Baseball	Pat McCormick, Diving
1957	Ted Williams, Baseball	Althea Gibson, Tennis
1958	Herb Elliott, Track and Field	Althea Gibson, Tennis
1959	Ingemar Johansson, Boxing	Maria Bueno, Tennis
1960	Rafer Johnson, Track and Field	Wilma Rudolph, Track and Field
1961	Roger Maris, Baseball	Wilma Rudolph, Track and Field
1962	Maury Wills, Baseball	Dawn Fraser, Swimming
1963	Sandy Koufax, Baseball	Mickey Wright, Golf
1964	Don Schollander, Swimming	Mickey Wright, Golf
1965	Sandy Koufax, Baseball	Kathy Whitworth, Golf
1966	Frank Robinson, Baseball	Kathy Whitworth, Golf
1967	Carl Yastrzemski, Baseball	Billie Jean King, Tennis
1968	Denny McLain, Baseball	Peggy Fleming, Skating
1969	Tom Seaver, Baseball	Debbie Meyer, Swimming
1970	George Blanda, Pro Football	Chi Cheng, Track and Field
1971	Lee Trevino, Golf	Evonne Goolagong, Tennis
1972	Mark Spitz, Swimming	Olga Korbut, Gymnastics
1973	O.J. Simpson, Pro Football	Billie Jean King, Tennis
1974	Muhammad Ali, Boxing	Chris Evert, Tennis
1975	Fred Lynn, Baseball	Chris Evert, Tennis
1976	Bruce Jenner, Track and Field	Nadia Comaneci, Gymnastics
1977	Steve Cauthen, Horse Racing	Chris Evert, Tennis
1978	Ron Guidry, Baseball	Nancy Lopez, Golf
1979	Willie Stargell, Baseball	Tracy Austin, Tennis
1980	U.S. Olympic Hockey Team	Chris Evert Lloyd, Tennis
1981	John McEnroe, Tennis	Tracy Austin, Tennis
1982	Wayne Gretzky, Hockey	Mary Decker, Track and Field
1983	Carl Lewis, Track and Field	Martina Navratilova, Tennis
1984	Carl Lewis, Track and Field	Mary Lou Retton, Gymnastics
1985	Dwight Gooden, Baseball	Nancy Lopez, Golf
1986	Larry Bird, Pro Basketball	Martina Navratilova, Tennis
1987	Ben Johnson, Track and Field	Jackie Joyner-Kersee, Track and Field

Associated Press Athletes of the Year (*Cont.*)

	MEN	WOMEN
1988	Orel Hershiser, Baseball	Florence Griffith Joyner, Track and Field
1989	Joe Montana, Pro Football	Steffi Graf, Tennis
1990	Joe Montana, Pro Football	Beth Daniel, Golf
1991	Michael Jordan, Pro Basketball	Monica Seles, Tennis
1992	Michael Jordan, Pro Basketball	Monica Seles, Tennis
1993	Michael Jordan, Pro Basketball	Sheryl Swoopes, Basketball
1994	George Foreman, Boxing	Bonnie Blair, Speed Skating
1995	Cal Ripken Jr, Baseball	Rebecca Lobo, Basketball
1996	Michael Johnson, Track and Field	Amy Van Dyken, Swimming
1997	Tiger Woods, Golf	Martina Hingis, Tennis
1998	Mark McGwire, Baseball	Se Ri Pak, Golf
1999	Tiger Woods, Golf	U.S. Women's Soccer Team
2000	Tiger Woods, Golf	Marion Jones, Track and Field
2001	Barry Bonds, Baseball	Jennifer Capriati, Tennis
2002	Lance Armstrong, Cycling	Serena Williams, Tennis
2003	Lance Armstrong, Cycling	Annika Sorenstam, Golf
2004	Lance Armstrong, Cycling	Annika Sorenstam, Golf
2005	Lance Armstrong, Cycling	Annika Sorenstam, Golf
2006	Tiger Woods, Golf	Lorena Ochoa, Golf
2007	Tom Brady, Pro Football	Lorena Ochoa, Golf

James E. Sullivan Award

Presented annually by the AAU to the athlete who "by his or her performance, example and influence as an amateur, has done the most during the year to advance the cause of sportsmanship."

1930	Bobby Jones, Golf
1931	Barney Berlinger, Track and Field
1932	Jim Bausch, Track and Field
1933	Glenn Cunningham, Track and Field
1934	Bill Bonthron, Track and Field
1935	Lawson Little, Golf
1936	Glenn Morris, Track and Field
1937	Don Budge, Tennis
1938	Don Lash, Track and Field
1939	Joe Burk, Rowing
1940	Greg Rice, Track and Field
1941	Leslie MacMitchell, Track and Field
1942	Cornelius Warmerdam, Track
1943	Gilbert Dodds, Track and Field
1944	Ann Curtis, Swimming
1945	Doc Blanchard, Football
1946	Arnold Tucker, Football
1947	John B. Kelly Jr, Rowing
1948	Bob Mathias, Track and Field
1949	Dick Button, Skating
1950	Fred Wilt, Track and Field
1951	Bob Richards, Track and Field
1952	Horace Ashenfelter, Track and Field
1953	Sammy Lee, Diving
1954	Mal Whitfield, Track and Field
1955	Harrison Dillard, Track and Field
1956	Pat McCormick, Diving
1957	Bobby Morrow, Track and Field
1958	Glenn Davis, Track and Field
1959	Parry O'Brien, Track and Field
1960	Rafer Johnson, Track and Field
1961	Wilma Rudolph, Track and Field
1962	Jim Beatty, Track and Field
1963	John Pennel, Track and Field
1964	Don Schollander, Swimming
1965	Bill Bradley, Basketball
1966	Jim Ryun, Track and Field
1967	Randy Matson, Track and Field
1968	Debbie Meyer, Swimming
1969	Bill Toomey, Track and Field
1970	John Kinsella, Swimming
1971	Mark Spitz, Swimming
1972	Frank Shorter, Track and Field
1973	Bill Walton, Basketball
1974	Rich Wohlhuter, Track and Field
1975	Tim Shaw, Swimming
1976	Bruce Jenner, Track and Field
1977	John Naber, Swimming
1978	Tracy Caulkins, Swimming
1979	Kurt Thomas, Gymnastics
1980	Eric Heiden, Speed Skating
1981	Carl Lewis, Track and Field
1982	Mary Decker, Track and Field
1983	Edwin Moses, Track and Field
1984	Greg Louganis, Diving
1985	Joan B.-Samuelson, T & F
1986	Jackie Joyner-Kersee, T & F
1987	Jim Abbott, Baseball
1988	Florence Griffith Joyner, Track
1989	Janet Evans, Swimming
1990	John Smith, Wrestling
1991	Mike Powell, Track and Field
1992	Bonnie Blair, Speed Skating
1993	Charlie Ward, Football, Basketball
1994	Dan Jansen, Speed Skating
1995	Bruce Baumgartner, Wrestling
1996	Michael Johnson, Track and Field
1997	Peyton Manning, Football
1998	Chamique Holdsclaw, Basketball
1999	Kelly and Coco Miller, Basketball
2000	Rulon Gardner, Wrestling
2001	Michelle Kwan, Figure Skating
2002	Sarah Hughes, Figure Skating
2003	Michael Phelps, Swimming
2004	Paul Hamm, Gymnastics
2005	J. J. Redick, College Basketball
2006	Jessica Long, Paralympic Swimmer
2007	Tim Tebow, College Football

The Sporting News Sportsman of the Year

1968	Denny McLain, Baseball
1969	Tom Seaver, Baseball
1970	John Wooden, Basketball
1971	Lee Trevino, Golf
1972	Charles O. Finley, Baseball
1973	O.J. Simpson, Pro Football
1974	Lou Brock, Baseball
1975	Archie Griffin, Football
1976	Larry O'Brien, Pro Basketball
1977	Steve Cauthen, Horse Racing
1978	Ron Guidry, Baseball
1979	Willie Stargell, Baseball
1980	George Brett, Baseball
1981	Wayne Gretzky, Hockey
1982	Whitey Herzog, Baseball
1983	Bowie Kuhn, Baseball
1984	Peter Ueberroth, LA Olympics
1985	Pete Rose, Baseball
1986	Larry Bird, Pro Basketball
1987	No award
1988	Jackie Joyner-Kersee, T & F
1989	Joe Montana, Pro Football
1990	Nolan Ryan, Baseball
1991	Michael Jordan, Pro Basketball
1992	Mike Krzyzewski, Basketball
1993	Pat Gillick/Cito Gaston, Baseball
1994	Emmitt Smith, Pro Football
1995	Cal Ripken Jr, Baseball
1996	Joe Torre, Baseball
1997	Michael Jordan, Basketball
1998	Mark McGwire, Baseball
1999	New York Yankees, Baseball
2000	Kurt Warner/Marshall Faulk, Pro Football
2001	Curt Schilling, Baseball
2002	Tyrone Willingham, Football
2003	Jack McKeon, Baseball Dick Vermeil, Pro Football
2004	Tom Brady, Pro Football
2005	Matt Leinart, College Football
2006	LaDainian Tomlinson, Pro Football
2007	Tom Brady, Pro Football

United Press International Male and Female Athlete of the Year

Year	MEN	WOMEN
1974	Muhammad Ali, Boxing	Irena Szewinska, Track and Field
1975	Joao Oliveira, Track and Field	Nadia Comaneci, Gymnastics
1976	Alberto Juantorena, Track and Field	Nadia Comaneci, Gymnastics
1977	Alberto Juantorena, Track and Field	Rosie Ackermann, Track and Field
1978	Henry Rono, Track and Field	Tracy Caulkins, Swimming
1979	Sebastian Coe, Track and Field	Marita Koch, Track and Field
1980	Eric Heiden, Speed Skating	Hanni Wenzel, Alpine Skiing
1981	Sebastian Coe, Track and Field	Chris Evert Lloyd, Tennis
1982	Daley Thompson, Track and Field	Marita Koch, Track and Field
1983	Carl Lewis, Track and Field	Jarmila Kratochvilova, Track and Field
1984	Carl Lewis, Track and Field	Martina Navratilova, Tennis
1985	Steve Cram, Track and Field	Mary Decker Slaney, Track and Field
1986	Diego Maradona, Soccer	Heike Drechsler, Track and Field
1987	Ben Johnson, Track and Field	Steffi Graf, Tennis
1988	Matt Biondi, Swimming	Florence Griffith Joyner, Track and Field
1989	Boris Becker, Tennis	Steffi Graf, Tennis
1990	Stefan Edberg, Tennis	Merlene Ottey, Track and Field
1991	Michael Jordan, Pro Basketball	Monica Seles, Tennis
1992	Mario Lemieux, Hockey	Monica Seles, Tennis
1993	Michael Jordan, Pro Basketball	Steffi Graf, Tennis
1994	Nick Price, Golf	Bonnie Blair, Speed Skating
1995	Cal Ripken Jr, Baseball	Steffi Graf, Tennis

Note: Award not given since 1995.

Dial Award

Presented by the Dial Corporation to the male and female national high school athlete/scholar of the year.

Year	BOYS	GIRLS
1979	Herschel Walker, Football	No award
1980	Bill Fralic, Football	Carol Lewis, Track and Field
1981	Kevin Willhite, Football	Cheryl Miller, Basketball
1982	Mike Smith, Basketball	Elaine Zayak, Skating
1983	Chris Spielman, Football	Melanie Buddemeyer, Swimming
1984	Hart Lee Dykes, Football	Nora Lewis, Basketball
1985	Jeff George, Football	Gea Johnson, Track and Field
1986	Scott Schaffner, Football	Mya Johnson, Track and Field
1987	Todd Marinovich, Football	Kristi Overton, Water Skiing
1988	Carlton Gray, Football	Courtney Cox, Basketball
1989	Robert Smith, Football	Lisa Leslie, Basketball
1990	Derrick Brooks, Football	Vicki Goetze, Golf
1991	Jeff Buckey, Football, Track and Field	Katie Smith, Basketball, Volleyball, Track
1992	Jacque Vaughn, Basketball	Amanda White, Track and Field, Swimming
1993	Tiger Woods, Golf	Kristin Folkl, Basketball
1994	Taymon Domzalski, Basketball	Shannon Miller, Gymnastics
1995	Brent Abernathy, Baseball	Shea Ralph, Basketball
1996	Grant Irons, Football	Grace Park, Golf
1997	Ronald Curry, Football	Michelle Kwan, Figure Skating

Note: Award not given since 1997.

Obituaries

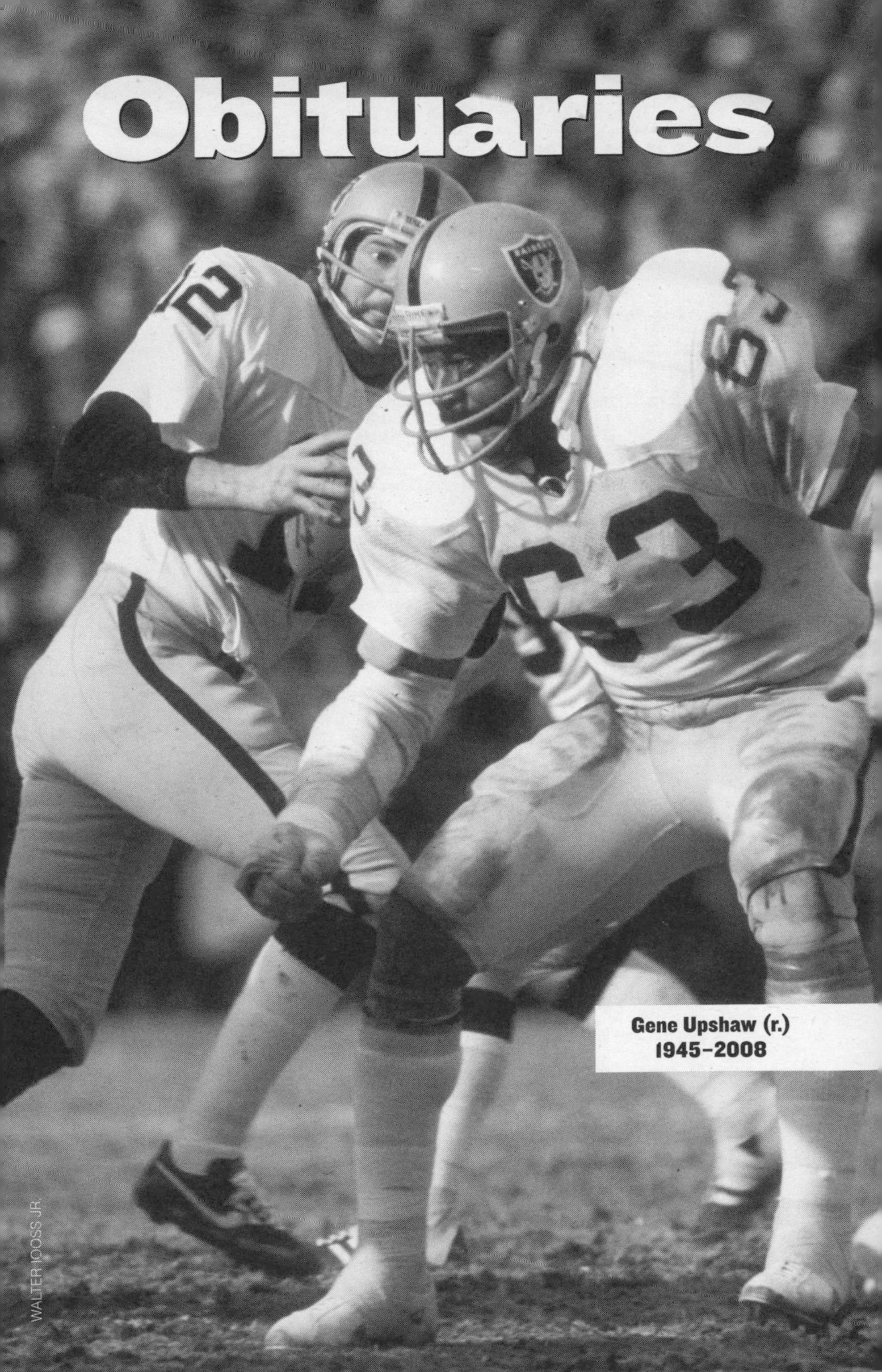

Gene Upshaw (r.)
1945–2008

WALTER IOOSS JR.

Max McGee, 75, football player. *SI writes:*

"Chosen by the Green Bay Packers in the fifth round of the 1954 draft, McGee didn't play his rookie season until three years later—he spent 1955 and '56 as a pilot in the Air Force. During his 11-year career, McGee snagged 345 receptions for 6,346 yards, scoring 51 touchdowns. But it wasn't until 1967 that McGee, by then an aging backup, became famous. Starting wideout Boyd Dowler suffered a separated shoulder on the Packers' second drive of Super Bowl I, forcing McGee into action. Although he had caught only four passes all season, McGee responded by having the game of his life, catching seven passes for 138 yards and two touchdowns in the big game, including the first TD scored in a Super Bowl. Even more impressive, McGee infamously did all this after staying out late drinking the night before. 'I set a record that will never be broken, McGee said a few years ago of his Super Bowl I performance. 'Most passes caught with a hangover.'"

In Deephaven, Minn., of injuries from a fall, on October 20, 2007.

John Woodruff, 92, track athlete. *Former Olympic gold medalist, SI writes:*

"Woodruff won the gold medal in the 800 meters at the 1936 Olympics in Berlin after pulling off one of the most unexpected maneuvers in track history—stopping dead in mid-race. Woodruff had failed to heed the warning of his coach and found himself hemmed in against the rail early in the race. Not knowing what else to do, the 21-year-old Pitt freshman hit the brakes, waited for the rest of the field to pass and then gunned past the best half-milers in the world."

In Fountain Hills, Ariz., of complications from heart and kidney disease, on October 30, 2007.

Joe Nuxhall, 79, baseball player and broadcaster. *Former Cincinnati pitcher. SI writes:*

"When he made his major league debut for the Reds on June 10, 1944, Nuxhall, a mere 15 years, 10 months, and 11 days old, became the youngest major leaguer in the modern era, a record that still stands. After a ground out, a walk, and a pop out, Nuxhall faced legendary Cardinals slugger Stan Musial and soon become unglued, walking three and giving up five runs before being pulled. After that disastrous outing, Nuxhall did disappear for a long while, but after some seasoning in the minors he returned to the Reds in 1952 and proved that he was no wartime novelty. He pitched until '66, mostly for Cincinnati, winning 135 games and twice making the All-Star Game. A year after he retired, he moved to the Reds' radio booth, and he spent the next 40 years—many of them with broadcast partner Marty Brennaman—delighting Queen City fans with his folksy style, unabashed homerism, and signature sign-off: "This the old left-hander rounding third and heading for home."

In Cincinnati, Ohio of pneumonia, on November 16, 2007.

Sean Taylor, 24, football player. *Washington Redskins defensive back. SI writes:*

"An All-American at the University of Miami, Taylor was drafted by the Redskins with the fifth overall selection in 2004. Coach Joe Gibbs called it "one of the most researched things" he's ever done, but Taylor soon began having problems. During his short NFL career, Taylor was charged with drunken driving (the case was later dismissed in court) and fined at least seven times for late hits, uniform violations and other infractions, including a $17,000 penalty for spitting in the face of Tampa Bay running back Michael Pittman during a playoff game in January 2006. Taylor also endured a yearlong legal battle after he was accused in 2005 of brandishing a gun during a fight near his home. He eventually pleaded no contest to two misdemeanors and was sentenced to 18 months' probation. On the field, Taylor's play was often erratic—he led the NFL in missed tackles in 2006 yet made the Pro Bowl that year because of his reputation as one of the hardest hitters in the league, one that earned him the nickname "Grim Reaper." Teammates and coaches often portrayed Taylor as misunderstood and in 2007 he seemed to have put his past problems behind him.

Taylor died after he was shot while protecting his wife and 18-month old daughter during a break-in at his home in the Miami suburb of Palmetto Bay."

In Miami, Fla., of a gun shot wound, on November 27, 2007.

Peter Davi, 45, surfer. *SI writes:*

"The 6'3", 240-pound big-wave man Davi drowned at Ghost Trees, a surf break off the Pebble Beach Golf Links. Davi helped popularize the spot, and he also made a name for himself on Hawaii's North Shore and at the treacherous Mavericks, a spot about 100 miles north of Monterey."

In Monterey, Calif., of drowning, on December 5, 2007.

Sir Edmund Hillary, 88, mountain climber.

"On May 29, 1953, Hillary and his Sherpa climbing partner Tenzing Norgay electrified the world when they became the first men to reach the summit of the world's tallest peak, Mt. Everest. Hillary, a former officer in the Royal New Zealand Air Force and an avowed beekeeper throughout his life, maintained a humility about his groundbreaking achievement, saying he was "an ordinary person with ordinary qualities." Soon after his famous climb, Hillary pioneered a new route to the South Pole. Later in life, Hillary used his celebrity to promote conservation efforts and to help aid the impoverished Nepalese people."

In Auckland, New Zealand, of a heart attack, on January 11.

Johnny Podres, 75, baseball player. *Former Brooklyn Dodger pitcher. SI writes:*

"Podres never lost the spirit—or the skills—that made him a Dodgers hero. The 23-year-old Podres gave the Dodgers their only championship before they moved to L.A. by beating the Yankees twice in the 1955 World Series, including a 2–0 masterpiece in Game 7. He was named *SI*'s Sportsman of the Year, and Podres's legend only grew when it later emerged that he had told his teammates before that game that if they scored one run, he'd take care of the rest.

As effective as Podres was as a pitcher—he was a four-time All-Star—he may have been a better teacher. After retiring in 1969, he worked as a pitching coach and instructor for five teams, ending with the Phillies in the late 1990s. He helped develop lefthander Frank Viola into a Cy Young Award winner and turned around Curt Schilling's foundering career when Schilling was traded to Philadelphia in 1992."

In Glens Falls, N.Y., of complications from a leg infection, on January 13.

Ed Vargo, 79, baseball umpire. *Former National League umpire. SI writes:*

"During a 23-year career that began in 1960, Vargo, a onetime minor league catcher, worked four World Series and four All-Star Games and officiated over several historic moments. He was behind the plate when Hank Aaron tied Babe Ruth's mark of 714 career home runs in 1974, and he worked the first World Series night game, in 1971. He is the only umpire to be behind the plate for a no-hitter and a perfect game by the same pitcher: He called Sandy Koufax's June 4, 1964 no-hitter and was there for Koufax's perfect game a year later."

In Butler, Pa., of congestive heart failure, on February 2.

Bob Howsam, 89, sports executive. *Founder of Denver Broncos. SI writes:*

"Howsam's six-decade career as a sports executive included founding the Denver Broncos and building the Cincinnati Reds into the Big Red Machine. With his family, Howsam bought the Denver Bears, a minor league baseball team, in 1948. He built a stadium for the team atop a garbage dump; it was eventually expanded into Mile High Stadium after Howsam founded the Broncos, an original AFL franchise, in1959. He sold the team in 1961 and turned his attention to baseball. After a stint as the Cardinals' G.M., he took over the same position with the Reds in 1967, assembling the roster that would dominate the National League in the 1970s."

In Sun City, Ariz., of heart disease complications, on February 19.

W.C. Heinz, 93, sportswriter.

For nearly three decades, Heinz, known to colleagues and friends as

"Bill," was one of America's foremost sports journalists, writing primarily about boxing and horse racing during the post-World War II era. His July 1949 newspaper article for the *New York Sun* entitled "Death of a Racehorse" is still considered a classic of the genre. Later in his career he turned to books, writing famous sports novels like "The Professional," and collaborating with Green Bay Packers coach Vince Lombardi to pen the legendary football book "Run to Daylight!" Heinz's storytelling skills were not confined merely to sportwriting, however. In 1968, he co-authored with H. Richard Hornberger—under the single pseudonym "Richard Hooker"—the well known Koren War novel "M*A*S*H," upon which a successful movie and long-running TV series were loosely based.

In. Bennington, Vt., of natural causes, on February 27.

Ken Reardon, 86, hockey player. *Former Montreal Canadiens defenseman. SI writes:*

"In a seven-year career with the Canadiens that was interrupted by World War II and shortened by injuries, the rugged Hall of Fame defenseman Reardon was twice a first-team NHL All-Star. (He made the second team three times.) Reardon helped the Canadiens win the 1946 Stanley Cup and spent more than a decade in the Montreal front office after retiring as a player in 1950."

In. Montreal, Quebec, Canada, of natural causes, on March 15.

Dick Nolan, 75, football coach. *SI writes:*

"In 1962, Nolan, a defensive back for the New York Giants, was traded to Dallas, where former teammate Tom Landry used him as a player-coach. Injuries forced Nolan to stop playing midway through the season; the secondary's loss was the coaching staff's gain. Nolan took over the defense and molded it into a unit that for years would remain one of the league's stingiest. In 1968, when he was 35, Nolan was hired away to be the head coach of the 49ers, a wide-open team that filled the air with footballs but seldom won. Under his leadership, San Francisco won three straight division titles.

Nolan later led the New Orleans Saints to their first nonlosing record (8–8 in '79) and returned to the Cowboys as an assistant in the '80s. Nolan's son Mike, went on to a coaching career and when he, too, was hired as the head coach of the 49ers in 2005, he successfully petitioned the NFL to let him wear a suit on the sidelines as his father had."

In Grapevine, Tex., of complications from prostate cancer, on April 9.

Cecilia Colledge, 87, figure skater *Former Olympic silver medalist.*

In 1932, at the age of just 11 years, 73 days, British figure skater Colledge became the youngest Olympian in history, a record that still stands today. Four years later, at the 1936 Games in Berlin, Colledge fell just short of defeating gold medalist and Norwegian skating legend Sonja Henie. A year later, Colledge went on to win the Ladies World Figure Skating Championship.

During her career, she was well known as a skating pioneer, becoming the first woman to execute a double jump (salchow), and she is credited with inventing the camel and layback spins as well as the one-foot axel jump. Colledge was inducted into the World Skating Hall of Fame in 1980.

In Cambridge, Mass., of natural causes, on April 12.

Darrell Garretson, 76, basketball referee. *SI writes:*

"Garretson was one of the NBA's most recognizable referees. During a career that lasted from 1967 to 1994, Garretson called more than 2,000 games, and for 17 years he served as the league's chief of officiating staff."

In Mesa, Ariz., of, natural causes, on April 21.

Buzzie Bavasi, 93, baseball executive. *SI writes:*

"In 1939 Bavasi, a native New Yorker, began working for the Brooklyn Dodgers as travelling secretary and publicity director. He replaced Branch Rickey as general manager in 1951 and built eight National League pennant winners around such future Hall of Famers as Jackie Robinson, Duke Snider, Roy Campanella and Sandy Koufax; during his 18-year tenure the Dodgers won four World Series—including their only title in Brooklyn, in '55. Bavasi left the Dodgers in 1968 to become president of the expansion Padres."

In San Diego, Calif., of natural causes, on May 1.

Frank Whiteley Jr., 93, horse trainer. *SI writes:*

"Whiteley trained two Horses of the Year: Damascus in 1967 and Forego in '76. But he is best remembered for training Ruffian, the filly who won her first 10 races, then was euthanized after breaking down in a '75 match race with Kentucky Derby champ Foolish Pleasure."

In Camden, S.C., of complications from pneumonia, on May 2.

Eight Belles, 3, thoroughbred.

Eight Belles, the first filly to run in the Kentucky Derby since 1999, broke down just moments after placing second in the race to the colt Big Brown. The dark filly appeared to be cooling down normally when she suddenly collapsed around the first turn, sending jockey Gabriel Saenz sliding to the ground. Her injuries included two severely broken front ankles as well as at least one broken sesamoid bone. Track veterinarians descended upon the horse and quickly made the determination to put her down, casting a tragic pall over the post-race festivities. Subsequent tests showed no pre-existing bone abnormalities or presence of steroids. Although the swiftness of Eight Belle's demise stood in marked contrast to 2006 Kentucky Derby winner Barbaro's extended battle to survive after breaking down at that year's Preakness, both track tragedies heightened concern about thoroughbred breeding and care as well as the future of horse racing.

In Louisville, Ky., euthanized after breaking two front ankles, on May 3.

Curtis Whitley, 39, football player. *Former NFL center. SI writes:*

"Whitley [was] found by friends dead in his home. Police say there was no sign of foul play. Whitely, who played for the Chargers, Panthers and Raiders from 1992 through '97, was suspended twice for violating the NFL's drug policy, and in 1994 he underwent treatment at the Betty Ford Center. In the 1997 book *Year of the Cat*, a recap of Carolina's '96 season, Whitley told authors Scott Fowler and Charles Chandler that he had been a frequent user of crystal methamphetamine."

In Fort Stockton, Tex., of an unattended accidental death, on May 11.

Luc Bourdon, 21, hockey player. *Vancouver Canucks defenseman. SI writes:*

"Bourdon suffered injuries in a motorcycle accident near his hometown of Shippagan, New Brunswick when his bike hit a tractor-trailer. He was the 10th pick of the 2005 draft and appeared in 27 games with Vancouver last year, scoring two goals."

In Shippagan, New Brunswick, Canada, of injuries sustained in a motorcycle accident, on May 29.

Herm Weiskopf, 74, sportswriter. *Former Sports Illustrated senior writer. SI writes:*

"After working as the editor of a small paper in Lock Haven, Pa., Weiskopf joined the magazine's staff in 1957 and stayed for 33 years. In addition to covering college football and college basketball, he wrote the Inside Pitch column."

In New Hope, Penn., of natural causes, on June 19.

Scott Kalitta, 46, race car driver. *Funny Car champion. SI writes:*

"Kalitta, who won the 1994 and '95 Top Fuel championships, was making a qualifying run for the Lucas Oil NHRA SuperNationals when his parachute failed to deploy; going 300 mph and unable to stop, he struck a pole anchoring the safety net at the end of the track. Kalitta was the son of legendary drag racer Connie Kalitta and had been a pro driver since '82."

In Englishtown, N.J, of injuries sustained in a racing accident, on June 21.

Daniel Bukantz, 90, fencer. *Four-time national fencing champion. SI writes:*

"Bukantz competed in four Olympics and later worked as an official in several Games. A member of the U.S. Fencing Hall of Fame, Bukantz is the father of Jeff Bukantz, 50, the captain of the U.S. fencing team."

In Queens, N.Y., of lung cancer, on July 26.

Skip Caray, 68, baseball announcer. *Former Atlanta Braves announcer. SI writes:*

"While his father, the late Hall of Fame broadcaster Harry Caray, was known for his ebullient personality, Skip was far more reserved, relying on a sharp, sardonic wit. "Skip Caray is as much a part of Atlanta Braves baseball as any of us," said Braves third baseman Chipper Jones. "We all grew up listening to Skip." Several health problems led Caray, who began broadcasting Braves games in 1976, to cut back his schedule; he only worked home games during his last season."

In Atlanta, Georgia., of complications from illnesses related to diabetes, on August 3.

John Challis, 18, fan. *SI writes:*

"In April Challis, who was diagnosed with terminal liver and lung cancer at age 16, made national headlines when, despite being too weak to run, he got a base hit in a game for his Freedom (Pa.) High baseball team. Over the next months he befriended several sports figures, including Penguins owner Mario Lemieux, Steelers quarterback Ben Roethlisberger and Alex Rodriguez, who met Challis when the teenager threw out the first pitch before a Pirates-Yankees game in June. Last month Challis visited Rodriguez's apartment in New York City. "He was a very brave boy," said Rodriguez. "I'll be inspired for the rest of my life."

In Pittsburgh, Penn., of cancer, on August 19.

Gene Upshaw, 63, football player and executive. *Former Oakland Raiders guard and executive director of the National Football League Players' Association.*

Upshaw's outstanding 15-season playing career was entirely with the Oakland/Los Angeles Raiders and included two Super Bowl wins and seven Pro Bowl appearances. Frequently listed as one of the most powerful men in U.S. sports, Upshaw was drafted in the first round by Oakland in 1967 out of Texas A&I—hardly a football factory. He was an NAIA All-American at center, tackle and end, but was switched to to left guard by the Raiders. He was part of one of the NFL's most dominant offensive lines, lining up between fellow Hall of Famers Art Shell at tackle and Jim Otto at center. Upshaw became the first player who was exclusively a guard to be enshrined in the Hall of Fame. In 1983, he became executive director of the players' association and guided it through the 1987 strike that led to replacement football.

His career was summed up Thursday by his close friend Art Shell, who played next to him on Oakland's offensive line.

"Gene was a true pioneer as one of the few African American leaders of a major union," Shell said. "He was the equal of owners in negotiations and made the league a better place for all players. Playing alongside of Gene was an honor and a privilege. He was a pillar of strength and leadership for our great Raider teams."

In Lake Tahoe, Calif., of pancreatic cancer, on August 20.

Kevin Duckworth, 44, basketball player. *Former Portland Trailblazers center. SI writes:*

"The 7-footer was a two-time All-Star for the Blazers in his 11-year career. One of the most popular players in Portland history—he made his off-season home in the city—Duckworth died in Glenden Beach, Ore., while on a goodwill tour for the team. An autopsy revealed an enlarged heart. "People talk about Clyde Drexler being the best player on the team, but I say it was Kevin Duckworth," said former teammate Buck Williams. "He was the X factor...the glue that [held] the team together."

In Glenden Beach, Oregon, of heart failure, on August 25.

Phil Hill, 81, race car driver. *Only American-born driver to win the Formual One Championship. SI writes:*

"Hill, who grew up in California, won his title under sad circumstances. In 1961 he was involved in a tight points race with Ferrari teammate Wolfgang von Trips. In the penultimate race of the season, the Italian Grand Prix, Von Trips died in an accident that also killed 15 spectators. Hill won the race and clinched the championship. An introspective man in a sport dominated by playboys—he spent much of his spare time in Europe in opera houses—Hill quit driving for a time in 1950 because of anxiety and ulcers. But in a 1961 piece he wrote for SI, he described how the thrill of climbing into a car drew him back: "All doubts, all anxieties, all memories of past painful struggles fade away before the magic of this occasional purity, and I am at one with the car."

In Salinas, Calif., of complications from Parkinson's disease, on August 28.

Walter "Killer" Kowalski, 81, pro wrestler. *SI writes:*

"Kowalski shot to fame in the 1950s as pro wrestler Killer Kowalski. In Montreal in 1954, Kowalski accidentally tore off part of the ear of opponent Yukon Eric. When he visited Eric in the hospital, the two laughed at how silly his bandages looked. The next day the papers reported that Kowalski had laughed at his victim, cementing his status as one of the leading heels of the day. the 6' 7", 275-pound Kowalski—in reality, a gentleman and longtime vegetarian—retired in '77 and ran a wrestling school in Massachusetts."

In Malden, Mass, of a heart attack, on August 30.

Tommy Bolt, 92, golfer. *1952 U.S. Open champion. SI writes:*

"Bolt had one of golf's prettiest swings and won 15 PGA Tour events after turning pro in 1946, but Terrible Tommy was best known for his volcanic temper. The Tour fined him on several occasions for breaking his clubs and using foul language on the course. Bolt's last Tour victory was in 1961, and he won the Senior PGA Championship in '69. "Now, I threw a couple of clubs," he once said. "But I threw them at the most opportune time...They always had the camera on me."

In Batesville, Ark., of liver failure, on August 30.

Don Haskins, 78, basketball coach. *SI writes:*

"In 38 seasons Haskins, who was inducted into the Basketball Hall of Fame in 1997 and retired in '99, led the UTEP Miners to 14 NCAA tournament appearances, but wins and losses don't measure his full impact on the game. In 1966 his team, then known as Texas Western, became the first with five black starters to win an NCAA title by beating heavily favored, all-white Kentucky; the story of that achievement was told in the 2006 movie *Glory Road.* The Miners' win paved the way for widespread recruiting of black players by NCAA schools. Said former Arkansas coach Nolan Richardson, who played for Haskins from 1961 to '63, "He was able to win without worrying about what color [his players] were."

In El Paso, Tex., of congestive heart failure, on September 7.

Mickey Vernon, 90, baseball player. *Two-time American League batting champion. SI writes:*

"The seven-time All-Star played for five teams from 1939 to '60. (with two years off for service in World War II), spending most of his career with the Washington Senators. He won batting crowns in 1946 and '53 with Washington, and in 1961 he became the first manager of the expansion Senators after the original franchise moved to Minnesota."

In Media, Penn., of a stroke, on September 24.

Paul Newman, 83, race car driver and team owner. *SI writes:*

"Known for some of the most searing performances in cinema history, Paul Newman preferred roles at the racetrack, where he was a driver and team owner. "I'll always talk about racing because the people are interesting and fun, the sport is a lot more exciting than anything else I do, and nobody cares that I'm an actor," he once said. Playing a driver in the 1966 film *Winning* sparked Newman's interest in racing, and his accomplishments behind the wheel included a second-place finish with two teammates in the 24 Hours of Le Mans in 1979."

In Westport, Conn., of lung cancer, on September 26.

Tom Tresh, 71, baseball player. *1962 American League Rookie of the Year. SI writes:*

"The versatile Tresh broke in with the Yankees as a switch-hitting shortstop and was an All-Star in his first full season, when he batted .286 with 20 home runs. The following year he moved to the outfield and was an All-Star again; he won a Gold Glove as a centerfielder in '65. He spent 8½ seasons with the Yankees before being traded to the Tigers midway through '69. He retired after that season."

In Venice, Fla., of a heart attack, on October 15.

2009 MAJOR EVENTS

JANUARY

Major College Bowl Games	Jan 1–5
NFL Wild-Card Playoffs	Jan 3–4
BCS Championship Game	Jan 8
NFL Divisional Playoffs	Jan 10–11
NFL Conference Championships	Jan 18
U.S. Figure Skating Championships	Jan 18–25
Australian Open	Jan 19–Feb 1
NHL All-Star Game	Jan 25

FEBRUARY

Super Bowl XLIII	Feb 1
World Cup Skiing Championships	Feb 3–15
Millrose Games	Feb 6
NFL Pro Bowl	Feb 8
NBA All-Star Game	Feb 15
Daytona 500	Feb 15
PBA World Championship	Feb 16–22

MARCH

World Baseball Classic	March 5–22
March Madness Begins	*March 19**
World Figure Skating Championships	March 22–29
Kraft Nabisco Championship	March 26–29
Major League Soccer Season Begins	*March 28**

APRIL

Major League Baseball Opening Day	*April 1**
NCAA Men's Basketball Final Four	April 4 & 6
NCAA Women's Basketball Final Four	April 5 & 7
NCAA Men's Hockey Frozen Four	April 8–11
NHL Playoffs Begin	*April 8**
The Masters	April 9–12
NBA Playoffs Begin	*April 18**
Boston Marathon	April 20
NFL Draft	April 25–26

MAY

Kentucky Derby	May 2
The Players Championship (Golf)	May 7–10
Preakness Stakes	May 16
NASCAR All-Star Race	May 16
Indianapolis 500	May 24
NHL Stanley Cup Final Begins	*May 25**

JUNE

French Open	May 24–June 7
NBA Finals Begin	*June 4**
MLB Draft	June 4–5
LPGA Championship	June 4–7
Belmont Stakes	June 6
U.S. Men's Open (Golf)	June 11–14
College World Series	June 12–22
NHL Draft	June 19–20
NBA Draft	June 25
U.S. Women's Open (Golf)	June 25–28

** Approximate date.*

JULY

Wimbledon	June 22–July 5
Tour de France	July 4–26
MLB All-Star Game	July 7
Men's British Open	July 16–19
FINA World Swimming Championships	July 19–Aug 2
Brickyard 400	July 26

AUGUST

Women's British Open	July 30– Aug 2
NFL Hall of Fame Induction	Aug 1
PGA Championship	Aug 6–9
PGA Tour Playoffs Begin	*Aug 13**
Little League World Series	Aug 14–23
World Track & Field Championships	Aug 15–23
Solheim Cup (Women's Golf)	Aug 20–23
College Football Season Begins	*Aug 29**

SEPTEMBER

U.S. Open (Tennis)	Aug 24–Sept 6
NFL Season Begins	*Sept 3**
NASCAR Chase for the Cup Begins	*Sept 13**
PGA Tour Championship	Sep 24–27

OCTOBER

MLB Divisional Series Begin	*Oct 1**
President's Cup (Men's Golf)	Oct 8–11
NHL Season Begins	*Oct 8**
MLB League Championship Series Begin	*Oct 9**
World Series Begins	*Oct 21**
NBA Regular Season Begins	*Oct 27**

NOVEMBER

New York Marathon	Nov 1
Women's Tour Championships (Tennis)	Nov 2–9
Breeders' Cup	Nov 6–7
Men's Masters Cup (Tennis)	Nov 8–15
NASCAR Chase for the Cup Ends	*Nov 15**
MLS Cup	Nov 22

DECEMBER

Heisman Trophy Presentation	Dec 5
Major College Bowl Games Begin	*Dec 18**

SOCCER

NCAA SPORTS

OLYMPICS

TRACK & FIELD

SWIMMING

MISCELLANEOUS SPORTS

AWARDS

OBITUARIES/ MAJOR EVENTS